The Essays of
Virginia Woolf

The Essays of Virginia Woolf

VOLUME II

1912–1918

EDITED BY

ANDREW McNEILLIE

Harcourt Brace Jovanovich, Publishers

San Diego   New York   London

Library of Congress Cataloging-in-Publication Data
(Revised for vol. 2)
Woolf, Virginia, 1882-1941.
The essays of Virginia Woolf.
Bibliography: v. 1, p.
Includes index.
Contents: v. 1. 1904-1912—v. 2. 1912-1918.
1. McNeillie, Andrew. I. Title.
PR6045.072.A6 1987   824'.912   86-29520
ISBN 0-15-129055-5 (v. 1)
ISBN 0-15-129056-3 (v. 2)

Printed in the United States of America

First edition

A B C D E

Contents

APPENDICES

Introduction

The marriage of Virginia Stephen and Leonard Woolf in August 1912 marked the beginning of one of the most notable collaborations in our recent cultural history. She was thirty; he would be thirty-two in November; and so they were not conspicuously young. Nor were they exactly untried in the world. Virginia Woolf had already displayed evidence of her genius, as those familiar with the first volume of this edition of her essays, with her early shorter fiction,[1] and who have read her first novel *The Voyage Out*, will know. On leaving Trinity College, Cambridge, in 1904, Leonard Woolf had 'spent 7 years in Ceylon, governing natives, inventing ploughs, shooting tigers'.[2] The Colonial Service had recently offered him 'a very high place' but he chose instead to resign: 'gave up his entire career' on the chance that Virginia Stephen might agree to marry him.[3] On his return, he had also begun his first novel, *The Village in the Jungle*, which was to appear in 1913. But at the same time, neither of the Woolfs could be described as being established in life. Indeed, Leonard Woolf ('He has no money of his own'[4]) was now positively disestablished. They resolved to live as inexpensively as they could, to write – their novels, and journalism – and also, in Leonard's case, 'to find out about labour and factories and to keep outside Government and do things on his own account'.[5] But during at least the first three years of their marriage, the question of how the Woolfs might live turned out to be a far more fundamental one, a matter, in fact, of Virginia Woolf's personal survival. For she suffered in that period two prolonged bouts of severe mental illness: first in 1913, when an attempted suicide brought her close to death, and then again in 1915, the year in which *The Voyage Out* was published.

These tragic circumstances are reflected in the composition of this volume, which contains no articles for the years 1914 and 1915 and three only for 1913. (The years 1910–12 were also relatively poor in journalistic output. But, although she certainly was ill in 1912 and required periods of seclusion and rest, this poverty had more to do with the fact that she was at that time almost exclusively occupied in writing and rewriting *The Voyage Out*, the completed manuscript of which she was to deliver to Duckworth & Co. in March 1913.)

The Woolfs lived first in rooms at Clifford's Inn in London and then in October 1914 removed to Richmond. There they remained, until the following March, amid extraordinary domestic turmoil at 17 The Green ('this House of Trouble'[6]), a number of Belgian refugees, compatriots of Mrs Le Grys, the landlady, among their fellow lodgers. From the diary Virginia Woolf briefly kept in January–February 1915, we may catch sight of the Woolfs in the interlude between the nightmare periods of her derangement: '. . . the evenings reading by the fire . . . reading Michelet & The Idiot & smoking & talking to L. in what stands for slippers & dressing gown',[7] the days spent 'scribbling',[8] reading, walking, attending concerts, house-hunting, going to the 'picture palace'[9] and the music hall, visiting libraries, seeing friends and in-laws, discussing the war, declaring oneself a Fabian.[10] Leonard Woolf wrote reviews for the *New Statesman*, *New Weekly*, *Co-operative News* and the *TLS*, lectured on co-operation and international subjects, worked at his highly influential book on *International Government* (1916) and at *Co-operation and the Future of Industry* (1919), a work begun in 1914. (In which year was published his second, and last, novel *The Wise Virgins* – 'very bad in parts; first rate in others'.)[11]

By March 1915 Virginia Woolf's condition was desperate. She seemed altogether to have lost her balance of mind. The Woolfs that month acquired Hogarth House, in Richmond, and Leonard took possession of it on the 25th. On the 26th *The Voyage Out* was published and in general the reviewers, discerning its distinction, received it with enthusiasm. But it was to be a long time before its author could fully appreciate her success. Not until the end of the year can she really be said to have emerged from her ordeal. Her association with the *TLS* recommenced in January 1916 with the appearance of her first review ('Queen Adelaide') in that journal, or, as far as we know, in any other journal, since she had reviewed *Les Copains* by Jules Romains in August 1913. By the end of 1916, as Quentin Bell has said, the Woolfs had 'evolved a pattern of life at Hogarth House to which they adhered more or less all their lives. They wrote in the morning, they walked in the afternoon, they read in the evening . . . once or twice a week Virginia would accompany Leonard to London and visit libraries, shops, concerts or friends'.[12] To this it should be added that they also divided their time between town and country (again, part of a lifelong pattern), migrating from Richmond periodically to stay in Sussex, at Asheham House, which Virginia had rented since before her marriage.

In April 1917 the Woolfs obtained a printing press and in July issued their first publication, *Two Stories*. This contained 'The Mark on the Wall' by Virginia Woolf and Leonard Woolf's 'Three Jews', and four woodcuts by Dora Carrington. They found the fascination of printing 'something extreme'[13] and at moments it seemed the press would completely take over their lives. But it did not quite do that. A year was to pass before the appearance of their second listed publication: *Prelude* by Katherine Mansfield. (They had also issued for private circulation, in about May or June 1918, *Poems* by Cecil Woolf, Leonard's brother, who had been killed in November 1917.) In the meantime, Virginia Woolf worked at her second novel, *Night and Day* (1919), which she had first conceived in July 1916. She also wrote a great amount of journalism, almost all for the *TLS*. (In the period covered by this volume only one of her articles appeared elsewhere, and that, 'Heard on the Downs', was published in *The Times* itself, 15 August 1916.) She was in great demand. Hardly had she time to declare herself 'rejected' by the *TLS*, than she must turn round and announce the revocation of her dismissal.[14] On occasion the *TLS* would 'shower'[15] her with books, and there is no doubt but that she thoroughly enjoyed it:

When I have to review at command of a telegram, & Mr Geal has to ride off in a shower to fetch the book at Glynde [a mile or so from Asheham House], & comes & taps at the window about 10 at night to receive his shilling & hand in the parcel, I feel pressed & important & even excited a little.[16]

She might receive '2 or even 3 books weekly':

& thus breast one short choppy wave after another. It fills up the time while Night & Day lies dormant; it gives me distinct pleasure I own to formulate rapid views of Henry James & Mr Hergesheimer; chiefly because I slip in some ancient crank of mine.[17]

And again we may see how by now she flourished, as she had not quite always done earlier in her career, when driven by the spur of the newspaper deadline:

... this sort of writing is always done against time; however much time I may have
... I write & write; I am rung up & told to stop writing till the messenger from the
Times appears; I correct the pages in my bedroom with him sitting over the fire here.

'A Christmas number not at all to Mr [Bruce] Richmond [Editor to the *TLS*]'s
taste, he said. Very unlike the supplement style.'

'Gift books, I suppose?' I suggested.

'Oh no. Mrs Woolf, its [sic] for the advertisers.'[18]

If Virginia's mental illness overshadowed the Woolfs' lives for a great part of the period spanned by this volume, their lives were also darkened by another lunacy: the war.

The war, and in particular the introduction of conscription in the spring of 1916, brought certain members of Bloomsbury into the public arena. Clive Bell, for one, knew his mind on the issue sooner than most of his friends. In 1915 he voiced his opposition to the confrontation in a pamphlet, calling for *Peace at Once*, a publication destroyed by order of the authorities. Maynard Keynes, although now a Treasury official actively engaged in organising war finance, became involved in the affairs of the No-Conscription Fellowship, as more directly did Virginia's brother Adrian Stephen, giving evidence on behalf of friends who had, as Conscientious Objectors, to appear before the Military and Appeal Tribunals. The 'private nightmare' of Virginia's illness prevented Leonard Woolf from considering, for some time, his own 'personal relation' to the war.[19] But when he did consider it, although convinced that the war was 'senseless and useless', he found that he could not be 'a complete pacifist'.[20] He was, however, exempted from military service, in June 1916, and again in October 1917. (He suffered from a congenital tremor of the hands.)

To Virginia Woolf the war was, artistically and otherwise, a subject almost unspeakable. She felt, as far as fiction was concerned, 'that the vast events now shaping across the channel are towering over us too closely and too tremendously to be worked [in] without a painful jolt in the perspective'[21] (and even in her later novels she treated it obliquely). She reported these and other events that brought the war closer to home, cursorily, in her diary. There she recorded incidents: casualties, ships sunk, air raids, the progress (or otherwise) at the Front. Patriotism she held to be, if not the last refuge of a scoundrel, a 'base emotion'.[22] On hearing the national anthem and a hymn at a Queen's Hall concert in 1915, all she could feel was 'the entire absence of emotion in myself & everyone else'.[23] For the non-participant, at least, life went on, and the inhumanity of war itself passed so far beyond common reality as to seem impossible to relate to. (Upon this point see the distinctly odd piece of writing 'Heard on the Downs'.) Relating to the war was perhaps especially difficult for one whose mental equilibrium had recently proved to be so disastrously unstable under even the most pacific external conditions.

The war, to propagate itself, also made away with the most ordinary kinds of truth. The 'peculiar irony' of Rupert Brooke's 'canonisation'[24] was for Virginia Woolf a supreme, personal example of this process. She remarked upon it when concluding her review ('The New Crusade', *TLS*, 27 December 1917) of John Drinkwater's *Prose Papers*. In this book Drinkwater had written on Brooke (who had died on active service in the Aegean in 1915), and, in recalling 'that volatile, irreverant, and extremely vivacious spirit before the romantic public took possession of his fame',[25] earned her gratitude. (She had known Brooke as a child on holiday at St Ives and in later years they were to enjoy a period of intimate acquaintance and to have many friends in common.) If she appreciated Drinkwater's account of Brooke, she failed to feel the same some eight months later about that by Edward Marsh. His memoir published with Brooke's *Collected Poems* she dismissed in the privacy of her diary as 'a disgraceful sloppy sentimental rhapsody'.[26] In the *TLS* ('Rupert Brooke', 8 August 1918), she necessarily tempered her feelings and, in her own words, 'trod out my 2 columns as decorously as possible'.[27] She agreed with the prefatory observations of the poet's mother that, as the work of someone not at all of Brooke's generation, Marsh's memoir was inevitably incomplete. His was more the Brooke of halcyon legend, who had 'died in the glory of public gratitude'.[28] Of Brooke's charming, ebullient, but also strangely flawed character, Virginia Woolf knew far more than she could begin to state in public. Her article, more an *éloge* than a review, nonetheless sought to provide, from her 'tantalising fund of memories',[29] a rounder picture of the man. She mentions the war directly only once, in asserting the inevitability of his prompt enlistment. On the subject of his famous war sonnets she is silent. (For other writings related to the war and its literature, see also 'A Cambridge V.A.D.', 'Two Irish Poets', 'War in the Village'.)

This is the period when, although engaged in writing the very traditional *Night and Day* (the likes of which Katherine Mansfield was to protest 'we had not thought to look upon ... again'),[30] Virginia Woolf was evolving, with gathering momentum, her modernist aesthetic. It is interesting to observe how, in speculating about Brooke, had he lived to fulfil his promise, she fancied that 'he would in the end have framed a speech that came very close to the modern point of view – a subtle analytic poetry, or prose perhaps, full of intellect, and full of his keen unsentimental curiosity'.[31]

She had already engaged in speculations as to the future promise of Siegfried Sassoon's poetry ('Mr Sassoon's Poems', *TLS*, 31 May 1917; see also the more muted appreciation in 'Two Soldier-Poets', *TLS*, 11 July 1918). But she also saw, immediately, how Sassoon had struck the authentic note in his war poems. Here she discerned 'realism of the right, of the poetic kind', saw how 'Yes, this [war] is going on; and we are sitting here watching it', and did so 'with a new shock of surprise, with an uneasy desire to leave [her] place in the audience . . .'[32] Her preoccupations in this article and some of her expressions (among them: 'moments of vision', 'shocks of emotion', 'moments of emotion') are those of her mature criticism. 'As it is the poet's gift', she begins, 'to give expression to the moments of insight and experience that come to him now and then, so in following him we have to sketch for ourselves a map of those submerged lands which lie between one pinnacle and the next'.[33] The language here, of 'moments' and concealed transitions, is concerned with what she refers to elsewhere as the artist's 'power to omit'.[34] It is also about the directness of vision which makes us unable to think of Sassoon 'putting down [his] thoughts in any form save the one he has chosen'.[35] To very few recent and still fewer contemporary English writers was she prepared to grant such accomplishment. (The most important native exception is Thomas Hardy, from whose poem and volume of poems – published in 1917 – the phrase 'moments of vision' derives. But she does not write on Hardy here. Samuel Butler is another significant exception – see 'A Man With a View'.)

Only to the Russians did she turn with similar applause to that bestowed upon Sassoon. The Russians were now, in an expression she applies to Dostoevsky ('More Dostoevsky', *TLS*, 22 February 1917), beginning to 'permeate'[36] the lives of English readers, above all in the steady stream of translations from Constance Garnett's pen. There was 'even something humiliating'[37] in the experience. The English nineteenth-century novel especially paled beside the Russian classics. They seemed to reduce such a writer as George Meredith ('On Re-reading Meredith', *TLS*, 25 July 1918) to the status of 'an insular hero bred and cherished for the delight of connoisseurs in some sheltered corner of a Victorian hothouse'.[38] But it was not just the Victorians. It was felt to be an open question whether any English novel could 'survive in the furnace of that overpowering sincerity'[39] of the Russians.

The Russian example had a profound influence upon the formulation of her later fictional method. We see this clearly in 'On Re-reading Meredith', and also in 'More Dostoevsky'. The latter, predating the piece on Sassoon by some three months, uses the same kind of critical language we find in the later article, only more extensively and in relation to fiction:

... if we try to construct our mental processes later [having stopped reading], we find that the links between one thought and another are submerged. The chain is sunk out of sight and only the leading points emerge to mark the course. Alone among writers Dostoevsky has the power of reconstructing these most swift and complicated states of mind, of rethinking the whole train of thought in all its speed, now as it flashes into light, now as it lapses into darkness; for he is able to follow not only the vivid streak of achieved thought, but to suggest the dim and populous underworld of the mind's consciousness where desires and impulses are moving blindly beneath the sod.[40]

We may be prompted by this to remember the tunnelling process Virginia Woolf described in writing about her approach to *Mrs Dalloway* (1925), at a time when 'the old post-Dostoevsky argument'[41] was very much in her mind. She was prompted to reflect upon the English and the method of 'most of our novelists' who 'reproduce all the external appearance – tricks of manner, landscape, dress, and the effect of the hero upon his friends – but very rarely, and only for an instant, penetrate to the tumult of thought which rages within his own mind'.[42] Such criticism, echoed in 'On Re-reading Meredith', recalls her later famous attack on Arnold Bennett and the 'Edwardians' in 'Character in Fiction' (*III VW Essays*) – which is more genially anticipated here in 'Books and Persons'.

Virginia Woolf took a more comprehensive view of the Russians than is represented by the classics – Tolstoy, Dostoevsky, Chekhov, Aksakoff (see 'Tolstoy's *The Cossacks*', 'More Dostoevsky', 'A Minor Dostoevsky', '*A Russian Schoolboy*', 'Tchehov's Questions'; and see also 'Mr Hudson's Childhood'). Of course to a large extent a reviewer's reading is determined by fashion and contingency, but Virginia Woolf was always keenly interested in uncanonised authors (contemporary or otherwise), and sought to see her literature, whether English, French, Russian or Greek, as a whole. A quotation for which she gives no source, in '*A*

Russian Schoolboy', reveals that she read, or used, Prince Kropotkin's survey of *Russian Literature* – a kind of literary guide – which Duckworth & Co. published in 1905. Her *Common Reader* essay 'The Russian Point of View' (*IV VW Essays*) derives in part from her review of *The Village Priest and Other Stories* by Elena Militsina and Mikhail Saltikov (see 'The Russian View'), the former a figure of considerable obscurity, the latter a relatively minor author and editor.

She first conceived her plan for *The Common Reader* (1st series: 1925) in 1921, its provisional title being 'Reading' or 'Reading & Writing'. The articles she drew upon directly in creating that book belong chiefly to the period 1919–24 (see *III VW Essays*). The two exceptions in this volume are 'The Russian View', already remarked upon, and 'Charlotte Brontë' (*TLS*, 13 April 1916), part of which is included in the essay '*Jane Eyre* and *Wuthering Heights*'. If the remainder of her articles here do not themselves surface in *The Common Reader*, a great many of them relate closely, in subject and argument, to the essays in both series of that work, and hence to Virginia Woolf's abiding literary interests. The essay 'Hours in a Library' (*TLS*, 30 November 1916), with its reader's-eye and exploratory view of literature, its emphasis upon 'pure and disinterested reading',[43] upon 'how it strikes a contemporary',[44] may be taken as a kind of condensed prototype for the later *Common Reader* volumes. The *Common Reader* essay 'How It Strikes a Contemporary' itself is again recalled in 'Mr Howells on Form' (*TLS*, 14 November 1918), not least in the review's deferential reference to the coming 'great critic'.[45] Here Virginia Woolf, ostensibly reviewing a novel by her contemporary Leonard Merrick (see also 'Mr Merrick's Novels'), uses the book's introduction by W. D. Howells as a springboard for an extended flight upon the subject of form, the problems and value of contemporary criticism, and the important historical function the reader may perform by continuing 'to frame tentative outlines of belief'.[46]

Among the contemporaries upon whom she writes, formulating her 'rapid views',[47] in this volume are: Gilbert Cannan ('*Mummery*'); Joseph Conrad ('*Lord Jim*'; 'Mr Conrad's "Youth" ', 'Mr Conrad's Crisis', all in a sense groundwork for her *Common Reader* essay 'Joseph Conrad'); John Galsworthy ('Mr Galsworthy's Novel'); Joseph Hergesheimer ('*The Three Black Pennys*'); L. P. Jacks ('Philosophy in Fiction'); Compton Mackenzie ('The "Movie" Novel'); Viola Meynell ('*Second Marriage*'); Elinor Mordaunt ('*The Park Wall*', '*Before Midnight*');

Frank Swinnerton ('Honest Fiction'); H. G. Wells ('The Rights of Youth', a review of *Joan and Peter* in which there occurs what proves to be an interesting 'Edwardian' diversion on Post-Impressionism and the Omega Workshops – see also 'Books and Persons'). 'Women Novelists', an account of a contemporary work of criticism, is additionally interesting in being germane to *The Common Reader*.

About as far away from the contemporary as, literary-historically, it is possible to be, we have Virginia Woolf's devotion to the 'peculiar magic'[48] of the Greeks. The *Common Reader* article 'On Not Knowing Greek' is obviously anticipated here in 'The Perfect Language' (*TLS*, 24 May 1917). In this piece she takes an almost Platonic view of Greek as the perfect linguistic form, 'the type of literature . . . the supreme example of what can be done with words'.[49] It is clearly an important essay, especially for readers interested in her aestheticism, and has not previously been collected.

Her similarly enduring interest in Richard Hakluyt's writings, and in the contents of 'The Elizabethan Lumber Room'[50] in general, is evidenced in 'Trafficks and Discoveries', as it was by the article of the same title in *I VW Essays*. Hakluyt turned out 'on mature inspection', as she observed in her diary on 7 December 1918, 'to justify over & over again my youthful discrimination'. She delighted in the 'great wealth of good reading' he provided, reciprocating in her own more utilitarian prose the 'sense of wonder unexhausted' of the Elizabethans.[51] Both her Elizabethan and wider historical curiosity may also be traced in '*The House of Lyme*' – *TLS*, 29 March 1917 – wherein she places something approaching a Yeatsean value on the 'great house' and its tradition, in time of war and strife. (See also '*Sir Walter Raleigh*'.)

Such an account as this, while drawing out certain unifying strands in her journalistic output, can only begin to suggest the diversity and range of the pieces in this volume or the speed with which she must have read and written to produce them. (Consider as a further indicator of her industry the joint occurrence in the *TLS*, 21 December 1916, of '*Social Life in England*' and 'Mr Symons's Essays'; in the *TLS*, 12 April 1917, of 'A Talker' and '*In Good Company*'; in the *TLS*, 10 October 1918, of 'Adventurers All' and 'Honest Fiction'.) There are, in addition to the pieces already mentioned, important essays here on a number of Americans: Edgar Allan Poe ('*Poe's Helen*'), Henry David Thoreau ('Thoreau'), Walt Whitman ('Visits to Walt Whitman'), and Henry James ('*The Method of Henry James*').

Most of the articles were produced in intervals while *Night and Day* lay dormant. Their vivacity is nonetheless undiluted. Perhaps we should expect nothing less from one who saw that 'Whether you are writing a review or a love letter the great thing is to be confronted with a very vivid idea of your subject'.[52] Her ideas are invariably vivid, and her memorable expressions abound: 'So queer and topsy-turvy is the atmosphere of these little stories that one feels . . . much as if one had been trying to walk over the bridge in a willow pattern plate' ('Chinese Stories'); 'to be always in love and always a governess is to go through the world with blinkers on one's eyes' ('Charlotte Brontë'); 'But, after reading . . . [*The Way of All Flesh*], we hardly dare inspect some of the masterpieces of English fiction; it would be as unkind as to let in the cold light of day upon a dowager in a ball dress' ('A Man With a View'); 'one native frog is of more importance than a whole grove of sham nightingales' ('A Talker'); 'A branch of learning suggests a withered stick with a few dead leaves attached to it. But Greek is the golden bough; it crowns its lovers with garlands of fresh and sparkling leaves' ('The Perfect Language'); 'when you do not read him he ceases to exist' ('*John Davidson*'); and so on.

By 12 March 1918 Virginia Woolf had written over 100,000 words of *Night and Day*. She completed it in the following November – the month of the Armistice – and it would be published by Duckworth & Co. in October 1919. In that same November The Hogarth Press began printing *Kew Gardens* (published in May 1919), and a start was made to the writing of the story 'Solid Objects' (first published in the *Athenaeum*, 22 October 1920). In 1917 Leonard Woolf had become a member of the editorial board of *War and Peace*, a political journal that evolved to become the *International Review*, of which he was appointed editor in September 1918. At the same time he was engaged in completing *Empire and Commerce in Africa. A Study in Imperialism* (1920). As proprietors of The Hogarth Press, the Woolfs had by now made the acquaintance of Katherine Mansfield, and of T. S. Eliot, whose *Poems* they published in May 1919. In 1918, Harriet Weaver approached them with a request that they consider publishing James Joyce's *Ulysses* (1922) – a task for which their small press was regrettably hardly adequate, even if it had been legally advisable to proceed. They were thus, whether they wished to do so or not, beginning to emerge upon the metropolitan cultural scene.

Elsewhere and earlier in Bloomsbury, the Second Post-Impressionist

Exhibition, with Leonard Woolf its secretary, had been organised by Roger Fry in October–December 1912. In the following July, the Omega Workshops opened at 33 Fitzroy Square. Clive Bell's book *Art*, in which he expounded the doctrine of 'significant form', was published in 1914; in May 1918 appeared a collection of his journalism, *Potboilers*. Vanessa Bell and Duncan Grant took up residence in 1916 at Charleston, a farmhouse under the Downs near the village of Firle, in Sussex, and there continued their lifelong collaboration as decorative artists. In 1918 was published Desmond MacCarthy's *Remnants*, a volume of journalism, and, far more momentously, Lytton Strachey's *Eminent Victorians* (both authors sought to have Virginia Woolf review their books in the *TLS*, but, for a variety of reasons, she did not do so).

The next decade would see a marked proliferation in the books and artefacts to come from the hands of Bloomsbury. Maynard Keynes would appear upon the literary and political stage. But no one in that illustrious group of friends stood, in relation to his or her life, quite as did Virginia Woolf at the close of 1918, upon the brink of the richest era in her authorial career.

1 –*The Complete Shorter Fiction of Virginia Woolf* (Hogarth Press, 1985), ed. Susan Dick.
2 – *I VW Letters*, no. 628, to Madge Vaughan, June 1912.
3 – *Ibid.*
4 – *Ibid.*
5 – *Ibid.*
6 – *I VW Diary*, 22 January 1915.
7 – *Ibid.*, 6 January 1915
8 – *Ibid.*, 2 January 1915.
9 – *Ibid.*, 25 January 1915.
10 – *Ibid.*, 23 January 1915.
11 – *Ibid.*, 31 January 1915.
12 – *II QB*, ch. ii, p. 35.
13 – *II VW Letters*, no. 840, to Vanessa Bell, 8 June 1917.
14 – *I VW Diary*, 12 and 14 March 1918.
15 – *Ibid.*, 23 September 1918.
16 – *Ibid.*
17 – *Ibid.*, 7 December 1918.
18 – *Ibid.*
19 – *II LW*, ch. iii, p. 127.
20 – *Ibid.*
21 – '*Before Midnight*', p. 87.
22 – *I VW Diary*, 3 January 1915.

23 – *Ibid.*
24 – 'The New Crusade', p. 203.
25 – *Ibid.*
26 – *I VW Diary*, 23 July 1918.
27 – *II VW Letters*, no. 959, to Katherine Cox, 13 August 1918.
28 – 'Rupert Brooke', p. 278.
29 – *Ibid.*
30 – *Athenaeum*, 21 November 1919.
31 – 'Rupert Brooke', p. 281.
32 – 'Mr Sassoon's Poems', p. 120.
33 – *Ibid.*, p. 119.
34 – 'Mr Howells on Form' p. 324.
35 – 'Mr Sassoon's Poems', p. 119.
36 – 'More Dostoevsky', p. 83.
37 – 'Tolstoy's *The Cossacks*', p. 77
38 – 'On Re-reading Meredith', p. 273
39 – *Ibid.*
40 – 'More Dostoevsky', p. 85.
41 – *II VW Diary*, 19 June 1923.
42 – 'More Dostoevsky', p. 85.
43 – 'Hours in a Library', p. 55.
44 – The title of the last essay in CR1.
45 – 'Mr Howells on Form', p. 324; and CR1, 'How It Strikes a Contemporary', pp. 232–5.
46 – 'Mr Howells on Form', p. 324.
47 – *I VW Diary*, 7 December 1918.
48 – 'The Perfect Language', p. 116.
49 – *Ibid.*, p. 118.
50 – The title of the third essay in CR1.
51 – Appendix I, 'Reading Notes', p. 357, and p. 358.
52 – 'Poe's *Helen*' p. 104.

Editorial Note

The first article in this volume, '*Frances Willard*', was published in the *Times Literary Supplement* on 28 November 1912, and is the earliest piece of journalism Virginia Woolf is known to have published following her marriage in the previous August (Volume I of these essays spanning the years 1904–1912 contains all of the articles up to her marriage). The final article in this volume, '*The Method of Henry James*', appeared in the *TLS*, 26 December 1918. In all, 98 articles are reprinted here, in chronological order, each, with the exception of 'Heard on the Downs' (*The Times*, 15 August 1916), from the pages of the *TLS*. Of these, 58 have not been collected before.

Annotations and other editorial interventions have been effected upon the same principles as those outlined in the Editorial Note to Volume I.

Two sets of Virginia Woolf's reading notes, relating to her essays 'Coleridge as Critic' and 'Trafficks and Discoveries' – the only such notes known to have survived from this period – have been transcribed from manuscripts in the Berg Collection, New York Public Library, and the Monks House Papers, Sussex University Library, and are reproduced in Appendix I.

Acknowledgements

I remain especially indebted to the directors of The Hogarth Press and to Professor Quentin Bell and Angelica Garnett, administrators of Virginia Woolf's Literary Estate, for retaining me to prepare this edition, and to the Leverhulme Trustees for the renewal of their original Research Grant. For her stalwart support throughout and for sharing in a large part of the reading required to annotate the essays, I owe a very great debt of gratitude to my wife, Diana McNeillie. I am also very grateful to Nicola Edwards, who, for no reward but the work itself has undertaken an immense amount of reading and researching for this volume. Christine Carswell of The Hogarth Press has again curbed my excesses, with great rigour and tact, for which I wish to thank her. I must also thank, once more, Professor S. P. Rosenbaum, for reading my introduction in its original draft, and for innumerable facts, words of advice, and other kindnesses conducive to the volume's completion. In addition, I wish to acknowledge the help and support of Professor Elizabeth Steele, Professor Quentin Bell, Anne Olivier Bell, Elizabeth Inglis, and of Colin Masters, Director and Secretary of the Thomas Coram Foundation for Children. I remain indebted to London University's Librarian and to the staff of the Library's periodicals department.

For permission to publish the material in Appendix I, I have to thank Professor Quentin Bell and Angelica Garnett, Sussex University Library, and the Henry W. and Albert A. Berg Collection, the New York Public Library, Astor, Lenox and Tilden Foundations.

Abbreviations

B&P	*Books and Portraits*, ed. Mary Lyon (Hogarth Press, London, 1977; Harcourt Brace Jovanovich, New York, 1978)
CE	*Collected Essays*, 4 vols ed. Leonard Woolf (vols 1–2, Hogarth Press, London, 1966, Harcourt Brace & World Inc., New York, 1967; vols 3–4, Hogarth Press, London, and Harcourt Brace & World Inc., New York, 1967)
CR	*The Common Reader*: 1st series (Hogarth Press, London, and Harcourt Brace & Co., New York, 1925; annotated edition, 1984) 2nd series (Hogarth Press, London, and Harcourt, Brace & Co., New York, 1932; annotated edition, 1986)
CW	*Contemporary Writers*, with a Preface by Jean Guiget (Hogarth Press, London, 1965; Harcourt Brace & World Inc., New York, 1966)
DNB	*Dictionary of National Biography*
DoM	*The Death of the Moth and Other Essays*, ed. Leonard Woolf (Hogarth Press, London, and Harcourt Brace & Co., New York, 1942)
G&R	*Granite and Rainbow,* ed. Leonard Woolf (Hogarth Press, London, and Harcourt Brace & Co., New York, 1958)
Kp	B. J. Kirkpatrick, *A Bibliography of Virginia Woolf* (third ed., Oxford University Press, Oxford, 1980)
LW	Leonard Woolf, *An Autobiography,* 2 vols (Oxford University Press, Oxford, 1980)
MoB	Virginia Woolf, *Moments of Being*, ed. Jeanne Schulkind

(2nd ed., Hogarth Press, London, 1985; Harcourt Brace Jovanovich, New York, 1985)

QB   Quentin Bell, *Virginia Woolf. A Biography. Volume One. Virginia Stephen, 1882–1912. Volume Two. Mrs Woolf, 1912–1941.* (Hogarth Press, London, and Harcourt Brace Jovanovich Inc., New York, 1972)

TLS   *Times Literary Supplement*

VW Diary   *The Diary of Virgina Woolf*, ed. Anne Olivier Bell (5 vols. Hogarth Press, London, and Harcourt Brace Jovanovich, New York, 1977–84)

VW Essays   *The Essays of Virginia Woolf*, 6 vols

VW Letters   *The Letters of Virginia Woolf*, ed. Nigel Nicolson (6 vols, Hogarth Press, London, and Harcourt Brace Jovanovich, New York, 1975–80)

W&W   *Women & Writing*, ed. Michèle Barrett (Women's Press, London, 1979; Harcourt Brace Jovanovich, New York, 1980)

The Essays of
Virginia Woolf

The Essays

1912

'Frances Willard'

The great merits of Mrs Strachey's life of Miss Willard,[2] its directness and candour and complete lack of padding, produce a very interesting picture of the famous philanthropist. They make one ask questions about her and her life which the ordinary biographer usually contrives to stifle, because his subject is dead. To begin with, Miss Willard was once young and very imperfect. Brought up in the West when the West was an untamed land, she loved shooting, climbing trees, and would rather saddle a cow than not ride at all; she hated housework, and had a passion for horse-racing. Very vivid is the account of their life in the middle of the last century at Janesville:

We see the hard work of the farm; the fencing and ploughing, the cutting of trees and rearing of cattle, the growing of the precious crops, and all the daily difficulties; how the house was banked up for fear of the winter hurricanes, and how the prairie fires were fought with fire; how the hogs escaped down the road, the gophers ate up the corn, and the rats got among the potatoes; how the apple trees died and the oxen were lost, and the milk froze in the churn by the fire and the blue-jays were caught in the quail traps.[3]

In those days she was no more interested in temperance than clever girls usually are. Her own culture was the object of her greatest enthusiasm. Although she loved her home, she insisted upon getting away from it to make experiments and have experiences of her own. Because the man[4] she loved and was to marry proved also a prig, though a worthy one, she broke off her engagement and lived the rest of her life independently. She

3

was, in short, a delightful and spirited American girl, and Mrs Strachey has surely done well to concentrate upon this period of her life and to devote less space to the years of immense success and celebrity. For Miss Willard did not remain, as she had become, a great schoolmistress.[5] The merest accident, a heavy fall of snow, induced a certain Dr Dio Lewis, who was lecturing about the country in 1873, to stay over the night and deliver another lecture upon temperance. It started a crusade which 'spread with the violence of a prairie fire'.[6] Women were the crusaders.

It must have been very strange ⟨writes Mrs Strachey⟩ to see the lines of women marching out from the churches into the snowy streets, singing their gentle hymns to warlike tunes, and strange to watch them halt before the saloons to kneel on the pavement to weep and 'pray for the soul of the proprietor that he might see the error of his ways'. And it must have been stranger still when these proprietors surrendered and rolled out their barrels into the streets to pour the 'poison' into the gutter, confessing their sins with tears, while the church bells rang, and the women wept for joy, and the roughs scooped up the rum-soaked snow and cursed the praying women.[7]

But the strangest thing of all was that Miss Willard gave up the profession which she loved to kneel upon the floors of public houses, too. She formed the women into a society, with herself for their leader. The story of the growth of that society is told briefly and competently by Mrs Strachey. Beginning with two or three women in a dingy little office, it spread over America, reached to England, rose in distant countries, India, China, Japan, culminating in a world society, with 'Do Everything'[8] for its motto, and world conventions with Miss Willard at their head. It is a wonderful story, and yet this part of the book is the least vivid. When one begins dealing with figures one is apt to be paralysed by them. Three hundred and sixty-five meetings a year – ten thousand letters – those facts are so startling that we forget to ask, What were they about? It is strange how little we know what Miss Willard believed, how vague her own creed was. Perhaps it is summed up as well in the message that her sister left her when she died as in other words: 'Tell everybody to be good.'[9] Miss Willard spent the best years of her life in doing that; in telling them, that is, not to drink, to be pure, to love each other, to enfranchise women, to help the poor. There is nothing very profound in that teaching, but consider the scale on which she did it. In 1881 she sent out ten thousand letters; 'forty different branches of work were carried on'; 'she averaged 365 meetings and many thousand miles of travel every year';[10] thirty million pages of literature were issued yearly from her office. So prolific was she that she put together 650,000 words of autobiography in three weeks.[11] It is all very American, but it is also very philanthropic. The modern philanthropist must also be an amazingly efficient machine. The reason is not far to seek. Their mission is not to create new ideas – Johnson, Shelley, Rousseau were not philanthropists – but to popularise, to make people practise as far as practicable the ideas of others, old ideas for the most part, ideas that have become rather dull and rather vague to most people. Of course their books, as Mrs Strachey says that Miss Willard knew her own to be, are 'horrible'.[12] Could they fulfil their mission if they were not? You must have bold phrases to slip in under people's doors, to force into their hands, to bawl into their faces. They must be phrases, too, about the most private of emotions. You must be ready to share all with crowds in the streets. Thus Miss Willard, when she heard of the death of her only brother, went to her meeting, told the audience 'all about it, and they cried together, praying, and talking of the heavenly life'.[13]

She shared everything; she died of sharing things, worn out, and glad to die long before she was an old woman. And the result? The result is as difficult to estimate as the number of letters she wrote is easy, for what things make people good, and what being good consists in are questions not easy to answer. Only no one who has read Mrs Strachey's book can doubt that Miss Willard was one of those rare beings, true, single-minded and courageous, above all of immeasurable powers of love, who may be said to be good, and therefore to do good whether we hold that telling people to be good on any possible scale of vastness is valuable or merely a kind of friction on the surface.

1 – A review in the *TLS*, 28 November 1912, (Kp C49) of *Frances Willard. Her Life and Work. With an introduction by Lady Henry Somerset. And eight illustrations* (Fisher Unwin, 1912) by Ray Strachey.
2 – Ray (Rachel Conn) Strachey, *née* Costelloe (1887–1940), pioneering feminist, married Oliver Strachey – an older brother of Lytton – in 1911. (Her sister Karin married VW's brother Adrian Stephen three years later.) Frances Willard (1839–98) was from 1879 president of the Women's Christian Temperance Union, which she had helped to found in 1874.
Lady Henry Somerset (1851–1921), who introduces the biography, was a daughter of Virginia Pattle, and so a relation of VW. Her friendship with Frances Willard, discussed in ch. xi, began when the two women met in Boston in 1891.
3 – Strachey, ch. i, p. 6, which has: 'the farm, the fencing', and 'and blue-jays'. The Willard family settled to farm on the banks of the Rock River in Wisconsin, near the then village of Janesville, in 1847.

4 – Rev. Charles H. Fowler (1837–1908), Methodist bishop, president of North-western University, 1873–6; see also next note.

5 – Frances Willard was president of Evanston College for Ladies when, in 1873, it became part of Northwestern University. She resigned from her new post as dean of women and professor of aesthetics in the following year, having been outman-oeuvred in a struggle for authority by the Rev. Fowler.

6 – Strachey, ch. VII, p. 173; Dr Dio (Dioclesian) Lewis (1823–86), author of *New Gymnastics* (1862) who from 1871 campaigned in aid of the Women's Christian Temperance Union.

7 – *Ibid.*, p. 177, which has: 'warlike tunes; and strange to watch', and ' "praying women"'.

8 – *Ibid.*, ch. IX, p. 211.

9 – *Ibid.*, ch. III, p. 108; Mary Willard died of consumption in 1862.

10 – For these two quotations, *ibid.*, ch. X, p. 252, and ch. IX, p. 228.

11 – *Glimpses of Fifty Years* (1889).

12 – Strachey, ch. III, p. 113.

13 – *Ibid.*, ch. VIII, pp. 206–7; Oliver Willard died in 1878.

1913

Chinese Stories

According to Mr George Soulié, the translator of these stories, we seriously mistake the nature of the ordinary Chinaman if we imagine him any more exclusively occupied with the great classics of his literature than we are with ours. If we see him with a book in his hand it is likely to be 'a novel like the *History of the Three Kingdoms* or a selection of ghost stories'.[2] Like us they have a hunger for novels and stories, which they read over and over again, so that, although in the West nothing is known about it, the influence of such light literature upon the Chinese mind 'is much greater than the whole bulk of the classics'.[3] They may resemble us in their craving for something lighter, nearer to the life they know than the old and famous books, but in all else how different they are! The twenty-five stories in *Strange Stories from the Lodge of Leisure*, translated from the Chinese by George Soulié, were written in the second half of the eighteenth century by P'ou Song-Lin, at a time, that is, when with Fielding and Richardson[4] our fiction was becoming increasingly robust and realistic. To give any idea of the slightness and queerness of these stories one must compare them to dreams, or the airy, fantastic, and inconsequent flight of a butterfly. They skim from world to world, from life to death. The people they describe may kill each other and die, but we cannot believe either in their blood or in their dissolution. The barriers against which we in the West beat our hands in vain are for them almost as transparent as glass.

Some people ⟨one of the stories begins⟩ remember every incident of their former existences; it is a fact which many examples can prove. Other people do not forget what they learned before they died and were born again, but remember only confusedly what they were in a precedent life. Wang, the acceptable of the yellow peach-blossom city, when people discussed such questions before him used to narrate the experience he had had with his first son.[5]

And the story which occupies three little pages tells how a boy had once been born a student, then a donkey, and then a boy again. Very often these stories are like the stories a child will tell of a sight which has touched its imagination for no reason that we can discover, lacking in point where we expect the point to come, suddenly breaking off and done with, but somehow memorable. Or it may be they are extravagantly sensational, or of the nature of fairy stories, where all is miraculously set right in the end, or again purposeless and callous as a child's stories, the good man being killed merely to make an end. But they all alike have a quality of fantasy and spirituality which sometimes, as in 'The Spirit of the River' or 'The River of Sorrows',[6] becomes of real beauty, and is greatly enhanced by the unfamiliar surroundings and exquisite dress. Take, for example, the following description of a Chinese ghost:

He went farther and farther: the moving lights were rarer; ere long he only saw before him the fire of a white lantern decorated with two red peonies. The paper globe was swinging to the steps of a tiny girl clothed in the blue linen that only slaves wore. The light behind showed the elegant silhouette of another woman, this one covered with a long jacket made in a rich pink silk edged with purple. As the student drew nearer the belated walker turned round, showing an oval face and big long eyes wherein shone a bright speck cruel and mysterious.[7]

So queer and topsy-turvy is the atmosphere of these little stories that one feels, when one has read a number of them, much as if one had been trying to walk over the bridge in a willow pattern plate.

1 – A review in the *TLS*, 1 May 1913, (Kp C49.1) of *Strange Stories from the Lodge of Leisures. Translated from the Chinese by George Soulié of the French Consular Service in China* (Constable & Co. Ltd, 1913).
2 – Soulié, Pref., p. v; *The History of the Three Kingdoms* or *San Kuo Chih yen-i*, an adventurous novel of the thirteenth century, set in the period 220–65, following the collapse of the Han dynasty.
3 – *Ibid.*, p. vi, which has: 'These works . . . have on the Chinese mind an influence much greater . . .'
4 – P'ou Song-Lin or P'u Sung-ling (1640–1715), whose stories and legends,

originally entitled *Liao-chaochih-i* and numbering more than three hundred, are usually attributed to actual localities, sometimes with a basis in fact; an edition of them was first published in 1766. Henry Fielding (1707–54), whose *Tom Jones* appeared in 1749, and Samuel Richardson (1689–1761), whose *Clarissa* was published in 1747–8.

5 – Soulié, 'Through Many Lives', p. 110, which has 'Wang The-acceptable of the Yellow-peach-blossom city, . . .'

6 – *Ibid.*, pp. 114–19; pp. 125–30.

7 – *Ibid.*, 'The Ghost in Love', pp. 2–3.

'Jane Austen'

In many ways Jane Austen must be considered singularly blessed. The manner in which from generation to generation her descendants respect her memory is, we imagine, precisely that which she would have chosen for herself – and she would have been hard to please. In 1870 the *Memoir* by her nephew[2] gave us not only the facts of her life, but reproduced the atmosphere in which that life was lived so instinctively that his book can never be superseded; and now once more the son and grandson of that nephew show themselves possessed to the full of the family taste and modesty. In this final biography, for surely no other will be possible, they have brought together all that is known about Jane Austen, basing their narrative, of course, upon the original memoir but completing it with the letters which appeared in Lord Brabourne's two volumes,[3] and adding certain other letters, traditions, and family histories. By doing so they have given depth and perspective to the figure which we see in our mind's eye; to say that they have told us anything fresh about her would not be true. Miss Cassandra Austen[4] put that effectively beyond their power. To her alone did Jane Austen write freely and impulsively; to her she must have expressed the hopes and, if the rumour is true, the one keen disappointment of her life; but when Miss Cassandra Austen grew old and suspected that a time might come when strangers would be curious about her sister's private affairs, she burnt, at great cost to herself, every letter which could gratify their curiosity. The letters which remain exist simply because she thought that no one, not even the nephews and nieces, would be sufficiently interested in Jane Austen to disturb them. Had she guessed that they would not only be read but published, that many thousands would enjoy the wit and ransack every sentence for revelations, we may be sure that she would have flung them also on to the flames with one sweep of her arm.

This being so, we are aware that it is a confession which is made when we say that we are sufficiently interested in Jane Austen to wish to know everything that it is possible to know about her. We are grateful to little Philadelphia Austen, who describes Jane 'not at all pretty and very prim, unlike a girl of twelve . . . Jane is whimsical and affected';[5] and to old Mrs Mitford, who remembered the Austens as girls and knew Jane as 'the prettiest, silliest, most affected, husband-hunting butterfly she ever remembers',[6] and to Miss Mitford's properly anonymous friend who

visits her now and says that she has stiffened into the most perpendicular, precise, taciturn piece of 'single blessedness' that ever existed, and that, until *Pride and Prejudice* showed what a precious gem was hidden in that unbending case, she was no more regarded in society than a poker or a firescreen . . . The case is very different now; she is still a poker – but a poker of whom everybody is afraid . . . A wit (the good lady exclaims, and we cannot help hoping with more reason than she knew of at the time), a delineator of character, who does not talk, is terrific indeed![7]

Of course these critics are wrong, but it is amusing to see as clearly as we do why they went wrong. Finally we are ready to bless Marianne Knight[8] perpetually for having recalled not very many years ago how 'Aunt Jane would sit very quietly at work beside the fire in the Godmersham library, then suddenly burst out laughing, jump up, cross the room to a distant table with papers lying on it, write something down, returning presently and sitting down quietly to her work again.'[9] Was it then that Mrs Norris gave William 'something considerable', or Lady Bertram had the happy idea of sending Chapman to help Miss Fanny?[10] We are grateful for trifles, in short, for it is by means of such trifles that we draw a little closer to the charm, the brilliance, the strength and sincerity of character that lay behind the novels. For the rest, we cannot grudge Jane and Cassandra the glance of satisfaction which they must cast at each other as after fresh scrutiny of that serene and smiling face we turn away baffled, and they know that their secrets are their own for ever. We need not be surprised that even the jealous Cassandra had no inkling of the curiosity of the generations to come. So lately as 1870 there was only one complete edition of the novels,[11] and the taste for them was a gift that ran in families and was a mark of rather peculiar culture. Today things have changed so far that the present biography is the third work about Jane Austen that has been published in the course of the year.[12] One, by Miss Brinton, takes the original form of continuing the fortunes of the characters and devising marriages between them – a work of great love and great ingenuity which, if taken not as fiction but as talk about Jane Austen's characters, will please that select public which is never tired of discussing them.

But the time has come, surely, when there is no need to bring witnesses to prove Jane Austen's fame. Arrange the great English novelists as one will, it does not seem possible to bring them out in any order where she is not first, or second, or third, whoever her companions may be. Unlike other great writers in almost every way, she is unlike them, too, in the very slow and very steady rise of her reputation: it has been steady because there is probably no novelist of the nineteenth century who requires us to make so little excuse for her, and it has been slow because she has limitations of a kind particularly likely to cramp a writer's popularity. The mere sight of her six neat volumes suggests something of the reason, for when we look at them we do not remember any page or passage which so burnt itself into our minds when we read it first that from time to time we take the book down, read that sentence again, and are again exalted. We doubt whether one of her novels was ever a long toil and stumble to any reader with a splendid view at the end. She was never a revelation to the young, a stern comrade, a brilliant and extravagantly admired friend, a writer whose sentences sang in one's brain and were half absorbed into one's blood. And directly one has set down any of the above phrases one is conscious of the irony with which she would have disclaimed any such wish or intention. We can hear it in the words addressed to the nephew who had lost two chapters of his novel. 'How could I possibly join them on to the little bit (two inches wide) of ivory on which I work with so fine a brush, as produces little effect after much labour?';[13] and again in the famous, 'Let other pens dwell on guilt and misery. I quit such odious subjects as soon as I can.'[14]

But however modest and conscious of her own defects she may be, the defects are there and must be recognised by readers who are as candid as Jane Austen herself would wish them to be. The chief reason why she does not appeal to us as some inferior writers do is that she has too little of the rebel in her composition, too little discontent, and of the vision which is the cause and the reward of discontent. She seems at times to have accepted life too calmly as she found it, and to any one who reads her biography or letters it is plain that life showed her a great deal that was smug, commonplace, and, in a bad sense of the word, artificial. It showed her a world made up of big houses and little houses, of gentry inhabiting them who were keenly conscious of their grades of gentility, while life itself consisted of an interchange of tea parties, picnics, and dances, which eventually, if the connection was respectable and the income on each side satisfactory, led to a thoroughly suitable marriage. It happens very seldom, but still it does happen, that we feel that the play of her spirit has been hampered by such obstacles; that she believes in them as well as laughs at them, and that she is debarred from the most profound insight into human nature by the respect which she pays to some unnatural convention. There are characters such as the characters of Elinor Dashwood[15] and Fanny Price which bore us frankly; there are pages which, though written in excellent English, have to be skipped; and these defects are due to the fact that she is content to take it for granted that such characters and conduct are good without trying to see them in a fresh light for herself.

But the chief damage which this conservative spirit has inflicted on her art is that it tied her hands together when she dealt with men. Her heroes were less the equals of her heroines than should have been the case, making allowance for the fact that so it must always be when a woman writes of men or a man of women. It is where the power of the man has to be conveyed that her novels are always at their weakest; and the heroines themselves lose something of their life because in moments of crisis they have for partners men who are inferior to them in vitality and character. A clergyman's daughter in those days was, no doubt, very carefully brought up, and in no other age, we imagine, were men and women less at their ease together; still, it rests with the novelists to break down the barriers; it is they who should imagine what they cannot know even at the risk of making themselves superbly ridiculous. Miss Austen, however, was so fastidious, so conscious of her own limitations, that when she found out that hedges do not grow in Northamptonshire she eliminated her hedge rather than run the risk of inventing one which could not exist. This is the more annoying because we are inclined to think that she could have run almost all the risks and triumphed. In proof of this we might quote two passages from *Mansfield Park* (the first is quoted by Professor Bradley in his lecture to the English Association),[16] where, forsaking her usual method, she suddenly hazards herself in a strange new atmosphere and breathes into her work a spirit of beauty and romance. Fanny Price standing at a window with Edmund breaks into a strange rhapsody, which begins, 'Here's harmony! here's repose! here's what may leave all painting and all music behind, and what poetry only can attempt to describe!'[17] &c. And, again, she throws a curious atmosphere of symbolism over the whole scene where Maria and Henry Crawford refuse to wait for Rushworth, who is bringing the key of the gate. 'But unluckily', Maria exclaims, 'that iron gate, that ha-ha gives me a feeling of restraint and hardship. I cannot get out, as the starling said.'[18]

But these limitations are noticeable only when Jane Austen is committing herself to saying seriously that such things and such people are good, which in the works of any writer is a dangerous moment, leading us to hold our breath; when she is pointing out where they are bad, weak, faulty, exquisitely absurd she is winged and inapproachable. Her heroes may be insipid, but think of her fools! Think of Mr Collins, Mr Woodhouse, Miss Bates, Mrs Norris, Mrs Bennet, and in a lesser degree of Mrs Allen, Lady Bertram, Sir William Lucas![19] What a light the thought of them will cast on the wettest day! How various and individual is their folly! For they are no more consistently foolish than people in real life. It is only that they have a peculiar point of view, and that when health, or economy, or ladies of title are mentioned, as must frequently happen in the world we live in, they give vent to their views to our eternal delight; but there are a great many circumstances in which they do not behave foolishly at all. Indeed, we are inclined to think that the most painful incident in any of the novels is when Miss Bates's feelings are hurt at the picnic, and, turning to Mr Knightley, she says, 'I must have made myself very disagreeable or she would not have said such a thing to an old friend.'[20] Again, when they are discussing the study of human nature and Darcy remarks, 'But people themselves alter so much that there is something to be observed in them for ever,' Mrs Bennet's reply is surely a stroke of genius. 'Yes, indeed,' cried Mrs Bennet, offended by his manner of mentioning a country neighbourhood, 'I assure you there is quite as much of that going on in the country as in town.'[21] Such is the light it throws upon the muddled vacuity of the poor lady's mind that she ceases to be ridiculous and becomes almost tragic in her folly.

It came so naturally to Jane Austen to describe people by means of their faults that had there been a drop of bitterness in her spirit her novels would have given us the most consistently satirical picture of life that exists. Open them where you will, you are almost certain to light upon some passage exquisitely satirising the absurdities of life – satirising them, but without bitterness, partly no doubt because she was happy in her life, partly because she had no wish that things should be other than they are. People could never be too absurd, life never too full of humours and singularities for her taste, and as for telling people how they ought to live, which is the satiric motive, she would have held up her hands in amazement at the thought. Life itself – that was the object of her love, of her absorbed study; that was the pursuit which filled those unrecorded years and drew out the 'quiet intensity of her nature', making her appear to the outer world a little critical and aloof, and 'at times very grave'.²² More than any other novelist she fills every inch of her canvas with observation, fashions every sentence into meaning, stuffs up every chink and cranny of the fabric until each novel is a little living world, from which you cannot break off a scene or even a sentence without bleeding it of some of its life. Her characters are so rounded and substantial that they have the power to move out of the scenes in which she placed them into other moods and circumstances. Thus, if someone begins to talk about Emma Woodhouse or Elizabeth Bennet voices from different parts of the room begin saying which they prefer and why, and how they differ, and how they might have acted if one had been at Box Hill and the other at Rosings,²³ and where they live, and how their houses are disposed, as if they were living people. It is a world, in short, with houses, roads, carriages, hedgerows, copses, and with human beings.

All this was done by a quiet maiden lady who had merely paper and ink at her disposal; all this is conveyed by little sentences between inverted commas and smooth paragraphs of print. Only those who have realised for themselves the ridiculous inadequacy of a straight stick dipped in ink when brought in contact with the rich and tumultuous glow of life can appreciate to the full the wonder of her achievement, the imagination, the penetration, the insight, the courage, the sincerity which are required to bring before us one of those perfectly normal and simple incidents of average human life. Besides all these gifts and more wonderful than any of them, for without it they are apt to run to waste, she possessed in a greater degree perhaps than any other English woman the sense of the significance of life apart from any personal liking or disliking; of the beauty and continuity which underlies its trivial stream. A little aloof, a little inscrutable and mysterious, she will always remain, but serene and beautiful also because of her greatness as an artist.

1 – A review in the *TLS*, 8 May 1913, (Kp C49.2) of *Jane Austen [1775–1817]. Her Life and Letters. A Family Record. With a Portrait* (Smith, Elder & Co., 1913) by

William Austen-Leigh, and of *Old Friends and New Faces* (Holden and Hardingham, 1913) by Sybil G. Brinton. 'Jane Austen was received,' VW wrote in late May to Violet Dickinson (*II VW Letters*, no. 670), 'with pleasure by some, hatred by others. It has won for me the friendship of a tawny bitch in South Kensington, Edith Sichel [1862–1914, writer on French history and culture, who lived at 42 Onslow Gdns] who is black to the 3rd finger joint in ink.' The other recipients of the article referred to are not identified. The same letter also announced the far more momentous news that Gerald Duckworth had accepted for publication *The Voyage Out* (1915).

See also 'Jane Austen and the Geese', 'Jane Austen Practising' and 'Jane Austen at Sixty', *III VW Essays*; and 'Jane Austen', *IV VW Essays* and CR1.

2 – J. E. Austen-Leigh, *A Memoir of Jane Austen* (Richard Bentley, 1870).

3 – Edward, Lord Brabourne, *Letters of Jane Austen. Ed with an introduction and critical remarks* . . . (2 vols, Richard Bentley & Son, 1884).

4 – Cassandra Austen (1772–1845), only sister of Jane Austen.

5 – *Life and Letters*, ch. IV, p. 58, Philadelphia Walter writing to her brother James, July 1788.

6 – *Ibid*., ch. VI, p. 84, Mary Russell Mitford (1787–1855), writing to Sir William Elford, 3 April 1815.

7 – *Ibid*., which has: 'a poker of whom everybody is afraid', and 'But a wit'.

8 – Jane Austen's niece. She was the daughter of Jane's brother Edward, who took the name Knight after a second cousin.

9 – *Life and Letters*, ch. XVI, p. 290.

10 – For the 'something considerable' given by Mrs Norris to William Price, *Mansfield Park* (1814), ch. 31 (ed. Tony Tanner, Penguin, 1966, p. 308); and for Lady Bertram's happy idea to send her own maid Mrs Chapman ('too late of course to be of any use') to help Fanny Price, *ibid*., ch. 27, p. 277.

11 – I.e., *Novels by Miss Jane Austen* (5 vols, Richard Bentley, 1833; reissued, 1856).

12 – The other work referred to, published in February 1913, was *Jane Austen. A Criticism and Appreciation* by Percy Fitzgerald. A fourth work, *Jane Austen* by Francis W. Cornish, appeared the following October.

13 – *Life and Letters*, ch. XX, p. 378, from a letter to Edward Austen, 16 December 1816.

14 – *Mansfield Park*, ch. 48, p. 446, which continues: 'as soon as I can, impatient to restore every body, not greatly in fault themselves, to tolerable comfort, and to have done with all the rest.'

15 – In *Sense and Sensibility* (1811).

16 – A. C. Bradley, 'Jane Austen. A Lecture' in H. C. Beeching (coll.), *Essays and Studies by Members of the English Association,* vol. II (O.U.P., 1911), p. 35, fn. 2.

17 – *Mansfield Park*, ch. 11, p. 139, which has: '"Here's harmony!" said she.'

18 – *Ibid*., ch. 10, p. 127.

19 – Of the characters listed here and not previously identified in either text or notes: Mr Collins, Mrs Bennet and Sir William Lucas appear in *Pride and Prejudice* (1813); Mr Woodhouse and Miss Bates in *Emma* (1816); Mrs Allen in *Northanger Abbey* (1818).

20 – *Emma* (1816), ch. 43 (ed. Ronald Blythe, Penguin, 1966, p. 364).
21 – *Pride and Prejudice* (1813), ch. 9 (ed. Tony Tanner, Penguin, 1972, p. 88).
22 – *Life and Letters*, ch. XIV, p. 240, which has: 'She was not only shy: she was also at times very grave. Her niece Anna is inclined to think that Cassandra was the more equably cheerful of the two sisters. There was, undoubtedly, a quiet intensity of nature in Jane for which some critics have not given her credit.'
23 – Box Hill, scene of the famous picnic in *Emma*; Rosings, seat of Lady Catherine de Bourgh, in *Pride and Prejudice*.

'Les Copains'

It is doubtful whether it would be possible to recall the names of half a dozen living novelists in England and France and honestly say to oneself in the case of each, 'He has not brought it off yet, but really his next book *might* be a masterpiece.' When M. Jules Romains[2] two years ago published *Mort de Quelqu'un*, for some people he certainly entered into this select and honourable band. The book was not only a good book, but it had that particular type of goodness which does not kill the hope that the author may produce one infinitely better; and a novel infinitely better than *Mort de Quelqu'un* would undoubtedly deserve some consideration from posterity. M. Romains has this year published *Les Copains*, and he would probably himself agree that, as far as posterity is concerned, his last book leaves him in the position he occupied in 1911. He has not attempted to fulfil the promise of two years ago; he has, in a sense, begun again. It would be impossible to imagine a more serious book than *Mort de Quelqu'un* or a less serious one than *Les Copains*. The former belonged to that class of modern French *roman* of which there is scarcely an equivalent in English fiction, in which there are no 'characters', no humour, no plot, only a few dramatised psychological and metaphysical theories. The latter is a farce – for the most part a broad-humoured, rather knockabout, and sometimes salacious farce.

There is, of course, no reason why a farce should not be a masterpiece, although the literature of all countries seems to show that it is easier to weep or preach or mock or even revile with genius than to fool with genius. It is rather refreshing, therefore, to find in a French novel so much honest fun as there is in M. Romains's book. It recalls in an odd

way the extravaganzas of Mr Chesterton.[3] No two writers have less in
common in style, feelings, opinions; and yet one can imagine a Latin Mr
Chesterton telling with the same genial gusto the story of the adventures
of the seven copains who set out to revenge themselves upon the two
provincial towns, Issoire and Ambert, for looking as they did upon the
map of the eighty-six departments of France. And, as in Mr Chesterton's
books, though there is plenty of fun for fun's sake, some of the best
things in Les Copains point a moral or possess a sting which take them
out of the province of farce into that of satire. M. Romains knows that it
is pleasant to laugh, but still pleasanter to laugh at someone. He does so
in the Rabelaisian sermon which Bénin preaches in the church at
Ambert. Sometimes his irony has the lightness and effectiveness of the
best French tradition. The copain Broudier is going to play a practical
joke upon the garrison of Ambert by pretending to be a cabinet minister;
he dresses up his three companions in full finery and decorates them with
orders to represent his 'commandant', 'mon cher directeur', and 'mon
secrétaire particulier';[4] then he addresses them as follows:

Quant à moi, vous le voyez, j'ai la mise savamment negligée et la bonhomie
autoritaire qui convient aux premiers serviteurs d'une démocratie. Vous êtes là pour
me garnir. Je porte moi-mème ma puissance; mais c'est vous qui portez mon
décorum, comme un larbin mon pardessus.[5]

In France they are at present fond of labels for writers as well as for
painters, and M. Romains's label is, of course, Unanimisme. There is
not, perhaps, at first sight a very great deal of the doctrine in Les
Copains; it does not dominate the book as it did Mort de Quelqu'un; but
the important thing which lies behind the label and the doctrine is
always with M. Romains. What really interests him is the feelings of
persons, not as individual characters, but as members of groups; what he
delights and excels in doing is to trace the mysterious growth, where two
or three are gathered together, of a kind of consciousness of the group in
addition to that of each individual of the group. It is probable that M.
Romains intended Les Copains to be the farce of Unanimisme; but it is
important, as showing where his powers and his future lie, that the best
things in the book are to be found, not where he is laughing at anything,
even his own doctrines, but where he makes us feel in subtle language
those kinds of feelings which peculiarly interest him. The following
passage could only have been written by the author of Mort de
Quelqu'un, and it makes one hope that M. Romains believes, as we do,

that he may write a much better book than *Les Copains*, but that it will not be a farce:

Le Saint-Péret mousseux débarbouilia les esprits. Il accrut l'ardeur, mais en l'épurant.

Les copains étaient envahis par un sentiment singulier, qui n'avait pas de nom, mais qui leur donnait des ordres, qui exigeait d'eux une satisfaction soudaine: on ne sait quoi qui ressemblait à un besoin d'unité absolue et de conscience absolue.

Ils en arrivèrent à comprendre qu'ils voulaient certaines paroles, qu'ils seraient assouvis par une voix.

Si plusieurs choses n'étaient pas dites, cette nuit même, il serait à jamais trop tard pour les dire.

Si plusieurs choses n'étaient pas constatées et manifestées, elles seraient à jamais perdues.[6]

1 – A review in the *TLS*, 7 August 1913, (Kp C49.3) of *Les Copains* (Eugène Figuière et Cie, 1913) by Jules Romains.

2 – Jules Romains (Louis Farigoule, 1885–1972), whose works at this date included the collection of poems *La Vie unanime* (1908) and the novel *Mort de quelqu'un* (1911), a translation of which, *The Death of a Nobody*, by Desmond MacCarthy and Sydney Waterlow, was to appear in 1914.

3 – G. K. Chesterton (1874–1936), among whose most recent works were *The Innocence of Father Brown* (1911) and *Manalive* (1912).

4 – For the first two companions, Romains, ch. V, p. 153; and for the last, *ibid.*, p. 154.

5 – *Ibid.*, p. 154.

6 – *Ibid.*, ch. VIII, p. 243, which has: 'Si plusieurs choses réelles'.

1916

Queen Adelaide

'I request not to be dissected nor embalmed, and desire to give as little trouble as possible,' wrote Queen Adelaide[2] characteristically when she was considering the disposition of her dead body; and all the industry of Miss Sandars has not been able to violate the privacy of her spirit. For if Queen Anne[3] is dead, we must invent some more absolute form of annihilation for Queen Adelaide. We cannot boldly affirm, after reading 289 pages about her, that she never existed; but we feel much as though we had been to visit someone in a large handsome house, and after wandering through all the state rooms and up the grand staircase and through the attics had heard only the swishing of a skirt and once – that was the most vivid moment of all – caught a glimpse of a 'wonderful red and grey parrot',[4] but never met the owner of the house, or heard more than the murmur of her voice in the next room. It is not Miss Sandars's fault. She has done her best to produce the Queen for us, and, as the Queen is dumb, has imagined what her feelings must have been on several very important occasions, as for example when she landed in England to marry a husband she had never seen.

The sea was rough . . . and the Princess Adelaide's spirits were doubtless at a low ebb . . . Nothing is reported of the interview between him and his future bride, and we can only guess the feelings of the Princess when, at the end of what must have been for one of her delicate physique a most exhausting fortnight, she was introduced to her middle-aged, garrulous, unpolished bridegroom. We may guess, however, that even were her agitation great, nothing of it appeared on the surface. Her manners were good, she was possessed of much reticence and self-control, and she doubtless behaved suitably and with the sense of propriety natural to her.[5]

That is the style of the volume. We are made to feel that it is not permitted in the case of a great lady so recently dead to impute to her any feelings save those that she might show to the public through the windows of her crystal coach on her way down the Mall when, although in constant fear of assassination, she made a point of sitting rather forward and very upright. She was always on her guard with the English, who disliked her, and she never lost the traces of her long girlhood in the pious secluded Court of Meiningen, where a paternal government issued decrees about coffins, and begging, and dancing on Sundays and wrestled, unsuccessfully it appears, with the problem of geese who stray from the flock. The Princess was well suited to pet and bully a state of devoted retainers, but only the arbitrary exigencies of politics could have forced a woman so trained to become the bride of William the Fourth, with his large family of illegitimate children, and given her the most corrupt court and the least reputable royal family in Europe for her circle and surroundings.

As fate would have it she became Queen Consort when England was struggling for reform. The mere thought of reform, were it merely the introduction of gas in a palace,[6] affected Queen Adelaide like an explosion of gunpowder, and suggested immediate death on a scaffold. She would accept William and George the Fourth, and a large impertinent family of FitzClarences with angelical sweetness and sub-mission, as part of the lot of womanhood, but the idea of giving power to the people stiffened her into something like self-assertion. All the influence she had she brought to bear on the King against the Reform Bill,[7] and drew on herself such hatred from the people that William paced the room anxiously if she were late home from the opera, and the newspapers bespattered her with names which nowadays would not be applied to any woman in the land.

But the Reform Bill passed and there was no martyrdom for Adelaide. Her head, that is, remained on her shoulders; but the discomforts of her lot surely amount in sum of agony to a beheading if it were possible to extract them and compute them. Doubtless, to borrow a very useful phrase from Miss Sandars, the manners of the Royal Family afflicted her considerably. They remind us of those astounding scenes in Dickens and George Eliot[8] when uncles and aunts behave in such a manner at the dinner table that we are inclined to think it is put on for the reader's benefit; but William the Fourth had exactly the same method. At a birthday dinner he took the occasion to jump up and abuse the Duchess of Kent, who was sitting next to him: 'I have no hesitation in saying that I have been insulted – grossly and continually insulted – by that person now near me'[9] upon which the Princess Victoria burst into tears, and the Duchess ordered her carriage. At another dinner party, to annoy the same lady's brother, he pretended to be deaf; and we have an appalling picture of the scene after dinner, when the chairs were placed in such a way that conversation was impossible, and the only diversion apparently for that silent company was to listen to the snores of the Duke of Somerset happily sleeping behind a pillar. But the domestic evenings of calm were no less trying, according to poor Lady Grey,[10] who hoped that she might never see a mahogany table again after sitting for two evenings round the one at Windsor, while the Queen netted a purse, and the King slept, 'occasionally waking for the purpose of saying, "Exactly so, Ma'am" and then sleeping again'. When he kept awake for any length of time, the King would pull out a 'curiosity'[11] for the company to look at, and then wander about signing papers, which a Princess blotted for him, while the Queen beckoned a small society of intimate friends into a corner and handed round her sketches. The nearest approach to the hypnotised boredom of that assembly is to imagine thirty people gathered nightly in a dentist's waiting room, with its round tables, and albums, its horsehair chairs, and diamond spotted carpet, and without even the excitement of the anticipated summons. This dreary scene dragged on until 1837, when the Queen found herself a widow, with an income of £100,000 a year. But her perpetual colds in the head and other indispositions had now developed into chronic ill-health, which made her 'rather fidgety about due attention being shown her',[12] and her chief interest seems to have lain in seeking health, in suppressing dissent and providing colonial bishops, in smiling graciously upon assembled multitudes and, let us hope, in admiring the gifts and cherishing the plumage of that remarkable bird, the red and grey parrot.

1 – A review in the TLS, 13 January 1916, (Kp c50) of *The Life and Times of Queen Adelaide* (Stanley Paul & Co., 1915) by Mary F. Sandars. Reprinted: *B&P*.
2 – Sandars, ch. xv, p. 285; Amelia Adelaide Louisa Theresa Caroline (1792–1849), Dowager Queen, was the eldest child of the Duke and Duchess of Saxe-Coburg

Meiningen. In 1818, she married William Henry, Duke of Clarence (1765–1837), who became William IV following the death of George IV in 1830.
3 – Queen Anne (1665–1714).
4 – Sandars, ch. xv, p. 279.
5 – For the matter before the second ellipsis, *ibid.*, ch. III, p. 46; and for the remainder, pp. 47–8.
6 – *Ibid.*, ch. VIII, p. 130; gas had been installed at Windsor but was cut off on the instructions of Queen Adelaide, who thought it a dangerous innovation.
7 – Introduced by Lord John Russell in 1831, to extend the franchise and bring about other electoral reforms, and passed by parliament in 1832.
8 – Charles Dickens (1812–70); George Eliot (1819–80).
9 – Sandars, ch. xIV, p. 258, slightly adapted; Victoria Mary Louisa, Duchess of Kent (1786–1861), daughter of the Prince and Princess of Saxe-Saalfield-Coburg. She married Edward, Duke of Kent (1767–1820), in 1818, and was the mother of the future Queen Victoria, who came to the throne on William IV's death in 1837.
10 – Henry Somerset, 7th Duke of Beaufort (1792–1853), sometime soldier, M.P., and, more famously, huntsman. Mary Elizabeth, *née* Ponsonby, Lady Grey (d. 1824), wife of the Whig statesman Charles, 2nd Earl Grey, Viscount Howick (1764–1845).
11 – For the king on waking, Sandars, ch. XIII, p. 229, quoting *Creevey Papers* (John Murray, 1903), p. 262; and for his 'curiosities' [sic], *ibid.*, ch. X, p. 162.
12 – *Ibid.*, ch. xv, p. 280.

A Scribbling Dame

There are in the Natural History Museum certain little insects so small that they have to be gummed to the cardboard with the lightest of fingers, but each of them, as one observes with constant surprise, has its fine Latin name spreading far to the right and left of the miniature body. We have often speculated upon the capture of these insects and the christening of them, and marvelled at the labours of the humble, indefatigable men who thus extend our knowledge. But their toil, though comparable in its nature, seems light and certainly agreeable compared with that of Mr Whicher in the book before us. It was not for him to wander through airy forests with a butterfly net in his hand; he had to search out dusty books from desolate museums, and in the end to pin down this faded and antique specimen of the domestic house fly with all her seventy volumes in orderly array around her. But it appears to the Department of English and Comparative Literature in Columbia

University that Mrs Haywood has never been classified, and they approve therefore of the publication of this book on her as 'a contribution to knowledge worthy of publication'.[2] It does not matter, presumably, that she was a writer of no importance, that no one reads her for pleasure, and that nothing is known of her life. She is dead, she is old, she wrote books, and nobody has yet written a book about her.

Mr Whicher accordingly has supplied not merely an article, or a few lines in a history of literature, but a careful, studious, detailed account of all her works regarded from every point of view, together with a bibliography which occupies 204 pages of print. It is but fair to him to add that he has few illusions as to the merits of his authoress, and only claims for her that her 'domestic novels' foreshadowed the work of Miss Burney and Miss Austen,[3] and that she helped to open a new profession for her sex. Whatever help he can afford us by calling Pope 'Mr' Pope or Pope Alexander, and alluding to Mrs Haywood as 'the scribbling dame',[4] he proffers generously enough. But it is scarcely sufficient. If he had been able to throw any light upon the circumstances of her life we should make no complaint. A woman who married a clergyman and ran away from him, who supported herself and possibly two children, it is thought without gallantry, entirely by her pen in the early years of the eighteenth century, was striking out a new line of life and must have been a person of character. But nobody knows anything about her, save that she was born in 1693 and died in 1756; it is not known where she lived or how she got her work; what friends she had, or even, which is strange in the case of a woman, whether she was plain or handsome. 'The apprehensive dame', as Mr Whicher calls her, warned, we can imagine, by the disgusting stanzas in *The Dunciad*,[5] took care that the facts of her life should be concealed, and, withdrawing silently, left behind her a mass of unreadable journalism which both by its form and by the inferiority of the writer's talent throws no light upon her age or upon herself. Anyone who has looked into the works of the Duchess of Newcastle and Mrs Behn[6] knows how easily the rich prose style of the Restoration tends to fall languid and suffocate even writers of considerable force and originality. The names alone of Mrs Haywood's romances[7] make us droop, and in the mazes of her plots we swoon away. We have to imagine how Emilia wandering in Andalusia meets Berinthus in a masquerade. Now Berinthus was really Henriquez her brother . . . Don Jaque di Morella determines to marry his daughter Clementine to a certain cardinal . . . In Montelupe Clementina meets the funeral of a young woman who has been torn to pieces by wolves ... The young and gay Dorante is tempted to expose himself to the charms of the beautiful Kesiah ... The doting Baron de Tortillés marries the extravagant and lascivious Mademoiselle la Motte ... Melliora, Placentia, Montrano, Miramillia, and a thousand more swarm over all the countries of the South and of the East, climbing ropes, dropping letters, overhearing secrets, plunging daggers, languishing and dying, fighting and conquering, but loving, always loving, for, as Mr Whicher puts it, to Mrs Haywood 'love was the force that motivated all the world'.[8]

These stories found certain idle people very ready to read them, and were generally successful. Mrs Haywood was evidently a born journalist. As long as romances of the heart were in fashion she turned out romance after romance; when Richardson and Fielding[9] brought the novel into closer touch with life she followed suit with her *Miss Betsy Thoughtless* and her *Jemmy and Jenny Jessamy*. In the interval she turned publisher, edited a newspaper called *The Parrot*[10] and produced secret histories and scandal novels rather in the style of our gossip in the illustrated papers about the aristocracy. In none of these departments was she a pioneer, or even a very distinguished disciple; and it is more for her steady industry with the pen than for the product of it that she is remarkable. Reading when Mrs Haywood wrote was beginning to come into fashion, and readers demanded books which they could read 'with a tea-cup in one hand without danger of spilling the tea'.[11] But that class, as Mr Gosse indicates when he compares Mrs Haywood to Ouida,[12] has not been improved away nor lessened in numbers. There is the same desire to escape from the familiar look of life by the easiest way, and the difference is really that we find our romance in accumulated motor-cars and marquises rather than in foreign parts and strange-sounding names. But the heart which suffered in the pages of the early romancers beats today upon the railway bookstall beneath the shiny coloured cover which depicts Lord Belcour parting from the Lady Belinda Fitzurse, or the Duchess of Ormonde clasping the family diamonds and bathed in her own blood at the bottom of the marble staircase.

In what sense Mr Whicher can claim that Mrs Haywood 'prepared the way for ... quiet Jane Austen'[13] it is difficult to see, save that one lady was undeniably born some eighty years in advance of the other. For it would be hard to imagine a less professional woman of letters than the lady who wrote on little slips of paper, hid them when anyone was near, and kept her novels shut up in her desk, and refused to write a romance about the august House of Coburg at the suggestion of Prince Leopold's librarian[14] – behaviour that must have made Mrs Haywood lift her hands in amazement in the grave. And in that long and very intricate process of living and reading and writing which so mysteriously alters the form of literature, so that Jane Austen, born in 1775, wrote novels, while Jane Austen born a hundred years earlier would probably have written not novels but a few exquisite lost letters, Mrs Haywood plays no perceptible part, save that of swelling the chorus of sound. For people who write books do not necessarily add anything to the history of literature, even when those books are little old volumes, stained with age, that have crossed the Atlantic; nor can we see that the students of Columbia University will love English literature the better for knowing how very dull it can be, although the University may claim that this is a 'contribution to knowledge'.

1 – A review in the *TLS*, 17 February 1916, (Kp C51) of *The Life and Romances of Mrs Eliza Haywood* [1693?–1756] (Columbia University Press, 1915) by George Frisbie Whicher, Ph.D., Instructor in the University of Illinois. Reprinted: *B&P*.
2 – Whicher, preliminary pages, from a declaration by A. H. Thorndike, Executive Officer, Columbia University Press.
3 – *Ibid.*, Pref., p. vii; Frances Burney (1752–1840); Jane Austen (1775–1817).
4 – *Ibid.*, ch. IV, p. 106; Alexander Pope (1688–1744) is referred to throughout by Whicher as Mr Pope, except at ch. I, p. 21, where the full name is used.
5 – For the 'apprehensive dame', *ibid.*, ch. I, p. 1, quoting David Erskine Baker's *Companion to the Play House* (1764); and for the 'disgusting stanzas', *ibid.*, ch. V, 'The Heroine of the "Dunciad"'; and see 'Eliza . . . / . . . yon Juno of majestic size, / With cow-like udders, and with ox-like eyes', Alexander Pope, *The Dunciad*, 1728, bk ii, ll.149ff; and 1743, bk ii, ll.157ff.
6 – Margaret Cavendish, Duchess of Newcastle (1624?–74), on whom VW wrote in 'The Duke and Duchess of Newcastle' (*I VW Essays*) and 'The Duchess of Newcastle' (*IV VW Essays* and *CR*1); and Aphra Behn (1640–89), author of plays, poems and novels, including *Oroonoko, or the History of the Royal Slave* (c. 1678).
7 – E.g., *Memoirs of a Certain Island adjacent to Utopia, written by a celebrated author of that country. Now translated into English* (1725), and a similar work, also with a key identifying the characters with well-known living persons, *The Secret History of the Present Intrigues of the Court of Caramania* (1727) – works which directly inspired Pope's attack on their author in *The Dunciad*.
8 – Whicher, ch. II, p. 76; the characters Berinthus, Emilia and Henriques occur in *The Lucky Rape* (1727); Don Jacques [sic] di Dorante and Kesiah in *The Fair Hebrew* (1729); Baron de Tortillee [sic] and Mlle la Motte in *The Injur'd Husband* (1723); Melliora in *Love in Excess* (1720); Placentia in *Philidore and Placentia: or L'Amour trop Delicat* (1727); Montrano and Miramillia in *The Fruitless Enquiry* (1727).

9 – Samuel Richardson (1689–1761); Henry Fielding (1707–54).

10 – *The History of Betsy Thoughtless* (1751); *The History of Jemmy and Jenny Jessamy* (1753); *The Parrot, with a Compendium of the Times*, 2 August–14 October 1746, which had been preceded by a similar publication, *The Female Spectator*, 1744–6.

11 – Whicher, ch. VII, p. 162.

12 – For the comparison by Edmund Gosse (1849–1928), *ibid.*, ch. I, p. 26; Ouida (Marie Louise de la Ramée, 1839–1908), whose works include *Under Two Flags* (1867), *Tricortin* (1869), *Two Little Wooden Shoes* (1874) and *A Village Commune* (1881).

13 – *Ibid.*, ch. VIII, p. 175, which has: 'preparing the way'; the ellipsis marks the omission of 'modest Fanny Burney and'.

14 – This suggestion was put to Jane Austen in 1816 by J. S. Clarke, librarian to Prince Leopold of the House of Coburg, the future king of the Belgians who that year had married Princess Charlotte, daughter of the Prince Regent. See *A Memoir of Jane Austen* (1870) by J. E. Austen-Leigh (ed. D. W. Harding, Penguin, 1965, p. 353).

Charlotte Brontë

The hundredth anniversary of the birth of Charlotte Brontë will strike, we believe, with peculiar force upon the minds of a very large number of people. Of those hundred years she lived but thirty-nine, and it is strange to reflect what a different image we might have of her if her life had been a long one. She might have become, like other writers who were her contemporaries, a figure familiarly met with in London and elsewhere, the subject of anecdotes and pictures innumerable, removed from us well within the memory of the middle-aged, in all the splendour of established fame. But it is not so. When we think of her we have to imagine someone who had no lot in our modern world; we have to cast our minds back to the fifties of the last century, to a remote parsonage upon the wild Yorkshire moors. Very few now are those who saw her and spoke to her; and her posthumous reputation has not been prolonged by any circle of friends whose memories so often keep alive for a new generation the most vivid and most perishable characteristics of a dead man.

Nevertheless, when her name is mentioned, there starts up before our eyes a picture of Charlotte Brontë, which is as definite as that of a living person, and one may venture to say that to place her name at the head of a page will cause a more genuine interest than almost any other inscription that might be placed there. What new thing, one may well ask, is to be said of so strange and famous a being? How can we add anything about her life or her work which is not already part of the consciousness of the educated man and woman of today? We have seen Haworth, either in fact or in picture; long ago Mrs Gaskell[2] stamped our minds with an ineffaceable impression; and the devotion of later students has swept together every trifle that may render back the echoes of that short and circumscribed life.

But there is one peculiarity which real works of art possess in common. At each fresh reading one notices some change in them, as if the sap of life ran in their leaves, and with skies and plants they had the power to alter their shape and colour from season to season. To write down one's impressions of *Hamlet* as one reads it year after year, would be virtually to record one's own autobiography, for as we know more of life, so Shakespeare comments upon what we know. In their degree, the novels of Charlotte Brontë must be placed within the same class of living and changing creations, which, so far as we can guess, will serve a generation yet unborn with a glass in which to measure its varying stature. In their turn they will say how she has changed to them, and what she has given them. If we collect a few of our impressions today, it is not with any hope of assigning her to her final position, or of drawing her portrait afresh; we offer merely our little hoard of observations, which other readers may like to set, for a moment, beside their own.

So many novels once held great have gone out of fashion, or are pronounced unreadable, that we may justly feel a little anxiety when the time comes to make trial of *Jane Eyre*[3] and the rest. We have suggested that a book, in order to live, must have the power of changing as we change, and we have to ask ourselves whether it is possible that Charlotte Brontë can have kept pace with us. Shall we not go back to her world of the fifties and find that it is a place only to be visited by the learned, only to be preserved for the curious? A novelist, we reflect, is bound to build up his structure with much very perishable material, which begins by lending it reality, and ends by cumbering its form. The mid-Victorian world, moreover, is the last that we of the present moment wish to see resuscitated. One opens *Jane Eyre* with all these half-conscious premonitions and excuses, and in ten minutes one finds the whole of them dispersed and the light shining and the wind blowing upon a wild and bracing prospect.

Folds of scarlet drapery shut in my view to the right hand; to the left were the clear panes of glass, protecting, but not separating, me from the drear November day. At intervals while turning over the leaves of my book, I studied the aspects of that winter afternoon. Afar, it offered a pale blank of mist and cloud; near, a scene of wet lawn and storm-beat shrub, with ceaseless rain sweeping away wildly before a long and lamentable blast.[4]

As a room full of people makes one who enters suddenly conscious of heightened existence, so the opening passages of this book make us glow and shiver as though we stood out in the storm and saw the rain drive across the moor. There is nothing here that seems more perishable than the moor itself, or more subject to the sway of fashion than the 'long and lamentable blast'. Nor is this exhilaration short-lived; it rushes us through the entire volume and scarcely gives us time to ask what is happening to us, nor in the end are we able to make out a very clear account of our adventures. We may reflect that this is exactly the opposite of our experience with certain other books justly numbered among the great. When we have finished *The Idiot*, or *Jude the Obscure*,[5] and even in the course of reading them, the plethoric state of mind which they induce is to be traced in a head resting on the hands, and oblivious eyes fixed upon the fire. We brood and ponder and drift away from the text in trains of thought which build up round the characters an atmosphere of question and suggestion in which they move, but of which they are unconscious. But it is not possible, when you are reading Charlotte Brontë, to lift your eyes from the page. She has you by the hand and forces you along her road, seeing the things she sees and as she sees them. She is never absent for a moment, nor does she attempt to conceal herself or to disguise her voice. At the conclusion of *Jane Eyre* we do not feel so much that we have read a book, as that we have parted from a most singular and eloquent woman, met by chance upon a Yorkshire hillside, who has gone with us for a time and told us the whole of her life history. So strong is the impression that if we are disturbed while we are reading the disturbance seems to take place in the novel and not in the room.

There are two reasons for this astonishing closeness and sense of personality – that she is herself the heroine of her own novels, and (if we may divide people into those who think and those who feel) that she is primarily the recorder of feelings and not of thoughts. Her characters are linked together by their passions as by a train of gunpowder. One of these small, pale, volcanic women, be she Jane Eyre or Lucy Snowe,[6] has but to come upon the scene, and wherever she looks there start up round her characters of extreme individuality and intensity who are branded for ever with the features she discerns in them. There are novelists, like Tolstoy and Jane Austen, who persuade us that their characters live and are complex by means of their effect upon many different people, who mirror them in the round. They move hither and thither whether their creator watches them or not. But we cannot imagine Rochester when he is apart from Jane Eyre, or rather we can only see him in different situations as she would have seen him in them, and to be always in love and always a governess is to go through the world with blinkers on one's eyes.

These are serious limitations, perhaps, and it may be true that they give her work a look of crudeness and violence beside that of more impersonal and more experienced artists. At the same time it is by reason of this marvellous gift of vision that she takes her place with the greatest novelists we have. No writer, that is to say, surpasses her in the power of making what she describes immediately visible to us. She seems to sit down to write from compulsion. The scenes in her mind are painted so boldly and in such strong colours that her hand (so we feel) drives rapidly across the paper, and trembles with the intensity of her thought. It is not surprising to hear that she did not enjoy writing her books, and yet that writing was the only occupation that could lift her up when the burden of sorrow and shame which life laid on her weighted her to the ground. Every one of her books seems to be a superb gesture of defiance, bidding her torturers depart and leave her queen of a splendid island of imagination. Like some hard-pressed captain, she summoned her powers together and proudly annihilated the enemy.

But although much has been said of her habit of describing actual people, and introducing scenes which had happened to her, the vividness of the result is not so easy to analyse. She had both an abnormal sensibility which made every figure and incident strike its pattern upon her mind, and also an extraordinary tenacity and toughness of purpose which drove her to test and investigate these impressions to the last ounce of them. 'I could never,' she writes, 'rest in communication with strong discreet and refined minds, whether male or female, till I had passed the outworks of conventional reserve and crossed the threshold of confidence, and won a place by their hearts' very hearthstone.'[8] It is by the 'heart's very hearthstone' that she begins her writing, with the light of it glowing on her page. Indeed, her production, whatever its faults, always seems to issue from a deep place where the fire is eternal. The peculiar virtues of her style, its character, its speed, its colour and strength, seem all of her own forging and to owe nothing to literary instruction or to the reading of many books. The smoothness of the professional writer, his ability to stuff out and sway his language as he chooses, was never learnt by her. She remains always unsophisticated, but with a power through sheer force of meaning of creating the word she needs and winging her way with a rhythm of her own. This mastery over language grew as she gained maturity as an artist; and in *Villette*, the last and greatest of her works, she is mistress not only of a strong and individual style, but of a style that is both variable and splendid. We are made to remember, too, her long toil with brush and pencil, for she has a strange gift, rare in a writer, of rendering the quality of colour and of texture in words, and thus investing many of her scenes with a curious brilliance and solidity.

Yet it was merely a very pretty drawing room, and within it a boudoir, both spread with white carpets, on which seemed laid brilliant garlands of flowers; both ceiled with snowy moulding of white grapes and vine leaves, beneath which glowed in rich contrast crimson couches and ottomans; while the ornaments on the pale Parian mantelpiece were of sparkling Bohemia glass, ruby red; and between the windows large mirrors repeated the general blending of snow and fire.[9]

We not only see that, we can almost touch it. She never heaps her colours, but lays a blue or a purple or her favourite crimson so rightly on the page that they paint the sentence as with actual pigment. Naturally, therefore, we should expect to find her a great landscape painter, a great lover of the air and the sky and all the pageant that lies between earth and heaven; nor may a student of hers tell whether he cares more for her people or for the keen air and the scent of the moor and the 'plumes of the storm'[10] which surround them with such light and atmosphere, and such overwhelming poetry. Her descriptions, too, are not separate visions, as they tend to be so often with writers of less powerful gift, but work themselves into the heart of the book.

It was a mile from Thornfield, in a lane noted for wild roses in summer, for nuts and blackberries in autumn, and even now possessing a few coral treasures in hips and haws, but whose best winter delight lay in its utter solitude and leafless repose. If a breath of air stirred, it made no sound here; for there was not a holly, not an evergreen to rustle, and the stripped hawthorn and hazel bushes were as still as the white worn stones which causewayed the middle of the path. Far and wide on each side there were only fields where no cattle now browsed, and the little brown birds which stirred occasionally looked like single russet leaves that had forgotten to drop.[11]

How beautifully that spreads the mood of the moment over the face of the land!

But these are the details of a great literary gift. We go back to her books, and sometimes this quality strikes us and sometimes that. But all the while we are conscious of something that is greater than one gift or another and is perhaps the quality that attaches us to books as to people – the quality, that is, of the writer's mind and personality. With their limitations and their great beauty these are stamped upon every page that Charlotte Brontë wrote. We do not need to know her story, or to have climbed the steep hill and gazed upon the stone house among the graves to feel her tremendous honesty and courage, and to know that she loved liberty and independence and the splendour of wild country, and men and women who are above all things passionate and true-minded. These are part of her as her imagination and genius are part of her; and they add to our admiration of her as a writer some peculiar warmth of feeling which makes us desire, when there is any question of doing her honour, to rise and salute her not only as a writer of genius, but as a very noble human being.

1 – An essay in the *TLS*, 13 April 1916, (Kp C52) commemorating the centenary of the birth, on 21 April 1816, of Charlotte Brontë (d. 1855), and which VW later incorporated in '"Jane Eyre" and "Wuthering Heights"', *IV VW Essays* and *CR*1. See also 'Charlotte Brontë' below, and 'Haworth, November, 1904', *I VW Essays*.
2 – Elizabeth Gaskell, *The Life of Charlotte Brontë* (1857). VW saw Haworth 'in fact' in 1904.
3 – *Jane Eyre* (1847).
4 – *Ibid.*, ch. 1 (ed. Q. D. Leavis, Penguin, 1966, pp. 39–40).
5 – Fyodor Dostoevsky (1821–81), *The Idiot* (1866); Thomas Hardy (1840–1928), *Jude the Obscure* (1895).
6 – Lucy Snowe, the heroine-narrator in *Villette* (1853).
7 – L. N. Tolstoy (1828–1910); Jane Austen (1775–1817).
8 – *Jane Eyre*, ch. 32, p. 400.
9 – *Ibid.*, ch. 11, p. 135.
10 – Apparently adapted from *Villette*, ch. 42 (ed. Mark Lilly, Penguin, 1979, p. 596): 'Not till the destroying angel of tempest had achieved his perfect work, would he fold the wings whose waft was thunder – the tremor of whose plumes was storm.'
11 – *Jane Eyre*, ch. 12, p. 142, which has: 'I was a mile'.

'Past and Present at the English Lakes'

We all know the charm of the country newspaper, in which columns are devoted to the flower show, or the trial of a poacher, or the wedding of the mayor's daughter, while the speeches of the Prime Minister and the agitations of the Empire are dismissed in very small type in some obscure corner. In reading Canon Rawnsley's book we feel something of this delightful change of proportion, as if a magnifying glass had been laid over the fells and dales of the north, and everything that happened beyond the rim of his glass had no existence at all.

Moreover, it is not the present time that his glass magnifies, but the summers of a century ago. We hear Hartley Coleridge murmur as he stops before each portrait in a friend's dining room, 'I wish you could give me a glass of beer.'[2] We see Wordsworth and Coleridge, De Quincey and Scott;[3] and so steeped is Canon Rawnsley in their thought that, though he travels in a motor-car, the landscape comes before him still as it was when Wordsworth looked at it. Shall we ever, we cannot help wondering, see these famous hills with our own eyes as though Wordsworth had never lived? And why is it that the art of describing places and skies in words is so seldom successfully accomplished? When Canon Rawnsley paints directly from the scene before him his sunsets and sunrises tend to remain merely an assembly of the names of colours – purple and gold, fawn and amber – without enough coherence in them to stir our imaginations into activity. But, on the other hand, in a charming paper called 'Crossing the Sands'[4] his method is different and far more successful. It is the narrative of a summer day's walk across the sand of Morecambe Bay. There are a great many facts, a certain amount of history, and a straightforward itinerary; but it is told in such a manner that we feel ourselves to be walking, too, upon the hard-baked sand with its wave-like ridges, fording the rivers and talking to the guide, and getting hot and blistered, and suddenly seeing the beauty of the whole, much as though we were there in the flesh. Perhaps then if you are not a Ruskin[5] or a Wordsworth, it is best not to look straight into the sunset but to rub along with humble facts until the mind at last is all of a glow and sees the sunset without its being described.

But the most interesting paper in the book is that on Gough and his dog.[6] Everyone remembers the story of the young man who was killed on Helvellyn and of the dog who watched beside his body until the shepherds found it three months later, for both Scott and Wordsworth have told the story in famous poems.[7] Canon Rawnsley desired to commemorate the event by placing a tablet on the spot. But almost by accident he was led to inquire into the facts, and now there came to him and to us a most cruel disillusionment. To us, living at a distance, it does not very much matter whether Gough fell at Striding Edge or at Swirrel Edge, so long as fall he did; but to read the heartless statement of a contemporary that the dog was found 'uncommonly fat' by her master's side, 'and the flesh of the latter was mostly consumed',[8] was of the nature of a catastrophe. For how many years, we exclaim, has not this impious creature robbed us of our sympathy!

But Canon Rawnsley's energy and faith were boundless, although at every step he was met by fresh disillusionments. For when once the story was examined each fact became doubtful, or was variously reported by different witnesses. Gough was certainly killed; but whether he fell or perished of starvation, whether he was fishing or making scientific observations, whether he was accompanied by two dogs or by one, nobody seemed to know. The breed of the dog varied as much as its character. Was it a spaniel or a terrier, a Dandie Dinmont or a 'laal yallow short-haired tarrier dog'?[9] The artists were consulted, but to no purpose. One has painted a huge white mongrel, another a black and tan collie, another a retriever, and another a small white terrier. Wordsworth would only say that it was not of mountain breed and barked like a fox. In his perplexity Canon Rawnsley sought out the descendant of the young man, and established the fact that he often went out with a dog and a walking-stick, and was fond of reciting poetry in the evening. Aged nurses and peasants tottering on the edge of the grave were consulted. The more anxious point of the dog's behaviour was submitted to a series of shepherds versed in the nature of dogs. Canon Rawnsley finds them unanimously of opinion that 'a dog wad nivver dea sic a thing; and he kenned dogs, t' naatur o' t' animal. But they did say that ravens had picked at him a bit.'[10] Still, as Canon Rawnsley says, 'better far does it seem that the poor traveller should have fallen a prey to the fowls of the air, those natural scavengers of the mountain side, than that the honour and fidelity of his faithful four-footed friend and mourner should be called in question'.[11] In the end it is pretty well established that Mr Gough was accompanied by two dogs, one of which left him, while the other remained, giving birth to puppies, and maintaining herself respectably upon the bodies of sheep, until she was discovered much emaciated and so wild that the hounds had to be set upon her before she could be taken. She was an Irish terrier, and her name was Foxey. But those who like to see the way in which the artist's mind works upon a subject cannot do better than compare the versions of the same story which have been given by a journalist, by Scott, by Wordsworth, and by De Quincey.[12]

1 – A review in the *TLS*, 29 June 1916, (Kp C52.1) of *Past and Present at the English Lakes* (James MacLehose & Sons, 1916) by the Rev. H. D. Rawnsley (1851–1920), honorary canon of Carlisle, author of numerous books on the Lake District. See also 'Wordsworth and the Lakes', *I VW Essays*.

2 – Rawnsley, 'Reminiscences of Hartley Coleridge', p. 19, which has: 'stopping before each picture and saying *sotto voce* to the picture, as if it were a living person, "I wish .."' Hartley Coleridge (1796–1849), the brilliant but tragically feckless eldest son of S. T. Coleridge.

3 – William Wordsworth (1770–1850); S. T. Coleridge (1772–1834); Thomas De Quincey (1785–1859); Sir Walter Scott (1771–1832).

4 – Rawnsley, pp. 230–69.

5 – John Ruskin (1819–1900), who settled at Coniston in 1871.

6 – *Ibid.*, 'Gough and His Dog', pp. 153–208; the remains of Charles Gough were found on Helvellyn in July 1805.

7 – *Ibid.*, pp. 154–5; Sir Walter Scott, 'Helvellyn' (1805); William Wordsworth, 'Fidelity' (1805).

8 – *Ibid.*, p. 167, from an account in the *Cumberland Pacquet*, 30 July 1805.

9 – *Ibid.*, p. 187. Dandy Dinmont, terrier-breeder in Scott's *Guy Mannering* (1815).

10 – *Ibid.*, p. 194.

11 – *Ibid.*, p. 174.

12 – *Ibid.*, pp. 174–8, which quotes De Quincey's extensive footnote on 'The case of Mr Gough' in 'Early Memorials of Grasmere', *Selections Grave and Gay* (1854).

A Man With a View

It is probable that any one who reads Samuel Butler[2] will wish to know more about him. He is one of those rare spirits among the dead whom we like, or it may be dislike, as we do the living, so strong is their individuality and so clearly can we make up our minds about their manners and opinions. Johnson[3] is of this company, and we can each add others according to our private tastes; but the number of people who will put Samuel Butler upon their list must be increasing every day. For this reason we would give a good deal to have a life of Butler, with plenty of letters and anecdotes and reports of those private sayings and doings in which surely he must have excelled. Mr Harris has had access apparently to no more information than is already before the public, so that he cannot gratify us in this respect; and at first there may seem little reason for another study of Butler's works when Mr Cannan's book[4] is scarcely a year old. But Mr Harris is quite strong enough to dispel our doubts. He writes clearly and with considerable force; he generates in us a desire to contradict him flatly, and again he makes us sigh, half with relief and half with annoyance, when he says something so true that we have always been on the point of saying it ourselves. His work has the merit, in particular the very clear chapter on the scientific books, of bringing out the main lines of thought which unite all Butler's work, so that instead of thinking him an eccentric who took up subjects much at random, we have a more serious picture of a man who built up solidly a house with many storeys. But the justification of Mr Harris's volume is that directly we have finished it we take down Butler to see what the change in our conception of him amounts to.

All this writing and disputing on his account is, of course, much what Butler himself expected of an intelligent posterity. But why is it that his lamp not only still shines among the living, but with a light that positively grows brighter and seems altogether more friendly and more kindling as the years go by? Perhaps it is that the other lights are going out. Certainly Mr Harris paints a very depressing picture of the great Victorians. There was George Eliot with her philosophic tea parties; and Tennyson declaiming pompously before the statues in the British Museum; and Pater with a style that Butler likened to the face of an enamelled old woman; and Arnold's 'odour which was as the faint sickliness of hawthorn'.[5] It was an age, according to Mr Harris, 'of false values and misplaced enthusiasms, unaccountable prejudices, astonishing deficiency in artistic perception, and yet with it a bewildering lack of real practical efficiency'.[6] Whether this is true or not, it represents very fairly Butler's own point of view. Further on, however, Mr Harris points out more suggestively that Butler was singular in being the spectator of his age, an amateur, 'a non-professional worker . . . as well as a lover'.[7] These words seem to us to indicate the most vital distinction that there was between Butler and his contemporaries. The Victorian age, to hazard another generalisation, was the age of the professional man. The biographies of the time have a depressing similarity; very much over-worked, very serious, very joyless, the eminent men appear to us to be, and already strangely formal and remote from us in their likes and dislikes. Butler, of course, hated nothing more than the professional spirit; and this may account for the startling freshness of his books, as if they had been laid up all these years in sweet-scented roots and pungent spices. Naturally his fellow men owed him a grudge (though we should like more evidence of what Mr Harris calls 'the conspiracy' against him),[8] as schoolboys set to do their sums in a dreary schoolroom have a grudge against a boy who passes the window with a butterfly net in his hand and nothing to do but enjoy himself.

But why, if they were imprisoned, was Butler free? Had the achievement been an easy one, we should not owe him the enormous debt of thanks which is his due. To free himself from the fetters which he found so galling it was not enough by a long way merely to refuse to be a clergyman. He had to preserve that kind of honesty, originality, or sensibility which asserts itself whether you are about to baptise a child or go to an evening party, and asks, 'Now why am I doing this? Is it because other people do it? Is it right? Do I enjoy doing it?' and is always preventing its possessor from falling into step with the throng. In Butler's day, at any rate, such a disposition was fatal to success. He failed in everything he took up – music and science, painting and literature; and lived the most secluded of lives, without need of dress clothes, in a set of rooms in Clifford's Inn, where he cooked his own breakfast and fetched his own water. But his triumph lay not in being a failure, but in achieving the kind of success he thought worth while, in being the master of his life, and in selecting the right things to do with it. Never, we imagine, did Butler have to plead that he was too busy for some pleasant thing, such as a concert or a play, or a visit to a friend. Every summer found him with sufficient pocket money to afford a trip to Italy; his week-end jaunts to the country were conducted with extreme regularity, and we should guess that he seldom put himself out to catch a train. But, above all, he had achieved a freedom of soul which he expressed in one book after another. In his obscurity he had wrought out a very clear notion of 'the Kingdom of Heaven'[9] and of the qualities needed by those who seek it; of the people who are the 'only people worth troubling about',[10] and of the things 'which nobody doubts who is worth talking to'.[11] He had, of course, a splendid collection of hatreds, just as he worshipped Handel and Shakespeare, Homer and the authoress of the

Odyssey, Tabachetti and Bellini,[12] so as to make him rather suspicious of other worshippers. In his isolation and idiosyncrasies he sometimes recalls Edward FitzGerald,[13] but with the great difference that whereas FitzGerald early realised the vanity of fighting the monster, Butler was always busy planting his darts in the flanks of his age, always pugnacious and always full of self-confidence. And against neglect and disapproval he had a private supply of most satisfactory consolations. It was much better fun, he said, to write fearlessly for posterity than to write, 'like, we will say, George Eliot, and make a lot of money by it'.[14] These reflections certainly kept his temper cooler than is usual in the case of a man who has so much to satirise, and also preserved in all its vigour his most uncompromising individuality. But perhaps his greatest fault as a writer springs from this irresponsibility, his determination, that is, to humour his own ideas in season and out of season, whether they serve to clog the story to stagnation, as sometimes happens in *The Way of All Flesh*, or to give it shade and depth. Very occasionally he reminds one of those eccentric and insistent people who persist in bathing daily in the Serpentine, or in wearing a greatcoat all the year round, and proclaim that such is the only road to salvation. But that trifling defect is the one drawback of the solitude to which he was condemned.

His many-sided training in art and music, sheep-farming[15] and literature, by exposing so many different sides of his mind to the light, kept him amazingly fresh to the end of life; but he achieved this freshness quite consciously also by treating life as an art. It was a perpetual experiment which he was for ever watching and manipulating and recording in his note-books; and if today we are less ambitious, less apt to be solemn and sentimental, and display without shame a keener appetite for happiness, we owe this very largely to Butler's example. But in this, too, he differed very much from his contemporaries.

All these qualities and a thousand more – for Butler is a very complex personality, and, like all great writers, finally inscrutable – are to be found in his books. Of these the most remarkable, perhaps, are *The Way of All Flesh*, and *The Note-books*. He had worked upon both for many years, and the novel he would have written yet again had he lived. As it is, it has all the qualities of work done almost as a hobby, from sheer love of it, taken up and laid down at pleasure, and receiving the very impress of the maker's hand. And yet it is easy to understand why it did not arouse enthusiasm when it first appeared – why it yields more upon the third reading than upon the first. It is a book of conviction, which goes its own way, passing the conventional turnings without looking at them. But, after reading it, we hardly care to inspect some of the masterpieces of English fiction; it would be as unkind as to let in the cold light of day upon a dowager in a ball dress. It would be easy to enumerate many important and splendid gifts in which Butler as a novelist was deficient; but his deficiency serves to lay bare one gift in which he excelled, and that is his point of view. To have by nature a point of view, to stick to it, to follow it where it leads, is the rarest of possessions, and lends value even to trifles. This gift Butler had in the highest degree; he gives a turn or a twist to the most ordinary matter, so that it bores its way to the depths of our minds, there to stay when more important things have crumbled to dust. If proof of this is wanted, read his account of buying new-laid eggs in *The Note-books*, or the story of 'The Aunt, the Nieces, and the Dog', or the anecdote of the old lady and her parrot in *The Humour of Homer*.[16] These *Note-books* of Butler's will certainly beget many other note-books, which will be a source of profound disappointment to their owners. It seems so simple a thing to have a note-book and to have ideas; but what if the ideas refuse to come, or lodge in the same place instead of ranging from earth to Heaven? We shall, at any rate, learn to respect Butler more highly. The truth is that despite his homeliness and his seeming accessibility, no one has ever succeeded in imitating Butler; to do so one would have to unscrew one's head and put it on altogether differently. At one time we think it is his humour that eludes us, that strange, unlaughing, overwhelming gift which compresses his stories at one grasp into their eternal shape; at another the peculiar accent and power of his style; but in the end we cease to dissect, and give ourselves up to delight in a structure which seems to us so entire and all of a piece; so typically English, we would like to think, remembering his force of character, his humanity, and his great love of beauty.

1 – A review in the *TLS*, 20 July 1916, (Kp c53) of *Samuel Butler: Author of Erewhon, the Man and His Work* (Grant Richards, 1916) by John F. Harris. VW wrote to Violet Dickinson, 26 May 1916 (*II VW Letters*, no. 759): 'Did you know old Samuel Butler? I have got to write about him. I wish I'd known him.' See also '*The Way of All Flesh*', *III VW Essays*, and 'The Two Samuel Butlers', *IV VW Essays*. Reprinted: *CW*.

2 – Samuel Butler (1835–1902), author of *Erewhon* (1872), *The Authoress of the Odyssey* (1897), *Erewhon Revisited* (1901) and *The Way of All Flesh* (1903).

3 – Dr Samuel Johnson (1709–84).

4 – Gilbert Cannan (1884–1955), *Samuel Butler. A Critical Study* (1915).

5 – For George Eliot (1819–80), Harris, intro., p. 12; for Alfred, Lord Tennyson (1809–92), *ibid.*, 'Conclusion', p. 273: 'Tennyson stood "bare-headed" and "imperial-looking". At length the party moved on to look at the sculpture. Tennyson led. "But the only remark," says Mr Gosse [in *Portraits and Sketches*, 1912], "which my memory has retained was made before the famous black bust of Antinous. Tennyson bent forward a little, and said, in his deep, slow voice: 'Ah! This is the inscrutable Bithynian!' There was a pause, and then he added, gazing into the eyes of the bust: 'If we knew what he knew, we should understand the ancient world'"'; for Walter Pater (1839–94) and for Matthew Arnold (1822–88), *The Note-Books of Samuel Butler*, ed. Henry Festing Jones (A. C. Fifield, 1912), p. 184: 'Mr Walter Pater's style is, to me, like the face of some old woman who has been to Madame Rachel and had herself enamelled. The bloom is nothing but powder and paint and the odour is cherry-blossom. Mr Matthew Arnold's odour is as the faint sickliness of hawthorn' (not quoted in Harris).

6 – Harris, intro., p. 16.

7 – *Ibid.*, ch. VIII, p. 257.

8 – *Ibid.*, intro., p. 17.

9 – Butler makes several allusions to 'The Kingdom of Heaven' and has one note so entitled in *Note-Books*, pp. 168–9.

10 – *Ibid.*, 'Art and Usefulness', p. 174, which has: 'Briefly, the world resolves itself into two great classes – those who hold that honour after death is better worth having than any honour a man can get and know anything about, and those who doubt this; to my mind, those who hold it, and hold it firmly, are the only people worth thinking about.'

11 – *Ibid.*, 'The Kingdom of Heaven,' p. 169, which has: 'Nobody who doubts any of this is worth talking with.'

12 – For Handel and Shakespeare, *ibid.*, 'Preparation for Death', p. 363; for Homer and the authoress, see n. 2 above, and *ibid.*, 'My Work', p. 376; for Tabachetti (the Flemish sculptor Jean de Wespin, so known in Italy) and for Giovanni and Gentile Bellini, *ibid.*, p. 376.

13 – Edward Fitzgerald (1809–83), author of *The Rubáiyát of Omar Khayyám* (1859).

14 – Harris, intro., p. 20, quoting Butler, *Note-Books*, 'Myself and My Books', p. 160.

15 – Having taken a first in classics at St John's College, Cambridge, in 1858, Butler emigrated the following year to New Zealand and made a very profitable living there as a sheep-farmer until his return to England in 1864–5.

16 – See *Note-Books*, 'New Laid Eggs', p. 249; Butler, *Essays on Life Art and Science* (1904), 'The Aunt, the Nieces and the Dog'; *The Humour of Homer* (1892), a lecture delivered at the Working Men's College, Great Ormond St, London, 30 January 1892.

Heard on the Downs: The Genesis of Myth

Two well-known writers were describing the sound of the guns in France, as they heard it from the top of the South Downs. One likened it to 'the hammer stroke of Fate'; the other heard in it 'the pulse of Destiny'.

More prosaically, it sounds like the beating of gigantic carpets by gigantic women, at a distance. You may almost see them holding the carpets in their strong arms by the four corners, tossing them into the air, and bringing them down with a thud while the dust rises in a cloud about their heads. All walks on the Downs this summer are accompanied by this sinister sound of far-off beating, which is sometimes as faint as the ghost of an echo, and sometimes rises almost from the next fold of grey land. At all times strange volumes of sound roll across the bare uplands, and reverberate in those hollows in the Downside which seem to await the spectators of some Titanic drama. Often walking alone, with neither man nor animal in sight, you turn sharply to see who it is that gallops behind you. But there is no one. The phantom horseman dashes by with a thunder of hoofs, and suddenly his ride is over and the sound lapses, and you only hear the grasshoppers and the larks in the sky.[2]

Such tricks of sound may easily be accounted for by the curious planes of curve and smoothness into which these Downs have been shaped, but for hundreds of years they must have peopled the villages and the solitary farmhouses in the folds with stories of ghostly riders and unhappy ladies forever seeking their lost treasure. These ghosts have rambled about for so many centuries that they are now old inhabitants with family histories attached to them; but at the present moment one may find many phantoms hovering on the borderland of belief and scepticism – not yet believed in, but not properly accounted for. Human vanity, it may be, embodies them in the first place. The desire to be somehow impossibly, and therefore all the more mysteriously, concerned in secret affairs of national importance is very strong at the present moment. It is none of our business to supply reasons; only to notice queer signs, draw conclusions, and shake our heads. Each village has its wiseacre, who knows already more than he will say; and in a year or two who shall limit the circumstantial narratives which will be current in the neighbourhood, and possibly masquerade in solemn histories for the instruction of the future!

In this district, for instance, there are curious ridges or shelves in the hillside, which the local antiquaries variously declare to have been caused by ice-pressure, or by the pickaxes of prehistoric man. But since the war we have made far better use of them. Not so very long ago, we say a hundred years at most, England was invaded, and, the enemy landing on the Down at the back of our village, we dug trenches to withstand him, much like those in use in Flanders now. You may see them with your own eyes. And this, somehow, is proof that if the Germans land they will land here, which, although terrifying, also gratifies our sense of our own importance.[3]

But these historical speculations are for the contemplative mind of the shepherd, or of the old cottager, who can almost carry back to the days of the great invasion. His daughter has evidence of the supernatural state of things now existing without going farther than the shed in which her hens are sitting. When she came to hatch out her eggs, she will tell you, only five of the dozen had live chicks in them, and the rest were addled. This she attributes unhesitatingly to vibrations in the earth caused by the shock of the great guns in Flanders. If you express a doubt she will overwhelm you with evidence from all the country round. But no one here limits the action of the guns to the addling of a few hen's eggs; the very sun in the sky, they assert, has been somehow deranged in his mechanism by our thunder on earth. The dark spell of cloudy weather which spoilt July was directly due to these turmoils, and the weather-wise at the cottage laid it down as a fact that we should see no more sun all summer. None could rightly divine the reason; but to offer a reason for such sublime transactions would be almost to cast a doubt upon them. The sun has shone fiercely since then and is shining still, and local wisdom has fastened with renewed hope upon the behaviour of the church bell. The bell belongs to a church which stands solitary upon a hill in the midst of wild marshes, and is gifted with the power of foretelling the return of peace by dropping from the belfry exactly three months before peace is declared. Thus, at least, did it testify to the advent of peace after the Boer War; and once again, on 3 May last, to the delight of all beholders, the rope broke and the bell fell to earth.

August is well on its way, but you may still hear the guns from the top of the Downs; the sun blazes in a cloudless sky, and the eggs are no longer addled; but we are by no means downcast, and merely turn our minds to the next riddle, with a deeper conviction than before that we live in a world full of mysteries.

1 – An article, 'from a correspondent', in *The Times*, 15 August 1916, (Kp c54). The Woolfs had spent most of the previous month, and were to spend the whole of August and up to 16 September at Asheham House, on the edge of the Downs, a short distance from Itford, near Lewes, in Sussex. The genesis of VW's article is not documented.
2 – Followed in *The Times* by the sub-heading: 'Borderland of Mystery'.
3 – Followed in *The Times* by the sub-heading: 'Portents at Home'.

'The Park Wall'

The Park Wall confirms us in our belief that Elinor Mordaunt takes a very high place among living novelists and also a very honourable one. The book, indeed, is good enough to make us cast our eyes back to the old novels of great reputation, not merely to make the old comparisons and declare that here at last we have a writer worthy, &c., &c.; but to see how far we have travelled and in what respects we differ. Mrs Mordaunt's books appear to us sufficiently original and therefore emphatic to serve as a landmark. She writes in her way, and they in theirs; and one writer may be more richly gifted than another: but that sometimes seems to be of less importance than to have, as only true artists have, a world of one's own; and we begin to think that, whether big or small, Mrs Mordaunt's world is certainly her own.

The Park Wall is a wall of solid bricks, for Alice Ingpen, the heroine, lives in a substantial country house, but it is also a wall of tough though immaterial prejudice. Although she is by nature very slow and diffident, Alice soon finds herself amazingly further outside her park wall than most young women of her station. In the first place, her marriage takes her to live at Terracine, an island which lies 'a species of blister on the hot face of the Indian Ocean'; and then her husband turns out to be 'a common low cad',[2] a speculator, a gambler, and, naturally, a completely unfaithful husband. By means of a stratagem he sends her back to England on the same ship with a man to whom she has no tie save that of friendship; and directly they land he proceeds to divorce her. Her family shut their park gates against her. A child is born to her, and she goes to live in the south of London, where eventually she finds work in a factory for making cheap dresses. We may add that the story, after many more complications than we have described, ends happily; but the story is not the important thing.

If it were the important thing there would be faults to find with it – the husband's stratagem, to begin with, is not a very convincing one; nor can we believe that a respectable family of country gentlefolk would bring themselves to desert their daughter, as the Ingpens deserted Alice. But does it very much matter? So long as the writer moves from point to point as one who follows the lead of his mind fearlessly, it does not seem to matter at all. Mrs Mordaunt's mind is an extremely honest one, and where it points, she follows. She takes us with her, therefore, our intelligence on the alert, uncertain what is to happen, but with an increasing consciousness that all that happens is part of a genuine design. The writer is sufficiently mistress of her art to hold this out firmly before us, without any of those sudden immersions in this character or that incident which overcome the ill-equipped writer and destroy his composition. Her mastery of her subject allows her to enrich it with reflections of real profundity:

In the romance of young lovers there is the bud; in marriage there is the real fruit, sweet or bitter, as the case may be. Those who have their teeth in the rind may be slow to discover its flavour, for there is a sort of shock of the taste which for a while conceals taste. But while they are still uncertain the onlookers know all about it; wait, with some interest, for the inevitable grimace, and then go away. The man or woman who thinks to keep them amused by going on grimacing is mistaken.[3]

This ability to withdraw slightly and see the picture as a whole and reflect upon it is very rare; it generally implies, as we think it does in the case of Mrs Mordaunt, a power to strike out characters with solid bodies and clear-cut features. Her men (unless we are merely hypnotised to think so by a woman's name on the title page) are less good than her women; but even they fill their spaces in the design satisfactorily, and Alice herself is extraordinarily successful. We feel ourselves thinking so closely with her that, as in the case of a living person, we almost anticipate her words. Mrs Mordaunt treats her without any of the self-consciousness and the random boldness which mark her portraits of men, and makes us wonder whether the most successful work in fiction is not done almost instinctively. Again, we find ourselves glancing back at the classics. But if anyone seeks proof that the moderns are attempting and achieving something different from the great dead, let him read the scene in the Bloomsbury hotel,[4] when the family spirit utters itself in scarcely articulate cries and curses, with a curious effect as of angry parrots fluttering in a cage round some mute dove with folded wings. Surely Mrs Mordaunt is here attempting something that the Victorians never thought of, feeling and finding expression for an emotion that escaped them entirely. But whether this is so or not, the fact remains that *The Park Wall* is separate and individual enough to be studied for itself.

1 – A review in the *TLS*, 31 August 1916, (Kp C55) of *The Park Wall* (Cassell & Co. Ltd., 1916) by Elinor Mordaunt (pseudonym for Evelyn May Mordaunt, *née* Clowes, 1877–1942), prolific author of fiction and travel books. 'I've just read Mrs Mordaunts latest novel "The Park Wall",' VW wrote to Molly MacCarthy on 26 August 1916, 'very good, I think, and if it weren't for you, I should again attempt to write to her.' (*II VW Letters*, no. 782; the reference to a previous attempt to write to Mrs Mordaunt is unexplained.) See also *'Before Midnight'* below. Reprinted: *CW*.
2 – Mordaunt, ch. VI, p. 54; ch. XVI, p. 153.
3 – *Ibid.*, ch. XI, p. 107; which has: 'cancels taste'.
4 – *Ibid.*, ch. XVII, pp. 174–88.

The Fighting Nineties

As the title indicates, this is not an autobiography or a book of ordinary recollections so much as the selection of a few memories dear to the writer. Mrs Pennell has never made notes – never, as it seems, had the time to stop and comment when life pressed such a succession of duties and delights upon her. She tells few anecdotes even of the dead, and leaves a wide space between herself and those living celebrities who are, she hints, ready to spring out with all their claws displayed at the least rattle upon the bars of their privacy. But her memories are much too personal and spontaneous to need such artificial ornaments. If 'Arnold at Venice'[2] catches your eye, you will read of a gentleman who 'found the café as comfortable a place to sleep in as any other', and 'the one thing that roused him was baseball',[3] from which we may deduce that he was not even related to Arnold the poet.

Mrs Pennell's day was one of strenuous bicycling and journalism; but this she cuts off and dwells almost exclusively upon a long series of nights in Rome and Venice, London and Paris, when the gilt mirrors of innumerable restaurants reflected little parties of very youthful artists discussing all things in life and art, until the proprietor had to produce candles for them to go home with. Mrs Pennell conveys very charmingly the impression of the wonderfully gifted beings who drifted round the table on those nights, with their eccentric adventures, and their casual way of upsetting all the traditions current in Spruce Street, Philadelphia, where she was brought up. At first she was continually surprised; they never mentioned 'history, dates, periods, schools', took no account of Ruskin, and considered living artists more interesting than dead ones. 'The vital questions were treatment, colour values, tone, mediums . . . There were nights when I went away believing that nothing mattered in the world except the ground on a copper plate or the grain of a canvas, or the paint in a tube.'[4] And they all believed consistently that in the whole world the only thing that matters is art.

Nights when the little tables in a café attract all the artists in a quarter have never flourished in London, although Mrs Pennell's pages give the lie once more to the notion that English people refuse to congregate and talk if they are given a comfortable private room, whisky and soda and a hospitable hostess. To judge by names, the best of all the nights, so far as brilliance of talk goes, must have been those in the Buckingham Street rooms overlooking the river. Henley came there, and R. A. M. Stevenson, Henry Harland, Whistler, Aubrey Beardsley[5] – all the stars, in short, of the last years of the nineteenth century. The rooms shook with Henley's robust roar, which drove timid spirits to seek far corners; or there was heard the 'Ha, ha!'[6] of Whistler, which also made certain guests thankful that the room was provided with many doors.

And here we must make what appears to be a confession. The little shelf of books bequeathed to us by the writers of that age has always seemed the fruit of an evening time after the hot blaze of day, when swift, moth-like spirits were abroad; a time of graceful talent and thin little volumes whose authors had done with life long before they were old. Nothing annoys Mrs Pennell more than such a description of her incomparable age. They were days above all of fighting and clamour. What they despised they called 'bleat'; what they loved they called 'human'.[7] 'The Fighting Nineties' she calls them in preference to any other description – fighting, it seems, 'Victorian sham prudery and respectability'.[8] Whether the historian will agree with her hardly matters. To the people who lived in them they were, mercifully enough, the one tolerable season of recorded time. If fortune has given us a different period, we may think Mrs Pennell mistaken, but we can sympathise. The difficulty is to sympathise with her in the later chapters, when she becomes so drastically exclusive that ninety-nine out of a hundred of her readers must feel themselves included in the vast herd of 'tourists', 'outsiders', or 'average Englishmen',[9] who, as they flounder about in cafés and galleries, have to be avoided, or, if they cannot be avoided, to be shocked. And from this artistic exclusiveness the step is very short to the worst exclusiveness of all – that which shuts itself up against youth and decries and belittles its work. The change from intense enjoyment of her own youth to disparagement of the youth of others is really surprising. What, one wonders, would Mrs Pennell have said if anyone had addressed her group as she addresses the artists of today?

I have watched with sympathetic amusement these late years one new movement, one new revolt after another, started and led by little men who have not the strength to move anything, or the independence to revolt against anything, except in their boast of it.[10]

Or again:

Their inability to take themselves with gaiety is what makes the young men of the twentieth century so hopelessly different from the young men of the eighteen-nineties. Their high moral ideal and concern with social problems would not permit them to see anything to laugh at in the experiment of feeding a peacock on cake steeped in absinthe.[11]

If such is the toll that time exacts from those who have tasted the best of life, one may surely be content to dine at all the wrong places and be shocked by all the right things.

1 – A review in the *TLS*, 12 October 1916, (Kp C55.1) of *Nights. Rome, Venice in the Aesthetic Eighties. London, Paris in the Fighting Nineties ... With sixteen illustrations* (William Heinemann, 1916) by Elizabeth Robins Pennell (1855–1936), art critic and writer on cookery, wife of the eminent American etcher and illustrator Joseph Pennell (1860–1926), several of whose pictures are reproduced in *Nights*; the Pennells collaborated on a number of books, including the authorised *Life of James McNeill Whistler* (1908).
2 – Pennell, an entry in the index.
3 – *Ibid.*, p. 86; p. 87.
4 – *Ibid.*, p. 46; John Ruskin (1819–1900), whose *Stones of Venice* was published in 1851–3.
5 – William Ernest Henley (1849–1903), poet, dramatist, critic and editor; Robert Alan Mowbray Stevenson (1847–1900), painter and art critic, champion of Impressionism, a cousin of R. L. Stevenson; Henry Harland (1861–1905), American novelist, who settled in England in the early nineties and became literary editor of the

Yellow Book; James McNeill Whistler (1834–1903), painter; Aubrey Vincent Beardsley (1872–98), artist, art editor of the *Yellow Book*.
6 – Pennell, p. 142.
7 – *Ibid.*, p. 136: 'Pretence of any kind was as the red rag; "bleat" was the unpardonable sin; the man who was "human" was the man to be praised. I would not pretend to say who invented this meaning for the word "human". Perhaps Robert Louis Stevenson . . . But however that may have been, "bleat" and "human" were the two words ever recurring like a refrain in the columns of the *National Observer* [ed. W. E. Henley] . . .'
8 – *Ibid.*, p. 118; p. 190.
9 – The terms 'tourist' and 'outsider' occur regularly *passim*, as do Englishmen; for the only reference to 'the average Englishman', *ibid.*, p. 284.
10 – *Ibid.*, p. 235.
11 – *Ibid.*, p. 265.

Among the Poets

On the face of it there is a great deal to be said in favour of such a book as this. For it is very pleasant to think of literature rather informally sometimes, and to be led about a library by some enthusiast who is always pulling out a volume and saying 'Listen to this'. And there is a real service to be performed by people who are not professors or specialists, but merely know good writing when they see it. The mass of new poetry is vast; every year hundreds of poems must sink to the depths and be lost for ever. We need, therefore, watchers with trained eyes who will go through book after book and extract what is worth keeping. And who, after all, is better qualified than Mr Coleridge to discharge the duties of an examiner or warden of letters? 'I have lived all my life in libraries,' he writes, 'first in my father's, which was magnificent, and afterwards in my own, which is precious.'[2] And, then, he is a Coleridge.

He begins with sufficient spirit to raise our hopes very high. Here, he says, taking down a book of poems by a young American, called Charles Henry Luders, 'is one of the most lovely things in the world'.[3] Naturally after hearing that we are disappointed by the poem itself. We are immediately prepared to cap it with something just as good by someone as little known. Next we have an extract from a prize poem on the Apollo Belvedere by Dean Milman;[4] and then, after a little discourse upon the value of classical study, a famous sonnet of Wordsworth's.[5]

What are the principles that guide Mr Coleridge in choosing selections for our improvement and delight? It is not difficult to discover them. The prize always goes to the poet of finish and scholarship, who observes the laws of prosody and elevates and refines the passions, which is, Mr Coleridge observes, the 'true function of the poet'.[6] And with this for his standard he moves his poets up and down like boys in a class. Walt Whitman and his admirers go to the very bottom. '. . . it is as impossible to argue with persons who admire tnis kind of flux from a dictionary ⟨The Song of the Broad Axe⟩ as it is to discuss principles of beauty in art with an admirer of the Cubists . . .';[7] and so on. There is more to be said for Lowell,[8] but Mr Coleridge pauses in his remarks upon him to observe rather plaintively that he wore a beard. On the other hand, Miss Anne Reeves Aldritch and Miss Lucy Larcom[9] get almost full marks. But Mr Coleridge's range is very wide and purposely haphazard. Here, for instance, he opens Swinburne, and remarks, 'In the later years of the nineteenth century Swinburne enjoyed a very considerable reputation.'[10] We may possibly be aware of that already; but other comments are more disputable and should make Mr Coleridge's library ring with argument. Pope, he says, 'never attains the grand style';[11] 'it is remarkable that even the finest work of Wordsworth appears to be generally quite uninspired';[12] 'the finest work is always perfectly simple';[13] of Walter Savage Landor, 'his excursions into poetry do nothing to enhance his fame'.[14] To all of which we can only reply that we do not agree with a word of it.

Living writers as a rule are not well represented in Mr Coleridge's library; or, if he admits them, there must be labels attached to them to warn off the public. Both Mr Masefield and Mr Bernard Shaw have 'projected upon the public the foul expletive which never passes the lips of any decent person'.[15] And Mr Yeats is by no means safe reading. He encourages a loose habit of mind – a confusion between beauty and vagueness. There is a line of his about evening which has been much admired by the young:

> And evening, full of the linnet's wings,

whereas the truth is that linnets 'go to roost no later than any other birds'.[16]

But these quotations show Mr Coleridge with the birch in his hand, driving intruders out of the sanctuary; and, that done, he falls down and worships with the most devout and thankful of hearts. His god – one need hardly say it – is Tennyson. And his final exhortation is to read through *In Memoriam* once a year at least; then he quotes 'Tears, Idle Tears',[17] and the beauty of it is so much greater than we remembered that we take down Tennyson at once. Enough has been said, perhaps, to show that, though we should not allow Mr Coleridge to choose our new poets for us, he is a very vigilant guardian of the old.

1 – A review in the *TLS*, 2 November 1916, (Kp c56) of *An Evening in my Library Among the English Poets* (John Lane, The Bodley Head, 1916) by the Hon. Stephen Coleridge.

2 – Coleridge, Preface, p. vii; Stephen William Buchanan Coleridge (1854–1936), clerk of assize, author, son of John Duke Coleridge (1st Baron Coleridge), the lord chief justice, and a graduate of Trinity College, Cambridge. His numerous publications include *New Poems* (1911), *Memories* (1913) and *A Morning in my Library* (1914).

3 – *Ibid.*, p. 4, referring to a poem, 'Wind of the North, wind of the norland snows', 'written by a young American over the grave of a beautiful girl that he had loved and lost and whom he soon followed'. Charles Henry Luders (1858–91), author of *The Dead Nymph and Other Poems* (1892) and *A Garden God* (1893).

4 – *Ibid.*, p. 5; Henry Hart Milman (1791–1868), dean of St Paul's, from 1849, had won the Newdigate Prize in 1812 with an English poem on the 'Apollo Belvidere' (sic); he was later to write historical dramas and religious histories.

5 – *Ibid.*, p. 8: the famous sonnet referred to is that beginning 'The world is too much with us . . .' William Wordsworth (1770–1850).

6 – *Ibid.*, p. 31, which has: 'It may be conceded that the chief function of the poet is to communicate pleasure, as that of the man of science is to communicate truth, but one of the poet's functions is to express in a perfect and soul-satisfying form the sorrows and losses that visit us all, and by clothing them with beauty, rob them of some of their crushing weight.'

7 – *Ibid.*, pp. 36–7; Walt Whitman (1819–92), *The Song of the Broad Axe* (1856).

8 – *Ibid.*, pp. 41–2; James Russell Lowell (1819–91).

9 – For Anne Reeve Aldritch (1866–92), author of *The Rose of Flame and Other Poems of Love* (1889), *Songs About Life, Love and Death* (1892), *ibid.*, p. 164; for Lucy Larcom (1824–93), author of *As It Is In Heaven* (1891), *At the Beautiful Gate and Other Songs of Faith* (1892), *ibid.*, p. 166.

10 – *Ibid.*, p. 180; Algernon Charles Swinburne (1837–1909).

11 – *Ibid.*, p. 144; Alexander Pope (1688–1744).

12 – *Ibid.*, p. 172.

13 – *Ibid.*, p. 135.

14 – *Ibid.*, p. 170; Walter Savage Landor (1775–1864).

15 – *Ibid.*, p. 163; John Masefield (1878–1967); George Bernard Shaw (1856–1950).

16 – *Ibid.*, p. 188, quoting from 'The Lake Isle of Innisfree' by W. B. Yeats (1865–1939).

17 – *Ibid.*, pp. 210–11; Alfred, Lord Tennyson (1809–92), *In Memoriam A.H.H.* (1850); 'Tears, Idle Tears', a song from *The Princess* (1847).

'London Revisited'

It is rather difficult to decide what section of the public ought to be advised to lay out six shillings upon Mr Lucas's book. If you want to look up information about a church or a building as you look up a train in the A B C, you will find nine times out of ten that there is no mention of that church or building. If, again, you want to contemplate London philosophically, humorously, or aesthetically, the lists of pictures, statues, and historic houses, delivered in the impersonal manner of a cathedral guide, will grate upon your teeth rather dryly. But if you belong to what is evidently no small section of the human race – that is, the public which reads whatever Mr Lucas writes[2] – the book may be recommended as a good example of his manner. He displays his neat, trim style, his love of old books, odd characters, cricket, Charles Lamb, collections, antiquities, water-colour paintings, curiosities, quotations – but the list threatens to be a long one; and the dominant interest in the present book is certainly London.

But if Mr Lucas had a million interests he could safely find pegs for them all in the streets of London. Personally, we should be willing to read one volume about every street in the city, and should still ask for more. From the bones of extinct monsters and the coins of Roman emperors in the cellars to the name of the shopman over the door, the whole story is fascinating and the material endless. Perhaps cockneys are a prejudiced race, but certainly this inexhaustible richness seems to belong to London more than to any other great city. By side of her Paris is small and frivolous; and, though all Continental cities have copied Paris, for Londoners, at any rate, there is only one real example of a town in the world – compared with her the rest are country villages. But each Londoner has a London in his mind which is the real London, some denying the right of Bayswater to be included, others of Kensington; and each feels for London as he feels for his family, quietly but deeply, and with a quick eye for affront.

Many of us, for instance, have never quite reconciled ourselves to the attempt which has been made of late to comb out her huddle of little streets and substitute military-looking avenues with enormous symbolical mounds of statuary placed exactly at the wrong spot – for we have no sense, like the French, for the outdoor dramatic. And the lavish use of white stone, though commended by Mr Lucas (it is, he says, 'the only true building material for London'),[3] lends itself too much in the hands of modern architects to scrolls and festoons, fit for the white sugar of a wedding cake rather than for the streets of a great city. But in the last two winters many of us must have realised the beauty of the white church spires for the first time; as they lie against the blue of the night in their ethereal ghostliness. There is room for all diversion of opinion about London; and, however often you may walk her streets, you are always picking up new facts about her. How many of us know two facts mentioned by Mr Lucas – that in St Giles's-in-the-Fields off the Charing Cross Road lie buried Marvell and Chapman, James Shirley and Lord Herbert of Cherbury?[4] and that all the lampposts in the parish of St Martin-in-the-Fields bear a relief of St Martin giving his cloak to the beggar?[5] The list of open-air statues which Mr Lucas has compiled is far longer than we should have expected. We own to finding ourselves completely outdone by Mr Lucas in appreciation of these works. But even the statues of London are lovable; and the sparrows find the top hats of statesmen good lodging for their nests. Finally, if Cleopatra's Needle is to count as a statue, why is there no mention of one of the few pieces of sculpture in the streets of London that is pleasing to the eye – the woman with an urn which fronts the gates of the Foundling Hospital?[6] In future editions of this book we hope that Mr Lucas will spare her a word of praise; and reveal the name of the sculptor.

1 – A review in the TLS, 9 November 1916, (Kp c57) of *London Revisited. With sixteen drawings in colour by H. M. Livens and sixteen other illustrations* (Methuen & Co. Ltd., 1916) by E. V. Lucas. (The book was issued as a companion to Lucas's *A Wanderer in London*, 1906.)

2 – Edward Verrall Lucas (1868–1938), journalist and critic, was a prolific author of light essays – of which he published about thirty collections – in the manner of Charles Lamb (1775–1834), of whom Lucas was both an editor and biographer, and whose essay 'Valentine's Day' (*Elia*, 1823), he discusses and quotes from at length in ch. II here.

3 – *Ibid.*, ch. I, p. 5.

4 – For the burial place of Andrew Marvell (1621–78), George Chapman (1559?–1634?), James Shirley (1596–1666) and Lord Herbert of Cherbury (1583–1648), *ibid.*, ch. III, pp. 51–3.

5 – *Ibid.*, ch. XXIII, p. 271.

6 – Lucas refers to the statue opposite the Foundling Hospital, at the end of Lamb's Conduit, of the philanthropist founder of the hospital Captain Thomas Coram (1668–1751) – see *ibid.*, ch. XIV, p. 163. The statue of 'the woman with an urn' which he neglected to mention is known as the Water Bearer and listed in A. Byron, *London Statues* (Constable, 1981), p. 272, as the Francis Whiting Fountain, 1870.

In a Library

We hope that the modesty of Professor Hudson's[2] preface will not mislead many of his readers into thinking that it is quite a simple matter to write such a book themselves. It is, he says, a by-product of 'more serious work in literature',[3] and unless we are much mistaken, behind each of the essays lies a background of extremely wide and serious reading. The learning is suppressed rather than obtruded; but it raises Professor Hudson to an eminence from which he can see his subject in the right proportions, and makes his treatment at once light and authoritative.

Anyone who chances to read an essay now and again upon such forgotten writers as Henry Carey and George Lillo[4] is aware how earnestly the essayist strains to prove the importance of his subject. Either he was the unacknowledged father of the novel or the forgotten originator of the essay – a claim we would willingly concede, for the most part, if by so doing we might escape the proofs of it. Professor Hudson, on the other hand, frankly acknowledges the obscurity of his heroes, and, by demonstrating that their writing was often extremely dull, persuades us to find a good deal of amusement in it. But, having all the facts at his fingers' ends, he can do what is more to the point – he can show us why it is that men like Carey and Lillo, while themselves unimportant, are yet interesting figures in the history of literature.

Carey, we all know, wrote 'Sally in our Alley'. But we do not know that he wrote it after 'dodging' a shoemaker's 'prentice who was taking his sweetheart to a 'sight of Bedlam, the Puppet-Shows, the Flying Chairs, and all the elegancies of Moorfields'.[5] We do not perhaps know that he was one of the first writers in that aristocratic age to see the 'beauty of a chaste and disinterested passion, even in the lowest class of human life'.[6] Before his time, chaste and disinterested passions were considered to be the monopoly of the peerage. It was only when you wrote a comedy or wanted to provide some comic relief that you could introduce the lower classes with propriety. This interesting theory is discussed at greater length in the paper upon George Lillo, whose play, *The London Merchant,* did much to bring middle-class men and women upon the stage not as butts, but as heroes and heroines – a piece of presumption which much offended 'the Town', although the play has been acted from 1731 down to our own time, when Sir Henry Irving used to play it in the provinces.[7] As a stout democrat Professor Hudson asserts that the prejudice which made an aristocratic hero essential is nowadays 'in the last degree unintelligible'.[8] But is that so? Considering the rarity of coronets, the number of lords and ladies in modern fiction is really notable, and must be supported by some demand on the part of the public. And the tendency is not quite so unintelligible or so vicious as Professor Hudson would have it. Without saying that certain kinds of emotion are actually made more dignified by the fact that they are felt by a king or a queen it is far easier to make them seem dignified. The associations are on the side of the peerage. And who shall say that a line like

Queens have died young and fair[9]

would have the same charm if it were merely girls, or maids, who had died young and fair?

The question, however, is not one of title or no title so much as the more interesting question of realism or romance. It is in this respect that Lillo was a great innovator. His heroes and heroines were not only merchants and clerks, but they felt like merchants and clerks. Their virtues were decency, honesty and thrift; and, however tragic they might be, they spoke in prose. And so, as Professor Hudson observes, we descend to the plays of Ibsen[10] and the modern development of prose fiction. But have we made things any easier for the novelist or the dramatist by widening their scope? Naturally not; for where everything may be written about, the difficulty is to know what to leave out. Our modern problem is that we want to preserve the beauty and romance of the heroic together with what is called character-drawing and likeness to life; and the peerage, if it tempts, tempts because it puts our characters a little further from us and invests them with a softer light. The whole subject of the middle-class drama and the growth of realism is a very interesting one, and we are glad to see that Professor Hudson proposes to treat it at length in a forthcoming book.[11]

1 – A review in the *TLS*, 23 November 1916, (Kp c58) of *A Quiet Corner in a Library* (G. G. Harrap & Co., 1916) by W. H. Hudson. Reprinted: *CW*.

2 – William Henry Hudson (1862–1918), an extension lecturer in English literature at London University. In the period 1897–1903, he had held professorial appointments in America at the universities of Stanford and Chicago.

3 – Hudson, Pref., p. vii.

4 – Henry Carey (d. 1743), poet and musician, author of burlesques, including, notably, *Chrononhotonthologos . . . the most tragical tragedy ever yet tragedised* (1734), and of 'Sally in Our Alley' and 'Namby Pamby' (*Poems*, 1729), verses written in ridicule of Ambrose Philips. George Lillo (1693–1739), dramatist, author of *The London Merchant, or the History of George Barnwell* (1731), *The Christian Hero* (1735), *Fatal Curiosity* (1736), *Elmerick, or Justice Triumphant* (1740). Hudson's other chapters are devoted to Thomas Hood (1799–1845) and to Samuel Richardson (1689–1761).

5 – Hudson, p. 68, quoting Carey's prefatory note to the poem.

6 – *Ibid*.

7 – *Ibid*., p. 122: '. . . strange as it may seem to those of us who remember him only in his later years, Sir Henry Irving [1838–1905] frequently performed in the character of Barnwell when a member of the Manchester Theatre Royal'.

8 – *Ibid*., pp. 126–7.

9 – Thomas Nashe (1567–1601), 'In Time of Pestilence':

> Brightness falls from the air;
> Queens have died young and fair;
> Dust hath closed Helen's eye.
> I am sick, I must die.
> Lord have mercy on us.

10 – Henrik Ibsen (1838–1906). And see Hudson, pp. 132–3, where it is argued that 'To us today, fresh from the perusal . . . of *Ghosts* [1881] or *Rosmersholm* [1886]', the idea that the impressiveness of tragedy, and its moral force, depend ultimately upon the rank and dignity of the characters seems monstrous and 'obviously . . . has no basis in fact'. And see p. 162 where Lillo's work is described as the forerunner of both melodrama and, 'more important than this, of that social play of realistic character and serious purpose which is so prominent a feature of our modern stage'.

11 – *Ibid*., Pref., p. vii: 'a volume on George Lillo and the Middle Class Drama of the Eighteenth Century, now nearing completion', but which was not published.

Hours in a Library

Let us begin by clearing up the old confusion between the man who loves learning and the man who loves reading, and point out that there is no connection whatever between the two. A learned man is a sedentary, concentrated solitary enthusiast, who searches through books to discover some particular grain of truth upon which he has set his heart. If the passion for reading conquers him, his gains dwindle and vanish between his fingers. A reader, on the other hand, must check the desire for learning at the outset; if knowledge sticks to him well and good, but to go in pursuit of it, to read on a system, to become a specialist or an authority, is very apt to kill what it suits us to consider the more humane passion for pure and disinterested reading.

In spite of all this we can easily conjure up a picture which does service for the bookish man and raises a smile at his expense. We conceive a pale, attenuated figure in a dressing-gown, lost in speculation, unable to lift a kettle from the hob, or address a lady without blushing, ignorant of the daily news, though versed in the catalogues of the second-hand booksellers, in whose dark premises he spends the hours of sunlight – a delightful character, no doubt, in his crabbed simplicity, but not in the least resembling that other to whom we would direct attention. For the true reader is essentially young. He is a man of intense curiosity; of ideas; open-minded and communicative, to whom reading is more of the nature of brisk exercise in the open air than of sheltered study; he trudges the high road, he climbs higher and higher upon the hills until the atmosphere is almost too fine to breathe in; to him it is not a sedentary pursuit at all.

But, apart from general statements, it would not be hard to prove by an assembly of facts that the great season for reading is the season between the ages of eighteen and twenty-four. The bare list of what is read then fills the heart of older people with despair. It is not only that we read so many books, but that we had such books to read. If we wish to refresh our memories, let us take down one of those old note-books which we have all, at one time or another, had a passion for beginning. Most of the pages are blank, it is true; but at the beginning we shall find a certain number very beautifully covered with a strikingly legible hand-writing. Here we have written down the names of great writers in their order of merit; here we have copied out fine passages from the classics; here are lists of books to be read; and here, most interesting of all, lists of books that have actually been read, as the reader testifies with some youthful vanity by a dash of red ink. We will quote a list of the books that someone read in a past January at the age of twenty, most of them probably for the first time. 1. *Rhoda Fleming*. 2. *The Shaving of Shagpat*. 3. *Tom Jones*. 4. *The Laodicean*. 5. Dewey's *Psychology*. 6. *The Book of Job*. 7. Webbe's *Discourse of Poesie*. 8. *The Duchess of Malfi*. 9. *The Revenger's Tragedy*.[2] And so he goes on from month to month, until, as such lists will, it suddenly stops in the month of June. But if we follow the reader through his months it is clear that he can have done practically nothing but read. Elizabethan literature is gone through with some thoroughness; he read a great deal of Webster, Browning, Shelley, Spenser, and Congreve; Peacock he read from start to finish; and most of Jane Austen's novels two or three times over. He read the whole of Meredith, the whole of Ibsen, and a little of Bernard Shaw. We may be fairly certain, too, that the time not spent in reading was spent in some stupendous arguments in which the Greeks were pitted against the moderns, romance against realism, Racine against Shakespeare,[3] until the lights were seen to have grown pale in the dawn.

The old lists are there to make us smile and perhaps to sigh a little, but we would give much to recall also the mood in which this orgy of reading was done. Happily, this reader was no prodigy, and with a little thought we can most of us recall the stages at least of our own initiation. The books we read in childhood, having purloined them from some shelf supposed to be inaccessible, have something of the unreality and awfulness of a stolen sight of the dawn coming over quiet fields when the household is asleep. Peeping between the curtains we see strange shapes of misty trees which we hardly recognise, though we may remember them all our lives; for children have a strange premonition of what is to come. But the later reading of which the above list is an example is quite a different matter. For the first time, perhaps, all restrictions have been removed, we can read what we like; libraries are at our command, and, best of all, friends who find themselves in the same position. For days upon end we do nothing but read. It is a time of extraordinary excitement and exaltation. We seem to rush about recognising heroes. There is a sort of wonderment in our minds that we ourselves are really doing this, and mixed with it an absurd arrogance and desire to show our familiarity with the greatest human beings who have ever lived in the world. The passion for knowledge is then at its keenest, or at least most confident, and we have, too, an intense singleness of mind which the great writers gratify by making it appear that they are at one with us in their estimate of what is good in life. And as it is necessary to hold one's own against someone who has adopted Pope, let us say, instead of Sir Thomas Browne,[4] for a hero, we conceive a deep affection for these men, and feel that we know them not as other people know them, but privately by ourselves. We are fighting under their leadership, and almost in the light of their eyes. So we haunt the old bookshops and drag home folios and quartos, Euripides in wooden boards, and Voltaire in eighty-nine volumes octavo.[5]

But these lists are curious documents, in that they seem to include scarcely any of the contemporary writers. Meredith and Hardy and Henry James were of course alive when this reader came to them, but they were already accepted among the classics. There is no man of his own generation who influences him as Carlyle, or Tennyson, or Ruskin[6] influenced the young of their day. And this we believe to be very characteristic of youth, for unless there is some admitted giant he will have nothing to do with the smaller men, although they deal with the world he lives in. He will rather go back to the classics, and consort entirely with minds of the very first order. For the time being he holds himself aloof from all the activities of men, and, looking at them from a distance, judges them with superb severity.

Indeed, one of the signs of passing youth is the birth of a sense of fellowship with other human beings as we take our place among them. We should like to think that we keep our standard as high as ever; but we certainly take more interest in the writings of our contemporaries and pardon their lack of inspiration for the sake of something that brings them nearer to us. It is even arguable that we get actually more from the living, although they may be much inferior, than from the dead. In the first place there can be no secret vanity in reading our contemporaries, and the kind of admiration which they inspire is extremely warm and genuine because in order to give way to our belief in them we have often to sacrifice some very respectable prejudice which does us credit. We have also to find our own reasons for what we like and dislike, which acts as a spur to our attention, and is the best way of proving that we have read the classics with understanding.

Thus to stand in a great bookshop crammed with books so new that their pages almost stick together, and the gilt on their backs is still fresh, has an excitement no less delightful than the old excitement of the second-hand bookstall. It is not perhaps so exalted. But the old hunger to know what the immortals thought has given place to a far more tolerant curiosity to know what our own generation is thinking. What do living men and women feel, what are their houses like and what clothes do they wear, what money have they and what food do they eat, what do they love and hate, what do they see of the surrounding world, and what is the dream that fills the spaces of their active lives? They tell us all these things in their books. In them we can see as much both of the mind and of the body of our time as we have eyes for seeing.

When such a spirit of curiosity has fully taken hold of us, the dust will soon lie thick upon the classics unless some necessity forces us to read them. For the living voices are, after all, the ones we understand the best. We can treat them as we treat our equals; they are guessing our riddles, and, what is perhaps more important, we understand their jokes. And we soon develop another taste, unsatisfied by the great – not a valuable taste, perhaps, but certainly a very pleasant possession – the taste for bad books. Without committing the indiscretion of naming names we know which authors can be trusted to produce yearly (for happily they are prolific) a novel, a book of poems or essays, which affords us indescribable pleasure. We owe a great deal to bad books; indeed, we come to count their authors and their heroes among those figures who play so large a part in our silent life. Something of the same sort happens in the case of the memoir writers and autobiographers, who have created almost a fresh branch of literature in our age. They are not all of them important people, but strangely enough, only the most important, the dukes and the statesmen, are ever really dull. The men and women who set out, with no excuse except perhaps that they saw the Duke of Wellington once, to confide to us their opinions, their quarrels, their aspirations, and their diseases, generally end by becoming, for the time at least, actors in those private dramas with which we beguile our solitary walks and our sleepless hours. Refine all this out of our consciousness and we should be poor indeed. And then there are the books of facts and history, books about bees and wasps and industries and gold mines and empresses and diplomatic intrigues, about rivers and savages, trade unions, and Acts of Parliament, which we always read and always, alas! forget. Perhaps we are not making out a good case for a bookshop when we have to confess that it gratifies so many desires which have apparently nothing to do with literature. But let us remember that here we have a literature in the making. From these new books our children will select the one or two by which we shall be known for ever. Here, if we could recognise it, lies some poem, or novel, or history which will stand up and speak with other ages about our age when we lie prone and silent as the crowd of Shakespeare's day is silent and lives for us only in the pages of his poetry.

This we believe to be true; and yet it is oddly difficult in the case of new books to know which are the real books and what it is that they are telling us, and which are the stuffed books which will come to pieces when they have lain about for a year or two. We can see that there are many books, and we are frequently told that everyone can write nowadays. That may be true; yet we do not doubt that at the heart of this immense volubility, this flood and foam of language, this irreticence and vulgarity and triviality, there lies the heat of some great passion which only needs the accident of a brain more happily turned than the rest to issue in a shape which will last from age to age. It should be our delight to watch this turmoil, to do battle with the ideas and visions of our own time, to seize what we can use, to kill what we consider worthless, and above all to realise that we must be generous to the people who are giving shape as best they can to the ideas within them. No age of literature is so little submissive to authority as ours, so free from the dominion of the great; none seems so wayward with its gift of reverence, or so volatile in its experiments. It may well seem, even to the attentive, that there is no trace of school or aim in the work of our poets and novelists. But the pessimist is inevitable, and he shall not persuade us that our literature is dead, or prevent us from feeling how true and vivid a beauty flashes out as the young writers draw together to form their new vision, the ancient words of the most beautiful of living languages. Whatever we may have learnt from reading the classics we need now in order to judge the work of our contemporaries, for whenever there is life in them they will be casting their net out over some unknown abyss to snare new shapes, and we must throw our imaginations after them if we are to accept with understanding the strange gifts they bring back to us.

But if we need all our knowledge of the old writers in order to follow what the new writers are attempting, it is certainly true that we come from adventuring among new books with a far keener eye for the old. It seems that we should now be able to surprise their secrets; to look deep down into their work and see the parts come together, because we have watched the making of new books, and with eyes clear of prejudice can judge more truly what it is that they are doing, and what is good and what bad. We shall find, probably, that some of the great are less venerable than we thought them. Indeed, they are not so accomplished or so profound as some of our own time. But if in one or two cases this seems to be true, a kind of humiliation mixed with joy overcomes us in front of others. Take Shakespeare, or Milton,[7] or Sir Thomas Browne. Our little knowledge of how things are done does not avail us much here, but it does lend an added zest to our enjoyment. Did we ever in our youngest days feel such amazement at their achievement as that which fills us now that we have sifted myriads of words and gone along uncharted ways in search of new forms for our new sensations? New books may be more stimulating and in some ways more suggestive than the old, but they do not give us that absolute certainty of delight which breathes through us when we come back again to *Comus*, or 'Lycidas', 'Urn Burial' or *Antony and Cleopatra*.[8] Far be it from us to hazard any theory as to the nature of art. It may be that we shall never know more about it than we know by nature, and our longer experience of it teaches us this only – that of all our pleasures those we get from the great artists are indisputably among the best; and more we may not know. But, advancing no theory, we shall find one or two qualities in such works as these which we can hardly expect to find in books made within the span of our lifetime. Age itself may have an alchemy of its own. But this is true: you can read them as often as you will without finding that they have yielded any virtue and left a meaningless husk of words; and there is a complete finality about them. No cloud of suggestions hangs about them teasing us with a multitude of irrelevant ideas. But all our faculties are summoned to the task, as in the great moments of our own experience; and some consecration descends upon us from their hands which we return to life, feeling it more keenly and understanding it more deeply than before.

1 – An essay in the *TLS*, 30 November 1916, (Kp C59). The title was used by Leslie Stephen for his collections of critical essays originally published in 1874 and 1876. Reprinted: *G&R, CE*.
2 – George Meredith (1828–1909), *Rhoda Fleming* (1865), *The Shaving of Shagpat: an Arabian Entertainment* (1856). Henry Fielding (1707–54), *Tom Jones, a Foundling* (1749). Thomas Hardy (1840–1928), *A Laodicean* (1881). John Dewey (1859–1952), *Psychology* (1887). William Webbe (fl. 1568–91), *A Discourse of English Poetrie* (1586). John Webster (1580?–1625?), *The Duchess of Malfi* (c. 1614). Cyril Tourneur (1575?–1626), *The Revenger's Tragedy* (1607).

3 – Robert Browning (1812–89); Percy Bysshe Shelley (1792–1822); Edmund Spenser (1552?–99); William Congreve (1670–1729); Thomas Love Peacock (1785–1866); Jane Austen (1775–1817); Henrik Ibsen (1828–1906); George Bernard Shaw (1856–1950); Jean Racine (1639–99); William Shakespeare (1564–1616).
4 – Alexander Pope (1688–1744); Sir Thomas Browne (1605–82).
5 – No volume of 'Euripides in wooden boards' is catalogued as having been owned by VW. The edition of the works of Voltaire (1694–1778) is probably that listed in Holleyman: *Oeuvres complètes de Voltaire*, ed. Caron de Beaumarchais, *et al* (70 vols, 1785–89), a set of which belonged to LW and which in 1904 he took to Ceylon – see *ILW*, p. 130.
6 – Henry James (1843–1916); Thomas Carlyle (1795–1881); Alfred, Lord Tennyson (1809–92); John Ruskin (1819–1900).
7 – John Milton (1608–74).
8 – Milton, *Comus, A Masque* (1634, published 1637), 'Lycidas' (1637); Sir Thomas Browne, 'Urn Burial' (1658); Shakespeare, *Antony and Cleopatra* (c. 1606–7).

Old and Young

We have one reason, not the only one by any means, for thinking highly of this book of essays: it makes us wish to write an essay of our own, for the old people. We believe that if they were treated to their share of sermons, in which youth reasoned with them and defined their temptations as frankly as Mr Paget has done it for the young in the present volume, the ordinary life of the household would be much improved. No doubt we have improved it already. The child who calls his mother Mary and his father John is not going to be tongue-tied with false reverence when he grows up; those parents may hope never to stiffen into tyrants living in a sacred, and presumably unhappy, isolation. But as things are the old are as mysterious as idols in a temple; we take off our shoes before we approach them. The whole of our tradition is against unpremeditated intercourse with them; before we speak we sort out what it is proper to say to them as if they were newly made acquaintances, although in fact they may be related to us by the closest ties.

Whether this tradition rests on some truth or is the relic of an age of ancestor worship we do not know; but the effect of such treatment is that we are curiously cut off from communication with the old. They are for the most part mute and scarcely ever the subject of imaginative speculation. And when they do emerge the result is strange. Three or four years ago there was an exhibition of Post-Impressionist pictures,[2] which acted, oddly enough, as a trumpet call to the elderly and consolidated their forces into one opaque block. Everyone of both sexes who was over sixty felt apparently that not only were the principles of art attacked, but also the sanctity of old age. The virulence of the grey-headed was a revelation of the passion that was, and no doubt still is, in them. It was not less puzzling than the pictures themselves. At that time some textbook dealing with the psychology of the old would have been of great assistance; and we suggest that Mr Paget should consider the composition of one. We would ask him to examine particularly the change of mind which takes place between the ages of fifty and sixty. It is when they reach that age, we note, that we begin to treat our elders with respect. Losing the stimulus of contradiction, and relaxing their minds now that they have climbed their ladders, they develop a strange jealousy, a pontifical attitude of mind, so that a celebrated surgeon thinks nothing of dictating laws to a painter, and a successful barrister defines the province of realism in music. Indirectly, Mr Paget's book throws some light on these problems; and his complete immunity from these vices at once makes us desire to qualify any suspicion of harshness in the above remarks. For the old, after all, are the deep mirrors of life, in whose depths we may see all the processions of the past, closely surrounded by the unknown, as the day by the darkness of night.

Mr Paget's book, however, is compact of so many things that we cannot pretend to lasso either it or him with one fling of the rope. We do not know that we can even prove him old as years go; fifty years ago, he tells us, he was a small boy learning Euclid; so that at the most he can lay claim to sixty years only. We accept his word that he is about to become a fossil, and also that his book contains sermons; our experience of the pulpit would not have suggested that particular word. And at the very start he amply proves his own contention that fossils 'are aggressive, contradictious creatures, always spoiling for a fight'.[3] Put him in a Devonshire garden in April and instead of fixing his eyes upon the nearest hedge with a critical stare which suggests the decadence of evergreens, he is off at once upon the beauty of nature and the kindness of his friends. No clergyman could wish for clearer signposts for a sermon; but as Mr Paget treats them they point many different ways. We never know what we may meet at the turn of the page. 'No need here for guide-book talk,' he says; and, indeed, we had settled down to expect something of the kind from him. 'If you want to pay a compliment to the beauty of nature . . . just say *Oh, my*! and expire.' And if Mr Paget talks about himself, he bids us not be offended, because 'every library is full of the beauty of nature and the loving-kindness of man. But so many of these descriptions are impersonal,' he adds, 'they look outside self, not into self.'⁴ One more quotation we may take from this essay:

We do feel, all of us, when we think steadily about it, that there must be some sort of limit to what is bad; some level of reality where it leaves off, some purpose which it does not prevent. In our common talk, our stock phrases, we admit this feeling. We explain away, as if we were in eternity – where, indeed, we are – the misconduct not only of ourselves but of others. *He didn't realise what he was doing, we say* . . . or, again, *One of his uncles is in a lunatic asylum.* [. . .] And I say these feelings are not only sane; they are as near the truth as we can get them.⁵

Now all this, we think, throws a little light upon the problems of old age. We see at once that the essayist is wonderfully at his ease, careless of what people may think of him, and convinced that any pretence is waste of time. All these good qualities spring from familiarity with life. But there are two other qualities which are present and which are even more significant. One is the happiness of old age, and the other is the certainty of the old as to what is right and what wrong. This happiness is quite consistent with a belief that things are very much worse than they were fifty years ago; that, indeed, may be one of the causes of it, though certainly it is not so in the case of Mr Paget. But the content of the old is much greater than their discontent, partly because they are for the most part irresponsible; and partly because they do not look ahead, but into the past and into the present. When we come to consider their certainty as to what is right and what wrong, however, we enter into the mystery of age.

It is clear that Mr Paget collects these essays in the hope that they will make young people in some way better. That, we think, is certain to be the result of so charming a book, but would anyone under sixty cherish such an aim? Until we reach that age those of us who are not moralists by profession have not made up our minds about our own lives, let alone the lives of other people. After that age we become, if we have a turn for thinking at all, full of concern for the soul. We lose the sense of separateness from others, and it becomes of great moment to us that people should understand the value of goodness. For evidently some kind of simplification takes place in the minds of the old. The soul rids itself of a multitude of cares and desires, and attaches itself with the greatest devotion to the one or two beliefs which survive. We think that for the most part these are beliefs in the goodness and badness of conduct, and that this is so is certainly confirmed by every one of Mr Paget's essays. Very active of mind, and having that mind stored with a great variety of knowledge, still the main question for him is always the moral question, whether he is discussing 'Moving Pictures', 'Handwriting', or 'The Beauty of Words'. He has no doubt at all that this is the important aspect of each subject, and therefore he calls us to consider it with an authority which is more impressive than any other of his gifts. By what combination of simplicity, sympathy and absolute sincerity he brings us to an attitude of open-mouthed attention we do not know. But though we cannot define it exactly this we take to be the peculiar gift of the old, which forbids us to be quite at our ease with them, but invests them with mystery and compels our reverence for a knowledge which we ourselves have not.

1 – A review in the *TLS*, 14 December 1916, (Kp C60) of *I Sometimes Think. Essays for the Young People* (Macmillan & Co., 1916) by Stephen Paget (1855–1926), surgeon, propagandist for modern medicine, and man of letters, author of works of biography and of several collections of essays for the young.
2 – The First and Second Post-Impressionist Exhibitions, 1910 and 1912, organised by Roger Fry at the Grafton Galleries.
3 – Paget, Pref., p. vii.
4 – For the three quotations, *ibid.*, 'The World, Myself and Thee', p. 2; p. 3; p. 6.
5 – *Ibid.*, p. 14, which has: 'And I say that'.

'Social Life in England'

These eight lectures were delivered in March 1916, by Dr Foakes Jackson before the Lowell Institute in Boston.[2] The audience apparently received them graciously, and the lecturer has now printed them for a wider audience under a title and inside a cover which seem to us both a little misleading. Dark blue books are not, it is true, necessarily profound; but the title seems to promise something more solid than we have here. That particular century[3] was a momentous one in our social history. The industrial revolution, which turned England from an aristocracy to a democracy, which drove the country people into the factories and raised a large and politically powerful middle class, and the passing of the Reform Bill[4] – to mention the most obvious events alone –

moulded England into a new shape. If Shakespeare had come to life again in the middle of the eighteenth century, he would very soon have understood his position; but if Shakespeare were to awake now! The thought of what he would see in the sky and on the earth is at once appalling and fascinating.

No one could expect an exhaustive account of such a transformation in eight lectures lasting presumably one hour each; but we might look for some grouping or emphasis which would bring a general theory to our attention. That is the kind of service which lectures, with all their disadvantages, tend to perform; and it is a real one. But in this readable little book with its amusing assembly of quotations from Creevey and Dickens, Trollope and Surtees,[5] the reader slips from one picture to another, and is left for the most part to make up his mind as to the kind of world they illustrate for himself. If he looks for guidance to Dr Foakes Jackson he will receive it, but that will not help him materially, because the lecturer does not seem to be altogether sure of his own opinion. In one place he seems to suggest that the society of the Regency was far more exclusive than the society of the present day; in another he asserts that the 'rift between classes'[6] is deeper in our own age than in any other. Now he is of opinion 'that the passions of men are much the same as formerly, and that, if the advantage is on either side, it is with the present rather than with the past'; and later he declares that we are living under a plutocracy which tends to 'substitute prudery and respectability for real Christianity'.[7] But there is no reason to be downcast; if we find these statements either contradictory or depressing we must lay the blame, if blame it is, upon the audience.

To Americans, we suppose, England is always something of an old curiosity shop; they rummage in our past with inquisitive affection, and even, one might suggest, with an eye for bargains. Dr Foakes Jackson dips here and there in our annals to provide his hearers with quaint tokens of the past, old rings, and bits of brocade; and he is careful not to go beyond the curiosity shop. He must not fatigue them with dates and details; he must not harrow their feelings, or offend their morals; he must, if possible, introduce some personal flavour into his discourse by informing them that his great grandparents entertained Crabbe,[8] and that he had a very bad cold when he went to Aldeburgh to prepare his lecture. All this is done very neatly and with a gentlemanly modesty which disarms criticism by advancing only the most temperate opinions and supporting them almost invariably by the authority of others. And so, very naturally, we have an account of the trial of Queen Caroline, taken from the pages of Mr Creevey, a sketch of John Wesley, the narrative of Margaret Catchpole,⁹ and so on. There is no need to tell our own public that Mr Creevey and John Wesley and Charles Dickens are all very good reading. But what Dr Foakes Jackson has given us, oddly enough, is not a picture of ourselves, but a picture of a cultivated American audience. They are, we gather, exquisitely urbane; they do not like outspoken criticism even of the poet Crabbe; the best way to lead them across the desert of the lecture hour is to bring a pocketful of sweetmeats and produce them one after another until the minutes are consumed. Read by this light, one of Dr Foakes Jackson's sentences has a pathetic ring in it. 'I hope,' he says, 'you will pardon the flippancy of the subject I am about to introduce; but I may say that it is not possible to understand English life without studying it.'¹⁰ Sweeping as the pronouncement is, we are inclined to agree with him.

1 – A review in the *TLS*, 21 December 1916, (Kp C61) of *Social Life in England 1750–1850* (Macmillan & Co., 1916) by F. J. Foakes Jackson.
2 – Frederick John Foakes Jackson (1855–1941), divine and author, Fellow of Jesus College, Cambridge, from 1886, honorary canon of Peterborough, 1910–27. During his visit to lecture at the Lowell Institute, Jackson was offered and accepted a professorship of Christian institutions at the Union Theological Seminary, New York, which he held until 1934.
3 – I.e. 1750–1850.
4 – Jackson, 'Creevey Papers – The Regency', p. 212: 'The Reform Bill of 1832 was the answer of the English middle class to the Bill of Pains and Penalties of 1820'; and 'Mid-Victorianism. W. M. Thackeray [1811–63]', p. 270: 'The ruling aristocracy came to an end when the Reform Bill was passed in 1832, but their prestige remained'.
5 – Thomas Creevey (1768–1838); Charles Dickens (1812–70), see *ibid.*, 'Social Abuses Exposed by Charles Dickens'; Anthony Trollope (1815–82); Robert Smith Surtees (1805–64), see *ibid.*, 'Sport, and Rural England'.
6 – Jackson, 'Mid-Victorianism. W. M. Thackeray', p. 301, and see next note.
7 – For the first quotation, *ibid.*, 'Creevey Papers – The Regency', p. 169; for the second, *ibid.*, 'Mid-Victorianism. W. M. Thackeray', pp. 300–1: 'This feeling of shame for having practised some perfectly reputable calling [trade] has had I believe very serious results ... It has destroyed a commercial aristocracy and put a plutocracy in its place. It tended for a time to substitute prudery and respectability for real Christianity; and, before the war at least, even these poor substitutes were growing so out of fashion as to be regretted. It has also deepened the rift between the classes.'
8 – *Ibid.*, 'George Crabbe [1754–1832]', p. 58: Jackson's maternal grandparents,

Mr and Mrs Burcham, had afforded Crabbe hospitality when, in 1780, he had gone to London to pursue a literary career.

9 – John Wesley (1703–91), see *ibid.*, 'Life in the Eighteenth Century Illustrated by the Career of John Wesley'. Margaret Catchpole (1773–1841) – an adventuress whose life was fictionalised by Rev. Richard Cobbold and published in 3 vols in 1845 – see *ibid.*, 'Margaret Catchpole'.

10 – Jackson, 'Sport, and Rural England', p. 302. For VW on English sporting life, see 'Jack Mytton', *V VW Essays* and *CR2*.

Mr Symons's Essays

Somewhere in the present volume Mr Symons quotes the saying of Charles Lamb, 'I love books about books', and adds that that is the test of the book-lover[2] – the test of him, we sometimes think, not because such books are boring or difficult, but rather because they are demoralising. Books about books are apt, one hardly knows why, to reduce Literature to a safe and comfortable pursuit for elderly valetudinarians by the fireside on winter evenings; and to love them seems to mean that such is our love of their subject that we can extract good even from these doubtful surroundings. But there is another sense in which we may take this remark – a sense in which it would certainly apply to the book before us – and that is that to be able to love and understand true criticism of writing is the final test of a love of books, and one of the sweetest rewards of it. Certainly, to be able to write such criticism is so rare a gift that one is inclined to doubt whether it is ever done save by the poets themselves. Our best criticism we owe to them. Coleridge and Lamb, Arnold and Sainte-Beuve[3] were all poets, either with the right hand or with the left. Indeed, it seems impossible for anyone who is not actually dealing with the problems of art to know the nature of them; or – and this is of greater importance – to have a lively enough passion for the artist's view to be in sympathy with the different forms of it.

Mr Symons is a very distinguished poet; as, indeed, we could have guessed from the character of his criticism. These papers are for the most part short: but they are aimed so directly at the heart of the subject that in each case they seem to show us something we had missed before. And it is always done as the poet knows how to do it: without display of knowledge or chain of argument, but directly, simply, and, in spite of the narrow bounds of the essay, fully. He has so fine an instinct for the aim and quality of each writer that the result seems effortless and brimming with truth. Naturally we do not accept all that Mr Symons says; but we must consistently pay homage to the spirit in which he approaches these different writers. It is the spirit of a man to whom art is as undoubtedly a part of life as bread, or air; but who, though his days are spent in the presence of it, never loses his sense of its divinity. In writing of Coventry Patmore he says:

... while he talked to me of the basis of poetry, and of metres and cadences, and of poetical methods, what meant more to me than anything he said, though not a word was without its value, was the profound religious gravity with which he treated the art of poetry, the sense he conveyed to me of his own reasoned conception of its immense importance, its divinity.[4]

'Profound religious gravity' expresses exactly the spirit of Mr Symons's essays; but there goes along with it a sense, most rare and refreshing, that to care for art is the most natural thing in the world. Very often it is the effect of criticism to make art appear so intricate and so remote from the interests of ordinary people that it is useless for them to try to care for it, let alone to attempt the practice of it. They persuade themselves that they are glad not to be artists, and make allowances for those who are. Mr Symons, on the other hand, treats literature with a kind of natural seriousness which should make even the least lettered aware that to write is the most normal occupation for man, or woman either; and we may study and love writing without being in the least queer ourselves. Those who care for literature already may repeat what Mr Symons has said of Coventry Patmore. If he had no other quality save this religious gravity, this reasoned conception of the immense importance, the divinity of poetry, we should be deeply grateful to him; as it is, we must also rejoice in the subtlety of his mind and in his brilliant intelligence. His work is more than a support to us; it serves to stimulate us to quicker feelings.

As to the brilliance, we do not suppose that Mr Symons cares to lay claim to much of that rather doubtful virtue. He has trained himself, as he says with perfect truth, to be 'infinitely careful in all matters of literature'.[5] But it is not seldom that his thought and language fuse themselves in a flash, perhaps a little to the surprise of the author and much to the delight of the reader. We may quote his saying about Meredith: 'In prose he would have every sentence shine; in verse he would have every line sparkle; like a lady who puts on all her jewelry at once, immediately after breakfast.'[6] This, too, is very true: 'To write poetry as if it had never been written before is to attempt what the greatest poets never attempted.'[7] And here is a comment upon Charles Lamb, so penetrating that we wonder, now that it is said, why it was never said before:

The quality which came to him from that germ of madness which lay hidden in his nature had no influence upon his central sanity. It gave him the tragic pathos and mortal beauty of his wit, ... and, also, a hard, indifferent levity, which, to brother and sister alike, was a rampart against obsession, or a stealthy way of temporising with the enemy. That tinge is what gives its strange glitter to his fooling: madness playing safely and lambently around the stoutest common sense.[8]

As we read through Mr Symons's essays we come to recognise, as is the case with all true critics, a certain vein of thought which underlies many of his judgments and gives them personality. He has so great a passion for beauty that he is a little hard upon work which has other qualities, perhaps more valuable than beauty. On this account he seems to us less than just to Ibsen and more than generous to Swinburne.[9] He can write of Ibsen – 'Given the character and the situation, what Ibsen asks at the moment of crisis is, What would this man be most likely to say? not, What would be the finest, the most deeply revealing thing that he could say? In that difference lies all the difference between prose and poetry'.[10] That, to us, is a complete misunderstanding. In such crises, we should say, Ibsen's attempt has been to give what is deeply revealing together with what is likely, and from that source springs his tremendous power. No doubt he failed often, and when he failed he produced either 'the language of the newspaper recorded with the fidelity of the phonograph',[11] or a fantastic symbolism which serves merely to throw dust in our eyes. But when he succeeds his success is based upon the fact that he has not flinched from the prosaic look of things as they are and yet has made them yield as true a poetry as any to be found in the plays of Swinburne. The danger of asking oneself, What is the finest, the most deeply revealing thing that I can make my character say? is demonstrated over and over again by Swinburne, and by most of our poetic dramatists. When their inspiration flags they continue automatically to produce fine words with the semblance of beauty on them; and that is a disease of which it will take many Ibsens and not a few Walt Whitmans[12] to cure us.

Probably Mr Symons intends his distinction between prose and poetry to refer only to the particular prose under discussion – that of Ibsen. But all through his volume there is an evident glory in the beauty of poetry, an exaltation of poetry as the most inspired form which literature can take. Perhaps we may account for this by the curious fact that it was not until he read Pater's *Studies in the History of the Renaissance* that he 'realised that prose also could be a fine art'.[13] And, unconsciously no doubt, he is led to lay stress upon this predilection of his because the temper of the age is impatient with beauty and the particular skill in which he delights. Too fine a critic not to feel worth where it exists, he will not admit the poetic power of Ibsen, and calls *Leaves of Grass* the 'most monstrous and magnificent failure of the nineteenth century'.[14] But the interesting point is not whether one style is bad and another good, or whether we exalt poetry or prefer prose, but that prose has been the chosen medium of the greatest writers of our time – of Dostoevsky, of Carlyle, of Tolstoy.[15] And modern poetry seems more and more to glance at prose and make trial of the methods of prose. Nor can we attribute this to a shallow impatience with tradition or to a failure of artistic power. It springs rather from the belief that there is a form to be found in literature for the life of the present day – for a life lived in little houses separated only by a foot or two of brick wall; for the complicated, intense and petty emotions of the drawing room; for the acts and sights of the streets, and for the whole pageant of life without concealment of its ugly surface. The language which shall express all this is neither the speech of the poets nor the speech of actual life, but it, too, is the result of that 'crystallisation in which direct emotion or sensation deviates exquisitely into art',[16] as Mr Symons puts it, writing of John Donne. The form of prose produces prolonged and cumulative effects; the form of poetry produces instant and intense effects; and for this, among other reasons, what we have to say now seems to shape itself more easily in the form of prose than in the form of poetry. But to place any limit upon either, or to predict that one will supersede the other, is to play with generalities and to force a living being between the walls of a rigid mould. The book of Mr Symons's essays should warn us against any excess of this kind; for whatever his own prejudices may be, he invariably brings all his imagination and all his skill to the understanding of the work before him.

1 – A review in the *TLS*, 21 December 1916, (Kp c62) of *Figures of Several Centuries* (Constable & Co., 1916) by Arthur Symons (1865–1945), poet, translator, critic and editor, friend of W. B. Yeats and of Walter Pater, and a considerable

influence on the young writers and artists of the 1890s. He was the author of several books of verse, including his first collection *Days and Nights* (1889), and also, notably, of *The Symbolist Movement in Literature* (1899).

2 – Symons, 'Charles Lamb [1775–1834]', p. 21, source unidentified.

3 – S. T. Coleridge (1772–1834); Matthew Arnold (1822–88); Charles Augustine Sainte-Beuve (1804–69).

4 – Symons, 'Coventry Patmore', p. 365; Coventry Patmore (1823–96), author of *The Angel in the House* (1854–62), *The Unknown Eros* (1877) etc.

5 – *Ibid.*, 'Walter Pater [1839–94]', p. 323: '...it was through his [Pater's] influence and counsels that I trained myself to be infinitely careful ...'

6 – *Ibid.*, 'George Meredith as a Poet', p. 142, which has: 'shine, in verse'; George Meredith (1828–1909).

7 – *Ibid.*, 'John Donne [c. 1571–1631]', p. 97.

8 – *Ibid.*, 'Charles Lamb', pp. 35–6.

9 – Henrik Ibsen (1828–1906); Algernon Charles Swinburne (1837–1909).

10 – Symons, 'Henrik Ibsen', pp. 266–7.

11 – *Ibid.*, p. 265.

12 – Walt Whitman (1819–92).

13 – Symons, 'Walter Pater', p. 322; *Studies in the History of the Renaissance* (1873).

14 – *Ibid.*, 'Coventry Patmore', p. 374; Walt Whitman, *Leaves of Grass* (1855).

15 – Fyodor Dostoevsky (1821–81); Thomas Carlyle (1795–1881); L. N. Tolstoy (1828–1910).

16 – Symons, 'John Donne', p. 104: 'It is always useful to remember Wordsworth's phrase of "emotion recollected in tranquillity", for nothing so well defines that moment of crystallisation in which direct emotion or sensation deviates exquisitely into art. Donne is intent on the passion itself, the thought, the reality; so intent that he is not at the same time, in that half-unconscious way which is the way of the really great poet, equally intent on the form, that both may come to ripeness together.'

1917

'Romance'

This little book entitled *Romance* contains two lectures, the first upon the origin of Romance, the second upon imitation and forgery. Each, the lazy reader may say, might well have split itself into another pair at least; but Sir Walter Raleigh has never had the interests of the lazy reader at heart. We must be prepared, then, to hold a slim little book in our hands and to find that each sentence holds enough matter to fill a page. The pleasure and the risk of such reading rather resemble the pleasure of finding oneself suddenly out of one's depth at sea. In the first place many of our most trusty props are removed. 'The best way', we are told, 'to restore the habit of thinking is to do away with the names.'² Is Romance, then, or the revival of Romance, to which heading our literary primers have accustomed us, merely a name? We mean something when we use it; but Sir Walter Raleigh is not going to tell us what we mean. He intends that we should find out for ourselves. Like all scholars who know what there is to be known and mix their learning with love, he discards those convenient but indigestible little pellets which between them have made the history of English literature about as interesting as Bradshaw,³ although of course not so accurate. He touches his subject with life, and invests it with all the uncertainty, the possibility, and the vagueness of a living thing.

You cannot define Romance; you cannot classify and explain the significance of men and books; 'to study the ascertained facts concerning men and books is to study . . . the only competent and modest part of the history of literature.'[4] The greater part of these lectures, therefore, is devoted to a sketch of the history of Romance, and there is only a tentative definition of Romance itself. But this sketch does much to define and clarify our ideas. For let us suppose that we have come into the lecture room believing rather vaguely that the romantic revival was a reaction against the school of Pope and Dryden; that it is chiefly marked by a return to nature; and that its most typical examples are to be found in 'Kubla Khan' and the 'Ode to a Nightingale'.[5] The lecturer knocks down our neat compartments one after another by observing that the great writers of all ages have always returned to nature, Pope no less than Wordsworth; that you may find the purest Romance in Virgil; that the Romance writers proper were distinguished by being actual, modern and realistic; that Romance became as bookish as decadent classicism. As for there being one period that is exclusively romantic, and another that is without romance, wherever we look in English literature we shall find Romance in the upper or in the under world. Further, even the age which we associate particularly with the revival of Romance contains Wordsworth, who 'drew straight from life' and 'shunned what is derived from other books',[6] and Scott, whose 'love for the knighthood and monkery was real but it was playful. His heart was with Fielding.'[7] Evidently it is a good thing to avoid, 'except for pastime, the discussion of tendencies and movements',[8] and stick as far as we can to the men and the books.

But there are some facts which may lead us to a clearer view. Many of our misconceptions about Romance may be attributed to a wrong understanding of another famous and ill-used name – the Renaissance. The study of Greek and Latin, for which that name stands, was consummated not in the fifteenth or sixteenth centuries, but in the eighteenth; thus the romantic revival was a reaction against the Renaissance. Fashion turned against the classics now that the classics were familiar and demanded a return to medieval Romance and chivalry. According to Sir Walter the strange thing about this movement was that it was not the supply which created the demand, but the demand which created the supply. Romance had to be made artificially in the forgeries of Ossian and at Strawberry Hill[9] before there arose a generation which could make the real thing.

So curious a state of things suggests speculations which will no doubt lead us to break our necks over another definition of Romance. For how does a country demand romantic poetry? And is it conceivable that sham castles and forged manuscripts, the products of a perfectly false feeling, had it in them to inspire certain little boys with the germs of some of the most genuine feelings that have ever existed? We cannot help thinking that the process was different, and infinitely complex, and that you make your poet as you make your demand for poetry, by a thousand influences which probably have very little to do with art. But the artistic influences are the easiest to trace. It is evident, as Sir Walter points out, that landscape painting, by inducing people to imagine themselves among mountains and sunsets and precipices, played an enormous part in the revival of Romance. We may also find matter for thought in those eighteenth-century gardens which were so strangely unlike the houses they surrounded. What did the gentleman in knee breeches and brocade think about when he stepped from his exquisitely civilised drawing room into a garden that was all green-covered ponds, ruins and blue distances? One may suppose that he thought a great deal about himself, and, removed from the constraint of furniture, rambled in a wilderness among the disorderly recesses of his own mind. To think about oneself is, of course, to think about a great many other things and people too; but perhaps there is truth in the distinction which Sir Walter draws between the 'modern romantic poet', who 'must keep himself aloof from life, that he may see it', and the epic poet 'who holds his reader fast by strong moral bonds of sympathy with the actors in the poem'.[10]

We mean a great many things when we say that a poem is romantic. We refer to an atmosphere of vagueness, mystery, distance; but perhaps we most constantly feel that the writer is thinking more of the effect of the thing upon his mind than of the thing itself. And up to a point there is nothing more real than the effect of things upon one's mind. The difficulty is to resist the temptation of conjuring up sensations for the pleasure of feeling them; and when he does that the writer is lost. For such a one,

> . . . lives alone,
> Housed in a dream, at distance from the Kind.[11]

The great poets, as Sir Walter Raleigh says, are those who 'face the discipline of facts and life'.[12] They may begin as Keats began, with a sense of the wonder of the visible world; of passion and love and beauty; but there comes a time when the passion turns to dream, and only the greatest wake themselves from that and make poetry with their eyes open. For, as Sir Walter says very finely, 'the poetry which can bear all naked truth and still keep its singing voice is the only immortal poetry'.[13]

1 – A review in the TLS, 18 January 1917, (Kp C63) of *Romance. Two Lectures* (Princeton, 1916) by Sir Walter Raleigh (1861–1922), Professor of English Literature, Oxford University, Fellow of Merton College. Raleigh, a relation by marriage of Lytton Strachey, whom he had taught at Liverpool University, delivered the Louis Clark Vanuxem Foundation Lectures ('The Origin of Romance' and 'Imitation and Forgery') at Princeton University on 4 and 5 May 1915. See also 'Trafficks and Discoveries', *I VW Essays,* and 'A Professor of Life', *IV VW Essays.*
2 – Raleigh, 'The Origin of Romance', p. 3.
3 – I.e., the *Railway Time-Tables, Monthly Railway Guide, Continental Railway Guide* etc, originally published by George Bradshaw (1801–53).
4 – Raleigh, 'The Origin of Romance', pp. 8–9; the ellipsis marks the omission of 'biography and bibliography, two sciences which between them supply'.
5 – S. T. Coleridge, 'Kubla Khan, a Vision in a Dream' (1816); John Keats, 'To a Nightingale' (1819). Alexander Pope (1688–1744); John Dryden (1631–1700).
6 – Raleigh, 'The Origin of Romance', p. 33; William Wordsworth (1770–1850).
7 – *Ibid.*; Sir Walter Scott (1771–1832); Henry Fielding (1707–54).
8 – *Ibid.*, p. 10.
9 – The poet Ossian and his Gaelic epics were the creation of James Macpherson (1736–96). Strawberry Hill: the gothic mansion near Twickenham created by Horace Walpole (1717–99), author of *The Castle of Otranto* (1764), whose name is also associated with that of Thomas Chatterton (1752–70), by whose gothic fabrications he was initially deceived.
10 – Raleigh, 'The Origin of Romance', p. 39; p. 40.
11 – William Wordsworth, 'Elegiac Stanzas – suggested by a picture of Peele Castle, in a storm, painted by Sir George Beaumont' (1807), ll. 53–4, not quoted by Raleigh.
12 – Raleigh, 'Imitation and Forgery', p. 84.
13 – *Ibid.*

Tolstoy's 'The Cossacks'

It is pleasant to welcome Tolstoy's *The Cossacks and other tales of the Caucasus*[2] to the World Classics. 'The greatest of Russia's writers,' say Mr and Mrs Maude in their introduction.[3] And when we read or re-read these stories, how can we deny Tolstoy's right to the title? Of late years both Dostoevsky and Tchehov[4] have become famous in England, so that there has certainly been less discussion, and perhaps less reading, of Tolstoy himself. Coming back to him after an interval the shock of his genius seems to us quite surprising; in his own line it is hard to imagine that he can ever be surpassed. For an English reader proud of the fiction of this country there is even something humiliating in the comparison between such a story as 'The Cossacks', published in 1863, and the novels which were being written at about the same time in England. As the lovable immature work of children compared with the work of grown men they appear to us; and it is still more strange to consider that, while much of Thackeray and Dickens[5] seems to us far away and obsolete, this story of Tolstoy's reads as if it had been written a month or two ago.

It is as a matter of fact an early work, written for the most part some years before it was published, and preceding both the great novels. He gathered the materials when he was in the Caucasus for two years as a cadet, and the chief character is the same whom we meet so often in the later books, the unmistakable Tolstoy. As Olenin he is a young man who has run into debt and leaves Moscow with a view to saving a little money and seeing a fresh side of life. In Moscow he has had many experiences, but he has always said to himself both of love and of other things, 'That's not it, that's not it.'[6] The story — and like most of Tolstoy's stories it has no intricacy of plot — is the story of the development of this young man's mind and character in a Cossack village. He lives alone in a hut; observes the beauty of the Cossack girl Maryanka, but scarcely speaks to her, and spends most of his time with Daddy Eroshka in shooting pheasants and talking about sport. At length he comes to know the girl and asks her to marry him, to which she seems inclined to consent; but at that very moment the soldier to whom she is engaged is wounded, and she refuses to have anything more to do with Olenin. He therefore gets himself put upon the staff and leaves the district. When he has said good-bye to them all, he turns to look back. 'Daddy Eroshka was talking to Maryanka, evidently about his own affairs, and neither the old man nor the girl looked at Olenin'.[7] Nothing is finished; nothing is tidied up; life merely goes on.

But what a life! Perhaps it is the richness of Tolstoy's genius that strikes us most in this story, short though it is. Nothing seems to escape him. The wonderful eye observes everything; the blue or the red of a child's frock; the way a horse shifts its tail; the action of a man trying to put his hands into pockets that have been sewn up; every gesture seems to be received by him automatically, and at once referred by his brain to some cause which reveals the most carefully hidden secrets of human nature. We feel that we know his characters both by the way they choke and sneeze and by the way they feel about love and immortality and the most subtle questions of conduct. In the present selection of stories, all the work of youth and all laid in a wild country far from town civilisation, he gives freer play than in the novels to his extraordinary keenness of physical sensation. We seem actually able to see the mountains, the young soldiers, the grapes, the Cossack girls, to feel the firmness of their substance, and to see the bright colours with which the sun and the cold air have painted them. Nowhere perhaps has he written with greater zest of the excitement of sport and of the beauty of fine horses; nowhere has he made us feel more acutely how fiercely desirable the world appears to the senses of a strong young man. At the same time the thought which unites these scenes and gives them so keen an edge is the thought which goes on incessantly in the brain of Olenin. He throws himself down in the middle of the hunt to rest under the brambles in a lair where a stag has just lain:

And it was clear to him that he was not a Russian nobleman, a member of Moscow society, the friend and relation of so-and-so and so-and-so, but just such a mosquito or pheasant or deer as those that were now living all round him. 'Just as they, just as Daddy Eroshka. I shall live awhile and die, and as he says truly: grass will grow and nothing more.'[8]

'But what though the grass does grow?' he continued thinking. 'Still I must live, and be happy, because happiness is all I desire . . . How then must I live to be happy, and why was I not happy before?' . . . and suddenly a new light seemed to reveal itself to him. 'Happiness is this!' he said to himself. 'Happiness lies in living for others' . . .[9] He was so glad and excited when he had discovered this, as it seemed to him, new truth, that he jumped up and began impatiently seeking someone to sacrifice himself to, to do good to, and to love. 'Since one wants nothing for onself', he kept thinking, 'why not live for others?'[10]

But Lukashka, to whom he gives a horse, suspects his motives for making such a valuable gift; and Eroshka, whom he treats as a friend and to whom he gives a gun, forgets him as soon as his back is turned. Perhaps then he is on the wrong tack after all. Here, as everywhere, Tolstoy seems able to read the minds of different people as certainly as we count the buttons on their coats; but this feat never satisfies him; the knowledge is always passed through the brain of some Olenin or Pierre or Levin,[11] who attempts to guess a further and more difficult riddle – the riddle which Tolstoy was still asking himself, we may be sure, when he died. And the fact that Tolstoy is thus seeking, that there is always in the centre of his stories some rather lonely figure to whom the surrounding world is never quite satisfactory, makes even his short stories entirely unlike other short stories. They do not shut with a snap like the stories of Maupassant and Mérimee.[12] They go on indefinitely. It is by their continuous vein of thought that we remember them, rather than by any incident; by thoughts such as that which comes to him in the middle of battle.

The spectacle was truly magnificent. The one thing that spoilt the general impression for me, who took no part in the affair, and was unaccustomed to it, was that this movement, and the animation and the shouting, appeared unnecessary. Involuntarily the comparison suggested itself to me of a man swinging his arms from the shoulders to cut the air with an axe.[13]

And thus we end by thinking again of the unlikeness between ourselves and the Russians; and by envying them that extraordinary union of extreme simplicity combined with the utmost subtlety which seems to mark both the educated Russian and the peasant equally. They do not rival us in the comedy of manners, but after reading Tolstoy we always feel that we could sacrifice our skill in that direction for something of the profound psychology and superb sincerity of the Russian writers.

1 – A review in the TLS, 1 February 1917, (Kp c64) of The Cossacks and Other Tales of the Caucasus . . . translated by Louise and Aylmer Maude (O.U.P., 1916) by Leo Tolstoy (1828–1910). See also Tolstoi's Love Letters and Talks With Tolstoi, both translated by S. S. Koteliansky and Virginia Woolf and published by the Hogarth Press in 1923.
2 – The stories concerned are: 'The Raid' (1853), 'The Wood-Felling' (1855), 'Meeting a Moscow Acquaintance in the Detachment (from Prince Nekhlyudov's Caucasian Memoirs)' (1856), 'The Cossacks' (1863).
3 – Tolstoy, Pref., p. viii.
4 – Fyodor Dostoevsky (1821–81), see 'More Dostoevsky' and 'A Minor Dostoevsky' below; Anton Chekhov (1860–1904), see 'Tchehov's Questions' below.
5 – W. M. Thackeray (1811–63); Charles Dickens (1812–70).
6 – Tolstoy, 'The Cossacks', ch. II, p. 13.
7 – Ibid., ch. XLII, p. 234, the story's final sentence.
8 – Ibid., ch. XX, p. 120.
9 – Ibid.
10 – Ibid., p. 121.
11 – Pierre Bezuhov in War and Peace (1865–72); Constantine Levin in Anna Karenina (1875–6).
12 – Guy de Maupassant (1850–93); Prosper Mérimée (1803–70).
13 – Tolstoy, 'The Raid', p. 263.

Melodious Meditations

The poets of the eighteenth century were fond of making their verse sound dignified by spelling certain qualities with a capital letter. It required a very good poet to make such personifications acceptable even then, and the habit has long been dropped. But we sometimes fancy that these antiquated ghosts merely took ship to America, lodged with the best families, and now walk abroad in those essays which the Americans write so frequently upon Old Age, Old Maids, On Being Ill, and Sorrow.[2] In those abstract contemplations we seem to recognise their nearly featureless faces, bloodless cheeks, and impeccable dignity of deportment. Life is difficult, but the good man triumphs; sorrow is not always evil; happiness depends upon what we are and not upon what we have; our truest friends are to be found among our books. If all these substantives began with capital letters, and if the lines were trimmed to the right length, we should at once have an eighteenth-century ode contributed by some country clergyman to the *Gentleman's Magazine*.[3]

And why this eternal commotion? Is all this turmoil the struggle of a baser element to attain self-realisation, to achieve psychic life? Is the whole universe seeking more life and fuller? Or is life our original sin, and death the great purifier? Is it beneficent death that is striving to cast out the vexing seeds of life and restore a universal calm? Is death the great ocean of peace to which all the rivers of existence flow? Is the blotting out of the universe, &c.[4]

This passage is taken at random from one of Mr Sedgwick's essays. Almost any novel, certainly any book of facts, seems to us better reading than these melodious meditations; and we say this emphatically in order to correct what we believe to be a misunderstanding on the part of Mr Wister. The American essayists, he says, unlike the novelists, 'save our face. We can point to them without blushing.' They show the stranger that 'some of us are writers and readers of civilised intelligence'.[5] Anyone who has read even a little of American literature hardly needs such assurance; there is nothing to blush at in the whole of it, except perhaps Walt Whitman;[6] and that is the worst we have to say of it. Their intelligence seems, oddly enough, more civilised, gentler, lower in tone than ours. And perhaps the studious refinement of their great writers is the result of this determination to show the stranger that they are people of civilised intelligence. Certainly Mr Sedgwick's essays carry out this theory, for they are not all as mild and melancholy as the above quotation would seem to show. When he writes upon Goethe, the Classics, Literature and Cosmopolitanism[7] he writes with a great deal of sense and energy, and enables us at least to understand the point of view of cultivated Americans towards their literature. He looks to literature to refine and restrain the boisterous spirit of democracy. He would give democracy supreme power over politics and economics; but then 'it must no longer seek to lay its hand on literature, art, higher education, pure science, philosophy, manners'.[8] The men of genius and learning are to constitute a priesthood, held in special reverence; and the intellectual traditions of generations of educated men should be taught by them as a special cult.

Was there ever a plan better calculated to freeze literature at the root than this one? We must imagine all our writers and artists properly pensioned and quartered in comfortable rooms in Oxford and Cambridge, where so long as they live the masses shall do them honour. In the Victorian age, which for all its faults was prolific of genius, this system was to some extent put into practice; the great men were secluded and worshipped, with the result that they wrote twice as much as they ought to have written, and, being geniuses all day long and every day, were for the most part extremely ill at ease and out of temper.[9] That seems to be the inevitable effect of a Priesthood upon the Priests who compose it; and though to reverence may be very good for the soul of the masses, still the best artistic work is done by people who mix easily with their fellows. Even with us art is far too much of a mystery and a luxury, but it is evidently still more beyond the reach of ordinary people in America. For the American critic attaches enormous importance to the appreciation of art, and seems to care very little for the making of it. It has been their misfortune perhaps to inherit our language with all those traditions which can hardly be taught, but must be felt naturally if they are to blossom into beauty. With a language of their own which would make its own traditions, they would have greater self-confidence, and would lose their excessive sensitiveness to the criticisms of those English professors who examine them from time to time and send them to the very bottom of the class. For no one can doubt that theirs is a splendid opportunity; or if any one is sceptical as to the future of American art let him read Walt Whitman's preface to the first edition of *Leaves of Grass*. As a piece of writing it rivals anything we have done for a hundred years, and as a statement of the American spirit no finer banner was ever unfurled for the young of a great country to march under:

There will soon be no more priests. Their work is done [. . .] A new order shall arise, and they shall be the priests of man, and every man shall be his own priest [. . .] They shall find their inspiration in real objects today, symptoms of the past and future. They shall not deign to defend immortality or God, or the perfection of things, or liberty, or the exquisite beauty and reality of the soul. They shall arise in America, and be responded to from the remainder of the earth.[10]

1 – A review in the *TLS*, 8 February 1917, (Kp c65) of *An Apology for Old Maids* . . . With a Preface by Owen Wister (Macmillan & Co., 1917) by Henry Dwight Sedgwick (1861–1957), American essayist and historian. 'We are going skating today,' VW wrote to Saxon Sydney-Turner on 3 February 1917 (*II VW Letters*, no. 821), 'on the Pen Ponds [Richmond Park] and tomorrow we have induced Lytton to come too . . . All the morning I have been reviewing with great labour an American essayist; and therefore I can't think of any good jokes.'

2 – Sedgwick's subjects include: 'An Apology for Old Maids', 'On Being Ill' (upon which VW was herself to write, see *IV VW Essays*), and 'The House of Sorrow', but not 'Old Age' as such.

3 – The monthly miscellany founded in 1731 by Edward Cave, to and upon which, during the period 1739–48, Dr Johnson was an important contributor and influence.

4 – Sedgwick, 'On Being Ill', p. 102, which continues: 'universe beyond the farm road, the reduction of it to a small sickroom, the diminution of the innumerable *dramatis personae* to one white-capped white-aproned nurse, a sample of the divine effort towards simplicity and peace?'

5 – *Ibid.*, Pref., p. xiii; Owen Wister (1860–1938), American lawyer and author, Overseer, Harvard University, 1912–18, 1919–25.

6 – Walt Whitman (1819–92), to whom no allusion is made in Sedgwick.

7 – Sedgwick writes on Goethe (1749–1832) – 'the great apostle of cosmopolitanism' (p. 211) – in 'A Forsaken God'. The other titles are: 'The Classics Again' and 'Literature and Cosmopolitanism'.

8 – *Ibid.*, 'A Forsaken God', pp. 162–3; the essay begins by addressing itself to 'certain frank opinions about America' expressed 'not long ago' (but otherwise unspecified) by Goldsworthy Lowes Dickinson (1862–1932), Fellow of King's College, Cambridge, Apostle, and friend of Bloomsbury.

9 – Cf. 'A Sketch of the Past', *MoB*, pp. 108–10, where VW expatiates upon Victorian 'genius', as the phenomenon affected her father Leslie Stephen; and note p. 109: 'Those who had genius in the Victorian sense were like the prophets . . . They were invariably "ill to live with".'

10 – *Leaves of Grass* (New York, 1855), p. xi, which has an ellipsis after 'past and future', and no comma after 'God', 'liberty', or 'America'.

More Dostoevsky

Each time that Mrs Garnett[2] adds another red volume to her admirable translations of the works of Dostoevsky we feel a little better able to measure what the existence of this great genius who is beginning to permeate our lives so curiously means to us. His books are now to be found on the shelves of the humblest English libraries; they have become an indestructible part of the furniture of our rooms, as they belong for good to the furniture of our minds. The latest addition to Mrs Garnett's translation, *The Eternal Husband*, including also 'The Double' and 'The Gentle Spirit', is not one of the greatest of his works, although it was produced in what may be held to be the greatest period of his genius, between *The Idiot* and *The Possessed*.[3] If one had never read anything else by Dostoevsky, one might lay the book down with a feeling that the man who wrote it was bound to write a very great novel some day; but with a feeling also that something strange and important had happened. This strangeness and this sense that something important has happened persist, however, although we are familiar with his books and have had time to arrange the impression that they make on us.

Of all great writers there is, so it seems to us, none quite so surprising, or so bewildering, as Dostoevsky. And although 'The Eternal Husband' is nothing more than a long short story which we need not compare with the great novels, it too has this extraordinary power; nor while we are reading it can we liberate ourselves sufficiently to feel certain that in this or that respect there is a failure of power, or insight, or craftsmanship; nor does it occur to us to compare it with other works either by the same writer or by other writers. It is very difficult to analyse the impression it has made even when we have finished it. It is the story of one Velchaninov, who, many years before the story opens, has seduced the wife of a certain Pavel Pavlovitch in the town of T———. Velchaninov has almost forgotten her and is living in Petersburg. But now as he walks about Petersburg he is constantly running into a man who wears a crepe hat-band and reminds him of someone he cannot put a name to. At last, after repeated meetings which bring him to a state bordering on delirium, Velchaninov is visited at two o'clock in the morning by the stranger, who explains that he is the husband of Velchaninov's old love, and that she is dead. When Velchaninov visits him the next day, he finds him maltreating a little girl, who is, he instantly perceives, his own child. He manages to take her away from Pavel, who is a drunkard and in every way disreputable, and give her lodging with friends, but almost immediately she dies. After her death Pavel announces that he is engaged to marry a girl of sixteen, but when, as he insists, Velchaninov visits her, she confides to him that she detests Pavel and is already engaged to a youth of nineteen. Between them they contrive to pack Pavel off to the country; and he turns up finally at the end of the story as the husband of a provincial beauty, and the lady, of course, has a lover.

These, at least, are the little bits of cork which mark a circle upon the top of the waves while the net drags the floor of the sea and encloses stranger monsters than have ever been brought to the light of day before. The substance of the book is made out of the relationship between Velchaninov and Pavel. Pavel is a type of what Velchaninov calls 'the eternal husband'.[4] 'Such a man is born and grows up only to be a husband, and, having married, is promptly transformed into a supplement of his wife, even when he happens to have an unmistakable character of his own . . . ⟨Pavel⟩ could only as long as his wife was alive have remained all that he used to be, but, as it was, he was only a fraction of a whole, suddenly cut off and set free, that is something wonderful and unique.'[5] One of the peculiarities of the eternal husband is that he is always half in love with the lovers of his wife, and at the same time wishes to kill them. Impelled by this mixture of almost amorous affection and hatred, he cannot keep away from Velchaninov, in whom he breeds a kind of reflection of his own sensations of attraction and repulsion. He can never bring himself to make any direct charge against Velchaninov; and Velchaninov is never able to confess or to deny his misconduct. Sometimes, from the stealthy way in which he approaches, Velchaninov feels certain that he has an impulse to kill him; but then he insists upon kissing him, and cries out, 'So, you understand, you're the one friend left me now!'[6] One night when Velchaninov is ill and Pavel has shown the most enthusiastic devotion Velchaninov wakes from a nightmare to find Pavel standing over him and attempting to murder him with a razor. Pavel is easily mastered and slinks away shamefaced in the morning. But did he mean to murder him, Velchaninov muses, or did he want it without knowing that he wanted it?

But did he love me yesterday when he declared his feeling and said 'Let us settle our account'? Yes, it was from hatred that he loved me; that's the strongest of all loves . . . It would be interesting to know by what I impressed him. Perhaps by my clean gloves and my knowing how to put them on . . . He comes here 'to embrace me and weep', as he expressed it in the most abject way – that is, he came here to murder me and thought he came 'to embrace me and to weep'. But, who knows? If I had wept with him, perhaps, really, he would have forgiven me, for he had a terrible longing to forgive me! . . . Ough! wasn't he pleased, too, when he made me kiss him! Only he didn't know then whether he would end by embracing me or murdering me . . .[7] The most monstrous monster is the monster with noble feelings . . . But it was not your fault, Pavel Pavlovitch, it was not your fault: you're a monster, so everything about you is bound to be monstrous, your dreams and your hopes.[8]

Perhaps this quotation may give some idea of the labyrinth of the soul through which we have to grope our way. But being only a quotation it makes the different thoughts appear too much isolated; for in the context Velchaninov, as he broods over the bloodstained razor, passes over his involved and crowded train of thought, without a single hitch, just, in fact, as we ourselves are conscious of thinking when some startling fact has dropped into the pool of our consciousness. From the crowd of objects pressing upon our attention we select now this one, now that one, weaving them inconsequently into our thought; the associations of a word perhaps make another loop in the line, from which we spring back again to a different section of our main thought, and the whole process seems both inevitable and perfectly lucid. But if we try to construct our mental processes later, we find that the links between one thought and another are submerged. The chain is sunk out of sight and only the leading points emerge to mark the course. Alone among writers Dostoevsky has the power of reconstructing those most swift and complicated states of mind, of rethinking the whole train of thought in all its speed, now as it flashes into light, now as it lapses into darkness; for he is able to follow not only the vivid streak of achieved thought, but to suggest the dim and populous underworld of the mind's consciousness where desires and impulses are moving blindly beneath the sod. Just as we awaken ourselves from a trance of this kind by striking a chair or a table to assure ourselves of an external reality, so Dostoevsky suddenly makes us behold, for an instant, the face of his hero, or some object in the room.

This is the exact opposite of the method adopted, perforce, by most of our novelists. They reproduce all the external appearances – tricks of manner, landscape, dress, and the effect of the hero upon his friends – but very rarely, and only for an instant, penetrate to the tumult of thought which rages within his own mind. But the whole fabric of a book by Dostoevsky is made out of such material. To him a child or a beggar is as full of violent and subtle emotions as a poet or a sophisticated woman of the world; and it is from the intricate maze of their emotions that Dostoevsky constructs his version of life. In reading him, therefore, we are often bewildered because we find ourselves observing men and women from a different point of view from that to which we are accustomed. We have to get rid of the old tune which runs so persistently in our ears, and to realise how little of our humanity is expressed in that old tune. Again and again we are thrown off the scent in following Dostoevsky's psychology; we constantly find ourselves wondering whether we recognise the feeling that he shows us, and we realise constantly and with a start of surprise that we have met it before in ourselves, or in some moment of intuition have suspected it in others. But we have never spoken of it, and that is why we are surprised. Intuition is the term which we should apply to Dostoevsky's genius at its best. When he is fully possessed by it he is able to read the most inscrutable writing at the depths of the darkest souls; but when it deserts him the whole of his amazing machinery seems to spin fruitlessly in the air. In the present volume, 'The Double', with all its brilliancy and astonishing ingenuity, is an example of this kind of elaborate failure; 'The Gentle Spirit', on the other hand, is written from start to finish with a power which for the time being turns everything we can put beside it into the palest commonplace.

1 – A review in the *TLS*, 22 February 1917, (Kp C66) of *The Eternal Husband, and Other Stories. From the Russian by Constance Garnett* (William Heinemann, 1917) by Fyodor Dostoevsky (1821–81). See also 'A Minor Dostoevsky' below; 'Dostoevsky in Cranford' and 'Dostoevsky the Father', *III VW Essays*; and see *Stavrogin's Confession* (Hogarth Press, 1922) by F. M. Dostoevsky, translated by S. S. Koteliansky and VW. Reprinted: *B&P*.

2 – Constance Garnett, *née* Black (1862–1946), took a first in classics at Newnham College, Cambridge, in 1883, and in the early 1890s began to learn Russian. Her classic translations from the Russian include the whole of Dostoevsky's oeuvre. The wife of the author and publisher's reader Edward Garnett, she was the mother of the novelist David Garnett (1892–1981), one of the younger generation in Bloomsbury.

3 – 'The Eternal Husband' (1870), 'The Double' (1846), 'The Gentle Spirit' (1876), *The Idiot* (1868–9), *The Possessed* (1872).

4 – Dostoevsky, ch. VII, p. 29: 'Velchaninov was convinced that there really was such a type of woman ['born to be unfaithful wives' p. 28]; but, on the other hand, he was also convinced that there was a type of husband corresponding to that woman, whose sole vocation was to correspond with that feminine type. To his mind, the

essence of such a husband lay in his being, so to say, "the eternal husband", or rather in being, all his life, a husband and nothing more.'

5 – *Ibid.*; the passage up to the ellipsis quotes Velchaninov's thoughts directly and is punctuated accordingly in the original, which also has: 'to have unmistakable character'.
6 – *Ibid.*, ch. VII, p. 57.
7 – *Ibid.*, ch. XVI, p. 125, which has: 'impressed him?'; and 'who knows? if I had wept'.
8 – *Ibid.*, p. 126.

'Before Midnight'

Before reviewing Mrs Elinor Mordaunt's new volume of short stories, *Before Midnight*, we ought to confess two, perhaps unreasonable, prejudices: we do not like the war in fiction, and we do not like the supernatural. We can only account for the first of these prejudices by the feeling that the vast events now shaping across the Channel are towering over us too closely and too tremendously to be worked into fiction without a painful jolt in the perspective; but, reasonable or unreasonable, this feeling is roused by one of Mrs Mordaunt's stories only. Better reasons for disliking the use of the supernatural might be given, especially in the case of a writer like Mrs Mordaunt, who has shown in her novels so great a gift for presenting the natural. Nobody can deny that our life is largely at the mercy of dreams and visions which we cannot account for logically; on the contrary, if Mrs Mordaunt had devoted every page of her book to the discovery of some of these uncharted territories of the mind we should have nothing but thanks for her. But we feel a little aggrieved when the writers who are capable of such delicate work resort instead to the methods of the conjurer and ask us to be satisfied with a trick.

As an example of what we mean let us take the second story, 'Pan'. Here a fashionable lady, who is recovering her health in the north meets a man out fishing who possesses himself of her heart in the most immediate and mysterious way, so that she follows him every day without knowing who he is, and is finally drowned at night in her endeavour to cross the river to reach him. All this is an allegory – but it is founded upon a theory which might form the basis of a deeply interesting study.

Yes, the country is a dangerous place if one once lets oneself become intimate with it, slipping one's soul free fom the stolid correctness of country folk, that correctness which has gained them the reputation of piety, and is, really, due to lack of imagination. For the fact is this: only the stolid, the unimaginative remain; the rest have gone back to the gods.[2]

That seems to promise extremely well. But to drag in the pointed ears, the shaggy hoofs, the strange music of the hemlock pipes in exchange for an analysis of the lady's state of mind seems to us equivalent to saying that the situation is too difficult to be pursued any further. Mrs Mordaunt has, as usual, so many shrewd and original things to say about the men and women of flesh and blood before she has recourse to magic that we resent the powers of darkness more than ever.

But it is not fair to say that she always avails herself of these short cuts. The first story in the book is rather a study in heredity than in magic, and so is the last;[3] and there are traces in both of them of that individuality which, whether it is the result of saying what one thinks or whether it is a special grace of nature, is certainly among the most refreshing of gifts. At the same time we must own that we like Mrs Mordaunt best when she is most resolutely matter-of-fact. Indeed, it is when she is keeping strictly to what she has observed that we catch sight of those curious hidden things in human life which vanish instinctively directly there is talk of ghosts or of gods.

1 – A review in the *TLS*, 1 March 1917, (Kp C67) of *Before Midnight* (Cassell & Co. Ltd., 1917) by Elinor Mordaunt (pseudonym for Evelyn May Mordaunt, *née* Clowes, 1877–1942), prolific author of fiction and travel books. In the original article in the *TLS*, but not in the earlier review of her novel *The Park Wall* (see above), she is referred to throughout as Miss rather than Mrs Mordaunt; the text here has been altered to accord with her married status and the earlier usage. Reprinted: *CW*.
2 – Mordaunt, 'Pan', p. 58.
3 – For the first story, 'The Weakening Point', *ibid.*, pp. 3–54; and the second, 'Parentage', pp. 269–326.

Parodies

A good parody is rather a complex thing, for it should be amusing in itself, and should also do the work of the critic with greater daring than the critic can usually display. Mr Squire's parodies are very good examples of what he terms 'a not wholly admirable art';[2] first they make us laugh, and then they make us think. Instead of analysing his author's gifts and fitting them as closely as he can with the right epithets, he makes a little model of the work in question and expresses his sense of the defects of that work by a few deft pinches and twists which bring out the absurdity without destroying the likeness. Although we may laugh we cannot deny that he tells us more about Mr Belloc, or Mr Wells, or Sir H. Newbolt[3] than many serious and industrious articles where the gifts and failings of these writers are scrupulously weighed to an ounce. Thus when we read,

> And as I watch bees in a hive,
>   Or gentle cows that rub 'gainst trees,
> I do not envy men who live,
>   No fields, no books upon their knees.
> I'd rather lie beneath small stars
> Than with rough men who drink in bars[4]

we recognise Mr Davies wearing an air of artless innocence only a little in excess of his natural expression. And if we read, very quickly,

> It was eight bells in the forenoon and hammocks running sleek
>   (It's a fair sea flowing from the West),
> When the little Commodore came a-sailing up the Creek
>   (Heave Ho! I think you'll know the rest)[5]

we get the same hearty feeling as of an old sea-dog rolling across the harbour in a salt sou'-wester which the genuine works of Sir Henry Newbolt are wont to produce. And it needs a second glance to assure us that it is all nonsense. Mr Wells is very good, too:

V

And then it was that Mary Browne came into my life ⟨...⟩ But now there was about her a certain quality of graciousness, very difficult to define, but very unescapable when it is present, that gave to her mouse-grey hair and rather weak blue eyes a beauty very rare and very subtle. She had spent, she told me, two years in the East End at some social work or other ...

VI

And then I met Cecilia Scroop . . .[6]

Of the parodies of modern writers, that of Mr Shaw[7] seems to us the least successful. His style is much too workmanlike to present any obviously weak points to the caricaturist; and to parody his matter you would have to be quicker and more agile of intellect than he is himself. Moreover, Mr Shaw parodies himself far better than anyone else could do it.

As a rule, we imagine, it is much easier to hit off one's own contemporaries, whose little foibles are as well known to us as those of our friends, than it is to dress up in the clothing of some old and famous poet so as to look precisely like him. This is really playing the sedulous ape as Stevenson prescribed it to those in search of a style,[8] and means that at one time or another you have done homage very humbly to the poet in question. If we had to teach children how to write English, no doubt this would be one of our instruments of torture. And Mr Squire complicates the exercise still further. He imagines how Gray would have written the *Spoon River Anthology*, or Lord Byron the 'Passing of Arthur' or Pope 'Break, break, break'.[9] We get the same sort of pleasure from noting his skilful translations from one style to another that scholars find in savouring Greek versions of English poetry. What could be more charming than,

> Nor the bright smiles of ocean's nymphs command
> The pleasing contact of a vanished hand[10]

as an Augustan version of mid-Victorian Tennyson? We can almost see the imperturbable good breeding and courtesy with which Pope, as Mr Squire presents him, receives the lyrical cry of his successor, contemplates it with a little distress, and smooths it out, into impeccable rhyming couplets. It is, indeed, a vivid little summary of a whole chapter of the history of literature.

---

1 – A review in the *TLS*, 8 March 1917, (Kp c68) of *Tricks of the Trade* (Martin Secker, 1917) by J. C. (John Collings) Squire (1884–1958), man of letters, literary editor of the *New Statesman*, 1913–19, and contributor to *Georgian Poetry 1916–1917* (1917) – 'that ridiculous Squire', VW was soon to call him (*I VW Diary*, 3 January 1918), a verdict she never felt inclined to revise.

See also 'Imitative Essays' and 'Bad Writers' below.
2 – From Squire's dedication to Robert Lynd.

3 – Hilaire Belloc (1870–1953); H. G. Wells (1866–1946); Sir Henry Newbolt (1862–1938).
4 – Squire, p. 10; from the first of two parodies of the work of W. H. Davies (1871–1940).
5 – *Ibid.*, p. 12; in which the last line is italicised.
6 – *Ibid.*, p. 35.
7 – For Squire's parody of George Bernard Shaw (1856–1950), 'Fragment from an Unwritten Play Mahomet the Prophet', *ibid.*, p. 39.
8 – Robert Louis Stevenson, *Memories & Portraits* (Chatto & Windus, 1887), 'A College Magazine', p. 59; 'Whenever I read a book or a passage that particularly pleased me, in which a thing was said or an effect rendered with propriety, in which there was either some conspicuous force or some happy distinction in the style, I must sit down at once and set myself to ape that quality . . . I have thus played the sedulous ape to Hazlitt, to Lamb, to Wordsworth, to Sir Thomas Browne, to Defoe, to Hawthorne, to Montaigne, to Baudelaire and to Oberman.'
9 – For Thomas Gray as the author of Edgar Lee Masters's *Spoon River Anthology* (1915), *ibid.*, p. 61; Byron as the author of Tennyson's 'The Passing of Arthur' (1869), *ibid.*, p. 71; and for Alexander Pope as the author of Tennyson's 'Break, Break, Break' (1842), *ibid.*, p. 59.
10 – *Ibid.*, p. 59.

'Sir Walter Raleigh'

To most of us, says Miss Hadow in her introduction to a book of selections from the prose of Sir Walter Raleigh, 'the Elizabethan Age stands for one of two things: it is the age of jewelled magnificence, of pomp and profusion and colour, of stately ceremonial and Court pageant, of poetry and drama; or it is the age of enterprise and exploration'.[2] But though we have every reason for being grateful to Miss Hadow for her part in the production of this astonishing little book, we cannot go with her in this initial distinction. If Shakespeare, as literature is the only thing that survives in its completeness, may be held to represent the Elizabethan age, are not enterprise and exploration a part of Shakespeare? If there are some who read him without any thought save for the poetry, to most of us, we believe, the world of Shakespeare is the world of Hakluyt[3] and of Raleigh; on that map Guiana and the River of the Plate are not very far distant or easily distinguishable from the Forest of Arden and Elsinore. The navigator and the explorer made their voyage by ship instead of by the mind, but over Hakluyt's pages broods the very same lustre of the imagination. Those vast rivers and fertile valleys, those forests of odorous trees and mines of gold and ruby, fill up the background of the plays as, in our fancy, the blue of the distant plains of America seems to lie behind the golden cross of St Paul's and the bristling chimneys of Elizabethan London.

No man was a truer representative of this Elizabethan world than Sir Walter Raleigh. From the intrigues and splendours of the Court he sailed to an unknown land inhabited by savages; from discourse with Marlowe and Spenser[4] he went to sea-battle with the Spaniard. Merely to read over the list of his pursuits gives one a sense of the space and opportunity of the Elizabethan age; courtier and admiral, soldier and explorer, member of Parliament and poet, musician and historian – he was all these things, and still kept such a curiosity alive in him that he must practise chemistry in his cabin when he had leisure at sea, or beg an old hen-house from the Governor of the Tower in which to pursue his search for 'the Great Elixir'.[5] It is little wonder that Rumour should still be telling her stories about his cloak, his pipe with the silver bowl, his potatoes, his mahogany, his orange trees, after all these years; for though Rumour may lie, there is always good judgment in her falsehood.

When we come to read what remains of his writing – and in this little book the indispensable part of it is preserved – we get what Rumour cannot give us: the likeness of an extremely vigorous and individual mind, scarcely dimmed by the 'vast and devouring space'[6] of the centuries. It is well, perhaps, to begin by reading the last fight of the *Revenge*,[7] the letters about Cadiz and Guiana, and that to his wife written in expectation of death, before reading the extracts from the *Historie of the World*, and to end with the preface to that work, as one leaves a church with the sound of the organ in one's ears. His adventures by sea and land, his quest of Eldorado and the great gold mine of his dreams, his sentence of death and long imprisonment – glimpses of that 'day of a tempestuous life'[8] are to be found in these pages. They give us some idea of its storm and its sunshine. Naturally the style of them is very different from that of the preface. They are full of hurry and turmoil, or impetuosity and self-assertiveness. He is always eager to justify his own daring, and to proclaim the supremacy of the English among other peoples. Even 'our common English soldier, leavied in haste, from following the Cart, or sitting on the shop-stall',[9] surpasses in valour the best of Roman soldiers. Of the landing in Fayal in the year

1597 he writes, 'For I thought it to belong unto the honor of our Prince & Nation, that a few Ilanders should not think any advantage great enough, against a fleet set forth by Q. Elizabeth'; although he had to admit that 'I had more regard of reputation, in that businesse, than of safetie.'[10]

But if we had to justify our love of these old voyagers we should not lay stress upon the boastful and magnificent strain in them; we should point, rather, to the strain of poetry – the meditative mood fostered by long days at sea, sleep and dreams under strange stars, and lonely effort in the face of death. We would recall the words of Sir Humfrey Gilbert, when the storm broke upon his ship, 'sitting abaft with a book in his hand . . . and crying (so oft as we did approach within hearing) "We are as near to Heaven by sea as by land."'[11] And so Sir Walter Raleigh, whose character was subject to much criticism during his lifetime, who had been alternately exalted and debased by fortune, who had lived with the passion of a great lover, turns finally to thoughts of the littleness of all human things and to a magnanimous contemplation of the lot of mankind. His thoughts seem inspired by a knowledge of life both at its best and its worst; in the solitude of the Tower his memory is haunted by the sound of the sea. From the sea he takes his most frequent and splendid imagery. It comes naturally to him to speak of the 'Navigation of this life', of 'the Port of death, to which all winds drive us'.[12] Our false friends, he says, 'forsake us in the first tempest of misfortune and steere away before the Sea and Winde'.[13] So in old age we find that our joy and our woe have 'sayled out of sight'.[14] Often he must have looked into the sky from the deck of his ship and thought how 'The Heavens are high, farr off, and unsearcheable';[15] and his experience as a ruler of uncivilised races must have made him consider what fame 'the boundless ambition in mortal men'[16] is wont to leave behind it:

They themselves would then rather have wished, to have stolen out of the world without noise, than to be put in minde, that they have purchased the report of their actions in the world, by rapine, oppression, and crueltie, by giving in spoile the innocent and labouring soul to the idle and insolent, and by having emptied the cities of the world of their ancient Inhabitants, and filled them againe with so many and so variable sorts of sorrowes.[17]

But although the sounds of life and the waves of the sea are constantly in his ears, so that at any moment he is ready to throw away his pen and take command of an expedition, he seems in his deepest moods to reject the show and splendour of the world, to see the vanity of gold mines and of all expeditions save those of the soul.

For the rest, as all fables were commonly grounded upon some true stories of other things done; so might these tales of the Griffins receive this moral. That if those men which fight against so many dangerous passages for gold, or other riches of this world, had their perfect senses . . . they would content themselves with a quiet and moderate estate.[18]

The thought of the passing of time and the uncertainty of human lot was a favourite one with the Elizabethans, whose lives were more at the mercy of fortune than ours are. In Raleigh's prose the same theme is constantly treated, but with an absence of the characteristic Elizabethan conceits, which brings it nearer to the taste of our own time; a divine unconsciousness seems to pervade it. Take this passage upon the passing of youth:

So as who-so-ever hee bee, to whome Fortune hath beene a servant, and the Time a friend: let him but take the accompt of his memory (for wee have no other keeper of our pleasures past) and truelie examine what it hath reserved, either of beauty and youth, or foregone delights; what it hath saved, that it might last, of his dearest affections, or of whatever else the amorous Springtime gave his thoughts of contentment, then unvaluable; and hee shall finde that all the art which his elder yeares have, can draw no other vapour out of these dissolutions, than heavie, secret, and sad sighs . . .[19] Onely those few blacke Swans I must except; who having had the grace to value worldly vanities at no more than their owne price; doe, by retayning the comfortable memorie of a well acted life, behold death without dread, and the grave without feare; and embrace both, as necessary guides to endlesse glorie.[20]

This is no sudden effort of eloquence; it is prefaced and continued by words of almost equal beauty. In its melody and strength, its natural symmetry of form, it is a perfect speech, fit for letters of gold and the echoes of cathedral aisles, or for the tenderness of noble human intercourse. It reaches us almost with the very accent of Raleigh's voice. There is a magnificence with which such a being relinquishes his hopes in life and dismisses the cares of 'this ridiculous world'[21] which is the counterpart of his great zest in living. We hear it in the deeply burdened sigh with which he takes his farewell of his wife. 'For the rest, when you have travailled and wearied all your thoughts, over all sorts of worldly cogitations, you shall but sitt downe by sorrowe in the end.'[22] But it is most evident in his thought upon death. The thought of death tolls all through Elizabethan literature lugubriously enough in our ears, for whom, perhaps, existence has been made less palpable by dint of much thinking and death more of a shade than a substance. But to the Elizabethans a great part of the proper conduct of life consisted in meeting the idea of death, which to them was not an idea but a person, with fortitude. And to Raleigh in particular, death was a very definite enemy – death, 'which doth pursue us and hold us in chace from our infancy'.[23] A true man, he says, despises death. And yet even as he says this there come to life before his eyes the 'mishapen and ouglye shapes'[24] with which death tortures the imagination. And at last, when he has taken the idea of death to him and triumphed over it, there rises from his lips that magnificent strain of reconciliation and acknowledgement which sounds for ever in the ears of those who have heard it once: 'O eloquent, just and mightie Death! whom none could advise, thou hast perswaded: what none hath dared, thou hast done.'[25]

1 – A review in the TLS, 15 March 1917, (Kp c69) of *Sir Walter Raleigh [1552?– 1618]. Selections from his Historie of the World, his Letters etc.* ed. with an introduction and notes by G. E. Hadow (O.U.P., 1917). See also 'Trafficks and Discoveries' below and the article of the same title in *I VW Essays*, and 'The Elizabethan Lumber Room', *IV VW Essays* and *CR1*. Reprinted: *G&R, CE.*

2 – Raleigh, intro., p. 7.

3 – William Shakespeare (1564–1616), Richard Hakluyt (1552?–1616), author of *Principal Navigations, Voyages, and Discoveries of the English Nation* (1589, 1598–1600).

4 – Christopher Marlowe (1564–93), Edmund Spenser (1552?–99).

5 – Raleigh, intro., p. 7: '[Raleigh] spent his leisure time at sea in the study of chemistry to such effect that he discovered "the Great Elixir" and was called upon to prescribe for the heir to the throne when the court physicians had given up all hope'; and p. 20: 'he had access to the governor's garden [at the Bloody Tower] and was allowed . . . to turn the hen-house into a chemical laboratory'.

6 – The origin of this phrase, which VW also quotes in 'Papers on Pepys' below, has resisted all attempts at discovery.

7 – Raleigh, 'The Last Fight of the Revenge', pp. 144–66, originally published as *A Report of the Truth of the fight about the Iles of Açores, this last Sommer. Betwixt the Revenge, one of her Majesties Shippes, And an Armada of the King of Spaine* (London, 1591).

8 – *Ibid.*, 'The Historie of the World', Pref., p. 36.

9 – *Ibid.*, 'A Comparison Between Roman and English Soldiers', p. 91.

10 – For these two quotations, *ibid.*, 'Concerning Naval Transport', p. 112; pp. 111–12.

11 – This description of the dying moments off the coast of Newfoundland of Sir Humphrey Gilbert (1539–83) – Sir Walter's half-brother – was also quoted by VW, though not as fully as here, in 'Trafficks and Discoveries', *I VW Essays,* from

Professor Walter Raleigh, *The English Voyages of the Sixteenth Century* (James MacLehose & Sons, 1906), p. 59.

12 – For both quotations, Raleigh, 'The Historie of the World', Pref., p. 51.

13 – *Ibid.*, p. 47.

14 – *Ibid.*, p. 54.

15 – *Ibid.*, p. 45, which continues: ': wee have sense and feeling of corporal things; and of eternall grace, but by revelation'.

16 – *Ibid.*, 'Of the Fall of Empires', p. 116.

17 – *Ibid.*, p. 115, which begins: 'Which were it otherwise, and the extreame ill bargaine of buying this lasting discourse, understood by them which are dissolved; they themselves . . .'; and has 'without noise;'; and 'Cities'.

18 – *Ibid.*, 'Of Griffins', p. 80, which has: 'things done:'; and 'Morall'. The ellipsis marks the omission of ', and were not deprived of halfe their eye-sight (at least of the eye of right reason and understanding)'.

19 – *Ibid.*, Pref., p. 54, which has: 'what ever'; and 'Spring-time'.

20 – *Ibid.*, p. 55, which has: 'Swannes I must except:'.

21 – *Ibid.*, p. 56: 'For seeing God, who is the Author of all our tragedies, hath written out for us, and appointed us all the parts we are to play . . . Certainly there is no other account to be made of this ridiculous world, than to resolve, That the change of fortune on the great Theater, is but as the change of garments on the lesse. For when on the one and the other, every man weares but his own skin; the Players are all alike.'

22 – *Ibid.*, 'Letters', 'The Copy of a Letter, written by Sir Walter Raleigh, to his wife, the Night before hee expected to be putt to death att winchester. 1603', p. 183.

23 – *Ibid.*, 'The Historie of the World', Pref., p. 54, which has: 'in chace, from our infancie'.

24 – *Ibid.*, 'Letters', p. 184.

25 – *Ibid.*, 'The Historie of the World', 'Of the Falls of Empires', p. 117, which has: 'perswaded;'; and continues '; and whom all the world hath flattered, thou only hast cast out of the world and despised: thou hast drawne together all the farre stretched greatnesse, all the pride, crueltie, and ambition of man, and covered it all over with these two narrow words, *Hîc iacet*'.

'The House of Lyme'

After reading Lady Newton's[2] history of the house of Lyme and looking at the pictures which adorn it we are inclined to think that the production of such works by the people who inherit such houses should be made compulsory by Act of Parliament. To have in one's possession this private door into the past, through which one can see back to the pale beginnings of English life four or five centuries ago, and to keep it locked against the public, is no less heinous an offence than to burn a portrait by Velasquez[3] once a year. It is true that we are still under the spell of Lady Newton's narrative, and her gifts, unfortunately, are by no means common ones. We are still looking through the door which she has thrown open at many generations of the family of Legh, at much of the history of England. Owing to her skilful arrangement and to a freshness of feeling which imparts a most delightful naturalness to her story, we are able for the moment to forget the substantial veil of the present and to gaze upon the lives which have receded from us but have not disappeared. To Lady Newton, we fancy, the veil is a very thin one, and to her the Leghs of the past are people of distinct character, tastes, clothing, appearances. She writes of them as if she had known them, and when she quotes their letters they take up the story with the most natural intonation. For although nothing, we imagine, would be more out of keeping with the family tradition than to rattle behind wainscots at dawn or indulge in other ghostly antics, we can scarcely believe that the dead Leghs have gone very far from their beloved possessions. No house can have a greater share of those happier ghosts who are with us in the daytime. It was surely at the prompting of one of these spirits that Lady Newton was led to open that 'fireproof cupboard the existence of which was unknown or had been forgotten', and take from it 'a large quantity of papers', tied up in bundles, labelled "Old Letters"'.[4] Certainly, if the ghosts felt the need of an interpreter, they could not have made a better choice.

On a high spot in the park of Lyme there stand two pillars of rough stone whose origin has never been accounted for, although it is agreed that they are of great antiquity. Beneath them spreads the plain of Cheshire and around them lie the hills of Derbyshire – 'an almost boundless view'[5] – and, in the days when those stones were set there, a view without sign of building or population. It is as if those old pagans had placed a mark here, and decreed that here a limit should be set to the wilderness of nature and man build himself a dwelling-place. The name of Lyme, indeed, stands for *limes*, a border, for the three counties of Cheshire, Lancashire, and Derbyshire come together at this point. And here, some time in the beginning of the fifteenth century, a house was built for the family of Legh; another house succeeded it in the middle of the sixteenth century, and the building and rebuilding of the house continued until the middle of the nineteenth century, when the designs of Leoni[6] were at last accomplished. If we consider these facts we shall see that Lady Newton has chosen her title well. Here in the same spot the same family has been building at the same house for something like five centuries. A son has succeeded a father, one tomb has been placed beside another, a new wing has been added to the house, or the windows have been altered. So slow is the growth of the house, so orderly the progress of life, that watching the gradual development we lose count of time and wake with a start to find that, while we have watched the house being built and one Sir Piers[7] succeed another, we have traversed the greater part of our English history. We have passed from the Middle Ages to the world as we know it now.

The Leghs were not a race to disturb the continuity of their history by any startling adventures. One, perhaps, fought at Flodden; another at Agincourt; a third sailed with Essex against the Spaniard and was knighted by Queen Elizabeth.[8] But for the most part they have been content to stay at home and do their duty; or, if compelled to serve in Parliament, have shown no anxiety to dictate the laws of the country, but hastened back to Lyme to shoot their stags or race their horses. The country might change its king or its religion without greatly disturbing the peace of mind of the master of Lyme; and by luck and wise conformity they lived through many troubled ages without losing their lives or their fortunes. The only one of the race who suffered a short term of imprisonment in the cause of the Stuarts[9] very soon came to his senses and, when the rising of '45[10] once more tempted the rasher heads of the county to venture their lives, sensibly refused to have anything to do with it. A set of Jacobite drinking glasses with the Stuart roses engraved upon them bears witness to a little post-prandial enthusiasm for the King over the water, and in congenial company a clock would chime out twelve Jacobite airs, as indeed it does to the present day.

The indifference of contemporaries to events which to us seem of the greatest, perhaps of the only, importance is one of the surprises which family letters generally hold in store for us. The Legh letters are no exception to the rule. Lady Newton tells us of a tradition that one of the Leghs, writing from London on the day that King Charles[11] had his head cut off, makes no mention of that fact; but this, of course, may be attributed to caution rather than negligence. Later, however, when news of the Plague and the Fire of London would, one thinks, have filled up a letter to the country very pleasantly, there is only one mention of either of them, and that, characteristically, introduces a compliment to Lyme, 'where health and wealth conspire to make you happy'.[12] To us this seems very right and fitting. The great value and interest of such letters as these lies in the fact that they drown the drums and trumpets of history with a deeper and subtler music of their own. We do not need the evidence of state papers or the eloquence of the College of Heralds to prove that Peter and Thomas and Richard Legh[13] were all gentlemen of the highest integrity and of the greatest importance to their corner of the world. By them the law was made and administered, they were the fountains of charity, the arbiters of right and wrong, the source of such influence as no one family in England wields today. We need not wonder that to go up to London and play a minute part in the passing of some Act of Parliament or even to take arms for a Cromwell[14] or a Stuart seemed to them of less importance than other work lying closer at hand. Their house was not only a house in every room of which traditions of their race had accumulated, but a law court, a theatre, a public building, and an hotel all in one; a self-sufficient community highly organised in each of its departments, and the centre of civilisation in that district. They did their duty also by their library, and at one time possessed a band of musicians. When visitors of importance came a play was provided.

Much labour and contrivance was continually needed to keep such an institution in working order. In the year 1607, for instance, eighty or a hundred people were employed in the house every day; the staff had to include brewers, spit-turners, glaziers, 'tincklers', carpet-makers, tailors, marlers, plasterers, gutterers, besides mole catchers, rat catchers, carters, and bricklayers.[15] The house, we must remember, was always being altered, furnished, and rebuilt, gardens dug and terraces levelled. In addition to the usual brewing, baking, and dairying, they slaughtered their own cattle, and made their own candles and soap. Besides the people regularly employed in these pursuits there was a floating population consisting of visitors from the great families in the neighbourhood, a sprinkling of poor relations who assisted at all births and marriages, and were expert at needlework and pastry making, and the squires who came for the racing and the hunting and stayed late to drink such toasts as 'May Aristocracy Rise on the Ashes of Democracy', or, 'A Fresh Earth and a High Metaled Terrier', or 'A Cellar well filled and a House Full of Friends'.[16] The Leghs were not a family to take to the pen without cause, and this is generally provided by some cock-fight or horse-race, or business connected with the famous herd of red deer. There is an amusing account of a hunt in Lancashire which tells how the writer returned after the fox was killed 'to drink a bowle of Hott Punch with ye fox's foot stew'd in it. Sr Willm drank pretty plentifully, and just at last perceiv'd he should be fuddled, "but," quoth he, "I care not if I am, I have kill'd a fox today."'[17] And whenever they are away they long that Parliament may rise and let them get back to 'sweet Lyme'[18] again and their wives and children. 'Dearest,' writes the delightful Richard, 'I want nothing this night to compleat the joy I am in but thy deare company and the brats.'[19]

Moving against this background of servants and dependents, household cares and country sports in the house which gradually changes and is rebuilt over their heads we see old Sir Piers[20] and the Peters and Richard discharging their businesses, making matches, settling disputes, doing their duty, and presiding over the life of the house, much to the satisfaction of their neighbours. The changes in the house correspond to a change which slowly transforms the race which lives in it. Nothing is more curious than to watch the gradual thawing of the human race from the monolithic isolation of Elizabethan days to the humanity and garrulity of the eighteenth century. The bare and comfortless rooms of the sixteenth century become furnished; the beds have cushions; the chairs are easy chairs; there are forks to eat with, and some regard for intimacy and privacy. Even the speech ceases to be the dialect of the district, and educated people have to observe the same laws of spelling. No longer can old Sir Peter thunder forth his commands and extort obedience from his grown-up sons; and by the time the book is finished the inaccessible House of Lyme is in close touch with the gossip and the shops of London.

But the most profound impression left upon us by this delightful and absorbing book is not one of change; it is one of continuity. The red deer have roamed the park for upwards of five hundred years; the famous mastiffs of Lyme, though 'now alas, threatened with extinction',[21] still exist whose ancestors followed their master in the Battle of Agincourt; the oak still stands beneath which the Duke of York killed a stag; the clock which Richard bought in 1675 is still keeping time for his descendants;[22] and the red hair for which the Leghs were marked five hundred years ago grows once more upon the head of their latest descendant. In a world which seems bent on ruin and oblivion we cannot refuse a feeling of affectionate respect for the courage with which such old houses still confront life, cherish its traditions, and are a sanctuary for the lovely wreckage of the past.

1 – A review in the *TLS*, 29 March 1917, (Kp C70) of *The House of Lyme. From its Foundation to the End of the Eighteenth Century* (William Heinemann, 1917) by the Lady Newton. 'I didn't honestly think that Lady Newton had made the best of her Lyme papers,' VW wrote to Violet Dickinson, 10 April 1917 (*II VW Letters*, no. 827), 'the truth was that the Legh's were almost invariably stupid – which accounts, I suppose, for their centuries of life on the same spot. Do you know them in the flesh? I should like immensely to write a book of that sort, if someone would trust me to tell the truth about their relations. It's so queer the sentiment she had for them.'

2 – Evelyn Caroline Newton, *née* Bromley-Davenport (d. 1931), wife of Thomas Wodehouse Legh, 2nd Baron Newton, diplomat and politician.

3 – Diego Rodríguez de Silva y Velasquez (1599–1660) – and see Newton, ch. III, p. 42: 'In the great picture by Velasquez of the children of Philip IV, the *Las Meniñas* . . . a large mastiff is seen in the foreground, one of the children rubbing its back with his foot. The dog is precisely the same as the Lyme mastiffs of the present day, having all their characteristics, and was no doubt a descendant of the pair presented by James I to Philip III in 1604.'

4 – *Ibid.*, intro, p. xiii, adapted.

5 – *Ibid.*, ch. II, p. 23.

6 – *Ibid.* ch. XXVII, 'Leoni's Alterations', pp. 370–82. Giacomo Leoni (1686–1764), Venetian architect, who settled in England in the early eighteenth century.

7 – For Sir Piers Legh (1360?–99), grantee of Lyme, who had the misfortune to be beheaded at Chester by Henry IV – and was 'the first of a long succession of Sir Piers' – see *ibid.*, ch. I, p. 1, and see the Legh family tree appended to Newton.

8 – For the Sir Piers (1455–1527) who possibly fought against James IV at Flodden Field, in 1513, *ibid.*, ch. I, p. 19; p. 21. For Sir Piers (or Peter) (d. 1422), who fought at Agincourt, 1415, *ibid.*, ch. I, p. 7. For the 'third' Sir Piers (1563–1635/6), knighted at Greenwich in 1598, *ibid.*, ch. IV, pp. 49–50. Robert Devereux, 2nd Earl of Essex (1567–1601).

9 – *Ibid.*, ch. XXVI, 'Imprisonment of Peter Legh [1669–1743/4]', pp. 360–9. Legh had become involved, in July 1694, in the so-called Lancashire Plot, one of a series of Jacobite conspiracies, and was arrested but discharged by the courts in the absence of substantial evidence against him. In 1696 he was once more apprehended, for high treason, and again discharged.

10 – *Ibid.*, ch. XXIX, p. 388; Peter Legh (1707–92) was the member of the family concerned at the time of the Jacobite Rising in 1745.

11 – *Ibid.*, ch. X, p. 158; Charles I was executed at Whitehall on 30 January 1649.

12 – *Ibid.*, ch. XVI, p. 237, Lady Anne Saville to her stepdaughter Elizabeth Legh, 16 October 1665: 'The general sicklynes of the yeare exempts few places but Lyme where . . .' The Great Fire raged 2–6 September 1666 and destroyed some two-thirds of London.

13 – VW appears to be referring here to Thomas Legh (1594–1639), doctor of divinity, rector of Sefton and Walton, father of Richard Legh (1634–87), M.P. for Cheshire, 1656, and for Newton, 1659–1678/9, and the latter's son Peter Legh (1669–1743/4), M.P. for Newton 1685.

14 – Oliver Cromwell (1599–1658).

15 – Newton, ch. IV, p. 61; p. 64.

16 – *Ibid.*, ch. XXVII, p. 369.
17 – *Ibid.*, ch. XXV, p. 357.
18 – *Ibid.*, intro., p. XIV, ch. XVIII, p. 263.
19 – *Ibid.*, ch. XVI, Richard to Elizabeth Legh, 19 February 1669/70, p. 242.
20 – VW is presumably referring to Sir Piers Legh (1513–90), original builder of the House of Lyme.
21 – *Ibid.*, ch. III, p. 42.
22 – For the oak, *ibid.*, ch. XIX, p. 283; and for the clock, *ibid.*, p. 281.

'Poe's Helen'

The real interest of Miss Ticknor's volume lies in the figure of Mrs Whitman,[2] and not in the love letters from Poe, which have already been published. It is true that if it had not been for her connection with Poe we should never have heard of Helen Whitman; but it is also true that Poe's connection with Mrs Whitman was neither much to his credit nor a matter of moment to the world at large. If it were our object to enhance the charm of 'the only true romantic figure in our literature',[3] as Miss Ticknor calls him, we should have suppressed his love letters altogether. Mrs Whitman, on the other hand, comes very well out of the ordeal, and was evidently, apart from Poe, a curious and interesting person.

She wrote poetry from her childhood, and when in early youth she was left a widow she settled down to lead a literary life in earnest. In those days and in America this was not so simple a proceeding as it has since become. If you wrote an essay upon Shelley,[4] for example, the most influential family in Providence considered that you had fallen from grace. If, like Mr Ellery Channing, you went to Europe and left your wife behind, this was sufficient proof that you were not a 'great perfect man',[5] as the true poet is bound to be. Mrs Whitman took her stand against such crudities, and, indeed, rather went out of her way to invite attack. Whatever the fashion and whatever the season she wore her 'floating veils'[6] and her thin slippers, and carried a fan in her hand. By means of 'inverting her lamp shades'[7] and hanging up bits of drapery her sitting room was kept in a perpetual twilight. It was the age of the Transcendentalists, and the fans and the veils and the twilight were, no doubt, intended to mitigate the solidity of matter, and entice the soul out of the body with as little friction as possible. Nature too had been kind in endowing her with a pale, eager face, a spiritual expression, and deep-set eyes that gazed 'beyond but never at you'.[8]

Her house became a centre for the poets of the district, for she was witty and charming as well as enthusiastic. John Hay, G. W. Curtis, and the Hon. Wilkins Updike[9] used to send her their works to criticise, or in very long and abstruse letters tried to define what they meant by poetry. The mark of that particular set, which was more or less connected with Emerson and Margaret Fuller, was an enthusiastic championship of the rights of the soul. They ventured into a sphere where words naturally were unable to support them. 'Poetry', as Mr Curtis said, 'is the adaption of music to an intellectual sphere. But it must therefore be revealed through souls too fine to be measured justly by the intellect . . . Music . . . is a womanly accomplishment, because it is sentiment, and the instinct declares its nature,' etc.[10] This exalted mood never quite deserted them when they were writing about matters of fact. When Mrs Whitman forgot to answer a letter Mr Curtis inquired whether she was ill 'or has the autumn which lies round the horizon like a beautifully hued serpent crushing the flower of summer fascinated you to silence with its soft, calm eyes?'[11] Mrs Whitman, it is clear, was the person who kept them all up to this very high standard. Thus things went on until Mrs Whitman had reached the age of forty-two. One July night, in 1845, she happened to be wandering in her garden in the moonlight when Edgar Allan Poe passed by and saw her. 'From that hour I loved you,' he wrote later. '. . . your unknown heart seemed to pass into my bosom – there to dwell for ever.'[12] The immediate result was that he wrote the verses 'To Helen' which he sent her. Three years later, when he was the famous poet of 'The Raven', Mrs Whitman replied with a valentine, of which the last stanza runs –

> Then, oh grim and ghastly Raven
> Wilt thou to my heart an ear
> Be a Raven true as ever
> Flapped his wings and croaked 'Despair'?
> Not a bird that roams the forest
> Shall our lofty eyrie share.[13]

For some time their meeting was postponed, and no word of prose passed between them. It might have been postponed for ever had it not been for another copy of verses which Mrs Whitman ended with the line

> I dwell with 'Beauty which is Hope'.[14]

Upon receipt of these verses Poe immediately procured a letter of introduction and set off to Providence. His declaration of love took place in the course of the next fortnight during a walk in the cemetery. Mrs Whitman would not consent to an engagement, but she agreed to write to him, and thus the famous correspondence began.

Professor Harrison can only compare Poe's letters to the letters of Abelard and Eloise or to the *Sonnets from the Portuguese*;[15] Miss Ticknor says that they have won themselves a niche among the world's classic love letters. Professor Woodberry,[16] on the other hand, thinks that they should never have been published. We agree with Professor Woodberry, not because they do damage to Poe's reputation, but because we find them very tedious compositions. Whether you are writing a review or a love letter the great thing is to be confronted with a very vivid idea of your subject. When Poe wrote to Mrs Whitman he might have been addressing a fashion plate in a ladies' newspaper – a fashion plate which walks the cemetery by moonlight, for the atmosphere is one of withered roses and moonshine. The fact that he had buried Virginia a short time before, that he denied his love for her, that he was writing to Annie[17] at the same time and in the same style, that he was about to propose to a widow for the sake of her money – all his perfidies and meannesses do not by themselves make it impossible that he loved Mrs Whitman genuinely. Were it not for the letters we might accept the charitable view that this was his last effort at redemption. But when we read the letters we feel that the man who wrote them had no emotion left about anything; his world was a world of phantoms and fashion plates; his phrases are the cast-off phrases that were not quite good enough for a story. He could see neither himself nor others save through a mist of opium and alcohol. The engagement, which had been made conditional upon his reform, was broken off; Mrs Whitman sank on to a sofa holding a handkerchief 'drenched in ether'[18] to her face, and her old mother rather pointedly observed to Poe that the train was about to leave for New York.

Cynical though it sounds, we doubt whether Mrs Whitman lost as much as she gained by the unfortunate end of her love affair. Her feeling for Poe was probably more that of a benefactress than of a lover; for she was one of those people who 'devoutly believe that serpents may be reclaimed. This is only effected by patience and prayer – but the results are wonderful.'[19] This particular serpent was irreclaimable; he was picked up unconscious in the street and died a year later. But he left behind him a crop of reptiles who taxed Mrs Whitman's patience and needed her prayers for the rest of her life. She became the recognised authority upon Poe, and whenever a biographer was in need of facts or old Mrs Clemm[20] was in need of money they applied to her. She had to decide the disputes of the different ladies as to which had been loved the most, and to keep the peace between the rival historians, for whether a woman is more vain of her love or an author of his work has yet to be decided. But the opportunities which such a position gave her of endless charity and literary discussion evidently suited her, and the good sense and wit of the bird-like little woman, who was extremely poor and had an eccentric sister to provide for, seem to justify her statement that 'the results are wonderful'.

1 – A review in the *TLS*, 5 April 1917, (Kp C71) of *Poe's Helen* (John Lane, 1917) by Caroline Ticknor. See also 'Thoreau' below, 'Emerson's Journals', *I VW Essays*; and see (for Caroline Ticknor) 'Glimpses of Authors', *III VW Essays*. Reprinted: *G&R*, *CE*.

2 – Sarah Helen Whitman, *née* Power (1803–78), poet, born at Providence, Rhode Island, was the widow of an inconspicuous lawyer, John Winslow Whitman (d. 1833). Her first volume of poems *Hours of Life* appeared in 1853; her other publications include *Edgar Poe and His Critics* (1860) and *Poems* (1879).

3 – This precise form of words has not been discovered, but see Ticknor, Pref., p. vii: 'After the lapse of half a century, Poe still remains the one romantic figure in the field of American Letters . . .'

4 – *Ibid.*, ch. III, p. 24, the essay is not identified; Percy Bysshe Shelley (1792–1822).

5 – *Ibid.*, ch. III, p. 27, quoting George William Curtis (1824–92), essayist, editor and reformer, who had been a student at Brook Farm. William Ellery Channing (1818–1901), poet, nephew of the unitarian minister W. E. Channing who exerted a considerable influence upon the Transcendentalists – members of the literary movement that flourished in New England, 1836–60, chief among whom were Ralph Waldo Emerson (1803–82), Henry David Thoreau (1817–62) and Margaret Fuller (1810–50). The younger Channing was a friend of Hawthorne and of Thoreau – of whom he wrote a biography, *Thoreau, the Poet-Naturalist* (1873) – and married Margaret Fuller's sister.

6 – *Ibid.*, ch. II, p. 15: 'In the matter of clothes she was entirely unconventional, dressing in a style all her own; she loved silken draperies, lace scarfs, and floating veils, and was always shod in dainty slippers'.

7 – *Ibid.*, ch. XV, p. 281, quoting Professor William Whitman Bailey: 'She had a trick of inverting her lamp shades so that a flood of light would be thrown upon and suffuse some particular painting or print, leaving the rest of the room in darkness . . .'

8 – Ticknor, ch. I, p. 5, quoting Mrs Whitman's friend Sarah S. Jacobs, which has: 'the dreamy look of deep-set eyes that gazed over and beyond, but never at you'.

9 – John Hay (1838–1905), writer and diplomat, author of *Pike County Ballads* (1871) and also of the 10-vol. *Abraham Lincoln: a History* (1890). Hon. Wilkins Updike (1784–1867), author of *Memoirs of the Rhode Island Bar* (1842) and of the *History of the Episcopal Church in Narrangansett* (1847).

10 – *Ibid.*, ch. III, p. 24, quoting G. W. Curtis to Mrs Whitman, letter 9 April 1845, which has: 'Music, so imperfect here, foreshadows a state more refined and delicate. It is a womanly accomplishment, because it is sentiment, and the Instinct declares its nature, when it celebrates heaven and the state where glorified souls chant around the throne. Poetry is the adaptation of music to an Intellectual sphere . . .'

11 – *Ibid.*, ch. III, p. 28, letter undated, which has: 'Autumn', and 'Summer'.

12 – *Ibid.*, ch. v, p. 60, letter 1 October 1848, which has: 'I cannot better explain to you what I felt than by saying that your unknown heart seemed to pass into my bosom – there to dwell forever – while mine, I thought, was translated into your own. From that hour I loved you.' Edgar Allan Poe (1809–40), poet and critic, found fame with the publication of *The Raven and Other Poems* (1845); the second of the two poems by Poe entitled 'To Helen' (published in November 1848) is addressed to Mrs Whitman.

13 – *Ibid.*, ch. IV, 'To Edgar Allan Poe', dated Providence, R.I., 14 February 1848, p. 46.

14 – *Ibid.*, ch. IV, p. 52.

15 – *Ibid.*, ch. v, p. 56; Professor James Albert Harrison author of *Life and Letters of Edgar Allan Poe* (1903). Pierre Abélard (1079–1142) and Héloïse (d. 1163), whose celebrated correspondence has been published in numerous editions. Elizabeth Barrett Browning (1806–61), *Sonnets from the Portuguese* (1850).

16 – George E. Woodberry, author of a biography of Poe in the American Men of Letters series, 1885, and of *The Life of Edgar Allan Poe. Personal and Literary* (2 vols, 1909). The source of his opinion on the publication of Poe's letters has not been traced.

17 – Virginia Poe, *née* Clemm (d. 1847), Poe's cousin, whom he married in 1836. Mrs Annie Richmond, of Lowell, Mass., another of Poe's passions, to whom he addressed the poem 'For Annie' (published in April 1849).

18 – *Ibid.*, ch. VIII, p. 120: 'The scene which ensued has been often described. Mrs Whitman herself quite ill, and worn out by worry and argument, returned to Poe certain letters and papers, then dropping upon a couch and placing a handkerchief drenched in ether to her face she relapsed into a semiconscious state.

Poe fell upon his knees beside her and continued his protestations, begging her to reconsider and to speak to him.'

19 – *Ibid.*, ch. XI, p. 174, Mrs Whitman to her friend Mrs Freeman, otherwise unidentified, letter dated March 1857.

20 – Maria Clemm, mother of Virginia.

A Talker

When one opens a book of poetry and discovers the lines:

> In 1863 Charles publishes
> How Orchid Flowers are Fertilized by Insects,

or

> In 1833 a man named Hallam,
> A friend of Alfred's, died at twenty-two,[2]

one may be either delighted or annoyed; one may feel that this method is the genuine, unhumbugging speech which poets would always use if they were sincere; or one may inquire with some asperity why, if Mr Masters wants to say this sort of thing, he does not run all his lines into one, and say it in prose. But this last seems to us a stupid criticism: the lines would be no better if they were all of the same length, and, moreover, they would not be prose. The lines we have quoted are not prose; the lines that follow are not prose.

> Up there in the city
> Think sometimes of the American village and
> What may be done for conservation of
> The souls of men and women in the village.[3]

The difficulty of describing Mr Masters lies precisely in the fact that if he is not a prose writer, still less is he a poet. And for this reason it is not necessary to consider him as a man who is making serious experiments in metre like the Imagists or the Vers Librists. He has none of the sensibility which, whether we think it irritable or perverted or inspired, is now urging them to break up the old rules and devise new ones, more arduous than the old. He seems to us to have little ear for the sound of words, and no poetic imagination. When he does an exercise in the classical style, such as 'Marsyas', or 'Apollo at Pherae', he is as smooth and dull and conscientious as a prize poet at one of our universities. His metaphors are then of this description:

> And looking up he saw a slender maid
> White as gardenias, jonquil-haired, with eyes
> As blue as Peneus when he meets the sea[4]

or,

> And once he strove with music's alchemy
> To turn to sound the sunlight of the morn
> Which fills the senses as illuminate dew
> Quickens the ovule of the tiger-flower.[5]

Whatever poetry may be, it is nothing at all like this; and although we very much prefer

> For when they opened him up
> They found his heart was a played out pump,
> And leaked like a rusty cup,[6]

we doubt whether that is any more in the right direction.

But if Mr Masters is neither a poet nor a prose writer, we must, after reading 280 pages of his work, find a name for him; and on the whole we think it nearest the mark to call him a talker. His jerky, creaking style, the inconsecutiveness of his thought, his slap-dash use of language, his openness and plain speaking (the best of his poems is too frank to be quoted)[7] all seem to mark him as a person who utters his ideas in talk, without stopping very long to think what he is saying. As the above quotations will have shown, when he stops to think he becomes the shadow of other respectable people; even the restraint of a rhyme seems to shackle him at once. But when he is most at his ease, and therefore at his best, we seem to see him in the corner of a New England public house, telling stories about Jerry Ott, Cato Braden, Malachy Degan, or Slip Shoe Lovey,[8] with considerable shrewdness, humour, and sentimentality. In this mood he resembles a very primitive and provincial Robert Browning.[9] And when there is a political crisis he gets upon his feet and delivers a harangue about life in general – for he is extremely didactic – more in the style of one of our village orators, save that his background is made of great advertisement hoardings, factory chimneys, and skyscrapers, instead of ancient churches and the oaks of ancestral parks.

> Suppose you do it, Republic.
> Get some class.
> Throw out your chest, lift up your head,
> Be a ruler in the world.
> And not a hermit in regimentals with a flint-lock.
> Colossus with one foot in Europe,
> And one in China,
> Quit looking between your legs for the reappearance
> Of the star of Bethlehem –
> Stand up and be a man![10]

To a stranger the familiarity of this colloquial style seems to show that Mr Masters is at any rate a true son of the house. The chief interest of his work, indeed, comes from the fact that it is self-consciously and self-assertively American; and it is for that reason we suppose that the American public hails it with delight, on the principle, with which we must agree, that one native frog is of more importance than a whole grove full of sham nightingales.

1 – A review in the *TLS*, 12 April 1917, (Kp C72) of *The Great Valley* (T. Werner Laurie, 1916) by Edgar Lee Masters (1869–1950), the poet of small-town America, whose *Spoon River Anthology*, published anonymously in 1915, found instant popularity.
2 – For the first quotation, Masters, 'The Great Valley, VII, Autochthon', p. 40; and for the second, *ibid.*, p. 36.
3 – Masters, 'Cato Braden', p. 119.
4 – *Ibid.*, 'Apollo at Pherae', p. 169.
5 – *Ibid.*, 'Marsyas', p. 157.
6 – *Ibid.*, 'Steam Shovel Cut', p. 177
7 – VW is possibly referring to the poem 'To a Spirochaeta', *ibid.*, pp. 104–5, in which acknowledgement is made of Robert Burns's 'To a Louse'.
8 – The character Jerry Ott appears in the poem 'Cato Braden'; for the other characters referred to see 'Malachy Degan' and 'Slip Shoe Lovey'.
9 – Robert Browning (1812–89).
10 – Masters, 'Come, Republic', pp. 74–5.

'In Good Company'

We have enjoyed Mr Kernahan's book so much that we find ourselves asking what the reason can be. For the most part snapshot reminiscences of celebrities, though we can no more help reading them than we can help turning the pages of a picture paper, leave us with a slight feeling of depression. The little pictures are so real, so authentic – and yet if Tennyson really said this or did that have we missed so very much by never having known Tennyson? And thus we determine to check our natural instinct of reverence, and come rather to disbelieve in great men. The impression that Mr Kernahan's book produces is the exact opposite of this. He is a good but by no means a blind hero-worshipper; he makes little use of stories or personalities; and some of his heroes are hardly to be counted among the great or even the celebrated. But he succeeds very singularly in making us feel that to all these men life was a rich and remarkable affair, and that, after all, is what we want to know about; that is what we cannot altogether get from their books. The average person is chiefly struck by the eccentricities of the great; Mr Kernahan, on the other hand, bears witness to the fullness, sincerity, and passion with which great men live compared with lesser men. It is our method, indeed, of passing time and spending money that should rightly be called eccentric – not theirs.

Consider, for instance, what the present of a bunch of flowers meant to Swinburne.[2]

In an ecstasy of delight, he took the flowers from my outstretched hand . . . He bent his head over them in a rapture that was almost like a prayer, his eyes when he looked up to thank me for the gift alight and brimming over with thoughts that were not far from tears . . . Then he turned to Miss Watts[3] with his courtly bow. 'As you have been as equally honoured as I, you will not think me robbing you if I carry my bunch away with me to put them in water and to place them in my own room. I want to find them there when I wake in the morning.'[4]

This was an important event to him; his next day would begin with a solitary ecstasy over a bunch of flowers. We must change our focus altogether if we want to understand how the day which begins with the contemplation of lilies is lived by the poet. Many incidents must be blurred; others brought out with a sudden and amazing intensity. And this impression of a change in the focus is still with us when Mr Kernahan writes of Watts-Dunton,[5] although, of course, it is a very different change. His day was spent not in ecstasies over bunches of flowers, but in a busy interminable traffic with ideas and literature. Never, as Mr Kernahan says, a professional literary man, he was steeped in every sort of literary knowledge and memory which somehow made it impossible for him ever to become an author himself. A book of some kind – on the first principles of literary criticism, a biography, a novel – was always impending over his head; every day his equipment became more stupendous; the fame of the unwritten masterpiece was such that publishers would come down in order to induce him at last to pluck the ripe fruit. '"Yes," he would say, "I cannot deny that I could write such a book. Such a book, I do not mind saying in confidence, has long been in my mind, and in the minds of friends who have repeatedly urged me to such work."'[6] He toyed complacently with the idea of fame and accomplishment. He would then telegraph to one or two of his friends for their advice, and in imagination the book was already completed.

But sitting down to write the first words of it, he was overcome by doubts; suddenly it seemed essential to use that particular hour for the composition of one of his innumerable letters, and so, although his intentions for books were enough to fill a large space in the British Museum, he left only two published volumes behind him.[7]

The study of Edward Whymper[8] gives us another view of the life which has got itself out of the rut, though in his case this was achieved by no bias of extraordinary genius, unless, as sometimes seems to be the case, to be a 'character' is to be an artist, although you produce no work of art. The account of this masterful, independent, and self-isolated man, who lived for choice at the top of a high house in Southend, with a house-keeper in the basement and the intervening storeys completely unfurnished, so that he might feel himself alone, interests us like one of those portraits of queer people painted to perfection by Borrow.[9] We would draw attention in particular to the delightful scene with the photograph of himself when he had already kept Mr Kernahan waiting from 8.30 to 12.30 for his supper.[10] Mr Kernahan was very hungry; he could see nothing remarkable in the photograph. At length Whymper tapped it with the stem of his pipe. 'What I wondered was whether you'd notice that the smoke coming from the bowl of the pipe has been painted-in upon the negative . . . When you get to know me better you'll find that I'm slow and methodical, but minutely accurate, even about little things.'[11] But, like all Mr Kernahan's studies, this is a portrait, and we have no right to spoil it by picking out a handful of eccentricities; for he makes us understand that the queer ways of the great are for the most part only an impatient short cut to a life beyond our reach.

1 – A review in the *TLS*, 12 April 1917, (Kp C73) of *In Good Company. Some personal recollections of Swinburne, Lord Roberts, Watts-Dunton, Oscar Wilde, Edward Whymper, S. J. Stone, Stephen Phillips* (John Lane, The Bodley Head, 1917) by Coulson Kernahan (1858–1943). See also 'Swinburne As I Knew Him', *III VW Essays*.

2 – Algernon Charles Swinburne (1837–1909), author of *Atalanta in Calydon* (1865) and *Poems and Ballads* (1st series, 1866; 2nd series, 1878), etc.

3 – Teresa Watts, sister of Theodore Watts-Dunton (see n. 5).

4 – Kernahan, pp. 26–7.

5 – Theodore Watts-Dunton (1832–1914), critic, novelist, poet, friend and protector of Swinburne, with whom he shared his home at The Pines, Putney, from 1879 until Swinburne's death.

6 – Kernahan, p. 92.

7 – His book of verse scenes, *The Coming of Love and Other Poems* (1897), and the

novel, *Aylwin* (1898), books with characters in common and dealing with gipsy life. Watts-Dunton's collection of literary portraits, *Old Familiar Faces,* and the novel *Vesprie Towers* were published posthumously, in 1916.

8 – Edward Whymper (1840–1911), wood-engraver and Alpinist, a friend of Leslie Stephen.

9 – George Borrow (1803–81), author of *Lavengro* (1851), *The Romany Rye* (1857), *Wild Wales* (1862), etc.

10 – Kernahan, p. 163.

11 – *Ibid.*

A Cambridge V.A.D.

The war, so people say, is breaking down barriers between the classes which seemed of adamant. Many individuals would have something of the kind to relate of havoc wrought within their own personalities by the same disaster. They have been made aware, to their delight, that they possess powers and desires which are entirely at variance with each other and with their accepted beliefs about themselves. Here we have the case of Miss Spearing, a late Fellow of Newnham, engaged when war broke out upon 'research work on certain Elizabethan dramas'.[2] Not even this war, one might have thought, would have disturbed an occupation so utterly alien to itself; and yet the proofs of her book sent to the Louvain University Press were among the first things to perish in the flames. She found compensation 'and much more'[3] for its loss by becoming a V.A.D. at Cambridge, and this little book consists of notes and diaries she wrote there and later when she was nursing at hospitals in various parts of France. She does not attempt to analyse her feelings very closely, as no doubt she had little time to indulge in them; but something of the excitement of a student plunged from books into practical work and finding herself quite capable of it is perceptible in her account and exhilarating to the reader.

Her first taste of camp life was not a mild one. The hospital camp was among chalk hills swept by the wind; the tents were blown down in the middle of the night; the camp was a sea of mud; the month November. When the snow came 'it was difficult to creep out of the tent without allowing a heavy mass of snow to fall in and overwhelm everything.' 'Yet most of us,' Miss Spearing adds, 'find camp life decidedly congenial.'[5] It is very healthy, for one thing; and then 'one makes friends quickly',[5] such conditions, one may suppose, providing a fine test of friendship. As for the soldiers, her patients, Miss Spearing has the usual story to tell – so usual that we have almost forgotten how remarkable it is. They are very gentle, very grateful, very much like children, and yet in some respects the conventional picture does not do them justice. Beneath a surface which is so much alike that it resembles a uniform assumed for convenience, 'the modern Tommy is often a highly strung individual, very sensitive to pain',[6] a man living in abnormal conditions, and showing naturally some qualities that one would not expect. Among them there is his taste, which Miss Spearing found a little puzzling, for highly sentimental songs, about 'home and mother and sweetheart', which he will get up and sing with 'the utmost seriousness'.[7] But this surely is of a piece with the desire for noise and merriment which breaks out unreasonably as a reaction from the strain of the trenches. 'We all,' she says, 'live very much for the day,'[8] and try to get as much into the day as possible, for it is a short one, and those who meet now may be moved elsewhere tomorrow.

This concentration of life is, perhaps, the secret of the fascination which so many people find in a hard and dangerous existence. The best qualities, and the most real, which might be hidden in the slow intercourse of normal life, come quickly to the surface. They find the readiest expression, so far as the English are concerned, in humour. But in the nurses, and in the soldiers, such experiences are forming deeper thoughts, of 'an underlying reality',[9] of a 'community of suffering';[10] and it is this which is in Miss Spearing's mind when she writes, 'I have had horrors enough to last me my whole life, but still I don't think I would have missed it if I had been given my choice.'[11] And yet she by no means shares the sentimental illusions about wounded soldiers and the effects of war on the character which she found rife in England on her return. A time in the trenches does not make bad men good; soldiers 'are very ordinary people, with an unfortunate weakness for getting drunk, and an inability to say "No" to a pretty girl.'[12] But among all these conflicting impressions there are two which in her case grow ever stronger – the love of poetry and the love of England. The poetry is the poetry of today, and England is the English country, the Cambridge country – 'the slow, quiet river ... the old Roman highway ... the yellow cornfields, the pleasant green meadows'.[13]

1 – A review in the TLS, 10 May 1917, (Kp C74) of From Cambridge to Camiers

Under the Red Cross (W. Heffer & Sons Ltd., 1917) by E. M. Spearing (Mrs Evelyn Mary Simpson, 1885–1963), associate and late Fellow of Newnham College, Cambridge. V.A.D. – Voluntary Aid Detachment, a nursing service auxiliary to the armed forces. (See *I VW Diary*, Saturday, 23 January 1915: 'Jean [Thomas] asked us to go & hear some V.A.D.'s sing; but the fire after tea was too tempting'.)

2 – Spearing, Pref., p. vii.

3 – *Ibid.*

4 – *Ibid.*, 'Winter in a Camp Hospital in France', p. 26.

5 – *Ibid.*, p. 27.

6 – *Ibid.*, 'The Aftermath of the Big Push (July, 1916)', p. 62.

7 – *Ibid.*, 'Songs in the Night', p. 79, slightly adapted.

8 – *Ibid.*, p. 75, which has: 'Moreover, we all live very much for the day and let the morrow take care of itself'.

9 – *Ibid.*, p. 75: 'Not that war may not, in many cases, have given men a new sense of underlying reality, and a deep steadiness of purpose. But on the surface, at any rate, the reaction from the strain of the trenches shows itself often in bursts of high spirits and a desire to make plenty of noise.'

10 – *Ibid.*, 'The Aftermath of the Big Push (July, 1916)', p. 59.

11 – *Ibid.*

12 – *Ibid.*, 'Cambridge Again', p. 80: '"Our demigods in the trenches," as I see one journalist calls them, know perfectly well that in ordinary circumstance they are very ordinary people . . .'

13 – *Ibid.*, pp. 83–4.

The Perfect Language

To those who count themselves lovers of Greek in the sense that some ragged beggar might count himself the lover of an Empress in her robes, the Loeb Library,[2] with its Greek or Latin on one side of the page and its English on the other, came as a gift of freedom to a very obscure but not altogether undeserving class. The existence of the amateur was recognised by the publication of this Library, and to a great extent made respectable. He was given the means of being an open and unabashed amateur, and made to feel that no one pointed the finger of scorn at him on that account; and in consequence, instead of exercising his moribund faculties almost furtively upon some chance quotation met in an English book, he could read a whole play at a time, with his feet on the fender. With such treatment, too, his little stock of Greek became improved, and occasionally he would be rewarded with one of those moments of instant understanding which are the flower of reading. In them we seem not to read so much as to recollect what we have heard in some other life.

Of course, no translation, as Mr Paton[3] would probably be the first to agree, is going to reproduce the bloom and scent, the natural poise and sequence, all that we feel before we understand the meaning, of the original words. No one is going to translate –

> O Proserpina,
> For the flowers now, that frighted thou let'st fall
> From Dis's waggon![4]

It is necessary perhaps to be English to understand that. But there are other qualities which can be rendered. A spirited version will give the movement and the form of a play so that a thousand suggestions can be received by a mind unable to grasp a fraction of them when weighed down with the labour of translation. It is important to read quickly, if only because the friction of speed creates in the reader the arrogant and, in this case, scarcely warrantable belief that he knows precisely what Aeschylus meant, that the misunderstood Aeschylus reserved a peculiar meaning for him, that he is for the first time building up a perfectly original figure of the poet. Without this conviction the reading of the classics is apt to become insipid, and the burden of other people's views a weight too heavy to be borne. But, once fired with the spirit of the partisan, it is wonderful what hardships no longer repel us, and how little respect is paid to the authority of the great. It is true that humiliation has generally to be faced at the end of these outbursts of zeal, for the reason that Greek is an immensely difficult language. A great deal of knowledge is essential for the moderate understanding of it, and not easy to come by. How many people in England can read Homer as accurately as a child of eight can read the morning paper? for example; and the few who read Sophocles perfectly are about as singular as acrobats flying through space from bar to bar.

To our thinking the difficulty of Greek is not sufficiently dwelt upon, chiefly perhaps because the sirens who lure us to these perilous waters are generally scholars of European reputation. They have forgotten, or never knew, or for reasons of their own choose to belittle, what those difficulties are. But for the ordinary amateur they are very real and very great; and we shall do well to recognise the fact and to make up our minds that we shall never be independent of our Loeb. And the more we own the difficulty, and confess the sense of unrewarded effort, the consciousness of pygmy understanding, the more we must testify to the miracle of the language. It will not let us go. It will not agree to be a respectable branch of learning which we are well content to admire in the possession of others. A branch of learning suggests a withered stick with a few dead leaves attached to it. But Greek is the golden bough; it crowns its lovers with garlands of fresh and sparkling leaves. We have only to open this volume of the anthology at haphazard to fall once more beneath the spell:

I Brotachos, a Gortynian of Crete, lie here, where I came not for this end, but to trade.[5]

The serene, restrained, and penetrating sound of that detaches itself at once from all others, even in the English version. What is added to it by the Greek words it is impossible to define. To appreciate them fully one would have, no doubt, to be born a Greek. But we are not aware of any affectation when we say that once having read them we know, even with our imperfect understanding, that there is a beauty in the Greek language which is unlike and beyond any that we have met elsewhere. Let us turn the page and read:

I am the tomb of a shipwrecked man; but set sail, stranger; for when we were lost other ships voyaged on.[6]

or,

If to die will be the chief part of virtue, Fortune granted this to us above all others; for striving to endue Hellas with freedom, we lie here possessed of praise that groweth not old.[7]

or,

Tears, the last gift of my love, even down through the earth I send to thee in Hades, Heliodora ...[8]

Here we have the peculiar magic, the lure that will lead us from youth to age, groping through our island fogs and barbarities towards that unattainable perfection. But perfection has a chill sound. It scarcely seems the right word for that extremely individual and definite spirit which is the flame of the Greek character. No one can read the few lines quoted above without feeling not only their extreme beauty, but also their extreme unlikeness to anything in any other language. It is an unlikeness that perpetually rouses our curiosity about them. These lines, in the first place, seem to be written neither in the infancy nor in the old age of the world, but in its maturity. There is no prettiness as there is no mysticism in them. We hear the voice of men whose outlook on life was perfectly direct and unclouded. There is, of course, that virtue of restraint so often praised in the Greeks that we tend to forget that it is most of all a virtue when, as in the present case, there is much to restrain. And although the present volume of the anthology is devoted to epigrams upon the dead, it is evident that this people had everything to restrain, a love of man or woman, a love of earth, a love of life itself more passionate, it seems, than ours. Nevertheless they are able to dismiss life with stoical clearness of sight, and of all their grief allow only one cry to escape them.

The difference between them and ourselves is made very clear in these epigrams where feelings of such depth and scope are concentrated into so small a space. They have to do with individual men and women; and we see, as in a vignette, a little view of the house, of the daily work, of the country outside the door. We can see the sharp lines of the mountains, the changing colour of the sea, the little vines stooping with grapes, and hear the harsh song of the crickets. It is the South, but it is not Italy. It is life, but it is not our life. When we attempt to visualise the Greek world we see it standing in outline against the sky without crowd or detail. One is inclined to think of their literature, too, as a succession of complete and perfect utterances; for (to the amateur at least) there are no schools in Greek literature, or imitations, no bad shots at great things which tend to blur the outline of the masterpiece when it is achieved. For us at least no chance saying in Greek, or association of words, opens up a view of irrelevant vulgarity such as it is well nigh impossible to exclude from the pages of those who write in a living tongue. On the contrary, we feel that if by chance the veil lifts in their writing it is to reveal something beautiful, something strong and sincere.

But we doubt whether it is right to use our English word beauty so perpetually when we speak of the Greeks, for they do not seem to have our conception of beauty, or of its rarity or of its value. Another power seems to be theirs – the power of gazing with absolute candour upon the truth of things, and beauty seems to come of its own accord, not as an ornament to be applied separately but as an essential part of the world as it appears to them. Theirs is a beauty of the whole rather than of parts; and although it would be possible, no doubt, to make a book of the beauties of their poets, we should miss much more by this treatment of them than we should if it were applied to our own Elizabethans. Among the epigrams of the anthology there are many examples of this flawless quality; save among the latest it would be hard to find one without a trace of it. It is a quality which has the likeness of impersonality were it not for that inflection of the voice with which they charge their words with all the sorrow, the passion, or the joy that words can say, or, more marvellously still, leave unsaid.

Now the white violet blooms, and blooms the moist narcissus, and bloom the wandering mountain lilies; and now, dear to her lovers, spring flower among the flowers, Zenophile, the sweet rose of Persuasion, has burst into bloom. Meadows, why·idly laugh in the brightness of your tresses? For my girl is better than garlands sweet to smell.[9]

The beauty of that seems to us incomparable and yet it is only a reflection of the beauty of the Greek.

But we could go on multiplying quotations and seeking and persuading ourselves that we find new reasons for our love of them indefinitely. For the truth is that, even to an amateur, Greek literature is not so much literature as the type of literature, the supreme example of what can be done with words. Even to him the words have their strong and unmistakable accent. Other words of other languages may come nearer to us, but what in Latin or English has this stamp of finality, what in any other literature so convinces us that the perfect form of human utterance has been found once and for all? Found easily, as we feel, almost unconsciously, such was the genius of the race for expression. And, although it seems ungracious to add this when we have owned so much indebtedness to translators, some knowledge of the language is a possession not to be done without. With the best will in the world the translators are bound to stamp their individuality or that of their age upon the text. Our minds are so full of echoes that a single word such as 'aweary'[10] will flood a whole page for an English reader with the wrong associations. And such is the power of the Greek language that to know even a little of it is to know that there is nothing more beautiful in the world.

1 – A review in the *TLS*, 24 May 1917, (Kp C75) of *The Greek Anthology*. With an English translation by W. R. Paton, vol. ii. The Loeb Classical Library (Heinemann, 1917). VW set immense store by Greek, which she saw as not only 'the perfect language' but also the privileged preserve of the educated male. Several of her friends were classical scholars, as indeed was LW. She began her own study of the language attending classes at King's College, London, in 1897, and took private lessons from Dr Warre, in 1898, and from Janet Case in 1902. See also 'On Not Knowing Greek', *IV VW Essays,* and *CR1*; and see *Jacob's Room* (1922), *passim.*

2 – Founded and endowed by James Loeb (1867–1933), American banker and philanthropist.

3 – William Roger Paton (d. 1921), classical scholar and archaeologist, educated at Eton and University College, Oxford, where he graduated in 1879.

4 – Shakespeare, *The Winter's Tale*, iv, 4, ll. 117–19.

5 – Paton, bk vii, no. 254A, by Simonides, p. 143, complete.

6 – *Ibid.*, no. 282, by Theodoridas, p. 155, complete.

7 – *Ibid.*, no. 253, by Simonides, p. 141, complete.

8 – *Ibid.*, no. 476, by Meleager, p. 259, which continues: '– tears ill to shed, and on thy much-wept tomb I pour them in memory of longing, in memory of affection. Piteously, piteously doth Meleager lament for thee who art still dear to him in death, paying a vain tribute to Acheron. Alas! Alas! Where is my beautiful one, my heart's desire? Death has taken her, has taken her, and the flower in full bloom is defiled by the dust. But Earth my mother, nurturer of all, I beseech thee, clasp her gently to thy bosom, her whom all bewail.'

9 – J. W. Mackail, *Select Epigrams from the Greek Anthology* (Longman's, Green & Co., 1890), no. xix, by Meleager, which has: 'mountain-wandering lilies'. VW possessed a 1907 edition of Mackail, probably the gift of Saxon Sydney-Turner, to which she alluded in a letter to Sydney-Turner on 31 December 1916 (*II VW Letters*, no. 813), announcing: 'Now I am going to read the Greek Anthology (in a copy you gave me once) which I find very hard and quite absorbing', and at its close, in Greek, quoted Meleager's epigram.

10 – E.g. Mackail, no. lxvii by Asclepiades, p. 117: 'I am not two and twenty yet, and I am aweary of living; O Loves, why misuse me so? why set me on fire; for when I am gone, what will you do? Doubtless, O Loves, as before you will play with your dice, unheeding.'

Mr Sassoon's Poems

As it is the poet's gift to give expression to the moments of insight or experience that come to him now and then, so in following him we have to sketch for ourselves a map of those submerged lands which lie between one pinnacle and the next. If he is a true poet, at least we fill up in thought the space between one poem and another with speculations that are half guesses and half anticipations of what is to come next. He offers us a new vision of the world; how is the light about to fall? What ranges, what horizons will it reveal? At least if he is a sincere artist this is so, and to us Mr Sassoon seems undoubtedly sincere. He is a poet, we believe, meaning by that that we cannot fancy him putting down these thoughts in any form save the one he has chosen. His vision comes to him directly; he seems almost always, before he began to get his words into order, to have had one of those puzzling shocks of emotion which the world deals by such incongruous methods, to the poet often, to the rest of us too seldom for our souls' good. It follows that this one slim volume is full of incongruities; but the moments of vision are interesting enough to make us wish to follow them up very carefully.

There are the poems about the war, to begin with. If you chance to read one of them by itself you may be inclined to think that it is a very clever poem, chiefly designed with its realism and its surface cynicism to shock the prosperous and sentimental. Naturally the critical senses rise in alarm to protect their owner from such insinuations. But read them continuously, read in particular 'The Hero' and 'The Tomb-Stone Maker', and you will drop the idea of being shocked in that sense altogether.

> 'Jack fell as he'd have wished,' the Mother said,
> And folded up the letter that she'd read.
> 'The Colonel writes so nicely.' Something broke
> In the tired voice that quavered to a choke.
> She half looked up. 'We mothers are so proud
> 'Of our dead soldiers.' Then her face was bowed.
>
> Quietly the Brother Officer went out . . .
>
> He thought how 'Jack', cold-footed, useless swine,
> Had panicked down the trench that night the mine
> Went up at Wicked Corner; how he'd tried
> To get sent home; and how at last he died,
> Blown to small bits. And no one seemed to care
> Except that lonely woman with white hair.[2]

What Mr Sassoon has felt to be the most sordid and horrible experiences in the world he makes us feel to be so in a measure which no other poet of the war has achieved. As these jaunty matter-of-fact statements succeed each other such loathing, such hatred accumulates behind them that we say to ourselves, 'Yes, this is going on; and we are sitting here watching it,' with a new shock of surprise, with an uneasy desire to leave our place in the audience, which is a tribute to Mr Sassoon's power as a realist. It is realism of the right, of the poetic kind. The real things are put in not merely because they are real, but because at a certain moment of emotion the poet happened to be struck by them and is not afraid of spoiling his effect by calling them by their right names. The wounded soldier looking out of the train window sees the English country again –

> There shines the blue serene, the prosperous land,
> Trees, cows, and hedges; skipping these, he scanned
> Large friendly names that change not with the year,
> Lung Tonic, Mustard, Liver Pills, and Beer.[3]

To call back any moment of emotion is to call back with it the strangest odds and ends that have become somehow part of it, and it is the weeds pulled up by mistake with the flowers that bring back the extraordinary moment as a whole. With this straight, courageous method Mr Sassoon can produce such a solid and in its way beautiful catalogue of facts as that of the train leaving the station – 'The Morning Express'.

But we might hazard the guess that the war broke in and called out this vein of realism before its season; for side by side with these pieces there are others very different, not so effective perhaps, not particularly accomplished, but full of a rarer kind of interest, full of promise for the future. For the beauty in them, though fitful, is of the individual, indefinable kind which comes, we know not how, to make lines such as we read over each time with a renewed delight that after one comes the other.

> Where have you been, South Wind, this May-day morning,
> With larks aloft, or skimming with the swallow,
> Or with blackbirds in a green, sun-glinted thicket?
>
> Oh, I heard you like a tyrant in the valley;
> Your ruffian haste shook the young, blossoming orchards;
> You clapped rude hands, hallooing round the chimney,
> And white your pennons streamed along the river.
>
> You have robbed the bee, South Wind, in your adventure,
> Blustering with gentle flowers; but I forgave you
> When you stole to me shyly with scent of hawthorn.[4]

Here we have evidence not of accomplishment, indeed, but of a gift much more valuable than that, the gift of being a poet, we must call it; and we shall look with interest to see what Mr Sassoon does with his gift.

---

1 – A review in the *TLS*, 31 May 1917, (Kp C76) of *The Old Huntsman and Other Poems* (Heinemann, 1917) by Siegfried Sassoon (1886–1967), by this date a captain in the Royal Welch Fusiliers. Sassoon had been injured in April 1917. He was currently convalescing in England and, while doing so, protesting, through the press and through parliament, at what he saw to be the deliberate prolongation of the war.

In August, declared by the under-secretary for war to be suffering from shell shock, he would be sent to Craiglockhart War Hospital, near Edinburgh, there to meet the young poet Wilfred Owen, who died in action on 4 November 1918.

A letter from Sassoon, which does not survive, expressing his appreciation of the review, was forwarded to VW by Lady Ottoline Morrell, to whom VW wrote on 5 June: 'I am so glad he liked the review. I've reviewed so little poetry that I was rather nervous, and I liked his poems very much.' (*II VW Letters,* no. 839; and see no. 860). See also 'Two Soldier Poets' below. Reprinted: *B&P.*

2 – Sassoon, 'The Hero', p. 48, the first stanza, the first line of the second stanza, and the whole of the final stanza.

3 – *Ibid.*, 'Stretcher Case' '[To Edward Marsh]', p. 50, which has: 'There shone the blue serene'; and 'Large, friendly'.

4 – *Ibid.*, 'South Wind', p. 87, the entire poem.

'Creative Criticism'

Mr Spingarn has some hard things to say of American criticism, of its dependence on the decayed and genteel tradition of Victorian England, of its 'hopeless chaos in the face of new realities of art',[2] which we admit that we have sometimes wished to say for ourselves, but they come with greater force and grace from the lips of an American. He demolishes more decayed and genteel traditions than the Victorians can justly be taxed with; and in the face of new realities his enthusiasm is so keen and clear-sighted that we wish that he would give us a few examples of the art besides this spirited defence of it. We wish indeed that he had written a longer book; for the subjects he deals with are very complex, and many of the interesting things that he says would be still more interesting if they were discussed more fully.

Mr Spingarn's chief object is to confute those people who still hold that the critic is an inferior being, and his art a base one. He sets out to show that his opinion is founded upon a misconception of the power that 'poets and critics share together';[3] for whatever the power is, he asserts that 'in their most significant moments the creative and the critical instinct are one and the same'.[4] This conception of the nature of criticism is of very modern date. It depends upon the assumption that the task of the critic is to ask himself – 'What has the poet tried to express and how has he expressed it?'[5] As Mr Spingarn shows, in a very interesting and suggestive summary of the history of criticism, this question was never asked with any unanimity until we come to the nineteenth century, and in particular to Coleridge, Carlyle, and Sainte-Beuve.[6] Horace asked whether there were more than three actors on the stage, or more than five acts in the drama; Dr Johnson whether the poet numbered 'the streaks of the tulip';[7] innumerable critics of less importance applied yet more arbitrary tests before they tied on the right label – epic, pastoral, tragedy, comedy as the case might be. It was little wonder that the critic and his art fell into disrepute, for the first act of any vigorous writer was to break all the laws and tear up all the labels. Nowadays, thanks to Sainte-Beuve and others, the conception of criticism has changed; we try to enter into the mind of the writer, to see each work of art by itself, and to judge how far each artist has succeeded in his aim. We do not think that our work is done when we have taken his measure by a standard roughly adapted to fit that particular class.

The important change of course, as we think that Mr Spingarn is right in saying, was the change which led critics to conceive of literature as an art of expression. A great deal might be said about this view of art, and about the statement that 'art has performed its function when it has expressed itself'.[8] But if you hold that view a great many questions that used to be taken into account have to be thrown overboard. Mr Spingarn makes a long and a bold list of them. In his phrase we have 'done with'[9] the old rules; we have done with the *genres*; we have done with technique as separate from art; we have done with the history and criticism of poetic themes; we have done with the race, the time, the environment of the poet; we have done with all moral judgment of literature; we have done with the 'evolution'[10] of literature. None of these questions, though each is interesting in itself, has anything to do with the value of a work of art. Possibly this may be so, although we cannot help thinking that of two poems the one with a higher morality is better aesthetically than the one with a lower morality. The critic then is confronted by the work of art in itself. He has to reproduce in his own mind the 'essence of unmixed reality',[11] if we like to call it so, and to say how completely it has been expressed. In order to do this, says Mr Springarn, 'aesthetic judgment becomes nothing more or less than creative art itself'.[12] That any writer capable of this feat is deserving of the highest praise is indisputable; but that his genius is of the same order as that of the poet we are not so certain. For criticism is not merely the re-creation of a work of art; the process of re-creation gone through by the critic is very different from the process which created the original work.

Criticism is largely the interpretation of art, and it is difficult to see how a work which contains the element of interpretation can be a work of art in the sense in which a poem is a work of art. There is a difference not of degree but of kind between Coleridge's *Lectures on Shakespeare* and the *Ancient Mariner*.[13] It does not seem possible to say of critical work, as it is possible to say of poetical work, that 'beauty is its own excuse for being'.[14] But to decide the exact amount of the difference, or the relative value of the two gifts, supposing them to be distinct, is not of great importance, even were it possible to do so. On the other hand, it is of very great importance to open the mind as widely as possible to see what each writer is trying to do, and in interpreting him only to frame rules which spring directly from our impression of the work itself.

For how in criticism are we to go altogether without 'rules'? Is not the decision to do so merely another rule? Although to feel is of the first importance, to know why one feels is of great importance too. There can be no doubt, however, that to be free to make one's own laws and to be alert to do it afresh for every newcomer is an essential part of any criticism worth having. And that criticism is worth having Mr Spingarn has proved conclusively; in another essay he might go on to tell us the reason why.

1 – A review in the *TLS*, 7 June 1917, (Kp c77) of *Creative Criticism: Essays on the Unity of Genius and Taste* (Henry Holt & Co., 1917) by J. E. [Joel Elias] Spingarn (1875–1939), professor of comparative literature at Columbia University, 1899–1911, author of *A History of Literary Criticism in the Renaissance* (1899) and *The New Criticism* (1911). From 1919 to 1932 Spingarn was a member of the publishing firm Harcourt, Brace and Company, VW's American publisher. A revised edition of *Creative Criticism* appeared in 1931.

2 – Spingarn, 'Prose and Verse', p. 99.

3 – *Ibid.*, 'The New Criticism', p. 4.

4 – *Ibid.*, pp. 42–3.

5 – *Ibid.*, p. 42.

6 – S. T. Coleridge (1772–1834); Thomas Carlyle (1795–1881); Charles Augustin Sainte-Beuve (1804–69).

7 – Spingarn, 'The New Criticism', p. 21, quoting Dr Johnson (1709–84), *The History of Rasselas, Prince of Abyssinia* (1759), ch. x (ed. D. J. Enright, Penguin, 1976, pp. 61–2): 'The business of a poet, said Imlac, is to examine, not the individual, but the species; to remark general properties and large appearances: he does not number the streaks of the tulip, or describe the different shades in the verdure of the forest.'

8 – *Ibid.*, p. 20: 'It was they [the Germans] who first realised that art has performed ...; it was they who first conceived of criticism as the study of expression.'

9 – *Ibid.*, p. 24.
10 – *Ibid.*, p. 40.
11 – *Ibid.*, p. 19.
12 – *Ibid.*, p. 42.
13 – S. T. Coleridge, *Notes and Lectures upon Shakespeare* ... (1849), most of which were first published in *Literary Remains* (1836–8); the lectures were originally given in 1810–11. *The Ancient Mariner* (1798).
14 – Spingarn, 'The New Criticism', p. 32.

'South Wind'

We have no quarrel with the shape or size or colour of this novel; but we believe that if, instead of being a brown, plump, freshly printed volume, it were slim, a little yellow, the date about 1818, the cover of a faded green, marked, perhaps, with the rim of an ancient tea cup – if, in short, it resembled the first edition of *Nightmare Abbey* or *Crotchet Castle*[2] – there would be people willing to sift the old bookstalls in search of it, to pay a sovereign for it: people fond of taking it from the shelf and reading their favourite passages aloud, and apt to remark, when they put it back again, 'What a pity it is that novelists don't write like this nowadays!' They very seldom do write like this. But when the reader, a few pages deep and beginning to feel settled in the new atmosphere, collects himself, his first comment is likely to be that it is a very strange thing that no one has thought of writing this book before Mr Douglas. The comment is a compliment, although there is a trace of annoyance in it. It signifies that the idea is one of those fresh and fruitful ideas that have been sailing just out of range on the horizon of our minds and now have been brought to shore and all their merchandise unladen by another.

Take all the interesting and eccentric people you can think of, put them on an island in the Mediterranean beyond the realms of humdrum but not in those of fantasy: bid them say shamelessly whatever comes into their heads: let them range over every topic and bring forth whatever fancy, fact, or prejudice happens to occur to them: add, whenever the wish moves you, dissertations upon medieval dukes, Christianity, cookery, education, fountains, Greek art, millionaires, morality, the sexes: enclose the whole in an exquisite atmosphere of pumice rocks and deep blue waves, air with the warm and stimulating breath of the South Wind – the prescription begins something in this way. But we have left out the most important element of all. We are at a loss to define the quality of the author's mind, his way of presenting these men and women, of turning his ideas. We glance at Peacock, and then, for a second, at Oscar Wilde.[3] Peacock is superbly eccentric and opinionated; Wilde is persuasive and lucid. Mr Douglas possesses these qualities, but they are his own. His book has a distinguished ancestry, but it was born only the day before yesterday. So individual is the character of his mind that as we read we frequently congratulate him upon having found the right form for a gift that must have been hard to suit. As frequently we congratulate ourselves on the fact that the whole affair is turning out so surprisingly and delightfully successful.

Upon the Island of Nepenthe, then, 'an islet of volcanic stone rising out of the blue Mediterranean',[4] are congregated for various reasons a great many people of marked idiosyncrasy – Mr Keith, Mr Eames, Miss Wilberforce, Mr and Mrs Parker, Count Caloveglia, Mme Steynlin, Mr Denis, and the Duchess of San Martino, to name only the most prominent. The Bishop of Bampopo, Mr Heard, alights here for a short stay on his way home from episcopal duties in the Equatorial Regions. He is introduced to them all one after another. We scarcely venture to attempt any summary of their characters or of their conversation. We may say, however, that Mr Eames was engaged in annotating Perrelli's *Antiquities*. But 'it is not true to say that he fled from England to Nepenthe because he forged his mother's will, because he was arrested while picking the pockets of a lady at Tottenham Court Road station, because he refused to pay for the upkeep of his seven illegitimate children'.[5] None of this is true at all. He once had a love affair, which left him chronically sensitive on the subject of balloons. But Mr Eames was the reverse of Mr Keith. Mr Keith collected information for its own sake. 'He could tell you how many public baths existed in Geneva in pre-Reformation days, what was the colour of Mehemet Ali's whiskers, why the manuscript of Virgil's friend Gallius had not been handed down to posterity, and in what year and what month the decimal system was introduced into Finland.'[6] His was a complex character; he held marked and peculiar views upon the origin of our English spleen; he was an epicure; and, 'chaster than snow as a conversationalist, he prostituted his mother tongue in letter-writing to the vilest of uses'. We are not surprised on the whole that 'friends of long standing called him an obscene old man'.[7] Of Mrs Parker we need only say that she treasured and displayed in her drawing room a piece of fine blue material fished from the floating *débris* of a millionaire's yacht, from which she deduced and expressed certain opinions as to the habits of travelling millionaires. Of the millionaire himself, what can be said? The Malthusian philosophy had no more distinguished supporter, and the part he played when in the opinion of the island it became necessary to protect Miss Wilberforce from herself was much to his credit. This poor lady, of unblemished descent and connections, having lost her lover at sea had taken to the bottle and given way to noctambulous habits, when she was liable to divest herself of her raiment. The Duchess, it is true, was not a duchess at all, but as she talked and behaved like one the right was conceded her. Mme Steynlin, on the other hand, 'cared little what frocks she wore so long as somebody loved her'.[8] The reader must imagine how they talked, and how one of them was induced incidentally to slip over the edge of a precipice.

But as we have left out all mention of the Alpha and Omega Club, of Buddha and the Little White Cows, together with innumerable other interesting and delightful facts, we must cease to summarise. Indeed, a summary of their conduct and conversation is too likely to give the impression that the characters are merely a gallery of whimsical grotesques, mouthpieces for the brilliant and well-informed mind of their author. That is far from the truth. There are an astonishing number of things that never get into novels at all and yet are of the salt of life; and the achievement of *South Wind* is that is has arrested a great number of these things and proved once more what a narrow convention the novelist is wont to impose on us. Meanwhile, although the hot season has dispersed the original party, Mr Keith is still in residence; Mr Roger Rumbold, the advocate of Infanticide for the Masses, and Mr Bernard, author of *The Courtship of Cockroaches,* have lately arrived. How often in the coming months will our thoughts seek relief if not repose in the Island of Nepenthe, and with what eagerness shall we await a further and even fuller report of its history!

1 – A review in the *TLS*, 14 June 1917, (Kp C78) of *South Wind* (Martin Secker, 1917) by Norman Douglas (1868–1952). Reprinted: *CW*.
2 – *Nightmare Abbey* (1818) and *Crotchet Castle* (1831) by Thomas Love Peacock (1785–1866).
3 – Oscar Wilde (1854–1900).
4 – Douglas, ch. 16, p. 193.
5 – *Ibid.*, ch. 3, p. 33, part of a longer sentence, which begins: 'It was not true to say'.
6 – *Ibid.*, ch. 9, pp. 120–1.

7 – For this and the preceding quotation, *ibid.*, p. 121; each is a complete sentence in the original.
8 – *Ibid.*, ch. 6, p. 72.

'Books and Persons'

There are two kinds of criticism – the written and the spoken. The first, when it gets into print, is said to be the cause of much suffering to those whom it concerns; but the second, we are inclined to think, is the only form of criticism that should make an author wince. This is the criticism which is expressed when, upon finishing a book, you toss it into the next armchair with an exclamation of horror or delight, adding a few phrases by way of comment, which lack polish and ignore grammar but contain the criticism which an author should strain all his forces to overhear. If criticism can ever help, he will be helped; if it can ever please, he will be enraptured; the pain, even, is salutary, for it will be severe enough either to kill or to reform. One or two writers there are who can put this criticism into prose; but for the most part the adjectives, the grammar, the logic, the inkpot – to say nothing of humanity and good manners – all conspire to take the dash and sincerity out of it, and by the time speech becomes a review there is nothing left but grammatical English.

Mr Arnold Bennett is one of the few who can catch their sayings before they are cold and enclose them all alive in very readable prose. That is why these aged reviews (some are nearly ten years old) are as vivacious and as much to the point as they were on the day of their birth. They have another claim upon our interest. They deal for the most part with writers who are still living, whose position is still an open question, about whom we feel more and probably know more than we can with honesty profess to do about those dead and acknowledged masters who are commonly the theme of our serious critics. At the time when Mr Bennett was Jacob Tonson of the *New Age*,[2] Mr Galsworthy, Mr Montague, Mrs Elinor Glyn, Mr W. H. Hudson, Mr John Masefield, Mr Conrad, Mr E. M. Forster, Mr Wells and Mrs Humphry Ward[3] were not exactly in the positions which they occupy today. The voice of Jacob Tonson had something to do with the mysterious process of settling them where, as we think, they will ultimately dwell. It is true that we are not going to rank any book of Mr Galsworthy's with *Crime and*

Punishment,[4] and we dissent a little from the generosity of the praise bestowed upon the novels of Mr Wells. But these are details compared with the far more important question of Mr Bennett's point of view. We have said that his is spoken criticism; but we hasten to add that it is not at all what we are accustomed to hear spoken at dinner tables and in drawing rooms. It is the talk of a writer in his workroom, in his shirt sleeves. It is the talk, as Mr Bennett is proud to insist, of a creative artist. 'I am not myself a good theoriser about art,'[5] he says. 'I . . . speak as a creative artist, and not as a critic.'[6] The creative artist, he remarks, on another occasion, produces 'the finest, and the only first-rate criticism'.[7]

We do not think that this is a book of first-rate criticism; but it is the book of an artist. Nobody could read one of these short little papers without feeling himself in the presence of the father of fifty volumes.[8] The man who speaks knows all that there is to be known about the making of books. He remembers that a tremendous amount of work has gone to the making of them; he is versed in every side of the profession – agents and publishers, good seasons and bad seasons, the size of editions and the size of royalties, he knows it all – he loves it all. He never affects to despise the business side of the profession of writing. He will talk of high-class stuff,[9] thinks that authors are quite right in getting every cent they can for it, and will remark that it is the business of a competent artist to please, if not *the*, certainly *a*, public. But it is not in this sense only that he is far more professional than the English writer is apt to be or to appear; he is professional in his demand that a novel shall be made absolutely seaworthy and well constructed. If he hates one sin more than another it is the sin of 'intellectual sluggishness'.[10] This is not the attitude nor are these the words of 'mandarins' or 'dilettanti'[11] – the professors and the cultivated people whom Mr Bennett hates much as the carpenter hates the amateur who does a little fretwork.

London swarms with the dilettanti of letters. They do not belong to the criminal classes, but their good intentions, their culture, their judiciousness, and their infernal cheek amount perhaps to worse than arson or assault . . . They shine at tea, at dinner, and after dinner. They talk more easily than ⟨the artist⟩ does, and write more easily too. They can express themselves more readily. And they know such a deuce of a lot.[12]

Whether we agree or disagree we are reminded by this healthy outburst of rage that the critic has not merely to deal out skilfully measured doses of praise and blame to individuals, but to keep the atmosphere in a right state for the production of works of art. The atmosphere, even seven years ago, was in a state so strange that it appears almost fantastic now. Canon Lambert was then saying, 'I would just as soon send a daughter of mine to a house infected with diphtheria or typhoid fever as'[13] let her read *Ann Veronica*. About the same time Dr Barry remarked, 'I never leave my house . . . but I am forced to see, and solicited to buy, works flamingly advertised of which the gospel is adultery and the apocalypse the right of suicide.'[14] We must be very grateful to Mr Bennett for the pertinacity with which he went on saying in such circumstances 'that the first business of a work of art is to be beautiful, and its second not to be sentimental'.[15]

But if we were asked to give a proof that Mr Bennett is something more than the extremely competent, successful, businesslike producer of literature, we would point to the paper on 'Neo-Impressionism and Literature'.[16] These new pictures, he says, have wearied him of other pictures; is it not possible that some writer will come along and do in words what these men have done in paint? And suppose that happens, and Mr Bennett has to admit that he has been concerning himself unduly with inessentials, that he has been worrying himself to achieve infantile realisms? He will admit it, we are sure; and that he can ask himself such a question seems to us certain proof that he is what he claims to be – a 'creative artist'.[17]

1 – A review in the *TLS*, 5 July 1917, (Kp c79) of *Books and Persons. Being comments on a past epoch 1908–1911* (Chatto & Windus, 1917) by Arnold Bennett (1867–1931) whose 'comments' were originally published in the *New Age*, under the pseudonym Jacob Tonson.

In dealing as it does with Bennett's article 'Neo-Impressionism and Literature', VW's review anticipates amicably the more heated controversy she was to pursue in 'Character in Fiction' ('Mr Bennett and Mrs Brown'), *III VW Essays*, in which volume see also the first of the two articles VW entitled 'Mr Bennett and Mrs Brown'.

The present review appeared in the same month as that in which VW published her experimental story 'The Mark on the Wall' and, probably, shortly before she began to write *Kew Gardens* (1919). Reprinted: *CW*.

2 – Edited by A. L. Orage, 1907–22.

3 – By the end of Bennett's period of activity as Jacob Tonson, in 1911, John Galsworthy (1867–1933) was chiefly known as the author of *The Man of Property* (1906) – discussed by Bennett in the *New Age*, 14 July 1910 (Bennett, pp. 214–16) – *The Country House* (1907), *Fraternity* (1909), *The Patrician* (1911), and the plays, *The Silver Box* and *Strife*, both produced in 1909. VW was shortly to review Galsworthy's *Beyond* (1917): see 'Mr Galsworthy's Novel' below.

C. E. Montague (1867–1928), author, dramatic critic, and journalist with the

Manchester Guardian, 1890–1914, 1919–25. Bennett reviewed Montague's first novel *A Hind Let Loose* (1910) in the *New Age,* 10 March 1910 (Bennett, pp. 201–3). Montague published a volume of criticism, *Dramatic Values* in 1911, and a second novel *The Morning's War* in 1913. After the 1914–18 War he made himself quite a different reputation as the author of anti-militaristic essays and fiction.

Elinor Glyn (1864–1943) wrote popular 'society' novels, one of which, *His Hour* (1910), Bennett reviewed in the *New Age,* 10 November 1910 (Bennett, pp. 271–7).

By 1911, W. H. Hudson (1841–1922) had published most of the works for which he is now known, including *The Purple Land* (1885), *Green Mansions* (1904) and *A Shepherd's Life* (1910), which was discussed by Bennett in the *New Age,* 24 November 1910 (Bennett, pp. 278–9). Hudson's autobiographical masterpiece *Far Away and Long Ago* appeared in 1918; for VW's review of it, see 'Mr Hudson's Childhood' below.

John Masefield (1878–1967) had published *Salt-Water Ballads* (1909), *Ballads and Poems* (1910), several collections of short stories, essays, plays, and a number of novels, including *The Street of To-day* (1911), on which Bennett wrote in the *New Age,* 20 April 1911 (Bennett, pp. 311–14).

Joseph Conrad (1857–1924) had published most of his major works by 1911. Bennett made several references to him in his *New Age* articles and wrote about him specifically, and his treatment at the hands of the *Athenaeum,* in the *New Age,* 19 September 1908 (Bennett, pp. 36–40).

E. M. Forster (1879–1970) had published *Howards End* in 1910 and this was discussed by Bennett in the *New Age,* 12 January 1911 (Bennett, pp. 292–3).

H. G. Wells (1866–1946) had also published most of his major works by 1911. Bennett frequently referred to Wells in his *New Age* column; he discussed his work in general in the issue for 4 March 1909 (Bennett, pp. 109–16), and his *The New Machiavelli* (1911), in that for 2 February 1911 (Bennett, pp. 294–9).

Mrs Humphry Ward (1851–1920) was the author of a great many popular novels, including *Robert Elsmere* (1888), *Eleanor* (1900), *Lady Rose's Daughter* (1903) and *The Testing of Diana Mallory* (1908). Bennett wrote about her heroines in the *New Age,* 3 October 1908 (Bennett, pp. 47–52).

4 – Bennett, 'John Galsworthy', p. 216; Fyodor Dostoevsky, *Crime and Punishment* (1866).

5 – *Ibid.,* 'Neo-Impressionism and Literature', p. 283 (*New Age,* 8 December 1910).

6 – *Ibid.,* 'W. W. Jacobs and Aristophanes', p. 56 (*New Age,* 24 October 1908); William Wymark Jacobs (1863–1943) was the author of several collections of stories.

7 – *Ibid.,* 'Artists and Critics', p. 158 (*New Age,* 21 October 1909).

8 – *Books and Persons* was Bennett's fifty-third published book.

9 – E.g., Bennett, 'The Literary Periodical', p. 243: 'High-class stuff is like radium.' (*New Age,* 8 September 1910).

10 – *Ibid.,* 'W. W. Jacobs and Aristophanes', p. 55.

11 – There are several references in *Books and Persons* to these phenomena.

12 – Bennett, 'The British Academy of Letters', pp. 229–30 (*New Age,* 18 August 1910).

13 – *Ibid.,* 'Censorship by the Libraries', p. 186 (*New Age,* 24 February 1910);

Canon Lambert was a member of the Hull Libraries Committee which banned H. G. Wells's *Ann Veronica* (1909).

14 – *Ibid.*, 'Unclean Books', p. 143 (*New Age*, 8 July 1910).

15 – *Ibid.*, 'The Length of Novels', p. 249 (*New Age*, 22 September 1910).

16 – 'Neo-Impressionism and Literature' (Bennett, pp. 280–5; *New Age*, 8 December 1910) was inspired by the First Post-Impressionist Exhibition (Manet and the Post-Impressionists), organised by Roger Fry at the Grafton Galleries, London, 8 November 1910–15 January 1911. It discussed the great British public's notoriously hostile reactions to the show and the possible implications of Post-Impressionism for the future of the novel.

17 – Bennett's concluding words (as revised in *ibid.*, pp. 284–5) were: 'The average critic always calls me, both in praise and dispraise, "photographic"; and I always rebut the epithet with disdain, because in the sense meant by the average critic I am not photographic. But supposing that in a deeper sense I were? Supposing a young writer turned up and forced me, and some of my contemporaries – us who fancy ourselves a bit – to admit that we had been concerning ourselves unduly with inessentials, that we had been worrying ourselves to achieve infantile realisms? Well, that day would be a great and disturbing day – for us.'

Thoreau

A hundred years ago, on 12 July, 1817, was born Henry David Thoreau, the son of a pencil-maker in Concord, Massachusetts.[2] He has been lucky in his biographers, who have been attracted to him not by his fame so much as by their sympathy with his views, but they have not been able to tell us a great deal about him that we shall not find in the books themselves. His life was not eventful; he had, as he says, 'a real genius for staying at home'.[3] His mother was quick and voluble, and so fond of solitary rambling that one of her children narrowly escaped coming into the world in an open field. The father, on the other hand, was a 'small, quiet, plodding man',[4] with a faculty for making the best lead pencils in America, thanks to a secret of his own for mixing levigated plumbago with fuller's earth and water, rolling it into sheets, cutting it into strips, and burning it. He could at any rate afford with much economy and a little help to send his son to Harvard, although Thoreau himself did not attach much importance to this expensive opportunity.[5] It is at Harvard, however, that he first becomes visible to us. A class-mate saw much in him as a boy that we recognise later in the grown man, so that instead of a portrait we will quote what was visible about the year 1837 to the penetrating eye of the Rev. John Weiss:

He was cold and unimpressible. The touch of his hand was moist and indifferent, as if he had taken up something when he saw your hand coming, and caught your grasp on it. How the prominent grey-blue eyes seemed to rove down the path, just in advance of his feet, as his grave Indian stride carried him down to University Hall. He did not care for people; his class-mates seemed very remote. This reverie hung always about him, and not so loosely as the odd garments which the pious household care furnished. Thought had not yet awakened his countenance; it was serene, but rather dull, rather plodding. The lips were not yet firm; there was almost a look of smug satisfaction lurking round their corners. It is plain now that he was preparing to hold his future views with great setness and personal appreciation of their importance. The nose was prominent, but its curve fell forward without firmness over the upper lip, and we remember him as looking very much like some Egyptian sculpture of faces, large-featured, but brooding, immobile, fixed in a mystic egoism. Yet his eyes were sometimes searching, as if he had dropped, or expected to find, something. In fact his eyes seldom left the ground, even in his most earnest conversations with you ...[6]

He goes on to speak of the 'reserve and inaptness'[7] of Thoreau's life at college.

Clearly the young man thus depicted, whose physical pleasures took the form of walking and camping out, who smoked nothing but 'dried lily stems',[8] who venerated Indian relics as much as Greek classics, who in early youth had formed the habit of 'settling accounts'[9] with his own mind in a diary, where his thoughts, feelings, studies, and experiences had daily to be passed under review by that Egyptian face and searching eye – clearly this young man was destined to disappoint both parents and teachers and all who wished him to cut a figure in the world and become a person of importance. His first attempt to earn his living in the ordinary way by becoming a schoolmaster was brought to an end by the necessity of flogging his pupils. He proposed to talk morals to them instead. When the committee pointed out that the school would suffer from this 'undue leniency' Thoreau solemnly beat six pupils and then resigned, saying that school-keeping 'interfered with his arrangements'.[10] The arrangements that the penniless young man wished to carry out were probably assignations with certain pine trees, pools, wild animals, and Indian arrowheads in the neighbourhood, which had already laid their commands upon him.

But for a time he was to live in the world of men, at least in that very remarkable section of the world of which Emerson was the centre and which professed the Transcendentalist doctrines.[11] Thoreau took up his lodgings in Emerson's house and very soon became, so his friends said, almost indistinguishable from the prophet himself. If you listened to them both talking with your eyes shut you could not be certain where Emerson left off and Thoreau began. '. . . in his manners, in the tones of his voice, in his modes of expression, even in the hesitations and pauses of his speech, he had become the counterpart of Mr Emerson.'[12] This may well have been so. The strongest natures, when they are influenced, submit the most unreservedly; it is perhaps a sign of their strength. But that Thoreau lost any of his own force in the process, or took on permanently any colours not natural to himself the readers of his books will certainly deny.

The Transcendentalist movement, like most movements of vigour, represented the effort of one or two remarkable people to shake off the old clothes which had become uncomfortable to them and fit themselves more closely to what now appeared to them to be the realities. The desire for readjustment had, as Lowell has recorded and the memoirs of Margaret Fuller[13] bear witness, its ridiculous symptoms and its grotesque disciples. But of all the men and women who lived in an age when thought was remoulded in common, we feel that Thoreau was the one who had least to adapt himself, who was by nature most in harmony with the new spirit. He was by birth among those people, as Emerson expresses it, who have 'silently given in their several adherence to a new hope, and in all companies do signify a greater trust in the nature and resources of man than the laws of the popular opinion will well allow'.[14] There were two ways of life which seemed to the leaders of the movement to give scope for the attainment of these new hopes; one in some cooperative community, such as Brook Farm;[15] the other in solitude with nature. When the time came to make his choice Thoreau decided emphatically in favour of the second. 'As for the communities,' he wrote in his journal, 'I think I had rather keep bachelor's quarters in hell than go to board in heaven.'[16] Whatever the theory might be, there was deep in his nature 'a singular yearning to all wildness'[17] which would have led him to some such experiment as that recorded in *Walden*,[18] whether it seemed good to others or not. In truth he was to put in practice the doctrines of the Transcendentalists more thoroughly than any one of them, and to prove what the resources of man are by putting his entire trust in them. Thus, having reached the age of twenty-seven, he chose a piece of land in a wood on the brink of the clear deep

green waters of Walden Pond, built a hut with his own hands, reluctantly borrowing an axe for some part of the work, and settled down, as
he puts it, 'to front only the essential facts of life, and see if I could not
learn what it had to teach, and not, when I came to die, discover that I
had not lived'.[19]

And now we have a chance of getting to know Thoreau as few people
are known, even by their friends. Few people, it is safe to say, take such
an interest in themselves as Thoreau took in himself; for if we are gifted
with an intense egoism we do our best to suffocate it in order to live on
decent terms with our neighbours. We are not sufficiently sure of
ourselves to break completely with the established order. This was
Thoreau's adventure; his books are the record of that experiment and its
results. He did everything he could to intensify his own understanding of
himself, to foster whatever was peculiar, to isolate himself from contact
with any force that might interfere with his immensely valuable gift of
personality. It was his sacred duty, not to himself alone but to the world;
and a man is scarcely an egoist who is an egoist on so grand a scale.
When we read *Walden*, the record of his two years in the woods, we have
a sense of beholding life through a very powerful magnifying glass. To
walk, to eat, to cut up logs, to read a little, to watch the bird on the
bough, to cook one's dinner – all these occupations when scraped clean
and felt afresh prove wonderfully large and bright. The common things
are so strange, the usual sensations so astonishing that to confuse or
waste them by living with the herd and adopting habits that suit the
greater number is a sin – an act of sacrilege. What has civilisation to give,
how can luxury improve upon these simple facts? 'Simplicity, simplicity,
simplicity!' is his cry. 'Instead of three meals a day, if it be necessary eat
but one; instead of a hundred dishes, five; and reduce other things in
proportion.'[20]

But the reader may ask, what is the value of simplicity? Is Thoreau's
simplicity simplicity for its own sake, and not rather a method of
intensification, a way of setting free the delicate and complicated
machinery of the soul, so that its results are the reverse of simple? The
most remarkable men tend to discard luxury because they find that it
hampers the play of what is much more valuable to them. Thoreau
himself was an extremely complex human being, and he certainly did
not achieve simplicity by living for two years in a hut and cooking his
own dinner. His achievement was rather to lay bare what was within
him – to let life take its own way unfettered by artificial constraints. 'I

did not wish to live what was not life, living is so dear; nor did I wish to practise resignation, unless it was quite necessary. I wanted to live deep and suck out all the marrow of life . . .'[21] *Walden* – all his books, indeed – are packed with subtle, conflicting, and very fruitful discoveries. They are not written to prove something in the end. They are written as the Indians turn down twigs to mark their path through the forest. He cuts his way through life as if no one had ever taken that road before, leaving these signs for those who come after, should they care to see which way he went. But he did not wish to leave ruts behind him, and to follow is not an easy process. We can never lull our attention asleep in reading Thoreau by the certainty that we have now grasped his theme and can trust our guide to be consistent. We must always be ready to try something fresh; we must always be prepared for the shock of facing one of those thoughts in the original which we have known all our lives in reproductions. 'All health and success does me good, however far off and withdrawn it may appear; all disease and failure helps to make me sad and do me evil, however much sympathy it may have with me or I with it.' 'Distrust all enterprises that require new clothes.' 'You must have a genius for charity as well as for anything else.'[22] That is a handful, plucked almost at random, and of course there are plenty of wholesome platitudes.

As he walked his woods, or sat for hours almost motionless like the sphinx of college days upon a rock watching the birds, Thoreau defined his own position to the world not only with unflinching honesty, but with a glow of rapture at his heart. He seems to hug his own happiness. Those years were full of revelations – so independent of other men did he find himself, so perfectly equipped by nature not only to keep himself housed, fed, and clothed, but also superbly entertained without any help from society. Society suffered a good many blows from his hand. He sets down his complaints so squarely that we cannot help suspecting that society might one of these days have come to terms with so noble a rebel. He did not want churches or armies, post offices or newspapers, and very consistently he refused to pay his tithes and went into prison rather than pay his poll tax. All getting together in crowds for doing good or procuring pleasure was an intolerable infliction to him. Philanthropy was one of the sacrifices, he said, that he had made to a sense of duty. Politics seemed to him 'unreal, incredible, insignificant',[23] and most revolutions not so important as the drying up of a river or the death of a pine. He wanted only to be left alone tramping the woods in his suit of Vermont grey, unhampered even by those two pieces of limestone which lay upon his desk until they proved guilty of collecting the dust, and were at once thrown out of the window.

And yet this egoist was the man who sheltered runaway slaves in his hut; this hermit was the first man to speak out in public in defence of John Brown;[24] this self-centred solitary could neither sleep nor think when Brown lay in prison. The truth is that anyone who reflects as much and as deeply as Thoreau reflected about life and conduct is possessed of an abnormal sense of responsibility to his kind, whether he chooses to live in a wood or to become president of the Republic. Thirty volumes of diaries which he would condense from time to time with infinite care into little books prove, moreover, that the independent man who professed to care so little for his fellows was possessed with an intense desire to communicate with them. 'I would fain,' he writes, 'communicate the wealth of my life to men, would really give them what is most precious in my gift . . . I have no private good unless it be my peculiar ability to serve the public . . . I wish to communicate those parts of my life which I would gladly live again.'[25] No one can read him and remain unaware of this wish. And yet it is a question whether he ever succeeded in imparting his wealth, in sharing his life. When we have read his strong and noble books, in which every word is sincere, every sentence wrought as well as the writer knows how, we are left with a strange feeling of distance; here is a man who is trying to communicate but who cannot do it. His eyes are on the ground or perhaps on the horizon. He is never speaking directly to us; he is speaking partly to himself and partly to something mystic beyond our sight. 'Says I to myself,' he writes, 'should be the motto to my journal,'[26] and all his books are journals. Other men and women were wonderful and very beautiful, but they were distant; they were different; he found it very hard to understand their ways. They were as 'curious to him as if they had been prairie dogs'.[27] All human intercourse was infinitely difficult; the distance between one friend and another was unfathomable; human relationships were very precarious and terribly apt to end in disappointment. But, although concerned and willing to do what he could short of lowering his ideals, Thoreau was aware that the difficulty was one that could not be overcome by taking pains. He was made differently from other people. 'If a man does not keep pace with his companions, perhaps it is because he hears a different drummer. Let him step to the music which he hears, however measured or far away.'[28] He was a wild man, and he would never submit to be a tame one. And for us here lies his peculiar charm. He hears a different drummer. He is a man into whom nature has breathed other instincts than ours, to whom she has whispered, one may guess, some of her secrets.

'It appears to be a law,' he says, 'that you cannot have a deep sympathy with both man and nature. Those qualities which bring you near to the one estrange you from the other.'[29] Perhaps that is true. The greatest passion of his life was his passion for nature. It was more than a passion, indeed; it was an affinity; and in this he differs from men like White and Jefferies.[30] He was gifted, we are told, with an extraordinary keenness of the senses; he could see and hear what other men could not; his touch was so delicate that he could pick up a dozen pencils accurately from a box holding a bushel; he could find his way alone through thick woods at night. He could lift a fish out of the stream with his hands; he could charm a wild squirrel to nestle in his coat; he could sit so still that the animals went on with their play round him. He knew the look of the country so intimately that if he had waked in a meadow he could have told the time of year within a day or two from the flowers at his feet. Nature had made it easy for him to pick up a living without effort. He was so skilled with his hands that by labouring forty days he could live at leisure for the rest of the year. We scarcely know whether to call him the last of an older race of men, or the first of one that is to come. He had the toughness, the stoicism, the unspoilt senses of an Indian, combined with the self-consciousness, the exacting discontent, the susceptibility of the most modern. At times he seems to reach beyond our human powers in what he perceives upon the horizon of humanity. No philanthropist ever hoped more of mankind, or set higher and nobler tasks before him, and those whose ideal of passion and of service is the loftiest are those who have the greatest capacities for giving, although life may not ask of them all that they can give, and forces them to hold in reserve rather than to lavish. However much Thoreau had been able to do, he would still have seen possibilities beyond; he would always have remained, in one sense, unsatisfied. That is one of the reasons why he is able to be the companion of a younger generation.

He died when he was in the full tide of life, and had to endure long illness within doors. But from nature he had learnt both silence and stoicism. He had never spoken of the things that had moved him most in his private fortunes. But from nature, too, he had learnt to be content, not thoughtlessly or selfishly content, and certainly not with resignation, but with a healthy trust in the wisdom of nature, and in nature, as he says, there is no sadness. 'I am enjoying existence as much as ever,' he wrote from his deathbed, 'and regret nothing.'[31] He was talking to himself of moose and Indian when, without a struggle, he died.

1 – A commemorative essay in the *TLS*, 12 July 1917, (Kp c80) based on Thoreau's works and on material in *The Life of Henry David Thoreau* (Richard Bentley & Son, 1890) by H. S. Salt. See also 'Poe's Helen', above, and 'Ralph Waldo Emerson', *I VW Essays*. Reprinted: *B&P*.

2 – Henry David Thoreau (1817–62), was the third child of John Thoreau and Cynthia Dunbar.

3 – Salt, ch. I, p. 24, quoting Thoreau writing to Daniel Ricketson, 1 February 1855.

4 – *Ibid.*, ch. I, p. 4.

5 – Thoreau was a student at Harvard, 1833–7: 'He is said to have refused to take his degree on the ground that five dollars was too high a price to pay for that honour' (Salt, p. 17).

6 – Salt, ch. I, p. 18, quoting Rev. John Weiss, *Christian Examiner,* Boston, July 1865, which has: 'grasp upon it', and 'sculptures'.

7 – *Ibid.*: 'He would smile to hear the word "collegiate career" applied to the reserve and inaptness of his college life.'

8 – *Ibid.*, p. 20.

9 – *Ibid.*, p. 23, quoting Thoreau's student theme 'Of Keeping a Private Journal', 1835.

10 – For Thoreau's leniency, Salt, ch. II, p. 26; and for his resignation, *ibid.*, p. 27, quoting William Ellery Channing, *Thoreau: The Poet-Naturalist* (Boston, Roberts Brothers, 1873).

11 – Ralph Waldo Emerson (1803–82), poet and essayist, leading light in the Transcendentalist movement, settled at Concord in 1834.

12 – Salt, ch. III, p. 57, quoting David Greene Haskins, *Ralph Waldo Emerson* (Boston, George H. Ellis, 1887).

13 – James Russell Lowell (1819–91), poet, essayist and diplomat, friend of Leslie Stephen and, effectively, VW's godfather; for his account of Thoreau see *My Study Windows* (Boston, James, R. Osgood and Company, 1871).

Margaret Fuller (1810–50), sometime editor of *Dial*, the Transcendentalist organ, author of *Summer on the Lakes in 1843* (1844), and *Woman in the Nineteenth Century* (1845); her memoirs, edited by R. W. Emerson, W. H. Channing and J. F. Clarke, were published in 1852.

14 – Emerson's observation does not occur in his biographical sketch of Thoreau (*The Writings of Henry David Thoreau*, xi vols, Houghton Mifflin Co., 1893, vol. x, *Miscellanies*, pp. 1–33), perhaps the most likely source, and its origin has not been traced.

15 – The so-called Institute of Agriculture and Education, 1841–7, established at West Roxbury in Massachusetts by the Transcendentalists George and Sarah Ripley.

16 – Thoreau's Journal, 3 March 1841, which has: 'these communities', and 'bachelor's hall', also quoted in Salt, ch. III, p. 79.

17 – Salt, ch. V, p. 128; original source untraced.

18 – *Walden* (1854).

19 – *Ibid.*, 'Where I Lived' (*Writings*, vol. II, p. 143); (also quoted in Salt, ch. III, p. 82).

20 – For the first quotation, *ibid.*, p. 144 (Salt, ch. IX, p. 236); and for the second, *ibid.*, pp. 144–5 (Salt, ch. IV, p. 93).

21 – *Ibid.*, p. 143 (Salt, ch. III, p. 82).

22 – For the three preceding quotations, *ibid.*, 'Economy', p. 125; *ibid.*, p. 39, which has: 'I say, beware of all enterprises that require new clothes, and not rather a new wearer of clothes'; *ibid.*, p. 116.

23 – Salt, ch. IX, p. 234.

24 – John Brown (1800–59), the abolitionist, whom Thoreau first met in 1857 and for whom he spoke in his 'Plea for Captain John Brown' at Concord Town Hall, 30 October 1859, following Brown's arrest at Harper's Ferry earlier in the month. (Brown was hanged at Charles Town, 2 December 1859.) See also, *Writings*, vol. x, 'The Last Days of John Brown' and 'After the Death of John Brown'.

25 – Journal, 26 March 1842 (the first two sentences only are quoted in Salt, ch. II, p. 33).

26 – *Ibid.*, 11 November 1851.

27 – *Walden*, 'The Village', p. 262.

28 – *Ibid.*, 'Conclusion', p. 502.

29 – Journal, 11 April 1852 (Salt, ch. V, p. 115).

30 – Gilbert White (1720–93) and Richard Jefferies (1848–87), to both of whom Salt alludes.

31 – Salt, ch. VIII, p. 213, quoting Thoreau writing to Myron B. Benton, 21 March 1862.

'Lord Jim'

This new edition of *Lord Jim* will be succeeded, we suppose, by the rest of Mr Conrad's works – those that are already published, and the many, as we hope, that are still to come. But will they all appear in the binding which disfigured *The Shadow Line*² and now afflicts us once more in *Lord Jim*? Will they all be of a sad green colour, and sprinkled with chocolate-brown nautical emblems such as might be stamped upon club note-paper, or upon some florid philanthropic pamphlet drawing attention to the claims of sea-captains' widows? As a general rule we submit to the will of publishers in silence, but it is time to cry out when they ask us to disfigure our shelves upon so large a scale as this. It is not a question of luxury, but of necessity: we have to buy Mr Conrad; all our friends have to buy Mr Conrad; and that Mr Conrad of all people should be robbed even of a shred of that dignity and beauty which he more than any living writer is able to create seems quite distressingly inappropriate.

Let us give thanks, however, for the portrait, and especially for the few words of introduction which Mr Conrad prefixes to the book. He tells us two facts of great interest: there is, or was, in existence a lady who does not like *Lord Jim*. That, though discreditable to her, is possible. But what are we to say of her reason? '"You know," she said, "it is all so morbid."' . . . 'The pronouncement,' writes Mr Conrad, 'gave me food for an hour's anxious thought.'³ That is sufficiently surprising, too. If Mr Conrad had taken this extravagantly bad shot into account for the space of a minute, we should have thought it an excessive compliment to the unknown lady; for is there any word in the language less applicable to *Lord Jim* than 'morbid'? In the second place, Mr Conrad has a few words to say about the origin of the story. He tells us that his first thought was of a short story concerned only with the pilgrim-ship episode; but after writing a few pages he became discontented, and laid them aside. But Mr Blackwood happened to ask him for a story, and 'it was only then that I perceived that the pilgrim-ship episode was a good starting point for a free and wandering tale'.⁴ A great many of his readers we think, will say that this statement explains a great deal: it explains that difficult break in the narrative; it explains the one criticism which we have ever formulated against this superb romance – that the second part of the book does not develop satisfactorily out of the first. The adventures at Patusan are not quite on a level with the rest.

Nevertheless, after reading *Lord Jim* again we are inclined to agree with what appears to be Mr Conrad's own opinion and to put *Lord Jim* at the head of all his works. There is *The Heart of Darkness*; there is 'Youth'; there is *Typhoon*;⁵ there is *The Shadow-Line*; for ourselves, we should claim a very high place for that beautiful fragment of *Reminiscences*⁶ still unfinished; but in *Lord Jim* Mr Conrad seems to have found once for all the subject that brings out his rare and wonderful qualities at their best. By a chance that does not come to every novelist, he has found his opportunity and made use of it to the very utmost. But it is not for us while he is still, happily, midway in his career to attempt to place Mr Conrad's books in order of merit or to weigh this famous work once more in our scales. Indeed, those critical susceptibilities which are set on edge by nine books out of ten and insist upon recording their complaints lie down happily and sleep in this case, and leave us with leisure to ruminate one or two ideas about Mr Conrad's work.

It is in *Lord Jim* that one of those passages occurs which interest us almost more for what they reveal of the writer than for any light they throw on the story. Marlow is drinking with that French naval officer who appears very distinctly for a few pages and then drops out altogether, and he remarks:

As if the appointed time had arrived for his moderate and husky voice to come out of his immobility, he pronounced 'Mon Dieu, how the time passes!' Nothing could have been more commonplace than this remark; but its utterance coincided for me with a moment of vision. It's extraordinary how we go through life with eyes half shut, with dull ears, with dormant thoughts . . . Nevertheless, there can be but few of us who had never known one of these rare moments of awakening, when we see, hear, understand ever so much – everything – in a flash, before we fall back again into our agreeable somnolence. I raised my eyes when he spoke, and I saw him as though I had never seen him before.[7]

That, so it strikes us, is the way in which Mr Conrad's mind works; he has a 'moment of vision' in which he sees people as if he had never seen them before; he expounds his vision, and we see it, too. These visions are the best things in his books. In *Lord Jim* particularly, how they crowd about us, these wonderful figures – Brierly, Chester, Stein – with their strange experiences all laid bare for an instant before, just as they come from darkness, they fade into darkness again! The gift of seeing in flashes is, of course, a limitation as well as a gift; it explains what we may call the static quality of Mr Conrad's characters. They change and develop very slightly; they are for the most part people whose characters are made up of one or two very large and simple qualities, which are revealed to us in flashes. But Mr Conrad's genius is a very complex one; although his characters remain almost stationary they are enveloped in the subtle, fine, perpetually shifting atmosphere of Marlow's mind; they are commented upon by that voice which is so full of compassion, which has so many deep and fine cadences in its scale. Mr Conrad has told us that it is his conviction that the world rests on a few very simple ideas, 'so simple that they must be as old as the hills'.[8] His books are founded upon these large and simple ideas; but the texture through which they are seen is extremely fine; the words which drape themselves upon these still and stately shapes are of great richness and beauty. Sometimes, indeed, we feel rather as if we were lying motionless between sea and sky in that atmosphere of profound and monotonous calm which Mr Conrad knows so strangely how to convey. There is none of the harassing tumult and interlocking of emotion which whirls through a Dostoevsky[9] novel, and to a lesser extent provides the nervous system of most novels. The sea and the tropical forests dominate us and almost overpower us; and something of their largeness, their latent inarticulate passion seems to have got into these simple men and these old sea-captains with their silent surfaces and their immense reserves of strength.

1 – A review in the *TLS*, 26 July 1917, (Kp c81) of *Lord Jim. A Tale* (J. M. Dent & Sons Ltd., 1917) by Joseph Conrad (1857–1924). See also *Youth* and 'Mr Conrad's Crisis', below; 'A Disillusioned Romantic', 'A Prince of Prose', 'Mr Conrad: A Conversation', *III VW Essays*; 'Joseph Conrad', *IV VW Essays* and *CR1*.
2 – *The Shadow-Line* (1917).
3 – Conrad, Author's Note, p. ix.
4 – *Ibid.*, p. viii, the first part of a sentence, which concludes '; that it was an event, too, which could conceivably colour the whole "sentiment of existence" in a simple and sensitive character'. William Blackwood, editor of *Blackwood's Magazine*.
5 – 'The Heart of Darkness', published in *Youth – A Narrative; and Two Other Stories* (1902); *Typhoon* (1903).
6 – *Some Reminiscences* (1912).
7 – Conrad, ch. XIII, p. 142, which begins: 'I kept him company; and suddenly, but not abruptly, as if . . .' VW's ellipsis marks the omission of 'Perhaps it's just as well; and it may be that it is this very dulness that makes life to the incalculable majority so supportable and so welcome'.
8 – *Some Reminiscences* (Eveleigh Nash, 1912), 'A Familiar Preface', p. 20.
9 – Fyodor Dostoevsky (1821–81).

'John Davidson'

If you write a thesis 'in partial fulfilment of the requirements for the degree of Doctor of Philosophy' upon a poet, it is inevitable perhaps that you should approach that poet solemnly and heavily, and, if he is not among the great, should attribute to him an importance which makes his familiar features appear strained and unnatural. Mr Fineman has not been able to avoid this common error. His essay opens with a cannonade of sonorous general statements about Victorian life and literature which it is difficult to bring into relation with actual books and facts. No doubt there is a connection between the discovery of electricity and the growth of realism in art, but it is a statement which puts a great strain upon the imagination; nor is it easy to make flesh and blood of an analysis of our modern view of romance, such as the following:

It either became symbolism; and this appealed to an age of increased intensity of commercial production because of the nerve-irritation that symbolic methods of double interpretation and aroused expectancy involved and implied; or else it became the romance of cruelty and tragic endings with occasional by-products of Wellsian science-romances and Davidsonian cosmological testaments.[2]

But when Mr Fineman gets on to Davidson[3] himself he is not so heavy-handed and he has plenty of interesting things to say. He takes Davidson from the point of view of the philosopher, and there is, of course, much in Davidson that the reader who is primarily interested in thought will find it worth his while to unravel. It is possible, and Mr Fineman's study lends support to this view, that to future generations Davidson will be interesting chiefly as the man who expressed most forcibly a material-istic view of the world in poetry. But Mr Fineman sends us back to Davidson's books and, leaving the views of future generations out of account, we try to take stock of our own.

It is less than ten years since Davidson died, leaving behind him the tragic preface in which, among other reasons for making an end, he stated that he had to 'turn aside and attempt things for which people will pay'.[4] His books came out in the last years of the nineteenth century and in the first years of this. The tragedy and whatever of achievement there is in the work are quite close to us; and yet already his voice has become a strange one. That is always so with a poet who is not great enough to be in the air as well as in print; when you do not read him he ceases to exist. But the neglect, at least in the case of Davidson, brings its compensation, for surprise is uppermost in re-reading him that anyone so good should be so little famous. And when we call him good, we mean, first and foremost, energetic, passionate, sincere, and master of his own method of expression. Take for example the first half of the *Testament of John Davidson*.[5] He wishes to do no less than re-fashion our conception of the universe. We are to admit no vision of another existence than ours; we are to realise that gods, centaurs, goblins, the lands of faery and romance, the whole 'wonderful Cosmogony of Other World',[6] are merely the reflections of man's unenlightened mind.

> Upon the mirror of eternity.[7]
> ... God and gods
> Are man's mistake; no brain exists
> Behind the galaxies, above them or beneath;

No thought inhabiteth eternity,
No reason, no intelligence at all
Till conscious life begins.[8]

The first half of the poem, in which man states his claim for supremacy to Hecate, has not only beauty in the poetic sense, but also a degree of interest which experience has scarcely led us to expect in such circumstances. It seems as if the fire of the new faith were to shrivel up finally those pallid and abstract gods and goddesses whose help is so often invoked by the academic poets for the sake of the poetic atmosphere which they create. Davidson is wholly in earnest; he sees and feels with remarkable force the vast conceptions which he is trying to express; and, above all, he is absolutely convinced of the paramount importance of his theme. And that, so we think, is his undoing. When man unrolls the whole origin, construction, and pageant of the universe, he is so burdened by all the facts which prove him right in his materialism that the poem breaks down beneath their weight; it becomes a lecture upon biology and geology delivered by an irate and fanatical professor. The facts which cumber his lines may be correct, but we do not want them stated as the following lines state them:

Secreted by the primal atom, all
The other atoms, the planets cooled,
Became; and all the elements, how much
So ever differing in appearance, weight,
Amount, condition, function, volume (gold
From iodine, argon from iron) wrought
Of the purest ether, in electrons sprang
As lightning from the tension filling space.[9]

Our quarrel is not at all with the words, which might very well take their place in poetry, or with the subject, which is magnificent, but with the proselytising spirit, which makes the truth of the facts of more importance than the poetry, and with the growing arrogance and acerbity of manner, as of one dinning the Gospel into the heads of an indifferent public. It is an open question how far Milton and Dante[10] believed the truth of the doctrines which they sang, and it is possible to enjoy them to the utmost without agreeing with them. But Davidson raises a spirit of controversy which makes it plain that if you do not agree with him you are damned.

Yet there are very few modern poets who need to be reduced to their proper stature by the august shades of Milton and Dante. The sturdy persistence with which Davidson thinks out his theme stands him in good stead now that the years have gone over him. He is always an interesting poet, and a far better spokesman for his time than others more mellifluous, although nature denied him the faculty of making even one of those little poems which everybody knows by heart. His shorter work, like the *Fleet Street Eclogues* and the *Ballads*,[11] has more chance of this form of popularity, but the chief interest of it, too, comes from the attitude of his thought; as Mr Fineman says, '. . . it is not the passing vision of ordinary joys and sorrows that haunts his imagination but rather the queries that lie back of it.'[12] His philosophy was no mood but a deep-seated conception which modified his views on language, on metre, on everything that had to do with his art. He thought that modern poetry has lost its strength because the poets still feign a belief in what they know to be false. '. . . the material forces of mind and imagination,' he wrote, 'can now re-establish the world as if nothing had ever been thought or imagined before.'[13] He meant to see the world anew, and to create an unliterary literature as if nothing had been written in the past, and the new poets were to be greater than Shakespeare. Literature, he said, is the greatest foe to literature.

> Lo! thirty centuries of literature
> Have curved your spines and overborne your brains![14]

And in order to lay the foundations of the new age he began by bringing into literature not only scientific words that were hitherto unknown there, but he took for his poems subjects that are superficially prosaic – Fleet Street, the Crystal Palace, Liverpool Street and London Bridge railway stations.[15] To our mind these are the best of his poems. They are original without being prophetic, they show his curious power of describing the quality of matter, and they are full of observation and of sympathy with the sufferings of man. The Bank Holiday scene at the Crystal Palace is a first-rate piece of description:

> Courageous folk beneath
> The brows of Michael Angelo's Moses dance
> A cakewalk in the dim Renascence Court.
> Three people in the silent Reading-room
> Regard us darkly as we enter: three
> Come in with us, stare vacantly about,
> Look from the window and withdraw at once.
> A drama; a balloon; a Beauty Show; –
> People have seen them doubtless, but none of those

> Deluded myriads walking up and down
> The north nave and the south nave anxiously –
> And aimlessly, so silent and so sad.[16]

The mood reminds us of that of Gissing[17] in his novels of middle-class life in London. Both men knew and felt the horror of the sordid and the squalid with peculiar intensity; Gissing because he was at heart a scholar, Davidson because he was by conviction, at least, an aristocrat. Indeed, here we come to that strange combination of different strands of thought which gives the poems of Davidson their very individual flavour. On the one hand we have:

> I see the strong coerce the weak,
> And labour overwrought rebel;
> I hear the useless treadmill creak,
> The prisoner cursing in his cell;
> I see the loafer-burnished wall;[18]

and on the other:

> Soul, disregard
> The bad, the good:
> Be haughty, hard,
> Misunderstood.[19]

Be an Overman,[20] be an Englishman, be a man of imperious imagination who stamps his will upon the world, be one of those dukes, marqueses, earls, or viscounts to whom the *Testament of John Davidson* is dedicated, and if that is impossible, submit to be ruled by your superiors. Having disposed of the gods of the old mythology, he sets up a new god, man himself, to rule over man. It may seem a harsh and insolent creed, but Davidson nevertheless lavishes beauty on it, and sings it not only with conviction, but with the sensibility of a poet:

> Stand up; behold
> The earth, life, death, and day and night!
> Think not the things that have been said of these;
> But watch them and be excellent, for men
> Are what they contemplate.[21]

---

1 – A review in the *TLS*, 16 August 1917, (Kp c82) of *John Davidson: A Study of the Relation of his Ideas to his Poetry*, 'A Thesis presented to the Faculty of the Graduate School in Partial Fulfilment of the Requirements for the Degree of Doctor of Philosophy' (University of Pennsylvania, 1916) by Hayim Fineman.
2 – Fineman, p. 3.

3 – John Davidson (1857–1909), Scottish poet, gave up schoolmastering and in 1889 settled in London where he associated with members of the Rhymers' Club, earned a scant living by journalism, and enjoyed friendships with such diverse literary personalities as Max Beerbohm and George Gissing. Davidson, who committed suicide, became a disciple of Nietzsche and a radical materialist.

4 – Fineman, p. 43, quoting Davidson, *Fleet Street and Other Poems* (1909), 'Prefatory Note'.

5 – *The Testament of John Davidson* (Grant Richards, 1908).

6 – *Ibid.*, p. 104:

> Till conscious life begins. The ouphs and elves,
> The satyrs, centaurs, goblins, gnomes and trolls,
> The ancient lands of faery and romance,
> Infernal and supernal domiciles,
> The dreadful dwellers there, and wonderful
> Cosmogony of Other World (perverse
> Reflexions of his unenlightened mind
> Upon the mirror of eternity,
> And on the mirrors of the sun and moon,
> The stars, the flowers, the sea, the woods, the wilds)
> With immaterial nothings deceived mankind,
> Even as his shadow on a darksome way
> Looms like a ghost and daunts the pilgrim still.

7 – *Ibid.*, see previous note.

8 – *Ibid.*, pp. 103–4, which has: 'Gods and God'; and 'mistake:'.

9 – *Ibid.*, pp. 98–9.

10 – John Milton (1608–74); Dante Alighieri (1265–1321).

11 – *Fleet Street Eclogues* (1893), second series (1896); *New Ballads* (1897); *The Last Ballad* (1899).

12 – Fineman, p. 17.

13 – *The Testament of John Davidson*, 'Dedication', p. 31.

14 – *The Testament of a Man Forbid* (Grant Richards, 1901), p. 9.

15 – 'Fleet Street', 'Railway Stations', 'The Crystal Palace' in *Fleet Street and Other Poems* (Grant Richards, 1909).

16 – *Ibid.*, 'The Crystal Palace', p. 37.

17 – George Gissing (1857–1903).

18 – *St George's Day. A Fleet Street Eclogue* (John Lane, 1895), p. 6, spoken by Menzies.

19 – *The Last Ballad and Other Poems* (John Lane, 1899), 'The Outcast', p. 153.

20 – For Davidson's version of Nietzsche's *Übermensch* see *The Testament of John Davidson*, 'Dedication', 'To the Peers Temporal of the United Kingdoms of Great Britain and Ireland', pp. 17–18.

21 – *The Testament of a Man Forbid*, p. 10.

A Victorian Echo

This reprint is, much to our pleasure, illustrated by the original wood-cuts of Arthur Hughes.[2] A reader who knows nothing of painting could scarcely fail to date these pictures within a year or two accurately enough; and, although literature is not so easy to classify as painting, we think we could give reasons for placing Dr Hake in the middle of the nineteenth century in spite of the claim that Rossetti made for him:

... Dr Gordon Hake is, in relation to his own time, as original a poet as one can well conceive possible. He is uninfluenced by any styles or mannerisms of the day to so absolute a degree as to tempt one to believe that the latest English singer he may have even heard of is Wordsworth.[3]

It is quite true, as Rossetti goes on to point out, that one thinks of a good many writers (Quarles, Bunyan, Pope and Gray[4] are the ones he selects) while reading Dr Hake, although his substance is remarkably his own. But there are two qualities which seem to us to stamp his date upon him very visibly – his simple way of accepting the current morality, and his Victorian method of describing Nature.

Turning to his pages after reading our Georgians we feel ourselves, as far as morality is concerned, back in the nursery. His imagination liked to work upon rather obvious themes rich in sentiment and rounded with a moral. We have the orphan child wandering in the woods to seek food for her starving grandparent and coming home to find him dead:

> No sound, no breath she heard above,
> 　Where grandsire in the garret lay.
> But one was there whose looks of love,
> 　'Poor little orphan,' seemed to say.
> She knew the chaplain's kindly face;
> The bearer of the lady's grace.[5]

Dr Hake believed in the chaplain, he believed in the noble lady and her stately pile, and when he had a heroine he called her quite seriously the Lady May of Alton Moor.[6] All this side of him is very charmingly represented by the minute story-telling woodcuts of Mr Hughes, where the more you peer into the shadows the more horn spectacles and family Bibles you discover. But the strange thing is that we only call either poems or pictures sentimental by an afterthought; and upon seeking a reason it seems to be that if you are going to tell stories about orphan girls, blind boys, and deserted children the way to do it is with the perfect sincerity and good faith of Dr Hake. It is an art known to the Victorians. They heard a sad story; they were genuinely moved by it; they wrote it down straightforwardly, asking no questions and without a trace of self-consciousness; and this is what we cannot do, and this is what we find most strange in them.

But the youngest of our critics could not dismiss Dr Hake as nothing more than a simple-minded and sentimental story-teller. He may have high-born ladies and maidens who, when asked their names, reply with 'looks that gave a sweetness out, "Lily of the Vale"',[7] but he is quite capable of sending the cripple child to the workhouse; his most indignant lines are about the evils of the public house; and the most remarkable poem in the book, 'Old Souls',[8] satirises one vice or humbug after another very deftly and with a neatness which recalls the satirists of the eighteenth century. Above all – and this is the quality which gave him his high repute with such critics as Rossetti and Mrs Meynell[9] – he was an artist; a writer with an exquisite sense of language, a strange and individual sense of humour, and a power, urged on we are told by a rigorous self-criticism, of working at his verse until nothing is left but terse original speech giving his meaning exactly and carrying the narrative on firmly and lightly. It is excellent story-telling. The ground is covered from one point to another without going round or going back or losing the way. And each one of his poems contains some beautifully accurate description of Nature. For example:

> Of loving natures, proudly shy,
>   The stock-doves sojourn in the tree,
> With breasts of feathered cloud and sky,
>   And notes of soft though tuneless glee;
> Hid in the leaves they take a spring,
> And crush the stillness with their wing.[10]

or,

> Before the sun, like golden shields,
>   The clouds a lustre shed around;
> Wild shadows gambolling o'er the fields
>   Tame shadows stretching o'er the ground.
> Towards noon the great rock-shadow moves,
> And takes slow leave of all it loves.[11]

Each of the quotations seems to us typically Victorian. Each is an example of the Victorian passion for getting Nature perfectly accurately, for her own sake, into poetry. And when, with much observation, much matching of words and of similes, the right description is found, down it goes, and the emotions of the poem pass round it as if it were an island in mid-stream and leave it unmoved.

1 – A review in the *TLS*, 23 August 1917, (Kp C83) of *Parables and Tales* by Thomas Gordon Hake. With a Preface by his son, Thomas Hake. Illustrated by Arthur Hughes (Elkin Mathews, 1917).

2 – Arthur Hughes (1832–1915), pre-Raphaelite painter, and illustrator, notably of works by William Allingham, Tennyson, Christina Rossetti, George MacDonald, and of the original edition of *Parables and Tales* (1872) by Thomas Gordon Hake (1809–95), physician and poet, friend of D. G. Rossetti (1828–82) and of George Borrow. Hake published several volumes of verse, including *Madeline and Other Poems* (1871) and *The New Day* (1890), and a volume of autobiography *Memoirs of Eighty Years* (1892).

3 – Hake, Pref., p. 13, quoting D. G. Rossetti on Hake's *Madeline* (1871), which continues: 'while in some respects his ideas and points of view are newer than the newest in vogue; and the external affinity frequently traceable to elder poets only throws this essential independence into startling and at times almost whimsical relief.'

4 – *Ibid.*; Francis Quarles (1592–1644), author of the book of devotional poems *Emblems* (1635); John Bunyan (1628–88); Alexander Pope (1688–1744); Thomas Gray (1716–71).

5 – *Ibid.*, 'The Lily of the Valley', stanza 40, p. 73.

6 – *Ibid.*, 'Mother and Child', stanza 23, p. 9.

7 – *Ibid.*, 'The Lily of the Valley', stanza 11, p. 64, which has:

> When folk who gossipped thereabout
>   Asked the child's name, – the child so pale, –
> With looks that gave a sweetness out,
>   She answered, 'Lily of the Vale'.
> Not then her eyes had dew-drops shed
> In early tribute to the dead.

8 – *Ibid.*, 'Old Souls', pp. 46–59.

9 – *Ibid.*, Pref., p. 15, quoting Alice Meynell in her preface to a selection of Hake's poems published in 1894.

10 – *Ibid.*, 'The Lily of the Valley', stanza 3, p. 61.

11 – *Ibid.*, 'The Blind Boy', p. 23.

Mr Galsworthy's Novel

Everyone, especially in August, especially in England, can bring to mind the peculiar mood which follows a long day of exercise in the open air. The body is tired out; the mind washed smooth by countless gallons of fresh air, and for some reason everything seems dangerously simple, and the most complex and difficult decisions obvious and inevitable. There is something truly or falsely spiritual about this state, and it is one which if prolonged may easily lead to disaster. In Mr Galsworthy's new novel the people fill us with alarm, because they appear all more or less under the influence of the great narcotic and therefore not quite responsible for their actions. They have been out hunting all day for so many generations that they are now perpetually in this evening condition of physical well-being and spiritual simplicity. With minds one blur of field and lane, hounds and foxes, they make sudden and tremendous decisions marked by the peculiar lightness and boldness of those who are drugged out of self-consciousness by the open air. Just before they drop off to sleep they decide that they must get married tomorrow, or elope with a housemaid, or challenge someone to fight a duel. This, of course, is an exaggeration, but some theory of the kind must be fabricated to explain this rather queer book, *Beyond*.

Charles Clare Winton, a major in the Lancers, was evidently in the condition described when he fell in love and had a child by a lady who was already the wife of a country squire, his friend. Nothing was more against all his ideas and, what is more important in the case of Major Winton, his tradition of good breeding than such behaviour. The child, a girl called Gyp, was left to his guardianship by the unsuspecting squire; and he salved his conscience to some extent by looking after her affairs and improving her investments. She lived with him and took his name. Being his daughter she was naturally extremely well-bred, loved dogs, and rode like a bird; but being a woman, very attractive, in an ambiguous position, and endowed with a passion for music, her lot was evidently to be complicated by queer sudden impulses on the part of others besides those which she felt for herself. At her first dance she was kissed on the elbow; by the time she was twenty-two she was involved in an affair with a long-haired Swedish violinist, called Fiorsen, whom she met when her father went to take the waters at Wiesbaden. In a second, as it seems to our apprehensive eyes, she is embraced by him; next minute she is actually married to a man whose past has been disreputable, and whom her father dislikes. 'That long, loping, wolfish, fiddling fellow with the broad cheek bones and little side whiskers (good God!) and greenish eyes, whose looks at Gyp he secretly marked down, roused his complete distrust.'² But he was a man of few words, and his own experience of love had convinced him that it was useless to interfere. The alarming thing was that Gyp herself had never given the matter any serious thought; her talks with Fiorsen, in spite of the embraces, had been of the most elementary and formal description. For example, coming home 'bone-tired'³ from a long day's hunting, she hears that Fiorsen is in the house; she has a hot bath and does for a moment consider what will happen if she refuses him. 'The thought staggered her. Had she, without knowing it, got so far as this? Yes, and further. It was all no good. Fiorsen would never accept refusal even if she gave it. But, did she want to refuse? She loved hot baths, but had never stayed in one so long. Life was so easy there, and so difficult outside.'⁴ She was not in love with Fiorsen; the only serious element in her decision was that, according to a certain Baroness, Fiorsen wanted saving from himself; and the task appealed to her. No wonder, then, that when she finds herself alone with her husband for the first time after the wedding, 'she thought of her frock, a mushroom-coloured velvet cord'.⁵

From these quotations it is not possible, perhaps, to gather that Mr Galsworthy is giving Gyp his closest and most serious attention. He represents her not only as a very finely organised being, fastidious, sensitive, and proud, but she lives her life and meets the harsh and inevitable blows of fate by a code of morality which has Mr Galsworthy's respect. It is by this time a matter of course that whatever Mr Galsworthy respects we must take seriously; whatever story he writes is likely to be not merely a story but also a point of view. But this time we must admit that we have not been able to get ourselves into that sympathetic state in which we read if not with agreement still with conviction. At every crisis in Gyp's fate, instead of feeling that the laws of society have forced her into positions where her passion and her courage vindicate her behaviour completely, we feel that she acts without enough thought to realise what she is doing – and therefore callously and conventionally; without enough passion to carry her triumphantly 'beyond'. She never forgets what the servants will think; and at a terrible moment she can remember that she is walking down

Baker Street without any gloves on and can forget her emotion in buying a pair. Behind her behaviour there is no code of morality; there is only a standard of manners which she was taught, no doubt, by the charming maiden aunt who lives in Curzon Street. This, of course, would be all very well if there were any trace of satire or of protest in Mr Galsworthy's portrait of her and her surroundings; but there is none. If you try to read the book as a satire upon honourable officers in the Lancers who hunt all day and sleep all night, to see in Gyp an amiable and innocent girl who has been flung disastrously from her dogs and ponies to sink or swim in the whirlpool of the world without any weapon save good manners, you are painfully at cross-purposes with your author. Gyp, he is careful to point out, is neither a 'new woman', nor is she a 'society woman';[6] she is a woman of temperament, or refinement, and of courage. And we are asked to believe that in the great things of life she was carried 'beyond' other people, and that these weapons of hers were good enough to fight her battles very finely, and to leave her in the end mistress of her soul and able to say, although her heart is broken and she can only find comfort in a Home for Poor Children, 'I wouldn't have been without it.'[7]

There are many other characters in the book, but they have, unfortunately, as we think, to comply with the standard which Gyp accepts. Fiorsen and Rosek are men of rather unpleasant character; Summerhay is a man of rather pleasant character. Gyp sums him up very well by her remark: 'I like men who think first of their dogs.'[8] Unfortunately she is led to exclaim more than once in the book also, 'What animals men are!'[9] Did she give them a chance, we wonder, of being anything much better? But the whole society seems to us to have had its sting, whether for good or for evil, for happiness or unhappiness, drawn long ago, and to be living rather a colourless than a vicious or beautiful life. There is nothing coarse or boisterous about this world; nobody seems to want anything very much, and when we think it all over at the end we remember, and this we mean sincerely and not satirically, a great many most delightful dogs.

1 – A review in the *TLS*, 30 August 1917, (Kp c84) of *Beyond* (William Heinemann, 1917) by John Galsworthy (1867–1933), among whose best-known works at this date were the novel *The Man of Property* (1906) and the play *Strife* (1909). See also 'Books and Persons' above and 'Character in Fiction', *III VW Essays*. Reprinted: *CW*.

2 – Galsworthy, pt I, ch. IV, pp. 43–4.

3 – *Ibid.*, ch. V, p. 55, which has: 'Ah, she was tired; and it was drizzling now. She would be nicely stiff to-morrow.'

4 – *Ibid.*, pp. 55–6, which has: 'It was all no good; Fiorsen would never accept refusal, even if she gave it!'

5 – *Ibid.*, pt. II, ch I, p. 65, which has 'Gyp thought of her frock'.

6 – For the first quotation, *ibid.*, ch. VII, p. 120; the second appears to be a paraphrase drawn fom *ibid.*, ch. V, p. 99, where Gyp is said to have felt she did not 'belong' either to 'high bohemia' or to 'that old orthodox, well-bred world' of her Aunt Rosamund.

7 – *Ibid.*, pt IV, ch. XII, p. 438.

8 – *Ibid.*, pt III, ch. I, p. 246.

9 – *Ibid.*, pt II, ch. XX, p. 227.

To Read Or Not To Read

There was once an old gentleman who could, if you gave him time, trace every evil of public and private life, and he thought them both in a bad way, to one and the same cause – the prevalence of the rat. He died, unfortunately, from the bite of one of the black or Hanoverian species before he was able to collect his arguments in a book, and the principles of his faith are lost to us for ever. Let us, therefore, make the most of Viscount Harberton while we have him; he has not rediscovered the lost theory of the rat, alas! but he has invented one that will do almost as well. Whenever our old friend would have wagged his head, looked very solemn, and ejaculated, 'Rats!' Lord Harberton goes through the same process and cries, 'Books!' What sin do you most abhor? Is it drunkenness or lying, cruelty or superstition? Well, they all come from reading books. What virtues do you most admire? Pluck them in handfuls, wherever you like, the answer is still the same; that is the result of not reading books. The trouble is that somehow or other the vicious race of readers has got the virtuous race of non-readers into its power. Wherever you look you find the readers in authority. 'Every administrative post throughout the Empire is being confined more and more to minds that can display a distorted faculty for reading and remembering what they are told, instead of judging for themselves what they care to read and remember.'[2] Worse than this, 'our scholastics' have 'managed

to acquire complete control in moulding the minds of the next generations'.[3] The vice is spreading daily, and things have come to such a pass
that if we do not look out the aristocracy will have forfeited their special
merit of 'disliking study and being more interested in their own opinions
than in those of their author'.[4]

But at this point the prophet's message seems capable of two interpretations, each capable of founding a different sect. We are told with great
emphasis that all the power is in the hands of the readers, but upon
another page we – the well-to-do gentry, that is – are warned that it is
owing to our vicious habit of reading that the Labour leaders have us at
their mercy. Let the Socialists and trade unionists have every opportunity for reading, Lord Harberton advises; but let us stop at once, for it is
only by so doing that we shall regain our lost ascendancy. It is really very
difficult to know what to do. And there is another source of confusion. It
is laid down on page 55 that the gift of writing is no more 'guarantee of
sense than the gift of song or the gift of the gab'. We are to remember that
'few men of letters are absolutely sane, and their silly side is the main
factor of their popularity'.[5] No sooner have we grasped this principle
and jeered where we used to do honour than we are presented with a list
of untaught, unread people, and bidden to own at once that 'in actual
writing, in drama, poetry, and fiction', in the art, that is to say, which
needs no gift and is best practised by insane people, 'they have more than
held their own'.[6]

In spite of these obscure passages it would be mere affectation to
pretend that there is any doubt about Lord Harberton's meaning. The
unread man is a kind of natural genius, nosing his way through the
world with an instinctive eye for the good and the right which is utterly
beyond the reach of thought, and can only be compared with the flick of
the wrist of a first-rate racquets player. Once common enough, these
creatures, owing to the spread of books, have become so rare that it will
be necessary in time for every household to keep one in its employ, so as
to preserve a contact with reality; Lord Harberton himself has one
already. The well-read man, on the other hand, is the 'champion bigot',[7]
the spirit of evil in our midst, who has endowed each one of the
professions with its long ears of pedantic absurdity. Look (merely to
look is enough) at Darwin; look at Lord Lister; look at Huxley, 'that old
bone-man';[8] look in the frontispiece at the faces of Swinburne,
Goldsmith, Wordsworth, and Gibbon, and compare them with the face
of William Whiteley, the Universal Provider. You will see that he is

'more alert, quite as intelligent, and with twice the vitality and character'.[9]

But though we have tried to show by these quotations that Lord Harberton makes good his claim for himself – 'education resisted, faith small; degrees none'[10] – there is a great deal in his book that might have been written by anyone. Take this, for example: 'There are plenty of minds who might read all the best authors at their own convenience and yet never be led to think at all; but when they are doing something practical the mind is alive and on the watch, and afterwards they think about it and how to do better, and they discover small improvements and inventions'.[11] That is almost the remark of a professor. And to say that the examination test has been a failure, and that letters after one's name are no proof of ideas within one's head – all this has been said by the schoolmasters over and over again. Nevertheless, such is the bustle and sprightliness of Lord Harberton's mind, such the audacity with which he flies from Tariff Reform to inoculation, from Party Government to Home Rule, to settle finally upon the flanks of the incorrigible reader, that we were just laying a faggot to our bookcase in the hope of catching his style, when we came upon the names of Schopenhauer and Herbert Spencer.[12] No praise is too high for them; in their books, we are told, we shall find the secret of the universe. After all, then, Lord Harberton is merely one of those cultivated people who play the innocent for a holiday. Still, one reader will give him the benefit of the doubt and take his advice to the extent of refraining for ever from the pages of Schopenhauer.

1 – A review in the *TLS*, 6 September 1917, (Kp c85) of *How To Lengthen Our Ears. An enquiry whether learning from books does not lengthen the ears rather than the understanding* (C. W. Daniel Ltd, 1917) by Viscount Harberton – Ernest Arthur George Pomeroy, 7th Viscount Harberton (1867–1944), soldier, educated at Charterhouse and Trinity College, Cambridge, formerly a captain in the Royal Dublin Fusiliers, author of *Salvation by Legislation; or Are We All Socialists?* (1908) and of works of classical scholarship.
2 – Harberton, ch. III, p. 26.
3 – *Ibid.*
4 – *Ibid.*, ch. VI, p. 82.
5 – *Ibid.*, ch. V, p. 55.
6 – For both quotations, *ibid.*; p. 68.
7 – *Ibid.*, p. 67.
8 – *Ibid.*, ch. VI, p. 72; Charles Darwin (1809–82); Joseph Lister, 1st Baron Lister (1827–1912); Thomas Huxley (1825–95).

9 – *Ibid.*, ch. XV, p. 197; Algernon Charles Swinburne (1837–1909); Oliver Goldsmith (1730–74); William Wordsworth (1770–1850); Edward Gibbon (1737–94). William Whiteley (1831–1907), founder of a chain of shops in London and of a mail order business which undertook to supply every kind of goods and by which Whiteley, the son of a Yorkshire corn factor, became a millionaire.
10 – *Ibid.*, p. 206.
11 – *Ibid.*, ch. IV, p. 37.
12 – Harberton frequently alludes to Arthur Schopenhauer (1788–1860) and to Herbert Spencer (1820–1903), and prefaces his book, and several of his chapters, with epigraphs from their works.

Mr Conrad's 'Youth'

Mr Arnold Bennett recently protested against those people who, when Mr Conrad is mentioned, exclaim 'Ah, Conrad!'[2] as if that were a different thing altogether, as if you were now talking about something that mattered. It is a form of exclusiveness that is very irritating, no doubt, particularly if you happen to be a novelist yourself; but when a new novel, or a reprint of an old novel, by Mr Conrad comes into our hands how can we suppress that exclamation? How can we help feeling that it is a different thing altogether – so different, indeed, that even our minute duties with regard to it attain a momentary dignity? There are two novelists in England today, so we feel spontaneously if wrongly, whom it seems no waste of time to criticise, whose work, we feel certain, is of such lasting importance that we are even serving a useful purpose when we try to value it, to make its shape a little more definite, its beauty a little more evident. Some naturalists, we are told, put their specimens into ant heaps to be eaten clean of unnecessary flesh – a humble office much like ours where these great men are concerned. Innumerable critics each armed with his pick and shovel do in the end, perhaps, clear away a few encumbrances. But Mr Hardy[3] and Mr Conrad are the only two of our novelists who are indisputably large enough to engage the services of a whole anthill. They are not men of one success, or one impression; they are men whose art has been large enough to develop now on this side, now on that, so that it is only by laying one book beside another that you can make out what the proportions and circumference of the giant really are.

'Youth' was first published in 1902; it is now republished by Mr Dent, with a note by the author. He tells us something of his relations with Marlow which we are glad to know:

He haunts my hours of solitude, when, in silence, we lay our heads together in great comfort and harmony; but as we part at the end of a tale I am never sure that it may not be for the last time. Yet I don't think that either of us would care much to survive the other . . . Of all my people he's the one that has never been a vexation to my spirit. A most discreet, understanding man. . .[4]

He has not very much to say about the three stories – 'Heart of Darkness' and 'The End of the Tether' are, of course, the other two – and that is what one might have expected; there is not much to be said. But he says that each one is the product of experience, pushed in the case of 'Heart of Darkness' 'a little (and only very little) beyond the actual facts of the case for the perfectly legitimate, I believe, purpose of bringing it home to the minds and bosoms of readers'.[5] He also says that the three stories lay no claim to unity of artistic purpose. And yet, though the mood is distinct and different in each, it is surely not difficult to see that these three stories are the work of one and the same period, just as *Chance* and *Victory*[6] are the work of another period. After reading them again one is inclined to say that here Mr Conrad is at his best; but it would be more just to say not that he is better, but that he is different. We probably mean that in these stories he gives us the most complete and perfect expression of one side of his genius – the side that developed first and was most directly connected with his own experience. It has an extraordinary freshness and romance. It is not so subtle or so psychological as the later mood. His characters are exposed far more to the forces of sea and forest, storm and shipwreck, than to the influence of other human beings. And these great powers, working in their large and inscrutable fashion, bring into action those qualities in mankind which always seem most dear to Mr Conrad's heart – courage, fidelity, magnanimity in the face of suffering. They are the qualities which mark those men who seem to have most of nature in them; they have been overlaid by civilisation and need the particular tests of nature to call them out, but they exist, so Mr Conrad seems to tell us, in the poorest and most apparently worthless of men. Those 'profane scallywags without a redeeming point'[7] plucked from the heart of a Liverpool slum, when tested by the supreme test of sea and fire, will be found to conceal these great possessions in the depths of their hearts. The ship is burning and 'we went aloft to furl the sails[8] . . . What made them do it?'[9] Was it praise, or sense of duty, or their most inadequate pay? 'No; it was something in them, something inborn and subtle and everlasting . . .'[10] There was a completeness in it, something solid like a principle, and masterful like an instinct – a disclosure of something secret – of that hidden something, that gift of good or evil, that makes racial difference, that shapes the fate of nations.'[11]

'There was a completeness in it.' Perhaps it is that quality which satisfies us so enormously in these stories. When the burning ship sinks, when Marlow adventures into the Heart of Darkness, and, most of all, when old Captain Whalley,[12] betrayed by nature and by man, fills his pockets with iron and drops into the sea we feel a rare sense of adequacy, of satisfaction, as if conqueror and conquered had been well matched and there is here 'nothing to wail'.[13] Mr Conrad, it is needless to say, has done other things supremely well; but in these first visions of life there is often a simplicity, a sense of perfect harmony, which is broken up as life goes on; and in the case of Mr Conrad we feel that this simplicity reveals the largest outlines, the deepest instincts.

1 – A review in the TLS, 20 September 1917, (Kp c86) of *Youth: A Narrative and two other stories* (J. M. Dent & Sons, 1917) by Joseph Conrad (1857–1924). See also '*Lord Jim*' above, 'Mr Conrad's Crisis' below; 'A Disillusioned Romantic', 'A Prince of Prose', 'Mr Conrad: A Conversation', *III VW Essays*; and 'Joseph Conrad', *IV VW Essays* and *CR1*.
2 – Arnold Bennett, *Books and Persons* (Chatto & Windus, 1917), 'The British Academy of Letters', p. 231. See also VW's review 'Books and Persons' above.
3 – Thomas Hardy (1840–1928).
4 – Conrad, 'Author's Note', p. viii.
5 – *Ibid.*, p. ix, which has: 'of the readers'.
6 – *Chance* (1914), *Victory* (1915).
7 – Conrad, 'Youth', p. 29.
8 – *Ibid.*, pp. 28–9, a complete sentence.
9 – *Ibid.*, p. 29, which has: 'What made them do it – what made them obey me when I, thinking consciously how fine it was, made them drop the bunt of the foresail twice to try and do it better. What?'
10 – *Ibid.*
11 – *Ibid.*, p. 30, which has: 'good or evil that makes'.
12 – For Captain Whalley see 'The End of the Tether'; for his death, *ibid.*, p. 363.
13 – John Milton, *Samson Agonistes* (1671), Manoa speaking, l. 1721:

> 'Nothing is here for tears, nothing to wail
> Or knock the breast, no weakness, no contempt,
> Dispraise, or blame; nothing but well and fair,
> And what may quiet us in a death so noble.'

Flumina Amem Silvasque

It is a proof of the snobbishness which, no doubt, veins us through that the mere thought of a literary pilgrim makes us imagine a man in an ulster looking up earnestly at a house front decorated with a tablet, and bidding his anaemic and docile brain conjure up the figure of Dr Johnson. But we must confess that we have done the same thing dozens of times, rather stealthily perhaps, and choosing a darkish day lest the ghosts of the dead should discover us, yet getting some true pleasure and profit nevertheless. We cannot get past a great writer's house without pausing to give an extra look into it and furnishing it as far as we are able with his cat and his dog, his books and his writing table. We may justify the instinct by the fact that the dominion which writers have over us is immensely personal; it is their actual voice that we hear in the rise and fall of the sentence; their shape and colour that we see in the page, so that even their old shoes have a way of being worn on this side rather than on that, which seems not gossip but revelation. We speak of writers; the military or medical or legal pilgrim may exist, but we fancy that the present of his heroes' old boots would show him nothing but leather.

Edward Thomas[2] was as far removed from our imaginary pilgrim as well may be. He had a passion for English country and a passion for English literature; and he had stored enough knowledge of the lives of his heroes to make it natural for him to think of them when walking through their country and to speculate whether the influence of it could be traced in their writing. The objection that most writers have no particular country he met in a variety of ways, which are all excellent, and many of them illuminating, because they spring from the prejudices and preferences of a well-stocked mind. There is no need to take alarm, as we confess to have done, at finding that the counties are distributed among the poets; there is no trace whatever of the 'one can imagine' and 'no doubt' style of writing.

On the contrary the poets and the counties are connected on the most elastic and human principle; and if in the end it turns out that the poet was not born there, did not live there, or quite probably had no place at all in his mind when he wrote, his neglect is shown to be quite as characteristic as his sensibility. Blake, for instance, comes under London and the Home Counties; and it is true that, as it is necessary to live somewhere, he lived both in London and at Felpham, near Bognor. But there is no reason to think that the tree that was filled with angels was peculiar to Peckham Rye, or that the bulls that 'each morning drag the sulphur Sun out of the Deep'[3] were to be seen in the fields of Sussex. 'Natural objects *always did and do* weaken, deaden, and obliterate imagination in me!'[4] he wrote; and the statement, which might have annoyed a specialist determined to pin a poet down, starts Mr Thomas off upon a most interesting discussion of the state of mind thus revealed. After all, considering that we must live either in the country or in the town, the person who does not notice one or the other is more eccentric than the person who does. It is a fine opening into the mind of Blake.

But the poets, as Mr Thomas shows, are an extremely capricious race, and do for the most part show a bird's or butterfly's attachment to some particular locality. You will always find Shelley near the water; Wordsworth among the hills; and Meredith within sixty miles of London. Matthew Arnold,[5] although associated with the Thames, is, as Mr Thomas points out in one of those critical passages which make his book like the talk of a very good talker, most particularly the poet of the garden and of the highly cultivated land.

> I know these slopes; who knows them, if not I?

'has the effect of reducing the landscape to garden scale'. There is, he points out, 'a kind of allegorical thinness' about Arnold's country, 'as if it were chiefly a symbol of escape from the world of "men and towns"'.[6] Indeed, if one takes a bird's-eye view of Arnold's poetry, the background seems to consist of a moonlit lawn, with a sad but not passionate nightingale singing in a cedar tree of the sorrows of mankind.[7] It is much less easy to reduce our vision of the landscape of Keats to something marked upon a map. We should be inclined to call him more the poet of a season than the poet of a place. Mr Thomas puts him down under London and the Home Counties because he lived there. But although he began as most writers do by describing what he saw, that was exercise work, and very soon he came to 'hate descriptions'.[8] And thus he wrote some of the most beautiful descriptions in the language, for in spite of many famous and exact passages the best descriptions are the least accurate, and represent what the poet saw with his eyes shut when the landscape had melted indistinguishably into the mood. This brings us, of course, into conflict with Tennyson.[9] The Tennysonian method of sifting words until the exact shade and shape of the flower or the cloud had its equivalent phrase has produced many wonderful examples of minute skill, much like the birds' nests and blades of grass of the pre-Raphaelite painters. Watching the dead leaves fall in autumn, we may remember that Tennyson has given precisely the phrase we want, 'flying gold of the ruin'd woodlands'; but for the whole spirit of autumn we go to Keats.[10] He has the mood and not the detail.

The most exact of poets, however, is quite capable of giving us the slip if the occasion seems to him to demand it; and as his theme is most often a moment of life or of vision, so his frozen stream, or west wind, or ruined castle is chosen for the sake of that mood and not for themselves. When that 'sense of England',[11] as Mr Thomas calls it, comes over us driving us to seek a book that expresses it, we turn to the prose writers most probably – to Borrow, Hardy, the Brontës, Gilbert White.[12] The sense of country which both Mr Hardy and Emile Brontë possess is so remarkable that a volume might be spent in discussion of it. We should scarcely exaggerate our own belief if we said that both seem to forecast a time when character will take on a different aspect under the novelist's hand, when he will be less fearful of the charge of unreality, less careful of the twitterings and chatterings which now make our puppets so animated and for the most part so ephemeral. Through the half-shut eyes with which we visualise books as a whole, we can see great tracts of Wessex and of the Yorkshire Moors inhabited by a race of people who seem to have the rough large outline of the land itself. It is not with either of these writers a case of the word-painter's gift; for though they may have their detachable descriptions, the element we mean is rubbed deep into the texture and moulds every part. Ruskin,[13] we observe, who did the description pure and simple to perfection, is not quoted by Mr Thomas; and the omission, which seems to us right, is a pleasant sign of the individual quality of the pilgrimage. We have seldom read a book indeed which gives a better feeling of England than this one. Never perfunctory or conventional, but always saying what strikes him as the true or interesting or characteristic thing, Mr Thomas brings the very look of the fields and roads before us; he brings the poets, too; and no one will finish the book without a sense that he knows and respects the author.

1 – A review in the TLS, 11 October 1917, (Kp c87) of *A Literary Pilgrim in England* . . . with eight illustrations in colour and twelve in monotone (Methuen & Co. Ltd., 1917) by Edward Thomas. The title of the article may be translated: 'Let

me adore the rivers and the woods.' See also, on the subject of literary pilgrimage, 'Haworth, November, 1904', 'Literary Geography', *I VW Essays,* and 'Great Men's Houses', *V VW Essays* and *The London Scene* (1982). Reprinted: *B&P.*

2 – (Philip) Edward Thomas (1878–1917), poet, essayist and critic, had been killed at Arras on 9 April 1917, serving with the Royal Garrison Artillery, having originally enlisted in the Artists' Rifles in July 1915. He was not at this date generally known to the public as a poet but as the author of prose studies of country life, including *Rest and Unrest* (1910), *Light and Twilight* (1911) and *The South Country* (1909). Thomas also published numerous critical pot-boilers and, notably, an account of *Richard Jefferies, His Life and Work* (1909).

3 – Thomas, 'William Blake [1757–1827]', p. 13, quoting Blake's poem 'Milton', bk 1, pt 21, l. 20.

4 – *Ibid.,* p. 12, quoting Blake's 'note to Wordsworth' [1770–1850], an annotation Blake made in his copy of Wordsworth's *Poems* (2 vols, 1815).

5 – Thomas discusses Percy Bysshe Shelley (1792–1822) and Matthew Arnold (1822–88) in the section on 'The Thames'; William Wordsworth (1770–1850) in 'The North'; and George Meredith (1828–1909) in 'London and the Home Counties'.

6 – Thomas, 'Matthew Arnold', p. 77, quoting and commenting on Arnold's poem 'Thyrsis', stanza 12, l. 1.

7 – This observation provoked some correspondence. See *TLS,* 18 October 1917, 'Arnold as a Poet of Nature', a letter from 'C.L.D.' who, having paraphrased VW's remark, commented: 'It is difficult to think of any other poet whose "backgrounds" and local "settings" have such variety as well as beauty . . . To speak of his muse as confined within garden walls, or clinging to cultivated land, is surely quite a mistake. His poetry is full of the fascination of mountain and forest and sea'. In which view 'C.L.D.' was supported two weeks later (*TLS,* 1 November 1917) by W. G. Waters of 7 Mansfield Street, W.

8 – *Ibid.,* 'Keats [1795–1821]', p. 36: 'Thus [by means of 'Hyperion'] Keats became "an old stager in the picturesque", as he said himself. Thus he learned to "hate descriptions", so that his poems thereafter contained no mere details verified from a notebook, but only broad noble features as suitable for heaven or hell as for the earth.'

9 – Thomas discusses Alfred, Lord Tennyson (1809–92) in the section on 'The East Coast and Midlands'.

10 – For the reference to Keats, *ibid.,* p. 38, where Thomas quotes from 'To Autumn'; the line by Tennyson, which Thomas does not quote, is from *Maud; A Melodrama,* pt I, iii, l. 12: 'And out he walk'd when the wind like a broken worldling wail'd, / And the flying gold of the ruin'd woodlands drove thro' the air'.

11 – *Ibid.,* 'Hilaire Belloc [1870–1953]', p. 155.

12 – Thomas discusses George Borrow (1803–81), in the section on 'The East Coast and Midlands'; Thomas Hardy (1840–1928) and Gilbert White (1720–93) in 'The South Downs and the South Coast'; and of 'the Brontës', only Emily (1818–48), in 'The North'.

13 – Thomas makes two passing references to John Ruskin (1819–1900). He also, incidentally, refers to Leslie Stephen (1832–1904) and the Sunday Tramps. Thomas

quotes (pp. 44–5) George Meredith on Stephen's 'unlimited paternal despotism' and his 'solicitous look of a schoolmaster'.

A Minor Dostoevsky

The second-rate works of a great writer are generally worth reading, if only because they are apt to offer us the very best criticism of his masterpieces. They show him baffled, casting about, hesitating at the branching of the paths, breaking into his true vein, and, misled by temptation, lashing himself in despair into a caricature of his own virtues and defects until the plan of his mind is very clearly marked out. The latest of Mrs Garnett's[2] translations, *The Gambler* (it includes also 'Poor People' and 'The Landlady'), will throw a good deal of light upon the processes of the mind whose powers seem almost beyond analysis in such works as *The Idiot* and *The Brothers Karamazov*.[3] If we call it second-rate compared with these, we mean chiefly that it impresses us as a sketch flung off at tremendous and almost inarticulate speed by a writer of such abundant power that even into this trifle, this scribbled and dashed-off fragment, the fire of genius has been breathed and blazes up, though the flame is blown out and the whole thing thrown to the ground in the same sudden and chaotic manner as that in which it comes into existence.

To begin with, all the characters – that is, a whole room full of Russian generals, their tutors, their stepdaughters, and the friends of their stepdaughters, together with miscellaneous people whose connection is scarcely defined – are talking with the greatest passion at the tops of their voices about their most private affairs. That, at least, is our confused and despairing impression. We are not certain whether we are in an hotel, what has brought all these people together, or what has set them off at this rate. And then, in the usual miraculous manner in the midst of ever-thickening storm and spray, a rope is thrown to us; we catch hold of a soliloquy; we begin to understand more than we have ever understood before, to follow feverishly, wildly, leaping the most perilous abysses, and seeming, as in a crisis of real life, to gain in flashes moments of vision such as we are wont to get only from the press of life at its fullest. Then the facts begin to emerge. The hero of the story is tutor in the General's family; he is in love with the General's stepdaughter Polina; she is involved with the French Marquis de Grieux; and her stepfather is in debt to the Marquis and in love also with a French adventuress. The stepfather's aunt, an old lady of seventy-five who should save them by dying, turns up in perfect health and proceeds to gamble away her fortune at the tables. They are all staying at Roulettenburg, and it is always possible to put everything to rights by a lucky spell at the tables. In order to save Polina the tutor begins to gamble, is sucked into the whirlpool, and never comes out again. All this is going at full speed at the moment of our first introduction to them; and to crowd the atmosphere still further, everyone is made to appear as if he or she had come upon the scene with all the preoccupations and tendencies which other circumstances have bred in them, so that we are speculating about all kinds of things that may happen in the spacious margin that lies on either side of Dostoevsky's page.

No one but Dostoevsky is able even to attempt this method successfully, and in 'The Gambler' where he is not completely successful one can see what fearful risks it entails – how often in guessing the psychology of souls flying at full speed even his intuition is at fault, and how in increasing the swiftness of his thought, as he always tends to do, his passion rushes into violence, his scenes verge upon melodrama, and his characters are seized with the inevitable madness or epilepsy. Every scene either ends or threatens to end with an attack of unconsciousness, or one of those inconsequent outbursts into which he falls, we cannot help feeling, when the effort to think is too exhausting. For example:

She cried and laughed all at once. Well, what was I to do? I was in a fever myself. I remember she began saying something to me – but I could scarcely understand anything. It was a sort of delirium – a sort of babble – as though she wanted to tell me something as rapidly as possible – a delirium which was interrupted from time to time with the merriest laughter, which at last frightened me.[4]

To control this tendency there is not in Dostoevsky, as there always is in Tolstoy, a central purpose which brings the whole field into focus. Sometimes in these stories it seems as if from exhaustion he could not concentrate his mind sufficiently to exclude those waifs and strays of the imagination – people met in the streets, porters, cabmen – who wander in and begin to talk and reveal their souls, not that they are wanted, but because Dostoevsky knows all about them and is too tired to keep them to himself.

Nevertheless, one finishes any book by Dostoevsky with the feeling that, though his faults may lie in this direction or in that, the range is so vast that some new conception of the novelist's art remains with us in the end. In this case we are left asking questions about his humour. There is a scene in 'The Gambler' where the General and the Marquis try to draw the old aunt from the gaming tables with visions of a little expedition into the country.

'There are trees there . . . we will have tea . . .' the General went on, utterly desperate. 'Nous boirons du lait, sur l'herbe fraîche,' added De Grieux, with ferocious fury.[5]

There is very little more, so little that when we come to re-read it we are astonished at the effect of humour that has been produced. Given the same circumstances, an English writer would have developed and insisted upon a humorous scene; the Russian merely states the facts and passes on, leaving us to reflect that, although humour is bound up with life, there are no humorous scenes.

1 – A review in the *TLS*, 11 October 1917, (Kp c88) of *The Gambler and Other Stories* (William Heinemann, 1917) by Fyodor Dostoevsky [1821–81]. From the Russian by Constance Garnett. See also 'More Dostoevsky' above; 'Dostoevsky in Cranford', 'Dostoevsky the Father', *III VW Essays*; and *Stavrogin's Confession* (Hogarth Press, 1922) by F. M. Dostoevsky, translated by S. S. Koteliansky and VW.
2 – Constance Garnett, *née* Black (1862–1946), for biographical details see 'More Dostoevsky', n. 2.
3 – *The Idiot* (1868–9), *The Brothers Karamazov* (1879–80).
4 – *The Gambler*, title story, ch. XV, p. 107.
5 – *Ibid.*, ch. XII, p. 80.

The Old Order

With this small volume, which brings us down to about the year 1870, the memories of Henry James break off. It is more fitting to say that they break off than that they come to an end, for although we are aware that we shall hear his voice no more, there is no hint of exhaustion or of leave-taking; the tone is as rich and deliberate as if time were unending and matter infinite; what we have seems to be but the prelude to what we are to have, but a crumb, as he says, of a banquet now forever withheld. Someone speaking once incautiously in his presence of his 'completed' works drew from him the emphatic assertion that never, never so long as he lived could there be any talk of completion; his work would end only with his life;[2] and it seems in accord with this spirit that we should feel ourselves·pausing, at the end of a paragraph, while in imagination the next great wave of the wonderful voice curves into fullness.

All great writers have, of course, an atmosphere in which they seem most at their ease and at their best; a mood of the great general mind which they interpret and indeed almost discover, so that we come to read them rather for that than for any story or character or scene of separate excellence. For ourselves Henry James seems most entirely in his element, doing that is to say what everything favours his doing, when it is a question of recollection. The mellow light which swims over the past, the beauty which suffuses even the commonest little figures of that time, the shadow in which the detail of so many things can be discerned which the glare of day flattens out, the depth, the richness, the calm, the humour of the whole pageant – all this seems to have been his natural atmosphere and his most abiding mood. It is the atmosphere of all those stories in which aged Europe is the background for young America. It is the half light in which he sees most, and sees farthest. To Americans, indeed, to Henry James and to Hawthorne,[3] we owe the best relish of the past in our literature – not the past of romance and chivalry, but the immediate past of vanished dignity and faded fashions. The novels teem with it; but wonderful as they are, we are tempted to say that the memories are yet more wonderful, in that they are more exactly Henry James, and give more precisely his tone and his gesture. In them his benignity is warmer, his humour richer, his solicitude more exquisite, his recognition of beauty, fineness, humanity more instant and direct. He comes to his task with an indescribable air of one so charged and laden with precious stuff that he hardly knows how to divest himself of it all – where to find space to set down this and that, how to resist altogether the claims of some other gleaming object in the background; appearing so busy, so unwieldy with ponderous treasure that his dexterity in disposing of it, his consummate knowledge of how best to place each fragment, afford us the greatest delight that literature has had to offer for many a year. The mere sight is enough to make anyone who has ever held a pen in his hand consider his art afresh in the light of this extraordinary example of it. And our pleasure at the mere sight soon merges in the thrill with which we recognise, if not directly then by hearsay, the old world of London life which he brings out of the shades and sets tenderly and solidly before us as if his last gift were the most perfect and precious of the treasures hoarded in 'the scented chest of our savings'.[4]

After the absence from Europe of about nine years which is recorded in *Notes of a Son and Brother*, he arrived in Liverpool on 1 March, 1869, and found himself 'in the face of an opportunity that affected me then and there as the happiest, the most interesting, the most alluring and beguiling that could ever have opened before a somewhat disabled young man who was about to complete his twenty-sixth year'.[5] He proceeded to London, and took up his lodging with a 'kind slim celibate',[6] a Mr Lazarus Fox – every detail is dear to him – who let out slices of his house in Half Moon Street to gentlemen lodgers. The London of that day, as Henry James at once proceeded to ascertain with those amazingly delicate and tenacious tentacles of his, was an extremely characteristic and uncompromising organism. 'The big broom of change' had swept it hardly at all since the days of Byron at least.[7] She was still the 'unaccommodating and unaccommodated city ... the city too indifferent, too proud, too unaware, too stupid even if one will, to enter any lists that involved her moving from her base and that thereby ... enjoyed the enormous "pull", for making her impression, of ignoring everything but her own perversities and then of driving these home with an emphasis not to be gainsaid'.[8] The young American ('brooding monster that I was, born to discriminate *à tout propos*')[9] was soon breakfasting with the gentleman upstairs (Mr Albert Rutson), eating his fried sole and marmalade with other gentlemen from the Home Office, the Foreign Office, the House of Commons, whose freedom to lounge over that meal impressed him greatly, and whose close questioning as to the composition of Grant's first Cabinet embarrassed him not a little.[10] The whole scene, which it would be an impiety to dismember further, has the very breath of the age in it. The whiskers, the leisure, the intentness of those gentlemen upon politics, their conviction that the composition of cabinets was the natural topic for the breakfast table, and that a stranger unable, as Henry James found himself, to throw light upon it was 'only not perfectly ridiculous because perfectly insignificant'[11] – all this provides a picture that many of us will be able to see again as we saw it once perhaps from the perch of an obliging pair of shoulders.

The main facts about that London, as all witnesses agree in testifying, were its smallness compared with our city, the limited number of distractions and amusements available, and the consequent tendency of all people worth knowing to know each other and to form a very accessible and, at the same time, highly enviable society. Whatever the quality that gained you admittance, whether it was that you had done something or showed yourself capable of doing something worthy of respect, the compliment was not an empty one. A young man coming up to London might in a few months claim to have met Tennyson, Browning, Matthew Arnold, Carlyle, Froude, George Eliot, Herbert Spencer, Huxley, and Mill.[12] He had met them; he had not merely brushed against them in a crowd. He had heard them talk; he had even offered something of his own. The conditions of those days allowed a kind of conversation which, so the survivors always maintain, is an art unknown in what they are pleased to call our chaos. What with recurring dinner parties and Sunday calls, and country visits lasting far beyond the week-ends of our generation, the fabric of friendship was solidly built up and carefully preserved. The tendency perhaps was rather to a good fellowship in which the talk was wide-sweeping, extremely well informed, and impersonal than to the less formal, perhaps more intense and indiscriminate, intimacies of today. We read of little societies of the sixties, the Cosmopolitan and the Century,[13] meeting on Wednesday and on Sunday evenings to discuss the serious questions of the times, and we have the feeling that they could claim a more representative character than anything of the sort we can show now. We are left with the impression that whatever went forward in those days, either among the statesmen or among the men of letters – and there was a closer connection than there is now – was promoted or inspired by the members of this group. Undoubtedly the resources of the day – and how magnificent they were! – were better organised; and it must occur to every reader of their memoirs that a reason is to be found in the simplicity which accepted the greatness of certain names and imposed something like order on their immediate neighbourhood. Having crowned their king they worshipped him with the most whole-hearted loyalty. Groups of people would come together at Freshwater, in that old garden where the houses of Melbury Road now stand,[14] or in various London centres, and live as it seems to us for months at a time, some of them indeed for the duration of their lives, in the mood of the presiding genius. Watts and Burne-Jones in one quarter of the town, Carlyle in another, George Eliot in a third,[15] almost as much as Tennyson in his island, imposed their laws upon a circle which had spirit and beauty to recommend it as well as an uncritical devotion.

Henry James, of course, was not a person to accept laws or to make one of any circle in a sense which implies the blunting of the critical powers. Happily for us, he came over not only with the hoarded curiosity of years, but also with the detachment of the stranger and the critical sense of the artist. He was immensely appreciative, but he was also immensely observant. Thus it comes about that his fragment revives, indeed stamps afresh, the great figures of the epoch, and, what is no less important, illumines the lesser figures by whom they were surrounded. Nothing could be happier than his portrait of Mrs Greville, 'with her exquisite good nature and her innocent fatuity',[16] who was, of course, very much an individual, but also a type of the enthusiastic sisterhood which, with all its extravagances and generosities and what we might unkindly, but not without the authority of Henry James, call absurdity, now seems extinct. We shall not spoil the reader's impression of the superb passage describing a visit arranged by Mrs Greville to George Eliot by revealing what happened on that almost tragic occasion.[17] It is more excusable to dwell for a moment upon the drawing room at Milford Cottage,

the most embowered retreat for social innocence that it was possible to conceive . . . The red candles in the red shades have remained with me, inexplicably, as a vivid note of this pitch, shedding their rosy light, with the autumn gale, the averted reality, all shut out, upon such felicities of feminine helplessness as I couldn't have prefigured in advance, and as exemplified, for further gathering in, the possibilities of the old tone.[18]

The drawn curtains, the 'copious service', the second volume of the new novel 'half-uncut' laid ready to hand, 'the exquisite head and incomparable brush of the domesticated collie'[19] – that is the familiar setting. He recalls the high-handed manner in which these ladies took their way through life, baffling the very stroke of age and disaster with their unquenchable optimism, ladling out with both hands every sort of gift upon their passage, and bringing to port in their tow the most incongruous and battered of derelicts. No doubt 'a number of the sharp truths that one might privately apprehend beat themselves beautifully in vain'[20] against such defences. Truth, so it seems to us, was not so much disregarded as flattered out of countenance by the energy with which they pursued the beautiful, the noble, the poetic, and ignored the possibility of another side of things. The extravagant steps which they would take to snare whatever grace or atmosphere they desired at the moment lend their lives in retrospect a glamour of adventure, aspiration, and triumph such as seems for good or for evil banished from our conscious and much more critical day. Was a friend ill? A wall would be knocked down to admit the morning sun. Did the doctor prescribe fresh milk? The only perfectly healthy cow in England was at your service. All this personal exuberance Henry James brings back in the figure of Mrs Greville, 'friend of the super-eminent'[21] and priestess at the different altars. Cannot we almost hear the 'pleasant growling note of Tennyson' answering her 'mild extravagance of homage' with 'Oh, yes, you may do what you like – so long as you don't kiss me before the cabman!'[22]

And then with the entrance of Lady Waterford,[23] Henry James ponders lovingly the quality which seems to hang about those days and people as the very scent of the flower – 'the quality of personal beauty, to say nothing of personal accomplishment as our fathers were appointed to enjoy it ... Scarce to be sated that form of wonder, to my own imagination I confess.'[24] Were they as beautiful as we like to remember them, or was it that the whole atmosphere made a beautiful presence, any sort of distinction or eminence indeed, felt in a way no longer so carefully arranged for, or so unquestionably accepted? Was it not all a part of the empty London streets, of the four-wheelers even, lined with straw, of the stuffy little boxes of the public dining rooms, of the protectedness, of the leisure? But if they had merely to stand and be looked at, how splendidly they did it! A certain width of space seems to be a necessary condition for the blooming of such splendid plants as Lady Waterford, who, when she had dazzled sufficiently with her beauty and presence, had only to take up her brush to be acclaimed the equal of Titian or of Watts.

Personality, whatever one may mean by it, seems to have been accorded a licence for the expression of itself for which we can find no parallel in the present day. The gift if you had it was encouraged and sheltered beyond the bounds of what now seems possible. Tennyson, of course, is the supreme example of what we mean, and happily for us Henry James was duly taken to that shrine and gives with extraordinary skill a new version of the mystery which in our case will supersede the old. 'The fond prefigurements of youthful piety are predestined, more often than not, I think, experience interfering, to strange and violent shocks ...'[25] Fine, fine, fine, could he only be ...'[26] So he begins, and so continuing for some time leads us up to the pronouncement that 'Tennyson was not Tennysonian'.[27] The air one breathed at Aldworth[28] was one in which nothing but the 'blest obvious, or at least the blest outright, could so much as attempt to live . . . It was a large and simple and almost empty occasion . . .'[29] He struck me in truth as neither knowing nor communicating knowledge.'[30] He recited *Locksley Hall* and 'Oh dear, oh dear . . . I heard him in cool surprise take even more out of his verse than he had put in.'[31] And so by a series of qualifications which are all beautifully adapted to sharpen the image without in the least destroying it, we are led to the satisfactory and convincing conclusion, 'My critical reaction hadn't in the least invalidated our great man's being a Bard – it had in fact made him and left him more a Bard than ever.'[32] We see, really for the first time, how obvious and simple and almost empty it was, how 'the glory was without history', the poetic character 'more worn than paid for, or at least more saved than spent',[33] and yet somehow the great man revives and flourishes in the new conditions and dawns upon us more of a Bard than we had got into the habit of thinking him. The same service of defining, limiting, and restoring to life he performs as beautifully for the ghost of George Eliot, and proclaims himself, as the faithful will be glad to hear, 'even a very Derondist of Derondists.'[34]

And thus looking back into the past which is all changed and gone (he could mark, he said, the very hour of the change) Henry James performs a last act of piety which is supremely characteristic of him. The English world of that day was very dear to him; it had a fineness and a distinction which he professed half-humourously not to find in our 'vast monotonous mob'.[35] It had given him friendship and opportunity and much else, no doubt, that it had no consciousness of giving. Such a gift he of all people could never forget; and this book of memories sounds to us like a superb act of thanksgiving. What could he do to make up for it all, he seems to have asked himself. And then with all the creative power at his command he summons back the past and makes us a present of that. If we could have had the choice, that is what we should have chosen, not entirely for what it gives us of the dead, but also for what it gives us of him. Many will hear his voice again in these pages; they will perceive once more that solicitude for others, that immense desire to help which had its origin, one might guess, in the aloofness and loneliness of the artist's life. It seemed as if he were grateful for the chance of taking part in the ordinary affairs of the world, of assuring himself that, in spite of his absorption with the fine and remote things of the imagination, he had not lost touch with human interests. To acknowledge any claim that was in the least connected with the friends or memories of the past gave him, for this reason, a peculiar joy; and we can believe that if he could have chosen, his last words would have been like these, words of recollection and of love.

1 – A review in the *TLS*, 18 October 1917, (Kp c89) of *The Middle Years* (W. Collins Sons & Co. Ltd. 1917) by Henry James (1843–1916). 'I have promised to write a long article upon Henry James,' VW wrote to Vanessa Bell at Charleston on 21 September 1917 (*II VW Letters*, no. 872), 'and the book may arrive in a day or two, in which case I should have to spend next week doing it, and it means such a lot of reading as well as writing that there wouldn't be much point in coming to you . . .'; and on Wednesday, 10 October, she confided in her diary: 'No air raid; no further disturbance by our country's need . . . Late last night, I was told to have my Henry James done if possible on Friday, so that I had to make way with it this morning, & as I rather grudge time spent on articles, & yet cant help spending it if I have it, I am rather glad that this is now out of my power.'

See also 'The Method of Henry James', below; 'Mr Henry James's Latest Novel', *I VW Essays*; 'Within the Rim', 'The Letters of Henry James', and 'Henry James's Ghost Stories', *III VW Essays*. Reprinted: *DOM, CE*.

2 – The person and occasion remain unidentified.

3 – Nathaniel Hawthorne (1804–64).

4 – Henry James, *Notes of a Son and Brother* (Macmillan & Co. Ltd, 1914), ch. v, p. 113.

5 – *Middle Years*, p. 3.

6 – *Ibid.*, p. 17.

7 – For 'the big broom', Henry James, *A Small Boy and Others* (Macmillan & Co. Ltd, 1913), ch. XII, p. 323: 'I liked for my own part a lot of history, but felt in face of certain queer old obsequiosities and appeals, whinings and sidlings and hand-rubbings and curtsey-droppings, the general play of apology and humility, behind which the great dim social complexity seemed to mass itself, that one didn't quite want so inordinate a quantity. Of that particular light and shade, however, the big broom of change has swept the scene bare; more history still has been after all what it wanted.' James does not refer here to Lord Byron (1788–1824).

8 – *Middle Years*, p. 23.

9 – *Ibid.*, pp. 104–5.

10 – *Ibid.*, p. 29; Gen. Ulysses S. Grant (1822–85), a Republican, became in 1868 the 18th president of the United States; he served, with scandalous ineptitude and disregard for the laws of the land, for two terms.

11 – *Ibid.*, p. 30.

12 – Alfred, Lord Tennyson (1809–92); Robert Browning (1812–89); Matthew Arnold (1822–88); Thomas Carlyle (1795–1881); J. A. Froude (1818–94); George Eliot (1819–80); Herbert Spencer (1820–1903); T. H. Huxley (1825–95); J. S. Mill (1806–73). (Another name VW might have added to this catalogue of eminent Victorians was that of her father, Leslie Stephen.)

13 – London clubs whose habitués tended to be of a radical and anti-clerical persuasion. (Leslie Stephen belonged for a period to both.)

14 – Farringford and, from *c.* 1874, The Briary, abutting properties at Freshwater in the Isle of Wight, were owned respectively by Tennyson and the painter G. F. Watts (1817–1904) – a milieu famously laughed at by VW in *Freshwater, A Comedy,* first performed in January 1935.

Melbury Road was the site in Kensington of the original Little Holland House, where Watts lived for about twenty-five years, from about 1850, with Henry Thoby Prinsep (1793–1878), of the Indian Civil Service, and his wife Sara, *née* Pattle (1816–67), a great-aunt of VW; and, less than 200 yards distant, of the new Little Holland House which Watts had built in the 1870s.

15 – Sir Edward Burne-Jones (1833–98), the painter, having first migrated from Bloomsbury to Kensington in 1864, finally settled in the following year at The Grange, North End Road, West Kensington; he was a frequent visitor at nearby Little Holland House. Carlyle lived in Chelsea, at no. 5 (now 24), Cheyne Row. George Eliot lived at The Priory, North Bank, Regent's Park, 1863–80.

16 – *Middle Years,* p. 74; Sabina Matilda (Mrs Richard) Greville, *née* Thellusson, of Milford Cottage, Surrey.

17 – *Ibid.,* pp. 79–82; the 'almost tragic occasion' refers to a visit James made, in the company of Mrs Greville, to Witley Villa, the Surrey retreat of George Eliot and G. H. Lewes (1817–78). The encounter ended with Lewes returning to James's hands 'a pair of blue-bound volumes' lent him by Mrs Greville. '". . . take them away, please, away, away!" I hear him unreservedly plead while he thrusts them at me,' James records (p. 82), 'and I scurry back into our conveyance, where . . . I venture to assure myself of the horrid truth that had squinted at me as I relieved our good friend of his superfluity. What indeed was this superfluity but the two volumes of my own precious "last" [*The Europeans* (1878).] – . . .'

18 – *Ibid.,* p. 76.

19 – For all three quotations, *ibid.,* p. 76.

20 – *Ibid.,* p. 75.

21 – *Ibid.,* p. 86.

22 – *Ibid.,* p. 102, which has: 'the pleasant growling note heard behind me, as the Bard followed with Mrs Greville'.

23 – Louisa, Marchioness of Waterford, *née* Stuart (d.1891), celebrated beauty and an accomplished painter, widow of the 3rd Marquess of Waterford (d.1859).

24 – *Middle Years,* p. 109, which has '"accomplishment"'.

25 – *Ibid.,* p. 88.

26 – *Ibid.,* p. 89.

27 – *Ibid.,* p. 90.

28 – Tennyson's second residence, near Haslemere in Surrey.

29 – *Middle Years,* p. 98, which has: 'it was a large'.

30 – *Ibid.,* p. 100.

31 – *Ibid.,* p. 104, from a more extensive sentence. *Locksley Hall* (1832).

32 – *Ibid.,* p. 105, from a more extensive sentence.

33 – For both quotations *ibid.,* p. 101, which has: 'If I should speak of this impression as that of glory without history, that of the poetic character more worn than paid for, or at least more saved than spent, I should doubtless much over-

emphasise; but such, or something like it, was none the less the explanation that met one's own fond fancy of the scene after one had cast about for it.'

34 – *Ibid.*, p. 85; George Eliot's *Daniel Deronda* was published in 1876.

35 – *Ibid.*, p. 114.

'Hearts of Controversy'

Although Mrs Meynell[2] is a true critic, courageous, authoritative, and individual, she will only consent to use her gift, publicly, in the cause of controversy. 'Exposition, interpretation,' she says, 'by themselves are not necessary. But for controversy there is cause.'[3] She sets no high value upon criticism – 'Poor little art of examination and formula!'[4] as she calls it. But we should suppose that no one today is more scrupulously careful than Mrs Meynell to determine what is to be said for and against any book that she thinks worth reading. We are conscious that she has made up her mind with unusual firmness, and that there is no writer of worth whom she has not by this time placed within a fraction of an inch of what she judges to be his right position. She, much more than most of us, knows what her standards are, and applies them as she reads. Her criticism, therefore, has a character and a definiteness which make it worth considering, worth testing, and worth disagreeing with.

The present volume of essays is an attempt to set right certain great reputations which, owing to our general habit of reading quickly and lazily accepting the current view of the case, are in danger of losing their proper proportions. The public version is a strange thing. It sways us much more than we are aware. We are swept along by an anonymous voice which alternatively debases Tennyson, exalts Swinburne, pits Thackeray against Dickens,[5] and bestows the laurel wreath and withdraws it on the impulse of the moment. Mrs Meynell's call to order is timely, and in many instances we come to heel with a good deal of contrition for our misdemeanours. The evident courage of her outspoken essay on Swinburne need not distract our attention from the profound though unwelcome truth of much of her criticism of him. But we have one complaint to lodge without entire confidence in its justness, so that we prefer to put it in the form of a question. Is it right that a critic should make his audience so conscious of their stupidity? May we not charge it partly to over-ingenuity on his part, although the main blame must rest with us? We were content in the belief that no one was going to say anything that we had not dimly foretold about Tennyson. And Mrs Meynell, with her precision and power of phrase, puts our dim foreboding perfectly. He is 'the poet with the great welcome style and the little unwelcome manner', she says. That is in the first place. But in the second he is, not so obviously, 'the poet who withstood France'.[6] Throwing out by the way the provocative remark that Matthew Arnold spoke of France as he spoke French, with 'an incurably English accent', she finally proclaims Tennyson 'our wild poet, . . . and wilder poet than the rough, than the sensual, than the defiant, than the accuser, than the denouncer'.[7] Wild is not the word we foresaw; but it is, of course, the exact word that Mrs Meynell means. Mrs Meynell never says a loose thing; and therefore we have to see, though we feel blind and blundering as we set about it, what we can do with this new ingredient in our conception. Then there is Dickens. Her distinction between exaggeration and caricature is admirably fine, and her reproof of our age in the person of Mr Lascelles Abercrombie is exquisite: 'My dear, you exaggerate.'[8] But then comes the queer shock that Mrs Meynell admires chiefly in Dickens, together with the humour and his dramatic tragedy, 'his watchfulness over inanimate things and landscape'.[9] The quotations she makes prove us partly in the wrong there too. If we give ourselves a bad mark for that oversight, must we have another because we are unable to trace the influence of Bolingbroke upon his style,[10] and a third because we cannot point directly to the two words that Dickens 'habitually misuses' although we are given the clue that Charles Lamb 'misuses one of them precisely in Dickens's manner'?[11] On the whole, we are inclined to make a distinction. Sometimes – the greater number of times by far – Mrs Meynell writes like a critic, and sometimes she writes like a specialist; sometimes she says the large sound thing, and sometimes she picks up the curious detail, puts it in the foreground, and lavishes upon it an attention which it does not deserve.

And where should we place the question of the English language – in the background or in the foreground? Our own prejudice would lead us to put it as far in the shadow of the background as possible. We prefer never to know, certainly never to mention, the pedigree of a word. We can see no reason for believing that a long pedigree makes a good word, or that there is any test of a word save the test of taste, which varies widely and should have every liberty to vary. The critic who brands certain words or phrases with the mark of his displeasure interferes with the liberty of the writer, and fetters his hand in the instinctive reach for what he wants. Let us then say nothing of words, let us leave grammar to right itself, and let us use them both as little consciously as possible. But here we are at variance with Mrs Meynell, whose sense of right and wrong in these matters is so clearly defined that she can make the question of Charlotte Brontë's use of English in the earlier books a cause of controversy. She wrote 'to evince, to reside, to intimate, to peruse'; she spoke of 'communicating instruction', 'a small competency', and so on.[12] It is quite true, and, to us, quite immaterial. A particle of dust, however, is not going to blind our eyes to the force and skill with which Mrs Meynell sends her arrow again and again to the heart of her target.

1 – A review in the *TLS*, 25 October 1917, (Kp C90) of *Hearts of Controversy* (Burns & Oates, 1917) by Alice Meynell. 'L[eonard]. out until 5 at his conference,' VW noted in her diary on Thursday, 18 October, '& the telephone rang constantly (so I thought, as I tried to pin Mrs Meynell down in a review)'.

2 – Alice Christiana Gertrude Meynell (1847–1922), poet and journalist, edited with her husband, Wilfrid Meynell, the *Weekly Register*, 1881–98, and the monthly *Merry England*, 1883–95, and contributed to the *Pall Mall Gazette*. Her work, both as essayist and poet, was admired and championed by Coventry Patmore, George Meredith and Francis Thompson, who addressed poems to her.

3 – Meynell, Intro., preliminary unnumbered page.

4 – *Ibid.*, 'Swinburne's Lyrical Poetry', p. 56.

5 – Alfred, Lord Tennyson (1809–92); Algernon Charles Swinburne (1837–1909); W. M. Thackeray (1811–63); Charles Dickens (1812–70).

6 – For Tennyson in the first and in the second place, Meynell, 'Some Thoughts of a Reader of Tennyson', p. 8.

7 – For Matthew Arnold (1822–88) and his French accent, *ibid.*, p. 9; and for Tennyson the wild poet, *ibid.*, pp. 21–2, slightly adapted, and which concludes: 'Wild flowers are his – great poet – wild winds, wild lights, wild heart, wild eyes!'

8 – *Ibid.*, 'Dickens as a Man of Letters', p. 28. The criticism of Lascelles Abercrombie (1881–1938) is directed at his poem 'Judith', published in *Emblems of Love* (1912).

9 – *Ibid.*, p. 29.

10 – *Ibid.*, p. 50; Henry St John, 1st Viscount Bolingbroke (1678–1751), statesman, friend of Pope and of Swift, and the author of brilliant political journalism, notably in the *Craftsman*, a periodical in which appeared his 'Remarks on the History of England by Humphry Oldcastle' (1730–1) and 'A Dissertation on Parties' (1733). His prose style is, according to Meynell, especially reflected in Esther Summerson's words in *Bleak House* (1852–3): 'There was nothing to be undone; no chain for him to drag or for me to break'.

11 – For the unspecified misuses of Dickens and of Charles Lamb (1775–1834), *ibid.*, p. 44.

12 – For Charlotte Brontë (1816–55) and her use of English, *ibid.*, 'Charlotte and Emily Brontë', p. 77; and see also 'Dickens as a Man of Letters', p. 45.

'A Russian Schoolboy'

The previous volumes of this chronicle, *Years of Childhood* and *A Russian Gentleman*,[2] left us with a feeling of personal friendship for Serge Aksakoff; we had come to know him and his family as we know people with whom we have stayed easily for weeks at a time in the country. The figure of Aksakoff himself has taken a place in our minds which is more like that of a real person than a person whom we have merely known in a book. Since reading the first volume of Mr Duff's translation we have read many new books; many clear, sharp characters have passed before our eyes, but in most cases they have left nothing behind them but a sense of more or less brilliant activity. But Aksakoff has remained – a man of extraordinary freshness and substance, a man with a rich nature, moving in the sun and shadow of real life so that it is possible, as we have found during the past year or two, to settle down placidly and involuntarily to think about him. Such words as these would not apply truthfully perhaps to some very great works of art; but nothing that produces this impression of fullness and intimacy can be without some of the rarest qualities and, in our opinion, some of the most delightful. We have spoken of Aksakoff as a man, but unfortunately we have no right to do that, for we have known him only as a boy, and the last volume of the three leaves him when he has but reached the age of fifteen. With this volume, Mr Duff tells us, the chronicle is finished; and our regret and desire to read another three, at least, is the best thanks we can offer him for his labour of translation. When we consider the rare merit of these books we can scarcely thank the translator sufficiently. We can only hope that he will look round and find another treasure of the same importance.

Ignorant as we are of the works of Aksakoff, it would be rash to say that this autobiography is the most characteristic of them; and yet one feels certain that there was something especially congenial to him in the recollection of childhood. When he was still a small boy he could plunge into 'the inexhaustible treasury of recollection'.[3] He is not, we think, quite so happy in the present volume because he passes a little beyond the scope of childhood. It deals less with the country; and the magic, which consists so much in being very small among people of immeasurable size so that one's parents are far more romantic than one's brothers and sisters, was departing. When he was at school the boys were on an equality with him; the figures were contracting and becoming more like the people whom we see when we are grown up. Aksakoff's peculiar gift lay in his power of living back into the childish soul. He can give to perfection the sense of the nearness, the largeness, the absolute dominance of the detail before the prospect has arranged itself so that details are only part of a well-known order. He makes us remember, and this is perhaps more difficult, how curiously the child's mind is taken up with what we call childish things together with premonitions of another kind of life, and with moments of extreme insight into its surroundings. He is thus able to give us a very clear notion of his father and mother, although we see them always as they appeared to a child. The effect of truth and vividness which is so remarkable in each of his volumes is the result of writing not from the man's point of view, but by becoming a child again; for it is impossible that the most tenacious memory should have been able to store the millions of details from which these books are fashioned. We have to suppose that Aksakoff kept to the end of his life a power of changing back into a different stage of growth at the touch of recollection, so that the process is more one of living over again than of remembering. From a psychological point of view this is a curious condition – to view the pond or the tree as it is now without emotion, but to receive intense emotion from the same sight by remembering the emotion which it roused fifty years ago. It is clear that Aksakoff, with his abundant and impressionable nature, was precisely the man to feel his childhood to the full, and to keep the joy of reviving it fresh to the end.

The happiness of childhood ⟨he writes⟩ is the Golden Age, the recollection of it has power to move the old man's heart with pleasure and with pain. Happy is the man who once possessed it and is able to recall the memory of it in later years! With many the time passes by unnoticed or unenjoyed; and all that remains in the ripeness of age is the recollection of the coldness or even cruelty of men.[4]

He was no doubt peculiar in the strength of his feelings, and singular compared with English boys in the absence of discipline at school and at college. As Mr Duff says, 'His university studies are remarkable; he learnt no Greek, no Latin, no mathematics, and very little science – hardly anything but Russian and French.'[5] For this reason, perhaps, he remained conscious of all those little impressions which in most cases fade and are forgotten before the power of expressing them is full grown. Who is there, for example, who will not feel his early memories of coming back to a home in the country wonderfully renewed by the description of the return to Aksakovo:

As before I took to bed with me my cat, which was so attached that she followed me everywhere like a dog; and I snared small birds or trapped them and kept them in a small room which was practically converted into a spacious coop. I admired my pigeons with double tufts and feathered legs ... which had been kept warm in my absence under the stoves or in the houses of the outdoor servants ... To the island I ran several times a day, hardly knowing myself why I went; and there I stood motionless as if under a spell, while my heart beat hard, and my breath came unevenly.[6]

Nor is it possible to read his account of butterfly collecting without recalling some such period of fanatical excitement. Indeed, we have read no description to compare with this one for its exact, prosaic, and yet most stirring reproduction of the succeeding stages of a child's passion. It begins almost by accident; it becomes in a moment the only thing in the world; of a sudden it dies down and is over for no perceptible reason. One can verify, as if from an old diary, every step that he takes with his butterfly net in his hand down that grassy valley in the burning heat until he sees within two yards of him 'fluttering from flower to flower a splendid *swallow-tail!*'[7] And then follows the journey home, where the small sister has begun collecting on her brother's account, and has turned all the jugs and tumblers in her room upside down, and even opened the lid of the piano and put butterflies alive inside of it. Nevertheless, in a few months the passion is over, and 'we devoted all our leisure to literature, producing [. . .] a manuscript magazine ... I became deeply interested in acting also.'[8]

All childhood is passionate, but if we compare the childhood of Aksakoff with our memories and observations of English childhood we shall be struck with the number and the violence of his enthusiasms. When his mother left him at school he sat on his bed with his eyes staring wildly, unable to think or to cry, and had to be put to bed, rubbed with flannels, and restored to consciousness by a violent fit of shivering. His sensitiveness to any recollection of childhood was such, even as a child, that the sound of a voice, a patch of sunlight on the wall, a fly buzzing on the pane, which reminded him of his past, threw him into a fit. His health became so bad that he had to be taken home. These fits and ecstasies, in which his mother often joined him, will hardly fail to remind the reader of many similar scenes which are charged against Dostoevsky as a fault. The fault, if it is a fault, appears to be more in the Russian nature than in the novelist's version of it. From the evidence supplied by Aksakoff we realise how little discipline enters into their education; and we also realise, what we do not gather from Dostoevsky, how sane, natural and happy such a life can be. Partly because of his love of nature, that unconscious perception of beauty which lay at the back of his shooting and fishing and butterfly catching, partly because of the largeness and generosity of his character, the impression produced by these volumes is an impression of abundance and of happiness. As Aksakoff says in a beautiful description of an uncle and aunt of his, 'The atmosphere seemed to have something calming and life-giving in it, something suited to beast and plant.'[9] At the same time we have only to compare him, as he has been compared, with Gilbert White to realise the Russian element in him, the element of self-consciousness and introspection.[10] No one is very simple who realises so fully what is happening to him, or who can trace, as he traces it, the moment when 'the radiance' fades and the 'peculiar feeling of sadness'[11] begins. His power of registering these changes shows that he was qualified to write also an incomparable account of maturity.

He gives in this book a description of the process of letting water out of a pond. A crowd of peasants collected upon the banks. 'All Russians love to watch moving water... The people saluted with shouts of joy the element they loved, as it tore its way to freedom from its winter prison.'[12] The shouts of joy and the love of watching both seem the peculiar property of the Russian people. From such a combination one would expect to find one of these days that they have produced the greatest of autobiographies, as they have produced perhaps the greatest of novels. But Aksakoff is more than a prelude; his work in its individuality and its beauty stands by itself.

1 – A review in the *TLS*, 8 November 1917, (Kp C91) of *A Russian Schoolboy. Translated from the Russian by J. D. Duff* (Edward Arnold, 1917) by Serge Aksakoff (1791–1850). Both VW and LW were to read Aksakoff in the original when, in 1921, they took lessons in Russian from S. S. Koteliansky – see *II VW Letters*, no. 1172, and *I LW*, p. 23. See also 'Mr Hudson's Childhood', below. Reprinted: *B&P*.

2 – Published in J. D. Duff's translation by Edward Arnold, in 1916 and 1917 respectively, and originally in 1856. J. D. Duff (d. 1940) was a fellow of Trinity College, Cambridge, and, incidentally, a member of the Conversazione Society (the Apostles).

3 – Aksakoff, ch. 1, p. 28.

4 – *Ibid.*, p. 7, which has 'that time'.

5 – *Ibid.*, 'Translator's Pref.', p. vii.

6 – *Ibid.*, ch. I, p. 6, which has: 'attached to me'; a comma where VW has an ellipsis between 'legs' and 'which'; and no comma between 'beat hard' and 'and my breath'.

7 – *Ibid.*, 'Butterfly-Collecting', p. 190.

8 – *Ibid.*, p. 214, which has: 'producing with much enthusiasm a manuscript magazine'.

9 – *Ibid.*, ch. III, p. 109, from a longer sentence.

10 – For the comparison with Gilbert White (1720–93), see Prince Kropotkin, *Russian Literature* (Duckworth & Co., 1905), p. 177.

11 – *Ibid.*, ch. II, p. 68: 'The radiance of some objects began to fade for me, and a peculiar feeling of sadness, such as I had never experienced before, began to cast a shadow over all the amusements and occupations I had loved so well.'

12 – *Ibid.*, p. 69, each extract is from a longer sentence.

Stopford Brooke

'As to Lord Selborne's Life, why do you read a book of that kind and done by a relation, too? One knows beforehand all that it will be, and that more than half will only be of interest to the relative and none to the world.'[2] Such was Stopford Brooke's opinion of the ordinary biography, and the reader who sits down to a couple of stout volumes dedicated to Brooke's own life, 'done by a relation, too',[3] may nurse a question of the same sort at the back of his mind. Judged by some of the standards which justify lavish and minute biography, Stopford Brooke may be found wanting. He left behind him no literary work of the first class. Time seems already to have withered a little the profusion and vitality of much that he wrote, and it is scarcely fair to read as literature much that he spoke.[4] But books are not the only test of greatness, even among those whose lives are spent in making them. The little circle of the great must be enlarged to include some of those who have spent themselves upon many things rather than concentrated upon a single one. But the question of greatness, always of little account in biography, need not trouble us at present. No reader of this book is likely to ask whether it was worth doing; and he will be wise, we think, not to attempt to sum up Stopford Brooke as this, that, or the other until he has read to the end, when the desire for such definitions may have left him.

For this biography has one quality at least which makes it very unlike the usual biography. It has the quality of growth. It is the record of the things that change rather than of the things that happen. Instead of knowing beforehand all that it will be, we constantly, as in life itself, find ourselves baffled and trying to understand. Much is due to the beautifully loving and alert skill with which Mr Jacks has done his work. Apart from the closeness of his relationship, he has by nature a singular insight into the qualities which made Stopford Brooke so memorable. He is peculiarly fitted to interpret the mass of documents which Brooke, with his passion for self-expression and his hatred of concealment, had written at all times of his life and left behind him. To our thinking, the result is a book not of revelations or confessions in the usual sense, but of spiritual development which carries the art of biography a step further in the most interesting direction now open to it – that of psychology.

The facts of Brooke's life are probably well known. Born in 1832, the son of a poor but well-born Irish clergyman, he was ordained in 1857, was curate at Kensington from 1859 to 1863, took the lease of St James's Chapel in 1865, and left the Church of England in 1880. From such a record we should expect to find conflicting strains at work in him. In his case they are so marked as to lie upon the surface, so profound as between them to rule his whole being.

One side of his nature ⟨says Mr Jacks⟩ belonged to religion; the other to art . . . He possessed a deep natural piety . . . but his feet were firmly planted on the earth; no pagan ever loved it better or received from contact with the things of sense a fuller current of the joy of life . . . and there is little doubt that had he lived in some age or society to which Christian culture was unknown he would have found satisfaction and won eminence . . . Between these two tendencies, the Christian and the Greek . . . the mediating power in Brooke was the impassioned love of beauty in all its forms, both natural and spiritual . . . His finest work, which ripened slowly and late, was the fruit of their union.[5]

In our age such a dual spirit is perhaps no uncommon inheritance; in the majority of cases one instinct triumphs and the other dies, or they both survive, imperfectly, in a state of chronic warfare. But it is extremely rare to find a mind open enough to widen year by year so that there is room for each different plant to come to flower. In the process the formal limitations devised by the hand of man might be swept aside, as indeed they were. Brooke, naturally enough, was marked down 'unsafe'[6] as a curate, and kept out of the danger of preferment by his superiors. He vacillated in the strangest way between Lisson Grove and Piccadilly, where he astonished the dowagers of that day by exclaiming, 'We must have more joy in life – I say, more joy!'[7] He found out in time that he was not meant to remain a curate. Nor would he go on acting as chaplain to the embassy at Berlin,[8] in spite of the opportunities which that position at one time seemed to promise of teaching future emperors of Germany the meaning of liberty. 'She ⟨the Crown Princess of Prussia⟩ wants an English tutor for her boys, to teach them, she said, "liberal principles, the English Constitution, and the growth of the nation into free government. Princes nowadays have no chance, Mr Brooke, unless they are liberal."'[9] He preferred to take his own chapel and preach his own message.

Then, after preaching for twenty-five years, he finds that the Church of England has become a fetter upon him, and he unloosens himself and passes on with no more effort, it seems, than a flower displays when it opens another bud. The faculty is puzzling and deserves our attention. 'No man,' says Mr Jacks, 'ever lived who was less in trouble about his soul than Brooke.'[10] 'His power of dismissing things,' said Mr Chesterton, 'is beyond praise'.[11] Mr Jacks's comment upon this is that when the issue was to be decided by argument Brooke's faculty of dismissing things 'would sometimes lead him to discharge the argument altogether and replace it with a bold statement of his own intuition'.[12] It is possible to suppose that if Brooke had been a deeper thinker this could not have been so; and, if, as Mr Jacks says, his position in the Church morally admitted of a very simple definition, 'that of a man who week by week publicly declares that he believes what he does not believe', it is strange that it should have taken him till he was nearly fifty to find that 'such a position is positively hateful'.[13]

But one must remember that Brooke attached very little importance to thinking – 'there is always the knowledge at the back of the mind that the secret of life is not in thinking, but in loving'.[14] And he spoke with impatience always of 'self-vivisecting souls ... twisting and turning incessantly in the labyrinth of their own spiritual entrails'.[15] But it is vain to attempt to summarise in a few words the many different intuitions and susceptibilities which resulted in Brooke's peculiar faith. It was the growth of his love of art, in which one may include the love of liberty and the love of humanity, his friendship with such men as Ruskin, Burne-Jones, Morris, and Holman Hunt, that chiefly made it impossible for him to wear 'an official uniform'[16] any longer. The story of a walk through the streets of London with his daughter illustrates in an amusing way his power of living in the world of imagination. They determined to

act the 'Seven Ages of Man' as they went along in order that 'the
Londoners might at last have the benefit of some really good
Shakespearean acting'. Having astonished the Londoners who
recognised their preacher, they burst at last into the room of J. R. Green,
shouting 'Here we are, Green, *sans* eyes, *sans* teeth, *sans* taste, *sans*
everything.'[17] Meanwhile, he was making a very beautiful house in
Manchester Square.[18] There were books in precious bindings, and
pictures everywhere, beautiful things which he loved to buy, loved to
explain, and loved to give away. A stranger to that house and to that talk
of literature and art would, says Mr Jacks, have guessed him to be an
artist, but on hearing that he was a clergyman 'there would have been no
ultimate surprise'.[19] And this we fancy is the point for the reader to hold
fast in his mind. We have spoken of growth and change, but the goal is
always towards some synthesis in which views generally found antagon-
istic are harmonised. The goal is pursued, moreover, down crowded
streets and in the thick of men and women. His week contained many
dinner parties and interviews and long delightful talks in the 'eagle's
nest'[20] at the top of the house; but for all that this is not a life in which
individual men and women are seen vividly or described intimately.
Famous though many of the names are, the 'good stories'[21] are few or
none. The aim was at some large community founded upon brotherhood
rather than towards the salvation of the individual soul.

Significantly enough Mr Jacks has recourse to the words of an Indian
writer and quotes from the *Sādhanā* of Tagore when he wishes to give
'the essential message' of Stopford Brooke. The passage, describing the
unity between man and nature, is too long to quote in full; and it is
difficult, we think, to understand it.[22] But even for those who are aware
of an impediment in their understanding of such philosophies the last
years of Brooke's life suggest many more ideas than can be dealt with at
all adequately in a review. The bare facts are that he withdrew from
London with powers unabated, ceased to work, and was completely
happy. So rare is happiness that it sometimes seems as if the desire for it
must be among the weakest of our desires. One has come to take it for
granted that the possession of great intellectual gifts is equivalent, in the
West at least, to unhappiness in manhood and an old age of resignation
or battered peace at the best. One saying of Brooke's throws, we think,
much light upon his reversal of the common experience. 'Green said, "I
die learning." I say I shall die un-learning, and, 'pon my word, it's the
wiser of the two sayings.'[23] We cannot help connecting the faculty of

'un-learning', which implies so much else, with that other power which is so marked and has such curious results in the memorable story of Brooke's old age. It happened that he found himself in 1898 at Homburg surrounded by people who reminded him of the characters in Ibsen – that is to say, people one would not touch 'even with a fishing rod ten yards long'.[24] As a way of escape he invented a myth in which the three springs of the place became people. Begun in play the story became something which he accepted as having actually taken place. We have not space to go into the details of this strange dream world, or of Mr Jacks's most interesting analysis of it. We call it strange because the expression of that state with anything like Brooke's degree of fullness is so rare; but we cannot help thinking that the experience in one shape or another is common enough, especially among those who are in the habit of putting their mental experiences into words. For the most part a moral objection of some sort tends to deny this side of the mind expression, and thus starves it of life. With Brooke the tendency is of the opposite kind. The whole story of his life is the story of a mind kept open in part by a powerful instinct of self-expression, and in part also by the tendency which became stronger and stronger in him against morality 'save as the expression of love'.[25] The record of the development of such a mind is one of the greatest interest, and one rarely attempted.

1 – A review in the TLS, 29 November 1917, (Kp C91.1) of Life and Letters of Stopford Brooke (John Murray, 1917) by Lawrence Pearsall Jacks. 'I don't like Sunday,' VW noted in her diary on 26 November 1917, 'the best thing is to make it a work day, & to unravel Brooke's mind to the sound of church bells was suitable enough.'
   See also 'Philosophy in Fiction', below; and 'Fantasy', III VW Essays.
2 – Jacks, vol. ii, ch. xxvi, p. 524. The work referred to is Memorials (4 vols., Macmillan & Co. Ltd., 1896–8) by Roundell Palmer, 1st Earl of Selborne (1812–95), Lord Chancellor, 1872–4, 1880–5, under Gladstone.
3 – Ibid.; Lawrence Pearsall Jacks (1860–1955), unitarian divine, principal of Manchester College, Oxford, 1915–31, was Brooke's assistant at Bedford Chapel and in 1889 married his daughter Olive Cecilia.
4 – Stopford Augustus Brooke (1832–1916) had won prizes for English verse while at Trinity College, Dublin, but his literary legacy, such as it is, consists chiefly in criticism. His Primer of English Literature (1876) was received enthusiastically by Matthew Arnold and sold widely; VW quotes from it, without identifying her source, in her essay 'I Am Christina Rossetti', V VW Essays and CR2.
5 – Jacks, vol. i, ch. IV, pp. 55–7, which has: 'But his feet'; and 'an impassioned love'.
6 – Ibid., vol. i, ch. VII, p. 114: 'Indeed, from the point of view of bishops and vicars in 1860 he was distinctly "unsafe", and his Broad Church views, extremely

moderate as they now seem, were a barrier which not even the influence of powerful friends could always overcome.'

7 – *Ibid.*, vol. i, ch. VI, p. 94; Brooke held his first curacy at St Matthew's, Lisson Grove, Marylebone, 1857–9, but enjoyed (*ibid.*, p. 92), at Piccadilly, Grosvenor Place, Portman Square, 'almost daily . . . meetings with Ministers of State, Ambassadors, artists, men of letters – and . . . other meetings too, "on a balcony, overlooking the Green Park", when Maud is quoted under the moon'.

8 – Brooke was chaplain at Berlin, 1863–4, ministering to the English court established around Victoria (1840–1901), the Princess Royal, who in 1858 had married Crown Prince Frederick of Prussia (1831–88), the future emperor of Germany.

9 – Jacks, vol. i, ch. XII, p. 219.

10 – *Ibid.*, ch. XI, p. 197, which has: 'But a man'.

11 – *Ibid.*, ch. XVI, p. 311, quoting G. K. Chesterton (1874–1936) on Brooke's *Browning* (1902), in the *Daily News*, 25 September 1902.

12 – *Ibid.*

13 – *Ibid.*, ch. XVI, p. 319, which has: 'believe; and it is not exaggeration to say that he found the position at this point positively hateful'.

14 – *Ibid.*, vol. ii, ch. XXX, p. 602.

15 – *Ibid.*, ch. XXIII, p. 481, adapted.

16 – *Ibid.*, vol. i, ch. XVI, p. 317; in addition to the personages cited by VW, Jacks also lists Tennyson, Arnold, the Earl and Countess of Carlisle, Giovanni Costa, the Italian painter, and Alphonse Legros, the French etcher, painter and sculptor.

17 – For both references to this Shakespearean episode, *ibid.*, vol. ii, ch. XX, p. 423. John Richard Green (1837–83), historian, author of a *Short History of the English People* (1874).

18 – No. 1 Manchester Square, Marylebone.

19 – Jacks, vol. ii, ch. XX, p. 413, which has: 'no ultimate incredulity'.

20 – *Ibid.*, p. 414.

21 – This phrase does not occur in Jacks.

22 – Jacks, vol. ii, ch. XXIX, p. 586; Brooke first became acquainted with the Indian poet and mystic Rabindranath Tagore (1861–1941) in 1911; Tagore's *Sādhanā*, addresses on life and its realisation, was published in 1913.

23 – *Ibid.*, p. 584.

24 – *Ibid.*, ch. XXVII, p. 554.

25 – *Ibid.*, ch. XXII, p. 454.

Mr Gladstone's Daughter

Those who say that the art of letter-writing is dead are not presumably the daughters of prime ministers.[2] We may make so bold as to suppose that these favoured people still sometimes sigh when their share of the postbag is meted out to them. The envelopes are not only numerous, but in some cases they are swollen beyond the scope of easy breakfast-table reading. In writing to Mrs Drew, Sir Mountstuart Grant Duff, for instance, would enclose a record of a twenty-six days' tour in India and proceed to make his statement about the condition of Hyderabad.[3] Lord Stanmore, then Sir Arthur Gordon, would give expression to the difficulties which beset a colonial governor conscious of a 'power of work and attention to detail with an ungrudging trust in my subordinates'.[4] Other correspondents remark that it is very important that the new Bishop (of London) shall be a Liberal;[5] and again someone pleads that a poet shall be given a pension, and does that pension last his lifetime or 'does it end if the country wants to be Tory'?[6]

That is the official side of Mrs Drew's correspondence, the inevitable privilege, or penalty, of being her father's daughter. But the men and women who came to Hawarden to see Mr Gladstone generally became almost independently of that the friends of Mrs Drew. The character of her correspondents makes it inadmissible to suppose that she was ever made use of – save with the completely open injunction. 'Please tell Mr Gladstone' – to take a message from the writer to her father. And yet some of the most amusing passages in these letters are amusing precisely because of the accident of her birth. People who, as we must feel, had no business in that sphere at all came fluttering through it in a delightfully audacious way. Ruskin had written an article which interested Mr Gladstone, and was invited to stay at Hawarden. He came, with a telegram of recall in his pocket, 'as suspiciously as a wild animal entering a trap'.[7] When he left he was on such cordial terms with them all that he wrote at once to his publisher to cancel certain strictures in *Fors*, being, as he put it, 'greatly dismayed'[8] to find how much more admirable Mr Gladstone was than he had expected to find him. All went well for two years. He was then moved to declare that he cared no more for Mr Gladstone or Mr Disraeli[9] than he did for two old bagpipes. This he could not retract, so he explained to Mrs Drew, because he meant it; nor would he mind if Mr Gladstone called him a 'broken bottle stuck on the top of a wall', upon which Mr Gladstone exclaimed with delight, 'He stands apart from and above all other men.'[10] Whether his further vociferations against Home Rule and in favour of land possession for all the world 'eternal as the mountains and the sea'[11] ever reached Mr Gladstone's ears we are not told; but when he and Burne-Jones talk about politics they do so with a freshness and a passion which might have made even Mrs Gladstone less bored by that subject than she was quite unashamed to be.[12]

Politics have their share in these letters, but no more than their share. The interest lies rather in the attitude of that particular group of highly privileged people towards the books and the pictures and the men and women of their time. The group ('chiefly drawn from the Gladstone, Balfour, and Lyttelton families')[13] was intimate, communicative, and honestly persuaded that nature as well as fortune had been generous at any rate to the others. They were alive to whatever went forward in a good many different worlds, and took their sides enthusiastically. The *Life of Carlyle* forms them into an anti-Froude society; *Progress and Poverty* goes the round from one earnest correspondent to another; *The Vulture Maiden* is 'devoured'; first impressions of *Robert Elsmere* are debated with extreme seriousness and not a little apprehension as to what the result of the book may be; the 'Maiden Tribute' crusade of Mr Stead is discussed passionately by Professor Stuart and gravely by Alfred Lyttelton.[14] And *Diana of the Crossways* and *The Minister's Wooing*, and 'Mme de Mauves' and the *Redemption of Edward Strachan*[15] are all coming out and getting inextricably mixed in importance and commendation.

Such was the nucleus of the larger group of the eighties 'styled, by those who did not belong to it, "The Souls"'.[16] Is there still, as the severity of these words implies, a public which impudently pretends to know more than it possibly can know about that gifted constellation, and in default of facts invents rumours? Here at any rate it is not going to be satisfied; here are only glimpses, not secrets. But these glimpses are certainly very pleasant. Mr Balfour stands at the top of a great double staircase and reflects, 'The worst of this staircase is that there is absolutely no reason why one should go down one side rather than the other. What am I to do?'[17] Joachim asks Miss Gladstone whether Wednesday would suit her 'to play with my accompaniment'.[18] In short, we can see quite enough to know that we should like to see more. The pity is that so little, not even the newspaper which was to advocate higher truths and at the same time let off the scum, survives for our edification. For although Mrs Drew's letters throw lights upon a past society significant even to the public and illuminating doubtless to friends, they are on the whole, and with the exception of Burne-Jones's letter, oddly inexpressive, oddly unformed and undistinguished, if you consider the names and the gifts of the writers. When it is a question of

Wyndhams and Lytteltons one can scarcely help considering their names and thinking of the eighteenth century, and remembering how Horace Walpole too was the son of a Prime Minister.[19]

1 – A review in the *TLS*, 6 December 1917, (Kp C92) of *Some Hawarden Letters. 1878–1913. Written to Mrs Drew (Miss Mary Gladstone). Before and after her marriage*. Chosen and arranged by Leslie March-Phillipps and Bertram Christian (Nisbet & Co. Ltd., 1917).

2 – William Ewart Gladstone (1809–98) was Prime Minister 1868–74, 1880–5, 1886, and 1892–4.

3 – *Letters*, ch. v, p. 153, 16 August 1884. Sir Mountstuart Elphinstone Grant Duff (1829–1906), statesman and author, Liberal M.P., 1857–81; he served under Gladstone as Under-Secretary of State for India, 1868–74, and for the Colonies, 1880–1, and was Lieutenant Governor of Madras, 1881–6.

4 – *Ibid.*, ch. IV, p. 98, 27 January 1882. Sir Arthur Charles Hamilton Gordon (1829–1912), created Baron Stanmore in 1893, had at one time been Gladstone's private secretary; he held several colonial governorships, including those of New Zealand, 1880–3, and Ceylon, 1883–90.

5 – *Ibid.*, ch. VI, p. 199, from Professor James Stuart of Trinity College, Cambridge, 10 January 1885. The new bishop of London, Frederick Temple (1821–1902), a future archbishop of Canterbury, was enthroned at St Paul's in April 1885; he was, indeed, a Liberal.

6 – *Ibid.*, ch. III, p. 85, from Edward Burne-Jones (1833–1898), concerning the pitman poet Joseph Shipsey, undated.

7 – *Ibid.*, ch. I, p. 6, editorial commentary. John Ruskin (1819–1900).

8 – *Ibid.*, ch. II, p. 21, John Ruskin, writing to his publisher, 18 January 1878: 'I have been greatly dismayed by the discovery to me of Mr Gladstone's real character, as I saw it at Hawarden: its intense simplicity and earnestness laying themselves open to every sort of misinterpretation – being unbelievable unless one saw him. I must cancel all my attack on him in *Fors*.' *Fors Clavigera* (1871–84), a series of letters addressed to the workmen and labourers of Britain.

9 – Benjamin Disraeli (1804–81), Tory Prime Minister, 1867–8, 1874–80.

10 – For the first quotation, *ibid.*, ch. III, p. 65, 23 October 1880; and for the second, *ibid.*, p. 63, editorial commentary, which continues: 'He is an exception and must never be judged by ordinary standards'.

11 – *Ibid.*, ch. IV, p. 102, 29 March 1882.

12 – *Ibid.*, Pref., pp. xii–xiii: ' "She contrived," Lady Lovelace says of her, "to combine the keenest interest and quick apprehension of all that concerned her husband's career with the most unashamed boredom with politics in general." '

13 – *Ibid.*, ch. IV, p. 135. Gladstone was an intimate friend of George William, 4th Baron Lyttelton (1817–76), who had married Mary Glynne, Mrs Gladstone's sister. Arthur James Balfour, 1st Earl of Balfour (1848–1930), philosopher and statesman, was intimate with Baron Lyttelton's extensive family and in 1875 had become engaged to his daughter May Lyttelton, who died a month or so after Balfour's proposal.

14 – J. A. Froude, *Thomas Carlyle: A History of his Life in London. 1834–1881* (1884); for its responsibility for the anti-Froude society, *ibid.*, ch. III, p. 91, editorial commentary. Henry George, *Progress and Poverty* (1879). For the devouring of *The Vulture Maiden* (1876), by Wilhelmine von Hillern, *ibid.*, ch. IV, letter from H. S. Holland, 1883, p. 133. For the agitation of W. T. Stead (1849–1912), editor of the *Pall Mall Gazette, 1883–90, ibid.*, ch. VI, pp. 200–1, 206–7. In July 1885 Stead published an attack on immorality in England entitled 'The Maiden Tribute of Modern Babylon', in which he indirectly implicated several public figures. As a result, parliament was galvanised into passing a Criminal Law Amendment Act, over which it had dragged its feet for some time, raising the age of consent to sixteen; and Stead, who had failed to substantiate some crucial evidence, spent three months in prison for libel.

15 – George Meredith, *Diana of the Crossways* (1885); Harriet Beecher Stowe, *The Minister's Wooing* (1859); Henry James, 'Mme de Mauves' (1873), collected in *A Passionate Pilgrim and Other Tales* (1875); W. H. Dawson, *The Redemption of Edward Strachan* (?1892).

16 – *Letters*, ch. IV, p. 135, editorial commentary.

17 – *Ibid.*

18 – *Ibid.*, ch. IV, p. 136, undated but of the period 1882–3. Joseph Joachim (1831–1907), Hungarian violinist and composer.

19 – The references, not previously noted, are to the family of George Wyndham (1863–1913), statesman and man of letters, sometime private secretary to Arthur Balfour, and chief secretary for Ireland, 1900–05; and to Horace Walpole (1717–97), fourth son of Sir Robert Walpole, prime minister, 1715–17, 1721–42.

'Charlotte Brontë'

Thirteen well-known writers,[2] twenty-eight illustrations and three maps here unite in testifying that Charlotte Brontë[3] is still a shining object to which the eyes of the living turn with love and question after a hundred years. Indubitably, she shines on, but it is also evident that no two people see the same star. Indeed, this book would be well worth reading were it only as a lesson in the meaning and nature of criticism. If we are ever inclined to think that the last word has been said and that our minds are made up for the rest of our lives, we may now change that opinion. Here are thirteen writers, all particularly fitted to define the character of this one woman and to pass judgment upon her three books, and each one of them is struck by a different quality, or values the same quality at a different rate. Nevertheless, although we must resign the comfort of depending upon an infallible support, by this means we get a much richer, more various, and finally, we believe, truer estimate than is usual. It is an example that might well be followed, were it not that few subjects lend themselves so happily to this particular treatment.

There are not many writers capable, after a century, of kindling such vivid sparks in such different minds. The essay by Mrs Humphry Ward[4] is on the whole the most comprehensive, not only because we read it before we have been disturbed, but because she is herself a novelist and has a wide knowledge of literature to lend authority to her view. She insists, quoting Renan, upon the Celtic nature of the Brontë genius;[5] the nature which grasps at passion and at poetry for their own sakes, which breaks all the rules and which neglects 'that shaping and fastidious instinct which is, in truth, the ultimate thing'. Charlotte Brontë, she says, lives because she is both dreamer and observer, 'bringing the poetic faculty to bear on the truth nearest to her'.[6] To this we should assent were it not that by doing so we must, according to Mrs Ward, sacrifice at least partially the curates in *Shirley*. Her art has not transmuted them from reality to literature, Mrs Ward explains; and yet if you cancel the first chapter of *Shirley* you lose, we think, the most convincing proof that Charlotte Brontë had a sense of humour.

But here already criticism has done part of its duty. It has revived our impression and given us the sense of possessing a live and combative conception of our author. Good criticism also is subtly suggestive; Mrs Ward whispers 'poetry, truth, feeling',[7] and sets us thinking how we too have felt the breath of the moors, and seen the purple sunset, and loved that angular honesty and rated it above wisdom. Still, Mr Gosse[8] interrupts, checking a mood which easily runs riot, have you ever thought how it would be to talk to Charlotte Brontë? 'It would probably have been disconcerting to the highest degree.'[9] She was without experience of the 'social amenities'. The atmosphere of Haworth was hard and dry; she lived in the 'blast of a perpetual moral east wind'.[10] 'She has the impatience, the unreasonable angers and revolts, of an unappreciated adolescent.'[11] All this, too, was latent in our conception, an important element, and one that has stamped itself irrevocably upon her work. If she had gone to Paris, not Brussels, if, as Mr Gosse suggests, she had studied Balzac,[12] if even she had enjoyed a few years of happiness, in what directions might she not have developed? It is tempting to speculate how humour and charity and genius itself would have ripened in the sun of a happy marriage. But such reflections are presently cut short by Bishop Welldon. 'If,' he says, 'Charlotte Brontë owed much to her own life, most of all did she owe to its sadness.'[13] For the moment this gives us pause; we grudge deeply any tribute to the value of sadness. The moral east wind and the anger bred of sadness are still too fresh in our minds. But then, after all, that intensity of passion which we honour most perhaps in Charlotte Brontë was only ground out by conflict; make her happy, make her amiable, make her fluent in society, and the writer we know has ceased to exist.

In spite of their diversities, however, these three critics have helped us to shape our conception and have not said anything which is so incompatible that we cannot make use of it. But there are more general questions to be considered, and upon these, too, the critics are at variance. Dr Garnett tells us that her principal shortcoming was that she could not create a character 'by sheer force of imagination',[14] and therefore, having to draw upon experience, had already exhausted her material. Completely though this verdict is reversed a few pages later by Professor Vaughan,[15] the question for us lies not in reconciling the critics, but in deciding what is meant by 'sheer force of imagination'. Tolstoy,[16] for example, drew far more accurately from life than Charlotte Brontë, but one can hardly charge him with a lack of creative power, or with poverty of material. Indeed, the opposite seems to be the truth; those who fix their eyes upon life itself depend more upon 'sheer force of imagination' than the purely subjective artists, if such there be, who create from their own resources. But the danger of using such ugly words as the old subjective and objective is illustrated by Dr Garnett, who, in spite of her dependence upon experience, puzzles us by placing Charlotte Brontë chief among those writers who are subjective.

But, although there are dangers, assumptions and questions of ill-defined scope leading us as far as we choose to go, the tenor of this book is unmistakable. She is the novelist of passion, of intensity, of revolt. Upon the general outlines all are agreed, but only one critic, Mr Chesterton,[17] makes, to our thinking, an unexpected contribution. An Irish friend of his, living in Yorkshire, 'once made to me the suggestive remark that the towering and over-masculine barbarians and lunatics who dominate the Brontë novels simply represent the impression produced by the rather boastful Yorkshire manners upon the more civilised and sensitive Irish temperament'.[18] That is all the more suggestive if you remember that the Brontës, being Irish and Cornish by birth, were as fanatical in their love of Yorkshire as adopted children are apt to be. There is, then, still much to ponder and much to guess; and yet, after all, the important thing after a hundred years is to feel what each of these writers feels, that whatever our differences we are all looking at a star. We have quoted Mr Gosse when he criticises Charlotte Brontë; let us end with his praise of her. 'She was, in her own words, "furnace-tried by pain, stamped by constancy", and out of her fires she rose, a Phoenix of poetic fancy, crude yet without a rival, and now, in spite of all imperfections, to live for ever in the forefront of creative English genius.'[19]

1 – A review in the *TLS*, 13 December 1917, (Kp C93) of *Charlotte Brontë 1816–1916. A Centenary Memorial.* Prepared by the Brontë Society. Edited by Butler Wood F.R.S.L. With a foreword by Mrs Humphry Ward and 3 maps and 28 illustrations (Fisher Unwin Ltd., 1918). See also 'Charlotte Brontë' above, 'Howarth, November, 1904', *I VW Essays*, '*Jane Eyre* and *Wuthering Heights*', *IV VW Essays* and *CR1*.

2 – Of whom the following are not mentioned by VW: Arthur C. Benson ('Charlotte Brontë: A Personal Sketch'); M. H. Spielmann ('Charlotte Brontë: in Brussels'); H. E. Wroot ('Story of the Brontë Society'); Sir Sidney Lee ('Charlotte Brontë in London'); Halliwell Sutcliffe ('The Spirit of the Moors'); J. K. Snowden ('The Brontës as Artists and Prophets'); Butler Wood ('A Brontë Itinerary').

3 – Charlotte Brontë (1816–55), author of *Jane Eyre* (1847), *Shirley* (1849), *Villette* (1853); her first novel, *The Professor*, was published posthumously, in 1857.

4 – Mrs Humphry (Mary Augusta) Ward (1851–1920), 'Some Thoughts on Charlotte Brontë'.

5 – Wood, p. 22: '"Never laugh at us Celts!... We shall not build the Parthenon... But we know how to seize upon the heart and soul..."'; and p. 23: '"In the heart of our race there rises... a spring of madness."' Ernest Renan (1823–92), Breton-born philologist and historian, best known as the author of *Origines du Christianisme* (1863–83).

6 – For the two preceding quotations, *ibid.*, p. 23, p. 29.

7 – *Ibid.*, p. 29.

8 – Edmund Gosse (1849–1928), 'A Word on Charlotte Brontë'.

9 – Wood, p. 43.

10 – For the two preceding quotations, *ibid.*, p. 42.

11 – *Ibid.*, p. 43.

12 – *Ibid.*, p. 44; Honoré de Balzac (1799–1850).

13 – *Ibid.*, J. E. C. Welldon (1854–1937), 'Centenary Address at Haworth', p. 74.

14 – *Ibid.*, Dr Richard Garnett (1835–1906), 'The Place of Charlotte Brontë in Nineteenth Century Fiction', pp. 166–7.

15 – Professor C. E. Vaughan (1854–1922), 'Charlotte and Emily Brontë: A Comparison and a Contrast'.

16 – L. N. Tolstoy (1828–1910).

17 – G. K. Chesterton (1874–1936), 'Charlotte Brontë as a Romantic'.

18 – Wood, p. 52.   19 – *Ibid.*, p. 45.

'Rebels and Reformers'

Mr and Mrs Ponsonby's[2] book is intended for children or for those who are too busy to read books in many volumes. But the interest of it lies not in the necessarily short and simple narratives giving the story rather than the ideas, although these are done clearly and with spirit, but in the reflections which lie about those stories and lodge here and there in the reader's mind. Like all books worth reading, this one is the outcome of a mass of judgments and beliefs which may be very briefly expressed in the work itself but lend it the gift which in the case of human beings we call personality.

When the writers remark how few lives there are of rebels and reformers compared with those of men of action, when they say that 'life is conflict',[3] that most famous men are of humble origin, that it is even more difficult to struggle against luxury than against poverty, that indifference and indolence are the worst of failings, that history has hitherto been the history of wars, then, to use a homely phrase, we prick up our ears and attend. If we sat among the children to whom this book will be read aloud in the winter evenings we should have guessed by this time what answer would please our teachers. As this book is meant primarily for children, it may be worth while to consider what the effect upon them of such stimulus is likely to be. Will it stir them from an early age to redress the wrongs of the world, or is there not in the human mind a curious tendency to go against the ideas suggested in childhood, so that the effect may be precisely the opposite of what Mr and Mrs Ponsonby intend? Tolstoy,[4] we remember, refused to force his views upon his children. The truth may be that if you want to breed rebels and reformers you must impress upon them from the beginning the virtues of Tories and aristocrats.

Mr Ponsonby enforces a point which the lives of these twelve heroes illustrate over and over again. It is 'the very struggle and continuous effort that is the making of them'.[5] What sort of future must we expect if the light of reason and humanity is lit in the earliest dawn of understanding in the nursery? Multiply the enlightened nurseries of the world and the race of rebels and reformers is extinct, until, indeed, the next wave of reaction sets in. The argument may throw a little light upon the very puzzling tendency of the human race to resist its reformers and to burn its rebels. The fact that rebels and reformers are a race of people who live by struggle and conflict may be some slight justification for the peculiar shrinking with which the normal mind regards them. For ourselves we are in agreement with many doctrines explicit and implicit in Mr and Mrs Ponsonby's book; and yet even from their straightforward pages the shadow of the spectre looks out and chills us against our will and against our reason. A strange melancholy pervades us. It may be that the element of denial and destruction enters more largely than that of creation or belief into the reformer's attitude. It may be that circumstances force him to dwell disproportionately upon the bad and the wrong and to draw a circle round the right which excludes many of the things we care for most. It may be that the average human mind, so far as it desires anything, desires to create and to like. At any rate by easy stages of 'indolence and indifference'[6] back we slip into a mood demanding poetry, music, fiction – Shakespeare, perhaps, most of all.

Now Mr and Mrs Ponsonby provide us with four men of letters, Cervantes, Voltaire, Hans Andersen[7] and Tolstoy; but they are careful to explain that although they wrote some famous books they are here for reasons not connected with their art. The reasons are good ones; yet what more living and prolific source of reform is to be found than the plays of Shakespeare? His claim to the title of reformer is no doubt obscured by the fact that he burnt no one and died presumably in his own bed; but, as every scribbler knows, each sentence wins its way to existence through a crowd of temptations or dies at their hands, and the most effective victory over evil seems to lie not so much in Acts of Parliament as in a song or two.

But these reflections, which certainly have not escaped Mr and Mrs Ponsonby, only go to prove the truth of their main contention that those who have won the title of rebels and reformers are never given their due of admiration. Either we feel ourselves in opposition to them for one of the above reasons, or the evils which they overcame seem too gross to call for heroic qualities in those who vanquish them. William Lloyd Garrison did more than anyone to abolish slavery, yet we find ourselves, as Mrs Ponsonby points out, less inclined to admire him than to be shocked that such views should be rare enough to demand admiration. Perhaps at the root of all our grudging hesitation lies the deep-seated human vanity which is wounded, after all these years, as the record of human cruelty and superstition is unrolled before us. But the struggle still continues; we find the rebel flame burning at its purest in the cry of little Ivan Tolstoy, who, when his mother told him that Yasnaya was his property, stamped his foot and cried, 'Don't say that Yasnaya Polyana is mine! Everything is everyone else's'.[8] No less true and persistent is the other cry which comes to us from the mouth of Countess Tolstoy. Her husband, she knows, goes ahead of the crowd, pointing the way. 'But I am the crowd [. . .] I live in its current, and see the light of the lamp which every leader, and Leo of course, carries, and I acknowledge it to be the light. But I cannot go faster; I am held by the crowd and by my surroundings and habits.'[9]

1 – A review in the *TLS*, 20 December 1917, (Kp C94) of *Rebels and Reformers. Biographies for Young People* (George Allen & Unwin Ltd., 1917) by Arthur and Dorothea Ponsonby.

2 – Arthur Augustus William Harry Ponsonby (1871–1946), Liberal M.P., since 1908, outspoken pacifist, and his wife Dorothea, *née* Parry. He later joined the Independent Labour Party and in 1930 was created 1st Baron Ponsonby of Shulbrede.

3 – Ponsonby, 'Savonarola' [1452–98, Italian religious reformer], p. 16.

4 – L. N. Tolstoy (1828–1910).

5 – Ponsonby, 'Tycho Brahe' [1546–1601, Danish astronomer], p. 86, which has: 'this very struggle'.

6 – *Ibid.*, 'William Lloyd Garrison' [1805–79, American opponent of slavery], p. 233, which has: 'sloth and indifference'.

7 – Miguel de Cervantes Saavedra (1547–1616); François Marie Arouet de Voltaire (1694–1778); Hans Christian Andersen (1805–75).

8 – Ponsonby, 'Tolstoy', p. 293

9 – *Ibid.*, p. 294.

Sunset Reflections

Mr Martin's little book will be welcomed, we believe, particularly by Americans. It comes from Stratford-upon-Avon in the first place; and that appeal is enforced by a gentle resignation of tone, a placid smoothness of utterance, a tendency to indulge in moralities and mysticisms, to harp wistfully upon the past, which are characteristic more of the essayists of that country than of ours. As a vision of England before the war, too, it will have greater interest for them than for us. The face of Europe, Mr Martin points out in his dedication, is being changed out of all knowledge by the war, and therefore 'it has seemed well to gather together these few peace pictures of a vanishing landscape and of those who once made it their home'. 'There is a mystery and a loveliness' he proceeds, 'in the sun's setting, distinct and apart from the wonder of his rising.'[2]

Whether it is that the light of sunset is on his face, or whether our memories are short ones, we certainly have difficulty in recognising Mr Martin's greengrocer's boy. It was a wet morning in October when he came in and told Mr Martin that, although wet here, it was shining 'in the happy fields'. When asked where these might be, 'he was puzzled and even a little distressed'. [. . .] 'The happy fields where men sing as they work.'[3] And he shouldered his basket and went off, leaving Mr Martin to a whole morning of what we may call in his own phrase 'the compelled silence of easeful meditation'.[4] He provided a title for the book, however, and therefore may be excused. But the old woman in the Welsh village with whom Mr Martin lodged has no such claim upon our charity. When, after trying for six weeks to get into a field which he saw from his window, Mr Martin asked her why the field for ever eluded him, and why he might not pass through that unguarded entrance, she replied, 'Fields and hedges can keep their secrets as well as we, but maybe things look different seen near to.'[5] If the war has put an end to such greengrocers' boys and taught such old ladies to give a plain answer to a plain question, we shall have something to thank it for.

The lower classes, as we know, may always be used more or less for purposes of allegory, but even upon the upper, the cultivated classes, the sunset, according to Mr Martin, has had the same transforming effect. Two grown people, for instance, would sit down seriously to discuss whether on the whole they preferred the sky or the earth. The lady explained, at greater length than we can grant her, how she liked the sky better 'because the sky stays unchanging in the beauty of its thousand shifting scenes . . .'[6] The gentleman replied that he preferred the earth, and as he has just exclaimed that the earth is his mistress, he has some right to be heard. 'We of the earth,' he wound up, 'would not change our wild wind-blown reeds for the faultless strings of Apollo.'[7] Again, before the war (and this we can verify from personal observation) poets were in the habit of saying that, given a crystal or allowed to make certain passes with the hands, they could make you see whatever vision they chose. In Mr Martin's version the lady holds an antique jewel in her delicate, thin-fingered hand, 'such a hand as Memling would have loved to paint', and her answer was always the same, 'I see a bright light,' until at last she said, 'I see flames everywhere, red flames burning like a great flower.'[8] The poet had meant her to see a lonely reed-covered lake. Now about the same time a poet was willing a lady of our acquaintance to see a burning rose; and to all his exhortations she would reply with the single word 'Frog.' We tell this story for the double purpose of showing that the visions presumably got mixed, and of assuring ourselves and any American readers that even in the time of the sunset we were occasionally monosyllabic.

But we are not altogether just to Mr Martin. Although devoted to every form of sunset himself, he recognises the fact that even in this land of decaying ruins, secular oaks, Shakespeare and the rest of it, some remain untouched. A case occurred in February 1912. There was then a sunset the like of which has never been seen and never will be seen by Mr Martin again. It affected even the spirits of his dog. But when he went about asking eagerly whether anyone else had seen the sunset, the replies were invariably disappointing. The dog then looked at him with 'grave silent reproach. What does it matter (so she seemed to say) what others have seen or think, when we two know; is it not enough that for us the heavens have been opened, and we have seen the glory of a new earth?'[9] She may have meant all that, but why not give the poor animal the benefit of the doubt?

1 – A review in the TLS, 20 December 1917, (Kp C95) of The Happy Fields. A Country Record (Shakespeare Head Press, 1917) by E. M. Martin, author also of Wayside Wisdom, a book for quiet people (1909) and Dreams in Wartime, a faithful record (1915).
2 – Martin, 'To Those Who Love the Country', preliminary unnumbered page, which has 'New beauty may come with this new harvesting of the nations; but there is . . .'
3 – Ibid., 'The Happy Fields', p. 4.
4 – Ibid., 'A Harrier of the Hedgeways', p. 49.
5 – Ibid., 'The Happy Fields', p. 10.
6 – Ibid., 'Weather Books', p. 28.
7 – Ibid., which has: 'It is the legend of Marsyas; but though stripped and flayed we of the earth . . .'
8 – Ibid., p. 22, which has: 'Memmling' [Hans Memling, c. 1430–94, Flemish religious painter].
9 – Ibid., p. 38.

The New Crusade

The process of making anything, whether it be a horseshoe, an ironclad, or a cigarette, has a fascination absent from the finished object, and of all creative processes that of the poet is the one we would give most to have the chance of watching were it possible. But of all makers poets are apt to be the least communicative about their processes, and, perhaps, owing in part to the ordinary nature of their material, have little or nothing that they choose to discuss with outsiders. The best way of surprising their secrets is very often to read their criticism. Thus, although Mr Drinkwater has many acute things to say about different poets in these papers, his most illuminating remarks are those which give us for a second a glimpse into his workshop. There we can see the unfinished stanzas, the litter of words, the chaos of conceptions from which at last the little poem of four lines is struck out by work 'colossal in its severity compared with that involved in any other kind of labour'.[2] Our fancy picture of Mr Drinkwater's workshop must represent a place without ornament or ease, but everywhere the signs of strife and austerity. His criticism bears the same stamp. He speaks of poets more as a soldier in a hard fought battle might speak of another soldier fighting with him or against him than as a critic looking from a distance and without share in the strife.

It is natural to consider further whether this point of view does not lie behind much of the best poetic work of our time, and in what directions that influence is making itself felt. When a poet speaks of poetry as the hardest labour in the world we may infer that he is up in arms against some popular fallacy which has at length goaded him to anger; nor does Mr Drinkwater leave us long in doubt as to the source of his irritation. 'We artists,' he writes in his dedication, 'have the world to fight. Prejudice, indifference, positive hostility, misrepresentation, a total failure to understand the purposes and the power of art, beset us on every side.'[3] The first few essays develop this position and are therefore extremely and almost wholly combative. Mr Drinkwater expresses with a certain stiffness, but with much honest eloquence, the view and the claims of the disinherited. Very possibly you will find the same sense of isolation in the artists of any period of the world's history; but it is no doubt more marked in such an age as ours where callings are sharply specialised and the artist cannot be a bank manager into the bargain. There is by nature, or there has come to be by custom, a deep gulf between the little body of visionaries and the great mass of practical people. But when we find Mr Drinkwater, who speaks for many of his generation, claiming his rights and asserting his capacities, we see that we are reaching a new phase in the old tacit hostility. The days of the truce which most of the poets of the past were quite content to observe are over, and there has gone with them perhaps a certain conception of the art of poetry. At least the conception of the artist himself has changed. It is we artists, says Mr Drinkwater, who are the strictly practical people, we 'who have our eyes set straight, not squinting; and so can see beyond our noses'.[4] Further, he threatens that if in the future, as in the past, no heed is paid to art, and it is treated as a luxury and not as a necessity, the work of civilisation is doomed. 'Here is the new crusade.'[5] The first step in the new crusade is to teach children to read poetry, and from that simple foundation all the civic virtues will grow of themselves. People who have learnt to love Shakespeare will, 'in less than a generation',[6] Mr Drinkwater insists, desire decent conditions to live in. Perhaps that does not overrate what, for brevity's sake, one calls poetry, but the possibility of teaching a love of poetry save by the indirect means of health and leisure seems to us problematical, to say the least of it.

But if Mr Drinkwater does not here discuss the practical part of the problem, we do not on that account accuse him of easy idealism or of irresponsible prophecy. This little book is solid testimony to the effect which such ideas have had upon his art. Tokens of the spirit which is inspiring the new crusade are scattered throughout Mr Drinkwater's pages. Poetry, he says, makes clarity and order out of vagueness and difficult confusion; it translates common simple life into the most exact and stirring beauty. As for the old taunt that a poet leads a life of luxury and indolence, Mr Drinkwater is almost too ready to enlarge upon the severity of discipline which he must be ready to undergo; but we must remark that the labour is of a special nature. It is not the labour of building up elaborate stanza structures, for 'the whole range of verse technique [...] may be covered in a perfectly regular five-foot quatrain'.[7] It is the labour rather of making what is vague clear, what is abstract concrete, what is common beautiful. Rightly or wrongly, we cannot help connecting these views of poetry with the belief that a capacity for the love of art is commoner than people allow. Mr

Drinkwater's anger is not the anger of the aristocrat who despises, but of the democrat who wishes to share. Whether such views are favourable to what used to be called inspiration we do not know; but we may prophesy that our age will be known not for one or two great poets, but because a large number of smaller men held such views as these and gave them the best shape they could.

Of the critical papers that on Rupert Brooke[8] will be read perhaps with most interest; and it is one of the few that do not inevitably suggest the question what Rupert Brooke himself would have said if he could come back to find himself thus idolised. To the loss of him his friends have had to add the peculiar irony of his canonisation; and any one who helps us to remember that volatile, irreverent, and extremely vivacious spirit before the romantic public took possession of his fame has a right to our gratitude. If the legend of Rupert Brooke is not to pass altogether beyond recognition, we must hope that some of those who knew him when scholarship or public life seemed even more his bent than poetry will put their view on record and relieve his ghost of an unmerited and undesired burden of adulation.

1 – A review in the TLS, 27 December 1917, (Kp c95.1) of *Prose Papers* (Elkin Mathews, 1917) by John Drinkwater (1882–1937), poet, dramatist and actor. See also 'Abraham Lincoln' below.

2 – Drinkwater, 'Frederick Tennyson', p. 131.

3 – From Drinkwater's dedicatory letter to William Rothenstein (1872–1945), painter and author.

4 – Drinkwater, 'The Value of Poetry in Education', p. 44.

5 – *Ibid.*, p. 45.

6 – *Ibid.*, p. 44: 'Let them use some of the money available for the purpose to send companies into the villages to play Shakespeare, and the work of other great or fine dramatists, and in less than a generation the people will desire decent conditions, and as soon as they desire them they will have them.'

7 – *Ibid.*, 'Frederick Tennyson', p. 136; the ellipsis marks the omission of ', from the veriest album incompetency to the most superb lyric mastery.'

8 – Rupert Brooke (1887–1915) on whom Drinkwater includes two papers: 'Rupert Brooke' and 'Rupert Brooke on John Webster'. See also VW on 'Rupert Brooke', below.

1918

'Visits to Walt Whitman'

The great fires of intellectual life which burn at Oxford and at Cambridge are so well tended and long established that it is difficult to feel the wonder of this concentration upon immaterial things as one should. When, however, one stumbles by chance upon an isolated fire burning brightly without associations or encouragement to guard it, the flame of the spirit becomes a visible hearth where one may warm one's hands and utter one's thanksgiving. It is only by chance that one comes upon them; they burn in unlikely places. If asked to sketch the condition of Bolton about the year 1885 one's thoughts would certainly revolve round the cotton market, as if the true heart of Bolton's prosperity must lie there. No mention would be made of the group of young men – clergymen, manufacturers, artisans, and bank clerks by profession – who met on Monday evenings, made a point of talking about something serious, could broach the most intimate and controversial matters frankly and without fear of giving offence, and held in particular the view that Walt Whitman was 'the greatest epochal figure in all literature'.[2] Yet who shall set a limit to the effect of such talking? In this instance, besides the invaluable spiritual service, it also had some surprisingly tangible results. As a consequence of those meetings two of the talkers crossed the Atlantic; a steady flow of presents and messages set in between Bolton and Camden; and Whitman as he lay dying had the thought of 'those good Lancashire chaps'[3] in his mind. The book recounting these events has been published before,[4] but it is well worth reprinting for the light it sheds upon a new type of hero and the kind of worship which was acceptable to him.

To Whitman there was nothing unbefitting the dignity of a human being in the acceptance either of money or of underwear, but he said that there is no need to speak of these things as gifts. On the other hand, he had no relish for a worship founded upon the illusion that he was somehow better or other than the mass of human beings. 'Well,' he said, stretching out his hand to greet Mr Wallace, 'you've come to be disillusioned, have you?'[5] And Mr Wallace owned to himself that he *was* a little disillusioned. Nothing in Walt Whitman's appearance was out of keeping with the loftiest poetic tradition. He was a magnificent old man, massive, shapely, impressive by reason of his power, his delicacy, and his unfathomable depths of sympathy. The disillusionment lay in the fact that 'the greatest epochal figure in all literature' was 'simpler, homelier, and more intimately related to myself than I had imagined'.[6] Indeed, the poet seems to have been at pains to bring his common humanity to the forefront. And everything about him was as rough as it could be. The floor, which was only half carpeted, was covered with masses of papers; eating and washing things mixed themselves with proofs and newspaper cuttings in such ancient accumulations that a precious letter from Emerson[7] dropped out accidentally from the mass after years of inter- ment. In the midst of all this litter Walt Whitman sat spotlessly clean in his rough grey suit, with much more likeness to a retired farmer who spends his time in gossip with passers-by than to a poet with a message. Like a farmer whose working days are over, it pleased him to talk of this man and of that, to ask questions about their children and their land; and, whether it was the result of thinking back over places and human beings rather than over books and thoughts, his mood was uniformly benignant. His temperament, and no sense of duty, led him to this point of view, for in his opinion it behoved him to 'give out or express what I really was, and, if I felt like the Devil, to say so!'[8]

And then it appeared that this wise and free-thinking old farmer was getting letters from Symonds and sending messages to Tennyson,[9] and was indisputably, both in his opinion and in yours, of the same stature and importance as any of the heroic figures of the past or present. Their names dropped into his talk as the names of equals. Indeed, now and then something seemed 'to set him apart in spiritual isolation and to give him at times an air of wistful sadness',[10] while into his free and easy gossip drifted without effort the phrases and ideas of his poems.

Superiority and vitality lay not in a class but in the bulk; the average of the American people, he insisted, was immense, 'though no man can become truly heroic who is really poor'.[11] And 'Shakespeare and suchlike' come in of their own accord on the heels of other matters. 'Shakespeare is the poet of great personalities.' As for passion, 'I rather think Aeschylus greater'.[12] 'A ship in full sail is the grandest sight in the world, and it has never yet been put into a poem.'[13] Or he would throw off comments as from an equal height upon his great English contemporaries. Carlyle, he said, 'lacked amorousness'.[14] Carlyle was a growler. When the stars shone brightly – 'I guess an exception in that country' – and someone said 'It's a beautiful sight,' Carlyle said, 'It's a *sad* sight' . . . 'What a growler he was!'[15]

It is inevitable that one should compare the old age of two men who steered such different courses until one saw nothing but sadness in the shining of the stars and the other could sink into a reverie of bliss over the scent of an orange. In Whitman the capacity for pleasure seemed never to diminish, and the power to include grew greater and greater; so that although the authors of this book lament that they have only a trivial bunch of sayings to offer us, we are left with a sense of an 'immense background or vista'[16] and stars shining more brightly than in our climate.

1 – A review in the *TLS*, 3 January 1918, (Kp C96) of *Visits to Walt Whitman in 1890–1891*. By Two Lancashire Friends. J. Johnston, M.D., and J. W. Wallace. With twenty illustrations. (George Allen & Unwin, 1917). Reprinted: *G&R, CE.*
2 – *Visits*, p. 20; Walt Whitman (1819–92).
3 – *Ibid.*, p. 259, Whitman writing to Dr Ducke, 25 June 1891, which has: 'I doubt if ever a fellow had such a splendid emotional send-back response as I have had f'm those Lancashire chaps under the lead of Dr J. & J.W.W. – it cheers & nourishes my very heart.'
4 – *Notes of a Visit to Walt Whitman . . . in July, 1890* (1890); *Diary Notes of a Visit to Walt Whitman and Some of His Friends* (1898).
5 – *Visits*, p. 90.
6 – *Ibid.*, p. 91.
7 – Ralph Waldo Emerson (1803–82).
8 – *Visits*, p. 137.
9 – John Addington Symonds (1840–93); Alfred, Lord Tennyson (1809–92).
10 – *Visits*, p. 222.
11 – *Ibid.*, p. 44: 'He quoted the saying of the Northern Farmer of "Lord Tennyson" as he called him: "Taake my word for it, Sammy, the poor in loomp is bad"; which he took exception to, saying that the poor in a lump were not bad. "And not so poor either; for no man can become truly heroic who is really poor. He must have food,

clothing and shelter, and," he added significantly, "a little money in the bank too, I think."'

12 – For the first allusion to Shakespeare, *ibid.*, p. 62, which has: 'Many of his visitors he said seemed to expect him to keep talking about "Shakespeare and poetry" and such-like, all the time; and Mr Whitman told him that he liked a little of the talk of everyday life occasionally – in fact, as Mr Whitman once put it, he "liked to be a sensible man *sometimes!*"' For the second allusion to Shakespeare, and Aeschylus, *ibid.*, p. 213.

13 – *Ibid.*, p. 47.

14 – *Ibid.*, p. 127; Thomas Carlyle (1795–1881).

15 – *Ibid.*, pp. 178–9.

16 – *Ibid.*, p. 219, quoting Whitman's friend and disciple Edward Carpenter (1844–1929).

Philosophy in Fiction

After one has heard the first few bars of a tune upon a barrel organ the further course of the tune is instinctively foretold by the mind and any deviation from that pattern is received with reluctance and discomfort. A thousand tunes of the same sort have grooved a road in our minds and we insist that the next tune we hear shall flow smoothly down the same channels; nor are we often disobeyed. That is also the case with the usual run of stories. From the first few pages you can at least half-consciously foretell the drift of what is to follow, and certainly a part of the impulse which drives us to read to the end comes from the desire to match our foreboding with the fact. It is not strange then that the finished product is much what we expected it to be, and bears no likeness, should we compare it with reality, to what we feel for ourselves. For loudly though we talk of the advance of realism and boldly though we assert that life finds its mirror in fiction, the material of life is so difficult to handle and has to be limited and abstracted to such an extent before it can be dealt with by words that a small pinch of it only is made use of by the lesser novelist. He spends his time moulding and remoulding what has been supplied him by the efforts of original genius perhaps a generation or two ago. The moulds are by this time so firmly set, and require such effort to break them, that the public is seldom disturbed by explosions in that direction.

These reflections arose when we try to account for the discomfort which so often afflicts us in reading the works of Mr Jacks.[2] We do not insinuate that he is therefore a great writer; he has not increased the stock of our knowledge very largely, nor has he devised a shape which seems completely satisfactory for his contributions; but nevertheless he is disconcerting. In the first place he has one distinction which we wish that more novelists shared with him, the distinction of being something besides a novelist. His bias towards philosophy and religious speculation leads him off the high road and carries him to blank spaces where the path has not been cut nor the name chosen. He is an explorer, and in view of that fact we can forgive him some wanderings which seem to lead nowhere and others which end, as far as our eyesight serves us, in a fog. We fancy that he reverses some of the common methods of those who write fiction. More often than not the seed which the novelist picks up and brings to flower is dropped in some congregation of human beings, from sayings, gestures, or hints; but we should guess that Mr Jacks most commonly finds his seed between the pages of a book, and the book is quite often a book of philosophy. That at once gives him a different method of approach and a different direction. He is acquainted with Moral Science:[3] he looks up from the page and wonders what would happen should some of its doctrines be put into practice. He conceives an undergraduate and sets him the task of atoning for the sins of a dissolute father according to the teachings he has learnt in the schools. The crisis of the story therefore takes the form of a philosophical argument between two undergraduates as to the morality of giving a shilling to a tramp, and the one who proves his case shall marry the lady. It seems to us extremely unlikely that anyone could hum the rest of that tune from hearing the first few bars. It is plain that if you are ordering your imaginary universe from this angle your men and women will have to adapt themselves to dance to a new measure. The criticism which will rise to the lips of every reader who finds himself put out by the unwonted sight is that the characters have ceased to be 'real' or 'alive' or 'convincing'. But let him make sure that he is looking at life and not at the novelist's dummy. Or he might do worse than reflect whether likeness to life is the prime merit in a novel; and, if that is agreed upon, whether life is not a much more ubiquitous presence than one is led by the novelist to suppose. Whether or not Mr Jacks has discovered a new vein of the precious stuff, some rare merit must be allowed a writer who through five volumes of stories lures us on to the last word of the last page.

He causes us to remember the exhilaration of driving by dusk when one cannot foresee the ups or the downs of the road. With Mr Jacks starting his story anywhere, following it anywhere and leaving it anywhere, as he is in the habit of doing, the incentive of the unexpected is constantly supplied to us. 'Oh, I'm nobody in particular,' he remarks in 'A Grave Digger's Scene'. 'Just passing through and taking a look round';[4] and anything that his eye lights upon may start a story, which story may be a parable, or a satire upon religious sects, or a ghost story, or a straightforward study of a farmer's character, or a vision, or an argument, with figures merely put in as pegs to mark the places. But although he disregards all the rules and effects a most arbitrary tidying up when he remembers them, there is one invariable partner in all his enterprises – a keen and educated intelligence.

Intelligence, with its tendency to acquire views and its impatience with the passive attitude of impartial observation, may be a source of danger in fiction should it get the upper hand; but even in a state of subjection it is so rare that we must welcome it on its own terms. The only reservation which we feel disposed to make in the case of Mr Jacks's intelligence is that it fills his mind too full with ideas derived from other sources to give him a wide and unprejudiced view of his subject. Instead of going on with his tale, he has views upon socialism, or sex problems, or education, or psychology which must be brought in and investigated at the expense of the individual. But even this reservation must be qualified. The portraits of Farmer Perryman, Farmer Jeremy and Peter Rodright[5] have the stuff in them of three-volume novels, and give the essence of different types without deviation into the mystical or the abnormal. On account of their solid truth we prefer them to the study of Snarley Bob in *Mad Shepherds*, whose portrait seems to have been made up from some cunning prescription found in the books rather than from direct observation. Yet as we make this criticism we are aware that it may merely represent the shudder of a conservative mind forced to consider what it has always shunned, invited to land upon one of the 'Desolate Islands'[6] not marked upon the map. Expectancy mingles itself in equal proportions with our distrust, for the things that Mr Jacks tries to bring into the light are among the deepest and the most obscure. 'Things from the abyss of time that float upwards into dreams – sleeping things whose breath sometimes breaks the surface of our waking consciousness, like bubbles rising from the depths of Lethe.'[7]

Inevitably it is extremely difficult to combine these new trophies of psychology with the old; and the results are often queer composite beings, monsters of a double birth, fit for the museum rather than the breakfast table. When, among other curiosities, we read of a mare which has mysteriously acquired the personality of a professor's lost love we can hardly help remarking, 'Piecraft is trying to live in two worlds, the world of imagination and the world of pure science; he will come to grief in both of them.'[8] But if we are more often interested than moved by Mr Jacks's stories, the balance is so seldom on that side that it would be churlish to demand a combination which only the very few can give us. For some reason or other intelligence is particularly rare in fiction. At first sight it seems that there must be something amiss with a story which is aimed at the reason; when we find sentence after sentence brief, pointed, and expressive we shiver at a nakedness that seems momentarily indecent. But when we have rid ourselves of a desire for the dusky draperies of fiction there is no small pleasure in being treated neither as child nor as sultan, but as an equal and reasonable human being. Mr Jacks uniformly achieves this wholesome result by writing with an exactness which gives a sharp idea of his meaning. Nothing is modified out of deference to our laziness. And occasionally, as in the remarkable paper called 'The Castaway', he writes what we may read not only for the light which it casts upon his methods, but for its own rare beauty. We quote the last passage:

Desolate Islands, more than I could ever explore, more than I could count or name, I found in the men and women who press upon me every day. Nay, my own life was full of them; the flying moment was one; they rose out of the deep with the ticking of the clock. And once came the rushing of a mighty wind; and the waves fled backward till the sea was no more. Then I saw that the Islands were great mountains uplifted from everlasting foundations, their basis one beneath the ocean floor, their summits many above the sundering waters – most marvellous of all the works of God.[9]

1 – A review in the *TLS*, 10 January 1918, (Kp C97) of *Mad Shepherds and other human stories* (1910), *Among the Idolmakers* (1911), *From the Human End* (1916). *All Men Are Ghosts* (1913), *Philosophers in Trouble* (1916), collected, 6 vols, Williams & Norgate, 1916–17, as *Writings* by L. P. Jacks. VW noted in her diary on Monday, 7 January 1918: 'To London today, L[eonard] with my Jack's article to the Times, I to Spiller about my spectacles; & I must get a new pair at a cost of £2.2. After that we met at the London Library . . .'

See also 'Stopford Brooke' above and 'Fantasy', *III VW Essays*. Reprinted: *CW*.

2 – Lawrence Pearsall Jacks (1860–1955), unitarian divine, principal of Manchester College, Oxford, 1915–31.

3 – *Philosophers in Trouble*, 'Bracketed First', p. 34: 'Those who are unfamiliar

with the ways of our University may learn with a gentle surprise that in the one subject which, from its nature, deals with Practice, the highest Degrees are obtainable without any Practical Examination whatsoever. That subject is Moral Science.'

4 – *Mad Shepherds*, 'A Grave Digger Scene' [sic], p. 213.

5 – For Farmer Perryman see *Mad Shepherds*; for Farmer Jeremy and Peter Rodright, *Among the Idolmakers*.

6 – *Among the Idolmakers*, 'The Castaway', p. 23; see also at n. 9 below.

7 – *Mad Shepherds*, 'Shepherd Toller O' Clun Downs', p. 140, which has 'Time', and forms part of a longer sentence.

8 – *All Men Are Ghosts*, the title story, p. 110.

9 – *Among the Idolmakers*, 'The Castaway', p. 23.

A Book of Essays

The order of the serious sixpenny weekly paper must originally have been evolved like the now almost extinct order of the meats and the sweets, in deference to some demand of the public appetite. It is a rule that after the politics we come to the lighter form of essay and so to the reviews; and as this order is never upset, it must have been devised either for our pleasure or for our good. We are confessing an abnormality, then, when we say that to us the essay is the superfluous part of the feast. To be honest, we can only bring ourselves to read it if the train has stopped for more than twenty minutes in a fog and it is no longer amusing to speculate upon the lost terrier for whom a reward is offered in the advertisements. We find our justification in the belief that there is nothing quite so rare as a good essay and nothing quite so dismal as a bad one. The very titles are enough to darken the landscape; the groan of the slave at his task is audible to our ears. Our gorge rises at the thought of all the turns and twists and devices which some fellow-creature is going through in order to persuade us to swallow a fragment of the truth without recognising it. For the essay is now chiefly employed to mitigate the severity of Acts, reforms, and social questions; it entices us to perform the operation of thinking under an anaesthetic. Worse still, there may be no question of thinking; the only question may be how best to amuse the public for the space of 1,500 or 2,000 words, in which case the essay is no more than a dance upon the tight rope, where if a single caper is cut clumsily the acrobat suffers death or humiliation before our eyes.

For these reasons there is one course in our weekly dinner which we invariably omit, and thus it comes about that we read Mr Robert Lynd for the first time. With reasons to back us we do not intend to climb down unreservedly, but we must admit that we might do better than read the advertisements next time the train stops in a fog. Mr Lynd is so competent a writer that we need have no fear that he is going to break his bones, and there are sure signs that he enjoys his work. Whether he writes upon the 'Horrors of War', or 'Grub', upon 'Taking a Walk in London', or 'Revenge' he seems to be following his own bent without too much anxiety either for our good or for our entertainment. The narrowness of his limits does not obviously constrict him, nor does he think it necessary because he has only fifteen hundred words at his disposal to make each one do the work of ten. The exigencies of the time may make it necessary to consider either 'Courage', or 'Treating', or 'Refugees', but that forbidding signpost is in his mind, the centre of all sorts of pleasant paths which lead either to the humours of the public house or, by way of a red omnibus and the Strand, to the top of a little eminence such as this:

We are exiles, if not fugitives, from the perfect city. We are sojourners and strangers under the sun; we build houses of a day in the valleys of death. There seems to be no patriotism of the earth for many of those, like St Paul, whose patriotism is in Heaven. Their psalms and hymns are like native songs remembered by those who will admit no citizenship here. The saint is still a foreigner in every land, a sorrowing refugee from skies not ours.[2]

In addition to the literary skill here displayed, which could be matched easily by other quotations, Mr Lynd has all the merits of an open and generous mind. He is always tolerant and for the most part sanguine, and would rather spoil his period than make a point at the expense of some charity or decency. The streets of London offer so many charming thoughts to one of his fertile fancy that it would be most excusable in him to find no room for his final reflection: 'We must never be allowed to enjoy walking in London till London has been made fit to walk in.'[3] Thus remembering the claims of humanity he no doubt willingly suppresses what we take to be the chief stock-in-trade of the essayist – himself. It is a most serious omission. Whether a first-rate essay has ever been written which is not the ripe fruit of egoism may be doubted. The essays of Elia[4] are so many confidences which impart to us the most private secrets of Lamb's heart. There is room in them for all sorts of facts about his whims and habits, but there is very little concern for the public good. The most delightful parts of Montaigne's essays[5] are those where he breaks from the consideration of some abstract quality to explore the peculiarities of his body or his soul. It is the same with Hazlitt, or with Thackeray in the *Roundabout Papers*.[6] None of these men has the least fear of giving himself away, and, perhaps, in a short piece that is the only thing of value that one can give away. In 2,000 words you cannot do much to reform society or inculcate morality, but you can tell us about your imperfect sympathies, your poor relations, or 'Mackery End in Hertfordshire'.[7] When we consider that this gift of intimacy is the most difficult of all to make, and that to convey anything so personal needs the impersonality of the highest art, we need not wonder that it is not often offered us between the politics and the reviews. We have reason indeed to be grateful when an essayist like Mr Lynd writes well enough to make us remember the possibilities of his form.

1 – A review in the *TLS*, 17 January 1918, (Kp c98), of *If The Germans Conquered England and Other Essays* (Maunsel & Co. Ltd., 1917) by Robert (Wilson) Lynd (1879–1949), literary journalist and essayist, editor of the *Daily News* (which in 1930 became the *News Chronicle*) and regular contributor, as Y.Y., to the *New Statesman*, 1913–39.
2 – Lynd, 'Refugees', p. 38.
3 – *Ibid.*, 'On Taking a Walk in London', p. 109.
4 – Charles Lamb (1775–1834), *Elia* (1st series, 1823; 2nd series, 1828) and *The Last Essays of Elia* (1833).
5 – Michel Eyquem de Montaigne (1533–92), *Essais* (1580, 1588); see also VW's 'Montaigne', *IV VW Essays* and *CR1*.
6 – William Hazlitt (1778–1830); see also VW's 'William Hazlitt', *V VW Essays* and *CR2*; W. M. Thackeray (1811–63), *The Roundabout Papers* (1863).
7 – As did Charles Lamb in *Elia*: 'Imperfect Sympathies', 'My Relations' and 'Mackery End, in Hertfordshire'.

'The Green Mirror'

In the drawing room, over the mantelpiece, there hung a green mirror. Many generations of the Trenchard family had seen themselves reflected in its depths. Save for themselves and for the reflection of themselves they had never seen anything else for perhaps three hundred years, and in the year 1902 they were still reflected with perfect lucidity. If there was any room behind the figures for chair or table, tree or field, chairs, tables, trees and fields were now and always had been the property of the Trenchard family. It is impossible to limit the pride of this family in itself.

Not to be a Trenchard was to be a nigger or a Chinaman[2] . . . The Trenchards had never been conceited people – conceit implied too definite a recognition of other people's position and abilities. To be conceited you must think yourself abler, more interesting, richer, handsomer than someone else – and no Trenchard ever realised anyone else.[3]

The reader who is acquainted with modern fiction will at this point reflect that he has met these people or their relations already; they must belong to that composite group of English families created by Mr Galsworthy, Mr Arnold Bennett and Mr E. M. Forster.[4] Very different in detail, they all share a common belief that there is only one view of the world, and one family; and invariably at the end the mirrors break, and the new generation bursts in.

This is said more in order to describe Mr Walpole's novel than to criticise it, although it is by this door that criticism will enter. There is no fault to be found with the theme. If the family theme has taken the place of the love theme with our more thoughtful writers, that goes to prove that for this generation it is the more fertile of the two. It has so many sides to it, like all living themes, that there is no reason why one book should repeat another. You may destroy the family and salute the dawn by any means at your disposal, passion, satire, or humour, provided that you are in love with your cause. But the danger of a cause which has had great exponents lies in its power to attract recruits who are converts to other people's reforms but are not reformers themselves. In so far as Mr Walpole presents the Trenchard family as a type of the pig-headed British race with its roots in the past and its head turned backwards he seems to us to fail. The place for the Trenchard type is the didactic stage. All the exaggerations of their insularity would hit the mark delivered from the mouths of actors, but from the mouths of people in a book with the merits of this book they sound forced and unreal. 'It was one of the Trenchard axioms that anyone who crossed the English Channel con-ferred a favour';[5] no Trenchard can marry a man who thinks 'Russia such a fine country'.[6] And quite in keeping with the limelight is the Uncle's well-known lecture upon the approaching break-up of his class. 'Nearly the whole of our class in England has, ever since the beginning of last century, been happily asleep . . . Oh, young Mark's just one of the advance guard. He's smashing up the Trenchards with his hammer the same way that all the families like us up and down England are being smashed up.'[7] The hammer is thrown and the mirror comes down with a crash. Upstairs a very old Mr Trenchard falls back dead; and out we pour into the street looking askance at the passers-by as though we ought to tell them too that another English family has been smashed to splinters and freedom is stealing over the roof-tops.

Mr Walpole's gift is neither for passion nor for satire, but he possesses an urbane observant humour. He has a true insight into the nature of domesticity. He can render perfectly the 'friendly confused smell of hams and medicine, which is the Stores note of welcome'.[8] The psychology of a lady charged with the exciting duty of buying three hot-water bottles is no secret to him. We have seldom met a better account of a long Sunday in the country and the cold supper with which it ends. On this occasion the servants were out, and there was no soup. These are the small things in which Mr Walpole is invariably happy, and in our view it is no disparagement to a writer to say that his gift is for the small things rather than for the large. Scott was master of the large method, but Jane Austen[9] was mistress of the small. If you are faithful with the details the large effects will grow inevitably out of those very details. In its way the portrait of the hobbledehoy brother Henry is a large achievement, based though it is upon a careful study of hot-water bottles and Sunday suppers. The aunts, too, when they are not drawn violently from their orbits by the young man who has spent some years in Moscow, prattle, squabble, and make it up again in the warm soft atmosphere of true imagination. There is no reason for Mr Walpole to apologise for what is slow, uneventful, and old-fashioned in the world which he portrays. We feel convinced that in these respects the war has done nothing to change it. The Trenchard family, far from having sprung apart when the mirror was unfortunately broken, had it mended at an expensive shop in Bond Street, and it was hanging as usual over the mantelpiece on 4 August 1914. Mrs Trenchard never did anything so hysterical as to turn her daughter from her house because she married a young man who talked rather superficially about Russia. Mother and daughter are at this moment knitting comforters together. The only person who turned out badly, as Mrs Trenchard said he would, was Mr Philip Mark – but it is no business of ours to write other people's novels. We confess that in this case we should like to, but that is only because Mr Walpole has done it in many respects so extremely well himself.

1 – A review in the *TLS*, 24 January 1918, (Kp C99) of *The Green Mirror. A Quiet Story* (Macmillan & Co. Ltd., 1918) by Hugh Walpole (1884–1941). See also 'A View of the Russian Revolution' below. Reprinted: *CW*.
2 – Walpole, bk. i, ch. III, p. 42.
3 – *Ibid.*, p. 43.
4 – John Galsworthy (1867–1933); Arnold Bennett (1867–1931); E. M. Forster (1879–1970).
5 – Walpole, bk i, ch. III, p. 59, part of a longer sentence.
6 – *Ibid.*, bk i, ch. VI, p. 129.
7 – *Ibid.*, bk ii, ch. VI, pp. 277–8.
8 – *Ibid.*, bk ii, ch. II, p. 167, which has: 'friendly, confused'; and 'medicines which'.
9 – Sir Walter Scott (1771–1832), of whose work, incidentally, Walpole was a devoted admirer; Jane Austen (1775–1817).

Across the Border

When Miss Scarborough describes the results of her inquiries into the supernatural in fiction as 'suggestive rather than exhaustive'[2] we have only to add that in any discussion of the supernatural suggestion is perhaps more useful than an attempt at science. To mass together all sorts of cases of the supernatural in literature without much more system or theory than the indication of dates supplies leaves the reader free where freedom has a special value. Perhaps some psychological law lies hidden beneath the hundreds of stories about ghosts and abnormal states of mind (for stories about abnormal states of mind are included with those that are strictly supernatural) which are referred to in her pages; but in our twilight state it is better to guess than to assert, to feel than to classify our feelings. So much evidence of the delight which human nature takes in stories of the supernatural will inevitably lead one to ask what this interest implies both in the writer and in the reader.

In the first place, how are we to account for the strange human craving for the pleasure of feeling afraid which is so much involved in our love of ghost stories? It is pleasant to be afraid when we are conscious that we are in no kind of danger, and it is even more pleasant to be assured of the mind's capacity to penetrate those barriers which for twenty-three hours out of the twenty-four remain impassable. Crude fear, with its anticipation of physical pain or of terrifying uproar, is an undignified and demoralising sensation, while the mastery of fear only produces a respectable mask of courage, which is of no great interest to ourselves, although it may impose upon others. But the fear which we get from reading ghost stories of the supernatural is a refined and spiritualised essence of fear. It is a fear which we can examine and play with. Far from despising ourselves for being frightened by a ghost story we are proud of this proof of sensibility, and perhaps unconsciously welcome the chance for the licit gratification of certain instincts which we are wont to treat as outlaws. It is worth noticing that the craving for the supernatural in literature coincided in the eighteenth century with a period of rationalism in thought, as if the effect of damming the human instincts at one point causes them to overflow at another. Such instincts were certainly at full flood when the writings of Mrs Radcliffe[3] were their chosen channel. Her ghosts and ruins have long suffered the fate which so swiftly waits upon any exaggeration of the supernatural and substitutes our ridicule for our awe. But although we are quick to throw away imaginative symbols which have served our turn, the desire persists. Mrs Radcliffe may vanish, but the craving for the supernatural survives. Some element of the supernatural is so constant in poetry that one has come to look upon it as part of the normal fabric of the art; but in poetry, being etherealised, it scarcely provokes any emotion so gross as fear. Nobody was ever afraid to walk down a dark passage after reading The Ancient Mariner,[4] but rather inclined to venture out to meet whatever ghosts might deign to visit him. Probably some degree of reality is necessary in order to produce fear; and reality is best conveyed by prose. Certainly one of the finest ghost stories, Wandering Willie's Tale in Redgauntlet,[5] gains immensely from the homely truth of the setting, to which the use of the Scotch dialect contributes. The hero is a real man, the country is as solid as can be; and suddenly in the midst of the green and gray landscape opens up the crimson transparency of Redgauntlet Castle with the dead sinners at their feasting.

The superb genius of Scott here achieves a triumph which should keep this story immortal however the fashion in the supernatural may change. Steenie Steenson[6] is himself so real and his belief in the phantoms is so vivid that we draw our fear through our perception of his fear, the story itself being of a kind that has ceased to frighten us. In fact, the vision of the dead carousing would now be treated in a humorous, romantic or perhaps patriotic spirit, but scarcely with any hope of making our flesh creep. To do that the author must change his direction; he must seek to terrify us not by the ghosts of the dead, but by those ghosts which are living within ourselves. The great increase of the psychical ghost story in late years, to which Miss Scarborough bears witness, testifies to the fact that our sense of our own ghostliness has much quickened. A rational age is succeeded by one which seeks the supernatural in the soul of man, and the development of psychical research offers a basis of disputed fact for this desire to feed upon. Henry James, indeed, was of opinion before writing *The Turn of the Screw* that 'the good, the really effective and heart-shaking ghost stories (roughly so to term them) appeared all to have been told ... The new type, indeed, the mere modern "psychical case", washed clean of all queerness as by exposure to a flowing laboratory tap ... the new type clearly promised little'.[7] Since *The Turn of the Screw,* however, and no doubt largely owing to that masterpiece, the new type has justified its existence by rousing, if not 'the dear old sacred terror',[8] still a very effective modern representative. If you wish to guess what our ancestors felt when they read *The Mysteries of Udolpho* you cannot do better than read *The Turn of the Screw.*

Experiment proves that the new fear resembles the old in producing physical sensations as of erect hair, dilated pupils, rigid muscles, and an intensified perception of sound and movement. But what is it that we are afraid of? We are not afraid of ruins, or moonlight, or ghosts. Indeed, we should be relieved to find that Quint and Miss Jessel[9] are ghosts, but they have neither the substance nor the independent existence of ghosts. The odious creatures are much closer to us than ghosts have ever been. The governess is not so much frightened of them as of the sudden extension of her own field of perception, which in this case widens to reveal to her the presence all about her of an unmentionable evil. The appearance of the figures is an illustration, not in itself specially alarming, of a state of mind which is profoundly mysterious and terrifying. It is a state of mind; even the external objects are made to testify to their subjection. The oncoming of the state is preceded not by the storms and howlings of the old romances, but by an absolute hush and lapse of nature which we feel to represent the ominous trance of her own mind. 'The rooks stopped cawing in the golden sky, and the friendly evening hour lost for the unspeakable minute all its voice.'[10] The horror of the story comes from the force with which it makes us realise the power that our minds possess for such excursions into the darkness; when certain lights sink or certain barriers are lowered, the ghosts of the mind, untracked desires, indistinct intimations, are seen to be a large company.

In the hands of such masters as Scott and Henry James the

supernatural is so wrought in with the natural that fear is kept from a dangerous exaggeration into simple disgust or disbelief verging upon ridicule. Mr Kipling's stories 'The Mark of the Beast' and 'The Return of Imray'[11] are powerful enough to repel one by their horror, but they are too violent to appeal to our sense of wonder. For it would be a mistake to suppose that supernatural fiction always seeks to produce fear, or that the best ghost stories are those which most accurately and medically describe abnormal states of mind. On the contrary, a vast amount of fiction both in prose and in verse now assures us that the world to which we shut our eyes is far more friendly and inviting, more beautiful by day and more holy by night, than the world which we persist in thinking the real world. The country is peopled with nymphs and dryads, and Pan, far from being dead, is at his pranks in all the villages of England. Much of this mythology is used not for its own sake, but for purposes of satire and allegory; but there exists a group of writers who have the sense of the unseen without such alloy. Such a sense may bring visions of fairies or phantoms, or it may lead to a quickened perception of the relations existing between men and plants, or houses and their inhabitants, or any one of those innumerable alliances which somehow or other we spin between ourselves and other objects in our passage.

1 – A review in the *TLS*, 31 January 1918, (Kp C100) of *The Supernatural in Modern English Fiction* (G. P. Putnam's Sons, 1917) by Dorothy Scarborough, Ph.D., Instructor in English Extension, Columbia University. See also 'Henry James's Ghost Stories', *III VW Essays*. Reprinted, as 'The Supernatural in Fiction', *G&R, CE*.
2 – Scarborough, ch. VIII, p. 310.
3 – Ann Radcliffe (1764–1823), author of *The Mysteries of Udolpho* (1794) etc.
4 – S. T. Coleridge (1772–1834), *The Rime of the Ancient Mariner* (1798).
5 – Sir Walter Scott (1771–1832), *Redgauntlet* (1824), and the tale of Willie Steenson, the blind fiddler.
6 – I.e. Willie Steenson's father.
7 – Henry James (1843–1916), *The Novels and Tales of Henry James* (New York Edition, Macmillan & Co. Ltd, 1908), vol. xii, 'The Aspern Papers', 'The Turn of the Screw' etc., pref., pp. x–xi.
8 – *Ibid*.
9 – Peter Quint and Miss Jessel in *The Turn of the Screw* (1898).
10 – *The Turn of the Screw*, ch. III ('The Aspern Papers' and 'The Turn of the Screw', ed. Anthony Curtis, Penguin, 1984, p. 165).
11 – Rudyard Kipling (1865–1936), whose 'The Mark of the Beast' (referred to by Scarborough, pp. 100–1, 167) and 'The Return of Imray' were published in *Life's Handicap. Being Stories of Mine Own People* (1891).

Coleridge as Critic

In his preface to the *Anima Poetae* Mr E. H. Coleridge[2] remarks that the *Table Talk*, unlike other of Coleridge's prose writings, still remains well known and widely read. We do not know that the brief article by Coventry Patmore prefixed to this new edition tells us much more than that Mr Patmore was himself a Conservative, but if the preface had any share in the republication of the *Table Talk*,[3] we owe it our thanks. It is always well to re-read the classics. It is always wholesome to make sure that they still earn their pedestals and do not merely cast their shadows over heads bent superstitiously from custom. In particular it is worth while to re-read Coleridge because, owing to his peculiarities of character and to the effect which they had upon such portrait painters as Hazlitt, De Quincey, and above all, Carlyle,[4] we possess a very visible ghost – Coleridge, a wonderful, ridiculous, impossibly loquacious old gentleman who lived at Highgate and could never determine which side of the path to walk on. The loquacity can hardly have been exaggerated, but read the *Table Talk* and you will get what no portrait painter can possibly catch – the divine quality of the old gentleman's mind, the very flash of his miraculous eye. Whether or no it is a test of true greatness, his own words give us at once not indeed a sense of perceiving the distinction between the reason and the understanding, but of knowing him as no second person can reveal him: there is a being in the book who still speaks directly to the individual mind.

The comparison between Coleridge and Johnson is obvious in so far as each held sway chiefly by the power of his tongue. The difference between their methods is so marked that it is tempting, but also unnecessary, to judge one to be inferior to the other. Johnson was robust, combative, and concrete; Coleridge was the opposite. The contrast was perhaps in his mind when he said of Johnson:

his *bow-wow* manner must have had a good deal to do with the effect produced . . . Burke, like all men of genius who love to talk at all, was very discursive and continuous; hence he is not reported; he seldom said the sharp, short things that Johnson almost always did, which produce a more decided effect at the moment, and which are so much more easy to carry off.[5]

Modesty may have required him to say Burke instead of Coleridge, but either name will do. The same desire to justify and protect one's type led him no doubt to perceive the truth that 'a great mind must be andro-gynous ... I have known strong minds with imposing, undoubting, Cobbett-like manners, but I have never met a great mind of this sort.'[6]

But the chief distinction between the talk of Coleridge and that of Johnson, or indeed, between the talk of Coleridge and that of most of the famous talkers, lay in his indifference to, in his hatred of, 'mere personality'.[7] That omission rules out more than gossip; it rules out the kind of portrait painting in which Carlyle excelled, or the profound human insight so often expressed by Johnson. One cannot suppose that Coleridge would ever have lifted a poor woman to his shoulders, but he could be 'pained by observing in others, and was fully conscious in himself of a sympathy' with the upper classes which he had not for the lower, until, hearing a thatcher's wife cry her heart out for the death of her child, 'it was given him all at once to feel' that, while sympathising equally with poor and rich in the matter of the affections – 'the best part of humanity'[8] – still with regard to *mental* misery, struggles and conflicts his sympathies were with those who could best appreciate their force and value. From this it is plain that if we seek Coleridge's company we must leave certain human desires outside, or rather we must be ready to mount, if we can, into an atmosphere where the substance of these desires has been shredded by infinite refinements and discriminations of all its grossness.

The incompatibility which certainly existed between Coleridge and the rest of the world arose, so the *Table Talk* persuades us, from the fact that even more than Shelley he was 'a beautiful and ineffectual angel'[9] – a spirit imprisoned behind bars invisible and intangible to the tame hordes of humanity, a spirit always beckoned by something from without. Very naturally, to his fellow prisoners behind the bars his interpretation was confused, and from a philosophic point of view inconclusive. But there has been no finer messenger between gods and men, nor one whose being kept from youth to age so high a measure of transparency. His criticism is the most spiritual in the language. His notes upon Shakespeare are, to our thinking, the only criticisms which bear reading with the sound of the play still in one's ears. They possess one of the marks which we are apt to discover in the finest art, the power of seeming to bring to light what was already there beforehand, instead of imposing anything from the outside. The shock, the surprise, the paradox, which so often prevail and momentarily illumine, are entirely absent from the art of Coleridge; and the purity of his criticism is further increased by his neglect here also of 'mere personality'. The possibility that one may throw light upon a book by considering the circumstances in which it was written did not commend itself to Coleridge; to him the light was concentrated and confined in one ray – in the art itself. We have, of course, to take into account the fact that he never produced any complete work of criticism. We have only imperfect reports of lectures, memories of talk, notes scribbled in the margins of pages. His views are therefore scattered and fragmentary, and it is usual to lament the ruin wrought by opium upon the vast and enduring fabric which should have been built from these broken stones. But this mania for size savours rather of megalomania. There is a great deal to be said for small books. It is arguable that the desire to be exhaustive, comprehensive, and monumental has destroyed more virtue than it has brought to birth. In literary criticism at least the wish to attain completeness is more often than not a will o' the wisp which lures one past the occasional ideas which may perhaps have truth in them towards an unreal symmetry which has none.

Coleridge's mind was so fertile in such ideas that it is difficult to conceive that, given the health of a coal-heaver and the industry of a bank clerk, he could ever have succeeded in tracking each to its end, or in embracing the whole of them with their innumerable progeny in one vast synthesis. A great number spring directly from literature, but almost any topic had power at once to form an idea capable of splitting into an indefinite number of fresh ideas. Here are some chosen for their brevity. 'You abuse snuff! Perhaps it is the final cause of the human nose!'[10] 'Poetry is certainly something more than good sense, but it must be good sense at all events.'[11] 'There is no subjectivity whatever in the Homeric poetry.'[12] 'Swift was *anima Rabelaisii habitans in sicco* – the soul of Rabelais dwelling in a dry place.'[13] 'How inimitably graceful children are before they learn to dance!'[14] 'There is in every human countenance either a history or a prophecy.'[15] 'You see many scenes which are simply Shakespeare's, disporting himself in joyous triumph and vigorous fun after a great achievement of his highest genius.'[16] A respectable library could be, and no doubt has been, made out of these ideas; and Coleridge, not content with carrying the stuff of many libraries in his head, had what in England is more remarkable, the germs of an equal susceptibility to painting and to music. The gifts should go together; all three are perhaps needed to complete each one. But if such gifts complete a Milton or a Keats[17] they may undo a Coleridge. The reader of the *Table Talk* will sometime reflect that although, compared with Coleridge, he must consider himself deaf and blind as well as dumb, these limitations, in the present state of the world, have protected him and most of his work has been done within their shelter. For how can a man with Coleridge's gifts produce anything? His demands are so much greater than can be satisfied by the spiritual resources of his age. He is perpetually checked and driven back; life is too short; ideas are too many; opposition is too great. If Coleridge heard music he wanted hours and hours of Mozart and Purcell;[18] if he liked a picture he fell into a trance in front of it; if he saw a sunset he almost lost consciousness in the rapture of gazing at it. Our society makes no provision for these apparitions. The only course for such a one to pursue is that which Coleridge finally adopted – to sink into the house of some hospitable Gillman[19] and there for the rest of his life to sit and talk. In better words, 'My dear fellow! never be ashamed of scheming! – you can't think of living less than 4,000 years, and that would nearly suffice for your present schemes. To be sure, if they go on in the same ratio to the performance, then a small difficulty arises; but never mind! look at the bright side always and die in a dream!'[20]

1 – A review in the TLS, 7 February 1918, (Kp C101) of *The Table Talk and Omniana of Samuel Taylor Coleridge* [1772–1834]. With a note on Coleridge by Coventry Patmore [1823–96] (O.U.P., 1917). See *I VW Diary*, Monday, 4 February 1918: 'Up to the Times with a Coleridge article; & once more I lost myself, owing to the multiplicity of Water Lanes . . .' See 'The Man at the Gate', 'Sara Coleridge', *VI VW Essays*; and (especially in the light of VW's remark in 'A Sketch of the Past') *MoB*, p. 115: 'I always read *Hours in a Library* by way of filling out my ideas, say of Coleridge, if I'm reading Coleridge', see also Leslie Stephen on Coleridge in both the *DNB* and *Hours in a Library* (vol. iv, 1904). Reprinted: *B&P*. Reading Notes (Berg xxx), reproduced in Appendix I.

2 – *Animae Poetae. From the unpublished Note-Books of Samuel Taylor Coleridge,* ed. Ernest Hartley Coleridge (William Heinemann, 1895), Pref., p. vii.

3 – Originally published as *Specimens of the Table Talk of Samuel Taylor Coleridge* (1835), with a preface by H. N. Coleridge.

4 – For William Hazlitt (1778–1830) on Coleridge: *The Spirit of the Age* (1825); for Thomas de Quincey (1785–1859): *Selections Grave and Gay* (vol. ii, 1854); and for Thomas Carlyle (1795–1881), *The Life of John Sterling* (1851).

5 – Coleridge, 'Table Talk', 4 July 1833, pp. 256–7; the ellipsis marks the omission of: '; – for no one, I suppose, will set Johnson before Burke – and Burke was a great and universal talker; – yet now we hear nothing of this except by some chance remarks in Boswell. The fact is, . . .' Dr Samuel Johnson (1709–84); Edmund Burke (1729–97).

6 – *Ibid.*, 1 September 1832, p. 201, which has: '. . . of this sort. And of the former,

they are at least as often wrong as right. The truth is, a great mind must be androgynous. Great minds – Swedenborg's, for instance – are never wrong but in consequence of being in the right, but imperfectly'; 'I have known *strong* minds'; and 'I have never met a *great* mind'.

7 – The origin of this phrase has not been traced, but for an example of Coleridge's strictures on 'this Age of Personality' see his 'Friend', no. 10.

8 – *Ibid.*, 'Allsop's Recollections', pp. 444–5: 'I have often been pained by observing in others, and was fully conscious in myself of a sympathy with those of rank and condition in preference to their inferiors, and never discovered the source of this sympathy until one day at Keswick I heard a thatcher's wife crying her heart out for the death of her little child. It was given me all at once to feel, that I sympathised equally with the poor and the rich in all that related to the best part of humanity – the affections; but that, in what relates to fortune, to mental misery, struggle, and conflicts, we reserve consolation and sympathy for those who can appreciate its force and value.'

9 – Matthew Arnold, *Essays in Criticism. Second Series* (Macmillan & Co., 1888), 'Byron', p. 203: 'But these two, Wordsworth and Byron, stand, it seems to me, first and preeminent in actual performance, a glorious pair, among the English poets of this century . . . I for my part can never even think of equalling with them any of their contemporaries; – either Coleridge, poet and philosopher wrecked in a mist of opium; or Shelley, beautiful and ineffectual angel, beating in the void his luminous wings in vain.'

10 – Coleridge, 'Table Talk', 4 January 1823, p. 41.

11 – *Ibid.*, 9 May 1830, p. 91, which continues: '; just as a palace is more than a house, but it must be a house at least.'

12 – *Ibid.*, 12 May 1830, p. 93.

13 – *Ibid.*, 15 June 1830, p. 116.

14 – *Ibid.*, 1 January 1832, p. 166.

15 – *Ibid.*, 'Omniana', p. 377, which continues: 'which must sadden, or at least soften, every reflecting observer'.

16 – *Ibid.*, 'Table Talk', 7 April 1833, p. 224, which has: 'You see many scenes and parts of scenes which are simply Shakespeare's, disporting . . .'

17 – John Milton (1608–74); John Keats (1795–1821).

18 – Coleridge, 'Table Talk', 6 July 1833, p. 258: 'Some music is above me; most music is beneath me. I like Beethoven and Mozart – or else some of the aerial compositions of the elder Italians, as Palestrina and Carissimi. – And I love Purcell.'

19 – The hospitable James Gillman lived with his wife at The Grove, Highgate, and there Coleridge resided and presided from 1816 until his death. Gillman was the dedicatee of the original edition of *Specimens of the Table Talk* . . . (1835) and the author of an unfinished *Life* of Coleridge (1838).

20 – The origin of this passage remains untraced.

Mr Conrad's Crisis

To possess a fuller account of the processes which have produced some notable books we should be willing to offer their distinguished authors liberal terms in the shape of our gratitude, or, if it suited them better, promise to forgo a chapter here, a volume there, in return for the gift of a few pages of spiritual autobiography. It is no impiety. We are not asking that the creator should dismember his own creatures. We ask only to be allowed to look more closely into the creative process and see those whom we know as Nostromo, Antonia, or Mrs Gould[2] as they were before they came into the world of Sulaco, while they existed merely in the rarer atmosphere of their maker's mind.

For whatever we learn of their pre-existence undoubtedly adds to our understanding of them when they come before us as men and women of established character and settled destiny. An artist like Mr Conrad, to whom his work is the life of his life, can only speak of his characters in the tone with which we speak of lives that have an existence independent of our own. There is a suggestive power in what he says about his intentions or his affections for these people which enables us to guess at more than is actually said. It is necessary to help out the words themselves with whatever power of intuition we may possess. In the Note, which is of course much too short for our satisfaction, Mr Conrad tells us that after writing *Typhoon* there occurred

a subtle change in the nature of the inspiration; a phenomenon for which I cannot in any way be held responsible. What, however, did cause me some concern was that after finishing the last story of the *Typhoon* volume it seemed somehow that there was nothing more in the world to write about.[3]

It is for us to guess what this check in the course of his development amounted to. We should like to fancy that we see how it happened that when one conception had worked itself out there was a season of seeming emptiness before the world again became full of things to write about; but they were not the same things, and we can guess that they had multiplied in the interval. The knowledge of this crisis, if such we can call it, lends vitality to an old dilemma into which it is common to find people plunging when *Nostromo* comes up for discussion. Is it 'astonishing', or is it a 'failure',[4] as critics according to Mr Conrad variously term it, or can one hold that it is both?

In either case it is illuminating to know that it is the work of a writer who has become aware that the world which he writes about has changed its aspect. He has not got used to the new prospect. As yet it is a world in which he does not see his way. It is a world of bewildering fullness, fineness, and intricacy. The relations of human beings towards each other and towards those impersonal ideals of duty and fidelity which play so large a part in Mr Conrad's scheme of life are seen to be more closely related and finely spun than had been visible to his youthful eye. From all this there results a crowding and suffocating superabundance which makes *Nostromo* one of those rare and magnificent wrecks over which the critics shake their heads, hesitating between 'failure' and 'astonishing', unable to determine why it is that so much skill and beauty are powerless to float the fabric into the main stream of active and enduring existence. The demon which attends Mr Conrad's genius is the demon of languor, of monotony, of an inertness such as we see in the quiescence of the caged tiger. In *Nostromo* the tiger broods superb, supine, but almost completely immobile.

It is a difficult book to read through. One might even say, had he not in later books triumphantly proved himself master of all his possessions, that the writer would have been better served by slighter gifts. Wealth of every sort pours its avalanche from different tributaries into his pages. It would be difficult to find half a dozen thin, colourless, or perfunctory sentences in the length of the book. Each is consciously shaped and contributes its stroke to the building up of a structure to which we are sometimes tempted to apply terms more applicable to the painter's art than to the writer's. ' . . . there was not a single brick, stone, or grain of sand of its soil that I had not placed in position with my own hands,'[5] he tells us in that passage of his *Reminiscences* where he records how for twenty months, 'neglecting the common joys of life,' he 'wrestled with the Lord'[6] for his creation. One may be aware, perhaps, of the extreme effort of this labour of construction, but one is also conscious of the astonishing solidity of the result. The sun is hot, the shadows profound, the earth weighted and veined with silver; the very plaster of Mrs Gould's drawing room appears rough to our touch, and the petals of her flowers are red and purple against it. But in a novel we demand something more than still life, and where the still life is thus superbly designed we want humanity as largely modelled and inspired by a vitality deep and passionate in proportion to the magnificence of the conception. As is apt to be the case with any work by Mr Conrad, his characters have the rare quality of erring upon the side of largeness. The gestures with which they move upon his wide stage are uniformly noble, and the phrases lavished upon them are beautiful enough to be carved for ever upon the pedestals of statues. But when critics speak of the 'failure' of *Nostromo* it is probable that they refer to something inanimate and stationary in the human figures which chills our warmer sympathies. We salute the tragedy with a bow as profound and deferential as we can make it; but we feel that nothing would be more out of keeping than an offering of tears.

1 – A review in the *TLS*, 14 March 1918, (Kp C102) of *Nostromo. A Tale of the Seaboard* (1904; J. M. Dent & Sons Ltd, 1918) by Joseph Conrad (1857–1924). 'A vile windy day,' VW noted in her diary on Sunday, 3 March 1918. 'Sent off my Conrad article, at last – & printed a few [honey pot] labels for Bunny [David Garnett], but we stayed in, & were very happy.'

See also 'Lord Jim' and 'Mr Conrad's *Youth*' above; 'A Disillusioned Romantic', 'A Prince of Prose', 'Mr Conrad: A Conversation', *III VW Essays*; and 'Joseph Conrad', *IV VW Essays* and *CR1*.

2 – For an account of these characters, see Conrad, 'Author's Note' (dated October 1917), pp. x–xiii.

3 – *Ibid.*, p. vii, which has: 'What however did'. *Typhoon* (1902).

4 – Conrad, *Some Reminiscences* (Eveleigh Nash, 1912), ch. v, p. 173: 'I was just then giving up some days of my allotted span to the last chapters of the novel *Nostromo*, a tale of an imaginary (but true) seaboard, which is still mentioned now and again, and indeed kindly, sometimes in connection with the word "failure" and sometimes in conjunction with the word "astonishing". I have no opinion on this discrepancy. It's the sort of difference that can never be settled.'

5 – *Ibid.*, p. 176, which has: 'of its soil I had not placed'.

6 – *Ibid.*, p. 173.

Swinburne Letters

It is possible that before opening this book of Swinburne's letters the reader may ask himself what pleasure, considering the poet's genius, he has a right to expect. The achievements of poets as letter writers in the past would warrant the highest hopes. There are people who would exchange all Byron's poems for half his letters, and upon many shelves *The Task* is spruce and virginal while Cowper's correspondence[2] has the dog's ears, the sloping shoulders, the easy, inevitable openings of a loved companion. Again, no one would wish to sacrifice a line that Keats ever wrote; but we cling as firmly to some of his letters as to some of his poems. So far as it is possible to judge at present, Swinburne is not with these men among the great letter-writers. Perhaps it may not be fantastic to seek some clue to his failure in this respect in the familiar portrait by Watts[3] which is reproduced as a frontispiece to the present volume. It is rather the portrait of a spirit than the portrait even of a poet's body. The eyes are set upon a distant vision. The mouth is slightly pursed in concentrated attention. The whole aspect is exquisitely poetical; but it is also strangely fixed and set. One can imagine how such a figure would take its way through crowded streets looking neither to right nor to left. One seems to perceive an underlying wholeness of nature in this man which would make it unusually hard to turn him from his purpose or to impress him with a different purpose of one's own. The authors[4] of the present book contradict these speculations in their suggestive recollections by dwelling upon the 'plastic and sensitive' nature of Swinburne's temperament. He 'speedily took on', they write, 'the colour (for good or ill) of his immediate environment', which statement they prove by the fact that he 'changed with almost miraculous alacrity' as soon as he came to live with Watts-Dunton.[5] This may be true and yet not exclude a rigidity of mental character which, while it increased the fervour of his admirations and the violence of his denunciations, did not lend itself happily to the give and take of familiar correspondence.

The letters in the present selection begin in 1869 and end some ten years before the poet's death. The early and more interesting letters are addressed chiefly to Rossetti,[6] but the greater number are written to Watts-Dunton in the years before they set up house together at Putney. It is safe to say that they will give a great deal of pleasure to lovers of Swinburne because, if they fail in the peculiar intimacies, abandonments and improvisations which mark certain famous letters, they by no means fail to conjure up the astonishing ghost of Swinburne. He appears in the beginning as the extremely careful and sagacious critic of poetry. In 1869 Rossetti asked him to criticise the proof sheets of his forthcoming volume.[7] He received the criticism which only a poet could give. In reading it we have a sense of watching a jeweller handling his diamonds and rubies. Here it is a question whether 'the break'[8] does not come too soon and suddenly; here it is a matter of sound – a choice between 'what's' and 'what is';[9] here 'I should unhesitatingly reject the five added lines in the Haymarket ... because they utterly deaden and erase the superb effect of the lines preceding . . .[10] The "yesterday's rose in the bosom" is better than beautiful, being so lifelike, but I would condense if I could the thought into a couplet.'[11] Many of the criticisms were accepted, suffused as they were with the glow of Swinburne's already rapturous commendation. 'I cannot tell you how ineffable in wealth of thought and word and every beauty possible to human work I see that set of sonnets to be . . . or how brutally inadequate I feel the best and most delicate comment possible on them to be.'[12] But at the age of thirty-two there was a mean between Swinburne's loves and his hates not so perceptible in later life, as a criticism upon *The Earthly Paradise* will prove. '⟨Morris's⟩ Muse is like Homer's Trojan women; she drags her robes as she walks. I really think any Muse (when she is neither resting nor flying) ought to tighten her girdle, tuck up her skirts, and step out . . . Top's is spontaneous and slow.'[13]

The impious wish must sometimes occur to us that some friend could have done for Swinburne's mind what Watts-Dunton did for his body. So much beauty and truth, such wit and insight seem to have been buried beneath the explosions of his amazing but in its later developments so sterile vocabulary. The talent, for instance, which is displayed in *Love's Cross Currents*[14] foretold the advent and indeed proclaimed the presence of a delightful and original novelist. But the prophecy was never fulfilled. The critic in his turn suffered the same extinction or dissipation; for Swinburne's praise or blame blots out the object of it as effectually as a dust storm conceals a daisy, and the verbal whirlwind of his later utterance becomes as monotonous as the smooth drone of a large humming top. In reading his letters, however, the criticism which we have impatiently uttered is disarmed. There is a gallantry about this enthusiastic figure which is irresistible. Moreover, it is impossible not to lay the blame for such catastrophe as there was upon a thousand circumstances which are hidden, as so much of Swinburne's life remains hidden, from our knowledge. The British public whom he delighted to flout and to tease did not surround their surprising fellow citizen with an atmosphere of sympathy. Perhaps, indeed, the man who could persuade the secretary of the Society for the Suppression of Vice to state in public that his Society did not, as the poet asserted, intend 'to burke' Rabelais, Shakespeare, and the Holy Bible,[15] deserved to do penance every Sunday of his life at Putney, shut up in his room because he dared not venture out in the midst of the holiday-making crowd. That day, according to the authors of this book, was the 'one prosaic time of Swinburne's life at the

Pines'.[16] The company of the Elizabethan dramatists was not sufficient; he was forced to extend his hours of sleep. On the other hand, Captain Webb had only to swim across the Channel and no voice was more vociferous in his praise. 'I consider it,' Swinburne wrote, 'the greatest glory that has befallen England since the publication of Shelley's greatest poem, whichever that may be.'[17]

But in truth the staple of these letters is composed neither of poetic meditation nor of invective against the public; matters of business provide the chief theme of the letters to Watts-Dunton, and would threaten them with dulness if that danger were not always averted by some delightful thrust or phrase or suggestion. When all the difficulties of his publishing affairs had been arranged, his landladies still had drunken husbands, his books were still left behind him in London, his letters still succeeded in getting lost, his tradesmen still insisted upon being paid.

'Such is the present excess of human baseness, and such the weltering abyss of social anarchy in which we live, that this demoralised Mammonite, whose all would be at my disposal – his life and his property alike – in a commonwealth duly based on any rational principle of order and good government, actually requires money for goods supplied to Me.'[18] In such crises of daily life Swinburne instinctively took up his pen and wrote a full and eloquent statement of the case to Watts-Dunton. In one such document, written, he declares, in great haste, it is possible to count seven separate commissions. Watts-Dunton is to draw up a form of subscription to the *Pall Mall*; to find an unfinished article in a drawer; to discover the lost letter of a Hungarian countess; to explain how to answer and direct it properly; to give an opinion upon both parties in a libel action; to forward a large number of books and manuscripts, and to order a variety of magazines. Finally, he need not trouble about the missing penholder; that has already been found.[19]

---

1 – A review in the *TLS*, 21 March 1918, (Kp C103) of *The Letters of Algernon Charles Swinburne. With some personal recollections* by Thomas Hake and Arthur Compton-Rickett (John Murray, 1918). Having pronounced herself 'rejected by the Times [Literary Supplement]' (*I VW Diary*, Tuesday, 12 March 1918), VW declared on the 14th, 'My dismissal is revoked. A large book on Pepys arrived ['Papers on Pepys', below], which I spent the evening reading, & now another on Swinburne awaits me at the Railway station. I'm divided whether one likes to have books, or to write fiction without interruption. But I may make a few shillings to pay for my

Baskerville [edition of Congreve].' See also 'Watts-Dunton's Dilemma', *III VW Essays*.

2 – For VW on the poet William Cowper (1731–1800), see 'Cowper and Lady Austen', *V VW Essays* and *CR*2; the essay, based on Cowper's correspondence (4 vols, Hodder and Stoughton, 1904), contains, incidentally, a single buried quotation ('thistly sorrow') from *The Task* (1785).

3 – The quarter-length portrait in oils by G. F. Watts (1817–1904) is in the National Portrait Gallery (no. 1542).

4 – Thomas Hake (d. 1917) and Arthur Compton-Rickett (1869–1937), literary journalist, university lecturer, and author of several works including *A History of English Literature* (1912) and, with Hake, *The Life and Letters of Theodore Watts-Dunton* (1916).

5 – For all three quotations, *Letters*, p. 171, which has: 'This is shown by the almost miraculous alacrity with which he shed the "old Adam" as soon as he had come to live with Watts-Dunton.' Walter Theodore Watts-Dunton (1832–1914), critic, poet, and author of the novel *Aylwin* (1898), had first met Swinburne (1837–1907) in 1872. Seven years later, when Swinburne was in a state of nervous collapse, he invited him to stay at his home at The Pines, Putney Hill; and there Swinburne remained, 'quiet and sequestered' (*Letters*, p. 173), until his death.

6 – Dante Gabriel Rossetti (1828–82), following the tragic death of his wife in 1862, had shared a house with Swinburne, a fervent admirer of his work both as painter and poet, and with George Meredith, at 16 Cheyne Walk, Chelsea.

7 – *Poems* (1870).

8 – *Letters*, 10 December 1869, p. 23; the poem under discussion, not identified in the text, is 'Jenny' (ll. 9–13).

9 – *Ibid.*, 24 February 1870, p. 45: 'And I wish for my ear's sake, which liked the over-syllable, you had not (in "John of Tours") written "What's the crying," etc.'. these sprucifications of structure injure the ballad sound and style, which ought *not* to be level and accurate.'

10 – *Ibid.*, 10 December 1869, p. 22, which has: 'on the Haymarket'.

11 – *Ibid.*, p. 23, which concludes'; it reads a little draggingly.' The reference is to 'Jenny', probably paragraph nine.

12 – *Ibid.*, 24 February 1870, p. 44; the work under discussion is the cycle of love-sonnets 'Towards a work to be called The House of Life'.

13 – *Ibid.*, 10 December 1869, p. 25, which continues '; and, especially, my ear hungers for more force and variety of sound in the verse.' William Morris (1834–96), known to his friends as 'Topsy', published his poem *The Earthly Paradise* in 1868–70.

14 – Swinburne's *Love's Cross Currents* (1905) was originally published as *A Year's Letters* in the *Tatler*, (25 August–29 December 1877) as by 'Mrs Horace Manners'.

15 – *Letters*, to Edward Harrison, 7 July 1875, pp. 56–7, referring to an earlier correspondence in the *Athenaeum*; the secretary concerned is not identified. To 'burke': 'to kill secretly by suffocation or strangulation, or in order to sell the victim's body for dissection, as Burke did' (*OED*).

16 – *Ibid.*, p. 191.

17 – *Ibid.*, to Watts-Dunton, 27 August 1875, p. 58; Captain Webb swam the

English channel from Dover to Calais in just under twenty-four hours on 24 August 1875.
18 – *Ibid.*, to the same, 30 January 1873, which has '*Me*'.
19 – *Ibid.*, 22 June 1879. The discovery of the 'penholder' is in fact recorded earlier in the letter, before the reference to the (unidentified) Hungarian countess.

Papers on Pepys

The number of those who read themselves asleep at night with Pepys[2] and awake at day with Pepys must be great. By the nature of things, however, the number of those who read neither by night nor by day is infinitely greater; and it is, we believe, by those who have never read him that Pepys is, as Mr Wheatley complains, treated with contempt. The Pepys Club 'may be considered', Mr Wheatley writes, 'as a kind of missionary society to educate the public to understand that they are wrong in treating Pepys with affection, tempered with lack of respect'.[3] The papers published in the present volume would not have suggested to us so solemn a comparison. A missionary society, however, which dines well, sings beautifully old English songs, and delivers brief and entertaining papers upon such subjects as Pepys's portraits, Pepys's stone, Pepys's ballads, Pepys's health, Pepys's musical instruments,[4] although it differs, we imagine, in method from some sister institutions, is well calculated to convert the heathen. Lack of respect for Pepys, however, seems to us a heresy which is beyond argument, and deserving of punishment rather than of the persuasive voices of members of the Pepys Club singing 'Beauty Retire'.[5]

For one of the most obvious sources of our delight in the diary arises from the fact that Pepys, besides being himself, was a great civil servant. We are glad to remember that it has been stated on authority, however well we guessed it for ourselves, that Pepys was 'without exception the greatest and most useful Minister that ever filled the same situation in England, the acts and registers of the Admiralty proving this beyond contradiction'.[6] He was the founder of the modern Navy, and the fame of Mr Pepys as an administrator has had an independent existence of its own within the walls of the Admiralty from his day to ours. Indeed, it is possible to believe that we owe the diary largely to his eminence as an official. The reticence, the pomposity, the observance of appearances which their duties require, or at least exact, of great public servants must make it more congenial to them than to others to unbend and unbosom themselves in private. We can only regret that the higher education of women now enables the wives of public men to receive confidences which should have been committed to cipher. Happily for us, Mrs Pepys[7] was a very imperfect confidante. There were other matters besides those naturally unfit for a wife's ear that Pepys brought home from the office and liked to deliver himself upon in private. And thus it comes about that the diary runs naturally from affairs of State and the characters of ministers to affairs of the heart and the characters of servant girls; it includes the buying of clothes, the losing of tempers, and all the infinite curiosities, amusements, and pettinesses of average human life. It is a portrait where not only the main figure, but the surroundings, ornaments, and accessories are painted in. Had Mrs Pepys been as learned, discreet, and open-minded as the most advanced of her sex are now reputed to be, her husband would still have had enough over to fill the pages of his diary. Insatiable curiosity, and unflagging vitality were the essence of a gift to which, when the possessor is able to impart it, we can give no lesser name than genius.

It is worth reminding ourselves that because we are without his genius it does not follow that we are without his faults. The chief delight of his pages for most of us may lie not in the respectable direction of historical investigation, but in those very weaknesses and idiosyncrasies which in our own case we would die rather than reveal; but our quick understanding betrays the fact that we are fellow-sinners, though unconfessed. The state of mind that makes possible such admission of the undignified failings even in cipher may not be heroic, but it shows a lively, candid, unhypocritical nature which, if we remember that Pepys was an extremely able man, a very successful man and honourable beyond the standard of his age, fills out a figure which is perhaps a good deal higher in the scale of humanity than our own.

But those select few who survive the 'vast and devouring space'[8] of the centuries are judged not by their superiority to individuals in the flesh, but by their rank in the society of their peers, those solitary survivors of innumerable and nameless multitudes. Compared with most of these figures, Pepys is small enough. He is never passionate, exalted, poetic, or profound. His faults are not great ones, nor is his repentance sublime. Considering that he used cipher, and on occasion double cipher, to screen him in the confessional, he did not lay bare very deep or very intricate regions of the soul. He has little consciousness of dream or mystery, of conflict or perplexity. Yet it is impossible to write Pepys off as a man of the dumb and unanalytic past, or of the past which is ornate and fabulous; if ever we feel ourselves in the presence of a man so modern that we should not be surprised to meet him in the street and should know him and speak to him at once, it is when we read this diary, written more than two hundred and fifty years ago.

This is due in part to the unstudied ease of the language, which may be slipshod but never fails to be graphic, which catches unfailingly the butterflies and gnats and falling petals of the moment, which can deal with a day's outing or a merrymaking or a brother's funeral so that we latecomers are still in time to make one of the party. But Pepys is modern in a deeper sense than this. He is modern in his consciousness of the past, in his love of pretty civilised things, in his cultivation, in his quick and varied sensibility. He was a collector and a connoisseur; he delighted not only in books, but in old ballads and in good furniture. He was a man who had come upon the scene not so early but that there was already a fine display of curious and diverting objects accumulated by an older generation. Standing midway in our history, he looks consciously and intelligently both backwards and forwards. If we turn our eyes behind us we see him gazing in our direction, asking with eager curiosity of our progress in science, of our ships and sailors. Indeed, the very fact that he kept a diary seems to make him one of ourselves.

Yet in reckoning, however imperfectly, the sources of our pleasure we must not forget that his age is among them. Sprightly, inquisitive, full of stir and life as he is, nevertheless Mr Pepys is now two hundred and eighty-five years of age. He can remember London when it was very much smaller than it is now, with gardens and orchards, wild duck and deer. Men 'justled for the wall and did kill one another'.[9] Gentlemen were murdered riding out to their country houses at Kentish Town. Mr Pepys and Lady Paulina[10] were much afraid of being set upon when they drove back at night, though Mr Pepys concealed his fears. They very seldom took baths, but, on the other hand, they dressed in velvet and brocade. They acquired a great deal of silver plate too, especially if they were in the public service, and a present of gloves for your wife might well be stuffed with guineas. Ladies put on their vizards at the play – and with reason if their cheeks were capable of blushing. Sir Charles Sedley[11] was so witty once with his companion that you could not catch a word upon the stage. As for Lady Castlemaine,[12] we should never persuade Mr Pepys that the sun of beauty did not set once and for all with her decline. It is an atmosphere at once homely and splendid, coarse and beautiful, of a world far away and yet very modern that is preserved in his pages.

The Pepys Club, which draws its life from so fertile a source, may well flourish and multiply its members. The portraits reproduced here, in particular a page of Mr Pepys's 'individual features',[13] are of themselves sufficient to make this volume of memorable interest. And yet there is one contribution which we would rather have left unread. It consists only of a little Latin, a few signs, two or three letters of the alphabet, such as any oculist in Harley Street will write you out upon half a sheet of note-paper for a couple of guineas.[14] But to Samuel Pepys it would have meant a pair of spectacles, and what that pair of spectacles upon that pair of eyes might have seen and recorded it is tantalising to consider. Instead of giving up his diary upon 31 May 1669, he might with this prescription have continued it for another thirty years.[15] It is some relief to be told that the prescription is beyond the skill of contemporary oculists; but this is dashed by Mr Power's statement that had Pepys chanced to sit upon the 'tube spectacall'[16] of paper which his oculist provided so that he must read through a slit,

he would then have found his eye strain removed; his acute mind would have set itself to determine the cause; he would have pasted slips of black paper on each side of his glasses, and the diary might have been continued to the end of his life; whilst the paper he would certainly have read upon the subject before the Royal Society would have added still greater lustre to his name, and might have revolutionised the laws of dioptrics.[17]

But our regret is not purely selfish. How reluctant Pepys was to close his diary the melancholy last paragraph bears witness. He had written until the act of writing 'undid' his eyes, for the things he wished to write were not always fit to be written in long-hand, and to cease to write 'was almost as much as to see myself go into my grave'.[18] And yet this was a writing which no one, during his life at any rate, was to be allowed to read. Not only from the last sentence, but from every sentence, it is easy to see what lure it was that drew him to his diary. It was not a confessional, still less a mere record of things useful to remember, but the store house of his most private self, the echo of life's sweetest sounds, without which life itself would become thinner and more prosaic. When he went upstairs to his chamber it was to perform no mechanical exercise, but to hold intercourse with the secret companion who lives in everybody, whose presence is so real, whose comment is so valuable, whose faults and trespasses and vanities are so lovable that to lose him is 'almost to go into my grave'.[19] For this other Pepys, this spirit of the man whom men respected, he wrote his diary, and it is for this reason that for centuries to come men will delight in reading it.

1 – A review in the *TLS*, 4 April 1918, (Kp C104) of *Occasional Papers Read by Members at Meetings of the Samuel Pepys Club*. Ed. by the late H. B. Wheatley, First President of the Club, vol. i, 1903–14 (Pepys Club, printed at the Chiswick Press, 1918). See 'Swinburne's Letters', n.1 above. Reprinted: *B&P*.

2 – Samuel Pepys (1633–1703) whose diary was first edited in 1825 and not published in its entirety until 1893–6, in an edition prepared by H. B. Wheatley – also the author of *Samuel Pepys and the World He Lived In* (1880), a work cited by Leslie Stephen in his *DNB* entry on Pepys.

3 – *Occasional Papers*, H. B. Wheatley, 'The Growth of the Fame of Samuel Pepys', p. 173.

4 – *Ibid.*, Lionel Cust, 'Notes on the Portraits of Samuel Pepys', and Samuel Pepys Cockerell, 'Notes on Some Distinctive Features in Pepys's Portraits'; D'Arcy Power, 'Who Performed Lithotomy on Mr Samuel Pepys'; F. Sidgwick, 'The Pepys Ballads'; D'Arcy Power, 'The Medical History of Mr and Mrs Samuel Pepys'; Sir Frederick Bridge, 'Musical Instruments Mentioned by Pepys'.

5 – *Ibid.*, p. 1, 'Beauty Retire' (words from Davenant's 'Siege of Rhodes') was sung at all the club's dinners – immediately after the toast to Pepys's immortal memory.

6 – *Ibid.*, Wheatley, 'The Growth of the Fame of Samuel Pepys', p. 160, an unattributed quotation.

7 – Elizabeth St Michel (d. 1669) whom Pepys had married in 1655, when she was aged fifteen.

8 – The origin of this phrase, which VW also quotes in 'Sir Walter Raleigh', above, has resisted all attempts at discovery.

9 – The source of this quotation has not been found.

10 – Lady Paulina, daughter of Edward Montagu, 1st Earl of Sandwich (1625–72).

11 – Sir Charles Sedley (1639?–1701), wit and dramatist, author of *The Mulberry Garden* (1668) and of *Bellamira* (1687). For his witticisms at the theatre see Pepys's diary, 4 October 1664 and 18 February 1667.

12 – Barbara Villiers (afterwards Palmer), Countess of Castlemaine and Duchess of Cleveland (1641–1709), the notorious mistress of Charles II.

13 – *Occasional Papers*, Cockerell, 'Notes on Some Distinctive Features in Pepys's Portraits', illustrations between pp. 36–7, with portraits drawn or otherwise executed after the manner of Hayls, by Kneller, by Cavallier, and attributed to Le Marchand, and showing details extracted from these of Pepys's eyes, nose and mouth.

14 – *Ibid.*, D'Arcy Power, 'Why Samuel Pepys Discontinued his Diary', p. 75: 'For Samuel Pepys Esq. Spectacles – +2 D.c. + 0.50 D. cyl. axis 90°'.

15 – *Ibid.*, which has: 'with these glasses the Diary might have been continued at any rate for several subsequent years. Such a prescription would, however, have been impossible'.

16 – *Ibid.*, p. 71, quoting the diary, 11 August 1668.

17 – *Ibid.*, pp. 76–7, quoting the diary, 31 May 1669.

18 – *Ibid.*, p. 74, which has: 'And thus ends all that I doubt I shall ever be able to do with my own eyes in the keeping of my Journal, I being not able to do it any longer, having done it now so long as to undo my eyes almost every time that I take my pen in my hand . . .'

19 – *Ibid.*, which has: 'And so I betake myself to that course which is almost as much as to see myself go into my grave; for which and all the discomforts that will accompany my being blind, the good God prepare me!'

'Second Marriage'

Fiction is probably the most living form of literature in England at the present moment, and for that reason it is the most difficult to judge. Far from having reached its full height, it is in a state of growth and development; we scarcely know on opening a new novel what to expect; the most sagacious has difficulty in deciding where to draw the line, and nowhere perhaps do our personal prejudices so confuse what should be our aesthetic judgments. To sit with crossed hands impartially observant when everything that is said or done rouses some irrational antagonism or sympathy, is like or unlike what we are accustomed to call life, conflicts with or ignores rules tentatively framed beforehand, requires more than the usual degree of infallibility. Nothing is so hard to criticise as a new novel, but nothing is more interesting than to make the attempt.

Miss Viola Meynell[2] is not likely to upset anyone by the obvious novelty of her methods. She does not plunge you beneath the surface into a layer of consciousness largely represented by little black dots. She does not experiment with phrases that recur like the motive in a Wagner opera. She has no animosity against adjectives, nor does she exterminate verbs upon principle. Her characters are related to each other in the normal way, and they live in a house which is definitely stated to be situated in the Fen country.[3] All the same you will probably find yourself stopping before you have read very far in *Second Marriage* to ask yourself what Miss Meynell is after; for the picture is sufficiently unlike life to forbid anyone to rest in the belief that it is a straightforward story with one simple knot which the last chapter will successfully untie. The reader has always to answer some such question when the writer is anything of an artist; he has to adjust his sight to the focus of another. If in this case we have found the adjustment more difficult than usual it is not because there is any special complexity in the story. The story is too simple to require much analysis. It is made out of the different engagements and marriages of Rose, Ismay, and Esther, the three daughters of Mr and Mrs Glimour, of Skirth Farm, in the Fens. Concurrently with their story runs the story of the farm and in particular the story of the pumping engine, the invention of Arnold Glimour, a young man who has quarrelled with his cousins at the farm. Ismay Hunt, the incredibly beautiful daughter of the Glimours, returns home, a widow, after a year of marriage, endowed with three thousand pounds. Instead of using this sum to facilitate her sister's marriage, she invests it in the pumping engine, saves the land from the floods which threaten it, and finally marries the inventor.

And now the question is what impression Miss Meynell's arrangement of this story makes upon us. If it is for her to carry out her design faithfully, it is for us to attempt to see what she has meant us to see. In our case we must admit that the attempt has been attended with more of groping and straining than is consistent with complete pleasure, or indeed with the certainty that we have seen aright. The impression is a little inconclusive. In the first place the introduction of men and women with some degree of detail at once incites us to do what we can to imagine them alive and real. But the process has hardly begun when it is checked; for some reason, possibly connected with the flatness and scarcity of the dialogue, our instinct is snubbed; we begin to suspect that Miss Meynell does not care very much for life or reality.[4] If we are not to bother about life we must cast about until we find another track. It may be a novel of still life, a novel, such as Miss Meynell is well qualified to write, about substance and texture, with a design of men and women indicated like a fresco upon a wall. But from this conception of the right point of view we are roused by snatches of slang, by the apparatus of breakfast, dinner and tea, and by sudden attempts at brutality such as the scene when Arnold Glimour ties his young brother to a tree, stamps a shilling into the earth and laughs to see him grub it out with his teeth. The scene has a curiously medieval taste about it. The fight between Arnold and Maurice, for all its parade of violence, is best conveyed to us by one of Miss Meynell's precise observations: 'Up in the dark, raftered roof the cobwebs shook and waved in the wind of their fight.'[5]

In the end, then, we settle to listen to the reflections which life in general has suggested to a curious and very fastidious observer, to whom the Glimour family was known not very intimately but with discernment, and to whom the characters of trees and skies are as well worth watching as the character of human beings. The different aspects of water, the effect of summer mist upon the trees, the sound of a storm, are described not only with care but with a sudden unexpected intensity as if the writer, having allowed the mass of obvious ideas and commonplace words to stream past her, suddenly saw and selected the single one of interest to her.

For the wind never came with a clean smooth edge; what it was doing it was never doing right – like a diver who does not cut neatly into the water but falls flat upon it, to his own violence and destruction. The shuddering blow it gave the house was like all the violent things done wrong and awkwardly in the world; and one could imagine that the reason why the wind grew in fury was because every blow it gave with such awkward violence was as hurtful to itself as to what it struck.[6]

Applied to the lives of people – Ismay, Rose, Maurice, Arnold – this method has the effect of telling you some recondite detail about them while leaving entirely unnoticed the substance of which they are made. Moreover, by this method everything is told you; it never happens, nor is it ever said. Indeed the dialogue is curiously timid, put into the mouth, not issuing from it, and losing in its colloquial reality the beauty of quality which Miss Meynell so frequently attains in her carefully wrought passages of description and analysis. The fifteen minutes after a book is finished recreate the impression of the whole in the reader's mind as upon reaching home the course of a walk comes before you from start to finish. At the end of *Second Marriage* we see no particular person, we remember no particular scene, but we have a general impression of having examined in a pleasing and quiet way rather an intricate pattern, full of ornament and detail, hidden in a secluded place where the sun, falling through greenish panes of old glass, has no longer any heat.

1 – A review in the *TLS*, 25 April 1918, (Kp c105) of *Second Marriage* (Martin Secker, 1918) by Viola Meynell. 'Then I went to Guildford,' VW wrote in her diary on Thursday, 18 April. 'I don't see how to put 3 or 4 hours of Roger [Fry]'s conversation into the rest of this page; (& I must stop & read Viola Meynell) . . .'

2 – Viola Meynell (1886–1956), a daughter of the poet and essayist Alice Meynell (see 'Hearts of Controversy' above), was the author of several novels, a study of George Eliot (1913) and a memoir of the soldier-poet Julian Grenfell (1917).

3 – Meynell, bk 1, ch. 1, p. 7: 'From the edge of the fen into its farthest places one family had for ages past inhabited the drowned lands.'

4 – A point VW touched on earlier in writing, about an unspecified work, to Lady Robert Cecil, 18 February 1916 (*II VW Letters*, no. 743): 'I have also been reading ... Miss Viola Meynell who depresses me with her lack of realism.'

5 – Meynell, bk 3, ch. III, p. 272.

6 – *Ibid.*, bk 1, ch, XI, pp. 132–3.

Two Irish Poets

That the song of a nightingale is sad and that a poet desires fame are two statements that have all the authority of legend behind them. Thus, Lord Dunsany will find room in a page or two of introduction to the *Last Songs* of Francis Ledwidge[2] to lament that the poet died before he saw his fame. The regret seems more fitting in the case of a poet than it would be in any other case, although at first sight the ungratified desire for fame seems merely pathetic and the attainment of the desire even a little ridiculous. Why should fame mean so much to anyone? The reason why it means so much to a poet will, perhaps, occur to the reader of these *Last Songs*. They seem to ask with a simplicity denied to poets of a richer or more powerful gift that we should be in sympathy with the singer. It is not praise that he wants, but that we should be on his side in liking what he likes.

Without some such assurance the task of writing the kind of poetry which this book contains must be difficult:

> I took a reed and blew a tune,
> And sweet it was and very clear
> To be about a little thing
> That only few hold dear.[3]

Most of Mr Ledwidge's poems are about those little things that only few hold dear not because they are rare or remote, but because they lie all about us, as common as grass and sky. There are poems about Spring, and Autumn, and Youth, and Love, and Home;[4] and with no obvious ecstasy to thrill you it is difficult at first to see why Francis Ledwidge

ventured to make poetry where most of us are silent. But either you are
caught by a phrase like that about a tree at evening:

> And when the shadows muster and each tree
> A moment flutters, full of shutting wings,[5]

or by a sense of completeness such as the following lines, 'With Flowers',
convey:

> These have more language than my song,
> Take them and let them speak for me.
> I whispered them a secret thing
> Down the green lanes of Allary.

> You shall remember quiet ways
> Watching them fade, and quiet eyes,
> And two hearts given up to love,
> A foolish and an overwise.[6]

And you come to believe in the end that you, too, hold these things dear.
Mr Ledwidge has not made them great, or passionate, or different; but
he has believed in the worth of his own feelings; and he has believed that
there was enough sympathy with such feelings for him to confide in a
world rather ostentatiously interested in other things. His belief was
deep enough to give him delight in stating it whether the world listened
or not, whether the Irish fields were before his eyes or seen in imagination through the smoke of battle.

Irish blood produces a likeness which it would be easy to exaggerate,
and yet, reading first Mr Ledwidge and then Mr Stephens,[7] you cannot
deny that the likeness exists. It is to be found in a common rightness of
feeling, as if, with whatever difference of gift, it came by nature to them
to say neither too much nor too little, but to keep well in the middle of
the note. The lilt of the voice which we believe we can detect in their
literature no less than in their speech is also easy to feel though difficult
to analyse. Synge[8] was the most potent master of it, and in the hand of
his imitators we must confess to have grown a little tired of the Irish style
in prose. But in poetry the natural charm and natural turn of voice give
quality and style to slight verses which without that grace would be
almost negligible. The 'Reincarnations' of Mr Stephens are very graceful, but by no means negligible. Having printed his note at the end of the
book – a habit to be commended to all authors – we read through the
poems in the belief tl.at they were entirely his own work, and in that
belief admired his range and variety of mood. As a matter of fact

everything in the book 'can be referred to the Irish of some one hundred to three hundred years ago'.[9] In two cases only is the translation exact, and in the rest of the poems Mr Stephens himself could hardly tell at what point and in what measure his words have mixed themselves with the words of Raftery, O'Rahilly, and O'Bruadhair.[10] We get a generalised impression that Raftery was a master of easy melody, that O'Rahilly was a satirist, and that O'Bruadhair was the most complex of them all, well endowed with words and inclined to run them into an 'unending rebellious bawl':[11]

> As lily grows up easily,
> In modest gentle dignity
> To sweet perfection,
> So grew she,
> As easily.
>
> Or as the rose that takes no care
> Will open out on sunny air
> Bloom after bloom, fair after fair,
> Sweet after sweet;
> Just so did she,
> As carelessly.[12]

That is the voice of Raftery.

> The lanky hank of a she in the inn over there
> Nearly killed me for asking the loan of a glass of beer.
> May the devil grip the whey-faced slut by the hair,
> And beat bad manners out of her skin for a year.[13]

That is the style of the witty, eloquent and truculent O'Bruadhair. However closely or loosely these versions may fit the originals, each seems to come from the mouth of an Irishman, who writes from his tradition and not from ours. These poems, like the translations from the Chinese, make you aware of another attitude towards poetry, of another civilisation. The difference in this case may not be very profound; it may only be as the change from the Cockney accent to broad Devonshire; but, even so, the sound is welcome in our ears.

1 – A review in the *TLS*, 2 May 1918, (Kp C106) of *Last Songs* (Herbert Jenkins Ltd, 1918) by Francis Ledwidge and of *Reincarnations* (Macmillan & Co., 1918) by James Stephens.
2 – Francis Ledwidge (1891–1917), poet, labourer, and Irish nationalist, had joined the Royal Iniskillin Fusiliers in 1914 'to fight "neither for a principle, nor a people, nor a law, but for the fields along the Boyne, for the birds and the blue sky over

them"' (*DNB*); he was killed in Belgium on 31 July 1917. His two previous volumes of verse, *Songs of the Field* (1915) and *Songs of Peace* (1916), were also introduced by Lord Dunsany – Edward John Moreton Drax Plunkett, 18th Baron of Dunsany (1878–1957), author of plays and novels, who served as a captain in the R.I.F., 1914–18, and took part in the suppression of the Easter Rising, during which he was wounded and captured by the nationalists.

3 – Ledwidge, 'The Find', p. 63.

4 – *Ibid.*, 'Spring', pp. 58–9; 'Autumn', pp. 26–7; 'Youth', pp. 22–3; 'Spring Love', p. 40; 'Home', pp. 71–2.

5 – *Ibid.*, 'The One Who Comes Now and Then' (dated: Belgium, 22 July 1917), p. 68.

6 – *Ibid.*, 'With Flowers' (dated: France, April 1917), p. 62.

7 – James Stephens (1880?–1950), author of the classic Irish fantasy *The Crock of Gold* (1912).

8 – John Millington Synge (1871–1909), author of *The Playboy of the Western World* (1907), etc.

9 – Stephens, 'Note', p. 61.

10 – Anthony Raftery (1784–1834); Egan O'Rahilly (fl. 1690–1726); David O'Bruadhair (fl. 1650–94).

11 – Stephens, 'Note', p. 66.

12 – *Ibid.*, 'Peggy Mitchell', p. 6.

13 – *Ibid.*, 'Righteous Anger', p. 37.

Tchehov's Questions

An anonymous American critic, introducing *Nine Humorous Tales* by Tchehov to his contemporaries, defines the Russian writer thus: 'If Tchehov is more humanly self-revealing than de Maupassant, he is on the whole more deep than O. Henry. If O. Henry may be called the American Tchehov with a "punch", Tchehov may equally be termed the Russian O. Henry with a caress.'[2] You look at that rather as you look at an advertisement cow standing in a field among real cows. The critic has tried to cut out a pattern of Tchehov with a very large, but, alas! a very blunt pair of scissors. The shape is so grotesque that it does not fit even the shadow of Tchehov preserved from past readings; and this is the more disappointing because Tchehov is still one of the nebulous, undefined writers of whom one is glad to have even an outline.

Everyone has read him by this time; one can foretell a large and inquisitive public for the fifth and sixth volumes of his stories, but it seems doubtful whether there will result from all this reading a unanimous verdict such as was passed in so short a space of time upon Dostoevsky.[3] That hesitation may be a sign that he is not on a level with the greatest of the Russian writers. He is at any rate not among the unmistakable and overwhelming geniuses who bend you, whether you are upstanding or flexible, in the way their spirit blows. He is more on a level with ourselves. He is not heroic. He is aware that modern life is full of a nondescript melancholy, of discomfort, of queer relationships which beget emotions that are half ludicrous and yet painful, and that an inconclusive ending for all these impulses and oddities is much more usual than anything extreme. He knows all this as we know it, and at first sight he seems no more ready than we are with a solution. The attentive reader who is on the alert for some unmistakable sign that now the story is going to pull itself together and make straight as an arrow for its destination is still looking rather more blankly when the end comes. Perhaps it comes in this way. 'With whom was he angry? Was it with people, with poverty, with the autumn nights?'[4] That is the end of a story called 'The Post'. The postman has to drive a student to the station, and all the way the student tries to make the postman talk, but the postman remains silent, and at last the student falls silent too. Suddenly, just before they reach the station, the postman says unexpectedly, 'It's against the regulations to take anyone with the post . . . Yes. It makes no difference to me, it's true, only I don't like it, and I don't wish it.'[5] And he walks up and down the platform with a look of anger on his face. But why was he angry?

The recurrence of this question, not only in the form of an actual note of interrogation but in the choice of incidents and of endings, produces at first a queer feeling that the solid ground upon which we expected to make a safe landing has been twitched from under us, and there we hang asking questions in mid air. It is giddy, uncomfortable, inconclusive. But imperceptibly things arrange themselves, and we come to feel that the horizon is much wider from this point of view; we have gained a sense of astonishing freedom. The method that at first seemed so casual and inconclusive, ordinary and upon the level of our own eyesight, now appears to be the result of an exquisitely fastidious taste, controlled by an honesty for which we can find no match save among the Russians themselves. There may be no answer to these questions, but at the same time let us never manipulate the evidence so as to produce something fitting, decorous, or agreeable to our vanity. Away fly half the conclusions of the world at once. Accept endlessly, scrutinise ceaselessly, and see what will happen.

But it is easy to make out a message that is momentarily satisfying, and to dwell too emphatically upon the philosophy of Tchehov. His philosophy is, of course, inseparable from all that he writes, but it has to blend itself with another element that springs with immense vigour and fecundity from a very deep source. He is a born story-teller. Wherever he looks, whatever he sees, wherever he goes, stories shape themselves quickly and with a sort of spontaneous directness which reminds one of an earlier age of the world's literature when story-telling was natural to man. The whole mass of Russia seems to be leavened with the spirit, instead of small patches or thin crusts. Frequently one of Tchehov's peasants will ask to be told a story, and his friend, who is also a peasant, will pour out a story which is not funny or an adventure, but the history of his life, told with coarseness perhaps, but with a subtlety and passion which we accept from him, though it would be impossible to imagine an English farmer speaking thus. '"It is interesting," said Savka (the watchman and scarecrow), "whatever one talks about is always interesting. Take a bird now, or a man . . . or take this little stone; there's something to learn about all of them." '[6] Or it is an account of a dinner in a small country house, where the local doctor is one of the guests. He leads a very dull life, and when he has the chance over-eats himself enormously. Yet he begins almost at once upon the nature of life. 'Yes! if one thinks about it, you know, looks into it, and analyses all this hotch-potch, if you will allow me to call it so, it's not life, but more like a fire in a theatre!'[7] He goes on to describe his sensations in this blazing theatre. And this is not by any means the speech of Tchehov through a mask: the doctor speaks; he is there, alive, himself, an ordinary man, but he looks at things directly; there is in him too a fibre of individuality which gives out its own sharp vibration to the touch of life.

Innumerable as Tchehov's characters seem to be, they are all different, and their differences are indicated by fine clean strokes dealt with astonishing celerity and certainty, for the whole story often occupies only a page or two. And yet, we ask again, what aim is there behind this certainty? What was his purpose in defining so many scores of men and women, who are for the most part so disagreeable in themselves or in their circumstances so degraded? Did he find no connecting link, no final arrangement which is satisfying and harmonious in itself, although the parts which compose it are painful and mean? It is difficult not to ask that question, and the very fineness and delicacy of Tchehov's mind make it unusually difficult to be sure of an answer. He seems able with one tap to split asunder those emotions that we have been wont to think whole and entire, leaving them scattered about in small disconnected splinters. How much of your mental furniture remains entire when you have read 'A Dreary Story'?[8] Even when the tale is apparently straight-forward, another view of it is reflected in some mirror in the background. But if he were merely cynical, brilliant, and destructive, we should have no question to ask; we should already know the answer. He is more profoundly disturbing than any cynic because his gifts are so rich and various. But among these gifts there are at least three which seem to contradict those who hold him the novelist of hopelessness and despair. There is no one who seems endowed, even through the necessarily coarse medium of a translation, with a keener sense of beauty. In some of the stories we may find that this beauty is by itself sufficient. Again, there is an originality in his choice of the elements that make up a story which sometimes produces an arrangement so unlike any we have met with before that it is necessary to consider whether he is not hinting at some order hitherto unguessed at, though perhaps never fully stated by him. 'Gusev'[9] is an example of this. And, finally, in his cruelty, in the harshness of his pictures, especially of the peasants and of their life is there not by implication a statement of the only sympathy which is creative?

1 – A review in the TLS, 16 May 1918, (Kp C107) of The Wife and Other Stories, The Witch and Other Stories ... translated by Constance Garnett (Chatto & Windus, 1918) and of Nine Humorous Tales (Boston: Stratford Publishing Co., ?1918) by Anton Tchehov. 'L[eonard Woolf] has gone to a [League of Nations] meeting at the House of Commons,' VW noted in her diary on Tuesday, 7 May 1918. 'I've had a rush of books as usual: three Tchekovs [sic], Logan, Squire and Merrick hanging over me.' See also 'The Russian Background', 'The Cherry Orchard', III VW Essays, and see 'The Russian Point of View', IV VW Essays and CR1.

2 – No copy of Nine Humorous Tales has been traced. Anton Chekhov (1860–1904). Guy de Maupassant (1850–93). O. Henry (William Sydney Porter, 1862–1910).

3 – Fyodor Dostoevsky (1821–81), see 'More Dostoevsky' and 'A Minor Dostoevsky', above.

4 – The Witch, 'The Post', p. 58; VW also quotes this passage in 'The Russian Point of View'.

5 – Ibid., p. 57; the first sentence here is also quoted in 'The Russian Point of View'.

6 – *Ibid.*, 'Agafya', p. 123.
7 – *The Wife*, the title story, p. 60, spoken by Dr Sobol.
8 – *Ibid.*, 'From the Notebook of an Old Man', pp. 131–219.
9 – *The Witch*, pp. 147–67.

Imitative Essays

It is always a misfortune to feel oneself out of sympathy with another person's taste. You cannot reason about a question of taste; you can only feel for yourself; you are bound to feel strongly, and yet your feeling may be quite unintelligible to a third person. Mr Squire's book of essays provides us with a case in point. The first essay, 'The Gold Tree', describes a tree in a college garden, whose leaves turn gold in a wonderful autumn, hang miraculously beautiful for a season, and then vanish. The essay, after gently meandering through moralities which seem a little obvious, ends with this passage: 'But may it not be, perhaps, that when I am an old man, near my grave, I shall some day wander into the gardens below my window and find a second time the tree of gold, still and perfect, under a consoling autumnal sky?'[2] The sentiment of that is one that makes us uncomfortable. The murmur of voices, singing in church, a few chords struck gently in the dusk – these things also make us uncomfortable. We grow more and more solemn as we read with that uneasy solemnity which suddenly turns to untimely laughter. Let us quickly find something that it is permissible to laugh at. We hastily turn the page and light on this:

The cook, when middle-aged, had married a daughter of the keeper of the Great Seal; but she unhappily was one day killed by that ferocious animal (it was as large as a walrus) . . . and left her husband a widower with an only son, a small boy, who spent much of his time wondering about vain and foolish things. He wondered, for example, why he often heard of aeroplanes turning turtle, but never of a turtle turning aeroplane; and also why it was that no one ever threw a third or a quarter of a brick at anyone else.'[3]

Our plight is worse than ever; we are as glum as an undertaker in the spring.

These are questions of taste, that must be decided by the individual judgment of each reader. But if you are so unhappy as to be neither charmed nor amused by such sentiment or such humour, you will find yourself asking how it comes about that a writer who has shown himself a vivacious satirist, and at least a serious writer of verse, can produce so insipid a volume of prose. The answer seems to be that he has failed because he has tried to write beautifully. The danger of trying to write beautifully in English lies in the ease with which it is possible to do something very like it. There are the old cadences humming in one's head, the old phrases covering nothing so decently that it seems to be something after all. Preoccupied with the effort to be smooth, rotund, demure, and irreproachable, sentimentality slips past unnoticed, and platitudes spread themselves abroad with an air of impeccable virtue. A quotation from one of the eighty-nine pages of this expensive and beautifully printed book will show what it is that we are objecting to:

As the long scroll of memory unfolded he felt that he had walked all his manhood among phantoms; and he derived no pain from the reflection that his friends were dead, and he himself already half-forgotten, save as a legend. For he knew, watching the stream, that it would have been better had he remained all his life in that garden with that river that did not change. The fountains of speech, now he would willingly converse with the river, were rusted and choked; why, when he was young had they been sealed? Why had he been compelled to go round the world to find himself?[4]

The fatal effect of such smoothing and mincing is that as you read on and on and on you gradually cease to feel or to think; edges are rounded, colours are faded, one trite simile follows another, and yet it is done so decorously that you can never put your finger upon a definite evil. A lover of literature will tolerate many varieties of failure and hold them fertilising in their season, but what good cause is served by a volume of plausible imitation? Is it worth making a protest, not only because Mr Squire is capable of doing much better work, but because, poured voluminously into a world too busy or too careless to discriminate, such writing does more harm, we fancy, than work which is marked all over with the stamp of the second-rate.

1 – A review in the *TLS*, 23 May 1918, (Kp C108) of *The Gold Tree* . . . with initials designed by Austin O. Spare and cut in wood by W. Quick (Martin Secker, 1917) by J. C. (John Collings) Squire (1884–1958), man of letters, literary editor of the *New Statesman*, 1913–19. See *I VW Diary*, 7 May 1918, and 28 May 1918: 'The rush of books [three Tchekovs, Logan, Squire & Merrick] was disposed of, & Squire was well drubbed too'.
2 – Squire, 'The Gold Tree', p. 7.
3 – *Ibid*., 'The Walled Garden', p. 11, which has: 'a small boy who'.
4 – *Ibid*., pp. 14–15, which has: 'river which did not change'.

Moments of Vision

To some readers the very sight of a book in which the plain paper so generously balances the printed paper will be a happy omen. It seems to foretell gaiety, ease, unconcern. Possibly the writer has written to please himself. He has begun and left off and begun again as the mood seized him. Possibly he has had a thought for our pleasure. At any rate, our attention is not going to be stretched on the rack of an extended argument. Here is a handful of chosen flowers, a dinner of exquisite little courses, a bunch of variously coloured air balloons. Anticipating pleasure of this rare kind from the fact that Mr Pearsall Smith's *Trivia* seldom do more than reach the bottom of the page and sometimes barely encroach upon its blankness, we deserve to be disappointed. We deserve to find moral reflections or hints for the economical management of the home. Perhaps our unblushing desire for pleasure of itself deserves to be disappointed. We can fancy that many of Mr Pearsall Smith's readers will placate their consciences for the sin of reading him by some excuse about going to bed or getting up. There are times, they will say, when it is impossible to read anything serious.

It is true that there is little to be got from this book except pleasure. It has no mission, it contains no information, unless you can dignify with that name the thoughts that come into the head, buzz through it, and go out again without improving the thinker or adding to the wealth of the world. The head of the author of *Trivia* contains, as he confesses, a vast store of book learning; but his thoughts have little serious concern with that; they may light upon some obscure folio as a robin might perch for a moment upon a book before flitting to the marble bust of Julius Caesar and so on to the shining brass head of the poker and tongs. This lightness, more justly to be compared to the step of a crane among wild flowers, is perhaps the first thing you notice. The second is that although Mr Pearsall Smith has preserved the freshness and idiosyncrasy of his idea he has done so by the unostentatious use of great literary skill. Nor can we long overlook the fact that his purpose is as serious as the purpose that fulfils itself in other books of more ambitious appearance. If we are not mistaken, it is his purpose to catch and enclose certain moments which break off from the mass, in which without bidding things come together in a combination of inexplicable significance, to arrest those thoughts which suddenly, to the thinker at least, are almost menacing with meaning. Such moments of vision are of an unaccountable nature; leave them alone and they persist for years; try to explain them and they disappear; write them down and they die beneath the pen.

One of the reasons which has led to Mr Pearsall Smith's success is that he has taken neither himself nor his thoughts too seriously. Most people would have been tempted to fill the blank pages. They would have strained to be more profound, more brilliant, or more emphatic. Mr Pearsall Smith keeps well on this side of comfort; he knows exactly how far his gift will carry him. He is on easy terms with what he calls 'that Masterpiece of Nature, a reason-endowed and heaven-facing Man' [. . .] 'What stellar collisions and conflagrations, what floods and slaughters and enormous efforts has it not cost the Universe to make me – of what astral periods and cosmic processes am I not the crown and wonder?'[2] Nevertheless, he is conscious of belonging to that sub-order of the animal kingdom which includes the orang-outang, the gorilla, the baboon, and the chimpanzee.[3] His usual mood towards himself and towards the rest of us is one of ironic but affectionate detachment, befitting an elderly Pierrot conscious of grey hairs. The poplar tree delights him and the 'lemon-coloured moon'.[4] 'After all these millions of years, she ought to be ashamed of herself!' he cries out, beholding the 'great amorous unabashed face of the full moon'.[5] As he listens to the talk of the thoughtful baronet:

I saw the vast landscape of the world, dim, as in an eclipse; its population eating their bread with tears, its rich men sitting listless in their palaces, and aged Kings crying, 'Vanity, Vanity, all is Vanity!' laboriously from their thrones . . .[6] When I seek out the sources of my thoughts, I find that they had their beginning in fragile chance; were born of little moments that shine for me curiously in the past . . . So I never lose a chance of the whimsical and perilous charm of daily life, with its meetings and words and accidents. Why, today, perhaps, or next week, I may hear a voice, and, packing up my Gladstone bag, follow it to the ends of the world.[7]

The voice may be the voice of Beauty, but all the same he does not forget to pack his Gladstone bag. Compared with the 'whimsical and perilous charm of daily life',[8] compared with the possibility that one of these days one may discover the right epithet for the moon, are not all the ends of serious middle-aged ambition 'only things to sit on'?[9]

We have marked a number of passages for quotation, but as it would be necessary to quote them only in part we refrain. But the mark was not in the margin of the book; a finger seemed to raise itself here and there as if to exclaim, 'At last! It has been said.' And, without making extravagant claims for a gift which would certainly refuse to bear a weight of honour, to cut these passages into two or otherwise mutilate them would be to damage a shape so fitting and so characteristic that we can fancy these small craft afloat for quite a long time, if not in mid stream, still in some very pleasant backwater of the river of immortality.

1 – A review in the *TLS*, 23 May 1918, (Kp C109) of *Trivia* (Constable & Co., 1918) by Logan Pearsall Smith (1865–1946), American-born man of letters, educated at Harvard and Oxford, and from 1913 a British citizen. The Hogarth Press published his *Stories from the Old Testament* in 1920; *More Trivia* appeared in 1922.

'I write expecting Philip Morrell to dinner – not that one need dwell upon that – Wind East & violent rain & grey sky again . . .' VW noted in her diary on Tuesday, 7 May 1918, 'I must read Logan's Trivia now.'

See also 'English Prose', *III VW Essays*. Reprinted: *CW*.

2 – Smith, 'My Portrait', p. 14.

3 – *Ibid.*, 'The Author', p. ix.

4 – *Ibid.*, 'The Poplar', p. 138, which has: 'Moon'.

5 – *Ibid.*, 'The Full Moon', p. 53, which has: 'great, amorous, unabashed'.

6 – *Ibid.*, 'The Sound of the Voice', p. 25, which has: 'populations', and 'lugubriously', not 'laboriously'.

7 – *Ibid.*, 'The Coming of Fate', p. 9, which has: 'sense', not 'chance'.

8 – *Ibid.*

9 – *Ibid.*, 'Human Ends', p. 46.

Dreams and Realities

Several years ago, turning the pages of a miscellany of some kind in which bad verses abounded, the present reviewer chanced upon a scrap of poetry signed with the name of Walter de la Mare.[2] The name was then unfamiliar, and the little poem, since we have never seen it republished, did not perhaps seem to Mr de la Mare worthy of preservation. Yet to us the shock of surprise with which we encountered this sharply and, considering its surroundings, almost improperly individual voice is still memorable. Reading the verses once more in the expectation of reducing them to harmony with the mediocrity of their companions, we were forced by their persistent assertion of merit to conclude that someone by a fluke or a freak had brought off a success which he would never repeat again. In the light of Mr de la Mare's subsequent achievements this judgment, if we think it discriminating, was certainly pessimistic. The voice which sounded so fine and distinct in that obscure gathering of the commonplace now speaks not only to a large audience, but to a great number of listeners it is a voice which has no fellow. The surprise, the sense of finding an unseized emotion reduced to its unmistakable form of words, possesses us when we read his latest volume, as it possessed us then.

Of the many proofs of the value of poetry, the conviction that the poet has said what was hitherto unsaid is among the most conclusive. In future for that emotion or mood, which he seems half to create and half to reveal, there is no other poet who serves instead of him.

> Far are those tranquil hills,
> Dyed with fair evening's rose;
> On urgent, secret errand bent,
> A traveller goes.[3]

Many readers could recognise the authorship of that simple statement of a characteristic theme without a name to it. The shapes of the day have lost their form; the low limits of the world stretch far on the horizon; the voice comes to us from just beyond the verge of light. He is the poet of hush and silence, of the deserted house, of flowers bowed in the moonlight.

> Speak not – whisper not;
> Here bloweth thyme and bergamot;
> Softly on the evening hour
> Secret herbs their spices shower,
> Dark-spiked rosemary and myrrh,
> Lean-stalked, purple lavender;
> Hides within her bosom, too,
> All her sorrows, bitter rue.[4]

He is the poet who wakes when the world sleeps, the poet of dreams, the poet who, when slumber is heavy upon the earth, hears faint stirrings and far murmurs and footfalls, for above all, perhaps, he is the poet who rouses us to an expectation of something that we can neither hear nor see.

> 'Secrets,' sighs the night-wind,
> 'Vacancy is all I find;
> Every keyhole I have made
> Wail a summons, faint and sad,
> No voice ever answers me,
> Only vacancy.'

'Once, once . . .' the cricket shrills,
And far and near the quiet fills
With its tiny voice, and then
Hush falls again.[5]

The poem ends in silence and hush, but, strangely, the sound goes on.
The quiet has become full of tremors and vibrations; we are still listening
long after the words are done. Possessed of this secret, Mr de la Mare is
able in a few verses to make full contact between the reader and some
intangible feeling of mystery, wonder or fear.

Those who delight in marking out as definitely as may be the
circumference of a poet's mind will not fail to point out that Mr de la
Mare has not proved himself capable of writing anything so sustained
as, shall we say, the *Prelude*.[6] A poet who is above all things personal is
closely limited by the bounds of that personality. We may defer to this
criticism to the extent of admitting that when Mr de la Mare takes upon
himself to discharge a patriotic duty, as in 'Happy England' he writes
what many others might have written. His verses to 'E.T.'[7] have also an
air of being written in a broad daylight to which the writer is ill
accustomed. But it is a mistake to suppose that because the whimsical
and fantastic are specially akin to him he is therefore to be banished until
the moon is up and the flowers of a June night are whispering with
phantoms. He proves once more that the essence of reality is only to be
reached through the substance.

Where blooms the flower when her petals fade,
Where sleepeth echo by earth's music made,
Where all things transient to the changeless win,
There waits the peace thy spirit dwelleth in.[8]

In poems like 'Vain Questionings', 'Eyes' and 'Life'[9] Mr de la Mare gives
clear enough evidence of mortality. Far from being rapt on some moonlit
island remote from human passion, he is conscious of 'an endless war
twixt contrarieties' of a 'livelong tangle of perplexities'[10] of a necessity
binding us to turn back from ecstasy to 'earth's empty track of leaden
day by day'.[11] Without that understanding of the gross body which
divides the seer from the seen his vision of the spirit in plant and man
could not be so distinct, nor his command to seek beauty and love it
above everything so imperious.

Look thy last on all things lovely,
Every hour. Let no night
Seal thy sense in deathly slumber
 Till to delight
Thou have paid thy utmost blessing;
Since that all things thou wouldst praise
Beauty took from those who loved them
 In other days.[12]

1 – A review in the *TLS*, 30 May 1918, (Kp c110) of *Motley and Other Poems* (Constable & Co. Ltd, 1918) by Walter de la Mare. See also 'The Intellectual Imagination', *III VW Essays*.
2 – Walter de la Mare (1873–1956), poet, novelist and anthologist; his publications to date included *Songs of Childhood* (1902), under the pseudonym Walter Ramal; *The Listeners* (1912) and *Peacock Pie* (1913).
3 – de la Mare, 'The Three Strangers', p. 60.
4 – *Ibid.*, 'The Sunken Garden', p. 3.
5 – *Ibid.*, 'The Empty House', p. 15.
6 – Wordsworth's *The Prelude* (1805–6, 1850).
7 – For 'Happy England', see de la Mare, pp. 47–8; and for 'To E.T.: 1917', *ibid.*, p. 55.
8 – *Ibid.*, 'Vain Questioning' [*sic*], p. 41.
9 – *Ibid.*, 'Eyes', p. 36; 'Life', p. 37.
10 – For both quotations, *ibid.*, 'Vain Questioning', p. 40, which has: 'An endless war'.
11 – *Ibid.*, 'Life', p. 37: 'Still out of ecstasy turn trembling back/ To earth's same empty track/ Of leaden day by day, and hour by hour, and be/ Of all things lovely the cold mortuary.'
12 – *Ibid.*, 'Fare Well', p. 75.

The Claim of the Living

Mr George[2] is one of those writers for whom we could wish, in all kindness of heart, some slight accident to the fingers of the right hand, some twinge or ache warning him that it is time to stop, some check making brevity more desirable than expansion. He has ideas and enthusiasms, prejudices and principles in abundance, but in his fluency he repeats himself, bolsters up good arguments with poor illustrations, and altogether uses more paper than the country can well afford. The following sentence shows how his ideas tend to overlap each other owing to the speed at which they are composed: 'Autobiography has had its way with him ⟨Mr E. M. Forster⟩ a little in *A Room with a View*, and very much more in that tale of schoolmasters *The Longest Journey*, but it was *Howards End*, that much criticised work, which achieved the distinction of being popular, though of high merit.'[3] Thus hooking one statement to another Mr George rambles over a great many ideas connected with novelists and their art, and abuses the public at great length for its insolent neglect of the artist. Proof is added to proof. When Lord Curzon, the Bishop of London, and Mr Conrad come into a room which of them causes 'a swirl in "the gilded throng"'?[4] The attitude of the State to the novelist defines itself most clearly when a royal commission is appointed.'[5] What novelist has ever been asked to sit upon a royal commission? What novelist has ever been welcomed as a son-in-law? To cut the matter short, if the present Lord Nelson owns 7,000 acres of land, what is the amount of pension enjoyed by Leigh Hunt's daughter?[6]

But Mr George's chief claim to attention lies not in this voluble and elementary satire, but in the courage with which he has faced his contemporaries. It is a courage that overshoots its mark, but still it needs considerable courage to declare that one has found 'more that is honest and hopeful in a single page of *Tono-Bungay* than in all the great Victorians put together'.[7] It needs, oddly enough, some quality rarer than courage and more desirable to have read all the novels mentioned in this book and to hold a serious opinion as to their merits. For it is extremely difficult to take the writings of one's contemporaries seriously. The spirit in which they are read is a strange compact of indifference and curiosity. On the one hand the assumption is that they are certainly bad, on the other the temptation assails us to find in them a queer and illicit fascination. Between these two extremes we vacillate, and the attention we grant them is at once furtive, intermittent and intense. In proof of this let anyone read over the list of seven young novelists accepted by Mr George as the most promising of their generation – Mr Beresford, Mr Cannan, Mr Forster, Mr Lawrence, Mr Compton Mackenzie, Mr Onions and Mr Swinnerton.[8] The list is fairly representative, but certainly if our income depended upon passing an examination in their works we should be sweeping the streets tomorrow. We feel sure that such a test would produce a large army of street-sweepers. It is not that we have neglected to order a certain number of their novels from the library. It is not that, on seeing them before us, we have neglected to read them. But our knowledge is perfectly haphazard and nebulous. To discuss the point of view, the growth, nature and development of any one of these writers in the same spirit that we discuss the dead proves impossible. The difficulty which lies at the root of this attitude affects Mr George too, in spite of his enthusiasm for modern fiction and his proud claim for the prose form. He does not find it at all easy to make out what is happening.

The literary tradition is changing and a new one is being made.[9] Perhaps we may divide these seven writers into three groups – self-exploiters, mirror-bearers and commentators . . .[10] They stand midway between the expression of life and the expression of themselves . . .[11] A new passion is born, and it is a complex of the old passions; the novelist . . . needs to be more positive, to aspire to know what we are doing with the working class, with the Empire, the woman question, and the proper use of lentils. It is this aspiration towards truth that breaks up the old form: you cannot tell a story in a straightforward manner when you do but glimpse it through the veil of the future.[12]

Fiction is becoming chaotic and formless and omnivorous. But the attempt at a general survey, or at any grouping of tendencies, is very vague; and Mr George turns not without relief to the criticism of the novels in detail, to biographical sketches, and even to memories of garden parties on Campden Hill.[13] The criticism is not bad criticism, but it has too great an air of the personal and provisional to be accepted with conviction. There is no perspective, no security about it.

But the fault hardly lies with Mr George and scarcely at all with the novelists. They must live before they achieve the repose which is so much more ornamental than life. They must appear at garden parties and achieve, or fail to achieve, the 'swirl' which Mr George thinks a proper tribute to their powers. But they must be content to forgo authoritative criticism until they are long past the age at which they can profit by it. They must put up with the random patronage of people who subscribe to libraries and to the snapshots of reviewers. Meanwhile they enjoy a kind of homage which is not altogether to be despised. We should judge it an immense calamity if all the writers whom Mr George speaks of were destroyed in a single night. Yes, in our condescending, indolent way we are proud of them; we need them; we have a dim consciousness of a band of light upon the horizon which is due to their incessant imaginative fervour, and sometimes we seem to see that from all this agitation and confusion something of great importance is taking shape.

1 – A review in the *TLS*, 13 June 1918, (Kp CIII) of *A Novelist on Novels* (W. Collins Sons & Co. Ltd, 1918) by W. L. George. Reprinted: *CW*.

2 – Walter Lionel George (1882–1926) was the author of several novels and of other miscellaneous publications, including *Labour and Housing at Port Sunlight* (1909), *Anatole France* (1915) and *Further Notes on the Intelligence of Women* (1916).

3 – George, 'Who is the Man', pp. 86–7; E. M. Forster, *The Longest Journey* (1907), *A Room With a View* (1908), *Howards End* (1910).

4 – *Ibid.*, 'Litany of the Novelist', p. 38; George Nathaniel Curzon, Marquess Curzon of Kedleston (1859–1925), statesman, Viceroy of India, 1898–1905, spent the years from 1905 in the political wilderness, until, in 1916, he became a member of Lloyd George's War Cabinet. Joseph Conrad (1857–1924).

5 – *Ibid.*, p. 39.

6 – For the unwelcome son-in-law, *ibid.*, p. 26; and for Lord Nelson and the daughter of Leigh Hunt (1784–1859), essayist, critic and poet, *ibid.*, p. 44.

7 – *Ibid.*, p. 60; H. G. Wells (1866–1946), *Tono Bungay* (1909).

8 – J. D. Beresford (1873–1947); for VW on his works, see 'Freudian Fiction' and 'Revolution', *III VW Essays*. Gilbert Cannan (1884–1955); see 'Mummery' below. E. M. Forster (1879–1970); see '*A Room With a View*', *I VW Essays*, and 'The Art of Fiction' and 'The Novels of E. M. Forster', *IV VW Essays*. D. H. Lawrence (1885–1930); see 'Postscript or Prelude?', *III VW Essays*. Compton Mackenzie (1883–1972); see 'The "Movie" Novel' below and 'Sylvia and Michael', *III VW Essays*. Oliver Onions (1872–1961); see 'A Practical Utopia', below. Frank Swinnerton (1884–1982); see 'Honest Fiction', below and 'September', *III VW Essays*.

9 – *Ibid.*, 'Who is the Man?', p. 67.

10 – *Ibid.*, p. 69, which has: 'If we wish to measure these dangers, then we must analyse the men one by one, and it will serve us best to divide them into three groups:'.

11 – *Ibid.*, p. 68, from a longer sentence.

12 – *Ibid.*, 'Form and the Novel', pp. 122–3.

13 – *Ibid.*, 'Three Young Novelists', pp. 101–2; the party-goer at the centre of George's account is the novelist Amber Reeves, a graduate of Newnham College, Cambridge, lover of H. G. Wells, and author of *The Reward of Virtue* (1911), *A Lady and Her Husband* (1914) and *Helen in Love* (1916). (The other two young novelists discussed are D. H. Lawrence and Sheila Kaye-Smith (1887–1956), author of *Starbrace* (1909), *Sussex Gorse* (1916) and other works.)

Loud Laughter

We have seen Mr Leacock[2] described both as Doctor and Professor; and his industry and success in making people laugh seem to entitle him to the brass plate, the variegated letters, and the consulting room of the specialist. If when Mr Leacock has applied all the batteries and tests of the most improved humorous science upon you you still remain grave and careworn in his hands, it is probable that you are hopelessly deficient – a chronic invalid. Upon us, we admit at once, his verdict was grave; he said that he had only been able to produce hearty laughter nine or ten times in the course of two hundred and forty pages; that our risible faculties were far too easily exhausted; and from the alert condition of the critical faculty under the process he could detect signs of premature decay. Possibly this was due to the enervating influence of an ancient civilisation; possibly the American climate might even now work wonders.

That is the worst that we have to say about Mr Leacock; he is a specialist in laughter. He is one of those people with an abnormal gift such as brings its possessor to celebrity upon the music-hall stage. His skill in producing the comic reminds us of the gentleman who whips off the tablecloth and turns it into Napoleon's hat; so Mr Leacock seems to delight in showing how he can make funniness out of anything. Humour, to judge by the reviewers' chorus of praise, is the right term to apply to his production; but to our thinking it is no more humour than the tablecloth is Napoleon's hat. It is a specialised product which, like a pug dog or a garden plant, has been bred so carefully that it no longer resembles the common stock. We have the hardihood to declare that the common stock flourishes naturally and profusely in these islands. With Falstaff and Mrs Gamp for parents it could not well be otherwise; but leaving them, as fairness requires, out of account, what we call humour in England seems to us a very different thing from the humour of *Frenzied Fiction*. Mr Leacock's method is probably too well known for it to be necessary to describe these fresh examples in great detail. They are almost without exception funny stories; and the fun consists in turning some foible or craze upside down by heaping exaggeration upon exaggeration, so that you laugh both at the absurdities of Mr Leacock's fancy and at the wretched ghost of reality thus nimbly travestied. A skit upon amateur agriculture opens in the following way:

I have hung up my hoe in my study; my spade is put away behind the piano; I have with me seven pounds of Paris Green that I had over. Anybody who wants it may have it. I didn't like to bury it for fear of its poisoning the ground. I didn't like to throw it away for fear of its destroying cattle. I was afraid to leave it in my summer place for fear that it might poison the tramps who generally break in in November. I have it with me now. I move it from room to room, as I hate to turn my back upon it. Anybody who wants it, I repeat, can have it.[3]

And so he goes on piling it up, one fantasy on top of another, until we hold our breath and wonder with what final perversion of sense he will cap the towering pyramid. The effect is cumulative, and fragmentary quotations give no true impression of the intensity and unreality which make this humour so different from the English variety. In candour we must admit that in certain of these skits, such as 'The Prophet in our Midst' and 'To Nature and Back Again',[4] Mr Leacock makes points a great deal quicker than we are used to take them. His lively sense of satire is never too deeply sunk in extravagances to cease to sting. But if laughter, if the degree in which we are soothed and expanded and persuaded into a mood of tolerant joviality are the tests of humour, we have no hesitation in bestowing our palm elsewhere. Ruling out the immortals, let us consider the claims of Mr Briggs[5] of Victorian *Punch*. Let us put in a word, too, for the humour that flourishes every night among a tangle of rubbish in the music halls. This humour is much slower and more cumbrous than anything in *Frenzied Fiction*; it can scarcely be said to have a point; but it has breadth, it has character; in its primitive way it has a good deal of human nature in it. It takes hold of the audience; it shakes them and seizes them and settles them down again in a mood of immense good temper. And then, quite slowly and deliberately and with an odd mixture of emotions, we begin to laugh.

Perhaps, after all, when we call Mr Leacock a specialist we mean that his emotions are not sufficiently mixed. He has isolated one from the rest, and each time he takes up his pen he goes straight for it, as if the human mind were a target with a golden bull's-eye in the centre and neat circles of different colours surrounding it. In truth, the book of humour is something of a prodigy, although custom has brought us to see nothing unnatural in it. But turn it the other way round; suppose that Mr Leacock had written, instead of *Frenzied Fiction, Funereal Fiction*. Suppose we began with a sob, went on to a tear, developed into a roar, and culminated in a paroxysm of uncontrollable lamentation – should we think that a desirable form of art? Would the critics be so eager then to acclaim him a master of tears?

1 – A review in the *TLS*, 20 June 1918, (Kp C112) of *Frenzied Fiction* (John Lane, The Bodley Head, 1918) by Stephen Leacock.
2 – Stephen Butler Leacock (1869–1944), English-born, Canadian-educated professor of political economy at McGill University, Montreal, author of *Elements of Political Science* (1906) and of several highly popular humorous works, including

Literary Lapses (1910), *Nonsense Novels* (1911) and *Sunshine Sketches of a Little Town* (1912).
3 – Leacock, xiv, 'Back from the Land', p. 178.
4 – *Ibid.*, iii, 'The Prophet in Our Midst', pp. 34–42; vi, 'To Nature and Back Again', pp. 76–90.
5 – The character created by the artist John Leech (1817–64) and based in part upon Leech's friend Millais. Mr Briggs's adventures were the inspiration for VW's juvenile serial story 'A Cockney's Farming Experiences' (see I QB, p. 30).

A Victorian Socialist

The reminiscences and reflections of Mr Belfort Bax² are distinguished from most of their kind by the conception which the writer has formed of his task. His aim has been to 'offer data and suggestions . . . for the due appreciation, now or hereafter, of the particular period of historic time in which my life has been cast – to wit, roughly speaking, the last third of the nineteenth and the opening years of the twentieth century'. The 'personal note' has been rigorously 'damped down',³ whether from shyness on the writer's part or because such matters do not seem to him likely to interest the historian of the future. However this may be, the method certainly produces a curious sense that the mid and late Victorian age, so near ours in point of time, is already distant and different enough to be summed up and judged as we sum up and judge the lives of the dead. As we read we feel ourselves exalted almost to the rank of that impartial observer to whom the England of the nineteenth century will appear as the Rome of the year 116 appears to an observer of the present day.⁴ Bating a certain unnecessary sensitiveness to possible disagreements and one or two beliefs whose fervour seems rather personal than universal, Mr Bax's book might very well stand for the book of the average thinking man of middle-class origin and socialist persuasion born in or about the year 1854. It is very sincere, very plain spoken, and very much in earnest.

An aged American gentleman⁵ who revisited England in 1901 told Mr Bax that he was astonished at the change between the English of that day and the English of 1848. When he compared the men and women he met in the Strand with their forebears they seemed to him to belong to a different race. Not only dress, but faces, ways, and manners had completely changed. In what the change consisted he unfortunately omitted to say; but the reader of Mr Bax's book will find a great deal to help him in framing an opinion upon that point. When, for example, Mr Bax was a boy the main topic of conversation in the family was religious dogma. Not only in his family but in most families of the Evangelical set Romanism and Latitudinarianism, preachers and the quality of their orthodoxy, were the staple of discussion, and upon all brooded equally the shadow of Sunday and the ban of social enjoyment. The theatres were especially condemned, save indeed as convenient signposts of destruction; for had not a lady, seeing the words 'To the Pit' emblazoned on the theatre door, read into them their right meaning and immediately sought salvation elsewhere?[6] The only permissible form of art, according to Mr Bax, was the oratorio. The *Messiah* and the *Elijah* were the only legitimate channels for aesthetic emotions, and the one piece of music that resounded from church, chapel and parlour indiscriminately was Mendelssohn's 'O rest in the Lord'.[7] How far this religious fervour was genuine, and how far it was the result of what Mr Bax calls 'unconscious hypocrisy'[8] it is hard to determine; but it is certain that those who were young enough to be coerced and sensitive enough to revolt 'preserved enduringly unpleasant reminiscences of that time'. Worse still, the memories of those who had held these 'morally repulsive and intellectually foolish beliefs', were held in no respect by their descendants, for 'their characters were poisoned and warped by the foulness and follies of their creed'.[9]

From such unpleasant reminiscences and early impressions sprang, no doubt, the drastic moral tone of Mr Bax's generation. No words seem to have been more often upon their lips than 'humbug', 'cant', 'sentimentalism' and 'superstition'. No generation has ever put more trust in reason, or rated more highly the powers of pure intellect. In an interesting passage Mr Bax traces the decline and death of his own belief in the supernatural, and is so sanguine as to suppose that reason has so far permeated the race that the modern child goes to bed without any fear of the dark. It seems probable that each generation of children will have its own fear of the dark, but we may certainly cede to Mr Bax's generation the credit of having marked out the boundary where light ends and darkness begins. This temper is notable in his remarks upon the Society for Psychical Research.[10] After examining some of the claims put forward by the Society, he comes to the conclusion that his own attitude may be described as 'an "agnostic" one, with a bias in favour of the negative opinion'.[11] The conclusion seems to us highly characteristic of his generation. With fairness, with honesty, with a display of reason before which emotion must shrink abashed, they tested the common objects of belief and proved them for the most part baseless, or, if judgment was suspended, they had a distinct 'bias in favour of the negative opinion'. Whether it is due to this spirit or to some temperamental quality of his own, the pervading atmosphere of this book would lead us to judge the mid and late Victorian period a dry, if wholesome, stage in our mental history. The moral earnestness which replaces and demolishes a too-easy credulity is bound in retrospect to seem a little excessive. Even when they took upon them to chide prigs or to denounce asceticism, one feels that the ghosts of the Evangelicals have inspired them rather than a pure delight in the joys of the senses. Mr Bax supports his advocacy of drink in moderation, or rather his attack upon the asceticism of doctors, by the statement that it 'is a noteworthy fact that the physical degeneration of the Scotchman of today is coincident with an increasing abstemiousness as regards whisky'.[12] It is hardly necessary to tell us that he has never 'gloried and drunk deep'.[13] One of the very few stories in the book of the great men with whom he has associated leaves us with an added impression of the seriousness which might attend even a walk in the country. He was walking with William Morris by the side of a stream.

Suddenly Morris became morose and unsociable in manner. A little while after again coming upon the high road we turned into an inn for luncheon. Sitting after the meal, I asked Morris the reason of his grumpiness. He replied that he was much exercised in passing through those fields in that he saw bulls regarding us in a more or less menacing manner, and that, although he himself could have escaped by swimming across the little river, knowing that I could not swim, he was perplexed as to what course to pursue in the event of a bovine attack. Hence his surliness.[14]

But these, after all, are trifles, little eccentricities that strike the eye as it rests upon the surface of an age. It need scarcely be said that the age was one that brought about an important change, and that if Mr Bax and his friends did their work of destruction, they also sought to establish what he calls 'the only true religion for human beings', that which has for its object 'the devotion to the future social life of Humanity'.[15] In this crusade Mr Bax has fought valiantly; upon that cause he has lavished all his passion. The only tears recorded in his book were shed 'in secret and in my own room'[16] for the martyrs of the Commune; his deepest source of gratification lies in the enlightenment of the working classes. His hope for the future is so deeply founded that it bridges the gulf cut by the war. The Socialist ideal reaches beyond 'any mere material transformation';[17] and, believing in its attainment, he looks forward to a time when the working classes of the world will be united in such an international society that the struggle of race with race will be for ever impossible.

1 – A review in the *TLS*, 27 June 1918, (Kp C113) of *Reminiscences and Reflexions of a Mid and Late Victorian* (George Allen & Unwin Ltd, 1918) by Ernest Belfort Bax.

2 – Ernest Belfort Bax (1854–1926), socialist and barrister, was an active member of the Social Democratic Federation and, with William Morris, co-founder in 1885 of the Socialist League. His several works of history and socialist philosophy include *Socialism: Its Growth and Outcome* (1893) written jointly with Morris.

3 – For both aims and personal note, Bax, Pref., p. 5.

4 – *Ibid.*, ch. XII, pp. 279–80: 'What would the modern classical scholar not give to have such an imperfect set of reminiscences and reflexions even as those contained in the foregoing pages, written in the year 116 by an inhabitant (say) of Rome, Alexandria, or Antioch, born in the year 54.'

5 – *Ibid.*, ch. X, p. 222: 'This gentleman, whose name was Hinton, had been one of the friends and companions of John Brown in the Harper's Ferry incident of 1857.'

6 – For the story of the converted playgoer, *ibid.*, ch. I, pp. 13–14.

7 – For Handel's *Messiah* (1742) and Mendelssohn's *Elijah* (1846), *ibid.*, p. 16.

8 – *Ibid.*, pp. 17–18; 'By unconscious hypocrisy I understand an attitude of mind which succeeds in persuading itself that it believes or approves certain things as it professes to do, while really *in foro conscientiae* this profession is dictated by a sense of its own interests, real or supposed.'

9 – For all three preceding quotations, *ibid.*, p. 20.

10 – For Bax on the Society of Psychical Research, founded in 1882, *ibid.*, pp. 25–7.

11 – *Ibid.*, p. 26.

12 – *Ibid.*, ch. XII, p. 267fn.

13 – *Ibid.*, pp. 278–9, quoting *The Rubáiyát of Omar Khayyám*, and remarking: 'I would certainly much rather think that the lion and the lizard keep the Halls where I had "gloried and drunk deep" (not that I ever did so), than that their sites should be reserved, not for the roar of the lion, but for the shriek of the steam whistle. Such is sentiment!'

14 – *Ibid.*, ch. V, p. 120.

15 – *Ibid.*, ch. I, pp. 29–30.

16 – *Ibid.*, p. 29.

17 – *Ibid.*, ch. IV, p. 93.

Mr Merrick's Novels

Twelve distinguished authors 'have fallen over each other', says Sir James Barrie, 'in their desire to join in the honour of writing the prefaces'[2] to the edition of Mr Merrick's collected works. At the present moment only the first of the twelve, Sir James Barrie, has appeared in the capacity of introducer, and he is in charge of *Conrad in Quest of his Youth*. Sir James, we need not say, makes the introduction in the most graceful terms, and leaves us to become better acquainted with the genial assurance that we shall get on splendidly; but, should it fall out otherwise, it will make no difference to his opinion of Mr Merrick. 'For long he has been the novelist's novelist, and we give you again the chance to share him with us; you have been slow to take the previous chances, and you may turn away again, but in any case he will still remain our man.' To start us on the right track he gives it as his opinion that *Conrad in Quest of his Youth* 'is the best sentimental journey that has been written in this country since the publication of the other one'. To leave us in no possible doubt of his meaning he adds, 'I know scarcely a novel by any living Englishman, except a score or so of Mr Hardy's, that I would rather have written.'[3]

The reader, thus advised and admonished, bethinks him perhaps of the *Sentimental Journey*,[4] conjures up the name of any novel by a living author that he might choose to have written, and conjectures that Mr Merrick will be first and foremost an artist whose gift has a rarity that specially appeals to connoisseurs. We maintain that this is the wrong way of approaching Mr Merrick. When Sir James suggests Sterne, when he talks of Mr Hardy, he is challenging us to make comparisons which we would much rather make in silence. He is putting us into the ungrateful position of the critic whose main business it is to find fault. Now the interest and value of the art of criticism lie more than anything in the critic's ability to seize upon what is good and to expatiate upon that. The only criticism worth having, we sometimes think, is the criticism of praise; but to give praise its meaning the standard of the first rate must be present in the mind, unconfused and unlowered, though kept in the background unless the merit of the work makes open reference to it worth while. Rightly or wrongly we cannot see that there is anything to be gained by naming the classics when we are discussing the interesting but unequal works of Mr Merrick.

Conrad in Quest of his Youth is an extremely readable book. More than that, it is sufficiently unlike other books to make you wish to take its measure, to account for its failure or its success. Here, evidently, is a novelist endowed with wit, with lightness of touch, with a sensitive quick-darting intelligence, and with just that turn of mind that is needed to give his work an unmistakable character of its own. Perhaps this last is the quality that has endeared him to his fellow writers. It is very rare, and yet, if unsupported by commoner gifts, it is apt to be thrown away, or at least completely ignored by the public. Competence, completeness and a dozen other virtues are negligible compared with the sensitive though perhaps ineffective handling of the artist. Within his limits Mr Merrick shows unmistakable traces of this endowment. Is not *Conrad in Quest of his Youth* an undoubted proof of it? From a dozen different scenes, precariously poised one on top of another, we get a charming irregular whole; we get a sense of the past; of deserted piers, of bathing places out of season, of barrel organs out of tune, of ladies past their prime. It has an atmosphere of its own. Mr Merrick possesses the cynicism peculiar to the sentimentalist; and in *Conrad* the mixture is extremely skilful, the sweet turning bitter, the sunset merging surprisingly into the daylight of three o'clock in the afternoon. His talent seems to lend itself peculiarly well to the faded distinction of the year 1880, when Piccadilly was blocked with hansom cabs and well-dressed people sat by Rotten Row and offered each other nicely turned phrases which already sound a little obsolete. Here is an example of this urbane dialogue; Conrad is talking to the lady whom he loved in his youth:

'You hurt me,' said Conrad, 'because for the first time I realise you are different from the girl I've looked for. Till now I've felt that I was with her again.' 'That's nice of you, but it isn't true. Oh, I like you for saying it, of course . . . If you had felt it really –' 'Go on.' 'No; what for? I should only make you unhappier.' 'You want comedy?' he demurred; 'you have said the saddest things a woman ever said to me!' She raised a white shoulder – with a laugh. 'I never get what I want!' 'It should have taught you to feel for me, but you are not "wondrous kind." ' 'Oh, I am more to be pitied than you are! 'What have I got in my life? Friends? Yes – to play bridge with. My husband? He delivers speeches on local option, and climbs mountains. Both make me deadly tired. I used to go in for music – God Save the King is the only tune he knows when he hears it, and he only knows that because the men take their hats off. I was interested in my house at the beginning – after you've quarrelled in your house every day for years it doesn't absorb you to make the mantelpiece look pretty. I

wanted a child – well, my sister has seven! . . . Voilà my autobiography up to date.'
'There is tomorrow,' said Conrad, moved. 'Tomorrow you must give me the comedy,' she smiled ⟨. . .⟩[5]

There is much that is up to that level, a good deal that is above it, and as his books are full of dialogue you may accuse Mr Merrick of airiness, perhaps of emptiness, but never of being a bore.

The success of *Conrad in Quest of his Youth* lies in the skilful balance of sweetness and bitterness, of romance and reality. But in the other novels the union is far more unequal, and in some of them the results appear to us to be more interesting. We can guess that Mr Merrick has tried, as most good novelists try, to shape a world bearing some resemblance to the world of his vision. Failure, the loss of ideals, the sacrifice of good to evil, and, above all, the degradation wrought upon the character by poverty, were some of the aspects of life that claimed Mr Merrick's attention. He did not master his theme, and perhaps he spoilt a book or two in trying; but it is evident that he was not content with a scene of brilliancy here, a character of vitality there, but aimed at something more complete. If you choose, as this characteristic makes it possible, to consider his books as one large composition, you must place in the centre a blazing fire, a radiance that casts its fictitious splendour to the furthest corners of the picture. This, of course, is the stage. Into that fire, from distant and obscure sources, come running heroes and heroines and other strange figures, who struggle to the light and pass out again into the dreary twilight of failure or disillusion, or remain hovering unsatisfied at a distance. And now we reach the dilemma by which Mr Merrick seems so often to have been posed. He feels the glamour of the stage in every nerve, he thrusts his men and women again and again into the furnace, but then at the last moment he repents and saves them alive. He bestows all sorts of gifts upon them. This one turns out to be a successful dramatist; that one earns £4,000 a year by painting pictures which are, incredibly enough, works of the highest merit. We do not believe with Sir James Barrie that Mr Merrick has frightened the public by his pessimism; we think it more probable that he has puzzled it by his compromises. His mediocrity is so strangely combined with his excellence. We have always to reckon with a lapse into melodrama as in the ending to *The Man Who Was Good*, or with the commonplace and conventional as in the climax of *The House of Lynch*.[6]

But we own to a grudge against the influence that has tried to spoil *Peggy Harper* or *The Quaint Companions*,[7] because, pruned of certain weaknesses, each of these books contains first-hand truth seized and set down with extraordinary vivacity. The proximity of the stage always revives Mr Merrick, and a second-rate actress never fails to put him on his mettle. Her cheap prettiness, her artistic incompetence, her vanity, her courage, her poverty, her makeshifts and artifices and endurance, together with the seduction of the theatre, are described not with mere truth of detail, though we guess that to be considerable, but with the rarer truth of sympathy. The description of Peggy Harper's home and of her mother, the decayed actress who has taken to drink but preserves the artistic instincts and passions, makes you feel that you have learned the truth about that section of humanity once for all. From each of Mr Merrick's books one could select a chapter or two possessing, often among second-rate surroundings, this stamp of first-hand quality. We find it most often when he has to deal with the seamy side of the stage; we find it oddly often in some minor character or in some little scene dashed off apparently by an afterthought. A touring company comes to grief, a girl stumbling through her part before the author, a troupe of actors trailing their draggled feathers and cheap tinsel across the windy parade of a seaside resort at Christmas time – into such scenes he puts so much spirit, so many quick touches of insight, that the precarious, flaring, tenth-rate life of the provincial stage has not only glamour and bustle, but beauty into the bargain. These are the scenes that we shall wish to read again.

The last of Mr Merrick's books, *While Paris Laughed,* should win a greater popularity than the others. Nothing in it is so good as certain passages that we should have liked to quote, from *Peggy Harper* in particular, but the quality is far more equal. It has all the quickness, lightness, and dexterity which scarcely ever fail him, and, in addition, the balance of this uneven talent is more successfully maintained. In recording the adventures of the poet Tricortin in Paris he is never quite serious, but he never laughs aloud; he hints at disagreeables and glances at delights; he suggests the divinity of art and the obtuseness of the public, but never for an instant does he pass from raillery to satire, or from suggestion to statement. It is a very skilful and craftsmanlike piece of work, and, if Mr Merrick still remains unpopular, we confess ourselves unable to guess the reason.

1 – A review in the *TLS*, 4 July 1918, (Kp C114) of *While Paris Laughed. Being Pranks and Passions of the Poet Tricortin* and of *Conrad in Quest of His Youth. An*

Extravagance of Temperament. With an introduction by J. M. Barrie (Hodder & Stoughton, 1918) by Leonard Merrick (1864–1939); the second work was originally published in 1903. 'Still, the classics *are* very pleasant, and even, I must confess, the mortals. I found great consolation during the influenza in the works of Leonard Merrick,' VW had written as early as 25 February 1918 to Saxon Sydney-Turner (*II VW Letters*, no. 910), 'a poor unappreciated second rate pot-boiling writer of stories about the stage, whom I deduce to be a negro, mulatto or quadroon; at any rate he has a grudge against the world, and might have done much better if he hadn't at the age of 20 married a chorus girl, had by her 15 coffee coloured brats and lived for the rest of the time in a villa in Brixton, where he ekes out his living by giving lessons on elocution to the natives – Now if this were about a Greek writer, it would be what is called constructive criticism, wouldn't it?' On Tuesday, 7 May, she noted in her diary that she had 'a rush of books' hanging over her, including Merrick; and on Thursday, 27 June, she wrote, 'I still find it difficult to make head or tail of Labour Party politics, or indeed of any other; but with practice I suppose it wouldn't be harder than reviewing Mr Merrick'.

See also 'Mr Howells on Form', below. Reprinted: CW.

2 – *Conrad*, intro., p. viii; J. M. Barrie (1860–1937).

3 – For all three quotations, *ibid.*

4 – Laurence Sterne, *A Sentimental Journey Through France and Italy* (1768).

5 – *Conrad*, ch., XII, pp. 159–60, which has: 'you *are* different'.

6 – *The Man Who Was Good.* With an introduction by J. K. Prothero, and *The House of Lynch.* With an introduction by G. K. Chesterton (Hodder & Stoughton, 1918), originally published in 1892 and 1907 respectively.

7 – *The Position of Peggy Harper.* With an introduction by Sir Arthur Pinero, and *The Quaint Companions.* With an introduction by H. G. Wells (Hodder & Stoughton, 1918), originally published in 1907 and 1903 respectively.

Two Soldier-Poets

It is natural to feel an impulse of charity towards the poems written by young men who have fought or are still fighting; but in the case of Mr Sassoon[2] there is no temptation to indulge in this form of leniency, because he is so evidently able-bodied in his poetic capacity and requires no excuses to be made for him. At the same time, it is difficult to judge him dispassionately as a poet, because it is impossible to overlook the fact that he writes as a soldier. It is a fact, indeed, that he forces upon you, as if it were a matter of indifference to him whether you called him poet or not. We know no other writer who has shown us as effectually as Mr Sassoon the terrible pictures which lie behind the colourless phrases of the newspapers. From the thousand horrors which in their sum compose one day of warfare he selects, as if by chance, now this of the counter-attack, now that of mending the front-line wires, or this again of suicide in the trenches. 'The General' is as good an example of his method as another:

> 'Good-morning: good-morning!' the General said
> When we met him last week on our way to the line.
> Now the soldiers he smiled at are most of 'em dead,
> And we're cursing his staff for incompetent swine.
> 'He's a cheery old card,' grunted Harry to Jack,
> As they slogged up to Arras with rifle and pack.
>
> *   *   *   *   *   *
>
> But he did for them both by his plan of attack.[3]

The vision of that 'hell where youth and laughter go'[4] has been branded upon him too deeply to allow him to tolerate consolation or explanation. He can only state a little of what he has seen, a very little one guesses, and turn away with a stoical shrug as if a superficial cynicism were the best mask to wear in the face of such incredible experiences. His farewell to the dead is spoken in this fashion:

> Good-bye, old lad! Remember me to God,
>   And tell him that our politicians swear
> They won't give in till Prussian Rule's been trod
>   Under the heel of England . . . Are you there? . . .
> Yes . . . and the war won't end for at least two years;
> But we've got stacks of men . . . I'm blind with tears,
>   Staring into the dark. Cheero!
> I wish they'd killed you in a decent show.[5]

There is a stage of suffering, so these poems seem to show us, where any expression save the barest is intolerable; where beauty and art have something too universal about them to meet our particular case. Mr Sassoon sums up that point of view in his 'Dead Musicians'. Not Bach or Beethoven or Mozart brings back the memory of his friends, but the gramophone does it bawling out 'Another little drink won't do us any harm.'[6] Mr Sassoon's poems are too much in the key of the gramophone at present, too fiercely suspicious of any comfort or compromise, to be read as poetry; but his contempt for palliative or subterfuge gives us the raw stuff of poetry.

No two poets could be more different than Mr Sassoon and Mr Dearmer;[7] the difference in point of view is unimportant, but the difference in expression is very interesting. Mr Dearmer writes of soldiers waiting in the trenches:

> We waited, like a storm-bespattered ship
> That flutters sail to free her grounded keel,[8]

and from that image it is at once evident that Mr Dearmer is trying to make a kind of poetry so different that the comparison with Mr Sassoon will serve us no longer. Reality is an accident that passes across the mirror of his mind and makes images that interest him far more than the object that caused them. While he unfolds his metaphor the scene that he is describing is over and done with. The cavalry and the batteries and the mules are tramping down the street, 'but all is dim' –

> Only my dreams are still aglow, a throng
> Of scenes that crowded through a waiting mind.
> A myriad scenes: For I have swept along
> To foam ashriek with gulls, and rowed behind
> Brown oarsmen swinging to an ocean song
> Where stately galleons bowed before the wind.[9]

Some of the loveliest poems in the language have been produced in the manner that Mr Dearmer attempts, and a young poet venturing once more as Keats[10] ventured commands our sympathy. But if the prize is of the greatest the undertaking is so perilous that it is no harsh criticism to say that Mr Dearmer's imagination is neither strong enough nor trained enough to do the work he asks of it. The romantic poet lays heavier tasks upon his imagination than any other. The vision alone is not enough; he must see it in detail as well as hold it in mass; he must know when to release and when to restrain the words which flock too fast and freely. Mr Dearmer has a wide range of language, but he trusts too much to chance, as if beauty could be captured by a random fling, and twenty words wide of the mark made no difference provided six or seven fall moderately near. He slips too often into the habit of imaginative inaccuracy; he compares men dashing to their holes to 'burrowing moles'; he says that gossamer clouds crossing the moon 'scurrying ran'; he makes glow-worms 'crawl excitedly'; he stuffs out his verse with such tags as 'glad tidings', 'laughter of the main', 'jewelled night'.[11] These instances may seem trivial, but they help to explain why it is that, though the effect of Mr Dearmer's longer poems is vaguely fine and vigorous, the whole seems to be slackly or numbly grasped, or, as in 'Gomme-court' to reel itself off into rhetoric. The war, perhaps, has brought these pieces forth before their time; for, where he is forced to concentrate, as in his 'Eight Sonnets', he comes much nearer to writing poetry.

1 – A review in the *TLS*, 11 July 1918, (Kp c115) of *Counter-Attack and Other Poems* (William Heinemann, 1918) by Siegfried Sassoon and of *Poems* (William Heinemann, 1918) by Geoffrey Dearmer. See also *I VW Diary*, 29 July 1918: 'a week end at Garsington . . . The string which united everything from first to last was Philip [Morrell]'s attack upon [J.M.] Murry in The Nation for his review of Sassoon . . . I was taxed with being on Murry's side . . .'; and see 'Mr Sassoon's Poems', above. Reprinted in part in 'Mr Sassoon's Poems', *B&P*.
2 – In May 1918, Captain Siegfried Sassoon (1886–1967) of the Royal Welch Fusiliers had rejoined his battalion in France. He was wounded in the head the following July and this brought his active military service to an end.
3 – Sassoon, 'The General', p. 26, the complete poem.
4 – *Ibid.*, 'Suicide in the Trenches', p. 31.
5 – *Ibid.*, 'To Any Dead Officer', p. 42.
6 – *Ibid.*, 'Dead Musicians', p. 59, italicised in the original.
7 – Geoffrey Dearmer was the son of the divine, Percy Dearmer. His brother Christopher had been killed at Gallipoli in 1915. Dearmer survived the war and later published a number of dramatic works.
8 – Dearmer, 'A Trench Incident', p. 54, which has 'keel;'.
9 – *Ibid.*, 'Reality', p. 55.
10 – Dearmer not only emulated Keats but wrote poems about him, e.g., 'Keats, Before Action' (*ibid.*, p. 41) and 'Keats' (*ibid.*, p. 74), in the last line of which he declares: 'Dear Keats your name is Paradise to me!'
11 – For the dashing moles *ibid.*, 'The Sentinel', p. 9; for the gossamer clouds, *ibid.*, 'Gommecourt', p. 28; for the excited glow worms, *ibid.*, 'Everychild', p. 63; for the three tags, *ibid.*, 'Resurrection', p. 23: e.g. 'Glad tidings to each clod, each particle of earth'; and 'Spring in the Trenches', p. 37: 'Glad tidings thrill the re-awakened earth'; *ibid.*, 'Eight Sonnets', V, p. 70; and 'The Strolling Singer', p. 86.

On Re-reading Meredith

This new study of Meredith is not a text-book to be held in one hand while in the other you hold *The Shaving of Shagpat* or *Modern Love*;[2] it is addressed to those who have so far solved the difficulties of the Master that they wish to make up their minds as to his final position in English literature. The book should do much to crystallise opinion upon

Meredith, if only because it will induce many people to read him again. For Mr Crees has written in a spirit of enthusiasm which makes it easy to do so. He summons Diana and Willoughby Patterne and Richard Feverel[3] from the shelves where they have fallen a little silent lately and in a moment the air is full of high-pitched, resonant voices, speaking the unmistakable language of metaphor, epigram, and fantastic poetic dialogue. Some readers, to judge from our own case, will feel a momentary qualm, as at meeting after the lapse of years some hero so ardently admired once that his eccentricities and foibles are now scarcely tolerable; they seem to preserve too well the faults of our own youth. Further, in the presence of so faithful an admirer as Mr Crees we may be reminded of some intervening disloyalties. It was not Thackeray or Dickens or George Eliot[4] who seriously tempted us from our allegiance; but can we say the same of the great Russians? Oddly enough, when Mr Crees is taking Meredith's measure by comparing him with his contemporaries he makes no mention of Turgenev, Tolstoy, or Dostoevsky. But it was *Fathers and Sons*, *War and Peace*, *Crime and Punishment*[5] that seduced multitudes of the faithful and, worse still, seemed for the time to reduce Meredith to an insular hero bred and cherished for the delight of connoisseurs in some sheltered corner of a Victorian hothouse.

The Russians might well overcome us, for they seemed to possess an entirely new conception of the novel and one that was larger, saner, and much more profound than ours. It was one that allowed human life in all its width and depth, with every shade of feeling and subtlety of thought, to flow into their pages without the distortion of personal eccentricity or mannerism. Life was too serious to be juggled with. It was too important to be manipulated. Could any English novel survive in the furnace of that overpowering sincerity? For some time the verdict seemed to go tacitly against Meredith. His fine phrases, his perpetual imagery, the superabundant individuality which so much resembled an overweening egotism seemed to be the very stuff to perish in that uncompromising flame. Perhaps some of us went as far as to believe that the process had already been accomplished and that it was useless to open books in which you would find nothing but charred bones and masses of contorted wire. The poems, *Modern Love*, *Love in the Valley*,[6] and some of the shorter pieces survived the ordeal more successfully and did perhaps keep alive that latent enthusiasm upon which Mr Crees now blows with the highest praise that it is possible to bestow upon literature.

He does not scruple to compare Meredith with Shakespeare. Shakespeare alone, he says, could have written the 'Diversion Played upon a Penny Whistle' in *Richard Feverel*.[7] Meredith 'illustrates better than any since Shakespeare that impetuous mental energy which Matthew Arnold deemed the source of our literary greatness'.[8] One might even infer from some statements that Meredith was the undisputed equal of the greatest of poets. 'No man has ever been endowed with richer gifts.'[9] He was the possessor of 'in some ways the most consummate intellect that has ever been devoted to literature'.[10] These, moreover, are not the irresponsible flings of a momentary enthusiasm but the considered opinion of a man who writes with ability and critical insight and has reached his superlatives by intelligible degrees of appreciation. We should perhaps alter his scale by putting Donne in the place of Shakespeare;[11] but however we may regulate our superlatives he creates the right mood for reading Meredith again.

The right mood for reading Meredith should have a large proportion of enthusiasm in it, for Meredith aims at, and when he is successful has his dwelling in, the very heart of the emotions. There, indeed, we have one of the chief differences between him and the Russians. They accumulate; they accept ugliness; they seek to understand; they penetrate further and further into the human soul with their terrible power of sustained insight and their undeviating reverence for truth. But Meredith takes truth by storm; he takes it with a phrase, and his best phrases are not mere phrases but are compact of many different observations, fused into one and flashed out in a line of brilliant light. It is by such phrases that we get to know his characters. They come to mind at once in thinking of them. Sir Willoughby 'has a leg'. Clara Middleton 'carries youth like a flag'. Vernon Whitford is 'Phoebus Apollo turned fasting Friar';[12] everyone who has read the novels holds a store of such phrases in his memory. But the same process is applied not only to single characters but to large and complicated situations where a number of different states of mind are represented. Here, too, he wishes to crush the truth out in a series of metaphors or a string of epigrams with as little resort to dull fact as may be. Then, indeed, the effort is prodigious, and the confusion often chaotic. But the failure arises from the enormous scope of his ambition. Let us suppose that he has to describe a tea party; he will begin by destroying everything by which it is easy to recognise a tea party – chairs, tables, cups, and the rest; he will represent the scene merely by a ring on a finger and a plume passing the window. But into the ring and plume he puts such passion and character and such penetrating rays of vision play about the denuded room that we seem to be in possession of all the details as if a painstaking realist had described each one of them separately. To have produced this effect as often as Meredith has done so is an enormous feat. That is the way, as one trusts at such moments, that the art of fiction will develop. For such beauty and such high emotional excitement it is well worth while to exchange the solidity which is the result of knowing the day of the week, how the ladies are dressed, and by what series of credible events the great crisis was accomplished. But the doubt will suggest itself whether we are not sacrificing something of greater importance than mere solidity. We have gained moments of astonishing intensity; we have gained a high level of sustained beauty; but perhaps the beauty is lacking in some quality that makes it a satisfying beauty? 'My love,' Meredith wrote, 'is for epical subjects – not for cobwebs in a putrid corner, though I know the fascination of unravelling them.' He avoids ugliness as he avoids dullness. 'Sheer realism,' he wrote, 'is at best the breeder of the dungfly.'[13] Sheer romance breeds an insect more diaphanous, but it tends perhaps to be even more heartless than the dungfly. A touch of realism – or is it a touch of something more akin to sympathy? – would have kept the Meredith hero from being the honourable but tedious gentleman that, with deference to Mr Crees, we have always found him. It would have charged the high mountain air of his books with the greater variety of clouds.

But, for good or for ill, Meredith has the habit of nobleness ingrained in him. No modern writer, for example, has so completely ignored the colloquial turns of speech and cast his dialogue in sentences that could without impropriety have been spoken by Queen Elizabeth in person. 'Out of my sight, I say!' 'I went to him of my own will to run from your heartlessness, mother – that I call mother!'[14] are two examples found upon turning two pages of *The Tragic Comedians*. That is his natural pitch, although we may guess that the long indifference of the public increased his tendency to the strained and the artificial. For this, among other reasons, it is easy to complain that this world is an aristocratic world, strictly bounded, thinly populated, a little hard-hearted, and not to be entered by the poor, the vulgar, the stupid, or that very common and interesting individual who is a mixture of all three.

And yet there can be no doubt that, even judged by his novels alone, Meredith remains a great writer. The doubt is rather whether he can be called a great novelist; whether, indeed, anyone to whom the technique of novel-writing had so much that was repulsive in it can excel compared with those who are writing, not against the grain, but with it. He struggles to escape, and the chapters of amazing but fruitless energy which he produces in his struggle to escape are the true obstacles to the enjoyment of Meredith. What, we ask, is he struggling against? What is he striving for? Was he, perhaps, a dramatist born out of due time – an Elizabethan sometimes, and sometimes, as the last chapters of *The Egoist* suggest, a dramatist of the Restoration? Like a dramatist, he flouts probability, disdains coherency, and lives from one high moment to the next. His dialogue often seems to crave the relief of blank verse. And for all his analytic industry in the dissection of character, he creates not the living men and women who justify modern fiction, but superb conceptions who have more of the general than of the particular in them. There is a large and beautiful conception of womanhood in Diana rather than a single woman; there is the fervour of romantic love in Richard Feverel, but the faces of the lovers are dim in the rosy light. In this lies both the strength and the weakness of his books, but, if the weakness is at all of the kind we have indicated, the strength is of a nature to counterbalance it. His English power of imagination, with its immense audacity and fertility, his superb mastery of the great emotions of courage and love, his power of summoning nature into sympathy with man and of merging him in her vastness, his glory in all fine living and thinking – these are the qualities that give his conceptions their size and universality. In these respects we must recognise his true descent from the greatest of English writers and his enjoyment of qualities that are expressed nowhere save in the masterpieces of our literature.

1 – A review in the *TLS*, 25 July 1918, (Kp C116) of *George Meredith. A Study of his Works and Personality* (B. H. Blackwell, 1918) by J. H. R. Crees, headmaster of the Crypt Grammar School, Gloucester.

See also 'Small Talk About Meredith' and 'Memories of Meredith', *III VW Essays*, and 'The Novels of George Meredith', *V VW Essays* and *CR2*. Reprinted: *G&R, CE*.

2 – George Meredith (1828–1909); *The Shaving of Shagpat, an Arabian Entertainment* (1856), *Modern Love* (1862).

3 – The references are to: Diana Warwick, heroine of *Diana of the Crossways* (1885); Sir Willoughby Patterne, a character in *The Egoist* (1879); and the hero of *The Ordeal of Richard Feverel* (1859).

4 – W. M. Thackeray (1811–63); Charles Dickens (1812–70); George Eliot (1819–80).

5 – Ivan Turgenev (1818–83), *Fathers and Sons* (1862); L. N. Tolstoy (1828–1910), *War and Peace* (1865–72); Fyodor Dostoevsky (1821–81), *Crime and Punishment* (1866).

6 – 'Love in the Valley', 1851 and 1878.

7 – Crees, ch. III, p. 40: 'In a pastoral modestly styled "a diversion on a penny whistle" we have a passionate outburst of soaring poetry which in the fervour of its impulse perhaps none else but Shakespeare could have written, and which in its appeal to natural beauty recalls us to Theocritus.'

8 – *Ibid.*, ch. VII, p. 183.

9 – *Ibid.*

10 – *Ibid.*, p. 190.

11 – Cf. 'Donne After Three Centuries', *V VW Essays* and *CR*2: 'He [Donne] is one of those nonconformists, like Browning and Meredith, who cannot resist glorifying their nonconformity by a dash of wilful and gratuitous eccentricity'; and 'The Novels of George Meredith', *ibid.*: 'Meredith's flamboyancy has a great ancestry behind it; we cannot avoid all memory of Shakespeare.'

12 – For Sir Willoughby, Crees, ch. II, p. 19; *The Egoist* (1879), ch. 2 (ed. George Woodcock, Penguin, 1968, p. 43). For Clara Middleton, Crees, ch. II, p. 31, and ch. VI, p. 138; *The Egoist*, ch. 4, p. 66: 'The young lady was outlined to Laetitia as tall, elegant, lively; and painted as carrying youth like a flag.' For Vernon Whitford, Crees, ch. II, p. 19; *The Egoist*, ch. 2, p. 42: 'And that [Mrs Mountstuart Jenkinson's portrait] of Vernon Whitford: "He is Phoebus Apollo turned fasting friar", painted the sunken brilliancy of the lean long-walker and scholar at a stroke.' The model for Whitford was VW's father, Leslie Stephen, leading figure in that fraternity of 'long-walkers' known as the Sunday Tramps, to which Meredith also belonged.

13 – For both quotations, Crees, ch. V, p. 107, Meredith writing to Frederick A. Maxse, 28 December 1865. Crees misquotes 'sheer Realism, breeder at best of the dung-fly!', according to *Letters of George Meredith* (2 vols, Constable, 1912).

14 – *The Tragic Comedians. A Study in a Well-known Story* (1880), ch. VIII (Memorial ed., Constable & Co., 1910, p. 95; p. 96).

Rupert Brooke

This memoir of Rupert Brooke has been delayed, in Mrs Brooke's words, because of 'my great desire to obtain the collaboration of some of his contemporaries at Cambridge and during his young manhood, for I strongly believe that they knew the largest part of him.'[2] But his contemporaries are for the most part scattered or dead; and though Mr Marsh has done all that ability or care can do, the memoir which now appears is 'of necessity incomplete'.[3] It is inevitably incomplete, as Mr Marsh, we are sure, would be the first to agree, if for no other reason because it is the work of an older man. A single sentence brings this clearly before us. No undergraduate of Rupert Brooke's own age would have seen 'his radiant youthful figure in gold and vivid red and blue, like a page in the Riccardi Chapel';[4] that is the impression of an older man. The contemporary version would have been less pictorial and lacking in the half-humorous tenderness which is so natural an element in the mature vision of beautiful and gifted youth. There would have been less of the vivid red and blue and gold, more that was mixed, parti-coloured, and matter for serious debate. In addition Mr Marsh has had to face the enormous difficulties which beset the biographers of those who have died with undeveloped powers, tragically, and in the glory of public gratitude. They leave so little behind them that can serve to recall them with any exactitude. A few letters, written from school and college, a fragment of a diary – that is all. The power of expressing oneself naturally in letters comes to most people late in life. Rupert Brooke wrote freely, but not altogether without self-consciousness, and it is evident that his friends have not cared to publish the more intimate passages in his letters to them. Inevitably, too, they have not been willing to tell the public the informal things by which they remember him best. With these serious and necessary drawbacks Mr Marsh has done his best to present a general survey of Rupert Brooke's life which those who knew him will be able to fill in here and there more fully, perhaps a little to the detriment of the composition as a whole. But they will be left, we believe, to reflect rather sadly upon the incomplete version which must in future represent Rupert Brooke to those who never knew him.

Nothing, it is true, but his own life prolonged to the usual term, and the work that he would have done, could have expressed all that was latent in the crowded years of his youth – years crowded beyond the measure that is usual even with the young. To have seen a little of him at that time was to have seen enough to be made sceptical of the possibility of any biography of a man dying, as he died, at the age of twenty-eight. The remembrance of a week spent in his company,[5] of a few meetings in London and the country, offers a tantalising fund of memories at once very definite, very little related to the Rupert Brooke of legend, presenting each one an extremely clear sense of his presence, but depending so much upon that presence and upon other circumstances inextricably involved with it, that one may well despair of rendering a clear account to a third person, let alone to a multiple of many people such as the general public.

But the outline at least is clear enough. So much has been written of his personal beauty that to state one's own first impression of him in that respect needs some audacity, since the first impression was of a type so conventionally handsome and English as to make it inexpressive or expressive only of something that one might be inclined half-humorously to disparage. He was the type of English young manhood at its healthiest and most vigorous. Perhaps at the particular stage he had then reached, following upon the decadent phase of his first Cambridge days, he emphasised this purposely; he was consciously and defiantly pagan.[6] He was living at Grantchester; his feet were permanently bare; he disdained tobacco and butcher's meat; and he lived all day, and perhaps slept all night, in the open air. You might judge him extreme, and from the pinnacle of superior age assure him that the return to Nature was as sophisticated as any other pose, but you could not from the first moment of speech with him doubt that, whatever he might do, he was an originator, one of those leaders who spring up from time to time and show their power most clearly by subjugating their own generation. Under his influence the country near Cambridge was full of young men and women walking barefoot, sharing his passion for bathing and fish diet, disdaining book learning, and proclaiming that there was something deep and wonderful in the man who brought the milk and in the woman who watched the cows. One may trace some of the effects of this belief in the tone of his letters at this time; their slap-dash method, their hasty scrawled appearance upon the paper, the exclamations and abbreviations were all, in part at least, a means of exorcising the devils of the literary and the cultured. But there was too much vigour in his attitude in this respect, as in all others, to lend it the appearance of affectation. It was an amusing disguise; it was in part, like many of his attitudes, a game played for the fun of it, an experiment in living by one keenly inquisitive and incessantly fastidious; and in part it was the expression of a profound and true sympathy which had to live side by side with highly sophisticated tastes and to be reported upon by a nature that was self-conscious in the highest degree. Analyse it as one may, the whole effect of Rupert Brooke in these days was a compound of vigour and of great sensitiveness. Like most sensitive people, he had his methods of self-protection; his pretence now to be this and now to be that. But, however sunburnt and slap-dash he might choose to appear at any particular moment, no one could know him even slightly without seeing that he was not only very sincere, but passionately in earnest about the things he cared for. In particular, he cared for literature and the art of writing as seriously as it is possible to care for them. He had read everything and he had read it from the point of view of a working writer. As Mrs Cornford says, 'I can't imagine him using a word of that emotional jargon in which people usually talk or write of poetry. He made it feel more like carpentering.'[7] In discussing the work of living writers he gave you the impression that he had the poem or the story before his eyes in a concrete shape, and his judgments were not only very definite but had a freedom and a reality which mark the criticism of those who are themselves working in the same art. You felt that to him literature was not dead nor of the past, but a thing now in process of construction by people many of whom were his friends; and that knowledge, skill, and, above all, unceasing hard work were required of those who attempt to make it. To work hard, much harder than most writers think it necessary, was an injunction of his that remains in memory from a chaos of such discussions.

The proofs of his first book of poems were lying about that summer on the grass. There were also the manuscripts of poems that were in process of composition. It seemed natural to turn his poetry over and say nothing about it, save perhaps to remark upon his habit of leaving spaces for unforthcoming words which gave his manuscript the look of a puzzle with a number of pieces missing. On one occasion he wished to know what was the brightest thing in nature? and then, deciding with a glance round him that the brightest thing was a leaf in the sun, a blank space towards the end of 'Town and Country' was filled in immediately.

Cloud-like we lean and stare as bright leaves stare.[8]

But instead of framing any opinion as to the merit of his verses we recall merely the curiosity of watching him finding his adjectives, and a vague conception that he was somehow a mixture of scholar and man of action, and that his poetry was the brilliant by-product of energies not yet turned upon their object. It may seem strange, now that he is famous as a poet, how little it seemed to matter in those days whether he wrote poetry or not. It is proof perhaps of the exciting variety of his gifts and of the immediate impression he made of a being so complete and remarkable in himself that it was sufficient to think of him merely as Rupert Brooke. It was not necessary to imagine him dedicated to any particular pursuit. If one traced a career for him many different paths seemed the proper channels for his store of vitality; but clearly he must find scope for his extraordinary gift of being on good terms with his fellow-creatures. For though it is true to say that 'he never "put himself forward" and seldom took the lead in conversation',[9] his manner shed a friendliness wherever he happened to be that fell upon all kinds of different people, and seemed to foretell that he would find his outlet in leading varieties of men as he had led his own circle of Cambridge friends. His practical ability, which was often a support to his friends, was one of the gifts that seemed to mark him for success in active life. He was keenly aware of the state of public affairs, and if you chanced to meet him when there was talk of a strike or an industrial dispute he was evidently as well versed in the complications of social questions as in the obscurities of the poetry of Donne. There, too, he showed his power of being in sympathy with the present. Nothing of this is in the least destructive of his possession of poetic power. No breadth of sympathy or keenness of susceptibility could come amiss to the writer; but perhaps if one feared for him at all it was lest the pull of all his gifts in their different directions might somehow rend him asunder. He was, as he said of himself, 'forty times as sensitive as anybody else,'[10] and apt, as he wrote, to begin 'poking at his own soul, examining it, cutting the soft and rotten parts away'.[11] It needed no special intimacy to guess that beneath 'an appearance almost of placidity'[12] he was the most restless, complex, and analytic of human beings. It was impossible to think of him withdrawn, abstracted, or indifferent. Whether or not it was for the good of his poetry he would be in the thick of things, and one fancies that he would in the end have framed a speech that came very close to the modern point of view – a subtle analytic poetry, or prose perhaps, full of intellect, and full of his keen unsentimental curiosity.

No one could have doubted that as soon as war broke out he would go without hesitation to enlist. His death and burial on the Greek island, which 'must ever be shining with his glory that we buried there',[13] was in harmony with his physical splendour and with the generous warmth of his spirit. But to imagine him entombed, however nobly and fitly, apart from our interests and passions still seems impossibly incongruous with what we remember of his inquisitive eagerness about life, his response to every side of it, and his complex power, at once so appreciative and so sceptical, of testing and enjoying, of suffering and taking with the utmost sharpness the impression of everything that came his way. One turns from the thought of him not with a sense of completeness and finality, but rather to wonder and to question still: what would he have been, what would he have done?

1 – A review in the *TLS*, 8 August 1918, (Kp c117) of *The Collected Poems of Rupert Brooke: With a Memoir* [by Edward Marsh] (Sidgwick & Jackson Ltd, 1918).

Rupert Chawnor Brooke (1887–1915), son of William Parker Brooke, a master at Rugby School, and Ruth Mary Cotterill, was educated at Rugby and King's College, Cambridge, where he read classics and English, 1906–9, and in 1913 became a fellow. Brooke was elected a member of the exclusive Conversazione Society (the Apostles) in 1908, and the following year became president of the University Fabian Society. On the outbreak of war he enlisted in the Royal Naval Division. He died of blood poisoning on active service in the Aegean on 23 April 1915. His published works include *Poems* (1911), the posthumous collection *1914 and Other Poems* (1915), and *John Webster and the Elizabethan Drama* (1916).

'[Bruce] Richmond rang up to offer me Rupert's Life for next week,' VW wrote in her diary on Thursday, 18 July 1918, 'I told him that I should like to explain Rupert to the public. He agreed that there was much misunderstanding. "He was a very jolly sort of fellow" . . .' VW had already remarked upon the 'peculiar irony', to his friends, of Brooke's 'canonisation', in the *TLS*, 27 December 1917 (see 'The New Crusade', above), and there expressed the hope that 'some of those who knew him when scholarship or public life seemed even more his bent than poetry will put their view on record and relieve his ghost of an unmerited and undesired burden of adulation.'

The Stephens had known Rupert Brooke as a child on holiday at St Ives in Cornwall. In later years he and VW were to have many friends in common and for a time they enjoyed an intimate acquaintance. She felt strongly that the memoir by Edward Marsh (1872–1953), now published with the poems, again failed to do Brooke justice. Private Secretary to Winston Churchill, and Brooke's literary executor, Marsh was a classical scholar, a patron of painters and poets, and editor of *Georgian Poetry*. He was a graduate of Trinity College, Cambridge, and, like Brooke, an Apostle. Marsh introduced Brooke to Lady Ottoline Morrell's circle and later drew him into more mundane London society, as frequented by the Asquiths and similar luminaries. His memoir, one hundred and fifty-nine pages in length, was written in August 1915.

'The book is a disgraceful sloppy sentimental rhapsody, leaving Rupert rather tarnished,' she wrote (*ibid.*, 23 July), after a 'great deal of talk' about Brooke with Lytton Strachey. She also consulted James Strachey who had been at preparatory school and afterwards at Cambridge with Brooke and knew him intimately. But as Strachey 'had a medical examination, we couldn't say much about Rupert, save that he was jealous, moody, ill-balanced, all of which I knew, but can hardly say in writing' (*ibid.*, 27 July).

In 1912, much to their unhappy incomprehension, Brooke had abruptly broken with his Bloomsbury friends – 'Spit on Bloomsbury for me' he was to urge his Old Rugbeian and Cambridge friend Geoffrey Keynes in 1913 – following a rift (for which, irrationally, he held Lytton Strachey responsible) in his troubled affair with Katherine Cox.

On 13 August 1918, we find VW writing about her review to Katherine Cox (*II VW Letters*, no. 959): '*I* wrote the article on Rupert in the Times. Bruce Richmond sent the book to me; but when I came to do it I felt that to say out loud what even I knew of Rupert was utterly repulsive, so I merely trod out my 2 columns as decorously as possible. It seemed useless to pitch into Eddy [Marsh]. James [Strachey] meant to try, but gave it up. I think it was one of the most repulsive biographies I've ever read (this, of course, is a little overstated!). He contrived to make the [Brooke] letters as superficial and affected as his own account of Rupert. We're now suggesting that James should write something for us to print. He's sending us the letters to look at. But if you tell Mrs Brooke would you ask her not to tell anyone else, as Richmond is always anxious it shouldn't get out who has done reviews.'

VW next heard from Mrs Brooke herself, on 21 August, and on the same day replied: 'It was a great pleasure to get your letter this morning. I had rather hoped that you would *not* see my review, as I felt that I had not been able to say what I wanted to say about Rupert. Also I am afraid that I gave the impression that I disliked Mr Marsh's memoir much more than I meant to. If I was at all disappointed it was that he gave of course rather his impression of Rupert than the impression which one had always had of him partly from the Stracheys and other friends of his own age. But then Mr Marsh could not have done otherwise, and one is very glad to have the Memoir as it is. Rupert was so great a figure in his friends' eyes that no memoir could possibly be good enough. Indeed, I felt it to be useless to try to write about him. One couldn't get near to his extraordinary charm and goodness. I was 5 years older than he was, and I saw him as one knows one's own family. I stayed a week with him at Grantchester and then he came down here [at Little Talland House, Firle, in Sussex], and we met sometimes in London. He was a wonderful friend. I married in 1912, and was ill for a long time afterwards and never saw him after he went to America [in 1913].'

See also 'The Intellectual Imagination', *III VW Essays*. Reprinted: *B&P*.

2 – *Collected Poems*, intro., p. ix.

3 – *Ibid.*

4 – *Ibid.*, Memoir, p. xxiv, a description of Brooke, as Marsh saw him for the first time, in the role of the Herald in a Cambridge undergraduate production of the Greek play *Eumenides*, in 1906.

5 – VW stayed with Rupert Brooke at The Old Vicarage, Grantchester, 14–19 August 1911, and the two had swum naked in the river together.

6 – Or *Neo-pagan*, as Bloomsbury dubbed the younger generation of mainly Cambridge friends – Katherine Cox, Gwen Darwin, Jacques Raverat, Justin Brooke, Dudley Ward, Gerald Shove, Geoffrey Keynes, David Garnett, the Olivier sisters – among whom Brooke was the leading spirit.

7 – *Collected Poems*, Memoir, p. xlii; Frances Crofts Cornford, *née* Darwin (1886–1960), poet, wife of the classical scholar and fellow of Trinity College, Cambridge, Francis Cornford, was one of Brooke's closest friends. Her first book, *Poems*, was published in 1910.

8 – *Ibid.*, p. 90, from the poem's penultimate stanza:

> Unconscious and unpassionate and still,
>   Cloud-like we lean and stare as bright leaves stare,
> And gradually along the stranger hill
>   Our unwalled loves thin out on vacuous air.

See also, *IV VW Diary*, 4 August 1934: 'Certainly bright leaves do glare [sic] as Rupert said'. And see Leonard Woolf, *II LW*, p. 8: 'Before his [Brooke's] quarrel with Lytton he was friendly both to me and to Virginia. He had a considerable respect for her, I think. He once stayed with her in Firle over a weekend and on Sunday morning they went and sat in Firle Park. He began to write a poem, his method being to put the last word of each line in rhyming quatrains down the sheet of paper and then complete the lines and so the poem. At one moment he said: "Virginia, what is the brightest thing you can think of?" "A leaf with the light on it," was Virginia's instant reply, and it completed the poem.'

9 – *Ibid.*, Memoir, p. xliii.

10 – *Ibid.*, p. cxv, Brooke writing to Marsh from Tahiti, in March 1914: 'The Game is Up, Eddie. If I've gained facts through knocking about with Conrad characters in a Gauguin *entourage*, – I've lost a dream or two. I tried to be a poet. And because I'm a clever writer, and because I was forty times as sensitive as anybody else, I succeeded a little . . . I am what I came out here to be. Hard, quite quite hard. I have become merely a minor character in a Kipling story.

I'll never be able to write anything more, I think . . .'

11 – *Ibid.*, p. lvii, from a letter to Frances Cornford, February 1911.

12 – *Ibid.*, p. xlii.

13 – *Ibid.*, p. clix, from a description by Brooke's friend and fellow naval officer Denis Browne of 'Rupert's island [Skyros] at sunset'.

A Practical Utopia

Mr Onions has undertaken a much more difficult task than that of making a Utopia. It is much easier to forecast what will happen in a hundred years' time than in ten years' time. A century gives you space in which to remould the world to your liking, but in ten years' time England will be much the same as she is now – or only a little different.

Leaving the exact date undetermined Mr Onions supposes that the war is over; the period of reconstruction is in full swing. Dick Helme, who was wounded in the war, is now a member of the Canals and Water Power Section of the Imperial Transport Service. He is taking a convoy of motor lorries to their headquarters on the Severn, when Miss Betty

Lygard, of the Sixth District of the Western Agricultural Area, asks him to give her a lift with her patent beehives and grindstones and bill-hooks. They have never met before, but by the time she is set down with her cases they have arranged to marry each other. You get the impression that these questions will be dispatched very plainly and efficiently in ten years' time, as, indeed, there is not a minute to spare and not a farthing to waste. For the same reason each individual seems to be badged, numbered, and graded in the service of the State. The period of the blood-letting had exhausted England so far that new fabric had to be made from the very beginning. Every living creature was put to use. Every yard of land was turned to advantage. The power of electricity threaded the whole country. A picture of the scene on one of the main roads will serve to show the activity of the hive:

Half the population seemed to have become mobile. The towns were being eviscerated of their slums . . . And wherever there was a settlement or the nucleus of one or the site for one, there was traffic. Steam tractors drew the wagons loaded with building materials, six, and eight, and ten at a time. Lorries followed them with separators and churns, egg crates, and cheese wrings for the dairy services. Reapers and binders and cultivators followed these again drawn by horses. Along the main road, bands of workmen and labourers walked on foot, splitting into detachments, and scattering as they went. Then there was the furniture, the chars-à-bancs with families, loaded with bedding and birdcages . . .[2]

It is a fascinating little model, but, as tends to be the case with all forecasts of this kind, too much stress seems to be laid upon the development of electricity and too little upon the development of humanity. The real triumph for the imagination would be to reveal the end that has been produced by these improved means. A conversation, for example, between a group of people in ten years' time might show us more of the condition of England, than any enumeration of mechanical changes. What things do they take for granted? What startling announcements fall from them naturally? It is comparatively easy to imagine a town clear of smoke, or dinner raised by touching a switch, or an entire house run by a competent engineer in the basement. Perhaps we are meant to infer that the ancient stuff of human nature changes with extreme slowness, and that ten years (if we choose that period) even of such prodigious surface development as we have beheld can do but little to modify the natures of men. If we are to take Mr Onions for a prophet the change is in the direction of briefness, bluntness, and efficiency, as if more than half the attention of the race still went to control the machinery they have devised for saving time. And, clogging the free sweep of every reformer's imagination are the masses of the uneducated upon whom no swift conjuring tricks of change can be performed. The form is necessarily rough and vague, but we can guess how Mr Onions intends his model to shape out. In the world of business there is to be the Amity, a confederation of business interests in alliance instead of competition; in the world of politics the machine is to be worked frankly by newspaper men as a business concern. We are to reach no Utopia in our time. We are to become more clear-sighted, more unselfish, and necessarily more hard-working. Those who find an absorbing interest in making models of the future will find a much greater store of raw material for their industry in *The New Moon* than we have been able to indicate. The solidity of the work is shown by the resentment with which in the last chapter we see the whole structure tumble down and dissolve into a dream.

1 – A review in the *TLS*, 15 August 1918, (Kp C118) of *The New Moon. A Romance of Reconstruction* (Hodder & Stoughton, 1918) by (George) Oliver Onions (1872–1961), author of several novels, including the semi-autobiographical *Little Devil Doubt* (1909) and *Good Boy Seldom* (1911). He was the husband of the popular novelist Berta Ruck, whose name VW was by chance to reproduce on a tombstone in *Jacob's Room* (1922), much to Onions's vexation (see *II QB*, pp. 91–2).
2 – Onions, pt ii, p. 124, which differs from VW's version in several minor points of punctuation.

'The Sad Years'

More than half of the poetry which flowers in England seems to be grown from the same seed – the desire for self-expression. The seed, happily, is as various as the self. But through the screen of language and metre one can see plainly enough that the origin of the poem was a personal experience, too personal and disconnected from other experiences to be projected into a story or wrought into an agument. The presence of this element is one reason for finding most poetry, even most bad poetry, worth reading, and for reading it with a confusion of spirit such as the narrative of the writer's experience if told in person would inspire. Nevertheless, we are inclined to attribute the unimportance of most verse to the same cause. There are the seeds of two poems, for instance, in the two statements that so-and-so was unhappy on Friday because it rained, and happy on Saturday because the sun was out; but unless our fount of sympathy is inexhaustible we get tired of a volume composed of these simple experiences of sunshine and rain. The mere fact of rhyming and scanning, like the fact of being in a confessional, somehow hallows what is written and said; so that all platitudes and confessions naturally seek the sanctuary of verse. Women are more prone than men to take refuge in this form of simple egotism, though for reasons, perhaps, that have more in common with modesty than conceit. They appear to be more shy of using their brains and of displaying their love of language in poetry than men of the same poetic gift. A simple statement, a mere cry, is enough, the argument seems to be, if you are writing poetry, and with luck it may turn out that you have written a masterpiece.

Something of this kind applies to Mrs Shorter's work, although she was frequently almost lucky enough to make it seem a wise policy. 'The gifts came to her out of the air, so to speak,' writes Katharine Tynan, 'real gifts and nothing acquired.'[2] We need not quarrel with the statement that her gifts were real. Every page of her book goes to prove it. The most severe of critics if asked for advice could only have advised her to go on writing poetry; and, indeed, it is likely that the woman who wrote the following verses would have written verses against all the dissuasion in the world:

> I saw children playing, dancing in a ring,
>   Till a voice came calling, calling one away;
> With sad backward glances she went loitering,
>   Hoping they would miss her and so cease to play.
>
> Pettishly and pouting, ''Tis not time to sleep,'
>   Sobbing and protesting, slowly she did go;
> But her merry comrades they all run and leap,
>   Feeling not her absence, heeding not her woe.[3]

The line that the critic might have taken would have been to urge her to concentrate, to enrich, to perfect, not to trust merely to 'passionate emotion to give it wings'.[4] For to arrive at art without any apprentice-ship may, as Mrs Tynan says, make the word genius not inapplicable to those who so arrive; but the difficulty is to name these fortunate people. Mrs Shorter, moreover, interests us partly because she was not content with her gift for singing songs that seem to sing themselves. The ideas behind several of her poems are subtle and difficult, and have evidently broken through her powers of expression so that they remain sketches rather than completed poems. One need not grudge an occasional stumble caused by an honest inability to get the meaning into words. But this faultiness of technique helps to make her verse seem unduly personal; she cannot give her melancholy or her indignation the impersonal stamp which perfect expression bestows, so that we forget the particular grief and the particular writer.

With these reservations one must give her a high place among those writers whose gift is such that one is almost afraid to advise them to concentrate, to finish or to perfect, lest in so doing they should spoil. They have virtues which seem to give their work the charm and intimacy of the living voice. To their own contemporaries they often seem more sympathetic, because they are more on our level of feeling, than the aloof and the contemplative. In reading Mrs Shorter's poetry, for instance, we are almost as much interested by her personality as we are by her poetry. We hardly know whether we like the verses we have quoted because they make us sympathise with her emotion or because we find them beautiful in themselves. The future of work marked by this twofold appeal is precarious, because its accent will scarcely be understood by a later age; but from that very reason arises much of its significance to us.

1 – A review in the *TLS*, 29 August 1918, (Kp C119) of *The Sad Years* (Constable & Co. Ltd, 1918) by Dora Sigerson (Mrs Clement Shorter). In a prefatory tribute to the author, who had died on 6 January 1918, Katharine Tynan relates that Dora Sigerson, daughter of an eminent Dublin doctor of medicine, had suffered a sudden breakdown in 1916 over the events that followed the Easter Rising and had died broken-hearted 'as she would have chosen to die, for the love of the Dark Rosaleen'.
2 – Sigerson, 'A Tribute and Some Memories' by Katharine Tynan, p. ix.
3 – *Ibid.*, 'I Saw Children Playing', p. 52, the first two of five stanzas.
4 – *Ibid.*, Tynan, p. xi.

The 'Movie' Novel

When we say that the adventures of Sylvia Scarlett are much more interesting than Sylvia Scarlett herself, we are recommending the book to half the reading public and condemning it in the eyes of the other half. There are people who require the heroines of their novels to be

interesting, and they know by experience that the adventurous heroine is apt to be as dull in fiction as she is in life. It is true that adventurers are not dull in the ordinary sense of the word; they are monotonous, self-centred, serious, rather than dull. They have spun all their substance into adventure, and nothing remains of them but a frail shell inhabited by a very small creature with an enormous egotism and an overweening vanity. The charge may be just, yet there is a great deal to be said in praise of adventures themselves, and not a little relief in finding occasionally that people are not quite so interesting as writers are in the habit of insisting, in novels, that we shall find them. Perhaps Sylvia might have been interesting if she had ever had the time to set about it. She had her moments of introspection, as upon that occasion when she announced 'I represent the original conception of the Hetaera – the companion. I don't want to be made love to, and every man who makes love to me I dislike. If I ever do fall in love, I'll be a man's slave.'² But perhaps she was aware that being interesting was not in her line, as we are inclined to agree with her that it was not. At any rate, this reflection occurs in a momentary lull, and directly Mr Mackenzie catches her in the lazy pose of self analysis he gives a crack of his whip and sends her flying, as merrily as if she had never heard the word Hetaera, through the next hoop.

We cannot begin even to count those hoops. They are so many and so variously designed that a bare programme of the entertainment or a catalogue of the actors' names would fill perhaps a score of columns. In very early youth Sylvia came to England dressed as a boy and christened Sylvester to share the shifts and adventures of her father, an absconding clerk, in the shadier suburbs of London. From the addresses of their lodgings and the names of their friends the experienced reader who has read, among other books, the novels of Dickens will gather what sort of life they led, and will even be able to improvise a certain amount of the conversation of Mrs Bullwinkle, Mrs Gowndry, Mr Monkley; and General Dashwood of Tinderbox Lane. But it is better and simpler to rely entirely upon Mr Mackenzie. He does it so fast and so deftly that merely to keep up with him is quite enough strain upon the faculties. He not only finds names for landladies, cabmen, mountebanks, actresses, tenors, managers, schoolmistresses, barons, clergymen, natives of Brazil, and maiden ladies living in villas appropriately named too, but he provides them with queer occupations, and clever things to say, let alone a number of surprising things to do. You can scarcely open the book anywhere without finding a cab bolting down Haverstock Hill with an eloping couple inside it, or a baboon escaping from Earl's Court Exhibition, or an actor dropping dead, or a curtain going up, or a landlady being funny. Here is a shop incident to show how quickly it rattles along:

The confusion in the shop became general: Mr Gonner cut his thumb, and the sight of the blood caused a woman who was eating a sausage to choke; another customer took advantage of the row to snatch a side of bacon and try to escape, but another customer with a finer moral sense prevented him; a dog, who was sniffing in the entrance, saw the bacon on the floor and tried to seize it, but, getting his tail trodden upon by somebody, he took fright and bit a small boy who was waiting to change a shilling into coppers. Meanwhile Sylvia ... jumped on to the first omnibus, ⟨&c., &c.⟩[3]

When we reached this point we seized the opportunity, not so much of being bored as of being out of breath, to reflect upon the propriety after all of using the word adventure. It is true that Sylvia is left on top of an omnibus bound for West Kensington without a penny in the world; she is young, beautiful, and friendless into the bargain; we have no idea what is going to become of her; why then do we refuse to call it an adventure? The obvious way to settle the question is to bring to mind Tom Jones, Moll Flanders, Isopel Berners, or the Flaming Tinman.[4] These people may not be interesting either, but when any one of them has not a penny in the world it is a serious matter. Compared with Mr Mackenzie's characters they are a slow-moving race – awkward, ungainly and simple-minded. But consider how many things we know about them, how much we guess, what scenes of beauty and romance we set them in, how much of England is their background – without a word of description perhaps, but merely because they are themselves. We can think about them when we are no longer reading the book. But we cannot do this with Mr Mackenzie's characters; and the reason is, we fancy, that though Mr Mackenzie can see them once he can never see them twice, and, as in a cinema, one picture must follow another without stopping, for if it stopped and we had to look at it we should be bored. Now, it is a strange thing that no one has yet been seen to leave a cinema in tears. The cab horse bolts down Haverstock Hill and we think it a good joke; the cyclist runs over a hen, knocks an old woman into the gutter, and has a hose turned upon him. But we never care whether he is wet or hurt or dead. So it is with Sylvia Scarlett and her troupe. Up they get and off they go, and as for minding what becomes of them, all we hope is that they will, if possible, do something funnier next time. No, it is not a book of adventures; it is a book of cinema.

1 – A review in the *TLS*, 29 August 1918, (Kp C120) of *The Early Life and Adventures of Sylvia Scarlett* (Martin Secker, 1918) by Compton Mackenzie (1883–1972) whose works at this date included *Sinister Street* (1913–14) and *Guy and Pauline* (1915). Mackenzie served in military intelligence during the war, chiefly in Greece, where he set part of his next novel *Sylvia and Michael* (1919), the sequel to the book reviewed here. See 'Sylvia and Michael', *III VW Essays*. Reprinted: *CW*.
2 – Mackenzie, bk II, ch. I, pp. 270–1.
3 – *Ibid.*, bk I, ch. V, pp. 151–2.
4 – Characters respectively in: Henry Fielding, *Tom Jones, a Foundling* (1749); Daniel Defoe, *The Fortunes and Misfortunes of the famous Moll Flanders* (1722); George Borrow, *Lavengro and the Romany Rye* (1858), and *Lavengro, the Scholar – the Gypsy – the Priest* (1851).

War in the Village

Nowadays many whose minds have not been used to turn that way must stop and ponder what thoughts the country people carry with them to their work in the fields, or cogitate as they scrub the cottage floor. It is a matter for speculation and shyness since the gulf between the articulate and inarticulate is not to be crossed by facile questioning, and silence may seem after all the best we can offer by way of sympathy to people whose lives seem so mysteriously and for such ages steeped in silence. Thus Mr Hewlett[2] has chosen one of the most difficult of tasks when he tries to think himself into the mind of the village wife, and to express thoughts 'which she may never have formulated, but which, I am very sure, lie in her heart too deep for any utterance save that of tears'.[3] He has succeeded, beyond doubt, in writing a terse, moving, and very sincere poem; but that it is the lament of a village woman for her shepherd husband killed in France, and for the baby whose death followed upon his death, we are not so sure.

Yet it would be difficult to say what quality we seek for in Mr Hewlett's poem and find lacking. Where it would have been easy to offend there is no ground for offence; the conception is very dignified and as completely without a touch of the sentimentality, which the theme invites, as the language is almost equally free from the taint of the professional writer. The village wife has nothing idyllic about her. From her birth upwards she takes her share in what Mr Hewlett calls 'the unending war'[4] waged from one generation to another by the sons and daughters of the poor. She scrubs and rinses and milks the cows year in and year out.

> On winter mornings dark and hard,
>   White from aching bed,
> There were the huddled fowls in yard
>   All to be fed.
> My frozen breath stream'd from my lips,
>   The cows were hid in steam;
> I lost sense of my finger-tips
>   And milkt in a dream.[5]

Very finely and truly Mr Hewlett bases her life deep down among the roots of the earth; she grows among the other growing things, and the hills and woods of her parish are England and the world to her, and she has inherited from generations of village women who lived this life and knew its perils the morality upon which their lives were founded.

> I learned at home the laws of Earth;
>   The nest-law that says,
> Stray not too far beyond the hearth,
>   Keep truth always;
> And then the law of sip and bite:
>   Work, that there may be some
> For you who crowd the board this night,
>   And the one that is to come.
> The laws are so for bird and beast,
>   And so we must live:
> They give the most who have the least,
>   And gain of what they give.
> For working women 'tis the luck,
>   A child on the lap;
> And when a crust he learn to suck,
>   Another's for the pap.[6]

This hard natural life scarcely shares in the changes of the self-conscious world. It has grown so close to the earth and so shaped itself to the laws of nature that it might well remain unshaken for ever. But one summer evening the village wife hears one stranger say to another as he passes, 'Then that means war'.[7] From that moment her security is troubled, and by November, to her inexpressible bewilderment, her own house and happiness are at the mercy of a force so remote that, though it has power to take her husband from her, she can hardly figure to herself what the nature of it is. Her husband feels it, and goes; more strangely it takes not only his body, but makes unfamiliar all that she knew in his spirit. She hears that he is missing, and exclaims:

> Missing! My man had been dead
> Before he went away.[8]

What, then, remains for her? Nothing but to ask perpetually those questions as to the reason and justice of these events which in the mind of a woman who has placed her trust in the rightness of the natural order have an extreme bitterness mixed with their bewilderment. She must puzzle out why the world has deceived her; why her right was not right after all.

The verses, as our quotations show, are plain, deeply felt, and often beautiful. But, for all their scrupulous care and regard for the truth, they strike us not so much as the thoughts and laments of the woman herself as the words of a very sympathetic spectator who is doing his best to express what he supposes must be there beneath the silence and at the heart of the tears. The argument has too much cogency, the thoughts follow each other in too orderly a fashion to be the cry of a woman bereft of husband and son. Perhaps it is coarseness – the quality that is the most difficult of all for the educated to come by – that is lacking. By coarseness we mean something as far removed from vulgarity as can be. We mean something vehement, full throated, carrying down in its rush sticks and stones and fragments of human nature pell-mell. That is what we miss in Mr Hewlett's poem, fine though it is.

1 – A review in the TLS, 12 September 1918, (Kp C121) of The Village Wife's Lament (Martin Secker, 1918) by Maurice Hewlett. Reprinted: CW.
2 – Maurice Henry Hewlett (1861–1923) regarded himself primarily as a poet – in 1916 he had published an epic poem The Song of the Plow – but he was far more successful as an author of romantic and historical fiction and had found fame and fortune overnight with his first book The Forest Lovers (1898). Early in her career as a reviewer, VW had referred to Hewlett, in a letter to Madge Vaughan, mid-December 1904, as an 'affected Dandy' and expressed a wish to give him his due (I VW Letters, no. 202).
3 – Hewlett, Note, p. 62.
4 – Ibid., p. 16: 'Watch you the same unending war/ Ontaken by your son.'
5 – Ibid., p. 26.
6 – Ibid., p. 15, which begins a new stanza at 'The laws are so for bird and beast'.
7 – Ibid., p. 36.   8 – Ibid., p. 55.

The Rights of Youth

The moralists of the nursery used to denounce a sin which went by the name of 'talking at', and was rendered the more expressive by the little stress which always fell upon the 'at', as if to signify the stabbing, jabbing, pinpricking nature of the sin itself. The essence of 'talking at' was that you vented your irritation in an oblique fashion which it was difficult for your victim to meet otherwise than by violence. This old crime of the nursery is very apt to blossom afresh in people of mature age when they sit down to write a novel. It blossoms often as unconsciously as we may suppose that the pearl blossoms in the breast of the oyster. Unfortunately for art, though providentially for the moralist, the pearl that is produced by this little grain of rancour is almost invariably a sham one.

In the early chapters of *Joan and Peter* there are a great many scenes and characters which seem to have been secreted round some sharp-edged grain which fate has lodged in the sensitive substance of Mr Wells's brain. Lady Charlotte Sydenham had some such origin; so, too, had Miss Phoebe Stubland; the sketch of Arthur Stubland was due to a disturbance of the kind, and certainly the schoolmistresses of St George and the Venerable Bede had no other begetter. We catch ourselves wondering whether Mr Wells is any longer aware of the grotesque aspect of these figures of his, burdened as they are with the most pernicious or typical views of their decade, humped and loaded with them so that they can hardly waddle across the stage without coming painfully to grief. The conscientious reader will try to refer these burlesques to some such abstraction as the Anglican Church, or the vagaries of aimless and impulsive modernism in the eighteen-nineties; but if you are indolent you will be inclined to give up playing your part in the game of illusion, and to trifle with idle speculations as to the idiosyncrasies of Mr Wells. But soon the very crudeness of the satire leads us to make a distinction, and directly we are satisfied of its truth our irritation is spent and our interest aroused. Mr Wells is not irritated with these people personally, or he would have taken more pains to annoy them; he is irritated with the things they represent. Indeed, he has been so much irritated that he has almost forgotten the individual. He is sore and angry and exaggerated and abusive because the waste, the stupidity, the senility of our educational system have afflicted him as men are, for the most part, afflicted only by their personal calamities. He possesses the queer power of understanding that 'the only wrongs that really matter to mankind are the undramatic general wrongs',² and of feeling them dramatically, as if they had wronged him individually. Here, he says, we have two children endowed with everything that the world most needs, and let us see what the world will make of them. What education have we to offer them? What are we able to teach them about the three great questions of sex and state and religion? First, he gluts his rage upon Lady Charlotte and Miss Phoebe Stubland, much to the detriment of the book, and then the matter is seriously taken in hand by Mr Oswald Stubland, V.C., a gallant gentleman with imaginative views upon the British Empire. He had believed that the Empire was the instrument of world civilisation, and that his duty in Central Africa was the duty of an enlightened schoolmaster. But when his health broke down he returned to the far more difficult task of educating two of the children of the Empire in the very metropolis of civilisation. He started off upon a pilgrimage to the schools and colleges of England, asking imaginative questions, and getting more and more dismayed at the answers he received.

Don't you *know* that education is building up an imagination? I thought everybody knew that . . . Why is he to *do* Latin? Why is he to *do* Greek? . . . What will my ward know about Africa when you have done with him? . . . Will he know anything about the way the Royal Exchange affects the Empire? . . . But why shouldn't he understand the elementary facts of finance?³

This is a mere thimbleful from the Niagara which Mr Wells pours out when his blood is up. He throws off the trammels of fiction as lightly as he would throw off a coat in running a race. The ideas come pouring in whether he speaks them in his own person or lets Oswald have them, or quotes them from real books and living authorities, or invents and derides some who are not altogether imaginary. He does not mind what material he uses so long as it will stick in its place and is roughly of the shape and colour he wants. Fiction, you can imagine him saying, must take care of itself; and to some extent fiction does take care of itself. No one, at any rate, can make an inquiry of this sort so vivid, so pressing, so teeming and sprouting with suggestions and ideas and possibilities as he does; indeed, when he checks himself and exclaims, 'But it is high time that Joan and Peter came back into the narrative,'⁴ we want to cry out,

'Don't bother about Joan and Peter. Go on talking about education.' We have an uneasy suspicion that Joan and Peter will not be nearly so interesting as Mr Wells's ideas about their education and their destiny. But, after all, we know that Mr Wells is quite right when he says that it is time to bring them in. He would be shirking the most difficult part of his task if he left them out.

Like his own Oswald Stubland, Mr Wells 'belongs to that minority of Englishmen who think systematically, whose ideas join on'. He has 'built up a sort of philosophy for himself',[5] by which he does try his problems and with which he fits in such new ideas as come to him. He is not writing about education, but about the education of Joan and Peter. He is not isolating one of the nerves of our existence and tracing its course separately, but he is trying to give that nerve its place in the whole system and to show us the working of the entire body of human life. That is why his book attains its enormous bulk; and that is why, with all its sketchiness and crudeness and redundancy, its vast soft, billowing mass is united by a kind of coherency and has some relation to a work of art. If you could isolate the seed from which the whole fabric has sprung you would find it, we believe, to consist of a fiery passion for the rights of youth – a passion for courage, vitality, initiative, inventiveness, and all the qualities that Mr Wells likes best. And as Mr Wells can never think without making a picture of his thought, we do not have youth in the abstract, but Joan and Peter, Wilmington and Troop, Huntley and Hetty Reinhart. We have Christmas parties and dressings-up and dances and night clubs and Cambridge and London and real people disguised under fictitious names, and very bright covers on the chairs and Post-Impressionist[6] pictures on the walls and advanced books upon the tables. This power of visualising a whole world for his latest idea to grow in is the power that gives these hybrid books their continuity and vitality.

But because Mr Wells's ideas put on flesh and blood so instinctively and admirably we are able to come up close to them and look them in the face; and the result of seeing them near at hand is, as our suspicions assured us that it would be, curiously disappointing. Flesh and blood have been lavished upon them, but in crude lumps and unmodelled masses, as if the creator's hand, after moulding empires and sketching deities, had grown too large and slack and insensitive to shape the fine clay of men and women. It is curious to observe, for example, what play Mr Wells is now constrained to make with the trick of modernity. It is as if he suspected some defect in the constitution of his characters and sought to remedy it with rouge and flaxen wigs and dabs of powder, which he is in too great a hurry nowadays to fix on securely or plaster in the right places. But if Joan and Peter are merely masquerading rather clumsily at being the heirs of the ages, Mr Wells's passion for youth is no make-believe. The sacrifice, if we choose to regard it so, of his career as a novelist has been a sacrifice to the rights of youth, to the needs of the present moment, to the lives of the rising generation. He has run up his buildings to house temporary departments of the Government. But if he is one of those writers who snap their fingers in the face of the future, the roar of genuine applause which salutes every new work of his more than makes up, we are sure, for the dubious silence, and possibly the unconcealed boredom, of posterity.

1 – A review in the *TLS*, 19 September 1918, (Kp C122) of *Joan and Peter. The Story of an Education* (Cassell & Co. Ltd., 1918) by H. G. Wells (1866–1946). As VW noted in her diary on Wednesday, 18 September 1918, Sidney and Beatrice Webb, who, like H. G. Wells, were founding members of the Fabian Society, had come to visit the Woolfs at Asheham House, Sussex, the previous Saturday, 'a pouring wet day . . . Next day, which was said to begin for the W[ebb]s at 5.30, when they begin tea-drinking in their bedrooms, I had to withdraw in order to do battle with a very obstinate review of Wells' "Joan & Peter". My ideas were struck stiff by the tap of Mrs W.s foot, up & down the terrace, & the sound of her rather high, a rather mocking voice, discoursing to L[eonard Woolf] while she waited either for W[ebb] to come or the rain to stop.' See also 'Character in Fiction', *III VW Essays*. Reprinted: *CW*.

2 – Wells, ch. XIV, p. 698: 'The country was at sixes and sevens because its education by school and college, by book and speech and newspaper, was confused and superficial and incomplete because its institutions were a patched-up system of traditions, compromises, and interests, devoid of any clear and single guiding idea of a national purpose. The only wrongs that really matter to mankind are the undramatic general wrongs; but the only wrongs that appeal to the uneducated imagination are individual wrongs.'

3 – *Ibid.*, ch. X, pp. 322–3, adapted.

4 – *Ibid.*, ch. IX, p. 284, which has: 'this narrative'.

5 – For both quotations, *ibid.*, ch. XII, p. 500.

6 – Post-Impressionism makes an early and, to students of Bloomsbury, an interesting appearance in *Joan and Peter*, as does Roger Fry, organiser of the Post-Impressionist Exhibitions at the Grafton Galleries in 1910 and 1912, in the character of Stubland, e.g., *ibid.*, ch. I, p. 6: 'From the last stage of Quakerism to the last extremity of decoration is but a step. Quite an important section of the art world in Britain owes itself to the Quakers and Plymouth Brethren, and to the drab and grey disposition of the sterner evangelicals. It is as if that elect strain in the race had

shut its eyes for a generation or so, merely in order to open them again and see brighter. The reaction of the revolting generation has always been toward colour; the pyrotechnic display of the Omega workshops in London is but the last violent outbreak of the Quaker spirit. Young Stubland, a quarter of a century before the Omega enterprise, was already slaking a thirst for chromatic richness behind the lead of William Morris and the Pre-Raphaelites. It took a year or so and several teachers and much friendly frankness to persuade him he could neither draw nor paint, and then he relapsed into decoration and craftsmanship.'

Mr Hudson's Childhood

Since in this account of his childhood Mr Hudson[2] speculates as to the origin of certain childish instincts, one may perhaps suitably begin what one has to say of his book by recalling a childish impression which his writing has brought to mind. Between or behind the dense and involved confusion which grown-up life presented there appeared for moments chinks of pure daylight in which the simple, unmistakable truth, the underlying reason, otherwise so overlaid and befogged, was revealed. Such seasons, or more probably seconds, were of so intense a revelation that the wonder came to be how the truth could ever again be overcast, as it certainly would be overcast directly this lantern-like illumination went out.[3] Somehow or other Mr Hudson writes as if he held his lantern steadily upon this simple, unmistakable truth, and had never been deluded or puzzled or put off by the confusions which overlay it. It is an effect that the great Russian writers produce far more commonly than the English, and may perhaps be connected with the surroundings of their childhood, so different both for Mr Hudson and for the Russians from the surroundings of the ordinary English childhood. Therefore one is reluctant to apply to Mr Hudson's book those terms of praise which are bestowed upon literary and artistic merit, though needless to say it possesses both. One does not want to recommend it as a book so much as to greet it as a person, and not the clipped and imperfect person of ordinary autobiography, but the whole and complete person whom we meet rarely enough in life or in literature.

But Mr Hudson himself provides one clue to the secret which we have clumsily tried to prise open. He has been saying that it is difficult not 'to retouch, and colour, and shade, and falsify' the picture of childhood by the light of what we have since become. Serge Aksakoff, he goes on to say, in his *History of My Childhood*, was an exception 'simply because the temper and tastes and passions of his early boyhood – his intense love of his mother, of nature, of all wildness, and of sport – endured unchanged in him to the end and kept him a boy in heart, able after long years to revive the past mentally and picture it in its true, fresh, and original colours'.[4] That is true also of Mr Hudson. When he writes of himself as a little boy he does not get out of his large body into a small different one, or fall into that vein of half-humorous and romantic reverie which the recollection of our small predecessor usually inspires. The little boy whom he remembers was already set with even fresher passion upon the same objects that Mr Hudson has sought all his life. Therefore he has not to reconstruct himself, but only to intensify. It seems, too, as if it must be the easiest thing in the world to remember clearly such a childhood as his was, spent not in some cranny, artificially scooped out of the grown-up world, but in a place naturally fitted and arranged for it. His father lived in a vast house on 'the illimitable grassy plain of South America',[5] at a little distance from a plantation of various kinds of trees which were the nesting-place of many different birds. A man upon horseback raised three or four feet above the surrounding level would see all round

a flat land, its horizon a perfect ring of misty blue colour, where the crystal blue dome of the sky rests on the level green world . . .[6] On all this visible world there were no fences and no trees excepting those which had been planted at the old estancia houses, and these being far apart the groves and plantations looked like small islands of trees, or mounds, blue in the distance, on the great plain or pampa . . .[7] The picture that most often presents itself is of the cattle coming home in the evening; the green quiet plain extending away from the gate to the horizon; the western sky flushed with sunset hues, and the herd of four or five hundred cattle trotting homewards with loud lowings and bellowings, raising a great cloud of dust with their hoofs, while behind gallop the herdsmen urging them on with wild cries.[8]

One is inclined to hold the view, indeed, that parents of children have no business to live anywhere except on the pampas of South America. For beyond the daily ecstasy of living out of doors, fate seems to have seen to it that the few human beings who wandered into the large house as guests, beggars or tutors summed up in their persons the most marked characteristics of humanity. There was Captain Scott, captain of what is unknown, but an Englishman of immense bulk, 'with a great round face of a purplish red colour', dressed always in a light blue suit, who would arrive with his pockets bulging with sweets from the distant land where sweets were made, and stand, 'looking [...] like a vast blue pillar,'[9] motionless upon the bank, rod in hand. Unknown in origin, he disappeared to an unknown fate, 'yet in my mind how beautiful his gigantic image looks!'[10] Then every seven or eight weeks the Hermit arrived, to beg not money but food, which he would take only in the form of flawless biscuits, for should they be chipped or cracked he would have none of them. He was supposed to have committed some terrible crime, which he expiated by wearing a very thick mattress stuffed with sticks, stones, lumps of clay, horns, and other heavy objects, enough to weigh down two men, which he dragged about with him, in penance for what no one knew, since he could speak no intelligible language and died under his mattress alone on the plains without confessing the nature of his crime. The supply of tutors in the pampas was also limited to men who had mysterious reasons of their own, whether it was a devotion to white Brazilian rum or difficulties with the Roman Catholic Church, for choosing a nomadic life and being unable to retain their employment for long. Mr Trigg, for example, 'followed teaching because all work was excessively irksome to him',[11] and was hired by the month, like the shepherd or the cowman, to teach children their letters, until his failing found him out, and in spite of his delightful social gifts and his passion for reading Dickens[12] aloud, he had to take his horse again and ride off with a bag containing all his possessions over the plains.

With reluctance one must resist the temptation of transcribing one such character sketch after another, not only because the transcription damages the pleasure of coming upon the page itself, but also because to give the impression that the book is mainly composed of such sketches would not be true. The remarkably handsome young gentleman with a wash-leather bag attached to his wrist who threw pebbles at small birds on the Parade at Buenos Aires, the immensely fat lady who sat perpetually on a cane chair attended by four hairless dogs, the three on the floor 'ever patiently waiting for their respective turns to occupy the broad warm lap',[13] the stranger who played divinely on the guitar but could not go on playing for thinking of his own family in Spain, Don Gregorio with his passion for breeding piebald horses and his rage against anyone possessed of such an animal who refused to sell it – all these figures met the eyes of the observant little boy, and are faithfully presented as the sort of thing that you saw if you looked up in South America from the absorbing business of life. For he was a child, almost a baby, when he discovered instinctively what was the business, or rather the spirit, of life, the string upon which all sights and thoughts and adventures were hereafter to be threaded. He begins as a small child who notices things in the bulk to gaze at the trees in the plantation. It was a 'wonderful experience to be among them, to feel and smell their rough, moist, bark, stained green with moss, and to look up at the blue sky through the network of interlacing twigs'.[14] Then those trees became full of birds, and Mr Hudson is constantly tempted to make 'this sketch of my first years a book about birds and little else'.[15] He resists the temptation, but, like all writers of strong individuality, a colour gets into his pages apart from the actual words, and even when they are not mentioned we seem to see the bird flying, settling, feeding, soaring through every page of the book. There are the immensely tall white-and-rose-coloured birds of earliest memory who stand feeding in the river and then shake out their wings, which are of a glorious crimson colour; then the resounding screams of the travelling parrots are heard, and they appear, flying at a moderate height, 'with long pointed wings and long graduated tails, in their sombre green plumage touched with yellow, blue, and crimson colour'.[16] These are the birds of earliest childhood, and from them his dreams spring and by them his images are coloured in later life. Riding at first seemed to him like flying. When he is first among a crowd of well-dressed people in Buenos Aires he compares them at once to a flock of military starlings. From watching birds comes his lifelong desire to fly – but it is a desire which no airship or balloon but the wings of a bird alone will satisfy. Later these first impressions were intensified by his habit of rambling off alone and standing motionless, staring at vacancy as his mother, following him in anxiety for his state of mind, supposed; but to her joy she found that he was not staring at vacancy, but observing 'an insect perhaps, but oftener a bird'.[17]

And yet if we were to say that on this account Mr Hudson's book is written chiefly for naturalists it would not be true. The naturalist will see the bird accurately enough, but he will not see it in relation to the tree, to the small boy, to the strange characters of the plain; nor will the bodies of birds represent for him that mysterious spirit which Mr Hudson, for some reason that psychologists must explain, finds in all nature, but in birds particularly. Because Mr Hudson is able to do all this, to read his book is to read another chapter in that enormous book which is written from time to time by Rousseau and Borrow and George Sand[18] and

Aksakoff among other people – a book which we can never read enough of; and therefore we must beg Mr Hudson not to stop here, but to carry the story on to the farthest possible limits.

1 – A review in the *TLS*, 26 September 1918, (Kp C123) of *Far Away and Long Ago. A History of my Early Life* (J. M. Dent & Sons Ltd., 1918) by W. H. Hudson. 'I went over to Charleston last Tuesday,' VW wrote in her diary on Monday, 23 September 1918, '& . . . sat with Nessa & laid bare my sorrows, which she can more than match . . . I walked home shoving my bicycle, too badly punctured to ride.

'Well then, the Times began to shower books upon me, & I was reduced at one point to writing my review in the afternoon, nor can I discover any reason why one's brains should be unavailable between 3 & 5. When the telegraph girl rode up with a telegram from Clive to put us off, owing to some disease of Mary's, we were both immensely relieved, & I threw down my pen, as they say, & ate a large tea, & found my load of writing much lessened. When I have to review at command of a telegram, & Mr Geal has to ride off in a shower to fetch the book at Glynde, & comes & taps at the window about 10 at night to receive his shilling & hand in the parcel, I feel pressed & important & even excited a little. For a wonder, the book, Hudson, was worth reading.'

Shortly after Hudson's death, on 18 August 1922, VW was to remark, in a letter to Katherine Arnold-Forster, dated 23 August (*II VW Letters*, no. 1276): 'I was to have been taken to see Mr Hudson this winter by [Dorothy] Brett, who adored him . . . Parts of his books are very good – only others are very bad; isn't that so? Anyhow, I wish I had seen him'. Later, in 'How It Strikes a Contemporary', *IV VW Essays* and *CR1*, she wrote: 'Passages in *Far Away and Long Ago* will undoubtedly go to posterity entire.' See also 'A Russian Schoolboy', above. Reprinted: *CW*.

2 – William Henry Hudson (1841–1922), naturalist and writer, was born at Quilmes, some ten miles from Buenos Aires, and came to England in 1869. His works include *The Purple Land* (1885), *A Naturalist in La Plata* (1892), *Green Mansions* (1904), and the classic *A Shepherd's Life* (1910), set in the downlands of Wiltshire.

3 – Compare 'A Sketch of the Past', *MoB*.

4 – Hudson, ch. VII, p. 226. Serge Aksakoff (1791–1850), *Years of Childhood* – published originally as part of *Family Chronicle*, 1856 – had appeared in English translation in 1916. See also 'A Russian Schoolboy', above.

5 – *Ibid.*, ch. IV, p. 45, which has: 'I remember – better than any orchard, grove or wood I have ever entered or seen, do I remember that shady oasis of trees at my new home on the illimitable grassy plain.'

6 – *Ibid.*, ch. V, p. 63, which begins: 'We see all round us'.

7 – *Ibid.*, p. 64, which has: 'On this visible earth'.

8 – *Ibid.*, ch. I, p. 10.

9 – *Ibid.*, p. 12.

10 – *Ibid.*, p. 13.

11 – *Ibid.*, ch. II, p. 26.

12 – Charles Dickens (1812–70).

13 – Hudson, ch. XI, p. 158.
14 – *Ibid.*, ch. IV, p. 45.
15 – *Ibid.*, p. 62.
16 – *Ibid.*, ch. VI, p. 86, which has: 'crimson colour!'.
17 – *Ibid.*, ch. VII, p. 93.
18 – Jean-Jacques Rousseau (1712–78); George Borrow (1803–81); George Sand (1804–76).

Caution and Criticism

One is inclined to say that if Mr Williams[2] had been less impartial and less conscientious he would have written a better, at least a more readable, book. If, like most historians of modern literature, he had written to prove a theory or impose a view of art, the 360-odd writers whose works he examines in these pages would have merged themselves magically in an orderly pattern, which, whether fallacious or not, we should have taken in at a glance. As it is each of these writers stands obstinately a little apart from his fellow; and when Mr Williams, drawing back and half closing his eyes, tries to resolve them into schools or tendencies he is forced to confess, being an honest man, that he can see nothing but individuals. That he set out in the hope of reducing them to some kind of order is obvious from the opening pages of his book. The year 1890, he does his best to insist, was the year in which the Victorianism of the Victorian age virtually, or practically, or to some extent, passed away; but as it was not of one texture, nor disappeared all at once, owing to the longevity of George Meredith[3] and other causes, nothing so dramatic as a fresh age could immediately succeed it. It was replaced gradually by a patchwork of influences – the significance of Oscar Wilde's aestheticism,[4] the aims of the *Yellow Book*, and the Savoy;[5] the influence of W. E. Henley;[6] and the ideals of the Celtic revival in Ireland. Under these banners we have with qualifications and exceptions, and, of course, with innumerable inter-alliances and reactions, fought until that other convenient date – August 1914.

This general statement being very guardedly and tentatively laid down, Mr Williams proceeds to examine into the cases of particular writers and finds before very long that it is impossible to keep them even within these sufficiently elastic boundaries. As early as page 68 he finds it necessary to content himself with the study of separate writers whose aims become increasingly individual and disconnected. Then a rough chronological order is attempted, and at one point it seems as if the novelists were to be grouped, not according to their age, but according to their worthlessness. It becomes, indeed, more and more evident, as Mr Williams says, that 'we are reading with our eyes too close to the book to see the print distinctly'.[7] Hampered by this drawback, and having no ulterior reward to offer himself in the shape of an aesthetic theory, Mr Williams is indefatigable and undaunted. His zeal is comparable to the zeal of the scientist who examines innumerable specimens and yet allows himself to draw no conclusions. The examination, too, seems to be equally thorough, whether the specimen is as rare and curious as Mr Conrad,[8] or as commonplace and abundant as writers whom we refrain from mentioning. His singular lack or disregard of personal preferences leads him to pronounce carefully balanced judgments upon books which, so far as we can see, no more deserve description than the dandelions of the year before last.

A forgotten writer called Henry Dawson Lowry[9] was once apparently compared by his admirers to Keats and Heine. Mr Williams in his careful way finds space to assure us that he has nothing 'of Heine's wayward strength, nothing of Keats's wealth of language and picturesque decorativeness,'[10] as if we were still in danger of wrecking ourselves upon that obsolete rock. Books whose writers alone can have any interest in their fate are carefully compared, their plots often analysed, and their final worth summed up in phrases which, if they censure, are generally moderately encouraging at the same time. 'Mr O'Sullivan has no affectation of startling originality, but he is rarely wholly commonplace.'[11] '*Auguries* (1913) contains grave and regular verse embodying the not too eager musings and emotions of a cultivated, thoughtful, but not original, mind.'[12] 'Her verse is never enhanced by those sudden and illuminating felicities of phrase and thought which mark greater poetry . . . but, on the other hand, she is not frequently disconcertingly empty of matter, and her sentiment rarely degenerates to insipidity.'[13] Such things have no doubt to be said in the world we live in, but we have always been sanguine enough to hope that the succeeding week strewed oblivion upon them.

But, making allowance for a certain formal remoteness of manner, which is, no doubt, inevitable considering the numbers to be surveyed, Mr Williams's judgment is uniformly fair and his mind singularly open.

He finds a good word not only for Mr Bennett and Mr Wells, but for Mr Tirebuck and Miss Milligan.[14] Most writers, again, set upon a task of such labour would by some means have deluded themselves into the belief that a good number of their vast flock of geese were swans. But Mr Williams is singularly without illusions. He reminds us that 'at the beginning of the twenty-first century, in all probability, the great number of the poets named in this book, with all their poems, will only be matter for comparative study by the literary expert'.[15]

As to the novelists. 'Of those who find a place here the greater number will be forgotten in a few decades.'[16] In a mood of intelligible pessimism he tells us indeed that it is better 'to read contemporary verse for the joy and inspiration it may afford us individually, untroubled by any desire to speak or write of it'.[17] Nevertheless, Mr Williams has been troubled to write, and to some purpose, for though the lack of complete bibliographies and the insufficiency of the biographies will not suit students who seek exact information, a foreigner wishing to take a bird's-eye view of modern English literature will find Mr Williams a safe guide.

1 – A review in the *TLS*, 3 October 1918, (Kp C124) of *Modern English Writers: Being a Study of Imaginative Literature 1890–1914* (Sidgwick & Jackson Ltd, 1918) by Harold Williams. Reprinted: *CW*.

2 – Rev. Harold Herbert Williams (1880–1964), a graduate of Christ's College, Cambridge, was a devoted university extension lecturer. His previous publications included a volume of poetry, a novel, and *Two Centuries of the English Novel* (1911). He joined the Royal Army Service Corps during the war and, according to the *DNB*, 'presumably' wrote the present work while on active service.

3 – Williams, p. xiii; George Meredith (1828–1909).

4 – *Ibid.*, p. xvi, discusses the aesthetic theories of Oscar Wilde (1854–1900) as expounded in the Preface to *The Picture of Dorian Gray* (1891) – in which Wilde asserted that 'All Art is quite useless' – and in the essay 'The Decay of Lying'.

5 – *Ibid.*, pp. xviii–xx; the *Yellow Book* (1894–7), a self-consciously 'new' and 'bizarre' little magazine, was edited originally by Henry Harland and Aubrey Beardsley. It soon became commercialised and was never as consistent as Arthur Symons's short-lived *Savoy* (1896), in which the public were given the purest distillation of Nineties decadence.

6 – *Ibid.*, pp. xxvi–xxvii; William Ernest Henley (1849–1903), poet, journalist and critic, a close friend of R. L. Stevenson, exerted considerable influence as the editor of the *Magazine of Art*, 1882–6, the *Scots* (later *National*) *Observer*, 1889–94, and the *New Review*, 1894–8.

7 – *Ibid.*, pt I, ch. III, p. 115.

8 – For Williams on Joseph Conrad (1857–1924), *ibid.*, pt IV, ch. III, pp. 387–96.

9 – Henry Dawson Lowry (1869–1906), poet and novelist, 'little known at any time' (*ibid.*, p. 117).

10 – *Ibid.*, pt I, ch. III, p. 117; Heinrich Heine (1797–1856); John Keats (1795–1821).

11 – *Ibid.*, pt II, ch. II, p. 181; Seumas O'Sullivan (James Starkey, 1879–1958), poet, in both English and Irish, whose most recent volume, *Requiem and Other Poems*, had appeared in 1917.

12 – *Ibid.*, pt I, ch. III, p. 85, discussing Laurence Binyon (1869–1943).

13 – *Ibid.*, pt II, ch. III, p. 192, discussing Dora Sigerson Shorter (d. 1918); see '*The Sad Years*' above.

14 – Arnold Bennett (1867–1931); H. G. Wells (1866–1946). William Edwards Tirebuck (1854–1900), author of several novels, generally depicting the life of the poor, and for which Tolstoy once expressed his admiration; he began his working life as an errand boy in Liverpool and was for some years a journalist with the *Yorkshire Post*. Alice Milligan (1880–1953), Irish poet, author of *Hero Lays* (1908).

15 – Williams, pt I, ch. III, p. 103.

16 – *Ibid.*, pt IV, ch. I, p. 279.

17 – *Ibid.*, pt. I, ch. III, p. 116.

Adventurers All

Miss Stuart[2] comes very near to being a poet, and if she fails it is, we believe, because she cherishes some old superstitious belief about the sanctity of inspiration; her Muse is an inspired figure with wild locks and a bandage round her eyes. The power of feeling emotion quickly and strongly is a great one and Miss Stuart has, in addition to this, an unusual power of putting her emotions, and also, for she thinks as well as feels, her ideas, into words that express them both beautifully and freely. For example, we might quote, although it is scarcely fair to quote single passages from a long poem, this from 'The Cockpit of Idols':

> And while these gods in the great shambles die,
>   Thrust on each other's spears,
> He, nameless and unchallenged, wanders by
>   In every tree that peers
> Into the wizard darkness of the hill,
>   And in each tarn most deeply contemplates
> The image of His beauty, lingers still
> To twist again the purfled clover's ears,

> World-weary feet He cools
> Where windless noons lie bathing in the pools,
>   Or takes His solitude
> Where, in the purple cloak of twilight, waits
> The moon to pierce the solitary wood.[3]

But too often at the height of her mood, when the utmost discretion and vigilance are needed, she seems to resign herself merely to utter words, herself accepting no responsibility for the sense or beauty or fitness of what is said. The common notion that poetry is something wild, emphatic, uttered in a shriek rather than in a singing or speaking voice, has persuaded her to pitch her normal tone so loud that when she wishes to be specially emphatic there is nothing for it but to coin monstrous superlative superlatives such as 'this most unquietest heart' or these 'most forlornest shells',[4] to rely upon the fortifying effect of capital letters, or upon a violence of imagery which jerks the whole stanza out of perspective. But faults of taste are not the worst of faults, and Miss Stuart proves, in such a poem as the quiet and beautiful 'Heliodore',[5] that she can free herself from them completely and remarkably.

The connection beween Miss Stuart and Mr Huxley[6] is the obvious one that they have nothing in common. The one is strong precisely where the other is weak. Miss Stuart has too many ideas and emotions, and is too careless as to what she does with them. But after reading the first few poems in Mr Huxley's little book it is clear that any idea or emotion that comes to him has the best possible chance of surviving beautifully. The criticism implied is, of course, that he is better equipped with the vocabulary of a poet than with the inspiration of a poet. He writes about the things he has thought and seen rather than about things he has felt, and in rendering them he shows a facility which begins by charming, but ends, as verse that relies so much upon happy adjectives is always apt to end, by running fluently to waste. The advice that one is inclined to give to an urbane and cultivated writer of his quality is to cease to use poetry in the serious, traditional manner, and to use it instead to explore those fantastic, amusing, or ironical aspects of life which can only be expressed by people of high technical skill and great sensibility. Mr Huxley proves himself, in verses like 'Social Amenities', 'Topiary', or 'On the 'Bus', quite capable of doing this:

> Sitting on the top of the 'bus,
> I bite my pipe and look at the sky.
> Over my shoulder the smoke streams out

> And my life with it.
> 'Conservation of energy,' you say.
> But I burn, I tell you, I burn;
> And the smoke of me streams out
> In a vanishing skein of grey.
> Crash and bump . . . my poor bruised body!
> I'm a harp of twittering strings.
> An elegant instrument, but infinitely second-hand,
> And if I have got phthisis it is only an accident.
> Droll phenomena![7]

If by a chance, which is not so improbable as at first sight appears, Miss Sitwell's[8] teapot reminded her first of the Tower of London and then of Joan of Arc she would say so without hesitation or consistency. The moon in one poem reminds her of a milk-white unicorn; in the next 'nurse's white gown' shines through the trees like a unicorn of unspecified colour.[9] For the most part we believe that Miss Sitwell is trying her best to be honest with her own conceptions, and, that being so, she is of course perfectly right not to care whether they appear outlandish, farfetched, or startling upon the printed page. But honesty of imagery is, after all, only the groundwork of writing. When you are sure that the sea is 'sequined with noisy light' or that 'colours like a parokeet Shrill loudly to the chattering heat',[10] you still have to decide what whole you wish to build up with these vivid or remarkable or unexpected phrases. By themselves they are little more than bright colours. But at this stage of her career the chief thing that Miss Sitwell has to tell us about the world is that it is extremely bright and very noisy. The air is brittle and bright as glass; 'plush mantles seemed to purr';[11] people are bright sparks; sound becomes substance, and sight becomes sound. There is almost invariably a brass band playing in the sun and tight green parasols reflect the blare of the brass. Miss Sitwell owes a great deal to modern painters, and until her optic nerve has ceased to be dazzled it is difficult to say how interesting her vision is.

> Green apples dancing in a wash of sun –
> Ripples of sense and fun –
> A net of light that waves as it weaves
> The sunlight on the chattering leaves;
>
> The half-dazed sound of feet,
> And carriages that ripple in the heat.
> The parasols like shadows of the sun
> Cast wavering shades that run

Across the laughing faces and across
Hair with a bird-bright gloss.
The swinging greenery cast shadows dark,
Hides me that I may mark

How, buzzing in this dazzling mesh, my soul
Seems hardening it to flesh, and one bright whole.
O sudden feathers have a flashing sheen!

The sun's swift javelin
The bird-songs seem, that through the dark leaves pass;
And life itself is but a flashing glass.[12]

That is proof that she can make charming ornaments already; in imitation of her manner we might liken them to the stiff china dogs that stand on farmhouse mantelpieces. But manner in the young is a form of paralysis, and already Miss Sitwell repeats her favourite adjectives and similes so often as to suggest that she is becoming prematurely imprisoned within the walls of her own style. She is too vigorous a writer to rest content with making china dogs indefinitely.

If you should buy the little anthology of recent poetry edited by Mr Jones[13] in the expectation of being brought into touch with the youngest and most revolutionary of modern poets you will, according to your temperament, be disappointed or relieved. Here is nothing to surprise and nothing to shock. The general attitude which we should have tried to define is very well expressed for us by Mr Earp:

I have been reading books
For about twenty years;
I have laughed with other men's laughter,
Wept with their tears.

Life has been a cliché
All these years.

I would find a gesture of my own.[14]

Of course there are exceptions. Mr Betts in 'The Pawns'[15] writes not only very well, but with a good deal of meaning; Mr Jones has an imagination which is trying to express itself; Miss Bridges[16] does exquisitely what it is no disparagement to say that her father has done more exquisitely still; and we can see no reason to think that Miss Sitwell has spent even a fraction of Mr Earp's twenty years in reading other people's books. But, speaking generally; the poets here represented in such modest quantities seem to be dealing with emotions received from books in language learnt from books. We must wait a little longer for that 'gesture of my own'.

1 – A review in the *TLS*, 10 October 1918, (Kp C125) of *The Cockpit of Idols* (Methuen & Co. Ltd, 1918) by Muriel Stuart; *The Defeat of Youth and Other Poems* (B. H. Blackwell, 1918) by Aldous Huxley; *Clowns' Houses* (B. H. Blackwell, 1918) by Edith Sitwell; and of *Songs for Sale. An Anthology of Recent Poetry* (B. H. Blackwell, 1918) ed. E. B. C. Jones.

'Roger [Fry], Duncan [Grant], Maynard [Keynes], Nessa [Vanessa Bell] & I all crammed in & padded along slowly across London to Chelsea,' VW recorded in her diary on Saturday, 12 October 1918. 'Somehow we passed Ottoline [Morrell], brilliantly painted, as garish as a strumpet, displayed in the midst of omnibuses under an arc lamp; & she reappeared in the Sitwells' drawing room. I had made acquaintance with the two Sitwell brothers the day before [at 46 Gordon Square], & been invited to the party. That very morning a review by me of Edith Sitwell's poems had appeared in the Times ... This group to which Gertler & Mary H[utchinson] are attached was unknown to me a year ago. I surveyed them with considerable, almost disquieting calm ... Edith Sitwell is a very tall young woman, wearing a permanently startled expression, & curiously finished off with a high green silk headdress, concealing her hair, so that it is not known whether she has any. Otherwise, I was familiar with everyone, I think.'

See also 'Cleverness and Youth' (a review of Aldous Huxley's *Limbo*, 1920), *III VW Essays*.

2 – Muriel Stuart was also the author of *Christ at Carnival, and Other Poems* (1916).

3 – Stuart, p. 24.

4 – For the first hyperbolical superlative, *ibid*., 'The Bastard', p. 9; and for the second, 'The Cockpit of Idols', p. 18.

5 – *Ibid*., pp. 43–6.

6 – Aldous Leonard Huxley (1894–1963) had published one other collection of poems, *The Burning Wheel*, in 1916, in which year he was also an editor of the annual anthology *Oxford Poetry*. Huxley was a contributor to *Wheels*, the anti-Georgian verse anthology edited annually, from 1916, by Edith Sitwell. VW had met him for the first time in April 1917, at Garsington Manor, the home of Philip and Lady Ottoline Morrell. There Huxley, unfit for military service, spent part of the war working on the land. (His first novel, *Crome Yellow*, was published in 1921.)

7 – Huxley, 'On the Bus', p. 39, the entire poem; for 'Social Amenities' and 'Topiary', p. 38.

8 – Edith Louisa Sitwell (1887–1964) published her first collection of poems, *The Mother*, in 1915, and in the following year there appeared a further volume, *Twentieth-Century Harlequinade*, a collaboration with her brother Osbert.

9 – For the first quotation, Sitwell, 'The Old Nurse's Song', p. 21; and for the second, 'Rocking-Horses', *ibid*.

10 – *Ibid.*, 'Minstrels', p. 8:

> Beside the sea, metallic-bright
> And sequined with the noisy light,
> Duennas slowly promenade
> Each like a patch of sudden shade,
>
> While colours like a parokeet
> Shrill loudly to the chattering heat;
> And gowns as white as innocence
> With sudden sweetness take the sense.

11 – *Ibid.*, 'Myself on the Merry-Go-Round', p. 19, which has: 'seem to purr'.

12 – *Ibid.*, 'Déjeuner sur l'Herbe', pp. 9–10, the complete poem, which has no stanza divisions.

13 – I.e., Emily Beatrice Coursolles ('Topsy') Jones (1893–1966) who, in 1917, had published with Christopher Jonson the collection *Windows*. In 1921 she was to marry Frank Laurence ('Peter') Lucas, a classical scholar of Trinity College, Cambridge, an Apostle, and a friend of Bloomsbury. *Songs for Sale* contains three of her poems, as well as pieces by Edith Sitwell and Aldous Huxley. In c. 1920 she published *Quiet Interior*, the first of several novels.

14 – Jones, 'Departure', p. 19. Thomas Wade Earp, author, of *Contacts and Other Poems* (1916) and an editor, 1918–20, of *Oxford Poetry*, later wrote books about art and artists.

15 – *Ibid.*, p. 8. Frank Betts had published *The Iron Age* (1916) and *Saga Plays* (1917).

16 – Jane Bridges, daughter of the then poet laureate Robert Bridges, is represented in Jones by one poem, 'Orpheus'.

Honest Fiction

Shops and Houses is one of those books which by their health and robustness should confute those who hold that English fiction is in a languid or degenerate condition. There can be no reason for despondency or for disparaging comparisons when novels of such care and conscience and ability are produced, not of course in any quantity, but still by a small and undaunted band of writers, among whom we must now place Mr Swinnerton. He is among the group of honest observers of contemporary life who filter their impressions sedulously and uncompromisingly through the intellect and suffer nothing to pass save what possesses meaning and solidity.

It is not necessary that Mr Swinnerton should say anything very strange or very unpleasant in *Shops and Houses*. He sets out to show us the life in a suburb not far from London where the men work in the city all day and the women spend their time ordering their households, going to tea parties, and buying things in shops. Mr Swinnerton takes up his position upon a little mound of intellectual honesty, from which he observes and according to which he judges. Perhaps there once happened to him what happened to his hero Louis Vechantor at the Hughes's tea party. '. . . He seemed for a moment to lose consciousness [. . .] The tea-table chatter sounded like a confused roaring of a crowd some distance away . . . Their laughter seemed to him like the grinning of skulls . . . Louis had never fainted, or he would have known that a curious sweet remoteness precedes the total loss of sensation. It was just that feeling of being apart and contemplative that had assailed him.'² *Shops and Houses* may well have had its origin in some such moment of remoteness at a tea party, but, having seen his vision, Mr Swinnerton set to work to search out and verify every detail that went to compose the large effect; and as each was received it was tested by a standard which we may roughly describe as the standard of intellectual honesty. How did they live, what did they live for, what were these healthy unemployed young women, these indolent elderly ladies, after? He has discovered an astonishing number of very minute facts as to the manner in which the ladies of Beckwith perform their chief occupation in life – the 'consumption of precious time'.³ He is with them when they wish to attract, and when they cease to wish to attract; he observes their attempts to marry or to prevent marriage; he sees them piecing together into interminable romances little shreds of gossip picked from the dust-heap. He examines the process by which the public opinion of Beckwith is formed, and traces it in operation upon a case specially submitted to it. How would Beckwith, he asks, deal with the case of a respectable resident's disreputable cousin who has the effrontery to set up a grocer's shop in Beckwith itself? By means of details and fragments he has set working a model Beckwith which performs all the functions of spending time with the regularity of an ant-heap; or, since the activity of an ant-heap has some direction, with the automatic accuracy of a decapitated duck. Moreover, he has created what he dissects. He is not only the 'disembodied and cruel spectator';⁴ he has enough sympathy to show us, at any rate through the eyes of Louis Vechantor, that there were possibilities and varieties among the people of Beckwith which make them momentarily attractive and intermittently pathetic.

But although there are passages of hope, Beckwith does not pass the test; Beckwith is shown up; as Dorothy Vechantor, who is appointed to wind up the spiritual affairs of Beckwith, says, 'I've been thinking whether perhaps Beckwith ... that it isn't altogether a place at all. I mean whether it isn't a sort of disease'.[5] In saying this she lays her finger not only upon the deficiency of Beckwith, but upon the deficiency which *Shops and Houses* shares with so many other novels of the intellectual school. Beckwith is proved to be a disease: it has failed to pass any of the tests which Mr Swinnerton so honestly and acutely applies; it is snobbish and vulgar, cruel, stupid, without worth, rhyme, or reason. Nevertheless, with all these proofs of its spiritual bankruptcy before us, we still remain unconvinced. Our lack of conviction is not, as at first sight appears, because of the incredible meanness and insignificance of the crimes cited against the inhabitants, although their minuteness certainly diminishes their power to affect us; we cannot believe that Beckwith is merely a disease because we cannot accept Mr Swinnerton's view of what constitutes health. Louis Vechantor and Dorothy, the daughter of the grocer, the grocer William, and the grocer's family are the representatives of sincerity and humanity. They are capable of thought and capable of love. They are the martyrs whom Beckwith half succeeds in pelting to death with its grains of spite; it is to them that we look with confidence to champion the human cause. And it is precisely these characters who fail us. Those scenes which should show us the honesty and energy of life removed from the burden of false convention are the weakest in the book. It is by their failure that we are led to doubt whether honesty and intelligence will really do all that the intellectual novelist claims for them, and whether because of their absence we are entitled to blot a whole suburb from the map. Perhaps there are other qualities, other aims, other desires which make even Miss Lampe of Station Road a little more complex than an agitated ant or a decapitated duck? Perhaps there is more in marriage, love, friendship, beauty than Mr Swinnerton altogether conveys? But, we repeat, it is a great thing that Beckwith should be destroyed; it is a most valuable work.

1 – A review in the *TLS*, 10 October 1918, (Kp C126) of *Shops and Houses* (Methuen & Co. Ltd, 1918) by Frank Swinnerton (1884–1982), novelist, critic and publisher's reader. Swinnerton was later to write unfavourably of VW's own fiction, and of Bloomsbury, in *The Georgian Literary Scene* (1935). For her reactions to his 'sneers' see *IV VW Diary*, 16 and 18 March 1935. See also 'September', *III VW Essays*. Reprinted: CW.

2 – Swinnerton, ch. IV, p. 60–1, slightly adapted.
3 – *Ibid.*, ch. II, p. 23.
4 – *Ibid.*, ch. IV, p. 60.
5 – *Ibid.*, ch. XXIV, pp. 290–1; the ellipsis is Swinnerton's.

Women Novelists

By rights, or, more modestly, according to a theory of ours, Mr Brimley Johnson should have written a book amply calculated, according to the sex of the reader, to cause gratification or annoyance, but of no value from a critical point of view. Experience seems to prove that to criticise the work of a sex as a sex is merely to state with almost invariable acrimony prejudices derived from the fact that you are either a man or a woman. By some lucky balance of qualities Mr Brimley Johnson has delivered his opinion of women novelists without this fatal bias, so that, besides saying some very interesting things about literature, he says also many that are even more interesting about the peculiar qualities of the literature that is written by women.

Given this unusual absence of partisanship, the interest and also the complexity of the subject can scarcely be overstated. Mr Johnson, who has read more novels by women than most of us have heard of, is very cautious – more apt to suggest than to define, and much disposed to qualify his conclusions. Thus, though his book is not a mere study of the women novelists, but an attempt to prove that they have followed a certain course of development, we should be puzzled to state what his theory amounts to. The question is one not merely of literature, but to a large extent of social history. What, for example, was the origin of the extraordinary outburst in the eighteenth century of novel writing by women? Why did it begin then, and not in the time of the Elizabethan renaissance? Was the motive which finally determined them to write a desire to correct the current view of their sex expressed in so many volumes and for so many ages by male writers? If so, their art is at once possessed of an element which should be absent from the work of all previous writers. It is clear enough, however, that the work of Miss Burney,[2] the mother of English fiction, was not inspired by any single wish to redress a grievance: the richness of the human scene as Dr Burney's daughter had the chance of observing it provided a sufficient stimulus; but however strong the impulse to write had become, it had at the outset to meet opposition not only of circumstance but of opinion. Her first manuscripts were burnt by her stepmother's orders, and needlework was inflicted as a penance, much as, a few years later, Jane Austen would slip her writing beneath a book if anyone came in, and Charlotte Brontë[3] stopped in the middle of her work to pare the potatoes. But the domestic problem, being overcome or compromised with, there remained the moral one. Miss Burney had showed that it was 'possible for a woman to write novels and be respectable',[4] but the burden of proof still rested anew upon each authoress. Even so late as the mid-Victorian days George Eliot was accused of 'coarseness and immorality' in her attempt 'to familiarise the minds of our young women in the middle and higher ranks with matters on which their fathers and brothers would never venture to speak in their presence'.[5]

The effect of these repressions is still clearly to be traced in women's work, and the effect is wholly to the bad. The problem of art is sufficiently difficult in itself without having to respect the ignorance of young women's minds or to consider whether the public will think that the standard of moral purity displayed in your work is such as they have a right to expect from your sex. The attempt to conciliate, or more naturally to outrage, public opinion is equally a waste of energy and a sin against art. It may have been not only with a view to obtaining impartial criticism that George Eliot and Miss Brontë adopted male pseudonyms, but in order to free their own consciousness as they wrote from the tyranny of what was expected from their sex. No more than men, however, could they free themselves from a more fundamental tyranny – the tyranny of sex itself. The effort to free themselves, or rather to enjoy what appears, perhaps erroneously, to be the comparative freedom of the male sex from that tyranny, is another influence which has told disastrously upon the writing of women. When Mr Brimley Johnson says that 'imitation has not been, fortunately, the besetting sin of women novelists',[6] he has in mind no doubt the work of the exceptional women who imitated neither a sex nor any individual of either sex. But to take no more thought of their sex when they wrote than of the colour of their eyes was one of their conspicuous distinctions, and of itself a proof that they wrote at the bidding of a profound and imperious instinct. The women who wished to be taken for men in what they wrote were certainly common enough; and if they have given place to the women who wish to be taken for women the change is hardly for the better, since any emphasis, either of pride or of shame, laid consciously upon the sex of a writer is not only irritating but superfluous. As Mr Brimley Johnson again and again remarks, a woman's writing is always feminine; it cannot help being feminine; at its best it is most feminine: the only difficulty lies in defining what we mean by feminine. He shows his wisdom not only by advancing a great many suggestions, but also by accepting the fact, upsetting though it is, that women are apt to differ. Still, here are a few attempts: 'Women are born preachers and always work for an ideal.' 'Woman is the moral realist, and her realism is not inspired by any idle ideal of art, but of sympathy with life.'[7] For all her learning, 'George Eliot's outlook remains thoroughly emotional and feminine'.[8] Women are humorous and satirical rather than imaginative. They have a greater sense of emotional purity than men, but a less alert sense of honour.

No two people will accept without wishing to add to and qualify these attempts at a definition, and yet no one will admit that he can possibly mistake a novel written by a man for a novel written by a woman. There is the obvious and enormous difference of experience in the first place; but the essential difference lies in the fact not that men describe battles and women the birth of children, but that each sex describes itself. The first words in which either a man or a woman is described are generally enough to determine the sex of the writer; but though the absurdity of a woman's hero or of a man's heroine is universally recognised, the sexes show themselves extremely quick at detecting each other's faults. No one can deny the authenticity of a Becky Sharp or of a Mr Woodhouse.[9] No doubt the desire and the capacity to criticise the other sex had its share in deciding women to write novels, for indeed that particular vein of comedy has been but slightly worked, and promises great richness. Then again, though men are the best judges of men and women of women, there is a side of each sex which is known only to the other, nor does this refer solely to the relationship of love. And finally (as regards this review at least) there rises for consideration the very difficult question of the difference between the man's and the woman's view of what constitutes the importance of any subject. From this spring not only marked differences of plot and incident, but infinite differences in selection, method and style.

1 – A review in the *TLS*, 17 October 1918, (Kp C127) of *The Women Novelists* (W. Collins Sons & Co. Ltd, 1918) by R. Brimley Johnson. Reprinted: *CW*.

2 – Frances Burney (1752–1840), later Madame d'Arblay, author of *Evelina* (1778), *Cecilia* (1782), *Camilla* (1796), and *The Wanderer* (1814); she was the daughter of Dr Burney, the musician and historian of music. (See also 'Dr Burney's Evening Party', *V VW Essays* and *CR2*.)

3 – Jane Austen (1775–1817); Charlotte Brontë (1816–55).

4 – Brimley Johnson, 'A Study in Fine Art (Jane Austen . . . 1775–1817)', p. 68.

5 – *Ibid.*, 'A Professional Woman (George Eliot 1819–1880)', p. 210; the source of these accusations is not given.

6 – *Ibid.*, 'A Picture of Youth', p. 53; the observation arises in a discussion of Dr Johnson's influence on Fanny Burney, who, he says, 'wrote Johnsonese fluently, and thereby mined her natural powers. We cannot estimate, by her foolishness, the influence of the Dictator.'

7 – *Ibid.*, 'A Professional Woman', p. 211; p. 207; both slightly adapted.

8 – *Ibid.*, p. 212.

9 – Becky Sharp and Mr Woodhouse, characters respectively in *Vanity Fair* (1847–8) by W. M. Thackeray and *Emma* (1816) by Jane Austen.

Valery Brussof

If we had no means of knowing that this book was the work of a Russian writer, should we guess from something indefinable in the quality of the writer's mind, from his style and his point of view, that he was at any rate not English? We think it very doubtful. Valery Brussof is, so Mr Graham tells us, 'a sort of Mediterraneanised Russian, with greater affinities in France and Italy than in his native land';[2] and besides, judging from this book of short stories, he is not a great writer: he does not hint at something more than he can state, or imply a whole of which he is only a part. Yet, though one could find his match for power within these islands, he has a quality which distinguishes him from the mass of good story-writers, in that he has a point of view. He has expressed his belief that 'there is no fixed boundary between the world of reality and that of the imagination, between the dreaming and the waking world, life and fantasy';[3] and the stories in the present volume all more or less give shape to his notion that the things commonly held to be visionary may be real, while the reality may equally well be a phantom. In England this train of thought is certainly not unknown in fiction; but we are apt to relegate it, a little nervously perhaps, to certain writers who make a study of the supernatural and by divorcing it from normal life envelop it in an atmosphere of emotional mysticism. Brussof's method is the exact opposite of this. As Mr Graham points out, he 'is not emotionally convinced of the truth of his writing, but wilfully persistent, affirming unreality intellectually and defending his conception with a sort of masculine impressionism'.[4]

Stated as he states it with hard intellectual power, there is no reason to question the truth of his assertion that the most vivid part of many lives is spent in a region invisible to the eyes of the rest of the world. The little Roman girl Maria, for instance, spent the greater part of her life dreaming that she was a reincarnation of Rhea Silvia, until she believed it so completely that she drowned herself in the Tiber; another woman lives her true life in communication with her own reflection in a mirror; a third endows the pens and papers in a stationer's shop with the qualities of living creatures, and loves them accordingly. In the literal and urgent way in which Brussof pursues his search through these shades there are signs that remind us that he comes of the race which approaches such subjects with magnificent seriousness and without sentimentality. Rather than invoke a supernatural power or any sensational agency, he explains these queer obsessions on the part of his characters by telling us that they were known to be weak-minded people or were actually confined to lunatic asylums. To doubt whether you are awake or dreaming, to be unable to decide whether you are real or a reflection, to get more pleasure from what you imagine than from what is true, is to be mad. But Brussof saw, of course, that this is no explanation at all. 'Is not our craziness,' he makes his Roman lovers ask, 'better than the reasonable life of other people?'[5] How does it differ, and who is to decide, after all, which things are real, which are unreal, what constitutes sanity and insanity?

But although it is interesting to find how firmly and even prosaically this creed is held by a mind which is neither emotional nor mystical, the theme has no special artistic merit, and easily becomes a formula which is not more interesting than any other. On the other hand, the stories which deal with the borderland between sanity and insanity are of far greater value, if only because they are more subtly graded and do not end in the convenient *cul-de-sac* of the mad house. They hint at least at the strange balancing and checking of dreams and realities that goes on in the minds of those who are able only by semi-conscious adjustments to behave in the same way as other people. There is the case of the old tramp who has stolen the bust of a woman's head because it reminded him of a woman he had once loved. He is asked whether he will not attempt to get an acquittal, and he answers, 'But why? . . . isn't it just the same where I shall think about Nina – in a doss-house or in a prison? . . . One thing worries me ⟨he adds⟩ What if Nina never existed?'[6] That is a dilemma which is always being dealt with by the mind: what is reality, and why are we so eager about things that are created for the most part chiefly by our own imaginations? Brussof does no more, and perhaps is unable to do more, than hint at the irrational element which, when we come to examine them, is so profoundly mixed with the most rational desires of ordinary people. But the fact that he has chosen to shift the weight of interest from the beaten track to this obscure and nebulous region of the mind's territory certainly makes him very well worth reading.

1 – A review in the *TLS*, 24 October 1918, (Kp C128) of *The Republic of the Southern Cross and Other Stories* ... with an introduction by Stephen Graham (Constable & Co. Ltd, 1918) by Valery Brussof (1873–1924).
2 – Brussof, intro. p. v.
3 – *Ibid*., p. vi, quoting Brussof's preface to the second edition of his *The Axis of the Earth*, publication date untraced.
4 – *Ibid*., p. xi.
5 – *Ibid*., 'Rhea Silver', p. 128, which has: 'And is not . . .'
6 – *Ibid*., 'The Marble Bust: a tramp's story', p. 40, which has: 'Only one thing . . .'; and continues: '. . . existed, and it was merely my poor mind, weakened by alcohol, which invented the whole story of this love whilst I was looking at the little marble head?'

'The Candle of Vision'

The reader may perhaps remember the experience of reading Thomas à Kempis, or *The Love Letters of a Portuguese Nun*[2] precociously before he was of an age to understand either religion or love. He will remember the inarticulate thunder of the words drumming so persistently and remorselessly upon the immature understanding that at length the book was thrown away not so much in boredom as a kind of exasperated humility. Occasionally *The Candle of Vision* produces the same desperate sense of obtuseness, as it reiterates passionately a belief which remains just beyond the doors of our perception. 'A. E.' has constant experience of certain spiritual states which are as remote from the ordinary person as the religious ecstasies of a saint are remote from a child. He is able by the exercise of his will to bring about some mental enlightenment in which perceptions and visions appear to him and dictate a different reading of life and a different relationship with other human beings. In the present book he desires, as he says, 'to be precise';[3] to analyse these experiences psychologically, and to induce others to make the same attempt.

All such revelations are at the present time bound to be inconclusive, to be contradictory, to make use of language which is highly metaphorical, and to be almost as unsatisfying as they are rich in suggestions. Where there is no argument and no proof one can only by quotation hint vaguely at the line 'A.E.' takes through the crowd of his spiritual experiences. At about the age of sixteen or seventeen 'the mysterious life quickening within my life'[4] began for him. Magical lights dawned and faded in him, as they do, he believes, in every one of us. He wished to obtain mastery over them, and for this purpose set himself the task of concentrating his mind upon some mental object, 'so that not for a moment, not for an instant, would the concentration slacken . . . Five minutes of this effort will at first leave us trembling as at the close of a laborious day.'[5] The habit of concentration having been won, he found himself in possession of a power of immense force for good or for evil.

But the ancients who taught us to gain this intensity taught it but as a preliminary to a meditation . . . The meditation they urged on us has been explained as 'the inexpressible yearning of the inner man to go out into the infinite'. But the Infinite we would enter is living. It is the ultimate being of us. Meditation is a fiery brooding on that majestical Self. We imagine ourselves into Its vastness. We conceive ourselves as mirroring Its infinitudes, as moving in all things, as living in all beings, in earth, water, air, fire, aether . . . We have imagined ourselves into this pitiful dream of life. By imagination and will we re-enter true being, becoming that we conceive of. On that path of fiery brooding I entered.[6]

Then there follow the dreams and the visions, the sudden illuminations of the text of a book, the cathedral filled with ancient worshippers, the spectral airship with its crew of prehistoric voyagers, scenes from the unknown lives of strangers – dreams and visions without end, and yet to what purpose? 'A. E.' will have it that the professed psychologists have been drawn from the ranks of the naturally unimaginative, and that their visions are caused neither by memories nor by the suppressed impulses and desires to which modern writers so confidently ascribe them. They come from outside, because, to use the inevitable metaphors, our minds are leaky boats upon the deep sea, cloudy panes obscuring the light, imperfect instruments for the conveyance of divine harmony; and step by step we proceed to spin round in the Dervish dance of unintelligible communion with the essential, the divine, the spirit of the universe, or whatever we choose to call it. That dance may be to us unintelligible, but we can witness the gyrations of 'A. E.' not only without a smile, but with confidence that for him the ceremony is sacred as well as absorbing.

There lies the value of his book as a record of ardent though stumbling conviction. But 'A. E.' does not escape what appears to be the inevitable penalty of any psychic experience, whereby it seems to be better, higher, more enlightened than any other; so that the world must be altered in accordance with it, and other minds must share the same experiences and come to the same conclusions. But let us imagine ourselves in that gaslit office where 'A. E.' spent some years of his boyhood, 'little heaps of paper mounting up before me'[7] and quick people flitting about with feverish faces and voices. One of his trances would come upon him, and he would find himself on a remote steppe, or exalted into communion with the spirits in a region of clouds and stars. Suppose, however, that this excursion had been not into the remote and invisible, but into the mind of the clerk, with his wrinkled face and blinking eyes, who sat beside him. According to some of us, that would have been a more exalted, difficult and imaginative affair altogether, a method no less true than the other of taking one's way out 'into the infinite'.[8] The drawback, as these papers perhaps show, of indulging too unreservedly in contact with the disembodied spirit is that it tends to become a monotonous process, lacking the humour and passion that diversify human inter-course, and too apt to end in a rapture of egotistic exaltation. 'A. E.'s' book helps to explain the curious transparency of modern Irish literature. But it is a mistake to read 'A.E's' book as if it were merely literature, and not to recognise the fact that in spite of difficulty and obscurity he has conveyed to us a fresh sense of the illimitable and inexplicable faculties which lie undisciplined and only half realised within the human mind.

1 – A review in the *TLS*, 31 October 1918, (Kp C129) of *The Candle of Vision* (Macmillan & Co., Ltd, 1918) by A. E., pseudonym of George William Russell (1867–1935), Irish poet, painter and mystic – also a man of more mundane affairs, who edited the *Irish Homestead*, 1904–23, and worked for the Irish Agricultural Society.

2 – Thomas à Kempis (1380–1471), German Augustinian monk, traditionally considered the author of the great devotional work on the soul's progress to perfection, *De Imitatione Christi*. Marianna Alcofcorado (1640–1723), the Portuguese nun whose letters have been published in numerous editions.
3 – A.E., 'The Many-Coloured Land', p. 27, which has: 'Spiritual moods are difficult to express and cannot be argued over, but the workings of the imagination may well be spoken of, and need precise and minute investigation.'
4 – *Ibid.*, 'Retrospect', p. 4.
5 – *Ibid.*, 'Meditation', p. 21.
6 – *Ibid.*, p. 23, which has: 'But that Infinite'.
7 – *Ibid.*, 'The Earth Breath', p. 10.
8 – See n. 6.

'Abraham Lincoln'

When upon page 57 of this play, Mr Drinkwater quotes Shakespeare,[2] a curious thing happens – or happened in one particular case. Instead of straining itself to visualise deal tables and top hats the mind begins with alacrity to conjure up cloud-capp'd towers and gorgeous palaces; as if a top hat were harder to imagine than a palace, as if clouds were our natural element. We are not therefore so foolish as to draw the conclusion that Shakespeare is a better dramatist than Mr Drinkwater, but only that Shakespeare's plays can be read, and we believe that *Abraham Lincoln* needs to be seen upon the stage to be seen at its best.

The first act represents the parlour of Lincoln's house at Springfield in the year 1860. Abraham Lincoln comes in wearing a 'greenish and crumpled top hat';[3] his pockets are stuffed with documents; a map of the United States hangs upon the wall; there is a cupboard which, when he looks to find a bottle in it, is found choked with papers instead. The mind is uncomfortably split up into perceiving that all this would tell upon the stage, and in realising that for some reason it is an obstacle to imagination upon the printed page. These cupboards and top hats are too real and prominent for their importance, just as we cannot help feeling that the dialogue is too thin and spare for its importance. The realistic dramatist is always faced with the difficulty that he can only allow his characters to say the barest abstract of what is in their minds; and for the dialogue to be further denuded of its scenery, deprived of its actors, and read as we read a book, with a mind hungry for a thousand details and comments which cannot possibly be put into the dialogue, is a test that, perhaps, Ibsen and Tchehov[4] alone of the moderns survive.

Mr Drinkwater is of course too serious and honest a writer for nothing to survive; a readable and interesting statement of the Northern case survives; but it is much like hearing played by one instrument – and that a piano – a piece which demands a whole orchestra of brass and strings. One seems to perceive long empty spaces when the piano keeps on strumming its homely chords in the bass and the melody is absent. President Lincoln comes out speaking good sense, good morality, and tolerable prose, but we wait in vain for any proof that besides the simplicity of genius he also possessed the inspiration. He is shown to be a very homely, uncouth, plain-spoken, sensible man; and when the great moments – such as the pardon of the boy sentry, or the last speech from the box at the theatre – arrive, they read, at least, with marked flatness. 'There, there; I believe you when you tell me that you couldn't keep awake. I'm going to trust you and send you back to your regiment.'[5] That sounds as if Mr Drinkwater were determined to prove that one of the remarkable things about Lincoln was that where smaller men said something striking he said something dull. But in the theatre the cumulative effect of sense, truth, honesty, and courage may have lent these speeches a force which it is impossible to perceive when we read them.

1 – A review in the *TLS*, 31 October 1918, (Kp C130) of *Abraham Lincoln: A Play* (Sidgwick & Jackson, 1918) by John Drinkwater (1882–1937). First produced in 1918 at the Birmingham Repertory Theatre, of which Drinkwater was the original manager, the play transferred in 1919 to the Lyric Theatre, Hammersmith. There it ran for over a year and, according to the *DNB*, 'established Drinkwater's fame at a blow'.
2 – Drinkwater, sc. iv, p. 57; Lincoln asks Slaney to read from *The Tempest*, IV, i, ll. 148ff: Prospero: 'Our revels now are ended . . .;' and himself concludes the extract speaking ll. 156–8: 'We are such stuff/ As dreams are made on . . .'
3 – *Ibid.*, sc. i, p. 11, stage directions.
4 – Henrik Ibsen (1828–1906); Anton Chekhov (1860–1904).
5 – Drinkwater, sc. v, p. 63, Lincoln addressing the sentry William Scott, 'a boy of twenty', court-martialled for sleeping on duty.

Mr Howells on Form

When Mr Howells[2] says that he is not going to define what he means by form in fiction, since it is 'one of those elusive things which you can feel much better than you can say',[3] we applaud his wisdom, and accept his decision. There may be truth as well as indolence in the remark that the less we seek to define art the more chance there is that we shall be able to produce it. At any rate let us leave these questions to be settled once in a generation, and meanwhile let us flatter ourselves that by continuing to frame tentative outlines of belief, always shifting and modifying their terms as we read, we are providing material for the great critic to build with when he comes.

Form, Mr Howells goes on to say, is very rare in English fiction, so that the public will probably not understand what he means when he singles out this quality in the novels of Mr Merrick for special praise. 'Our public might very well enjoy form,' he adds, 'if it could once be made to imagine it.'[4] Here we think he does us some injustice. We need neither persuasion nor force to make us enjoy the form of Pope or Peacock, Jane Austen or Gray;[5] one might go farther and say that half our pleasure in reading the writers of the eighteenth century comes from the delight we take in their sense of form. In the case of the Victorians it is more difficult; in the case of our own generation it is almost impossible to see that such a thing as form exists. But it seems likely that this is in part the result of trying to squeeze our voluminous moderns into the finely shaped mould of *The Rape of the Lock*, or of the *Princesse de Clèves*.[6] When we talk of form in the loose fashion confessed above we probably mean more than anything the form not of the Elizabethans but of the eighteenth century. It is very natural. Who, after all, can resist the fascination of their writers or refuse at some time or another to make such sacrifices as may enable him to attempt at least to write what would have satisfied their ears? For perhaps the most striking of their qualities is one that seems to demand some sacrifice: it is their power to omit. Take down, for instance, the letters of Gray, freely written to intimate friends, and you will be struck by the way in which almost nothing is said and almost everything is suggested. He has to write a letter of condolence:

I break in upon you at a moment, when we least of all are permitted to disturb our friends, only to say, that you are daily and hourly present to my thoughts. If the worst be not yet past, you will neglect and pardon me: but if the last struggle be over; if the poor object of your long anxieties be no longer sensible to your kindness, or to her own sufferings, allow me (at least in idea, for what could I do, were I present, more than this?) to sit by you in silence, and pity from my heart not her, who is at rest, but you, who lose her. May He, who made us, the Master of our pleasures and of our pains, preserve and support you! Adieu.[7]

Eloquence might embellish that theme for page upon page and yet in the end the few formal words would still say more. In contemplating them one is led to imagine an art of suggestion, a shorter, denser, richer form of literature refusing to waste itself in repetition or explanation, an art recognising the ludicrous incapacity of words to repeat even a simple emotion exactly, but the magical power of the right words to do more – to abstract and exalt it.

But the sense of form which seems to have prevailed in the eighteenth century may be much more perceptible to us than to them. It may be that they stand at precisely the right degree of distance from us to appear in the light most becoming to their peculiar qualities. The repose, the distinction, the reserve of their manner are precious to us – enviable, almost incredible. Perhaps we endow them with more of substance than really belongs to them; perhaps we admire them partly because we find them so easy to understand, so definite, so assured that their version of life and of art is the right one. Such admiration on our part is a tribute to the completeness with which they triumphed, imposing shape upon the tumult of their material, so that after more than a century their masterpieces appear to us shaped with a flawless simplicity, as if the task had been easier then, the material less complex and stubborn.

But, granting them every grace and perfection of art, did they not perhaps leave out too much, and sacrifice so devoutly at the shrine of form that some very important qualities were excluded along with those that they rightly judged to be superfluous? Perhaps we feel the form of the eighteenth century so sharply because it is not merely beyond our reach but utterly opposed to our temper. When Mr Howells speaks of the neglect or absence of form in modern fiction we should more hopefully assert that it is everywhere scattered about us but that we are as yet unable to see it. Whether this particular quality is ever visible to the generation that is engaged in creating it seems very doubtful. We cannot recognise among ourselves a conception of the art of fiction such as Jane Austen seems to have held so surely and unquestioningly; we are only now beginning to make out with hesitation and difficulty the form concealed in what still appears to many the formlessness of Mr Hardy's novels.[8] It is not that life is more complex or difficult now than at any other period, but that for each generation the point of interest shifts, the old form puts the emphasis on the wrong places, and in searching out the severed and submerged parts of what to us constitutes form we seem to be throwing fragments together at random and disdaining the very thing that we are trying our best to win from chaos.

1 – A review in the *TLS*, 14 November 1918, (Kp C131) of *The Actor-Manager* . . . With an Introduction by W. D. Howells (Hodder & Stoughton, 1918) by Leonard Merrick (1864–1939). The work was originally published in 1898. See also 'Mr Merrick's Novels' above.

2 – William Dean Howells (1837–1920), American novelist, playwright, critic and editor. See also '*The Son of Royal Langbrith*', *I VW Essays*.

3 – Merrick, intro., p. v, which continues: 'better than you can say; to define it would be like defining charm in a woman, or poetry in a verse'.

4 – *Ibid.*, from a longer sentence.

5 – Alexander Pope (1688–1744); Thomas Love Peacock (1785–1866); Jane Austen (1775–1817); Thomas Gray (1716–71).

6 – Alexander Pope, *The Rape of the Lock* (1714); Mme La Fayette, *La Princesse de Clèves* (1678).

7 – Thomas Gray to William Mason, 28 March 1767, no. ccxcvi in vol. iii of *The Letters of Thomas Gray. Including the correspondence of Gray and Mason.* Ed. Duncan C. Tovey (3 vols., G. Bell & Sons Ltd, 1900–12), which has 'you. Adieu!' William Mason (1724–97) was a poet and a fellow of Pembroke College, Cambridge; his wife Mary, *née* Sherman, had died of consumption at Clifton on the previous day.

8 – Thomas Hardy (1840–1928); for VW's views on his novels, see 'Half of Thomas Hardy', *IV VW Essays,* and 'The Novels of Thomas Hardy', *V VW Essays and CR 2.*

Bad Writers

Perhaps it is unnecessary to feel a slight pang of commiseration for Solomon Eagle when he talks of papers 'contributed weekly, without intermission, to the *New Statesman* since April, 1913'.[2] But it is difficult when a writer hopes that he has produced a book to read in 'without tedium, for ten minutes before one goes to sleep'[3] not to feel slightly ashamed of oneself, as a single head of the many-headed beast, for not having gone to sleep hours ago. Here we have kept him at it, flattering us, wheedling us, telling us funny stories, never boring us, or making us think, or making us cry, for five years and a half; and we are still awake, and as exacting and capricious as a pampered Sultan sunk among cushions on a divan. Books of essays somehow have a tendency to make us feel autocratic and oriental. We are conscious of retinues of slaves. Numbers of them have had their heads cut off and been thrown into the moat for failing to please us already; but Solomon Eagle amuses the Sultan; he has made the Sultan laugh; therefore we grant him permission to go on living on condition that he makes us laugh every night before we go to sleep for ever and ever.

Solomon Eagle has made a discovery which bids fair to enable him to fulfil this condition very easily: he has discovered that English literature is funny. On hearing this, the well-read reader runs over the scale from Chaucer to Robert Bridges in the space of a second or two and raps out something about Falstaff or Mrs Gamp. Anyone can do that. But who save Solomon Eagle, can begin the scale with John Lyly and end it with Mrs Barclay?[4] Have you any conception of what he calls 'the beauties of badness'? Are you aware that 'peculiar poetic treasures'[5] lie uncollected and unappreciated in every bookshop in the Charing Cross Road? Do you, in short, know the look of literature the wrong side out? From a brief and increasingly anxious inspection of one's bookcase the probability seems to be that one knows nothing whatever about it. There are Shakespeare and Shelley and Keats and Matthew Arnold and Gibbon and Walter Pater – a rabbit-run through the ages – a path absolutely dusty with the traffic of culture. The sole possibility of badness is provided by the works of one's friends, and that hope fades soon enough. Which of them would have the imaginative abandonment to write —

> I have found thee there, in a world of rest,
>   In the fair sweet gardens of sunlit bliss,
>   Where the sibilant sound of an Angel's kiss
> Is the sanctioned seal of a Holy quest?[6]

Which of them has sufficient passion to make his hero speak thus over the telephone to an unknown lady? 'Speak to me again,' he said, 'you, who spoke to me last night. Speak to me again. What wait I for? I wait for you! Just now – in my utter loneliness, in my empty solitude – I wait for you.'[7] They lack passion; they lack abandonment.

327

These are by no means the best of Solomon Eagle's discoveries; for the best bad writers often take a page at a stride, but even from them you can judge, perhaps, the sort of quality that bad literature possesses. It is the quality of unfettered imagination. Bad books are written in a state of boiling passion, with a complete certainty of inspiration. Language and grammar are impediments which are disregarded if they become troublesome; and thus you get in the best bad writers that sense of quickly following the half-articulate words of nightmare which is so exciting or so bewildering, as the case may be. The process is not one of thought but one of intuition, and as in this they seem to follow such great examples as Scott, if we are afraid to claim Shakespeare also, let us inquire into the reason of their badness. Why do they invariably suggest not only the incoherence but the unreality of nightmare? The bad writer seems to possess a predominance of the day-dreaming power, he lives all day long in that region of artificial light where every factory girl becomes a duchess, where, if the truth be told, most people spend a few moments every day revenging themselves upon reality. The bad books are not the mirrors but the vast distorted shadows of life; they are a refuge, a form of revenge. Should you feel, however, that these reflections are tending to become melancholy or dull, you have only to shuffle Solomon Eagle's pages and make your choice of something more pleasant to think about. Shall we consider whether Wordsworth, the divine poet, was a dull man?[8] Shall we ask who wrote the worst sentence in the English language? Shall we re-write it in the manner of Henry James,[9] and so dreaming fall asleep?

1 – A review in the *TLS*, 21 November 1918, (Kp C132) of *Books in General* (Martin Secker, 1918) by Solomon Eagle (i.e. J. C. Squire). For VW's private opinion of the 'omnivorous & callous throated Eagle . . . that cheap & thin blooded creature, (I speak of his journalism) & his methods of running the paper, his lack of power judgment & competence', see *I VW Diary*, 5 April 1918. She did not herself contribute to the literary pages of the *New Statesman* under Squire's editorship, but LW did.

See also 'Parodies' and 'Imitative Essays', above.

2 – Squire, Pref., p. 7; John Collings Squire (1884–1958), poet and critic, was literary editor of the *New Statesman* from 1913 to 1919, when he left to found the *London Mercury*; he was succeeded at the *New Statesman* by Desmond MacCarthy ('Affable Hawk'). Squire issued two further selections from his 'Books in General' column, in 1919 and in 1921.

3 – *Ibid.*, p. 7.

4 – For Squire on John Lyly (1554?–1606), author of *Euphues: the Anatomy of Wit*

(1578) and *Euphues and his England* (1580), *ibid.*, 'The Worst Style in the World',
pp. 214–20; and for Mrs (Florence Louisa) Barclay (1862–1921), author of
romances, including *The Rosary* (1909), and *The White Ladies of Worcester*
(1917), *ibid.*, 'Mrs Barclay Sees It Through', pp. 79–85.
5 – *Ibid.*, 'The Beauties of Badness', p. 48.
6 – *Ibid.*, p. 45; the author is unidentified.
7 – *Ibid.*, 'Mrs Barclay Sees It Through', p. 82.
8 – *Ibid.*, 'Wordsworth's Personal Dullness', pp. 174–9.
9 – *Ibid.*, 'Henry James's Obscurity', pp. 179–84.

Trafficks and Discoveries

Most people have only time to ask whether history is readable, not to
seek further whether it is true. But in one sense the most readable
histories are also the most true, in so far as their vivid and spirited
qualities arise from the force with which the historian himself has
believed in his narrative; and perhaps no one can write with fire and
conviction unless he has got hold of some form of the truth. It is partly
this sense of conviction, partly the great artistic skill with which, having
decided upon his interpretation, he shapes his narrative in conformity
with it that makes Froude among the most readable of historians. His
history was, as he said that it ought to be, 'as interesting as a novel'.[2] His
account of the English seamen of the sixteenth century tells itself rather
than is told. The knots of the narrative dissolve in his fingers as he
touches them. The figures of the Queen, of Philip of Spain, of Drake, of
Medina Sidonia[3] and the rest, stand out as clear-cut in feature and as
inevitably placed in relation to each other as if Froude spun the story
from his own imagination. It has the force and directness of fiction. He
was helped, of course, by those famous prejudices and opinions which
colour all his writing. He believed fervently in the English Reformation;
he believed that the English seamen were its most sturdy disciples; he
believed emphatically that Drake, Hawkins,[4] and their fellows were the
best and bravest of mankind; and he came forth not as an apologist for
their deeds, but as the champion of heroes who needed a Homer to sing
them in strains befitting their merit. For all these reasons the story, as he
told it, would have been a good one, had it not been intrinsically one of
the best in the world. Nothing is lacking that poet, novelist, or historian
could desire. In the first place, there is the sea, washing the shores of

unknown lands; then, for adversary, there is the pride of the Spaniard, his mastery still undisputed; the prize itself is virgin land of untold capacity, or caraques heavy with bars of silver and gold; the spirit which inspires the whole is love of religious freedom and love of country; and the catastrophe, as Froude develops it with superb dramatic power, is the complete overthrow of the usurper by a handful of private gentlemen on the threshold of victory. The very titles of his lectures might serve for the books of an epic poem, as grand, so Froude declared, as the *Odyssey*.[5]

The heroic figures which Froude has extracted and shaped are not, however, in the least visionary. Indeed, in the shaping process they lose inevitably something of the humanity which we discern in them obscurely engaged with their forgotten comrades upon those traffics and discoveries which are recorded in the volumes of Hakluyt.[6] Their destiny was not always by any means so patently to the glory of God and the confusion of the Spaniard as would appear from the vantage-ground of the historian. They had, as we have, a mixture of motives in their undertakings, among which the desire to justify the Protestant faith was not always to the fore. But what they lose in symmetry, when studied in the rough, they gain in richness, depth and variety. They gain to such an extent, indeed, that it seems worthwhile to exhort those who have not read to read, those who do not possess to buy, the principal navigations, traffics and discoveries of the English nation made by sea or overland to the remote and farthest distant quarters of the earth, as Richard Hakluyt, preacher and some-time student of Christ Church, in Oxford, collected and set them forth.

As good a starting-place as another is provided by the letter which Hakluyt drew up in the year 1582, and gave to a friend 'that was sent into Turkey'.[7] Here we have set forth in urgent and eloquent language the great need of establishing a trade between England and the East. The chief English commodity was wool. The English wool is the most fine, most soft, most strong, most durable of any wool in the world, and the least subject of any to the moth, as the old Parliament robes of the king and noble peers plainly testify. If he can find a market for wool, he will give 'an infinite sort of the poor people occasion to pray' for him, since through their misery they were forced to crime and 'daily consumed with the gallows'.[8] Next, the English traveller is to look about him curiously, and, in particular, to make inquiry whether 'Anile that coloureth blue be a "natural commodity of those parts"' . . . and if it be compounded of an herb to send the same into this realm by seed or by root in barrels of earth, with all the whole order of sowing, setting, planting, replanting, and with the compounding of the same.'[9] Needless to say, immortal fame would be his if he could discover a method of producing oil in England, since the method of making it from radish seed has failed. He is reminded how the stock of English commodities has been gradually improved by the adventure and generosity of bygone travellers. Dr Linaker, in the time of Henry VII, brought the damask rose, and lately 'flowers called tulipas' have been introduced from Austria, to say nothing of bull, cow, sheep, swine, horse, mare, cock, hen, and a thousand other beasts and plants, without which 'our life were to be said barbarous'.[10] In short, this journey is not only to bring profit to himself, but to increase knowledge, and, in particular, to benefit the poor 'ready to starve for relief'[11] more than by building them almshouses or by giving them lands and goods. Many voices at that time were urging the same plea; and nothing more strikes the imagination than the readiness with which some gentleman from the West Country, perhaps, hears the summons, lays his case before the rich men of his acquaintance, fits out his little band of ships, collects his company, and sets sail, 'having saluted their acquaintance, one his wife, another his children, another his kinsfolk, and another his friends dearer than his kinsfolk'.[12] At Greenwich the courtiers come running out at the news that the ships are in the river; 'the Privy Council looked out of the windows of the Court ... the ships thereupon discharge their ordnance ... and the mariners they shouted in such sort that the sky rang again with the noise thereof'.[13] Considering that the ship in which Drake sailed round the world was no bigger than 'a second-rate yacht of a modern noble lord',[14] and that the voyage was generally a voyage to an unknown land, over seas made dangerous by hostile Spaniards, Portuguese, and French, the solemn leave-taking is accounted for. Well might the mariners walk upon the hatches, climb the shrouds, stand upon the mainyard to wave their friends a last farewell. Many would come back no more; let alone the risk that a wave would swamp the little ship, as happened to Sir Humfrey Gilbert, or that they might be 'congealed and frozen to death', like Sir Hugh Willoughby, or hung up by adverse winds off the coast of Cornwall for a fortnight, until, in their thirst, they licked the muddy water off the deck, as happened to the Earl of Cumberland.[15]

There was also the terror of the supernatural. The spiritual atmosphere was very cloudy, though pierced in a manful way by the sense and piety of the sailors. Sea lions, sea serpents, evaporations of fire and whirlpools that cast ships upon shore, 'as Richard Chancellor told me that he had heard Sebastian Cabot report',[16] were at all times possible, and might well be the disguise of the Devil himself. The survivors of some of these early voyages came home to England in such a state that 'Sir William, his father, and my Lady, his mother, knew him not to be their son, until they found a secret mark, which was a wart upon one of his knees'.[17] Significantly, the articles and orders to be observed by the ships often begin with the injunction to lead a holy life on board, and 'serve God twice a day'.[18] Encompassed with such perils and obscurities, they might well have cause to call upon Divine help before the voyage was out. The Divinity may be addressed much as if He were a temporal prince scarcely hidden by the clouds; but their piety is real enough. Down they fall upon their knees before doing battle with the Turkish galleys; the owner of the vessel preaches his sermon, bidding them not repine, nor do as 'the citizens of Bethulia did';[19] after which drums, flutes, and trumpets sound, and the *Three Half Moons* engages eight of the enemies' vessels.

Then stood up one Grove the master, being a comely man, with his sword and target, holding them up in defiance against his enemies ... But chiefly the boatswain showed himself valiant above the rest; for he fared among the Turks like a wood lion; for there was none of them that either could nor durst stand in his face, till at the last there came a shot from the Turks, which brake his whistle asunder, and smote him on the breast, so that he fell down, bidding them farewell and to be of good comfort.[20]

For thirteen years John Fox and his companions served in captivity to the Turks, until, being weary thereof, 'he lift up his bright, shining sword of ten years' rust,'[21] and struck his keeper such a blow that his head clave asunder, the sword which did the deed being claimed by the abbot and monks of Gallipoli and hung for a monument upon their convent walls.

But the hopes and expectations of these adventurers more than counterbalanced their sufferings. There was the chance of the North-West Passage, and gold, perhaps, in the commonest black stone. They went not only to dispose of merchandise, but as ambassadors from the Queen of England, taking a present with them to the sovereign of the land, 'three fair mastiffs', perhaps, 'in coats of red cloth', together with a sonorous letter, 'the paper whereof did smell most fragrantly of camphor and ambergris, and the ink of perfect musk'[22] from Elizabeth herself. Strange and splendid were the ceremonies that the English sailors newly landed from their voyage were invited to behold. They saw the Emperor at Moscow 'sitting in his chair of estate, with his crown on his head and a staff of goldsmith work in his left hand', and beheld 'the great Turk where he sumptuously sate alone'.[23] Marvellous was the richness of the earth and the shapes of the creatures seen, as John Locke saw the elephant, 'not only with my bodily eyes, but much more with the eyes of my mind and spirit'.[24]

So the different companies established themselves in different quarters of the globe, and lonely little groups of Englishmen began doing trade with the natives, bartering their wool and cloth for wax and tallow in Russia, tempting the African savages to give them ivory and gold in exchange for hawks' bells, horses' tails, hats, and unwrought iron. The letters of instructions sent by merchants in London to their agents, and the agents' replies, abounding in detail and preserving the names of many forgotten adventurers, make as good reading as the more heroic passages which have become famous. But to abstract is idle. The only possible course to take with Hakluyt's voyages, whether you own them in the convenient Everyman edition or in the five quarto volumes published about 1810,[25] is to read them through; to read dedications, ambassages, letters, privileges, discourses, advertisements; for only thus will you become possessed of the unity of the whole. Different people write the book, but they have the same outlook, the same manner of speech. Beauty of phrase, astonishing and scattered impartially, is frequent enough; the average of their writing is full of freedom and melody; but beyond that lies what is more difficult to define, something common to them all – an attitude of mind, large, imaginative, unsated. There is a sort of nobleness about them; seen through their eyes, the world appears fresh and flowing, unexplored, and of infinite richness.

1 – A review in the TLS, 12 December 1918, (Kp C133) based on English Seamen in the Sixteenth Century (Longmans, Green & Co., 1895), and, as stated at the head of the article, 'The Hakluyt's Voyages, Travels, and Discoveries of the English Nation', for which VW used Hakluyt's Collection of the Early Voyages, Travels and Discoveries of the English Nation. A New Edition, with Additions (5 vols., R. H. Evans, 1809–12), making certain modifications to the original spelling.

On Saturday, 7 December 1918, she wrote in her diary: 'For some reason, not connected with my virtues I think, I get 2 or even 3 books weekly from the Times, & thus breast one short choppy wave after another. It fills up the time while Night & Day lies dormant . . . I have spent the week (but I was interrupted 2 days, & one cut short by a lunch with Roger) over Hakluyt: who turns out on mature inspection to justify over & over again my youthful discrimination. I write & write; I am rung up & told to stop writing; review must be had on Friday; I typewrite till the messenger from the Times appears; I correct the pages in my bedroom with him sitting over the fire'.

See 'Sir Walter Raleigh' above; 'Trafficks and Discoveries', *I VW Essays*; *'Richard Hakluyt', III VW Essays*; 'The Elizabethan Lumber Room', *IV VW Essays* and *CR* 1. Reading Notes (MHP, B.2d), reproduced in Appendix I.

2 – The origin of this phrase has not been discovered. James Anthony Froude (1818–94), historian and man of letters, whose *English Seamen* ... consists of lectures originally given at Oxford, where, in 1892, he was appointed regius professor of modern history.

3 – Elizabeth I (1533–1603); Philip II of Spain (1527–98); Sir Francis Drake (1540?–96); Alonso Pérez de Guzmán, duque de Medina Sidonia (1550–1615), who commanded the Spanish Armada.

4 – Sir John Hawkins (1532–95).

5 – Froude, Lecture iv, 'Drake's Voyage Round the World', p. 80. The other lectures are: 'The Sea Cradle of the Reformation'; 'John Hawkins and the African Slave Trade'; 'Sir John Hawkins and Philip the Second'; 'Parties in the State'; 'The Great Expedition to the West Indies'; 'Attack on Cadiz'; 'Sailing of the Armada'; 'Defeat of the Armada'.

6 – Richard Hakluyt (1552?–1616), geographer, educated at Christ Church, Oxford, 1570–4, actively promoted English discovery and colonisation and became a member of the London or South Virginian Company. A one-volume version of *The Principal Navigations* ... first appeared in 1589, and a three-volume edition in 1598–1600.

7 – Evans, vol. ii, 'A brief Remembrance of things to be indevoured at Constantinople, and in other places in Turkie ... drawn by M. Richard Hakluyt of the Middle Temple, and given to a friend that was sent into Turkie 1582', p. 279.

8 – For both quotations, *ibid.*, vol. iii, 'A discourse written by Sir Humphrey Gilbert Knight, to prove a passage by the Northwest to Cathaia and the East Indies', p. 45.

9 – *Ibid.*, vol. ii, 'What you shall do in Turkie, besides the businesse of your Factorship', p. 282, which has: 'And in any wise, if Anile that coloureth blew be a naturall commodity of those parts, and if it be compounded of an herbe, to send the same to this realme by seed or by root in barrell of earth ... compounding of the same, that it may become a naturall commodity in this realme as Woad is, to this end that the high price of forreine Woad (which devoureth yeerely great treasure) may be brought downe.'

10 – For both quotations, *ibid.*, 'Other some things to be remembered', p. 284. Dr Thomas Linacre (1460?–1524), English humanist and physician, founder of the Royal College of Physicians.

11 – *Ibid.*, p. 285.

12 – *Ibid.*, vol. i, 'The booke of the great and mighty Emperor of Russia, and Duke of Muscovia, and of the dominions orders and commodities thereunto belonging; drawn by Richard Chancelour', p. 272.

13 – *Ibid.*

14 – Froude, 'Drake's Voyage Round the Worlde', p. 107.

15 – Sir Humfrey Gilbert (1539?–83). For the quotation regarding Sir Hugh Willoughby (d. 1554), Evans, vol. iii, 'Certaine other reasons, or arguments to proove a passage by the Northwest, learnedly written by M. Richard Willes Gentleman',
p. 47. George Clifford, 3rd Earl of Cumberland (1558–1605).

16 – Evans, vol. ii, 'The second voyage to Guinea . . .', p. 478.

17 – *Ibid.*, vol. iii, 'The voyage of M. Hore and divers other gentlemen, to Newfoundland, and Cape Briton, in the yeere 1536 and in the 28 yere of king Henry the 8', p. 169: 'They arrived at S. Ives in Cornewall about the ende of October. From thence they departed unto a certaine castle belonging to Sir John Luttrell, where M. Thomas Buts, and M. Rastall and other Gentlemen of the voyage were very friendly entertained: after that they came to the Earle of Bathe at Bathe, and thence to Bristoll, so to London. M. Buts was so changed in the voyage with hunger and miserie, that Sir William his father and my Lady his mother knew him not to be their sonne, untill they found a secret marke which was a wart upon one of his knees, as hee told me Richard Hakluyt of Oxford himselfe . . .'

18 – E.g., *ibid.*, 'Articles and orders to be observed for the Fleete . . .', p. 106: 'Inprimis, to banish swearing, dice, and card-playing, and filthy conmunication [sic], and to serve God twice a day, with the ordinary service usuall in Churches of England, and to clear the glasse, according to the old order of England.'

19 – *Ibid.*, vol. ii, 'The woorthy enterprise of John Foxe an Englishman in delivering 266. Christians out of captivity of the Turkes at Alexandria, the 3. of Januarie 1577', p. 246.

20 – *Ibid.*, which concludes: 'encouraging them likewise to winne praise by death, rather then to live captives in misery and shame.'

21 – *Ibid.*, p. 248.

22 – For the three mastiffs, *ibid.*, vol. ii, 'The voyage of the Susan of London . . .', p. 291; and for the fragrant letter, *ibid.*, 'A letter written by the most high and mighty Empresse the wife of the Grand Signior Sultan Murad Can to the Queenes Majesty of England, in the yeere of our Lord, 1594', p. 453.

23 – For the Emperor, *ibid.*, vol. i, 'The voyage, wherein Osep Napea the Moscovite Ambassadour returned home . . .', p. 352, which has 'goldsmiths worke'; and for the Turk, *ibid.*, vol. ii, 'The Voyage of the Susan . . .', p. 291.

24 – *Ibid.*, vol. ii, 'The second voyage to Guinea set out by Sir George Barne, Sir John Yorke, Thomas Lok, Anthonie Hickman and Edward Castelin, in the yeere 1554. The Captaine whereof was M. John Lok', p. 474: 'At this last voyage was brought from Guinea the head of an Elephant, of such huge bignesse, that onely the bones or cranew thereof, beside the nether jaw and great tusks, weighed about two hundred weight, and was as much as I could well lift from the ground . . . This head divers have seene in the house of the worthy marchant Sir Andrew Judde, where also I saw it, and beheld it, not only with my bodily eyes, but much more with the eyes of my mind and spirit, considering the worke, the cunning and wisedome of the workemaister: without which consideration, the sight of such strange

and wonderfull things may rather seeme curiosities, then profitable contemplations.'
25 – *The Principal Navigations, Voyages, Traffiques and Discoveries of the English Nation* ... With an introduction by John Masefield (8 vols., Everyman's Library, 1907).

'The Three Black Pennys'

The obvious thing to say about Mr Joseph Hergesheimer's novel *The Three Black Pennys* is that it possesses form as undoubtedly as a precious stone shaped to fit exactly into a band of gold possesses form. The comparison with something hard, lustrous and concrete is not altogether fanciful. In recollection, the last sentence being read, the reader's impression of the book as a whole assumes something of the smooth solidity of a well-fashioned gem. When the last sentence is finished nothing vague or superfluous is left to blur the outline; the substance is all neatly packed into the form, rounded off, disposed of, completed. The sense of conclusiveness is so satisfactory, and also so rare, that we could enjoy it separately from any feeling of pity or pleasure aroused by the fortunes of the characters, as a blind man might enjoy the shape of a stone though unable to see its colour.

Mr Hergesheimer's story, the story of a family owning a great ironworks in Pennsylvania from the middle of the eighteenth century to modern times, had need of this shaping if only to compress it within a volume of moderate size. Each of the Pennys whom he has selected to represent his theme stands out from the rest of his family because the Welsh blood mixed with the English blood centuries ago asserts itself in him. It produces, Howat's father says, 'a solitary living, dark lot. Unamenable to influence, reflect their country, I suppose, but lovers of music ... it sinks entirely out of sight for two or three and sometimes four generations; and then appears solid, in one individual, as unslacked as the pure, original thing.'[2] It appears in Howat; in his grandson Jasper; in Jasper's grandson Howat, the last of the Pennys. The black Pennys did not take to life easily; there was something unmalleable in their composition which stayed unmelted in the common furnace. They did not run into the ordinary social mould. In their obdurate ways of impressing themselves upon other people they more resembled the great hammer at Myrtle Forge, persistently and relentlessly beating out iron, than the iron itself. 'If the hammer stops,' Howat told his wife in the eighteenth century, 'all this, the Pennys, stop, too.'[3] The last Penny was unable even to make one of those marriages which his ancestors had achieved with so much difficulty; the hammer had stopped in his father's time; the Pennys made iron no longer.

But the story cannot, as this summary might suggest, be read as a discourse upon heredity with a satiric motive; Mr Hergesheimer is too much of an artist to insist that human life is capable of any such forced solution. If, curiously enough, a certain type of character occurs at intervals in the same family, it occurs as a blue or a green might repeat itself beautifully in a pattern. The beat of the great hammer recurs too; when it stops we know that something more important has ceased; the raccoon hunt repeats itself; for, as we began by saying, Mr Hergesheimer has a strong sense of form, and these are some of the more obvious devices used by him to hold his story together, to secure continuity, to bind his gem in a circle of gold. An attentive reader will discover others less obvious. Whether he has succeeded equally in another direction is more open to doubt. The entrances and exits of the Pennys and of the women allotted them as partners are so carefully timed and regulated that they would tend to be mechanical were they not more obviously pictorial. There is no room here for license or for the larger sweep and expressiveness of human character. Perhaps Mr Hergesheimer is a little hampered in this direction by his keen susceptibility to material objects. He handles, for the concrete term is justified, his blue decanters and cut-glass decanters, holds them to the light, relishes their grain and texture with a gusto which is sometimes excessive. He cannot resist observing. We can remember no novel in which women's dresses are more frequently and carefully described. This is not done, however, to give atmosphere or local colour, but because the beauty of still life makes part of the writer's vision. We owe to this individual gift some remarkable scenes at the forge and descriptions of American landscape. It is one of the qualities that make the *Black Pennys* an unusual novel, to be read slowly, thoughtfully and with a sense of luxury.

1 – A review in the *TLS*, 12 December 1918, (Kp C134) of *The Three Black Pennys. A Novel* (William Heinemann, 1918) by Joseph Hergesheimer (1880–1954). On 7 December 1918, VW wrote in her diary: 'No sooner had I done a little type setting,

& ruled off the hour & a half before dinner in which to read my distinguished American novelist [Hergesheimer] recommended by Mr Galsworthy [unelucidated], than Lottie admitted Sydney Waterlow.'

See also '*Java Head*', '*Gold and Iron*', 'The Pursuit of Beauty' and 'Pleasant Stories', *III VW Essays*. Reprinted: *CW*.

2 – Hergesheimer, I, 'The Furnace', ch. III, pp. 30–1.

3 – *Ibid*., ch. VII, p. 92; Howat Penny to Mrs Ludowika Winscombe, whom, at this stage in the story, he has yet to marry, her husband being still alive.

A View of the Russian Revolution

Mr Hugh Walpole[2] in his short foreword to this volume seems to us to be doing its writer rather a disservice than a service. Invoking that blessed word 'atmosphere', he sets out a claim which, we think, Miss Buchanan could hardly wish to put forward on her own behalf. 'I believe,' says Mr Walpole, 'that I am speaking without any exaggeration when I say that this book of Miss Buchanan's is the first attempt of any writer in any language to give to the world a sense of the *atmosphere* of Russia under the shock and terror of those world-shaking events', the war and the Revolution. Mr Walpole explains that by 'atmosphere' he means in this connection the general outlook upon events of the sort of people whom in English we should refer to as 'the man in the street'.[3] In our opinion this frank and vivacious diary of 'Sir Buchanan's'[4] daughter cannot claim to represent this outlook. The book sets out to be an account of Petrograd in the last four years as it appeared to a young lady moving in the diplomatic 'set', and the result does not pass beyond this modest aim.

At the outbreak of the war Miss Buchanan volunteered as a nurse in one of the Petrograd hospitals; in order to discharge her duties more efficiently she set to work to learn Russian – a study in which, we gather from the few sentences quoted in this book, she is not yet very proficient. The first half of her book describes in vivid fashion the outbreak of the war and Miss Buchanan's and her friends' experiences with the wounded, the refugees and their children – '"Meriel, his head was absolutely alive," she said, with a little gasp'[5] – and there are also descriptions of the Russian Court and its ceremonies as Miss Buchanan saw them. The following passage is a typical example of her method; it has the merits and defects of descriptions which rest wholly upon shrewd but sympathetic personal observation:

Looking back at my diary, I see that it was this winter also that I met General Polivanov, the new Minister of War. We dined yesterday evening with the Sazonoffs, and I sat next to Polivanov. Politically I know really nothing about him, but personally I immediately took a great sympathy to him. He is one of those grand old Russians, enormously tall, with a wonderfully commanding, imposing presence. A rugged face framed in a short dark beard, and deep-set grey eyes, keen and very bright and yet unspeakably kind. He asked me all about the hospital and my work, and when I said I loved the soldiers beamed on me delightedly, and promised me very soon to come and visit them himself.[6]

Miss Buchanan leads up to the outbreak of the Revolution with one of the more particularly fearsome accounts of Rasputin's death. After drinking nearly a whole bottle of poisoned wine and eating a dish of poisoned cakes and being shot through the heat, the 'priest'[7] (as Miss Buchanan inaccurately calls him) still recovers consciousness, hurls himself at Prince Yusupov, and tries to escape through the garden. Three months later Miss Buchanan returned to Petrograd from a holiday just in time for the outbreak of the Revolution. 'Shut up now in the house and forbidden to go out, I think I spent most of my time that morning sitting on the big staircase of the Embassy, gleaning what information I could from the various people who came and went.'[8] Her account of the summer and winter of 1917 follows the usual path; like so many other observers, she notices the indiscriminate enthusiasm of the Russian soldiery and peasants for even the most contradictory doctrines, and the facility with which skilful orators were able to manipulate the sympathy of the crowds they addressed. The British Embassy was faced across the river by Lenin's stronghold, and whenever there was a prospect of a Bolshevist rising the members of the Embassy staff were pressed either to leave the building altogether or to take safety in the more protected part of it. Miss Buchanan's desire not to miss any of the excitement led to General Knox's assuring her that she 'was more trouble than all the Russian Army'.[9] Her descriptions of the Bolshevist *émeutes*, as seen from the Embassy windows, are the best thing in the book.

It is unfortunate that the writer has allowed herself to enter upon the troubled sea of the Russian revolutionary politics of last year. Certainly she does not profess to be qualified to pass final judgments, but even in the vague outline of events which she gives there are too many traces of gossip accepted as fact. In the Kornilov affair, for example, it is hardly fair to M. Kerensky, for whose intentions Miss Buchanan expresses her admiration, to say that 'the papers published a telegram of Kerensky's proclaiming himself Dictator and commanding Kornilov to resign at once'.[10] It was not Kerensky himself, but the Provisional Government which gave him special powers to deal with the liquidation of the Kornilov affair, and he was not thus or otherwise invested with dictatorial powers. When, again, Miss Buchanan says, 'What seems, however, certain is that, fearing a Bolshevik rising, the Government negotiated with Kornilov to send troops up to Petrograd to quell the insurrection under the command of General Krimov',[11] she should remember that one of the Government's main accusations against General Kornilov was not that he sent the troops to Petrograd, but that he sent them, as he had been particularly requested not to do, under the command of General Krimov. When Miss Buchanan assumes that her statement 'seems certain', she is unintentionally begging one of the most vexed questions of an intensely complicated business. Unlike personalities, politics cannot always be elucidated by the clever intuition which Miss Buchanan in her purely descriptive chapters shows herself well able to command.

1 – A review in the *TLS*, 19 December 1918, (Kp C135) of *Petrograd. The City of Trouble 1914–1918* by Meriel Buchanan. Daughter of the British Ambassador (W. Collins Sons & Co. Ltd, 1918).

2 – Hugh Walpole (1884–1941), the popular novelist, had served during the war with the Russian Red Cross and was head of Anglo-Russian propaganda in Petrograd during the February Revolution of 1917. His experiences in Russia inform a number of his works, including *The Green Mirror* (1918) – see '*The Green Mirror*', above – from which Buchanan quotes, ch. XXXII, pp. 251–2.

3 – Buchanan, Foreword, p. 1.

4 – Sir George William Buchanan (1854–1924) was ambassador at St Petersburg, 1910–18. (The misappellation does *not* occur in *Petrograd*.)

5 – Buchanan, ch. VII, p. 49.

6 – *Ibid.*, p. 51, which has quotation marks round 'We dined . . . himself.'; and also has 'gray' eyes.

7 – *Ibid.*, ch. XI, p. 82; p. 83. Grigori Yefimovich Rasputin (b. 1872) was killed in December 1916.

8 – *Ibid.*, ch. XIII, p. 97.

9 – *Ibid.*, ch. XX, p. 152.

10 – *Ibid.*, ch. XXII, p. 165. Alexander Fordorovich Kerensky (1881–1970), head of the provisional government from July 1917, in September ordered the arrest of the army's commander-in-chief, General Lavr Georgyevich Kornilov (1870–1918), who had attempted to seize Petrograd and establish a military dictatorship.

11 – *Ibid.*, ch. XII, p. 169.

The Russian View

When, in one of Mr Galsworthy's latest stories one of the characters addresses a stranger as 'Brother'[2] you rub your eyes and wonder whether it is possible that you are reading a translation from the Russian. It is true that both the characters are at the moment in a condition of great misery, but in a book about English people written by an Englishman such a word seems out of keeping. 'Mate', perhaps, would be the English equivalent; but mate does not mean brother, and it would be wisest to accept the fact that, however much we may wish to follow the Russian example, we cannot say 'brother' to a stranger in England. Turning to the pages of Elena Militsina and Mikhail Saltikov[3] in the belief that we have met the word over and over again, we do not, as a matter of fact, find a single example of it. We have found it in the atmosphere, then; it is the word which expresses, not only the attitude of the characters to each other, but the writer's attitude towards the world. Saltikov died in the year 1889; Elena Militsina is still apparently a young woman. Half a century lies between the appearance of the first book of the one and the first book of the other; but, as Dr Wright notes, 'the unity of outlook and the kindred sympathies shared by these two writers of successive generations show that the aspirations uttered in 1847 were still unfulfilled in the first decades of the twentieth century...[4] ⟨The stories⟩ should help us to realise ⟨he adds⟩ that a change in the government of Russia was inevitable.'[5] But the unity which we feel in both writers lies deeper than that – it will outlive a change of government; roughly stated, it seems to consist in their sense of brotherhood. It is for the sake of the outlook which they have in common that we translate and publish and read with interest stories which are not of themselves of great artistic importance.

Call it what we like, the quality which we recognise at once as the Russian quality in the stories before us is hardly to be found in English literature. The impulse to write has come to us from a different direction – from so many different directions, indeed, that it is impossible to say that there is any one quality supremely characteristic of English literature. The impulse which urges the Russians to express themselves seems more simple, and is more easily detected in the lesser writers than in the great; they have been driven to write by their deep sense of human suffering and their unwavering sympathy with it. An able English writer treating the theme which Elena Militsina has treated in *The Village Priest*, would have shown his knowledge of different social classes, his intellectual grasp of the religious problem. His story would have been well constructed and made to appear probable. All this seems irrelevant to the Russian writer. She asks herself only about the soul of the priest, and tries to imagine what was in the hearts of the peasants when they prayed or came to die. As for the story, there is none; there is no close observation of manners; her work shows very little sense of form; she leaves off anywhere, as it seems, without troubling to finish. And yet, in spite of its formlessness and flatness, she produces an effect of spirituality. It is as if she had tried to light a lamp behind her characters, making them transparent rather than solid, letting the large and permanent things show through the details of dress and body. She is not a writer of remarkable gift, so that, having produced this sense of transparency, with its strange power to make us imagine that we are on the threshold of something else, she stops short; she cannot show us what goes on in the souls thus unveiled. Saltikov is more penetrating and more masterly; but he, too, approaches his work in the same spirit of sympathy with suffering rather than in a spirit of curiosity, or amusement, or intellectual interest. It is sympathy that enables him to draw in so short a space so remarkable a picture of the Russian peasant toiling in the immense field of Russia.

There is no end to the field; you cannot get out of it anywhere. Konyaga has drawn the plough afar and across it, yet he never reached the boundary of this land. Whether it is bare or flowery, or benumbed under a snowy winding sheet, it stretches far and wide in its might; it does not provoke to strife with itself but straightway leads captive. It is not possible to guess its secret, nor to overcome, nor to exhaust it; as soon as it dies, it is alive again ... The land crushes him, takes away his last powers, and yet will not confess itself satisfied.[6]

Both writers seem to be saying to us constantly, in the words of Militsina's priest:

Learn to make yourself akin to people. I would even like to add: Make yourself indispensable to them. But let this sympathy be not with the mind – for it is easy with the mind – but with the heart, with love towards them.[7]

In some such words one might sketch roughly the nature of the gift made us by the Russian writers. More than any others they seem impressed with the profound suffering of human beings; and perhaps it is common

suffering rather than common happiness or effort or desire that produces the feeling of brotherhood. 'Deep sadness,'[8] says Dr Wright, is
typical of the Russian people. Whether or not they are more sad than
other people, it is certain that they never attempt to conceal their
sadness. There is none of that effort so common in England to appear
better off than you are; there is no disgrace in poverty and failure; the
feeble-minded are called with reverence 'the Slaves of God'.[9] On the
other hand there is none of that instinct to rebel against sorrow, to make
something brave, gay, romantic, intellectual, out of life, which the
literatures of France and England so splendidly express. The gulf
between us and them is clearly shown by the difficulty with which we
produce even a tolerable imitation of the Russians. We become awkward and self-conscious, or worse, denying our own qualities, we write
with an affectation of simplicity and goodness which soon turns to
mawkish sentimentality. The truth is that if you say 'brother' you must
say it with conviction, and it is not easy to say it with conviction. The
Russians themselves produce this sense of conviction not because they
acquiesce or tolerate indiscriminately or despair, but because they
believe so passionately in the existence of the soul. Konyaga, the worn-
out horse who typifies the Russian peasant, may be beaten, harassed,
hardly alive, 'but a sound core lives in him, neither dying, nor dismembered, nor destroyed. There is no end of this living core, that alone is
clear.'[10] And that alone is important; that living core which suffers and
toils is what we all have in common. We tend to disguise or to decorate
it; but the Russians believe in it, seek it out, interpret it, and, following its
agonies and intricacies, have produced not only the most spiritual of
modern books but also the most profound.

1 – A review in the *TLS*, 19 December 1918, (Kp C136) of *The Village Priest and
Other Stories* from the Russian of Militsina & Saltikov. Translated by Beatrix L.
Tollemache. With an introduction by C. Hagberg Wright (Fisher Unwin Ltd, 1918).
VW later adapted and made use of part of this review when writing 'The Russian
Point of View', *IV. VW Essays* and *CR1*.
2 – John Galsworthy (1867–1933), 'The First and the Last', in the collection *Five
Tales* (Heinemann, 1918), p. 18: 'A surge of feeling came up in Laurence for this
creature, more unfortunate than himself . . . "Well, brother," he said, "*you* don't
look too prosperous!"'
3 – Elena Dmietrievna Militsina, dates untraced, is represented in the present
volume by the title story and by 'The Old Nurse'. Mikhail Evgrafovich Saltikov
(1826–89), better known under his pseudonym Schédrin, author of *Provincial*

Sketches (1857–8) and editor of the *Fatherland Review* from 1878, until its
suppression by the authorities in 1884. The present volume contains three of his
stories: 'Konyaga', 'A Visit to a Russian Prison' and 'The Governor'.
4 – *Village Priest*, intro., p. viii; Sir Charles Hagberg Wright (1862–1940), librarian
and specialist in Russian literature, educated privately in Russia, France and
Germany, and at the Royal Academical Institution, Belfast, and Trinity College,
Dublin. From 1893 until his death he was secretary and librarian of the London
Library.
5 – *Ibid.*, p. xxii; see also n. 9 below.
6 – *Ibid.*, 'Konyaga', p. 75; the ellipsis marks the omission of: 'You cannot grasp
which is death and which is life. But in life or in death the first and unchangeable eyewitness is Konyaga. For others these fields represent abundance, poetry, and vast
spaces; but for Konyaga – they mean servitude.'
7 – *Ibid.*, 'The Village Priest', p. 34.
8 – *Ibid.*, intro., p. xxii: 'They [Saltikov's sketches] reveal his love of humanity and
his greatness of heart, while giving us a typical picture of the Russian people, their
deep sadness, their inherent simplicity and kindliness. They should help us to realise
that a change in the government of Russia was inevitable.'
9 – *Ibid.*, 'The Village Priest', pp. 8–9: 'Beside her were the two old maids – Slaves of
God she called them – the foolish, simple-minded Theckla and the crazy Mokrena.
They were winding thread, or else knitting or sewing something.'
10 – *Ibid.*, 'Konyaga', p. 77, which has: 'A sound core'.

'Mummery'

Mummery, which is apparently the nineteenth volume from Mr Cannan's[2] pen, is a clever readable novel, as we have some reason to expect
that an author's nineteenth book should be. Nineteen volumes cannot be
brought from start to finish without learning whatever you are capable
of learning about writing books; but the risk of learning your lesson so
thoroughly is that you may become in the process not an artist, but a
professional writer. You may learn to write so easily that writing
becomes a habit. Mr Cannan has to tell the story of two men of genius,
one a painter, the other a dramatist; both would reform the stage, one by
his designs, the other by his plays; but they are both frustrated, so far as
the present is concerned, by the British public and by Sir Henry Butcher,
the actor-manager, who serves that public faithfully or with only an
occasional disloyalty. The theatrical world is very vivaciously and very
literally represented by Mr Cannan, so that many of the characters in it

seem to belong as much to the actual world as to the world of fiction. But whether or not he has his counterpart in life, Sir Henry Butcher is certainly the most imaginative character in the book. One can believe that actor-managers famed for their sumptuous representations of Shakespeare, as illustrious in society as upon the stage, in whom strangely enough the dramatic genius burns up by fits and starts, are much as Mr Cannan depicts them. The wealthy peer who supports the higher drama, the manager's wife who regards the theatre 'as a kind of salon' and hates any attempt 'to divert Sir Henry from the social to the professional aspect of the theatre',[3] the atmosphere of the Imperium behind the scenes and in the boxes, are all done skilfully and with humour.

So long as Mr Cannan is noting down what he has observed he shows himself a shrewd though not a very subtle observer. But when he draws conclusions from what he has seen and becomes the intellectual satirist, he writes as if from habit, repeating what he has learnt by heart from writers of what he calls 'the Sturm and Drang period'[4] in whom the intellect was often very keen and the satiric gift very fine. Mr Adnor Rodd is their representative. The name is sufficient to show us that, let alone the distinguished appearance and the abrupt manner. But Mr Adnor Rodd, though he is a very conscientious man and writes plays which no one will produce, is not, so far as our experience goes, a very clever man. 'Money!' he exclaims. 'That is the secret of the whole criminal business. Money controls art. Money rejects art. Money's a sensitive thing too. It rejects force, spontaneity, originality. It wants repetition, immutability, things calculable. Money . . . '[5] He is, in short, what the conventional idea of an artist is supposed to be, 'demoniac and challenging';[6] just as Charles Mann, the painter, is the irresponsible and non-moral variety of the same type. Sir Henry Butcher and the Imperium theatre are quite proof against attacks levelled at them by people of this calibre, and deserve to be so. But it is a misfortune from the point of view of the book, in so far as it is a book of criticism and ideas. Mr Cannan has every right to criticise society in his books, but, like everything else in a novel criticism must be the expression of a writer's own convictions; the conventions of the intellectual are at least as sterile as the conventions of the bourgeois. Mr Cannan seems to be falling into the habit of being intellectual in a perfectly conventional way, so that his criticism is more and more a stereotyped complaint and his remedy more and more a nostrum made up for him by other people. If he had thought out his position afresh and for himself, he would scarcely have spoilt Clara Day by making her half a natural nice woman and half the embodiment of somebody's theory upon the function of the female sex in human society. 'Her childish detestation of her womanhood was gone. She accepted it, gloried in it as her instrument, and knew that she could never be lost in it. For ever in her mind that crisis was associated with Kropotkin's escape from prison [. . .]'[7] On the advice, no doubt, of some distinguished writer, she saw 'that being a woman, she must work through a man's imagination before she could become a person fit to dwell on the earth with her fellows',[8] and married Rodd; but a marriage so cordially vouched for by the best authorities has no need of our commendation. It is in Mr Cannan's interest, and not in Mr and Mrs Rodd's, that we recommend him to find some means of destroying the careful selection of books, including six volumes of Ibsen, which they took with them on their honeymoon.

1–A review in the *TLS*, 19 December 1918, (Kp C137) of *Mummery. A Tale of Three Idealists* (W. Collins Sons & Co. Ltd, 1918) by Gilbert Cannan. Reprinted: CW.
2 – Gilbert Cannan (1884–1955), novelist, dramatist and dramatic critic; his works include the *roman à clef Mendel* (1916), based on the life of the painter Mark Gertler (1891–1938) and dedicated to (Dora) Carrington (1892–1932), a book that VW had thought 'rather interesting' (*II VW Letters*, no. 805, to Saxon Sydney-Turner).
3 – Cannan, ch. x, p. 127.
4 – *Ibid.*, ch. xI, p. 142; the writers are listed as: 'Shaw, Barker, Galsworthy, Ibsen, Schnitzler, Hauptmann, Tschekov, Andreev, Claudel, Strindberg, Wedekind'.
5 – *Ibid.*, ch. xII, p. 160, which has: 'You! You talk of money! That is the secret', and 'a sensitive thing, too'.
6 – *Ibid.*
7 – *Ibid.*, ch. vIII, pp. 103–4, which has a paragraph at 'For ever'.
8 – *Ibid.*, ch. xVIII, p. 243, which has: 'and being a woman'.

'The Method of Henry James'

Henry James[2] is much at present in the air – a portentous figure looming large and undefined in the consciousness of writers, to some an oppression, to others an obsession, but undeniably present to all. In either case, whether you suffer from the consciousness of Henry James or rejoice in it, you can scarcely do better than read what Mr Beach has to say about him. He has seen we will not say the, but certainly a, figure in the carpet, which, considering the width of the fabric and the complexity of the pattern, is something of an achievement. But further and more remarkably, considering his race, it is not to Mr Beach a mere diagram to be committed to memory in order to win the prize, whatever that may be, of accurate culture. You will not come out top through reading Mr Beach, but you will be made to enjoy thinking about Henry James and stimulated to frame theories to account for him; you may in the end find yourself with a pattern of your own.

Mr Beach is far too fruitful and cogent a writer to lend himself to summary, nor can we develop a fraction of the things which tempted us to amplify them as we read; but we may perhaps brood for a moment upon the question in general. It is a commonplace to say that no other writer causes his readers to ask so many questions or has a following more sharply divided among themselves than Henry James. Mr Beach is a Jacobean – that is to say he believes that in *The Wings of the Dove*, *The Ambassadors*, and *The Golden Bowl* Mr James produced 'the beautiful fruits'[3] of a method which he had invented and perfected through a long series of failures and experiments. Other admirers cease to admire at or about the year 1889 – the year of *The Tragic Muse*.[4] Both these sects can make out a good case for their beliefs, and are happy in their convictions. But more difficult to define and less enviable is the position of a third group, which cannot accommodate itself to either camp. The trouble with them is that they admire both periods, but with inexplicable lapses, almost unknown in the case of other writers, when from the extreme of admiration they turn to something like contempt. A sudden chill in an atmosphere of cordiality, a hint of callousness beneath the show of affection – by some such figures alone can they describe the insidious sensation which converts them from enthusiasts to outcasts. The worst of it is that they scarcely dare formulate their meaning, since any plain statement seems so grievously an over-statement. If you woke in the night and found yourself saying, 'Henry James is vulgar – Henry James is a snob', you would annihilate these words, lest the very darkness should overhear them. In the light of day the utmost you can bring yourself to murmur is that Henry James is an American. He had the American love of old furniture. Why these characteristics should at moments appear capable of such devastating effects is one of those puzzles that so often destroy the peace of mind of the fickle Jacobeans. His characters, so they say, are somehow tainted with the determination not to be vulgar; they are, as exiles tend to be, slightly parasitic; they have an enormous appetite for afternoon tea; their attitude not only to furniture but to life is more that of the appreciative collector than of the undoubting possessor.

But somehow none of this seems of importance compared with the other fact, which becomes increasingly clear, that Henry James, whatever else he may have been, was a great writer – a great artist. A priest of the art of writing in his lifetime, he is now among the saints to whom every writer, in particular every novelist, must do homage. His pursuit of his method was religious in its seriousness, religious in its sacrifices, and productive, as we see from his prefaces and sketches, of a solemn rejoicing such as one can imagine in a priest to whom a vision of the divinity has been vouchsafed at last. A glimpse of the possibilities which in his view gather round every story and stretch away into the distance beyond any sight save his own makes other people's achievements seem empty and childish. One had almost rather read what he meant to do than read what he actually did do. Merely as the writer who could make words follow his bidding, take his inflection, say what he wished them to say until the limit of what can be expressed seems to be surpassed, he is a source of perpetual wonder and delight. That is one side of him which is of perennial fascination, but perhaps it is not the most important side. The important side is suggested by the design which he made in order to explain his conception of *The Awkward Age*. He drew on a sheet of paper

the neat figure of a circle consisting of a number of small rounds disposed at equal distances about a central object. The central object was my situation, my subject in itself, to which the thing would owe its title, and the small rounds represented so many distinct lamps, as I liked to call them, the function of each of which would be to light with all due intensity one of its aspects.[5]

One has to look for something like that in the later books – not a plot, or a collection of characters, or a view of life, but something more abstract, more difficult to grasp, the weaving together of many themes into one theme, the making out of a design.

1 – A review in the *TLS*, 26 December 1918, (Kp c138) of *The Method of Henry James* (Yale University Press, 1918) by Joseph Warren Beach, Associate Professor of English, University of Minnesota. 'For some reason, not connected with my virtues I think,' VW wrote in her diary on 7 December 1918, 'I get 2 or even 3 books weekly

from the Times, & thus breast one short choppy wave after another. It fills up the time while Night & Day lies dormant; it gives me distinct pleasure I own to formulate rapid views of Henry James & Mr Hergesheimer [see '*The Three Black Pennys*' above]; chiefly because I slip in some ancient crank of mine.'

See also 'Mr Henry James's Latest Novel', *I VW Essays*; 'The Old Order', above; 'Within the Rim', 'The Letters of Henry James', 'Henry James's Ghost Stories', *III VW Essays*.

2 – Henry James (1843–1916).

3 – Beach, pt II, p. 255; *The Wings of the Dove* (1902), *The Ambassadors* (1903), *The Golden Bowl* (1904).

4 – *Ibid.*, 'Explanations', p. 4.

5 – *Ibid.*, pt I, pp. 19–20, quoting *Harper's Weekly*, vol. ix, 1898, pp. xvi–xvii.

Appendices

APPENDIX I

Reading Notes

The reading notes reproduced here relate to the articles 'Coleridge as Critic' and 'Trafficks and Discoveries'. They are the only such notes from the period 1913–18 known to have survived. Those on Coleridge were originally made, with others, at the opposite end of a notebook later used by Virginia Woolf as part of her diary for 1918 and 1919 (Reading notes: Berg, xxx, 4pp. numbered 7–10). They are based upon two works: *Omniana* in vol. i of *The Literary Remains*, ed. H. N. Coleridge (2 vols., Pickering, 1836); and: *The Table Talk and Omniana of Samuel Taylor Coleridge. With a note on Coleridge by Coventry Patmore* (OUP, 1917).

The notes for 'Trafficks and Discoveries' are transcribed from MHP (B. 2d., 7pp and 2pp.). They are based upon two works: vols. i–iii of *Hakluyt's Collection of the Early Voyages, Travels and Discoveries of the English Nation. A new edition, with additions* (5 vols., R. H. Evans, 1809–12); and: *English Seamen in the Sixteenth Century* (Longmans, Green, & Co., 1895) by J. A. Froude.

The transcriptions retain the original haphazard punctuation, with two exceptions: single rather than double quotation marks are used and have been supplied, with the help of the texts concerned, wherever Virginia Woolf has failed either to close or to open these; a full point has been inserted in two or three instances after page references. Virginia Woolf's insertions are indicated by ⟨angled brackets⟩; her cancellations are marked through with a fine line. Dubious readings have been enclosed in square brackets and queried [thus?].

Coleridges Table Talk & Omniana

OMNIANA (in my edition) _____

Reading this through, I was struck by C's greater than ⟨re-membered⟩ humanity & ~~subtlety~~ humour. His discrimination of course very subtle, but often fine into the bargain:

335. a good passage upon the falseness of sympathy: how it comes from insincerity. No doubt he saw much into character —— more than one has come to think, owing to his character. always heard of as a spout of words, not as a person with insight.

343. 'in every face a history or a prophecy.'

356. It is unworthy to do nothing but enjoy poetry.

369. Evils of procrastination.

385. The handsome hypocricies that spring from the desire of distinc-tion.

Table Talk – Oxford Edition. 1918.

C. thought Old Mortality, Guy Mannering the best of Scott.

41. Euripides like a modern Frenchman – never so happy as when giving a slap at the Gods altogether.

41. Snuff the final cause of the human nose.

56. 'If you take from Virgil his diction & metre, what do you leave him'?

65. 'I have a smack of Hamlet myself.'

73. definition of prose & poetry: prose = words in their best order; poetry = best words in best order.

74. genius can't exist with envy.

86. liked Jane A's novels.

91. 'poetry must be good sense.'

93. 'no subjectivity in Homeric authors' – argument for their being many authors.

103. had been flogged into being a Christian.

106. Mrs Barbaulds criticism of the A.M. lacked a moral.

108. works of imagination should be written in very plain language.

115. on Rabelais (good). Swift compared with R.

117. C. a post Imp: '~~th~~ overcoming difficulties the way of decadence.'

117. C. a post Imp: 'th overcoming difficulties the way of decadence.'
118. Everyone born an Aristotelian or a platonist.
132. 'I have no ear whatever; – but intensest delight in music, & can detect good from bad.'
135. Col. in favour of adult suffrage.
141. C. at pictures.
163. on Home rule.
166. Children graceful before they have learnt to dance.
182. Old Greek & Latin same order as English: Virgil & Tibullus not.
184. on beauty of Greek language.
185. America. slang.
189. W<u>th</u> greatest phil. poet since Milton.
190. great things done by individuals, not Acts of Parl.
194. English habit of praising foreigners to their own cost.
195. Milton's love of music greater than of painting.
198. Keats. 'The school is your father &c'.
201. Great minds androgynous.
209. Home rule to be an absolute division.
213. one can't imitate Sh<u>re</u>: has no manner.
239. The Sonnets written to a woman: in So<u>y</u>.
252. As a boy Aeschylus; youth & middle age Euripides; now in declining years Sophocles, the most perfect.
256. when Johnson's talk the bow-wow manner.
258. Coleridge seems to have been a mass of sensibilities. I love Purcell —— the effect of music in helping him to write poetry.
260. no pleasure from associations with places – living collaterally.
261. philanthropists hostile to the individual but benevolent to the race.
262. C<u>l</u>had memory for words.
263. against Gibbon.
267. greatest pleasure in Milton's poetry comes from his egoism. M: himself that you see.
269. Tristram Shandy scarcely readable by women – higher powers can only act with help of lower.
284. Scotts novels the only books he could *read* when ill.
286. Landor cd. not make his poetry into a whole. Chronological order best for poems.
293. I take no interest in facts —— they must refer to something else.
~~261. philanthropists always wrong; in heart hostile to individuals, but benevolent to the race.~~

293. Sh^{res.} way of creating sentences – not seeing them entire first.

293. & Crabbe gives one little or no pleasure.

295. Sh^{re} not more intelligible to his own time than to ours.

318. Excellence of verse to be untranslatable – 'printers devils personifications' (Gray).

344. 'The impossibility of any man's being a great poet without being first a ~~grea~~ good man' Ben Jonson. Dedict Volpone.
(*Allsops recollections*).

416. on Scotts novels. less indecent than Sterne, but none of his characters so good: in all subjects there is a struggle between opposites.

421. Lamb essentially a Xtian, tho' a sceptic.

430. good description of Cobbett.

437. Works written upon 'Scraps of Sibylline leaves, including margins of books & blank pages.'

440. – strange that no great poet has come from the lower classes except Burns.

441. Crashaw & St Theresa perhaps suggested the first thought of Christabel.

445. his discrimination between one's feelings for poor & rich.

447. Greater part of L.B. sold to seafaring men, who thought that A.M. must have relation to Nautical matters.

452. Shelleys wish to consult Co.

470. Wordsworth <u>all</u> man: least femininity in his mind.

Hakluyt. Vol. I.

how H. looked at maps when a boy.

v. Strange that natives of Japan &c. shd. be seen here.

xii. Records lie recklessly hidden in misty darkness.

258. Sir H. Willoughby frozen to death in 1553 'for pickerie ducked at the yards arm & so discharged.' Thomas Nash. Queer names rescued.

271. Sir H.W. of goodly personage (for he was of tall stature).

271. Master Sidney's discourse – all shareholds in the discovery of Muscovy. Chancelor did it 1553.

272. The ships leave; crew in watchet; privy council on the towers to see; men ran up the masts.

273. if the cruelty of death hath taken hold of them God send them a Christian grave & sepulchre.
list of native words given – all directions for finding

326. your way. Ambassador wrecked off Scotland; how he was treated by the Lord Mayor in London.

323. & sent back with a male & female lion for the Czar.

306. Cabot comes to Greenwich to say goodbye to Burrough.

330. little companies of ships setting fourth to trade with Muscovy.

332. coloured cloths sent to Russia; cables & rope & furs bought wax flax tallow & train oils.

323. gifts sent by King & Queen to Russia:

347. whales ingendering time. superstitions & habits of natives.

356. merchants 'dining' with Emperor.

415. what the merchant adventurers have discovered, & hope to discover. 'not commonly by seas frequented'

416. English merchants for discovery of new trades – monopolies

vol.2.

the great wealth of good reading in H: even dedications & addresses worth something

ix. wollen [sic] cloth the natural commodity of the realm

216. the vermin of Cyprus. Takes note of religious practises.

210. man had hold of cable by his teeth; 217. the cat wh. swam.

219. how the natives charm away the water spout

222. fine [leisured?] reading: the Vulture.

246. John Fox meets ~~the~~ eight gallies of Turks: his address to his sailors.

246. Then stood up John Grove the master .. with his sword & target (being a comely man) beauty held in esteem. 'fared among the Turks like wood lion'.

247. Fox 13 years prisoner to the Turks.

250. the Christian God helpful: Turk God very dull. howsoever their God behaved himself, our God showed himself a ~~very~~ God indeed.

250. The sword ⟨248⟩ with wh. Fox killed the keeper hung up by the Monk of Gallipoli.

253. Elizabeth 'Cloud of most pleasant rain & sweetest fountain of noblenesse & virtue.'
256. Certain of our subjects slaves in your gallies
261. E. apologises for evil doers.
268. Their sense of wonder unexhausted: canary birds.
268. The women of Venice rather monsters than women.
270. Protestant brings bad luck to the ship.
272. trusting gallies of Turks
279. to sell knit socks of Norwich yarn in Con‑ᵖˡᵉ
280. The special virtue of English wool, testified by condition of old Parliament robes. no moth in them
 — 'turning to hag & wallet' of the poor people.
281. 'apt young men' always sent out.
282. passion for Anile: to grow it in England. The Turkish dies [sic].
 — They cd. dye yellow & green. Anile made blue.
282. if any man cd. discover oil in England he wd. have immortal fame. oil from radish seed.
284. What discoveries of plants & fruits a m traveller may make for his country — Dr Linaker brought in the damask rose, & tulipas from Vienna; seed of Sabacco from West indies 'many have been eased of the rheumes'. the good of the poor.
287. trumpets drum & flute on board.
291. present of dogs made to the Turk. magnificence with wh. the English sailors are entertained.
 — the prophet '(a fool) who cried Hough!
307. falsehood seldom known among merchants.
422. ships setting out together because of Spanish threats. Turkish flowers of speech.
452. a garden of nightingales — a flock of phasant birds
453. The Queen's letter smelt of camphor & ambergris. ink of musk
474. saw the elephant not only with bodily eyes but with the eyes of my sy spirit. admiring the workmaster.
475. habits of the elephant: debate with dragon: mixture of their blood produces vermilion.
478. what Chancellor said that Cabot reported about whirlpools.
479. worms & shells on the ships.
595. to observe the daily order of Common Prayer.
607. the nature of the prize: sugar, phants teeth &c.

620. commodities include horsetails hats; brought back pepper, phants teeth, oil

656. Sailors imagining what running at tilt there wd. be at Whitehall on the Queen's day.

656. how they lay off Cornwall for 14 days without drink. Good account of rain caught.

657. how they gave the T<u>rk</u> to drink, to teach them humanity

659. talks of Irish habits as of a completely strange country.

662. The leaders of the gallies dressed in silk, with silver whistles & plumes of feathers.

676. whole key covered with silver & gems.

682. Sir R.G. very unquiet in his mind [is?] greatly affected to war.

Hakluyt vol. 3.

9. E. withdraws her consent to R's going: he misunderstands

14. the cargoe of spices & calicoes. Her majesty chief among adventurers.

28. Cabot came to London as a merchant 'to sail by the West into the East where spices grow .. more divine than human.'

31. desire of discovery inherited like sickness.

45. Egg in moonshine – need makes the old wife to trot.

47. Sir HW. congealed & frozen to death.

45. one of the reasons for the N.W. passage: 'needy people of our country wh. now trouble the commonwealth & through want here at home are inforced to commit outrageous offences, whereby they are daily consumed with the gallowes'.

53. the Queen waving her hand to Frobisher.

<u>59</u>. Frobishers Prayer. natives to be made Xtian.

<u>94</u>. unicorns horn given to the Queen.

106. articles & orders drawn up by Frobisher.

98. how the captive savages met each other.

168. desirous to see the strange things of the world.

169. The men eat each other – How Mr Buts was only known by a mark on his arm.

189. music, morris dancers, hobby horses, & maylike concerts to delight the savage people–

Froude. English Seamen.

10. Cabot looked for passage to Cathay. Henry 7th.

12. Henry 8th. Hawkins went to Guinea.

12. Thorne (H.8th) went for NW passage.

12. Hore – to Newfoundland.

22. Spirit of enterprise grew with reformation.

24. the privateers a force to put down the Inquisition

28. how the west country families took to the sea.

46. Stukeley.

54. An African co. formed by Hawkins.

55. Got slaves in Sierra Leone & sold them at St Domingo

64. Drake comes in.

65. reasons of Philips dislike.

70. Drakes 3rd. voyage 1567.

84. Very good story teller – impossible to re-tell Froude.

95. the story reads like a chapter from Monte Christo.

104. shd. be an epic as grand as the Odyssey.

117. how they were puritans. Drake taking communion with Doughty.

122. her ballast was silver, her cargo gold, – emeralds & rubies

123. Capture of the Cacafuego.

124. Drake dined alone with music.
     ⟨[Pelican]⟩

138. vessel no larger than a second-rate yacht of a modern noble lord.

178. Drakes largest expedition starts 1585 to revenge the corn ships taken by Spain. Froude spins out a fine coherent story from the mass of H.

224. Drake sent to Cadiz on the Bonaventura.

236. takes the San Philip.

241. Safety of England rested on adventurers.

APPENDIX II

Notes on the Journals

All but one of the articles in this volume appeared in the *Times Literary Supplement*, which continued to be edited by Bruce Lyttelton Richmond (1871–1964), who had taken over the newly-founded paper in 1902. The exception is the essay 'Heard on the Downs: The Genesis of Myth', contributed to *The Times*, 15 August 1916.

The *TLS* articles are listed here by year and date of publication.

1912: *'Frances Willard'* (28 November); *1913*: 'Chinese Stories' (1 May); *'Jane Austen'* (8 May); *'Les Copains'* (7 August); *1916*: 'Queen Adelaide' (13 January); 'A Scribbling Dame' (17 February); 'Charlotte Brontë' (13 April); *'Past and Present at the English Lakes'* (29 June); 'A Man With a View' (20 July); *'The Park Wall'* (31 August); 'The Fighting Nineties' (12 October); 'Among the Poets' (2 November); *'London Revisited'* (9 November); 'In a Library' (23 November); 'Hours in a Library' (30 November); 'Old and Young' (14 December); *'Social Life in England'* (21 December); 'Mr Symons's Essays' (21 December); *1917*: *'Romance'* (18 January); 'Tolstoy's *The Cossacks*' (1 February); 'Melodious Meditations' (8 February); 'More Dostoevsky' (22 February); *'Before Midnight'* (1 March); 'Parodies' (8 March); *'Sir Walter Raleigh'* (15 March); *'The House of Lyme'* (29 March); *'Poe's Helen'* (5 April); 'A Talker' (12 April); *'In Good Company'* (12 April); 'A Cambridge V.A.D.' (10 May); 'The Perfect Language' (24 May); 'Mr Sassoon's Poems' (31 May); *'Creative Criticism'* (7 June); *'South Wind'* (14 June); *'Books and Persons'* (5 July); 'Thoreau' (12 July); *'Lord Jim'* (26 July); *'John Davidson'* (16 August); 'A Victorian Echo' (23 August); 'Mr Galsworthy's Novel' (30 August); 'To Read Or Not To Read' (6 September); 'Mr Conrad's *Youth*' (20 September); *'Flumina Amem Silvasque'* (11 October); 'A Minor Dostoevsky' (11 October); 'The Old Order' (18 October); *'Hearts of Controversy'* (25 October); *'A Russian Schoolboy'* (8 November); 'Stopford Brooke' (29 November); 'Mr Gladstone's Daughter' (6 December); *'Charlotte Brontë'* (13 December); *'Rebels and Reformers'* (20 December); 'Sunset Reflections' (20 December); 'The New Crusade' (27 December); *1918*: *'Visits to Walt Whitman'* (3 January); 'Philosophy in Fiction' (10 January); 'A Book of Essays' (17 January); *'The Green Mirror'* (24

January); 'Across the Border' (31 January); 'Coleridge as Critic' (7 February); 'Mr Conrad's Crisis' (14 March); 'Swinburne letters' (21 March) 'Papers on Pepys' (4 April); *Second Marriage* (25 April); 'Two Irish Poets' (2 May); 'Tchehov's Questions' (16 May); 'Imitative Essays' (23 May); 'Moments of Vision' (23 May); 'Dreams and Realities' (30 May); 'The Claim of the Living' (13 June); 'Loud Laughter' (20 June); 'A Victorian Socialist' (27 June); 'Mr Merrick's Novels' (4 July); 'Two Soldier-Poets' (11 July); 'On Re-reading Meredith' (25 July); 'Rupert Brooke' (8 August); 'A Practical Utopia' (15 August); *The Sad Years* (29 August); 'The "Movie" Novel' (29 August); 'War in the Village' (12 September); 'The Rights of Youth' (19 December); 'Mr Hudson's Childhood' (26 September); 'Caution and Criticism' (3 October); 'Adventurers All' (10 October); 'Honest Fiction' (10 October); 'Women Novelists' (17 October); 'Valery Brussof' (24 October); *The Candle of Vision* (31 October); *Abraham Lincoln* (31 October); 'Mr Howells on Form' (14 November); 'Bad Writers' (21 November); 'Trafficks and Discoveries' (12 December); *The Three Black Pennys* (12 December); 'A View of the Russian Revolution' (19 December); 'The Russian View' (19 December); *Mummery* (19 December); *The Method of Henry James* (26 December).

Bibliography

This list does not include information about the several collections of Virginia Woolf's writings to which reference is made in the annotations. For this information, and for certain other bibliographical references, the reader should consult the list of Abbreviations at p. xxv

ESSAYS

The Moment and Other Essays, ed. Leonard Woolf (Hogarth Press, London, 1947; Harcourt Brace & Co., New York, 1948)

The Captain's Death Bed and Other Essays, ed. Leonard Woolf (Hogarth Press, London, and Harcourt Brace & Co., New York, 1950)

The London Scene (Frank Hallman, New York, 1975; Hogarth Press, London, and Random House, New York, 1982)

OTHER WORKS

The Complete Shorter Fiction of Virginia Woolf, ed. Susan Dick (Hogarth Press, London, and Harcourt Brace Jovanovich, New York, 1985)

WORKS OF REFERENCE

Virginia Woolf's Reading Notebooks (Princeton University Press, Princeton, New York, 1983) by Brenda R. Silver

Virginia Woolf's Literary Sources and Allusions. A Guide to the Essays (Garland, New York, 1983) by Elizabeth Steele

BIBLIOGRAPHY

CRITICAL STUDIES

Victorian Bloomsbury. The Early Literary History of the Bloomsbury Group. Volume One (Macmillan Press, London, St Martin's Press, New York, 1987) by S. P. Rosenbaum

INDEX

This index is not exhaustive: references to fictional characters in the ephemeral popular novels which VW reviewed are not entered and minor characters in other works are also omitted, unless the reference has been judged to be of special interest; fictional characters are otherwise identified in this way: 'Quint, Peter, H. James's character...' Place names are indexed on a selective basis, according to the frequency of reference and also to their significance to VW. Works are indexed under their author and in the case of biographies, their subject. The notes are indexed selectively, generally only in relation to references in the text. Thematic entries have been included under the following heads: American Literature; Aristocracy; Biography; Character; Contemporaries; Criticism; Democracy; Drama; Eighteenth Century, the; Essay, the; Elizabethans, the; Greek; Latin; Letters; Literary Pilgrimage; Moment, the; Novel, the (and fiction); Poetry; Post-Impressionism; Prose; Reader, the (and reading); Realism; Romance; Russian Literature; Victorian Era; War, the; Women. General references under a given subject are cited last, unless written works are involved, in which case these conclude the entry concerned.

Acknowledgements

It is a pleasure to record my gratitude to many friends, colleagues, and librarians, to my contributors, whose patience has matched that of Griselda, to my equally patient and helpful editors at the Oxford University Press, Frances Whistler, Sophie Goldsworthy, and Sarah Hyland, and to my painstaking copy editor, Mary Worthington.

Contents

List of Illustrations

Frontispiece: Chaucer the Pilgrim (from the Ellesmere MS, MS EL 26 c 9, fo. 153v, Huntington Library)

Between Pages 260 and 261

1. Chaucer (from a copy of Hoccleve's *Regiment of Princes*, BL MS Harley 4866 fo. 88)
2. The Wife of Bath (from the Ellesmere MS, MS EL 26 c 9, fo. 72, Huntington Library)
3. The Pardoner (from the Ellesmere MS, MS EL 26 c 9, fo. 138, Huntington Library)
4. Scenes from *The Pardoner's Tale*: the buying of the poison and the death of the rioters, from a carved wood panel, ?1400–1401 (The Museum of London)
5. The Pardoner (Cambridge University Library MS Gg. 4.27, fo. 306)
6. Criseyde leaves Troy and Troilus for the Greek camp (from a manuscript of the French translation of Boccaccio's *Filostrato*; Bodleian Library, MS Douce 331, fo. 52)
7. The Wife of Bath (Cambridge University Library MS Gg. 4.27, fo. 222)
8. Frontispiece to a manuscript of *Troilus and Criseyde* (the Parker Library, Corpus Christi College, Cambridge, MS 61, fr.)
9. Jupiter, Mars, and Venus (from *The Complaint of Mars*; Bodleian Library, MS Fairfax 16, fo. 14v)
10. The Garden of the Rose: the dreamer is admitted by Idleness; on the walls can be seen Covetousness, Avarice, Envy, Sorrow, inside, Narcissus, and on the left Daunger with his club (from a manuscript of the French *Roman de la Rose*, British Library, MS Egerton 1069, fo. 1)
11. Griselda, her father, and Walter, in *The Clerk's Tale* (Charles Cowden Clarke, *The Riches of Chaucer* (1835); Bodleian Library, 35.216, vol. I, facing p. 203)
12. Criseyde sees Troilus ride past (from the Kelmscott Chaucer (1896), Bodleian Library, Kelmscott Press b.1, p. 482)
13. Criseyde and Diomede in the Greek camp (from the Kelmscott Chaucer (1896), Bodleian Library, Kelmscott Press b.1, p. 536)

Illustration Acknowledgements

Permission to reproduce is gratefully acknowledged: Frontispiece and figs. 2–3: The Huntington Library, San Marino, California; figs. 1, 10, 14: The British Library (fig. 14 © courtesy of the artist's estate/Bridgeman Art Library); fig. 4: The Museum of London; figs. 5, 7: The Syndics of Cambridge University Library; figs. 6, 9, 11–13: The Bodleian Library, University of Oxford; fig. 8: The Master and Fellows of Corpus Christi College, Cambridge; fig. 15: © Alberto Grimaldi Productions SA and MGM CLIP + STILL, print supplied by the British Film Institute.

Contributors

[RB]	Ron Bedford, Armidale
[PB]	Piero Boitani, Rome
[JAB]	John Burrow, Bristol
[HC]	Helen Cooper, Oxford
[SG]	Stephen Gill, Oxford
[RFG]	Richard Firth Green, Ohio
[JCH]	John C. Hirsh, Georgetown
[AH]	Anne Hudson, Oxford
[JDN]	John North, Groningen, Oxford
[DP]	Derek Pearsall, York
[PS]	+Patricia Shaw Urdiales, Oviedo
[EGS]	Eric Stanley, Oxford
[HW]	Hanneke Wilson, Oxford

(All unsigned entries are the work of the Editor)

List of General Entries

This *Companion* contains numerous topical entries—including Chaucerian terms such as 'daunger' and 'maistrye', literary categories such as 'aubade', 'Breton lay', 'prologues', and historical events such as 'Hundred Years' War' and 'Peasants' Revolt'—and the list below is necessarily selective. It consists of the most substantial topical entries, and others which risk being overlooked, either because the reader will not necessarily guess at their existence (e.g. 'ejaculations and interjections', 'hunting', 'recognition scenes') or because they occur infrequently in cross-references. In the interests of brevity the more self-evident subjects—for example, the occupations of the Canterbury pilgrims—are not listed.

ages of man
alchemy
ale
allegory
alliterative verse
allusion
angels
animals
architecture
astrology and astronomy
auctour and auctoritee
audience
beauty
birds
book
canon of Chaucer's works
Canterbrigge, Cantebregge
Caunterbury
characters and characterization
Chaucer, Geoffrey: life
Chaucer, Geoffrey: reading
children and childhood
chivalrie
chronology of Chaucer's works

classical antiquity
classical literature
clothes
comedy
cosmology
courtly love
criticism of Chaucer's works
Crusades
curteisie
dance
death
debate
devil
dialogue
digression
diversity
drama
dreams
dream vision
drunkenness
editing and editions
ejaculations and interjections
emotion
Engelond

Reader's Guide

The Oxford Companion to Chaucer aims to present in attractive form a range of information which will help readers and students in the understanding of England's greatest medieval poet. It contains entries on Chaucer's life, his family and friends, his works and the characters in them, his reading and the use he made of it. There are entries on persons and places mentioned by him. Apart from his known sources, there are entries on some contemporary English and European writers. His scientific knowledge is fully treated by Professor John North. There are entries on his language and versification, and on some of the topics and ideas that are prominent in his work. Other entries illustrate the reception of Chaucer from his death up to the early 20th century. The extensive later criticism is surveyed in a separate entry (criticism of Chaucer II). Earlier discussions of Chaucer have more than antiquarian interest: they frequently draw attention to aspects of his work neglected in contemporary criticism. It is hoped that the mingling of longer discursive entries with the more factual notes will encourage the reader to browse as well as to search for information, and find in the combination of 'sentence' and 'solaas' something of the special delight that the reading of Chaucer brings.

The arrangement is alphabetical, with the headwords normally in their Chaucerian form. (**It should be noted that in Middle English words the letter *y* when it represents a vowel is treated as *i*:** thus *fyssh* and *Fysshestrete* come before 'Fitzralph'.) Quotations from Chaucer and references to his works are from *The Riverside Chaucer*, edited by Larry D. Benson (OUP, 1988). Where a book and line reference is not preceded by the abbreviated name of the work, it refers to *The Canterbury Tales*. Chaucerian quotations are in Middle English, with glosses for difficult words. In other early English quotations the spelling has been modernized. Readers without access to the Riverside edition may sometimes encounter problems in finding the quotation or reference, but these are soluble. The most obviously troublesome is the arrangement of the 'Fragments' of *The Canterbury Tales*, where that of the Riverside and most modern editions differs somewhat from that found in the older edition of W. W. Skeat and a few others that follow it. These differences are set out on pages 73–74. In the case of the Prologue to *The Legend of Good Women* quotations are from the F version; any from the G version are indicated.

The bibliographical references which follow many of the entries are of necessity brief and selective. This is especially the case in the entries for Chaucerian works, where there is now a large mass of information and commentary. Here, a typical pattern will be a reference to the relevant pages of the Riverside edition, and occasionally to another smaller edition which will prove useful; to a work of reference (such as one of the Oxford Guides to Chaucer) which will provide further discussion; and to one or two critical studies. All references are listed in the References at the back of the book. Those preceded by '(ed.)' or 'trans.' refer to a scholarly edition or translation of a primary source and are listed under the name of the editor or translator rather than the author of the work being studied or translated.

This book differs from the other sort of 'companion' which is a collection of modern critical essays and follows the longstanding Oxford concept of an alphabetically arranged companion. Its format allows a number of suggestive points to emerge, some of which are not always highlighted in recent academic Chaucerian criticism. The impressive range of Chaucer's reading and of his interests, for instance, is acknowledged, but sometimes underestimated. As Gabriel Harvey remarked, poets 'must be exquisite artists, and curious universal scholars', and commended Chaucer for his 'astronomy, philosophy, and other parts of profound or cunning art'. His knowledge of science, and especially astronomy, was indeed remarkable. It is not often pointed out that of all the great English poets Chaucer is the most skilled in science. His curiosity is also seen in a delight in the 'thisness' of things and people: 'every thing in Chaucer has a downright reality,' said Hazlitt. He treats with precision and imagination the circumstances of everyday life and matters of common experience, the 'repeated experience and regular feelings' of common humanity that Wordsworth noted: the 'objects of the Poet's thoughts are every where'.

Abbreviations

adj.	adjective
adv.	adverb
Aen.	*Aeneid*
Anel	*Anelida and Arcite*
Astr	*A Treatise on the Astrolabe*
astr.	astrological
astron.	astronomical
AV	Authorized Version
BD	*The Book of the Duchess*
Bo	*Boece*
CH	*Chaucer: The Critical Heritage* ed. D. S. Brewer, 2 vols. (London, 1978)
ChR	*Chaucer Review*
ClT	*The Clerk's Tale*
CT	*The Canterbury Tales*
CYT	*The Canon's Yeoman's Tale*
DNB	*Dictionary of National Biography*
ed., edn.	editor, edition
EETS	Early English Text Society
El.	Ellesmere Manuscript
Fort	*Fortune*
Fr.	French
FrT	*The Friar's Tale*
FranT	*The Franklin's Tale*
GP	*General Prologue* (of *The Canterbury Tales*)
Her.	*Heroides*
HF	*The House of Fame*
Hg	Hengwrt Manuscript
KnT	*The Knight's Tale*
L.	Latin
LGW	*The Legend of Good Women*
LR	*Chaucer Life Records* ed. M. M. Crow and C. C. Olson (Oxford, 1966)
m.	metrum, metre

MancT	*The Manciple's Tale*
MchT	*The Merchant's Tale*
ME	Middle English
MED	*Middle English Dictionary*
Mel	*Melibee*
Met.	*Metamorphoses*
MilT	*The Miller's Tale*
MkT	*The Monk's Tale*
MLN	*Modern Language Notes*
MLR	*Modern Language Review*
MLT	*The Man of Law's Tale*
MS, MSS	manuscript(s)
MP	*Modern Philology*
NPT	*The Nun's Priest's Tale*
NS	New Series
NT	New Testament
OE	Old English
OED	*Oxford English Dictionary*
orig.	original(ly)
OT	Old Testament
PardT	*The Pardoner's Tale*
ParsT	*The Parson's Tale*
PF	*The Parliament of Fowls*
PhysT	*The Physician's Tale*
PL	*Patrologia latina*
PMLA	*Publications of the Modern Language Association of America*
PQ	*Philological Quarterly*
pr.	prosa, prose
PrT	*The Prioress's Tale*
Prol LGW	Prologue to *The Legend of Good Women*
RES	*Review of English Studies*
Rom	*The Romaunt of the Rose*
Rv	*The Riverside Chaucer* ed. Larry D. Benson (Oxford, 1988)
RvT	*The Reeve's Tale*
S&A	*Sources and Analogues of Chaucer's Canterbury Tales* ed. W. F. Bryan and Germaine Dempster (London, 1958) (page references in square brackets are to the 2nd edn., vol. 1, ed. R. Correale and M. Hamel (Cambridge: Brewer, 2002))
SAC	*Studies in the Age of Chaucer*
ShipT	*The Shipman's Tale*

SNT	*The Second Nun's Tale*
SqT	*The Squire's Tale*
STC	*Short Title Catalogue* ed. A. W. Pollard and G. R. Redgrave, 2nd edn. ed. W. A. Jackson, F. S. Ferguson and K. F. Pantzer (London, 1986)
STS	Scottish Text Society
SumT	*The Summoner's Tale*
Theb.	*Thebaid*
Tr	*Troilus and Criseyde*
WBProl	*The Wife of Bath's Prologue*
WBT	*The Wife of Bath's Tale*

Chronology

1327	Accession of Edward III (1327–77)
1328	Philip of Valois becomes king of France, as Philip VI
late 1330s	Boccaccio, *Il Filostrato*
1337	Edward sends letter to 'Philip of Valois, who calls himself King of France'. Beginning of The Hundred Years War. Giotto d.
1339–41	Boccaccio, *Teseida*
1340	Edward assumes title of 'King of England and of France'
early 1340s	Geoffrey Chaucer born
1341	Laureation of Petrarch at Rome
1345–7	Edward III campaigns in France
1346	English victory at Crécy
1347	English capture Calais
1348–9	The Black Death in England. In Europe Flagellant movements, persecution of Jews
1349	Edward III establishes Order of the Garter. Richard Rolle d. Bradwardine d. William of Ockham d.
1350	Philip VI of France d. John II, 'the Good', succeeds
early 1350s	Boccaccio, *Decameron*
1350–69	Peter the Cruel of Castile
1351–82	Under Winrich of Kniprode, Grand Master, the Teutonic Order at the height of its power
1354	Scottish alliance with France. Turks capture Gallipoli
1355–7	English campaigns in France
1356	The Black Prince victorious at Poitiers. King John captive in England (1357–60, and 1363–4). French States-General under Étienne Marcel, Provost of the Paris merchants, demand reform
1357	Chaucer a page in household of the Countess of Ulster, wife of Lionel, a son of Edward III Turks take Adrianople
1358	Rebellion of French peasants (the Jacquerie) put down, as were the burghers of Paris; their leader Étienne Marcel killed

1359–60	English campaigns in N. France, Champagne and Burgundy. Chaucer a 'valettus' in the company of Prince Lionel, captured near Réthel, and ransomed
1359–89	Murad I, Emir of the Turks
1360	(May) Treaty of Brétigny; uneasy peace in France, formalized later in peace of Calais
1361	Froissart arrives in England to serve in Queen Philippa's household
1360s–1380s	Langland at work on *Piers Plowman*
1364	King John of France d. Charles V, 'the Wise', succeeds (1364–80). Duchy of Burgundy granted to Charles's brother, Philip 'the Bold' (–1404)
1365	Peter of Cyprus captures Alexandria but has to abandon it
1366	(February–May) Chaucer in Navarre on a diplomatic mission. The French expel Peter the Cruel from Castile and (for a short time) make Henry of Trastamara, his illegimate brother, king in his place
	Chaucer's father d. His mother remarries. Chaucer married to Philippa de Roet (by September)
1367	(January) Richard of Bordeaux (later Richard II) b
	(April) The Black Prince defeats Henry of Trastamara at Nájera and restores Peter the Cruel
	(June) Chaucer granted annuity as esquire of the king's household
1368	Chaucer abroad on the king's service. (12 September) Blanche, Duchess of Lancaster, first wife of John of Gaunt d. At some point (soon?) after this Chaucer writes *The Book of the Duchess*
1369	Henry of Trastamara defeats Peter the Cruel at Montiel. Peter is murdered. (August) Queen Philippa d.
1369–73	The war in France is renewed. French capture most of the lands ceded to Edward III at Brétigny
1369–1405	Timur (Tamburlane) ruler of the Mongols
1370	(June) Chaucer given letters of protection for going to parts beyond the sea in the king's service
	The Black Prince sacks Limoges. Du Guesclin made Constable of France
1372–3	Chaucer on mission to Italy (Genoa and Florence)
1374	Lease to Chaucer of a dwelling above the gate of Aldgate. Chaucer appointed controller of customs in the port of London Petrarch d.

1375	Boccaccio d. Coluccio Salutati Latin Secretary of Florence
1376	The Black Prince d.
1377	Chaucer on various missions to France. Edward III d. Richard II, aged 11, succeeds (1377–99). Machaut d.
1378	Beginning of Great Schism in Western Church. The Italian Urban VI elected at Rome, supported by England, Italy, Bohemia, Hungary. The French Clement VII at Fondi (moving to Avignon in 1379), supported by France, Spain, Sicily, Scotland. (May–September) Chaucer on mission to Lombardy
?c.1379–80	*The House of Fame*
1380	Charles V of France d., succeeded by Charles VI (1380–1422)
1381	Richard II m. Anne of Bohemia. Chaucer's mother d. (June) The Peasants' Revolt. Anglo-French truce for six years
early 1380s	*The Parliament of Fowls*
1382	Wyclif's opinions officially condemned by London Synod Turks capture Sofia
?1382–7	*Troilus and Criseyde*. *Boece* perhaps about the same time.
1384	Wyclif d.
1385	Chaucer a member of the commission of the peace in Kent
1386	Chaucer gives up Aldgate lease. MP for Kent at one session. The 'Wonderful Parliament', where there is an attempt to curb the king's power. In December retires from the controllership of customs
?c.1386–7	*The Legend of Good Women* (after *Troilus*)
1387	Philippa Chaucer d.
?late 1380s	Chaucer begins *The Canterbury Tales*
1388	The 'Merciless Parliament'. The Lords Appellant cause the removal of a number of Richard II's closest advisers. Some of his supporters are put to death. Scots defeat the English at Otterburn
1389	Richard II regains power. Chaucer made clerk of the king's works. Turks defeat the Serbs at Kosovo. Murad I murdered. Bajazet I Emir of the Turks (1389–1403)
1390	Chaucer robbed at the 'Fowle Ok'
1391	Chaucer resigns as clerk of the king's works
1392	Madness of Charles VI of France.
1393	(?) *A Treatise on the Astrolabe*. (?) *The Equatorie of the Planetis*. Bajazet subdues Bulgaria
1394	Queen Anne d.

1396	Richard II m. Isabella, daughter of Charles VI. Truce with France but the kings cannot conclude a peace. Walter Hilton d.
1397	Richard II takes revenge on the Appellants
1399	(February) John of Gaunt d. (September) Richard II deposed by Henry of Lancaster, Gaunt's son: he reigns as Henry IV (1399–1403). (December 24) Chaucer takes lease on a house near the Lady Chapel of Westminster Abbey
1400	Geoffrey Chaucer d. (?25 October)

E

The Sea of Ocean

The Sea of Ocean

The
Earthly
Paradise

China

Inde

Carrenar
The Drye Se

ASYE

The Rede See

Araby

o *Babiloigne*

N

Black Sea

Turkeye

⊕ Jerusalem

S

Constantinople

Cipre

Orkades

Egypt

EUROPE

Grece

Crete

AFFRIKE

Ytaille

The Grete See

Scotland
Engelond

France

Spaigne

The Sea of Ocean

W

MAP 1: Sketch of a Mappemounde, or Mappa Mundi, a medieval map of the whole
world, simplified from the early 14th-c. one at Hereford (see p. 309).
Italic place-names are in Chaucer's spelling, roman ones modern.

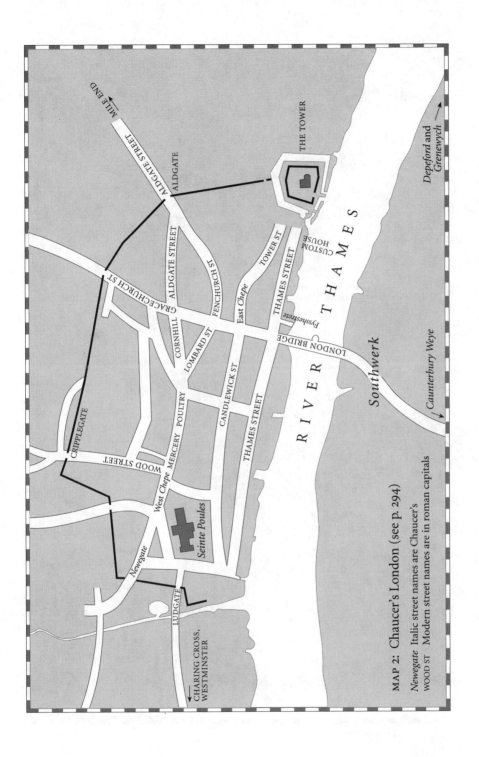

MAP 2: Chaucer's London (see p. 294)

Newegate Italic street names are Chaucer's
WOOD ST Modern street names are in roman capitals

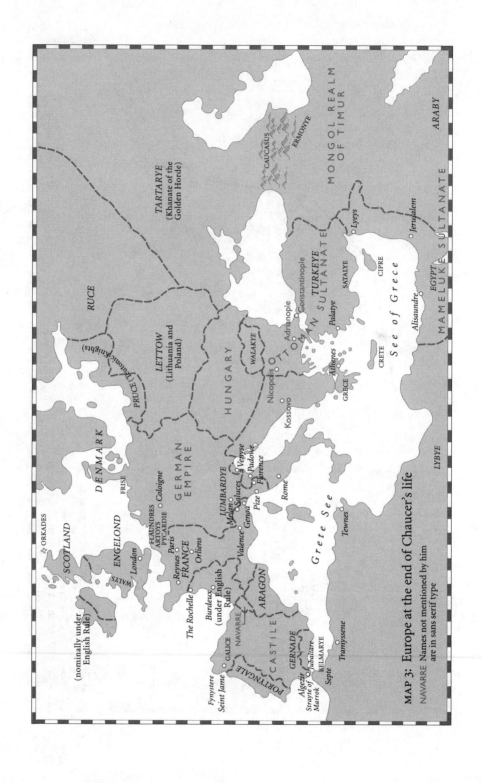

MAP 3: Europe at the end of Chaucer's life NAVARRE Names not mentioned by him are in sans serif type

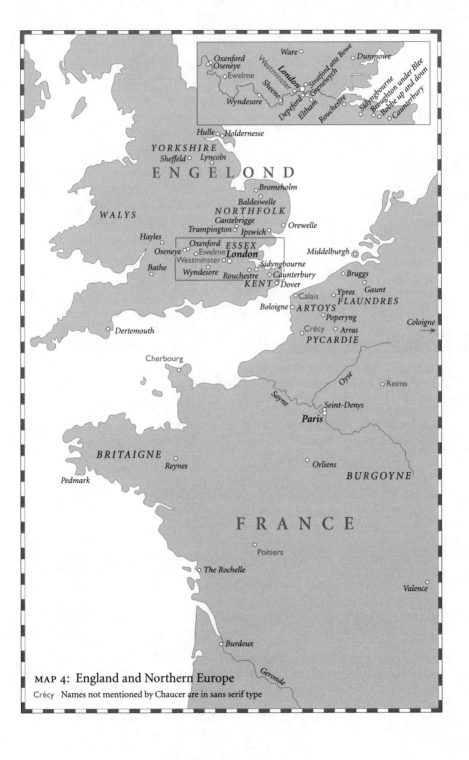

Inset map (upper right):

Oxenford
Oseneye
Ewelme
Westminster · London
Sheene
Wyndesore
Depeford
Eltham
Stratford atte Bowe
Grenewych
Rouchestre
Ware
Dunmowe
Sidyngbourne
Broughton under Blee
Boobe up and doun
Caunterbury

Main map:

Hulle · Holdernesse

YORKSHIRE
Sheffeld · Lyncoln

ENGELOND

Bromeholm
Baldeswelle
NORTHFOLK
Cantebrigge
Trumpington · Ipswich · Orewelle
WALYS

Hayles
Oxenford ESSEX
Oseneye · Ewelme
London
Westminster
Bathe
Wyndesore · Rouchestre · Caunterbury
Sidyngbourne
KENT · Dover
Middelburgh
Bruggs
Calais · Ypres · Gaunt
Boloigne · ARTOYS · FLAUNDRES
Poperyng
Crécy · Arras
PYCARDIE
Coloigne →

Dertemouth

Cherbourg

Sayne
Oyse · Reims

Seint-Denys
Paris

BRITAIGNE
Reynes
Orliens
BURGOYNE
Pedmark

FRANCE

Poitiers

The Rochelle

Valence

Burdeux
Geronde

MAP 4: England and Northern Europe

Crécy Names not mentioned by Chaucer are in sans serif type

A

Aaron, the brother of Moses (*Moyses), a priest, is cited by the friar in *The *Summoner's Tale* (III.1894) as an example of abstinence (according to Exod. 34:28, he fasted for forty days and forty nights).

ABC, one of Chaucer's shorter poems (184 lines, in eight-line stanzas). It is a translation of a prayer to the Virgin (Seinte *Marie) in the *Pelerinaige de la vie humaine* (1331; second redaction 1335) by Guillaume de *Deguilleville. Like its original, it is an alphabetical poem, each stanza beginning with the letters from A to Z in order. Alphabetical poems were quite common, and neither Deguilleville nor Chaucer found the form constricting (even the last three stanzas find introductory names in 'Xristus', 'Ysaac', and 'Zacharie'). The *ABC* is less intensely lyrical than the invocations to Mary made by the *Prioress and the Second Nun, but it makes eloquent use of traditional Marian images, and achieves a nice balance of learned diction (legal terms like 'acquitaunce'; and Latinate words with solemn liturgical or biblical suggestions—like 'ancille' [maidservant] or 'misericorde' [mercy]) and of more homely vocabulary— 'thee whom God ches [chose] to mooder'. It is usually thought to be an early work, but the evidence is not certain—if a note in the 1602 edition of *Speght, that it was made, 'some say', at the request of *Blanche, duchess of Lancaster, represents a genuine medieval tradition, the poem would have been written before 1368, the year of her death.

(ed.) *Rv* 637–40, 1076–8; Scattergood (1995), 462–65.

Abigayl. Abigail, the wife of Nabal in the Old Testament, saved her husband (I Sam. 25:1–35) from the wrath of King David. In the Middle Ages she was often cited as a type of the good wife giving good advice (as in *Melibee* VII.1100); since her intercession involved not telling her husband what she was doing it may be that the reference to her 'good conseil' in *The *Merchant's Tale* (IV.1369) is in that context somewhat ironic.

Abraham, the Old Testament patriarch whose story is told in Genesis 11:27–25:18. He was traditionally held to be the image of faith; however, the only reference to him in Chaucer concerns his marital arrangements—the *Wife of Bath cites him (III.55) as one of those holy men who 'hadde wyves mo [more] than two'.

Absolon (1) in the Old Testament, the son of King David (2 Sam. 13–19:8), whose beauty and whose splendid head of hair (2 Sam. 14:26) were famous. In medieval literature he became a traditional example of male *beauty (an elaborate rhetorical description by *Peter of Riga gave him golden hair); thus he figures in the *ballade sung by the ladies in the Prologue to *The *Legend of Good Women* 'Hyd, Absolon, thy gilte tresses clere'.

Absolon (2), the Oxford parish clerk in *The *Miller's Tale*, the rival of the clerk Nicholas for the affections of Alison. We are given a formal *portrait of him (I.3312–80). He has something in common with his biblical namesake—good looks and flowing locks (he probably ought to have been tonsured). He is something of a dandy, who takes great care over his appearance, and he is *jolif* (amorous, lusty), fancying himself as a wooer. Besides being a parish clerk (with an eye for the wives of the parish), Absolon is also a barber-surgeon, and skilled in conveyancing; he is a musician, a dancer, and an actor (see also **parody, and burlesque**).

accident is used to mean 'chance happening' or 'occurrence', but in medieval *philosophy it also had a more technical sense, deriving from *Aristotle: the outward quality or appearance, the attributes of a thing, as opposed to its essential nature or 'substance'. This distinction was commonly used in late medieval theology to explain transubstantiation, the transformation of the substance of the bread and wine when it was consecrated in the Eucharist into the substance of the Body and Blood of Christ, while the 'accidents'—the appearance of the bread and wine—remained. It lies behind a couple of comic uses in Chaucer: the Pardoner (VI.538–9) remarks that cooks 'turnen substaunce into accident' and Troilus says (*Tr* IV.1505) that it is 'a gret folie | For accident his substaunce ay [ever] to lese [lose]', punning on the other senses of *accident* 'an uncertain happening' and *substaunce* 'wealth'.

Accidie, Sloth; one of the *Seven Deadly Sins.

Achademycis, 'the scoles of . . . Achademycis' [L. *Academicis studiis*], the 'Academy', the school of philosophy founded by *Plato (in a grove of olive trees near Athens sacred to the hero Academus), mentioned in *Boece* (I pr.1: 68).

Achate(s), a faithful friend of Aeneas (*Eneas), 'a knyght', mentioned in *The *House of Fame* 226, and in the legend of Dido in *The *Legend of Good Women*.

Acheloys, Archeleous, Achaleous (Acheloys is the possessive form), the river Achelous in Greece. Achelous the river god in the form of a bull fought Hercules (*Ercules), had one of his horns broken, and 'for schame hidde hym in his ryver' (*Bo* IV m.7; VII.2106).

Achemenye, Persia (and Armenia), from the mountains of which the Tigris and the Euphrates flow (L. Achamaenes, founder of the first Persian royal house, the Achaemenidae), mentioned in *Boece* (V m.1).

Achille(s), son of Peleus and Thetis, the greatest of the Greek heroes in the siege of *Troy, is mentioned a number of times (e.g. *BD* 329). The 'queynte spere' (actually a sword) with which he wounded *Thelophus, and which had the power

to heal the wound it made, is alluded to in *The Squire's Tale* (V.239–40). In the Middle Ages he was also a famous lover: in *The Parliament of Fowls* 290 he appears in a list of lovers, along with Paris, Helen, and Troilus; there is a reference (*BD* 1067–71) to the story that his death was the result of his love for Polyxena (*Polixena), and (*HF* 398) to his falseness to *Breseyda. He is fierce and implacable: 'fierse Achille' (*Tr* V.1806) and 'cruel Achilles' (*HF* 1463). In *Troilus and Criseyde* he 'despitously' (cruelly) slays Troilus (who, earlier (III.374), has sworn 'If I lye, Achilles with his spere | Myn herte cleve'); and he is (*Tr* V.1558–61) the slayer of Hector (Ector). But the death of Achilles, like that of Hector, was 'written in the stars' (II.197–8).

Achitofel, Ahitophel, the wicked counsellor of King David, who incited *Absolon (1) to rebel against his father (2 Sam. 15–17), cited as a famous traitor in *The *Book of the Duchess* (1118).

Actaeon, see *Attheon.

Adam (1) the first man according to the Book of Genesis, made by God from earth; the husband of *Eve, and the father of mankind ('the seed of Adam', *ABC* 182). Chaucer's references to him concern his creation, that of Eve as his consort (in varying tones: cf. VII.1103 and IV.1325–9), and, especially, his part in the Fall, which brought original sin into the world (later to be washed away by the sacrifice of Christ (*Jhesus Crist), the 'second Adam'). The Monk gives Adam a very brief '*tragedy': he was driven out of 'hys hye prosperitee | To labour, and to helle, and to meschaunce' (VII.2013–14) for 'mysgovernaunce'. According to the Pardoner (VI.505–11), it was because of gluttony; according to the Nun's Priest (VII.3257–8) it was because of 'woman's counsel'. The Wife of Bath does not deliver an opinion on this, but she remarks (III.693–6) that if women had written stories like male clerks have done, they 'wolde han writen of men moore wikkednesse | Than al the mark of Adam [i.e. the whole male sex] may redresse'.

Adam (2), Chaucer's scribe (see *book), the subject of the poem *Adam* (sometimes called 'Adam Scriveyn' or, from the rubric in the only surviving

MS, 'Chaucers Wordes unto Adam, His Owne Scriveyn), a witty seven-line epigram remonstrating with him, and urging him to 'wryte more trewe' so that Chaucer will not need 'to correcte and eke to rubbe and scrape' (i.e. scrape the old ink off the parchment, and rub the surface smooth). It must have been written after *Boece and *Troilus, which are mentioned in it. No one has ever discovered Adam's second name. He seems to have lived on in proverb: in Jonson's *Bartholomew Fair* (iv. 4) a character says of Adam Overdo, a Justice of the Peace, 'I knew Adam, the clerk . . . when he was Adam scrivener, and writ for twopence a sheet'.

(ed.) *Rv* 650, 1083; Pace and David (1982), 133–7; Scattergood (1995), 501–3.

Admetus, see *Amete.

Adoon, Adoun, Adonis, the son of Myrrha (*Mirra). His beauty captivated Venus. When, in spite of her warnings, he went hunting and was killed by a boar, she caused the anemone to spring from his blood. The story is told by *Ovid (*Met.* 10). In Chaucer, two lovers allude to the love of Venus for Adonis: Palamon (*KnT* I.2224), and Troilus (*Tr* III.721).

Adrastus, legendary king of Argos, who led the army of the Seven against *Thebes (1). He returned home (*Anel* 61) when the expedition was defeated.

Adriane. Ariadne, daughter of King Minos of Crete, fell in love with *Theseus, and gave him a thread so that he could find his way out of the Labyrinth (*Laboryntus) after killing the Minotaur (*Mynotaur). He carried her away with him, but abandoned her on the island of Naxos—'He lefte hir slepynge in an ile | Desert allone, ryght in the se' says Chaucer (*HF* 416–17, upbraiding the false Theseus. Her story was told by *Ovid (*Met.* 7 and 8, and *Her.* 10), and by several medieval poets. Chaucer tells it in *The Legend of Good Women* (1886–2227) with considerable eloquence and feeling, making, as Ovid had done, the scene of her abandonment a finely pathetic one: as she stood on the shore calling to her deceiver, 'the holwe [hollow] rokkes answerde hire agayn'.

Aeneid; **Aesop**; *Aetas Prima.* See *Eneyde, *Eneydos*; *Isope; *Former Age.

AFFRICAN (1), Publius Cornelius Scipio Africanus Major (236/5– *c.*183 BC), Roman consul at the beginning of the Second Punic War and a great general who drove the Carthaginians out of Spain, invaded Africa, and ended the war by his victory at Zama. In Cicero's *Somnium Scipionis* (*Drem of Scipioun*), he appears in a dream to his grandson, Scipio Africanus Minor (*Scipio(n)*), foretells his future, urges him to virtue rather than to human fame, and explains the nature of the universe to him. In *The *Parliament of Fowls* Chaucer reads this book, falls asleep, and in his dream meets 'Affrican', who becomes his guide.

AFFRIKAN (2), (the) (Scipio Africanus Minor), see *Scipio(n).

Affrike, Auffrike, Africa (see Map 1). Until the Portuguese voyages of the 15th c., medieval Europe knew little of Africa except those northern areas along the Mediterranean which had been (more or less) familiar since classical times. One medieval map, the Hereford Mappa Mundi (see *Mappemounde) shows Egypt, the Nile, the Atlas mountains, and the Fortunate Isles (the Canaries, Madeira, and Teneriffe) but the centre of the Continent is empty, peopled only by grotesque figures derived from ancient legendary geography. According to *Bartholomew, Africa is 'more rich and wonderful' than Asia or Europe, with gold and precious stones, and fruit, corn, and olives. It has fewer trees than other lands, and in many places it is barren because of 'heaps of gravel'. It has many wonderful kinds of men and beasts— 'cokatryces', apes, dragons, ostriches, and elephants. In Chaucer's time northern Africa was under Muslim rule (see *Belmarye), but his brief references are usually to it as the setting for events in classical stories, like that of *Dido, or of the ' *Drem of Scipioun'. He once mentions it (*HF* 1339) as one of the three continents: 'Auffrike, *Europe, and *Asye'.

Agameno(u)n. Agamemnon, son of Atreus (hence called *Attrides), the king of Mycenae and brother of Menelaus, the husband of Helen (*Eleyne), led the Greek forces at the siege of

Agaton

*Troy. Troilus (*Tr* III.382) calls him 'cruel kyng Agamenoun'. In *Boece* (IVm.7) there is a reference to his sacrifice of his daughter Iphigenia.

Agaton, Agathon or Agatho, who in *The *Legend of Good Women* (F 526) is said by the narrator to have told how *Alceste was turned into a constellation. His identity is uncertain. It has been suggested that he is the 5th-c. Greek tragedian of that name (mentioned by Dante), and that the reference may be to the *Symposium* of *Plato (sometimes known as 'Agatho's feast' because it was held in his house). But although Alcestis appears there, there is no mention of this transformation.

Agenores doghter, see *Europe (1).

Ages of Man (see *children, *Nature, *old age, *youth). In his work on old age, Cicero (*Tullius) remarks that nature has a single path which is run only once, and to each stage in it there are allotted appropriate qualities. Medieval writers had a strong sense of the appropriate qualities and the appropriate behaviour, based both on experience and on tradition. Many of these become proverbial: 'wine and youth' says the Physician (VI.59) cause Venus (i.e. sexual desire) to increase; 'old age' says Criseyde (*Tr* IV.1369) is 'full of covetousness'. There were various schemes for dividing the 'stages' of life: sometimes a simple binary opposition of young/old, sometimes various scientific and philosophical schemes. That of three ages, from *Aristotle, is a biological pattern of rise and fall through growth, stasis, and decline (reflected perhaps in *The *Knight's Tale* with the pattern of Egeus (old), Theseus (mature), and the young Palamon, Arcite, and Emily, and among the gods, Saturn (grandfather), Jupiter (father), and Venus (daughter). We also find four ages, a physiological pattern with the four seasons, the four elements, and the four *humours; or, following Isidore (*Ysidre), six ages (which is sometimes associated with the influential Augustinian six ages of temporal history), giving a series of infancy (up to 7), childhood (up to 14), 'youth' (up to 50), advanced age (*aetas senioris, gravitas,* up to 70), and old age (up to death); or seven ages, sometimes forming an astrological pattern with the planets. A fine example of a (non-astrological)

seven-age system is found in the mural painting (*c.*1330) at Longthorpe Tower, near Peterborough, where the series shows Infans (in a cot), Puer (with a top), Adolescens, Juvenis (with a hawk), Senior (with a sword), Senex (with a bag of money), and Decrepitus (with crutches).

Isidore's generous and rather modern-sounding allowance of up to 50 years for 'youth' raises the question of what actual medieval people thought of as 'young' and 'old'. The accepted lifespan is the biblical 'three score years and ten'—thus *Dante begins the *Commedia* at the age of 35, 'in the middle of the journey of our life'. There are no exact statistics about life expectancy in the Middle Ages, but in spite of the dangers of infancy and childhood, and later of plague, war, or accident, many seem to have enjoyed a reasonable lifespan. Chaucer lived for about sixty years, more or less the same as that of his Italian literary contemporaries, Dante (56), Boccaccio (62), and Petrarch (70), and of his king, Edward III (65). He is not forthcoming with information about his own age at the time of writing poems, unlike Dante, but as far as his fictional creations are concerned he follows the standard pattern of expectation. There are cases where he does not give an age (or refuses to—in the case of *Criseyde). The characters whose ages are given cover the whole range. There is an infant of six months in the cradle in *The *Reeve's Tale* (I.3971–2), the 7-year-old school boy in *The *Prioress's Tale* (VII.503), the maiden *Virginia of 'twelve yeer . . . and tweye' in *The *Physician's Tale* (VI.30), the 18-year-old *Alison in *The Miller's Tale*, a number of 'young' 20-year-olds—the *Squire (I.82), *Malyne in *The Reeve's Tale* (I.3970), *Anelida, the *Wife of Bath's *Jankyn (III.600), etc. The lustful monk of *The *Shipman's Tale* is 30, the Wife of Bath—of unspecified age at the time of the pilgrimage—is 40 at the time she cast her eye on Jankin, her last husband. In *The *Merchant's Tale* January has passed 60 years and describes himself as old and grey when he insists on marrying a young wife not above 20 ('I wol no woman thritty yeer of age'); the old man of *The Pardoner's Tale* is of unspecified age, but has a staff like Decrepitus, and is looking to die, though he still has his wits about him.

Some of these characters seem to be deliberately placed in transitional phases in the Isidorean scheme—the young schoolboy, Virginia, and possibly the Wife of Bath and old January with his youthful desires. However, medieval writers are not usually as interested as their modern counterparts (the heirs of a tradition of literary realism) in the *development* of personality or individuality. The interest seems rather to be on how the character's thoughts and actions reflect the stage of his or her journey through life. An individual's behaviour or qualities can be appropriate or inappropriate to his or her age. The Physician speaks approvingly of the modesty, humility, and moderation of the young Virginia, who always spoke according to her 'degree', and avoided going to the feasts, revels, and dances of her elders. But 'inappropriate' qualities were not necessarily always wicked or comic. They might be evidence of what John Burrow has called the 'transcendence' of the particular stage of life. A child might show the wisdom of age, usually through the grace of God, as in the widespread topic of the *puer senex*, a frequent pattern for a saint, and sometimes for a young hero (see *children and childhood, *Ypotys). Chaucer makes use of this, but he also derives much comedy from the lusty old lovers who will not admit that they are nearing the end of their path.

Burrow (1986).

Aglawros, Aglauros the sister of Herse (*Hierse) (*Tr* III.730). In *Ovid's *Metamorphoses* 2 she provoked the wrath of Minerva (*Mynerva) by prying into one of her secrets. Minerva made her envious of her sister, whose beauty had aroused the love of Mercury (*Mercurye). When Aglauros tried to prevent Mercury from entering her sister's room, he turned her into a stone. Chaucer's allusion suggests that it was Mercury's love for Herse which made the goddess angry with Aglauros.

Alayn; Alan of Lille, Alanus de Insulis; Alba. See *Aleyn (2), *Aleyn (1); *Aubade.

ALBERTANUS OF BRESCIA (?1193–1270), the author of the very popular *Liber consolationis et consilii* (The Book of Consolation and Counsel), which in a French version by Renaud de Louens was the source of *Melibee. The *Liber* was one of three moral works which Albertanus presented to

his three sons, the others being the *De arte loquendi et tacendi* (which is used in *The *Manciple's Tale*—possibly Albertanus is one of the 'clerkes' mentioned in IX.326), and the *De amore et dilectione Dei* (which is used in *The *Merchant's Tale*).

Albyn, in *Boece (I pr.4) Albinus, 'a conseiller of Rome', who was defended by Boethius against a charge of treason.

Albyon, Albion, an old name for Britain (see *Engelond). It appears only in the phrase 'conquerour of *Brutes Albyon' in *The Complaint of Chaucer to his *Purse*, almost certainly a reference to *Henry IV.

Albon, daun, one of the names given to the *Monk by the Host (VII.1930).

'Albricus Philosophus', the name of a popular handbook of *mythography, sometimes called *De deorum imaginibus libellus* (?late 14th c.), an epitome of the first chapter of the *Ovidius moralizatus*, part of the large *Reductorium morale* of the 14th-c. writer *Bersuire. It has been suggested as a source for the portrait of *Venus in *The Knight's Tale* (I.1955–66).

Alchabitius, see *Alkabucius.

Alcathoe, *Ovid's 'Alcathoe, the city of Megara' (*Met.* 7. 443), besieged by Minos (*LGW* 1902) so called after its founder Alcathous. Megara is on the isthmus of Corinth in Greece, near Salamis.

ALCEBIADES, ALCYPIADES, Alcibiades (*c.*450–404 BC) an Athenian of great beauty, a friend of Socrates, a general, and a politician of uncertain trustworthiness (cf. *Bo* III pr.8). A story that his faithful mistress buried his body after his death is alluded to in *The *Franklin's Tale* (V.1439). In *The Book of the Duchess* (1057) he is cited (as elsewhere in medieval literature) as an example of *beauty.

Alceste, Alcestis, the wife of Admetus (*Amete), king of Pherae in Thessaly. Apollo persuaded the Fates to allow him a longer lifespan than they had allotted to him if he could find someone who was willing to die for him. His father and mother refused, but his devoted wife agreed. Hercules (*Ercules) brought her back from Hades. In the Middle Ages, she becomes a standard type of faithfulness (*trouthe*) and wifely devotion ('Lo, which a wyf was Alceste' says *Dorigen, V.1442). Troilus (*Tr* V.1527–33) makes an extended allusion to her sacrifice; and after concluding the story of Criseyde's 'falsing' of Troilus Chaucer says apologetically to 'every lady bright of hewe, | And every gentil womman' that he would 'gladlier' write '*Penolopees trouthe and good Alceste'. The most prominent appearance of the 'good Alceste' is with the God of *love in the Prologue to *The *Legend of Good Women,* where her legend is firmly recalled to the poet accused of heresy against love. Here she is associated not only with love ('she taught al the craft of fyn lovynge, | And namely [especially] of wyfhod the lyvynge') but with the daisy, into which flower, according to Chaucer, she was turned. She shows her kindness by intervening on behalf of Chaucer, and it is she who proposes his 'penance' of writing 'a glorious legende | Of goode wymmen'.

alchemy. Various derivations have been offered for the Arabic word (out of Greek) that describes proto-chemistry. The leading contender, 'the Egyptian art', certainly agrees with a common romantic medieval view of its pedigree. Many writers, medieval and modern, have been at pains to emphasize the subject's spiritual character, over and above the aim to transmute base metals into gold, but it can be defined in many ways, and indeed the outlook of its practitioners changed considerably over the centuries. It can be seen as the combination of a suitable theory of matter (until well after Chaucer this was at root *Aristotle's) with common empirical knowledge.

The smelting of ores was one of the most prized but difficult of the practical arts. Metals were often confused, and alloys not clearly distinguished from pure metals. By late antiquity there was a standard list of elemental metals: gold, silver, copper, lead, iron, tin, and mercury. The list was artificially limited, to the extent that each metal was made to correspond to a different planet. This is one aspect of a tendency for the early alchemists to value symmetries above empirical observations, and to draw them from many other

disciplines—astrology, theology, the crafts of the jeweller, the painter, the metal-worker, the pharmacologist, and so on. In time, Hermetic mystery entered the vacuum created to some extent by practical failure.

In 1652 Elias Ashmole included *The *Canon's Yeoman's Tale* in a published collection of English alchemical treatises. He ranked Chaucer among the 'Hermetick Philosophers', and asserted that the poet 'fully knew the *Mistery'.* The Canon closes by expatiating at length on the making of the philosopher's stone, earlier called 'elixer', and he names as his sources *Arnold of the Newe Toun and *Senior. The vocabulary is arcane—'dragon' is mercury, dragon's 'brother' is sulphur, and so forth—and was derived from Arabic Hermetic treatises. Like all the natural sciences, alchemy had been greatly expanded in the Arab world. The most famous name of Arabic alchemical writers was Jâbir ibn Hayyân (*fl.* early 9th c.), although the writings ascribed to him were fairly certainly produced by a school rather than by one man. Jâbir made much use of numerology and astrology, the theory of talismans and the invocation of spirits through prayer. He supplemented the Greek list of 'spirits'—sulphur, mercury, arsenic—with a fourth, sal ammoniac. The theory that the metals are compounds of mercury and sulphur was one of the most widely diffused of all in medieval alchemy, and is that alluded to by the Canon's Yeoman. Another Muslim alchemist was the famous physician al-Râzî (*Razis), in whose extensive summaries use is made of such ideas. A third influential writer was Ibn Umail, the Canon's Yeoman's 'Senior'.

Alchemy reached the Latin West in the mid-12th c., when Robert of Ketton translated a work of Morienus (a Christian alchemist working in 7th-c. Damascus) from Arabic into Latin. Between that time and Chaucer, a vast body of alchemical material appeared in Latin, but it was never included in the standard university curriculum, despite many pseudo-Aristotelian texts, and despite the reputations of such scholars as Roger *Bacon and Albertus Magnus (see *Lapidaire) both of whom had worked at alchemical transmutation. Part of the reason is to be found in a section of a work by Avicenna (*Avycen), translated by Alfred of Sareshall around 1200, that became attached to Aristotle's *Meteorology*. The text included much useful alchemical information (on the mercury–sulphur theory of metals, for example), but then it went on to attack alchemy, and was later much quoted by sceptical writers glad to have—as they thought—Aristotle's backing. Avicenna argued that art is essentially inferior to nature; and that although we might change the accidents of a substance, such as its colour or taste, we can never know the specific natures of metals, for those are beyond our senses. We can never know, therefore, whether we have taken them away or not. The drift of this is that art can never reproduce nature's achievements in the production of metals.

The alchemists' rejoinders were various: it was said that art is often *superior* to nature. The question of the possibility of inter-specific transmutation gave rise to much barren scholastic discussions of substance and form, genus and species. *Vincent of Beauvais entered this debate rather ineffectually, with some speculations on the mercury–sulphur theory. Albertus Magnus attacked those who said that all metals share the form of gold in various degrees of completeness. He still believed that one specific form could be destroyed and another substituted for it. Like Albertus, Bacon was anxious to distinguish between the speculative and the operative science. He spent considerable sums of money on experiments. He went as far as to maintain that alchemy offered one of the chief ways of reforming natural science as a whole, for he believed it to be even more basic than Aristotle's matter-theory.

Further attacks on the subject were launched at the end of the 13th c. by Giles of Rome, who followed Aristotle and Aquinas in maintaining that the generation of metals requires a power that is to be found only in the depths of the earth. There was a succession of Dominican condemnations of alchemy—the first had been in 1272—and the movement culminated in a papal bull of 1317 (by John XXII) prohibiting alchemy. The reasons behind this bull, it has to be said, were more monetary than theoretical: it was directed against counterfeiting, and the papal advisers were hedging their bets on the possibility of using transmuted gold for this purpose. The ban is an important part of the context of *The Canon's Yeoman's Tale*.

Western alchemists followed their predecessors' example in attempting to prepare elixirs, substances capable of inducing chemical transformation merely by their presence. (The notion of an elixir is not very different from that of a catalyst in modern chemistry.) Elixirs were not merely aimed at the production of gold: they were thought capable of inducing longevity, and in the West especially were discussed by many medical writers, notably John of Rupescissa (*fl.* 1350), a Catalan mystic.

From a modern perspective, the most lasting achievements of the Western alchemists were the preparation of alcohol and the mineral acids. These discoveries were made possible by an improvement in the apparatus for distillation. Once the mineral acids were available (nitric, sulphuric, and hydrochloric—but not properly differentiated) they could be used for the decomposition of most substances then known. By Chaucer's time there was in principle ample scope for the practice of alchemy in a style more closely resembling modern chemistry than the mysticism of John of Rupescissa and the chicanery of the Canon's Yeoman. In practice alchemical style did not shun the mystical approach for another two centuries. [JDN]

Curry (1960); Halleux (1979); Holmyard (1957); Manzaloui (1974).

Alcione, Alcyone, daughter of Aeolus, wife of King Ceyx (*Seys). Their story is told by *Ovid (*Met.* 11). Ceyx is drowned in a terrible storm. His devoted wife constantly prays for his return, and the goddess Juno asks the God of Sleep to send the shape of the dead Ceyx to Alcyone in a dream so that she may know the truth. The distracted queen determines to join him, goes down to the sea, and finds his dead body floating nearby. As she leaps into the waves she finds herself flying: they have both been transformed into birds (the halcyon or kingfisher). The story was a great favourite in the Middle Ages: it is told by *Gower and by *Froissart. In *The *Book of the Duchess*, Chaucer, unable to sleep, reads it in a book, 'a romaunce', and relates the tale (62–230), omitting the final transformation.

Alcmena; Alcypiades. See *Almena; *Alcebiades.

Aldeberan Aldebaran (Arabic *al-dabarân*, 'the follower'). Alpha Tauri, the brightest star in the constellation of Taurus. In the usual representation, this is the eye of the bull, one of the Hyades. It is mentioned with *Algomeysa in *A Treatise on the Astrolabe* as a star that does not rise to the south of the astrolabe's east line. (See also *astrology and astronomy; *Bole.)   [JDN]

Aldgate, one of the gates in the city wall of *London. It was on the east side, and through it came a busy thoroughfare. Chaucer had a dwelling over Aldgate from 1374 to 1386, and must have written some of his poems there. The gate probably had two circular towers, and still had a defensive role. In 1377, because of the fear of a French attack, the gates of London were ordered to be fortified with portcullises and chained (*Stow in his *Survey of London* (1598) says that the Aldgate 'hath had two pair of gates, though now but one; the hooks remaineth yet. Also there hath been two portcullisses; the one of them remaineth, the other wanteth, but the place of letting down is manifest'). After the *Peasants' Revolt, when the rebels broke into London through Aldgate, it was guarded. Its neighbourhood, Aldgate Ward, was home to many trades, and was filled with shops and tenements (many of them with gardens)— still in Stow's time, 'divers fair houses for merchants and other'. Its churches included the Priory of the Holy Trinity, St Katherine, St Andrew, and a house of the Crutched Friars (whose memory survives in the street name Crutched Friars); nearby, says Stow, 'of old time [presumably before the expulsion of 1290] were certain tenements called the poor Jewry, of *Jews dwelling there' (now Jewry St).

Aldiran, a star in the constellation of *Leo, described in some medieval star lists as *in fronte Leonis*. In *The *Squire's Tale*, the 'gentil Leon with his Aldiran' rose over the horizon as Cambyuskan rose from the table. It is not immediately clear precisely which star Chaucer intended, since many medieval star lists are confused, but it may be shown that he had indeed accurate data in front

of him for what was described by Ptolemy as 'the southernmost of the two stars in the head of Leo'. (See also *astrology and astronomy.)   [JDN]

ale. The ancient word [OE *ealu*] for the alcoholic drink made from an infusion of malt by fermentation is found in Chaucer, but he never uses the equally old word *beer* (used to distinguish the variety of ale flavoured with hops). Ale seems to have been a common drink of all classes of society, but Chaucer's references are mostly found in exchanges with or in the tales told by 'churls' or non-noble folk (especially *MilT, RvT, PardT*; though the *Franklin served good ale). In medieval England ale was a basic commodity, brewed in larger households as well as in taverns; many brewers were women. As with bread, the quality and the price were controlled: in the case of London ale (I.382) every ward of the city had 'aleconners' to test it. Some of Chaucer's adjectives refer to its quality in a rather general way: thus we find 'myghty' ale (of which a large quart is brought to *Nicholas by the carpenter in *The Miller's Tale* who stocks up against the impending flood with 'breed and chese and good ale in a jubbe [jug]'); or 'strong ale atte beste' (I.4147); or a 'draughte of moyste and corny ale' (VI.315) i.e. 'new' and tasting strongly of the corn or malt. Like other drinks it was sometimes spiced (some is sent by *Absolon (2) to Alison along with spiced wine and mead (I.3378)). When a tavern's brew was ready it put out an 'ale stake', a pole with a branch or bush of leaves at its end—hence the remark that the garland which the *Summoner wears on his head is 'as greet as it were for an ale-stake' (I.667). It is at an 'alestake' (unless again this is a joking allusion to the Summoner's headgear) that the *Pardoner insists on pausing to 'drynke and eten of a cake' before telling his tale (VI.321). The power of ale is sometimes much in evidence (see *drunkenness). The *Wife of Bath uses the imagery of ale to give a homely twist to the ancient topic of the 'bitter cup' (fortune can give a person either sweet or bitter drink; cf. *Bo* II pr.2:74–6). She silences the interruption of the Pardoner (III.170–7) by saying that she is going to broach a different barrel which will taste worse than ale, and after he has heard her tale of the tribulations of marriage, he can choose which one he will sip from (see also *wine).

ALEYN (1), referred to in *The *Parliament of Fowls* (316 ff.), is Alan of Lille or Alanus de Insulis (*c.*1120–1202/3), a famous master of the schools of Paris whose Latin writings, imbued with the Platonism of the 'school of Chartres' (especially influenced by the *Timaeus* with its mythopoeic account of the cosmos), were widely known. Like other 12th-c. writers (see *Bernardus Silvestris) he was interested in myths and fables with hidden meanings, and wrote cosmological poetry, with heavenly journeys through the spheres revealing the nature of the universe, its pattern of creation, degeneration, and renewal, and the celestial beings who inhabit and control it. For Alan the central figure is the goddess Natura (*Nature); his cosmological vision is not explicitly referred to any Christian scheme. Chaucer was deeply influenced by his thought. The *De planctu Naturae*, 'The Complaint of Nature' or 'the Pleynt of Kynde' as he calls it (*PF* 316), describes Nature's great beauty and her robe of many colours which celebrates the variety of the created world—her mantle is adorned with fishes, her robe with the different species of birds. As in Chaucer, she is an intermediary, a mediatrix, who maintains order and 'accord'. The virtues associated with her are temperance or moderation, chastity, generosity, and humility. The stars and the planets obey her, and perform their duties in accordance with her command.

Like Chaucer, Alan was interested in the role of *love in the universe. Hymenaeus, the god of weddings, is Natura's brother, and Venus has her duties under her governance, but obedience does not come easily to her, and she turns to adulterous and secret loves. Nature's 'complaint' concerns the ways in which mankind has failed to live by her laws. The *Anticlaudianus*, a philosophical epic, is explicitly referred to in The *House of Fame*: as Chaucer is carried up through the heavens he thinks upon 'Anteclaudian' (986). In this poem Prudentia (or Fronesis) also made a celestial journey, and saw the daemons (*aerios cives, cives superi*) in the air (where clouds, mists, and storms are engendered)—the source of the passage in *The House of Fame* (925–34) where Chaucer himself sees 'the eyrryssh bestes' and 'many a citezeyn' of that region. In the *Anticlaudianus* Nature has the paradisal setting which Chaucer used in *The Parliament of Fowls* (though the house he gives her is made of branches, not of gold and precious gems). Mankind is urged to avoid vice by an eager obedience to Nature's laws. Among many topics, that of *Fame is discussed: the virtuous man should not make it his object, but to reject it altogether is too austere. Prudentia returns to earth to re-create Nature's paradise there.

Anticlaudianus, ed. Bossuat (1955); trans. Sheridan (1973); *De planctu Naturae*, ed. Häring (1979); trans. Sheridan (1980); Dronke (1974).

Aleyn (2), one of the Cambridge clerks in *The *Reeve's Tale*.

Alete, Alecto, one of the *Furies, invoked at the beginning of book IV of *Troilus and Criseyde* (IV.24).

Alexander; Alexandria, see *Alisa(u)ndre.

Algarsyf, son of Cambyuskan in *The *Squire's Tale*; This Arabic-sounding name (and those of his mother *Elpheta, his brother *Cambalo, and sister *Canacee (2)) has provoked a number of speculative etymologies and interpretations (including a supposed similarity to that of Yaroslav I, the father of Alexander Nevsky). If, as has been plausibly suggested, the tale has an astronomical structure, Algarsyf may be an analogue for *Jupiter, and his name may be derived from an Arabic name for a lunar mansion.

Algezir, Algeciras, a town and seaport in southern Spain, which, when it was in Christian hands, the sultan of Fez and a large Merenid army besieged in 1340; he was, however, roundly defeated at the battle of the River Salado in the same year, by the combined forces of Alfonso XI of Castile and Afonso IV of Portugal, the former going on to capture Algeciras in 1344, after a prolonged siege witnessed by the Knight (I.57). [PS]

Algomeysa (Arabic *al-gumaysâ*'), Procyon, alpha Canis Minoris; the brightest star in the Lesser Dog. This is mentioned with *Aldeberan in *A Treatise on the *Astrolabe* as a star that does not rise to the south of the astrolabe's east line. (See also *astrology and astronomy.) [JDN]

9

Algus, see **Argus (3); *Augrym.

Alhabor (Arabic *al-'abûr*), Sirius, the Dog Star, alpha Canis Maioris. This 'faire white sterre', by far the brightest of the fixed stars, is used in *A Treatise on the *Astrolabe* to judge the hour of the night. It is conspicuous on the retes of astrolabes of the type illustrated in the Chaucer manuscripts, since it is represented by a dog's head, or more precisely by the tip of the dog's tongue. (See also **astrology and astronomy.)   [JDN]

Alys (1), the name of the **Wife of Bath (III.320; also called Alisoun, III.804).

Alys (2), the name of the Wife of Bath's 'gossip' or close friend (III.548).

ALISA(U)NDRE, ALYSAUNDER, ALEX- ANDER, ALIXANDRE MACEDO.

Alexander the Great (356–323 BC) of Macedon (**Macedoyne), son of Philip II and Olympias, was educated by **Aristotle, and soon showed himself to be a brilliant military commander. He invaded Asia, conquering Persia, Syria, and Egypt. His campaigns took him as far as what is now Samarkand and Afghanistan, and finally India; he had hoped to reach the Ganges, and what he thought to be the end of the world, but his men refused. After reaching the delta of the Indus in 325, he set off homewards, but died of fever in Babylon (**Babiloigne). The fame of his remarkable achievements lived on and grew still more remarkable in later history and legend. The story of Alexander became one of the most popular subjects of medieval **romance. He was transformed into a chivalric hero, one of the **Nine Worthies. His extraordinary life, from a birth marked by prodigious signs to a death (in legend) by treachery and poison, involved all the wonders of the East (which were detailed in such works as the so-called 'Letter of Alexander to Aristotle', often, like other Alexander books, sumptuously illustrated). In some stories Alexander goes up in a heavenly journey, carried up by four griffins (an incident which the Eagle (*HF* 915) alludes to while he is bearing Chaucer aloft), and down in the sea in a glass diving-bell, a kind of early submarine; he meets the noble Brahmans, who explain their religion and their virtuous way of life, and finds the Trees of the Sun and the Moon, which foretell his end. As the **Monk, who briefly tells his **'tragedy' (VII.2631–70), says, his story is so 'commune' that everyone 'hath herd somwhat or al of his fortune'. His 'fortune' there is a panegyric of his achievements and his knightly nobility ('he was of knyghthod and of fredom [nobility] flour') and a lament for his fall, 'empoysoned' by his 'owene folk'. Elsewhere, he is cited as an example of 'worthinesse' and fame (*BD* 1060, *HF* 1413); and the Manciple records a common anecdote about him—that he was told that the difference between a tyrant (called a 'capitayn') and an outlaw (called a 'theef') resides only in the strength of the forces at their disposal (IX.226–34).

Cary (1956); Dronke (1997); D. J. A. Ross (1963).

Alisa(u)ndre. Alexandria, a city on the north coast of Egypt (**Egypte), founded by Alexander the Great in 331 BC. It was the capital of the Ptolomies (see **Tholome (2)) and a great intellectual centre of the Hellenistic world, and later of Eastern Christianity (legend has it that St **Mark, its first bishop, was martyred there; and St Catherine of Alexandria who was probably unhistorical, was widely venerated). It declined in size and importance after its capture by the Arabs. It was known to the medieval West because of its earlier illustrious history, and through the **Crusades (Chaucer's **Knight (I.51) was at its bloody and short-lived capture in 1365 by Peter of Cyprus (**Petro kyng of Cipre); cf. VII.2392). It remained a commercial centre, especially for the spice trade. In Chaucer it is mentioned as an example of a 'greet' town—with Nineveh, Rome, and Troy (VIII.975), and in a list of exotic distant and dangerous places in *The Book of the Duchess* (1026).

Aliso(u)n (1), the young wife of the carpenter in *The *Miller's Tale*, desired by both **Nicholas and **Absolon (2). The formal **portrait of her (I.3233–70) has been much admired, and is often quoted as an example of the physical naturalism which pervades the Tale. Her animal vitality is suggested by a series of rustic images: her body is compared to that of a weasel, the colour of her brows to that of a sloe, she is softer than 'the wolle is of a wether'; her song is like that of a swallow, she skips like a kid or a calf, and so on (all this makes her *clothes, which are also described in some detail seem highly erotic as well). It is noteworthy that at the end of the tale, although her night of bliss with Nicholas in her husband's bed is comically curtailed, she is the only one of the main characters to escape without pain or punishment.

Aliso(u)n (2), the name of the *Wife of Bath (III.804; also called Alys, III.320).

Aliso(u)n (3) the name of the Wife of Bath's 'gossip' or close friend (III.530).

ALIXANDRE, see *Alisa(u)ndre.

ALKABUCIUS, Abû al-Sakr 'Abd al-'Azîz ibn 'Uthmân ibn Alî al-Qabîsî (*fl. c.*950), astrologer, and adept in Ptolemaic *astronomy. Born near either Mosul or Samarra (both now Iraq), he worked mostly at the court in Aleppo (Syria). His *Introduction to the Art of Astrology* drew on standard authorities from many periods and cultures. It was much copied, both in its original Arabic and in John of Spain's Latin translation (1144). Cecco d'Ascoli (before 1327) and John of Saxony (Paris, 1331) wrote commentaries on it. It was translated into French by Pélerin de Prusse (1362) and into English in the early 15th c. or before. Alkabucius is quoted by Chaucer in his *Treatise on the *Astrolabe* (1.8, 13), to the effect that the subdivision of degrees is potentially infinite. This is his only reference to a strictly astrological writer by name. There are very many instances where Chaucer's use of astrology conforms with the doctrines set out in the *Introduction*. (See also **astrology and astronomy**.) [JDN]

Alkaron, the Koran, the sacred book of Islam, referred to by the mother of the sultan in *The Man of Law's Tale* (II.332–3).

ALLA, the king of Northumbria in *The Man of Law's Tale* (the name is that of an historical 6th-c. Anglo-Saxon king).

allegory appears in such a variety of shapes and forms that it is not easy to pin it down by a definition. The germ is found in the ancient rhetorical figure of *allegoria*, 'when we speak one thing and mean another'. As Dr Johnson says, it is 'a figurative discourse, in which something other is intended, than is contained in the words literally taken; as, wealth is the daughter of diligence, and the parent of authority'. We might now be inclined to call this example a metaphor, and to restrict the term allegory to an extended metaphor, in which the 'figurative discourse' is elaborated into a narrative, as in the story of a lover-knight (Christ) who wooed a lady (Man's soul) but was rejected, and finally died to win her love. Another kind is what is often called 'personification allegory', in which a personification of a virtue, a vice, or some other mental or moral quality will be involved in a dramatic narrative or conflict—as in the *Roman de la Rose*, for instance, the most famous example of this kind in the Middle Ages. Some medieval commentators and writers like to find more recondite meanings under the veil of the allegory. This is sometimes carried to such extremes that a modern critic has used the term 'imposed allegory'. Sometimes an author writing on the literal level will be confronted in a dream by the personification of some quality like Old Age or Death or an institution like Holy Church.

Allegorical thinking was certainly encouraged by the idea that the created universe and the course of history mirrored the ordering providence of God: they were 'books' written by his finger, which could be 'read'; by penetrating into their mysteries, man could discern something of divine truth. Examples of allegory can be found as far back as the Old Testament (cf. Isa. 5:1–7), and New Testament writers found prophecies of the New Covenant under the words of the Old Testament. This method of interpretation was much extended by Christian commentators in later centuries. The discovery of prophetic 'figures' or 'types' of the New Covenant in the persons or the scenes of the Old (often called 'typology') was especially widespread. An Old Testament book like the Song of Solomon (or Song of Songs) was taken to have various spiritual significances, such as Christ's love for man or for the Church.

And in the Middle Ages there were more elaborate schemes of biblical interpretation (usually of individual verses) at various 'levels of meaning' (often, but by no means always, four): the literal; the allegorical (applying it to Christ and the Church Militant); the tropological or moral (referring it to the soul and to virtues or vices); and the anagogical (applying it to the heavenly realities).

Classical literature and mythology could also be read allegorically: the *Ovide moralisé*, for instance, offered a series of such interpretations of Ovid's stories. The idea was that even in these pagan writers one could find figures and shadows of the redemptive plan of the true God. And the world of nature could also be interpreted in this way (see *Lapidaire, *Bestiary).

Given that allegory was so common and so pervasive, it is striking that Chaucer uses it so little. (This has been challenged by one school of modern criticism (see *Criticism of Chaucer II) which claims that he meant his narratives to be read in an allegorical way, revealing, in the manner of St Augustine, the conflict between cupidity and charity, but this view has not won widespread support.) He translated part of the *Roman de la Rose*, but never himself attempted anything so elaborate. His only consistently allegorical poem is the short *Complaint unto *Pity*, where Pity is dead 'and buried in a heart', and her contrary, Cruelty, is triumphant.

In his religious writing, he alludes to two very common old Testament 'types': in the *ABC* (169) he says that Isaac (whom his father Abraham was ordered to sacrifice) was a 'figure' of Christ's death; and in the Prologue of The *Prioress's Tale* the Virgin Mary is addressed as 'bussh unbrent, brennynge in Moyses sighte'—a reference to the miraculous burning bush of Exodus 3:2 which was taken to be a prophetic figure of the Virgin Birth (cf. *ABC* 92–4). In a passage in The *Second Nun's Tale* in which the significance of the name 'Cecilia' is expounded (VIII.85–119), he uses the phrase 'in figurynge' (similarly, Troilus's symbolic dream of the boar 'was shewed hym in figure' (*Tr* V.1449)). Chaucer uses personifications as easily as any medieval poet, but only in certain limited contexts. In his dream vision poems, for instance, the dreamer will meet figures like Nature or Fame,

but in these the narrative is not allegorical in any thoroughgoing way: it seems often to be neither wholly literal nor wholly metaphorical. In *The Canterbury Tales* allegory is even more sparse and incidental. A personified Death is sought by the rioters in The *Pardoner's Tale*, but they find 'him' only in the form of a pile of gold florins (and the mysterious old man who directs them to it may be a 'symbolic' figure, but is not a narrowly 'allegorical' one). The framework of the story of *Melibee* and the names—especially *Prudence and *Sophie—can certainly be called allegorical, though the tale as a whole works rather through *debate rather than as a formal allegory. Perhaps calling the old husband and the young wife in The *Merchant's Tale* January and May is using a technique of allegorical generalization to balance the particularity of some of the scenes. And it may be that some other names (like *Absolon (2) in *MilT*) are allusive and are chosen to suggest a (comic or ironic) parallel with their 'figures' in scripture or in history. In general, however, Chaucer seems to prefer the 'thisness' of persons and things.

Lewis (1936); Piehler (1971); Tuve (1966).

alliterative verse has as its metrical principle the recurrence of the same sound at the beginning of a number of (usually stressed) words within the line. It was the distinctive form of Old English poetry. Strictly, the term is used of verse written in unrhymed lines, but it is often used to describe verse where consistent alliteration is used in combination with rhyme (which can occasionally be found in OE, but is much more frequent in ME, where the rhyme patterns can be very complicated). The term 'Alliterative Revival' is often used to describe a group of poems, many of them from the north or the north-west Midlands, written in alliterative verse (of a looser, less strict kind than in OE) in the 14th c. The origins of this are uncertain. It does not seem to have been a revival in the sense of a conscious imitation of pre-Conquest models; it may be that popular, sub-literary types of alliterative verse survived the Conquest, and that out of this was developed a more literary form. However, there is certainly no doubt about the distinction of much ME alliterative poetry (*Piers Plowman, *Sir Gawain and the Green Knight*, and *Pearl* are only the best known of its masterpieces) nor about its variety—we have visions, satires and political poems, and romances. Alliteration and alliterative patterns are common in other kinds of verse (e.g. in the northern plays). In the north and in Scotland especially, alliterative poetry continued to be written long after Chaucer's death.

It is not clear how familiar Chaucer was with such works. In The *Squire's Tale a strange knight rides into the hall, rather as the Green Knight does in Sir Gawain and the Green Knight, and speaks in a way that even the courteous Gawain could not improve—in such a high style, the narrator jokingly says, that he cannot climb over it. It would be nice to think that this is directed at the rather recondite northern diction of that romance, but the evidence is not absolutely convincing. However, the remark of the Parson, 'trusteth wel, I am a Southren man; | I kan nat geeste [tell a tale in verse] "rum, ram, ruf," by lettre' (X.42–3) is certainly a reference to alliterative verse (he mentions the alternative, 'rym', in the next line). What is not so certain is what implications are to be drawn. Alliterative poetry, while it is found in abundance in the north, was certainly not restricted to that area. *Langland, in one passage, says that he lived in London, and some of the other satirical alliterative poems show a knowledge of what is going on in the capital. Perhaps the Parson comes from even further south than London, but that is perhaps being over-literal. In fact, Chaucer (like other southern writers) has alliterative formulaic phrases. He uses strongly alliterative patterns, within his normal metrical scheme, on two occasions (both battle scenes, where the acoustic possibilities of alliterative verse had often been demonstrated). In the tournament in The *Knight's Tale we have lines like 'ther shyveren shaftes upon sheeldes thikke' or 'ther stomblen steedes stronge, and doun goth al', and in the description of the battle of Actium in The *Legend of Good Women 'With grisely soun out goth the grete gonne, | And heterly they hurtelen al atones', etc. He does not himself seem to have minded the occasional 'rum, ram, ruf'.

Oakden (1930, 1935); Turville-Petre (1977).

allusion is defined by Dr Johnson as 'that which is spoken with something supposed to be already known, and therefore not expressed'. This is a sensible definition, but the topic raises some interesting questions. It is obvious that what is 'supposed to be already known' will vary from age to age—thus the opening lines of the *General Prologue assume that we know something about *Zepherus and the astronomical sign of the *Ram, and the identity of the unnamed 'hooly blisful martyr' associated with Canterbury. This is the kind of knowledge which most members of Chaucer's *audience probably carried around in their heads, but what of more recondite allusions? Sometimes Chaucer will expand these, or at least give a little explanatory comment—Adonis (*Adoon), who was slain by the boar (Tr III.721) —but sometimes he does not. In The *Parliament of Fowls, the dreamer sees the god *Priapus standing 'in swich aray as whan the asse hym shente | With cri by nighte' (255–6). Here the audience needs to know its Ovid. The much-discussed question of how far the audience (as a whole or individually) could have been expected to pick up such allusions will never be finally resolved.

In a poet's creative work, there are different kinds of echoes or allusions. Sometimes perhaps a line or two has stuck in his memory, sometimes he is recalling a whole scene or a whole context. One useful (though not watertight) distinction which has been made is between 'quotation' (obviously conscious—a Chaucerian example would be the sonnet of Petrarch (*Petrak) which is given to Troilus as a song), 'allusion' (intentional in varying degrees), and 'echo' (which does not depend on conscious intention).

In Chaucer classical allusions represent a very important and extensive group (he refers to ancient stories and heroes, to nymphs and satyrs and fauns, with an easy familiarity), but it is only one group. There are allusions to common school texts, to Aesop (*Isope) and Cato (*Catoun (2)), as well as to the *Bible and Boethius. Allusions are by no means always literary; some are recognizably contemporary (*Jakke Straw, for instance), and there were no doubt others to which we have lost the key. More important, though, is a stream of allusion to a wide variety of communal experience and lore (to the man in the moon—cf. Tr I.1024; to games of dice or chess; to *proverbs and to common symbolism—e.g. that blue signifies constancy).

Chaucer's use of allusion is sophisticated and intelligent, varying in tone (sometimes ironic or parodic) and in density (allusions are especially prominent in *Troilus and Criseyde*, but are also frequently used in *The Canterbury Tales*—especially in the discourse of, for instance, the Wife of Bath, the Merchant, and the Nun's Priest). Allusion sometimes serves to heighten the style, as in the invocation at the end of book III of *Troilus* ('Thou lady bryght, the doughter to *Dyone, | Thy blynde and wynged sone ek, daun *Cupide, | Yee sustren nyne ek [see *Muses], that by *Elicone | In hil *Pernaso listen for t'abide'). But there is always flexibility. The lamentation at the fall of *Troy is used as a 'pitous' hyperbole in *The Man of Law's Tale* (II.288–92) and as a mock-heroic one in *The Nun's Priest's Tale* (VII.3355–60). Sometimes an allusion provides a kind of exemplary expansion: in the love scene in *Troilus* book III, 'Mida [*Myda] ful of coveytise' and *Crassus are mentioned (1387–93) as examples of the covetous folk opposed to the 'perfit joie' of love and '*gentilesse' (an 'echo' may well be involved here since the two are linked together by *Dante (*Purgatorio* 20. 106–8), who deeply influenced Chaucer's views on these subjects). At other points, allusions to things supposed to be already known are used to give a sense of local and contemporary actuality (as when the Host exclaims 'Lo *Depeford, and it is half-wey pryme! | Lo *Grenewych, ther many a shrewe is inne!' (I.3906–7)), or when Pandarus, trying to persuade Troilus to carry off Criseyde, uses an allusion to the taking of Helen—'Artow in Troie, and hast non hardyment [daring] | To take a womman which that loveth the' (*Tr* IV.533–4)—an allusion which Troilus recognizes and rejects.

In *Troilus and Criseyde* allusions are consistently used to intensify the larger dramatic or tragic pattern: references to the parallel story of *Thebes (1); to the underworld and its denizens in books IV and V; and an allusion to the story of two parallel tragic lovers, *Orpheus and Eurydice (IV.788–90), expresses at once a sad and pathetic hope of reunion and a bleak certainty of separation. A fine passage near the beginning of book IV shows Chaucer's technique of literary allusion at its best. Troilus in despair at the impending loss of Criseyde lies on his bed in his darkened room. Chaucer adds a simile: 'And as in wynter leves ben biraft, | Ech after other, til the tre be bare, | So that ther nys but bark and braunche ilaft [left], Lith Troilus, byraft of ech welfare, | Ibounden in the blake bark of care' (225–9). This is an allusion to a famous simile in Dante's *Inferno* when the crowd of the damned are gathered on the shore by Charon: 'as in autumn the leaves drop off one after the other until the branch sees all its spoils on the ground.' This itself is a conscious allusion to a simile of *Virgil describing the dead pleading with Charon to carry them across the stream. The recollection of these grim contexts reinforces Chaucer's sombre image. At the same time we can see here how the best allusion has a transforming power. Chaucer has made the image still more bleak by his 'winter' and his emphasis on the stripping bare of the tree. The phrase 'ibounden in the blake bark of care' boldly changes simile into metaphor—of the cruel and oppressive imprisonment of despair—which is at once an echo of the wood of the suicides in Dante and an intimation of an image used later in *Troilus*, that of the 'woful *Mirra' transformed into a tree, and weeping bitter tears through its bark. Perhaps the most interesting aspect of allusion is the insight it gives into the creative imagination.

Hollander (1981); Gray (1984).

Alma redemptoris mater ('O gracious mother of the Redeemer'), an antiphon to the Virgin Mary, sung by the little schooboy in *The *Prioress's Tale*.

Almache, Almachius, the pagan Roman prefect in *The *Second Nun's Tale*.

Almageste, see *Ptholomee.

Almena, Alcmena, the mother of Hercules (*Ercules) by *Jupiter, who by his power extended the night on which he slept with her. In the *aubade scene in *Troilus and Criseyde* Criseyde alludes to this event in her invocation to night: 'O nyght, allas, why nyltow over us hove | As longe as whan Almena lay by Jove?' (III.1427–8).

Almenak, almanac. This word of obscure (but seemingly Arabic) origin is used of various sorts of astronomical *table (usually those now called ephemerides) that give the 'true places' of the Sun, Moon, and planets, at regular intervals of time. The true places are usually the *ecliptic coordinates *latitude and *longitude. The intervals are usually days, or groups of days (typically five or ten). The word 'almanac' is often used of any calendar (see *kalendere) with tabulated planetary positions.

There is a class of so-called 'perpetual almanacs' that depend for their validity on the fact that the planets repeat their cycles of longitude after certain intervals of time. (Venus, for example, repeats her cycle every eight years.) There is no doubt that Chaucer often worked to much higher accuracy than could have been the case had he made use only of perpetual almanacs. This does not mean that he refrained from using all almanacs: on the contrary, he probably owned and used an Oxford set compiled in 1348; and there are explicit references to lunar almanacs in both *A Treatise on the *Astrolabe* and *Equatorie of the Planetis*.

Almanacs are to be distinguished from tables that serve only as intermediaries for the calculation of true places. Almanacs are much less commonly found in medieval manuscripts, since those of the non-perpetual sort become outdated, and involve great labour in calculation. It was for this reason that astronomers made equatoria. (See also *astrology and astronomy*.)   [JDN]

Almycanteras, almucantar (Arabic *al-muqantara*, pl. *-at*). (The *-at* ending was often regarded as sing. in medieval Latin.) A parallel of constant altitude above (occasionally below) the horizon, as inscribed on an astrolabe plate. The function of almucantars is explained in *A Treatise on the *Astrolabe*. (See also **clymat**; **heyte**; **oriso(u)nte**.)   [JDN]

Alnath (Arabic *al-nath*), Alpha Arietis, the brightest star in the *Ram. In the star lists associated with *A Treatise on the *Astrolabe*, a gloss states that according to Ptolemy the star marks the head of Aries. The name was also used as the name of the first lunar *mansion, the beginning of which the star had once marked, and it occurs in this context in *The *Franklin's Tale*. By his choice of words there, Chaucer shows familiarity with the

doctrine of the movement of the eighth sphere. (See also *astrology and astronomy*; *sper(e)*.)   [JDN]

ALOCEN, Alhazen, Abû 'Alî al-Hasan ibn al-Hasan ibn al-Haytham (965–*c*.1040, also called al-Basrî and al-Misrî. Ibn al-Haytham, or Alhazen (to use the usual Latinized form of his name al-Hasan), was the greatest of Arabic writers on optics, and also made important contributions to mathematics and astronomy. Born in Iraq, he settled in Egypt, perhaps after working in Basra and Baghdad. His most influential work, the *Optics*, owed much to *Aristotle, *Euclid, and Ptolemy (*Pthilomee), but in its experimental and mathematical content it went far beyond any of them, especially on the subject of vision. The *Optics* was translated into Latin by Gerard of Cremona (1114–87), and was much quoted by Robert *Grosseteste and Roger *Bacon, as well as by two other standard Western writers on optics, Witelo (*Vitulon) and John Pecham (*c*.1230–92). The Stranger-Knight in *The *Squire's Tale* carried with him a mirror in which the future could be seen, and the Squire relates how this prompted Cambyuskan's guests to speak of 'Alocen, and Vitulon, and Aristotle'. They had, he adds, all written of ingenious mirrors and optical theory (perspective). (See also *science*.)

[JDN]

Amadrides, Hamadryads, tree nymphs, dispossessed by the preparations for *Arcite's (1) funeral pyre in *The *Knight's Tale* (I.2928).

Amazones, Amazons, a legendary nation of women fighters (the name means 'breastless ones', because it was said that when they were girls they burned off one of their breasts in order to use their bows more effectively). Their land *Femenye (i.e. the land of women) was placed either on the south shore of the Black Sea or further north in the region of the Don, and in either case was called Scythia. They were the object of much curiosity. *Bartholomew, following Isidore (*Ysidre), recounts that they were originally the wives of Goths, and when their husbands were treacherously killed, they took their weapons, and rushed on their foes 'with manly heart' to avenge them.

No men were allowed to live in their land. They chose husbands in neighbouring regions and went to them to beget children; male offspring were either killed or sent back to their fathers later, but daughters were kept and taught to shoot and hunt. Under a series of famous queens—Thamyris, Penthesilea (who was killed at *Troy), and others—they made their land into a great empire, and were much feared by the Greeks because of their skill in war. In The *Knight's Tale Chaucer simply records that Theseus laid siege to the land of the Amazons and married Hippolita, their queen (I.880).

AMBROSE, SEINT, St Ambrose (339–97), bishop of Milan (where the church he founded, which became the Romanesque basilica of San Ambrogio, containing his bones, could have been seen by Chaucer). An influential theologian, and a writer of hymns, he was one of the four learned doctors of the early Church (the others being St *Jerome, St Augustine (*Austyn(e))—whose conversion was partly due to Ambrose—and St Gregory the Great (*Gregorie)). He is quoted by the Second Nun (VIII.271) and by the Parson (X.84).

Amete, Admetus king of Pherae and husband of Alcestis (*Alceste).

Amphiorax, Amphiaraus (the -ax is probably a French spelling for -aus), an Argive hero who had taken part in the Calydonian boar hunt (see (*Meleagre) and the expedition of the Argonauts (see *Jason), and a great seer. His wife Eriphyle (*Eriphilem) was bribed into persuading him to become one of the Seven in their expedition against *Thebes (1), even though his foreknow-ledge told him that none of the Seven apart from *Adrastus would return alive. When he left he instructed his children to avenge his death by killing their mother and mounting another exped-ition. He was swallowed up in the earth and was later avenged by his son. It is his spectacular end which figures most prominently in Chaucer's allu-sions to him: he 'fil thorugh the grounde' in *Troilus and Criseyde (V.1500). Earlier, in the 'romaunce . . . of Thebes' which Criseyde and her ladies are reading, he has become a 'bisshop' and 'fil thorugh the ground to helle' (II.104–5).

Chaucer found the story in the *Thebaid of Statius (*Stace) and in the Fr. *Roman de Thèbes*—which also calls him a bishop (perhaps because this was the nearest Christian equivalent, and/or the head-dress thought to be worn by ancient high priests resembled a mitre). Because the treachery of his wife caused his death, her 'legend' is one of the stories that *Jankin (4) enjoyed telling the *Wife of Bath (III.740–6).

Amphioun, Amphion, son of Jupiter and Antiope, king of *Thebes (1) (with his twin brother), and husband of *Nyobe. He was a celebrated harper, who could make the stones move from their places. He is referred to in *The Canterbury Tales* both as a founder of Thebes (I.1546) and as a musician (IV.1716), who 'with his syngyng walled that citee' (IX.116).

ANAXAGORE. Anaxagoras (c.500–c.428 BC), was supposedly the first philosopher to live in Athens, having perhaps arrived there with Xerxes' army. With the aid of Pericles his friend, he sur-vived a charge of impiety and fled to Lampsacus, where he founded a school. He advocated what could be described as an organic equivalent of atomism. Fragments of his teaching were known largely from the writings of *Aristotle. A reference in *Boece* is only to his harassment and exile, for which the source was Diogenes Laertius. [JDN]

Anchises, the father of Aeneas (*Eneas), was car-ried by his son from the burning city of *Troy, and accompanied him on his journeyings, dying in Sicily. His escape is mentioned in the account of the *Aeneid* (see *Eneyde) given in The *House of Fame* (168–73) and again in the legend of *Dido in *The Legend of Good Women*, as is his meeting with his son in the underworld (HF 441–2).

ANDREAS CAPELLANUS is often thought (without certain evidence) to have been a chaplain at the court of Marie de Champagne in the 12th c. It now seems likely that he flourished in the fol-lowing century. His book *De arte honesti amandi* (or *De amore*) seems to have been popular. A mod-ern English translation calls it 'The Art of Court-ly Love', and it has often been taken as a straightforward guide to what has been termed the 'code' of *courtly love. This is misleading. It is very much in the tradition of *Ovid's writings on how to win love and how to get over it. The tone is witty and sceptical (bringing Ovid up to date, he says that he 'is not ignorant of the art of soliciting nuns'). Book I (addressed to an unidentified 'Walter') discusses the nature of love ('love is a certain inborn suffering derived from the sight of and excessive meditation upon the beauty of the opposite sex, which causes each one to wish above all things the embraces of the other and by common desire to carry out all of love's precepts in the other's embrace), and how to proceed. Book II is about how to retain it, concluding with a number of judgements made by the countess of Champagne in questions of love and a list of the rules of love (such as 'marriage is no real excuse for not loving', 'love is always a stranger in the house of avarice', 'every lover regularly turns pale in the presence of his beloved', 'real jealousy always increases the feeling of love'). Book III is a rejection of love, listing (with at least a show of seriousness) the reasons why a wise man should avoid it: it causes dissension and war, no woman can keep a secret, woman is fickle, every woman in the world is wanton, etc. Walter should prepare himself for his heavenly Bridegroom, of whose coming we know neither the day nor the hour.

(ed.) Trojel (1892); (trans.) J. J. Parry (1941); P. G. Walsh (1982); Dronke (1994).

Androgeus the son of Minos and Pasiphae (*LGW* 1896), sent to school in Athens, was killed there 'lernynge philosophie'—out of envy, says Chaucer. *Gower says it was because of his pride in his achievements.

Andromacha, Andromache, the wife of Hector (*Ector). The story of her prophetic dream of her husband's death (VII.3141-8) comes from *Dares, not from ancient sources.

Anelida and Arcite, a poem of 350 or 357 lines on Anelida, the queen of Armenia (*Ermony) and 'fals Arcite'. After an elaborate invocation to *Mars and *Pallas as the armed goddess of war, the *Muse Polyhymnia (*Polymya), and a description of the triumphant return of *Theseus to Athens, the scene shifts to *Thebes (1), where Anelida is

dwelling. Arcite wins her love, but is false to her 'of his newfangelnesse', and cruelly overbearing. He abandons the devoted faithful Anelida for another lady (who turns out to be cruel and disdainful towards him). Anelida in despair makes a *complaint, a formal lament of fourteen intricate stanzas, which in its emotional intensity and eloquence is probably Chaucer's most successful piece of writing in this kind. A further stanza which appears in only four of the twelve MSS seems to move us back to the story, and promise a continuation, but the authenticity of this stanza has been strongly questioned. If it is simply a scribal addition, the poem would have the form of a complaint with a brief introductory narrative setting (as *The Complaint unto *Pity* and *The Complaint unto *Mars*). The introduction to the 'pitous' love situation asserts the function of the art of poetry in preserving (as does *memory) material which would otherwise be lost through time and age 'which that al can frete [devour] and bite | As hit hath freten mony a noble story'. Most critics are agreed that it was written before *The Canterbury Tales,* possibly in the 1370s, but it has elements in common with *Troilus and Criseyde* and *The Legend of Good Women,* and may have been written in that period. The opening uses *Boccacio's *Teseida,* the source of *The *Knight's Tale*; it may well be that Chaucer invented the central story.

(ed.) *Rv* 375-81, 991-3; Scattergood (1995), 469-73; Norton-Smith (1981).

angels (Greek 'messenger'), spiritual beings enjoying the vision of God in heaven. (After their creation, *Lucifer, the brightest of the angels, because of his pride challenged God and was cast down with his followers, the 'fallen angels', to become the *devil.) Traditionally, there were 'orders' of angels: three hierarchies each containing three choirs (Seraphim, Cherubim, Thrones; Dominations, Virtues, Powers; Principalities, Archangels, Angels). The two lowest orders acted as God's messengers to men. Angels are above the vicissitudes of the sublunary world and of *Fortune ('Fortune may no angel dere [harm]' says the Monk, VII.2001). In the Middle Ages there was much interest in them (they belonged mysteriously both to the world of heaven and that of earth, and in appearance had attributes both of men and of birds) and an intense belief in them as spiritual powers working in the world (like their adversaries the evil demons). A 'guardian angel' was assigned to each individual as protector. Angels were frequently represented in art, worshipping in heaven (singing and playing instruments) or taking part in great spiritual events on earth. Especially endowed with spiritual power were the great archangels *Gabriel who came to Mary (*Marie) in the Annunciation (see *Angelus ad Virginem*), *Raphael, and Michael (see *Michelmesse*), a mighty warrior against the devil and a mighty intercessor (often shown slaying the dragon or weighing souls at the Last Judgement). They were often depicted with feathered wings 'angels that ben fethered brighte' *Rom* 742), and sometimes with peacock feathers (hence the allusion in *PF* 356 'the pecok, with his aungel fetheres bryghte'). It is not clear that the 'fyr-reed cherubynnes face' of the *Summoner (I.624) is a reference to any particular iconographic tradition or specific illustration, but it is possible that Chaucer was thinking of the gleaming gold ('red' gold, or gold applied over a red ground), faces they were sometimes given in pictures or in play masks. In Chaucer's narratives angels rarely make an appearance: one comes to *Cecilia and Valerian in *The *Second Nun's Tale*, and gives them crowns of roses and lilies which he has brought from Paradise; in a rather different context, the *Summoner refers merrily (III.1676–703) to another who showed a *friar in a vision how twenty thousand friars lived under the devil's tail in hell. The God of Love (see *Cupide), when he appears in *The *Legend of Good Women*, looks like an angel (and is frequently so depicted in art)—'aungelyke hys wynges saugh I sprede' (236). Because angels were constantly associated with heavenly harmony and beauty, the word and its derivatives were commonly used as hyperbole. This is not always simply proverbial or formulaic—there are cases where the word may be fully meaningful or at least have strong undertones. In *The *Parliament of Fowls* the harmony of the birds' song is angelic ('with voys of aungel in here armonye', 191). This detail and the whole scene is reminiscent of the visions of the Otherworld, where the heavenly noise of the birds is often noted. Similarly, the natural beauty of

*Criseyde was 'so aungelik . . . That lik a thing inmortal semed she' (*Tr* I.102–3), and *Emelye in *The Knight's Tale* (whom Palamon at first sight thinks to be a goddess) 'as an aungel hevenysshly . . . soong'.

Angelus ad Virginem, a religious song on the Annunciation which *Nicholas in *The *Miller's Tale* (I.3216) likes to sing at night in his chamber. Like a number of these songs to the Virgin Mary, it has affinities with songs of secular love ('the angel secretly entering her chamber, softly overcoming the virgin's fear, says to her "Hail!"'). It is tempting to suppose that Nicholas warms as much to this element in the song as to the devotional content (though he does not go as far as Frate Alberto, who in a famous story in the *Decameron* wins the favours of a lady by pretending to be the angel Gabriel).

animals (see also *birds, *Nature). Medieval people, like the people of traditional societies today, lived close to the animal world. A firmly non-romantic attitude to animals produced examples of cruelty, but there is also evidence of understanding and even affection. Man was superior, since he had reason, but he had an intimate and mysterious relationship with the animal world, since there was no human quality (whether courage or timidity or meekness or malice) which did not have its equivalent in animals. Familiarity with animals often brought a precision of observation which finds expression in many sketches, marginal drawings, and carvings in the later Middle Ages, and a curiosity which could be scientific. Medieval popular science took over animal lore from the ancient world. *Bartholomew gives a long account of the diverse qualities of animals: some are gentle, like the sheep, some wild like the tiger, some bold and proud like the lion, others guileful like the wolf or the fox. There is the same diversity in their food and in their cries. Popular tradition handed on these stereotyped animal 'characters'. Since animals were both close to man and yet unalterably different, it is not surprising that they could be charged with symbolism or significance in folklore, in homely similitudes and proverbs, and in works like the *Bestiary* which interpreted them as part of the book of nature.

Animals could be heraldic or astronomical, magical (e.g. they were used for foretelling the future), or mystical (some have a particular affinity with *saints, whom they help in various ways).

The natural world had been created for the use of man. Animals provide food, and remedies for human infirmities. Others are there to remind man of his own weakness and of the power of God; or are created for man's amusement, 'as apes and marmosets and parrots'. Even these, however, can carry messages to man, and not necessarily flattering ones. That animals provide entertainment as well as instruction helps to account for the popularity of animal stories, especially those that feign that 'beestes and briddes koude speke and synge' (VII.2881) (see *fable; *Renard).

Animals of diverse species are everywhere in *Chaucer, as are the dissensions and hostilities of the animal world, the ancient principle of 'contraries' in nature—'For natureelly a beest desireth flee | Fro his contrarie, if he may it see, | Though he never erst had seyn it with his ye' (VII.3279–81).

Tame animals include those animals common in and about medieval houses or farms. Significantly the *Pardoner claims that one of the relics he is selling will cure the illnesses of any domestic cow, calf, or sheep (VI.352–60). That names are given to some of the animals—the sheep Malle ('Molly'), the dogs Colle, Talbot, and Gerland, the horses Brok (= badger, because it was grey) and Scot (III.1543; see also *Bayard)—is another testimony to the closeness of man and beast. The familiarity can be seen in various colloquial remarks and locutions: alchemists, says the Canon's Yeoman, can be recognized by their strong smell—'they stynken as a goot', their smell is 'rammyssh' (VIII.886–7).

Of the domestic animals, the *sheep* is traditionally inoffensive, and the *lamb* especially has a strong symbolic charge: 'among all the beasts of the earth' says Bartholomew, 'the lamb is the most innocent, soft, and mild' (cf. II.617–18; IV.538; *Former Age* 50). It was the image of Christ 'the white Lamb, that hurt was with a spere' (II.459; cf. VII.581–4). Tradition was less kind to the *pig*, accounted 'foul and unhonest'. Two men fighting (I.4278) 'walwe [wallow] as doon two pigges in a poke [bag]', and both the Wife of Bath and the Parson quote the Old Testament proverb 'as a

jewel of gold in a swine's snout, so is a fair woman which is without discretion' (Prov. 11:22). One of the more unusual domestic disasters depicted in the temple of *Mars in *The Knight's Tale* is the sow devouring the child in the cradle (I.2019). *Dogs* appear in a number of domestic references or similitudes: they eat the crumbs that fall from the lord's table (VIII.60) or fight over the proverbial bone (I.1177). More fashionable are the hounds used for hunting (as in *The *Book of the Duchess*, or the swift greyhounds owned by the Monk, I.190). The puppy which acts as a guide in *The Book of the Duchess* is associated with the hunt, but its friendly fawning suggests a household pet or a lapdog—like those which the *Prioress fed with exquisite food (I.146–9). (In early literature she is an unusually devoted pet-lover.) Chaucer does not use stories of the dog's high-minded faithfulness. The *cat* is a more ambiguous creature, belonging to the world of the wild as well as to that of the house, in which, as a mouse-catcher, it had made itself at home: the carpenter peers into Nicholas's room through a hole 'ther as the cat was wont to crepe' (I.3441); another cat is rudely swept off the bench by a visiting friar (III.1775). Its passion for its natural 'contrary' the *mouse* is remarked on by the Manciple to illustrate the workings of natural desire: even if the cat has been nourished with milk and tender meat and given a bed of silk, 'lat hym seen a mous go by the wal, | Anon he weyveth [refuses] milk and flessh and al . . . | Swich appetit hath he to ete a mous' (IX.176–80). (The medieval mouse was proverbially 'drunken' (I.1261, etc.), and was then, as later, thought to be 'cow'rin' and 'tim'rous'—hence the expression 'mouse's heart' (*Tr* III.736; cf. III.572).) If the cat did not catch it, it might be caught in a trap—to the distress of the tender-hearted Prioress (I.144). The *horse*, like the dog, was an animal which came in more and less fashionable grades, and a variety of shapes for differing purposes. Chaucer uses a number of words (e.g. *capul*, *stede*, *stot*) for different varieties: *amblere* ambling horse (on which the Wife of Bath sat 'easily'); *courser* or *dextrer* a charger, a warhorse; *hakeney* a 'hackney' or small riding horse; *jade* a nag, a horse of poor quality (ridden by the Nun's Priest); *palfrey* a riding horse; *rouncy* another riding horse (used by the Shipman; possibly a big horse). Chaucer assumes a knowledge of horses in his audience: they will not be surprised that there are wild horses in the Cambridgeshire fens (I.4059–66), and they will understand the allusion when the *Pardoner is called 'a geldyng or a mare' (I.691).

The horse drew carts (cf. the scene in The *Friar's Tale*, III.1539 ff.), and was used for travel, hunting (hence the prized horses in the Monk's stable (I.168)), and in tournaments and war. The old association of a knight with his most significant piece of equipment is preserved in the word 'chivalry' (*chivalree). When Troilus rides back from battle on his 'baye steede' in *Troilus* II.624–51 it is a fine knightly sight. In sharp contrast with a practised rider's skill demonstrating man with his reason in control of the animal world, is the drunken Cook falling off his horse. Legendary horses mentioned include the Trojan horse, the horses of the Sun (*Bo* III m.1) and of Cynthia (*Tr* V.1018), the winged horse Pegasus (*Pegasee), and the horse of brass in *The Squire's Tale* (which is so well made that it is 'horsly' and 'quyk of ye'). Many of the horses of the pilgrims in the *General Prologue* seem appropriate to their riders—the Knight has a good horse, while the horsy Monk's bridle jingles louder than a chapel bell, and the Clerk's animal actually resembles its owner in its gauntness (I.287–8). Not surprisingly, similitudes involving horses are common, and range from the simple— the drunken miller snores ('as an hors he fnorteth in his sleep' (I. 4163; cf. II.790) and the Wife of Bath says (III. 386) 'as an hors I koude byte and whyne')—to the elaborate image of Bayard in *Troilus* (I.218–24).

Wild animals include those that are hunted (see *hunting): the *hare*; the *deer* (as in *BD*); the *wild boar* (a standard image of ferocity) (cf. I.1658, III.2160, etc.), which also appears in a symbolic dream (*Tr* V.1238 ff.). Others intrude on the shelter of the yard, like the *polecat* (VI.855) or the *fox*— well known in literature and legend as a false trickster—which almost finishes off *Chauntecleer. Without the ingenuity of the more ambiguous fox is the *wolf*, lurking 'in the briars' (X.720), fairly easily outwitted as a *fable shows (I.4055). Some creatures are singled out in the symbolic structure as particularly evil or venemous, like the *toad* (cf. X.636). The *serpent* (associated with Satan (cf. VII.558), and inheriting the bad

reputation of its antecedents in classical myth (*Idra, *Phitoun)) 'slily crepeth' under the grass and 'styngeth subtilly' (III.1994–5; cf. V.512–13). It is used to describe the wicked sultaness in *The Man of Law's Tale* (II.360–1). The *scorpion* 'deceyvable', which ancient proverbial lore thought to be pleasant and flattering in appearance while preparing to sting with its tail, is a common figure of treachery, and is applied to Fortune (IV.2057–64 and *BD* 636–41) and to treacherous people (II.404, IX.271).

Apes were a source of entertainment and of instruction. Bartholomew says that they love to imitate the actions of men (whom they resemble in certain respects), and can be kept to amuse them with their grimaces and tricks. They can also be used as patterns of ugliness or folly. The skull of the miller in *The Reeve's Tale* is 'piled [bald] as an ape' (I. 3935). And the word *ape* in Chaucer's English can mean 'fool' or 'dupe': the Pardoner made the parson and the people his 'apes' (I.706; cf. also X.650, *Tr* I.913). A man can be 'ape-drunk' (IX.44), one of the stages of drunkenness. The ape provides one of the Parson's few jokes (though a highly satirical one): he notes (X.423) that men's short jackets reveal tightly cut hose 'and eek the buttokes of hem faren as it were the hyndre part of a she-ape in the fulle of the moone' (when apes were thought to display themselves thus).

Among more exotic wild animals are the *camel* (only referred to in IV.1196, where wives are urged to be 'strong as is a greet camaille'); the *leopard* (particularly exotic, cf. I.2186, VII.2261); and the *tiger* (especially 'cruel' and fierce). The *lion* (or the 'wilde lyonesse' which in the story of Thisbe (*Tisbe) leaves the marks of its 'steppes brode') is fierce (providing a standard similitude, e.g. I. 1598, VIII.198; the Wife of Bath was 'stubborn as a lioness', III.637). It brings from antiquity a reputation for courage (VII.2646) and nobility. It has a 'gentil kynde' which makes it a pattern for a good king or lord (see *LGW* 391–6). Exotic wild animals are the neighbours of the legendary and the monstrous: the *mermaid*, which could not sing as merrily as Chauntecleer (cf. *Rom* 679–84); the *griffin* (I.2133); the *centauris; or the *Mynotaur. Chaucer also knew stories of humans transformed into beasts (see *Attheon, *Calistopee, *Circes), and of Midas (*Myda) with his long asses' ears.

Chaucer makes good use of this extensive menagerie. His animal fables in *The Nun's Priest's Tale* and *The Manciple's Tale* stand out, but there are less obvious examples. He does not give us an abstract discussion of the relationship of humans to animals (though there is a striking moment when Palamon, imprisoned, asks the 'cruel gods', 'What is mankynde moore unto you holde | Than is the sheep that rouketh [cowers] in the folde?' (I.1307–81)), but prefers to use the traditional symbolism in a more allusive way. There are the proverbial metaphors of ordinary colloquial speech—'Fox that ye ben!' says Criseyde to Pandarus (*Tr* III.1565) alongside the occasional more recondite image (as when 'fawns' in *Tr* I.465 are apparently 'young desires'; cf. also *Tr* II.964). In the animal world Chaucer finds some of his most vivid and intense images or similes: Troilus in agony like a wild bull in its death throes (*Tr* IV.239–45), the Pardoner's eyes staring wide like those of a hare (I.684), the glutton 'fat as a whale, and walkynge as a swan' (III.1930), or Absolon lusting after Alison—'if she hadde been a mous, | And he a cat, he wolde hire hente anon' (I.3346–7). Sometimes he will point a description with a startlingly precise detail: an old husband's face, newly shaven, is like the skin of a dogfish (IV.1825), a miller's beard red 'as the brustles of a sowes erys' (I.556).

Janson (1952); Klingender (1971); Rowland (1971); Yamamoto (2000).

Anne (1), St Anne the mother of the Virgin Mary (often shown in paintings teaching the Virgin to read). She became a popular saint in the later Middle Ages; the patron of various religious guilds in England, she had an important shrine at Buxton. In honour of the marriage of *Richard II and *Anne of Bohemia (Jan. 1382) Pope Urban VI ordered her feast day to be observed throughout England. In Chaucer she is simply mentioned as the Virgin's mother (II.641, VIII.70), and is once used in an *oath (III.1613).

Anne (2), the sister of *Dido.

ANNE OF BOHEMIA, first wife of Richard II, whom she married in January 1382; she was the daughter of the Emperor Charles IV; she died 7 June 1394. Lydgate in *Fall of Princes* (I.330 ff.)

states that Chaucer wrote 'at request off the queen, | A legende off parfit hoolynesse, | Off Goode Women', who must from the date of *The Legend of Good Women* have been Anne; this may be an unwarranted deduction from the more modest indication by Chaucer himself (Prologue F 496–7), where he relates Alceste's command to write the book of *goode women* and 'whan this book ys maad, yive it the quene, | On my byhalf, at Eltham or at Sheene'.   [AH]

anni collecti, expansi, see *yere.

ANSELM, SEINT, archbishop of Canterbury 1093–1109; originally from Lombardy, but for thirty years before his consecration to Canterbury he had been prior of Bec. Nowadays chiefly remembered for his theological works, including the *Monologion*, *Proslogion*, and *Cur Deus Homo*, but in the medieval period his devotional writings (including apocryphal texts) were as frequently cited. One of the latter is quoted in the *Parson's Tale* (X.169–73).   [AH]

Antaeus; Anteclaudian. See *Antheus; *Aleyn (1).

Antecrist. The Antichrist, the leader of Christ's enemies mentioned in the New Testament, was early identified with various persecutors and enemies of the faithful—Antiochus Epiphanes (*Anthiochus) from the Old Testament, *Nero, *Simon Magus, etc. Using imagery from the Book of Revelation (such as the dragon with seven heads) and Apocalyptic tradition (see *Apocalips(e)), medieval legends made him into a combination of persecutor-tyrant and pseudo-Christ. As the end of the world draws near, Antichrist will pretend to be the Messiah, deceive the ignorant, and persecute the faithful before he is finally destroyed by Christ. In Chaucer, he is referred to only once, linked with *Lucifer, by the *Parson (X.788).

Emmerson (1984).

Antenor(e), Anthenor, Antenor, one of the elders of *Troy, who was in favour of restoring Helen to the Greeks because she had been taken treacherously. Later legend made him into a traitor who betrayed the city to the Greeks by sending the Palladium (*Palladion), on which the city's safety depended, to Ulysses. He appears in a list of famous traitors in *The Book of the Duchess* 1119, and is several times mentioned in *Troilus and Criseyde*: he was captured by the Greeks, and it is a bitter irony (underlined by the narrator (IV.197–210) that the Trojans decide that he should be brought back in exchange for Criseyde.

Antheus, Antaeus, a giant, the son of *Neptune and Ge or Gaia, the Earth. A great wrestler, formidable because each time he was thrown and touched his mother his strength increased. He was killed by Hercules (*Ercules), who lifted him up and crushed him (VII.2108, *Bo* IV m.7:51).

ANTHIOCHUS, Antiochus Epiphanes, king of Syria and surrounding territories (reigned 175–163 BC); desiring to unify his people and resist Rome, he tried to abolish the Jewish religion, which provoked the revolt of the Maccabees. In the Middle Ages he was frequently taken to be a prefiguration of the Antichrist (*Antecrist). The Book of Daniel (*Danyel) comes from his time. His story (from the Book of Maccabees (*Machabee (2))) is told in The *Monk's Tale (VII.2575–630). He is presented as an 'overreacher' who in his pride thought that he could reach the stars, weigh every mountain, and restrain all 'the floodes of the see', besides persecuting God's people. God punished him with an invisible and incurable wound; further torments included 'wikked wormes' creeping through his body, so that he stank so horribly that no one could endure the smell, and he died 'ful wrecchedly'.

Anticlaudianus, see *Aleyn (1).

Antigone, the niece of Criseyde. (Chaucer seems to have invented her, perhaps taking the name from one of the heroines of antiquity, either the Antigone of the story of *Thebes (1) or the Antigone in *Ovid's *Metamorphoses* who was changed into a bird.) In *Troilus and Criseyde* II.824–96 she reassures Criseyde, answering her doubts about committing herself to love by singing (so 'that it an heven was hire vois to here') a 'Trojan song' in praise of *love, its power, its virtue, and its joy.

Antylegyus, a companion of *Achilles, slain with him in a temple to which they had gone for the marriage of Achilles and Polyxena (*BD* 1069). (The name is a corruption of Antilochus, which itself is an error for Archilochus.)

Antiochus (1), king of Antioch in the story of Apollonius of Tyre (*Appollonius); the 'cursed kyng' who 'birafte his doghter of hir maydenhede' (II.82–5).

ANTIOCHUS (2), see *Anthiocus.

ANTONY, ANTONIUS, Mark Anthony (Marcus Antonius, *c.*82–30 BC), the Roman general who became the lover (husband, according to Chaucer and a couple of other medieval sources) of Cleopatra (*Cleopatre). In The *Legend of Good Women* (580–705) he is presented as a 'ful worthy, gentil' warrior, but 'rebel unto the toun of Rome', and a man who 'falsely' left his wife, 'the suster of Cesar' (Octavia). Defeated at the battle of Actium by Octavius (*Octovyan), he took his own life.

ANTONY, SEINT, OF EGYPT (251–356), an ascetic and abbot, who endured a series of spectacular temptations, became a very popular saint in the Middle Ages, renowned especially for his healing powers. His relics were taken to Alexandria (*Alisaundre), but other places claimed them, like La Motte in France, where there was a pilgrimage centre for sufferers from 'St Anthony's fire' or erysipelas, a severe inflammation of the skin, causing a deep red colour. The hospitallers would ring small bells as they rode about asking for alms; these bells were later hung around the necks of animals to protect them from disease. Their pigs were allowed to roam freely in the streets. Hence the iconography of the saint includes both bells and pigs (and in 16th–17th c. English the smallest pig in the litter was called a 'tantony'). The only reference in Chaucer is to the disease and its colour: the *Parson, railing against tightly cut male clothes which reveal the 'shameful privee membres', singles out for special mention those which accentuate this by being particoloured (white and black or white and blue or black and *red*)—'thanne semeth it . . . that half the partie of hire privee membres were corrupt by the fir of Seint Antony, or by cancre, or by oother swich meschaunce' (X.427).

ANTONYUS. Antoninus (Caracalla), the Roman emperor (188–217), mentioned in *Boece* (III pr.5:49) not because of his famous Baths in Rome, but because his action in having the jurist Papinian thrown to the soldiers' swords, is an example of the uncertain position of the friends of kings.

Apennyn, the Apennines, the mountain range in Italy, the 'hilles hye' which mark the boundary of Lombardy (*Lumbardye) (IV.45).

Apes; Apelles. See *animals; *Appelles.

Apius, Appius, the false judge in *The Physician's Tale.*

Apius and Virginia, a play by 'R. B.' (registered in 1567) reworks the story of *The *Physician's Tale* in the manner of a late morality play (see *drama), with a nimble, wicked Vice, Haphazard, who disputes with Conscience for the soul of the unjust judge.

Apocalips(e), the biblical Book of Revelation (the meaning of the Greek word), a series of visions traditionally but probably wrongly attributed to St John the Apostle. Its vivid but enigmatic revelation of hidden things made it a favourite with people fascinated by *prophecy and the coming end of the world. Its striking images were well known and were often depicted in art—the four beasts 'full of eyes' around the throne of God, the vision of the New Jerusalem, etc. It inspired other apocalyptic writing, which developed the notion of six ages of the world, and drew attention to key events which represented cataclysmic points of change from one age to another or were signs of the end (e.g. the ravages of the Tartars (see *Tartarye)). Chaucer does not show any interest in apocalyptic or millenarian prophecy, but he refers to the vision of the four beasts and their eyes in *The House of Fame (1381–5), and the book is quoted once by the Parson (X.136) (see *Antecrist).

Apocryphal works, see *Canon of Chaucer's Works; *Chauceriana.

Apollo, Appollo, the Greek god, conceived to embody almost every manly virtue associated with high civilization—for example a mastery of music, philosophy, archery, justice, religion, and medicine. (Isidore of Seville (*c.*570–636) made him out to be the inventor of medicine, and Aesculapius his son to have continued in the art. Cf. Chaucer's 'olde Esculapius', *General Prologue* I.429.) As early as the 5th c. BC it was argued that Apollo was the Sun, and this association continued in Greek and Roman literature, to be passed on to the Middle Ages. Apollo had several oracles, the chief being at Delphi. (From *The *Franklin's Tale* as well as *Troilus and Criseyde*, it appears that Chaucer thought 'Delphos' to be the location of Phebus' (Apollo's) temple, perhaps confusing it with Delos, the god's birthplace. See **Cynthea**.) In Roman art Apollo is generally a god of healing, and in *The Franklin's Tale* Chaucer seems to be taking from Ovid's *Metamorphoses* the notion that he is a god of herbs. In late antiquity and the Middle Ages he is, however, usually depicted or described as a youth with bow or lyre, often together with the huntress Artemis (the Roman Diana (*Dyane)) his sister.

From early times Apollo was associated with the solar deity Phoebus (in Greek 'the shining one'), and as a result the name Phœbus Apollo occurs often. Chaucer uses the names more or less indifferently of the god, but prefers 'Phebus' for the Sun. Apollo is mentioned in the penultimate line of the (interrupted) *Squire's Tale,* there being a personification of the Sun, and described in accordance with standard medieval iconography as drawn in a chariot. [JDN]

Appelles, Apelles, according to the 12th-c. *Alexandreis* of Walter of Chatillon, a legendary Jewish sculptor who made an elaborate tomb for Darius (*Daryus (1)). He is cited as a great artist (and it is possible that he has been conflated with the historical Greek painter Apelles, a favourite of Alexander the Great). The *Wife of Bath refers to him (III.499), saying that her fourth husband's tomb is less 'curyus' than the one he made so 'subtilly'; and he appears (with *Pigmalion and

Appollonius

*Zanzis (1)) in Nature's list of the great artists of the ancient world, who are still not skilful enough to 'countrefete' her.

Appollonius, the hero of the story of *Apollonius of Tyre*. This tale, briefly alluded to by the Man of Law (II.81–5), seems to go back to a Greek *romance (typically involving separated families, supposed deaths, and shipwrecks). It was very popular in the Middle Ages, circulating in many versions in Latin and the vernaculars. It is used by *Gower as the final story in his *Confessio Amantis*, and his version is the basis of Shakespeare's *Pericles*. A wicked king of Antioch lies with his beautiful daughter, and keeps her for himself by requiring any suitor to answer a riddle or die. Apollonius, the prince of Tyre, comes to the country, understands the riddle (which refers to the incest), but because the answer would reveal the king's guilt, and fearing the king's treachery, he flees. After many adventures and sorrows he finally finds happiness.

Aquarie, Aquarius, the eleventh sign of the Zodiac. (See also *signe; *Zodiak.)

Aquilon, Aquilo (in *Boece*), the north wind (see *Boreas).

Arabe, Araby, Arabia, 'a province of Asia' according to *Bartholomew, who mentions its spices and gems, which were important to Western Europe, as well as that it is the home of the mythical *bird, the Phoenix (see *Fenix). The inhabitants of the Arabian peninsula were the first converts to Islam in the 7th c. and began the great waves of Arab expansion along the coasts of North Africa, to Sicily and southern Italy and to Spain (*Spaigne). The Arabs had a great influence on Western cultural history, especially in the rediscovery of Greek philosophy, science, and medicine, to which they added their own contributions (see *science, *medicine). The Arabian peninsula itself by the 14th c. was ruled by the Mamelukes of *Egypt. The few references to Arabia (or Arabs, or Arabic) in Chaucer are either scientific (in the *Astrolabe), or to it as an exotic land. Thus it is mentioned in *The Book of the Duchess* 982 as the home of the phoenix, and in

*The *Squire's Tale* (V.110) the stranger knight announces that the steed of brass is a present from his liege lord, 'the kyng of Arabe and of *Inde'. This land seems to be what was sometimes called 'Middle India', i.e. southern Arabia or Aden.

Aragon, province in north-east Spain, formerly the kingdom of Aragon, which was united, by royal marriage, with Catalonia in 1137, a union which lasted until 1410. The trumpeting referred to by Chaucer in *The *House of Fame* (III.1248), was apparently a characteristic feature both of Aragonese and Catalan ceremonial.   [PS]

Arcadye, Arcadia in Greece, a mountainous region in the Peloponnese, mentioned in *Boece* (IV m.3:18) as the birthplace of Mercury.

Archymoris, possessive form of Archemorus (or Opheltes), the infant son of King Lycurgus of Nemea. On the way to Thebes (1), he was killed by a serpent while his nurse, *Hypsipyle, was directing the Greeks to the river Langia. His funeral rites (the 'brennynge' referred to in *Tr* V.1499) are described in the *Thebaid* of Statius (*Stace).

architecture (see also *visual arts). Chaucer's was an age of great architecture, and one in which building was extensive and ambitious. As Joan Evans says, 'to the men of the fourteenth and fifteenth centuries building was in itself a good act; if ecclesiastical, it glorified God, if secular, it was part of good administration.' A medieval builder could become a rich and important man. In 14th-c. England, William Wynford, the architect of the nave of Winchester, and Hugh Herland, the king's carpenter, are commemorated in the east window of Winchester College. They and Henry Yevele—perhaps the most famous English architect of the century, who worked at Canterbury and Westminster Abbey (for which he received payments from Chaucer, the Clerk of the Works, from 1389 to 1391)—were in close contact with the powerful *William of Wykeham during the construction of his foundations New College, Oxford, and Winchester College.

The buildings Chaucer could see around him—and not only in England, but on his journeys to

France, Italy, and Spain—included palaces and great halls, civic and defensive buildings, churches in the Romanesque or Norman styles, and newer edifices in the Gothic style which had developed in the 12th c. In these the weight of stone vaulting was carried on pointed arches and ribs, buttressed outside to permit slender columns within, and the building could soar to a great height. Windows became very large, and were filled with stained glass glorifying God with a radiance of light. England in the 14th c. was beginning to adapt French Gothic in distinctive ways, both in the 'Decorated' style (c.1290–1350) and in the later, distinctively English 'Perpendicular' style with its high soaring lines and its fan-vaulting (as in the choir of Gloucester Abbey, the choir at York, and the naves of Winchester and Canterbury.

In the more prosperous areas of the country, parish churches were being built (or rebuilt or extended, like St Mary Redcliffe at Bristol). These churches, large and small, were filled with fine woodwork, rood-screens, stained glass, wall-paintings, and brasses. There were also the large churches of the preaching friars, and private chapels (like St George's Chapel, Windsor, repairs to which were supervised by Chaucer as Clerk of the Works in 1390), chantries (where masses were sung for the souls of the dead), and academic halls and hostels, like the 14th-c. quadrangle (Mob Quad) and library of Merton College, Oxford, or New College (built in the last twenty years of the century).

Castles were beginning to differ in conception and appearance from their predecessors, although they usually retained some defensive function. Some older castles were modified: at Kenilworth a very grand domestic hall, some 90 feet (30 m) long, was built for *John of Gaunt (c.1392). The gatehouse was still a necessary defensive building, found also at abbeys (as that of Bury St Edmunds, which has been described as 'half fortress and half church'), and in city walls, as at London's *Aldgate, where Chaucer lived for a time. Even a building built for domestic use, like Broughton Castle in Oxfordshire (begun c.1300) had a moat and a gatehouse. Smaller manor houses which did not have to house a great retinue, had, in addition to the living quarters of the lord and his family, a hall where many of the household used to eat, be

entertained, and sleep. It sometimes had a fire-place in the wall, sometimes simply a hearth in the centre of the floor (with the smoke escaping through a louvre in the roof). At one end, a screen would protect the hall from the entrance; on the outer side of it were doors for the pantry, the but-tery, and the kitchen (if this was not in a separate building), above it often a gallery, which could be used by minstrels at feasts. At the other end was the dais and the high table, at which the lord and his family ate. This design survives in the halls of the older Oxford and Cambridge colleges.

There were other types of domestic and secular buildings—royal palaces, episcopal palaces, mer-chants' houses like that of the wool merchant William Grevel (d. 1401), which still survives at Chipping Camden, Glos., or the smaller ones scattered around in the Cotswolds. Humbler dwellings have not usually survived, but there is, for instance, the Fish House at Meare, Somerset, built in the early 14th c. by the Abbot of Glaston-bury for his fisherman. By continental standards, many English civic buildings probably looked modest, but there was the very large and impres-sive Westminster Hall, where parliaments and great feasts and pageants were held. The recon-struction of this ancient palace was begun in 1393, with Yevele and Wynford as master masons. Hugh Herland's famous hammerbeam roof (c.1399) was the largest in Europe. A very great deal has been lost—not simply the small, humble timber-built houses, but a number of the most important buildings that Chaucer saw, such as the royal palace at Sheen (*Sheene), old St Paul's, a fine Gothic cathedral, or the royal palace at Woodstock.

All this is part of the landscape of Chaucer's narratives; he refers to abbeys and parish churches (like the Wife of Bath's, where her fourth husband lay buried under the rood-beam), cottages, houses, castles, and palaces. Sometimes the layout of a building is important for the plot: in The *Miller's Tale the carpenter's Oxford house is commodious, providing a separate room for his lodger, an open-roofed hall, a bower (for the carpenter and his wife) with a 'shot-window' (probably a case-ment), rooms (perhaps under the roof) for the ser-vants, and a stable in the garden; in The *Reeve's Tale the miller's Trumpington house is decidedly incommodious. We are told in some detail how *Pandarus arranged his rooms for the meeting of the lovers: Criseyde is to sleep in a 'closet', a small inner room (normally Pandarus's bedroom) with a fireplace, opening out of the hall; the hall is divided by a 'travers', a screen or curtain, into two rooms—the 'myddel chaumbre' for her women, and an 'outer hous' where Pandarus will sleep. Sometimes the larger social function of the house is central: the *fabliaux in Fragment I of *The Canterbury Tales* make comic use of the idea of '*herbergage'—lodging and lodgers. The contrast of humble cottage and royal palace is sharply pointed in *The *Clerk's Tale*. Some more exotic buildings which Chaucer mentions also have a larger significance. The elaborate description of the huge amphitheatre ('a noble theatre'), a mile in circumference, which is created for the tournament in *The Knight's Tale* is taken from the *Teseida*. (*Boccaccio may well have had the Colosseum in mind.) However, there are significant differences: in Chaucer, it is specially built for the occasion; it is even grander, incorporating other structures, the temples of the gods; and Theseus has deliberately placed it on the spot at which the two young knights have been discovered earlier in disorderly combat, as if, as Kolve says, 'he proposes to lay down upon these woods a vast circle of marble, measured and shaped by the human mind, within whose perfect form he will ordain the most ceremonial and highly structured of all forms of human combat' (p. 112). Whether or not Chaucer ever saw an amphitheatre, the lists set up inside it were a construction with which he was very familiar—in May 1390 he supervised the building of scaffolds for jousts at Smithfield.

Chaucer does not share the interest of religious writers in the allegorical House or Castle of the Soul, but he is aware of the symbolic or metaphorical possibilities of buildings. At the end of Book I of *Troilus and Criseyde* he quotes the comparison which Geoffrey of Vinsauf (*Gaufred) makes between the architect, who does not rush hastily into the work of construction, but creates in his mind the whole idea before he begins, and the poet. The most obviously 'meaningful' buildings are to be found in his dream visions. The chamber in which the dreamer in *The *Book of the Duchess* finds himself, with its painted walls and (unusually for a secular building) its stained glass, at first seems luxurious and strange rather than symbolic: it seems primarily to contrast with the beautiful temperate natural world into which he passes. It is a brief example of the rhetorical device of ecphrasis (the detailed description—especially of a work of art): the dreamer is leaving the images of art (the story of Troy and Jason on the walls, that of the *Romance of the Rose* in the windows) for the world of '*experience'. In *The *Parliament of Fowls* there is an even stronger contrast between the temperate world of *Nature (whose 'halls' and 'bowers' are made of branches) and the magnificently 'artful' temple of *Venus, made of brass set on pillars of jasper, in the interior of which is a wall painted with the stories of unhappy lovers.

More elaborate still is the use of buildings in *The *House of Fame*. Here, the structure is, in part at least, determined by three allegorical houses. The dreamer first finds himself in a temple made of glass, richly decorated with golden images: its canopied niches ('tabernacles'), pinnacles of precious stones, and finely wrought pictures suggest a kind of dreamlike and heightened version of an elaborately decorated late medieval church or civic building. On one wall he finds written in a table of brass the story of the *Aeneid* (*Eneyde). The building is the temple of Venus; it is set, as he discovers when he goes outside, in the midst of a desert. The general idea for it comes from *Virgil's account of the citadel of Juno (*Aeneid* 1), which contains incidents from the fall of Troy. Chaucer's building is made of glass, that fragile product of art, as easily broken as is the kind of love that Aeneas has for Dido (cf. the contrast made between appearance ('apparence') and reality ('existence') in 265–6). In the celestial regions to which he is taken by the Eagle, the dreamer finds the House of *Fame. It is built entirely of beryl, which shines 'ful lighter than a glas'—and makes things look bigger than they are. It has gold plating, and like the Temple of Venus, it is ornamented elaborately. The edifice is set upon a gleaming rock of ice, a weak foundation (as the dreamer calls it, 1132). Even stranger (more wonderful than the Labyrinth (*Laboryntus)) and more unstable is the House of Rumour or Aventure, which stands below the castle of Fame in a valley. This grotesque, huge building

(60 miles (72 km) in length) is made of twigs like those used to make wicker baskets; it is full of holes (to let the sound out), like a cage; and it whirls about at great speed. Chaucer has blended *Ovid's house of Rumour (*Met.* 12) with descriptions of the house of Fortune in Alan of Lille (*Aleyn (1)) and *Jean de Meun, and seems to be thinking of a rough, ruined building covered with thatch and with gaping holes—perhaps, it has been suggested, because 'Rumour is a low, primitive type of Fame, just as the rude rustic dwelling is the primitive original of the palace'. Again, all three buildings are in striking contrast to the orderly world of Nature as seen by the dreamer in Book II and expounded by the Eagle, where everything has its proper, natural 'house' or place ('a kyndely stede', 731): rivers flow into the sea, fish dwell in the water, trees in the earth—'thus every thing | Hath his proper mansioun'.

Evans (1949); Kolve (1984); Norton-Smith (1974), 45–61.

Arcite (1), one of the heroes of The *Knight's Tale.

Arcite (2), the false lover of Anelida in *Anelida and Arcite.

Arctour, Arcturus, Arcturus. Where Boethius used 'Arcturus' ambiguously, for the star (the brightest in the constellation Boötes) and for its constellation, Chaucer in *Boece distinguishes the latter with 'Arctour'. (See also *astrology and astronomy.)   [JDN]

Ardea, capital of the Rutuli in Latium, besieged by the Romans under *Tarquinius (*LGW* 1694).

Arge, Argon, Argos, a city and kingdom in the Peloponnese, the country of the Argeyes (*Tr* V.1501). It is mentioned in the legend of Hypermnestra (*LGW* 2682), and in Troilus and Criseyde *Diomede, the son of King *Tydeus, was heir to Argos and Calydon (V.805; cf. V.934).

Argyve (1), Argia, the wife of Polynices (*Polymyte(s)), who wept for his death (*Tr* V.1509).

Argyve (2), the mother of Criseyde (*Tr* IV.762); she is not named in Chaucer's sources.

Argon, see *Arge.

Argonautycon (referred to in the legend of *Hypsipyle (*LGW* 1457), as a source for the names of Jason's companions) seems to be the *Argonautica*, an epic on the quest of the Argonauts for the Golden Fleece by Valerius Flaccus, a Latin poet of the 1st c. AD. (Other poems with this title are those of Apollonius Rhodius, a Greek epic which Chaucer would not have known at first hand, but which was the source of the others, and of Varro 'Atacinus', a free Latin version of Apollonius which has not survived complete.) Perhaps Chaucer was following a vague reference in *Dares: if a reader wants to know their names 'let him read the "Argonauts"'; but the quoting of the title in a correct form makes this unlikely. The work of Valerius Flaccus seems to have been virtually unknown in Europe until one MS was discovered by the Italian humanist Poggio Bracciolini in the early 15th c. It has been suggested, however, that at least one early MS may be traced back to Britain, so that it might have been possible for Chaucer to have found a MS in England. A more likely alternative, perhaps, is that he saw an excerpt or excerpts from the work, or simply found a reference to the title elsewhere.

(ed.) Kramer (1913); (ed. and trans.) Mozley (1934).

Argus (1), the builder of the ship *Argo* (*LGW* 1453).

Argus (2), Argos Panoptes (having many eyes— one hundred, set around his head), son of Jupiter and Niobe (*Nyobe). He was set by the jealous Juno to watch over the beautiful Io, who had been transformed into a heifer by Jupiter to conceal her. Mercury tricked him into sleeping and killed him, and his eyes were placed in the peacock's tail. Chaucer knew the story from *Ovid's Metamorphoses 1, and alludes to it (e.g. I.1390; *Tr* IV.1459), twice with reference to the deception of husbands (by May in The *Merchant's Tale (IV.2111); and by the *Wife of Bath (III.358)).

ARGUS (3), Abû Ja'far Muhammad ibn Mûsâ al-Khwârizmî (pre 800–post 847), mathematician, astronomer, and geographer; member of an important scientific academy at Baghdad. The name 'al-Khwârizmî' was rendered as 'Alchorismi' or 'Algorismi' by his Latin translators (beginning with Adelard of Bath, Robert of Chester, and Gerard of Cremona in the 12th c.), and this was later often shortened to 'Algus', 'Algo', 'Argo Philosophus', and the like. His works were of an importance in the West far outstripping their intrinsic merits: his *tables, and the *canons to them, introduced advanced astronomical techniques (with a strong Indian element); his algebra was the first of any importance written in Arabic, and determined the general style of Western algebra; but his arithmetical treatise on Hindu numerals (our 'Arabic' numerals) literally changed the face of Western science, leading eventually to the abandonment of Roman numerals. (In astronomy this was more or less complete by the end of the 13th c. In commerce the old forms continued long after the Middle Ages.) The new arithmetic immediately gave rise to numerous treatises, and the subject took the generic name *algorismus*, giving us our word 'algorithm'. The *augrym stones of the clerk Nicholas in The *Miller's Tale took their name from the same root. Algorismus was an essential part of the university curriculum (see *Quadrivium), and many hundreds of medieval manuscripts on the subject are still extant. (See also *astrology and astronomy.) [JDN]

Ariadne, see *Adriane.

Aries, Ariete, the first sign of the Zodiac, the Ram. Chaucer's 'heved of Aries', the head of Aries (L. *caput Arietis*), is where the Sun is to be found at the spring equinox. He shows familiarity with the astrological properties of the sign when, at the beginning of The *Squire's Tale, he lists several of them: it is a *face, of Mars; the Sun has its *domicile and exaltation there (see *mansioun; *exaltacioun); and its properties are choleric and hot. Chaucer uses '*Ram' as a synonym, and does not refer by either name to the stars of the *constellation* of Aries. (See also hed; signe; Zodiak.) [JDN]

Aryn, Ujjain (Madhya), a place on the zero meridian, according to the Hindu tradition. The name entered Western astronomy with the *tables of al-Khwârizmî (*Argus (3)). The city was supposedly in the middle of the habitable world, and by Latin writers was sometimes mistakenly said to lie on the equator. (It is actually close to the Tropic of Cancer.) The name *centre aryn* is used in *Equatorie of the Planetis for the centre of the main plate. This corresponds to the centre of the world, but in a (deliberately) different sense from that originally intended by Hindu astronomers. [JDN]

Arionis harpe, the constellation Lyra. In *The *House of Fame, the constellation is so mentioned, while in the following book the harper '*Orion' is named, suggesting that Chaucer believed the constellation Orion to be mythologically linked with Lyra. Arion was a historic person. The chief star in Lyra is Vega, known also as Vultur Cadens, and to this star the falling bird in The Squire's *Tale corresponds. [JDN]

Aristoclides, the tyrant of Orchomenos, who pursued the maiden *Stymphalides (V.1387).

ARISTOTLE (384–322 BC), Greek philosopher, who wrote and taught on almost every science practised in his time. Although Chaucer's explicit references to Aristotle are few, he shared the indebtedness of all medieval scholarship to the man who was then often simply known as 'the Philosopher', the name by which he is known in The *Parson's Tale and The *Legend of Good Women. The Clerk of Oxenford in the *General Prologue to The *Canterbury Tales would rather have had twenty volumes of Aristotle and his philosophy than rich robes, fiddle, or psaltery. Although *Plato's name is mentioned with Aristotle's in The *House of Fame, the cosmological survey there offered is thoroughly Aristotelian. Several doctrines in *Boece* are ascribed to the philosopher, as are materials Chaucer took from Martianus Capella (*Marcian) and Macrobius (*Macrobes), but to dwell on them would be to overlook the fact that Aristotelian influences were present in almost all contemporary scholastic writings.

Aristotle was born in Stagira (in Macedon), the son of the physician to the king. He studied and worked at Plato's school in Athens for nearly twenty years. Opposed to the mathematization of philosophy advocated by Plato's successor Speusippus, he left for a succession of teaching posts on various Greek islands, where he pursued his important zoological researches. From 342 he became tutor to the future Alexander the Great. In 335 he returned to Athens, where he spent twelve years as head of a school he set up in the Lyceum. Anti-Macedonian feeling after the death of Alexander led him to retreat to Chalcis in 323, and there he died a year later.

Aristotle's principal writings were: (1) the *Organon*, a series of logical treatises; (2) writings on the physical sciences, including the *Physics* and *On the Heavens*; (3) several long biological works; (4) treatises on psychology; (5) the *Metaphysics*; (6) treatises on ethics and politics; (7) two works on literature, the *Rhetoric* and *Poetics*, these last being without importance in the Middle Ages.

Aristotle's philosophy was continued after his death by other members of his school, and was the subject of very many expositions and commentaries, especially in Alexandria after an edition of his writings was produced by Andronicus of Rhodes (*c.*50 BC). After the closing of the schools there in the 6th c., Aristotelian learning was preserved by Arab, Syrian, and Jewish scholars, being translated into Latin largely from those sources but partly from Greek, especially in the 12th and 13th c. Before then, the logical texts were known through translations by Boethius and the *Introduction* by Porphyry. Thomas Aquinas (1225–74) had William of Moerbeke (*c.*1220–86) translate from Greek virtually the whole of what was then known. There was a certain degree of Christianization (as there had been of Plato by Augustine long before), and the end of the 13th c. saw much tension between elements of the ecclesiastical establishment and the new Latin Averroists with their Aristotelian learning (see *Averrois). These controversies centred on the problems of the unicity of the intellect and the eternity of the created world. Another problem, with a clear Chaucerian echo, concerned determinism, and predestination. (See also *astrology and astronomy; *Avycen; *Bacon; *Boece; *cosmology; *Grosseteste; *Nature; science; *Seven Liberal Arts.)

[JDN]

Jaeger (1948); W. D. Ross (1945); (for medieval Latin tradition, *Aristoteles Latinus* (1952–); (trans.) W. D. Ross et al. (1909–52); collected editions in Budé, Loeb, and Oxford Classical Texts series).

Arithmetic, see *arsmetrik; *Argus (3); *augrym; *Seven Liberal Arts; *Quadrivium.

Armorike, 'that called is *Britayne' (1), Armorica, the ancient name of Brittany. It is the setting of *The *Franklin's Tale*, notable for its dangerous rocks (see *Pedmark, *Kayrrud), and for the 'layes' which the 'olde gentil Britouns' made (see *Breton lay). In *The *Monk's Tale* (VII.2388) it is mentioned once as the home of Oliver de Mauny.

ARNOLD OF THE NEWE TOUN, Arnald of Villanova (*c.*1240–1311). A native of Aragon, Arnald was sometime master of medicine at Montpellier, where he had studied. He held many posts involving papal and royal patronage, was conservative in his techniques but successful, and earned renown for this fact as well as for his extraordinarily prolific writings. In *The *Canon's Yeoman's Tale* Chaucer quotes at length from a much-copied alchemical work usually ascribed to Arnald, the *Rosarius philosophorum* (Chaucer's *Rosarie*). Its authenticity has been questioned, but the argument is inconclusive. (See also *alchemy.)

[JDN]

ARNOLD, MATTHEW (1822–88), poet, educational reformer, critic, and man of letters, an important force in Victorian cultural life. In spite of his statement that Chaucer lacked high seriousness, he praised him eloquently. In his General Introduction to T. H. Ward's *The English Poets* (1880, repr. as 'The Study of Poetry' in his *Essays in Criticism*, 2nd ser., 1888) he says that Chaucer has an enduring power of fascination: 'he is a genuine source of joy and strength, which is flowing still for us and will flow always'. He praises his style and analyses his 'divine liquidness of diction, his divine fluidity of movement' in a discussion which is unusually detailed for the time. Chaucer is superior to the earlier 'romance-poetry' of France because 'he has gained the power to survey the world from a central, truly human point of view'. 'And yet'—for all his excellent qualities—'Chaucer is not one of the great classics'. He fails the severest Arnoldian test, that the greatest poetry has 'the high and excellent seriousness' which, according to Aristotle, makes it superior to history. To discover what poetry 'belongs to the class of the truly excellent, and can therefore do us most good', we should have always in our mind 'lines and expressions of the great masters' which may be applied as 'touchstones' to other poetry. Thus the 'accent' of such a verse as Dante's 'in la sua voluntade è nostra pace' [in His will is our peace] 'is altogether beyond Chaucer's reach'. Chaucer's poetry has 'largeness, freedom, shrewdness, benignity; but it has not this high seriousness'—which is found in Homer and in Shakespeare.

Arpies, Arpiis, the Harpies (orig. 'snatchers') in ancient mythology were monsters in the shape of birds with the faces of women, who ate human flesh. They were destroyed by Hercules (*Ercules). Chaucer calls them 'the cruel bryddes felle' (VII.2100; cf. *Bo* IV m.7).

Arras, a city of Artois (*Artoys) in northern France, celebrated for its tapestries and its cloth—in *The Romaunt of the Rose* 1234 it is said of the frock worn by Fraunchise that 'so fair was noon in all Arras'.

Arrius, a character in a story mentioned by the *Wife of Bath (III.758), which Chaucer probably found in Walter Map. When his friend Latumyus told him that in his garden he had a tree on which his three wives had hanged themselves, he asked for a shoot of 'that blessed tree'.

ARSECHIELES, Abû Ishâq Ibrahîm ibn Yahyâ al-Naqqâsh ibn al-Zarqâlî (d. 1100), astronomer. (He has been known by many names, Ibn az-Zarqellû, Azarchel, Arzachel, Azarquiel, etc.) Azarchel was a renowned scientific instrument-maker and maker of water-clocks in Toledo who became learned in astronomy. For reasons of security he moved to Córdoba at some time after 1078, and continued his astronomical researches there. His writings include treatises on a universal astrolabe (a more difficult instrument than Chaucer's), an almanac (*almenak), and an equatorium in the same tradition as that described in *Equatorie of the Planetis*. Azarchel's fame owes most, however, to his *canons to the Toledan *tables. The original Arabic is lost, but Latin versions by Gerard of Cremona and John of Seville(?) circulated and survive in large numbers. The tables were mostly drawn from the work of other astronomers and only reduced to the Toledan meridian by Azarchel; many others were subsequently based on them. They continued in general use until the mid-14th c., and later in some places—Chaucer put them into the hand of the clerk of Orleans in *The *Franklin's Tale*. They were eventually superseded by various versions of the Alfonsine tables, which were also assembled in Toledo, c.1270, although not widely diffused until fifty years later. Chaucer himself used the Alfonsine tables. (See also *Astrolabie; *astrology and astronomy; *Toletanes.) [JDN]

arsmetrik, arithmetic. The word is from a standard medieval L. word for arithmetic, *arsmetrica*, not derived from the Greek *arithmetike*, but by a mistaken etymology compounded from L. *ars* and Greek *metron*. It occurs innocently enough in *The *Knight's Tale*, but in keeping with the humour of *The *Summoner's Tale* is perhaps there a pun on *ers*, 'arse'. (See also *augrym; *Quadrivium.) [JDN]

art(e). This word (L. *ars*) is sometimes used in unfamiliar ways in medieval English. It can mean skill, or art as against nature (cf. V.197)—as in Dr Johnson's example 'to walk is natural, to dance is an art'. Hence the 'art poetical' referred to in *The *House of Fame* (1095). But it can also mean the 'arts curriculum' of a medieval *university (see *Seven Liberal Arts). The clerk Nicholas was learning 'art' at Oxford (I.3191); the anti-intellectual miller tells the Cambridge clerks that though his house is small, they know how to make twenty feet into a mile by arguments, since they have learned 'art' (I.4122–4)—a reference to the disputations of the schools. It can also mean 'craft', 'principles and practice', 'technique', or 'science': thus there is an 'art' of astronomy (I.3209) and of alchemy and medicine. It was sometimes used for a codified set of rules or instructions: thus there were 'arts' of rhetoric (cf. V.38–9, 104), of letter-writing, of grammar, of memory, of war, and (especially) of love (cf. I.476)—with its own explanatory manuals like

'Ovides Art' (III.680), the *Ars amatoria* of *Ovid. That expert seducer Jason, however, knew all the 'art and craft' of love 'withoute bok' (*LGW* 1607–8).

ARTHEMESIE, Artemisia, the widow of Mausolus, the ruler of Caria and Lycia on the eastern coast of Turkey. When he died in 353 BC a splendid tomb was built for him (hence the word 'mausoleum') by Artemisia, who succeeded him. She is cited by *Dorigen in The *Franklin's Tale* (V.1451–2) as an example of perfect wifehood.

Arthour, Artour, Arthur, son of Uther Pendragon, legendary king of Britain. Geoffrey of Monmouth (*Gaufride) told the story of his rise to power with the help of the prophet Merlin, his marriage to Guinevere, his establishment of a mighty empire, and how he was mortally wounded in battle against Mordred and carried off to the Isle of Avalon. It became the subject of many *romances. A few medieval chroniclers expressed doubts about the historicity of Geoffrey's story, but even after the legend had been finally demolished by sceptical historians, the fame of Arthur (now an ancestor of the Tudor monarchs) lived on. Chaucer does not show much interest in this area of medieval literature. The *Wife of Bath's Tale* is set in 'th'olde dayes of the Kyng Arthour', but the king himself has a less important role than his (unnamed) queen.

Artoys, Artois, a province of northern France. It is mentioned (along with the neighbouring *Flaundres and *Pycardie) as one of the places in which the *Knight had fought valiantly (I.86). This whole area was one which was fought over again and again in the *Hundred Years War—and Chaucer himself saw service here (see Geoffrey *Chaucer: life). This particular reference may be to the campaign of Henry Despencer, bishop of Norwich, in 1383, which ended in failure.

Arveragus, a knight of Brittany, and husband of Dorigen in The *Franklin's Tale*. His name is probably meant to sound like the Latinized form of a Celtic name (it is possible, but not certain that the idea came from Arviragus, the son of

Cymbeline, king of Britain, a great warrior, who appears in Geoffrey of Monmouth (*Gaufride).

Ascalaphus, see *Escaphilo.

ascendent, the degree of the *ecliptic that is rising on the horizon, this being of especial interest to an astrologer in the casting of *horoscopes in general and nativities in particular. The twelve mundane houses are reckoned from this point. In his *Treatise on the *Astrolabe* Chaucer gives rules for discovering the ascendent. He notes the custom of taking a planet to be ascendent with all ten degrees of the *face in which it is found, and he notes a possible error that can result. He introduces the reader to another traditional extension of the rules, whereby an additional interval of five degrees might be included in the first house.

Chaucer uses 'horoscopum' as a synonym for 'ascendant' in his *Treatise*. (See also *astrology and astronomy; *mansio(u)n; *nativitee; *oriso(u)nte. [JDN]

ascensioun, ascencioun, ascension. Ascensions are of two sorts, right (*ascensio in circulo directo,* that is, measured along the equator) and oblique (*ascensio in circulo obliquo,* that is, the arc between the vernal point and the east point of the horizon). These quantities are of importance in matters of time-keeping and the casting of *horoscopes. (See also *astrology and astronomy.) [JDN]

Asye (1), Asia, one of the three continents recognized in the Middle Ages (and mentioned as such, along with Africa (*Affrike) and *Europe (2) in *HF* 1339). It is 'the half part of the world' according to *Bartholomew (and appears thus on medieval maps (see *Mappemounde and Map 1), as the top half of a circle which has Jerusalem in the centre). Beyond the Holy Land, the maps will show such places as Babylon (*Babiloigne) on the Euphrates, India (*Inde) with the river Ganges, Ceylon, and in the extreme East the Garden of Eden or Earthly Paradise, traditionally placed on a mountain, with its four rivers running down. Exotic animals and creatures figure prominently—unicorns, elephants, Bactrian camels with two humps, giants, and dragons. From ancient history and legend (like the stories of Alexander (*Alisa(u)ndre)) medieval Western Europe derived a strange and heady mixture of fact and fiction, added to by later travellers' tales and embellished by armchair travellers such as *Mandeville. It was a natural setting for any medieval tale of wonder. (See also *Barbarie.)

Asye (2), the country in which *The *Prioress's Tale* is set (VII.488), is usually taken to be Asia Minor, which in Chaucer's day was controlled by the Ottoman Turks (see *Turk(e)ye). It is possible that the Tale is simply set in an unspecified town in remote and exotic Asia, but Asia Minor would more readily perhaps produce a 'greet citee' with Christian folk in some numbers (with a magistrate and an abbot), as well as a Jewish ghetto. If so, the reference to 'Seint *Nicholas' (VII.514), who was bishop of Myra in south-western Turkey (and according to legend performed miracles in that area) might be an appropriate piece of local colour.

Askanius, Ascanius son of Aeneas, who led him from *Troy 'in his ryght hand' (*LGW* 942); he is also mentioned in *The House of Fame* 178 and *The Legend of Good Women* 1138. (See *Eneyde*; *Iulo.)

Aspect, the angular separation (measured in *ecliptic longitude) of two planets, astrologically interpreted; literally, the way the planets look at one another (L. *adspicere*). If the planets are 60° apart they are in sextile (friendly) aspect; if 90° apart the aspect is quadrile (hostile); if 120° the aspect is trine (friendly). Aspects are often marked on *horoscopes. (See *astrology and astronomy.)

[JDN]

Assembly of Ladies, The. A *dream vision (written c.1475?) of 756 lines in rhyme royal (see *versification). Its appearance in *Thynne's edition of Chaucer (1532) is the only reason for its attribution to Chaucer (see *Chauceriana). It was removed from the *canon by *Tyrwhitt in the 18th c., but continued to appear in some 19th-c. editions. As in *The *Floure and the Leafe*, the narrator quite clearly says that she is a woman, and there seems to be no good reason not to believe her. She relates to a knight how one afternoon she and her friends came to a beautiful arbour and fell asleep. In her dream Perseverance appears and summons her and her companions to a council which is soon to be held by her mistress, Loyalty. They are to come dressed in blue (the colour of constancy and fidelity), and Loyalty will hear their grievances. Diligence will be their guide. But no men are to come ('Nat one?' says the dreamer, in a rather Chaucerian tone, 'ey, benedicite! | What have they don?'— but Perseverance will not say). She arrives at the palace of Plesaunt Regard ('Pleasant Looks'), and with her companions is led by the chamberlain, Remembraunce ('Memory'), to a chamber with its walls adorned with the stories of martyred heroines. The petitions (concerning broken promises, instability in love, loving in vain, etc.) are read out by her secretary, Avisenesse ('Prudence'). After she has listened to them, Loyalty says she will shortly hold a judicial assembly to remedy them. The dreamer awakes, and her tale is warmly praised by the knight. *The Assembly of Ladies* is an attractive poem, with a distinctive and lively persona, characterized by a colloquial turn of phrase ('Abide . . . ye be an hasti one' she says to the knight), by curiosity and independence. It is both serious in its celebration of ideal womanhood (in the spirit of *Christine de Pisan's *Cité des dames*, though much less overwhelmingly encyclopaedic) and a light-hearted and deft contribution to a courtly war of words.

(ed.) Pearsall (1962).

ASSUER(E), ASSUERUS, Ahasuerus (actually Xerxes I, reigned 486–465 BC), king of the Persians, and husband of Esther (*Ester).

astralabie, astrelabie, astrolabie (planispheric) astrolabe.

Astrolabe, A Treatise on the, a work written by Chaucer in fulfilment (as he says) of a request by his 10-year-old son Lewis. It was probably composed in the early months of 1393. The treatise was largely drawn from a work that was wrongly ascribed to *Mâshâ'allâh. Chaucer's announced plan was for five parts, but only two were written. The first amounts to a description of the components of the astrolabe and the lines and scales engraved on them. The whole instrument would have been of brass, about 10 or 20 cm across. It comprised a circular tray-like disc (the '*moder', mother) holding a stack of circular plates, one for each '*clymat' (geographical latitude), only the topmost of the stack showing through the pierced '*riet' above it. The riet was essentially a star map. All these elements, and rules on front and back (one for sighting the stars), were held together by a 'pyn' through the centre, secured by a horse-shaped wedge (the 'hors'). The plates of an astrolabe are fixed in position; the riet is free to rotate, and the two in combination are capable of simulating the movements of the stars over the fixed network of local coordinates as used in spherical astronomy. On the back of the mother a calendar scale was engraved, allowing the user to estimate the Sun's position in the *ecliptic on any day of the year. A more or less superfluous horary quadrant was also often engraved there.

The whole assembly is suspended from the thumb by a ring and shackle; it then hangs vertically under its own weight. The stars can be observed through holes in a pair of vanes on one of the rules (or the Sun by the shadow of one vane on the other), and by following the instructions offered in the second part of Chaucer's treatise, and using the star map and plate as a calculating device to reduce the observations, conclusions of some two score different sorts could be drawn.

The (pseudo-)Mâshâ'allâh treatise was not of course meant for a 10-year-old, and included another part, dealing with the construction and engraving of an astrolabe, using a method of stereographic projection now thought to have originated with the astronomer Hipparchus (*c*.140 BC). Accompanying this was a table with a list of coordinates for the stars that were to be included on the riet. Such star tables were not strictly necessary for Lewis, with his own ready-made astrolabe, but Chaucer planned such a table for Part III of his treatise. He promised, too, to include material 'after the *kalenders of the reverent clerkes, Frere J. *Somer and Frere N. *Lenne'. Chaucer made use of at least one of those two calendars in writing The *Canterbury Tales.

Parts IV and V were to be each a '*theorike': Part IV to explain and predict lunar and planetary motions, Part V to teach the rules of astrology. Chaucer's astrological intentions here are quite explicit, for he speaks of the tables of equations of houses (for the latitude of Oxford; see *hous) and tables of planetary dignities.

There is good reason to believe that Chaucer

was adept at the use of the astrolabe, and that it assisted him greatly in those places where he worked astronomical calculations into his poetry. The *Squire's Tale in particular lends itself to interpretation as an exercise in the use of the instrument. (See also *astrology and astronomy; label; midnyght; myle-wey.)   [JDN]

Michel (1947); North (1990); Pintelon (1940).

astrology and astronomy. By his treatises on the two most important astronomical instruments of the Middle Ages, the astrolabe and the equatorium, by the example of his poetry, with its often transparent use of astronomical and astrological allegory, and by the high precision with which he introduces celestial events into many of his poems, Chaucer shows how seriously he took these twin subjects. He inherited two traditions that were vigorously continued in his day, and both owed much to Ptolemy (*Ptholomee) the Alexandrian astronomer of the 2nd c. The first had at its root the synthesis of astronomy in Ptolemy's *Almagest*; in the second, Ptolemy's astrological work *Tetrabiblos* left many traces.

Although *Almagest* made use of earlier Greek geometrical constructions and Babylonian data, and although the parameters of the Ptolemaic theory had been revised by astronomers in the Islamic and Iberian worlds, to the writer of the Middle Ages Ptolemy was the prime source of astronomical knowledge. The clerk Nicholas in The *Miller's Tale possessed an *Almageste* and an astrolabe. The astronomical system underlying the *Equatorie of the Planetis* was thoroughly Ptolemaic. It was one aimed at the calculation of planetary *longitudes and *latitudes, rather than at explaining planetary movement on the basis of physics: Aristotelian *cosmology was regarded to a great extent as a different subject.

The Ptolemaic scheme was entirely geocentric. (Aristarchus, in the 3rd c. BC, had proposed a heliocentric system, but it was not generally adopted.) The geometrical models for planetary motion varied from planet to planet. The simplest was for the Sun, where uniform motion around a simple eccentric circle sufficed (that is, a circle whose centre was at a distance from the centre of the Earth). Essential to each of the models for the remaining planets was a deferent circle (this was also eccentric; see *defferent) carrying an *epicycle, which in turn carried the planet. The epicycle moved uniformly only with respect to an *equant. The planet's position was found as the point where the Earth-planet line met the *ecliptic. There were additional complications, especially with the models for the Moon and Mercury.

The geometrical models are considerably easier to appreciate than the derived techniques of calculation, which proceeded in many stages from the determination of mean motions to true places by the incorporation of certain so-called equations. The vocabulary of the *Franklin on this subject in regard to the clerk of Orleans is accurate and correctly used. It seems likely that some of Chaucer's own astronomical tables survive, bound together with the unique manuscript copy of *Equatorie of thePlanetis*. (See *aux; *equacio(u)n; *Mercurye; *Mone; *mote(e); *radix; *retrograd; *Sonne; *table; *Tolletanes.)

Astronomy was the basis of time reckoning. For periods of days and years, and the feasts of the Church, the calendar was the appropriate instrument, its structure being taught in the *Quadrivium under the name of *computus*. Numerous astronomical instruments apart from the astrolabe were used for the recording of hours and minutes. The 'chilyndre' of The *Shipman's Tale* was a portable cylindrical sundial, and dials of many other sorts were in use, including various sorts of horary quadrant with a wider astronomical value. The mechanical clock was available by Chaucer's time: this too was a by-product of astronomy. (See *clokke; *day; *hour; *kalendere; *myle-wey; *months and seasons; *pryme; *yer(e).)

The clerk Nicholas 'had lerned *art', that is, had studied the arts curriculum of *Trivium and Quadrivium, but had also turned to astrology. He owned an astrolabe. Had he read Chaucer's work on the instrument he would have learned much basic astrology. This was not formally a part of the Quadrivium, but was certainly studied in universities, not least as a part of *medicine. As related in the *General Prologue*, the Doctour of Phisik (*Physician) was grounded in astronomy, and could calculate ascendents for use in natural magic on his patients' behalf. Chaucer makes much use of the subject, but leaves us in some doubt as to his sources. Apart from Ptolemy's *Tetrabiblos* (known

in the West as *Quadripartitum*) other important ancient sources of medieval doctrine were by such as Dorotheus, Firmicus Maternus, and Rhetorius. Chaucer mentions *Alkabucius on a trivial point in *A Treatise on the *Astrolabe*, and the '*Haly' mentioned in the *General Prologue* might have been the astrologer. Astrological doctrine reached the West with so many accretions and inconsistencies, however, that it is hard to describe it briefly and systematically. (For a further important intermediate writer see *Mâshâ'allâh.)

The chief aim of the art was prognostication on the basis of the state of the heavens at certain times. (See *ascendent; *horoscope; *hous; *nativitee.) The basic astronomical calculation would have been done with the help of tables, in some cases an equatorium, and very probably an astrolabe. Undoubtedly one of the chief reasons for learning astronomical techniques in the first place was to apply them astrologically. The planets were deemed to have qualities of their own (see *Saturne; *Jupiter; *Mars; *Sonne; *Venus; *Mercurius; *Mone) but also in relation to one another (see *aspect and in relation to the ecliptic (see *dignitee). Even in the absence of the planets, the signs of the Zodiac could have significant properties (see *signe, and the signs by name). Much of the mystique of the subject came from its complex rules, for which—authority apart—only impressionistic arguments could ever have been offered in justification. A case in point is the concept of *atazir,* used in The *Man of Law's Tale*.

Contrary to common belief, astrology was doctrinally safe within the orbit of the Christian Church during the Middle Ages. Although several leading clerics preached against it—most of them only after learning it at first hand themselves—it was generally thought to lead into spiritual danger only when alloyed with such arts as were related to nigromancy. It was not wholly concerned with the fortunes of the human individual: its branches considered meteorological questions (see *weather), questions of the rise and fall of religions and sects, epidemics, plagues, the fortunes of nations, and matters of history generally. It was frequently used to make an 'election', that is, to decide (on the basis of a *horoscope) whether to undertake an enterprise; and this use encompasses many of its medical uses, for

instance, deciding as to suitable times for bleed-ing. (See also *medicine.) [JDN]
Curry (1960); Manzatoui (1974); North (1990); North (1976); Wood (1970).

astrologien, astronomer, astrologer. Chaucer draws no clear distinction between the two. When in *Troilus and Criseyde the cock is called 'commune astrologer', Chaucer is rendering the Latin of Alanus de Insulis (*Aleyn (1)), as was recognized in several early glosses to the manuscripts. (See also *astrology and astronomy.) [JDN]

Athalante, Atthalante, Atalanta, a great huntress who took part in the Calydonian boar hunt (see *Calydoigne) with Meleager (*Meleagre), who was in love with her. His action in giving the head of the boar to her caused a fatal feud. The story is told by *Ovid (*Met.* 8). The scene of Atalanta hunting the wild boar is one of those painted on the temple of the virgin huntress Diana (*Dyane) in The *Knight's Tale (I.2070). In The *Parliament of Fowls (286) the story of Atalanta is painted in the temple of Venus. The reference there suggests the story told (by Venus) in *Met.* 10 of how the beautiful Atalanta lived in the woods and rejected her suitors. She would accept only the man who could beat her in a foot-race. Any challenger who failed was put to death. Hippomenes defeated her by dropping the golden apples of the Hesperides, but though Venus had helped him, he showed no gratitude, and she punished the two by exciting Hippomenes to make love to Atalanta in a sacred temple. As a result they were transformed into lions.

Athalantes doughtres, the (seven) Pleiades, the best known of all star clusters. In Greek myth-ology the seven daughters of Atlas and Pleione. Virgil calls them *Eoæ Atlantides.* Chaucer's spelling (*HF* 1007) might indicate a confusion with *Athalante. [JDN]

ATHALUS, Attalus III Philometor, king of Pergamum in north-western Turkey (reigned 138–133 BC). He is cited in The Book of the Duchess (663) as the inventor of *chess.

Athamante, Athamas, son of Aeolus and king of *Thebes (1). Juno, jealous of Ino, his wife (the nurse of the child of Semele, beloved of Jupiter), went down into the underworld and persuaded Tisiphone (*Thesiphone) to drive Athamas mad. He killed one of his children and Ino leapt into the sea with the other. Chaucer read the story in *Ovid, *Met.* 4, and in *Dante (*Inferno* 30), and alludes to it in *Troilus and Criseyde (IV.1539).

Athenes, Athenys, Atthenes. Athens, the city of ancient Greece, is frequently mentioned in Chaucer. It is the setting of *Anelida and Arcite and of The *Knight's Tale, where it has knights and tournaments and is ruled by 'duke' Theseus. This may not be simple anachronism: possibly Chaucer was thinking of contemporary Athens, where there was in fact a duke (a Latin duchy was set up by the crusaders after the capture of Constantin-ople in 1204; it did not fall to the Turks until the 15th c.). *Demophon the false lover of Phyllis is also 'duk and lord' of Athens (*LGW* 2442; cf. *HF* 388). Once it appears rather mysteriously as the setting for the temple of Isis (*Ysidis) which was burnt (*HF* 1844–5). In *Boece (not surprisingly) it is more recognizably like the ancient city: there are references to its democracy ('governement of mul-titude', I pr.5:18) and to its Stoa Poikile or painted colonnade in the marketplace (which gave its name to the philosophy of Stoicism—the 'porche', 'that is to seyn a gate of the toun of Athenis there as philosophris hadden hir congre-gacioun to desputen' (V m.4).

Atiteris appears among the pipers and minstrels in The *House of Fame (1227). The name is often explained as a corruption of *Virgil's Tityrus, the shepherd-singer of the first Eclogue. But since the neighbouring performers (*Pseustis, *Marcia) seem to be figures of folly, and Tityrus was closely associated, and sometimes identified, with the great poet of antiquity, it has been suggested that Chaucer simply made the name up for the context (possibly even from a/ab 'unlike' *Tityrus.*, i.e. a practitioner of bad verse).

Atropos, see *At(t)ropos.

Attheon. Actaeon, the grandson of Cadmus, founder of *Thebes (1); came upon Diana (*Dyane) bathing naked with her nymphs, and was transformed into a stag, and destroyed by his own hounds (*Ovid, *Met.* 3). In *The *Knight's Tale* (I.2065–6) the scene of his transformation is depicted in the temple of Diana ('an hert ymaked, | For vengeaunce that he saugh Diane al naked'), and when Emily prays to the goddess she refers to his fate (I.2303).

ATTILLA, Attila king of the Huns (reigned 434–53). He devastated the Balkans, invaded Germany and France (reaching Orleans) and Italy, where after plundering Milan and Pavia, he was turned away from Rome by the prayers of the Pope and the promise of tribute. The widespread early story that he died from a nosebleed brought on by a drunken orgy on his wedding night is cited by the *Pardoner as an example of *drunkenness— this great conqueror died in his sleep 'with shame and dishonour, | Bledynge ay at his nose in dronkenesse' (VI.579–81). Chaucer did not know the tales in earlier heroic literature of the death of Attila at the hands of an avenging Germanic woman.

Attrides, Agamemnon (*Agamenoun) son of Atreus (*Bo* IV m.7:1).

At(t)ropos, Atropos, one of the three Fates (*Parcas): Clotho, *Lachesis, and Atropos, who cut the thread of life (cf. *Tr* IV.1208, 1546).

Aubade (aube), the French equivalent of the Provençal *alba*, a 'dawn-song' usually expressing the sorrow of two lovers at their enforced separation. It is a lyrical form (often associated with *'courtly love'), common in Provençal, French, and German medieval literature, but is not by any means confined to Western Europe. The coming of the dawn is signalled by the crowing of the cock or the warning cry of the watchman—'see the dawn breaking!'; the lovers wish to deny that day is coming or to prolong the night—'the daybreak! how soon it comes!'. As Dronke says, 'the alba shows a secret meeting; the lovers meet by night ... they know that the coming of day will cut short their joys, and that the very quality and poignancy of their love is conditioned by this. Daylight brings back the claims of the real, waking world, which both lovers must acknowledge; it is the

background against which secret love has beauty'. It is clear that Chaucer had it in mind when in *Troilus and Criseyde* (III.1415–526) he extended Boccaccio's scene of the parting of the lovers. He begins it with the crowing of the cock; Criseyde laments the coming of the day which will part them, urges the night to linger, and complains that it is performing its 'office' too quickly, while Troilus reproaches the 'cruel day' and the sun. (Chaucer is also thinking of *Ovid's story of Hero and Leander in *Heroides* 18.) The lovers become aware of the demands of time and of the larger world which is beginning to press in on their own small paradise—as it does in the farewell of the lovers in Shakespeare's *Romeo and Juliet* 3.5. There are briefer examples of it or allusions to it in *Troilus and Criseyde* (III.1695–711), and in *The Complaint of *Mars* (87–91); and a deliciously parodic one in *The *Reeve's Tale* (I.4234–48), where after a night of uncourtly passion, the clerk Aleyn takes leave of Malyne when 'the third cock began to sing' with the words 'Fare weel, Malyne, sweete wight [creature]! | The day is come; I may no lenger byde'.

Dronke (1978), 167–85; Hatto (1965).

Auchinleck MS, now in the National Library of Scotland, named after its former owner, Alexander Boswell of Auchinleck, the father of the biographer of Dr Johnson. It was written 1330–40, and contains an important collection of *romances, religious poems, and other material. It has been suggested that it was produced in a London lay scriptorium or 'bookshop'. It has also been suggested that Chaucer may have read it, but this is far from certain. The MS, however, contains a range of the popular romances which he makes fun of in *Sir Thopas*, including copies of some which he echoes or mentions: *Guy of Warwick, Bevis of Hampton* (*Beves), and *Horn child.

(facsimile) Pearsall and Cunningham (1977).

auctour and auctoritee (L. *auctor* and *auctoritas*). The ME words can mean respectively 'creator, originator' as well as 'author', and 'authority' in its legal, political, and ecclesiastical senses. However, when used of literature they often have a stronger or more precise sense than they do now. An *auctour* was an 'author', but of a special and important kind. He was an 'authoritative' writer, often almost a sage, from whose work wise sayings (*sententiae* or 'sentences') and examples could be taken and used. He could be a technical authority—so that for information on the art of medicine, for instance, one would turn to an *auctour* such as Galen (*Galyen (1)). His *auctoritee* was normally supported by its antiquity, for 'out of olde bokes . . . cometh al this newe science' (*PF* 24–5). Some idea of the veneration given to an *auctour* can be seen when a medieval writer imagines a meeting with one of his illustrious predecessors, like the famous encounter in the *Inferno* when *Dante meets his master Virgil, who is to act as his guide. A set of canonical Latin *auctores*, pagan and Christian, were studied in medieval schools, and were furnished with commentaries and explanatory *prologues. The basic idea is that the *auctor* is the original and trustworthy source of the material in question. The Roman fabulist Phaedrus says that Aesop is his *auctor*, who invented the material, and that he has polished it in verse. In later medieval times a rather obvious distinction was made between an *auctor*, a *compilator* or compiler, who simply collected and arranged the material of other writers (in the *Astrolabe*, Chaucer says that he is an ignorant 'compilator' of the work of 'old astrologers'), a *scriptor* or scribe, who copied it, and a *commentator*, who provided the commentary.

The relationship of the moderns to the ancients was not always one of straightforward veneration. In the 12th c., the teacher Bernard of Chartres is reported as saying that the moderns are as dwarfs standing on the shoulders of giants; that they can see further is because of the greatness of the ancients. Some medieval writers seem happy to forgo any claim to 'authority', while others seem to think of themselves as 'authors' and take a self-conscious interest in literary *fame. Many remain anonymous; some give their name with some expression of humility; some are concerned to establish their identity and the list of their works. Writers find different ways of claiming 'authority'—they have found their material in a chronicle or in a dream, for instance. Sometimes, while remaining outwardly reverential to the words of their 'authors' they find ways to change or challenge them.

Chaucer seems to share his contemporaries' reverence for 'thise olde auctours', but is not always reverential. He uses the words in the traditional manner. 'And auctours shal I fynden' says the old hag in *The *Wife of Bath's Tale* (III.1212), to support the view that old people should be honoured. 'Auctoritee' is sometimes not quoted, whether because there is no need, since we know from *experience (e.g. I.3000–1), or because it is not appropriate to the *game (see III.1276–7). The degree of 'authority' may be questioned: in *The *Nun's Priest's Tale*, Chauntecleer (himself a great quoter of 'authorities') tries to put down Pertelote when she quotes 'the wise Cato' (one of the *auctores* of the elementary curriculum) by airily remarking that in old books one can find many a man of greater *auctorite* than Cato ever was (VII.2975). Authorities can be used with a certain degree of 'game'. 'Rede auctours', says the Nun's Priest (VII.3263)—after some remarks on the disastrous counsels of women, which he says he has spoken in 'game'—and listen to what they say about women. This technique, of citing an authority in order to absolve the speaker from blame or responsibility for his statements, is one of which Chaucer is very fond, and which plays a large part in creating the Protean and elusive character of his narrative voice. In a passage near the end of the *General Prologue* he excuses the 'plain' speaking of some of the pilgrims (citing two major authorities, Christ who himself spoke plainly in holy writ, and Plato who advised appropriate diction) on grounds of 'realism'. He must simply 'reherce' the words that they actually speak—thus by implication casting himself in the role of the 'compiler'. The technique can be used for other purposes. In *Troilus and Criseyde*, he constantly refers to his 'auctour' (whom he feigns to be the Latin writer *Lollius'). He will only speak 'as myn auctour seyde' (II.18), so he should not be blamed. This is used in expressions of serio-comic humility—'I kan nat tellen al' (the scene of the lovers' union) 'as kan myn auctour'; or sometimes to mystify by claiming that certain knowledge is not possible—no author states how long it was before Criseyde forsook Troilus for Diomede (V.1086–8). Sometimes the 'auctour' is cited for statements or passages which are Chaucer's own invention. No doubt this sometimes 'lends an air of authority' to what he is saying, but a private game is involved as well. In *The *House of Fame*

(314), where he says that he will cite no other author (than Virgil) for the lament of Dido which he has read in his dream: he has in fact invented most of the sixty lines. His starting point is Virgil, but he has amplified the words, and changed the view of that *auctor*. Perhaps surprisingly, the word 'auctour' is used by the *Manciple when he warns against telling tales: 'Be noon auctour newe of tidynges, wheither they been false or trewe'. It is intriguing that (as *The Canterbury Tales* survive) this is followed by the Parson who rejects all 'fables'. Chaucer's attitude to literary fame remains elusive. But in spite of many asseverations of humility and some apparent demonstrations of it—he does not, like Dante, meet the great poets of antiquity and be asked to walk in their company, but tells his 'litel bok' of *Troilus* to kiss the steps 'where as thou seest pace | Virgile, Ovide, Omer, Lucan, and Stace'—he seems to regard himself as their disciple, and perhaps as a modern 'auctour'. (See *poets and poetry.)

Curtius (1953), esp. 48–62; Minnis (1984); Minnis and Scott (1988).

audience. There have been some very confident assertions and speculations about the nature of Chaucer's audience (in the narrow sense of the group of people who first heard or read his poems), and about his relationship with it. In fact, there is very little reliable external evidence. Chaucer is often described as a 'court poet', but he was not a court poet in the sense of one who was supported at a court because of his poetry. The records relating to his offices and salaries show that these came because of his administrative qualities, not because of his literary ones. One of the MSS of *Troilus and Criseyde* (now Corpus Christi College, Cambridge, MS 61) has a famous frontispiece which has often been reproduced with the title 'Chaucer reading to the Court of Richard II', and has sometimes been used to suggest that his immediate audience consisted of the king and the high nobility. The splendid (outdoor) scene indeed shows a king, queen, and nobles around a figure (resembling some other 'portraits' of Chaucer) at a lectern or pulpit. (See Fig. 8.) However, the literal interpretation of this scene as the representation of an actual occasion has been seriously questioned. The scene is stylized; the noble listeners are not identified. It has been suggested—and it is certainly possible—that the frontispiece may be due to the manuscript's editor, publisher, or recipient, and that it may be an attempt to give the impression of the sumptuous occasion that the poem might seem to demand. There is, of course, no evidence that Chaucer did not read *Troilus* to the royal court: we simply do not know. He certainly had court connections, from his early service with Lionel, earl of Ulster and in the royal household (see Geoffrey *Chaucer: life); and a few of his poems have some association with the higher nobility or with royalty, although the closeness of the association, and the exact nature of any possible patronage remain obscure. It is from the wider administrative circles of the 'court', the officials, civil servants, and lawyers, that Chaucer's familiar friends seem to come. Men such as *Gower, *Strode, *Clanvowe, *Usk, or the recipients of the verse letters *Bukton and *Scogan probably form the earliest group of his known readers. After his death, the 15th-c. owners of MSS of his works include aristocrats, landowners, and merchants; and he was read with varying degrees of attention by his imitators and literary successors (see *criticism of Chaucer I).

In Chaucer's day, books could be both read and heard. Some of his references clearly imply an audience of readers: 'Thow, redere' he says in *Troilus and Criseyde* V.270; and in *The Canterbury Tales* tells his readers that if they do not wish to read the churls' tales, they should 'turne over the leef' and choose another tale (I.3177). It is quite possible that some of his work was circulated in MS among his friends before it was 'published'. It is also possible that he sometimes read some of it to them. Reading aloud to a group was still a normal method of presenting literary works. In *Troilus and Criseyde* there is a scene where the ladies are sitting in a paved parlour and a maiden is reading the romance of Thebes to them. Chaucer's works could well have been read aloud in this way. No doubt this practice of reading aloud helped the medieval author to achieve a closeness and intimacy with his audience, a relationship which became increasingly difficult for authors in the age of print and mass production.

But internal references also demonstrate that he was thinking (like most authors) of an audience wider than his immediate circle of readers or hearers. The suggestion of possibly 'turning over the leaf' (I.3177) is obviously meant for all readers of MSS of *The Canterbury Tales*. He likes to give the impression of spontaneity, of a closeness with his readers. He will speak directly to one part of the audience—to 'lovers', or to those interested in questions of love. He will anticipate the objection of a particular person—some 'lover' might think, 'I would not win love in this way' (*Tr* II.29–35); some envious person might think 'this was a sudden love' (*Tr* II.667); and so on. He was constantly experimenting with *narrators and narrative voices. As Dieter Mehl says, 'he creates the illusion of a lively and mutual relationship between the fictional narrator . . . and the fictional audience with which we are asked to identify ourselves'. And, of course, in *The Canterbury Tales*, he provides a fictitious audience of pilgrims and some lively and vivid audience reactions. The narrators there can speak very directly to their hearers. There is a very dramatic example in *The *Man of Law's Tale* (II.645–51) when the narrator, describing the plight of his heroine, suddenly asks his audience whether they have not seen the pale face of a man being led to his death. Like his narrators, Chaucer has this quality of intimacy with his audience, whoever they are.

Giffin (1956); Green (1980); Mehl (1974); Pearsall (1977); Strohm (1977).

Auffrike; Augustyn. See *Affrike; *Austyn(e).

augrym, arithmetic (cf. modern *algorism, algorithm*; Old Fr. *augrisme*). The clerk Nicolas in *The *Miller's Tale* had 'augrym stones', counters as used for calculation with an abacus board. Chaucer's 'noumbres of augrym' were the Hindu-Arabic numerals. (See *Argus (3)) [JDN]

AUGUSTUS CESAR, CESAR AUGUSTUS. 'Augustus' was the honorary title conferred in 27 BC on the first Roman emperor, Octavian (see *Octovyan). This form is only used by Chaucer in *A Treatise on the *Astrolabe* (1.10) to explain the name of the month of August (see *months and seasons).

AURELIAN, the Roman emperor (Lucius Domitius) Aurelianus (270–5), the conqueror of Queen Zenobia (*Cenobia) in *The Monk's Tale* (VII.2351–74).

Aurelius, Aurelie, the squire in *The *Franklin's Tale*. The name is probably meant to be a touch of local colour: it was a Roman name used by the Britons (cf. e.g. the King Aurelius Ambrosius in Geoffrey of Monmouth (*Gaufride)).

Aurora (1), goddess of the dawn (*LGW* 774).

Aurora **(2),** see *Peter of Riga.

Auster, the south wind (*Bo.* I m.7:3, II m.3:11; see *Nothus).

AUSTYN(E), AUGUSTYN, St Augustine of Hippo (354–430), doctor of the Church and the most influential patristic writer on medieval theology. Apart from about five years in Italy, he spent all his life in North Africa where from *c*.396 to his death he was bishop of Hippo. His theology was set out in many forms: biblical commentary (e.g. on Genesis, Psalms, and on the gospel of John), sermons (some 300 survive, plus numerous apocryphal additions), polemical writings (against the Manichean, Donatist, and Pelagian heresies), and tracts (e.g. *De Trinitate)*. Most influential were the *De Civitate Dei* (written 413–26), an extended analysis of the opposition between the kingdom of God and the kingdom of the world, provoked by the fall of Rome in 410, and the *Confessions*, an autobiographical account of his early life and conversion together with extended meditations on the relation of the soul to God. Augustine's influence spread to every nook and cranny of medieval theological and religious writing. His most important role for Chaucer was perhaps as one of the authorities on *free will and predestination (mentioned in *NPT* VII.3241), but a wide range of his writings are quoted or referred to in *The Parson's Tale* and elsewhere. Augustine in the medieval period was regarded as the writer of a monastic rule used by the Augustinian canons; hence the references to *Austyn* in *GP* I.187–8. [AH]

Aux, apogee, most distant point of an *epicycle of *deferent, circle from the centre of the Earth (or in the case of *Equatorie of the Planetis*, from what is there called 'centre *Aryn'). (See also *astrology and astronomy*.) [JDN]

AVERROIS. Averröes, Abû'l-Walîd Muhammad ibn Ahmad ibn Muhammad ibn Rushd (1126–98), known to Western scholastics as Commentator. Averroes was born at Córdoba. He studied Islamic theology, law, medicine, and mathematics, and after serving as judge and physician at court—moving often between Seville and Córdoba—he was instructed to write a commentary on the works of *Aristotle. Accused of unorthodoxy, in 1195 he was banished, his books were ordered to be burned, and study of his philosophy was forbidden. The edicts were cancelled when his prince, al-Mansûr, returned to Morocco and recalled the philosopher, but he died there soon afterwards.

Although mentioned by Chaucer only in the *General Prologue* as one of many learned writers known to the Doctour of Physik (*Physician), Averroes' influence on Chaucer's and the previous century was much more than that of an eminent physician. Latin Averroism became a powerful intellectual force, introducing a logical and scientific approach to certain problems (of the soul, creation, and truth) that aroused much theological hostility. One notorious idea (perhaps not actually held by Averroes) was that a proposition may be philosophically true although theologically false. Whether or not Chaucer knew the details of the controversy, its relevance to any medieval writer who introduced multiple levels of meaning into his poetry would have been plain enough. (See also *medicine*.) [JDN]

AVYCEN, Abû 'Alî al-Husayn ibn 'Abdallâh ibn Sînâ (980–1037), Avicenna. Born in Bukhara, Avicenna taught in Isfahan and served as physician to a succession of Persian princes. A prolific philosophical writer in the tradition of *Aristotle (but much influenced too by *Plato and the Neoplatonists), he was greatly admired as such in the West in the 13th c. His reputation as a philosopher, however, was shorter-lived than that as a physician. It is not surprising that he is mentioned by Chaucer in the *General Prologue* as one whose writings were known to the *Doctour of Physik (*Physician). (See also *medicine*.) [JDN]

Avysioun, see *dream vision*.

AYALA, PERO LÓPEZ DE, Chancellor (1332–1407). Spanish diplomat, politician, poet, and prose writer, whose life and work offer certain parallelisms with those of his immediate contemporary, Chaucer (see *Spaigne). Generally considered the first Spanish humanist, with a special interest in *Boccaccio and the Troy story, López de Ayala studied and translated a number of Latin works, including Boethius's *Consolatio philosophiae* and parts of Livy, an author whose influence is apparent in the prose *Chronicles* in which López de Ayala narrates the principal events of the reigns of the different kings he served in his long lifetime: Peter the Cruel (*Petro (1)), Henry II, John II, and Henry III of Castile. Captured both at the Battle of Nájera in 1367 by the Black Prince, and at that of Aljubarrota (*Portyngale) in 1385, by the Portuguese, López de Ayala composed almost certainly during the latter imprisonment perhaps his most famous work, the long and didactic *Palace Verses,* a social manifesto in the first part of which he criticizes the corruption of the Church, from Pope to parish priest, and satirizes all classes of men, from the king downwards, except the very poor, expressing at the same time his own ideas concerning war, justice and the administration of the kingdom. The work, like Juan *Ruiz's *Book of Good Love,* contains a medley of styles and subject matter, the second part being composed of lyrical poems to the Virgin, and the third, consisting of a long commentary on the story of Job and the doctrine of the *Moralia* of St Gregory. [PS]

azemutz, azimutz (pl.), azimuths. (From Arabic *samt,* 'direction'.) These may be lines on an astrolabe plate radiating from the observer's zenith and dividing the horizon line into equal intervals. The intervals are typically of 5, 6, 10 or 30 degrees, but in *A Treatise on the *Astrolabe* 1.19.7 Chaucer mentions twenty-four divisions (thus each is of 15 degrees), and some MS diagrams show thirty-two divisions, corresponding to a compass rose. (See also *astrology and astronomy*; *Cenyth*.) [JDN]

B

Babiloigne, Babiloyne, Babilan, the ancient city of Babylon, on the river Euphrates. It is marked prominently on medieval maps, and was regularly associated with the tower of Babel. In the Middle Ages Babylon was also the name of old Cairo. Chaucer's references are all to the ancient city, (in legend) built and fortified by Semiramus (*Semyrame) who had it 'ditched all about' and its walls made of hard well-baked tiles—i.e. bricks (*LGW* 706–9); the 'sovereyn see' [seat of empire] of Nebuchadnezzar (*Nabugodonosor; VII.2149); and the home of Thisbe (*Tisbe) in *The Legend of Good Women*. It is cited as an example of a rich and great city (*BD* 1061).

BACON, Roger (*c*.1219–*c*.1292), English Franciscan, an influential writer on natural philosophy, *alchemy, optics, and calendar reform. Bacon played an important part in promoting experimental and mathematical methods in the natural sciences. These interests of his were acquired in his studies at the university of Paris, but more especially at Oxford under the influence of *Grosseteste (after 1247), and he lectured in the Faculty of Arts in both places on much of the Aristotelian corpus. He claimed to have spent more than two thousand pounds on his researches. He entered the Franciscan order only around 1257, and within two or three years had incurred the displeasure of the master general, Bonaventure, on questions of astrology and alchemy. His European reputation was assured when Pope Clement IV asked for his philosophical writings. He replied with three famous encyclopaedic works: *Opus maius, Opus minus,* and *Opus tertium.* In these he set forth his aim to bring about the intellectual renewal of the Church. He argued for the pragmatic value of learning, especially of languages, in the advancement of the Christian cause. Bacon had a fertile imagination, and some of his utterances were in later ages seen as visionary—as foretelling the microscope and telescope, for example, the ever-burning lamp, the flying machine, the self-powered vehicle, explosive powders, and so forth.

Bacon's subsequent writings were mingled with such intemperate observations on almost all classes of society that in retrospect his downfall seems inevitable. Perhaps his affinities with Averroism were also partly responsible for his condemnation and imprisonment in Paris, from 1277 or so, possibly until his death. (See also *Alocen; *Averrois; *Grosseteste; *science; *Vitulon.)   [JDN]

Crombie and North (1970), 377–85; Crowley (1950).

Bacus, Bachus, Bacchus, the god of wine, son of Jupiter and Semele. He gave his gifts to Autumn, the time for pressing the grapes (*Bo* I. m.6:15). In *The *Legend of Good Women* (2376) Procne (*Progne) feigned to go on 'pilgrimage' to the temple of Bacchus, but Chaucer does not reproduce Ovid's remarks about the frenzied rites. Bacchus is closely associated with *Venus: he sits beside her in her temple in *The *Parliament of Fowls* (275); he pours the wine at January's wedding in *The *Merchant's Tale* (IV.1722) while she dances. The association is too close for some moralists—the *Physician says that the virtuous Virginia did not allow Bacchus to have 'mastery' of her mouth (VI.58), 'for wyn and youthe dooth Venus encresse'. But the god can drive away care: after the Manciple has given the already drunken Cook a draught of wine, the Host blesses the name of Bacchus, who can turn 'earnest' into '*game' (IX.99), an important role for him to play in *The Canterbury Tales* (see *wine; *drunkenness).

Bagpipes, see *musical instruments.

Bayard, a name for a horse (cf. I.4115, *Tr* I.218). It was originally the bay-coloured magic horse given by Charlemagne to Renaud, one of the four sons of Aymon, and a prominent figure in romance. In the proverbial phrase 'as bold as blind Bayard', it is used as the type of over-bold recklessness (VIII.1413).

Bailly, see *Host.

Balade of Complaint, a *ballade of three stanzas, which has sometimes been thought to be by Chaucer, and is usually included among the 'dubious' short poems. There is no external evidence for his authorship (the poem appears in a MS of John *Shirley, but he did not attribute it to Chaucer); the internal stylistic evidence is inconclusive: the poem is a polished amatory complaint, which may have been an imitation of Chaucer.

(ed.) *Rv* 660, 1091; Scattergood (1995), 477.

Baldeswelle, Bawdeswell (Norfolk), 15 miles (24 km) north-west of Norwich. The *Reeve came from near this town (I.620).

BALE, JOHN (1495–1563), bibliographer and Protestant polemicist. As a young man Bale was a member of the Carmelite order, but left in 1530 or soon after following his conversion to Protestantism. He left England for Germany in 1540, but returned in the reign of Edward VI and in 1552 became bishop of Ossory. He had to flee in 1553 after Mary's accession, but returned after Elizabeth came to the throne. Bale included Chaucer in both his *Illustrium Magnae Britanniae scriptorum . . . summarium* (1548) and his *Scriptorum illustrium Maioris Brytanniae . . . catalogus* (1557–9). Bale's biography of the poet in these two works is unreliable, even grotesquely so (his date of death is variously given as 1458, 1402, and 1400); much of his information derived from John *Leland. His listing of poems in the *Catalogus* contributed to the consolidation of the 'Chaucerian apocrypha': Bale included *The *Plowman's Tale*, *Assembly of Ladies*, *Testament of Cresseid*, (*Lydgate's) *Flower of Curtesye* and *Complaynt of the *Black Knight*, (*Usk's) *Testament of Love*, (*Clanvowe's) *Cuckoo and the Nightingale* and other works unidentifiable from their titles. Bale also included Chaucer's works in his notebook, unpublished till modern times, known as *Index Britanniae scriptorum*. Bale seems primarily to have used one of the printings of the edition by William *Thynne (1532, reprinted 1542 and 1550, *STC* 5068–74), but certainly encountered Chaucer manuscripts in his extensive searches.

[AH]

ballade, a French *lyric form very common in the 14th and 15th c. Among the many poets who used it were *Guillaume de Machaut, *Deschamps, *Christine de Pisan, Charles d'Orléans, and (outstandingly) Villon. Strictly, it consists of three seven- or eight-line stanzas, each using the same rhymes throughout, and ending with the same line as a refrain. It is usually concluded with an *envoy addressed to a prince, a lady, or another person. Chaucer may have been the first writer to use this French form in English. He wrote a number, varying in form and in content. (See *To *Rosemounde*, *Womanly Noblesse*, *Fortune* and *The Complaint of *Venus* (both triple ballades—three ballades connected, with an envoy), *Against *Women Unconstant*, *Truth*, *Gentilesse*, *Lak of *Stedfastnesse*, *Lenvoy de Chaucer a *Scogan* (a double ballade), *Lenvoy de Chaucer a *Bukton*, *The Complaint of Chaucer to his *Purse*, and 'Hyd, Absolon, thy gilte tresses clere' in the Prologue to *The *Legend of Good Women* (F 249–69, G 203–23).

Ballenus. Belinous or Belenos (Balanus), a disciple of Hermes Trismegistus, appears among the magicians in *The *House of Fame* (1273). He is said to have discovered underneath a statue of Hermes a book which contained the secrets of the universe.

Balthasar, Belshazzar, king of Babylon (*Babiloigne), son of Nebuchadnezzar (*Nabugodonosor). The *Monk tells his 'tragedy' (VII.2183–246), following the account in Daniel 5 of the great feast interrupted by the mysterious hand writing its prophetic message.

Barbarie, the (V.1452; cf. 'the Barbre nacioun', II.281) seems to be used for heathendom generally—the lands in question are Asia Minor and Syria. (The restricted sense of Barbary as the North African coast (the land of the Berbers) appears in English later, in Shakespeare's day.)

BARNABO VISCOUNTE, Bernabò Visconti, lord of Milan (d. 1385), 'god of delit and scourge of Lumbardye', is the subject of a one-stanza tragedy told by the *Monk (VII.2399–406). He was ousted from power in May 1385 by his nephew and son-in-law Gian Galeazzo, and died mysteriously and suddenly in prison. Chaucer's lines attribute his death to Gian Galeazzo, but profess ignorance of the reason and the manner of it (he was popularly thought to have been poisoned). Chaucer had met Bernabò (and the English commander *Hawkwood) on his embassy in 1378 (see Geoffrey *Chaucer: life). There had been a previous connection between the English and the powerful Visconti family. Desirous of increasing their status, a marriage was arranged between Violante, the daughter of Galeazzo Visconti, Bernabò's brother, and Lionel, duke of Clarence, an early patron of Chaucer, and it was celebrated with great pomp in Milan in June 1368 (though the happiness and the political benefit were short-lived, since Lionel became ill and died in October, before he returned to England). And in 1378 Bernabò's daughter Caterina was offered in marriage to Richard II, but nothing came of this. It is clear that the news of Bernabò's fall would have been of interest to the English court. The Visconti remained in power for the rest of the century.

BARTHOLOMEW THE ENGLISHMAN (*fl.* 1220–50), Bartholomæus Anglicus. An Englishman who studied at Paris, he entered the French Province of the Franciscan Order. Bartholomew earned fame as a lecturer on theology in Paris before being sent to the Saxon Province of his order. His greatest work became one of the best known of all encyclopaedias of natural science in the Middle Ages: *De proprietatibus rerum* (*On the Properties of Things*). This synoptic work in nineteen books, covering medicine, natural history, astronomy, cosmography, and cosmology, became extremely popular for well over three centuries, and was translated into French, English (by *Trevisa), Dutch, Italian, and Spanish during the 14th and 15th c.   [JDN]
(ed.) Seymour (1975).

BASILIE. St Basil the Great (*c.*330–379), monk,

hermit, and bishop of Caesarea, is quoted once by the Parson (X.221).

Basilius, one of Boethius's (*Boece) accusers, apparently of dubious reputation—he was 'chased out of the king's service' (*Bo* I pr.4:110); his identity is not certain.

Bathe, Bath, Somerset. The medieval town, which is now overwhelmed by later developments, both elegant and inelegant, was a centre of the wool trade. The *Wife of Bath is actually said to have come from 'biside' Bath (I.445). This may well mean a village near Bath, but it has been suggested that it refers to the parish of St Michael's *juxta Bathon* outside the north gate of the town's walls.

BEAUCHAMP, SIR WILLIAM, Captain of Calais (and later Lord Abergavenny), a friend of Chaucer, who accompanied him to Calais in July 1387.

BEAUMONT, FRANCIS (*c.*1550–1624—to be distinguished from the more celebrated dramatist Beaumont (1584–1616))—was the Master of Charterhouse, and had been a fellow student of Thomas *Speght at Peterhouse, Cambridge. In his edition of Chaucer (1598), Speght published a letter (dated 1597) from Beaumont, which is an interesting piece of Elizabethan literary criticism of the poet. It defends Chaucer against two contemporary complaints: that his words have grown 'too hard and unpleasant'; and that he is 'somewhat too broad in some of his speeches'. Chaucer's language was in its own day pure, and still is worthy of imitation (as *Spenser has shown), he says. The 'incivility' can be excused on grounds of literary decorum. Chaucer's *Canterbury Tales* is his own invention ('without following the example of any that ever writ before him'): 'his drift is to touch all sorts of men, and to discover all vices of that age.' In such works as *Troilus and Criseyde*, *The Legend of Good Women*, and *The Book of the Duchess*, Chaucer 'soareth much higher'. *Troilus*, in particular, is praised for being 'sententious' ('there be few staves . . . which are not concluded with some principal sentence, most excellently imitating Homer and Virgil'). Chaucer may be called 'the pith and sinews of eloquence; the very life itself of all mirth and pleasant writing', and he excels in descriptions, possessing 'his readers with a stronger imagination of seeing that done before their eyes, which they read, than any other that ever writ in any tongue'. He makes an interesting reference to 'those ancient learned men of our time in Cambridge' who read Chaucer and commended him to the younger sort, and brought Speght and himself 'in love with him'.

CH i. 135–9.

beauty. In medieval writings on aesthetics, which are mostly to be found in the works of philosophers and theologians, God is the essence and the source of beauty: beauty can be seen in Christ, the Virgin Mary, the angels, or heaven. However, the sources of medieval ideas of beauty are not exclusively Christian. Some are inherited from classical antiquity—for instance, the association of the beautiful and the good, and the way this is expressed in number, harmony, and order. Boethius (*Boece) (III m.9), echoing Plato's *Timaeus*, says that God bears the pattern of the beautiful world in His mind, and shapes it in that ideal likeness, ordering the parts to frame a perfect whole, constraining the elements by harmony. Unity is sometimes a principle of beauty: then, *diversity may suggest something fallen or incomplete. However, there is also the idea that diversity is ordained by God from the unity and simplicity of His divine mind, and that therefore there is beauty in diversity.

Beauty is characteristically expressed in terms of light, the splendour and perfection of all embodied things, according to *Grosseteste. God is the source of Light, brighter than the sun's rays, and if proportion gives harmony and order to created things, light endows them with a transcendent quality of 'nobility'. This aesthetic principle underlies the passion which medieval writers have for light and luminosity, and their delight in shining, glowing things and colours and scenes such as spring landscapes. In ME the word *bright* is very commonly used (in a way it is not in Modern English) of the beauty of a lady ('Emelye the brighte' (I.1737), 'Criseyde the brighte' (*Tr* V.516), etc.). Others are 'bright of hue' (IV.377; cf. *Anel* 41). That the word is not entirely formulaic is shown by its

opposition to *pale*: cf. *Troilus and Criseyde* IV.740 'hire hewe, whilom bright, that tho was pale' and V.708. Although moralists insisted on the transitory nature of the beauty of created things and the potential deceptiveness and falseness of earthly beauty, piety and aesthetic delight could coexist.

These abstract ideas appear in stereotyped forms and formulae in rhetorical precept and practice (see *rhetoric). There are exemplary figures of beauty (like *Absolon (1) or Helen (*Eleyne)). There are patterns for the literary description of ideal female or male beauty; of the ideal *landscape (often genuinely ideal in that it is not meant to represent reality, so that olives and cedars and palms will appear in northern poetry); of the grove, of the forest, with its different species (the listing of which may be not so much a display of rhetorical virtuosity as a tribute to *Nature's creative diversity), of the *locus amoenus*, which recalls the *garden of Paradise. Literary examples are found in travel books, visions of the other world, and romances. These evocations of ideal beauty are often contrasted with examples of *ugliness, e.g. deserts, grotesques, or misshapen creatures. As the Middle Ages progressed, there was in literature, and especially in the visual arts, an increasing interest in individualized portraiture, in the illusion of reality, in 'lifelike' representation, as evidenced, for instance, in the sculptures of the prophets on the 'Well of Moses' at the Chartreuse de Champmol near Dijon by Claus Sluter (1395–1406). These prophets are awesome, but no longer hieratic; they are impressive figures of old men.

Chaucer has a range of aesthetic terms, some of them still in modern use—*faire* (or the n. *fairnesse*), commonly used in the quite general sense of 'beautiful' or 'pretty' (of clothes, forests, gardens, flowers, steeds, cities, etc. as well as of human physical beauty); *fyne, swete, gay, comlynesse*—but others which are now unfamiliar—*gent* (noble, slender); *tretys* 'graceful, well-formed'; *fetys* 'elegant' (used e.g. of a cloak, I.157) or 'elegantly shaped' (of dancing girls, VI.478) and its adverb *fetisly* (I.273; cf. I.3319, 4369), or *joly* (I.3316). An interesting group of words is used of works of art and the like: *delitable* ('many another delitable sighte' IV.62; 'delitable ditees' [poems] *Bo* I m.1);

curious 'skilfully made' (of a pin, a tomb, the 'arraying' of a garden, or of pictures (*HF* 125)) and *curiosite* 'intricate workmanship' (of the palace of Fame, *HF* 1178)—though this is a quality not prized by all: the Parson speaks severely (X.828) of the 'curiosity' of the elaborate preparation of food.

Descriptions of beautiful places and people are clearly related to traditional rhetorical patterns, but show interesting variations. The *Romaunt of the Rose* opens with a beautiful spring landscape, and the dreamer is soon admitted to an even more beautiful garden, a *locus amoenus* (he thought to 'have ben in Paradys'); in it there is a carefully tended and shady 'mixed grove' (see Fig. 10). Trees of different kinds appear in profusion in the landscape of Chaucer's own dream visions, and in the forest in The *Book of the Duchess* (cf. 416–33) and The *Parliament of Fowls* (172–82) the profusion is designed to express and celebrate the abundance and plenitude of Nature.

Formal descriptions of beautiful men are rare, and are not as straightforwardly eulogistic as that of Myrthe in *The Romaunt of the Rose* (817–46, who is tall, with broad shoulders but 'smalish in the girdilstede', has bright hair and grey eyes, a face as round as an apple, and all his features elegantly formed, so that 'he semed lyk a portreiture'). In his own poems Chaucer liked to vary the stereotypes. The description of Absolon probably echoes that of the biblical examplar of beauty and the famous rhetorical description of him by *Peter of Riga, but it is fitted to the Oxford context of The *Miller's Tale* and to his unheroic role in the story. Features suggestive of a dandified and perhaps slightly effeminate appearance are picked out with a combination of faintly absurd exaggeration and homely detail—his hair is curled and stretched out like a fan; his eyes are fashionably grey, but grey 'as a goose'. Similarly, Sir *Thopas has the pink and white complexion of Myrthe (and the standard female beauty), but the redness is absurdly compared to scarlet cloth (and contrasts with his fair hair—here 'saffron'); and we are told abruptly that he had a 'semely nose'.

In the *Romaunt* a female personification of Beauty appears with the God of Love. She is of high rank; she is not 'dark' or 'brown', but glowing and 'bright'. She is as white as a lily or a rose; she has no need to use make-up; her yellow tresses reach down to her heels; her nose, mouth, eye, cheek, and all her members are 'wel wrought'; she is young, elegant ('fetys'), and slender. Another personified Beauty is seen by the dreamer in *The *Parliament of Fowls* (225) among the attendants of Cupid outside the temple of *Venus: this one is 'withouten any atyr'. In The *Book of the Duchess* (817–1032) the lady's beauty is being recalled by the grieving man in black. The details are conventional—derived from French versions of the traditional rhetorical stereotype (golden hair, beautiful *eyes, a face 'whit, rody, fressh, and lyvely hewed', etc.—with some that were not always to remain in fashion—each limb rounded and shapely ('fattysh, flesshy, not gret therewith'), hips of 'good breadth', and a straight flat back. But the description is enlivened by comments, questions, recollections of her actions, and speech, so that a sense of personality and freshness is created. The whole is informed by *'mesure'—moderation—and her physical beauty is matched by her moral beauty.

This is the image of the beautiful lady as she might be depicted in a MS illustration of a courtly scene (and perhaps of the actual courtly beauty, assisted by simple cosmetic equipment such as hair dyes). And these are in general the characteristics of other beautiful women in Chaucer. They do not all have a long body (Anelida and Criseyde are 'middle' in stature), but they are slender (cf. I.3234, IV.1602); they have long golden hair ('yellow', I.1049, *LGW* 1747; 'sunnish', *Tr* IV.736, 816—sometimes with a further specific detail: Criseyde's is *ounded* 'wavy'). The Prioress has the fashionable grey eyes—and a 'tretys' nose (I.152). The slender arms mentioned by the Wife of Bath (III.261) as a feature which attract men are possessed by Criseyde (*Tr* III.1247), who also has a straight back and 'sydes longe, flesshly [well shaped], smothe, and white'. Breasts are round—and small (*Tr* III.1250), and white (*Tr* IV.752, V.219). The whiteness of complexion which was so obviously prized can be related to the aesthetic of light, and also, no doubt, has a social significance, since a sunburned complexion would suggest an outdoor, labouring life. Chaucer has no brown girls, but among the male pilgrims, the Yeoman and the Shipman are sunburned. Above all it is the eyes and the face which reveal beauty most splendidly (Criseyde's face is like the 'image of Paradise', *Tr* IV.864).

Chaucer uses the traditional techniques of emphasis, sometimes declaring beauty to be 'inexpressible' (V.34–41), or comparing it favourably with celebrated exemplars of beauty (Criseyde is (*Tr* I.454–5) fairer than *Eleyne or *Polixene). He also uses much of the more general lore concerning beauty. It is 'natural' (*LGW* 1749); the Physician, extolling the beauty of *Virginia, imagines Nature exulting in her work (VI.7–29; cf. *BD* 1195–8). Beauty is associated with *youth (cf. *Tr* I.982 and *The *Merchant's Tale*), and it will not last, as Pandarus repeatedly says (*Tr* II.337 ff.) as he urges Criseyde to 'go love' before age will devour her. At other times, the proverbial 'beauty without bounty [goodness] is never good' is exemplified (as in May in *MchT*). The ideal combination of goodness and beauty is found in *Custance (II.158, 162), *Griselda (IV.211–12), and Virginia (VI.112).

There are again variations on the stereotypes. The *portrait of the attractive 18-year-old *Alison (1) in *The Miller's Tale* is as carefully fitted to her role in the narrative as that of her admirer Absolon, her beauty being expressed through a series of rustic images. In a more ironic context, January is moved to address the beauty of his lady May in the language of the Song of Songs: 'Com forth now, with thyne eyen columbyn! | How fairer ben thy brestes than is wyn!'.

Chaucer does not usually elaborate an opposition of beauty and ugliness. The contrast in *The Wife of Bath's Tale* between the ugliness of the old hag and the beautiful young woman into whom she is transformed is simply but dramatically registered ('a fouler wight ther may no man devyse' | 'she so fair was, and so yong therto'); and the contrast between May and January in *The Merchant's Tale*, although it uses details like January's thick bristles and slack skin around his neck in contrast to his wife's 'tendre face', is related to be a more general opposition of age and youth. Chaucer seems rather to endorse the principle of *Boccaccio that the beauty of a flock of white doves is more enhanced by the presence of a black crow than by that of a pure white swan. Criseyde's only 'lack'—that her brows were joined together (*Tr.* V.813)—seems to make her eyes even more beautiful. In *The Canterbury Tales* we sometimes

find creations which differ completely from the courtly and rhetorical patterns of beauty. The merry apprentice in *The *Cook's Tale*, for instance, who is 'broun as a berye, a propre short felawe, | With lockes blake, ykembd ful fetisly' (I.4369–70), seems to have no difficulty in attracting the girls. Other descriptions have a teasing overlap. The miller's daughter in *The Reeve's Tale* is a sturdy country girl ('thikke and wel ygrowen') but has the grey eyes of the fashionable beauty (perhaps appropriate to the 'noble kyn' of her mother); along with her father's snub nose; she has 'brestes rounde and hye', but broad buttocks. Such descriptions, like the portraits of the *General Prologue*, suggest that Chaucer was in no way confined to the idealizing aesthetic patterns of beauty, but found a different kind of beauty in human diversity and 'lack', rather like the realistic sculptors of the later Middle Ages. (See also *visual qualities.)

Brewer (1955); de Bruyne (1946); Curtius (1953), 180–2; Frappier (1976); Glunz (1937).

BECKET, ST THOMAS, see *Thomas of Kent, Seint**.

Belial (an OT Hebrew word (?'wickedness'), applied by St Paul to Satan), a common medieval name for the devil; used once by the *Parson (X.897).

Belle, the. The Bell, near the *Tabard in Southwark (*Southwerk), mentioned in the *General Prologue* (I.719), is probably one of the several taverns of that name which existed in Southwark. It has been suggested that it may rather have been one of the licensed brothels in the area.

Belle Dame sans Merci, La, an early 15-c. French poem by Alain Chartier, translated into English by Sir Richard Roos or Ros (?*c.*1410–82). It is a dialogue between an importunate lover and his lady, who parries his advances with wit and good sense—well before Shakespeare's Rosalind, she remarks of the sickness of love that 'but few peple it causeth for to dye'. But at the end of the poem the lover, in spite of all his pleading, is not granted 'mercy', and dies. The original poem seems to have caused a *scandale* in French courtly literary circles, provoking a series of 'answers' and a continuing debate. The result of the lady's '*daunger' was taken by some to be an attack on love. The English version is an elegant and highly polished piece of work. Although certainly not by Chaucer, it was included in *Pynson's 1526 edition, and even though removed from the canon by *Tyrwhitt, continued to appear in some 19th-c. editions. Because of its association with Chaucer it was widely read, and gave its title to a well-known poem by Keats.

(ed.) Skeat (1897).

Bellona. The Roman goddess of war is alluded to at the beginning of *Anelida and Arcite*, where she is equated with the armed goddess *Pallas.

bells, see *musical instruments.

Belmarye, a Moorish state in North Africa (Benmarin, now Morocco; see Map 3), ruled in the 14th c. by the Banu Merin or Merenids, a Berber dynasty. The Knight had campaigned here (I.57)—perhaps with the Christian privateers who attacked towns there—and mentions it in his tale as a place where lions are found (I.2630).

BENEIT (BENEDIGHT), SEINT, St Benedict (*c.*480–*c.*550) the father of Western monasticism. Born in Nursia (the region of Norcia in Umbria), he abandoned his studies in Rome to become a hermit. He organized his disciples into small communities, and founded the monastery at Monte Cassino, between Naples and Rome. In the influential 'Rule of St Benedict' or 'Benedictine Rule' he adapted traditional ascetic teaching in a moderate and orderly way, and set out a daily pattern of prayer, worship, and labour. The monks should live in a community, totally obedient to their abbot, and not wander about. Chaucer's *Monk, with his love of hunting and travelling, found his Rule old and somewhat strict (I.173), and preferred to follow the practice of 'the newe world'. In *The *Miller's Tale*, a Benedict from popular lore appears (I.3483) in the carpenter's magic charm—the form of the name there, Benedight, perhaps suggests a confusion with the word *benedight* 'blessed'. He was a saint of particular spiritual power, to whom many miracles were attributed.

BENOÎT DE SAINTE-MAURE, a 12th-c. French poet, probably from Sainte-Maure in Touraine. He wrote a verse history of the dukes of Normandy for Henry II of England, but his most influential work was the *Roman de Troie* (see *Troy). This long verse *romance is based on the books of *Dares and Dictys (*Dite), but for the first time incorporates the love story of Troilus and Criseyde. He probably invented the episode of the separation of the lovers and Criseyde's infidelity. Benoît's book was abridged in a Latin version by Guido (*Guydo) delle Colonne, which was presented as a newly discovered and independent account, and was widely used by later writers on Troy. Chaucer, however, made use of Benoît at first hand in *Troilus and Criseyde*.

(ed.) Constans (1904–12).

Bere, bear, constellation of the (Greater) Bear, *Ursa Major, *or* the brightest star in it. The name probably has a prehistoric ancestry, and the tradition that 'the Wain' is a vulgar alternative is also extremely ancient. *Boece* has the often-repeated tradition that it never sets—although of course at low geographical latitudes it does so. The *Iliad* and *Odyssey* limit the Bear to seven stars. The *House of Fame* speaks of 'eyther bere', so including the Lesser Bear, for which see *Septemtryones.   [JDN]

Beryn, The Tale of, a poem of just over 4,000 lines, is found in one MS of *The Canterbury Tales*. It was printed in *Urry's Chaucer of 1721, but the authenticity was doubted even then in the preface (see *Chauceriana). *Tyrwhitt excluded it from the canon. It is a 15th-c. work claiming some affinity with *The Canterbury Tales*. A lively introduction describes the arrival of the pilgrims at Canterbury, their visit to the cathedral and sightseeing, and their sojourn at an inn, where the Pardoner is discomfited by Kit the tapster. When the pilgrims leave early the next morning, the Merchant offers to tell the first tale. The story itself is based on a section of a 14th-c. French prose romance, the *Roman de Bérinus*, which seems to go back to an oriental tale of the Merchant and the Rogues. Beryn, the spoilt son of a Roman senator, is forced to repent, and becomes a merchant. He comes to a town where the inhabitants are the most deceitful people in the world (the schemes and the ensuing litigations become increasingly fantastic). Finally, an old beggar gives him good legal advice—to answer the charges with even bigger falsehoods. Beryn wins the favour of the king, who rewards him with his daughter. The English author adapted the legal proceedings so as to provide a satirical commentary on contemporary English practice.

(ed.) Furnivall (1909).

BERNARD, St Bernard of Clairvaux (1090–1153), born in Burgundy, became a Cistercian monk and (in 1115) abbot of Clairvaux. He became an important figure in the intellectual and political life of the 12th c. His eloquent and passionate sermons and spiritual writings made him a major influence on contemporary and subsequent spirituality. He stressed the grace and the love of God, and fostered an intense devotion to the humanity of Christ and to the Virgin Mary (*Marie). Thus the Second Nun in her invocation to the Virgin 'of whom that Bernard list so wel to write' (VIII.30) uses the famous prayer to Mary which *Dante puts into the saint's mouth in *Paradiso* 33. As a great 'authority', he is several times quoted by the Parson (e.g. X.256–9, X.723). Not all the 'sentences' attributed to him are actually his; some come from the extensive body of 'Pseudo-Bernardine' works. He is probably that 'Bernard the monk' who 'did not see everything' referred to in the proverb quoted in the *Prologue* to The *Legend of Good Women* (16).

BERNARD GORDON (*fl.* 1294–1308), Master of Medicine. It is not known whether Bernard Gordon was of French or Scottish origins. His chief work was his *Lilium medicinæ*, begun in 1303 when he was in his twentieth year of teaching at the University of Montpellier. He is one of the three modern physicians named in the description of the Physician in the *General Prologue* to The *Canterbury Tales*, the others being John of Gaddesden and Gilbertus Anglicus (*Gatesden and *Gilbertyn). (See also *medicine.) [JDN]

BERNARDUS SILVESTRIS, a scholar and commentator who wrote in the 1140s, was interested in Platonism (he was profoundly influenced by the *Timaeus*) and the interpretation of myths.

Like Alan of Lille (see *Aleyn (1)), he was the author of a cosmological epic with Natura playing a central role. His *Cosmographia* (also called *De mundi universitate* or *Megacosmos*) was known to Chaucer, who used it in the passage at the beginning of The *Man of Law's Tale* on the destiny which is 'perhaps' written in the book of heaven with the stars. Chaucer shared his fascination with the question of how human affairs are controlled and conditioned, and the relationship of this to freedom of choice.

(ed.) Dronke (1978); (trans.) Wetherbee (1973).

BERSUIRE, PIERRE (Petrus Berchorius), author of the *Ovidius moralizatus* (*c.*1340–2), which is book 15 of his very large *Reductorium morale* (written probably 1335–40, and revised 1359), but circulated separately. Bersuire made at least two redactions of it, incorporating in the second some details from the (quite separate) French 14th-c. poem the *Ovide moralisé*. There were many adaptations and abridgements (see *Albricus). The *Ovidius moralizatus* and its tradition furnished Chaucer with extensive mythographical information, notably in the description of *Venus in The *Knight's Tale*.

Monfrin and Samaran (1962); Twycross (1972), 3–45.

Berwyk, Berwick-upon-Tweed, a town on the Northumberland coast. It was a border town, repeatedly fought over by Scots and English. It is used in the phrase 'fro Berwyk into *Ware' (I.692) to indicate the 'whole of England'.

Bestiary, a collection of moralized accounts of *animals, *birds, and other creatures derived from the Greek *Physiologus, a book of about fifty anecdotes from natural history followed by moralities, dating from between the 2nd and the 4th c. AD. This is a curious blend of Christian allegory and the mystical science of late antiquity. Under the veil of the 'properties' of creatures there is revealed the pilgrimage of the life of man, and the dangerous wiles of the devil—'as the woodpecker, when he finds a hollow tree, builds his nest in it, so also does the devil with man'. Yet it contains some serious natural history. The Latin prose *Physiologus* proved very influential, producing versified, expanded (and sometimes splendidly illustrated) versions, which eventually found their way into many vernacular translations. In England, there are OE fragments, on the Panther and the Whale, versions in Anglo-Norman, and another in ME from the 13th c. The *Bestiary*'s interpretations were well known: for instance, the phoenix (*fenix), which rises from the ashes of its pyre (Christ's Resurrection); or the whale mistaken by mariners for an island, which, when they light a fire on it, plunges down into the depths and destroys them (as the devil does with those who place their trust in him).

Klingender (1971).

Bethulia, Bethulie, an unidentified 'strong city' of the Jews, which was saved from the assault of Holofernes (*Oloferne) by the heroine *Judith (VII.1099, 2565).

Beves, mentioned in *Sir Thopas* (VII.899), the hero of the English romance *Bevis of Hampton*, of which the earliest surviving version is in the *Auchinleck MS. Like *Guy of Warwick* (*Gy) it is ultimately derived from an Anglo-Norman romance. The evil wife of Guy, the earl of Southampton, has her husband murdered by her lover. Her child Bevis is protected by a faithful steward, Saber, but is carried by pirates to the Saracen king of Armenia. There Josian, the king's daughter, falls in love with him, promises to become Christian, and gives him a warhorse. But Bevis is imprisoned, and Josian is made to marry the king of Mombrant (but preserves her virginity by magic). Eventually Bevis escapes, rescues her, and overcomes the giant Ascopart, who becomes his servant. The three of them flee as far as Cologne. After many further adventures the family is reunited: Bevis kills the king of Mombrant; one of his sons becomes king of Armenia, and the other heir to the throne of England. Saber is made earl of Southampton, while Bevis and Josian retire to Mombrant for a holy death. It is an extremely lively romance, and remained popular, finding its way into early printed versions, and surviving in chapbook form for centuries.

(ed.) Kölbing (1885–9).

Bible. 'The Bible was the most studied book of the middle ages. Bible study represented the highest branch of learning' (Beryl Smalley). The standard version in medieval Western Europe was the Latin translation of St *Jerome in the 4th c. (the 'Vulgate'). In spite of his misgivings about them, he included apocryphal Old Testament books like the story of *Judith or the Maccabees (*Machabee) which were eventually banished from most post-Reformation Bibles. The Bible was used in schools, and in the cloisters, where the *lectio divina* or divine reading was part of the monastic pattern of life. It was a set book for theologians. Its 'sacred page' was used for teaching and preaching, for commentary and for meditation. From the time of the Fathers through the Middle Ages there was a series of important and influential commentaries on its books—by St Augustine (*Austyn), St *Gregory, Hugh of St Victor (d. 1141), Andrew of St Victor, Peter Comestor (d. *c.*1169), and many others. The standard commentary, the 'Glossa ordinaria', is a large work of composite authorship from the 12th c.; Anselm of Laon was a central figure in its inception, but others made contributions; it was expanded by Gilbert de la Porrée and Peter Lombard.

The effects of this intense study were diverse. Contrary to popular opinion, medieval Catholic theology and spirituality is strongly biblical in its inspiration. The technique of biblical exegesis (often using *allegory) developed a number of distinctive features: glossing (***glose, glosyng***) became a continuous commentary rather than a series of linear notes; the *quaestio* or 'question' to be debated (a rhetorical term, the most celebrated literary example of which is Hamlet's 'To be, or not to be: that is the question') increasingly involved extended discussion which could become systematic dogmatic teaching. Old Testament studies sometimes involved consultation with Jewish rabbis and the learning of Hebrew. Biblical patterns affected the writing of history, especially of 'universal history' from the creation to the present day. Biblical books and stories were also frequently paraphrased in the vernaculars. Preachers often supplied their own versions of the gospel for the day or of other texts they referred to, and probably many ordinary layfolk acquired their knowledge of the Bible in this way (and through depictions in the visual arts) rather than through the concentrated 'Bible study' of later periods. But under the influence of *Wyclif (who does not himself appear to have been a translator) and the *Lollards, late 14th-c. England saw an attempt at a complete vernacular translation in the 'Wycliffite' versions of the Vulgate. The Council of Oxford (1407) forbade the making of any fresh translations and the use of Wycliffite versions, although they seem to have been common in the 15th c.

In Chaucer, the Bible is frequently mentioned incidentally and sometimes ironically: the *Physician was not a great student of it (I.438); the *Wife of Bath quotes it for her particular purposes (e.g. that 'gentil text' that bids us wax and multiply)—and her husband *Jankin (4) hunts in it for a proverb which can be used against her (III.650). Biblical verses are also often quoted (by such ill-assorted figures as the *Pardoner (VI.578, 586) and the *Parson), and there are echoes of biblical phraseology.

Smalley (1952).

Biblis. Byblis, mentioned among the ill-fated lovers in the temple of *Venus in *The Parliament of Fowls* (289), the daughter of Miletus, fell passionately in love with her twin brother Caunus. When she confessed her desire, he was horrified, and when she approached him again, he fled to a foreign land. Byblis went mad, and followed her brother, howling like a Bacchante. But she collapsed in the woods, and was transformed by her own tears into a fountain. *Ovid tells the story in *Metamorphoses* book 9.

Bilyea, Bilia, wife of Duillius (a Roman general in 256 BC), who was famous for being able to tolerate his bad breath ('I thought the mouths of all men smelt like that' she said, according to St *Jerome). She is cited as an example of wifely chastity by Dorigen in *The *Franklin's Tale* (V. 1455).

birds (see also *animals, *Nature). Chaucer shares with other medieval writers and artists an interest in birds and a delight in their variety. The beauty of their song is sometimes likened to that of the *angels. They supply figures for the fabulists, and lessons for the moralists and preachers: the crow cries 'cras, cras [tomorrow, tomorrow]' like a reluctant penitent (see *Bestiary). And they supply familiar and homely subjects for the visual

artist: a window at Yarnton, Oxon, shows an owl ringing a bell, with the inscription 'we must pray for the fox', and a tit as a cellarer saying 'who blameth this ale?' Accurate drawings of birds adorn the pages of a number of late medieval English MSS. Like animals, birds were close to men. Cockcrow—if not always the splendid performance given by *Chauntecleer—was a familiar way of marking the time—the cock is the *orloge* (clock) of small villages, we are told in *The *Parliament of Fowls* (350; cf. *CT* I.3357, 3675, 3687, 4233; VI.362; *Tr* III.1415). Around a medieval house were the domestic fowl—hens, ducks, and geese (as in *NPT*)—and the ruddok or robin redbreast, called 'tame' in *The Parliament of Fowls* (349). Inside were sometimes pet birds or caged birds (which, proverbially, desired liberty (cf. IX.163–74), and could be an image of human imprisonment (VII.2414)).

The song of birds is frequently mentioned in descriptions of ideal landscapes—in *The *Book of the Duchess* Chaucer dreams that he is wakened by the 'noyse and swetnesse' of the song of the small birds; in *The *Parliament of Fowls* they sing 'with voys of aungel in here armonye'—until some of them become noisily impatient with the debates; Chaucer then reproduces the sounds of the goose, the cuckoo, and the duck: 'Kek kek! kokkow! quek quek!' Other characteristics are used for standard similes: birds are proverbially 'glad' ('as glad as bird of day', 'as blithe as bird on briar', etc.; cf. VII.38, 50–1), and swift in flight (cf. I.190). Sometimes they flutter—as Venus's doves 'flikerynge' in *The *Knight's Tale* (I. 1962), a word nicely used of Criseyde's spirit in *Troilus and Criseyde* (IV.1221–2). Familiarity can produce a witty simile—in *The *House of Fame* there are as many writers of old tales 'as ben on trees rokes [rooks] nestes' (1516)—or a bold metaphor—as when Troilus calls on his soul to 'unneste, | Fle forth out of myn herte' (IV.305–6). And, since birds were both hunted and used in *hunting, there are references on the one hand to hostile fowlers and their equipment (cf. e.g. *LGW* 132–3; to bird-lime, III.934, *Tr* I.353; to the 'lime-rod', VII.2384), and on the other to hawking and its techniques and equipment (cf. e.g. *Tr* III.1779; to the *lure* or bait (III.415, 1340, etc.); to the *muwe*, the 'mew' or pen (*Tr* III.1784, etc.); or to the *sours* or swift upward flight of a bird of prey (*HF* 544, III.1938)). In spite of the exhortations of moralists against divination from the flight or noise of birds (see *The *Parson's Tale*, X.604), this was widely practised, and left its mark in some traditional 'properties' of birds: 'the raven wys' (*PF* 363) (cf. *Tr.* V.382, where the croaking of ravens is linked with the prophetic shrieking of owls) and 'the crowe with voys of care' (*PF* 363), because it cries out when rain is approaching (though Isidore and others insist that one should not believe that God 'shows his privy counsels to crows'). Legendary birds, like the Harpies (*Arpies) or the Phoenix (*Fenix) are only briefly alluded to.

Birds provide Chaucer with some of his most vivid and lively characters: most obviously, the *Eagle in *The House of Fame* and *Chauntecleer and *Pertelote in *The Nun's Priest's Tale*; but also the falcon in *The *Squire's Tale* and the crow whose transformation from white to black is the subject of *The *Manciple's Tale*. They play an especially prominent role in *The Parliament of Fowls*, where they gather on St *Valentine's Day to choose their mates, and to attend the parliament of Nature, where they listen to the debate between the noble eagle-suitors for the beautiful female eagle. They sit in their orders: the birds of prey in the highest position, the worm-eating birds, the water-birds 'lowest in the dale', and the seed-eating birds on the green. The long catalogue of the species present (330–64) is itself a celebration of the diversity of Nature's creatures. Personalities and attitudes soon emerge and clash—the goose's impatient 'but she wol love hym, lat hym love another' provokes the scornful laughter of the 'gentil foules', and a plea for lifelong service in love from a blushing turtle dove. In the end, Nature has to silence the quarrelling birds, and deliver her verdict.

An extensive 'aviary' is found in Chaucer's works: over fifty species are mentioned. Some names are very familiar; others more mysterious (the *waryangles* (shrikes; III.1408) or the *tydif*, a small and allegedly inconstant bird (?titmouse); *LGW* 154, V.648). Sometimes we have an old form, as *heysoge* (*PF* 612) for hedge sparrow, a word which survived in dialect as *haysuck*. Vultures, the birds 'called "voltoris"', which torture Tityus (*Ticius) in the underworld (*Tr* I.788) sound perhaps a little unfamiliar to Chaucer (who appears to be reusing his own translation of a passage in Boethius).

The characteristics that are noted seem to come from genuine natural history (the 'frosty' *fieldfare* (*PF* 364; cf. *Tr* III.861) is so called either because of its white underside, or, more probably because it is a winter visitor to England), bestiary lore, and popular belief. Thus we have 'the royal *egle*' that 'with his sharpe lok perseth the sonne' (*PF* 330–1), a detail regularly found in encyclopaedias and bestiaries, and a reference to the soaring of eagles (V.123). Eagles are always 'noble' birds (hence a white eagle appears in Criseyde's dream in *Tr* II.925–31, and King Emetreus of 'Inde' carries a tame white eagle on his hand (I.2178)). Several other kinds of birds of prey are mentioned (*merlin, peregrine, goshawk, sparrowhawk, falcon*—with the technical name for a particular variety used in hunting herons, a *faucoun heroner* (*LGW* 1120) or *heroner* (*Tr* IV.413; cf. V.1197)). The *kite* is called 'the coward kyte' in *PF* 349. *Bartholomew explains that it is bold among small birds, but cowardly and fearful among great ones, hunting tame birds and chickens, and eating carrion (thus it carries off the bone over which two dogs were fighting (I.1177–9)).

The *magpie* (*pie*) is 'jolif' or 'pert' (forward, impudent), and provides a simile applied to both women (the Miller's wife in *The *Reeve's Tale*) and men (the Wife of Bath's fourth husband, the 'revelour'). It is full of 'jargon' (IV.1848)—a good word for its unmelodious chattering cry—and 'the janglynge pye' (*PF* 345) is used as an image of the gossipers with their 'jangling' tongues who are the enemies of love (*Tr* III.527). Its relative, the *jay*, is also 'light' and 'jolif' (cf. I.4154, of *Alison); it also 'jangles' (II.774) or chatters (VIII.1397), and is called 'the scornynge jay' (*PF* 346). The jay was sometimes caged and taught words (cf. I.642, IX.132). The *chough* is 'thieving' (*PF* 345), and can also be taught to talk (cf. III.232).

The *goose* is proverbially witless: hence, 'as lewed as gees' (IV.2275), 'goosissh' people (*Tr* III.584); and when in *The Parliament of Fowls* her 'kakelynge' produces an uncourtly thought, it is rejected by the sparrowhawk ('lo, here a parfit resoun of a goos!' (568)). But it is also traditionally watchful—'the waker goos' of *The Parliament of*

birds

Fowls 358. It produces the proverbial simile 'as grey as goose' (I.3317), and the proverb 'there is no goose so grey that it will be without a mate', used in the Wife of Bath's *Prologue* (III.269–70). Its other distinction is gastronomic. In *The Reeve's Tale* the miller roasts a goose for the clerks (I.4137), and the Cook is famous, or notorious, for his 'stubble goose' (I.4351), a fat goose fed on stubble, traditionally eaten at Michaelmas or Martinmas. Roast *swan* was also a favourite dish (cf. I.206); more romantically, the swan was thought to sing 'against his death' (*Anel* 346–7; *PF* 342; *LGW* 1355–6). The *heron*, 'the eel's foe', and the '*heronsew*' (young heron) were also hunted for food. The *stork* was thought to punish adultery (*PF* 361) by beating and sometimes killing its unfaithful mate.

Sometimes the moral 'charge' which the bird carries has an obvious origin. The splendid *peacock* is 'proud', and the voracious *cormorant* is 'the hote cormeraunt of glotenye' (*PF* 362)—cf. Shakespeare's 'insatiate cormorant'. But why is the *lapwing* 'false' (*PF* 347)? It seems to have been a traditional idea: Bartholomew describes it as 'ungentle' and 'unclean', and a flock of lapwings was called a 'deceit' in the 15th c. It may be because the seducer Tereus in the story of Philomela (*Philomene) was changed into a hoopoe, sometimes translated as lapwing (as in *Gower, who says it is the 'falsest of all birds'). Or perhaps there is a less literary explanation: it may be because of the wiliness it shows in luring away visitors to its nest. The *owl* is traditionally the prophet 'of wo and of myschaunce' (*LGW* 2253–4; cf. *Tr* V.319, 382), 'that of deth the bode [presage] bryngeth' (*PF* 343). Its habits are also alluded to—the knight in *The Wife of Bath's Tale* 'al day after hidde hym as an owle' (III.1081; cf. *PF* 599–600). The *cuckoo* is the image of foolishness (I.1810, *PF* 505). It is also 'unkind' (*PF* 358), because contrary to nature it lays its eggs in other birds' nests; hence, its association with cuckoldry: the crow in *The Manciple's Tale* sang 'cuckoo!' before it revealed the adultery of Phoebus's wife (IX.243).

More straightforward is the symbolic significance of the *dove*, which is associated with Venus (I.1962: *PF* 237; *HF* 137). It has 'meek eyes' (*PF* 341), an idea alluded to by January in *The Merchant's Tale* (IV.2139, in a parody of the Song of Songs). The turtle dove is traditionally 'true' (cf. *PF*

582–8): 'if she loseth her mate, she seeketh not the company of others, but goeth alone and hath mind of the fellowship that is lost, and groaneth' says Bartholomew. The *sparrow*, on the other hand, 'Venus sone' (*PF* 351), is (from antiquity) associated with lechery: the Summoner is 'lecherous as a sparwe' (I.626). The intriguing mixture of tradition and observation is well illustrated by the *swallow*, which is called (*PF* 353) the 'murderer of small fowls' (prob. = bees, then often classified among the birds), or, in two MSS, 'of small flies'. In *The Miller's Tale*, Alison sang as loudly and eagerly as a swallow on a barn (I.3258). The swallow's insistent twittering ('cheterynge') wakes up Pandarus in *Troilus and Criseyde* (II.68–70). And because of the story of Procne (*Proigne), its song can be heard as a 'sorowful lay' (*Tr* II.64). The same legend (Philomene) gave a melancholy tone to the song of the *nightingale* (that 'clepeth forth the leves grene', *PF* 351–2), a bird which had powerful literary associations, especially with love—and which was also far more common than it is now. The beauty of its song is several times referred to: the Wife of Bath when she was young could sing 'as any nyghtyngale' (III.458) (cf. also VIII.1343, IX.294); and there is an allusion to its distinctive 'brokkynge' or trilling (I.3377). The amorous young *Squire slept 'namoore than doth a nyghtyngale' (I.98). In a much more serious context in *Troilus and Criseyde* (II.918–24), sitting on a green cedar under Criseyde's chamber wall, a nightingale sings 'peraunter in his briddes wise a lay: Of love'. Later in that poem (III.1233–7) Chaucer uses its observable habit of indulging in trials of its voice before bursting into full song in an extended simile for Criseyde's hesitant opening of her heart:

> as the newe abaysed nyghtyngale,
> That stynteth first whan she bygynneth to synge,
> Whan that she hereth any herde tale,
> Or in the hegges any wyght stirynge,
> And after siker doth hire vois out rynge.

What is perhaps most distinctive is the way that Chaucer uses precise details to make vivid similes which illuminate human behaviour. In *The Wife of Bath's Tale*, the wife of Midas puts her mouth down to the water and speaks her secret to it: 'as a bitore bombleth in the myre, | She layde hir mouth unto the water down' (III.972–3). (The *bittern* lives in reed-beds, and its booming call, says a modern guidebook, 'often heard at dusk in breeding season, has been compared to blowing in a bottle, or a distant foghorn, and may be heard for up to three miles'.) The Pardoner describes how he preaches: stretching out his neck 'est and west upon the peple I bekke [nod], | As dooth a dowve sittynge on a berne' (VI.396–7). The apprentice Perkyn, who liked to sing and dance and hop, is 'gaillard [merry] as goldfynch in the shawe [wood]' (I.4367), a brightly coloured and lively bird, which skips about and sings gaily. A delicious combination of observation and traditional lore is used to reveal the nature of the friar in *The *Summoner's Tale* (III.1803–5) when he embraces the wife tightly, kisses her sweetly, 'and chirketh [chirps] as a sparwe | With his lyppes'.

Armstrong (1956); Harrison (1956); Klingender (1971).

Black Death, the name given to the 'plague', a pandemic which spread from the East in the 1340s, and reached England in the winter of 1348–9. It was apparently carried by the fleas of rats, and was a lethal type of bubonic fever (with distinctive swellings) which also appeared in pneumonic form and was communicated from one person to another. Death occurred within days. There were further regular outbreaks throughout the century, and later. It is difficult to estimate the exact extent of the mortality, but it was considerable. Contemporary chroniclers present it as a great catastrophe, and while their estimates may be exaggerated, there is not much doubt that it was traumatic. The most vivid literary account is that of the ravages of the plague at Florence (and of its emotional results) at the beginning of *Boccaccio's Decameron.

It is also difficult to estimate the economic and social effects of the devastation. In most cases it seems to have sharply intensified already existing tendencies, as the growing shortage of labour or the depopulation of villages and hamlets in certain areas. In Europe messianic and apocalyptic preachers saw in it signs of the end, and emotional religious movements like those of the Flagellants sometimes caused outbreaks of civil violence. It may be that it intensified an already existing 'macabre' tendency in some religious art and literature (like the 'Dance of Death', for instance, which seems to appear in Europe at the end of the 14th c. and continues throughout the 15th). It certainly produced a small group of distinctive images— that of the Virgin Mary sheltering her faithful from the plague under her protective mantle, or those of the 'plague saints' like St Roch, St Sebastian, or St *Anthony of Egypt—and literary works with particular purposes such as medical tracts on the plague, or prayers for protection against it.

As a child in London, Chaucer was fortunate to survive the Black Death. Although in his writings he does not dwell obsessively on *death and mortality in the manner of Villon, the action of *The *Pardoner's Tale* is set against the background of a plague, in which Death slays 'all the people' in a district ('he hath a thousand slayn this pestilence'), silently, like a 'privy thief' (VI.670–9). Elsewhere he makes one or two general references to (e.g.) 'corrupt pestilence' (IV.2252); and alludes to the traditional astrological and mythographical idea that *Saturn's 'lookyng' is the 'fader of pestilence' (I.2469). But there is a rather pointed satirical remark in the *General Prologue* about the Physician's prudent handling of his money: 'he kepte that he wan [gained] in pestilence' (I.442).

Gottfried (1983); Platt (1996); Shrewsbury (1970); Ziegler (1969).

Black Knight, *The Complaint of the Black Knight* (also called 'A Complaint of a Lover's Life', 'A Complaint of an Amorous Knight', or 'The Maying and Disport of Chaucer'), a poem long attributed to Chaucer because it appeared in the early printed editions (it was still accepted by *Tyrwhitt, and was removed from the canon by *Bradshaw). It is in fact a poem by *Lydgate (and was attributed to him by *Shirley), inspired by Chaucer's The *Book of the Duchess. The sorrowful poet goes out into the woods in May, and finds a park surrounded by a wall of green stone. In a glade there is an arbour, and there he sees the prostrate figure of a man, who makes a piteous lament because his lady will show him no mercy. The traditional sufferings of love are expressed with some rhetorical power ('the dedely face lyke asshes in shynyng, | The salte teres that fro myn yen [eyes] falle'), and the whole is suffused with an elegant *melancholy. In the twilight, as the poet begins to record the man's lament, he sees the planet *Venus rising in the sky, and prays that the goddess may have mercy on this faithful man and lighten the heavy hearts of all sorrowing lovers. The poem is learned and allusive, and is one of Lydgate's best works.

(ed.) Norton-Smith (1966), 47–66.

BLACK PRINCE, Edward the Black Prince (1330–76), the eldest son of *Edward III. He commanded part of the king's army at Crécy (1346), and led the English to victory at Poitiers (1356). In 1367 he made an expedition to Spain, and after winning the battle of Nájera, restored Pedro the Cruel (*Petro) to the throne of Castile. The prince contracted a sickness from which he never fully recovered. There is a fine effigy of him in Canterbury Cathedral. He married (1361) Joan, the 'Maid of Kent'; their son was the future King *Richard II.

BLAKE, WILLIAM (1757–1827), poet and artist. He produced a series of engravings of the Canterbury Pilgrims (see *illustrations) which he describes in his 'Descriptive Catalogue' (1809). They are leaving the *Tabard Inn just before sunrise. His remarks are highly individual and interesting. He was fascinated by their characters: he says they are 'the characters which compose all ages and nations'; the names or the titles may change, but not the substance. According to Blake, 'every age is a Canterbury Pilgrimage; we all pass on, each sustaining one or other of these characters; nor can a child be born, who is not one of these characters of Chaucer.' Among the individual pilgrims, the Knight is 'a true hero, a good, great, and wise man', whereas the Friar is a 'complete rogue, with constitutional gaiety enough to make him master of all the pleasures of the world'. He warms to the ideal Parson—'an Apostle, a real Messenger of Heaven, sent in every age for its light and its warmth'. The Pilgrims are fitted into Blakeian mythology—the Pardoner is 'the Age's Knave' ('this man is sent in every age for a rod and a scourge . . . to divide the classes of men . . . and he is suffered by Providence for wise ends'), and the Summoner is 'also a Devil of the first magnitude, grand, terrific' (the Devil and the Angel, both sublime, are perhaps equally useful to society: they are embodiments of the 'eternal Principles that exist

in all ages'). Chaucer 'has divided the ancient character of Hercules between his Miller and his Plowman': the Plowman is 'Hercules in his supreme eternal state, divested of his spectrous shadow; which is the Miller, a terrible fellow, such as exists in all times and places for the trial of men, to astonish every neighbourhood with brutal strength and courage, to get rich and powerful to curb the pride of Man'. Chaucer separates the characters of women into two classes—the Prioress and the Wife of Bath; one predominates in some ages, one in others. He ends with a defence of his picture, and an attack upon that of his rival Stothard: 'when men cannot read they should not pretend to paint'. It is full of errors (e.g. the Wife of Bath is a 'young, beautiful, blooming damsel'); 'all is misconceived, and its mis-execution is equal to its misconception'.

(selection) *CH* i. 249–60; Bindman (1978), nos. 477–8.

BLANCHE, DUCHESS OF LANCASTER, wife of John of Gaunt. The daughter of Henry, duke of Lancaster, she married her cousin on 19 May 1359, when he was 19. She was the mother of the future king, *Henry IV. She died—young and beautiful, according to *Froissart—probably on 12 September 1368 (not, as previously thought, 1369), while Gaunt was absent in Spain, campaigning with his brother the *Black Prince. He married again in 1371, but paid for memorial masses for Blanche in 1379 and 1382. In 1374 he ordered alabaster for a tomb to be made for her in St Paul's by the master mason Henry Yevele (see *architecture), and in his will directed that his body should be laid by that of his 'beloved former wife Blanche where she is buried'. Chaucer's *Book of the Duchess*, which he calls 'the Deeth of Blaunche the Duchesse', seems certainly to have been written to commemorate her death.

Palmer (1974–5).

Blaunche the Duchesse, Deeth of, see *Book of the Duchess*.

Blee. 'The Blee' (orig. perhaps 'rough ground' or 'broken ground overgrown with scrub'), mentioned in *The Manciple's Prologue* (IX.3) is Blean Forest in Kent, near Canterbury.

Bobbe-up-and-down, 'a litel toun | Under the *Blee, in Caunterbury Weye', mentioned in *The Manciple's Prologue* (IX.2), is probably Harbledown, two miles from Canterbury, on the old London road. 'Up and down field' in the neighbouring parish of Thannington has also been suggested, as has Bobbing, near Sittingbourne, but that is too far away and not 'under the Blee'. It sounds like a joke on the up and down movement of a pilgrim on horseback, and, if 'up and down field' was well known, perhaps represents a conflation of that and Harbledown.

BOCCACCIO. Giovanni Boccaccio (1313–75) was the son of a Florentine merchant who worked with the Bardi company. Boccaccio probably spent his childhood in *Florence (and in the nearby village of Certaldo), but was then sent to Naples for his apprenticeship with the local branch of the company. In Naples, he frequented the highly cultivated, international court of King Robert of Anjou, began to study canon law, and finally devoted himself to literature and learning, becoming acquainted with the classics, with French romances and lyric, with the work of such scholars as Paolo da Perugia, Andalò del Negro, and Dionigi da Borgo San Sepolcro, with the poetry of Cino da Pistoia, *Dante, and possibly Petrarch (*Petrak), as well as with popular literary forms. In an attempt at constructing his own fictional autobiography on the model of, for instance, Dante's *Vita nuova*, he purported to have fallen in love at this time with a lady called 'Fiammetta' (whom 19th-c. scholars mistakenly identified with Maria d'Aquino, the king's natural daughter). In 1340–1 increasing political and financial difficulties prompted Boccaccio's return to Florence, whose authorities frequently employed him on important diplomatic missions and official duties at home (later, nostalgia for his past experiences made him try to settle back in Naples on three different occasions). In 1360, Pope Innocent VI gave Boccaccio, who had already taken minor orders, permission to receive Church benefice (which included the 'cure of souls'). He first met Petrarch in 1350, and his admiring friendship for the poet and humanist ten years older than himself—exchanges with whom became very intense afterwards both by letter and

personal visits—stimulated him to pursue further the study of the classics, of ancient history and mythology, and to compose massive scholarly works in Latin. His prominence on the Florentine cultural scene was acknowledged when, on 25 August 1373, the City entrusted him with the task of expounding Dante's *Comedy* in a series of public *lecturae Dantis*. These began on Sunday, 23 October in the church of Santo Stefano in Badia, but ill health forced Boccaccio to put an end to his lectures when he reached Canto XVII of *Inferno*. He had in the meantime retired to Certaldo. His death there on 21 December 1375 was lamented by the humanist Coluccio Salutati and by the 'novelliere' Franco Sacchetti, who recalled that Boccaccio had been 'so well known and so much in demand even in France and England that he had been translated into their languages'.

Boccaccio's contribution to Italian and European literature is immense. From the very beginning of his career as a writer he experiments in different genres, forms, and subject matters, often inventing, renewing, or consecrating them for good. He employs the Dantean *terza rima* in what is generally accepted as his earliest poem, the *Caccia di Diana*, and then again in the *Amorosa visione*. In the pastoral *Comedia delle ninfe fiorentine* (or *Ameto*), we have a mixture of prose and verse (*terza rima*) on the model of Boethius's *Consolatio* and Dante's *Vita nuova*. *Filostrato*, *Teseida*, and *Ninfale fiesolano* (the latter a pastoral idyll on the story of Affrico and Mensola) consecrate the use of *ottava rima* in narrative poems. With the *Filocolo*, the *Elegia di Madonna Fiammetta*, the *Decameron*, and the treatises on Dante (*Trattatello in laude di Dante* and *Esposizioni sopra la Comedia*), Italian prose acquires long-lasting models. In his massive Latin writings, Boccaccio interprets, sums up, and reorganizes ancient myth (*Genealogie deorum gentilium*), and exemplary history and biography (*De casibus virorum illustrium* and *De claris mulieribus*), and propounds an important 'defence of poetry' (*Genealogie* XIV–XV). His work in the field of vernacular narrative is decisive. Already in the *Filocolo*, he greatly amplifies the traditional story of Floris and Blanchefleur, and inserts within it an episode in which Floris listens to a series of 'questions of love' being debated at the Neapolitan court. *Filostrato* and *Teseida* launch the 'roman d'antiquité' on a grand and newer scale. In the former, what had been only an episode of the Trojan cycle (as in Benoit de Sainte Maure's *Roman de Troie* and in Guido delle Colonne's *Historia destructionis Troiae*) becomes a romance entirely devoted to the passionate and ultimately tragic love story of Troiolo and Criseida. With the latter—the account of Arcita's and Palemone's love and struggle for Emilia—Boccaccio creates the first Italian epic romance, the ideal descendants of which will be Ariosto's *Orlando furioso* and Tasso's *Gerusalemme liberata*. In the *Amorosa visione*, he precedes Petrarch in exploiting the conventional dream-poem of love to celebrate the 'triumph' of Wisdom, Glory, Riches, Love, and Fortune. The *Elegia di Madonna Fiammetta* constitutes the first 'psychological novel' where a lady is made to recount her own unhappy love story. Finally, the *Decameron* offers a collection of novellas so far unique in Europe. Its frame (the fiction by which a 'brigata' of young ladies and men decide to escape plague-stricken Florence and retire to the country, where they entertain each other by narrating ten stories a day for ten days), its overall design (the 'themes' of each 'giornata' seem to be arranged in an ideal order, from a representation of vices in the first to a celebration of virtues in the last, through days devoted to the interplay of fortune, love, and human ingenuity), its use of cultured and popular material, its peculiar realism, the mixture and renewal of all genres of storytelling, the extraordinary flexibility and precision of the style, the memorable portrayal of characters (from the evil Ser Ciappelletto in the first novella to the noble Griselda in the last), and situations (from the description of the Florentine plague in the 'Introduzione' to romantic, comic, and piquant love scenes), the gusto for conversation and quip—all this makes of Boccaccio's masterpiece a model of narrative, a human 'comedy' to be set by the side of Dante's 'divine' one.

Chaucer's knowledge of Boccaccio has long been a puzzle to scholars. The two writers may even have met personally (when Chaucer was in Florence in 1372–3 Boccaccio's fame, his connection with Petrarch, and his prominence in Dante studies might have prompted the English author to seek an encounter), but no evidence of this has yet been found. In fact, Chaucer never mentions

Boccaccio by name, and at times seems deliberately bent upon confusing matters related to Boccaccio's identity. In *The House of Fame* (1468) he lists '*Lollius*' as one of the writers of the Trojan cycle, and this name recurs twice in the *Troilus* (I.394; V.1653) as that of Chaucer's authority for the poem, which is actually based on Boccaccio's *Filostrato*. Yet the first time Chaucer mentions 'Lollius' in *Troilus*, he seemingly attributes to him a sonnet written by Petrarch which has no place in the *Filostrato* such as we know it. In recounting the story of Zenobia, for which Chaucer draws on Boccaccio's *De mulieribus claris* and *De casibus virorum illustrium*, the Monk of the *Canterbury Tales* again refers his audience back to his 'maister Petrak . . . That writ ynough of this' (VII.2325–6).

Moreover, Chaucer does not explicitly mention any of the works by Boccaccio from which he borrows extensively. However, the rubric 'De Casibus Virorum Illustrium', which accompanies the beginning or end of *The Monk's Tale* in several MSS might be considered—if indeed it were due to Chaucer himself—as an indication of his acquaintance with at least that Boccaccian title. Furthermore, in *The Knight's Tale* (which is based on the *Teseida) Chaucer has Arcite call himself 'Philostrate' when (I.1428) he returns to Athens to be a 'page of the chambre of Emelye the brighte'. As Arcita's alias in the *Teseida* is 'Penteo', Chaucer's change looks like an oblique, but deliberate allusion to the title of Boccaccio's *Filostrato*. And this gesture appears as even more poignant when one thinks that Chaucer is at this point using another poem by the same writer; that the meaning of 'filo-strato' as proclaimed by Boccaccio himself, 'vanquished by love', can be applied to Arcite as well as to Troiolo: and that in the *Troilus* Chaucer borrows at least one key passage from the *Teseida* (the ascent of Troilus's soul, adapted from that of Arcita). In short, the name 'Philostrate' seems to imply an awareness on the part of Chaucer that *Filostrato* and *Teseida* are the product of the same man. Finally, it would be difficult for Chaucer not to come upon Boccaccio's name while using at least five of his works. To speculate that the writer who, as Sacchetti says, was translated even in France and England did not carry enough 'authority' for Chaucer to acknowledge him is clearly wrong.

As far as Chaucer's knowledge of, and relationship with Boccaccio is concerned, we are left, then, with a fascinating enigma. Chaucer's use of Boccaccio's works is less mysterious and more rewarding to critics, although they may not know when, how, and which kind of Boccaccian MSS Chaucer acquired. The extent and the quality of his borrowings from *Filostrato* and *Teseida* seem to indicate that he owned copies of at least these two poems. The first he may have come upon, and to which he kept returning in his career as a writer, was the *Teseida*. Echoes from it seem to inspire one of the poetic invocations of *The House of Fame* (II.518–22), and several lines are translated in the *Anelida and Arcite* (1–21). Twelve stanzas from *Teseida* VII (50–62), describing the garden and temple of Venus, are adapted in *The Parliament of Fowls* (211–94). The poem as a whole provides the plot of *The Knight's Tale*, to which it also contributes iconographic details, similes, and entire lines. Finally, Chaucer increasingly draws upon the *Teseida* in Book V of *Troilus*, to which he appends the ascent of the hero's soul from Book XI of Boccaccio's poem (he eliminates this, Arcita's 'apotheosis', from *The Knight's Tale*).

It seems clear, then, that the first aspect of the *Teseida* which struck Chaucer was its style (in particular, the high, 'classicizing' diction of its poetic invocations, which he reproduced in the *Anelida*); that the mythological and iconographic apparatus caught his eye next (to the point of making him 'translate' Boccaccio's Temple of Venus in the *Parliament*); and that at some stage Chaucer decided to use the *Teseida* for what it was, a narrative of love, strife, death, and final conciliation. While fully exploiting it as such, Chaucer also modified it profoundly by shortening his version (in what we now know as *The Knight's Tale*), tightening up the structure, changing some incidents in the plot and some features of characterization, and deepening the philosophical dimension. Finally, it was an episode of the *Teseida* (the ascent of Arcita's soul to the eighth sphere after his death) that gave Chaucer the opportunity of radically altering the end of Troilus's story.

Chaucer based his own version of this story, *Troilus and Criseyde*, upon Boccaccio's *Filostrato*. Here, he had a plot with all the ingredients of a tragic romance. He seized upon them eagerly and,

translating large chunks of the original, worked them up to a grander scale. He greatly lengthened the narrative, heightened it by adding proems to each of the first four books and a long 'epilogue' to the fifth, gave it a touch of comedy by brilliantly recasting the character of Pandarus as well as dialogues and scenes and the narrator's attitude to his own material and audience. He intensified Boccaccio's lyricism, explored the psychology of his characters more deeply, and used the story to raise important philosophical questions.

There are similarities between Boccaccio's *Amorosa visione* and Chaucer's **House of Fame*, and parallels between the *Decameron* and the *Canterbury Tales* (the closest analogue for *The *Shipman's Tale* is *Decameron* 8,1), but direct borrowing is very doubtful. The description of January's lovemaking in *The *Merchant's Tale* may be indebted to the *Comedia delle ninfe fiorentine*. Most scholars agree that *Filocolo* IV.31–4 (Menedon's story of Tarolfo, his wife, and Tebano, with his concluding 'question') constitutes the primary source of *The *Franklin's Tale*, although Chaucer changes the names of his protagonists and modifies setup, plot, atmosphere, and themes (apparently conforming to an 'ideal' or actual Breton lay).

Chaucer's knowledge of Boccaccio's early vernacular romances was, then, extensive and deep (in fact unique among non-Italian writers of the 14th c.), and it affected all of his major works in such a way that only a sophisticated blend of verbal, structural, situational, contextual, cultural, and historical analysis can account for it. While study of the *Decameron* and *The Canterbury Tales* must be a matter of purely comparative criticism, there is enough evidence to conclude that the impact of Boccaccio's Latin works on the English writer was less strong than that of *Teseida*, *Filostrato*, and *Filocolo*. His acquaintance with the *Genealogie* is uncertain, although claims have been made that some details in *The *Legend of Good Women* (Ariadne, Phyllis, and Hypermestra) derive from Boccaccio's mythological encyclopaedia. The idea of the *Legend*, on the other hand, may owe something to the layout of Boccaccio's *De claris mulieribus*, and in the first story of the collection, that of Cleopatra, Chaucer seems to be borrowing from this work. What is certain is that he draws on *De claris mulieribus*, for the episode of

BOECE, BOECIUS

Zenobia in *The *Monk's Tale*. Here, however, he also uses *De casibus* 8,6: and it is to the *De casibus* that he may have turned for the general frame of the Monk's 'tragedies' about the 'fall' of people from 'heigh degree', as well as for details in the episodes of Adam, Sampson, and Nero. The *De claris mulieribus* and the *De casibus virorum illustrium*, in other words, may have prompted Chaucer to put together collections of exemplary, tragic tales of ladies and men, supplied him with information regarding them, and provided him with a model of highly elaborate phrasing (as in the Zenobia story). Whether the proto-humanistic features of Boccaccio's Latin writings was (or indeed could be) perceived by him remains a matter of speculation.   [PB]

(ed.) Branca and others (1964–).

BOECE, BOECIUS. Anicius Manlius Severinus Boethius (*c.*480–524), Roman senator and philosopher, was born into an ancient noble family. He was brought up in the house of the patrician Symmachus, and was steeped in the Greek-inspired literary and philosophical culture of late antiquity. He entered the service of the Ostrogothic King Theodoric, who from 493 was the ruler of Rome. He was made consul in 510, and his two sons together in 522. But he fell from favour, was accused of treachery, imprisoned, and bludgeoned to death. In spite of his busy public life he found time to translate Porphyry's *Introduction to the Categories of Aristotle* and Aristotle's works on logic, and to produce treatises on arithmetic, geometry, and music, and (probably) some tractates on theology. However, his most famous work was written in prison at the end of his life. *The Consolation of Philosophy* was immensely influential throughout the Middle Ages. It was the subject of many commentaries, and was sometimes paraphrased or translated into the vernaculars—by, for instance, King Alfred in England and *Jean de Meun in France.

It was read as a *consolation, and, significantly, lies behind much of the 'prison literature' of the Middle Ages (cf. Chaucer's account of the imprisoned Arcite and Palamon in *The *Knight's Tale*). It is also a philosophical work, 'an invitation to the philosophic life', a dialogue in the manner of Plato, but with a heavenly interlocutor, Philoso-

phy, a woman of awe-inspiring appearance, with burning eyes, and variable height, being sometimes of human size, sometimes so tall that her head pierces the heavens. She is the ancestor of a number of formidable heavenly ladies who reveal hidden wisdom to later poets in their dreams. In a somewhat Platonic way she banishes the Muses of Poetry from the bedside of the sorrowful and ailing Boethius. However, the verses which from time to time she speaks or sings (in a variety of sophisticated metres) are often excellent. The form of a medley of alternating verse and prose was also imitated by later writers.

In a series of arguments the problem of why it is that the innocent suffer false accusations and evil is explored, and the discussion moves on to consider the nature of true happiness and the way in which God governs and controls the created universe. Since God is all-knowing as well as all-powerful and benevolent, there is, says Boethius, an incompatibility between divine foreknowledge and freedom of the human will. Philosophy argues that the quality of knowledge depends on the capacity of the knower to know, and that in this respect God's capacity is of a different kind from man's. God is eternal, and sees all things simultaneously, whereas man knows only in part, and cannot see clearly the ways in which the events planned in the mind of God are mediated through the constantly changing acts of *Fortune. Providence, the divine reason, disposes all things, and Fate is the planned order working in things subject to change. Philosophy offers a vision of cosmic harmony, in which the warring elements are held together by love, and the problem of evil finds a mystical solution in a vision of divine peace and love. It is essentially a Platonic scheme, in which the soul, freed from darkness and false goods, ascends to God the true Light, whence originally it came, though it has only dim recollections of its former true nature. Boethius writes as a philosopher, not as a theologian, and the work is without specifically Christian references to the Church, to redemption, or to grace.

Its stress on the ascent of the individual soul through philosophical reflection and separation from the false goods of the mutable world, its literary quality, and its wide and deep human sympathy (as, for instance, in the fine lyric on the story of *Orpheus, who turned his eyes back and downwards from the true light) made it a major source for the pious *humanism of the Middle Ages. It also influenced the writing of history (especially of secular history) and secular narrative (where the philosophical concepts of God, Providence, Fate, Fortune, and Man are dominant)—rather than the Augustinian theological narrative, where God's providence is responsible for everything that happens in time, a view which has no room at all for Fortune.

Chaucer's close reading of Boethius and his work of translation (see *Boece*) profoundly influenced his views over a whole range of topics. The influence can be seen in his discussions of *love, of *fortune, of *free will and predestination, of the vicissitudes of man's life, of the blindness of mortal minds, and so forth. It is most obvious in the clearly 'Boethian' speeches—of Arcite, Palamon, and Theseus in *The Knight's Tale* or of Troilus in *Troilus and Criseyde* (IV.958–1078), or in a favourite topic, like '*gentilesse' (III.1168, and *Gentilesse*), but it is in fact pervasive. Everywhere there are echoes or quotations (e.g., *HF* 972–8). And these may well occur in comic contexts. In *The Nun's Priest's Tale* the imminent fate of Chauntecleer provokes the citation of Boethius as an expert on the question of free will and predestination (VII.3242), and a little later (VII.3293–4) the fox quotes him as an expert on music. Since Boethius's discussion of music is exclusively theoretical, the remark 'or any that kan synge' is probably a joke. When Pandarus in Book I of *Troilus and Criseyde* attempts to comfort his friend, a number of echoes and allusions may suggest that he is a kind of comic Lady Philosophy.

(ed.) Bieler (1957); (ed. and trans.) Stewart and Rand (1918); (trans.) Watts (1969); Chadwick (1981); Gibson (1981); Jefferson (1917).

Boece. Chaucer's translation of *The Consolation of Philosophy* is mentioned in the list of works that he gives himself (X.1088, *LGW* F 425; cf. *Adam* 2). Its date is uncertain, but it is usually thought to be the 1370s or early 1380s. For his translation of the Latin he also used the French version of *Jean de Meun and the commentaries of William of Conches and Nicholas *Trivet. The work has no explanatory preface, but the extensive glosses

which he gives seem to imply that his intention was to make Boethius available to readers with little or no Latin, rather than a private exercise in translation. His version is entirely in prose, careful and literal. It is not easy to read, but is of considerable interest to students of early translation, particularly in the way it deals with philosophical vocabulary. The number of surviving MSS and the fact that it was printed by *Caxton and *Thynne suggests that it was reasonably popular.

(ed.) *Rv* 395–472, 1003–19; Minnis (1993).

Boetes, the constellation Boötes (see *Arctour).

Boethius, see *Boece.

Boghtoun under *Blee. Boughton under Blean, about five miles from Canterbury, on the pilgrim road coming from Ospringe (a standard stopping place). Here, after riding 'fully five miles' after the end of the Second Nun's story, the pilgrims are joined by the Canon and his Yeoman (VIII.556).

Bole, the Bull, Taurus, the second sign of the Zodiac. Chaucer usually preferred the Latin name (see *Taur). Called the 'White Bole' in *Troilus and Criseyde*, where also Troilus alludes to the abduction of Europa by Jupiter, in the form of a bull. (See also *Jupiter (1); *signe; *Zodiak.)   [JDN]

Boloigne (1), Bologna, the town in Italy, with an ancient university famous for the study of law. It is several times referred to in *The *Clerk's Tale*. Griselda's children are sent there by Walter, to be cared for by his sister, the countess of '*Panik'.

Boloigne (2), Boulogne-sur-Mer in northern France, which had a miraculous image of the Virgin Mary. It was visited by the *Wife of Bath (I.465).

book. Chaucer lived in the age of the manuscript book (printing with movable type was invented in the 15th c., and was brought to England by *Caxton). There were other forms of written *documents—individual sheets, used for *letters or what Chaucer calls 'bills' (formal documents containing pleas, petitions, complaints, etc.) or a 'paper' (I.4404, perhaps a written certificate of release); or rolls, which had been the standard form of the book before the triumph of the bound codex AD *c.*400, and were still in use for some purposes (the Pardoner enters the names of those who make offerings in a roll (VI.911)). The MS book, although it varied greatly in size and in shape, was a volume consisting of sheets of parchment (usually sheepskin or goatskin, dressed and prepared for writing), vellum (superior parchment, sometimes made from calfskin), or paper (apparently a Chinese invention, which was brought to Europe, and began to be manufactured in Italy in the 13th c.), folded into quires, and stitched and bound. The text was written (in one or two columns) on lines which had been ruled with a lead point or ink. Sometimes paragraphs or sections were begun with larger letters or decorated initials. Books could be sumptuously illuminated and illustrated. There was a marked difference in quality between de luxe copies of books and ordinary 'working' MSS (notarial accounts, etc.) or cheap copies of devotional texts or vernacular literary works. In the earlier Middle Ages manuscripts were usually copied in monastic scriptoria; but secular scriptoria and a secular book trade developed. The production of an elaborately illustrated volume involved cooperation between scribes, painters with various specialized skills, and binders.

The literate were a very small percentage of the total medieval population (and those able to read Latin were even fewer in number), and books were expensive. They were therefore more usually read in libraries than at home as personal possessions. During the Middle Ages, libraries became widespread. In the earlier period, they were normally found in religious institutions. Such a library would normally contain the works of the Latin fathers, some more modern works of theology and biblical commentary, some ancient literature, technical works of law, medicine, and science, and some chronicles, especially those of local interest. The books were often kept in cupboards or chests, but in the later Middle Ages library rooms were built with reading desks or lecterns and chained books. The growth of *universities and colleges led to an increased demand for books, and eventually these institutions developed their own collections (Merton College, Oxford (*Oxenford), for instance, had an impressively varied array by the 14th c.). A growing number of wealthy laymen also collected books. Notable late medieval secular libraries were those of the kings of France, the dukes of Burgundy, and the Visconti of Milan. (For a 14th-c. English bibliophile, see *Richard of Bury.)

Chaucer uses the word *librarye* only in his translation of Boethius (for L. *bibliotheca*; I pr.4:14, pr.5:39). In his works, books seem to be stored in various places. The God of Love reminds Chaucer (*LGW* 510) that he has a book lying 'in a chest'. His clerk Nicholas keeps his books 'on shelves couched at his beddes heed' (I.3211)—which is where the Clerk of the *General Prologue* would keep his (I.293). This was probably common. However, the clerk in *The *Franklin's Tale* keeps his (V.1207, 1214) in a 'studie' ('study, library'), which is where, according to the Eagle, Chaucer is wont to spend his nights writing (*HF* 633). Wherever he kept it, there has been much discussion of the extent of Chaucer's library (see Geoffrey *Chaucer: reading). In the *Prologue* to *The Legend of Good Women* (G 273), the God of Love says that he possesses 'sixty bokes olde and newe' containing stories of women, but this is almost certainly a comic exaggeration, since such a number on one topic would imply an enormous private library. Even the 'twenty bokes . . . | Of Aristotle and his philosophie' which the Clerk would prefer to have than rich robes (I.294) would be beyond the reach of all but the richest collector.

The book had a central importance in medieval culture. Christianity (like its nearest rivals Islam and Judaism) was a 'religion of the book' (see *Bible). Its sacred book sometimes played a dramatic role in the spiritual life of individuals. St Augustine's (*Austyn) famous account in the *Confessions* of his conversion moves to its climax when he hears the voice of a child saying 'take it and read', and he returns to his Bible and reads the first passage on which his eyes fall—'and all the darkness of doubt was dispelled'. And there was the divine Judge's book of reckoning which would be used on Doomsday. The book in general became a very significant symbol. The figure of Christ on the cross may be interpreted as a book. The world is a book created by God. History and nature are books for humankind.

Chaucer makes many references to the book or to books (of many kinds, including books of magic and merchants' books of reckonings), and frequently applies the word to his own writings—thus in his '*Retractions' (X.1085) he speaks of 'the Book of Troilus', 'the Book of Fame', etc. And he makes as many references to reading. He assumes an audience of readers (telling them to 'turn over the leaf' (I.3177), sending them off to read Solomon, Virgil, Dares, or various other authors, and addressing 'thow redere' (*Tr* V.270; *PF* 132)) —though he also assumes that books may be read aloud to others. Although he presents himself as a very bookish person, not many of his characters are 'reading men'. Even among the 'clerks', the *Monk was not accustomed to pore over a book in his cloister (I.185). In *The *Prioress's Tale* we have a glimpse of the beginning of the learning process, with the little child 'his litel book lernynge, | As he sat in the scole at his *prymer' (VII.516–17). This would eventually have led to the acquisition of skill in what Chaucer calls *lett(e)rure* 'book learning, literature' (VII.2296, 2496).

Books are associated with authority (*auctoritee) (sometimes in opposition to *experience, sometimes complementing it: 'men sen [see] alday, and reden ek in stories' (*Tr* III.1063)). In *The *Man of Law's Tale* a book containing the Gospels is used for the solemn swearing of an *oath (II.662–72). Chaucer and his narrators will frequently quote an authority with the phrase 'the book seith' (where the 'book' in question can range from the Bible to the 'book of *Launcelot de Lake' (VII.3212), or indeed be non-existent), or 'as bokes us declare', 'as olde bokes tellen us', etc. There is an entertaining and illuminating incident in *The *Wife of Bath's Prologue* (III.627ff.) when her Jankin, one of those clerks who write so disparagingly of women, uses his book of wicked wives for his wife's edification, reading it to her by the fire. Three leaves are torn from 'this cursed book', and after the ensuing violence the Wife 'made hym brenne [burn] his book anon'—an act which can be seen variously as a victory over patriarchal authority or as an example of outright censorship, or both.

Symbolic or metaphorical books are not as significant in Chaucer's work as in that of some medieval authors, but in *The *Second Nun's Tale*

(VIII.200–17) a book appears (as in Augustine's *Confessions*) to signal a spiritual climax, that with the text written in letters of gold which Valerian receives from the mysterious old man (probably St *Paul). (The Pauline opposition of the letter and the spirit is also alluded to by the friar in *The *Summoner's Tale* (III.1794) in his defence of *glosynge.) In *The Man of Law's Tale* (II.190–2) we have the book of the heaven written with stars, and although Chaucer does not have the book of the face (as Shakespeare's 'Read o'er the volume of young Paris face'), the behaviour of young *Virginia provides an improving tome—'For in hir lyvyng maydens myghten rede, | As in a book, every good word or dede | That longeth to a mayden vertuous' (VI.107–9).

There are many references to writing, both as the act of composition (cf. e.g. *Tr* I.7, 394) and in its most literal sense: Pandarus cautions Troilus not to write his love letter 'scryvenyssh', i.e. like a professional scribe, in a formal hand. Chaucer is concerned about the 'miswriting' of scribes (*Tr* V.1795), and his verse to *Adam (2) is exact in its detail: he has to correct his work 'and eke to rubbe and scrape', i.e. scrape off the old ink and rub the parchment clean. There are references to pen and ink as the writer's instruments of composition (cf. IV.1736; *Tr* III.1693; *Tr* IV.13; *LGW* 2357, 2491, etc.).

Chaucer also alludes to the appearance of the book (its binding, I.294), and to the appearance and disposition of its text (to the rubric, words written in red as a heading to a section)—'ne after thy text, ne after thy rubriche' (III.346), or, even more precisely, 'we stynten at thise lettres rede' (*Tr* II.103)—or to the chapters (VII.3065; *PF* 32). In *Troilus and Criseyde* he shows himself to be conscious of the structural division into 'books' (see II.10; III.1818; IV.26)—whereas when he is imitating popular romance in *Sir Thopas* he uses the older minstrelish word for a section, a 'fit'. The text may be a scriptural or authoritative statement, or the text of a book in general (II.905; and 'textuel' (IX.235, 316; X.57) is used of one who is well versed in texts, well read, learned). As in actual medieval books, the text may be accompanied by an interpretative gloss (cf. *BD* 333; *Tr* IV.1410); or it may appear without gloss as a 'naked text' ('the naked text'; 'in pleyn text, withouten nede of glose', *LGW Prol* G 86, F 328).

The most characteristic and entertaining image of all, however, is that presented of himself as one totally wrapped up in books, constantly reading—in bed 'to drive the night away' (*BD* 46–9); out of bed with a book written 'with lettres olde' (*PF* 19), an 'olde bok totorn' (*PF* 110). He has the Eagle (*HF* 647–60) describe him as a hermit-like recluse going home after his day's work to sit at another book 'as domb as any stoon', until his look is fully dazed. Chaucer suggests the same of himself (*LGW* 30–4):

On bokes for to rede I me delyte,
And to hem yive [give] I feyth and ful credence,
And in my herte have hem in reverence
So hertely, that ther is game noon
That fro my bokes maketh me to goon.

Book of Cupid; Book of Decrees; Book of Fame. See *Cuckoo and the Nightingale*; *Decrees, Book of*; *House of Fame*.

Book of the Duchess, The. This poem (of 1,334 four-stress lines) is probably the earliest of Chaucer's surviving major works. In his *Retractions* he calls it 'the book of the Duchesse'. The title he gives it in another list of his works (*LGW* F 418), 'the Deeth of Blanche the Duchesse', is strong evidence that its occasion was to commemorate the death (probably on 12 September 1368) of *Blanche, duchess of Lancaster, the wife of *John of Gaunt, earl of Richmond (until 1372) and duke of Lancaster. This is supported by what seem to be references to her and her husband in word-plays (e.g. White, Richmond, Lancaster) within the poem. Its date of composition, however, is not certain. It was probably written in the period 1369–72, before the influence of Italian literature on Chaucer's writing becomes evident. John of Gaunt remarried in 1371, but it has been suggested that the poem may have been written for one of the later commemorations of the death of Blanche. Chaucer's wife was in the service of Gaunt's second wife, but we know nothing certain about the nature of the poet's relationship with Gaunt. He is sometimes said to have been Chaucer's 'patron' or to have commissioned the work; this may have been the case, but there is no direct evidence for it. The poem's Man in Black and Lady White have similarities with the duke

and duchess, but are not replicas of them. Its concerns are general as well as specific, and the treatment of the bereavement is symbolic and mirror-like (giving what seems to be a tactful detachment), rather than directly biographical.

The poem survives in three MSS and *Thynne's 1532 edition of Chaucer. It is deeply influenced by French courtly literature, in particular by the *Roman de la Rose* and by its 14th-c. successors, the *dits amoureux*—poems like *Guillaume de Machaut's *Jugement dou roy de Behaigne* (where the poet overhears a knight and a lady lamenting and arguing whether the faithlessness of his beloved is a greater cause for grief than the death of her lover), *Jugement dou Roy de Navarre*, and *La Fonteinne amoureuse* (which like *BD* has the tale of Ceyx (*Seys) and *Alcyone, *Froissart's *Le Paradys d'Amours*, or the anonymous *Le Songe vert*. There are verbal echoes of some of these poems, and they provide Chaucer with details, motifs, and suggestions for form and structure (for instance, in the way in which *complaint is transformed into *consolation). But Chaucer's poem is more complex and ambitious than any of them. It is a *dream vision which is made to seem positively dream-like, recounted by a narrator who is given a distinct individuality, and who plays an important role in the action.

The work opens with the poet complaining of his insomnia in a passage which both establishes a distinctive narrative voice and sets (in a semi-comic way) a mood of perplexity and grief. The narrator does not know what is happening to him and involves the reader in this uncertainty. There are hints of themes which become significant later (e.g. the linking of melancholy and death (23–7) and the idea that Nature is opposed to excessive sorrow (16–21)).

(44–269) Since he is not able to sleep, the narrator reads a book in bed. Among the 'fables' which it contains is the Ovidian story of Ceyx and Alcyone, which he tells at some length. (Chaucer has carefully adapted the story to its new context, concentrating on Alcyone's emotional state, omitting Ovid's final scene of metamorphosis, and adding a touch of comedy with the attempt of Juno's messenger to awaken *Morpheus, the god of sleep.)

(270–442) The poet promptly falls asleep over his book, and dreams a wonderful dream. It seems to be May, and the birds are singing sweetly in accord. The windows of his chamber portray the story of Troy, and the walls are painted with the Romance of the Rose. The sound of a horn summons him outside to a scene of *hunting, presided over by the emperor Octavian (*Octovyen). They ride into the *forest, but the hart evades the hounds. The poet meets a small whelp, which acts as if it knows him, but which refuses to be caught, and leads him down a flowery green path into another part of the wood, full of flowers and very green ('Hyt had forgete the povertee | That wynter, thorgh hys colde morwes [mornings], | Had mad hyt suffre'), with huge trees growing closely together, under and in which are a multitude of animals. (443–1310) Here he becomes aware of a man in black, sitting against an oak tree, and speaking a complaint—'my lady bryght', he says, 'is fro me ded and ys agoon [gone]'. (The question has been raised whether, since the dreamer later asks the man in black 'where is she now?', Chaucer has been careless here, or whether he intended the narrator to assume a deliberate obtuseness for the sake of his therapeutic attempts to console the knight by encouraging him to express his grief and so 'ease' his heart (556). The latter seems more likely, and perhaps it should also be noted that a 'complaint' in the Middle Ages would not necessarily be expected to provide a precise autobiographical statement, but could be a generalized, or indeed conventional, expression of grief.)

When the sorrowing man in black notices the presence of the dreamer, the two engage in a discussion which continues almost to the end of the poem. In answer to the request to reveal his sorrow (549), the man in black gives a long lament and a tirade against *Fortune. Concerned at his extreme sorrow and apparently fearful that he may commit suicide, the dreamer remonstrates with him. The man in black continues with a long account of how he fell in love, and with an elaborate description of his lady's *beauty and virtue. He recounts how he first met her, how he first made a song for her, how he was first rejected, but at last accepted—'and thus we lyved ful many a yere'. The dreamer presses him with questions—where is she now?—and, when the man in black still evades a direct answer, saying 'I have lost more than thow wenest', asks 'what may that be?' The final answer

is simply 'she ys ded!', and the dreamer can only express human sympathy and fellow feeling—'be God, hyt ys routhe!' Abruptly we return to the hunt, and when the king rides homeward to 'a long castell with walles white . . . on a ryche hil', the dreamer is wakened by its bell ringing twelve o'clock, and finds himself in bed with his his book. He resolves to put this curious dream into rhyme.

In the earlier 20th c., *The Book of the Duchess* was criticized for looseness of construction, and was generally seen as an immature first step on a road to maturity, with the comic aspects giving a premonition of the more ambitious comedy of *The Canterbury Tales*. Increasingly it has been recognized as a sophisticated and imaginative work, with an intricate structure, which uses parallel figures and images to produce a 'pattern of desire and loss', a haunting and delicate dream poem which has its own inner logic as well as the abrupt shifts of direction and the frustrating 'dead ends' characteristic of actual dreams. It clearly shows some characteristic Chaucerian techniques (such as the balancing of widely differing tones and registers or the use of a naive, passive, often puzzled narrator) and themes (authority *(auctoritee) and *experience, *Nature, *love, and *death). It tactfully avoids the admonitory tone of much medieval writing on death, and, more surprisingly perhaps, the Christian consolatory topic of the reunion of mortals in the next life. The consolation it offers is a simple human statement of '*pite', an acceptance of mortality ('to lytel while oure blysse lasteth'), and a suggestion that the working of *memory may recall love and ease sorrow.

(ed.) *Rv* 329–46, 966–76; Phillips (1984); Minnis (1995), 73–160; Bronson (1952); Clemen (1963), 22–36; Kean (1972), i. 31–66; Spearing (1976); Wimsatt (1968); Windeatt (1982).

Book of the Lion ('book of the Leoun'), a lost and unidentified work. Chaucer refers to it in his 'Retractions' (X.1087), immediately after *The Canterbury Tales*. It has been suggested that it may have been a version or adaptation of either *Guillaume de Machaut's *Dit dou Lyon* or *Deschamps's *Dit du Lyon*.

Book of the Twenty-five Ladies, see **The *Legend of Good Women.**

Boreas (in *Boece* (I m.3:12, m.5:24), the north wind. In Greek mythology he was a descendent of Erechtheus, a legendary king of Athens (see *Aquilon).

BRADSHAW, HENRY (1831–86), scholar, was educated at Eton and King's College, Cambridge. In 1856 he gave up a teaching post in Ireland to work in the Cambridge University Library. He became a great expert on manuscripts and a famous bibliographer. Increasingly he turned to the study of the MSS of Chaucer. He used rhyme tests to establish the *canon of Chaucer's works, and projected an edition, but this never appeared. However, he gave his name to the 'Bradshaw Shift' which places Fragment VII of *The *Canterbury Tales* (in the order of the *Ellesmere MS) as B² following Fragment II (or B), followed by VI (C). This order (which places Rochester (*Rouchestre), mentioned in VII.1926, before Sittingbourne (*Sidyngbourne) mentioned in III.847, and closer to Canterbury) is adopted in the edition of *Skeat.

BRADWARDYN, THOMAS (c.1290–1319). Bradwardine first gained eminence as a mathematician at Merton College Oxford, and subsequently as a theologian; in 1335 he joined the household of *Richard of Bury, bishop of Durham, and shortly before he fell victim to the Black Death was consecrated archbishop of Canterbury. His most influential work was the *De causa Dei contra Pelagium* (completed by 1344), in which he discussed the issues of *free will and predestination, and affirmed (following Augustine (*Austyn) but contrary to the dangerous revival of Pelagianism he perceived in early 14th-c. theology) both the absolute foreknowledge of God, and the impotence of the human will to act well without divine prevenient grace; it is for this reason that he is mentioned in *The Nun's Priest's Tale* (VII.4432). [AH]
Oberman (1957).

BRATHWAIT, RICHARD (c.1588–1673), poet, born of a Westmoreland family, studied at Oriel College, Oxford, and later at Cambridge. After a brief period in London, devoted to the writing of poetry and plays, he returned to live on the family estates. In a poem in *The Smoaking Age* (1617) Chaucer's 'incensed Ghost' complains that his muse 'was fed | With purer substance than your Indian weede', and of the treatment given to him by the 'barren brain-worms of this time' who 'disrelish' his tongue, and indulge in pruning, purging, and polishing, The 'pleasing comments' that Brathwait promised appeared in 1665, as 'A Comment upon the Two Tales of our Ancient... Poet Sir Jeffray Chaucer', a collection of discursive comments on *The *Miller's Tale* and *The *Wife of Bath's Prologue and Tale*, with some entertaining paraphrases. He says of the climax of the quarrel between the Wife of Bath and Jenkin, 'while poor Jenkin is thus labouring in all humble manner to compose his own Peace, the dead Coarse [corpse] revives, and fetcheth him such an overthwart Blow, as his Head rings again', and 'to confirm, that she is near Death, she concludes, "I may no longer speak": A dangerous Sign that she is past all hope of Recovery. For when a woman is laid speechless, the Bell may well ring out.'

CH i. 145–8; Spurgeon (1901).

BRENBRE, NICHOLAS. Brenbre (or Brembre) was a collector of the wool custom and subsidy during the years 1374–7, for part of which Chaucer was controller; Chaucer must certainly have known him in this capacity, and perhaps later. He became prominent in London politics, and was mayor in 1377 and again in 1383–5; his time in this office seems to have been marked by corruption and factionalism. Brenbre was knighted by *Richard II in 1381, and was one of the five leading supporters of the king (the others being Robert de Vere, earl of Oxford, Michael de la Pole, the chancellor, Alexander Nevill, archbishop of York, and Chief Justice Robert Tresilian) against whom an appeal of treason was brought in 1387 by *Thomas of Woodstock, duke of Gloucester, Richard, earl of Arundel, Thomas Beauchamp, earl of Warwick, Thomas Mowbray, earl of Nottingham and *Henry, earl of Derby. The latter group, the 'Appellants', gained the upper hand, and in the 'Merciless Parliament' of 1388 Brenbre, along with other friends of the king, was condemned and executed. [AH]

LR 153–5.

Breseyda, Brixseyde, Briseis, a Trojan girl captured by Achilles, taken from him by Agamemnon. The story is told in the *Iliad*, but Chaucer knew it from *Ovid's *Heroides* (3) and from *Benoît de Sainte-Maure, who made her the beloved of Troilus, and thus the literary ancestor of *Criseyde. In Chaucer her falseness to Achilles is alluded to in *The *House of Fame* (397–8). The list of the heroines whose stories are told in Chaucer's 'the Seintes Legende of Cupide' (i.e. *The *Legend of Good Women*) includes her name (II.71), but no trace of this story has survived. Possibly it was one of the legends which he intended to write, or which he had written and intended to revise.

Mapstone (2000).

Bret, Welshman (*HF* 1208).

Breton lay, A type of short verse *romance in French or English usually treating a single adventure and usually dealing with love and the supernatural. Some similar story patterns can be distinguished, but there is much variety in the subject matter, and a Breton lay is often identified simply by the fact that it claims in its prologue that it is based on a 'lay' sung by the ancient Bretons. (It has been suggested that the original 'lay' in the Breton language, of which no example survives, may have been a lyrical poem set within or connected with a narrative story.) In French, the best (though probably not the first) examples are those of *Marie de France in the 12th c.; the earliest surviving English examples seem to come from the 14th (see *Sir Launfal; *Sir Orfeo). The *Franklin's Tale* signals itself as a Breton lay, and has a genuinely Breton setting. Its very different treatment of love and the supernatural, however, and its concern with ideas like '*gentilesse'—as well as the fact that its source seems to be *Boccaccio—set it quite apart from other surviving Breton lays. Its distinctiveness makes very doubtful the theory once advanced that Chaucer revivified a form which had become old-fashioned, and caused a revival of the English Breton lay in the 15th c. The later English examples seem to owe nothing at all to *The Franklin's Tale*.

Britaigne (1), Britayne, Briteyne. Brittany, or 'Little Britain' (in former times called Armorica

(*Armorike)), a predominantly Celtic-speaking region, was in Chaucer's day a duchy under the overlordship of the kings of France (*Edward III, who had occupied part of it, had to give up his claims by the treaty of Brétigny in 1360, though the English continued to control parts of the south and west). Chaucer's *Shipman was familiar with its ports, and with every inlet in its coast (I.407–9), and *The *Franklin's Tale* is set there (see *Kayrrud; *Pedmark).

Britaigne (2), Briteyne, 'Greater' Britain, the home of King Arthur (*Rom* 1199). In *The *Franklin's Tale* the knight *Arveragus went from Brittany (*Britaigne (1)) to 'Engelond, that cleped [called] was eek Briteyne' (V.810).

Brito(u)n (1), Breton (V.709, 711, III.858).

Brito(u)n (2), Briton, Celt (II.545, 547, etc.).

Brixseyde, see *Breseyda.

Brok, the name of a horse (III.1543).

Bromeholm. Bromholm Priory in Norfolk possessed a *relic of the true cross, brought from Constaninople in the 13th c. Pilgrims visited it because of its miraculous powers. It is mentioned in *Piers Plowman,* and in *The *Reeve's Tale* (set in East Anglia), when the miller's wife, startled by her husband's body falling on her, cries out 'Help! hooly croys of Bromeholm!' (I.4286).

'Brooch of Thebes'. In a list of Chaucer's works given by *Lydgate in the Prologue to *The Falls of Princes* there is a mention 'of the broche which that Vulcanus | At Thebes wrought'. This has sometimes been taken to be a lost work, but it probably refers to the striking image in *The Complaint of *Mars* (244–62), and is a description of that poem.

Brugges, Bruges, the administrative centre of Western Flanders (*Flaundres), and an important mercantile and artistic centre. It came under the rule of dukes of Burgundy (*Burgoyne) in 1384. Its commercial dominance gradually passed to Antwerp, but it remained a fine and prosperous town, with important monuments and works of art. The merchant of Saint-Denis (*Seint-Denys) in The *Shipman's Tale made a business trip there to buy goods, and Sir Thopas's brown stockings came from Bruges (VII.733).

Brutes (possessive form of) 'Brut', i.e. Brutus, the great-grandson of Aeneas, the legendary Trojan founder of Britain, to which he gave his name (Complaint of Chaucer to his *Purse 22).

Brutus (1), Lucius Junius, the nephew of Tarquin (*Tarquyn). After the death of Lucretia (*Lucrece) he 'swore by her chaste blood' (LGW 1862–3) that Tarquin should be banished, and led the rising against him.

BRUTUS (2), Marcus Junius Brutus (78?–42 BC), Roman politican who with Gaius Cassius joined the conspiracy against Caesar (*Cesar (2)) for idealistic reasons, and took part in the assassination. He killed himself after his defeat in the second battle of Philippi. His wife Portia (*Porcia) committed suicide rather than live without him (V.1449). In the Renaissance Brutus was sometimes seen as the heroic defender of republican values; in the Middle Ages, however, the tyrannicide is generally regarded as a traitor to his temporal lord (Dante places him with other traitors in the bottom of hell). The *Monk in his 'tragedy' of Julius Caesar calls him 'this false Brutus' (VII.2706). In the same story (VII.2697) there also appears a figure called 'Brutus Cassius', a conflation of the two famous tyrannicides. (Apparently Chaucer was not the first medieval writer to confuse the two, an error presumably arising from the omission of the abbreviation for et ['and'] in a Latin text.) The Brutus mentioned in an *Ubi Sunt passage in Boece (II m.7:19) along with *Fabricius and Cato (*Catoun (1)) is probably Marcus Junius Brutus, but could conceivably be Lucius Junius *Brutus (1).

Brutus Cassius, see **Brutus, Marcus Junius**.

Bukton, Lenvoy de Chaucer a Bukton, a short poem surviving in one MS (where it is given this title) and in one early print. It is (like *Scogan) a verse

*letter with an *envoy. Chaucer has promised to talk of the 'sorwe and woo that is in mariage'; he will not say (he says) that it is the chain of Satan at which he continually gnaws, but he will dare to say that if he were out of his pain he would never wish to be bound. He quotes St Paul's advice to take a wife for it is better to wed than burn, but balances this with the saying of the 'wise' that he will have sorrow and be his wife's thrall. It may well be that he would rather be taken prisoner in Frisia (*Frise) than fall again into the trap of wedlock. The envoy puts a moral ('unwys is he that kan no wele endure'), advises Bukton to read the Wife of Bath on the question, and prays that God may grant him to lead his life 'frely . . . in fredam'—'for ful hard is to be bonde'. The tone is light-hearted and jesting, and the poem plays wittily with 'authoritees' (*auctoritee) (including Holy Writ) and traditional images of marriage as a chain and a prison. The suggestion that here (as in Scogan) Chaucer is imitating the easy, urbane, conversational tone of the Horatian epistle has much to commend it.

There are two possible recipients; Sir Peter Bukton of *Holdernesse in Yorkshire, who had strong Lancastrian connections, and was steward to the earl of Derby, later *Henry IV; and Sir Robert Bukton, a squire of Queen Anne and later of *Richard II, probably a less likely contender. The poem is generally placed in the 1390s. The reference to being a prisoner in Frisia has been taken to imply a date in 1396, when there was an expedition against the Frisians (who, according to *Froissart, treated prisoners with particular brutality), but this is not certain. That to the Wife of Bath indicates that the Prologue to her tale had been written, at least in some form.

(ed.) Rv 655–6, 1087–8; Pace and David (1982), 139–48; Scattergood (1995), 497–500; Norton-Smith (1966).

Bull (astron.), see *Bole.

Bulle, papal bull, a *document or charter issued by the pope, so-called from the bulla or seal which authenticated it. The *Pardoner says that he shows 'bulles of popes and of cardynales, | Of patriarkes and bishops' (VI.342–3) which he claims give him authority to preach and to sell his relics and pardons, and asks the pilgrims to bow their heads 'under this hooly bulle' (VI.909). In *The *Clerk's Tale* (IV.739–49) the word is used for the counterfeited papal edicts allowing Walter to leave his wife.

Burdeux. Bordeaux (under English control in Chaucer's time), the capital of Gascony, was then a great fortified city not much smaller than London, and the trading centre of the large and important *wine-growing area of south-western *France. The *Shipman (I.397) contrived to steal wine 'fro Burdeux-ward [as it was coming from Bordeaux]'; and the *Pardoner mentions the town when he refers to the practice of mixing cheaper Spanish wine into others (VI.571).

Burgeys, burgess, a citizen of a town or borough (strictly, one who had full municipal rights, e.g. a *merchant or a master craftsman). In the *General Prologue*, Chaucer uses the word of the Guildsmen (I.369–70), 'wel semed ech of hem a fair burgeys | To sitten in a yeldehalle [guildhall] on a deys', and of the *Host, 'a fairer burgeys was ther noon in *Chepe' (I.754). In *Troilus and Criseyde* (IV.345) it is used of the citizens who meet with the lords in the parliament.

Burgoyne, Burgundy, the rich agricultural region in eastern *France around the river Saône. It grew in political and cultural importance under the Valois dukes of the late 14th and 15th c. It is mentioned only in the *Romaunt* (554).

BURLEY, SIR JOHN, knight and former captain of Calais, received with Chaucer in 1376 a payment for a journey on the king's secret affairs. The nature of this mission is not known.

BURLEY, SIR SIMON, brother of John, a friend of the Black Prince, and an influential man in *Richard II's court. He was a garter knight, JP for Kent, constable of Dover, and warden of the Cinque Ports. With Chaucer he was a fellow witness at the Scrope-Grosvenor trial (see **Geoffrey *Chaucer: life**) and was associated with the poet as a member of the commission of peace for Kent from 1385. As a result of the accusations of the Appellants, he was impeached for misuse of power and responsibility for corrupting the court, and, in spite of pleas from the queen and others, was executed in 1388. *Froissart calls him a wise and gentle knight. He left twenty-one books, and seems to have been a man of some literary tastes, who shared Froissart's liking for chivalric romance.

Burnel the Asse, Daun; Bury. See *Speculum Stultorum*; *Richard of Bury*.

Busirus, Busyrides, Busiris, a son of Poseidon and a legendary king of Egypt. In order to avert drought he was advised by a seer to sacrifice all visiting strangers. This he did, beginning with the seer. Unfortunately for him, one of his later guests was Hercules (*Ercules) (cf. *Bo* II pr.6:67). In *The *Monk's Tale* he is a 'cruel tyrant' killed by Hercules, who made his horses eat him (VII.2103–4). Here Busirus has been conflated (perhaps before Chaucer) with the Thracian King Diomedes, who fed his mares on human flesh, and was destroyed by Hercules and fed to the horses.

C

Cacus, Kakus, Cacus, a legendary giant who stole some of the cattle which Hercules (*Ercules) was bringing back from Geryon, and was slain by the hero in his 'cave of stoon' (VII.2107). By this killing Hercules 'appeased the wrath' of *Evander (*Bo* IV m.7:52, 54), whose land had been ravaged by the monster.

Cadme, Cadmus, Cadmus, son of Agenor, king of Tyre, and brother of *Europa (1), the founder and first king of *Thebes (1) (I.1546, 1547).

Caesar, see *Cesar.

Caym, Cain, the son of *Adam, who murdered his brother Abel (Gen. 4:1–16), and was driven out by God. Many legends clustered about him, but in Chaucer he is mentioned only by the Parson (X.1015), as a man who despaired of Christ's mercy.

Calcas; Calendar. See *Calkas; *Kalendere.

Calydoigne, Calydoyne. Calidon, the kingdom of *Tydeus, father of *Diomede (*Tr* V.805, 934).

Caliope, Callyope, Calliope, chief of the *Muses, and muse of epic poetry, the mother of *Orpheus (*Bo* III m.12:23), 'the myghty Muse' (*HF* 1400), invoked at the beginning of book III of *Troilus and Criseyde* in words which allude to a traditional etymology of her name as 'best voice' or 'excellent voice'.

Calipsa, Calypso, a daughter of Atlas, who by her magic detained Odysseus for seven years on the island of Ogygia. Chaucer could have found the story in *Ovid. In *The House of Fame* 1272 she appears in a list of magicians.

Calistopee, Calyxte, Callisto, a nymph of Diana, who was seen, desired, and possessed by *Jupiter. Driven out by Diana, she bore a son, Arcas. The angry *Juno transformed her into a bear. Later, her son met the bear, which seemed to recognize him, and would have killed her had not Jupiter intervened and changed them both into constellations,—*Ursa and Arcturus (*Arctour). *Ovid's story (*Met.* 2) is referred to twice in Chaucer—in *The Knight's Tale*, in the temple of Diana (I.2055–9, where she is transformed into the 'loode-sterre'), and in *The Parliament of Fowls* 286.

Calkas, Calcas, Calchas, the father of *Criseyde in *Troilus and Criseyde*, a soothsayer, who learning of the impending destruction of Troy, fled from the city, leaving his daughter to face the anger of the people (I.64–98). Later, his demand that she should be exchanged for *Antenor (IV.64–134) brings about the separation of the lovers.

Cambalo, Cambalus the son of *Cambyuskan in *The *Squire's Tale*. His name has been variously derived from Cambaluc, the capital of Kublai Khan, Kambala, Kublai's grandson, and Cembalo (Balaclava) in the Crimea.

CAMBISES, the son of Cyrus (*Cirus) the Great, king of Persia (reigned 529–522 BC), and conqueror of Egypt. He is quoted by the friar in *The *Summoner's Tale* (III.2043 ff.) as an example against anger and drunkenness.

Cambyuskan, the noble Tartar king in *The *Squire's Tale*, a virtuous pagan, a paragon of kingship, and a great warrior and conqueror. He celebrates his birthday with a sumptuous feast in his palace. He is probably based on Genghis (Chingis) Khan ('Camius Can' in the Latinized form of the name, c.1154–1227), the founder of the Mongol empire (see *Tartarye). Some details, however, may be drawn from the descriptions of the splendid court of his grandson Kublai Khan at Cambaluc (Beijing) given by travellers such as Marco Polo and Odoric of Pordenone. It was yet another grandson, Batu or Sain Khan, the Khan of the West or the 'Golden Horde', who devastated Russia (cf. V.10) and destroyed Kiev. The astronomical references at the beginning of the Tale suggest a close association between Cambyuskan and *Mars.

Cambridge, see *Cantebrigge.

Campayne, Campania (the modern Campagna), a province in Italy, a fertile area south of Latium (*Bo* I pr.4:88).

Campaneus, see *Capaneus.

Canaan, son of Ham, cursed by Noah (Gen. 9:22–7), referred to once by the *Parson (X.766) as an example of thraldom because of sin.

Canace(e) (1), the daughter of King Aeolus, bore a child as the result of an incestuous relationship with her brother, Macareus, and took her own life. The passionate lament given to her by *Ovid in the *Heroides* was well known in the Middle Ages, and was used by *Gower and *Lydgate. Chaucer mentions the story twice. In the *ballade, 'Hyd, Absolon, thy gilte tresses clere', in the Prologue to *The Legend of Good Women,* Canace is mentioned in a group of tragic lovers (F 265, G 219), and in the Introduction to *The Man of Law's Tale,* which refers directly to heroines whose stories are told in *The Legend of Good Women* it is pointed out that Chaucer has avoided two tales of incest, those of *Ap(p)ollonius and of Canacee: 'thilke wikke ensample of Canacee, | That loved hir owene brother synfully' (II.78–9). The implications of this apparently straightforward remark are uncertain. It is unlikely to be a slighting reference to Gower, although it might be a private joke. Various ingenious interpretations have been suggested.

Canace(e) (2), the beautiful heroine of *The *Squire's Tale,* presented by the stranger knight with a magic mirror and a ring which allows her to understand the speech of birds. It has been suggested that she may be associated with Canace(e) (1), and that the tale was to have been one of incest, and was therefore abandoned. But there is no real evidence for this. It has also been argued that she is the analogue of a star.

Cananee, the womman, the Canaanite woman (Matt. 15:22–8) who convinced Christ of her great faith. She is alluded to in the prayer to the Virgin in the Prologue to The *Second Nun's Tale (VIII.59–61).

Cancre, Cancro, Cancer, the fourth sign of the Zodiac. Named in The *Merchant's Tale and alluded to in The Parson's Prologue as the exaltation of Jupiter. The Sun is at its head at the commencement of summer. It is the *domicile of the Moon and the dejection of Mars. (See also * exaltacioun; *hed; *signe; *Zodiak.) [JDN]

Candace (1), Candace, a queen of India, who lured Alexander into her power, and (in the romances) became his mistress. In Against *Women Unconstant (16) she is linked with Delilah (*Dalyda) and *Criseyde as an example of instability.

Candace (2), who appears in a list of tragic heroines in The *Parliament of Fowls (288), remains unidentified. She may be Candace (1) or Canace(e) (1).

Cane, Cana in Galilee, where the wedding took place (John 2:1–11). It is mentioned by the *Wife of Bath (III.11).

Canyos (*Bo* I pr.3:57 (L. *Canios*)) either 'the followers of Canius (*Canyus)' or (as Boethius intended) 'men like Canius'.

CANYUS, Julius Canius (or Canus), a Stoic philosopher condemned to death by Caligula (*Bo* I pr.4:180–3). He is cited as an example of philosophical tranquillity by Seneca (*Senek).

Canon of Chaucer's Works (see also entries for individual works). It is not always easy to establish the authentic works of a medieval writer. They often exist in MSS copied after the author's death, sometimes without ascription, or wrongly ascribed. In the case of Chaucer, a number of apocryphal works (see *Chauceriana) were associated with him either by scribes or by early printers and editors, and many of them appeared in his 'collected works' until *Skeat's *Oxford Chaucer* at the end of the 19th c. However, the canon of his genuine works can be fairly clearly established. The evidence consists (1) of lists of his works provided by the poet himself; (2) lists or references given by later medieval poets; (3) those attributions to him by scribes or editors which seem to have some authority, tested by (4) linguistic and stylistic evidence.

In fact, most of the important literary works are secured by (1) Chaucer's own lists, of which there are three. (*a*) The Prologue to The *Legend of Good Women* contains two groups: a mention of two works which have caused offence, a translation of the *Roman de la Rose* and *Troilus and Criseyde;* and later (F 417 ff., G 405 ff.), a list offered in the poet's defence, of various works most of which can be identified: The *House of Fame*, The *Book of the Duchess*, The *Parliament of Fowls*, and the translation of Boethius. Also listed are 'the love of *Palamon and Arcite*', and 'the lyf ... of Seynt *Cecile*', usually thought to be early versions of The *Knight's Tale* and The *Second Nun's Tale*, '*Origenes upon the Maudeleyne*', and (G text only) 'Of the *Wreched Engendrynge of Mankynde*'. (*b*) The Introduction to The *Man of Law's Tale* mentions 'Ceys and Alcione' (the story used in The *Book of the Duchess*) and 'the Seintes Legende of Cupide' (*The Legend of Good Women*). (*c*) In the '*Retraccions*' Chaucer lists *Troilus*, The *House of Fame*, The *Book of the Duchess*, The *Parliament of Fowls*, The *Canterbury Tales*, the translation of Boethius, and The *Book of the Leoun*.

(2) Of the later lists, that of *Lydgate in the Prologue to The *Fall of Princes* is the most important, because of his closeness in time to Chaucer. This confirms the preceding items, and adds the *Astrolabe* and the mysterious '*Trophe*' and 'Daunt in English' (see The *House of Fame*). Of the scribal attributions (3), the most trustworthy are those of John *Shirley. He, for instance, records Chaucer's authorship of The *Complaint of *Mars*, an attribution which is confirmed by an item in Lydgate's list (see *Brooch of Thebes**).

The process of critical revision which removed the apocryphal works that appeared in the early printed editions began in the 18th c. with *Tyrwhitt. He rejected The *Plowman's Tale*, *Gamelyn*, *Beryn*, *Jack Upland*, The *Lamentation of Mary Magdalene*, The *Assembly of Ladies*, and other poems. He also pointed out that some were clearly attributable to other writers—as, for instance, The *Testament of Cresseid*, La *Belle Dame sans Mercy*, or The *Letter of Cupid*. He still accepted the whole *Romaunt*, The *Court of Love*, The *Complaint of the *Black Knight*, The *Isle of Ladies*, The *Floure and the Leafe* (with doubts), The *Cuckoo and the Nightingale*, and The *Testament of Love*. Most of these were rejected by *Bradshaw, and with the editions of *Skeat the canon as we have it today took final form.

There are still, however, some questions. Firstly, there are some lost works, most notably The *Book of the Leoun*, *Origenes upon the Maudeleyne*, and *Of the Wreched Engendrynge of Mankynde*. Various attempts have been made to identify these, and some existing ME works have been advanced as contenders. And, presumably, we have lost some (or many) of the love lyrics which Chaucer refers to in general terms in the Prologue to The *Legend of Good Women* and the Retracciouns. A number of the surviving *lyrics which have been attributed to him present a particularly difficult case, since they are often conventional in content and style, and scribal attributions can be very uncertain. Modern editors are still divided, for instance, on the authenticity of *Proverbs*, Against *Women Unconstant*, or *Womanly Noblesse*. There seems no doubt that Chaucer translated part at least of the *Roman de la Rose*, but the authorship of the three surviving fragments of the ME *Romaunt* is still in question. Finally, a strong case has been made for his authorship of The *Equatorie of the Planetis*, and it is often, but not universally, accepted as his.

Canon, The, whose experiments with *alchemy form the subject of The *Canon's Yeoman's Tale*, does not appear in the *General Prologue*, and it is not clear whether his sudden arrival (and departure) was part of Chaucer's original conception of the *Tales* or an idea which came to him in the course of composition. The Pilgrims have reached

*Boghtoun under Blee when he and his yeoman gallop up at great speed. He is not heavily burdened, and his dress is described in some detail: a cassock with a surplice, a black cloak with a hood attached, a hat hanging by a lace, and a burdock leaf under his hood as a kind of sweat-band. He may be an Augustinian (or Black) Canon. It has been suggested that Chaucer may have had some particular individual in mind. In 1374 William de Brumley, a chaplain, confessed to the making of counterfeit gold coins, following the instructions of William Shuchirch, a canon of Windsor. If the latter was still alive in 1390, he might well have been known to Chaucer as the Clerk of the Works for St George's Chapel (and, it has been suggested, Chaucer may have lost money in his dealings with him). However, this identification remains completely uncertain, as does the question of whether the Tale arose from what *Tyrwhitt called 'some sudden resentment'.

Canon's Yeoman, The. Like the *Canon, this figure, the narrator of The *Canon's Yeoman's Tale*, is not mentioned in the *General Prologue*.

Canon Yeoman's Prologue and Tale, The, follow The *Second Nun's Tale* (to which it is linked) to form the final part of Fragment VIII of The *Canterbury Tales*. Prologue and Tale together amount to just over 900 lines in couplets. The Prologue describes how the Pilgrims are suddenly joined by the *Canon and his Yeoman, who engages in conversation with the *Host. He begins by praising the Canon's qualities and skills—he is greater than any 'clerk', for by his craft he could pave the road with silver and gold. But, he is too clever by half. In response to further prompting, the Yeoman begins to describe their dwelling and their way of life: his discoloured face comes from blowing at the fire, but all to no avail, so that they will soon be reduced to the state of beggars. At this point the Canon 'draws near' and overhears what is being said, and tells the Yeoman to be quiet. The Host insists that he should carry on, and when the Canon realizes that his secrets will be revealed, he flees 'for verray sorwe and shame'. The Yeoman now gleefully promises to tell all.

The Tale itself falls into two sections (in the *Ellesmere MS they are headed *prima pars* and *secunda pars*, but, since most MSS copy them continuously, this does not necessarily represent Chaucer's division). Both are linked in that they are a satirical representation of *alchemy. In the first, the Yeoman describes his life as an alchemist, in the second he tells a story about a fraudulent alchemist. He has been with the Canon for seven years, and in his long monologue he mixes lamentation and bitter asides with a detailed account of the 'elvysshe craft', using its technical terminology (its 'termes been so clergial and so queynte' that they make the practitioners seem wise). With much scorn he describes a spectacular failure in which a pot explodes and various explanations are advanced to account for it. He brings the section to a conclusion with some proverbial reflections: appearances are deceptive; 'he that semeth the wiseste . . . | Is moost fool, whan that it cometh to the preef; | And he that semeth trewest is a theef' (VIII.967–9).

The second section tells (in a discursive manner, with exclamations, asides, and digressions) of a canon of 'infinite falsnesse'. He borrows a mark from a rich priest, promising to repay him after three days, which he does. Having thus won the priest's confidence, he sets about deceiving him. The priest is encouraged to take part in an elaborate experiment in which, by a sleight of hand, quicksilver is apparently transmuted into silver. The canon extracts 40 pounds for the formula, and is never seen by the priest again.

The Canon's Yeoman's Tale is unusual in a number of ways. It is not found in the important *Hengwrt MS. The theory that this indicates that it is not a genuine work is very unlikely, since it seems thoroughly Chaucerian, but the omission may indicate that it was a very late work, or that it was placed in the sequence at a late date. The dramatic quality of the Prologue, with the unexpected arrival of two totally new characters, is also noteworthy. It may indicate a tendency to experiment further with the framework, or represent a bold way of introducing new material at a late stage. The structure of the Tale has also occasioned some discussion. The two parts are complete in themselves (with a different canon in each), but although it has been argued that the second part was distinct and independent, the MSS treat the whole as a unity. And the Yeoman's consistent and vehement attack on alchemy gives it a satisfying coherence. It is a type of 'occupational satire' rather like The *Friar's Tale or The *Summoner's Tale. No clear source is known (though there are a number of fabliau-like stories about alchemists' tricks). The material is drawn rather from Chaucer's extensive reading in the scientific literature of alchemy. The satire is intensified by the placing of the tale next to the purity and the spirituality of The Second Nun's Tale. The Canon's Yeoman's Tale is not one of the better-known Canterbury Tales, but deserves attention. It contains some excellent dramatic writing, and 'a sheer density of *things* unparalleled elsewhere in Chaucer's work' (Cooper); and it is an interesting example of the extended confessional monologue (cf. the *Wife of Bath and the *Pardoner).

(ed.) *Rv* 270–81, 946–51; *S&A* 685–98; Cooper (1989), 368–81.

Cano(u)n, rule (L., from Greek *kanon*). A common name (sing. or pl.) for a scientific text embodying a series of procedural rules. The *Pardoner's remark that '*Avycen wrote never in no canon more wondrous symptoms of poisoning' refers to Avicenna's widely circulated *Canon Medicinæ*. In the prologue to A Treatise of the *Astrolabe Chaucer promises to include in Part IV a lunar *table with a canon to explain its use. In Part II he writes as though Lewis (Lewis *Chaucer) already possessed a calendar with a table of conjunctions and explanatory canon. (See also *astrology and astronomy; *conjunccio(u)n; *kalendere; *medicine.) [JDN]

Cantebrigge, Cantebregge. Cambridge, the university town in East Anglia, is the general setting for The *Reeve's Tale (the main action of which takes place in the nearby village of *Trumpington). It is a deliberate parallel to the setting of The *Miller's Tale in Oxford (*Oxenford). The Cambridge of Chaucer's day lacked some of the landmarks so familiar now, such as the Chapel of King's College (begun in the 15th c.) and only a few corners and buildings of the older colleges give a feeling of the 14th c.—for example, Old Court in Corpus Christi College, the chapel of Caius (then Gonville), or the hall of Peterhouse. As in Oxford there were numerous halls which have not survived or were later made part of other, newer foundations—thus the 14th c. institutions of Michaelhouse and King's Hall (probably the '*Soler Halle' of *RvT*) became part of Trinity College in the 16th c. The university was smaller than Oxford. Its scholars came mainly from Britain, and especially from the north and east of England. Cambridge was a busy market town. As in Oxford, there was rivalry between Town and Gown, which occasionally erupted into riots, and which is reflected in the miller's scornful references to 'clerks' (cf. I.4049–54, 4096–7, 4122–4) as well as in his habit of defrauding the college. Chaucer shows some local knowledge: that, for instance, King's Hall had a high proportion of northerners, and that Trumpington had a parson (one of the parsons may have been known to him personally).

Bennett (1974).

Canterbury, see *Caunterbury.

Canterbury Tales, The, survives in an unfinished form, consisting of about 17,000 lines of prose and verse. It is found in part or as a whole in a large number of MSS, a testimony to its popularity. Just over eighty remain (of which fifty-five seem to have once contained all the Tales), ranging in date from about 1400 to the late 15th c. The earliest is the *Hengwrt MS, in the National Library of Wales, which has a text apparently close to what Chaucer wrote, but a disjointed ordering of the Tales; the slightly later *Ellesmere MS, in the Huntington Library, San Marino, California, probably written by the same scribe, has most often been used as the base text for modern editions (see *editing and editions). Other important MSS are MS Dd.4.24 and MS Gg.4.27 in Cambridge University Library, and Corpus Christi College, Oxford, MS 198. The Canterbury Tales was printed (by *Caxton, *Pynson, and *Wynkyn de Worde) before the end of the 15th c., and has been in print continuously ever since, in the editions of Chaucer's works by *Thynne, *Stow, *Speght, and *Urry, through to the *Tyrwhitt edition of the Tales and its successors in the 19th and 20th c.

The date of the work's inception is not certain. The fact that it does not appear in the list of Chaucer's writings given in the Prologue to The *Legend of Good Women (probably 1386–7) suggests that it was not then written, at least in a complete form. Its composition probably occupied most if not all of the remaining years of Chaucer's life. Some of the individual Tales, however, were probably in existence earlier in some form or other. This is almost certainly the case with *The *Knight's Tale* and *The *Second Nun's Tale*, which seem to be referred to in the list in the Prologue to *The Legend of Good Women*. Other Tales—for example, *The *Monk's Tale*—have been said, often on stylistic grounds, to be early work, but there is no general agreement. *The Legend of Good Women* shows that Chaucer was already interested in a collection of short narratives; it may be that the idea of using the Canterbury pilgrimage as a framework for another and more varied collection of stories told by different narrators came to him in the late 1380s. The ancient device of the 'framed' collection of stories is by no means uncommon in the Middle Ages (The *Seven Sages of Rome* and *Gower's *Confessio Amantis* are English examples; the *Libro del buen amor* of Juan *Ruiz a Spanish one), and it is probably not necessary to search for a particular 'source'. It has, however, been suggested that Chaucer may have known of one or more Italian collections of *novelle*, such as *Boccaccio's *Decameron* or the *novelle* of Giovanni Sercambi. The latter (which uses the device of a pilgrimage) is now thought likely to date from after 1400. The question of the *Decameron* has been much debated: in the opinion of many it is possible, or probable that Chaucer knew it (but see *Boccaccio). Although there are striking similarities in outlook and ideas as well as in some individual stories, the handling of the framework is different (there the young men and ladies who tell the stories have retired from Florence to the country in order to escape the plague). The common medieval practice of *pilgrimage provides Chaucer with his framework—even though he does not attempt to give a detailed account of an actual one (there is, for instance, no mention of the shrines which were often visited on the way to Canterbury).

The *General Prologue* describes the meeting of the Pilgrims in the *Tabard Inn at Southwark, and the agreement (suggested by the *Host, Harry Bailly) that they should tell stories on their way to and from Canterbury, with a dinner as the prize

for the best story. There are thirty pilgrims, including Chaucer (assuming that the 'preestes three' of the Prioress are an error, or an unrevised first thought, for the single unnamed 'Nun's Priest' who in fact tells a tale)—and they are later joined by the *Canon and his Yeoman. The original suggestion (I.790–4) is that each should tell two stories going and two on the way back, but in the work as we have it only twenty-two pilgrims tell a single tale each, and Chaucer himself tells two. There is no reference either to arrival at Canterbury or to any return to Southwark. It may be, as some think, that Chaucer was simply unable to complete the grand scheme (the 15th-c. 'continuations' in *Lydgate's *Siege of Thebes* and *The Tale of *Beryn*, which both begin a supposed journey back from Canterbury, seem to be assuming this). Many, however, think that the plan (which involved a very large number of stories) has been changed, with the homeward journey being abandoned, and the number of required tales reduced (in V.698 there is a reference simply to 'a tale or two', and just before the Parson begins his tale, the Host remarks, with every sign of intended closure, 'now lakketh us no tales mo than oon', X.16).

The work exists in ten Fragments (designated either by Roman numerals or, following the earlier editions of the Chaucer Society and *Skeat, by letters of the alphabet). These are units defined by internal links of one kind or another. They are (in the order of the Ellesmere MS):

Fragment I (or Group A). The *General Prologue*; *The Knight's Tale*; *The *Miller's Prologue and Tale*; *The *Reeve's Prologue and Tale*; *The *Cook's Prologue and Tale*.

Fragment II (B¹). *The *Man of Law's Introduction, Prologue, Tale and Epilogue*.

Fragment III (D). *The *Wife of Bath's Prologue and Tale*; *The *Friar's Prologue and Tale*; *The *Summoner's Prologue and Tale*.

Fragment IV (E). *The *Clerk's Prologue and Tale*; *The *Merchant's Prologue, Tale and Epilogue*.

Fragment V (F). *The *Squire's Introduction and Tale*; *The *Franklin's Prologue and Tale*.

Fragment VI (C). *The *Physician's Tale*; *The *Pardoner's Introduction, Prologue, and Tale*.

Fragment VII (B²). *The *Shipman's Tale*;

The**Prioress's Prologue and Tale*; *The Prologue and Tale of* *Sir Thopas; *The Tale of* *Melibee; *The* **Monk's Prologue and Tale*; *The* **Nun's Priest's Prologue, Tale, and Epilogue*.

Fragment VIII (G). *The* **Second Nun's Prologue and Tale*; *The* **Canon's Yeoman's Prologue and Tale*.

Fragment IX (H). *The* **Manciple's Prologue and Tale*.

Fragment X (I). *The* **Parson's Prologue and Tale* and 'Chaucer's Retraction' (*Retracciouns).

The Ellesmere order makes good sense of what remains (all MSS, whatever their ordering of II–IX, begin with the *General Prologue* and end with *The Parson's Tale*, and Fragments IX and X are explicitly linked), but what Chaucer had in mind for the final structure remains unknown. A few modern editions favour the alternative order of Skeat noted above, which gives us: I, II, VII, VI, III, IV, V, VIII, IX, X. This makes use of the "*Bradshaw shift', which attempts to rationalize the topographical and chronological references indicating the progress of the journey to Canterbury. However, while Chaucer might have had such a scheme in mind, and while it is reasonable to suppose that he might well have eventually put all the topographical references into the correct order, the existing MSS give no support to the 'Bradshaw shift'.

There are other signs of incompleteness and indications of revision in progress. *The Cook's Tale* and (in the opinion of most) *The Squire's Tale* are not finished. Chaucer's plan seems to have been to bind the different stories together by narrative exchanges between the pilgrims and by prologues and epilogues, but this is only partially completed (see *epilogues, *links). Thus, while some of the Fragments begin with an exchange in which the Host invites a particular pilgrim to tell a tale, in others a pilgrim simply begins talking. There are one or two oddities: in the Manciple's Prologue (IX.II), the words 'Is that a cook of Londoun . . . ?' to some seem to imply that the Cook is being introduced as if for the first time, and certainly when the Host calls on him to tell a tale (IX.13), it is strange that there is no reference to his earlier attempt in Fragment I. It may be that the Manciple's Prologue was written later, and Chaucer meant to cancel the Cook's Prologue and Tale,

and perhaps introduce him at another point, or that the Cook's Prologue and Tale were written after the Manciple's Prologue and Chaucer intended to adjust the latter. Again, there is some evidence which suggests that Chaucer had been moving a tale from one teller to another. That the Man of Law says 'I speke in prose' (II.96) just before he begins his tale in verse may imply that he was originally meant to tell a prose tale, perhaps *Melibee*. Similarly, it has been claimed that *The Shipman's Tale* was first intended for the Wife of Bath.

The evidence quite clearly shows that *The Canterbury Tales* exists in an unfinished state. However, there has been considerable disgreement about how complete it is as a work of art, and a lively debate about its unity and structure. At one extreme are those who insist that it is work in progress, a series of fragments, and that our modern desire for a unified book should be resisted, at the other those who are convinced that it has a clear integrity and a unifying 'idea'—though there has not always been agreement in describing what that is. Furthermore, some have stressed the dramatic quality of the work, emphasizing the interplay between one teller's tale and the next, and that each tale should be taken as a dramatic statement from a particular pilgrim, not as a generalized 'Chaucerian' view. Those who carry this to extremes often use the framework narrative as series of clues to the 'real' meaning of the tale, so that, for instance, *The Prioress's Tale* is said to expose its teller's hypocrisy, or *The Man of Law's Tale* to reveal the inadequacies of the teller's grasp of the religious and moral questions raised by it. More moderate views accept the authorial presence of Chaucer the creator of the fiction, while recognizing that from time to time in narrative passages he will make us aware of a self-consciously contrived 'voice' of a particular pilgrim narrator. At times the author seems to move almost imperceptibly in and out of the voice and mind of one of his creations. As to the question of unity, the majority of critics have tended to prefer a middle ground, recognizing that, although the work was not 'published' in any final, revised form, there are a number of unifying factors—such as the metaphoric function of the pilgrimage, the recurring motifs, patterns of ideas and themes (like *marriage, '*gentilesse', etc.) which suggest an elaborate (if unfinished) structure of debate or discussion, or the sense of a distinct authorial presence—which are sufficient to give form to the evident *diversity of the Fragments.

There has been less argument concerning the literary quality of *The Canterbury Tales*. It has been a popular work for centuries, and is acknowledged as one of the masterpieces of English literature. The excellence of individual narratives and the vividness of the Pilgrims (both in the formal *portraits in the *General Prologue* and in the way they behave in the 'framework') are immediately obvious. The work is infused with an extraordinary diversity and dramatic life. The group of Pilgrim narrators is strikingly unlike that of the *Decameron*—a group of young beautiful people of similar background and taste. The Canterbury Pilgrims are from a variety of social classes and callings, thrown together by chance ('by aventure yfalle | In felawshipe', I.25–6). Not surprisingly, there are disagreements, quarrels, and conflicts. The Reeve is angered by the Miller's story; the Host has a violent argument with the Pardoner. There are interruptions—the Miller interrupts the Host and insists on telling his own 'noble tale'; the Monk's ceaseless flow of stories about the fall of those in high estate is politely but firmly interrupted by the Knight, and the Host joins in, less politely; Chaucer himself is stopped in mid-career in his account of the adventures of Sir Thopas. There are unforeseen events—the Cook falls off his horse; the Canon flees when his Yeoman is about to reveal his secrets. The framework in which the stories are placed is one of diverse and jostling humanity. However, the group has something of that sense of community which is developed among any group of travellers with some common purpose. This is suggested by the frequency with which the narrator refers to 'we', 'us', and 'our', as well as by the manner in which the Host presides over the company: 'Greet chiere made oure Host us everichon, | And to the soper sette he us anon' (I.747–8). The bond, however, is fragile, and moments of embarrassment and unease are never too far away. Thus, for instance, when the Pardoner announces that he will have a drink, 'right anon thise gentils gonne to crye, | 'Nay, lat hym telle us of no ribaudye!' The

Pardoner's tale is far from 'ribaudye', but at the end of it he strains the social bonds even more severely. All this has the effect of providing built-in audience reactions, with the Pilgrims offering a flow of comments, interpretations, and applications to their own lives.

In the *Decameron* the pattern of the storytelling is carefully organized. Each of the group takes turns as president for the day, and announces the topic for the stories. Ten days of storytelling produce exactly one hundred stories. The Host finds it much more difficult to maintain control. All the time Chaucer keeps up the pretence of simply reporting what he sees and hears. Some tales arise directly out of quarrels—like those of the Reeve, or the Friar and the Summoner. Some are fitted so closely to their tellers that they seem like dramatic monologues or soliloquies. Questions are raised, then picked up and debated further or alluded to in passing. The succession of tales gives a shifting perspective. One tale will sometimes comment, obliquely or directly, on its predecessor, or offer a different point of view—thus the aristocratic noble love of *The Knight's Tale* gives way to the more earthy passions of *The Miller's Tale* and *The Reeve's Tale*. These strong contrasts of attitude and tone have sometimes suggested the cultural contrast of Lent and Carnival, with the 'unofficial' voice being allowed to make fun of the 'official' culture. There is some truth in this, provided that we do not set up a rigidly black and white opposition. *The Knight's Tale* has its own irony and touches of comedy, and *The Miller's Tale* its own kind of seriousness—and the fabliau is by no means the exclusive property of 'unofficial' culture any more than the romance belonged only to high 'official' culture.

It is variety above all which is characteristic of *The Canterbury Tales*, a variety of stories and styles and of *language and form. It offers a veritable anthology of medieval literary genres, and in this it differs markedly from *The Legend of Good Women*, and even from the *Decameron* (although that has considerable diversity of topic and tone). Chaucer's quiet remark about the audience reaction at the end of *The Miller's Tale*—'diverse folk diversely they seyde'—is profoundly true of the work as a whole. From it serious ideas and matters of 'earnest' emerge, but in the spirit and setting of *game'. The game of storytelling has rules, but it enjoys a carnival licence. Significantly, it begins with eating and drinking, with the promise of free and uninhibited table talk. The final end of the prize dinner is never realized, but *The Canterbury Tales* itself presents a feast, a *satura* or satire in its etymological sense of a mixed dish—of verse and prose, of high and low, of earnest and game. (See *imitations; *modernizations and translations; *editing and editions; *Criticism of Chaucer.)

(ed.) *Rv*; Blake (1980); *S&A* 1–81 [1–22]; (numerous studies include:) C. D. Benson (1986); Cooper (1983); Howard (1976); Kean (1972) vol. ii, Kittredge (1915); Norton-Smith (1974); Pearsall (1985); Phillips (2000).

Capaneus, Cappaneus, Campaneus, Capaneus, one of the Greek champions who assisted *Adrastus and Polynices (*Polymytes) in the expedition of the Seven against *Thebes (see *Tr* V.1485–1510). 'Proud Capaneus' (*Tr* V.1504, *Anel* 59) was destroyed by a thunderbolt. In *The *Knight's Tale* (I.912–47), his widow leads the lamentations of the company of black-clothed women who appeal to *Theseus for mercy and for vengeance on the tyrant *Creon, who had refused the burial of their husbands' bodies.

Capitolie, the Capitol (in Rome), the south-west summit of the Capitoline hill, overlooking the Forum, with a great temple of Jupiter, the city's guardian. Chaucer, like some other medieval writers, places the assassination of Julius Caesar here (VII.2703–10). (He was killed in the Curia of Pompey in the Campus Martius.)

Capricorn(e), Capricornus, the tenth sign of the Zodiac. The Sun is at its head (*hed) at the commencement of winter. The sign is a *domicile of Saturn, the dejection of Jupiter, and the exaltation of Mars. (See also *exaltacioun; *signe; *Zodiak).

[JDN]

Caribdis. Charybdis, a dangerous whirlpool off the coast of Sicily in the straits of Messina. Troilus alludes to it in a song of despair (*Tr* V.644).

carole, karole, in French and ME often means a round *dance with singing (and the verb *carole*: dance and sing). Such *caroles* are frequently mentioned in medieval courtly literature, and there are references also to popular round dances and dance songs. It has been suggested that the dancers moved round hand in hand singing the refrain or 'burden', and then stood still while an individual singer sang the stanza. However, the choreography of the courtly *carole* is not completely certain: often the participants clearly form a ring and move to the movement of their soloist leader, yet other references suggest a processional dance (and it would obviously be possible for one to turn into the other). Songs quoted in French texts are very similar to or identical with *rondeaux. Probably, as John Stevens says, the *carole* 'is not in the formal sense a genre' but rather 'a set of constituents which may be fitted together in a number of ways to make a dance-song'. In the ME *Romaunt of the Rose* (742 ff.) there is a description of the 'fair folk' who went 'upon a karole'. A lady (Gladnesse) 'karolede hem'—i.e. sang the song accompanying the dance—with a voice 'ful clere . . . and ful swete'. 'Carolynge' brings delight to ladies (VIII.1345), and is one of the skills of the courtly lady in *The *Book of the Duchess* (848–9). The company of ladies in the Prologue to *The Legend of Good Women*, as they danced around the daisy, 'songen, as it were in carole-wyse, | This balade' (G 199–202). The word 'carol' is also applied in English to a type of *lyric (presumably descended from the *carole*) which became very common in the 15th c., a 'fixed form' characterized by a 'burden' alternating with the stanzas. Some of the later carols have elaborate music and seem far removed from ring-dances.

Greene (1977); Stevens (1986).

Carrenar (*BD* 1029, where it is linked with 'the *Drye Se') is probably Kara-Nor (Black Lake), a lake on the eastern edge of the Gobi Desert or desert of Lop, beside an ancient highway.

Cartage (1), Carthage, a city on the northern coast of Africa, near the modern Tunis. It was founded by Phoenicians in the 9th c. BC (according to legend, by Queen *Dido), and became pre-eminent among the independent cities of North Africa, a notable Mediterranean maritime power. It came into conflict with Rome in the Punic Wars (264–261 BC and 218–202 BC), during the second of which the Carthaginian general Hannibal

(*Hanybal) invaded Italy, but which ended with the defeat of the Carthaginians by Scipio Africanus Major (*Affrican (1)). Chaucer alludes to it as a rich city (*BD* 1062), and refers to the wars (VII.3365); the majority of his references are to it as the setting of the story of Dido (*BD* 732; *HF* 224, 236; *LGW* 1000).

Cartage (2), in the phrase 'from Hulle to Cartage' used to suggest the great extent of the *Shipman's journeys (I.404) may be the Tunisian Carthage (*Cartage (1)) or the port of Cartagena (Cartago Nova) in the Spanish Levant. (There is also a small southern Spanish town Cartaya in the province of Huelva.) [PS]

Ca(a)s, see *Fortune.

Cassandra, Cassandre, Cassandra, in Greek legend the daughter of Priam (*Priam(us)) and Hecuba (*Ecuba), who, because she refused the advances of *Apollo, was punished by having her gift of prophecy rendered useless because no one would ever believe her predictions, as when she foretold the destruction of Troy. In the story as told by Guido delle Colonne (*Guydo) she makes a long and sorrowful lament over the city; this is referred to in The *Book of the Duchess (1247–8). Her most important appearance in Chaucer is in *Troilus and Criseyde, where as the sister of Troilus (III.410; also called *Sibille, V.1450), she is asked to explain his dream of the boar kissing Criseyde (V.1450–535). She interprets his prophetic dream correctly as signifying Criseyde's shift of loyalty to Diomede (the descendent of Meleager (*Meleagre), who slew the Calydonian boar). This provokes a statement of angry disbelief from Troilus. This episode has been changed from its equivalent in the *Filostrato, where Troiolo interprets his own dream, and Cassandra taunts him for loving Criseida, suggesting that Chaucer was interested both in registering Troilus's tense psychological state and in making use of the tradition of Cassandra as the prophetess doomed never to be believed.

CASSIDORE, CASSIODORIE, CASSIO-DORUS. Flavius Magnus Aurelius Cassiodorus (*c.*480–*c.*575), a younger contemporary of Boethius (*Boece), spent the first part of his life as an important administrator in the service of *Theodoric the Ostrogoth and his successors. In 540 he retired to his estates at Vivarium, where he founded a monastery. By collecting and preserving much pagan as well as Christian literature he ensured the survival of a significant body of ancient learning. Of his works the most influential was the *Institutes* (*Institutiones divinarum et saecularium litterarum*). Written for his monks, it expounds the study of scripture, and discusses learning in general, based on the *seven liberal arts. Cassiodorus is quoted several times in *Melibee*: these are proverbial remarks (e.g. 'it is signe of a gentil herte whan a man loveth and desireth to han a good name') taken over from the French original of the tale.

(ed.) Mynors (1937); (trans.) L.W. Jones (1949).

Cassius, see *Brutus.

Castor and Pollux, the sons of Leda (*Pollux* is a L. form of the Greek *Polydeuces*). The father is variously given as Zeus or Tyndareus. Stellified (as mentioned in The *House of Fame) they become the brightest stars in the constellation of *Gemini, the Twins, Castor being the brighter. (See also *astrology and astronomy; *sterre.) [JDN]

Cataloigne, Catalonia, a province in north-eastern Spain united to the Crown of Aragon between 1137 and 1410. The trumpeting referred to by Chaucer in The *House of Fame (III.1248) was apparently a characteristic feature of Catalan and Aragonese ceremonial. [PS]

CATOUN (1), Marcus Porcius Cato Uticensis (i.e. 'of Utica') (95–46 BC) a man of rigid and unbending integrity, an opponent of Julius Caesar and the triumvirate, who after the death of Pompey (*Pompe) continued his resistence in Utica (near Carthage) until it became clear that his cause was hopeless, whereupon he committed suicide. He was praised by Cicero, and is one of the heroes of *Lucan's *Pharsalia*. He is mentioned in *Boece* IV pr.6:233, and is perhaps also the 'stierne Catoun' (*rigidus Cato*) who is linked with *Brutus in II m.7:19, although this may be his grandfather, 'the censor', equally famed for his uprightness and morality. (See also *Marcia Catoun.)

CATO(U)N (2), Dionysius Cato, supposed author of the *Distichs* (*Disticha Catonis*), a collection of sententious sayings composed about the 3rd c. AD. It was used in the Middle Ages as a schoolbook, was translated into the vernaculars, and was widely known. Chaucer refers to 'Cato' twelve times in *The *Canterbury Tales* as an 'authority' (see *auctour) who may be quoted to support or prove a point in argument. Thus the old Carpenter in *The *Miller's Tale* 'knew nat Catoun, for his wit was rude, | That bad [bade] man sholde wedde his simylitude' (I.3227–8; cf. also IV.1377; VII.2940–1, 2971–6; VIII.888).

(ed.) Boas and Botschuyver (1952); (ed. and trans.) Wight and Duff (1934); Hazelton (1960).

cats, see *animals.

CATULLUS. Gaius Valerius Catullus (*c.*84–*c.*54 BC), the famous Roman poet, is mentioned once in *Boece* III pr.4:11. However, he was not widely known in the Middle Ages, and there is no evidence that Chaucer read him.

Caucasus, Kaukasous, the mountain range which extends for about 700 miles (1,120 km) from the Black Sea to the Caspian, including such high peaks as Ararat. Medieval writers sometimes call the range a 'mountain': Chaucer refers to it as the limit of the world—'the montaigne that highte Caucasus' in *Boece* (II pr.7:63), and, more poetically, in *The *Wife of Bath's Tale* in the course of a similitude for inherent nobility: 'Tak fyr and ber it in the derkeste hous | Betwix this and the mount of Kaukasos' (and it will still continue to burn, which is its 'office natureel').

Caunterbury, Canterbury, in Kent, a great religious centre from the arrival of the missionary St Augustine in 597. Its distinguished archbishops included Lanfranc, *Anselm, *Bradwardine, and of course Thomas Becket (see *Thomas of Kent), whose martyrdom in 1170 made it a place for *pilgrimage. The town has many ancient churches, but is dominated by the great Cathedral (Christ Church) raised by Lanfranc on the ruins of St Augustine's church, and several times rebuilt and reconstructed. The choir was begun by the French master mason William of Sens in 1175 in

the Gothic style and completed by William the Englishman in 1179–84. A new nave was built during Chaucer's time by Henry Yevele in the Perpendicular style (see *architecture). The elaborate shrine of Becket, at which healing miracles were regularly reported, stood in Trinity Chapel behind the high altar from 1220 until 1538, when it was destroyed by Henry VIII.

Pilgrims entered by the West Gate of the walled town (probably built under the direction of Yevele), and approached the Cathedral by Mercery Lane (probably so called because it had stalls and booths where objects of devotion, pilgrim badges, 'ampulles' of healing water from Becket's well in the crypt, and mementoes could be purchased). The 15th-c. tale of *Beryn* imagines the arrival of Chaucer's pilgrims: they go to the Cathedral to make their offerings, and are sprinkled with holy water. The Knight goes straight to the shrine, but the Pardoner and the Miller 'and other lewd sots' wander around peering at the glass and attempting to interpret the stories and the coats of arms, and have to be packed off by the Host to the shrine to kiss the relics. After the service, they go out and buy 'Canterbury brooches' to put in their caps. In the afternoon, after dinner, some of them go sight-seeing in the town.

Like all pilgrimage sites, Canterbury had many hostelries and lodgings. One of the most interesting survivals is the Hospital of St Thomas or Eastbridge Hospital, founded in the 12th c. as a hostel for poor pilgrims. Inns have often been absorbed into surrounding houses, but something is known about the one at which, according to *Beryn*, Chaucer's pilgrims stayed. It was called the Chequer of the Hope, perhaps because its sign had a chessboard and a barrel hoop indicating the entertainment which it provided. It was in a handsome timbered building with over hanging eaves on the corner of Mercery Lane and High Street, not far from the Cathedral; it had an oblong courtyard and was furnished with a large dormitory supported on wooden pillars and extensive cellars. (See also *Caunterbury weye.)

Caunterbury, Tales of, see *Canterbury Tales*.

Caunterbury weye, the road from London to Canterbury, referred to in the Manciple's

Prologue (IX.3). The old Kent Road ran through various places mentioned in *The *Canterbury Tales*—the '*Wateryng of Seint Thomas', Deptford (*Depeford), Greenwich (*Grenewych), past Rochester (*Rouchestre) to Sittingbourne (*Sidyngbourne), Boughton under Blean (*Boghtoun), and Harbledown (*Bobbe-up-and-down). Chaucer's name for the latter perhaps suggests the movement of a horse: the riding of pilgrims to Canterbury is enshrined in the English word 'canter'. The passage of large groups of pilgrims must have often been a busy and a noisy affair. In the early 15th c., William Thorpe, a *Lollard and no lover of pilgrimages, complains that some pilgrims 'will have with them bagpipes, so that in each town that they come through, what with noise of their singing and with the sound of their piping and with the jingling of their Canterbury bells [small bells on the horses] and with the barking out of dogs after them, these make more noise than if the king came thereaway with his trumpeters and many other minstrels'.

CAXTON, WILLIAM (probably born between 1415 and 1424; d. 1492), the first English printer and an important merchant and publisher. He was apprenticed to a London mercer, and was engaged in the wool trade, spending about thirty years in the Low Countries, and rising to the position of governor of the English 'nation' of merchant adventurers in Bruges. The new technique of printing with movable type had been developed by Gutenberg at Mainz about 1450, and in 1471 Caxton went to Cologne to acquire a press and skilled workmen. He published his first book in 1473 or 1474, and in 1476 moved to England, setting up his press in the precincts of Westminster Abbey, from where he produced a steady flow of translations and of editions of English texts. His particular interest in printing English vernacular works (which made good business sense, since Latin and French books could be obtained ready-made abroad) set a pattern for later English printers, and was of great importance in the development of the idea of a distinctive national literary tradition. He printed *Gower, *Lydgate, and Malory, but his extensive production of Chaucer's writings is especially remarkable. It marked the beginning of a continuing series of editions and reprintings, and helped to establish Chaucer's 'canonical' position as a great English poet. His first edition of *The *Canterbury Tales* is now thought to date from 1476. A second followed some years later (1484), with woodcuts of the pilgrims. From 1477 to 1484 he also printed *Anelida and Arcite* together with *Purse; The *Parliament of Fowls; Boece; The *House of Fame; *Troilus and Criseyde; and the shorter poems *Fortune, *Truth, *Gentilesse, and *Scogan. In short, he published all of Chaucer's poetry except for The *Book of the Duchess, The *Legend of Good Women, the *ABC, the *Romaunt, and some lyrics. He also printed the Latin elegy on the poet by the humanist Surigone. Caxton warmly endorsed the high contemporary opinion of Chaucer. He calls him 'the worshipful fader and first foundeur and enbelissher of ornate eloquence in our Englissh' and a 'noble and grete philosopher', and remarks 'he excellyth in myn oppynyon alle other wryters in our Englyssh, for he wrytteth no voyde wordes, but alle hys mater is ful of hye and quycke [lively] sentence'.

CH i. 74–9; Boyd (1984); Hellinga (1982).

Cecilie, Cecilia, the heroine of the *Second Nun's Tale*, St Cecilia, supposedly a Roman martyr of the 3rd c. Almost nothing is certainly known about her, although the martyrs associated with her—Tiburtius, Valerian, and Maximus—do seem to have been historical. However, a vivid legend of the 5th c., and its later retellings, made her a popular saint. From the Renaissance she has traditionally been the patron saint of musicians.

Cecile, lyf of Seynt, see *Second Nun's Tale*.

Cedasus, Scedasus of Leuctra in Boeotia. In her lament in The *Franklin's Tale* Dorigen refers (V.1428) to his daughters who (according to St *Jerome) slew themselves because they had been raped by two drunken young guests.

Ceys, Seys, Ceyx, son of the morning star and husband of Alcyone. His story is told in The *Book of the Duchess* (62–220). (See *Alcione*.)

Ceys and Alcyone. The remark in the Introduction to The *Man of Law's Tale* (II.57) that Chaucer 'in youthe . . . made of Ceys and Alcione' probably refers to his telling of their story in *The *Book of the Duchess* rather than to a lost work.

Cenyth, (1) zenith, in the common modern sense: the point of the heavens directly above the observer (medieval L. from Arabic samt *al-ra's.*). This corresponds to medieval L. *zenith capitis,* echoed in *A Treatise on the *Astrolabe* 1.18.15–17; (2) Chaucer also uses the word, fully in keeping with Arabic and medieval L. precedents, as a synonym of azimuth (*samt,* direction, is the root of both words). See *A Treatise on the Astrolabe* 1.19.10 and 2.31.23. (See also *astrology and astronomy; *azemutz.) [JDN]

CENOBIA, CENOBIE, Zenobia, queen of Palmyra (*Palymerie) in Syria, who succeeded her husband Odenathus (*Odenake) in AD 266 or 267 and, in spite of the fact that her city had long enjoyed the protection of Rome, invaded Asia Minor and Egypt, provoking its hostility. She was deposed by *Aurelian in 272, and Palmyra was destroyed. Her story forms one of the 'tragedies' of *The *Monk's Tale* (VII.2247–374). It is based on the account in *Boccaccio's *De claris mulieribus* (although Chaucer attributes it to 'Persians', and later refers the reader to Petrarch (*Petrak)). Zenobia is a mighty warrior and huntress, wise and skilled in languages. In this eloquent and pathetic story she is the innocent victim of *Fortune. Aurelian determines to take vengeance on this apparently unconquerable adversary, and finally captures her and her two sons, and makes her walk before him in his triumph, with gold chains hanging on her neck.

centauris, centauros, the centaurs, a tribe of proud monsters (Boethius's *Centauros superbos*) with the upper part a human and the lower a horse. Hercules fought off an attack by them when he visited the Centaur Pholus. The episode is mentioned in *Boece* (IV m.7:29) and *The *Monk's Tale* (VII.2099). [JDN]

Cerberus, the monstrous three-headed watchdog of Hades. In *Troilus and Criseyde* Pandarus once swears 'to Cerberus yn helle ay be I bounde' (I.859). Other allusions are to legends in which he is overcome. He was 'al abasschid' by the song of *Orpheus (*Bo* III m.12:31); and brought by

Hercules (*Ercules) to the upper world (VII.2102)— 'by his treble cheyne' (*Bo* IV m.7:36).

Cerces, see *Circes.

Ceres, Roman goddess of corn, agriculture and plenty. In *The *Parliament of Fowls* (276) Ceres, 'who brings remedy for hunger' sits together with Bacchus (*Bachus) the god of wine in the temple of Venus—a visual representation of the proverbial idea that 'without Ceres and Bacchus Venus is cold'. She is also linked with them in a line in *Troilus and Criseyde* (V.208). (See also *Cibella.)

CESAR (1) (Caesar), a ruling prince (*ProlLGW* F 358–60, G 333–6).

CESAR (2) (Julius Caesar) see *Julius; **CESAR (3)** (Octavius Caesar) see *Octovyan; **CESAR (4)** (Caligula) see *Gaius Cesar; **CESAR AUGUSTUS,** see *Augustus Cesar.

Cesiphus. Sisyphus, a legendary king of Corinth, of immense cunning, who for his misdeeds on earth was condemned to spend his time in Hades pushing a great stone up to the top of a hill only to see it roll down again. Chaucer seems to allude to him in *The Book of the Duchess* (589), but the form 'Cesiphus' here is a modern editorial emendation, the MSS having 'Thesiphus' or 'Tesiphus'. In medieval handwriting 't' and 'c' are easily confused, but the phrase 'that *lyeth* in helle' may suggest rather the giant Tityus (*Ticius), who was tortured as he was stretched out on the ground. Perhaps there has been a confusion, either on the part of Chaucer or of a scribe.

'Ch'. These letters in a 14th-c. French MS seem to indicate the authorship of a series of fifteen lyrics in French. The intriguing possibility that they might be by Chaucer has been suggested, but there is no certain proof.

Wimsatt (1982).

Chaldeye. Chaldea or Babylonia (*Babiloigne). In *The *Monk's Tale* (VII.2157) there is no 'clerk' in Chaldea (famous for its astrological and occult learning) who can interpret the dream of Nebuchadnezzar (*Nabugodonosor).

Chano(u)n, see *Canon.

characters and characterization. These words, so often used in discussions of Chaucer, are never used by him. In the English of his day *character* simply had its original sense of an engraved or impressed mark or stamp, and seems to have developed such senses as (Johnson) 'a representation of any man as to his personal qualities', 'the person with his assemblage of qualities' or 'personal qualities; particular constitution of the mind' centuries later. *Characterization*, a 16th-c. word, seems to be first found in the sense of the 'creation of fictitious characters' in Fielding. Medieval literary theory represents the Aristotelian concept of character by *consuetudo* ('custom, habit'), a typical pattern of behaviour rather than a set of personal idiosyncracies. The notion of 'playing the part of' or a writer speaking 'in the person of' makes use of the L. *persona*. Such *personae* may also be exemplary—examples, for instance, of steadfastness or fortitude. Medieval rhetorical books offer advice rather on how to describe a person's appearance and behaviour effectively or on how to render the 'circumstances' of a scene or an action in a vivid way. That early critical terminology differs from modern in this area does not of course mean that Chaucer was incapable of achieving what a modern critic might call 'characterization', but it suggests that we need to be careful in our use of the term.

In the history of Chaucer criticism, an emphasis on his 'characters' seems to appear from the time of *Dryden, to flourish in the 18th c., a period which saw the development of a similar interest in Shakespeare's characters, and even more in the 19th and early 20th c., influenced by the practice and theory of the realistic novel and a growing scientific interest in psychology and psychological motivation, again in parallel with Shakespearian criticism. Dryden's words (1700) are still in the older rhetorical tradition: 'Not a single Character escaped him. All his pilgrims are severally distinguish'd from each other; and not only in their inclinations, but in their very physiognomies and persons.' While a sense of the general or 'universal' aspect of his characterization is sometimes expressed, increasingly critics warmed to the perceived individuality of some characters—'In

Chaucer, Cressida is represented as a grave, sober, considerate personage ... who has an alternate eye to her character, her interest, and her pleasure: Shakespear's Cressida is a giddy girl, an unpractised jilt' (*Hazlitt, 1817)—or to their realism, or to a 'rounded' or 'three-dimensional' quality.

At its best such criticism has proved illuminating and interesting, and conscious of the more exemplary aspects of Chaucer's characterization and of the way 'character' emerges from narrative situations, but it was easily vulgarized, and has sometimes been taken to extremes, resulting in 'character sketches' entirely separated from the text, or has encouraged a confusion between fictional 'characters' and living persons. This has provoked a strong reaction in recent Chaucer criticism, with attempts to replace 'round' or 'three-dimensional' characters with rhetorical configurations or allegorical figures. Thus, instead of the many attempts at a psychological interpretation or explanation of the *Pardoner, he has been presented as an exemplification of sin; it has been urged that the *Wife of Bath has no 'personality' but is rather a universalized image of some aspect of Woman. Or, less extremely, that the personages in *Troilus and Criseyde 'possess no individual psychology in the modern sense at all', but 'think of themselves as exemplifying kinds of behaviour or moral paradigms of actions after ethical configurations', as *exempla of the kind which 'would have been familiar to Cicero or Seneca' (Norton-Smith).

The truth probably lies between the two extremes. Medieval literature does sometimes show some interest in 'psychology', or at least in the inner life of the mind or the soul—witness the treatment of love in some courtly *romances, or the self-examination demanded by some mystical or penitential books. Some readers at least were encouraged to have a sense of their own self (what Chaucer calls one's 'propre persone'); in *Melibee we are told that having a 'good name' depends both on good reputation and on 'good conscience to thyn owene persone inward' (VII.1644). On the other hand, in the simpler forms of narrative— exempla, ballads, popular romances—it is usually impossible to speak of 'characterization' at all: the figures here are the anonymous figures of folk tale (a king, a queen), or are given the simplest degree of individuation by being named. And even in the most sophisticated literature any 'characterization' is indissolubly linked to narrative action and context.

Like other medieval writers, Chaucer makes use of traditional literary character types—the noble knightly hero, the suffering heroine, the aged lover, etc.—sometimes straightforwardly, but more often with variations or differentiating details. Sometimes he will use the simple narrative figure (as in the case of St Cecilia (*Cecile) or of *Sir Thopas), but he will often make various suggestions concerning motivation or 'character'. These may take the form of remarks about a person's 'temperament' in terms of *physiognomy or *astrology (the *Miller's great mouth, that the *Reeve is 'a sclendre colerik man'; the Wife of Bath herself suggests that it is significant that she is Venerian 'in feelynge' and that her heart is Martian). For some personages he will use the formal rhetorical *portrait, detailing physical or moral characteristics (e.g. the *Parson is 'holy' and 'virtuous'). The technique here is far from simple. In the *General Prologue, Chaucer uses 'the fiction of reportage'—that he has just met all the pilgrims—so that his unsystematic remarks apparently tossed off both give a sense of immediacy and suggestiveness. Ironies and omissions involve the reader in attempts at interpretation. The impression is strongly given that, as Hazlitt puts it: 'Chaucer had an equal eye for truth of nature and discrimination of character; and his interest in what he saw gave new distinctness and force to his power of observation. The picturesque and the dramatic are in him closely blended together, and hardly distinguishable; for he principally describes external appearances as indicating character, as symbols of internal sentiment.'

At other times the dramatic aspect is much the most important. In the narrative the figure will be shown reacting to exterior or interior stimuli through speech or *gesture or some other expression of *emotion. Sometimes a character will be given a monologue, whether private (as with Criseyde, *Tr* II.701–63, 771–808) or public and 'dramatic' (as when the Wife of Bath or the Pardoner harangue the pilgrims).

In any discussion of 'characterization' in Chaucer, due attention must be paid to the narrative and rhetorical contexts, to the importance of ethical or exemplary patterns, and to the influence of traditional literary types. In the end, however, a character like the Wife of Bath is much more lively and memorable than her literary ancestors like 'La Vieille [the Old Woman]' in the *Roman de la Rose*, and seems more complex than any rhetorical or ethical 'configuration'. She is not a 'character' from a realistic novel, and we cannot isolate all of her motivations, but Chaucer has endowed her with a dramatic vitality and a remarkable individuality. It seems reasonable to describe this process as 'characterization'. (See also *criticism of Chaucer.)

Hazlitt, *CH* i. 280; Norton-Smith (1974), 204.

Charing Cross. The stone cross in Westminster erected by Edward I in memory of his queen, Elinor. Nearby was a building used as the mews for the king's falcons, for which Chaucer was responsible when he was Clerk of the Works in 1389–91. In the 16th c. the house was rebuilt to stable the king's horses. Also close to Charing Cross was the hospital of St Mary of Rouncesval (*Rouncivale). (See also *London.)

Charite(e), see *love.

CHARLES, Charlemagne (768–814), king of the Franks and emperor, an impressive figure both in history (as an effective ruler and a patron of learning) and in legend, where he and his barons became prominent characters in the Old French epics, the *chansons de geste*. The most famous, the *Chanson de Roland* (the Oxford MS of which dates from *c.*1100) describes the last battle of Roland (*Rowland) and Oliver (*Olyver) against an attack by a huge Saracen army instigated by the treachery of Ganelon (*Genelloun), and of Charlemagne's vengeance. This and other stories were widely diffused from a variety of sources. Chaucer briefly alludes to Charles in The *Monk's Tale* (VII.2387).

CHAUCER, AGNES, the poet's mother, appears in documents as the wife of John Chaucer from October 1349 to May 1367. Her husband died in 1366, and she married another London vintner called Bartholomew Chappel.

CHAUCER, ALICE (d. 1475), the daughter of Thomas *Chaucer, the poet's son. She was three times married, finally to William de la Pole, earl, and later duke of Suffolk (d. 1450), whose grandfather had opened the parliament of 1386 in which Geoffrey Chaucer took part. She died at Ewelme in Oxfordshire, where her splendid tomb, with those of her parents, can still be seen in the church.

CHAUCER, GEOFFREY: life. Neither the date nor the place of Chaucer's birth are known for certain. Since in 1386 he described himself as 'forty and more', it is usually assumed that he was born in the early 1340s. His parents, Agnes and John *Chaucer, had property in London, including one in Thames Street (Vintry Ward), and it is possible that Geoffrey was born there. He was born into a prosperous merchant family, which had been engaged in the export of wool and the import of wine in Ipswich. His father was a vintner, a wholesale wine dealer. There were three schools near Thames Street, but nothing certain is known about his early education; there is no evidence that he ever went to a *university. The first surviving record which names him (in 1357, as the recipient of clothes and a small gift 'for necessaries at Christmas') is the account book of the household of Elizabeth de Burgh, Countess of Ulster and wife of Prince *Lionel, one of Edward III's sons. He seems to have been one of her retainers, possibly a page, and to have kept a connection with the Ulster household until at least 1360. In 1359 he saw military service in France, probably with Prince Lionel's company, possibly in the *Black Prince's division. He was at the town of Réthel, near the city of Reims which Edward was besieging at the end of 1359 and the beginning of 1360. At some point in the campaign (which took the English army as far as Burgundy (*Burgoyne)) he was captured, but was released by 1 March 1360 (with the king making a contribution of £16 towards his ransom).

He appears in 1366 in a safe-conduct from Charles II (the Bad) of *Navarre permitting him to travel across his country with three companions. He may have been on pilgrimage to Compostela (Seint-*Jame), or his journey may have had something to do with the arrangements for the Black Prince's campaign in Castile to restore

Pedro the Cruel (*Petro (1)) to his throne. In 1366 Chaucer's father died, and his mother remarried; by this year too he himself was married to Philippa Roet (see Philippa *Chaucer). In 1367 he appears as a member of the royal household, being described as an *esquier* or a *valettus*, one of a company of men who were dispatched on administrative or diplomatic missions in England or sometimes in Europe. He received wages and allowances, gifts, and appointments to various offices. The suggestion that he may also at this time have been studying law at the Inner Temple, one of the Inns of Court, depends on the later testimony of Thomas *Speght, who claimed to have seen an Inner Temple record of Chaucer being fined for beating a Franciscan friar in Fleet Street, and is not supported by other extant records.

Between 1367 and 1374 Chaucer made a number of journeys abroad. In 1368 he was given a royal warrant to pass through Dover. He may have been away for as many as 106 days, and it has been suggested that he may have gone to Milan (*Melan) where Prince Lionel had married one of the Visconti, but there is no evidence for this. He was probably away again in 1369, when he was among the members of the household to receive £10 for accompanying *John of Gaunt on an expedition to Picardy (*Pycardie). And in 1370 he had a letter of protection to go in the king's service (for some unspecified purpose) to 'parts beyond the sea' (*ad partes transmarinas*). In 1372–3 he made his first recorded journey to Italy (*Ytaille) together with two Italian merchants to negotiate for the king with the doge of *Genoa over the use of an English port. He also visited *Florence, perhaps to discuss the king's financial arrangement with the Bardi bankers. It seems unlikely that this was Chaucer's first contact with Italian culture. He may well have been chosen for the mission because he already had some knowledge of the language. However, the visit was almost certainly significant for his literary development. It is not known if, while he was at Florence, he met Petrarch (*Petrak) or *Boccaccio, who were living in the area or nearby, but he may well not only have heard about them, but found MSS of their works. And at Florence the writings of *Dant(e) were the subject of intense veneration and study. Chaucer's own career as a poet had begun before he set off for

Italy (see *chronology of Chaucer's works). His *Book of the Duchess* commemorates the death of John of Gaunt's wife *Blanche in late 1368, and it is quite likely that even before this he was writing courtly lyric poetry.

The next few years of his life are reasonably well documented, and seem to have been a period of prosperity. In 1374 the king, who was celebrating the feast of St George at Windsor (*Wyndsore), granted him a gallon pitcher of wine daily for the rest of his life. This was renewed in 1377 by *Richard II, and in 1378 it was commuted for an annuity of 20 marks. In the same year he was appointed controller in the port of London, responsible for the customs or export tax on wool, skins, and leather, a considerable volume of revenue. Also in 1374 he leased a dwelling over *Aldgate, close to the customhouse. It was here that he wrote The *House of Fame, The *Parliament of Fowls, and *Troilus and Criseyde. He also went on several royal missions: in 1376 on 'the king's secret affairs', and several times in 1377 to 'divers parts beyond the seas', and to Paris and Montreuil. In 1378 he was again sent to Italy, to Lombardy, to treat with Bernabò Visconti (*Barnabo Viscounte), the ruler of Milan, and Sir John *Hawkwood, his general and son-in-law, on 'matters touching the king's war'.

After his return he was involved in a mysterious lawsuit involving a charge of the *raptus* (which may mean either abduction or physical rape) of one Cecilia Chaumpaigne, who seems to have been the daughter of William Champain or Champneys, a baker. All that is known for certain is that he was cleared of responsibility, being released on 1 May 1380 (acknowledged by Cecilia on 4 May) of all actions seeking redress. What Chaucer's relationship was with the two other citizens involved in the case, Robert Goodchild and John Grove, remains unclear. The witnesses who supported him were his friends and men of high standing—Sir William *Beauchamp, chamberlain of the king's household, Sir John *Clanvowe and Sir William Nevill, knights of the king's chamber, John *Philipot, collector of customs, and Richard Morel, a London grocer. He certainly seems to have taken trouble to find weighty support. There has been much speculation concerning the case but nothing has been proven. In 1381 he may have

witnessed in London the violence of the *Peasants' Revolt, to which he makes one apparently joking reference (VII.3393-6).

In 1386 he retired from the controllership, and gave up the lease of his dwelling in Aldgate. He moved to Kent (possibly to Greenwich (*Grenewych))—or had already done so, since in October 1385 he joined a commission of peace for Kent, and in 1386 was elected as a knight of the shire to represent the county in parliament. In that year he gave evidence before the High Court of Chivalry for his friend Sir Richard Scrope against Sir Robert Grosvenor in a controversy over the right to bear certain arms. He said that when he was in serving in France before the town of Réthel he had seen the arms in question borne by Sir Richard and his nephew, and that they were commonly agreed to be those of the Scropes. While walking along Friday Street in London he saw them displayed outside a house and was surprised to be told that they were the Grosvenor arms. His involvement in this celebrated trial indicates that he had some very well-connected acquaintances, and perhaps suggests that he had a greater interest in 'chivalry' than some modern critics are prepared to allow him. The name of his wife Philippa is not found in the records after 18 June 1387, presumably because of her death. In the same year he made his last recorded mission abroad, to Calais. The year 1388 saw the death of three men with whom he had worked closely—Sir Nicholas *Brenbre, Sir Simon *Burley, and Chief Justice Tresilian—because of the accusations made by the Appellants, hostile to the king's favourites.

Chaucer's official career was by no means over, however. In July 1389 Richard II, now back in control, appointed him clerk of the king's works at Westminster, the Tower of London, other castles (such as that at Berkhamstead) and seven manors (including *Eltham and Sheen (*Sheene)). He also had the duty of overseeing parks, hunting lodges, the mews for the royal falcons at *Charing Cross, and a variety of other tasks—the building of a wharf, the erection of scaffolds for a joust in Smithfield, etc. It was an important position, and Chaucer was assisted by a controller and a staff of deputies and clerks. His work ranged from the rebuilding of a wharf near the Tower of London to the repair of St George's Chapel, Windsor, and brought him into contact not only with humble craftsmen but with some prominent figures in contemporary *architecture, like the master mason Henry Yevele. In September 1390 Chaucer was waylaid and robbed by highwaymen at least once, at the 'Foule Oke' in Kent. He may well have been carrying wages from Westminster to Eltham.

In June 1391 the clerkship of the works was transferred to John Gedney. The reason for Chaucer's retirement (or removal?) are not known. Suggestions such as that it may have been connected with the robbery (whether because he feared another attack or because he was thought to have carelessly allowed himself to be robbed), or with his discontent with unsatisfactory financial arrangements (at the end of his term his audit showed £87 still owing to him), or with advancing years and a desire to have more time for writing, or because he had not proved very energetic in carrying out his duties, must all remain conjectures. At some point during the 1390s he found another appointment as deputy forester of the royal forest of North Petherton (Somerset). Gifts and annuities from Richard II were continued after his fall, by *Henry IV—though, apparently, slowly and partially (a situation which may be referred to in his *Complaint to his *Purse*). Towards the end of his life Chaucer was living on a leased property in the garden of the Lady Chapel of Westminster Abbey (probably on the site of the present Lady Chapel or Chapel of Henry VII). No record of him survives after June 1400; the traditional date of his death, 25 October 1400, depends upon an inscription placed on a tomb in the Abbey in 1556. It probably contains his remains, since *Caxton says that he was buried at the entrance to the chapel of St Benedict, which is nearby. He seems to have left two sons (see Lewis and Thomas *Chaucer). It is sometimes claimed that he also had two daughters—an 'Elizabeth Chaucy' and an 'Agnes'—but they are not certainly identified as his offspring in the surviving records.

The fairly extensive records of his life (in comparison, we know nothing about the Gawain-poet, and almost nothing about *Langland) survive because of his varied public administrative career, not because of his fame as a writer. However, there is evidence that his work was admired in his own day. Thomas *Usk praises him for 'goodnes of manliche speche' and calls him a 'noble philosophical poet', and his friend *Gower says (1390) that he had filled England with 'ditees' and 'songes glade'. And his work was known even outside England. The French poet, *Deschamps, at about the same time wrote a eulogistic *ballade to the 'great translator, noble Geoffrey Chaucer'. The records show that he was a successful man of affairs, but give no sense whatever of his personality. Nor do the surviving 'portraits' in MSS, although the venerable bearded figure of the poet may well be some sort of 'likeness' (and that these depictions are relatively common—eight survive, and others have been cut out—suggests a strong tradition of portraiture) (see frontispiece, Fig. 1).

Even more tantalizing are the remarks Chaucer makes or causes others to make about himself in his own works. These are usually comic or self-deprecating. In The *House of Fame the *Eagle, who familiarly calls him 'Geffrey', describes him as a bookish recluse (652–60). The *Man of Law, before listing his works, remarks 'thogh he kan but lewedly | On metres and on rymyng craftily' (II.47). The *Host says that he stares at the ground 'as if he wanted to find a hare', that he 'semeth elvyssh by his contenaunce' (see *Elf-queene), and clearly implies that his waist is not slender (VII.695–704)—Chaucer himself jokes about his stoutness in *Scogan (31) and in *Merciles Beaute (27). Most readers also sense a strong and distinctive personality emerging from his work as a whole, or at the very least a highly distinctive narrative voice (see *narrators). This is particularly the case in The *Canterbury Tales, where he likes to present himself as a naive pilgrim-observer. What connection these various personae have with Chaucer the man can never be established. As has often been pointed out, it is highly unlikely that a civil servant of Chaucer's experience and skill would have been as naive as Chaucer the pilgrim pretends to be—though he might well have shared his persona's ironic detachment and sense of humour. But any sense of personality remains a literary construct, and any attempts at 'psycho-criticism' or biographical criticism must remain highly speculative. We simply do not know exactly what lies behind the reference to the mysterious sickness in The Book of the Duchess which he says has afflicted him for eight years and which can be cured by only one physician (30–40), any more than we can be sure about the remark that the Eagle said 'awak!' in the same voice used by 'one I could name' (*HF* 560–2)—is this a reference to his wife, or, since the Eagle spoke in 'a man's voice', to some friend or servant? Such allusions are teasingly similar to his habit of occasionally making use of other real people, like Roger de Ware (see *Cook) or Harry Bailly (see *Host). The temptation to construct a biographical personality has been a strong one. In the 18th-c. Life of Chaucer which accompanies *Urry's edition, John Dart finds from all the references a poet very like an ideal contemporary literary gentleman:

as to his temper, he had a mixture of the gay, the modest, and the grave . . . His course of living was temperate and regular; he went to rest with the sun, and rose before it, and by that means enjoyed the pleasures of the better part of the day, his morning walk and fresh contemplations . . . His reading was deep, and extensive, his judgment sound, and discerning . . . In one word, he was a great scholar, a pleasant wit, a candid critick, a sociable companion, a steadfast friend, a grave philosopher, a temperate oeconomist and a pious Christian.

Some later 20th-c. 'Chaucers' tend to be more ironic, more liberal, more 'subversive'. The problems with attempting to discover Chaucer's 'personality' are similar to those encountered with Shakespeare—that we are dealing with a chameleon-like dramatic writer, who can produce many persons and voices, and that the bland surface of portraits and of public records give no hint of his intense inner imaginative life.

LR; *Rv*, pp. xi–xxii; Howard (1987); Kane (1984); Pearsall (1992); Brewer (1978); Cannon (1993, 2000); Ferris (1967); Loomis (1965), 1–6.

CHAUCER, GEOFFREY: reading (see also *book). If the poet's private life remains much more elusive than his public life, we can trace his development as a writer (see *chronology), and there is a good deal that can be said about his reading. It is not, however, a straightforward subject. It must be remembered that some literary works which we may take for granted were not always available to him (so that references to Homer (*Omer) or *Catullus are not based on direct

knowledge). Not every work which was available would be known to a particular author. Some references may be to a body of vague or diffused 'general knowledge' forming part of a writer's 'mental furniture'—rather in the way that in the 20th c. a reference to Freud or to a Freudian theory would not necessarily imply a profound or even a direct knowledge of his writing. In particular, we may have to make allowance for the medieval passion for quoting 'authorities' (see *auctour and auctoritee): in medieval religious writing there is a tendency to ascribe to 'Augustine' or 'Bernard' or some other authority remarks which are not always by them; secular writers will sometimes give 'authenticity' to their work by referring to 'my author' or to an old book, whether or not they are actually following some such source. Sometimes there may be genuine confusion or apparent obfuscation involved (see '*Lollius'). References or quotations can sometimes come not from complete texts but from *florilegia, collections of sayings or 'sentences', or from anthologies and collections of extracts (see *Argonautycon). Knowledge of one work need not imply a knowledge of other works by the same writer. Thus, the fact that in *Troilus and Criseyde* Chaucer translates a single sonnet of Petrarch (*Petrak) does not necessarily mean that he had read the whole collection of Petrarch's lyrics, nor (without further evidence) that he had an extensive knowledge of Petrarch's other works. Even if a medieval author is translating or paraphrasing a known original, other possible intermediaries may be involved: thus Chaucer in adapting the story of *Griselda from Petrarch's Latin also used a French translation, whereas in the case of *Melibee* he seems to have been using a French translation of a work by *Albertanus of Brescia and not the original Latin. When we have 'analogues' rather than sources everything becomes much less clear. The *Prioress's Tale* shows that Chaucer had read one or more *miracles of the Virgin Mary, but we do not know exactly which ones. Similarly, he had obviously read (and probably heard) a number of *fabliaux, but it is impossible to draw up any certain list of his reading in this area.

Even with all these caveats, it is clear that the breadth of Chaucer's reading was impressive. It ranges from authors he probably encountered at school—like 'Cato' (*Catoun) or 'Aesop' (in Latin, see *Isope)—to those which he later found for himself, and to which, as he makes the *Eagle in *The *House of Fame* say, he would return after his 'rekenynges' and pour over, 'domb as any stoon' (quite possibly at this time an indication of a constant reader, who did not need to form the words with his lips) until his eyes were dazed. It covers a variety of types and genres, from satirical works to penitential and instructive treatises, from anti-feminist tracts to the literature of love. Most remarkable of all, perhaps, is his extensive reading of works of *science, especially of medicine and astronomy.

The linguistic range is equally impressive. He read widely in Latin, French, and Italian. Oddly enough, it is more difficult to establish a 'list' of his reading in his mother tongue, English, than it is in the case of these other languages. There are a number of possible (and not mutually incompatible) explanations which may be suggested for this: perhaps he had so thoroughly assimilated the English books that no explicit reference was needed; perhaps he assumed that they would be part of the 'general knowledge' of his readers; perhaps for him they did not have the 'authority' of some of the books written in the other languages (in his day the rise in status of the English *language was a relatively recent one). They certainly did not play such an obvious role in his imaginative work as the writings of *Ovid or *Dante or *Jean de Meun. But his knowledge of them was probably extensive. It is clear from the *parody in *Sir Thopas* that he had read or heard a good number of popular English *romances—he refers there explicitly to the heroes of *Guy of Warwick*, *Bevis of Hampton* (*Beves), *Lybeaus Desconus* (*Lybeux), *Sir Perceval of Gales*, *Horn child*, and *Ypotys*; and similarities have been detected with *Sir Launfal*, *Sir Eglamour*, and *Thomas of Erceldoune*. He certainly knew something about *alliterative poetry. We cannot be sure how much of the English *lyric tradition was known to him, outside the songs he refers to. *The *Miller's Tale* clearly alludes to the *drama, but in its vernacular forms this was something seen rather than read. Similarly, he would certainly have heard *sermons in English.

Chaucer was a poet whose roots were in the European tradition. He was, it seems, reasonably well versed in Latin, the language of '*clerks' and of learning (see also *classical literature, *Latin) Opinions about his learning have varied from an enthusiastic belief that it was *very* extensive to the ultra-cautious view that he had not read any Latin work outside those which he demonstrably made use of. There is no evidence that he was fluent enough to write in Latin, as *Gower did. While his interests and attitudes were never narrowly 'neo-classical' he brought to the retelling of stories from antiquity an enthusiasm which is characteristic of medieval *humanism, using both Latin originals and vernacular versions. *Ovid was a major source for him, especially the *Metamorphoses* (*Methamorphosios) and the *Heroides* (*Episteles of Ovyde). He had probably also read the French *Ovide moralisé* and an Italian version of the *Heroides*. From the *Aeneid* (*Eneyde) of Virgil (*Virgile(e)) he took, most notably, the story of *Dido, making her, as other medieval writers (like the author of the French *Roman d'Eneas*) had done, into a tragic heroine and the central figure in the episode. He also made use of the *Thebaid* of Statius (*Stace)—and again the story of *Thebes (1) was available in the French *Roman de Thèbes*. Other poets whom he mentions, and whom he probably used (although to what extent is a matter of debate) are *Juvenal, *Lucan, and *Claudian. It has been claimed that some of his poetic epistles were influenced by *Horace, and a number of critics have detected an 'Horatian' quality in his satire. It is also difficult to estimate how much of Seneca (*Senek), who is frequently cited, he had actually read. Seneca was a favourite author in the Middle Ages, whose works were copied, anthologized, and quoted. Chaucer may have been interested in Senecan stoicism, and he certainly uses Senecan material in the discussion of 'gentilesse' in *The *Wife of Bath's Tale*; it is possible, but not certain, that he knew some of the plays, Cicero (*Tullius) is also quoted (frequently in *Melibee*); Chaucer had certainly read the *Somnium Scipionis* (*Drem of Scipioun), with the commentary of Macrobius (*Macrobes). Livy (*Titus Livius) too is mentioned, but it is far from certain that Chaucer had actually read him.

Among later Latin writers, Boethius (*Boece), whom he translated, clearly had a profound influence on him. Not surprisingly, Chaucer shows a knowledge of the Latin *Bible and liturgy. He refers to *Dares (perhaps the epic of *Joseph of Exeter) and Dictys (*Dite) for the matter of *Troy; and causes the Wife of Bath to make good use of *Jerome's epistle against *Jovinian; he refers to the encyclopaedic writer Martianus Capella (*Marcian). His reading in medieval Latin was very wide. He knew the 9th-c. Eclogue of '*Theodulus' and the *Historia destructionis Troiae* of Guido (*Guydo) delle Colonne. He had a particular interest in the cosmological and philosophical poets of the 12th c., Alan of Lille (*Aleyn (1)) and *Bernardus Silvestris, and in the satirical writers, like *Nigel Wireker (or Whiteacre), the author of the *Speculum Stultorum*. His reading included scientific treatises, mythographical and rhetorical writings and commentaries; he refers to the 12th-c. encyclopaedist Vincent of Beauvais (see *Estoryal Myrour). He translates Petrarch's story of Griselda, and says that he has translated the *De miseria condicionis humane* (or *De contemptu mundi*) of Pope Innocent III (see *Wrecched Engendrynge of Mankynde*).

It is quite possible that, like Gower, Chaucer may have written in French—although nothing attributed to him has survived (see '*Ch'). French medieval literature was extremely varied, and far from exclusively 'courtly'. We have already seen how many French translations from Latin works were available in Chaucer's day. He made extensive use of these, and of other writings of a practical or religious kind—the plot of The *Man of Law's Tale* comes from the Anglo-Norman chronicle of Nicholas *Trevet (or Trivet); the *ABC is translated from *Deguilleville. Besides the *romans d'antiquité* (like *Benoît's *Roman de Troie*), he probably knew some chivalric and courtly romances, and something of the very rich French lyrical tradition. Chaucer's creative imagination was clearly excited by the long 13th-c. allegorical poem the *Roman de la Rose*, begun by *Guillaume de Lorris and completed by Jean de Meun. He says that he translated it (see *Romaunt of the Rose*), and he certainly knew it thoroughly: echoes of it, allusions to it, motifs and ideas derived from it recur throughout his poetry. He seems to have been particularly intrigued by the techniques and ideas of Jean de Meun. Chaucer was also very well read in the French love poetry of

the 14th c. He was much influenced by the works of *Guillaume de Machaut, *Deschamps, *Froissart in particular (though he also knew some of the work of more minor poets like *Nicole de Margival and Oton de *Graunson). The influence can be seen in both style and subject matter, and is most evident in (though not confined to) the early dream visions like The *Book of the Duchess*.

Chaucer's knowledge and use of Italian literature (see also *Ytaille) is much more remarkable and unusual. Indeed, as far as we can tell, it was not only exceptional in English literary circles in his own day, but remained so throughout the following century. It is not clear when or where his reading of Italian writers began: their influence becomes evident in his work from the late 1370s. It seems likely that he learnt some Italian (perhaps from merchants in London) before he first visited the country. The extent of his reading in Italian cannot be charted exactly. If, as seems likely, he used an Italian translation of the *Heroides*, this suggests a knowledge extending beyond the three great writers with whose work we know him to have been to some extent familiar—Dante, *Boccaccio (though he is never named) and Petrarch. The results of Chaucer's reading of Boccaccio and Dante are very clear. Boccaccio's *Teseida* and *Filostrato* gave him the plots—and much else—for The *Knight's Tale* and *Troilus and Criseyde* (whether or not Chaucer had read the *Decameron*, a work which offers many parallels both in detail and in general spirit with The *Canterbury Tales* remains a matter of argument). He frequently quotes and echoes Dante (he knew the *Convivio* as well as the *Commedia*), and takes from him the story of Ugolino (*Hugelyn of Pyze). It is probable too that Dante influenced his ideas about *fortune, '*gentilesse' and *love. The contribution of Petrarch's Italian writing seems much less extensive, but the sonnet which is made into Troilus's song (*Tr* I.400–20), with its characteristic fusion of passion and logic, is beautifully fitted both to the character and the context.

It is evident that Chaucer's reading was not only wide but deep, and the use which he made of it is far more complex than a list of his 'books' can suggest. His reading gave him much more than stories and plots; it moulded his style and his ideas.

He is in the best sense a learned poet, a *doctus poeta*, who has made his reading part of his creative imagination, and blended the authority of his books with *experience. For particular local effects he may portray himself as 'bookish', or make a character—like the Wife of Bath—display the extent of his reading. He will sometimes use *quotation—like the speech of Troilus on predestination in the fourth book of *Troilus*—but carefully fitted to the context—as is the Dantean prayer which brings the fifth book to an end. More usually, however, although we may detect an *allusion or an 'echo', the evidence of his reading remains hidden beneath the surface of the new work into which it has been transformed by a creative alchemy.

Boitani (1983); Brewer (1974); Lowes (1934); Phillips (1993); Shannon (1929); Wimsatt (1968).

CHAUCER, JOHN. The poet's father was probably born in 1312 or 1314, and died in 1366. In 1324 he was abducted by an aunt in order to be married to her daughter, but he was freed and the aunt and her collaborators were fined. He took part in some military campaigns—against the Scots; in the earl of Lancaster's rising against Queen Isabella and Mortimer (for which he was outlawed in 1329); and possibly in Flanders in 1338. Like his father before him he became a vintner (he appears in the records as such from the beginning of 1337), and prospered. By October 1349 he had married Agnes Copton. They accumulated property, especially in London—including the Vintry tenement in Thames Street (later 177 Upper Thames St, a property destroyed in the Second World War).

CHAUCER, LEWIS, son of the poet. *A Treatise on the *Astrolabe* is addressed to 'lyte [little] Lowys my sone' who has reached the 'tendir age of ten yeer'. It has usually been assumed that 'little Lewis' was the poet's son (the suggestion that he was the son of Chaucer and Cecilia Chaumpaigne (see Geoffrey *Chaucer: life) is not supported by firm evidence); but it has been argued that he was rather the son of Chaucer's friend Sir Lewis *Clifford, and Chaucer's godson. It has also been suggested that he may have been a fiction, perhaps

invented to justify the simple style of the treatise. However, the fact that a 'Ludowicus Chaucer' is mentioned along with a 'Thomas Chaucer' in a retinue roll of 1403 seems to establish him as the poet's son (perhaps he was Lewis Clifford's godson). The 15th-c. poet *Lydgate thought that Lewis was Geoffrey's son.

CHAUCER, PHILIPPA, the wife of the poet (by September 1366). She was probably the daughter of Sir Gilles (called 'Paon' or Payne) de Roet, a knight of Hainault who had accompanied Queen Philippa to England. He later became Guienne King of Arms. Another of his daughters was Katherine Swynford (see *John of Gaunt). Philippa was 'domicella' or lady in waiting to Elizabeth, countess of Ulster, Edward III's daughter-in-law, to Queen Philippa, and later to Constance of Castile, John of Gaunt's second wife. She received annuities from Edward III, Richard II, and John of Gaunt. In 1386 she was admitted to the fraternity of Lincoln Cathedral (which included Henry, earl of Derby, later Henry IV, and her nephews Thomas Swynford and John Beaufort; and, from 1387 King Richard and Queen Anne). She probably died in 1387 (the last record of her is on 18 June 1387).

CHAUCER, ROBERT, the poet's grandfather, Robert le Chaucer (or Robert Malin le Chaucer), the son of Andrew de Dinnington of Ipswich, became a vintner and citizen of London; he had settled there with his wife Mary by the late 13th c.

CHAUCER, THOMAS (d. 1434), the son of the poet. He is first named as a son of Geoffrey Chaucer in a London lawsuit of 1396. He became a wealthy landowner and an influential figure in early 15th-c. England. His early marriage to Maud Burghersh brought him large estates, including the manor of Ewelme in Oxfordshire. He received annuities from John of Gaunt, Richard II, and Henry IV, and served as chief butler to three successive kings. Henry IV made him constable of Wallingford Castle and steward of the honours of Wallingford and St Valery and of the Chiltern Hundreds. In 1405 he became forester of North Petherton Park, as his father had been, and a

Chauceriana

farmer of the forests of Somerset. In 1411 the queen gave him the manor of Woodstock and other estates. He sat as MP for Oxfordshire in successive parliaments, and was chosen Speaker of the House of Commons in 1407, 1410, 1411, and 1414. He served with Henry V in France, and was present at the battle of Agincourt. In 1424 he was made a member of the council. His only daughter, Alice *Chaucer, became duchess of Suffolk; her grandson John, earl of Lincoln, was designated heir to the throne by Richard III, and continued to maintain his claim even after Richard's defeat at Bosworth. Thomas Chaucer was the recipient of an eloquent poem by *Lydgate on the occasion of his departure (possibly for France in 1414, when he was sent to treat with the ambassadors of the duke of Burgundy); Lydgate pays him a nice compliment by an allusion to his father's generous Franklin ('Saynt Julyan . . . come hoome ageyne'; cf. I.340).

Norton-Smith (1966a) 4–6; Ruud (1926).

Chauceriana, the name sometimes given to a group of works which, although not by Chaucer (see *Canon of Chaucer's Works), have at various times and for various reasons been attributed to him or associated with him. It is a heterogeneous group, which includes the many apocryphal works attributed to Chaucer by scribes and early editors, or included in printed collections of his works as 'additions'. The list includes both works by known authors (e.g. Lydgate's *Siege of Thebes or Henryson's *Testament of Cresseid) and anonymous pieces. Some of the latter (like The *Flower and the Leaf or La *Belle Dame sans Merci) because of their supposed connection with Chaucer were better known in earlier times than they are now. It begins to develop fairly early: thus *Thynne's edition includes The *Plowmans Tale, La Belle Dame sans Merci, the *Black Knight (by Lydgate), The *Testament of Love (by Usk), The Letter of Cupid (by *Hoccleve), and The *Cuckoo and Nightingale (by Clanvowe); and *Speght has The *Isle of Ladies, The Flower and the Leaf and *Jack Upland. Many of these works are printed in volume vii of *Skeat's edition of Chaucer ('Chaucerian and Other Pieces'). The following list, though not complete (in particular it does not include many lyrics and short poems), gives some idea of the range of the material (further information can be found under the individual entries): The *Assembly of Ladies, *Balade of Complaint, The Tale of *Beryn, Black Knight, The *Court of Love, The *Craft of Lovers, The Cuckoo and the Nightingale, The Flower and the Leaf, *Gamelyn, The Isle of Ladies, Jack Upland, La Belle Dame sans Merci, *Lamentation of Mary Magdalen, The Letter of Cupid, The *Letter of Dido to Aeneas, The *Pilgrim's Tale, The Plowman's Tale, *Proverbs of Chaucer, The *Siege of Thebes, The Testament of Cresseid, The Testament of Love.

'Chaucerians, English', the name sometimes applied to those poets in 15th-c. and early 16th-c. England who praise and imitate Chaucer and whose work is obviously influenced by him. It is rather too general a term for a varied group of writers, whose indebtedness to Chaucer shows itself in different ways. It usually includes such writers as *Hoccleve, *Lydgate, Ashby, Walton, the authors of some of the '*Chauceriana', and, later, *Hawes, Barclay, and *Skelton. Most express their admiration of Chaucer, and many regularly use Chaucerian diction and phraseology or poetic forms—especially the love allegory. They may take up a favourite Chaucerian topic, or show their indebtedness to Chaucer even when they are translating from French—as in La *Belle Dame sans Merci or Hoccleve's Letter of Cupid (which has an allusion to The *Legend of Good Women). Allusions to Chaucer's poems are usually reverent compliments to the master; only infrequently are they used to give an imaginative depth to the new context. Attempts to imitate the intellectual flexibility and the range of linguistic register characteristic of Chaucer's major work are very rare. However, the better writers are in no way limited by the 'Chaucerian' tradition; indeed, poets like Hoccleve and Skelton often find their voice by moving away from Chaucer's forms and ideas. Those poems which remain closest to the tradition—like The *Floure and the Leafe or The Temple of Glass—are attractive minor works.

'Chaucerians, Scottish'. If the term 'English Chaucerians' is unfair to the variety of late medieval English courtly poetry, this title, traditionally given to some Scottish poets of the same period (to James I, the probable author of

The *Kingis Quair, *Henryson, *Dunbar, *Douglas, and sometimes to Lindsay), obscures even more seriously the diversity and vitality of the literary traditions of medieval *Scotland. Indeed, it is arguable that it should not be used at all. Not only is the list of poets far too narrow—the anonymous fabliau, The Freiris of Berwick, for instance, was rightly praised by C. S. Lewis as 'above all other attempts to continue the tradition of the comic Canterbury Tales'—but the word 'Chaucerian' suggests an exaggerated degree of dependence. Much of Dunbar's work is hardly 'Chaucerian' at all; and even King James and Henryson, the two poets who seem most deeply involved with Chaucer, treat him in an original and distinctive way. One of the earliest enthusiasts for medieval Scottish literature, the 18th-c. antiquary John Pinkerton, defended the autonomy of the Scottish tradition and the achievement of the Scottish poets: 'Dunbar, having a genius at least equal to Chaucer, and perhaps more original'— and even more extremely—'Chaucer was in the highest admiration in Scotland . . . but not one Scottish poet has imitated him; or is in the least indebted to him.' His patriotism carried him away. The Kingis Quair is a 'Chaucerian' poem, which manipulates Chaucerian ideas and style deftly—and differently. Henryson read Chaucer with great care and imagination. The allegorical poetry of Dunbar and Douglas is full of echoes of Chaucer. These poets were indebted to Chaucer, sometimes in technique (as Henryson's use of a *narrator), often in style (as in the allusive texture of The Kingis Quair), sometimes in ideas (Chaucerian views on *love, *nature, etc.). What is distinctive about this group of writers is the way in which they make this Chaucerian strand in the literary tradition which they inherited entirely their own. Thus Dunbar's 'Tua Mariit Wemen and the Wedo' is indebted to The *Wife of Bath's Prologue, but is quite different in tone—and in its *alliterative verse form.

Chaucer's Dream; Chaucer's language; Chaumpaigne, Cecilia; Chaunce. See *Isle of Ladies; *language; Geoffrey *Chaucer: life; *Fortune.

Chauntecleer, the cock, the hero of The *Nun's Priest's Tale. The name (Fr. chantecler, from chante(r) 'sing' + cler 'clear') is that of the cock in the Roman de Renart (see *Renard). It is found in ME before Chaucer. Chauntecleer struts out of the world of the animal *fable to become, with the *Eagle in The *House of Fame, Chaucer's most entertaining *bird character, formed with an exquisite blend of affectionate observation and mock-heroic detachment. He lives up to his name, since he has no equal in crowing in 'all the land'—his voice is 'merrier' than the church organ. And his crowing marks the time exactly, for he is a natural astronomer. Chauntecleer is a well-read bird who can quote Boethius (*Boece) and other *authorities, and has strong views on *dreams. He is also a handsome creature, very masculine in behaviour and outlook. He has an entourage of seven hens on whom to 'doon al his plesaunce', which he does with considerable vigour and enjoyment, befitting a servant of *Venus ('moore for delit than world to multiplye', as the clerical narrator slyly remarks (VII.3345), alluding to a well-known ecclesiastical statement of the purpose of *marriage). (At the end of the tale the Host is moved to remark that had the strongly built priest who tells it been secular, he would have been 'a trede-foul aright' and would have needed more than 'seven tymes seventene' hens.) This sensuous hero is susceptible to flattery, and he can be a little over-solemn, but as nothing compared with some of the critics who have attempted to interpret him, and in so doing afford almost as much entertainment as he does. Some have attempted to identify his actual breed: the Golden Spangled Hamburg has been suggested. Others have taken flight into allegory and symbolism: in his fall he is parallel to Adam; sitting on his beam he is a figure of the crucified Christ; for one he is the holy man, for another the slothful priest. This entertaining and learned creature surely deserves to be left in peace in his yard (and in his tale).

Chepe. The modern Cheapside was in medieval *London a busy thoroughfare with many shops. The ward of Cheap (the name is an old word for market) contained the city's great markets, and among its inhabitants were mercers, cordwainers, bakers, fishmongers, poulterers, and cheesemongers. This is reflected in the names of some of

Chess

the streets: Poultry St, Ironmonger's Lane, Cordwainer St (now Bow Lane). The ward also contained some fine churches and chapels. Chaucer's various allusions to it (all in *The *Canterbury Tales*) are easy and familiar: it is associated with citizens and tradesmen (of the Host it is said that 'a fairer burgeys was ther noon in Chepe' (I.754)); it is where wine is sold (VI.564, 569; and IX.24). Cheapside was a favourite place for processions and festivals. Perkyn the apprentice victualler in *The *Cook's Tale* runs out of his shop to see a 'riding' there (I.4377).

Cherubynnes face, see ***angels**.

Chess and related board games were popular in the Middle Ages. Chess was thought to have been invented by Attalus (*Athalus), the king of Pergamos. Pieces and sets of pieces have occasionally survived (the most famous being the 12th-c. Scandinavian pieces now in the British Museum). The game's terminology had already found its way (via French) into the English language by Chaucer's time. Some words are of oriental origin: thus, 'checkmate' comes from an Arabic (originally Persian) expression meaning 'the king is dead' (in ME the word *maat* (mate) is also widely used in the sense of 'defeated, exhausted'); and *fers*, which in Europe had come to mean the 'queen' comes from an Arabic word for 'wise man' or 'counsellor'. Some of the terms were obviously very familiar: *Criseyde says (*Tr* II.754) 'shal noon housbonde seyn to me "Chek mat!"'. Medieval writers frequently found analogies between chess and human life. Chaucer's only extended use of the symbolism of chess is in *The *Book of the Duchess* 652–84), where the Man in Black complains that Fortune has cheated him in a game by taking his queen (*fers*). Here the technical terms abound: Fortune 'seyde "Chek her!" | And mat in the myd poynt of the chekker [chess-board] | With a poun errant [moving, or mating, pawn]'.

Cooley (1948); French (1949); Golombek (1976); H. J. R. Murray (1913).

CHESTERTON, G. K. (1874–1936), journalist, controversialist, and author. He became a Roman Catholic in 1922. One element in his diverse writings is a distinctive kind of medievalism, very different from that of the Pre-Raphaelites, in which a nostalgia for many aspects of the Middle Ages is transformed by a hearty vigour of thought and expression into a set of political and religious values opposed to those of his own time. He produced a book on Chaucer (1932), out of the conviction that 'it is as easy for an ordinary Englishman to enjoy Chaucer as to enjoy Dickens'. He made good use of the scholarly information which had by then become available (while making satiric remarks about the pedantry and aridity of some of the scholarship), and gave it all a very Chestertonian emphasis. Medieval logic, faith, guilds, and chivalry are brought into play as part of a witty attack on the aberrations of the modern world. He praises Chaucer as an Englishman (while pointing out that he 'drew on the traditions of about four European literatures' and that he had the 'central and civilised character' of the medieval poet). He also praises him as a Christian poet, not as a poet with a 'Message', but rather as one with a spiritual largesse or generosity ('the charity of Chaucer towards Cressida is one of the most beautiful things in human history'), and with a sense of delight and wonder in the created world. In 'All I Survey' (1933) he returns to this 'most human of human beings', who flatly contradicts all that the moderns have been told is 'medieval'— Chaucer is sane, liberal, tolerant, humorous, social, and at ease with men. He was 'one of that fairly large and very happy band of artists who are not troubled with the artistic temperament'. There is a special Chaucerian 'mood' and it is essentially 'merry', a distinctive Chaucerian atmosphere—'a sort of diffused light which lies on everything, whether tragic or comic, and prevents the tragedy from being hopeless or the comedy from being cruel'.

Chesterton (1932); *CH* ii. 486–9.

chevalrie, see ***chivalrie**.

Chichevache (Fr. 'lean cow', orig. *chicheface* 'lean face'), a legendary monster which fed on patient wives, mentioned in the Envoy to *The *Clerk's Tale* (IV.1188). It is contrasted with the well-fed Bicorne, whose diet consists of patient husbands. The pair are the subject of a later poem by *Lydgate; and are vividly represented in a 15th-c.

wall-painting in the castle of Villeneuve-Lembron (Puy-de-Dôme) in France.

Loomis (1965), 161–2.

children and childhood (see also *families, *Ages of Man, *youth; 'childhood' covers *infantia, pueritia,* and *adolescencia* in the seven-age scheme). There is nothing in Chaucer to match the lively account which *Froissart gives of his own boyhood in *L'espinette amoureuse*—making dams, mud pies, chasing butterflies, collecting shells, rolling nuts, spinning tops, and fighting—but children and childhood have an important role in his poetry. Neither the vocabulary of childhood nor the dominant contemporary ideas about it correspond exactly with modern usage and thought. While some of the words which Chaucer uses (like 'son' or 'daughter') are thoroughly familiar to modern readers, others may sometimes have unfamiliar meanings. Thus *boy* in ME can also mean 'a servant' (as it probably does in The *Pardoner's Tale* (VI.670), though the person in question sounds as if he is young), and can sometimes have more strongly pejorative senses, ranging from 'urchin' or 'brat' (VII.562) to 'rogue' (III.1322). For 'boy' Chaucer uses the older word *knave* (e.g. VII.310; a word which could then also mean 'servant', 'peasant', or 'villain') or *knave child* (e.g. II.715). And in the language of his day 'girl' could be applied to a young person of either sex (e.g. I.664; though in I.3769, given *Absolon's sexual tastes, the 'gay gerl' is probably female). More specifically, Chaucer will use *mayde child* (e.g. IV.446). The word *child* itself is applied to an unborn baby (X.576), a child, or a youth: Absolon is described as 'a myrie child' (I.3325); and *Sir Thopas is called 'child' (VII.809, etc.), an old popular romance locution for 'noble youth, knight' (cf. *Horn child). *Childhede* is his abstract term.

The medieval family was probably much less 'child-centred' than its modern counterpart. At home and at school (for those who went there) a strict discipline was recommended, and, it seems, was usually inflicted. Children probably made most of their own entertainment—there are references to and illustrations of various children's games. There was not, as there was from the later 18th-c. on, a 'children's literature' in the sense of books written explicitly for this particular age group. Children probably shared in the literature available for their elders, listening to songs, fables, proverbs, romances, and tales. As is still the case in 'traditional' societies, much common lore was picked up from elders ('thus taughte me my dame', as the 'boy' in *The Pardoner's Tale* says when he gives the rioters some proverbial advice; cf. also IX.317 ff.) and from friends (as the schoolboy in *The *Prioress's Tale* learns about the *Alma recemptoris* from his school-mate, VII.530–45).

The question of how close the emotional attachments between parents and their children actually were is impossible to answer with certainty. Some modern social historians have perhaps too readily assumed that in an age of severe infant mortality parents were less ready to make a heavy emotional investment in their children. In letters, sons and daughters address their parents with some formality. However, literary evidence often suggests a stronger emotional bond. For instance, in *Pearl,* which may have an autobiographical basis, the bereaved father's feeling for his daughter seems to be a very intense one. That this is thought to be natural seems also to be implied by a number of Chaucer's incidental remarks and images. He, for instance, uses a striking simile to express the grief of *January: 'he yaf a roryng and a cry, | As dooth the mooder whan the child shal dye' (IV.2364–5). The warning of the Parson against loving a child before God (X.860) suggests that this actually happened, and his urging of the need to suffer patiently the loss of goods, wife, or child (X.1055) suggests that this was not the automatic reaction (cf. also VII.983). In medieval religion, alongside the idea of the child tainted with original sin which had to be washed away in baptism, there was also that of the child as a symbol of innocence. Supporting this were the powerful images of the Christ child, of the young Virgin Mary, and of the Holy Innocents.

As with the other *ages of man there was a strong sense of what was fitting and appropriate for childhood. Children according to *Bartholomew 'lead their life without care and business', only prizing games and delight, 'and fear no peril more than beating with a rod'; 'they love an apple more than gold'. They are quickly angered, quickly pleased, and quick to forgive. Some—like the *puer/puella senex* transcend these expectations. Such exceptional qualities, associated with the wisdom of age, are often the result of God's grace. In Chaucer's *Monk's Tale* there is a well-known biblical example: the boy Daniel 'that was the wiseste child of everychon' who could interpret the dreams of Nebuchadnezzar when the learned Chaldean clerks could not (VII.2151–8). In *The *Clerk's Tale* the young Griselda belongs to this category: 'But thogh this mayde tendre were of age, | Yet in the brest of hire virginitee | Ther was enclosed rype and sad corage' (IV.218–20). In Chaucer words like *childly* or *childishly* often have the idea of 'appropriate' behaviour lurking behind them (see *BD* 1095, or the childish jealous man, *Tr* III.1168). *Old age can show in a ridiculous and inappropriate way the qualities proper to childhood (*Rom* 399, 402). And a worldly-wise miller dismisses the young clerks whom he has outwitted with the derisive remark 'Ye, lat the children pleye' (I.4098).

Chaucer's work is full of familiar allusions to children and childhood. At the beginning of the *Astrolabe* he remarks on the proper style to be adopted in writing for a 10-year-old: he apologizes for the 'superfluity' of words because 'curious endityng and hard sentence is ful hevy . . . for such a child to lerne' and remarks 'me semith better to writen unto a child twyes a god sentence, than he forgete it onys'. There are allusions to most of the joys and dangers of childhood: the Parson, after speaking against contraception, goes on to rebuke those mothers who murder their children for fear of worldly shame (X.577), but also remarks that there is nothing that a child relishes so much as his nurse's milk (X.121); there are references to 'child's play' (IV.1530), to a friendship going back to childhood (I.1192–3), to the fear which the *Summoner's face aroused in children (I.628). There are also references to the bringing up of children: the miller's wife in *The *Reeve's Tale* 'was yfostred in a nonnerye' (I.3946); although Griselda was 'povreliche yfostred up', she had learnt to work hard and to reverence her old father (IV.213–31); children are taught to hold their tongue, says the *Manciple (IX.334). Absolon in his mortification wept 'as dooth a child that is ybete [beaten]' (I.3759). This reference is perhaps not simply proverbial. There are one or two hints that

Absolon was a rather 'childish' youth (cf. for instance his remark 'I moorne as dooth a lamb after the tete' (I.3704): it is possible that *Alison's scornful rejoinder 'it wold nat be "com pa [kiss] me"' (I.3709) is a deliberate use of childish language).

References to children are sometimes used to give a circumstantial realism, and in a number of tales children have some part in the plot. The six-month-old baby in *The Reeve's Tale* in its cradle set at the foot of the bed so that the mother could rock it and suckle the child fulfils both functions. In two of the Canterbury Tales—*The *Prioress's Tale* and *The *Physician's Tale*—children are central. The 7-year-old schoolboy in *The Prioress's Tale* (VII.503), who is about to move from *infantia*, the age of innocence and *pueritia*, is treated with some naturalism; he is childishly curious to find out about the antiphon he has heard sung, and is determined to learn it. He becomes an innocent martyr, but even in this deeply devotional work it is interesting that Chaucer concentrates on a family relationship (in this case between the child and his widowed mother), and uses the child as a focus for pathos and *pite. The same is true of the maiden *Virginia of 'twelve yeer . . . and tweye' in *The *Physician's Tale*, between child and young woman, who also dies a violent death.

Children are important even in 'supporting roles'—and sometimes even when they are only briefly mentioned (see *LGW* 1323) or appear in the briefest narrative (as in the terrible story of Ugolino (*Hugelyn) and his three small children in *The *Monk's Tale*). The sufferings and joys of *Griselda and *Constance are deeply involved with their children. In *The Clerk's Tale* carefully selected details which suggest ordinary life (when Griselda's daughter is born, she would, says the narrator, have preferred a son (IV.444); her son was taken when he was two years old 'and fro the brest | Departed of his norice' (617–18)) are used to build up the suspense and heightened pathos of the scenes of parting, in which Chaucer shows the terrible conflict between obedience and natural motherly 'pite'. Her anguish (as great as that of the mothers of the Innocents) expresses itself not in shrieking but in the piteous request 'atte leeste | Burieth this litel body in som place | That beestes ne no briddes it torace [tear it apart]' (570–2; cf. 681–3). In *The *Man of Law's Tale* Constance's young son shares in her tribulations ('hir litel child lay wepyng in hir arm' as she is cast adrift in her ship (II.834)), and again increases the pathos in these very emotional scenes, seeming to share in her sorrow: 'hir childe cride, and she cride pitously' (919). Here a Christian religious image of child and mother offers some consolation: Constance prays to the Virgin Mary who saw her own son rent on a cross. In both tales the children figure prominently in the concluding recognition scenes of 'pitous joye', and in both the emotional attachment of parents to children is not in doubt. Griselda clasps hers so hard that they can hardly be taken from her arm. In such stories Chaucer uses children and their parents to explore, as Jill Mann says, 'not only the relations of human beings to each other . . . but also their relation to the universe in which they find themselves and to the forces governing it'.

Ariès (1962); Brewer (1964); Mann (1983); Orme (2001); Shahar (1990).

Chiron, see *Eacides Chiron.

chivalrie (see also *knight, *courtly love). Chaucer's word for 'chivalry' or 'knighthood', and for 'knightly deeds' or 'knightly pursuits'. 'Chivalry' has been described as an ethos in which martial, aristocratic, and Christian elements were fused. One element might sometimes be stressed at the expense of another, but they were intertwined. Although it was essentially an aristocratic set of ideals, true knightliness and courtesy ('*curteisie') did not simply depend on noble birth but on worth and virtue (see *gentilesse'). Chivalry flourished in Western Europe between the 12th and 16th c. Some men attempted to live up to its ideals, and some succeeded; others, as was well known, did neither. However, it had a wide and deep influence on medieval culture and society.

Its origins are secular (the word is connected with *cheval* 'horse', the 'noble beast' which carried the mounted elite of a feudal society to battle), but its ideals were profoundly affected by religion. As in many areas of medieval life, 'earnest' and '*game' coexisted. War was part of the knight's calling, and it had its own elaborate rules and ceremonies. But one of the most characteristic chivalric institutions, the tournament, which

flourished in spite of ecclesiastical disapproval, was its 'game' equivalent, affording training for young warriors, a splendid and exciting spectacle, and a courtly pastime. The *Knight's Tale has memorable examples of both—the battlefield with its grim heap of dead bodies at the beginning, and the spectacular and violent tournament at the end.

The ladies who watched these demonstrations of male strength and skill played an increasingly important role in the concept of chivalry. They were also part of the audience for the distinctively chivalric forms of literature which developed—most notably the courtly *romance. There were other forms of 'chivalric' literature; books on the art of war, and romantic biographies of the 'flowers of chivalry', men who seemed to their friends and followers to embody its ideals, like the later French knight Bayard, the 'chevalier sans peur et sans reproche' (*Alexander is called 'of knyghthod and of fredom [nobility] flour', VII.2642). The ideals of chivalry were honour and loyalty, the defence of ladies and the service of God; or, as the dying *Arcite says, 'trouthe, honour, knyghthede, | Wysdom, humblesse, estaat [rank], and heigh kynrede, | Fredom, and al that longeth to that art' (I.2789–91).

The ideals as well as the splendid ceremonies of chivalry continued in the more urban and mercantile world of the later Middle Ages. It enjoyed the patronage of kings, sometimes Arthurian enthusiasts, who set up feasts of the 'round table' or founded new chivalric orders, like that of the Garter in England or the Golden Fleece in Burgundy. It is too easy to dismiss late medieval chivalry as superficial, decadent, or simply nostalgic. It has been said, with much justification, that it enjoyed an 'Indian Summer' in early Tudor England.

Chaucer's own attitudes are difficult to ascertain. It is true that his own romances are not straightforwardly 'chivalric', but it is hard to accept the extreme view that The Knight's Tale is entirely ironic or comic, or that The *Squire's Tale represents the decline of court culture. Indeed, The Knight's Tale seems to present the splendours and the miseries of the chivalric life in an even-handed and realistic manner appropriate to its teller, who was, like Chaucer, a 'knight of the shire' or Member of Parliament. The knights in Chaucer's narratives are a diverse group, both in time (some living in the ancient world, where, it was thought, chivalry had originated) and in behaviour. Beside the worthy *Arveragus and the upright *Virginius, we have the treacherous and false knight who murdered Alla's wife and accused Constance in The *Man of Law's Tale (II.582–689), the lecherous old *January, the knight in The *Wife of Bath's Tale who raped a maiden, and that comic knight errant Sir Thopas.

Much of the language and the world of chivalry seems to be taken for granted. There are words or phrases which had become part of the common vocabulary: recreant 'cowardly' (Tr I.814); hommage (to Christ in The *Parson's Tale X.313; to Love in BD 770). Sometimes the reference is more pointed; chyvachie or chevache, which means 'a cavalry expedition' (I.85), 'riding' or 'feat of horsemanship' (used ironically of the Cook, IX.50). Sometimes we have a direct allusion to a chivalric ritual: the Parson (X.766) says that 'the swerd that men yeven first to a knyght, whan he is newe dubbed, signifieth that he sholde defenden hooly chirche'. Such references give a circumstantial feel to the knightly settings of The Knight's Tale or *Troilus and Criseyde, where Troilus rides in from battle 'so lik a man of armes and a knyght' (II.631), with his helm hanging down behind him and his shield 'todasshed . . . with swerdes and maces' (II.638–40), and where the sight of 'a manere cote-armure' (V.1651) leads to his desperate attempts to kill *Diomede ('with many a cruel hete | Gan Troilus upon his helm to bete', V.1761–2). Chaucer is not a narrowly 'chivalric' writer, but chivalry is still an important part of his world.

Brewer (2000); Ferguson (1960); Keen (1984); Painter (1940).

Chorus, Corus, or Caurus, the north-west wind in *Boece (I m.3:7; IV m.5:24).

CHRÉTIEN DE TROYES, a distinguished and influential poet who flourished c.1170–1190 in northern France, and who at one time enjoyed the patronage of Marie de Champagne. He is a figure of the greatest importance in the development of *romance. His surviving romances—Erec and Enide, Cligès, Yvain, Lancelot, and the unfinished Perceval—are remarkable for their narrative skill, their dramatic dialogue, and their treatment of love and lovers (see *courtly love). There has been some speculation that Chaucer's technique in Troilus and Criseyde may owe something to Chrétien, but there is no certain evidence that he had read the French writer.

(ed.) Foerster (1884–99); (trans.) D. D. R. Owen (1987).

CHRISTINE DE PISAN, (1365–after 1429), French writer, was born in Venice. As a small child she was taken to France, where her father, Tommaso da Pizzano, a scholar, physician, and astrologer, had been invited to join the court of Charles V. She was fortunate (and unusual) in having a father who insisted on giving her an excellent education. At the age of 15 she married Étienne de Castel, a nobleman and courtier. With the death of Charles V in 1380, Tommaso lost favour at court and died a few years later. Then in 1390 her husband died, and she was left with three children to support. There followed an intense writing career, in the course of which she produced many works in verse and prose. That she was successful in gaining patronage and popularity is shown by the number of surviving MSS, some of them splendidly illustrated. Several of her works were translated into English in the 15th and early 16th c. She wrote a series of fine lyrics, and took a leading part in a French literary debate over the *Roman de la Rose. Her Livre de la Cité des Dames (Book of the City of Ladies, 1405) is a witty defence of women against the attacks of misogynistic writers. It includes interesting remarks on a number of women mentioned in Chaucer (*Dido, *Zenobia, the *Amazons, and others). She also wrote a life of Charles V, and a number of works on moral and political matters. Her reading was wide: unusually among her French contemporaries she knew *Dante; and her interest in ancient stories is characteristic of the older 'medieval *humanism'.

(ed.) Roy (1886–96); Curnow (1975); (trans.) Richards (1983); Willard (1984).

Christopher (I.115), an image or medal of St Christopher worn by the *Yeoman. St Christopher was a popular saint (famous especially for having carried the Christ-child across a river), the patron saint of travellers, and a protector against plague and sudden death.

chronology of Chaucer's works. Because of the paucity of clear contemporary references and the absence of external evidence, the dating of the works is only approximate (for fuller details, see the individual titles). Even where such references exist, they are not exact enough to give a certain date. Thus, while it is agreed that The *Book of the Duchess* is occasioned by the death of *Blanche in September 1368, there is no general agreement about how much time elapsed between that event and the writing of the poem. Chaucer also seems to have sometimes revised his works (as the Prologue to The *Legend of Good Women*) and sometimes to have used earlier material (as in some Canterbury Tales). The lists he gives of his works in the Prologue to The *Legend of Good Women* and in the Introduction to The *Man of Law's Tale* are of some help in fixing a relative chronology. Arguments based solely on stylistic 'development' have not won general approval. The old division of his literary career into 'French', 'Italian', and 'English' periods is oversimplified. It can be argued that he was always an English poet, and that while French influence is certainly very strong in his earlier works, it never completely died. The influence of his Italian reading appears in the 1370s, but while *Troilus and Criseyde* is based on an Italian poem, it also makes extensive use of Chaucer's reading in Latin and French.

Most Chaucerian scholars would agree at least in general with the following rough outline. One certain 'early work' is The Book of the Duchess (1368–72?). Others might be the *ABC and The *Romaunt of the Rose* Fragment A (if that is by Chaucer). The *House of Fame* was written while Chaucer was Controller of the wool custom (1374–85), perhaps in 1378–80. Possibly also from the 1370s come some tragedies later adapted for The *Monk's Tale*, and some lyrics. The *Second Nun's Tale* (or a version of it) and *Anelida and Arcite* have also been placed in the 1370s, but there is no certain evidence. In the period from 1380 to 1387 are usually placed The *Parliament of Fowls* (?1380–2), *Boece*, and Troilus and Criseyde (?1384–7). After Troilus comes *Adam Scriveyn and The Legend of Good Women (at least in its present form). In this period may belong also The Complaint of *Mars (?c.1385), The Complaint of *Venus, possibly an earlier version of The *Knight's Tale,

and possibly the 'Boethian' short poems. The *Canterbury Tales* was begun in the late 1380s and continued in the 1390s. From the 1390s also probably come the *Astrolabe*, some short poems— *Lenvoy de Chaucer a *Scogan, *Lenvoy de Chaucer a Bukton, *Complaint of Chaucer to his Purse—and the '*Retracciouns'.

Church, see *piety, *religion.

Cibella, Cybele, a Phrygian goddess of nature and fertility. In The *Legend of Good Women (F 531) she is said to have made the daisy and given it its white crown. (This may have been suggested by a passage in *Froissart in which *Ceres receives the daisies made from the tears of Heres.)

Cicero, see *Tullius.

Cylenios, Cylenius, Cyllenius, Mercury. For the origin of the name, see *Mercurye (1). In The Complaint of *Mars, when Venus is said to flee to 'Cilenios tour', the reference is to the sign of Gemini, with 'toure' an interval of 30° on the *ecliptic (but not understood as a *domicile in the ordinary sense). [JDN]

Cymerie, the Cimmerians, according to the ancients a people living at the end of the world where the sun never shone, near the entry to the underworld (this is alluded to in The *House of Fame 73).

Cynthea, Cynthia the Moon. Cynthus is a mountain of Delos, celebrated as the birthplace of *Apollo, and also of *Diana, for whom Cynthia was therefore an alternative name. It is best known in classical literature from the poems to Cynthia by the Roman elegist Propertius (fl. 15 BC). In Book IV of *Troilus and Criseyde, Criseyde swears by Cynthia that she will return to Troilus before the *Moon (named as *Lucina) leaves the sign of *Leo, and that event is recounted in Book V with much additional astronomical detail, using Cynthia as the name of the Moon now. (See also *Latona.) [JDN]

Cipioun, see *Scipio(n).

Cipre, Cyprus, in the 14th c. the realm of Pierre de Lusignan (*Petro (2) mentioned in *The *Monk's Tale* (VII.2391)).

Cyprian, a Roman of noble birth who was one of Boethius's accusers (*Bo* I pr.4:103).

Cypride, Cipris, the Cyprian i.e. *Venus, who, according to legend, landed in Cyprus (*Cipre) when she came from the sea, and was worshipped there. Chaucer uses this alternative name several time (*HF* 518; *PF* 277; *Tr* III.725, etc.).

Circes, Cerces, Circe, daughter of the Sun, and an enchantress who turned the companions of Ulysses into swine. Chaucer would have known the story from *Ovid's *Metamorphoses* 14, and from Boethius (IV m.3). She is mentioned as a famous sorceress in *The Knight's Tale* (I.1944) and *The House of Fame* (1272).

Circo, 'the place that highte [was called] Circo' in *Boece* (II pr.3:59) is the great Roman Circus, a place for spectacles and ceremonies, where Boethius saw his two sons made consuls. Chaucer has kept the inflected form of the Latin word from his original.

Cirrea. Cirra (modern Kyrra), near Delphi, is associated with Helicon (*Elicon(e)) and Mt. Parnassus (*Parnaso), the home of the *Muses, in *Anelida and Arcite* (17).

CIRUS, Cyrus the Great (d. 529 BC) the founder of the Persian empire. He extended his rule over Lydia (*Lyde). Babylon (*Babiloigne), and the Greek cities of Asia Minor. His conquest of Croesus (*Cresus) king of Lydia is mentioned in *The *Monk's Tale* (VII.2728) and in *Boece* (II pr.2:59–61). In *The *Summoner's Tale* (III.2079) he appears as an example of an 'irous' (wrathful) man; he destroyed the river Gyndes (*Gysen) because one of his horses drowned in it.

Cithe, see *Scithia.

Citherea, Citheria, Cytherea, one of the names of *Venus (from the island Cythera off the southern coast of Greece, where according to one legend she landed after being formed in the sea; cf. *Cypride). Chaucer uses it three times (I.2215; *PF* 113; *Tr* III.1255).

Cithero(u)n, Mt. Cithaeron in Greece. In *The *Knight's Tale* it is said to be the principal dwelling of *Venus, and she is called 'gladere of the mount of Citheron' (I.1936, 2223). This seems to be a confusion with the island Cythera (see *Citherea).

Cithia, see *Scithia.

civitate, de, the *De civitate Dei* (*The City of God*) of St Augustine (*Austyn) referred to by the *Parson (X.754).

CLANVOWE, SIR JOHN (*c.*1341–1391). His family lived on the borders of Herefordshire and Wales; as a young man he fought in various French campaigns between 1364 and 1378; he entered the service of Humphrey Bohun, earl of Hereford, and on his death in 1373 into the service of Edward III and later into the service of Richard II. He was used on various diplomatic missions, including one on behalf of *John of Gaunt; he died on an expedition in October 1391 near Constantinople. Clanvowe was one of Richard II's chamber knights, and was in close association with a number of those named like himself by Thomas *Walsingham as Lollard knights. Clanvowe's sympathy with some of the views forwarded by the followers of John *Wyclif is probably assured by his authorship of a religious tract called *The Two Ways*. Clanvowe's other work, *The Boke of Cupide* (or *The *Cuckoo and the Nightingale*) was regarded as a genuine Chaucer poem until the late 19th c. Clanvowe was one of the witnesses to the deed releasing Chaucer from all action against him by Cecily Champaigne in 1380, and seems for the 1370s and 1380s to have been one of the court circle in which Chaucer moved.   [AH]

(ed.) Scattergood (1975); MacFarlane (1972).

CLARE, SEYNTE. St Clare of Assisi (1194–1253), a disciple of St Francis, and a great contemplative. Her name is used in an oath by the *Eagle in *The *House of Fame* (1066) just after Chaucer has asked him about the great noise coming from the House of Fame. Perhaps there is a joking allusion to her contemplative silence; perhaps the name was simply chosen for the rhyme. (Her 20th-c. function as patron of television would be curiously appropriate.)

Clarre(e), see *wine.

classical antiquity (see also *classical literature). Medieval illustrations of the siege of *Troy show a walled town (sometimes with a drawbridge) and battles between knights in armour (see Fig. 8). Modern readers of *Troilus and Criseyde are surprised to find not only knights but also a 'bishop' (see *Amphiorax). Neither artists nor writers attempted to portray the exterior appearance of an ancient setting in the manner of a 19th-c. historical novelist. There is evidence for an interest in the ancient world in many places: a 12th-c. guide to ancient *Rome, the *Mirabilia Romae Urbis* or 'wonders of the city of Rome', for instance, but here legend takes over from history, and the book was adapted for the use of pilgrims. Classical archaeology as we know it is the product of the Renaissance.

Medieval popular literature, if it uses the ancient world at all, transforms it into an exact replica of the medieval world. More sophisticated writers, however, are aware of differences (especially of religion), and draw the attention of their readers to them, creating a strange world in which past and present are intermingled, and in which figures from the pre-Christian world are endowed with contemporary feelings and problems as well as contemporary dress, and act out their destiny in a kind of 'eternal present'. Such 'anachronism' may be less a manifestation of naivety than a way of heightening and intensifying scenes and characters.

Chaucer has this kind of interest in the ancient world. In *Troilus and Criseyde* he produces perhaps the greatest medieval 'romance of antiquity', and finds many other stories in his old books. These are set around the Mediterranean from Rome to Athens (*Atthenes) and from Troy to Egypt. He seems to have been especially interested in *mythography (as in the descriptions of the gods and their temples in The *Knight's Tale and The *Parliament of Fowls), but he refers also to history, and to legend. From his sources he takes many local details: thus he alludes to the Capitol

(*Capitolie), to the theatre (I.1885, 1901, 2091), and several times to a triumph (II.400; VII.2363, 2696; *Anel* 43), which he knows involves captives walking beside the laurel-crowned victor's chariot. Rome has senators. In The *Second Nun's Tale, set in the Rome of early Christianity, a less well-known rank is mentioned: Maximus, an 'officer | Of the prefectes, and his corniculer' (VIII.369). 'Corniculer' (adjutant, subordinate officer) from L. *cornicularius* (the soldier wore a horn-shaped helmet) seems to appear here in English for the first time. This is also the case with 'urn', rather self-consciously introduced in *Troilus*, where the hero thinking of his death requests that the ashes of his heart should be kept 'in a vessell that men clepeth [call] an urne' (V.311). This body of knowledge, limited though it is by the standards of later classicists, is used to great effect in *allusions. These come very naturally in those tales which are set in the ancient world, but are not restricted to them. In The *Nun's Priest's Tale, for instance, there are several, usually in mock-heroic contexts, a clear sign of his (and presumably a significant part of his audience's) familiarity with them.

In his 'ancient' stories Chaucer uses this material to give a sense of 'actuality'. Troilus is made to refer to a number of other details of the ancient funeral: the pyre ('the fir and flaumbe funeral | In which my body brennen shal to glede [glowing coal]'); the festival at his 'vigile' (wake); 'and pleyes palestral' (the athletic games at the funeral—another word apparently appearing for the first time in English). At the beginning of *The Knight's Tale* Theseus gives back to the ladies the bones of their husbands 'to doon obsequies, *as was tho [then] the gyse [custom]*' (I.993): they are burnt accompanied by great lamentations. At the end of the tale there is an elaborate description of the building of Arcite's pyre, the burning of the bodies, and the lamentation and festivities (including the 'wake-pleyes' which involve wrestling 'naked with oille enoynt'). There are frequent references to ancient religious rites (e.g. 'alle the rytes of his payen [pagan] wyse', I.2370) and the sacrifices at the temples of the gods in *The Knight's Tale* are made into powerful and eerie scenes.

In the narrative of *The Second Nun's Tale* (VIII.392–9) Christian faith comes into direct conflict with a pagan demand to sacrifice. The total antagonism of paganism to Christianity, characteristic of the early Christian period, sometimes returns in later times, when the threat of pagan religion had disappeared. It will sometimes haunt even those medieval writers who are normally happy to explore the ancient world and to use its mythology in their poetry. Probably Chaucer's remark at the end of *Troilus and Criseyde* (V.1849) about the 'cursed old rites' of the pagans is an example. Usually, however, he is content to use the old gods, the *Furies, and other creatures of antiquity (the 'satiry [satyrs] and fawny more and lesse, | That halve goddes ben of wildernesse' (*Tr* IV.1544–5), etc.) without evident strain and with enjoyment. His delight in classical antiquity is not at all antiquarian, and in this it is characteristic of a kind of medieval *humanism.

Fyler (2000).

classical literature (see also *classical antiquity; *Latin; Geoffrey *Chaucer: reading**). Medieval writers did not make as strict a distinction between classical and later Latin literature as did the humanists of the Renaissance. The list, for instance, of those who have written about *Troy which Chaucer gives in *The *House of Fame*, includes, besides Homer (*Omer), the much later authors *Dares, Dictys (*Dite), Guido delle Colonne (*Guydo) and Geoffrey of Monmouth (*Gaufride). And although Homer is called 'great', it is indicated that there is some doubt about the accuracy of his version of events (since he was favourable to the Greeks). Indeed, Homer's Greek text was not known to the great majority of medieval Western readers, who depended on the 'Ilias Latina' (the 12th-c. Latin 'Iliad' of Simon Chèvre d'or), on the Trojan stories of the other writers listed by Chaucer, and on the accounts in *Virgil and *Ovid. Classical Greek literature in general was only known through Latin sources (thus Chaucer finds the name of Euripides (*Euripidis) in Boethius (*Boece), but could only have found anything like Greek tragedy in the Latin plays of Seneca (*Senek)). And a number of Latin writers and works were not widely available.

Classical Latin literature was not lost at the end of the Roman empire. It had a lively, and sometimes strange 'after-life'. Texts were copied, and studied, and supplied with commentaries. Much ancient literature owed its very survival to the activity of Cassiodorus (*Cassidore); the encyclopedic writings of Isidore of Seville (*Ysidre) and Martianus Capella (*Marcian) preserved cosmological, mythological, and literary lore. Boethius, the last great representative of late antique literary culture, handed some of it on to his medieval successors.

Classical texts formed part of the medieval school curriculum. The 12th-c. *Dialogue on the Authors* of Conrad of Hirsau lists the names of twenty-one ancient and modern writers, arranged in ascending order of difficulty. They include the elementary texts: the grammarian Donatus, 'Cato' (*Catoun), Aesop (*Isope—in Latin), and Avianus, another fabulist. Then come Christian poets from late antiquity (e.g. Prudentius); prose writers—Cicero (*Tullius), Sallust, and Boethius—and finally the pagan poets—*Lucan, *Horace, Ovid, *Juvenal, 'Homer' (in Latin), Persius, Statius (*Stace), and Virgil. Other authors (e.g. Terence) are mentioned in other lists. Conrad's work discusses the title, subject matter, and intention of each work, its method of treatment, and the part of philosophy to which it pertains; it often has notes on the life of the author. In schools the texts were given close grammatical study. In Chaucer's time an inventory of books (1358) left by William de Ravenstone, a master at the almonry school of St Paul's Cathedral, included Virgil's *Georgics*, Claudian's *Rape of Proserpina*, Lucan, Statius, and Ovid's *Metamorphoses* (*Rv* p. xiii).

Classical literature (or some of it, in some forms) was an important element in medieval literary culture. Its reception was not simply a case of passive acceptance. It was a living tradition which a number of medieval writers found challenging and inspiring. They did not feel that it was a remote monument from the past. The result was that though ancient texts and contexts were sometimes misunderstood, they were also often transformed into new works of art, relevant to the 'present day'. There is nothing stiffly 'neo-classical', for instance, about the medieval 'romance of antiquity': it produced such subtle and imaginative works as the French *Roman d'Eneas* or *Troilus and Criseyde*. Retellings, paraphrases, adaptations, and translations of ancient writings are to be found throughout the later Middle Ages: cf. such diverse works as the *Roman de Thèbes*, the *Ovide moralisé*, Caxton's *Boke of Eneydos*, the *Eneados* of Gavin *Douglas. Some ancient writers were especially influential. Virgil, 'the poet', was *Dante's master and guide; Ovid was a source of inspiration for Chaucer; Cicero and Seneca were constant favourites.

During the Middle Ages there were various attempts to 'renew' classical antiquity, and to rediscover and imitate its literary works in a more conscious way (see *humanism). The last and greatest of these was the Italian humanism of the 14th and 15th centuries, always associated with the name of Petrarch (*Petrak), which brought to light lost texts, strove to improve latinity, and with its new ideal of 'authenticity' ushered in the period of neo-classical imitation.

Curtius (1953); Dronke (1974); Fleming (1990); Friend (1953); Harbert (1974); McCall (1979); Minnis (1982); L. D. Reynolds, Marshal, and Mynors (1983); Shannon (1929).

CLAUDYAN, CLAUDIAN. Claudius Claudianus (?b. *c*.370, d. early in 5th c.), one of the last Latin poets of the empire, was probably born in Alexandria (*Alisa(u)ndre), where he spent his childhood. He was in Rome from *c*.395–404, and wrote a number of works for patrons, including poems in praise of the young Emperor Honorius, and his general Stilicho, and an epithalamium for Honorius and Maria, Stilicho's daughter. His best-known work is the *De raptu Proserpinae* or 'Rape of Proserpina', an unfinished poem in three books (probably written 395–7). Claudian was much admired and widely read in the Middle Ages, becoming a 'curriculum author'. Readers warmed to his vigour and rhetorical skill, to his picturesque and vivid descriptions, and to his treatment of cosmology. Chaucer uses or mentions him several times. It has been suggested that he read him in a school anthology, the *Liber Catonianus*, which contains all the poems or passages he seems to know. The lines in *The *Parliament of Fowls* (99–105) on the way in which people dream about what they have been doing in the course of their day's work are closely based on the opening of his panegyric on the sixth consulship of Hono-

rius (*De sexto consulatu Honorii*). It is as the author of the *De raptu Proserpinae* that he is most frequently mentioned. The *Merchant refers readers eager to know the stories about how Pluto carried off Proserpina to Claudian. Chaucer regards him as an *authority on the underworld. In *The *House of Fame* (1509–11) 'Daun Claudian . . . that bar up al the fame of helle, | Of Pluto, and of Proserpyne' stands on a pillar (appropriately of sulphur), 'as he were wood [mad]', an interesting reference to his poetic 'furor' or divine frenzy which Claudian mentions at the beginning of his poem.

(ed. and trans.) Platnauer (1922); Pratt (1947); Shannon (1929).

CLAUDIUS (1). Claudius Gothicus, the Roman emperor (AD 268–70) before *Aurelian, is mentioned in the story of Zenobia (*Cenobia) in *The *Monk's Tale* (VII.2335).

Claudius (2), Marcus Claudius, the servant of *Appius in *The *Physician's Tale*.

Clemence, Clementia, the goddess of mercy, mentioned in *The *Knight's Tale* (I.928).

Cleo, Clio, the *muse of history, invoked at the beginning of the second book of *Troilus and Criseyde*. A gloss in one MS calls her 'mistress of eloquence' (*domina eloquencie*): in the Middle Ages she was also associated with *rhetoric.

CLEOPATRE, CLEOPAT(A)RAS, Cleopatra (68–30 BC), queen of Egypt, daughter of Ptolemy Auletes (*Tholome (2)), renowned for her beauty and her disastrous love for Mark Antony (*Antonius), which led to her suicide after the defeat at Actium. She is mentioned as an exemplary figure in the *ballade in the Prologue to *The *Legend of Good Women*, and her story is told later in the work (580–705). Chaucer's exact source is not known. His Cleopatra is a martyr of love, who is praised for her great 'trouthe' or fidelity. The battle of Actium is vividly described as if it were a medieval sea battle. She dies by plunging herself into a snake-pit. She is mentioned also in the list of unfortunate lovers in the temple of *Venus in *The *Parliament of Fowls* (291).

clerk; clergy

Clere Laude, see *Laude.

clerk; clergy (see also the *Clerk; *religion; *university). The word 'clerk' (L. *clericus*) in Chaucer's time meant 'a scholar, a man of learning', and, more specifically, an ecclesiastic, whether already in holy orders or intending to take them—as, for instance, a student at a medieval university. 'Clergy' meant 'the clerical order, the body of clerics', and also 'clerkly skill' or 'learning' (Chaucer uses it only in this sense). A 'clerk' (ideally, if not always in practice) was an initiate in the elite Latin literary and intellectual culture, a member of the 'lerned', as against the 'lewed' [unlettered, lay, ignorant]. The medieval clergy, the whole body of ministers and officials of the Church, was a very large group, heterogeneous, but sharing obligations and privileges. It was hierarchically organized. The 'minor orders' (which increasingly came to be regarded as a period of probation) were those of the porter, lector (who read or chanted the lessons), exorcist, and acolyte (who had to carry the candlesticks in procession and light the altar candles). The 'major orders' were those of the subdeacon (whose duties included the preparation of the water used in the Mass, the bringing of the chalice to the altar), the deacon (who could serve at the altar, baptize, and preach), the priest (who alone could celebrate the Mass), and bishop. Clerks were not required to wear a special dress (although the orders of monks and friars had their distinctive clothes or 'habits'). Tonsure, the cutting of the hair, was required, certainly for the major orders, but practice seems to have been lax. Clerks were expected to live an honest and chaste life, and celibacy was obligatory for those in major orders, but here too practice was lax. Some occupations and pastimes were forbidden, like soldiering, playing games of chance, or hunting. Clerks were expected to recite the divine office. Their privileges included protection from physical attack, and from being tried in a lay court.

Since 'clerks' were so prominent in medieval life, it is not surprising that they appear so frequently in Chaucer. His clerks are as varied a group as their real-life counterparts, not least in their learning and chastity. They range from the *Parson and the *Clerk, through the students of the university towns of Oxford and Cambridge, to the *Friar, the *Pardoner, and others. Because the word was synonymous with 'scholar', it appears in non-Christian settings. There are 'clerks' in Chaldea, for instance (VII.2157); Seneca (*Senek) is a 'clerk' (III.1184), and *Ovid is 'Venus clerk' (*HF* 1487). Even the 'tonsure' (which Chaucer wittily applies to himself in his *Complaint to his *Purse* ('I am shave as nye as any frere [friar]' (19)) is transferred to the ancient world by Troilus when he cites the opinions on predestination of those that have their 'top ful heighe and smothe yshore [shaven]' (IV.996). They are associated with learning and wisdom. They have old books, and sometimes they are old themselves, or even dead ('thise wise clerkes that ben dede | Han evere yet proverbed to us yonge', *Tr* III.292–3). Other non-clerical characters are even less convinced of their wisdom, especially those practical men of the world whose anti-intellectual prejudices have been formed in the 'university of life', for whom 'the greatest clerks are not the wisest men' (I.4054). That proudly 'lewed' man, the carpenter in The *Miller's Tale* tells his clerkly lodger an *exemplum of a clerk who was so intent on watching the stars that he fell into a pit (I.3454–61). (The interest of clerks in astronomy and magic (cf. the clerk of Orleans in The *Franklin's Tale*) seems to have suggested to some people a kind of dark power.) They are not noted for praising women, as the Wife of Bath points out (III.688–91; cf. IV.935).

Clerk, The. The *portrait of the poor Clerk of Oxford in the *General Prologue* (285–308) is both idealized and memorable. The last line, 'and gladly wolde he lerne and gladly teche', has almost achieved proverbial status. Two elements are stressed—his leanness and his learning—and the two are connected. He is a student of logic, destined perhaps to become a distinguished schoolman. His love of *books in preference to rich robes or musical instruments and the remark that he was a devoted student who did not waste what he received from his friends or relatives sets him clearly apart from that other Oxford clerk, *Nicholas in The *Miller's Tale* (see especially (I.3211–15, 3219–20). Students are often called 'poor clerks', but here the epithet is not formulaic. This clerk is genuinely poor and genuinely otherworldly. Nor does he waste words. His speech 'sownynge [in accord with] in moral vertu', and the admirable brevity of his style, 'short and quyk [lively] and ful of hy sentence' is exemplified in the Tale he tells.

Rv 810; Cooper (1989), 43; Mann (1973), 74–85.

Clerk's Tale, The, is the first tale in Fragment IV of the *Canterbury Tales, and is followed immediately by the *Merchant's Tale. In the Prologue (in couplets) the Clerk is asked to tell 'som myrie tale', avoiding the figures of rhetoric. He says that he will tell a story he learnt at Padua from Petrarch (*Petrak). The Tale (in rhyme royal—see *versification) just over 1,100 lines in length, is divided into six parts. (I) The young marquis Walter of Saluzzo (*Saluces), in northern Italy, lives only for the present moment, and, to the distress of his people, will not marry. Eventually he yields to their urging, but insists on making the choice himself. (II) In a nearby hamlet lives Janicula, old and very poor, but blessed by God with a young daughter of 'vertuous beautee' called *Grisilde (Griselda). The marquis decides to marry her. On the day set for the wedding he rides there with a great retinue and asks her father for her hand. He makes one stipulation—she must always be obedient to his will. She humbly promises that she will never disobey him. Her old clothes are left behind, and she rides in splendour to his palace. She is loved and admired for her goodness by the people. Soon she has a daughter. (III) Walter is seized with a 'merveillous desir' to test his wife; he tells her that the 'gentils' are loth to be subject to one of such low estate, especially since the birth of her daughter. An officer takes the daughter away. Walter secretly arranges for the girl to be cared for by his sister, who is married to the earl of *Panik (Panico), near Bologna. (IV) After four years Griselda bears a male child, and when it is two years old Walter decides once again to test her, again citing the supposed murmurings of the people. Again, Griselda is totally obedient, and again the child is removed by the officer and taken to Bologna. The marquis marvels at her patience, but still continues in his 'crueel purpos'. He arranges a divorce, and he sends for the two children (the daughter is now aged 12). (V) He now begins his final test. He says that since the people are demanding that he should take another wife, he will send her back to her father's house. In a dignified speech (in which her emotions, barely controlled, only once break out: 'O goode God! How gentil and how kynde | Ye semed by youre speche and youre visage | The day that maked was oure mariage!') she reiterates her humble obedience and love for him. Clad in her smock, and followed by the people cursing Fortune, she makes her way back to the house of Janicula. (VI) When the earl of Panik is about to arrive with what the people suppose to be the new wife, Walter summons Griselda to help with the preparations, and she assents willingly. The girl and her brother arrive, and Walter asks Griselda what she thinks of the girl's beauty. 'A fairer saugh [saw] I nevere noon than she', she says, but warns him against tormenting such a tenderly raised girl. Seeing this extraordinary patience and lack of malice, Walter at last takes pity on her, and explains that the children are hers. Griselda swoons 'for pitous joye', and there is an emotional scene of reunion. She is restored to her former state, and all live happily.

This story, says the Clerk, is not told to urge wives to follow Griselda in humility, for that would be impossible, even if they wished to, but to show that every creature should be constant in adversity as she was. God allows us to be scourged with adversity to test us. But since it would nowadays be very hard to find 'in al a toun Grisildis two or three', the Clerk will end with a song for love of the *Wife of Bath, 'whos lyf and al hire secte [sex] God mayntene'—and he gives an *envoy (in six-line stanzas of identical rhyming pattern): 'Griselde is deed, and eek hire pacience'. Wives should not follow her, but Echo 'that holdeth no silence', and they should fight back.

As the Clerk says, the story is based on Petrarch: the *De obedientia ac fide uxoria mythologia* (a fabile of wifely obedience and faithfulness; written 1373–4), which is itself a version of the last story in the *Decameron. Ultimately it is probably a *folk tale. Chaucer also used a French translation of Petrarch's Latin. The date at which he wrote *The Clerk's Tale* cannot be established with certainty. It is usually assumed that it belongs to the period of the composition of the *Canterbury Tales. There are similar medieval stories of oppressed heroines, such as The *Man of Law's Tale, the *Lai le freine* of *Marie de France, or the romance *Emare. That the story of Griselda was also problematic is evident from the Clerk's words. It continues to excite considerable argument. Many modern readers find it completely reprehensible, and it has been said that Chaucer's attempts to add realistic details or criticisms of Walter only make a revolting story worse. But there have been more sympathetic readings (and the more it is studied the less straightforward and simple it seems). It is certainly not an exercise in modern 'realism': there is no attempt, for instance, to explain (much less analyse) the origin of Walter's 'merveillous desir'. It may well be that this sudden, apparently arbitrary action is a reflection of the story's folk-tale origin. There have been attempts to read the tale as an allegory, but these are not very convincing— it is hard to take Walter as God, or even as a divinely sanctioned tempter like Satan in the story of Job. His arbitrariness might rather suggest *Fortune, the power that the Clerk himself draws attention to. It has been called 'a secular saint's legend. Religious symbols and allusions may be present, but the main drift of the tale seems to be exemplary: it is 'sownynge in moral vertu'. The Clerk's stress on constancy in adversity, and his reference at the end to the Epistle of St James, may suggest that one element in it is related to the widespread medieval literature of *consolation.

Although it does not have the marvellous adventures of The Man of Law's Tale, it is similar to that kind of tragicomical *romance in which a separated family is at last wonderfully reunited. Like that tale, it is one in which Chaucer takes every opportunity for a scene of *pite or pathos. At these moments Chaucer is boldly attempting to appeal to common human and 'realistic' emotions in the midst of an extraordinary folk-tale-like situation. At other times he seems to be deliberately setting up tensions by allowing his narrator to express vehemently his horror at Walter's cruelty. It is notable that the theme of *gentilesse or true nobility which underlies the story here quite clearly sets the virtuous peasant against the wicked nobleman. Griselda is probably not simply the passive heroine that modern readers sometimes take her to be. *Patience in the Middle Ages was regarded as a positive and sometimes heroic virtue, rather like fortitude. Its supreme religious manifestation was in the suffering Christ, from whose mouth 'nevere cam . . . a vileyns word . . .: whan men cursed hym, he

cursed hem noght; and whan men betten hym, he manaced hem noght' (VII.1503). Griselda is perhaps 'imitating' Christ when she describes Walter to her children as 'youre benigne fader'. In its dramatic context, the tale clearly has a bearing on the *Wife of Bath's remarks on *maistrye, *marriage, and *women. As she had said, and as the Clerk admits, clerks were notoriously prone to speak ill of women. Although he insists on a general moral of patience in adversity, the wifely patience of Griselda which he quietly but firmly underlines is in obvious contrast to the Wife's behaviour. How double-edged is the merry envoy in which he apparently endorses her views? This narrator is intellectually agile, and can match the Wife herself in the ironic blending of 'earnest' and '*game'.

(ed.) Rv 137–53, 879–84; S&A 288–331 [101–67]; Cooper (1989), 185–201; Pearsall (1985), 265–77; Kittredge (1912); Mann (1983); Salter (1962); Sledd (1951); Spearing (1972).

CLIFFORD, SIR LEWIS (c.1330–1404). Clifford's family came from Devon. By 1360 he was in the service of the *Black Prince, and after his death served his widow Joan and his son Richard II; he increased his wealth and landholding by marriage, and took part in a number of military campaigns in France and elsewhere. He was named by *Walsingham and Henry Knighton as a *Lollard knight, and was certainly in close association with others of that group; the claim by Walsingham that Clifford abandoned his Lollard beliefs in 1402 may be questionable. Clifford brought Chaucer the poem written in his honour by Eustache Deschamps in 1385 or 1386, along with some of the French poet's balades, and Clifford's son-in-law Philip la Vache is the addressee of Truth; it has been suggested that Clifford was godfather to Chaucer's son Lewis (*Lewis Chaucer).   [AH]

Brusendorff (1925), 175–7; MacFarlane (1972).

Clymat, climate (Greek klima), a region of the Earth's surface lying between two parallels of *latitude. On Ptolemy's system there are seven such regions. In A Treatise on the *Astrolabe Chaucer uses the word simply to mean a single (terrestrial) latitude (2.39, 25), and 'tables of the clymates' (1.3, 4) refers to the plates of the astrolabe, each of which is strictly valid at only one latitude. The word used of a region in relation to its weather is seemingly later than Chaucer. (See also *astralabie; *astrology and astronomy.) [JDN]

Clitermystra, Clytemnestra, wife of Agamemnon (*Agamenoun), who 'for hire lecherye . . . falsly made hire housbonde for to dye' appears in *Jankyn's book of wicked wives (III.737). He read this story to the *Wife of Bath 'with ful good devocioun'.

clokke, clock (L. *clocca*, bell). The mechanical clock was invented, probably in East Anglia, about 1280, and was at first made of iron for use in churches. The first mechanical clock of which we know the constructional details was that designed and built at St Albans by abbot Richard of Wallingford (*c.*1292–1336), an Oxford astronomer. It was extremely intricate, and its prime purposes were to ring the hours (to regulate the monastic day) and to show the state of the heavens, on a large astrolabe-type dial with a twenty-four hourly rotation. (The first clocks rarely had dials, and none had a dial of the simple twelve-hour type.) In Chaucer's day there were several large public clocks of a similar sort in London, for example at St Paul's and Westminster Palace, and there was one at Windsor Castle. The astronomically precise *Chauntecleer was more precise in his crowing 'than is a clokke or an abbey orlogge' (Lat. *horologium*, timepiece). In *A Treatise on the* *Astrolabe* Chaucer uses 'houres of the clokke' interchangeably with 'houres equales'. Expressions like 'ten of the clokke' were becoming commonplace: they occur in the Introduction to *The Man of Law's Tale* (II.14) and the Parson's Prologue (X.5), both places echoing usage in tables from Nicholas of Lynn's calendar. (See also *astrology and astronomy; *day; *hour; *Lenne; *pryme; *technology.) [JDN]

clothes. For those who could afford it, Chaucer's age was one of sartorial magnificence, in which the men dressed as splendidly as the women. There is a delight in exquisite materials and in finery and display. Clothes were social 'signs'. They could indicate class, membership of a guild or profession, or of the following of a nobleman, or of a religious order. There were sumptuary laws which regulated what should be worn by various groups and ranks (in the mid-14th c., for instance, London prostitutes were forbidden to wear 'noble hoods' or fur-lined cloaks so as to suggest that they came from a nobler rank of women). Clothes could also be symbolic signs. The vestments of a priest and the various pieces of a knight's armour could be given symbolic significances. Clothes were also signs which could reveal personality, or a carefully constructed self-image. The satirists make much fun of the swaggering 'gallant', overdressed and out to impress, or men wearing wide gowns of scarlet, furred, with sleeves hanging down to the ground.

Chaucer gives great prominence to clothes, both in formal descriptions and in narrative. We find the basic medieval garments: *sherte* 'shirt' or 'smock'; *smok* similarly a simple garment (worn for instance by the poor *Griselda, IV.886); *kirtel* 'tunic' or 'frock'; *breche* 'drawers' (in colloquial, slangy contexts, VI.948) and *hose(n)* 'stockings, leggings'. There is the *cote*, a long high-necked garment which could be drawn in at the neck, on top of which could be worn an overdress, or a cloak or cape. Other over-garments are the *mantelet* 'short cloak' (I.2163); *courtepy* 'jacket' or 'short coat' (I.290), the *surcote* 'outer coat' (I.617), and the *tabard*, a loose garment worn by the *Ploughman. These references are sometimes accompanied by details of colour or style (the Canon's cloak is 'sewed to his hood', VIII.571), or with comments on their quality (the *Prioress's cloak is 'ful fetys', I.157). The *Squire's gown has sleeves fashionably 'longe and wyde' (I.93), and the Monk's sleeves are 'purfiled (embroidered) at the hond | With grys (expensive grey squirrel fur)' (I.193–4).

There are references to ornaments, to brooches (like the large one *Alison had on her 'low collar' (I.3265), or that of gold and azure set with a ruby, which Criseyde pinned on Troilus's 'sherte' (*Tr* III.1370)), to rings (I.3794, *Tr* III.1368), and to the elaborately worked belts and girdles worn by both men and women (I.329, 358, 3250, etc.). From these would hang various ornaments, or in the case of men, weapons (e.g. I.3929). Shoes are laced high (I.3267); boots are 'clasped faire and fetisly' (I.273). Gloves are associated with nobles (I.2874, *Tr* V.1013). The Pardoner has a humbler (but allegedly magical) mitten (VI.372–3).

clothes

Hats were so common that they figure in colloquial expressions. Some men, says Pandarus, boast about women though they knew them no more 'than myn olde hat' (*Tr* III.320), and the duck swears 'by myn hat!' (*PF* 589). Caps were frequently worn—as by the *Pardoner, who rode 'dischevelee [with hair hanging loose], save his cappe' (I.683). More elaborate kinds of headgear include the *Merchant's 'Flaundryssh bever hat' (I.272; hats of beaver-skin were considered grand and elegant), and the *Wife of Bath's hat (worn over a wimple) which was as broad 'as is a buckler or a targe' (I.470–1). Noteworthy too is the hat with black fringes worn by the mysterious yeoman who accosts the summoner in *The *Friar's Tale* (III.1382). Hoods were also worn by women and men for protection and for display (see I.103, 195, 564, 612). The *typet* or dangling point of the hood could be wound around the head for display (I.3953), or used to hold things (it is where the Friar keeps his store of knives and pins to be used as gifts, I.233). The tipet with a bell on it (*HF* 1841) is part of the dress of a court fool. Female headgear includes the wimple, the kerchief, a linen head-covering, and the *calle* or hair-net (III.1018). People wear various kinds of garlands on their heads (I.666, 1054, 2176).

In bed the night-cap is worn: in *The *Merchant's Tale* old January sits up 'in his sherte, | In his nyght-cappe' (IV.1852–3). (Night-caps seem to have been worn more frequently it seems than 'shirts' in bed.) In *The *Reeve's Tale* (I.4303) there is a comic night-time misunderstanding when the wife thinks that one of the clerks is wearing a *volupeer* or cap.

There are also numerous references to the materials from which the clothes are made. These are usually splendid fabrics (often called 'fine' or 'gay') like satin, silk, samite (a rich silk fabric), scarlet (another rich fabric), 'clooth of *Tars' (silk from Turkestan), or 'cloth of *Gaunt' (Ghent), but sometimes humbler stuff like 'falding' (coarse woollen cloth) or 'fustian' (another coarse fabric). The *Friar's *semycope* (short cloak) is of expensive 'double worstede'; he does not have a threadbare cope like a poor scholar (I.259–62). That genuine 'poor scholar', the *Clerk, has an 'overeste courtepy [jacket]' which is 'ful thredbare' (I.290; the deliberate repetition of 'threadbare' emphasizes the contrast with the Friar).

Clothes are usually an instant indication of wealth or poverty. The Clerk is in striking contrast to the *Physician, who is dressed in cloth which is blood red and Persian blue, 'lyned with taffata and with sendal [thin rich silk]' (I.439–40). But the rich do not always choose to spend their money on clothes or choose to wear splendid clothes on all occasions. The rich Sergeant of Law 'rood but hoomly in a medlee [of mixed colour] cote' (I.328), though it does have a silk belt.

Examples of clothes as a sign of social rank or occupation include the splendid livery of the Guildsmen, 'clothed alle in o [a single] lyveryee | Of a solempne and a greet fraternitee' (I.363–4), and the *Yeoman, dressed as a forester or huntsman 'in cote and hood of grene' (I.103). When Arcite in *The *Knight's Tale* escapes from prison, he disguises himself: 'right anon he chaunged his array, | And cladde hym as a povre laborer' (I.1408–9).

Overtly symbolic or allegorical clothes are rarely found in Chaucer. His Parson refers to St Paul's advice to 'clothe yow . . . in herte of misericorde, debonairetee [meekness], suffrance, and swich manere of clothynge' (X.1053), but Chaucer usually prefers to work by allusion or suggestion. Criseyde wears the black of the widows. St Cecilia in *The *Second Nun's Tale* wears a hairshirt under her robe of gold (VIII.132–3). In *The *Legend of Good Women* Alceste is arrayed in the likeness of a daisy (213–25). Probably the most extensive symbolic or semi-symbolic use of clothes in a narrative is to be found in *The Clerk's Tale*, where they 'point' various rises and falls in the fortune of the heroine, and sometimes emphasize the contrast between her poor attire and her innate nobility of soul. The references are surprisingly frequent: the marquis has rich clothes measured and ornaments prepared for his new bride (IV.253–9), and comes 'richely arrayed' (267) to find her. She is 'despoiled' of her old attire (with a touch of satire it is noted that the 'ladyes' were not 'right glad | To handle hir clothes, wherinne she was clad'), and clothed 'al newe' (372–85). When her ultimate test comes, and she is required to give way to a new queen, Griselda alludes to this transformation ('ye dide me streepe [strip] out of my povre weede, | And richely me cladden'), restores the clothes to Walter ('heere agayn your clothyng I restoore'), and asks simply that she should be allowed to cover herself with a smock. And 'in hir smok, with heed and foot al bare, | Toward hir fadre hous forth is she fare'. The 'pitous' scene is heightened by her father's attempt to cover her with hir 'olde coote' which has now become so old that he cannot get it on her body (862–917). Finally, when the 'new queen' arrives, Griselda ('noght . . . abayst of hire clothyng, | Thogh it were rude and somdeel eek [also somewhat] to-rent') goes with glad face to welcome her (1011–15). When the truth is revealed, she is once again stripped of her 'rude array', and clad in 'a clooth of gold that brighte shoon' (1114–20). This seems to blend the moral pattern with a folk-tale one in which splendid clothes signal a recognition of true beauty and virtue.

In some descriptions clothes are imaginatively used to create a memorable visual image or to suggest something about an individual's personality or character, as with the Wife of Bath, 'ywympled wel' and with a superfluity of cloth of fine texture, with her large hat, her 'foot-mantel' or overskirt reaching to the feet, her tightly laced hose 'of fyn scarlet reed', her shoes 'ful moyste and newe', and the sharp spurs on her feet (I.470–3). In The *Miller's Tale* (I.3233–54) the youthful animal attractiveness of *Alison's body is emphasized by the loving attention given to the details of her clothes, such as her girdle, decorated with silk and with an elegant purse hanging from it, a white apron with 'many a goore [flare]', a white smock, embroidered with coal-black silk, and matching ribbons on her white cap, her shoes laced high upon her legs. Her admirer *Absolon (2) is also a colourful figure. His beautiful golden hair is set off by a kirtle of light blue, a brilliantly white surplice, and red hose. His elaborate latticed shoes, cut so that they resembled the windows of St Paul's Cathedral, are the final dazzling accompaniment.

Chaucer will often use a reference to clothes as a circumstantial detail to give a sense of familiar 'ordinary life' in a narrative ('don [put] this furred cloke upon thy sherte') or in a formal *portrait. This is most obvious in those of the *General Prologue, where almost everyone has at least one item of clothing specified, often appropriate in one way or another to the character, like the *Knight's fustian gypon (tunic) stained by his coat of mail, or the fashionable dress of the *Squire or sometimes revealingly inappropriate, as in the case of the *Monk or the *Friar.

The most direct and vehement sartorial satire comes from the Parson, when he reproves excess in clothing. Clothes began with the Fall, he says, when Adam and Eve were moved by their new shame to sew 'of fige leves a maner of breches to hiden hire membres' (X.325–9). Pride shows itself in fashionable dress (X.415–30), with 'superfluity' of clothing. He laments the expense involved in the embroidering, the notching of borders, the ornamenting with stripes and bars, the costly furring, the cutting and 'dagging' of garments. He criticizes the length of gowns 'trailynge in the dong and in the mire, on horse and eek on foote, as wel of man as of womman'. He is even more severe on the opposite sin of 'the horrible disordinat scantnesse of clothyng': those fashionable tight-fitting and parti-coloured garments which draw attention to the 'horrible swollen membres'. As in some later moralists, revealing and closely-fitting dress (here it is male) unleashes a flood of eloquence: 'thise kutted sloppes [short outer coats], or haynselyns [short jackets], that thurgh hire shortnesse ne covere nat the shameful membres of man . . . Allas, somme of hem shewen the boce [bulge] of hir shap, and the horrible swollen membres . . . and eek the buttokes of hem faren as it were the hyndre part of a she-ape in the fulle of the moone.'

Fairholt (1840); Hodges (2000); Newton (1980).

Cobler of Canterburie, The. This interesting attempt at a collection of 'Chaucerian' stories was printed in 1590 (and in an expanded form as *The Tinker of Turvey* in 1630). The unknown author praises the example of 'old father Chaucer'. Six stories in prose (mostly of the fabliau type) are told by a cobbler, a smith, a scholar, and old woman, and a summoner, who are travelling from Billingsgate to Gravesend on a barge.

coins, coinage; *coitu, De.* See *money; *Constantyn.

Colatyn, Lucius Tarquinus Collatinus, the husband of Lucretia (*Lucrece).

Colcos

Colcos, Colchis, a country at the eastern end of the Black Sea, the home of the Golden Fleece and of *Medea. It appears (as an 'isle') in *The *Legend of Good Women* (1425).

Colle (1), (*tregetour) an English illusionist of the late 14th c. mentioned in *The *House of Fame* at the end of a list of magicians (1277–81). The narrator says that he saw him perform a strange thing on a 'table of sycamore': he carried a windmill under a walnut shell.

Colle (2), the name of a dog in *The *Nun's Priest's Tale* (VII.3383).

Coloigne. Cologne, on the Rhine, is one of the pilgrimage sites which the *Wife of Bath had visited (I.466). It was famous for the shrines of the three Magi (the 'Three Kings of Cologne'), whose relics were taken there by the Emperor Frederick Barbarossa in the 12th c., and of St Ursula and her eleven thousand virgins, who were believed to have been martyred there by the Huns.

Colossenses (ad), St Paul's Epistle to the Colossians, cited by the *Parson (X.634).

comedy. Chaucer uses the word only once, at the end of *Troilus and Criseyde*, where he takes leave of his *'tragedye' and prays that he may be given power 'to make in [probably 'compose'] som comedye' (V.1788). He seems to be using the word in the wider sense it has in medieval literary theory of a story which ends happily ('comedy is a narration in poetic form which at the beginning portrays the harsh reality of some miserable condition, but its material has a happy ending, as one can see from Terence's comedies' says Guido da Pisa (Minnis and Scott, 475)). It was etymologized as 'village song', and was associated with lowly subjects and with 'humble' style.

The comic seems to have had an important role in medieval culture in general and in literary culture in particular. There is evidence for an almost insatiable appetite for entertainment and games; for festivals of reversal or the 'world upside down'; for comic and parodic reversals of serious rituals and forms. The doctrine that literature should contain both the 'useful' and the 'sweet' was given

a particular application to justify man's need for '*game' in a story of St Anthony which uses the image of the bow that needs to be 'unbent' in order to maintain its efficiency. 'Relaxation' and 'refreshment' were necessary for the life of man, and literature (and especially comic literature) found a place here. That Chaucer enjoys and portrays 'game' as well as 'earnest' is in no way surprising; what is remarkable is the imaginative skill with which he does it.

A very general definition of comedy as a story which ends happily does not do justice to the variety and diversity of Chaucer's comic writing, the quality of which seems to have been recognized from the earliest times. Happy endings are common but not universal. The ending of *The *Merchant's Tale* has often been thought to be dark and bitter. Even in *The *Reeve's Tale* the element of revenge is strongly felt at the end—as the *Cook correctly says (I.4338) the miller 'hadde a jape of malice in the derk'. Even if a group of 'comic tales' is isolated it is striking in its variety. It will include *fabliaux, but other types as well, such as the animal fable of *The *Nun's Priest's Tale* and satirical anecdotes like *The *Friar's Tale* or *The *Summoner's Tale*. And Chaucer uses a whole range of techniques and modes—satire, *parody, the mock-heroic, *irony. His comedy is sometimes normative, but it is 'constantly undercut through recurrent questioning of both the social norms and the simpler aspects of the satiric process' (Pearsall, 166). Sometimes the only positive qualities seem to be cleverness and ingenuity. Sometimes we have a 'festive comedy' with carnivalesque fantasy and topsyturveydom; at other times the comedy is sharp and edged with satire.

Brewer (1972, 1996); Minnis and Scott (1988); Olson (1974); Pearsall (1985).

commune profit, a phrase used in *The *Parliament of Fowls* (47), where virtuous men who loved common profit, says *Affrycan (1), go into a place of everlasting joy. Chaucer has adapted the *patria* and the *res publica* of the *Somnium Scipionis* (see *Drem of Scipioun) to contemporary political thought. The term 'common profit' (or its French equivalent) occurs in accounts of the proceedings of Plantagenet parliaments. Chaucer uses the phrase in the account which Boethius gives of his service to the state (*Bo* I pr.4), and again in a discussion of order in society in *The *Parson's Tale* (X.773). However, it has for him wider suggestions of peace, charity, and general harmony. The virtuous Griselda in *The *Clerk's Tale* brings this to her realm: she promoted 'the commune profit' so that there was no discord, rancour or 'hevynesse' in the whole country which she could not pacify (IV.430–4). It seems to be opposed to the 'singuler profite' which *Dido laments as a driving force in men (*HF* 310). (See also *politics.)

complaint can mean simply 'lamentation' or 'complaint', but it is also used with specific senses. It is used to describe speeches of lamentation or sorrow made by characters within a narrative. These are often rhetorically well formed and eloquent. Examples range from relatively short monologues, like that of Criseyde in *Troilus and Criseyde* IV.757–98, to Dorigen's extended lament in *The *Franklin's Tale* (V.1355–456). In *The *Nun's Priest's Tale* (VII.3338–73) the narrator makes a mock-heroic lamentation over the unfortunate Chauntecleer. It also refers to a genre of *lyric poetry, a song or poem of complaint or grief. Like the French *complaincte* or *complaint*, from which it probably derived, it was a very loosely defined form, of almost any length, but usually a monologue about *love. Chaucer refers to it several times: in *The *Merchant's Tale* Damian 'in a lettre wroot . . . al his sorwe, | In manere of a compleynt or a lay' (IV.1881), and in *The Franklin's Tale* 'compleintes' are listed with 'layes, songes' and 'roundels, virelayes' (V.948). He uses the term of short lyrics like that which is spoken by the Man in Black in *The *Book of the Duchess* (475–86), and of *Oenone's epistle in Ovid's *Heroides*. It is his own favourite lyric type, and he makes a number of interesting experiments. In *Complaint unto *Pity* he uses an autobiographical fiction—'a compleynt had I, writen in myn hond, | For to have put to Pite as a bille [?a legal bill of petition]' (43–4). Elsewhere he combines lyric and narrative, uses his distinctive narrator's voice, and generally increases the complexity of the type (see especially *Mars*, *Venus* and *Anelida and Arcite*).

Davenport (1988); Norton-Smith (1974), ch. 2.

Complaynt d'Amours, a lyrical *complaint which survives in three MSS. No MS attributes it to Chaucer, but *Skeat thought that it could be by him. It is smooth and eloquent, and has an allusion to *The *Parliament of Fowls*, but few scholars have accepted it as certainly genuine.

(ed.) *Rv* 658–9, 1090; Scattergood (1995), 477.

Complaint of the Black Knight; Complaint of Chaucer to his Purse, Complaint of Mars; Complaint of Venus; Complaint to His Lady; Complaint unto Pity; Complexioun. See *Black Knight*; *Purse*; *Mars*; *Venus*; *Lady*; *Pity*; *humour.

Confessio Amantis, the major English work of John *Gower. It is a poem of over 30,000 lines in eight books. As the title implies, the framework is a confession, of a lover Amans to Genius, a priest of Venus. The *Seven Deadly Sins form the structure of Genius's instruction of the lover. He illustrates his doctrine with a large number of excellently told short exemplary stories, many of them from *Ovid. At the end the lover is told that he is too old for love, and goes 'homward a softe pas'. Several of the stories are parallel to stories in Chaucer: Florent (book 1), *The Wife of Bath's Tale*; Constance (2), *The *Man of Law's Tale*; Phebus and Cornide (3), *The *Manciple's Tale*; Pyramus and Thisbe (3), Legend of Thisbe (*LGW*); the story of Ceix and Alcyone (4) appears in *The *Book of the Duchess*; Tarquin (7), Legend of Lucrece (*LGW*).

(ed.) Macaulay (1899–1902); (selections) Bennett (1968).

conjunccio(u)n, conjunction, an (apparent) joining of two heavenly bodies; or an occasion when both have the same *longitude, but are possibly separated in *latitude. Chaucer gives no definition. In *A Treatise on the *Astrolabe* he speaks of conjunctions without qualification, but means conjunctions of the Sun and Moon (new moon). (See also *astrology and astronomy.) [JDN]

Connigaste, Conigast or Cunigast, a Gothic minister of *Theodoric, said by Boethius to have been an oppressor of the poor (*Bo* I pr.4:56).

consolation or 'comfort' (which is Chaucer's preferred word) is an important element in medieval literature, especially in religious and didactic works. The formal *consolatio* goes back to pagan antiquity. Examples from Roman times which were influential in the Middle Ages are some of the writings of Seneca (*Senek) and of Cicero (*Tullius). The techniques and topics of the ancient *consolatio* (discussions of *Fortune, commonplace *solacia* or 'solaces' (all men must die; earthly fame is transitory and deceitful, etc.), or the use of *exemplary figures or stories) are found in the *Consolation of Philosophy* of Boethius (*Boece), and in later works. The most famous 'book of comfort' in English is More's *Dialogue of Comfort against Tribulation*, written in the Tower of London in 1534, but long before then there were many treatises which attempted to provide consolation for suffering and *death. There are also more ambitious literary attempts at dealing with the mysteries of suffering and death, like the poem *Pearl. Consolatory passages are found sometimes in religious writing, sometimes in secular narratives. Providing comfort was one of the functions of *friendship (thus Pandarus attempts to console the lovesick and despairing Troilus). At the end of The *Knight's Tale *Theseus gives a rather stoic speech of consolation (I.2987–3074).

One of Chaucer's narratives is a clear example of the typical 'book of comfort', his own *Tale of *Melibee*, a translation of a French version of a Latin *Liber consolationis*. It is full of proverbial and sententious topics of consolation from both ancient and Christian sources. It is an exemplary story, showing how a man should patiently accept suffering, and forgive his enemies with a 'gentil' heart. *Patience was regarded as a defence against adversity—the Parson was 'in adversitee ful pacient' (I.484). The suffering heroines Constance and Griselda demonstrate the anguish and the strength that it brings. Constance finds strength in the traditional Christian images of consolation, the suffering Christ and the Virgin *Mary ('queen of comfort' in *ABC 77; 'thou confort of us wrecches' in VIII.32). The narrator of The *Clerk's Tale says that the story is a model for every person to be as constant in adversity as Griselda, and refers to the Epistle of St James, itself a little book of comfort. In The *Book of the Duchess*, which has a strongly consolatory element, Chaucer ignores the usual Christian topics in favour of an indirect

approach through images and suggestions, through the power of memory to recall lost happiness, and through expression of human pity ('*pite').

Barratt (1983); Gray (1986).

Constance, see *Custance*.

CONSTANTYN, Constantinus Africanus (*fl.* 1065–85). Born in Carthage, Constantine was the first important translator of medical treatises from Arabic into Latin. His early biography is obscure, but he is known to have converted to Christianity and joined the Benedictines at Monte Cassino, where he died. He translated parts of Hippocrates and Galen and various Græco-Arabic compendia, often introducing his own material. He greatly influenced the 12th-c. medical school at Salerno. Constantine is listed in the *General Prologue* (I.433) as one of the *Doctour of Phisik's authorities, and in *MchT* (IV.1810–11) is 'the cursed monk, daun Constantyn', who composed a work *De coitu* (this has information on aphrodisiacs). (See also *medicine.) [JDN]

Constellacio(u)n, configuration of planets, in particular in a *horoscope. In The *Knight's Tale* (I.1084–91), Arcite asks Palamoun whether an unfriendly planetary configuration at their birth was not responsible for their imprisonment. The same usage is to be found in at least five other poems by Chaucer. He does not use the word in our modern sense of a grouping of *fixed* stars. (See also *astrology and astronomy; *planete; *signe; *sterre.) [JDN]

Cook, The. The Cook has been brought on pilgrimage by the Guildsmen. In the *General Prologue* his brief *portrait (I.379–87) consists largely of a list of his dishes and culinary skills, but it all becomes somewhat unsettling when we are suddenly informed that he had a *mormal* (ulcer) on his shin. We discover more about him later. He is called Roger, or Hogge of *Ware, and he is a cook 'of London'. It seems quite likely that Chaucer had a real person in mind. There was a Roger Knight de Ware of London, cook, who appears in one or two legal cases. The *Host jokingly (or apparently jokingly) makes some rude allusions to his warmed up pies and to the many flies in his shop (I.4345–54). His skill in strong London ale (I.382) leads to an unfortunate fall later, when his horse throws him, and he has to be lifted back, with considerable difficulty (IX.46–55).

Rv 814; Cooper (1989), 48; Mann (1973), 168–70.

Cook's Tale, The, which follows The *Reeve's Tale and concludes Fragment I, is apparently unfinished. There is no way of establishing its date: it is very closely fitted to its predecessor, and may well have been written at the same time. Nor can any source for the story be identified.

The Cook is delighted with the Reeve's story, and promises to tell 'a litel jape' which happened in 'oure citee', i.e. London. In response to the Host's critical remarks about his cooking he says that he hopes he will not be angry because the tale is about an innkeeper. It begins with the introduction of Perkyn Revelour, an apprentice victualler, who loved the tavern better than the shop. He is a dicer and a reveller, and his master is glad to give him permission to leave. Perkyn moves in with a companion of his own kind, who had a wife who kept a shop for appearance sake and fornicated for a living. At this point the scribe of the *Hengwrt MS, leaving the rest of the page blank, wrote 'Of this cokes tale maked Chaucer na moore'.

There are a couple of 15th-c. attempts at ending the tale—both with a severe punishment for Perkyn. Some MSS insert The Tale of *Gamelyn, but this is certainly not by Chaucer and does not seem appropriate to the Cook. Most scholars believe that the tale is in fact unfinished, although it has been argued that it is complete as it stands, bringing to conclusion the theme of *herbergage or 'lodging' which has been prominent in the two preceding *fabliaux. The last couplet is neat and pointed, but it does give a very abrupt ending. Perhaps an inconsistency in the Prologue to The *Manciple's Tale, where the Cook is introduced as if for the first time, may suggest that Chaucer had not finally decided what to do at this point in the composition of the Tales. Perhaps he might have cancelled the Cook's present prologue and fragment. It is also very difficult to guess how the story might have been continued, since there is no source to give guidance. Most critics have assumed that it would have been a fabliau to match the preceding two, and

sharing their interest in 'riot'. But the sententious remarks about Perkyn may indicate a different kind of story. It has been suggested, for instance, that it could have become a prodigal son type of story. Not enough remains for us to be sure. It does seem, however, that the London setting is a deliberate foil to Oxford and Cambridge—and it is a long way from the Athens of The *Knight's Tale.

(ed.) Rv 84–6, 853; S&A 148–54 [75–86]; Cooper (1989), 118–21; Kolve (1984), 257–84; Stanley (1976).

Coribantes. Corybantes, the priests of Cybele, are mentioned in *Boece (IV m.5:16, 19) as beating their tabors and basins of brass when the moon is in eclipse in order to rescue it from enchantment. Boethius himself simply referred to a 'general error' (i.e. a common pagan practice): Chaucer's Corybantes have come in from his French translation and *Trevet's commentary.

Corynne, Corinna, referred to as a source in *Anelida and Arcite (21), Corinna's identity is not certain. She may well be the Greek lyric poet of Tanagra or Thebes (6th c. BC), who is mentioned by Statius (*Stace), who is himself cited along with 'Corynne' in Chaucer's line. Or it may be the name of *Ovid's mistress Corinna (to whom the Amores were addressed) taken as an authority because she was associated with a lament.

Corynthe, Corinth, in Greece, referred to in one of the *Pardoner's stories (VI.604).

cosmology. The Greek word *kosmos* originally meant 'order', and according to tradition was first applied to the world as a whole by Pythagoras (see *Pictagoras), whose mathematical and musical studies had impressed on him the order and regularity in the world. It was often used thereafter (like *ouranos*) to denote the visible world and the heavens. The word 'cosmology' is not as old as Chaucer, but aptly describes a branch of medieval study that was distinct from astronomy, although owing much to it. Most of the basic problems in this subject are pre-Socratic in origin, but are first collected in one place by *Plato, in his Timaeus, and then more systematically by *Aristotle in his Physics, On the Heavens, Metaphysics, and other writings.

There was among the Greeks a general belief in a universe limited in space and governed by a set of unalterable laws. Aristotle considered the existence of the universe in time, past and future, to be potentially infinite—a doctrine that required either careful exegesis or a straight denial by the medieval Christian. On the question of creation, Plato was generally the easier of the two to accept, and the Platonic idea that it is soul that carries round the Sun, Moon, and planets was likewise not unattractive. Aristotle, however, had from an early date taken over from the pre-Socratics a concept of Nature as having a source of motion within itself, and his later doctrine of a Primum Mobile (*First Moeving) had the additional attraction to later Christians (not to mention Jews and Muslims) of a parallel with the actions of God. Whatever the appeal of Platonic and Neoplatonic cosmology in the later Middle Ages, in the last resort it was the sheer coherence and systematic character of the Aristotelian version, and of rigorous commentaries by such as Averroes (*Averrois), that eventually won the day.

The concept of natural motion is applied, in On the Heavens, to the four elements: earth and water move naturally to the centre of the universe (the centre of the earth) and air and fire away from that centre. A fifth element, æther, moves with a circular motion, and is the element of which the celestial regions are composed. The movement of all things presented a problem: Aristotle had argued that even a self-moved mover requires an outside cause to initiate movement. If infinite regress is to be avoided, there must be at least one prime mover that is unmoved; that is, in regard to which one ceases to insist on a mover. This is the outermost heaven. The planets and all below were moved as it were by a force transmitted down from this unmoved mover.

The physical basis for the observed planetary motions was in a broad sense complete, but the details were still to come. Eudoxus, an early contemporary, had put forward a geometrical scheme of unparalleled ingenuity for explaining the general pattern of planetary motions, in particular retrogradations (*retrograde); Callippus improved this somewhat; and finally in his Metaphysics, Aristotle revised the theory so as to give it, as he thought, physical plausibility. Whatever its virtues, with fifty-five spheres his theory was certainly cumbersome. In a sense, this was now the 'official' Aristotelian system, but in point of fact, the simple system, where each planet was assigned a single sphere (from the Moon's, the nearest, to Saturn's and that of the stars at the outermost), was good enough for most natural philosophers in the Middle Ages. Even Ptolemy (*Ptholomee), who lived half a millennium later than Aristotle, and who had a vastly superior system of epicyclic astronomy at his disposal (that found in Almagest), wished to combine his own system with Aristotle's, which he thought physically correct. (Ptolemy achieved his ambition in his Planetary Hypotheses, but this was known only indirectly in the Middle Ages.) Medieval cosmology had thus in a sense been fixed in character seventeen centuries before Chaucer, and was loosely based on a system of planetary astronomy that had been superseded for more than a millennium of that time.

Chaucer learned basic Aristotelian cosmology in many ways: it permeates *Boece, and is behind Cicero's Dream of Scipio and Macrobius' commentary on it (and so provides part of the frame for The *Parliament of Fowls). He no doubt picked up material from Martianus Capella, and Sacrobosco's On the Sphere; he might even have read some of Aristotle's works himself. The Eagle in The Parliament explains the doctrine of natural place in an intelligent way. (See also *astrology and astronomy; *Macrobes; *Marcian; sound; *Tullius.) [JDN]

North (1990); Thorndike (1923–41).

counse(i)l is a common word in Chaucer, and an important theme. In the narratives there are naturally many cases of persons seeking or being given advice. The idea that sharing of counsel is part of *friendship lies behind the reproaches of Palamon to Arcite in The *Knight's Tale (I.1146–51). Many of the remarks about 'counsel' are proverbial. A particular favourite is the biblical 'work all by counsel and you shall not rue' (attributed to *Solomon, but in fact from Ecclesiasticus 32:24). In *Melibee (VII.1003) it introduces a scene in which Melibee literally takes counsel from a 'greet congregacion of folk'. In this tale the theme of 'counsel' is central: it is ultimately based on a Latin book 'of *consolation and counsel'. It demonstrates the value of listening to good advisers. But the value and importance of good counsel is everywhere acknowledged. It informs some philosophical or monitory lyrics: Chaucer's poem *Truth* for instance is called in some MSS 'Balade de bon conseyl'.

'Counsel' however is not without its problems. In The *Merchant's Tale* (where again it is an important idea) January 'takes counsel', but ignores the good counsel of Justinus ('the upright man'), and prefers the advice of Placebo (whose name means 'I shall please'), who tells him what he wants to hear. In The *Miller's Tale*, Nicholas also quotes a proverb of 'Solomon' in order to ensnare the carpenter in his ingenious plotting (I.3526–33). In *Melibee* the supreme giver of good counsel is a woman, Prudence (who lists a number of illustrious predecessors: *Rebekka, *Judith, *Abygail and *Hester (VII.1097–100)). But there is a certain amount of disagreement in proverbial lore about the status of 'women's counsel'. That women (allegedly) find it hard, as the Wife of Bath admits, to 'keep counsel' (see III.980 ff.) is eagerly seized on by some males. The Monk (speaking of Samson) warns: 'beth war by this ensample oold and playn | That no men telle hir conseil til hir wyves' (VII.2091–2). And the Nun's Priest points out gleefully (but with some justification in the circumstances) that the counsel that they give can lead to disaster: 'Wommenes conseils been ful ofte colde; | Wommanes conseil broghte us first to wo | And made Adam fro Paradys to go' (VII.3256–8), although he takes care to add 'thise been the cokkes wordes and nat myne'.

Court of Love, The, a 15th-c. poem which found its way into the early editions of Chaucer (see *Chauceriana) and was only rejected in the 19th c. by Bradshaw and Skeat. Although the text is corrupt, it is a lively and entertaining work. The young narrator, Philogenet, a clerk of Cambridge, visits the court of love, where he is guided by Philobone. He sees the true lovers, clad in blue, and reads the statutes of love's court (the sixteenth of which is to please the lady seven times at night). There is much vivid and witty writing (the friars, monks, and nuns lament that they 'so sone went to religion') and there is a fine descriptive passage when the birds sing the Matins of Love.

(ed.) Skeat (1897).

courtesy, see *curteisie.

'courtly love' or 'amour courtois'. The term is a modern one, used originally to describe the conception of love in the poetry of the Occitan troubadour poets of the 12th c. in southern France, then in the lyric and narrative courtly poetry of northern France and elsewhere, including England. There has been much controversy about the term and its usefulness. It has been claimed that courtly love was an entirely literary conception which had no relationship with actual society or life, but this view has been fiercely denied. It has been claimed that it represents a complete change of consciousness in Western Europe in the 12th c. (and various theories about its possible origins have been put forward). At the other extreme it has been claimed that it was possible in any age or place, and some examples have been produced. Others have argued that it is simply a modern invention of little or no value in the understanding of medieval literature. Since Chaucer never uses the term and seems happy with the word 'love', it is tempting to say that that should be good enough for us. Yet he is the inheritor of a distinctive though varied literary tradition in Western love literature, marked by a semi-technical terminology and by certain patterns of ideas.

Courtly love is in the Middle Ages often called *fin' amors* (or some similar term in other vernaculars, such as Chaucer's 'fyn lovynge' (*LGW* 544)). It is essentially a 'noble' or 'exquisite' love, in contrast to the crude passion of 'churls' or those of high birth who do not have noble souls; it is opposed to venial or inconstant love, and to ignoble passions like jealousy (see *jalousie). Although traditional patterns of ideas or behaviour may be recognized, we do not have a rigidly fixed 'code' with 'rules' (see *Andreas Capellanus). There are examples of adulterous or extramarital love in courtly love stories (those of Lancelot or Tristram, for instance), but there are also cases where love and marriage coexist (in Chrétien de Troyes as well as in Chaucer). What seems to interest the poets primarily is not whether the love is inside or outside marriage, but the *quality* of the love itself.

We might safely distinguish the following patterns, which are commonly, though not universally found. Love comes from the sight of the lady; the male lover's heart is pierced by her eyes. There are examples of a distant love (*amour lointain*) based on hearsay or reputation (as that of the Sultan in *MLT*), but typically love comes from an actual encounter. It is an overwhelming passion, which turns the lover's world upside down, like a 'conversion' (as in *Troilus and Criseyde*). The lover then humbly serves his lady, who is for him the sum of all excellence. He serves her with a religious devotion (religious language is often used: the lady is sometimes mistaken for a goddess, or is sometimes the 'figure' of a goddess; sometimes the first falling in love occurs in a church or a temple). It is a voluntary service which involves suffering. Typically, the unrequited lover will grow pale with sleepless nights, tremble at the sight of his lady, suffer from melancholy, from lovesickness, 'the loveris maladye | Of Hereos' (I.1373–4). There is an exquisite blend of pain and *joy. But through suffering love ennobles the lover. He grows in the virtues of noble love, *gentilesse', *curteisie', dignity and honour, courage and worth. He will not imagine that he will ever be fully worthy of his lady, but love will make him less unworthy. The lady, for her part, has free choice. She may give her 'grace' if and when she wishes. It is assumed that she should show 'mercy' to her suppliant lover if he has served her nobly and constantly, but the choice is hers. She will, however, run the risk of being stigmatized as a cruel and heartless mistress, like the lady in *La *Belle Dame sans Merci* (see *daunger). Typically, the affair will be secret and discreet. It will usually end in physical consummation, in which the fullest 'joy of love' will be experienced. *Fin' amors* is associated with youth, and beauty, and joy.

Chaucer was obviously completely familiar with this kind of love literature. However, for him it is usually only one kind of love which forms part of a varied and mysterious spectrum (see *love, *marriage). He will make his own adaptations, like blending it with a philosophically based marriage in *The *Franklin's Tale*, where Arveragus is his lady's 'servant in love, and lord in mariage' (V.793). Or he will use its ideas or terminology with come-

dy or irony, as when in a very non-courtly context in *The *Miller's Tale*, Nicholas in the throes of 'deerne [secret] love' for Alison, finally wins favour when he 'gan mercy for to crye' (I.3288). But there are a number of poems in which the language or concepts of *fin' amours* figure prominently and seriously. The Man in Black's recollection of his wooing of the Lady White in *The *Book of the Duchess* is a case in point: after a long service, his lady gave him 'the noble yifte of hir mercy'. In *The *Knight's Tale*, Palamon is wounded through the eye by the beauty of Emily, and thinks that she is the goddess *Venus. Arcite, who is hurt as much as he is, finally dies with the words 'mercy, Emelye!' on his lips. In *Troilus and Criseyde* especially, we have a dramatic presentation of an overwhelming passion, of the sufferings of 'this wondre maladie', and the ennobling power of love: 'for he bicom the frendlieste wight, | the gentilest, and ek the mooste fre . . .'. But Troilus is more than a 'typical courtly lover', and the love story that is unfolded is far more than a typical story of *fin' amors*.

Dronke (1965–6); Lewis (1936); Newman (1968); Wack (1990).

Craft of Lovers, The, a 15th-c. verse dialogue between two lovers, which was included in the early editions of Chaucer (see *Chauceriana). It was rejected from the canon by *Tyrwhitt, but was still included in some early 19th-c. editions.

CRASSUS. Marcus Licinus Crassus (d. 53 BC), a member (with Caesar and Pompey) of the 'first triumvirate' to rule Rome, was defeated by the Parthians in 53 BC. Because of his greed, he was murdered by having molten gold poured into his throat. He is cited along with Midas (*Myda) as an example of avarice—the opposite of the *gentilesse of true lovers—in *Troilus and Criseyde* (III.1391).

Creon, a legendary king of *Thebes (1), refused to allow the bodies of the defeated Greeks to be buried, and was overcome by *Theseus and killed in the great battle at the beginning of *The *Knight's Tale*. He is alluded to elsewhere (*Anel* 64, *LGW* 1661). He is described as 'old' and a 'tyrant'.

Creseyde; Cresseid, Testament of; see *Criseyde; *Testament of Cresseid.

CRESUS, Croesus, the last king of Lydia (*Lyde) (*c.*560–546 BC), whose wealth was proverbial. He was defeated by the Persian king Cyrus (*Cirus). According to the *Monk, who tells his story (VII.2727–66), when he escaped from being burnt alive he began a new war because of his pride. He had a prophetic dream (apparently a medieval invention) in which he was on a tree being attended by Jupiter and Phoebus. His daughter explained to him that it signified the gallows, and indeed, the proud king was hanged. He was a well-known exemplary figure. Chaucer probably took the story from *Jean de Meun's discussion of *Fortune in the *Roman de la Rose,* Croesus is referred to elsewhere (I.1946 *HF* 105, *Bo* II pr.2:58–60); and the Nun's Priest recalls his dream in a more comic context (VII.3138–40).

Crete, the island in the Mediterranean Sea, the setting for Theseus's adventure with the Minotaur (*Mynotaur) (I.980, III.733, *LGW* 1886, 1894).

Creusa, the wife of Aeneas (*Eneas), who was lost at Troy, and whose spirit warned him to flee to Italy, is mentioned in *The* *House of Fame* (175–92) and *The* *Legend of Good Women* (945).

Criseyde, Criseyda, Cre(i)seyde, Criseda. Criseyde, the heroine of *Troilus and Criseyde*. Her name derives ultimately from Homer's 'Chryseida', the accusative form of Chryseis, daughter of Chryses. It seems that *Boccaccio applied the name Criseida to another ancient heroine, Briseida or Briseis (*Breseyda), who had been made the beloved of Troilus by *Benoît de Sainte-Maure. In the medieval literature of *love, it was obviously problematical that a lady of beauty and loving disposition should be unfaithful to her devoted lover (see the accusations made against Chaucer in the *Prol. LGW* 331 ff.). And there has been extensive modern discussion of her behaviour and of her '*character'. Attitudes have ranged from the severely judgemental to the generous and sympathetic. Chaucer himself seems to find it difficult to relate the terrible end of the story, constantly referring to the 'books' or the 'story' as if he is being forced to record the event of her betrayal. He refuses to chide her 'forther than the storye wol devyse', and expresses 'pite' and 'routhe'. At the

end of the poem (V.1828 ff.) the epithet *villana* ('wicked', 'ill-bred') applied to her by Boccaccio is removed. Throughout the poem his tone has been consistently sympathetic, and indeed defensive (cf. II.666–79), rather as if he is aware of the anti-feminist interpretation, which had been and could be put upon her subsequent behaviour. At the same time one or two remarks seem to be deliberately designed to give an air of mystery or uncertainty. He says, for instance, that he does not know whether she had children or not, although he knew that Boccaccio had said that she did not have any. There are certain aspects of her personality to which he gives particular emphasis. Her fearfulness, is stressed at the moment she is first introduced (the Trojans' desire for vengeance is made stronger than in Boccaccio, so that 'of hire lif she was ful sore in drede . . . | For bothe a widewe was she and allone.' We are reminded of it throughout, and near the end of the story (V.1023 ff.) as she broods on the pressing words of *Diomede, it is not only 'his grete estat', but the 'perel of the toun' and 'that she was allone and hadde nede | Of frendes help' that are noted as dominant. Consistent with this are her caution and prudence and her concern for her good name (which is constantly stressed). Her steps towards love and its consummation are much more hesitant and uncertain than those of Boccaccio's more sensual heroine.

It is Criseyde herself who comes nearest to a judgement in the lament she gives when she 'falsed' Troilus (V.1054–85). In this remarkable speech, Chaucer has simplified and heightened Benoît's long monologue in which Briseida reproaches herself, selecting some details and investing them with great pathos. What she says has the ring of her own personality—her concern for her 'name', a brief flash of self-justification ('al be I nat the first that dide amys'), her awareness of circumstances ('syn I se ther is no betre way'), and her strong sense of the instability of the world. (For the treatment of her by later writers, see *Troilus and Criseyde*; *The* *Testament of Cresseid*; *Troilus and Cressida*.)

Crisippus. Chrysippus, probably an anti-feminist writer mentioned by St *Jerome, appears in the list of the contents of *Jankyn's (4) book in *The* *Wife* *of Bath's Prologue* (III.677). He is otherwise unknown. It has also been suggested that Chaucer may have had in mind the stoic Chrysippus who is mentioned by Cicero.

CRISOSTOM, see *John (3) Crisostom, Seint*.

criticism of Chaucer I (to the earlier 20th c.). 'No other author has been commented on in English so regularly and extensively over so long a period', says D. S. Brewer. The quality of Chaucer's writing was acknowledged early, and he soon came to occupy a 'canonical' position as the 'father' of English poetry. In the earlier period he is usually associated with *Gower and *Lydgate. The great flood of comments about him is fascinating in what it reveals about changes in emphasis, attitudes, and taste, but it is a very heterogeneous mass of material, ranging from the briefest of comments, some of them apparently offhand remarks, to more carefully thought out pieces. The comments of other creative writers will often have a close relationship to their own work (see e.g. *Blake, *Wordsworth).

In the 15th and early 16th c. we have a series of laudatory statements by English and Scottish writers which frequently single out for praise his eloquence and rhetorical skill.

As his work and the historical context in which it was produced gradually receded into the past, his language became increasingly difficult for readers (in spite of the lists of 'hard words' in editions), and is often noted as 'ancient'. Similarly his metre (see *versification) became unfamiliar, because of changes in pronunciation, and was thought to be limping. Cultural and social changes also had an effect. It is arguable that Chaucer (who certainly satirized the vices of the clergy) may have had some sympathy for some of the early Lollard criticisms of the ecclesiastical establishment, but in the 16th c. and later we find him firmly enrolled as a proto-Protestant. In the 16th c. there seems to be a preference for his courtly and aristocratic works. The poet's moral aspects rather than his comic tales are emphasized, and his 'bawdiness' becomes a problem. As early as 1591, Sir John Harington defends his translation of Ariosto against those who would condemn him but 'admire our Chawcer, who both in words and

sence incurreth far more the reprehension of flat scurrilitie . . . not onely in his millers tale, but in the good wife of Bathes tale, and many more, in which only the decorum he keepes is that excuseth it and maketh it more tolerable'. Comments in the 16th and 17th c. are usually brief, usually laudatory, though sometimes apologetic or defensive, but of considerable interest (see *Beaumont; *Brathwait; *Harvey; *Sidney; *Spenser). In 1700 appeared Dryden's *Fables, Ancient and Modern*, the preface to which was by far the most sophisticated and extended criticism of Chaucer to date, and which still remains impressive. It is sympathetic and independent. *Dryden compares Chaucer with Ovid, and defends him against the Latin poet. He writes with spirit and vigour, and clearly with fellow feeling ('I found I had a soul congenial to his'). Yet he was uneasy with ribaldry, and his sense of decorum was much stricter than Chaucer's, who 'sometimes mingles trivial things with those of greater moment'. He has problems with the metre, deciding that Chaucer's verse is not harmonious but was thought musical in his day. He follows many of the older views: Chaucer is the father of English poetry, instrumental in the adorning and amplification of the language. However, some of the qualities he singles out are not so traditional. Chaucer followed nature closely, and his work has a certain realism. He points out that Boccaccio and Chaucer wrote 'novels' (i.e. short stories). He is interested in *characters. Chaucer was 'a man of a wonderful comprehensive nature' who created a variety of characters, all differentiated. He sums this up in the famous phrase 'here is God's plenty'.

The influence of Dryden remains strong throughout the 18th c. Chaucer is praised as 'a diligent observer of nature', and for his characterization. The great revival of interest in medieval literature in the second half of the century brought even more sympathetic and more informed accounts of Chaucer's work. Thomas *Warton, for instance, in his *History of English Poetry* (1774–81) remarks that he was 'a universal reader', and that while 'it is certain that Chaucer abounds in classical allusions . . . his poetry is not formed on the ancient models'. An impressive foretaste of the scholarship of the 19th c. is found in *Tyrwhitt's edition of *The *Canterbury Tales* (1775–8) (see also *Gray).

The Romantic period produces some interesting criticism of Chaucer (see especially *Wordsworth; *Blake; *Godwin; *Hazlitt; *Hunt). There is a characteristic interest in imagination, individuality, feeling, and sincerity. There is a greater emphasis on popular elements in Chaucer's style, but sometimes a feeling that his writing lacks mystery and grandeur. A liking for simplicity of style may sometimes lead to a dislike of *rhetoric, and a misunderstanding of its nature and functions. Simplicity is sometimes associated with an essential Englishness, and in the 19th c. Chaucer becomes pre-eminently the poet of the English people.

Chaucer criticism in the middle and later 19th c. is diverse and various, showing both a clear continuity with the past and its own newer interests. It sometimes has the rich, splendid, and colourful quality of Victorian medievalism. It can sometimes now seem rather over emotional, or over gentlemanly, but at its best it is humane and sympathetic, conveying both enthusiasm and pleasure. The century saw great advances in Chaucerian scholarship and in the understanding of ME texts and of medieval literature in general, and some of this begins to filter through to the literary critics. They were (as in the previous century) writers and men of letters, both English (see *Arnold), and now American (see *Emerson). They were later joined by academic critics, professors and teachers in the new schools of English. The qualities of Chaucer which are most often stressed are his humanity and his humour, his realism (and sometimes his rationalism). He is often 'genial', and sometimes 'childlike'. The vividness of his descriptions, the dramatic quality of his work, and its likeness to the novel are often commented on. There is a growing interest in his *irony.

The same interests continue into the earlier 20th c. The comments of writers and men of letters are usually brief but often illuminating (see *Huxley, *Chesterton, and especially *Woolf), but increasingly the mass of the criticism is produced by academics. There is by now a notable and well-established American tradition of Chaucer scholarship and criticism. In England, the wide-ranging W. P. *Ker produced criticism of medieval literature which was both learned and humane. The critic William Empson, while not a professional

medievalist or Chaucerian, made a typically original and suggestive contribution on the 'ambiguity' of Chaucer (1930). Already something of the variety and diversity of later Chaucer criticism is beginning to appear.

Brewer (1978); (contains extensive extracts from critics up to 1933); Spurgeon (1925).

criticism of Chaucer II: since 1930. The year 1933 can be taken, conveniently if rather arbitrarily, as the date when 'modern' criticism of Chaucer came into being. It was the date of publication of the edition of Chaucer's *Complete Works* by F. N. Robinson: this was the edition almost universally used for citation by scholars and critics in subsequent years, its place being taken by Robinson's second edition when it came out in 1957, and by the 'third' (the *Riverside Chaucer*, edited by L. D. Benson) in 1987.

The view of Chaucer's writings that prevailed in the 1930s was fundamentally that inherited from *Dryden and *Arnold. It was the neo-classical view of Chaucer as a great and primarily comic realist, a portrayer of general human nature, and an expert delineator of character. The work of J. M. Manly (1926) on the historical actuality of Chaucer's pilgrims, and on the real-life models that Chaucer might have used, had been the classic exposition of this fallacy, fulfilling in its way the 19th-c. dream of a dramatic realism so close to life as to be almost indistinguishable from it. Reinforced by the still-persuasive reading by G. L. *Kittredge (1913) of the *Canterbury Tales* as principally governed by the 'dramatic principle' (the tales exist to characterize their tellers), and of *Troilus and Criseyde* as a kind of psychological novel, the idea of Chaucer as the supreme poet of realism persisted and still persists as a dominant approach to his writing. The full-length study of the *Canterbury Tales* by W. W. Lawrence (1950) is a sober reading of the *Tales* in terms of dramatic realism; the study of the *Tales* by R. M. Lumiansky (1955) is a less sober version of the same, in which few constraints are placed upon the fantasizing, outward into the tales, of the pilgrimage drama and the pilgrims' characters; C. A. Owen (1977) shows, in an astute reading of individual tales, the residual strength of the tradition. The classic study of *Troilus and Criseyde* in

C. S. Lewis's *The Allegory of Love* (1936), though framed in the context of a study of a literary tradition, accepts as given that the dominant interest of the poem is in the psychologically realistic depiction of the three main characters.

A particular temptation in the 'dramatic' reading of the *Canterbury Tales*, the excesses of which are well analysed in the narrative-stylistic study of C. D. Benson (1986), is the tendency to read individual tales not just as expressions of the character of the pilgrim-narrator, but as indications of the speaker's inadequacy. Tales that are in some way unsatisfactory to the modern reader, by reason of their apparent endorsement of opinions that such a reader finds alien, can thus be 'ironized', their unsatisfactoriness, whether it has to do with opinions on war, women or Jews, blamed on their narrators, and Chaucer recruited to good modern causes. Much writing on the religious tales, especially the Prioress's Tale, takes this line, and Terry Jones's book on the Knight (1980) is a lively and idiosyncratic example of the general tendency.

More important, however, in the history of modern Chaucer criticism has been the New Criticism. Developed in the 1930s, partly in response to the erosion of that older community of shared values that was assumed in neo-classical reading, the New Criticism takes as its basic assumption that literary works are structures in which meaning is embodied in local detail and texture of style and in larger kinds of formal patterning as much as in traditional representational content. The first visitation of the New Criticism upon Chaucer, and still its masterpiece, is the study by Muscatine (1957), whose account of the blending and conflict of 'bourgeois' and courtly stylistic techniques in Chaucer's poetry seems to demonstrate just that quality of unresolved dialectic that late 20th-c. readers specially desire in poetry. Studies of Chaucer by Payne (1963) and Jordan (1967) work according to similar principles of stylistic and structural analysis, though to somewhat different effect, while Howard (1976) and David (1976) attempt a combination of 'dramatic' and 'new critical' readings.

A particular development has been the elucidation of the role of the Chaucerian 'narrator' in creating the ambiguities and multiple meanings that are the stock-in-trade of the New Criticism. The most influential work in this field has been that of Donaldson (1954, 1958), whose analysis of the fallible first-person narrator has been enthusiastically taken up, whether in relation to 'Chaucer the dreamer' in the dream-poems, 'Chaucer the narrator' in *Troilus*, or 'Chaucer the pilgrim' in the *Canterbury Tales*. The direction of such work has often been towards a simplification of Donaldson's subtleties, and particularly the substitution of a rather rigidly conceived persona for the unnamable author. But later writers, such as Lawton (1986) and Leicester (1990), working with postmodern concepts of the 'author', have been able to develop more sophisticated models for the understanding of the role of Chaucer's first-person narrators.

At some polar extreme from the New Criticism stands the so-called 'Historical Criticism' of Robertson (1962) and his followers, which was influential in North America during the 1960s and 1970s. The claim of the Historical Criticism was, not unreasonably, that medieval poetry should be understood in the context of medieval rules and conventions of interpretation. In practice, this meant the imposition upon Chaucer of a dogmatically allegorical reading in accordance with Augustinian doctrine of Charity and Cupidity. Much that needed to be understood was revealed in this process, particularly in relation to the significance of biblical allusion in Chaucer, but the general approach has come to seem both doctrinaire in its techniques and monolithically rigid in its assumptions. Nevertheless, it provides still the momentum for full-length studies of *Troilus* by Wood (1984) and Fleming (1990). The modified 'historical' criticism of Allen (1982) and Minnis (1984), who exploit a range of sources for medieval critical theory much wider than the biblical exegesis almost exclusively used by Robertson, has greater flexibility, and these scholars are aware, or try to be, that medieval academic theories concerning the interpretation of literature are not historical precepts for the interpretation of particular literary works.

The influence of the Historical Criticism was largely confined to North America. England had its own kind of dogmatic moralism, inspired by F. R. Leavis, in which the serious moral business of Chaucer's poetry as a 'criticism of life' was proclaimed, as in books by Speirs (1951), Whittock (1968), and Robinson (1972). But Chaucer criticism in England has tended to work more within the tradition of humane eclecticism most fully and richly represented by C. S. Lewis, and to have at the same time a particular regard for the social and cultural and literary-historical contexts in which his writing can be placed. Brewer (e.g. 1984) has been prolific in this English tradition, while Burrow (1971) and Kean (1972) have concentrated on Chaucer's position at the centre of a web of formal and stylistic practices, Salter (1983) on his cultural and especially his European inheritance, and Mann (1973), in a classic study, on the miracle that Chaucer worked in the *General Prologue* upon the traditional materials of estates satire. It is from America, however, that has come the fullest account of the context of Chaucer's poetry in the pictorial traditions and images of his day (Kolve 1984).

Chaucer criticism has begun in recent years to be responsive to the ferment of change and innovation in modern theories of literary interpretation. In this ferment, the cult of ambiguity, always something of a short-term tactic in the New Criticism, gives way to the assertion of indeterminacy of meaning as a hermeneutic principle. Ferster (1985), taking her cue from the German phenomenologists, argues for an interest in interpretation as a persistent theme in Chaucer's poetry, and for the uninterpretability of his poetry except in terms of a more or less subjective construction of meaning. Sklute (1984) takes as his theme the inconclusive and open-ended nature of Chaucer's poems, which he relates to 14th-c. debates about the referentiality of language, the potential of language, that is, to represent reality in any but a partial and subjective manner. (Burnley (1979), by contrast, sees the possibility of developing an architectonics of Chaucer's language which will make meanings more objectively recoverable.) The surprising juxtapositions and disjunctions of Chaucer's poetry, its bringing together of the popular and the courtly, the sacred and the obscene, have been examined by Kendrick (1988) and Ganim (1990) in terms of 'play' and 'theatricality': both writers derive much from the ideas of Bakhtin. Jordan (1987) has attempted a reading of Chaucer in the light of structuralist and post-structuralist theories of narrative, and there have been tentative

moves towards a deconstruction of whatever of his poetry Chaucer himself left undeconstructed.

On a different plane of significance, the evident need for a more sophisticated account of the relation of Chaucer's poetry to the political, social, and economic realities of his day, more sophisticated, that is, than the simple neo-classical model of 'reflectionism' (literature 'reflects' historical reality), has produced some important studies. The conflicts between social groups, the shifting nature of individual identity within those groups, the disruptive effects of social and economic change, and the conflicts within Chaucer's representation of this rapidly changing world, are the subject matter of books by Aers (1980, 1986, 1988) and Patterson (1987, 1991). Strohm (1989), meanwhile, writes a 'social biography', in which Chaucer's own station in life, his career, and his political affinities, are written into the conflicts and conciliations of his poetry. The essays in the collection edited by Patterson (1990) show the influence of Renaissance 'New Historicism' in the manner in which they attempt to picture Chaucer's poetry as embedded in the political, social, and economic practices of his time.

Finally, one of the richest veins in Chaucer criticism has been that opened up by feminist readers and critics. There are a few, such as Delany (1983), who see Chaucer writing cleverly about women but working mostly within the constraints of a male-dominated and generally misogynistic society and official culture. Others, such as Kiser (1983), in her account of the *Legend of Good Women*, find both a representation and a critique of that society and culture, and some see in Chaucer a kind of proto-feminist. Mann (1991) gives a measured account of Chaucer's manipulations of the anti-feminist tradition, while Dinshaw (1989) considers that Chaucer, though he cannot stand outside the masculine discourse through which his world is construed, yet gives unusually full recognition to alternative feminine viewpoints.   [DP]

Aers (1980, 1986, 1988); J. B. Allen (1982); C. D. Benson (1986); Brewer (1984); Burnley (1979); Burrow (1971); David (1976); Delany (1983); Dinshaw (1989); E. T. Donaldson (1954, 1958); Ferster (1985); Fleming (1990); Ganim (1990); Howard (1976); T. Jones (1980); Jordan

Crusades

(1967, 1987); Kean (1972); Kendrick (1988); Kiser (1983); Kittredge (1915); Kolve (1984); Lawrence (1950); Lawton (1986); Leicester (1990); C. S. Lewis (1936); Lumiansky (1955); Manly (1926); Mann (1973, 1991); Minnis (1984); Muscatine (1977); C. A. Owen (1977); Patterson (1987, 1990, 1991); Payne (1963); Robertson (1962); Robinson (1972); Salter (1983); Sklute (1984); Speirs (1951); Strohm (1989); Whittock (1968); Wood (1984).

Crusades, military expeditions proclaimed by the Pope against the enemies of Christendom. The name comes from the cross which was worn as an emblem. The most famous and prestigious crusades were those against the Muslims in the Holy Land. Jerusalem was taken in the First Crusade (1099), and the Latin kingdom of Jerusalem was established. In 1187 Saladin captured the city of Jerusalem, and subsequent expeditions, though sometimes marked by great feats of arms, were not military successes. There were crusades against the Muslims in Spain, and against the pagans along the Baltic. Crusading was involved with the ideals of *chivalry and with religion and *pilgrimage. Some crusaders took vows based on those of pilgrims, and were given indulgences. As in the case of pilgrimages, no doubt people participated for a variety of reasons. There were some adventurers, and booty could sometimes be found (though not as easily as on the battlefields of France), but the usual motives seem to be to acquire honour and merit, both secular and religious.

Chaucer's supreme crusader is the *Knight, whose campaigns are listed in his portrait in the *General Prologue (I.43–78). He has had crusading experience in three areas—in Spain, the Mediterranean, and Prussia (*Pruce). In Spain he fought in Granada (*Gernade) and at the siege of Algeciras (*Algezir) in 1344—like *Henry of Grosmont, the earl of Salisbury, and other Englishmen. Around the Mediterranean, there were a series of expeditions (there was no full-scale crusade in the Holy Land in this period). The Knight was at *Alisaundre, the Alexandrian crusade of 1365 led by Peter of Cyprus (*Petro (2) kyng of Cipre), who also led the attacks on Antalya (*Satalye) in southern Turkey (1361) and on Ayash (*Lyeys) near Antioch (1367), at which a number of English knights were present. There were continuous crusading expeditions in Prussia in the 14th c. These were the *reisen* (expeditions or forays) into Lithuania (*Lettow) and Russia (*Ruce) by the Order of the Teutonic Knights, usually led by the Grand Master (the famous Winrich von Kniprode in the second half of the 14th c.) or his Marshal. In these arduous campaigns in the 'wilderness' across the river Memel the Teutonic Knights encouraged the participation of Western knights. These foreign knights were martial pilgrims who could not expect material gain in terms of lands or booty, but did gain military experience and glory, and were lavishly entertained by the Teutonic Knights. The famous *Eretisch* (table of honour) was a great feast usually held at the end of a *reise*, to which distinguished foreign visitors were invited as a sign of honour, and at the end were given special badges with the motto 'Honneur vainc tout! [honour conquers all]'. It may be that the statement that the Knight 'hadde the bord bigonne (i.e. sat in the place of honour) | Aboven alle nacions in Pruce' is a reference to this. Certainly, English nobles frequently took part in the campaigns: among the more illustrious were Henry of Grosmont, Henry Bolingbroke (the future *Henry IV), and the Beauchamps of Warwick.

No single Englishman has been discovered who took part in all of the Knight's campaigns, but Englishmen were to be found on all of them. It seems that Chaucer has taken what was not uncommon military experience for noblemen of the time and presented it in a heightened form. At the Scrope-Grosvenor trial of 1386 at which Chaucer was a witness, no less than four out of the six families involved had had crusading experience. The Scropes in particular had a proud crusading record. Members of the family had fought in Prussia, and at Alexandria and 'Satalye' with Peter of Cyprus. It has been suggested that their collective experience could have offered the model for Chaucer's Knight. He may also have been thinking of one of the 'flowers of chivalry', like Henry of Grosmont, the father of the Duchess Blanche.

Christiansen (1980); Keen (1983); Mayer (1972); Riley-Smith (1987).

Cuckoo and the Nightingale, The, a poem now attributed to Sir John *Clanvowe. It was influenced by

Chaucer's early poems, chiefly *The Parliament of Fowls,* probably some version of *The Knight's Tale* and possibly the F Prologue to *The Legend of Good Women*; this would point to a composition date after 1386. The poem is preserved in five manuscripts along with genuine works of Chaucer, Gower, Lydgate, and Hoccleve, and was printed in *Thynne's 1532 edition of Chaucer; until the present century it was regarded as a work of Chaucer.   [AH]

   (ed.) Scattergood (1975).

Cupide, Cupido, Cupid, the son of *Venus and the god of *love. In the Middle Ages, the Roman winged boy-god is not depicted as a naked child. In the illustrations to the *Roman de la Rose* he is shown as a beautiful youth, winged, wearing splendid garments and a crown or wreath. It is likely that Chaucer visualized him in this way. He appears in the two descriptions of the temple of Venus, with details taken from the *Roman,* and from the *Teseida* of *Boccaccio. In *The *Parliament of Fowls* (211–17) Cupid 'our lord' is seen under a tree beside a spring. In the *Roman de la Rose* this is the 'fontaine d'amors' ('the Welle of Love', *Rom* 1627), where Cupid is forging and filing his arrows, and Wille (Desire) his daughter is tempering the heads. In *The *Knight's Tale* (I.1963–6) he stands before Venus. He has two wings on his shoulders, and carries a bow with arrows 'brighte and kene'. He is blind 'as it is often seene'. Evidently, Cupid's blindness was proverbial by Chaucer's day (see *HF* 137–8; *Tr* III.1808).

   In the Prologue to *The *Legend of Good Women* (226–40) Chaucer sees Cupid dressed in silk, embroidered with green sprays, his golden hair crowned with a sun. He holds two fiery darts 'as the gledes rede'. He has wings like an angel, and looks sternly on the poet, whose heart turns cold, and who remarks that although men say that he is blind, it seems that he can see very well. This god of love has awesome power, like *Dante's 'lord of terrible aspect'. The presumptuous young Troilus feels his wrath: the god of love looks angrily on him, and shows that 'his bowe has naught broken; | For sodeynly he hitte hym atte fulle' (*Tr* I.206–10). The allusive way in which yet another iconographic detail is used here does not obscure the fierceness of the passion that the god seems to embody. Even the detail in *The Legend of Good Women* of Cupid spreading his wings like an *angel—'so aungelyke his wynges saugh I sprede' (236)—suggests that he is a spiritual force. And the familiar 'Cupide, oure lord' (*PF* 212) suggests that all mankind is subject to the power of *love.

   Panofsky (1939), ch. 4.

curteisie and the adjective *curteis,* both of French origin, and derived ultimately from the word 'court', are used in various senses in Chaucer. They are usually glossed respectively as 'courtly conduct, courtliness, civility; graciousness', and 'courteous, chivalrous; gracious', but the concept of 'courtesy' is a wide one which covers a range from table manners (as expounded in the 'courtesy books', manuals of instruction found from the 12th to the 16th c.) to spiritual grace. The words and ideas which cluster around it in Chaucer include *debonaire* ('gracious; meek; kind, gentle, courteous'), *debonairetee* ('graciousness, kindness'); *benygne* ('gracious, kind, gentle, considerate'), *benignyte* ('goodness, graciousness'); *pite*; and *large* ('liberal, generous'), with *largesse* ('generosity'). Thus Prudence describes her lord as 'debonaire and meeke, large, curteys' (VII.1757).

   Most obviously, however, it often overlaps with *gentilesse.* 'Courtesy' represents the characteristic values and virtues of the knight, and like *chivalry it is regularly opposed to *vilenie* or churlishness. But it is also used in more general senses. It can denote a nobility of behaviour, with values which are both personal and social. It is closely linked with *love (and especially with that variety sometimes called *courtly love). In the world of Guillaume de Lorris's *Roman de la Rose* only the *courtois* can become Love's vassals. There the God of Love instructs the lover in the necessary courteous behaviour, rather in the manner of a 'courtesy book' (he must dress neatly, and keep his nails clean, etc.). The injunction to be cheerful at all times is not an easy one for a lover, since his emotions make him into a solitary figure, subject to melancholy. But the sufferings which love imposes bring an ennobling and virtuous *curteisie*—in *Troilus and Criseyde* Love makes the hearts of her servants 'worthy', 'corteys . . . fresshe and benigne' (III.26). All the characteristics of *curteisie* which pierced the heart of the lover are found in the courtly lady. In *The *Book of the Duchess* (850–2) the lover remembers how his lady looked 'so debonairly', and spoke in so goodly and friendly a manner.

Courtesy (like *gentilesse*) may have undertones which belong less to social or courtly life than to religion. This is not surprising in an age in which the exemplars of chivalry include not only Lancelot but the Grail heroes Galahad and Percival. In *Pearl* the Virgin *Mary is called 'quene of cortaysye'; courtesy, says one 'courtesy book' came down from heaven when Gabriel greeted our Lady. The *Parson refers to 'the curteis Lord Jhesu Crist' (X.245). Like *gentilesse,* courtesy was sometimes thought not to be dependent on noble birth, though it was regarded as the ideal to be expected of those of noble birth. This idea lived on beyond the Middle Ages—as Milton's Lady says to Comus: 'honest-offered courtesy . . . oft is sooner found in lowly sheds | With smoky rafters than in tap'stry halls | And courts of princes, where it first was named | And yet is most pretended'.

In the *General Prologue* the *Knight 'loved chivalrie, | Trouthe and honour, fredom and curteisie' (I.45–6), and the *Squire (as befitted a lover) was 'curteis', humble, and willing to serve (I.99). However, the 'curteisie' on which the *Prioress set her pleasure (I.132) is not the high chivalric or courtly virtue, but the exquisite manners associated with the court (which she took pains to imitate; I.139–40). Different again is the 'curteisie' of the *Friar. Although he did not regard it as respectable to bother with sick lepers, wherever there might be any profit, 'curteis he was and lowely of servyse' (I.250), perhaps a deliberately ironic echo of the description of the Squire. These different but interrelated strands are found throughout the *Canterbury Tales. Chaucer seems more ready to use *curteis* or *curteisie* in an ironic way than *gentil* or *gentilesse*. Friars with their wheedling ways are always targets. There is a deliberate repetition in The *Summoner's Tale: the friar addresses Thomas 'curteisly and softe' (III.1771), and a few lines later rises to greet the wife 'ful curteisly' (III.1802)—and embraces and kisses her 'sweetly'. There is an excellent ironic use in The Reeve's Tale, where the Miller's stealing increases: 'for therbiforn he stal but curteisly, | But now he was a theef outrageously' (I.3997–8). In The Miller's Tale the language of high 'courtesy' is placed in more earthy surroundings: 'do wey youre

handes, for youre curteisye!' exclaims Alison (I.3287) to the importunate Nicholas. And the parish clerk Absolon, who enjoyed censing the wives of the parish, would not take an offering from them—'for curteisie, he seyde, he wolde noon' (I.3351). In the mock-heroic description of Chauntecleer's beloved hen, 'faire damoysele Pertelote' we find the phrase 'curteys she was, discreet, and debonaire' (VII.2871).

Courtesy in behaviour and manners is often alluded to (not always with total seriousness). The Prioress's notable presence has an effect on the Host, who speaks to her 'as curteisly as it had been a mayde' (VII.446). The drunken Miller would not doff his hood or hat, 'ne abyde no man for his curteisie' (I.3123), but shouts—unlike the dreamer in The *Book of the Duchess* who stands quietly before the Man in Black, doffs his hood, and greats him 'debonayrly, and nothyng lowde' (515–18). The strange Knight in The Squire's Tale (V.93–7) greets the assembled nobles with greater 'reverence and obeisaunce' than *Gawayn, with his olde curteisye', a famous exemplar of courtesy. The courtly virtue appears also as an allegorical figure (in Rom, PF, Pity).

The truly courteous figures in Chaucer's narratives are an interesting group. There is, for example, the lover *Troilus, with his 'gentil' heart. He is always generous, kind, and attentive to his lady's honour. He convincingly provides the answer to her first question about him—can he well speak of love? (II.503). He can maintain a 'glad cheer' on public occasions even when he is under great emotional strain. When Criseyde leaves for the Greek camp, Troilus 'in wyse of curteysie' accompanies her with a troop of knights (V.64–6). On one rare occasion (and it seems to be a private one) his control breaks and extreme anguish causes him to forget his courtesy. At the moment when his sister *Cassandra gives the (correct) interpretation of his prophetic dream, confirming his deepest fears, he bursts out: 'thow seyst nat soth . . . Thow sorceresse, | With al thy false goost of prophecye!' (V.1519 ff.). In *Custance 'the mirror of all courtesy' (II.166) the virtue shows itself as a kind of inner grace—she is 'ful of benygnytee' (II.446; cf. 615). This is a quality she shares with Griselda (IV.411, 554, 929, 1025). (Perhaps the phrase in *SqT* (V.486) 'verray wommanly benignytee' suggests that this aspect of courtesy, like 'pite' is especially associated with women. Unlike Constance, who is an emperor's daughter, Griselda is a poor peasant, whose innate courtesy is contrasted with the behaviour of her husband, who is introduced at the beginning of the tale as 'ful of honour and of curteisye' (IV.74). She demonstrates the truth of the view that true courtesy 'oft is sooner found in lowly sheds | With smoky rafters'.

Nicholls (1983); Zumthor (1972), 466–72.

Custance. Constance, the heroine of The *Man of Law's Tale.

CUTBERD, SEINT, St Cuthbert (d. 687), bishop of Lindisfarne, whose shrine was in Durham Cathedral, but who was a popular saint throughout England. He appears only in an oath in The *Reeve's Tale (I.4127), perhaps appropriately placed in the mouth of a northern clerk.

D

DAFYDD AP GWILYM (b. *c*.1320), the Welsh poet, one of the finest writers of the later Middle Ages and an older contemporary of Chaucer, with whom he has sometimes been compared. His poems, written with immense technical skill, cover a wide range of subjects. The most famous are concerned with nature and love—and adventures in love—but he also wrote religious poems. Sometimes, like Chaucer, he presents himself in a self-deprecating and ironic way. Sadly, there is no evidence (and almost certainly no likelihood) that either poet knew the work of the other.

(ed. and trans.) Bromwich (1985); Knight (1989).

Dalida, Delilah, the woman loved by Samson (*Sampson) in the Old Testament (Judges 16), who betrayed him to his enemies by having his hair, in which his strength lay, cut off while he slept. She is referred to in The *Monk's Tale (VII.2063 ff.), The *Book of the Duchess (738), and in Against *Women Unconstant (16), where she is linked with *Criseyde and *Candace.

Damascien, listed as one of the authorities on *medicine known to the *Physician (I.433). John of Damascus (d. *c*.749) was an important Eastern theologian, but the name was also given to works by Arabic physicians, such as *Serapion.

DAMASIE, SEINT, Pope Damasus I (d. 384), who commissioned St *Jerome to revise the Latin text of the Bible. A quotation attributed to him is used by the *Parson (X.788).

Damyan, the squire who falls in love with May in The *Merchant's Tale.

Damyssene (adj. 'of Damascus'). According to the *Monk, Adam was made by God's own finger 'in the feeld of Damyssene' (VII.2007), i.e. where Damascus later stood. This idea is found in a number of medieval works.

Danao, Danaus, in Greek mythology the brother of Aegyptus (*Egiste). Danaus had fifty daughters and Aegyptus fifty sons. Because of a quarrel between the brothers Danaus and his daughters fled to Argos (*Arge). The sons of Aegyptus pursued them and married them, but Danaus ordered his daughters to kill their husbands on their wedding night. They did so, except for Hypermnestra (*Ypermistra). In his version of her story in The *Legend of Good Women Chaucer has reversed the two brothers, making Danaus the one who 'many a sone hath of his body wonne', and the father of Lynceus (*Lyno). The source of the error is not known. It may possibly have come from some commentary on Ovid.

dance. In the Middle Ages there were many kinds of dances, from the antics of jugglers, tumblers, and dancing bears to dances with more solemn movements which underlie images of the dance as the harmony of heaven, the dance of the angels and the heavenly hosts. There were 'professional' dances, done by paid performers for entertainment, and 'social' dances in which anyone might join. These were found at all levels of society, although, as usual we know much more about the pastimes at the 'courtly' end of the scale. In some parts of Europe there were dances in churches, and some ecstatic religious dancing. There were dance mimes and dancing games. Dance was always associated with *music, and very often with song (see *carole).

Chaucer does not allude to the whole range of medieval dancing, but his references are frequent and various. Dancing is associated with festivals and festivities (and jousts, I.2486): 'there feste they, there daunce they and synge' (*LGW* 2157; cf.

1269, 2255). It is a joyous scene in both art and literature. In The *Romaunt of the Rose (759 ff.) in the middle of a *carole* Mirth has set two young damsels, clad only in kirtles, who danced 'queyntely'. One would come 'al pryvyly' towards the other, and when they were almost together, they 'threw together their mouths', so that it seemed as if they were constantly kissing. Dancing is associated with spring, with May and Maying. In *Troilus and Criseyde*, Pandarus says to Criseyde (II.111–12), 'do wey youre book, rys up, and lat us daunce, | And lat us don to May som observaunce'. The close connection with mirth and joy (and youth) explains why in The *Franklin's Tale dancing is part of the efforts Dorigen's friends make to cheer her up (V.900 ff.). Indeed, dancing is often virtually identified with joy and happiness: in The *Man of Law's Tale the sorrowful Custance 'liste nat to daunce' (II.1048), and the forsaken *Anelida says (214) 'turned is in quakyng al my daunce'. The idea becomes proverbial: 'daunseth he murye [merrily] that is myrtheles?' (*PF* 592).

Dancing takes place at marriage festivities (II.707, IV.1769). At the wedding in The *Merchant's Tale *Venus herself is said to have danced before the bride and all the company with her fire brand in her hand (IV.1727–8). It is usually associated with love and with Venus's children ('dauncen lusty Venus children deere', V.272; ladies dance around the temple of Venus in *PF* 232). Its erotic associations are sometimes noticed by moralists: the *Physician says that dances can be the occasion of flirtations (VI.65); and the *Pardoner (VI.465–7) links them with 'riot' and mentions 'tombesteres [dancing girls] Fetys and smale [elegant and slim]' (477–8). However, there is very little denunciation of dancing in Chaucer.

It is a pastime of courtly ladies; 'I sawgh hyr daunce so comlily, | Carole and synge so swetely' recalls the Man in Black (*BD* 848–9; see also *Tr* V.565; *KnT* I.2201–3). But other women also enjoy dancing: 'wives' do, according to The Shipman's Tale (VII.7, 14); the poor widow in The *Nun's Priest's Tale is still able to dance ('the goute lette [prevented] hire nothyng for to daunce', VII.2840). The *Wife of Bath lists dancing as one of the skills for which women may be desired (III.259), and recalls that when she was young and 'ful of ragerye' she could dance to a small harp (III.457).

But men are not far behind. Dancing is one of the *Squire's skills (I.96), as it is of another squire, *Aurelius in The Franklin's Tale (V.925–30). An energetic style is practised by Absolon in The *Miller's Tale ('in twenty manere koude he trippe and daunce | After the scole of Oxenforde tho, | And with his legges casten to and fro' (I.3328–30)). This may be a reference to a local style of dancing—perhaps even to the Morris dancing for which the area was later famous. The apprentice Perkyn in The *Cook's Tale was also a keen dancer.

Fairies dance, or used to dance, according to the Wife of Bath: 'the *elf-queene, with hir joly compaignye, | Daunced ful ofte in many a grene mede' (III.860–1); and the knight in her Tale sees twenty-four ladies dancing at the edge of a *forest, who then suddenly vanish (III.990–6). And in The Merchant's Tale Pluto and Proserpina and their 'fayerye' dance around the well in the garden (IV.2038–41).

We even find a dancing horse: the magic horse in The Squire's Tale 'bigan to trippe and daunce, | Whan that this knyght leyde hand upon his reyne' (V.312–13). And in that exotic land of *Tartary, the humans do strange kinds of dances ('the forme of daunces | So unkouthe', V.283–4). In The *House of Fame the dreamer sees pipers 'of the Duche tonge' 'lerne love-daunces, sprynges, | Reyes, and these straunge thynges' (1234–6). This may be an allusion to some new fashion; both words, *reyes* (probably of Dutch origin) and *sprynges*, seem to be attested here for the first time. *Reyes* are round dances; *sprynges* presumably sprightly and lively dances (in the 15th c. *spring* had the sense of 'a lively tune').

Not surprisingly, 'dance' is used in a number of metaphorical senses. Chaucer does not refer to the 'Dance of *Death' (in which Death carries off all estates in a processional dance), which was probably not known in England in his day. But he does refer to the 'dance of love' ('loves daunce', *Tr* II.1106; 'th'amorouse daunce', *Tr* IV.1431) and its variant, 'the olde daunce' (I.476; cf. VI.79, *Tr* III.695), Chaucer seems to have been the first to use this expression (which he found in the *Roman de la Rose*) in English. A person's heart can 'dance' for joy (*Tr* II.1304, V.1136).

Stevens (1986); Gougaud (1914); Sahlin (1940).

Dane. Daphne, a nymph, the daughter of Peneus (*Penneus), a river-god, was loved both by the god *Apollo and the mortal Leucippus. Leucippus was killed by the nymphs, but Apollo kept on pursuing her. She was turned by her father into a laurel tree, which became sacred to Apollo. Chaucer read the story in Ovid (*Met.* 1). It is depicted in the temple of *Diana in The *Knight's Tale* (I.2062–4): 'ther saugh I Dane, yturned til a tre'. Troilus refers to the story in his prayer to the gods to assist him in his love: he calls on Phoebus to remember how 'Dane hireselven shette [enclosed] | Under the bark, and laurer wax [became] for drede' (*Tr* III.726–7).

Danyel, Daniel the Old Testament prophet, famous in the Middle Ages as an apocalyptic writer and an authority on *dreams, and as an example of the way in which God cares for his suffering servants. In The *Man of Law's Tale* there is an allusion to his adventure in the lions' den (Daniel 6), which was a common exemplum of God's providential help (II.473–5). He appears in the Monk's story of Nebuchadnezzar (*Nabugonosor, VII.2143 ff.) as the 'wiseste childe' (see *children) who could expound the meaning of the dreams (cf. VII.3128).

DANT(E), DAUNTE. Dante Alighieri (1265–1321) perhaps the greatest of medieval poets, was born in *Florence of an old and propertied family. Little is known of his early life. In 1277 he was betrothed to Gemma Donati, who became his wife (probably *c.*1283). At some point he fell in love with the girl he calls 'Beatrice' (probably Bice Portinari, who became the wife of Simone de' Bardi). When she died in 1290, he was overwhelmed with grief, and turned to the study of philosophy, and (1295) to an active political life.

Florence had been divided by the rivalry of the Guelfs, traditionally the supporters of the power of the Pope in Italy, and the Ghibellines, who supported the German emperor. The Guelf party split into two factions, which came to be called 'Blacks' and 'Whites'. Dante was associated with the 'Whites'. In 1300 he was a Prior—one of the men who held power in the commune. In this office he had to confirm the city's objections to papal interference, and was included in the papal condemnation of the rulers of Florence. In November, Charles of Valois, the brother of the king of France, and an agent of Pope Boniface VIII, entered Florence with an army, enabling the Blacks to seize power. In January 1302 Dante was condemned for financial corruption and for conspiracy against the Pope, first to exile and later to death. He felt bitterly that he had been a victim of injustice, but had to spend the rest of his life as exile, and died at Ravenna.

The exact dating of his works is disputed, but the general pattern of his creative life is clear. His early lyric poems, in the tradition of *courtly love in its Tuscan variety (the *dolce stil nuovo*, or 'sweet new style') were followed by the *Vita Nuova* or 'New Life' (1290–4), a collection of lyrics linked by a prose narrative, which tells the story of his love for Beatrice. Love brings a 'new life', as if in a conversion. Beatrice's beauty is a reflection of divine wisdom and goodness, and she draws her lover's soul heavenward. She reappears as the central figure in the *La *Divina Commedia*.

From the period of exile comes, first, an unfinished Latin treatise *De vulgari eloquentia* (probably 1303–4), a discussion of the role and nature of the vernaculars descended from Latin. They do not have the stability and glory of Latin, but Dante sees the possibility of finding an 'illustrious vernacular' which will be a fit vehicle for poetry. This is followed (1304–8) by the unfinished *Convivio* or 'Banquet', which gives a commentary on three allegorical or philosophical poems. In one he argues that nobility (*gentilezza*) is not based on riches or birth but is a quality implanted in the soul by God (see '*gentilesse'). From 1309 to 1312 comes the *Monarchia*, a Latin treatise on the temporal power of the empire and the papacy, which was condemned by Pope John XXII in 1329. It is not certain when Dante began the writing of his greatest work, *La Divina Commedia* (possibly as early as 1304–8). It seems to have been finished just before his death. This is a work of great complexity and imaginative range, showing an extraordinary variety of register and style, a vividness of simile and metaphor, and scenes of intense pathos and grandeur.

Chaucer names Dante several times. In *The Wife of Bath's Tale* (III.1126) he is described as 'the wise poete of Florence | That highte [was called] Dant', and as 'the grete poete of *Ytaille' in *The Monk's Tale* (VII.2461). In *The Friar's Tale* (III.1520) he is referred to as an authority on hell (as in *HF* 450), and in the Prologue to *The Legend of Good Women* (F 360) he is cited as the author of a remark about envy. These references alone suggest familiarity and admiration: Dante is associated not merely with Italy, but also with Florence; and he is given the honour of being designated by the special title of a '*poet', and described as 'great'.

Dante's influence on Chaucer was considerable, but it manifests itself in ways very different from that of *Boccaccio. Dante does not provide the source for long narrative poems. Those passages in Chaucer which are translations or adaptations are very much briefer. The longest are the 'pitous' story of Ugolino and his children (see *Hugelyn), nicely adapted to its new context in *The Monk's Tale* (VII.2407–62), and the invocation to the Virgin Mary in the *Second Nun's *Prologue* (VIII.36–56), which is based on St Bernard's prayer in *Paradiso*, the third part of the *Commedia*.

Evidence of a reading of Dante is first seen in *The *House of Fame*. It is unlikely that this poem is, as has been suggested, a '*parody' (in a strict sense) of the *Divine Comedy*, but there are some general correspondences: the division into three books, the use of invocations, the dating of the visions, the heavenly journey. Certainly the *Eagle, and the desert in which the dreamer finds himself, seem to be reminiscences of Dante. In addition, there are some close verbal echoes: the invocation at the beginning of Book III is based on that at the beginning of the *Paradiso*. From this time on Dante's influence can be found throughout Chaucer's writing.

It varies in its nature and its extent. In *The *Parliament of Fowls*, for instance, the inscription over the gate which 'speaks' to the dreamer (120–48) is clearly suggested by the inscription in black over the entrance to hell: 'through me men go to the woeful city; through me men go to the eternal sorrow; through me men go among the lost souls . . . abandon every hope, ye who enter' (*Inferno* 3.1ff.). However, that on Chaucer's gateway consists of two contradictory inscriptions in gold and black, suggesting the different fates of lovers rather than the destined one of sinners.

Dante influenced Chaucer's views on some major questions—*Fortune, *love and '*gentilesse' (where the influence of *Convivio* IV can be seen). Chaucer also seems to respond to Dante's poetic, where there is an easy and rapid movement from high to low style, and where no word or image is too common or too homely. The effect seems to have been to liberate Chaucer's own imagination.

Dante's influence may be seen in such diverse matters as the treatment of planetary allusions or the concept of the *Furies as goddesses who both inflict torment and suffer it (from *Inferno* 9). There are many echoes and *allusions. Sometimes Dante will suggest a striking word, phrase, or image. Thus, in *The *Knight's Tale* the phrase 'al the orient laugheth of the light' (I.1494) is Dante's 'rider l'oriente' (Chaucer makes the sun cause this, in a scene of May and love, but perhaps remembers that in *Purgatorio* 1.20 it is caused by Venus); and later, the phrase 'ministre general' used to describe destiny (I.1663) is Dante's 'general ministra' in a discussion of Fortune (*Inferno* 7). Perhaps the bold word 'unsheath' in ''til I my soule out of my breste unshethe' (*Tr* IV.776) was suggested by *Paradiso* 1.20–1, and 'the double sorwe' at the beginning of the poem by the 'doppia tristizia' of Jocasta (*Purgatorio* 22.56). In the fourth book of *Troilus* especially, Chaucer seems to be using echoes of the *Inferno* to intensify the pain and sorrow of his lovers.

Sometimes Chaucer thinks of Dante at a moment of great emotion, as in the lines (1863–5) which introduce the prayer with which he concludes *Troilus and Criseyde* which are taken from the *Paradiso*. At other times, he seems to be thinking of an episode or a moment in Dante and producing his own variation on it. In the invocation to Apollo at the beginning of the third book of *The House of Fame* he says that he will go to the next laurel tree and kiss it—where Dante says that he will crown himself with its leaves. Here at least he does not seem to present himself as a Dantean *vates* or prophet. (See also ***Boccaccio**; ***Guinizelli**, ***Ytaille**.)

(eds.) Foster and Boyde (1976); Petrocchi (1966–7); Simonelli (1966); (trans.) B. Reynolds (1969); Sinclair (1939–46); Wickstead (1903); Bennett (1977); Boitani (1983).

Dardanus

Dardanus, the ancestor of the kings of Troy. 'The yate ... of Dardanus' (*Tr* II.617–18) was one of the gates of the city, through which Troilus makes a triumphal entry.

Dares, Dares Frygius. Dares the Phrygian, a Trojan priest who is mentioned by *Homer (Iliad 5.9), was thought in the Middle Ages to have been the author of an account of the fall of *Troy. This is extant only in a Latin prose version, the *De excidio Troiae historia*, written probably in the 5th or early 6th c. AD. It is possible that there was a version in Greek from the 1st century AD. The story is told from a Trojan viewpoint. Chaucer refers to 'Dares' four times as an authority on the Trojan War (*BD* 1070, *HF* 1467, *Tr* I.146, V.1771). It has been convincingly argued that the 'Dares' which Chaucer used was in fact the *Frigii Daretis Ylias* of *Joseph of Exeter, which was widely known as 'Dares'.
    (ed.) Meister (1873); (trans.) Frazer (1966); Roberts (1970); Root (1917–18).

Daryus (1). Darius III Codomanus (d. 330 BC), the king of Persia overthrown by Alexander (*Alisa(u)ndre; VII.2648). His tomb, reputedly the work of *Appelles, is alluded to by the *Wife of Bath (III.498).

Daryus (2). Darius the Mede (Daniel 5:31–6:28), who overthrew Belshazzar (*Balthasar), is referred to in *The *Monk's Tale* (VII.2237).

daughters, see *families; *children.

Da(u)n, a title of respect (literally 'lord' or 'master', from L. *dominus*). In Chaucer it is used of priests (who were also called 'Sir'), and especially of monks—e.g. the *Monk himself (VII.1929–30), and (with satiric frequency) of Daun John, the monk in *The *Shipman's Tale*: of ancient writers, sages, and heroes, and of ancient gods. Sometimes it is an ironic or comic term of respect (as perhaps in the case of the smith in *MilT* whom 'men cleped daun Gerveys', I.3761, and certainly in the case of 'Daun Burnel the Asse' and 'daun Russell the fox' in *NPT*, VII.3312, 3334).

daunger (n.) and daungerous (adj.) have a variety of senses in Chaucerian English. Only once, it seems, do we find the modern meaning of 'danger' or 'peril' (in the 'daungers' (I.402) which threaten the *Shipman at sea). 'Danger' is one of those words which have changed their meaning considerably. It came into English from French, and derives ultimately from a (hypothetical) late Latin *dominiarium*, from *dominium* 'lordship, sovereignty'. In Chaucer's language, the word can still mean 'power, dominion, control' (I.663, *Rom* 1049). Related to this is the sense of 'resistance' (*withouten daunger*: without objection, freely; *with daunger*: reluctantly, with reluctance (e.g. III.521)). (Similarly, the adjective can mean 'niggardly, stingy', or 'unwilling'.)
    The most distinctive sense of *daunger*, however, is 'disdain, reserve' (and of the adjective 'haughty, disdainful'). This is characteristically used of a lady's attitude to her lover. Thus, in *Anelida and Arcite* the *daunger* of Arcite's new lady 'made him bothe bowe and bende' (186), and in *Troilus and Criseyde* Pandarus pleads with Criseyde 'lat youre daunger sucred [sweetened] ben a lite' (II.384). It is virtually a technical term of *courtly love; the quality which is opposed to mercy and '*pite'. It is found in a variety of contexts: 'Elde [old age] daunteth [overcomes] Daunger at the laste' says Pandarus to Criseyde (*Tr* II.399). More sensitively, the narrator in his prayer or conjuration at the moment of the union of the lovers ('Awey, thow foule daunger and thow feere' (III.1321)) associates it with fear: both are lost at this joyful moment. It is often personified: 'al [although] founde they Daunger for a tyme a lord. | Yet Pitee, thurgh his stronge gentil myght, | Forgaf, and made Mercy passen Ryght [Justice]' (*LGW* 160; see also *PF* 136; *Tr* II.1376). Daunger's most memorable appearance is in the *Roman de la Rose* of Guillaume de Lorris (where his companions are Wicked Tongue, Shame, and Fear). Bialacoil (Fair Welcome) has encouraged the lover to approach his rose, but a dreadful churl, black, hairy, with red eyes (and, in the illustrations, armed with a great club—see Fig. 10) leaps out and frightens Fair Welcome away. In *Jean de Meun's continuation *Pite* overcomes Daunger with a flood of tears.

Daunte, see *Dant(e).

David, Davit, King David in the Old Testament (1 Samuel–1 Kings 2:10 in the Authorized

Version; 1 Kings–3 Kings 2:10 in the Vulgate) is referred to or cited a number of times. There are allusions to events from his life; as the young slayer of the giant Goliath (*Golias, II.934–7), as an example of the way God's grace gives extraordinary strength and courage; of his anger against *Nabal, which was turned away by Abigail (*Abygail, VII.1099). He is cited as 'the prophet David', and as the author of the Psalms. The 'sentences' quoted as his sometimes come from the Psalms (e.g. VII.1301) but sometimes from a different writer altogether.

day, natural, artificial, or vulgar. There are over 800 uses of the word 'day' in Chaucer's writings, and few of them diverge widely from our own. The chief difference concerns the distinction between calendar day and daylight; and there are consequences for the *division* of the day into hours. (1) With *houres equates* or *houres of the clokke*, the astronomer's day of twenty-four hours beginning at midnight or (more usually) midday was appropriate. Chaucer knew both conventions. He calls this the *day naturall*. Little attention was given to defining the precise moments of midnight and noon, or to our distinction between the true Sun and the astronomer's Mean Sun; and time was local time, and not based on a distant standard meridian. (2) *Houres inequales*, unequal hours, were derived as twelfth parts of the *day artificall*, measured from sunrise to sunset. Again, this was not a particularly well-refined concept, but twilight was definitely excluded. (Hours of the night were the twelfth parts of the remaining part of twenty-four hours, and so generally differed from day hours.) (3) The *day vulgar* included daylight as well as morning and evening twilight. Chaucer speaks of the remaining part of the full natural day as the *vulgar nyght*. (See also *astrology and astronomy; *hour.) [JDN]

Deadly Sins, see *Seven Deadly Sins.

death in the Middle Ages was often a more public affair than it is in the modern world. The great plagues of the 14th c. produced some gruesome scenes, and the sight of a public execution was a common one (cf. *MLT* II.645–7). Yet it is a dangerous oversimplification to say that the later Middle Ages were 'obsessed' with death. Nor was there a single medieval attitude to death. The Christian ascetic tradition of the contempt of the world *(contemptus mundi)* produced penitential works which elaborated the idea that the body is the 'food of worms', and this and related 'macabre' topics were given visual expression. But there were other traditions. Attempts to shock the living into repentence by the fear of death and the contemplation of the misery of the human condition were balanced by ideas which emphasized rather the dignity of man as the child of God, or attempted to find consolation and even harmony in the fact of death. People were urged to make careful preparation for it, and to accept it calmly, with faith and hope. In the ideal death scene, which is sometimes depicted in medieval MSS, the dying man lies in his bed attended by a priest holding the crucifix before his eyes, and surrounded by his kinsfolk.

The Church provided rituals for death and patterns of consolation for the dying. Commonly, after a visit by the priest, and the making of a confession and a will, the priest would ring the church bells, and carry the last communion to the dying person, often in a solemn procession with members of the community. After the administration of 'extreme unction' (anointing with oil) and of the last communion, the body was carefully prepared, washed and clothed, and placed on a bier. It sometimes remained in the house for a wake, sometimes it was immediately carried in procession to the church for a funeral mass. Finally it was taken to the place of burial and solemnly interred in a coffin, sometimes of stone, more usually of wood. The rich and powerful might be buried in church, and were commemorated in various ways. In 14th-c. England incised brasses were very common, with the images of priests, knights and their wives, and later, merchants and their wives. Funeral effigies of the important nobility were also common (a famous example is that of the *Black Prince). Sometimes elaborate canopied tombs were constructed.

There were powerful Christian patterns of *consolation. The crucifix held before the dying person's eyes recalled the last sufferings of Christ, who by his death had destroyed death. Death could be seen as the gateway to a new life, as the sleep of those awaiting the resurrection of the body, as the joyous end of the earthly pilgrimage of the soul to its true home in 'Jerusalem celestial'. There was probably a widespread acceptance of death as God's will. After death the dead were still close to the living, who prayed for their souls. Medieval intellectual writers were also able to draw on the literature of the ancient world, where they found shared proverbial material (that death levels all estates, for instance), suggestive attitudes and topics (stoic fortitude, or fame living on after death).

Death is an important theme in Chaucer's work. His narratives produce a variety of deaths, many of them violent. These range from death in battle (in The *Knight's Tale *Arcite, who is destined to die a violent death, is first discovered with his friend *Palamon in a heap of dead bodies on the battlefield (I.1005–14)) to murder (as in The *Pardoner's Tale). We find allusions to the contemporary lynching of Flemings in London (VII.3394–6) and to sudden death by pestilence (VI.661–79). There are many references to the usual practices of burial. The 'herse', a frame for holding lights around the coffin, appears in the Complaint unto *Pity, where the central image is that of Pity 'buried in a heart'. Biers appear in both Christian (VII.625) and ancient contexts (I.2871, 2877, 2900). In *Troilus and Criseyde (IV.1182–3), Troilus, thinking that Criseyde is dead, 'gan hire lymes dresse in swich manere | As men don hem that shal ben layd on beere'. Stories which are set in antiquity sometimes have references to classical funeral practices: to the pyre (in KnT), the funeral urn for the ashes (Tr V.311), or the funeral games (Tr V.304; I.2959–62). Cleopatra has the body of Mark Antony embalmed and enclosed in a magnificent shrine made of rubies and gems, and 'ful . . . of spicerye' (LGW 672–7)—but this sounds like a more exotic version of what might have happened in the Middle Ages. An image in The *Squire's Tale seems to allude to a medieval carved tomb, perhaps with a funeral effigy: 'as in a toumbe is al the faire above, | And under is the corps', (V.518–19). People are carried to the grave with the bell 'clinking' before the corpse (VI.664). Petrarch (*Petrak) is nailed in his 'chest' (i.e. a wooden coffin, IV.29); and the *Wife of Bath's fourth husband is 'in his grave and in his cheste'

(III.502)—he is the one buried beneath the rood beam of the church (496).

There is proverbial material: 'Deeth is an ende of every worldly soore', I.2849; 'Deeth, that wol nat suffre us dwellen heer, | But as it were a twynklyng of an ye, | Hem bothe hath slayn, and alle shul we dye' (IV.36–8); 'deeth manaceth every age, and smyt | In ech estat' (IV.122–6). There are references to popular lore (e.g. PF 179, 343). The *Parson eloquently expands the biblical 'shadow of death' in the Prayer of *Job and speaks of the pains of hell, but does not dwell on the dissolution of the human body. Saints and martyrs achieve a glorious Christian death: in The *Second Nun's Tale. St Cecilia laughs in the face of death, and the young 'clergeoun' of The *Prioress's Tale achieves heavenly glory (in stark contrast to the 'shameful death' meted out to his persecutors). We find classical stories ending in suicide, and that of *Virginia slain by her father to avoid dishonour. The association of love (described as 'quike deth', Tr I.411, 420) and death is found in a number of places—in The *Book of the Duchess, *Troilus and Criseyde (e.g. the deathly swoon of Criseyde in book IV or the despair of Troilus in book V), in the legends of *Cleopatra, and of Pyramus and Thisbe (*Tisbe) who wish to lie together in a single grave (LGW 903).

In The *Pardoner's Tale, Death is described as a 'privee theef', and although his sinister presence is felt throughout the exemplum, he works silently, through men's cupidity, and when his work is done, goes his way 'withouten wordes mo'. Chaucer here exploits the irony latent in the folly of men and the unexpectedness of death. In The Book of the Duchess he seems interested not only in death and how it is to be faced, but in its relationship to love, and in other penumbral states, sleep and melancholy, which seem to parallel or foreshadow it. From early in the poem he establishes patterns of images which suggest both death and sorrow and life and rebirth. When the man in black is encouraged to reveal the story of his love, memory seems to bring some comfort, but at the end he is 'as ded as ston'. The dreamer simply offers a heartfelt expression of human sympathy and pite—'be God; hyt ys routhe'. The need for mankind to accept the unalterable fact of death, which is implicit here is made explicit at the end of

The Knight's Tale. The description of Arcite's death blends grim physiological details ('the pipes of his longes gonne [lungs began] to swelle', etc.) with ironic or joking remarks from the narrator about the approach of death ('fare wel phisik! go ber the man to chirche!'). In this complex scene, at the very moment of death, something of the earlier harmony and friendship is found again, but his final words express a deep sadness: 'What is this world? What asketh men to have? | Now with his love, now in his colde grave | Allone, withouten any compaignye' (I.2777–9). The bringing together of the survivors by Duke Theseus after the passage of 'certain years' with a consolatory speech of a distinctly stoic cast, urging the courageous acceptance of mutability achieves a new kind of harmony which does not forget the 'worldly soore' of death but tries to contain it.

Daniell (1997); A. Murray (1998, 2000); Tristram (1976).

debate, a common form in medieval life, used in scholastic disputations, in the law courts, and as a rhetorical exercise. The literary verse debate, in which stanzas or speeches are given alternately by two disputants (sometimes human, sometimes animal or avian, sometimes opposed abstract qualities) was very popular. It is found in, or underlies, a number of the poems formerly attributed to Chaucer (e.g. *The *Cuckoo and the Nightingale*, *The *Flower and the Leaf*). *The Consolation of Philosophy*, which he translated, owes much to the Platonic dialogue. Chaucer himself does not write a formal debate. There are passages of 'debate'—the 'stryf' between Placebo and Justinus in *The *Merchant's Tale*, the discussion in the council in *Melibee*, or the arguments between the rival suitors in *The *Parliament of Fowls*, and a good example of an 'internal debate' in Criseyde's monologue in *Troilus and Criseyde* (II.703–812), but Chaucer prefers to represent the clash of ideas through contrasting stories, scenes, or images.

Decameron, *Boccaccio's collection of 100 stories in prose, which he found in diverse sources and probably gathered together in the early 1350s. It is set in 1348 when Florence was devastated by the plague. A group of seven young women (Pampinea, Fiammetta, Filomena, Emilia, Lauretta, Neifile,

and Elissa) and three young men (Panfilo, Filostrato, and Dioneo) leave the city for a neighbouring villa and entertain each other by telling stories for ten days (whence the title of the book). Each of them tells one story on each day. Each day one of them is elected leader, to direct the course of the storytelling. The *Decameron* is one of the greatest medieval comic works, and a magnificent example of the art of narrative. There is a mixture of earnest and game, and scepticism and irony are blended with humanity—'to take pity on people in distress is a human quality which every man and woman should possess' are its opening words.

It is likely, as some have claimed, that Chaucer knew the *Decameron*, but it has not been conclusively proved. The *Decameron* provides a number of analogues to the stories of *The *Canterbury Tales*, some of them remote (e.g. 3.4 (*MiLT*), 9.6 (*RvT*), 5.2 (*MLT*)), some rather closer, as *The *Shipman's Tale* (8.1), *The *Merchant's Tale* (7.9), and *The *Franklin's Tale* (10.5). The *Clerk's story of *Griselda is first found as the concluding tale of the *Decameron* (10.10). There are plenty of hypocritical friars, foolish husbands, and independent women, and there are certainly profound similarities in outlook and interests. The topics of *women, *marriage, *love, '*gentilesse' seem to have fascinated both writers.

(ed.) Branca (1951–2); (trans.) McWilliam (1972); N. Thompson (1996).

DECORAT, Decoratus, quaestor in 508, is mentioned in *Boece* (III pr.4:23, 26). Boethius speaks scathingly of him as a parasite and an informer.

Decrees, Book of, the general name for the body of canon law, comprising primarily the *Decretum* put together by *Gratian, and the *Decretals*, but also often covering the later appended books, the *Clementines* and *Sext*. Chaucer's quotations from it (in *Mel* 1404 and *The Parson's Tale*) are readily identifiable. [AH]

ed. Friedberg (1879–81).

Dedalus, Didalus, Daedalus, a legendary craftsman and a descent of Hephaestus or Vulcan, who built the *Labyrinth in Crete for King Minos. The king tried to confine him there, but he made wings for himself and his son Icarus (*Ykarus) and they flew away. Chaucer (who read the story in *Ovid and the *Roman de la Rose) refers to him several times: to his skills in The *Book of the Duchess (570), to his flight in The *House of Fame (919, as he is carried up by the Eagle), and to his maze (HF 1920; Bo III pr.12:156). See also *Domus Dedaly.

Deeth of Blaunche the Duchesse, see *Book of the Duchess.

Defferent, deferent (L. deferens, 'carrying'). The deferent circle (centred on the 'centre defferent') is the circle around which the epicycle is carried, in the standard Ptolemaic explanation of planetary motion. The deferent circle was usually eccentric, that is, its centre was not identical with the Earth's. (See *astrology and astronomy.)

[JDN]

DEGUILLEVILLE, GUILLAUME DE, a 14th-c. French Cistercian monk, the author of a popular allegorical trilogy: the Pelerinaige de la vie humaine or Pilgrimage of Human Life (first redaction 1331, second 1355), the Pelerinaige de l'âme (of the Soul), and the Pelerinaige de Jésus Christ. The first two poems appear in English versions in the 15th c. But before then Chaucer had translated a prayer from the Pelerinaige de la vie humaine as his *ABC.

Deiphebus, Deiphebe, Deiphobos, the third son of Priam, the king of Troy. He is mentioned in The House of Fame (444), and appears as a prominent character in Troilus and Criseyde. He is Troilus's favourite brother (II.1394–8) and Pandarus's great friend (II.1403–4). He generously offers to help Criseyde when Pandarus tells him that she is being persecuted by the false *Poliphete (II.1422 ff.). It is in his house that Criseyde is taken by Pandarus to visit the supposedly sick Troilus. He appears once later at a more bitter moment, when the tunic which he has taken from *Diomede in battle is carried before him as a sign of victory, and Troilus recognizes the brooch on its collar (V.1650–61).

DEYSCORIDES, Dioscorides (fl. c. AD 50–70), a Greek physician who wrote a pharmaceutical book on the medical properties of plants, the Materia medica. He was one of the authorities known to the *Physician (I.430).

Delphyn, Delphinus, the small constellation Dolphin, mentioned in The House of Fame (1006). (See also *astrology and astronomy.) [JDN]

Delphos, Delphi in Greece, which had a famous temple of *Apollo and an oracular shrine, where a priestess gave ecstatic and often obscure replies to the questions put by suppliants. There is a reference to Delphi as the site of Apollo's temple in The *Franklin's Tale (V.1077), and to the oracle in *Troilus and Criseyde (IV.1411).

demande d'amour, a 'love-problem' posed for discussion in courtly conversation and *debate. These were commonly found in medieval love literature in various languages. There were collections of such questions (a later English example is called The Demaundes off Love). Chaucer uses variations of the demande d'amour within his narratives for a variety of literary purposes: to engage the audience, to set it thinking, debating, or analysing, and as a device to indicate the closure of a poem or a section of narrative, to emphasize the theme or question in hand, and to blend it with the movement of the plot. At the end of the first part of The *Knight's Tale, when Palamon is condemned to perpetual imprisonment, but is still able to see Emily, and Arcite is set free, but exiled, so that he cannot see her, the narrator asks: 'Yow loveres axe I now this questioun: | Who hath the worse, Arcite or Palamoun?' A rather different question is put by the queen to the condemned knight in The *Wife of Bath's Tale: 'I grante the lyf, if thou kanst tellen me | What thyng it is that wommen moost desiren' (III.904–5). Yet another example is the question put to the audience at the end of The *Franklin's Tale about the behaviour of the characters: 'Lordynges, this question, thanne, wol I aske now, | Which was the mooste fre [generous, noble], as thynketh yow?' (V.1621–2).

DEMETRIUS, king of Sparta (139–127 BC), to whom the king of the Parthians sent a pair of golden dice in scorn, is mentioned by the *Pardoner (VI.621). Chaucer probably found his story in *John of Salisbury's *Policraticus*. (See also *Stilboun*.)

Demociones daughter, mentioned by *Dorigen in The *Franklin's Tale* (V.1426) as one of those who slew themselves rather than be defouled. She is taken from a list given by St *Jerome to demonstrate the ancient regard for chastity. He says that the virgin daughter of Demotion, prince of the Areopagites, killed herself when her betrothed died rather than marry another.

Demopho(u)n, Demophon, the 'duke of Athens', who was loved by *Phyllis (see The *Legend of Good Women*, 2393–561), but wickedly betrayed her, and she hanged herself in grief. An example of male falseness, he is mentioned in connection with her elsewhere in Chaucer (II.65; *BD* 728; *HF* 388–96; *LGW* F 264).

DENYS, SEINT, St Denis (Dionysius, d. 250), the patron saint of France. His preaching helped to convert Gaul, and he became bishop of Paris, where he was martyred. Over his body and that of his companion martyrs was built the abbey of Saint-Denis, where his remains were preserved, and which later became the burial place of the French kings. His cult spread widely because he was wrongly identified with Dionysius the Areopagite, a 5th-c. Neoplatonist and mystical writer, who claimed to be Dionysius the disciple of St Paul, who was converted at Athens. He appears in an oath by the monk in The Shipman's Tale (VII.151)—appropriately, since the tale is set in the town of Saint-Denis (*Seynt-Denys).

Denmark in the 14th c. was suffering from the commercial competition of the German merchants, who in effect came to dominate the Baltic. In 1397 it became part of a federation of Scandinavian kingdoms. If Chaucer's '*Gootland' (I.408) is Gotland, then the *Shipman would have sailed past; if it is Jutland, then he would have visited Denmark. Otherwise it is mentioned only (by the widely travelled *Wife of Bath) in a phrase indicating the whole extent of the world: 'I was to hym as kynde | As any wyf from Denmark unto *Ynde' (III.824).

Depeford, Deptford, now part of south-east

*London, then a small town about 5 miles from London, just before Greenwich (*Grenewych) on the Dover road. 'Lo Depeford, and it is half-wey pryme! [about 7.30 a.m.]' announces the Host (I.3906) just before the *Reeve begins his tale.

DERBY, see *Henry IV, Henry of Derby.

Dertemouthe, Dartmouth, the port in Devon from which the *Shipman came (I.389). Its estuary afforded a safe harbour for merchant ships, fleets, and pirates. Chaucer visited the town in 1373 on official business, three months after his return from Italy (with which trip the business may be connected). He was sent to deliver a Genoese ship, *La Seinte Marie et Seint George*, which had been placed under arrest there (for some unknown reason), to her master, John de Nigro. Some years earlier John had been transporting goods and men in this ship for a Genoese merchant John de Mari (who accompanied Chaucer on the journey to Italy, and seems to have been acting as an agent for Edward III in hiring Genoese crossbowmen). A prominent merchant acquiring property in Dartmouth at this time was John Hawley (whose brass (1408) is in the church of St Saviour). He was a powerful shipowner and a buccaneer, and one of his ships might well have had something to do with this affair. A possible model for the Shipman has been found in one of his captains, Piers Risseldon, perhaps the Peter Risshenden who was master of a ship called the *Maudelayne* sailing from Dartmouth in the 14th c.
LR 40–2.

DESCHAMPS, EUSTACHE (*c.*1344–1404 or 1405) a French poet, and contemporary of Chaucer. A native of Champagne, he studied at the university of Orléans, entered the royal service in 1368, and became bailiff of Senlis in 1389. Like Chaucer he had a successful administrative career, and travelled widely, sometimes on diplomatic missions. He was a disciple of *Guillaume de Machaut. His own literary output was immense—in lyric, narrative, dramatic poetry, and prose. He wrote the first treatise on poetry in French, the *Art de Dictier* (1392), and a long poem against marriage, the *Miroir de Mariage*. His favoured lyric form was the *ballade, of which he produced over 1,000 examples, but he wrote voluminously in a variety of other lyric forms. He also wrote moral and satirical pieces on the decadence of the world. Many of his poems are filled with personal, autobiographical material, or with his own observations on human follies. The variety of subject matter is matched by a variety of attitude and tone.

Although his allegiance to the French cause was firm, he had some connections with England: he knew the poet *Graunson (who took the English side), and one of his patrons was Wenzel of Luxemburg, himself a poet, the uncle of *Anne of Bohemia. In 1385–6 Sir Lewis *Clifford, Chaucer's friend, brought back from France a poem by Deschamps in praise of the English poet. The balade is a panegyric, with the refrain 'Grant translateur, noble Geoffroy Chaucier'. It characterizes Chaucer's achievements by exempla (he is Socrates, Seneca, Ovid, etc.) and images: Chaucer is an eagle of philosophy (perhaps an allusion to The *House of Fame?), a gardener who has transplanted a rosebush to England (presumably a reference to The *Romaunt of the Rose), an 'earthly god of love in Albion', the lord of the spring of Helicon, a noble poet in whose garden Deschamps would only be a nettle. Chaucer is praised for his brevity of speech and his wisdom. Even allowing for its hyperbole, it is a valuable testimony to Chaucer's literary reputation.

At the end of this ballade, Deschamps asks Chaucer to accept graciously the 'schoolboy works' which he is sending by Clifford. It is not known whether Chaucer ever responded, as he was asked to. Nor is it easy to establish firmly how much of Deschamps's poetry he read or used. It is thought that Chaucer used the *Miroir de Mariage* in The *Wife of Bath's Prologue* and the early part of The *Merchant's Tale*, although much of the anti-feminist material is found elsewhere, and it is not absolutely certain that he had seen this unfinished work. Similarly uncertain is the use of the *Lai de Franchise* (1385) in the Prologue to The *Legend of Good Women*, though the phrase 'erthly god' (95) could well be an echo of 'déesse mondaine'. It has been suggested that this poem might have been one of those brought by Clifford. Deschamps has similar verses to the *Proverbs, but again the material is widespread. Parallels have also been detected in other short poems (*Lak of Stedfastnesse), and

there is a general similarity between Chaucer's poetic epistles and those which Deschamps wrote, either in the form of ballades, or in that of longer and looser intimate verse letters.

(ed.) Queux de Saint-Hilaire and Raynaud (1878–1903); *CH* i. 39–42.

despair; destiny. See *melancholy; *Fortune, *freewill and predestination.

devil. The devil (called Satan or Satanas (Hebrew 'adversary')) was prominent in medieval theological discussion, in penitential and homiletic literature, and in popular religion and folklore. He was the first of the *angels, excelling in beauty (and called Lucifer i.e. 'light-bearer', from the combination of two scriptural verses, Isaiah 14:12 and Luke 10:18), who rebelled against God because of pride, and with his companions fell from heaven to hell. He was the serpent who seduced *Eve, causing the Fall of man and the bringing of death into the world. His power over man was destroyed by Christ, who according to legend, before his Resurrection went down to hell and led the righteous patriarchs of the Old Testament out from Limbo, the place where they had waited since their death. At the Last Judgement, according to the New Testament (Matthew 25:41), the devil and all his followers will depart into eternal fire. In the Middle Ages he presided over the torments of the wicked in hell, and was an active force of evil in the world, working against Christ and his followers. In both of these activities he was assisted by many other demons and malignant spiritual beings.

In Chaucer the devil appears frequently. The usual words for him are *devel* and *fe(e)nd*. He is called variously *Sathan(as), *Lucifer, and *Belial. The references to him reflect both the fear and familiarity with which he was treated in the Middle Ages. Naturally, they cluster most thickly in specifically religious works like The *Parson's Tale, which portrays man's life as a continual struggle against the devil and his wiles. Here he appears as the tempter of Eve (X.330 ff.), and of all men (he even makes a little speech explaining how he goes about it, X.355 ff.). But he trembles when he hears the name of Jesus (X.597–8). Memorable images are used to drive home the moral points: the five fingers of one of the devil's hands illustrate the kinds of Gluttony, those of the other hand illustrate the types of Lechery (X.830, 850 ff.); ire is the devil's furnace (545); flatterers are the devils' enchanters (615) or chaplains (617); scorners are partners with the devil (637); japers are his apes (651). (The *Pardoner also uses this kind of imagery: the rioters 'sacrifice to the devil', in his 'temple', and their entertainers are 'the verray develes officeres' (VI.470–82).) More learnedly, the Parson refers to Belial 'that is, the devel' (and offers an odd etymology for the name, 'withouten juge', X.896–7). St Paul's remark that 'Sathanas transformeth hym in an aungel of light' is applied to wicked priests (894).

Other religious tales use the traditional images and ideas easily and allusively: 'Oure firste foo, the serpent Sathanas' urged the Jews to murder (VII.558 ff.), St Cecilia's martyrdom won victory over the fiend (VIII.34), in The *Man of Law's Tale Christ's power helps 'folk out of the feendes snare' (II.571). In this tale Satan has a prominent role. He is 'envious' since he was 'chaced from oure heritage', and eager to lead the sultaness astray as he did Eve (II.365–71), and he continually seeks an opportunity to beguile us (II.582), and plots against Constance, stirring a knight to murder (598). He is associated with traitors and treachery (II.780–1; cf. X.616). But Christ who died for our redemption bound Satan—and he still lies there (II.634).

The fall of Lucifer, 'brightest of angels alle', and his transformation into Satan is the *Monk's first tragedy (VII.1999–2006). Elsewhere, we find his traditional roles simply alluded to: the devil tempts and moves the heart to wickedness (e.g. VI.130–2). In The *Pardoner's Tale it is the 'feend, oure enemy' who puts the thought of buying poison into the mind of one of the rioters (VI.844–8). The devil knows what goes on in the hypocrite's mind (V.522).

We occasionally catch a glimpse of a more 'popular' devil. In one of Constance's prayers the fiend has 'claws' (II.454). The carpenter in The *Miller's Tale uses a charm against the evil spirits (I.3478 ff.). When the miller falls on his sleeping wife in The *Reeve's Tale she cries out 'the feend is on me falle!' (I.4288), alluding to the incubus, a demon in the form of a human who lay with women or, as a 'nightmare', with men. The more

learned word is used by the Wife of Bath (III.880), but according to her now that *elves have vanished the only incubus remaining is the wandering friar. Chaucer himself makes a distinctly light-hearted reference to the chain which binds Satan in hell when he associates it with the chain of marriage in *Bukton: 'I wol nat seyn how that yt is the cheyne | Of Sathanas, on which he gnaweth evere' (9–12).

Some of the colloquial expressions of popular speech suggest a certain familiarity. The devil (or the fiend) features very prominently in *oaths, whether they are curses or simple *ejaculations. The common pattern of 'the foule feend hym quelle [kill]!' (VIII.705), or 'the foule feend hym fecche!' (VIII.1159), sometimes has picturesque variants: 'the devel out of his skyn | Hym terve [flay]' (VIII.1273), 'the devel be hys soules bane!' (HF 408), 'the devil sette here [their] soules 'bothe afyre!' (LGW 2493), or (provoked by a gaping mouth): 'the devel of helle sette his foot therin!' (IX.38; cf. also Tr I.805; Tr IV.630; II.1064; I.3750; VII.924, etc.). Some of the phraseology has a modern ring: 'the devel go therwith!' (III.476), 'thus goth al to the devel' (III.262), 'how devel maistow brynge me to blisse?' (Tr I.623), 'what, devel of helle, sholde it elles be?' (VIII.1238); and 'in the devil's way' (tel on, a devel way! I.3134; a twenty devel wey! I.3713).

There are proverbs and proverbial expressions (e.g. I.3903; V.602–3) and similes or comparisons (Nero is as vicious 'as any feend that lith ful lowe adoun', VII.2464; the crowd pursuing the fox 'yolleden as feendes doon in helle', VII.3389). Similar phrases used for hyperbole are 'fouler than the devel was' (HF 1638), 'worse than a feend' (VII.3286, IX.320; cf. the adj. feendly 'devilish, monstrous', which Dorigen uses of the black rocks). The *Merchant improves on this; his wife is the worst that can be, 'for thogh the feend to hire ycoupled were, | She wolde hym overmacche' (IV.1218–20). An old husband 'chides like a fiend', according to the *Wife of Bath (III.244). The *Canon's Yeoman brings his recital of the sinister terms of alchemy (a science he regularly associates with fiends) to an end with a diabolic flourish: 'I have yow toold ynowe | To reyse a feend, al looke he never so rowe [no matter how ugly he looks]' (VIII.860–1).

The devil was obviously alive and well in

popular lore and language. Perhaps the most spectacular demonic intervention in a Chaucerian narrative is by the classical 'furie infernal' which burst from the ground in The *Knight's Tale (I.2684), but by far the most entertaining is by the devil himself in The *Friar's Tale, in which he appears as a yeoman in green wearing a hat with black fringes. His exchanges with the Summoner are superb examples of sustained quiet irony. He remarks that his dwelling is 'fer in the north contree', a traditional setting for the infernal regions, and that he hopes to see his companion there, for a very long time. And there is a moment of extreme hilarity when the devil reveals (or attempts to reveal) his true identity. Taking an oath ('the devel have al') literally becomes central to the plot, but the devil is a sophisticated theologian and knows the importance of 'intention', and he takes his proper prey in the end (III.1639–41). The Summoner's response is to quote the proverb 'freres and feendes been but lyte [little] asonder', and to illustrate their true 'heritage' by the grotesque vision of the multitude of friars under the devil's tail in hell.

devotion, see *piety.

dialogue is extensively used by Chaucer to give a sense of vivid actuality. It can range from formal *debate to familiar conversation, covering all kinds of emotional situations and encounters. He uses dialogue to introduce characters, to allow them to reveal (or conceal) their motives and thoughts, and to control the development of the action. In The *Reeve's Tale, for instance, after the characters have been introduced, the two students meet the miller, and greet him in a familiar 'hail, fellow, well met' style which suggests old acquaintance, and, perhaps, old suspicion: 'Al hayl, Symond, y-fayth! | Hou fares thy faire doghter and thy wyf?' | 'Aleyn, welcome . . . | And John also, how now, what do ye heer?' (I.4022–5). Under the jovial talk which ensues it is not hard to sense the contradictory desires—of the students to keep their eyes on the grinding at every moment so that they will not be cheated, and of the miller, who is equally determined to cheat them. 'What wol ye doon whil that it is in hande?' he asks, with apparent innocence. 'By God, right by the hopur wil I stande . . . and se howgates the corn gas

[goes] in', replies John, claiming that he has never watched the process before. This does not deceive the miller, who smiles, and 'thinks' (in a little interior monologue) 'all this is only done for a trick'.

Chaucer excels at this sort of conversation, which flows easily along in an apparently artless way, and gives a powerful impression of realism. It is often marked by colloquial diction, *ejaculations and *oaths, and frequent calls to attention (e.g. Tr I.1030). Yet it is at the same time integral to the movement of the action. Quite often a change in direction occurs as a result of dialogue. Arguments turn into angry exchanges, like that between Palamon and Arcite in The *Knight's Tale as they discover that they are rivals in love (I.1123 ff.). More subtle variations in *emotion also emerge in dialogue—as often in the exchanges between Pandarus and Criseyde in Troilus and Criseyde. At the beginning of book II there is a relaxed conversation between them, in which Criseyde's playful and joking expressions of incredulity and outrage at Pandarus's attempts to persuade her to go 'Maying' gradually turn into more serious questions as he teases her curiosity.

The passages of dialogue are artfully placed within the narrative. A stretch of narrative will suddenly erupt in a burst of conversation. At the beginning of The Miller's Tale, for instance, the carefully described *portraits of Nicholas and Alison immediately spring into life when Nicholas takes advantage of the husband's absence to begin to 'rage and pleye' with his young wife (I.3271–300) in a lively exchange in which *gestures emphasize the words. Later, just before the denouement, the three characters put themselves to bed in their tubs with a brief exchange (in a tale in which all the characters, and the narrator, are very talkative, the brevity is comically effective): '"Now, Paternoster, clom [hush]!" seyde Nicholay, | And "Clom!" quod John, and "Clom!" seyde Alisoun' (I.3638–9). Among the longer narratives, Troilus is notable for the way in which long scenes conducted almost entirely in dialogue alternate with passages of direct narrative and exclamations or reflections from the narrator. Always there is a careful mixing of familiar dialogue with more formal speeches or laments.

Chaucer seems to be especially interested in dialogue as a subtle means of revelation. He sometimes uses it to reveal another hidden pattern of meaning. A hilarious example of 'pillow talk' in *The Miller's Tale* between the carpenter, awakened by Absolon's singing outside the window, and his wife ('What! Alison! Herestow nat Absolon, | That chaunteth thus . . . ?' . . . 'Yis, God woot, John, I heere it every deel', I.3364–9) is like a Joycean 'epiphany' revealing the carpenter's sublime simplicity and the knowingness of Alison. In *The *Summoner's Tale* much of the comedy and satire comes from the conversations between the *friar (a member of a group renowned for persuasive and insinuating talk) and Thomas and his wife. This is matched in *The *Friar's Tale* by the gloriously ironic undertones of the conversations the summoner has with the *devil.

Dialogue can also be used to 'point' a tragic scene, as in the brief, emotionally charged exchange between Ugolino (*Hugelyn) and his children in *The *Monk's Tale* (VII.2429–52); and it is prominent in 'pitous' scenes in *The *Clerk's Tale* and *The *Man of Law's Tale*. There are serious discussions, in which advice is given (as in *Melibee). However, outside these, '*game' tends to mingle with 'earnest', and the advice is not entirely serious (as in some of the exchanges between Chauntecleer and Pertelote in *The *Nun's Priest's Tale* or that between Nicholas and John on the coming Flood in *The Miller's Tale* (I.3487 ff.)). When instruction or 'sermoning' begins to take over in an exchange, as with Chaucer and the *Eagle in *The House of Fame*, the dialogue may become comically 'one-sided' ('and y answered and seyde, "Yis"'). This can lead to an equally comic irritation in the talkative partner, sometimes reciprocated: when Pandarus stirs the inattentive Troilus by crying 'Awake!', Troilus remonstrates, 'Frend, though that I stylle lye, | I am nat deef. Now pees, and crye namore, | For I have herd thi wordes and thi lore' (*Tr* I.752–4).

Dyane, Diana, the Roman goddess (identified with the Greek Artemis) of women, chastity, and the Moon. She is the chaste huntress of the woods, and is associated with the lower world. In Chaucer she appears in all of these aspects. When the great warrior Theseus goes hunting in *The Knight's Tale* it is said that 'after *Mars he serveth now Dyane' (I.1682). Later in the tale there is a description of the temple of 'Dyane the chaste' (I.2051–88; cf. *PF* 281). On the walls are depictions of hunting and modest chastity, though the stories mentioned (see *Calistopee, *Dane, *Attheon, *Atthalante, *Meleagre) show the goddess as rather less than benign. Diana herself is shown sitting on a hart, with small hounds about her feet, and a moon beneath. Her statue is clothed in green, as befits a huntress, and she carries in her hand a bow and a sheathful of arrows. She looks down towards the dark region of *Pluto. A woman in childbirth calls upon her. Later (I.2273 ff.) Emily sacrifices to her, addressing her as 'chaste goddesse of the wodes grene | . . . Queene of the regne of Pluto derk and lowe, | Goddesse of maydens' but receives no grace. In *The *Franklin's Tale* there is a reference to the story of a maiden *Stymphalides, who takes sanctuary in Diana's temple (V.1388–94). The story of her wrath against the Greeks and her punishment of them by the Calydonian boar is told in *Troilus and Criseyde* (V.1464 ff.). Troilus prays to her as goddess of the Moon to be favourable to his *viage* (journey = undertaking; III.731–2 (cf. II.74–5)). (See also her other names: *Cynthea; *Latona; *Lucina; *Mone.)

Dianira, Dianyre, Deianira, daughter of Oeneus of Calydon, and wife of Hercules (*Ercules). She had been told by *Nessus, a dying Centaur, that his blood would regain the affection of her husband if he was ever unfaithful to her. When he carried off Iole (*Yole) she sent him a robe smeared with the blood, but it had been poisoned by the blood of the Hydra, the water snake which he had slain, and clung to his flesh painfully. He had himself carried to a pyre on Mt. Oeta and burned. Chaucer read her story in Ovid's *Heroides* (9) and *Metamorphoses* (book 9). She is several times mentioned as the wife of Hercules (e.g. *HF* 402). Although Chaucer lists 'the pleinte of Dianire' in the Introduction to *The *Man of Law's Tale* (II.66) as appearing in his '*Seintes Legende of Cupide', it is not found in *The *Legend of Good Women* as we have it. One of the stories of wicked wives which *Jankin reads to the *Wife of Bath is 'of Hercules and of his Dianyre, | That caused hym to sette hymself afyre' (III.725–6). In *The *Monk's Tale*, however, where the story is told (VII.2119–35), the narrator says that some clerks excuse Deianira, 'fressh as May', because Nessus made the shirt, and that 'be as be may' he will not accuse her.

Dictys Cretensis, see *Dite.

Dido, the widow of Sychaeus (*Sytheo), and the legendary founder and queen of Carthage. In*Virgil's *Aeneid* she receives Aeneas (*Eneas) and his company with great kindness, and is filled with passion for the hero. When a storm interrupts a hunting expedition the two of them take refuge in a cave and become lovers. Her rejected suitor Iarbas (*Yarbas) comes to hear of it and appeals to Jupiter, who orders Aeneas to leave Carthage. His preparations are discovered by Dido, who pleads with him to stay. His excuses provoke a bitter outburst. A last piteous entreaty is of no avail. When she sees the fleet leaving, Dido takes her own life. Ovid, in *Heroides* 7, gives her a passionate epistle, which tells the story from her point of view. In medieval literature she becomes a heroine of romance, the tragic victim of Aeneas's lack of fidelity, his 'untrouthe'. Chaucer gives the story in *The *Legend of Good Women* (924–1367) and in *The *House of Fame* (239–432), using the accounts of both Virgil and Ovid. Like other medieval writers he is very sympathetic to Dido (though noting her folly in loving too quickly) and critical of Aeneas.

In *The Legend of Good Women* we have an eloquent story of passion and pathos. Dido is a woman of great beauty and virtue; she feels 'routhe and wo' for the exile ('and, for he was a straunger, somwhat she | likede hym the bet'). Her love is suffused with '*pite' and '*gentilesse'. Love brings the traditional medieval symptoms; she becomes pale, and 'waketh, walweth [twists and turns], maketh many a breyd [sudden movement], | As don thise lovers'. Her speech to her sister Anna (*Anne (2)) demonstrates love's overwhelming power—'in hym lyth al, to do me live or deye'. In spite of Anna, who 'somdel it withstod', love 'may nat ben withstonde; | Love wol love'. There are no excuses for Aeneas; he proves the dictum that in love 'oon shal laughen at anothers wo'—'now laugheth Eneas'. The narrator addresses 'sely wemen, ful of innocence . . . pite . . . trouthe', and laments men's unkindness, bitterly repeating the word 'gentil' ('this grete gentil-man . . . | That

feyneth hym so trewe and obeysynge, | So gentil' (1264–6)). After a tense exchange between them, the story moves to a sudden and violent end: 'upon the fir of sacrifice she sterte, | And with his swerd she rof hyre to the herte'.

In *The *House of Fame* the dreamer finds her story written in the temple of Venus. Again, it takes a severe view of Aeneas who betrayed her 'and lefte hir ful unkyndely', but here it is recorded that the 'book' offers some explanation of his behaviour—'the book seyth Mercurie . . . | Bad hym goo into Itayle' (427–8). Chaucer refers his readers to both Virgil and Ovid, but he treats Dido in a distinctive way. She is not only an entirely sympathetic figure, but a more introspective one: she discusses the causes of men's infidelity (300–10), noting that 'oon . . . wolde have fame | In magnyfiyinge of hys name'. Her passionate (and greatly expanded) lament on the workings of 'wikke Fame' underlines the central questions concerning Fame and Rumour which the poem poses. Dido's death is also alluded to in *The Man of Law's Tale* (II.64), *The Book of the Duchess* (731–3), and *The Parliament of Fowls* (289).

dignite(e), dignity, honour (astrology). Chaucer reters to the doctrine in *A Treatise on the *Astrolabe*. To take an illustration from *The *Squire's Tale*: there the Sun is in Mars' *domicile ('mansioun'; when Mars is there he has five dignities thereby). The Sun, however, is near its own exaltation (giving it four dignities), and is in its triplicity (implicit; three dignities). It is not in its own term (so missing two dignities) or its own face (it is in that of Mars, worth one dignity). (See also *astrology and astronomy.)   [JDN]

digression. In a very self-conscious way Chaucer frequently draws attention to a digression which he is avoiding, or, more often, indulging. The *Clerk briefly describes the prohemium (proem or *prologue) to Petrarch's story of Griselda, and remarks that a full topographical account of the Po valley would seem 'a thyng impertinent [irrelevant]' (IV.54). At the beginning of *Troilus and Criseyde* the narrator says that he is not going to tell the story of the fall of Troy: 'how this town com to destruccion | Ne falleth naught to purpos me to telle, | For it were a long digression | Fro my matere' (I.141–4). Even here, it will be noted, he contrives to insert the idea of the destruction of Troy, which is not altogether 'a thyng impertinent' in the poem.

It seems appropriate that this is the first recorded occurrence of the word 'digression' in English, for Chaucer is a superb practitioner of this rhetorical and narrative technique. An instructive example occurs a little later in *Troilus* (I.211–61), where in the midst of the account of how Troilus was pierced by the god of love, the narrative is literally frozen for some fifty lines, while the narrator muses and reflects—on the sudden fall of this proud detractor of love, and on its exemplary nature in a passage which suggests other patterns of ideas and images which are to be significant. The narrator marks the 'return' to his principal 'matter': he will 'tellen forth' his tale, and leave 'other thing collateral' (a sort of modest disclaimer, which by apparently denying in fact emphasizes the relevance of the digression). Here digression (a form of rhetorical amplification) is clearly being used to develop a pattern of ideas, to give variety to the tone, and to give variety to the rhythm of the narrative by playing with the reader's expectations—our desire to 'get on with the story' is both frustrated and increased.

Chaucer's use of digression was probably encouraged by the example of other writers (notably *Jean de Meun and *Ovid) and by the discussions in rhetorical treatises. Geoffrey of Vinsauf (*Gaufred), for instance, is aware of the effect of 'delays' or *morae* on the reader's eagerness to reach a conclusion. Chaucer often uses it to provide a 'commentary' on the narrative, sometimes explanatory or opinionative, sometimes unsettling, so that the reader has to see things from a quite different perspective. And he likes to play games with his readers, in the 'return' from a digression, or by using the rhetorical device of *occupatio* or 'refusal to tell'. This can be a kind of 'frustrated digression' (as in the 'long digression' on the destruction of Troy which we are not given). There are longer examples, like the refusal to 'make mention' of all the minstrelsy at Theseus's feast, the gifts, the ladies, the hawks, the hounds, etc. (I.2197–207). Nor will he describe the making of Arcite's pyre from different kinds of trees (twenty-one are mentioned), the effects on

the wood spirits, the mortals, etc. (I.2919–64). After nearly fifty lines listing items and actions which are not going to be told, the narrator announces: 'But shortly to the point thanne wol I wende | And maken of my longe tale an ende'.

The many examples of digression show a considerable variety, ranging from brief 'asides' ('But whether that she children hadde or noon, | I rede it naught, therfore I late it goon'. *Tr* I.132–3) through more extended interventions (e.g. *Tr* II.666 ff.) to some very long examples. Such is the narrative skill that even these can be disguised from an unwary reader. Not everyone notices that the description of the pilgrims in the *General Prologue* is an extended digression. The easy, conversational style disguises it, but it is clearly marked:

> But natheless, whil I have tyme and space,
> Er that I ferther in this tale pace,
> Me thynketh it accordaunt to resoun
> To telle yow al the condicioun
> Of ech of hem . . .
> And whiche they weren, and of what degree
>
> (I.35–40)

After nearly 700 lines there is an elegant and complicated 'return'. The narrator announces 'Now have I toold you . . . | Th'estaat, th'array, the nombre', etc. (I.715). But this apparently closural remark is a feint. We move instantly into another digression (725 ff.)—do not blame me if I speak plainly and broadly—which is both a *captatio benevolentiae* and a complex rhetorical statement about the language and technique of the ensuing tales. It is not until l. 747 that the small action of the *Prologue* resumes.

Individual tales afford an amazing number of digressions. In The *Wife of Bath's Tale* we have the story of Midas's (*Myda) wife, and the old hag's disquisition on '*gentilesse', which seems at first to be a digression (and is certainly a narrative 'delay') but which turns out to be an integrated part of the story, fitted both to the plot and to the concerns of the narrator. Digressions are used as 'delays' to make an even more complicated narrative rhythm in other tales. In The *Pardoner's Tale* the story begins rapidly, setting the scene of the company of young rioters in Flanders. But after about twenty lines the Pardoner begins a long and entertaining homiletic discourse on gluttony (especially drunkenness), dicing, and swearing (VI.483–660). Then, with a traditional signal of 'return' ('But, sires, now wol I telle forth my tale'), the story resumes and moves quickly to its grim conclusion.

Most complicated of all, however, is *The *Nun's Priest's Tale*. The intricate pattern is established at the beginning, with a teasingly roundabout introduction of the main character, Chauntecleer. The narrative does not begin until some sixty lines after the opening of the tale. Its first stage, the account of Chauntecleer's prophetic dream of the terrible beast, quickly turns into an extended formal disputation on the significance of dreams in general as well as of this one in particular, supported by *exempla (which suggest different ways in which the narrative might develop). *The Nun's Priest's Tale* is remarkable in not only being filled with digressions, but constantly keeping alive the possibility of yet more digressions (and keeping the reader uncertain about what is digressive and what is not). After nearly 300 lines, the narrative seems about to begin to move again, with Chauntecleer flying down from his beam, but we are frustrated by an elaborate *chronographia* (or setting of time) and narratorial comments. When it does move ('Now wol I torne agayn to my sentence' VII.3214)—with the entry of the fox into the yard, it hovers on the edge of digression with a series of expansive narratorial comments. Finally, an elegant transition with an ironic disclaimer ('Thise been the cokkes wordes, and nat myne; | I kan noon harm of no womman divyne' (3265–6)) takes us back into the narrative. But even here there are explanatory asides on *Physiologus and 'contraries' in Nature. It is by now clear to all readers that the fox will pounce, but the moment is delayed by a series of exclamations and remarks on free will and necessity. Chauntecleer begins to beat his wings (3322), but there follows an exclamation about flattery and flatterers. When the sudden attack comes (3334) (after some teasingly descriptive circumstances 'strecchynge his nekke, and heeld his eyen cloos') it unleashes a veritable barrage of exclamations and laments (3338–73), including a tongue-in-cheek invocation to Geoffrey of Vinsauf and a little *occupatio* or 'frustrated digression' on that terrible day Friday which the rhetorician had so fervently addressed. And the passage continues with more exclamations and mock heroic laments until

(with 'now wol I turne to my tale agayn', 3374) the narrative takes up the pursuit of the fox and his victim. (See also *narratives; *rhetoric.)

Gray (1996).

dinner, see *food.

DIOGENES. The Greek Cynic philosopher (4th c. BC), who espoused a virtuous simple life (reputedly in a large earthenware tub) is quoted (probably from St *Jerome or *John of Salisbury) in *The *Former Age* (35) as saying that tyrants are not eager to try to conquer poor regions.

Diomede in **Troilus and Criseyde* (V.15 ff.), the Greek who escorts Criseyde from Troy, and eventually becomes her lover. In Homer Diomedes, the son of *Tydeus, is a famous warrior who led the men of Argos (*Arge) against Troy. Chaucer gives a brief description of him (V.799–805): he has a 'sterne vois and myghty lymes square', he is bold, and 'chivalrous | Of dedes', and some say that he is 'of tonge large [free of speech]'. He is once called, significantly, 'this sodeyn [forward, impetuous] Diomede' (V.1024).

Diomedes, the king of the Bistones in Thrace was killed by Hercules (*Ercules), who fed his flesh to his man-eating mares. This is mentioned in *Boece* (IV m.7:40).

Dyone, the mother of Venus (*Tr* III.1807).

Distichs **of Cato,** see *Cato(u)n (2).

DITE, TYTUS. Dictys Cretensis (the Cretan) was regarded in the Middle Ages, with *Dares, as one of the leading authorities on the Trojan War. The preface by Lucius Septimus to the influential Latin *Ephemeridos belli Troiani* (4th c. AD) claims that it is a translation of a work in Greek. A fragment of a Greek Dictys (1st c. AD) has been found. According to Lucius Septimus the text was originally written in Phoenician characters. Dictys himself says that he was present at the siege on the Greek side as a companion of Idomeneus. Chaucer refers to Dictys twice as an authority on the war (*Tr* I.146, *HF* 1467).

(ed.) Eisenhut (1958); (trans.) Frazer (1966).

diversity. The *Miller's Tale* meets with a slightly mixed reception from the Pilgrims: 'Diverse folk diversely they seyde, | But for the moore part they loughe [laughed] and pleyde' (I.3857–8). Chaucer is fond of using this proverbial idea, a version of 'quot homines, tot sententiae' or 'so many heads so many wits'. In The *Man of Law's Tale* the Sultan's advisers cannot agree: 'Diverse men diverse thynges seyden; | They argumenten, casten up and doun' (II.211–12). Nor can the friends of January in The *Merchant's Tale*: 'Diverse men diversely hym tolde | Of mariage manye ensamples olde. | Somme blamed it, somme preysed it, certeyn' (IV.1469–71). The magic horse in The *Squire's Tale* provokes a similar diversity of opinion: 'Diverse folk diversely they demed; | As many heddes, as manye wittes ther been' (V.202–3). It is obvious that much of the dramatic interest of The *Canterbury Tales* arises directly from diversity and disagreement. However, the principle of diversity is central to all of Chaucer's work, and is put to a variety of uses. The *Wife of Bath* uses it in an appeal to the value of *experience: 'diverse scoles maken parfyt clerkes, | And diverse practyk in many sondry werkes | Maketh the werkman parfyt' she says (III.44c–e)—she has had 'schooling' through five husbands. Pandarus, distinguishing between his role in bringing Troilus and Criseyde together and that of a bawd or go-between, uses the scholastic 'diversity requires a distinction': 'ther is diversite required | Bytwixen thynges like' (*Tr* III.405). Earlier in the poem, he had applied the proverbial remark that 'a wheston [whetstone] is no kervyng [cutting] instrument, | But yet it maketh sharpe kervyng tolis' (*Tr* I.631–2) to himself as a justification for his role as Troilus's adviser and friend in love (a fool can guide a wise man). Pandarus uses the principle that 'by his contrarie is every thyng declared' ('whit by blak, by shame ek worthinesse') to suggest, in a comic mode, a decorous idea of concord. And indeed, the attitudes and personalities of the two friends make a pleasing *coincidentia oppositorum*—together they form one of the great *pairs* of fiction.

Although there is an evident delight in diversity, it is by no means always presented as a necessarily good thing. The 'diversity' between the Muslim and the Christian religions (II.220) which causes disagreement among the Sultan's counsellors leads to a massacre. The jostling throng which the dreamer sees in the House of Rumour (*HF* 2034–109) handing on (with improvements) every new tiding is an image of confusion and disorder. Uncontrolled diversity may threaten aesthetic form. Pandarus in telling Troilus how to write a love letter (*Tr* II.1023–43) stresses appropriateness and concord ('Ne jompre [jumble] ek no discordant thyng yfeere [together]'), otherwise what will emerge will be monstrous like a grotesque. The 'gret diversite' in the English language and in the 'writyng of oure tonge' (*Tr* V.1793–4) may lead to misunderstanding and the ruining of the metre.

The diversity of *Nature's created species, however, is both orderly and beautiful, and is celebrated in The *Parliament of Fowls* and elsewhere (see *beauty). Ultimately, in the way it contains 'contraries' and enmities, it reflects the divine harmony and order. The ancient world valued the union of contrasts in a beautiful scene, like the Vale of Tempe, which combined a quiet river valley with a wild and rugged gorge. This principle, similar to that which Pandarus advocates more light-heartedly, is clearly germane to Chaucer's creative aesthetic. But he also likes to use extreme contrasts in a bold way, and sometimes to revel in the uncertainty, the confusion, or the disorder which diversity can bring, in all the perplexities and animosities of 'sondry folk, by aventure yfalle', and in the diversity of the opinions they express.

Dives, the rich man who is taken to hell (unlike the beggar, Lazarus (*Lazar)) in the gospel story (Luke 16:19–26) is referred to in The *Summoner's Tale* (III.1877).

Divina Commedia, La (or ***Commedia***), the greatest poem of *Dante. Its verse form is the *terza rima* (lines arranged in groups of three, rhyming aba bcb cdc, etc.). Its basis is the common medieval literary form of a journey in a dream or vision to hell or to the otherworld, but this is completely transformed into an intricately structured philosphical work which combines allegory and political commentary.

The poem consists of three long sections divided into cantos. At the beginning of the first, the

documents

Inferno (Hell), the poet, fearful in a dark wood, meets Virgil, who has been sent by Beatrice to be his guide in a spiritual odyssey. They enter the gate of hell, and begin their descent down through the successive circles where the sinners are punished. The virtuous heathen are placed in Limbo in the first circle. Among the 'forest' of spirits, Dante meets the shades of four great poets of antiquity (Homer, Horace, Ovid, and Lucan) and sees the ancient heroes and philosophers (canto 4). He then comes to the place 'where no light shines', to hell itself. In the second circle are the lustful, including the tragic lovers Paolo and Francesca, their shades borne on the winds like the cranes flying in a long line. The third circle, presided over by Minos (*Mynos (1)) contains the gluttonous. In the fourth are the avaricious; in the fifth the wrathful. Still lower are the violent (including the suicides, transformed into trees), and the fraudulent (including Pope Nicholas III), planted like a post upside down. Among the evil counsellors is the great and defiant spirit of Ulysses (*Ulixes), who led his men to destruction in the ocean (canto 26). The traitors are in the ninth circle. Here Ugolino (*Hugelyn), a victim of treachery as well as a traitor, tells his story. At the very bottom are the great traitors, Judas, Brutus, Cassius, and Satan himself, standing in the ice. The beating of his great bat-like wings makes freezing winds; from the six eyes of his three heads flow tears and bloody foam. 'Now it is time to go', says Virgil, 'for we have seen everything'. Through a secret path they return to the 'bright world' and come out to see the stars again.

In the *Purgatorio* the journey continues as the dawn rises. Purgatory is a high mountain with circular ledges on which are groups of penitent sinners. Dante first meets some souls who have repented only at the last hour, whose ascent is slow and lethargic. They meet the impressive figure of the poet Sordello, who had urged the princes of Europe to rule with nobleness and courage. He leads them through the Valley of the Princes, rulers who were long distracted by ambition from noble actions. Dante and Virgil finally come to the gate of purgatory and enter. The terraces rising upward are filled with penitents who have shown in different ways love perverted or inadequate or excessive (love is the seed of every virtue and of every action which deserves punishment). At the top, Virgil makes his farewell. Dante now enters the Earthly Paradise (canto 28), and meets a beautiful lady (later named as Matilda), who leads him to the chariot of the church and to Beatrice, who will henceforth be his guide.

The *Paradiso* offers a series of visions of light, joy, and song, as Dante is led upwards through the ten heavenly spheres: the Moon, Mercury, and Venus (these three and their inhabitants still to some degree in the shadow of the earth), the Sun (associated with the wise, theologians like Thomas Aquinas, St Francis and his beloved Poverty, St Bonaventura and St Dominic), Mars (the home of the courageous warrior saints who form a cross of souls as a sign of victory), where Dante's ancestor, Cacciaguida, praises the ancient virtues of Florence, laments its decline, and prophesies Dante's life in exile, Jupiter (the place of just rulers), and Saturn (the sphere of temperance, where the contemplatives are set). Then Dante is taken to the fixed stars (the Church triumphant), where he is examined by St Peter, St James, and St John on Faith, Hope, and Charity. He ascends to the Crystalline sphere, where he sees the Angelic circles turning, and finally to the Empyrean, where he sees the river of light and the eternal celestial Rose, made up of the angels and the saints. St *Bernard prays to the Virgin Mary, and signals Dante to look upward to the light. With this ecstatic vision the poem ends: 'now my desire and my will, like an evenly moving wheel, was turned by the Love that moves the sun and the other stars.'

(ed.) Petrocchi (1966–7); (trans.) Sinclair (1939–46).

Docto(u)r, see *Physician.

documents of various kinds were an important part of daily life for many in the Middle Ages. They were written by the literate, but were also used by or on the illiterate. Apart from *books and *letters, the majority of those mentioned in Chaucer have to do with the *law in one of its various forms. At one end of the spectrum is the *Man of Law, with his royal letter of appointment (*patente* I.315), and his skill in drawing up legal documents (I.325); at the other is the *Summoner, an officer of the ecclesiastical court, with his

Significavit or writ (I.662). The summoner in *The *Friar's Tale* (who is keen in the punishing of violations of wills and marriage contracts, III.1307–8) produces a 'bill of summons' (III.1586); however, his prospective victim, the old woman, knows her way around, and asks for a *libel*, a written statement of the charge (III.1595). The *Pardoner has a wallet stuffed with pardons (indulgences), and he too is armed with a *patente* with the bishop's seal. He flourishes his 'bulles of popes and of cardynales' (VI.342), and apparently records the names of his 'customers' in a roll (VI.911). The *papir* which the apprentice in *The *Cook's Tale* seeks from his master (I.4404) is a mercantile or legal document, perhaps a written certificate of service and release. There are references to a *registre* (I.2812), to *scrit and bond* (writs for a marriage contract, IV.1697). The *bille* in *The *Physician's Tale* (VI.166 ff.) is a legal charge or petition. This word can also be used of a private letter; and it appears in *Complaint unto *Pity* as the document of a lover's complaint: 'A compleynt had I, writen in myn hond, | For to have put to Pite as a bille' (43–4). It is also used in religious works: the *ABC* says that Christ 'with his precious blood . . . wrot the bille | Upon the crois as general acquitaunce [acquittal]' for mankind (59), an image which recalls the 'charters of Christ', devotional texts drawn up in legal form, recording a grant of heaven's bliss to mankind, sealed with Christ's wounded heart, and witnessed by those present at Calvary.

dogs, see *animals.

domicile, a technical term of astrology (not used by Chaucer) used to refer to any sign of the Zodiac regarded as a planetary house. This is distinct from the notion of a house as a subdivision of the Zodiac in a horoscope. In both cases there are twelve houses. (See also *horoscope; *hows; *signe.) [JDN]

Domus Dedaly, the Labyrinth (*Laboryntus) in Crete (*HF* 1920) built by Daedalus (*Dedalus).

Donegild, the mother of *Alla in *The *Man of Law's Tale*.

Dorigen, the heroine of *The *Franklin's Tale*. The

origin of the name, which is evidently meant to sound Celtic, is unknown.

DOUGLAS, GAVIN (?1475–1522), a late medieval Scottish poet, educated at St Andrews, and probably at Paris. He became Provost of St Giles in Edinburgh, and later bishop of Dunkeld. He was a member of one of the most powerful families in Scotland, and became increasingly involved in politics. He was exiled and died in London. His early poem *The Palice of Honour* is a learned dream vision which owes much to the example of Chaucer, and in particular to *The *House of Fame*. He had learnt from him the art of projecting an easy and apparently confidential narrative voice. In the Prologue to his splendidly energetic translation of Virgil's *Aeneid*, the *Eneados* (1513), he reacted strongly against the common medieval view of Aeneas as a faithless betrayer of *Dido, and after an eloquent praise of his master Chaucer ('principal poet but peir [without peer]') he ventures, cautiously and humbly, that in this case 'my mastir Chauser gretly Virgill offendit' by calling Aeneas 'traytour'. He then puts forward a famous exculpation: Chaucer should be excused for the reproach he 'set on Virgill and Eneas . . . For he was evir (God wait [knows]) all womanis frend'.

 Palice of Honour (ed.) Bawcutt (1967); *Eneados* (ed.) Coldwell (1957–64); Bawcutt (1976).

Dover, Jakke of, see *Jakke.

Dragon, (1) the Dragon, whose head and tail mark the lunar nodes, the points of intersection of the Moon's path with the ecliptic. In *Equatorie of the Planetis* the Latin is retained: *Caput Draconis* (for the ascending node) and *Cauda Draconis* (for the descending node). The nodes are crucial for the determination of eclipses. They have a pseudo-planetary character in astrology, and it seems likely that they have a role in the story of the blinding of *Januarie. In the *Astrolabe* the 'Tayl of the Dragoune' is reckoned with Mars and Saturn as one of the 'wicked planetes' (2.4, 36). (See also *astrology and astronomy.) (2) the metal mercury; in this alchemical parlance (*CYT* VIII.1435–40), the dragon's brother is sulphur. (See also *alchemy.) [JDN]

drama. It is difficult to ascertain the extent of Chaucer's knowledge of the drama of his day. Though much has been lost, medieval drama was evidently rich and varied. There were 'mystery plays' (plays on biblical subjects often arranged in a 'cycle'), parish plays, Latin liturgical plays, 'interludes', saints' plays and the earliest examples of the allegorical 'morality plays', and, probably, folk plays and 'games', as well as 'semi-dramatic' forms: mummings, pageants, royal entries, processions and 'ridings' (cf. I.4377), and chivalric ceremonials like tournaments and jousts. The *Wife of Bath says that she enjoyed processions and 'pleyes of myracles,'—presumably plays representing the miracles worked by saints. In *The* *Miller's Tale* Chaucer is more specific. The Oxford parish clerk, *Absolon, played '*Herodes upon a scaffold hye' (I.3383–4). This seems to be a reference to the blustering tyrant of the mystery plays, who, in one surviving stage direction, is said to 'rage in the pageant and in the street also'. The 'scaffold hye' may be an outdoor stage or the upper story of a pageant wagon. Oxford was large enough to mount a cycle of mystery plays, but no text has survived. It is quite likely that later in the tale there is a further reference to the comic scene between Noah (*Noe) and his shrewish wife (I.3538–40). In the Middle Ages there was some knowledge of the Roman drama, and ancient theatrical metaphors (the 'stage of life' or 'theatre of the world') were in use. Chaucer came across such references in Boethius, e.g. the 'theatre' (*Bo* I pr.1:49) and the 'stage of life' (II pr.3). It may be that he himself had this image in mind at the end of *Troilus and Criseyde* when the hero's soul looks down like a spectator on 'this wrecched world'. The amphitheatre of Boccaccio's *Teseida* becomes the 'noble theatre' for the jousting in *The *Knight's Tale* (I.1885 ff.). There were medieval Latin imitations of Roman comedies, and some classical Latin drama was read or studied in schools—the plays of Terence, Plautus, and Seneca (*Senek), who probably influenced medieval ideas of *tragedy, and perhaps Chaucer's *Troilus*.

What is certain is that Chaucer's work has a markedly dramatic quality. This is particularly evident in *Troilus and Criseyde*, of which a high proportion consists of direct speech and *dialogue. The speeches of the characters range from realistic colloquial exchanges to formal rhetorical laments, almost in the manner of operatic arias. Chaucer seems to have given much thought to the construction of expressive dramatic scenes, many of which are his own invention (like the dinner party at the house of Deiphebus in books II–III which Pandarus arranges and where, like a master of ceremonies, he makes sure that everyone is playing the correct role; see II.1710–11). Careful attention is given to entrances (Pandarus comes into Troilus's room unexpectedly, and hears him groan (I.549), in book II he discovers Criseyde and her ladies listening to a romance, in book IV, after the news that Criseyde is to be exchanged, he hastily comes to comfort Troilus 'in a rees [rush]'), and to exits, as that of Troilus at the end of the fourth book, or in the scene of the exchange at the beginning of book V, where 'to Troie homward he wente' after seeing Criseyde ride off, with the new character Diomede leading her by the bridle of her horse. Even the characters sometimes seem to regard themselves as figures in a play. Troilus in particular sees himself as an exemplary figure in a tragedy (see e.g. IV.270–3, 323–9, V.295–322). The three main characters are each given what sounds like a formal speech of leave-taking: Criseyde in V.1054–85 (ending 'but al shal passe; and thus I take my leve', after which we are given only the text of her last letter), Troilus in V.1673–722, to which Pandarus uncharacteristically finds it hard to reply (his brief speech (V.1731–44) ends 'I kan namore seye'). It has often been noted that a dramatic principle is also at work in *The *Canterbury Tales*. Within the individual narratives we find many excellent miniature examples of expressive scenes—the carpenter and his servant trying to rouse Nicholas in his locked room, and finding him gaping in the air (I.3419 ff.), or the nocturnal bedroom farce in *The Reeve's Tale*. In some cases the tellers of the tales (notably the *Wife of Bath and the *Pardoner) are given long soliloquies or dramatic monologues in which they discuss themselves and their dealings with others. Even though the whole work is not completed, it is evident from the descriptions of the individual pilgrims in the *General Prologue* and from the way that they interact with each other or with the Host in the surviving *links between the tales that Chaucer envisaged a large-scale dramatic interplay between the tales. Enough has survived to give a powerful effect of continuing debate and dramatic *diversity. Finally, in all of his works Chaucer shows that—like the early English vernacular drama—he loves to mix comic and serious scenes.

Not surprisingly, some of these dramatic narratives were later turned into stage drama, and, again not surprisingly, it is *Troilus and Criseyde* which provided the most famous example (see *Troilus and Cressida*). Even before Shakespeare's play, the story had been turned into some kind of interlude or playlet as part of a Tudor court entertainment. The festivities at Epiphany in 1516 began with a play about 'Troylous and Pandor'. It has not survived. Perhaps the title might suggest that its interest lay in the wooing and in the comic aspects rather than the philosophical concerns of the poem, but it would be rash to speculate. Calkas appeared in it. His role was taken by the musician William Cornish, whose Children of the Chapel Royal performed the play. It was followed by a pageant involving a combat in which knights defended a castle placed in the hall; at the end the queen and other ladies descended from the pageant and gave speeches, and minstrels appeared on the castle to accompany the noble maskers in their dances. And long after Dryden's less distinguished dramatic version, the story was made the basis of an opera in Walton's *Troilus and Cressida* (performed first in 1954). Some of the Canterbury Tales were also turned into plays— mostly in the 16th and 17th c. by dramatists avid for plots. The best known is a derivative of *The Knight's Tale*, *Two Noble Kinsmen*. But before that there was the *Palamon and Arcite* in two parts (1566) of Richard Edwards; and another *Palamon and Arcite* is recorded in 1594. The *Clerk's Tale* was turned into a play (now lost) by Radclif (*c.*1550) for his school (he also did *Melibee*—also lost, which must have made an instructive if not a gripping piece). Later plays use other versions of the (widespread) Griselda story—e.g. *Patient Grissil* by Dekker and others (1599–1600) (see **Grisild(e)**). The *Physician's Tale* is the basis of *Apius and Virginia* (1567). Other dramatists used sections of Chaucer's Tales: an early example is Heywood, *The Pardoner and the Frere* (?before 1521), a later is *Shakespeare, in *Midsummer Night's Dream*. In the 20th c., a musical of *The Canterbury Tales*,

based on a dramatic version of Nevill Coghill's translation, ran successfully in London in the late 1960s, and the Italian film director Pier Paolo Pasolini used some of the tales in his *I racconti di Canterbury* (1972) (see Fig. 15).

Beadle (1994); Conrad (1995); Cooper (1989), 420–7.

dream vision. The name given to a common medieval literary type in which the action is said to take place within a dream and/or vision experienced by a dreamer-narrator. It is a reflection of an ancient fascination with *dreams. The classical *Somnium Scipionis* (see *Drem of Scipioun) and the 13th-c. *Roman de la Rose* were especially influential. The use of a dream framework is found in such later works as Bunyan's *Pilgrim's Progress* or William Morris's *News from Nowhere*.

Dream visions sometimes take the form of a journey to the next world, but the settings in which the dreamer or visionary may find himself are varied. Often it is a scene from the natural world which has been strangely transfigured, a temple, or a beautiful grove or garden. The process of illumination can be through symbolic or allegorical scenes or events or through rational discourse and argument, or, most commonly, a combination of the two. The dreamer, always a central figure, is often in some state of anxiety, perplexity, or spiritual crisis. In his dream he will meet various guides or figures of authority. These may appear as personifications, but are often active cosmic powers (like *Nature or *Fortune or *Fame). The dreamer will sometimes be an onlooker in some symbolic scene, or, frequently, he will become engaged in a dialogue or disputation. Enlightenment will come through the images he sees and through question, answer, and argument: 'the spiritual forces are identified in the form of personifications, analysed in dialogue, and then either accepted or rejected for absorption into the personal psychic entity of those who participate in the spiritual processes the allegory embodies' (Piehler).

Dreams present all kinds of literary possibilities. The dream or vision itself will usually have a clearly marked beginning and end, although this is not always the case (Boethius (*Boece) suddenly becomes aware of the strange figure of Philosophy in his room, and *Dante simply 'finds himself' in a dark wood). But many writers delight in the challenge of introducing the dream and of finding ways in which to wake the dreamer up (very often by some noise) and bringing the whole experience to a conclusion. 'Dream narrative' can be marked by abrupt transitions or by mysterious juxtapositions or digressions of a labyrinthine kind. Some writers exploit the possible effect of having a dreamer who is sometimes the same as the author and sometimes quite distinct. The composition of dream visions often arouses a self-conscious interest in the nature of imaginative fiction and art. In his commentary on the *Somnium Scipionis* *Macrobius notes the similarities of the dream to the literary work: the latter, like the dream, may employ several levels of reference at the same time. The poem like a dream may be at once both private and public, having both 'a personal area of reference and a more public and generalized rhetorical aim' (Norton-Smith). The dream also offered a solution to the problem of 'fiction'. Where a modern author will have no difficulty in assuming his readers' agreement with the idea that his fiction though invented is somehow 'true', medieval writers seem not always to have been able to do so. They like to claim that the truth of their work has some authentication. A very useful alternative to the assertion that a story has been found in an old book by some recognized author (*auctour) is the claim that the strange experience came in a personal dream or vision.

Chaucer wrote a number of dream visions: *The *Book of the Duchess, The *House of Fame, The *Parliament of Fowls*, and the *Prologue* to *The *Legend of Good Women*, which introduces the tales (and in the F version, since there is no statement that the dreamer woke up, perhaps we are to assume that he is writing them in his dream). His treatment of the kind is highly original. He may have invented the episode of the poet reading at bedtime, and reading a work which has direct or indirect links with his state of mind and with the dream narrative that follows. He seems to have enjoyed the interplay between reality and dream, in the sudden and mysterious transitions and dreamlike links possible in this kind of narrative.

In *The Book of the Duchess* he exploits the combination of the private and the public, the subjective and the objective, for psychological purposes. The Man in Black is a 'figure' of John of Gaunt and at the same time is a projection of the poet's imagination, binding together the two characters and the writer of the poem and its recipient. From this dream vision poem general ideas—concerning Love, Nature, Fortune, Death—emerge. In *The House of Fame* and *The Parliament of Fowls* such philosophical ideas occupy a more central position. Here we can see a deliberate dialectical method, both in the juxtaposition of contrasting symbolic images or scenes (e.g. the temple of *Venus and the vision of *Nature on her hill of flowers) and in an underlying conflict (which is subtly resolved) between *experience and authority (*auctoritee). In all of the poems (but most obviously in *The House of Fame*) Chaucer seems self-consciously concerned with his own poetic art.

His treatment of ideas is not grimly didactic, but combines seriousness and humour. The figure of the dreamer-*narrator appears as a naive, bewildered person, with a reverence for authority and a decided tendency to bookishness coupled with an apparent ignorance or uncertainty. He does not seem to be an intense pilgrim of the mind: things simply seem to happen to him (he is carried aloft by an eagle or pushed in through a gate). Yet he is an alter ego of the poet, with an insatiable curiosity, both about experience and about authority.

The guides and authority figures which he meets are also treated in an original way. No guide in other dream visions can match the talkative Eagle; Dame Nature speaks with homely force. There is a characteristic liveliness in the *dialogues. The symbolic landscapes and settings of the dream visions are traditional, but are imaginatively treated, with a careful attention to detail. Chaucer's dream visions usually have elaborate introductions, establishing not only the distinctive narrative voice of the dreamer to be, but also adumbrating patterns of images and ideas. The endings are abrupt. In *The Book of the Duchess* the dreamer is wakened by a bell, in *The Parliament of Fowls* by the 'shouting' of the birds, *The House of Fame* breaks off with the appearance of one who seemed to be 'a man of gret auctorite'. Chaucer likes to leave his readers not with any neat conclusion or summary or even suggestion of the completion of a process of enlightenment, but with a teasing remark or a question. 'This is such a curious dream', he muses at the end of *The Book of the*

Duchess 'that I will try to put it into rhyme'; at the end of *The Parliament* he turns back to his books in the hope of finding something which will make him 'fare the bet [better]'. What the dreams were really about, and what he has learnt from them are left for his readers to discover.

P. Brown (1999); Hieatt (1967); Lynch (1988); Norton-Smith (1974), 5; Piehler (1971); Spearing (1976); Windeatt (1982).

dreams. Medieval writers inherited ancient traditions concerning the nature and significance of dreams. They knew from the Bible that God could speak to men in dreams and visions (Job 33:15–16), as in those of Pharaoh (*Pharao), *Joseph (1), Nebuchadnezzar (*Nabugodonosor), and others. They could find in Virgil (*Aeneid* 6) the Homeric image of the two gates of sleep, one made of ivory and one of horn, through which came respectively false and true dreams, and in Ovid (*Met.* 11) the god *Morpheus, surrounded by the forms of dreams. Aristotle's remarks about dreams are quoted. Cicero's *Somnium Scipionis* (*Drem of Scipioun) is an influential text.

The commentary (*c.* AD 400) of Macrobius (*Macrobes) on the *Somnium Scipionis* offers an elaborate classification of the varieties of dreams. There are, he says, five principal types. Two of them are without significance (because they are not prophetic): the *insomnium* or nightmare which is caused by anxiety or bodily distress, and the *phantasma* or *visum*, an apparition, which occurs in the 'first mist of sleep' between wakefulness and sleep, when a person thinks he is awake and seems to see strange forms moving about or rushing in at him. Three are significant, having prophetic value: the *somnium* or enigmatic dream, which conceals its significance with figures and ambiguity, and cannot be understood without an interpretation; the *visio* or prophetic vision; and the *oraculum*, the oracular dream in which a relative or some revered or sacred person, like a priest or even a god, appears to give prophetic information or advice.

There were other schemes of classification and explanations. Medical treatises point out that the derangements of the body's 'complexion' might be reflected in dreams. One scheme distinguishes the *somnium naturale*, originating from bodily complexions and humours, the *somnium animale*, caused by anxieties of the waking mind, and the *somnium coeleste*, consisting of impressions implanted by celestial intelligences. Astrologers may distinguish visions sent by God, dreams coming from planetary influences (of varying reliability, depending on the power or position of the planets), and dreams coming from the humours of the body. A theologian like St Augustine distinguishes different categories of visions: those which come through the natural senses, those which are impressed by spiritual powers on the imagination in sleep or in trance, and those in which divine mysteries are directly and intuitively discerned by the intellect. Visions or dreams may be the work of evil spirits as well as of good ones. Around this much popular lore gathered. There was for instance the 'nightmare', originally a female demon which settled on people while they slept there was widespread curiosity about dreams and visions which revealed the future or the mysteries of life after death. Dreams were a form of divination (opposed by the Parson (X.604)). Dream books offered advice on the interpretation of dreams (often, as in their modern equivalents, of a cautiously general kind).

Much of this material was common knowledge. The encyclopaedia of *Bartholomew gives a summary (book 6). Animals have dreams (dogs bark and horses neigh in their sleep). We dream of things which we experienced by our senses when awake. True dreams may be open and plain, or may be 'wrapped in figurative, mystic, and dim and dark tokenings and bodings'—as in the case of Pharoah's dream. Dreams may be revelations from God or deceptions by Satan. They may be caused by the complexion: a sanguine person has 'glad and pleasant dreams', a melancholic dreams of sorrow; the choleric dreams of fire and fiery things; the phlegmatic of rain and snow. Sometimes dreams come from 'appetite, affection and desire': the hungry man dreams of food, and the more he dreams of food, the hungrier he is when he wakes. A covetous man dreams of gold. They may come from an evil disposition of the brain (those disposed to frenzy and madness have strange and wonderful dreams), from corrupt blood, or the changing of air. They may differ with age: small children do not dream.

dreams

In spite of all the learned commentary and almost obsessive discussion (the Middle Ages took dreams very seriously indeed), there was no simple answer to the question which for most people was central: were dreams 'true'? A pair of opposed proverbs expressed the dilemma: on the one hand 'dreams are false' (did not Cato (*Catoun) say 'ne do no fors of [pay no attention to] dremes', VII.2941)?, but, on the other, 'dreams are true' (as evidenced by *Daniel). The argument rages seriously and comically throughout Chaucer's works.

The opening of The *House of Fame offers a typical avowal of ignorance—and at the same time a scintillating display of oneiric terminology:

> ... hyt is wonder ...
> To my wyt, what causeth swevenes ...
> .   .   .   .   .   .
> Why that is an a vision
> And why this a revelacion,
> Why this a drem, why that a sweven ...
> Why this a fantome, why these oracles,
> I not [do not know];

This breathless virtuoso performance continues for another forty or more lines, touching on the difficulties concerning kinds, times, significances, and causes (mentioning the familiar complexions, disorders like melancholy, devotion and contemplation, the cruel life of lovers, spirits, and a possible intrinsic foreknowledge in the soul) before finally throwing the problems back to the 'grete clerkys'.

This proem demonstrates the range of Chaucer's vocabulary concerning dreams. The basic words are dre(e)m (both 'dream' and 'vision') and the older sweven which has a similar range, and usually overlaps with dre(e)m. The apparent distinction made here (and only here in Chaucer) may be a comic one, since the difficulties involved in the (often overlapping) categories laid down by the theorists seem to be part of the joke. Fantome is a 'delusory dream'; avisioun a vision or a dream. Chaucer also uses the word traunce for very powerful emotional reactions, but in his works these do not result in 'visions'.

Chaucer had read widely in ancient and medieval dream literature. Remarks and allusions show a knowledge of the general lore concerning dreams. See, for instance, The Man of Law's Tale

(II.804) (Custance's anxiety may cause her to suffer in her dreams), The Squire's Tale (V.357–9) (after revelry, heads are full of 'fumositee' [fumes from wine] which causes dreams of no significance), The Wife of Bath's Prologue (III.581–2) (dreaming of blood betokens gold). In The Parliament of Fowls (99–105) we are told people often dream of things experienced during the waking hours: the wery huntere ... | To wode ayeyn his mynde goth anon. The dreams of the judge, the carter, the rich man, the sick man, and the lover are similar reflections (99–105). (Behind these lines lie a number of literary examples, going back ultimately to the Somnium Scipionis itself, where Scipio suggests that he dreamed of his grandfather because he was the subject of the conversation he had with Masinissa the previous night.) In The Second Nun's Tale dreams are associated with unreality (cf. Tr III.584–5, 1342), and, perhaps, the idea that earthly life is a dream. When Tiburce hears the account of the visit of the angel, he asks, 'Seistow | In soothnesse, or in dreem I herkne this?', and receives the reply 'In dremes ... han we be | Unto this tyme ... | But now at erst [first] in trouthe [truth], oure dwellyng is' (VIII.260–4). There is one case (from Boethius) where 'dream' echoes the Platonic notion of 'recollection': earthly men dream of their beginning, though nor clearly nor perfectly (Bo III pr.3:1 ff.).

In his own *dream visions Chaucer likes to present himself as naively proud of the wondrous quality of his dreams. In The House of Fame his 'avisyon' is more marvellous than those of Isaiah, Scipio, Nebuchadnezzar, Pharoah, *Turnus, or '*Elcanor' (512–16). And in The Book of the Duchess he sounds like a connoisseur when he describes his dream as 'so ynly swete', as well as so 'wonderful' that none of the great experts—Joseph, Pharoah, Macrobius—could interpret it (275–89). The Book of the Duchess and The Parliament of Fowls seem to be examples of the somnium animale, since our attention is drawn to the perturbations or concerns of the dreamer's mind; in The House of Fame, however, the suggestion (however light-hearted) is that the dream is a somnium coeleste.

Several types of dream occur in Chaucer's narratives: a 'celestial vision' in The Second Nun's Tale (VIII.200–16); less reverent examples in The Summoner's Tale (III.1675–703, 1854–93). The *Monk's

Tale, with its rather determinist view of *Fortune, makes notable use of dreams which foretell the future. It refers to the prophetic dreams of Nebuchadnezzar (VII.2156), and describes the visions of Belshazzar (*Balthasar) and Croesus (*Cresus) together with their interpretations and their predictable outcome (2202–35, 2740–56).

The most interesting use of dreams within a narrative is to be found in *Troilus and Criseyde* and The *Nun's Priest's Tale. In *Troilus* dreams are used to mark emotional climaxes, and to allow glimpses into the hidden emotional currents of the story. When Troilus returns from the temple where he has first seen Criseyde, he has a brief waking dream (I.362–4) in which his memory recalls the scene and her appearance. In the second book (925–31) Criseyde dreams of a white eagle which tears out her heart and places his heart in its place. This is the culmination of a sequence invented by Chaucer: the sight of Troilus riding in the street, Criseyde's anguished interior arguments, Antigone's song of love, the nightingale singing beneath her chamber. As in medieval dream lore her waking experiences are echoed in her dream. The bird image takes the form of the noble eagle, its whiteness suggesting Troilus's goodness and nobility of soul. The exchange of hearts comes from an impression printed in Criseyde's mind by Antigone's words (869–73), and is a symbolic fulfilment of them.

In book V terrible dreams afflict the sorrowing Troilus. He dreams (246–61) of 'The dreadfulleste thynges | That myght ben', that he is alone in a horrible place, lamenting, or that he is alone among his enemies and has fallen into their hands (again, there is a connection with waking experience, and again there is a symbolic, prophetic level). Troilus takes them to be a sign that he must die (317–18). Pandarus, however, takes a robustly sceptical view of dreams (which Chaucer has much expanded from what he found in his source). The dreams 'and al swich fantasie' arise simply from melancholy. Pandarus lists the traditional explanations: they are revelations or infernal illusions (so the priests), they come from physical causes, from 'complexiouns' (so the physicians), or from fasting or gluttony (who therefore can know what they signify?). Others say they come from 'impressions' (372 ff.); others

that 'th'effect goth by the moone'. He sweeps them all briskly aside—leave them to 'thise olde wives' with other kinds of auguries.

Later in the book (1233 ff.) Troilus, not yet aware that Criseyde has yielded to Diomede, has a symbolic dream like that of Criseyde in book II. As he walks through a forest, he sees a boar sleeping in the sun and embracing Criseyde. There is an equivalent scene in Boccaccio's poem, but Chaucer has changed it apparently to differentiate it from the earlier dream to which it is formally parallel (and for which it obviously supplied some suggestions). In Boccaccio it is violent and erotic. The boar charged through the wood and tore out Criseida's heart, but she cared little for the hurt, and almost took pleasure in it. Chaucer has made it into a static scene which the dreamer 'comes upon', an 'unkind', unnatural scene, as if from a depiction of some mythological story. Troilus instantly interprets it symbolically ('my lady bryght, Criseyde, hath me bytrayed') and Pandarus again says that dreams beguile men, though now he changes his ground slightly by claiming that this happens because people interpret them incorrectly (it could here signify Criseyde's father on the point of death and his daughter weeping and kissing him). Cassandra (*Cassandre) interprets the dream as Troilus did. Troilus finally confronts Pandarus ('that in dremes for to triste | Me blamed hast') with the proof of Criseyde's 'falsing' and states his conviction that 'the goddes shewen bothe joie and tene | In slep, and by my dream it is now sene' (1714–15).

In The *Nun's Priest's Tale* dreams are treated in a spirit of 'game'. The cock Chauntecleer has a terrifying dream, of a creature shaped like a hound, of colour between yellow and red, his tail and ears tipped with black, with narrow snout, glowing eyes, and a fearsome look (VII.2898–907). Pertelote reproves him sharply for being frightened by dreams, and urges rational and medical explanations: dreams come from overeating, from complexions. Superfluity of the red choleric humour causes people to dream of fire, red beasts, and whelps, just as the black humour of melancholy causes fearfulness of black bears, black bulls, black devils. She quotes Cato's proverb 'Ne do no fors of dremes', and prescribes a list of purgative herbs. Chauntecleer appeals to greater authorities, to exempla and to some notable prophetic 'avisions'. The consequences of his decision to 'diffye bothe sweven and dreem' seem likely to make him analogous to one of those unfortunate princes in *The Monk's Tale* who were warned by prophetic visions or misled by women's counsels, but in the end Fortune is favourable to him. And the whole question of the 'truth' of dreams seems to be left in the balance. Chaucer never tells us whether we should side with Chauntecleer and Troilus or with Pertelote and Pandarus.

P. Brown (1999); Curry (1960); Kruger (1992).

Drem of Scipioun, the *Somnium Scipionis* of Cicero (*Tullius). Originally the closing section of *De re publica*, it was preserved in the Middle Ages through the commentary which Macrobius (*Macrobes) wrote on it, with which it was usually read. It is modelled on the vision of Er which ends Plato's *Republic*. In it Scipio Africanus the younger (*Scipio(n)) describes how on a visit to Masinissa (*Massynisse), an ally of Rome in the Second Punic War, the aged king talked at length about his famous grandfather, Scipio Africanus Major (*Affrican (1)), and his deeds in that war. When Scipio goes to bed he dreams that his grandfather stands before him, and speaks to him. He foretells his future and urges him to virtue and the service of the state. From a point high in the heavens he sees the littleness of earth, the greatness of the heavens, and the planetary spheres in motion, causing by their movement a wonderful harmony. His grandfather explains the nature of the cosmos to him, and tells him to condemn earthly fame. The reward of the noble soul is to be taken to the heavens. Those who are enslaved by bodily pleasures will hover close to the earth and return to the heavens only after long ages of torment. 'He departed, and I awoke from sleep'. The *Somnium Scipionis* was a seminal text. Chaucer knew it well, referring to it in *BD* (284–7) and *HF* (916–18). He gives a fine poetic (and slightly Christianized summary) at the beginning of *PF* (36–84).

(trans.) Stahl (1952); Windeatt (1982).

drunkenness (see also *ale; *wine). In Chaucer drunkenness is not a major preoccupation, but when it occurs the effects can be dramatic. Medieval literature is rich in descriptions of convivial and roistering scenes. The period also produced some splendid drinking songs. Literary tavern scenes often seem to blend disapproving satire with the evocation of a kind of disorderly vitality. Actual tavern brawls as recorded in the legal records could themselves be spectacular. Preachers and moralists disapprove of drunken excess, and of the tavern as the 'church of the Devil'. The *Parson calls drunkenness 'the horrible sepulture [burial-place] of mannes resoun' (X.821). A number of contemporary drunkenness proverbs take this high moral line: 'in whom that drynke hath dominacioun | He kan no conseil kepe' (quoted by the Pardoner, VI.560–1; cf. VII.1192). More moderate is that quoted by Criseyde 'For though a man forbede dronkenesse, | He naught forbet that every creature | Be drynkeles for alwey' (*Tr* II.716–18). And there is a rather charming proverbial comparison 'drunken as a mouse' (presumably from the erratic darting movements of that small creature (see I.1261, III.246–7)).

In *The *Canterbury Tales* there is a certain interest in the characteristic symptoms of drunkenness. Already in the Middle Ages there were colloquial expressions and euphemisms for these. In *The *Reeve's Tale*, for instance, the miller goes to bed at midnight after drinking much strong ale (I.4146–67): he had 'varnished his head' (i.e. his head was shining with sweat; cf. modern 'well oiled'?), he is 'ful pale' (commonly noted as a sign of drunkenness; cf. I.3120); he belches, and speaks through his nose as if he had a cold. His wife has also 'wet her whistle' (4155), and her snoring forms a *burdon* (ground-bass) to the noises of her husband: 'as an hors he fnorteth [snorts] in his sleep, | Ne of his tayl bihynde he took no keep'. The snoring, says the Reeve, could be heard for two furlongs, and their daughter completes the ensemble: 'the wenche rowteth [snores] eek, *par compaignye*'. The drunken messenger in *The *Man of Law's Tale* (II.771 ff.) has the usual strong breath and faltering limbs, and 'jangles'. He is an example of the old maxim that 'ther dronkenesse regneth ... | Ther is no conseil hyd'. While he is snoring false letters are substituted for those he bears. Drink has a more bizarre effect on the *Summoner, who will then speak nothing but Latin (I.638).

Drunkenness has a dramatic role in *The Canterbury Tales*. If the pilgrimage is to end at a martyr's shrine it begins in a tavern; and it is presided over by a *Host who is not only generous with drink ('strong was the wyn, and wel to drynke us leste', I.750; cf. I.819) but is skilled in handling those who have had too much. The conviviality established at the beginning is the source of some truth-telling and of some 'lewednesse' and folly, and of some disorder.

This begins with the drunken *Miller interrupting the Host, and loudly insisting on telling a tale instead of the Monk. The Host, realizing his condition, handles the situation calmly until he is finally irritated by the unstoppable Miller ('Tel on, a devel wey! | Thou art a fool; thy wit is overcome', 3134-5). In contrast, the infuriated *Reeve himself interrupts the Miller's stately and self-conscious 'protestacioun' ('I am dronke; I knowe it by my soun') with 'Stynt thy clappe! | Lat be thy lewed dronken harlotrye' (3144-5). The Miller's response is a marvellous display of exaggerated courtesy and tolerance, spiced with some preacherly morality (3151-66). The change of tone carefully prepares us for the quite undrunken telling of the tale itself, an effortless transition from an exercise in local 'realism' to the conventions of narrative. But the Miller's interruption serves as a neat introduction to the first *fabliau of the collection, and establishes its framework of '*game'. For the Reeve, however, he is still 'this dronke Millere' (3913), and in his Tale he gets his own back with the strange night music at the house in Trumpington.

The Pardoner causes a stir by insisting on having a drink before he begins his tale (VI.321 ff.). The fact that the folk of his tale are 'rioters' who 'drynken over hir myght' gives him the opportunity for a preacher's diatribe against drunkenness. With some relish he lists the famous drunks of ancient times: Lot (*Looth), Herod (*Herodes), and *Attila (two others found elsewhere in the Tales are Holofernes (*Oloferne) and *Cambises). He warns against the subtle power of Spanish wine, and creates a vivid picture of the drunken man—'O dronke man, disfigured is thy face, | Sour is thy breeth, foul artow to embrace, | And thurgh thy dronke nose semeth

the soun | As though thou seydest ay, "Sampsoun, Sampsoun!"' (VI.551-4), and, as he continues, we hear the traditional topics of the moralists: 'thy tonge is lost, and al thyn honeste cure, | For dronkenesse is verray sepulture | Of mannes wit and his discrecioun'. The tale begins in the tavern (where Death had taken off the rioters' friend 'for-dronke, as he sat on his bench upright'), and although they find Death under a tree, two of them find death in a bottle. The Pardoner's own drink does not seem to impair his narrative powers (although his self-correction, 'nat Samuel, but Lamuel seye I' (585), may suggest a tipsy desire for precision). Whether it affects his judgement in his ill-fated attempt to sell relics to the Host we are not told. Later, the *Cook causes an even greater stir when he falls off his horse (IX.48). As the Manciple sharply notes, he has all the symptoms. The Host handles the situation with his usual aplomb. A kind of order is restored, which prompts him to remark (with some irony) on the healing powers of good wine. There is not much room in *The Canterbury Tales* for the vehement condemnations of the moralists. It is no doubt a deliberate irony that the person who reviles drunkenness most emphatically is the drunken Pardoner.

DRYDEN, JOHN (1631-1700), poet, dramatist, and critic, has a special place in the history of Chaucerian studies. At the end of his life he produced *Fables Ancient and Modern* (1700), an impressive collection of narrative poems translated or adapted from earlier stories. Besides the first book of the *Iliad*, stories and passages from the *Metamorphoses*, and from Boccaccio, it contains 'Palamon and Arcite or, The Knight's Tale', 'The Cock and the Fox or, the Tale of the Nun's Priest', 'The Wife of Bath, her Tale', and 'The Character of a Good Parson imitated from Chaucer, and inlarg'd'. He also included an adaptation of *The *Flower and the Leafe*, then thought to be by Chaucer. He translated Chaucer with vigour and sympathy (see *modernizations), and expressed his great admiration for him in the Preface. Chaucer is not without fault: 'he writes not always of a piece, but sometimes mingles trivial things with those of great moment. Sometimes also, tho' not often, he runs riot, like Ovid, and knows not when he has said enough.' But 'he is a perpetual fountain of good sense, learn'd in all sciences, and therefore speaks properly on all subjects'. This intelligent and subtle preface proved very influential in the history of Chaucer criticism (see *criticism of Chaucer I).

CH I. 160–72 (part of Preface).

Drye Se. The lady in The *Book of the Duchess did not require her admirers to 'goo hoodles into the Drye Se | And come hom by the *Carrenar' (1028). The 'drye se' is probably the Gobi desert, which was sometimes called 'the sea of sand' or 'the gravelly sea'. *Marco Polo describes the Gobi, or desert of Lop, as consisting entirely of mountains and sand and valleys; arid and haunted by spirits. It has been suggested that in Chaucer's day it may have been confused with the great shoals at the mouths of the rivers Dvina and Pechora in Russia, the beginning of another trade route to Asia.

Dulcarnoun, proposition I.47 of Euclid's Elements, the theorem of Pythagoras. From the Arabic for 'two-horned', presumably because this was thought to describe the familiar diagram. In *Troilus and Criseyde, Pandarus says that Dulcarnon is called flemyng of wrecches, and so evidently confuses it with proposition I.5, known in Latin as fuga miserorum. [JDN]

Dun is in the myre. At the beginning of the Manciple's Prologue, the Host begins to 'jape and pleye' and says 'Sires, what! Dun is in the myre!' (IX.5). This is apparently a proverbial colloquial expression meaning 'things have got stuck'. It is frequently found after Chaucer. 'Dun' (i.e. a dark coloured horse) is used as a name for any horse. The reference seems to be to a game (sometimes called 'drawing Dun out of the mire'), in which the participants competed by trying to move and carry off a heavy log, representing the horse in the mire (cf. Mercutio, in Romeo and Juliet (1.1.41) 'If thou art Dun, we'll draw thee from the mire').

DUNBAR, WILLIAM (?c.1460–?1513; see '*Chaucerians, Scottish'), may have been a graduate of the University of St Andrews. He was a cleric, and was associated with the court of James IV.

He produced a great variety of mostly non-narrative poetry—satires, lyrics both secular and religious—which reveal an extraordinary linguistic energy and a sharp, macabre imagination. 'The noble Chaucer of makaris flour' heads the list of poets taken by death in his well-known 'Lament for the Makars'. His 'Tretis of the Tua Mariit Wemen and the Wedo' is reminiscent of the *Wife of Bath's Prologue, but his most obvious indebtedness to Chaucer is seen in his allegorical poems, 'The Thrissill and the Rois', and 'The Goldyn Targe', which praises him as the 'rose of rethoris all' and 'all the lycht' of 'oure Inglisch'.

(ed.) Bawcutt (1998); Kinsley (1979); Bawcutt (1992).

Dunmowe, Little Dunmow, near Chelmsford in *Essex. When the *Wife of Bath says of her suffering husbands (III.218) 'the bacon was nat fet [fetched] for him . . . | That som men han in Essex at Dunmowe' she is alluding to a custom of the manor in which a side of bacon was presented to a couple who could prove (originally, before the Prior) that they had lived in conjugal harmony for a year and a day'. It is said to have begun in 1244, and to have continued to the 20th c.

DUNSTAN, SEINT (909–88) was born near Glastonbury of a noble family. He is said to have been expelled from the household of his uncle, the archbishop of Canterbury, accused of 'studying the vain poems and futile stories of the pagans and of being a magician'. He became a monk, and was later abbot of Glastonbury, and made the monastery into a famous and influential school. Later still he became bishop of Worcester, then of London, and eventually archbishop of Canterbury (960). His greatest achievement was the reform of the monastic movement. In his old age and after his death an extensive cult grew up around him. Visions, prophecies, and miracles were attributed to him. He is said to have been a painter, a musician, and a worker in metals. Legend claimed that he had power over devils. He is sometimes depicted holding the devil by the nose with a pair of tongs. It is this tradition which Chaucer remembers when in The *Friar's Tale (III.1501–2) the fiend says that devils are sometimes 'servant unto man, | As to the erchebisshop Seint Dunstan'.

E

Eacides Chiron (Eacides, possessive form of Aeacides = Achilles, grandson of Aeacus), Chiron the centaur, skilled in music, medicine and prophecy, the tutor of Achilles, mentioned in a list of harpers in *The *House of Fame* (1206).

Eagle. The golden eagle, who appears at the end of Book I of *The *House of Fame*, and carries the dreamer up through the heavens, may have been suggested to Chaucer by the eagle in *Dante (*Purgatorio* 9. 19–20). In the *Bestiary, the eagle is noted for its soaring flight and keen gaze, and sometimes for its rigorous education of its young. It could be used as a symbol of contemplative thought, but Chaucer's eagle (one of his earliest comic creations) is an enthusiastic and loquacious instructor, lecturing his taciturn and amazed companion on the wonders of sound and stars.

EBRAYK JOSEPHUS, see *Josephus, Ebrayk.

Ecclesiaste, the author of the apocryphal Old Testament book Ecclesiasticus (apparently written or compiled by Jesus the son of Sira (*Jhesus Syrak)), seems to be referred to by the Wife of Bath (III.651) and as a general proverbial authority by the *Nun's Priest.* (VII.3329). There is perhaps a confusion with Ecclesiastes, the Old Testament wisdom book of the 'Preacher'.

Echo, Ecquo, Ekko. Echo, a nymph who fell in love with the beautiful but cruel *Narcissus, was rejected, and wasted away until only her voice remained. Because of enchantment by Juno she could only repeat the words of others. This story of hopeless love is told by *Ovid (*Met.* 3. 380–99). It is used as an exemplum by Aurelius in *The *Franklin's Tale* (V.951), who says that he must die like Echo who dared not tell her 'wo'. Echo appears in lists of those who died for love in *The*

*Book of the Duchess (735). But the idea of the 'everlasting voice' is found in the Envoy to *The *Clerk's Tale* (IV.1189), where 'noble wyves' are urged to follow the example of Echo and 'evere answereth at the countretaille [in reply]'.

Eclympasteyr, 'the god of slepes heyr' in *The *Book of the Duchess* (167), a son of *Morpheus. Chaucer took the name from *Froissart's Enclimpostair (possibly a witty formation from *enclin* + *postere* 'lying flat') in the *Paradys d'amours*.

Ecliptic, eclyptik, ecliptic (as in 'lyne ecliptik of hevene', *A Treatise on the *Astrolabe* 1.21, 24). The apparent path of the Sun on the celestial sphere, traversed in the course of its annual motion. Celestial *longitude is measured along the ecliptic, from the head of Aries as origin. (See also ***Aries**; ***astrology and astronomy**; ***hed**.)   [JDN]

Ecquo, see *Echo.

Ector. Hector, son of *Priam and brother of Troilus. This Trojan hero, who had become for the Middle Ages one of the legendary champions of *chivalry (see the *Nine Worthies), appears as a noble and generous figure in **Troilus and Criseyde*. In Book I, when Criseyde appeals to him for protection, Hector 'pitous of nature' consoles her, and remains her friend (cf. II.1450–5). He opposes the proposed exchange of Criseyde for Antenor. His death (V.1548–68) at the hands of Achilles introduces a sombre and elegiac note, foreshadowing the death of Troilus (called 'Ector the secounde') (II.158; cf. II.739–40) and the destruction of the city. He is elsewhere referred to as one of the heroes of Troy (*BD* 328) and an example of outstanding courage (*BD* 1064). The death of Hector was a famous scene. In *LGW* (934) there is an allusion to the appearance of his ghost to

Ecuba

Aeneas. All four references in *The *Canterbury Tales* are to his death: the lamentation that accompanied it (I.2832), the fact that it was written in the stars (*MLT*, II.198), and twice (in a mock-heroic context) in *The Nun's Priest's Tale* (VII.3142, 3144) in connection with the prophetic dream of his wife Andromache (*Andromacha).

Ecuba, Hecuba, *Priam's wife, the mother of *Troilus (*Tr* V.12).

Edippe, Edipus, Oedipus, the son of Laius, king of Thebes, who blinded himself when he learnt that he had killed his father and married his mother. Chaucer knew the story not from Greek tragedy, but from the *Thebaid* of Statius (*Stace) and the *Roman de Thèbes* (see *Thebes (1)). He refers to it twice in *Troilus and Criseyde* (II.102; IV.300): in the account of the 'romaunce' of Thebes which is read to Criseyde and her ladies; and in the lament of Troilus after he has heard the news that Criseyde is to be sent back to the Greeks, when he compares his fate to that of Oedipus ('but ende I wol, as Edippe, in derknesse | My sorweful life, and dyen in distresse', IV.300–1).

editing and editions. An 'edition' (derived from a word meaning 'put forth' or 'publish') is (*OED*) 'one of the differing forms in which a literary work (or a collection of works) is published, either by the author himself, or by subsequent editors'. Since none of Chaucer's literary works survives in a copy written by himself, we are heavily dependent on the 'subsequent editors', whether medieval scribes or modern scholars. We now read Chaucer in 'critical' editions provided by the latter, which give us a corrected text, presented with modern punctuation and layout (and often in a spelling which has been to some extent standardized or modernized), and usually with explanatory glosses and notes and critical introductions. These editions differ markedly in appearance from the copies left by the medieval scribes and early printers on which they are based. The vagaries of some medieval scribes are notorious (see Chaucer's 'Wordes unto *Adam (2), his owne scriveyn'), and, not surprisingly, these early copies contain many errors. Some are very obvious. But in cases where variant readings make good sense

and/or are found in authoritative MSS—such as 'Gret rumour gan' | 'The noise up ros' (*Tr* I.85) or 'the bryghte goddes sevene' | 'the blisful goddes sevene' (*Tr* III.1203)—how are we to say which is erroneous? It may well be that either or both cases give us evidence of Chaucer revising his text.

The editorial process by which the modern critical edition is derived from the surviving early evidence for Chaucer's texts is far from simple. Its traditional aim is to attempt to restore as nearly as possible the words which the author actually wrote (though, of course, what he wrote could exist in different forms or stages). The surviving textual evidence has to be carefully evaluated, with the aim of establishing which manuscripts or which individual readings seem closest to the supposed 'original'. The editor is then faced with a number of choices. He may decide to present the text of one individual MS, simply correcting what seem to be self-evident errors, and in his notes citing variant readings from other MSS and suggesting further possible emendations. Such an editor might be criticized for evading his fundamental task of reconstruction. Or he may opt for an 'eclectic' or composite text, taking 'better' readings from a number of different MSS. This method (found in the 18th-c. edition of the *Tales* by *Tyrwhitt) is obviously open to the charge of being subjective or arbitrary. The great majority of modern editors have preferred to attempt to establish a critical text. This can be done in a number of ways. That based on the editing of classical texts attempts to construct a 'family tree' or *stemma* of the textual witnesses, determining their relationship to each other by the way in which errors are shared and transmitted. Theoretically, the resulting emended text is that of the editor (it is his version of the author's text), and would not need to correspond exactly with that of the best manuscript or manuscripts in the *stemma*. In practice, most editors have chosen a 'good' MS as their base (e.g. in the case of the *Tales* the *Ellesmere MS or the *Hengwrt MS) and have emended it (with varying degrees of freedom) from other MSS which their textual analysis has shown to have some authority.

Argument has raged over the general questions involved here—how far the editor's 'personal judgement' may be allowed to run, as against 'objective' or 'scientific' (or mechanical?) applications of a technique; and even whether the notion of an original 'text' can be justified. And such problems continue to haunt the editor in matters of detail. How far, for instance, is one justified in emending a text (such as *The Book of the Duchess*) so as to restore (or impose) a regular metrical pattern? And all kinds of questions concerning Chaucer's stylistic usage, the influence of the works he is adapting or translating, as well as of the precise tone of the particular context must be borne in mind. The examples from *Troilus and Criseyde* quoted above illustrate this. It can be argued that 'the bryghte goddes' should be preferred because the phrase occurs in another poem, *Scogan*, and because a precisely astral reference is appropriate. But it would be possible also to make a contextual case for *blisful*. It can be argued that in the other case *rumour* should be chosen because it corresponds to the *romor* or *rumor* of his Italian source, and because it is more likely to have originated with Chaucer himself than to have been introduced by a scribe. Against this, it might be speculated that in revision Chaucer decided to substitute for the literal (and possibly recondite) term a more vigorous, homely and favourite word. On such matters argument is likely to continue.

Editions of Chaucer's complete Works
(for editions of separate works see the entries under individual titles)

In 1526, Richard *Pynson printed a work in three parts perhaps intended to be sold separately; there is no general title page, but it contains *Troilus, The Canterbury Tales, The House of Fame, The Parliament of Fowls*, and *Truth*, as well as some non-Chaucerian works (see *Chauceriana). But the first edition of the complete works to present itself as such is that of William *Thynne (1532, and later editions). This contained some apocryphal works. It was followed in 1561 by John *Stow's *The workes of Geffrey Chaucer, newlie printed with diuers addicions, whiche were neuer in print before*. As the title indicates, still more apocryphal works were added. *Speght's *The Workes of our Antient and Learned English Poet, Geffrey Chavcer* appeared in 1598 (and a second edition in 1602, reprinted in 1687). In the 18th c. came the edition of *Urry (1721), which was criticized by Tyrwhitt (see also *Morell).

Dr *Johnson projected an edition but it never appeared. However, the contemporary enthusiasm for collections of English poets produced the editions (simply following Urry and Tyrwhitt) of John Bell (1782), Anderson (1795), Chalmers (1810), and others. Robert Bell's edition in his *Annotated Editions of the English Poets* (1854–6) has rather more in the way of commentary, but the first truly scholarly edition is the six-volume Oxford Chaucer of W. W. *Skeat (*The Complete Works of Geoffrey Chaucer*, 1894–7). Although we now know much more about the MSS than Skeat did, his edition is remarkable for its learned commentary, its glossary, and the way in which it distinguished the genuine works from the spurious. Other 19th-c. editions include the beautiful Kelmscott Chaucer (1896), and the Globe edition of 1898. The 20th c. produced the elaborate eight-volume work of Manly and Rickert (1940); F. N. Robinson's *The Works of Geoffrey Chaucer* (1933, with a second edition in 1957) became the standard scholarly text, now replaced by *The Riverside Chaucer* (1987) under the general editorship of Larry D. Benson.

Ruggiers (1984).

EDWARD, SEINT. Before embarking on his 'tragedies' the Monk (VII.1970) offers 'the lyf of Seint Edward' as a possible tale, without further elaboration. He is usually taken to be Edward the Confessor, king of England 1043–66, who was venerated as a saint. In Chaucer's day there was a magnificent shrine for his relics in Westminster Abbey. He seems to have been regarded as a patron saint of England, and there are many depictions of him and a number of 'Lives' were written in Latin, Anglo-Norman, and ME. It is just possible that the Monk's story could have been of another saintly pre-Conquest English king, St Edward the Martyr, murdered at Corfe in 979. Although not as prominent as Edward the Confessor, he enjoyed a wide and continuing devotion in the later Middle Ages. It would be tempting to speculate that the suddenness and the violence of his demise might have appealed to the Monk. According to William of Malmesbury, his beautiful but wicked stepmother 'allured him with female blandishment' so that a servant was able to stab him as he drank eagerly from a cup—and later made atonement by becoming a nun. If the 'or ellis' with which the Monk introduces his alternative suggestion of 'tragedies' is taken as strongly adversative, 'Seint Edward' is likely to be the Confessor. It has also been suggested that there is a possible allusion to the murdered king Edward II, whose canonization was supported by Richard II. Astell (2000).

EDWARD III (b. 1312), king of England 1327–77. The early years of his reign were marked by his absence on numerous campaigns in France, though after 1360 these wars were carried on by his eldest son, the Black Prince. During Chaucer's membership of the royal household from 1367 Edward's powers were failing, and during his last years corruption at court was notorious. In March 1360 Edward ransomed Chaucer after his capture in France; subsequently Chaucer went on various missions on the king's behalf; numerous payments were made by the king to Chaucer and to his wife Philippa *Chaucer. Edward fathered numerous children: in addition to the Black Prince (who predeceased his father, and whose son succeeded as *Richard II), Chaucer had dealings with *John of Gaunt, duke of Lancaster from 1362, and Lionel, duke of Clarence from 1362. Edward's active patronage of literature seems to have been limited, but he owned a number of books, many of which were inherited by Richard II. It was at Edward's instigation that St Stephen's Chapel Westminster was completed and decorated, Windsor Castle refurbished, and the Chapel of St George reconstructed.   [AH]
  LR; (books) Cavanaugh (1985), 278–80.

Egeus, Aegeus, king of Athens, father of Theseus, mentioned in The *Legend of Good Women (1944). In a brief appearance in The *Knight's Tale (I.2838, 2905) (where he is twice called 'old') he comforts the people after the death of Arcite with 'ensamples and liknesse', reminding them in proverbial lines that no man ever lived in this world who did not die.

Egypt (e) in Chaucer's day was part of the Muslim world, ruled by the dynasties of the Mamelukes (originally slave bodyguards). His references, however, are to earlier historical periods: of the 'Kyng, daun Pharao' (NPT VII.3133), BD 281, and

the plagues, BD 1206; or the Egypt of Antony and Cleopatra (LGW).

EGIPCIEN MARIE, see *Marie, Egipcien.

Egiste(s), Egistus, Aegyptus, in The Legend of Good Women the father of Hypermnestra. In Ovid she was one of the fifty daughters of Danaus, whose brother Aegpytus had fifty sons. The reason for Chaucer's error or substitution is not known: possibly it was suggested to him by some commentary on Ovid.

Eglentyne, Madame, the *Prioress (the name means 'briar rose').

ejaculations and interjections. The word ejaculation, now used to mean 'the hasty utterance of words expressing *emotion', once meant a short prayer 'darted up' to God (like that of the miller's wife in a comic rather than devotional context in The *Reeve's Tale (I.4286): 'Help! hooly croys of Bromeholm'). In grammar it is usually called 'interjection' ('a natural ejaculation, expressive of some feeling or emotion, used or viewed as a part of speech' (OED)), because it is 'thrown in' between sentences, clauses or words, mostly without grammatical connection. The function of ejaculations is rhetorical, symbolic, and dramatic. Palsgrave in the 16th c. says that they 'serve to expresse the passyons and the affections of the mynde'. They cover (and crystallize) a wide variety of emotional states, which may often be complex and ambiguous. They elude the grasp of the lexicographer and the glossator because their significance is highly contextual and often depends on intonation. It is not surprising that Chaucer, with his dramatic imagination and his liking for local realism in speech, makes extensive use of them.
  They may sometimes be 'vocal gestures' of onomatopoeic or imitative origin, like buf (used only once, in the SumT, III.1934), which probably represents the sound of a belch. 'Wehee' (I.4066) represents the whinny of the stallions as they gallop off to the mares, provoking a volley of human cries of alarm. A celebrated example occurs at the climax of a scene in MilT (I.3740) when Alison expresses her delight and exultation: '"Tehee!" quod she, and clapte the wyndow to.' Others,

however, have a respectable, or once respectable, etymology: such are the numerous examples of *oaths involving the names of saints—often in the form 'by Seynte *Clare', sometimes simply with the saint's name ('"*Peter!" quod he'); or such locutions as the very common *pardee* (Fr. 'by God' = 'certainly, to be sure'), or *by my fey* (orig. Fr. 'faith'), or, more rarely, the apparently more vulgar *by/for Goddes bones*, and its euphemism *for cokkes bones*, or *by corpus bones* (which is perhaps a confusion of *Corpus Domini* and *Goddes bones*).

Very common ejaculations include: *A!* which covers a very wide range of emotions, from the delectable pain caused by the stroke of love (as the vision of Emily (*Emelya) affects *Palamon in *The Knight's Tale* I.1078: 'he bleynte and cride, "A!"') to extreme anger (as of the miller in *The Reeve's Tale* I.4269: '"A, false traitour!" quod he'), and much else. It also varies considerably in intensity: it may express surprise, alarm, excitement in thought ('"A!" thoghte this frere, "That shal go with me!"', III.2144) or reflective musing, as that of Chaucer in *The House of Fame* (470), when he has seen all the images in the temple—'"A, Lord", thoughte I, "That madest us."' It is sometimes combined with *ha* ('A ha! By God, I have my tale ageyn' says the *Wife of Bath, III.586), or *benedicite* ('bless you/us'), a locution which like the modern French *ça alors*! may sometimes express the bewilderment of the ordinary man confronted by an apparently meaningless cosmos.

ey! (occasionally spelt *I*, and also strengthened by words such as *benedicite, Goddes foo/mercy/ mooder*, etc.) is another 'natural ejaculation' expressing surprise or incredulity, which tends to appear in colloquial or familiar contexts. Thus the wife in *RvT* says to herself as she finds her way back to her own bed 'I hadde almoost goon to the clerkes bed. | Ey, benedicite!' (I.4219–20), or the Host's vehement reaction to the behaviour of January's young wife (IV.2419–20): 'Ey! Goddes mercy! ... | Now swich a wyf I pray God kepe me fro!' Criseyde uses it several times, usually when talking to her uncle Pandarus (e.g. 'Ey, uncle myn, welcome iwys', *Tr* II.87), as he does.

O! is a very common vocative, often used with a noun in formal rhetorical exclamations, 'O deth, that endere art of sorwes alle' (*Tr* IV.501), but also in ordinary address, as when the wife in *The *Ship-*

man's Tale* greets the monk (VII.98): 'O deere cosyn myn, daun John'. It is also frequently used as an ejaculation 'expressing, according to intonation, various emotions as appeal, entreaty, surprise, pain lament etc.' (*OED*). So the *Wife of Bath cries out to her husband Jankin (III.800) '"O! hastow slayn me, false theef?"', and the narrator of the story of Griselda (*Grisilde) exclaims (IV.621) 'O nedelees was she tempted in assay!'.

Other ejaculations indicate various kinds of reproach, indignation or repugnance, like the common *fy!* or *fy (up)on*, or the less common *straw!* used to express contempt (the noun *straw* was one of a number of ME words sometimes used as types of things of little value). The *Host says to the *Franklin 'Straw for youre gentilesse!' (V.695). Distress or alarm can be expressed by *harrow!* (Old French *haro*, of obscure origin). Alison (I.3285–6) fends off the importunate Nicholas: '"Why, lat be!" quod she. "Lat be, Nicholas, | Or I wol crie 'out, harrow' and 'alas'"'. *Out!* (from the adverb = 'away') similarly expresses various combinations of lamentation, indignation, and reproach, and is often combined with *alas!* or *harrow!*, as in the previous example, or in the exclamation uttered by old *January in the *Merchant's Tale* (IV.2366) when he sees his young wife up in the tree with her lusty squire: '"Out! Help! Allas! Harrow!" he gan to crye'. *Allas!* (Fr.) is the most common ejaculation for expressing a variety of states of unhappiness, grief, sorrow, pity, or concern. Also common is *weylawey* (from OE), which is often combined with *allas!*, or strengthened in other way, as in the phrases *weylawey the whyle*, or *welawey that I was born!*

The very common *lo!* ('look, see, behold') is used to direct attention to the presence or approach of something, or to what is about to be said: 'Lo Depeford, and it is half-wey pryme!' (I.3906) or 'Lo, thus byjaped and bigiled was he!' (VIII.1385). Sometimes its meaning is vaguer (more like the modern 'Oh'), but there is usually some deictic or demonstrative element, as in 'Lo, who may truste on Fortune any throwe?' (VII.3326), a remark which arises from examples of great men hurled down by Fortune. *How!* (like modern 'ho', 'hi') also attracts attention: in *MilT* (I.3437) the carpenter tries to rouse Nicholas, '"What, how! What do ye, maister Nicholay?"'

Elcanor

Later (I.3576) Nicholas imagines himself calling out to the others as they float about in the flood, 'thanne wol I clepe, "How, Alison! How, John!"' *Hust* ! (cf. 'hush', 'hist' 'a sharp whispered sound enjoining silence' (*OED*): in *The Miller's Tale* (I.3722) 'And unto Nicholas she seyde stille, | "Now hust, and thou shalt laughen al thy fille."'

Many of the above are regularly used in close imitations of colloquial language in the ordinary flow of discourse or social encounters. Other exclamations or interjections thus used include *gramercy* or *gra(u)nt mercy* ('thank you') (from Fr., originally 'may God reward you greatly'). There are exclamations of warning or encouragement like *lat be!* or *com of!* (used by the clerks in *RvT* (I.4074), '"Step on thy feet! Com of, man, al atanes!"', or the impatient birds in *PF* (494), '"Com of!" they criede, "allas, ye wol us shende!"'). There are calls for silence or order like *pees!* (much used by the Host, and Dame Nature) or *hoo!* (with which the Knight interrupts the Monk (VII.2767): '"Hoo!" quod the Knyght, "good sire, namoore of this!"'. Finally, we have signals of greeting, like *hayl* or *welcome* ('Al hayl, Symond, y-fayth!' . . . 'Aleyn, welcome', I.4022–4), and parting, like *far(e)wel* or *adieu* (as Pandarus takes leave of Troilus (*Tr*. I.1040–1): '"But farewel, I wol go. | Adieu! Be glad! God spede us bothe two!"').

Ekko, see *Echo.

Elcanor, mentioned in a list of famous dreamers at the beginning of Book II of *The *House of Fame*, has not been certainly identified, but may be Helcana, the heroine of a French story who in disguise took the name Helcanor and appeared to her lover in dreams. She is not, however, a dreamer herself.

Eld, see *old age.

Eleaticis. 'The scoles of Eleaticis' (L. *Eliaticis . . . studiis*), the Eleatic school of philosophy founded by Parmenides (*Parmanydes) and *Zeno at Elea on the coast of Lucania in southern Italy, mentioned in *Boece* (I pr.1:68).

Eleyne, Helen of *Troy, the wife of king Menelaus of Sparta, whose abduction by Paris

provoked the Greek expedition to besiege the city—'the ravysshyng to wreken [avenge] of Eleyne, | By Paris don' (*Tr* I.62–3). In this poem she appears at the dinner (i.e. lunch) party at the end of Book II, where she generously offers to help Criseyde, and speaks in 'goodly softe wyse' to Troilus. Other characters mention her in casual allusions: her influence over Paris (II.1447–9) or her abduction and its consequences (IV.548–9, 1347; V.890). Elsewhere she appears in a list of figures from the story of Troy (*BD* 331), and of ill-fated lovers (*PF* 291). She was an exemplary figure of *beauty (cf. *Tr* II.454–5; *Prol. LGW* F 254). (Although Chaucer says (II.70) that in his 'Seintes Legende of Cupide' (i.e. *The Legend of Good Women*) he treated 'the teeris [tears] of Eleyne', there is no other reference to her in that poem as we have it.) For a more earthy reference see *The *Merchant's Tale* (IV.1754), where old Januarie, looking on the beautiful face of May, dreams of how he will that night 'in armes . . . hire streyne [clasp her] | Harder than evere Parys dide Eleyne'.

ELEYNE, SEINT, St Helen(a) (d. 330) empress and mother of Constantine, the first Christian emperor. According to legend, she found the wood of the true cross at Jerusalem, 'the croys which that Seint Eleyne fond' (VI.951), which the *Host swears by in his attack on the *Pardoner, the purveyor of false *relics.

Elf-queene in *Sir Thopas* (VII.788, 795) a creature of magical beauty whom the hero hopes to make his mistress; the 'queene of *Fayerye' mentioned a few lines later seems to be identical in kind. Chaucer has in mind the mysterious encounters between mortals and fairy women in romances. In King Arthur's day, says the Wife of Bath (III.859–61), when this land was 'fulfild of fayerye', the 'elf-queene, with hir joly compaignye, | Daunced ful ofte in many a grene mede'. But elves are dangerous as well as beautiful: she associates 'elf' with 'incubus'; the Carpenter in *The *Miller's Tale* includes them in his charm against evil spirits (I.3749); and *Custance in *The *Man of Law's Tale* (II.754) is once accused of being an 'elf' and producing a child who is a horrible 'feendly creature'. Similarly 'elvish' is ambiguous: it is used slightingly of *alchemy in *The *Canon's Yeoman's Tale* ('oure elvysshe craft', 'this elvysshe nyce loore', VIII.751, 842), presumably with the sense 'magical' or possibly 'mysterious', but it is also applied to the appearance of Chaucer himself in the Prologue to *Sir Thopas* ('He semeth elvyssh by his contenance, | For unto no wight dooth he daliaunce') where it seems to mean something like 'as if he had come from the Otherworld', 'abstracted' and 'unsociable'.

Burrow (1995).

Eliachim (AV Joachim), a high priest of Bethulia (Judith 4:7), who opposed Holofernes (*Oloferne) (VII.2566).

Elicon(e), Helicon, properly a mountain in Boeotia, Greece, which was sacred to the *Muses; it had on it the springs of Hippocrene and Aganippe. It is about 25 miles (40 km) southeast of the higher Mt. Parnassus (*Parnaso). Chaucer's reference to it in *The *House of Fame*, probably inspired by Boccaccio's *Teseida* ('on Parnaso . . . | Be Elicon, the clere welle', 522) shows that he thought of it there as a spring or fountain on Mt. Parnassus, and the same is probably true of his other two less explicit references (*Tr* III.1809; *Anel* 17). This confusion is found elsewhere in medieval literature.

Elye, Elijah, the Old Testament prophet. Like Enoch (*Ennok) he did not die, but was raised bodily into heaven by a whirlwind (2 Kings 2:1–18). This is ruefully alluded to by the dreamer in *The *House of Fame* (588). There was a widespread belief that he and Enoch would return from the Earthly Paradise to challenge Antichrist (*Antecrist) before the establishment of the Messianic kingdom. The *friars were fond of associating themselves with Elijah and Elisha—the Carmelites, established in the early 13th c., named them as their founders—and this claim was sometimes used against them in anti-fraternal satire. In *The *Summoner's Tale*, the friar likens 'the clennesse and the fastynge of us freres' to Elijah's fasting on Mt. Horeb (III.1890; cf. 1 Kings 19: 8); and later—after a hyperbolic apocalyptic warning—refers to 'Elye and Elise' (2116) as friars.

Elise, Elisha, an Old Testament prophet, the successor of Elijah (*Elye), and the leader of the enthusiastic 'sons of the prophets' (cf. 1 Kings 19–2 Kings 13). Like Elijah, he is claimed as a friar by the friar in *The *Summoner's Tale*.

Elisos, Elysium, in ancient mythology, the place where those favoured by the gods lived on happily after death. Sometimes it was a meadow in the West by the stream Oceanus which encircled the earth, sometimes in the 'islands of the blest', or in the lower world (as in *Virgil). Chaucer's conception of it was probably influenced by *Dante (see especially *Inferno* 4). His only reference to it (*Tr* IV.789–91) is an allusion by Troilus to the separated lovers *Orpheus and Eurydice (*Erudice): 'though in erthe ytwynned be we tweyne, | Yet in the feld of pite, out of peyne, | That highte Elisos, shal we ben yfeere, | As Orpheus and Erudice, his feere.' The 'feld of *pite, out of peyne' may echo Ovid's *arva piorum* (*Met.* 11. 62). It was also sometimes associated with 'eleison' ('pity'; cf. *kyrie eleison* (Lord, have mercy)), and a L. gloss on *Lucan's *Pharsalia* explains it as *campi misericordiae* ('fields of pity') 'where the pious rest'; or as *extra lesionem* 'beyond injury'. In the *Ovide moralisé*, it is the place of rest for souls who have not deserved torment (*paine*), where Orpheus finds Eurydice among the 'piteous company' (*en la piteuse compaignie*).

Elixir, in *alchemy the agent which transmutes base metals to silver or gold.

Ellesmere Manuscript. MS Ellesmere 26. C. 9 (from the beginning of the 15th c.), formerly in the possession of the earl of Ellesmere, now in the Henry E. Huntington Library, San Marino, California, is the most famous and the most elegant of the manuscripts of *The Canterbury Tales*. Its attractive miniatures of the pilgrim storytellers have often been reproduced (see frontispiece, Figs. 2, 3). Like other MSS of the Tales, it contains some glosses and marginalia. It was probably written by the scribe of the earlier *Hengwrt manuscript, and is a major source for the text of *The Canterbury Tales*. The majority of modern editors have used it as the base text even though its individual readings may not be as good as those of Hengwrt, and the order of the Tales which it uses has been very widely adopted. The result has been that what most modern readers think of as *The Canterbury*

Tales is in fact an edition of this manuscript, and they suppose that its rubrics (e.g. 'the wordes of the Hoost to the compaignye'), the layout of the Tales (e.g. the four-part structure of The *Knight's Tale* or the two-part structure of The *Canon's Yeoman's Tale*) are Chaucer's own, although this is not at all certain. The question of the early history of the work is complicated and mysterious (see The *Canterbury Tales*).

(facsimile edn.) Egerton (1911); Hanna (1989); Pearsall (1985), 10–13; Samuels (1983).

Elongacioun, the angular separation (in ecliptic *longitude) of one planet from another; when unqualified this is usually of the Moon from the Sun. (See also *astrology and astronomy.)

[JDN]

Elpheta, wife of Cambyuskan, in The *Squire's Tale*, the mother of *Algarsyf and *Cambalo, and of *Canacee. If Elpheta is to be associated with a star of the same name, this is the brightest star in the Crown of Ariadne, *Corona Borealis* (a star that is in *Scorpio, a mansion of Mars). [JDN]

Eltham, a royal residence 7 miles (5 km) from London, mentioned (together with *Sheene) in the Prologue to The *Legend of Good Women* (F 497). The reference is not in the G text. Perhaps it was omitted to avoid any reference to the lately dead Queen *Anne of Bohemia (d. 1394). It was one of the manors which Chaucer had to oversee when he was Clerk of the King's Works (1389–91).

Embelif, oblique(ly). See *oriso(u)nte.

Emele(-ward), (towards) Emilia, a province in northern Italy, mentioned in the Prologue to The *Clerk's Tale*.

Emelya, Emelye, the young and beautiful sister of Queen Hippolyta in The *Knight's Tale*, with whom Palamon and Arcite fall in love.

EMERSON, RALPH WALDO (1803–82), American man of letters, lecturer and philosopher, who propounded the doctrine of Transcendentalism ('nature is the incarnation of thought. The world is the mind precipitated'). In 'The American Scholar' (1837) he cites Chaucer as one of the timeless English poets whose work can be read with 'the most modern joy'. He saw that Chaucer was 'a huge borrower'. In *Representative Men* (published 1850) he is an example of the great 'traditional' poet: 'a great poet, who appears in illiterate times, absorbs into his sphere all the light which is anywhere radiating'. Such poets 'are librarians and historiographers, as well as poets. Each romancer was heir and dispenser of all the hundred tales of the world.' Chaucer also has the 'cheerfulness' of the true poet, and seems to be enrolled as a Transcendentalist: 'Shakspere, Homer, Dante, Chaucer, saw the splendour of meaning that plays over the visible world; knew that a tree had another use than for apples, and corn another than for meal, and the ball of the earth, than for tillage and roads: that these things bore a second and finer harvest to the mind, being emblems of its thoughts, and conveying in all their natural history a certain mute commentary on human life.' Emerson's remarks on Chaucer represent the beginnings of American criticism of the poet.

CH ii. 33–6 (selection).

Emetreus, 'kyng of *Inde' in The *Knight's Tale* enters the lists with his retinue to support Arcite as *Lygurge does for Palamon. The character is apparently Chaucer's invention. There is an elaborate description (I.2156 ff.) of his exotic appearance (yellow hair, lemon-coloured eyes, 'sangwyn' colour, freckles) and he is accompanied by 'ful many a tame leon and leopart'. Like Arcite, he seems to be associated with *Mars.

emotion. Chaucer does not use the word *emotion*, which appears first in English in the late 16th c. In the Middle Ages its modern senses are covered by such words as 'passion' or L. *affectus*. It was thought that the 'appetites' or desires of the 'sensitive' or 'sensible' (as against the 'rational') soul produced the 'passions'; these were analysed by philosophers and preachers as well as by poets. As in antiquity, it was widely recognized that emotions affect the body as well as the mind and have physical symptoms. There is also a good deal of evidence that emotions were powerfully felt, and that their expression (in weeping, wringing of hands; etc.) was more open and public than in the modern Western world. Writers were often drawn to stories of men and women in whom the power of emotion threw off the restraint of reason and led to a disastrous excess or lack of '*mesure'. There was also an awareness of the affective power which literature could exercise. Some kinds of medieval literature particularly set out to move the emotions, such as the sermons which are intended, as the Host says, 'to make us for oure olde synnes wepe', or tragic or 'pitous' stories.

Chaucer uses a wide range of vocabulary to describe or express emotion, sometimes using the same words as Modern English, though often with a different meaning or range of meanings. An obvious example is *sad*, which usually has the sense of 'steadfast, calm, serious'. He uses *sentement* (personal feeling, personal experience; passion), or *felyng*. Some of the words are the technical terms of medieval psychology: *passioun* (cf. *Tr* IV.704–7), *affectes* 'desires' (*Tr* III.1391), *affectioun*, which can mean 'emotion' as well as 'affection' (its power memorably described in *The *Miller's Tale*, I.3611), *appetyt* 'desire', *sensibilitees*, used in *Boece* in its more technical sense of 'impressions' or sensations imprinted in the soul (V m.4), or *sensualitee* 'that part of man's nature concerned with the senses', as against reason (only in *ParsT*). Words used to describe emotions felt by characters may sometimes have a strong charge (e.g. *grisly*, or be strengthened with an intensifying prefix-*forwery*). Sometimes a neutral word for 'appearance' or 'expression' (*che(e)re* or *countenaunce*) is modified by a descriptive adjective (*mery*, *glad*, *deedly*, etc.). Sometimes an ordinary word may be used in a vivid metaphorical way: sorrow may 'gnaw' a heart (*Tr* IV.621), or joy cause it to be opened (*Tr* III.1239).

To build up an emotional scene Chaucer uses a variety of structural, dramatic, and rhetorical devices (repetition, apostrophe, imagery, etc.). Emotional intensity or emotional nuance can be expressed through songs, through music, through various noises (from the sound of bells to the sound of farts), and through straightforward silence, as when at the end of *Troilus and Criseyde* (V.1725–29), Pandarus is so 'sory', 'shamed', and 'astoned' that he stands 'as stille as ston; a word ne kowde he seye', or when the Pardoner is speechless with fury (VI.956–7) and 'answerde nat a word; | So wrooth he was, no word ne wolde he seye.'

An emotional reaction is often 'pointed' by a *gesture or a physical reaction (cases where the face or the body will reveal through signs the workings of the soul). Sorrow or compassion will cause tears to flow (e.g. *MLT* II.659–61), but when Absolon wept 'as dooth a child that is ybete' (*MilT* I.3759) it seems to be from a mixture of distress, mortification, and venemous hatred. We find sighing, or the voice quavering because of extreme emotion (as when Troilus first speaks to Criseyde, *Tr* III.93), smiling or laughing, usually for joy, but sometimes for scorn, turning pale (most commonly for fear or grief, but also as a symptom of *drunkenness), quaking (for fear or for anger), swooning, wringing hands; hiding the face, kissing, embracing (with a variety of emotional intentions) (e.g. IV.1100–3 or VII.202–3).

Chaucer's characters also feel 'inwardly' or 'inly'. Sight or imagination may set an *impressioun*, an image or an imprint on the heart (e.g. *Tr* I.295–8; II.899–900). The heart can be 'tickled' (a word twice used by the Wife of Bath (III.395, 471), it can 'quappe [throb]' or 'quake', it can be 'pierced' or 'slain', or 'melt' or suddenly grow cold (V.1023).

They feel a great variety of emotions: among the most prominent are *love or desire (not always solely directed to a human object ('Desir of gold shal . . . his soule blende [blind]' (*Tr* IV.1399)), and earthy passions like *ragerie* 'wantonness' (e.g. *MchT* IV.1846–7), that strong emotion '*pite* which overlaps with *compassioun* and other 'kindly' or natural emotions, *joy and its less solemn relatives, *jolitee* ('pleasure; love, passion' as well as 'cheerfulness') and *mirthe* ('joy, gladness' as well as 'mirth, amusement'). These are often expressed through laughter, at a variety of objects or situations, and of a varying intensity: the Host began 'to laughen wonder loude' (IX.94), whereas in *BD* (850) one of the admirable qualities of the lady is to 'laughe and pleye so wommanly'. Yet Criseyde, amused by Pandarus, laughs more wholeheartedly so that 'it thoughte hire herte brest' and that she 'wende [thought] for to dye' (II.1108, 1168–9). More etherial is the laughter of the spirit of Troilus looking down from the eighth sphere (*Tr* V.1821–2). St Cecilia laughs with Christian certainty at her pagan judge (VIII.462)). Or we find anger (with its distinctly physical symptoms, e.g. I.3745), which may overlap with hate or with various kinds of indignation, irritation, loathing or revulsion, scorn or contempt (the Miller's wife in *RvT* was 'ful of hoker and of bisemare' [disdain or scorn]'. I.3965), envy, grief and sorrow, jealousy (*jalousie), and various forms of *hevinesse* or dejection, or *melancholy. Characters feel varying degrees of shame, bewilderment, amazement (e.g. II.526–7), or wonder (a 'merveille' will cause the spectators to be 'agast' or fall silent). There are some interesting examples of fear and terror (*fere*, *drede*, etc). Criseyde, 'the ferfulleste wight | That myghte be', is 'wel nigh out of hir wit for sorwe and fere' (I.108; cf. II.449–50). Fear is presented as a most powerful emotion (which can drive one 'out of one's wit') with extreme physical results—falling, thinking to die, shuddering, or quaking (see e.g. *LGW* 2310 ff.; *KnT* I.2342). That kind of sudden terror in which the heart suddenly 'grows cold', and the effect is that of stunned horror, bewilderment, and prostration is found in *The *Franklin's Tale* when Dorigen is confronted by Aurelius with the news that he has achieved the seemingly impossible condition she set for him: she 'astoned stood; | In al hir face nas a drope of blood. | She wende nevere han come in swich a trappe' (V.1339–41).

Sudden movements or moments of emotion or emotional release may sometimes stand out dramatically: when January looked at his young wife May, he was 'ravysshed in a traunce' (IV.1750), but so was the squire Damyan (IV.1774–5). For such moments, Chaucer sometimes uses the word *surprised* (in its older sense of 'seized, violently affected'). When Melibee's enemies hear the sweet and gentle words of the generous Prudence: 'they weren so supprised and ravysshed and hadden so greet joye of hire that wonder was to telle' (VII.1733). And the phrase used of the delight of Troilus forgiven by Criseyde (*Tr* III.1184)—'This Troilus, with blisse of that supprised'—may well lie behind the 'surprised by joy' of *Wordsworth and C. S. Lewis.

Chaucer is also interested in nuances and ambiguities, and in the coexistence of different emotions (especially in the emotional paradoxes of the 'dredful joye' of Love and in the conflicting emotions of lovers), in the stirring of emotion, in indecision, and in reflection or pondering (as when the youngest 'riotour' in *The Pardoner's Tale*

(VI.838–9) 'ful ofte in herte . . . rolleth up and doun | The beautee of thise floryns newe and brighte'). There is a similar variety in his larger emotional scenes. Sometimes he will give us a straightforwardly 'pitous' scene, like the story of Ugolino (*Hugelyn), where all our attention is focused on the pathos, but in other very characteristic cases a word from the narrator will make all ambiguous— Malyne's farewell to the clerk Aleyn in *The *Reeve's Tale* (I.4248) seems to achieve a strange and delicate blend of irony and pathos: 'and with that word *almoost* she gan to wepe'. (See also *gestures.)

Endlinks. See *Epilogues.

Eneas, Enyas, Enee, Aeneas, son of Anchises, the hero of the *Aeneid* (*Eneyde) and the lover of *Dido.

Eneyde, Eneydos, the *Aeneid* of *Virgil, the twelve books of which are summarized in *The *House of Fame* 151–382, where the dreamer finds it written 'on a table of bras'. Aeneas has escaped from the ruin of Troy and after wandering for seven years finds himself on the coast of Libya. He and his men are received with kindness by *Dido, queen of Carthage (*Cartage (1)), to whom Aeneas relates (II–III) the fall of Troy and his later adventures. Venus fills her with a passionate desire for Aeneas, and when (IV) their hunting party is interrupted by a storm, the couple take shelter in a cave, where Dido 'becam hys love and let him doo | Al that weddynge longeth too'. Jupiter orders Aeneas to leave Carthage and in spite of Dido's pleas and recriminations the Trojans leave, and Dido kills herself. In Sicily, Aeneas celebrates the anniversary of the death of his father Anchises (V). Later (VI) he visits the Cumaean Sibyl, and with her descends to the underworld, where he sees the ghosts of Anchises, Dido, and others, 'and every turment eke in helle'. The Trojans come to Latium (VII), where their descendents will found Rome, and are opposed by the Italian tribes. The wars are described in the following books, and the epic ends with the death of their leader Turnus at the hands of Aeneas.

Like other medieval poets Chaucer finds the Dido episode of especial interest, and treats Dido as an abandoned heroine. Aeneas is 'the false

Enee' (*CT* II.64) especially in her story as told in *The* **Legend of Good Women*. In the *House of Fame* there is some attempt to excuse him, but though there is one reference to 'the fame of Pius Aeneas' (1485), Chaucer responded less to the Roman concept of *pietas*, the maintenance of a proper relationship with gods and family, than to the romantic pathos of Dido's fate.

The *Aeneid* was a well-known text in the Middle Ages, studied at school, furnished with commentaries (that of the 4th-c. grammarian Servius being the most famous), and often retold in whole or in part in the various vernacular languages (e.g. in the *Roman d'Enéas*). It was the main source for knowledge of *Troy and the Trojan War. The familiarity of the story may be illustrated by the way in which the mock-heroic description of the lamentations over the plight of *Chauntecleer seized by the fox in The **Nun's Priest's Tale* (VII.3356–9) alludes to those made at the destruction of Troy.

(ed.) Mynors (1969); (ed. and trans.) Fairclough (1930–2); trans. C. Day Lewis (1986); Baswell (1995).

Engelond, England. In the 19th c. the quintessential 'Englishness' of Chaucer was singled out for praise. Not only was he the 'father of English poetry' (an earlier idea), but he was, according to Ruskin, 'the most perfect type of a true English mind'. There may be some truth in this, but his was as much a European mind, since medieval England culturally was part of Western Europe. The source of much of his work 'imaked was in Fraunce' (and in other countries, Mediterranean as well as Northern), and those English figures of the *General Prologue, who are going like their compatriots, 'from every shires ende | Of Engelond' to Canterbury, tell stories which are often set 'abroad'. The England of the 14th c. which produced Chaucer was a less self-consciously patriotic place and a rather more excitingly tumultuous one than Victorian or even Shakespearian England. And 'Engelond, that cleped was eek Briteyne' had a fascinating legendary past.

It is, according to *Bartholomew, the largest island in the Ocean, once called *Albion from the white rocks which are still seen in the sea cliffs.

The Trojans came here and fought with the giants, and called it Britain after *Brutus. Later (and here we move into real history) came the Saxons, who slew or drove out the Britons, and called the land Anglia. (The name in fact comes from the Germanic tribe of the Angles, but more fantastic derivations are suggested, e.g. that it is from L. *angulo*, because it is set in the corner of the world.)

In the 14th c. its borders included Wales (*Walys), Ireland (but in name only, outside Dublin and the surrounding area), but not *Scotland, an independent kingdom, which had reaffirmed its independence at Bannockburn in 1314. At the beginning of the century, the dominions of the English king also included a large section of *France: part of the duchy of Aquitaine in the south-west with its capital Bordeaux (*Burdeux), the Channel Islands, and the county of Ponthieu in the north. England was still an agricultural country, with no more than about four and a half million inhabitants in all. After *London (?*c*.35,000 inhabitants), the larger towns included York, Bristol, Plymouth, and Coventry, but by modern standards no town was very large, and the distinction between town and country was much less sharp than it later became (even London had its fields, and it was easy to walk into the countryside). Chaucer expects his readers to assume this: in a town mentioned in one story there is at the west gate 'a dong-carte' ready to carry dung to the fields (VII.3035–6); and even at Troy the 'warden of the gates' at night calls to the people outside the walls to bring in their animals (*Tr* V.1177–80). In the countryside there were contrasts in the *landscape, most obviously between those areas where the woods had been cleared for agricultural land and the moorlands or the great tracts of *forest which still covered much of England. In some areas the 'many sheep' were farmed for the good wool which was the country's most important export; no doubt the proverbial expression 'as thick as sheep in fold' was often literally true. In the more populous regions people lived in villages, the houses gathered around a church, sometimes with a mill and a manorhouse.

The country's communications system was a network of paths and roads, some of them going back to Roman times (in the phrase 'by wey and eek by strete', *strete* was originally the paved

Engelond, England

Roman road, *via strata*). Rivers were crossed by bridges, whether large and famous like London Bridge, or small and local like that which crossed the brook at Trumpington (I.3922). In bad weather especially, travel could be arduous. In *The *Friar's Tale* a cart loaded with hay gets stuck in the mud on a road (III.1538–65, and the casualness of other allusions to 'slough' (VII.2798; IX.64)) suggest that it is part of everyday experience. And there were other dangers for travellers; in 1390 Chaucer himself was held up and robbed. People journeyed 'riding by the way' (the rich might have carriages or horse-litters), or walking: in *The *Pardoner's Tale* the three rioters set off on a footpath (which has a stile) to the 'grete village' where Death has been busy. Travellers of all kinds found lodging (*herberwe) and sustenance in the many inns, hostels, and ale-houses.

It seems already to have become proverbial to describe England as 'merry', but this meant 'pleasant, delightful', not the joviality unconfined of the later 'merrie' England. Indeed, other contemporary proverbial remarks are less flattering: Englishmen are unstable (they 'are born under the moon'), or 'when they see their advantage they forget truces and good faith' (this early version of 'perfidious Albion' is quoted by a Scottish chronicler), Englishmen are envious, Englishmen love 'gift'. In fashion, the English are 'the apes of every nation', Englishmen have tails (a taunt much used by adversaries). Their soldiers were called by the French (for obvious reasons) 'god-damns'.

In England the 14th c. was a period of tension and strain, and of profound economic and social change. The system whereby peasants were bound to the land was gradually disintegrating, a process probably intensified by depression and by labour shortages after the *Black Death. The older self-sufficient economy of the manor gradually gave way to a mercantile one based on money. Markets and market towns had long been important but the increase of trade needed capital and larger commercial centres, which London became, especially for the cloth trade with Europe. Merchants became more numerous, more important, and sometimes very rich (Chaucer's *Merchant was 'sownynge alwey th'encrees of his wynnyng').

Englishmen had also to contend with natural disasters, with famine, and with plague. The Black Death of 1349 returned in later years. And there was endemic violence in the form of fighting and rioting. The most effective form of policing seems to have been the neighbours' 'hue and cry', of which we have a comic example in the pursuit of the fox in *The Nun's Priest's Tale* (VII.3375–400) (though that also has a grimmer allusion to *Jakke Straw and his company killing Flemings in the *Peasants' Revolt of 1381). English political life in this century was also violent. Edward II, in conflict with his barons, was murdered in 1327. The long reign of *Edward III (1327–77) brought more stability at home, but saw the beginning of the *Hundred Years War. The troubled reign of the young king *Richard II (1377–99) ended with his deposition and death, and left a legacy of internecine strife to the following century. A French observer, Jean Juvenal des Ursins, remarked that the English did not think twice about killing their kings.

Many Englishmen spent a good deal of their time at war, whether in local strife in the Marches or on the Borders, or in full-scale campaigns against the Scots or the French. Some took part in *Crusades. The long war with the French had far-reaching consequences. It was to end a long period of Anglo-French culture (going back to the Norman Conquest), a past which in the 14th c. was of immediate political importance mainly to the king and the higher nobility, but which had been and still was of great significance in the cultural history of the whole nation. Early victories gave way to defeat and disillusionment. By 1377 the English held only the towns of Calais, Cherbourg, Brest, Bordeaux, and Bayonne, and the areas around them. Eventually, in the 15th c. all the English possessions in France were lost, including, saddest of all, the *wine-producing area of the south-west.

It was a period when ecclesiastical and spiritual life (see *religion, *piety) had its share of disillusionment also. There was widespread criticism of the worldliness of the Church and of churchmen, and an acknowledgement of the need for reform. There is evidence of anti-clericalism and anti-papalism (no doubt intensified by the great Schism of 1378 which produced two rival Popes). Direct attacks on orthodox doctrine were made by *Wyclif and the *Lollards. But not everything was in a state of breakdown or crisis. There is evidence of spiritual vitality in enthusiastic piety and mysticism. And the medieval ideal of order was enacted in the practices of religion and in the steady progress of the seasonal and the liturgical calendar.

The cultural history of the period is lively and exciting. Magnificent surviving monuments testify to its achievements in *architecture. The other *visual arts can show tapestries and embroidery (the *opus anglicanum* which was renowned throughout Europe), illuminated Psalters, wall-paintings, and tomb sculptures. There were advances in education and learning. New colleges (like *William of Wykeham's college of that name) were founded in Oxford and Cambridge. London saw the development of a 'lawyers' university' in the Inns of Court. And we can see evidence of a medieval *humanism.

The English *language, depressed in status at the Norman Conquest, was becoming increasingly important in political, legal, and administrative life. Its vocabulary was by now enriched with a multitude of words of French origin. Its dialects were still markedly diverse (cf. Chaucer's reference to 'diversity' in *Tr* V.1793–4) and still produced fine literary works, though the English of London was beginning to share in the city's growth in importance. The literature written in English in this period is varied and distinguished. There are excellent examples of *romance, lyric, drama, and *alliterative verse (e.g. *Pearl*, *Sir Gawain and the Green Knight*). There are lively narratives, and collections of stories like *Handlyng Synne* or the *Confessio Amantis* of Chaucer's friend *Gower. Some of the visionary and mystical writing, like that of his contemporaries *Langland and *Julian of Norwich, is outstanding. Chaucer is not the 'father of English literature', but he is the 'father' of one kind of English poetry, that written by his successors and admirers, *Hoccleve, *Lydgate, *Henryson, *Dunbar, *Skelton, *Spenser, and others. They rightly praise him for his embellishment of English. He brought the poetic modes and the poetic thought of a diversity of European writers into the English literary tradition, and made them at home. And he realized the full potential of contemporary English. His self-conscious awareness of language (he even notes a linguistic trick like the friar lisping 'to make his Englissh sweete upon his tonge' (I.265)) is matched by the boldness with which he uses English in all registers. Perhaps this is where his true Englishness lies.

Du Boulay (1970, 1974).

Enyas, see *Eneas.

Ennok, Enoch, the Old Testament patriarch, the father of Methuselah, who 'walked with God and he was not; for God took him' (Gen. 5:24). In the Middle Ages he was associated with Elijah (*Elye), as he is by the dreamer in *The *House of Fame* (588). Various books of revelations and visions were attributed to him.

Ennopye, Oenopia, the large island Aegina, in the Saronic Gulf, south of Piraeus, the 'country' to which Theseus went after the slaying of the Minotaur (*LGW* 2155).

Ensa(u)mple, exemple, see *exemplum.

Envoy, the 'sending forth' of a poem (cf. the traditional 'go, litel bok' formula used at the end of *Troilus and Criseyde* (V.1786) and before Chaucer by Ovid and others, and after him by many more), the conclusion or concluding stanza(s), the author's parting words. In *lyrics it is often a short stanza addressed to the recipient, which differs in form from the rest of the poem. An envoy is not necessarily the logical conclusion to the work but often is rather a means of connecting the ideas or the action to some contemporary context. The word is also used as the title of some of Chaucer's verse epistles. Sometimes in MS copies of longer works an 'envoy' is indicated, e.g. the lines at the end of *The *Clerk's Tale* are labelled by a scribe 'Lenvoy de Chaucer'. They are Chaucer's own invention, but are said in the text to be sung by the Clerk. It is a formal envoy: in a different stanza form, in fact a double *ballade.

Envoy de Chaucer a Bukton; Envoy de Chaucer a Scogan. See *Bukton; *Scogan.

Eolus, Aeolus, 'the god of wyndes', several times referred to in *The *House of Fame*.

Ephesios, 'Seint Paul *Ad Ephesios*' in *The Parson's Tale* (X.748), Paul's Epistle to the Ephesians.

epicicle, the small circle that carries the planet in Ptolemaic astronomy. Its centre moves round the deferent (**defferent) circle. The name is used of an appropriate component part of the equatorium described in **Equatorie of the Planetis*. See also **astrology and astronomy; *riet*.)   [JDN]

Epycuriens, the followers of Epicurus (referred to in *Boece*).

EPICURUS, the Greek philosopher (341–270 BC), the founder of the Epicurean school of philosophy, was born in Samos of Athenian parents, and settled in Athens. He stressed the importance of the evidence of the senses, holding that pleasure (or the absence of pain) is the only good, since it is the only good known to the senses, and that it should be found in virtuous living and the harmony of body and soul. In *Boece* (III pr.2:78) he is said to have 'juggid and establissyde that delyt is the soverayn good'. Somewhat unjustly his views were associated with a delight in good living: thus the **Franklin is described (I.336) as 'Epicurus owene sone'. This idea seems also to be glanced at in *The *Merchant's Tale* (IV.2021 ff.) where old January's habit of living 'ful deliciously' is said to illustrate the view of 'somme clerkes' that 'felicitee | Stant in delit'.

Epilogues (to Tales), the title given by critics to passages which occur at the end of some of the surviving fragments of *The *Canterbury Tales*. These are sometimes called 'Endlinks'. (Within the fragments the tales are often carefully linked together (see **links).) The Epilogue to *The *Merchant's Tale* (at the end of Fragment IV) is straightforward, consisting of about twenty lines from the Host, commenting on the tale and complaining about his own wife. The others, however, are all in some way problematic. They indicate the unfinished nature of *The Canterbury Tales*, and are sometimes possible evidence for earlier stages of composition and revision. The Epilogue to *The *Man of Law's Tale* (at the end of Fragment II, not found in over twenty MSS, including **Ellesmere and **Hengwrt) is a brief exchange between the Host, who

describes the preceding story as a 'thrifty tale', the Parson, whom he asks to tell a tale and who reproves him for swearing, and (in the great majority of the MSS which have it) the Shipman, who interrupts the Host's rejoinder, and says that he will tell one. It has been argued that this comes from a period when *Melibee* was assigned to the Man of Law, and that it was possibly intended to introduce *The *Shipman's Tale*, and that the phrase 'my joly body' ['myself'] which he uses of himself would be more appropriate to a female narrator and may be a relic from an even earlier stage when Chaucer intended having the Wife of Bath tell what is now the Shipman's Tale. The passage seems certainly Chaucerian, but is probably one for which he had not found a final home. Modern scholarly editions often print these lines within square brackets, as they do with the Epilogue to *The *Nun's Priest's Tale* (at the end of Fragment VII), sixteen lines in which the Host praises the tale, comments on the virile and sexual qualities of the priest, and speaks 'with ful merie chere' to another unspecified pilgrim. These lines occur only in a small group of MSS of inferior authority and may have been cancelled by Chaucer when he wrote lines 1941–62 of the Prologue to *The *Monk's Tale*, where he describes the Monk in very similar, and sometimes identical terms ('thou woldest han been a tredefowl aright'). On the other hand, it has been argued that it should be kept, because repetition is not un-Chaucerian and because there is a possibility that the best MSS, striving to suggest completeness, might have omitted passages which suggest discontinuities. It certainly seems intended to fit *The Nun's Priest's Tale*, and Chaucer might well have been able to find a place for it in a finished version of the whole work. A similar problem is presented by the stanza at the end of *The *Clerk's Tale* in which the Host says that he wishes his wife had heard it (IV.1212a–g). This seems to interrupt the repetition of the final line in the first line of the Merchant's Prologue. Finally, there are some spurious links which seem to have been invented by later scribes dissatisfied with the lacunae: thus some MSS attempt to link Fragments VI–VII (*Pardoner's Tale–Shipman's Tale*), and in the Epilogue to *The Nun's Priest's Tale*, mentioned above, some put in the name of a pilgrim. (See also ***Prologues**.)

Episteles (**of Ovyde**), The *Heroides* or *Heroidum Epistulae* ('Letters of Heroines') of *Ovid, a series of letters in elegiacs supposedly addressed by the heroines of ancient legend to their lovers or husbands (and in three cases by the lovers to the heroines). These are passionate and eloquent complaints from women suffering distress of various kinds (betrayed, deserted, abused, or anxious for the safety of their husbands) and form a remarkable exploration of love from the woman's viewpoint. It was a popular work in the Middle Ages, and Chaucer knew it well. He refers to it in *The *House of Fame* (379), and in the Prologue to *The *Man of Law's Tale* (II.55) is said to have 'toold of loveris . . . | Mo than Ovide made of mencioun | In his Episteles, that been ful olde'. His other two references to it are in *The *Legend of Good Women* (G 305, 1465), a work which is deeply indebted to it (in the stories of Thisbe, Hypsipyle, Medea, Ariadne, and especially those of Phyllis and Hypermnnestra).

(ed. and trans.) Showerman and Gould (1977).

Equacio(u)n, a small angle in the Ptolemaic theory of planetary motion, by which a mean value is corrected to produce a true. There are two chief sorts: equations of the centre and of the argument. In modern astronomy these are usually called 'anomalies'. (See also *astrology and astronomy.)
[JDN]

equant, the name of a point (or of a circle centred on it) in Ptolemaic planetary theory. The motion of the centre of the *epicycle moves uniformly around this point. Each planet has its own equant on the equatorium described in *Equatorie of the Planetis*. (See also *astrology and astronomy.)
[JDN]

Equatorie of the Planetis, a treatise describing the construction and use of an equatorium, an astronomical instrument for determining the *ecliptic positions of the Sun (*Sonne), *Moon and planets (*Planete). The title was supplied by D. J. Price, who first argued that Chaucer was both author and scribe of the equatorium text, found in a single manuscript (Peterhouse, Cambridge, MS 75.I). Further arguments have been offered in support of these conclusions, which are now widely accepted.

The script of the codex is unusually large, presumably to ensure that the scrivener, using this from which to make a fair copy, make no mistakes (cf. *Adam* (2)). From evidence internal to the text and certain astronomical *tables bound with it, the treatise seems to have been written around June 1393, shortly after the *Treatise on the *Astrolabe*. The name 'Chaucer' is used of a certain *radix in the astronomical tables.

To calculate the position of each of the planets for a given time, using standard tables, would have occupied an astronomer for several hours. The use of an equatorium would have greatly shortened the task, say to twenty minutes, although with a certain loss of accuracy, depending on the size of the instrument. (Chaucer's recommendation was for an unusually large main disc, 6 foot across.)

Equatoria were of various designs, but these fell into two broad classes. In the first, graduated discs (of parchment, wood, or metal) were used to simulate the circles of planetary theory—the epicycles (*epicicle), deferents (*defferent), and so forth, to which Chaucer alludes in *The *Franklin's Tale*. The second type of equatorium was intuitively less obvious, and demanded a greater mastery of the intricacies of the theory. It was essentially a collection of scales and other devices for simplifying the computation of the subsidiary stages in a standard calculation, and then combining them. The best-known example of the first class in the Latin West was by Campanus of Novara (*c.*1220–1296), and the best example of the second by Richard of Wallingford (*c.*1292–1336). Chaucer's was in the first class. There are precedents for most of the ideas it embodies, and he was perhaps indebted to a lost Oxford work on the subject. It does show signs of real originality, however; and since Chaucer invested much time and effort in planetary computation, it is likely that he had some familiarity with the use of equatoria when he composed his own treatise on the subject. (See also *astrology and astronomy.)
[JDN]

(ed.) Price (1955); North (1990).

Equinoxiall, equinoctial, celestial equator (L. *(circulus) æquinoctialis*). The spring and autumn equinoxes, when day and night are equal, occur when the Sun is where the *ecliptic crosses the celestial equator, the great circle mid-way between the north and south celestial poles. For this reason the celestial equator is often called 'the equinoctial'. The word is used on the astrolabe for the corresponding circle. Spring is astronomically defined as commencing when the Sun crosses from the southern to the northern hemisphere; and autumn when the reverse change takes place. (See also *months and seasons; *solsticioun; *yere.) [JDN]

Ercules, Hercules (Greek Herakles), the Greek hero, son of Alcmene and Zeus/Jupiter, famous for his strength, courage, and fortitude, in the 'harde travailes'—the Labours of Hercules—which are enumerated in *Boece IV m.7. Chaucer refers to him and his 'grete strengthe' a number of times. With *Jason (he was one of his companions, the Argonauts, in the expedition to recover the golden fleece), he appears in the story of Hypsipyle (LGW 1480–1558). He helps the false Jason to win her love, seeming (but only seeming) 'sad, wys, and trewe'. (The source of his role here is not known: it was perhaps suggested by an accusing letter from Deianira (*Dianira) to Hercules in Ovid's Heroides, but it may simply be that Chaucer was attempting to suggest that like some other great champions who were brought down by the wiles of a woman he had a less admirable side.) He is the subject of one of the 'tragedies' in The *Monk's Tale (VII.2095–142), where we are told the story of his death by the poisoned shirt which his 'lemman' Deianira gave him. In the temple of Venus in The *Parliament of Fowls he appears among the lovers who have died because of their love; and his fate is one of the examples of the wickedness of women in the book that *Jankyn (4) read to the Wife of Bath (III.724–5).

Eriphilem, Eriphyle, wife of Amphiarus (*Amphiorax). She was bribed by Polynices to persuade her husband to take part in the campaign of the Seven against *Thebes (1). He did so even though as a seer he knew that none of the Seven would return. His son Alcmeon carried out his command for vengeance by slaying his own mother. She figures among the wicked wives (III.743) whose stories the Wife of Bath's husband Jankin delights in telling her.

Ermony, Armenia. Anelida, the heroine of *Anelida and Arcite, is 'the quene | Of Ermony' (72). The ancient Christian country was devastated by the Seljuks in the 11th c., and in the 14th c. it fell to the Mamelukes. For an English audience it would have been remote and exotic, filled with 'wonders and things wonderly shaped' (*Bartholomew). It was famous for Mt. Ararat, where Noah's ark rested.

Erro, see *Herro.

Erudice, Eurydice wife of *Orpheus, alluded to in Bo III m.12, and (by Criseyde) in Tr IV.791.

Escaphilo. Ascalaphus, the son of Acheron, revealed that Persephone, who had been carried off to the lower world by Hades, had eaten some pomegranate seeds there. As a result, although the lamentations of her mother Demeter had moved Jupiter to intervene, she could not be entirely released. For this he was turned into an owl by Persephone. Chaucer could find the story in *Ovid and *Claudian. He makes a brief *allusion to the owl, that is called Escaphilo' in Troilus V.319–20.

Esculapius, Aesculapius, god and founder of medicine. In the Middle Ages, a number of medical books were attributed to him. He appears (as 'the olde Esculapius') at the head of the list of authorities with which the *Physician in the General Prologue (I.429) is said to be acquainted. (See *medicine.)

Eson, Aeson, the father of *Jason.

Esperus, see *Hesperus.

Essex, the English county (between Suffolk and the Thames). Chaucer's family had been merchants in Ipswich nearby, but he mentions the county only once (III.218), in connection with the town *Dunmowe.

estates satire is the name given to the kind of satire which portrays representative types of various 'estates' i.e. classes and occupations, demonstrating the vices or follies considered to be typical of each. It is concerned with the characteristics and characteristic shortcomings of particular social groups. An 'estate' was a social, political, or occupational class or group. Three principal 'estates of the realm' were distinguished (divinely ordained, and going back to an ancient tripartite division into those who prayed, those who fought, and those who worked): clergy, nobles, and commons. During the Middle Ages the last 'estate' became increasingly differentiated into various occupational groups, but although it was hardly adequate as a political description of a society with a growing money economy, the traditional three-fold division persisted for a long time.

Chaucer's own use of estates satire is most evident in the *General Prologue* of *The Canterbury Tales*, where he uses the traditional form of a list of estates (going well beyond the 'three estates of the realm', who would be represented by the Knight, the Parson, and the Ploughman). Such lists could be varied according to taste or purpose, but some figures were very commonly found—notably, monk, friar, priest, lawyer, doctor, or knight. Shortcomings are lamented, remedies proposed for defects. This kind of satire does not offer exact sociological observation, but makes extensive use of social stereotypes (to the development and continuation of which it also contributes) and proverbial matter. Thus it is likely that a *friar will be characterized by persuasiveness, '*glosing', a proclivity for wenching, and the giving of easy confessions. The *General Prologue*, although it is an original and distinctive creation, keeps the conceptual form of estates satire. It has been argued by Jill Mann that it is a literary form as much as, or more than, 'an exhaustive survey of medieval English society' (thus its small number of women may have something to do with the fact that 'estates literature rarely listed more than two estates of women—religious and secular'). It gives a list of estates (mostly from the 'third estate') which are referred to by their occupation (Miller, Reeve, etc.) rather than by name. The clerical figures are deeply influenced by Latin estates satire, but in general in the treatment of professional characteristics there is a distinctive stress on work. The various *portraits sometimes evoke the idealized version of the estate, sometimes the real-life version, with all its perversions and inadequacies.

Mann (1973); Mohl (1933).

Ester, Hester. Esther, the Jewish heroine of the Old Testament Book of Esther (which has been described as a 'popular romance'). As consort of the Persian king Ahasuerus (*Assuer(e)) (in fact, Xerxes I, who reigned 486–465 BC), she used her influence to save her countrymen and in particular her kinsman Mordecai (*Mardochee) from the violent persecution of the vizier Haman. This was a popular exemplary story in the Middle Ages. Esther became a proverbial figure of womanly grace. Thus she appears as a model of goodness and 'debonairte' [gentleness of manner] in *The *Book of the Duchess* (985–7), of meekness (*Prol LGW* F 250), and as one who 'by hir good conseil [*counseil] enhaunced greetly the people of God' (*Mel.* VII.1101). In *The Merchant's Tale* she appears in a list of wives who gave 'good conseil' (IV.1371), and later (1744) as a figure of meekness in a comparison with the 'benyngne . . . chiere' that the young wife May showed at her wedding ('Queene Ester looked nevere with swich an ye | On Assuer, so meke a look hath she').

Estoryal Myrour, the *Speculum historiale* of *Vincent of Beauvais, mentioned in *Legend of Good Women* (G 307). Several versions appeared. The subject is the history of mankind from Creation to 1254.   [JDN]

Ethiocles, Eteocles, son of Oedipus, who was to rule *Thebes (1) alternately with his brother Polynices (*Polymytes), but refused to make way for him, and in the ensuing war 'each of them slew the other' (as Cassandra tells the story in *Tr* V.1485–1510).

Ethiopeen, Ethiopian. The inhabitants of Ethiopia, for the Middle Ages a land of deserts and wondrous beasts, were renowned (as in the ancient world) for their blackness ('for the sun is nigh and roasteth and toasteth them' says *Bartholomew); the Parson remarks (X.345) that after his sojourn in the desert St Jerome's 'flessh was blak as an Ethiopeen for heete'.

Ethna, Mt. Etna, the volcano in Sicily, mentioned in *Boece (II m.5, pr.6), 'the fyer of the mountaigne Ethna that ay brenneth', and (since it was one of the entrances to the underworld) in a probable allusion in *The *Merchant's Tale*

(IV.2230) to Pluto's ravishing of Proserpina (actually in the fields of Enna).

Etik, quoted as an authority in the Prologue to *The *Legend of Good Women* ('vertu is the mene, | As Etik seith', F 166), remains unidentified. Probably it refers to *Aristotle, author of the *Ethics*, perhaps to some other moral author, such as Horace, who is called *ethicus* by *John of Salisbury.

EUCLIDE, Euclid (*fl. c.*295 BC), Greek mathematician. Author of the *Elements* (of geometry), as well as of important works in conic sections, optics, and music. Virtually nothing is known of Euclid's personal life, even though he was by far the best known of all ancient mathematicians, with a name synonymous with geometry itself. He taught in Alexandria. His *Elements* are set out in a deductive style that (with the philosophical support of *Aristotle) moulded Western views on the essential character of a true science. Boethius (*Boece) is known to have made a translation into Latin. The problem of the transmission of the *Elements* to the Latin Middle Ages through Arabic and Greek intermediaries is complex. One important translator was Adelard of Bath. In *The *Summoner's Tale* Euclid is named (with Ptolemy (*Phtholomee)) as a model of subtlety. (See also ***Dulcarnoun**; ***Quadrivium**.) [JDN]

Eufrates, the river Euphrates in Mesopotamia, referred to in *Boece (V m.1).

EURIPIDIS, Euripides (*c.*408–406 BC), the Greek tragedian. The only reference to him is in *Boece (III pr.7:25), as the disciple of Philosophy, who said 'that he that hath no children is weleful by infortune [fortunate in his misfortune]' (cf. *Andromache* 420). Chaucer himself would not have read Euripides.

Eurippe, the strait Euripus which separates the island of Euboea on the eastern side of Greece from Boeotia, used to refer to any strait with a violent tidal flow. *Boece (II m.1:3) compares Fortune to 'the boylynge Eurippe'.

Europe (1). Europa the daughter of Agenor, king of Tyre, wooed by Zeus in the form of a white bull

(see also *Taur) and carried off to Crete. The story is told by *Ovid in *Metamorphoses* 2.833–75. In Chaucer she is mentioned in Troilus's invocation to Jove in **Troilus and Criseyde* III.722, and, as 'Agenores doghtre' in an astronomical reference in the Prologue to the **Legend of Good Women* (F 113).

Europe (2), One of the three continents of medieval cartography (HF 1339, II.161; see Maps 1, 3).

Eurus, the east or south-east wind (referred to in *Boece* II m.4:4; IV m.3:1).

Eva, Eve, the first woman, wife of Adam, and mother of all humankind. According to the story in Genesis, she was tempted by the serpent to eat the forbidden fruit of the tree of knowledge, and when she and Adam did so they were driven from Paradise. The Virgin Mary (see *Marie), the 'second Eve', by her obedience in carrying out the will of God in the incarnation of Christ, restored the loss caused by the first Eve. Eve is prominent in discussions and diatribes concerning the relative status of men and woman from St Paul through medieval didactic and misogynistic writings. Chaucer has a number of references, relating in one way or another to the Fall: Satan made Eve 'brynge us in servage' (II.368); she appears first in the book of wicked women that Jankin read to the Wife of Bath (III.715) ('Of Eva first, that for hir wikkednesse | Was al mankynde broght to wrecchednesse'), and with some irony figures in the praise of marriage in *The Merchant's Tale* (IV.1329). The pattern of Eve lies behind some female figures whose counsel brings disaster or near-disaster (*NPT* VII.3256–9). The Parson once allegorizes her as the 'flesh' (X.331), but though he takes the story of her creation to signify the lower status of *women (X.925 ff.) (God made the first woman 'nat of the heved of Adam, for she sholde nat clayme to greet lordshipe') this does not mean that they are completely inferior: 'Also, certes, God ne made nat woman of the foot of Adam, for she sholde nat been holden to lowe; for she kan nat paciently suffre. But God made woman of the ryb of Adam, for woman sholde be felawe unto man.'

Evander (literally 'good man'), an Arcadian who

founded a colony on the banks of the Tiber in the place where Rome was to stand (mentioned in *Boece* IV m.7:53, 55).

Evaungiles, the Gospels: in the *Man of Law's Tale* (II.666) 'a Britoun book, written with Evaungiles' is used to swear an *oath on.

exaltacioun, exaltation (of a planet, in astrology). Exaltation occurs in the Zodiac at a point opposed to the planet's *dejection* (Chaucer speaks only of its 'falling'). Exaltation is the second most important dignity of a planet, the first being its *domicile. (See also *Aries; *Cancre; *dignite(e); *Pisces; *signe.) [JDN]

exemplum, the Latin form (pl. *exempla*) of Chaucer's *ensa(u)mple*, an example, an exemplary or illustrative story (like *example* and *sample*, the word originally meant something 'taken out' as a specimen). *Exemplum* is used in a technical sense to describe a genre of medieval literature, the short tale or anecdote designed to point a moral, but usually vivid and entertaining. These seem to have been very popular, and were gathered together in collections. They were frequently used by *friars and other preachers addressing a popular audience (and some, no doubt, were made up for the purpose). The friars were sometimes criticized for relying too heavily on such entertaining tales. It is against this background that we should see the *Parson's austere rejection of the telling of 'fables and swich wrecchednesse'; he will offer 'moralitee and vertuous mateere'. However the *Pardoner is a great user of exempla in his preaching, as he explains: (VI.435–8) 'Thanne telle I hem ensamples many oon | Of olde stories longe tyme agoon. | For lewed peple loven tales olde; | Swich thynges kan they wel reporte and holde'. And the 'moral tale' which he tells is a particularly fine extended example. Chaucer uses *ensa(u)mple* both in this specialized sense and in the more general sense of exemplar, pattern, illustration, or analogy. These are quoted as authorities (*auctoritee) in arguments or persuasions of others or of one's self, sometimes in lists or catalogues (as in Dorigen's complaint in The *Franklin's Tale*, V.1355–456). 'Of Sampson now wol I namoore sayn,' says the *Monk, 'Beth war by this ensample oold and playn

| That no men telle hir conseil til hir wyves' (VII.2090–2). He is a great user of 'ensamples trewe and olde'. And their use tends to encourage a certain long-windedness. *Chauntecleer, after a speech of about 130 lines to his wife Pertelote which contains two exempla, seems to be coming to a conclusion (VII.3105–8), but he is just pausing for breath. Auditors are usually silent, but Troilus grows impatient with Pandarus (*Tr* I.759–60) and exclaims 'Lat be thyne olde ensaumples, | the preye.' However, Chaucer seems to have enjoyed them. (See also *fable; *proverb.)

Mosher (1911); Scanlon (1994); Welther (1927).

Exodi, Exodus, the Old Testament book (L. possessive sing. in a reference in the *Parson's Tale*, X.750).

experience, from L. *experiri* 'to put to the test, try', can mean 'observing or undergoing' and (in science) 'observation, ocular proof', as well as its more familiar general sense of (Johnson) 'knowledge gained by trial and practice'. (Only the noun is found in Chaucerian English: the verb appears in the early 16th c. It is often alluded to, by the *Eagle in an enthusiastic scientific way ('Thou shalt have yet, or it be eve, | Of every word of thys sentence | A preve by experience') (*HF* 876–8), and by others (as it still is) in offhand generalizations. Lecherers know 'by experience', says the Wife of Bath (III.468), that 'in women vinolent [full of wine] is no defence'. It is closely linked with *auctoritee, with which it is not (in the widest sense) incompatible (counsellors who are 'trewe, wise, and of oold experience' have 'auctoritee'; cf. *Mel* VII.1164–8). But 'authorities' (in the sense of authoritative texts or authors quoted in argument) can differ. *Chauntecleer demonstrates this in refuting his wife. (VII.2974–83) and arguing that the significance of dreams is shown by experience, 'verray preve'. In its sense of 'verray preve' it is sometimes contrasted with 'auctoritee'. Theseus, speaking of the fixed term of created things, remarks 'Ther nedeth noght noon auctoritee t'allegge, | For it is preeved by experience' (I.3000–1); and the Parson, like other contemporary preachers, invokes everyday 'experience' (X.927): 'ther as the womman hath the maistrie, she maketh to muche desray [disorder]. Ther neden none ensamples of this; the experience of day by day oghte suffise.' This is most memorably expressed in the opening lines of the Wife of Bath's Prologue: 'Experience, though noon auctoritee | Were in this world, is right ynogh for me | To speke of wo that is in mariage' (III.1–3). (It may well be a private Chaucerian joke that this defiant statement is an allusion with a traditional literary background: it echoes the *Roman de la Rose* 12804–5—'I know all by practice: experience has made me wise'.) The opposition also lurks behind some of the remarks of practical men of the world (like the carpenter in *MilT* and the miller in *RvT*) who have to do with scholars, and attempt to prove (without complete success) that 'the gretteste clerkes been noght the wisest men'. The opposition if 'experience' and 'authority' has been taken up by critics, who point out Chaucer's characteristic balance of the observation of life (perhaps encouraged the offices he held (see Geoffrey *Chaucer: life)) and the fruits of his extensive reading. Perhaps we should see them as two ways to wisdom, sometimes comically opposed, sometimes complementary.

eye. Chaucer's interest in eyes was not confined to those of humans. Unlike them, the small birds in the *General Prologue* sleep with 'open ye'. (It is not absolutely clear whether this suggests 'lightly', or whether it is a reference to the set of transparent eyelids which birds have.) The sinister fox which appears to Chauntecleer in a dream has 'glowynge eyen tweye' (VII.2905), and though the wonderful steed in The *Squire's Tale* is made of brass, its essential 'horsliness' is shown in its eye (it was (V.194) 'so horsly and so quyk of ye'). But it is the appearance and the significance of the human eye which account for such figurative uses as *hevenes ye* 'sun', *brestes ye* 'heart'—and Alison's 'nether ye' (I.3852). More spiritual are the 'eyes of thought' in *Boece* (III pr.9) which should be turned, in a Neoplatonic way, towards Light (a number of the images of the blindness of mortal men (e.g. *Tr* I.211) have distinctly Boethian overtones).

In his encyclopaedia, *Bartholomew discusses sight and the eyes. Sight enables us to apprehend and recognize colours, shapes, and outer properties. Each eye has a 'crystalline humour': it is clear, and round, so as to avoid damage. (In *HF*

658 there is a reference to the 'daswed [dazed? dimmed?] look' which Chaucer's avid reading produces, and the eye-glass or spectacle was familiar enough for the Wife of Bath to use it figuratively: 'Poverte a spectacle is . . . | Thurgh which he may his verray freendes see' (III.1203–4).) Three of Bartholomew's points are of particular interest: (1) Sight is more subtle and lively than the other senses. A 'quyk' eye is a sign of life: when *Arcite is dying, 'dusked his eyen two'. (2) Of all the senses the eyes are nearest to the soul, and show the working of the mind and the *emotions. (3) Nature has set the eye on the highest place of the body as a watchman (see also *Prudence).

The second of these ideas—that the eyes are the 'token' or the 'mirror' of the soul—lies behind many of Chaucer's uses. Sometimes the 'token' is simply indicated by a descriptive adjective (eyes may be 'friendly' or 'meek' or 'cruel'). At other times (notably in the *portraits in the *General Prologue*) we are given a precise detail which may have significance in *physiognomy, the art of attempting to read character from the face. Thus the *Pardoner (I.684) has 'glarynge eyen' 'as an hare' (which has large, protuberant eyes, and was thought to sleep with them open—and was thought to be hermaphroditic). Possibly the *Friar's 'twinkling eyes' (I.267) indicate a propensity to malice and craft. But the eyes are the index of the mind in a variety of ways, some of them quite complex. Sorrow causes tears to spring from the eyes. In *Troilus* IV.869 the eyes of the sorrowful Criseyde are encircled by 'a purpre ryng'. Arcite's sorrow makes his eyes 'holwe [sunk deep] and grisly to behold' (it has robbed them of 'lifeliness' and made them suggestive of death 'hollow eyed'). Or the eyes may show mercy or '*pite'. The exemplar here is the Virgin Mary (*Marie) with her 'pitous eyen cleere' (*ABC* 88). That her 'blissful eyen' saw all her son's torment is recalled by another suffering mother in The *Man of Law's Tale* (II.845). This little scene (II.834–67) shows how important the eyes can be in this kind of narrative: Constance's little child is weeping (834); in a maternal *gesture of comfort, she lays her kerchief 'over his litel eyen' (838), and raises her eyes to heaven (840). She prays to the Virgin, twice referring to her eyes (845, and 848 'thow sawe thy child yslayn bifore thyne yen'), and the scene draws to its conclusion with Constance looking backward to the land (862).

The eyes betray both lust and love. Whereas the wicked judge in The *Physician's Tale (VI.123–9) is seized with passion, Walter inspects Griselda (IV.236–8) more soberly: 'noght with wantown looking of folye | His eyen caste on hire, but in sad wyse | Upon hir chiere he wolde hym ofte avyse'. The beautiful eyes of the lady in The *Book of the Duchess (859–77) ('debonaire, goode, glade, and sadde') reveal her '*mesure' or moderation, 'for were she never so glad, | Hyr lokynge was not foly sprad, | Ne wildely'. But Alison in The *Miller's Tale (I.3244) has 'a likerous ye'. The beautiful lady of courtly literature traditionally has 'grey' eyes (Rom 546, 862; whether or not this is exactly equivalent to the modern colour, or whether it means 'greyish', 'hazel', or 'grey with shades of blue' has been much discussed). The well-bred *Prioress shares this features (as does a less courtly lady, the Miller's daughter in RvT) (Some handsome men also have grey eyes (Myrthe, Rom 822, and, with a more homely simile 'greye as goos', the less courtly Absolon in The Miller's Tale I.3317)). Chauntecleer's praise of Pertelote's eyes ('so scarlet reed aboute youre yen', VII.3160–1) is clearly making fun of this courtly topic. *Love is 'first learned in a lady's eyes', often with a devastating pain: 'ye sleen me with youre eyen, Emelye' says Arcite (I. 1567). Troilus in the temple, unaware that 'Love hadde his dwellynge | Withinne the subtile stremes of hire yen' suddenly feels his spirit 'die' (Tr I.304–7) 'right with hire look' (a phrase that is repeated several times during the scene). In terms of medieval psychology, from the 'stremes' of the eyes the lady's 'figure' is imprinted on the heart: 'in his herte botme gan to stiken | Of hir his fixe and depe impressioun.'

But, as the proverb says, 'he is blind in both eyes that does not see into the heart.' At the climax of The *Merchant's Tale we find an interesting case involving both literal and metaphorical blindness

caused by love and by folly. The blind January (Fortune 'biraft hym bothe his yen' (IV.2067)) is at the mercy of his young wife—'as good is blynd deceyved be | As to be deceyved whan a man may se' remarks the narrator (2107–10). An allusion to Argus who, though he had a hundred eyes, 'yet was he blent' (2113) introduces her trick to get her squire Damyan into January's garden of delights. The old man calls upon his fair spouse to come forth 'with thyne even columbyn [dovelike]' (2141), a parodic echo of the Song of Songs. Thanks to Pluto, he is miraculously given back the sight of his eyes (2355) so that he may see his wife's harlotry. His outcry when 'up to the tre he caste his eyen two' (2360) is not assuaged by May's attempt to explain all. January is sure of what he saw: 'he swyved thee; I saugh it with myne yen.' At first unmoved by her attempt to argue that he had 'som glymsyng, and no parfit sighte', he repeats the phrase 'I se . . . as wel as evere I myghte | . . . with bothe myne eyen two' (2385) before he finally accepts her explanation: 'it is al another than it semeth. | He that mysconceyveth, he mysdemeth' (2409–10). The eye, as Bartholomew said, can see the 'outer properties', but as a proverb has it, 'al thyng which that shineth as the gold | Nis nat gold . . . | Ne every appul that is fair at eye | Ne is nat good' (VIII.962–5). Forgetful of prudence and watchfulness, Chauntecleer does not emulate the small birds of the General Prologue: deluded by the fox into crowing (VII.3332), 'strecchynge his nekke,' he 'heeld his eyen cloos'.

Collette (2001); Klassen (1995).

Ezechie, Ezechias, King Hezekiah, whose words to God after his sickness ('I wol remember me all the yeres of my lyf in bitternesse of myn herte') (Isaiah 38:15) are twice quoted in the Parson's Tale (X.135, 983).

Ezechiel, the Old Testament prophet, quoted several times in the Parson's Tale (X.140, 143 etc.).

F

fable. A fable, says Dr Johnson, is 'a narrative in which beings irrational, and sometimes inanimate ...are for the purpose of moral instruction feigned to act and speak with human interests and passions.' The word (orig. 'story') is often used in the Middle Ages in its more general senses (e.g. by the Parson, X.31, 34) and what we now call animal fables are sometimes called 'fables', but sometimes 'stories' or 'tales'. Animal fables form part of a larger group of animal stories, some of which are less concerned with 'moral instruction' (as some of the stories of *Renard). The European fable tradition is associated with the name of Aesop (*Isope). Greek Aesopic fables were not, however, directly known in the medieval West. Aesopic material was transmitted through the Latin fable of late antiquity and its later derivatives. The fable is usually a short narrative, succinct and memorable, leading to a moral point which is made explicit. The fable was regarded as a humble form but also as the vehicle for wise teaching. It appealed to a number of sophisticated writers (*Marie de France, Chaucer, and later *Henryson and La Fontaine) who found in it various kinds of literary possibilities and challenges. Characteristically, the *animal protagonists exist in full autonomy, but their relationship with human life and behaviour is a shifting and delicate one, which can be the source of both 'earnest' and 'game'. Now they will act or speak like humans, and now like animals. Thus *Chauntecleer quotes Boethius (*Boece) and other 'authors' in his learned discourse, but he summons his hens with a 'chuk' to the corn he has found in the yard (VII.3174–5).

Chaucer alludes to a number, e.g. to the fable (found in Marie de France) of the lion and the peasant ('who peyntede the leon, tel me who? III.692). Two of the *Canterbury Tales* are, or are closely related to, fables. The *Manciple's Tale* is based on the fable of the 'tell-tale bird' which he

found in Ovid, an aetiological narrative explaining why the crow is black. He makes it into something much more than this, but gives a formal 'morality' at the end, which he attributes to his 'dame'. The proverbial moral 'kepe wel thy tonge' is one of expediency: the man who keeps his mouth shut survives. This kind of self-interested morality is not at all unknown in the Aesopic tradition, but the Manciple expresses it with remarkable cynicism.

The well-known story of the cock and the fox was found both as a separate fable (in, for instance, Marie de France) and in the *Roman de Renart*, which was probably Chaucer's main source. In The *Nun's Priest's Tale* it is given its most brilliant literary treatment. Chaucer transforms the simple fable form into a rich texture of elaboration, amplification, and allusion. The setting is detailed. The traditionally rapid forward movement of the story is constantly delayed by *digressions, elaborate descriptions, or exclamations, which allow all kinds of mock heroic and parodic games. The narrator's explicit acknowledgement that the story belongs to the genre of the animal fable ('for thilke tyme, as I have understonde, | Beestes and briddes koude speke and synge', VII.2880–1) comes some sixty lines after its opening, as a comment on Chauntecleer and Pertelote's delightful habit of singing together the song 'My lief is faren in londe'. At times the story seems almost on the point of turning into something else—like the Monk's kind of 'tragedy' which it is making fun of. There are allusions to other kinds of animal literature and lore (mermaids can sing, according to Physiologus, and the wicked fox has read the *Speculum Stultorum* ('Daun Burnel the Asse')). The human interests and passions which exercise the birds include some of the questions closest to Chaucer's heart, and the high-spirited treatment of them gives an extraordinary complexity to the narrative. But somehow the underlying structure of the fable form remains intact. The climax is an action of choice, when Chauntecleer 'ravysshed' by the fox's flattery agrees to crow with his eyes closed (and the first cause of this is not only his vanity and susceptibility at this point, but his earlier choice to ignore his conviction that his dream was a prophetic one). Unlike many fables, this one ends in '*game', and in a scene in which both fox and cock make speeches showing that they have learned something. The narrator, deftly reminding us of the paradoxical nature of the fable, both humble and profound, brings it to a conclusion with a morality which is very appropriate— though whether this is the only 'moral instruction' that it offers is another matter.

fabliau (plural **fabliaux**). The word (which seems to have meant 'a little story') is related etymologically to '*fable'. It is now used to designate a short comic tale in verse, often involving sexual deception and outwitting, often scurrilous or bawdy. (The medieval usage is not consistent, and other words are sometimes used to describe such tales.) This is a kind which flourished in France in the 13th c. The only surviving example in English before Chaucer is the 13th-c. *Dame Sirith*. The term 'fabliau' is sometimes used in a looser, more general sense to cover similar comic tales in prose, both the literary *novella* (found, for instance, in the *Decameron*), and the oral bawdy anecdote, which had existed for centuries. A number of *The *Canterbury Tales* (in verse) are often called fabliaux: *The *Miller's Tale*, *The *Reeve's Tale*, *The *Merchant's Tale*, *The *Shipman's Tale*, *The *Summoner's Tale*, and (by some) *The *Friar's Tale*. Perhaps the unfinished *Cook's Tale* would also have been one.

The fabliau (in both the narrow and wider senses) characteristically gives vigorous expression in terse and simple style to a decidedly non-idealistic view of life. Its setting is non-courtly, its characters tradesmen or merchants (and their wives and daughters), clerics, students. It is sometimes praised for its realism (like the marital scenes depicted in the misericords—see *visual arts**). However, while there is often realism in the setting (e.g. the cat's hole in *The Miller's Tale*),

the plot is often far from realistic, indeed (as in that Tale) more fantastic than that of a courtly *romance.

The French fabliau operates with stereotyped characters and stereotyped expectations (e.g. of the marriage of an old man and a young wife). Women are both objects of desire and intent on fulfilling their own desires. Clerks are ingenious and inventive—and amorous. Characters are often not given names, but are simply figures, referred to as 'the clerk', 'the miller', etc. And they are not usually seen in isolation, but in relationship to some adversary in a conflict or competition which helps to define them in terms of the action's unexpected—or expected—turns and events. In this kind of fabliau the plot is of cardinal importance. The success of the fabliau stands or falls by the quality of the action. The concentration on the action is partly responsible for the precision of detail. As in a farce some essential information (e.g. in *The Reeve's Tale*, the fact that the baby's cot is at the foot of the wife's bed) has to be neatly and unobtrusively worked in in readiness for the part it will later play. Even the cat's hole has its part in the action of *The Miller's Tale*.

The fabliau is often entirely self-contained, presenting itself as pure entertainment. It is often amoral, although it may sometimes be possible to detect a kind of comic justice, in which vanity and folly receive appropriate punishment and intelligence emerges as the most positive and valuable quality. There is a delight in clever tricks or ruses—like the wife's 'suffisant answere' given to her by Proserpina in *The Merchant's Tale*—even if they are not always successful. There often seems to be a kind of naturalism at work, celebrating carnal (and usually youthful) passion. The fabliau can be irreverent or subversive, making fun of religion, or the mores of self-important citizens. Its satire and comedy can be abrasive and cruel.

Proverbial wisdom is both quoted and enacted: 'a gylour [deceiver] shal hymself bigyled be' is the 'moral' of *The Reeve's Tale*. And the fabliau is close to popular literature in other respects. It is often very similar to the 'jesting' type of *folk tale. On the other hand the fabliau may sometimes overlap with the fable, or even with the *exemplum or the moral tale. A comic story of a priest and a peasant and his cow appears as the French fabliau

'Brunain', and is also used as a moral exemplum illustrating 'how mercy may increase temporal goods'.

There has been much discussion concerning the origin of the French fabliau. The older view—that it came into being *c*.1200 as an expression of an emerging middle class which wanted a less exclusive and idealized literature than that provided for courtly circles has been strongly challenged. If we move outside the confines of the French verse fabliau the question of origins becomes more difficult: indeed it is one which can hardly be put. Dronke has pointed out how fabliau-like material is found not only over wide geographical areas, but over great tracts of time. The fabliau-like story of 'The Widow of Ephesus' is found in Petronius (1st c. AD). The story of the 'Snow Child'—a merchant returning home after a long absence finds that his wife has a small son, which she explains as the result of her swallowing a snow-flake; later the father takes the boy abroad and sells him into slavery, and when he returns explains the disappearance as the result of the very hot sun—is found in medieval Latin, later as a French fabliau, and later still in collections of 'merry tales'; it is even alluded to in an English religious mystery play. 'Fabliau', Dronke says, 'is one of the great constants in European literature', and can take a variety of forms.

Chaucer's handling of the fabliau stories in *The Canterbury Tales* is sophisticated and original. Each of them is given a distinctive treatment which transforms them from a simple 'cherles tale' into something different and more complex. Even *The Shipman's Tale*, where the simple structure brings it close to the typical French fabliau, contrives to conceal beneath its smooth surface some uneasy views of the bourgeois mercantile ethos and of the ways of monks. With the Friar and the Summoner, Chaucer seems to be playing with the genre. *The Friar's Tale* sounds as if it is going to be a fabliau, but in fact turns out to be a satirical exemplum; *The Summoner's Tale*, however, is a splendidly scurrilous example of the kind. Much more complicated is the treatment of *The Merchant's Tale*, where the favourite triangle situation of the fabliau—old husband, young wife, and young squire—is the basis for a deeply ironical treatment of blindness, folly, and marriage, and

much else, in a narrative structure that is far more intricate than any usual fabliau, elaborated by literary allusion, rhetorical expansion, formal debate, homily, mythology, and parody. In *The Miller's Tale* and *The Reeve's Tale* Chaucer takes the opportunity to set the stories with the kind of local detail that is found in this tradition only in the *Decameron*. He treats the stories both with a greater rhetorical expansiveness—in the formal *portraits of the characters, for instance—and with a greater dramatic awareness, using all his skill in *dialogue and the construction of scenes. Although French analogues can be found for the separate parts of the plot of *The Reeve's Tale*, none of them shows anything of the skilfulness with which Chaucer unites action and character. The way in which the tale is fitted to the character of the misanthropic narrator, and made into an exercise in concentrated venom, is both brilliant and unique. Furthest, perhaps, from the 'typical fabliau' is the more genial *Miller's Tale*, with its ingeniously elaborated plot, and its developed characterization. In short, Chaucer transformed the fabliau so that it is hardly recognizable. He seems to expect these stories to cause embarrassment to some in his audience, and ingenuously asks not to be blamed—'men shal nat maken ernest of *game'. But the artistic pleasure he shows in reworking them forbids anyone to 'turn over the leaf'.

Cooke (1978); Dronke (1973); Jodogne (1975); Levy (2000); Richardson (1970).

FABRICIUS, Gaius Luscinus Fabricius, a Roman general of the 3rd c. BC, and a figure of exemplary honesty, austerity, and incorruptibility. Chaucer calls him 'trewe Fabricius' in *Boece* II.m.7 (L. *fidelis*).

Face, face (astrological). Each sign of 30° into which the *ecliptic is divided may be further divided into three equal parts, or faces, and each then assigned to a planet. Chaucer explains that 'somme folk' take it that a planet rises with the entire face in which it is situated, and he points out that failure to take a planet's *latitude into account can here mislead. He was not however, averse to using the concept of face: at the beginning of *The *Squire's Tale*, for example, he places the Sun in a face of Mars. (See *ascendent; *astrology and astronomy; *dignite(e); *horoscope; *signe.)

[JDN]

fayerye, fairye, in Chaucer a collective noun meaning 'the fairies' or 'fairyland' (he once uses the pl., III.872). It is also used to mean 'magic' or 'enchantment' in general (*May's beauty was such that simply to behold her 'it semed fayerye', IV.1743), or 'a piece of magic, a marvel' (in The *Squire's Tale the horse of brass seemed to the people to be 'a fairye', V.201).

There was a widespread belief in fairies. They were beautiful, and fairy ladies are often described dancing. Fairyland seems to be outside time and is far away, and difficult for a searcher to find; and yet the fairies are close to men and can intervene in their lives at will. Fairyland is a beautiful place, and yet a dangerous one, from which it may be impossible to return. Fairies have a very prominent role in some *Breton lays (like *Sir Launfal or *Sir Orfeo). Chaucer's Sir Thopas, who is avid for a fairy adventure, comes to the 'contree of Fairye | So wilde' (VII.802–3) where the 'Queene of Fayerye' lives, but we never get to the end of his story. Chaucer's fairies are somewhat peripheral. They are most prominent in The *Wife of Bath's Tale, set in the magical days of King Arthur (*Arthour), when the land was filled with 'fayerye' (before the arrival of the multitudes of friars). In the tale a knight riding 'under a forest syde' comes upon a group of ladies dancing. The dance vanishes before he can reach it leaving only the mysterious ugly old woman who presides over the remainder of this tale of magic. In a more unlikely context in The *Merchant's Tale Pluto and *Proserpina 'and al hire fayerye' made melody and danced around the well in January's garden (IV.2039–41). Pluto is 'kyng of Fayerye' (2227, 2234), and she is the 'queene of Fayerye' (2316). In The *Squire's Tale (V.96), a remark suggests that Sir *Gawain is living on in fairyland—perhaps because his 'olde curteisye' was 'out of this world', perhaps because he was related to Morgan la Fay, perhaps simply because he was associated with King Arthur. Chaucer does not seem to be much interested in the varieties of magical creatures. Elves and fairies seem to overlap (see *elf-queene). He has no dwarves, and his giants, apart from the one who

guards the fairy queen and challenges Sir Thopas (VII.807ff.), come from classical antiquity (*Anteus, or those who attacked the gods, Boece III pr.12:133ff.). (See also *magic.)

fairs (which take their name from the *feriae*, ecclesiastical festivals and holidays, on which they were held) were a very important feature of medieval life. These perodical opportunities for buying and selling (less frequent than the regular markets) could be very large, and could last for several days or several weeks. They sometimes became noted for particular products. They had special privileges, and were carefully regulated. Famous English fairs included that of St Bartholomew in Smithfield, London; St Giles in Oxford and Winchester; and Stourbridge (which later was the model for Bunyan's Vanity Fair). They also provided meeting places for the exchange of news and stories and were centres of entertainment, visited by pedlars and jugglers.

Chaucer alludes to them as part of the texture of everyday life. The merchant in The *Shipman's Tale returns home from Bruges 'whan that ended was the faire' (VII.325). And the Wife of Bath trained her husbands well, so that they were eager, she says, 'to brynge me gaye thynges fro the fayre' (III.221). Because of their limited duration, fairs were commonly taken as a figure of something which is quickly past and gone. A proverb which was a favourite with preachers—'this world is but a fair'—is used by Chaucer at the end of *Troilus and Criseyde: 'thynketh al nys but a faire, | This world that passeth soone as floures faire' (V.1840–1).

He uses markets in the same allusive way. The 'common market-place' is where people are always passing by (IV.1583). The miller in The *Reeve's Tale was a 'market-betere' (I.3936) i.e. a quarrelsome loiterer around a marketplace. And the Wife of Bath quotes an appropriate proverb— 'great press at market makes dear ware' in support of her doctrine that women should not be too generous with their distinctive wares (III.522–3).

Fame (see also *House of Fame). The word (like its original, L. *fama*) had a number of related senses which Chaucer plays with. (1) It can mean 'renown': thus, the 'fame' of Virginia's virtue (VI.111) and of Griselda's goodness (IV.418) spread far and wide. In this sense it has a number of near-synonyms—*glorie* (in the sense of 'renown' etc.), *laude* 'praise, honour', *renomee* 'renown' (or the past participle of the verb, *renomed*), or *renoun*. Closely related is the sense of 'repute, reputation' (whether good or bad). In *The House of Fame* we hear both of 'good fame' (1545) and of 'a shrewed fame' (1619). This overlaps with *name* in the sense of 'reputation' and with *reputacioun*. (2) It retained its L. sense of 'rumour'. It is this sense that is dominant in *Dido's exclamation against 'wikke Fame' (*HF* 349), which is based on Virgil. It merges into the senses 'talk, tidings, news'—the 'fame' that king Alla had come on pilgrimage was carried through Rome (II.995)—and is synonymous with *rumour* 'rumour, general talk; uproar'. (3) It may also mean 'ill-repute', as when the *Reeve reproaches the *Miller for bringing 'wyves in swich fame' (I.3148), and linking it with the words *apeyren* ('injure') and *defame* (verb: 'slander, disgrace'; noun: 'bad reputation, dishonour, disgrace'). Overlapping in a number of senses is the word *loos* 'praise, fame', 'reputation', 'rumour' (it is linked with 'tidings' in *LGW* 1424), and *honour*, which can mean 'fame', 'reputation', or 'good name'.

Fame is the central topic of *The House of Fame*, where we meet it personified as a goddess. Outside this work the references are usually brief—thus, in *Troilus and Criseyde* the news that Criseyde is to be handed over to the Greeks is quickly spread when 'the swifte Fame' (who reports falsehoods and truths equally) 'was thorughout Troie yfled with preste [swift] wynges | Fro man to man' (IV.659–62). Theseus in *The *Knight's Tale* gives a stoic, soldierly view of fame—'thanne is it best, as for a worthy fame, | To dyen whan that he is best of name' (I.3055–6), linking it with 'honour' and 'good name'.

For his treatment of Fame in *The House of Fame* Chaucer used the descriptions of Fama in *Virgil (*Aeneid* 4) and *Ovid (*Met.* 12), supplemented by other authors. He knew the *Somnium Scipionis* (*Drem of Scipioun) with its stress on virtue rather than worldly fame as the proper motive for action. And he was clearly influenced by the discussion in Boethius (*Boece) (II pr.7), in which Philosophy, following the views of Cicero, Seneca, and Pliny, argues strongly against the

pursuit of fame: 'if you think of the infinite spaces of eternity what cause do you have to rejoice in the continuation of your name?' The soul, freed from its earthly prison, cares not for worldly glory. Biblical and Christian thoughts on the vanity of worldly glory chimed well with this view. At the same time, Chaucer was aware of the possibilities of literary fame—that monument more lasting than bronze which the poet could erect. In this he was not alone among medieval poets. *Dante echoes Boethius—'the world's noise [*il mondan romore*] is but a breath of wind, which blows this way and that' (*Purgatario* 11.100–1); in *Paradiso* (22.134–5) he looks down at the earth and smiles 'at its paltry appearance'. However, with this goes a belief in the lasting glory of poetry, and in the sublimity of the poet's calling. At the beginning of *Paradiso* he prays to Apollo for inspiration—if the power divine grants him to show forth the shadow of the divine kingdom, he will come to the god's laurel tree, and crown himself 'with those leaves of which the theme and thou will make me worthy'.

The goddess whom Chaucer meets in *The House of Fame* is a grotesque and extraordinary figure. Her size varies—sometimes she seems shorter than a cubit, sometimes her head touches the heavens. She has innumerable eyes, ears, and tongues. These iconographical details are based on Virgil's description of Fama (Rumour), a terrible and monstrous creature who by day perches on a rooftop or a high turret and by night flits swiftly around, spreading scandal. Chaucer gives Fame the golden hair of the traditional stereotype of female *beauty, and the terms in which it is described ('as burned gold hyt shoon') are in accord with the gorgeous splendour of her house. The final visual detail is the most odd and puzzling: on her feet are partridges' wings (1392). It is usually thought that this represents a misreading by Chaucer or by the scribe of his copy of Virgil of *pernicibus alis* ('with swift wings') as *perdicibus alis*. It is curious though that he gives the correct translation in *Troilus*. There he was following Boccaccio's version, but it seems clear that he knew the Virgil passage, and it is tempting to suppose that this may be a deliberate change. Whether or not this is so, the detail adds to the grotesque quality by replacing the sinister bat-like image of Virgil by a much humbler one: the partridge whirs low over the ground or walks rapidly; its grating song turns into a rapid cackle.

Chaucer's Fame is the sister of *Fortune (*HF* 1547), and her actions in awarding good or bad reputation show the same arbitrariness. The unstableness of Fame is emphasized by placing her castle on a hill of ice (a detail from *Nicole de Margival's description of the house of Fortune). The magnificent fittings of Fame's House also suggest deception or distortion (see *architecture). Her role as Rumour is explored in the latter part of the third book. Here Ovid's house of Rumour, which has a thousand apertures and countless entrances, and is never silent, but filled with constant murmurs and whisperings as 'a thousand rumours, false mixed with true . . . flit about', is transformed into a strange building made of twigs, and to the disembodied rumours are added throngs of human beings who bring rumours, and tidings, and lies—shipmen, pilgrims, pardoners, couriers, messengers. It might be aptly called the House of Aventure, 'that is the moder of tydynges' (1983). Unlike *Nature (with whom she is implicitly contrasted) Fame seems as much the goddess of discord as of concord.

The uncertain and arbitrary nature of Fame is evident. Within this rather Boethian view of fame is set another strand of thought, often submerged but still central, concerning 'literary fame', the poet's position, his inspiration, and his art. The images of the *Aeneid* (supplemented by the citing of other authors) in the temple of Venus in the first book is paralleled by the sight of the great writers standing on their columns in Fame's palace (1429–1512). There is some dissension ('one said that Homer made lies'), yet there is a strong suggestion of the power of poetry and the poets who 'bear up' the fame of a topic or subject.

Chaucer seems concerned with the validity of his own art of poetry. The first part of his answer to the person who asked him if he had come to have fame—'Nay . . . I cam noght hyder . . . For no such cause' (1873–5)—is sometimes quoted as an example of his lack of concern with literary fame. However, while showing a due caution in committing himself to the arbitrary whims of the goddess, he goes on to speak in a quietly confident tone: 'I wot myself best how y stonde; | For what I drye [experience, feel], or what I thynke, | I wil

myselven al hyt drynke . . . | As fer forth as I kan myn art'. And he gives the reason for his coming—to find 'matter' for his art: 'somme newe tydynges for to lere, | Somme newe thynges, y not what'. This seems consistent with the way at the beginning of the third book he has adapted Dante's invocation to Apollo. Here there is a modest disclaimer, and with pointed humility Chaucer says that if he is helped he will go and kiss the next laurel that he sees. But underneath there can be felt a certain confidence. As J. A. W. Bennett says, he is 'the first Englishman to share Dante's sense of the worth of poetry and of the act of poetic creation'.

Bennett (1968); Boitani (1984).

Fame, the Book of, see *House of Fame.

families (see also *children; *mothers). The importance of families in Chaucer has rather been obscured by a single-minded concentration on his treatment of love, marriage, women, etc., as if these were entirely isolated entities. It is true that he does not describe family life in the detailed manner of the 19th-c. novel. It is also true—and more surprising to the modern reader—that he never uses the word 'family'. In his English that word was normally used (like its L. original *familia*) in the sense of 'household', the whole group of parents, children, other relatives, dependants, servants, and retainers living together. Even a very elaborate household—that of a king or of a bishop—was thought of as a *familia*. Lower in the social scale it was fairly simple. The prosperous Oxford carpenter and his wife in The *Miller's Tale* have two servants and a lodger, whereas the household of the Cambridge miller in The *Reeve's Tale* consists only of the parents and their two children. At all levels the household was a centre of government headed by a paterfamilias, whose duty was to feed, clothe, and protect the members of the family, who in turn owed obedience and loyalty to him. The 'family', however, was not simply a legal or political unit: that there was a special intimacy connected with it is shown by the development of some related English words. Chaucer uses the adj. *famulier, famil(i)er* which means 'belonging to the household' (IV.1784), but also 'intimate' (I.215) or 'courteous' (*LGW* 1606). In *Boece* there is the noun *familier* 'a member of the household', but also 'a close associate', and the abstract noun *familiarite* 'association with; friendship; intimacy' (as in 'flaterynge famylarite').

In Chaucer's narratives there are plenty of servants both true and treacherous (like the squire in *January's household who carved before his master in the approved manner, but was a 'famulier foo', 'a servaunt traytour', IV.1784–5). But he seems to have been particularly interested in the relationship between parents and children. A study by Jill Mann shows how Chaucer uses this to explore not only the relationships of humans to each other but also to the universe in which they find themselves (God's governance of which is ideally mirrored in the human family), and 'the mystery of the relation between power and love'. Chaucer is drawn to narratives which show family relationships under stress in extreme situations, like that of the anguished mother searching for her child in *The *Prioress's Tale*, or the father Ugolino (*Hugelyn) starving with his children in the tower, or of families cruelly divided and finally joyously reunited (*The *Man of Law's Tale* and *The *Clerk's Tale*). He tells these in a way which excites '*pite' and also raises questions about suffering, justice, and authority. The stories depict cruelty within the family, but show that the cruelty, has a cause or some motivation, and that even the most tyrannical man is subject to some kind of power he may be what Mann calls an 'enthralled lord'. The two cruel mothers-in-law of *The Man of Law's Tale*, who take power into their own hands, bring vengeance upon themselves or their people. They seem related to the mothers-in-law of *folk tale: they both persecute their innocent daughter-in-law; one of them kills her son; the other is killed by her son.

Closer to the ideal parent–child relationship is the touching scene in *The Clerk's Tale* (IV.901–17) where Griselda's old father comes out to help his distressed daughter on her way from the palace. He is responding in kind to the dutiful way she had looked after him in his poverty (221–2, 229–31). Janicula is a rare case in Chaucer where the ideal, benevolent father is given any extended treatment (and he is made very human by the revelation that he had always been suspicious of this marriage—he has no high opinion of gentlefolks).

In comic and satiric contrast is the image of family pride and pretention presented at the beginning of *The Reeve's Tale*, where 'haughty' Symkyn the miller, inordinately proud of his wife 'of noble kyn', the daughter of the parson, and his daughter, destined to be married into 'som worthy blood of auncetrye', parades with them on holy-days.

In all the narratives there are many allusions to family relationships or family settings. The *Franklin is at odds with his son; the fox in *The Nun's Priest's Tale* touches the vanity of Chauntecleer by praising the incomparable crowing of his father; Melibee has to be persuaded not to take vengeance for the attack on his wife and daughter. There are famous family situations from antiquity: the sisters *Dido and Anna (*Anne (2)); or Philomena (*Philomene) and Procne (*Progne) (when Philomena is raped she cries out 'Sister!' with a loud voice, and 'father dear!'). Criseyde, although a widow, is not a solitary lady: besides a somewhat problematic father, and an uncle, she has three nieces (II.814), as well as ladies in waiting. Even that merry widow the *Wife of Bath, whose family concerns seem largely restricted to husbands and prospective husbands, has a niece whom she 'loved weel' (III.383, 537).

We are given glimpses of family life at different levels of society, from the Trojan nobility at a dinner party or Criseyde and her ladies listening to a romance to the convivial drinking and the domestic meal in the cramped surroundings of the miller's house in *The Reeve's Tale*. At all levels, family life lacks the privacy so prized in the modern Western world. People lived close together, often squeezed into one or two rooms (as in *The Reeve's Tale*); even in more sumptuous surroundings servants are constantly about—Pandarus wishing to speak confidentially to Criseyde has to wait until he 'saugh wel that hire folk were alle aweye' (II.1194). Brief allusions show families engaged in the normal medieval occupations. Nicholas, the student lodger in *The Miller's Tale* is being 'put through college'—'after his freendes fyndyng and his rente'—by funds provided by friends or relatives. In *The *Summoner's Tale* the friar, 'penetrating a house' as *friars were supposed to do, finds the goodman sick on a couch, and from the wife picks up the family news—that her child has just died. The rich merchant in *The

Shipman's Tale, whose household even includes pages, is going off to Bruges (*Brugges) on business like any 14th-c. merchant, and rashly (it turns out) leaves his wife at home.

Du Boulay (1970), ch. 6; Mann (1983); Spearing (1983).

Fate; fathers; feasts. See *Fortune, free will and predestination; *families; food.

Fawny, fawnes (L. *faunil*) Fauns, in Roman antiquity deities or spirits of the countryside, (in form partly human, partly goatlike) and often associated with the satyrs (*Satiry), are mentioned in *Troilus* (IV.1544) and *The Knight's Tale* (I.2928).

Femenye ('the land of women'), the country of the Amazons in 'Scythia' (see *Amazones) in *The *Knight's Tale*.

Fenix, the Phoenix, a legendary bird of great beauty thought to live in Egypt or 'Arabia'. There was only one alive in the world at any one time. When its time came to die it prepared a pyre for itself, and the next phoenix rose from its ashes. It was often taken as a symbol of the Resurrection. In *The *Book of the Duchess*, however, it represents the unique beauty of the lady. The Man in Black says 'Trewely she was, to myn ye, | The soleyn [solitary] fenix of Arabye, | For ther livyth never but oon' (981–3).

Ferrare, Ferrara in Emilia, Italy, close to which flows the river Po (IV.51).

Filocolo, an early prose work of *Boccaccio, which retells the old French romance story of Floris and Blanchefleur. It illustrates the irresistible power of love: in spite of the opposition of his parents, Florio is passionately united with his Biancafiore. In the narrative a series of 'questions of love' or '*demandes d'amour' are debated, producing a number of inset tales. One of these, Menedon's story of Tarolfo, his wife, and Tebano, seems to be the source of *The *Franklin's Tale*. There are also echoes of the *Filocolo* in *Troilus and Criseyde*.

(ed.) Quaglio (1964); (trans.) Hutton (1927).

Filostrato, an early poem of *Boccaccio's, written in the late 1330s in ottava rima, is the main source of *Troilus and Criseyde*. In this the story of the lovers Troiolo and Criseida and their friend Pandaro, set in the doomed city of *Troy, is told in a vivid narrative, with fine psychological detail. It is an exciting and lyrical work, full of dramatic scenes. Boccaccio hints at parallels with a (probably fictitious) love affair of his own. It provided Chaucer with more than story material; quite clearly, it excited his creative imagination. While keeping the general outline of the plot, he transformed the work completely. Long scenes are added, altering the tempo of the story; the characters of the main personages are differently conceived; the autobiographical and personal hints are replaced by a narrator who purports to be simply a servant of the servants of love, a complex passion which he affects not to comprehend. Comedy is added, but at the same time the philosophical interests of Boccaccio are extended. It is possible that Chaucer also used a French translation of the Italian.

(ed.) Branca (1964); (trans.) Griffin and Myrick (1929).

Fynystere (I.408), Cape Finisterre in the province of Galicia (*Galice), north-western Spain, one of the westernmost promontories of Europe (*finis terrae*). [PS]

First Moeving, First Moevable, First Mover, Primum Mobile (L.). In Aristotelian *cosmology this was conceived to be the motive power of the entire universe, its effect being transmitted inwards from one set of planetary spheres to the next. As Chaucer explains in *A Treatise on the *Astrolabe*, it is what moves the eighth sphere; and the equinoctial is its girdle. (See also *Spere; *Equinoxiall. [JDN]

Fyssh, fish (astr.), one of the two in the constellation of *Pisces. (See also **astrology and astronomy; *Pisces; *signe.** [JDN]

Fysshestrete, a street near *London Bridge, close to the river, mentioned by the *Pardoner as a place where Spanish *wine is sold (VI.564). In the time of *Stow, there were still 'fishmongers and fair taverns' on Fish Street Hill and New Fish Street.

FITZRALPH, RICHARD (*c.*1300–1360). Of Anglo-Irish extraction from Arnagh, FitzRalph was educated at Oxford and later became canon and dean of Lichfield, and in 1347 archbishop of Armagh. His writings fall into three groups, an influential commentary on the *Sentences* of Peter Lombard, a survey of the issues dividing Christendom *Summa de questionibus Armenorum* that followed his discussions with representatives of the Eastern Church, and his anti-fraternal writings. The last group was by far the most influential in England, and includes the 1350 *Proposicio*, various other long sermons, and the *De pauperie Salvatoris* in which he paved the way towards Wyclif's more extreme views on dominion. Though Chaucer never names him, his anti-fraternal satire directly or indirectly owes much to FitzRalph's development of the charges against the mendicant orders.   [AH]
    K. Walsh (1981).

Flaundres, Flanders, a region in the south-west of the Low Countries, north of Artois (*Artoys). By the 14th c. it had become extremely prosperous, especially through its cloth trade with England. Urban development meant that a number of its towns were great centres of trade. By the 15th c. it had become the centre of a brilliant school of painters and illuminators. In the 14th c. some of the Flemish towns, especially Ghent (*Gaunt), asserted their autonomy against the claims of the Count of Flanders, who sided with his French liege lord, while the towns, heavily dependent on English wool, favoured the English. On the death of Louis de Mâle (1384) Flanders passed to the duke of Burgundy (*Burgoyne). Throughout the century there were diplomatic overtures and treaties. In 1377 Chaucer himself was given funds to go with Sir Thomas Percy on a mission to Flanders, though Chaucer's account of expenses specifies only Paris and Montreal. Flanders was important to the English economy, and trade links across the routes on the Channel and the North Sea were close. Merchants made regular trips. Wool was the most important English commodity, but other produce went as well: the poet's father, John Chaucer, received a permit to ship 40 quarters of wheat from Ipswich to Flanders. In return came textiles, richly coloured cloth, and fashionable *clothes. The *Merchant wears 'a Flaundryssh bever hat' (I.272).

The common family name 'Fleming' is a testimony to the number of Flemish traders and workmen who settled in England, especially in London. Chaucer's wife was the daughter of a Flemish knight; and when he makes his *Cook quote a proverb ('sooth pley, quaad pley [a true jest is a bad jest]', as the Flemyng seith (I.4357)) the use of the Flemish word *quaad* ('bad') suggests that he knew it in its original form. Foreigners, especially those who were, or were thought to be prosperous could be the victims of violence. In *The *Nun's Priest's Tale* there is a reference to *Jack Straw's mob lynching the Flemings who lived near to the river Thames in London during the *Peasants' Revolt in 1381 (VII.3396). This was a particularly ruthless affair: according to one chronicler, 'in the Vintry . . . there was a very great massacre of Flemings, and in one heap there were lying about forty headless bodies of persons who had been dragged forth from the churches and from their houses; and hardly was there a street in the city in which there were not bodies lying of those who had been slain.'

Chaucer's *Squire had campaigned in Flanders (I.86; possibly a reference to the events of 1383, see *Artoys), and the merchant in *The *Shipman's Tale* goes there on business, to Bruges (*Brugges) for a *fair. Other references are probably more lighthearted. Sir Thopas was born there (at *Poperyng, VII.720)—perhaps a comically mercantile birthplace for a romantic hero. The *Pardoner's Tale* is set in Flanders (VI.463), although no more specific details are offered.
    Wallace (1997).

Flegitoun Phlegethon ('the fiery'), one of the rivers of Hades, referred to by Troilus as 'the fery flood of helle' (*Tr* III.1600). Chaucer found the name in *Virgil and in *Dante.

Flemyng, see ***Flaundres**.

Flexippe, the name of one of Criseyde's nieces (*Tr* II.816).

Flymyng, see ***Flaundres**.

Flora, the Roman goddess of flowers and fertility.

She is mentioned in *The Book of the Duchess* (402) and the Prologue to *The *Legend of Good Women* (F 171), linked both times with Zephyrus (*Zepherus).

Florence, in Tuscany, was in Chaucer's day a powerful republican city-state, turbulent and creative. Its textile industry and its commerce and banking had made it a wealthy urban centre. The English word *florin* preserves the memory of its international commercial success. The gold florin, first issued in the mid-13th c., became an international coin (see *money). It was a pile of 'floryns fyne of gold ycoyned rounde' which led the rioters in *The *Pardoner's Tale* to destruction.

Florence's politics, like those of other Italian states, were marked by factionalism. The internal struggles of the Ghibelline and Guelph parties (see *Dante) were succeeded by tensions between nobles and sections of the non-noble 'popolo', and between the well-off members of the great guilds and the poorer artisans. This was reflected in the various changes of government throughout the century. The 1370s in particular were troubled years, and the long-standing discontent among the 'ciompi', the poorly paid cloth workers erupted in a briefly successful revolt in 1378. In the period after 1382 the republic expanded its territories. The Medici family, which dominated Florence in the 15th c., was just beginning to lay the foundations of its power. Giovanni di Bicci de' Medici (1360–1429) devoted himself to the development of the banking business. His son Cosimo, later to be called 'father of the country', was born in 1389.

The city was not then dominated by the great 15th c. dome of the cathedral, although the main work of the cathedral had been completed in 1378. But many of its churches and well-known landmarks—the Campanile, the Palazzo Vecchio, the Ponte Vecchio, etc.—were either completed or in course of construction in the 14th c.

Chaucer visited Florence on his Italian journey of 1372–3. The reason for his visit is not known—quite possibly it was because of Edward III's negotiations with Florentine bankers, notably the Bardi. Nor is it known what literary or artistic contacts he may have made. It is virtually certain that he at least heard about *Dante, *Boccaccio, and Petrarch (*Petrak), but whether he met either

or both of the two latter writers is not known. His only reference to Florence (III.1125) shows that he knew of Dante's connection with the city. (See also **Geoffrey *Chaucer: life**; *Ytaille.)

Florilegia. Literally 'collection of flowers', the term is given to the numerous collections of *quotations from classical and patristic authors that were put together in the medieval period. Such collections were by Chaucer's day usually arranged alphabetically under headings, these headings being chosen according to the interest of the compiler; the range of authors from which any *florilegium* drew also depended upon the aim and access of the compiler. Many *florilegia* drew heavily upon earlier similar collections, rather than returning to original sources. A medieval author's quotations from, or allusions to, earlier writers often came from these *florilegia*; this was particularly true in regard to passages from Greek authors whose works were not accessible in full in Latin. The source of Chaucer's tale of Melibee is known itself to have drawn on several *florilegia*, including the widely disseminated *Manipulus Florum*. Jankyn's *book of wikked wyves* (III.669) was evidently a *florilegium* of anti-feminist writings.   [AH]

Rouse and Rouse (1979).

Floure and the Leafe, The (*The Flower and the Leaf*), a 15th c. allegorical poem of about 600 lines in rhyme-royal stanzas, apparently (like *The *Assembly of Ladies*) written by a woman. It has many echoes of Chaucer and was included in the edition of *Speght (see *Chauceriana). Before it was banished from the canon in the 19th c., it was much admired. It was paraphrased by *Dryden and *Wordsworth, and provided scenes for the Chaucer window in Westminster Abbey. It is an elegant poem. The narrator sees a company of knights and ladies approach, dressed in white, with chaplets and branches of laurel, oak, woodbine, and hawthorn. There is singing, dancing, and jousting, and they then go under a huge laurel tree, 'with great reverence . . . enclining low' to it, and dancing around it. Then there appears a second company clad in green, with chaplets of flowers, who do reverence to a flowery mound in the meadow. The sun becomes hot; their flowers fade, and they faint. Then a strong wind blows down all the flowers, except those of the company under the tree. A storm of rain and hail drenches those in green, while those in white are safe beneath their laurel tree. One of the ladies explains the significance of the scene: those in white are the company of the Leaf, the chaste, the faithful, and the noble, with their queen *Diana; the others are the company of the Flower, the servants of *Flora, who love hunting and hawking 'and many other such idle dedes'. The narrator is asked which she will honour 'this yeere', suggesting an actual courtly game in which everyone was to choose at a May festival whether to serve the Flower or the Leaf. (See also *The *Legend of Good Women.*)

(ed.) Pearsall (1962).

folk tale (variously called 'international popular tale', 'tale of magic', 'fairy tale' or by the German word 'Märchen') is a type of short narrative circulating in popular oral form. The most famous collection in modern times is the *Kinder- und Hausmärchen* of the brothers Grimm (first published in 1812). There are earlier collections by Straparola, Basile, and Perrault. Many such tales are of great antiquity (the *Odyssey*, for instance contains some), although in some cases it is impossible to say if examples in the post-medieval collections go back to the Middle Ages, or, if so, in precisely what form. They are also widely dispersed. Some Eastern tales found in *The Thousand and One Nights* and other similar collections find their way into medieval literature. Folk tales appear in collections of *exempla, and sometimes form the basis of *romances, lays, and other literary narratives. There have been many interesting attempts to define and analyse the folk tale—in terms of its symbolism, its narrative pattern, and 'motifs'. It is important to remember that folk tales are not fixed and unchanging stories. They are traditional narratives, using traditional formulae and story patterns. Over the centuries they have evolved and changed, as generations of tellers have adapted them to specific audiences in different cultures. Some patterns are found across different cultures, but the tales also show a variety deriving from the particular linguistic and social groups in which they are embedded.

Some of the characteristic patterns of the Western European folk tale were almost certainly found in their medieval predecessors. The heroes and heroines are involved in dangerous journeys and quests. Their world is a dangerous one, full of magic (which is simply accepted without any surprise or explanation). They meet antagonists and magic helpers. There is much apparently arbitrary behaviour (it is sometimes provoked by mysterious supernatural powers in the background, but this is not always made clear). It is a world marked by extremes of behaviour—and by extreme clear-cut oppositions. If rash promises are made they must be kept. Goodness and kindness are valued, but so are cleverness and cunning. There is a great deal of violence and brutality, but it is set in an emotional pattern which is satisfying and even comforting. The tale will normally have a happy ending. The action is central and all-important. It takes place in a strange isolation, free from historical or geographical specificity, which gives an eerie translucent quality (what has been called 'a transparent and clear view of reality'). The central figure who is both the means and the end of the narrative is also isolated, often abandoned or cast out. Such figures are one-dimensional. The style is simple and unelaborated. This clear, isolated world is the perfect setting for magic events and for traditional devices of narrative excitement and suspense—like the favourite 'recognition scene' in which the true hero/heroine is revealed.

Folk tales underlie a number of Chaucer's *Canterbury Tales*—most obviously *The *Clerk's Tale*, *The *Man of Law's Tale*, *The *Wife of Bath's Tale*, *The *Franklin's Tale*, and *The *Pardoner's Tale*—although he derives his material primarily from literary sources. It is easy to recognize a motif (like the rash promise in *The Franklin's Tale* or a whole story type:—in *The Pardoner's Tale* 'The treasure hunters who murder one another'). Underneath the literary story of *Griselda is a folk tale (see *The Clerk's Tale*), which may go some way to explaining the sudden and arbitrary actions of Walter—cf. the father in 'The Twelve Brothers' in the Grimms' collection: 'Once upon a time there was a king and a queen who lived peaceably together and had twelve children, but the children were all boys. Then the king said to his wife, 'If the thirteenth child you are going to have is a girl, then all the twelve boys shall die, because I want her to have great wealth and the kingdom to be inherited by her alone.' *The Wife of Bath's Tale* is in some ways a similar story, though with an actual physical 'disenchantment', a kind of feminine version of 'The Frog Prince'. While Chaucer usually keeps the traditional narrative opening ('whilom' (once upon a time)) he quickly sets about fleshing out the tales with specific details of place and personality: 'in Surrye whilom dwelte . . .', 'In th'olde dayes of Kyng Arthour', 'In Armorik, that called is Britayne', 'In Flaundres whilom was a compaignye', etc. Transforming a folk tale into a literary work with greater realism and characterization, or into an exemplary story illustrating some moral virtue like '*gentilesse' or *patience is not always without problems.

Aarne and Thompson (1964); K. Jackson (1961); Luke (1982); Lüthi (1970); Zipes (2000).

food in the Middle Ages was varied. Local seasonal produce was supplemented by imported delicacies like spices or wines (there was as yet no tea or coffee). In noble halls it was elaborately prepared and served with considerable ceremony. There was music and minstrelsy. The most distinguished persons sat at a high table and dais, the rest at side tables. After the washing of hands, the food was served in a series of courses. It was eaten with knives and the fingers (there were no forks) according to the requirements of etiquette (books of table *manners and of recipes have survived). At great feasts there would be highly elaborate 'subtleties', sculptured confections of pastry or sugar. There was a liking for spices and spiced drinks and food. Food and the serving of food involved a complex pattern of significance. Its social functions, for instance, included the bonding of households and groups, the demonstration of status, magnificence, or lordly generosity (*largesse*); it was affected by the demands of *medicine (which recommended or advised against certain foods or diets) and *religion (which prescribed seasons of fasting or abstinence).

A number of types of food are mentioned by Chaucer. The description of the *Cook (I.379–87) lists his basic skills ('he koude rooste, and sethe [boil], and broille, and frye')—he could 'boille the chiknes with the marybones [marrow bones]'. Besides baking a pie, he produced dishes more

unfamiliar to the modern reader: *poudre-marchant tart* (a sharp spice or flavouring powder), *galyngale* (a sweet spice), *mortreux* (spiced stews of meat or fish), and *blankmanger* (a kind of thick stew or mousse made of chopped chicken or fish, richly spiced). Later, however, Harry Bailly is less than complimentary about his pies (see *Jakke of Dovere), pasties, and parsley stuffing (I.4346–52). In *The *Miller's Tale* Absolon sends Alison 'pyment [spiced wine], meeth [mead], and spiced ale, | And wafres, pipyng hoot' (I.3378–9)—the wafers were thin cakes baked in wafer irons over a fire. May in *The *Merchant's Tale* tells her husband that she has a great desire to eat small green pears (with the suggestion that she is pregnant, IV.2329–37). In his balade *To *Rosemounde* (17) Chaucer compares himself, twisting and turning in the throes of love to a 'pyk walwed in galauntyne', a pike steeped in galantine, which seems to be either an aspic or a pickling sauce made of bread, vinegar, salt, and pepper.

The types range from the 'deyntees' of noble feasts to the humblest fare of the poor, like 'hawebake' ('baked haws or hawthorn berries', II.95). The poor eat 'potage' (broth), bacon, cheese, and bread, which is the most basic foodstuff (as is shown by the common proverbial remark 'I shall never more eat bread'). Bread is regularly linked with *ale (e.g. I.341) and cheese (I.3628). It was sometimes baked in the form of a 'cake', a round flat loaf (I.668, 4094; VI.322). There were different grades of bread, ranging from the fine white bread or *payndemayn* (to which Sir *Thopas is compared, VII.725) and *wastel-bred* (I.147), the most expensive ordinary bread, to the cheapest 'broun breed' (VII.2844).

Common kinds of food are so familiar that they can be used allusively. The *Wife of Bath says 'I nyl envye no virginitee. | Lat hem be breed of pured whete-seed, | And lat us wyves hoten [be called] barly-breed' (III.142–4). Food may be linked with sex: the Wife refers to 'bacon' (old meat, III.418); and the knight in *The *Merchant's Tale*, arguing for the desirability of a young wife, remarks 'bet than old boef is the tendre veel' (IV.1420; cf. 'hony deere', 'hony-comb', or 'sweete cynamome' as terms of endearment (I.3617, 3698–9)). Other expressions are more general: 'in his owene grece I made hym frye' (III.487); 'ye han cast alle hire wordes in an hochepot' (i.e. hotchpotch, stew, VII.1256). The 'table' is used by the Wife of Bath, who is fond of food-related metaphor: 'I wolde nat spare hem at hir owene bord' (III.421); it is a symbol of the family as well as of husbandly power (Jankyn came down from Oxford 'and wente at hom to bord | With my gossib', III.528). There are descriptions of noble feasts. In The *Squire's Tale Cambyuskan, sitting on his dais, is served a succession of dishes including swans and young herons—and some more exotic Mongol dishes which are not described (V.69–72). Minstrels play before the table. This is a display of royal magnificence or 'nobleye'. In The Merchant's Tale there is a sumptuous wedding feast (IV.1710–67). In general, however, Chaucer prefers to single out some well-known detail or practice. There are references to carving at the table or to sitting in the place of honour (I.52). There is the dinner party in *Troilus and Criseyde. 'Dinner' was the first full meal of the day, taken between 9 a.m. and noon (here it is an hour after 'prime', i.e. at 10 a.m.). After dinner was a time for relaxation (V.918), for confidential talk (VII.255 ff.) or private business: it is then that May goes to see Damian (IV.1920–45), just as Criseyde visited the sick Troilus. There are references to 'soper', the last meal of the day ('they spedde hem fro the soper unto bedde', Tr II.947; see also V.518), to 'after-soper' (V.302), and to the 'voidé' or nightcap of spiced wine taken with comfits before retiring (Tr III.674).

Chaucer makes use of the associations and significances attached to food and eating to place his characters in a social and moral setting. The temperate diet recommended by medical books, for instance, is endorsed by the *Physician (I.435–7) and by the monk in The *Shipman's Tale—'especially in this heat'—(VII.261–2). The 'attempree diete' of the poor widow in The *Nun's Priest's Tale (VII.2832–46) keeps her healthy. She drinks water instead of wine, and eats bread, broiled or grilled bacon, and sometimes an egg or two. She has no need of the 'poynaunt sauce' of the kind made by the Cook (I.352).

The idea of a temperate diet pre-dates Christianity. In The *Former Age Chaucer treats the myth of the Golden Age, when men were content with the fruit of the fields, ate nuts, haws 'and swich pounage [food for pigs]' and drank water from the cold well: 'no man yit in the morter spyces grond | To clarre [spiced wine] ne to sause of galantyne. (In later ages, 'human food' is strictly distinguished: Nebuchadnezzar, smitten by God, ate hay like an ox (VII.2172), and the men transformed by Circe into swine ate acorns (Bo IV m.3).) Temperance was reinforced by Christianity and its teachings on gluttony. On this the *Pardoner speaks vehemently (VI.512 ff.), waxing sarcastic at the work of the cooks, knocking the marrow out of bones, and making elaborate sauces at great expense. The *Parson discusses 'pride of the table' (X.443–5) (those banquets to which rich men are invited, and the poor 'put awey and rebuked') and alludes to the 'sotiltes' or elaborate confections at medieval feasts: 'excesse of diverse metes and drynkes, and namely swich manere bake-metes and dissh-metes, brennynge of wilde fir and peynted and castelled with papir, and semblable wast'.

The ways in which food and its consumption reveal a style of life or even a person's inner being are obvious weapons for the satirist. Chaucer's satire varies in intensity, and the variations are subtle. The good-living *Franklin with his supplies of baked meat and fish (he keeps partridges, and bream and pike in fishponds, and has all 'deyntees' according to the different seasons) and his table dormant (i.e. permanently set up and not taken down after use), is a gourmet not a glutton. More piquent is the emphasis on the exquisite table manners of the *Prioress (I.127–36). She is not an entirely unworldly person. Much less gentle is the satirical treatment of the friar in The *Summoner's Tale (III.1836–47), who, professing the ideal of poverty (1881–2), lists the delicacies he would like for dinner: capon's liver, a silver of soft bread 'and after that a rosted pigges heed'—'I am a man of litel sustenaunce'.

In the narratives feasts and eating are put to varied uses. In The *Reeve's Tale the miller makes a great show of hospitality to the clerks (after all, he has something to celebrate)—besides bread and ale, a roast goose is provided—but hospitality can pose its own problems, as we see. The motif of the 'interrupted feast' is an effective and a favourite narrative device (as in *Sir Gawain and the Green Knight). The splendid feast in The Squire's Tale is interrupted after the third course by the entry of a knight on a horse of brass. A comic example is found in The Summoner's Tale (III.2162 ff.), where the angry friar rushes into the lord's hall as he is sitting at table. A spectacular and bloody example occurs at the beginning of The *Man of Law's Tale. At the wedding feast (with 'deyntees mo than I kan yow devyse') the Christian guests and the Sultan himself are all 'tohewe and stiked [hacked to pieces and stabbed] at the bord' (II.430). At the end the recognition scenes are set in feasts (1009 ff., 1093 ff.), symbolizing the restoration of fellowship and family harmony. Something similar happens at the end of The *Clerk's Tale (IV.1027 ff.).

Appropriately for a work in which food figures so prominently, The Canterbury Tales begins with a supper ('with vitaille at the beste'), and has the promise of another at the end. (See also *Ale; *wine.)

Mead (1931); (examples of recipes) Hieatt and Butler (1976); Hodgett (1972).

forest was an important element in the medieval *landscape. When in The *House of Fame Chaucer looks down on the world he notices 'feldes and playnes, | And now hilles, and now mountaynes, | Now valeyes, now forestes' (897–9). He had first-hand experience of looking after them. As Clerk of the Works he had to oversee hunting lodges and parks, and was made deputy forester of the royal forest at North Petherton (see Geoffrey *Chaucer: life). Forests were important sources of revenue; they included cultivated land and villages as well as woods. The terminology of Chaucer's time is not quite the same as in Modern English. The OE word wood is used generally, and overlaps with the newer term forest. Forest was the French term for what lay outside (L. fores) the walled park. Its technical legal sense was a woodland area set apart for the hunting of animals and game, usually belonging to the king, and subject to the forest law. It could also be used more generally to refer to extensive wooded areas. (English place-names with forest are late and rare, those with wood early and common.) A park was an enclosed tract of woodland for keeping animals of the chase, distinguished by having walls and gates (e.g. that in The *Parliament of Fowls is 'walled

with grene ston') and by not being subject to the forest law.

The association with *hunting is close: the 'wery huntere' dreams of the wood (PF 100). The *Yeoman of the *General Prologue is a forester (I.117), clad in the traditional green; he is a game-keeper, skilled in wodecraft (hunting practice and ceremonial). He, like the foresters in The *Book of the Duchess (361) who assist the hunt as trackers, is the sort of person with whom Chaucer as a forest administrator would have had to deal. Forests were also the home of outlaws (like Robin Hood) living off the king's venison, and a refuge for rob-bers and other fugitives. Chaucer quotes an early version of the 'poacher turned gamekeeper' proverb: 'a theef of venysoun' who has given up his trade makes the best keeper of a forest (VI.83–5). 'Ye looken as the wode were ful of thevys' says the lord in The *Summoner's Tale to the friar who has just stormed in in a state of agitation (III.2173).

A long literary tradition added other associ-ations and expectations. Characters in a medieval story who go into the forest may expect to meet outlaws, madmen (or melancholy lovers), fairies and monsters and other wonders—and wild ani-mals. The fox carries off the cock 'toward the wode' (VII.3336); birds prefer freedom in the for-est 'rude and coold' (IX.170; cf. Bo III m.2:21–31). Some are more dangerous and more exotic, like the tiger or other cruel beast 'that dwelleth outher in wode or in forest' in The *Squire's Tale (V.419–20), or the lioness who makes a dramatic appearance 'out of the wode' in the tale of Thisbe (LGW 805–6). These ancient forests had other dangers too: Philomena is raped in a cave in a for-est (LGW 2310 ff.). They were also the haunt of gods and goddesses, like *Diana, 'chaste goddesse of the wodes grene' (whose devotee, the young Amazon Emily, loved 'huntynge and venerye, | And for to walken in the wodes grene', I.2308–9), or Venus who appears as huntress in the forest in the story of Dido (LGW 1971 ff.). This forest is a 'wilderness', but there is a grimmer classical forest (in the cold region of Thrace) depicted in the tem-ple of Mars in The *Knight's Tale, 'with knotty, knarry, bareyne trees olde, | Of stubbes sharpe and hidouse to biholde' (I.1975–80).

The medieval literary forest is often a much more pleasant place, exhibiting the plenitude of *nature in its multitude of trees, animals, and birds. But it is a mysterious place in which marvels and perils may be found. This is especially so in the *romance, where the forest (beyond the boundaries of courtly civilization) is the setting for adventures and tests. It may be enchanted, the home of fairies, the passage to the otherworld. There are a few suggestions of this in Chaucer. It is 'under a forest syde' (III.990) that the knight in *The *Wife of Bath's Tale* sees the dance of the mysterious four and twenty ladies, and it is 'under a forest syde' (III.1380) that the summoner in *The *Friar's Tale* meets the mysterious yeoman clad in green. Like other questing knights in romances, Sir *Thopas rides 'thurgh a fair forest' (VII.754 ff.). In which he finds not only wild beasts, but a giant and the promise of an '*elf-queene'.

Chaucer's most extensive and imaginative use of woodland settings, however, occur in *dream visions. The walled park in *The Parliament of Fowls* with its trees 'clad with leves that ay shal laste' is a *locus amoenus* and the appropriate place for the goddess Nature to hold her annual assembly of birds. In *The Book of the Duchess* the forest is the setting for the mysterious dream adventure. Its huge trees growing closely together and its flowery glades suggest the life and plenitude of nature, but it is also like the enchanted forest of romance. The dreamer is drawn into it by the noise of a hunt, which turns out to be a strange dream-hunt in which no hart is killed, and he is led (by a magical animal guide) to a contrasting scene which has its own strange contrasts. In a densely shaded grove completely filled with animals he finds a solitary human being, a melancholy lover, sitting at the foot of a huge oak. In both poems the woodland setting is perfectly matched to the symbolic action.

Former Age, The, one of Chaucer's philosophical or 'Boethian' lyrics. It survives in two MSS, both of which attribute it to him. The modern title is taken from the beginning of the poem: 'A blissful lyf, a paisible and a swete, | Ledden the peples in the former age.' One MS calls it 'Aetas Prima', the other 'Chaucer upon the fyfte metur of the second book'. This is a reference to its main source in Boethius (*Boece), metrum 5 of book II. Chaucer also knew treatments of the idea in other works,

notably *Ovid's *Metamorphoses* (Books 1 and 15) and the *Roman de la Rose*. The poem gives a very eloquent exposition of the traditional topics. In those days people were content with what the fields provided. They ate nuts, shelled the corn which grew unsown, and drank water. They had no fire, no dyes, no swords, no coins, no ships, no commerce; no trumpets for war nor towers nor walls (the lost paradise is traditionally defined by negatives). There was no need for strife, because there were no profits or riches. Cursed was the time 'that men first dide hir swety bysinesse | To grobbe up metal, lurkynge in derknesse. | And in the riveres first gemmes soghte'. This was the beginning of covetousness, 'that first our sorwe broghte'. There were then no palace-chambers or halls: this blessed folk slept in caves on grass or leaves instead of sheets and feathered down. They lived in simple virtue, without quarrelling. There were no lords, no taxes, and no tyranny. Whereas nowadays . . . The contrast with the present day is of course also traditional. However the vehemence of Chaucer's ending—'Allas, allas, now may men wepe and crye! | For in oure dayes nis but covetyse, | Doublenesse, and tresoun, and envye, | Poyson, manslawhtre, and mordre in sondry wyse'—is remarkable, and it has been suggested that he may be thinking of particular events in the last years of the reign of Richard II.

(ed.) *Rv* 650–1, 1083–4; Pace and David (1982), 91–101; Scattergood (1995), 486–9; Norton-Smith (1963); Schmidt (1976).

fortitude, see *patience.

Fortune. In Roman religion there was a goddess Fortuna (of fortune, luck, or fate), with temples dedicated to her. She was already endowed with many of her later characteristics (she is called blind, inconstant, and variable) and attributes (the ball, and especially the wheel). In spite of attempts by the early Christian Fathers to destroy her, she lived on in the poetic mythography of the Middle Ages, frequently described or depicted with her wheel, elevating a man on it to the topmost point of glory, then ruthlessly casting him down.

Chaucer frequently refers to the personified goddess (e.g. in his set of ballades called *Fortune, or in *The *House of Fame*, where she is the sister of

*Fame), but he does not repeat the elaborate formal description of her and her wheel which is so common in medieval literature, but prefers to allude to this familiar iconographical image: 'thus Fortune on loft | And under eft, gan hem to whielen bothe' (*Tr* I.138–9; cf. VII.2445–6).

He also alludes to her characteristics (many of which had already become proverbial). She gives gifts, but then takes them away: as the Parson says, it is foolish to trust in them. This can be the source of narrative irony, as when the rioter in The *Pardoner's Tale*, finding the gold, says 'this tresor hath Fortune unto us yiven' (VI.779). Fortune is unstable, and fickle, treacherous, deceitful, and vindictive. In The *Book of the Duchess* she has defeated the Man in Black as in a game of *chess, and checkmated him. In his tirade against her (618 ff.) she is called a 'trayteresse fals and ful of gyle', 'fals, and ever laughynge | With oon eye, and that other wepynge'; she is like the scorpion which (according to tradition) has a fair face but a venomous tail.

She casts men down suddenly, without warning; and when she does this, she is implacable, without '*pite' even delighting in her work. We are reminded of this at the beginning of the fourth book of *Troilus and Criseyde*. Fortune seems 'trewest whan she wol bygyle': when she throws someone down from her wheel 'than laugheth she, and maketh hym the mowe [grimace]' (IV.3–7). She turns her 'bright face' from Troilus. The same image is used at the end of The *Monk's Tale*: 'for whan men trusteth hire, thanne wol she faille, | And covere hire brighte face with a clowde' (VII.2765–6).

The condition of man subject to Fortune's reign beneath the moon is a very uncertain one. Chaucer uses Boethian images to express this: a blind man or a drunk man who cannot find his way home (I.1260–7). Some large philosophical and theological questions are implied here (see **free will and predestination**), often complicated by the medieval interest in prophetic *dreams and in *astrology. In the discussions of such questions Boethius (*Boece) is especially influential. His *Consolation of Philosophy* deals with the ways in which man should respond to Fortune, with the questions of the freedom of the will, and of the injustice found in a world under God's 'purveiaunce' (providence, foresight). *Dante also

influenced Chaucer. In the *Inferno* (7) Virgil explains to Dante that Fortune is one of the heavenly 'intelligences': a 'general minister and guide' (*general ministra e duce*) who presides over the movement of power and prosperity from one nation to another and from one family to another. She never ceases her work of permutation. She is cursed by those who ought to praise her. She is wrongfully blamed, for she is one of the blessed. That Chaucer knew this passage is shown by his use of the phrase 'ministre general' in a remark made by the narrator of The *Knight's Tale* which draws attention to an apparent coincidence (I.1663–72). It is there applied to *Destinee* or 'fate' ('the planned order', according to Boethius (IV pr.6), 'inherent in things subject to change, through the medium of which Providence binds everything in its own allotted place'). There is a similar passage (again at a turning point in the narrative) in *Troilus*, where Fortune is called 'executrice of wierdes [probably the fates]' and is linked with 'influences of thise hevenes hye': they are our 'shepherds' beneath God (III.617).

Both Dante's Virgil and Boethius's Lady Philosophy see Fortune as it were from beyond the grave. Their views are not usually shared by the wretched mortals who suffer her whims and deceptions. In Chaucer, the characters involved in Fortune's reign are sometimes sceptical about 'purveiaunce'. Examples are to be found in the questioning speeches by Dorigen in The *Franklin's Tale* about the 'black rocks', or by the two knights in their Athenian prison in The *Knight's Tale* (I.1251 ff.; the remarks about destiny mentioned above are placed significantly in the mouth of the Christian narrator).

From time to time there are mentions of various traditional 'remedies' against Fortune (this was a topic of much interest in the Middle Ages: Petrarch's (*Petrak) Latin treatise on the 'remedies of Fortune' seems to have been extremely popular). These include fortitude or *patience (as demonstrated by *Griselda), deriving 'virtue' from 'necessity' in a Stoic manner; and forethought and *prudence. In Chaucer's tale of *Melibee*, the aptly named heroine Prudence gives her husband extensive advice on how to deal with Fortune. He should not tempt Fortune, nor trust her, no matter how attractive she seems: '*Senec seith, "What man that is norissed [nourished] by Fortune, she maketh hym a grete fool"' (VII.1446–54).

However, it is through narrative action that Chaucer prefers to explore such ideas. He is always fascinated by the flux of narrative, and likes to draw attention to the working of Fortune, as at the beginning of *The Canterbury Tales*, where the lot fell to the Knight 'were it by aventure, or sort, or cas'. Fortune and chance play a dominant role in most narratives, with the exception of a tale like the Man of Law's, which is, in the manner of a saint's life, built upon an Augustinian, providential pattern (in it the solitary reference to Fortune, significantly, occurs in a prayer to God: 'He that is lord of Fortune be thy steere [guide]', II.448). The gloomy role of Fortune in *The Monk's Tale* is delicately mocked in *The Nun's Priest's Tale* with its version of a proud 'prince' ready to fall, a prophetic dream, etc. For good measure we are also given there a brief account of the varying views about foreknowledge and predestination. And at the climaxes of the tale we find tell-tale references to Fortune—'but sodeinly hym fil a sorweful cas, | For evere the latter ende of joye is wo' (VII.3204–5)—and to the way she turns her wheel—'Lo, how Fortune *turneth* sodeynly | The hope and pryde eek of hir enemy!' (VII.3403–4). Typically, Fortune has tricked and cast down both the cock and the fox in succession. Chauntecleer is a comic example of a 'fallen prince', yet at the same time the knight, who had had quite enough of fallen princes, has been given the kind of story he wanted: 'as whan a man hath been in povre estaat, | And clymbeth up and wexeth fortunat' (VII.2775–6).

Patch (1927).

Fortune, one of Chaucer's 'Boethian' lyrics, is a triple *ballade, surviving in ten MSS. It is sometimes entitled 'Balades de Visage sanz Peinture', a rather mysterious description. It may mean 'ballades which present portraits without using paint', i.e., presumably, a poem which presents a verbal image of *Fortune rather than the well-known visual one, which seems rather recondite. Among other suggestions, the most convincing is that this title conceals a mistake for 'deux visages', i.e. a dialogue between two characters (*Guillaume de Machaut wrote some 'balades à deux visages').

The poem is a dialogue between the 'plaintiff' (as in a court of law) and Fortune. It uses a number of traditional topics and ideas, most obviously from Boethius (*Boece). The first ballade is the complaint of the 'plaintiff', with the refrain 'fynally, Fortune, I thee defye [deny (your power), repudiate]!'. He laments the absence of Fortune's favour, but remarks that he still has the light of his reason to distinguish friend from foe in her 'mirror'. In the second (with the refrain 'and eek thou hast thy beste frend alyve'), Fortune responds: 'no man is wrecched but [unless] himself it wene [supposes]'. She has taught him to distinguish real friends from false ones. His 'anchor' (an image of hope) still holds fast. She is a queen; he is born in her 'regne of variance' and must 'drive' about the wheel with others. The third is shared between the two speakers. 'Thy lore I dampne', says the plaintiff. Fortune defends her mutability by using Dante's argument, that she is carrying out the execution of God's will: 'this world hath ever resteles travayle', and her work will continue until the plaintiff's last day. The poem is concluded by an *envoy in rime royal, in which Fortune asks 'princes' not to let this man complain: 'and but you list [please] releve him of his peyne. | Preyeth his beste frend of his noblesse | That to som beter estat he may atteyne'. This unusual envoy has been taken as an appeal to the dukes of Lancaster, York, and Gloucester, who in 1390 controlled gifts given in Richard II's name. This would give a very precise date for the poem, although the envoy could have been added at a time well after the poem was written. Nor is it certain that 'the best friend' must be the king. Some quite different personal reference may be involved, or, indeed, the whole poem could be a quite general consolatory work. Whatever the context is, the poem is an intricate and eloquent piece of work, with interesting imagery and a display of high technical skill.

(ed.) *Rv* 652–3, 1084; Pace and David (1982), 103–19; Scattergood (1995), 504–6; Norton-Smith (1976).

Fragments (of *The Canterbury Tales*) see *Canterbury Tales*.

France, Fraunce. The 'realm of France', as Chaucer calls it (VII.116), was the most powerful neighbour and rival of *England. It was not then a highly centralized and homogeneous state, and, although it extended from the Channel to the Atlantic, the Pyrenees, and the Mediterranean, its land boundaries were not as precisely drawn as in later periods (see Map 3). A 'Frenchman' might be a man who owed allegiance to the king of France, or he might be a person who spoke one of the varieties of the French language—and possibly owed allegiance to the king of England, whose domains included Aquitaine, and who had some claim to the French throne (see *Hundred Years War). During Chaucer's lifetime it was ruled by the Valois kings Philip VI (d. 1350), John II 'the Good' (1350–64), Charles V 'the Wise' (1364–80), and Charles VI (1380–1422). It was a predominantly rural country, but a rich and populous kingdom. It has been estimated that its population was perhaps five times greater than that of England, and that its largest city, *Paris (2), was twice as large as *London. Its other large towns—Rouen, Bordeaux (*Burdeux), Toulouse, and the cloth towns of Flanders (*Flaundres) were bigger than English towns. Its great lords—the dukes of Brittany, Burgundy, and Guyenne, and the count of Flanders were in effect princes, ruling over very extensive domains through a machinery of government modelled on that of the king. The king ruled through and with his council; but because of internal and external strife, the central authority was sometimes very weak.

In the cultural history of Western Europe, France had played (and continued to play) a dominant role. In religious and intellectual history it was the cradle of such influential developments as the growth of Cistercian monasticism and the revival of theological studies. Here Paris, with its schools and university, had been the intellectual centre of Europe (*Bartholomew in the 13th c. compares it to Athens, the 'mother of liberal arts and of letters').

French medieval literature was rich, varied, and influential. Its famous stories—of Roland, Tristan, Lancelot, the Grail, etc.—were translated and adapted; its genres and forms, its styles and techniques were imitated all over Europe. There were epics, the *chansons de geste* like the *Chanson de Roland*, written in assonanced lines; courtly *romances in rhyming couplets (like those of *Chrétien de Troyes) or later in prose; *Breton lays; satirical works like the *Roman de *Renard*; allegories both secular (like the *Roman de la Rose*) and religious (like the *Pèlerinages* of *Deguilleville); plays, lyrics, religious poetry and prose, chronicles, *fabliaux. Outside France, the romance and the courtly lyric in its various forms (*ballade, *roundel, *virelay, etc.) most obviously bear the imprint of French originals, but French influence is pervasive.

There are many indications of the influence of French culture and literature in Chaucer's works. He refers familiarly to the notorious traitor of the Roland story, '*Genylon of France' (VII.194). The tune of the roundel sung at the end of The *Parliament of Fowls 'imaked was in Fraunce' (it sounds as if Chaucer has an actual tune in mind); and the *Parson refers to the 'new French song' (*Jay tout perdu mon temps et mon labour* 'I have totally wasted my time and effort') which Chaucer himself quotes in *Fortune. An earlier 'song of *Chaunte-pleure*' is mentioned in *Anelida (320); it had become proverbial for something that began happily and ended sorrowfully. The *Shipman's Tale (a fabliau) is set in France, at Saint-Denis (*Seint-Denys); The *Franklin's Tale (a Breton lay) is set in Brittany, and contains a visit to Orléans (*Orliens) to an expert in magic.

Chaucer himself had done military service in France, and had travelled to it and through it on the king's business (see Geoffrey *Chaucer: life). It is probable that for him French was a second tongue, which he would use constantly in business and diplomacy and in court circles. He may, like *Gower, have written poetry in French. It seems likely that he spoke the 'Frenssh of Parys' (I.126), a phrase he uses in a joke about the *Prioress's French 'after the scole of Stratford atte Bowe' (probably an Anglicized French, perhaps thought of as slightly old-fashioned; but perhaps her convent's French was that of Hainault, a dialect presumably spoken by Chaucer's wife).

French words and phrases are sometimes used in his narratives: 'Seynt Julyan, loo, bon hostel [(grant) good lodging]!' says the *Eagle (HF 1022). Many seem to be standard and common, but some are clearly deliberately used, though it is not always easy to isolate the precise undertones. In 'fyn blak satyn doutremer' (BD 253) the last

Franklin

word simply means 'foreign, from abroad', but probably adds a suggestion of the exotic; the *Wife of Bath's 'bele chose' (III.447, 510) is a delicate euphemism. When in The *Reeve's Tale 'the wenche rowteth eek, par compaignye' (I.4167), the French phrase brings a hint of sarcasm to the description of an uncourtly scene. Similarly, when the Host calls the Pardoner 'thou beel amy' ('fair friend', VI.318) it sounds derisive. The Friar in The *Summoner's Tale twice uses the phrase 'je vous dy' to Thomas (III.1832, 1838). The phrase is not uncommon, but here it seems that the friar is out to impress—and is convicted of 'affectedness' out of his own mouth. When the merchant in The Shipman's Tale answers 'Quy la?' to his wife's knock (VII.214), it seems that Chaucer is giving a little French local colour.

Chaucer had immersed himself in French literature (see Geoffrey *Chaucer: reading). He translated and adapted French works, used French translations, and was familiar with the ideas developed in French literary culture. It may well be, as Clemen has suggested, that it was his deliberate intention 'to give the idiom of English poetry the entrée to the court, to ennoble it after the French pattern'. But from his earliest attempts we can see him transforming his French books into something new.

Clemen (1963); Fowler (1967); Muscatine (1957); Phillips (1993); Wimsatt (1974 and 1991).

Franklin, a landed member of the minor gentry. The Franklin of the *General Prologue is presented as a well-to-do country gentleman, famous for his good living and hospitality. He is a son of *Epicurus, who delights in his *food, and is generous in dispensing it to others—he was like St *Julian the Hospitaller. He is prominent in local administration: he has been a knight of the shire (like Chaucer) and a sheriff; he rides with the *Sergeant of Law, who is also involved in public administration. The *portrait has only two physical details: he has a white beard and a sanguine complexion (which would suggest a good digestion). We learn more about him from an exchange with the *Squire and the *Host at the end of The *Squire's Tale. He praises the squire for speaking eloquently, and expresses the wish that his son, who prefers dicing to the pursuit of virtue, had his

'discrecioun', and would learn '*gentilesse' (which is an important theme of The *Franklin's Tale). The portrait is usually taken to be a good-natured and tolerant one. Some critics, however, have argued that it is more satiric, even to the extent of suggesting that he is a social climber or *parvenu* with an intellectual limitation which is reflected in his tale. But there seems to be no compelling reason to take this jaundiced view. Certainly, one early 15th-c. reader, the poet *Lydgate, seems not to have done so, since in a poem addressed to Thomas *Chaucer, the poet's son, he echoes the allusion to St Julian.

Rv 812; Cooper (1989), 45–6; Mann (1973), 152–9; Pearsall (1985), 148; Saul (1983).

Franklin's Tale, The, the second and final tale in Fragment V of The *Canterbury Tales, following the apparently unfinished *Squire's Tale. It is introduced by an exchange between the *Franklin and the *Squire on the idea of '*gentilesse'—at too great length for the *Host, who exclaims 'straw for youre gentillesse!'. The Franklin replies courteously, and begins with a brief Prologue. He will tell one of those 'lays' which the 'olde gentil' Bretons made. After an elaborate apology for his lack of skill in rhetoric, he moves into his tale (of about 900 lines in couplets).

*Arveragus, a knight of Brittany woos and marries *Dorigen, a lady of great beauty from a very noble family. He swears to renounce '*maistrie' (mastery, dominion) and to obey her as a lover, but will keep 'the name of soverayntee' as befits his status. In return, she promises to be his 'humble trewe wyf'. They live in great happiness for a year and more. Arveragus then decides to go to England to win honour in arms. He is away for two years, and Dorigen is griefstricken. Her friends persuade her to walk with them to drive away her 'derke fantasye [imaginings]'. But the sight of the sea, and especially of the 'grisly rokkes blake' on the coast, brings back her sorrow. The rocks provoke a powerful lament, which questions how a 'parfit wys God' could create such a terrible and dangerous thing. One day when they are in a beautiful garden, a young squire, Aurelius, who has long loved her in secret, approaches and pleads for 'mercy'. She firmly rejects him, but in pity promises that if he can remove all the rocks, she will love him. Aurelius is in despair. Arveragus returns and he and Dorigen live in great joy while Aurelius continues in torment. His brother, a clerk, remembers that when he was a student at Orléans he once saw a book of natural magic; he is convinced that there are sciences used by *tregetoures (illusionists) which will be of help. With Aurelius he sets out for Orléans in search of a clerk who can cause the rocks to disappear. They find a young clerk who demonstrates his skill in magic, and agrees to help—for a thousand pounds. They set off for Brittany.

It is now the 'colde, frosty seson of Decembre', and the turning point of the year. The magician finds the propitious time, and through his magic 'for a wyke or tweye | It seemed that alle the rokkes were aweye'. Aurelius now reminds Dorigen of her promise. She is overwhelmed by this totally unexpected news and in a long *complaint she berates *Fortune for facing her with the choice of either death or dishonour, and recalls examples of virtuous women who preferred death to dishonour. Arveragus, who has been out of town, returns to find her weeping. She tells him all, and he listens calmly and patiently, 'with glad chiere, in freendly wyse'. He insists that she should keep her word, for 'trouthe is the hyeste thyng that man may kepe'; but, as he says this, his emotions break out ('with that word he brast anon to wepe'), and he forbids her to speak of 'this aventure' to anyone or to show any sign of grief—he will endure his woe as best he can. Dorigen goes to the garden to give Aurelius her answer, but meets him on the way. When he learns her purpose, he begins to feel compassion for her and for her husband, and decides that it would be better to forgo his desire than to commit a 'cherlyssh wrecchednesse | Agayns franchise [nobility] and alle gentillesse', and releases Dorigen from her promise, saying 'thus kan a squire doon a gentil dede | As wel as kan a knyght'. While Dorigen and Arveragus can now live happily, Aurelius faces poverty because of his promised payment. However, when the clerk hears the full story, he too is moved to release Aurelius from his agreement, and to demonstrate that a clerk is also capable of a 'gentil dede'. The tale ends by putting a question: 'which was the mooste fre [noble, generous], as thynketh yow?'

There is no clear indication of the date at which *The Franklin's Tale* was written. It has been suggested (North) that astrological datings can be discerned within the tale—that Aurelius prays to the Sun on 22 July 1385, and that the rocks were removed on 25 December 1387, after 'two yeer and moore'. The G version of the Prologue to *The *Legend of Good Women* (usually dated 1394 or later) contains a similar passage on virtuous women. Most scholars assume that it was written during the period of the composition of the majority of the Tales, especially those concerned with marriage. Nor is there a clear source. The closest analogue is a story told by *Boccaccio in two versions, once in the *Decameron* (10.5), and once in the *Filocolo*. There the story is told in the context of a series of 'questions of love' (see *demande d'amour), and is followed by a debate, in which Fiametta argues strongly for the husband who was prepared to give up honour and especially the honour that comes from having a chaste wife. Chaucer prefers to leave the question open, perhaps in order to invite debate in his audience. There are other differences: in Boccaccio the lady promises her love if her admirer can make a garden bloom in winter and there is nothing like Chaucer's emphasis on the emotional attachment of Dorigen to Arveragus or on Arveragus's concern for *trouthe*. Underlying the story is a *folk tale of the type sometimes called 'The Damsel's Rash promise'.

The opening indicates the genre to which the Tale belongs: it is that type of short *romance known as the *Breton lay. The Breton place-names (*Pedmark, *Kayrrud) and the Breton- or Roman-sounding personal names (*Arveragus, *Dorigen, *Aurelius) give an unusual sense of authenticity to the setting; at the same time they suggest a remote and magic world appropriate to the events of the story. It is not however, written in the simple style of the Breton lay. In spite of the Franklin's disclaimer, there is a considerable display of rhetorical skill, and the distinctive narrative 'voice' often uses Chaucer's apparently offhand or sceptical asides. The narrator leaves the woful Aurelius lying in his bed with the remark 'let him choose, as far as I am concerned, whether he lives or dies' (1086). At the same time, scenes of pathos are treated with considerable feeling.

free will and predestination

Besides being a well-constructed tale, *The Franklin's Tale* is also concerned with ideas. A number of the questions or themes which interest Chaucer particularly are very prominent: for example, *love, the question of maistrye or sovereignty in *marriage, gentilesse, *patience, and trouthe. However, the interpretation of the Tale has provoked a good deal of controversy. Some critics have expressed disquiet at the treatment of the ethical issues involved, often taking an unsympathetic view of the character of the Franklin. It is possible, however, to argue that, as in *The *Clerk's Tale*, Chaucer takes an extraordinary situation as a kind of test case. Here he carefully suggests the motivation of her rash action in her 'trewe' love for her husband and her fear for his safety. The same is true of Arveragus and his concern for trouthe and honour. Again, this is an extreme case—as is underlined by a remark from the narrator (which may have been added in revision): 'paraventure an heep of yow . . . | Wol holden hym a lewed [foolish] man in this, | That he wol putte his wyf in jupartie [at risk]' (1493–5). His motivation is rooted in love and a concern for Dorigen's 'trouthe' which reflects his view of marriage as companionship rather than 'maistrye'. Chaucer seems to delight in the challenge of making a folk tale with its strange absolutes into a literary moral story, with dramatically conceived characters who have human emotions. He gives 'to a romantic fairy tale a degree of dramatic realization which takes us at least momentarily out of the realm of romance into that of domestic tragedy' (Pearsall). Its optimistic ending is entirely appropriate to its genre of romance. The virtues of gentilesse and trouthe seem to have a spiritual power which can transform men's hearts. It is as if a spiritual grace overcomes self-seeking passion and the magician's illusion.

(ed.) *Rv* 178–89, 895–901; *S&A* 377–97 (211–65); Cooper (1989), 230–45; Pearsall (1985), 144–60; Mann (1991), 111–20; North (1990), 422–42.

Fraunce, see ***France.**

free will and predestination. In the history of Christian thought few issues have caused greater controversy: the problem may in simple terms be put: 'How can the prescience, beneficence and

omnipotence of God be reconciled with man's free will?', 'If God already knows that a man will eventually go to hell, in what sense does that man have any freedom of will to choose persistently good acts rather than evil? and, if he has no such freedom of will, can God be regarded as beneficent?', 'If a man acts well because God knows beforehand that he will do so, what moral virtue (or its reward) accrues to the human thereby?', 'What is the purpose of a man's contrition, or of preaching and the advice of the confessional, if a man's eventual destiny is already known to God at birth?' The traditional answer to these problems in the medieval period attempted to differentiate between God's omniscience and his omnipotence, and to insist that to God all time was constantly present: thus, because at a man's birth God was aware of everything that would affect him throughout his life, he knew that man's eventual destination but did not compel it—at each choice man could exercise his own free will to choose good or evil, but God knows before the decision is made what it will be. Such was the basis of the thought put forward by Augustine (*Austyn), and coupled by him with stress upon the complete dependence of man upon the prevenient grace of God to choose the good. Boethius (*Boece) in his *Consolation of Philosophy* argues a similar line, though expressed in terms drawn from Neoplatonic philosophy rather than in expressly Christian language; Chaucer in his translation grappled with the problem of expressing these ideas in the vernacular. Prolonged debate in the medieval period produced variations, especially in stress, upon these ideas; during Chaucer's lifetime notable contributions were made by bishop *Bradwardine and by John *Wyclif, both diminishing the stress upon free will.

The notion of *fate* is obviously relevant to many of Chaucer's tales (e.g. the *Man of Law's Tale*, or the *Monk's Tale* tragedies), but Chaucer has three extended discussions of predestination and free will. The most important is in *Troilus and Criseyde*, where both Criseyde and Troilus speculate on the extent to which their action is predestined or within their own control, but where most explicitly Troilus debates the question in IV.958–1078. The passage, which has been suggested by Root and other critics to have been added by Chaucer at a late stage in the revision of the whole because of its absence from certain manuscripts, is dependent closely upon Boethius V pr.2 and pr.3. Notoriously, Troilus omits Boethius's ensuing invocation of God's timelessness to protect human free will, concluding in terms the same as he had begun: 'Thus to ben lorn, it is my destinee' (IV.959). Chaucer in the poem as a whole also investigates, through irony and through the narrator's awareness that the audience knows the story's outline from the start, the effects of foreknowledge for the foreknower—he has, in fact, put the reader in the place of God. He also, through the narrator's bumbling attempts to exonerate Criseyde (e.g. V.1050), effectively contributes to the contemporary debate on whether God can undo the past, and seems to conclude that he cannot (or at least will not). That Chaucer was aware of the philosophical interest of his poem is evident from his dedication of it to *Strode. The relation between the *purveiaunce of God* and *fortune* is the subject of much speculation in Chaucer's writing, as it was throughout the medieval period, but comments are particularly pervasive in *The Knight's Tale*. Arcite and Palamon both comment extensively on the cruelty of fortune and the unknowable will of the gods, when one is released and the other remains in prison. As pagans their dilemma does not include the need to incorporate the Christian concept of a beneficent deity, though little change would be needed for an audience contemporary with Chaucer to apply Palamon's question to their own situation: 'What governance is in this prescience, | That giltelees tormenteth innocence?' (I.1313–14). Destiny here is seen as the 'ministre general | That executeth in the world over al | The purveiaunce that God has seyn biforn' (I.1663–5), and hence is like God, immutable. Chaucer's third discussion is much more light-hearted, being placed in the context of the fox's fulfilment of the cock's dream in *The *Nun's Priest's Tale*; it is indeed itself rather an allusion to the contribution of Augustine, Boethius, and Bradwardine to the discussion than a full examination of the issues (*NPT* VII.3230–66). [AH]

Oberman (1967); Root (1926).

Friar, The (ME *frere*, orig. 'brother')—and friars.

The portrait of the Friar in the *General Prologue* (I.208–69), which immediately follows that of the *Monk, is one of most vivid in the whole series. From the outset it is teasingly ambiguous: he is 'a wantowne and a merye' and also 'a ful solempne man [of great dignity]'. He is not identified as a Franciscan or indeed as a member of any specific order. That he is a representative of the whole genus is suggested by the remark that he had greater persuasive skill ('daliaunce and fair langage') than any of the 'ordres foure' (i.e. Carmelites, Augustinians, Dominicans and Franciscans). Friars were expected to live a life of poverty, subsisting through begging. So this friar is a mendicant, a *lymytour* ('limiter', a friar licensed to beg within certain fixed limits). He is particularly skilful in raising money: he is an easy confessor ('he was an esy man to yeve penaunce, | Ther as he wiste to have a good pitaunce'). Ingratiation has other rewards apparently. He carries trinkets as presents for 'faire wyves'. And he arranges marriages for young women (possibly, though this is not explicitly said, for his own victims). He is an accomplished musical performer: he sings and plays the *rote* (a stringed instrument). He knows the taverns in every town. It is clear that the life of this 'worthy' man is hardly conducted according to the ideal of apostolic poverty. He is more familiar with innkeepers and barmaids than with the sick and needy. There is no profit to be made there. His dress is not the threadbare gown of a poor scholar, but reflects his 'worthiness'; his cloak is of double worsted: 'he was lyk a maister or a pope'. Precisely chosen details fill out the description: he is as strong as a champion; he has a fair white neck; he lisps 'somwhat' to 'make his Englissh sweete upon his tonge': 'in his harping . . . | His eyen twynkled in his heed aryght | As doon the sterres in the frosty nyght'. And in the very last line of the description he is, unusually, given a name Hubert.

In the background of this *portrait is the figure of Faus Semblant (False Seeming) in the *Roman de la Rose*. And Chaucer makes use of traditional stereotypes and topics from the extensive antifraternal satire of the Middle Ages. For instance, the propensity for cultivating the rich rather than the poor, the giving of easy penance, the liking for fine clothes, the skill in winning confidence and worming their way into people's houses are all common charges, often very fiercely expressed. Chaucer's technique, however, is more indirect and subtle. He deliberately refrains from explicit moral condemnation. His friar is a genuinely convivial and jovial man (and is influential in establishing the later image of the 'merry friar'). But the uses to which his bland pleasantness is put inevitably give an ironic undertone to words like 'plesaunt' or 'curteis'. And there are more sinister undertones, clear suggestions of avarice and lechery, and hints of blackmailing and 'fixing'.

The widespread use of the stereotypes of antifraternal satire in the late Middle Ages suggests that for a variety of reasons friars were felt to be hypocritical. (They had made great contributions to the spiritual and intellectual life of medieval Europe from the 13th c., in piety, preaching—notably by the Franciscans (founded by St Francis of Assisi) and the Dominicans (founded by St Dominic)—, and to scholarship (Chaucer names two learned friars, *Nicholas of Lynn and John *Somer, in the *Astrolabe).) The friars were open to criticism on a number of counts. There was early hostility because they could present a threat to well-established and stable ecclesiastical structures. They came into conflict with the monks, and were seen as competitors by the parish clergy. When the Franciscans modified their founder's insistence on strict apostolic poverty, the way was open for what moralists saw as an abandonment of early ideals and a surrender to worldliness.

Other friars appear in the background of Chaucer's tales. In *The *Miller's Tale* their singing in the chancel marks the end of a night of passion (I.3656); the Host alludes to their Lenten preaching (IV.12); according to the *Wife of Bath they have supplanted the fairies (III.864–81); in his *Complaint to his *Purse* Chaucer laments that he is 'shave as nye [closely, i.e. stripped bare of money] as any frere'. But the Friar of the *General Prologue* still has an important role to play. He irritates the *Summoner and by telling a story about a wicked summoner, provokes the telling of a story against friars (see *Summoner's Tale). Here we find many of the old topics of satire, and some new ones. The preaching of Friar John produces money for requiem masses (to be sung by friars, who are more effective than priests) and for the construction of holy houses. The building of rich and elaborate churches (rather than the humble ones recommended by St Francis) is a standard criticism. The Friar is shown begging, interrupting his sales talk with the remark (III.1752) that he is recording the benefactor's name (which, we are told, is quickly erased). He meets his match, but not before he has revealed himself as a splendidly unctuous character whose hypocrisy has no bounds. He embraces and kisses the wife with evident enjoyment, orders a fine meal while praising abstinence and poverty, warns against wrath, but flies into a passion when he is tricked.

Rv 807–8; Cooper (1989), 40–2; Mann (1973), 37–54; Szittya (1986); A. Williams (1953).

Friar's Tale, The, follows *The *Wife of Bath's Tale* in Fragment III. It is introduced by a short prologue in which the *Friar announces that he will tell 'a *game' about a *Summoner. His description of a summoner as 'a rennere [runner] up and doun | With mandementz [summonses] for fornicacioun. | And is ybet [beaten] at every townes ende' leads the Host to urge him to be courteous as befits his estate, and the Summoner to threaten revenge. The tale he tells (364 lines in couplets) sounds as if it is going to be a *fabliau, but turns out to be a satirical *exemplum.

An archdeacon who is energetic in the prosecution of offenders, especially lechers, is assisted by a cunning summoner, 'a theef, and eek [also] a somonour, and bawde'. One day as he is going to summon an old widow (in order to extract a bribe), he meets a yeoman at the edge of the *forest. He is wearing a green jacket and a hat with black fringes. They exchange greetings, and when the yeoman learns that his companion is a summoner, he says that he too is a bailiff although he is 'unknowen as in this contree'. He promises the summoner gold and silver if he ever visits him. They become sworn brothers, and ride together. The summoner is talkative and inquisitive, and asks the yeoman where he may be found. He answers softly, 'far in the north'. The summoner then asks for advice on how to perform his office to the greatest profit. The yeoman says that he has a hard and demanding master, and that he lives by extortion. 'So do I!', exclaims the summoner, and announces with enthusiasm that he has neither compassion nor conscience. The yeoman smiles 'a litel', and reveals who he is: 'I am a feend [*devil]; my dwellyng is in helle.' This dramatic announcement is met with a comic absence of surprise. The summoner is more curious about his companion's human shape—and his shape in hell, and the other shapes he assumes. He is assured that later he will know all the answers from experience, and will be a greater authority on it than *Virgil or *Dante.

As they both ride off together on their parallel missions of making profit by any means, the summoner proposes that they share their winnings. At the edge of a town they find a hay cart is stuck in the mud, and hear the carter angrily consign his horses to the fiend. 'Take them', says the summoner to the yeoman. But the fiend, who is something of an intellectual, points out that this was not his 'entente' (intention). This is proved true, for when the horses begin to pull, the carter commends them to God and to St *Loy. At the other end of town is the old widow from whom the summoner wants to get 12 pence. He knocks on her gate, and after an exchange in which the summoner relentlessly refuses to accept her pleas of poverty, and threatens to take her new pan for payment of an earlier (alleged) offence, she consigns both him and the pan to the devil 'blak and rough of hewe'. The yeoman asks her politely if she really means it. She does, she says, unless the summoner repents. This he angrily refuses to do: 'Nay, olde stot, that is nat myn entente.' After this double statement of intention, the fiend claims the summoner and carries him off 'where as somonours han hir heritage'. We should, concludes the Friar, beware of the fiend, and pray that summoners should repent of their misdeeds before he seizes them.

The Friar's Tale is not one of the best known of the *Canterbury Tales*, but it is one of the most successful comic stories in the whole collection. It contains some of Chaucer's most brilliant *dialogue, and the *characterization of the summoner and the fiend is superb. It fits perfectly into its context, being both a teasing echo of the meeting with a supernatural creature in The *Wife of Bath's Tale and a full-blooded and clever satirical assault on the Summoner. Stories of the damnation of an unpopular official and the motif of the heartfelt curse are common, but no immediate source for

the tale is known. The analogues (of which the closest is found in Caesarius of Heisterbach's collection of exempla) do not have Chaucer's deft and witty dialogue.

(ed.) *Rv* 122–8, 875–6; *S&A* 269–74 (87–99); Cooper (1989), 167–75; Pearsall (1985), 217–22; Szittya (1975).

FRYDESWYDE, SEINTE, St Frideswide (*c.*680–735), a princess who fled from marriage to found a monastery at Oxford. She appears in an oath by the carpenter in *The Miller's Tale* (I.3449) when he finds his Oxford student lodger apparently in a trance. It is appropriate, since she was noted for her healing powers, especially the casting out of devils, as well as being the patron saint of the town.

friendship. The ancient ideal of friendship was known to the Middle Ages especially through Cicero's *De amicitia* (44 BC). Cicero argues that the noblest friendship cannot exist without virtue. Its cause is to be found in Nature itself; the word *amicitia* comes from *amor* (love). It is concord, as against discord: 'friendship is nothing else than an accord in all things, human and divine, conjoined with mutual goodwill and affection,' Friendship surpasses simple *propinquitas* or 'closeness' (as with neighbours or relatives). The 'mutual goodwill of a friend' involves the sharing of both joy and adversity. There should be no feigning or hypocrisy. Among friends there is equality. Friendship is generous and outgoing, and altruistic: 'the effect of friendship is to make, as it were, one soul out of many'.

Such ideas seem to have appealed both to monastic writers on spiritual friendship and to love poets. In the *Roman de la Rose*, for instance, there is a character called Amis or Friend, who comforts and advises the lover, and rejoices like a true companion when Danger (*Daunger) grants him pardon. In *Jean de Meun's part he gives rather Ovidian advice: the lover should try bribing the guards or using some deceit in order to release Fair Welcome.

Classical ideas were fused with biblical and Christian ones ('greater love hath no man than this, that a man lay down his life for his friends', etc.). One result was the development of a large

friendship

proverbial corpus concerning friendship, in which the advice ranged from the altruistic to the self-interested: 'a friend (is proved) in need'; 'assay your friend ere you have need'; 'a friend in court is better than penny is purse'; 'a friend may become a foe'; 'leave not an old friend for a new'; 'no friendship is so perilous as feigned friendship', etc.

In his treatment of friendship, Chaucer uses an extensive range of vocabulary. Besides his words *fre(e)nd* and *fre(e)ndshipe* he has the more general *felawe* ('comrade, companion') and *felaweshipe* ('band of associates, company', but which is also associated with friendship of cameraderie, and can overlap in sense (cf. *Tr* II.204–6)), or *fere* ('companion'). *Gossip* (originally a 'spiritual relative'—a sponsor at baptism, or a child of one's godfather) had become generalized to mean also a familiar acquaintance (of either sex). (The further extension of meaning to the type of conversation associated with such acquaintances is post-Chaucerian.) 'Friend' does not of course always have the larger and more intense connotations of the *De amicitia*. It is frequently used simply as a polite term of address (e.g. VIII.593, 1181, etc.), and greater intimacy is given by prefixing the adjectives *de(e)re* or *le(e)ve* ('dear'). As the *Parson says, there is no friendship in hell (X.205). In Chaucer there is often an evident delight in a 'company'—'so myrie a compaignye' (I.764; see also I.2105, III.860). Friendship's range can be seen from Chaucer's own proverbial lore. There is much of this in his tale of *Melibee*, where the importance of true friends is constantly stressed, with advice from Solomon (VII.1158–9) or Cato (1306–7); there are biblical and Senecan thoughts on grieving for the death of a friend, and one or two cautionary remarks: 'neither to thy foo ne to thy frend discovere nat thy secree ne thy folie' (1141). Prudence warns of the dangers to friendship: Fortune changes and you become poor, 'farewell friendship and fellowship' (VII.1558; cf. *Bo* III. pr.5: 66–8). Elsewhere the dangers of anger (X.561) or an unguarded tongue (IX.342) are noted. Most dangerous perhaps, is flattery. Prudence quotes Cicero, 'amonges alle the pestilences that been in freendshipe the gretteste is flaterie' (VII.1176). Examples are to be seen in the fox in *The Nun's Priest's Tale* and *Placebo in The Merchant's Tale*. In *The Canterbury Tales* the pilgrims

are a company, 'by aventure yfalle | In felaweshipe' (I.25–6). Within this 'compaignye' (III.189; cf. 1278) there are stronger friendships. The Franklin rides in the company of the *Man of Law (I.331), and the *Pardoner is the 'freend' and 'compeer' (companion) of the *Summoner (I.670). In the Tales, characters typically have their sets of friends (like the Wife of Bath, III.243, 529–30). (The importance of having friends is highlighted in *Troilus and Criseyde* when Criseyde is abandoned by her father and is vulnerable—'for bothe a widewe was she and allone | of any frend to whom she dorste hir mone [complain]', I.98.) In The *Man of Law's Tale*, when Constance is isolated by her experiences, the mention of friends heightens the sorrow of her situation (II.268–9; cf. 658). *Griselda is an even more isolated figure: there is no mention of her friends at all.

There are familiar references to people's behaviour with their friends. The Wife of Bath goes walking with Jankyn and Alisoun. In The *Shipman's Tale* the merchant goes to the monk Dan John 'to pleye', to find out how he is doing, 'and for to tellen hym of his chaffare [business]', | As freendes doon whan they been met yfeere [together]', and is received with 'feeste and murye cheere' (VII.337–42)—cf. Criseyde and Pandarus (*Tr* II.150–2).

There are 'sets' or 'gangs': the 'compaignye | Of yonge folk that haunteden folye' in The *Pardoner's Tale* (VI.463–4), or Troilus's group of young knights (I.183–9). A much more intense form of friendship is found in 'sworn brotherhood'. This formal, legally binding relationship obliged the two friends to help each other in war and all kinds of danger throughout their lives. There are examples in classical as well as in medieval literature. It is prominent in the *Knight's Tale*, where Palamon and Arcite are bound by ties of kin (they are cousins, the sons of two sisters); they wear the same heraldic device, and they are sworn brothers (I.1012, 1019, 1131–2). It also appears in a more comic and satirical context in The *Friar's Tale*, where the summoner eagerly agrees to the suggestion of the mysterious yeoman, and each 'in ootheres hand his trouthe leith, | For to be sworne bretheren til they deye' (III.1398–1405).

Cicero's ideal has connections with such topics as '*gentillesse*, *lore, and *marriage. *Venus is said (*Tr* III.29–30) to be 'sothfast cause of frend-ship', and (III.1748–9) Love 'knetteth lawe of compaignie'. Friendship is one of the effects of love: Troilus became 'the frendlieste wight, | The gentilest . . .' (I.1079–80) and in the social behaviour of lovers friendliness is a quality that is praised (e.g. *BD* 919–21).

Three works are especially interesting in their treatment of friendship. In *The Knight's Tale* Venus seems to be far from the 'sothfast cause of frendship', but rather a cause of discord. The friendship of the two knights gives way to rivalry in a love which has nothing to do with altruism. 'Ech man for himself, ther is noon other' says Arcite 'proudly' (I.1182), though he still addresses Palamon as 'brother' and 'leeve brother' (1181, 1184). The change in their relationship is pointed by the reference to the ideal friendship of Pirithous and Theseus (1199–1200). Even after Arcite revokes their oath of brotherhood (1604–7), there are echoes of their old friendship (1652, 1722, 1740). Theseus forgives them and orders them to be his 'friends' (1825). The conflicting patterns of discord and concord come to their climax in the scene of reconciliation between the dying Arcile and Palamon. At the moment of death the generous qualities of friendship reassert themselves.

*Pandarus in *Troilus and Criseyde* is in many ways similar to Amis in the *Roman de la Rose*. He advises Troilus, consoles him, and helps him by intrigue and persuasion. Like Jean de Meun's Amis he is worldly and Ovidian. His efforts and 'engyn' (contrivance) put some strain on his relationship with his niece Criseyde, with whom he enjoys an affectionate friendship (see III.604–6). At one emotional point she says sorrowfully that she thought him 'my beste frend' (II.412). Troilus reassures him about his role telling him that what he has done was done for friendship. Pandarus's friendship for Troilus can also be related to the ancient ideal of altruistic friendship. He is called a 'friend' at his first appearance (I.548), and the word is constantly applied to him. He takes friendship seriously: he remarks (I.591–2) that it is a friend's right to share both sorrow and joy. Chaucer often reminds us of his involvement: 'to ese his frend was set al his desir' (III.486; cf. 489–90). The friendship is reciprocated (see III.1590–1, 1597). And for all Pandarus's jesting, the intensity of his

feeling for Troilus is never in doubt. In book I, he 'neigh malt [almost melted] for wo and routhe [pity]' at the sight of his friend's sorrow; in book IV the news that Criseyde is to be sent to the Greeks causes him almost to take leave of his senses (IV.348), and he hurries to his friend 'in a rees [rush]' (in *Boccaccio's version Troilus sends for him)—and 'ful tendreliche wepte'. For Criseyde, friendship for Troilus is the first stage of love (II.962; cf. II.371, 379–80). It is a sombre moment later when Diomede offers friendship to her (V.135; cf. 185) and when they begin to speak 'of this and that . . . as frendes don' (V.853–4). One of the causes suggested for her final yielding to Diomede is that 'she was allone and hadde nede | Of frendes help' (V.1026–7). When she sadly decides that there is no other course, she says to herself that Troilus shall have 'frendes love' (V.1080), and repeats this in her last letter to him (V.1622, 1624).

The connection of ideal friendship with the generous impulses of the heart in love underlies the noble but doomed love of Criseyde and Troilus (who indeed proved to be her 'fulle frend' (II.1552)). But what is hinted at there is made explicit in *The Franklin's Tale*, where it is shown to be an essential quality in marriage. This is set against a background which is full of various kinds of friendship. Dorigen's friends 'conforten hire in al that ever they may'; Aurelius is helped by the friendship of his brother; and the clerk asks after student companions he knew at Orléans in 'the old days' (1179–82). The marriage of Dorigen and Arveragus is based on 'gentillesse' (cf. V.754) and an absence of '*maistrye' (cf. 745–9). The narrator emphasizes this in a passage (761–98) which, interestingly, begins with a statement about friendship: 'freendes everych [each] oother moot obeye, | If they wol longe holders compaignye.' 'Obedience' and 'patience' are necessary rather than sovereignty. In her crisis Dorigen turns to her husband, who listens patiently, and answers 'with glad chiere, in freendly wyse'. That they have both 'learned to suffer' gives them the strength to withstand and to conquer. This marriage, based on mutual trust and consideration, has much in common with Cicero's friendship—'an accord in all things'.

(*De amicitia* ed. and trans.) Falconer (1923); Keen (1962); Mills (1937).

Frise, Frisia, on the northern coast of Holland and the neighbouring part of Germany. The addressee of *Bukton* is warned that experience will make him prefer to be captured in Friesland than to fall into the trap of wedding. This may be an allusion to the brutal treatment meted out by the Frisians to their captives, but 'Frise' is a convenient rhyme-word. It seems simply to be a tag in the *Romaunt of the Rose* when the precious stone in Rychesse's girdle is said to be worth 'all the gold in Rome or Frise' (1093).

FROISSART, JEAN (*c.*1337–after 1404). French poet and chronicler, was born at Valenciennes to a bourgeois family. From 1361 to 1369 he was in England in the service of Philippa of Hainault, the wife of *Edward III. He travelled and made many friendships. After Philippa's death he returned to Hainault, finding new patrons, and eventually becoming a canon of Chimay. In 1394–5 he briefly revisited England. His prolific writings include a large body of lyric verse, a number of allegorical dream visions (*Le Paradys d'Amours, L'espinette amoureuse, Le joli buisson de jonece,* etc.), a long verse romance (*Méliador*), and his most famous work, *Les chroniques de France, d'Engleterre, et des païs voisins.* These chronicles cover the period 1325–1400 (up to 1361 he relied on an earlier chronicle). They give a vivid narrative of the events, and are especially notable for the way in which they convey the excitement of the wars and great deeds of *chivalry. It seems very likely that Chaucer knew Froissart. He certainly knew and used some of his works. In *The *Book of the Duchess* the opening lines are based on their equivalent in the *Paradys d'Amours*, where the sorrowful lover describes his condition; it is also indebted to it for the prayer to *Morpheus, and for the name *Eclympasteyr. The Prologue to *The *Legend of Good Women* also has echoes of Froissart's poetry or parallels to it, notably the *Joli buisson de jonece*, and the *Paradys d'Amours*, Chaucer had also read his praises of the marguerite or daisy. There are many other interesting parallels. The elegance and grace of Froissart's style and his handling of the love vision were useful models for him, but his treatment of the French poet's work is notably independent.

(ed.) Kervyn de Lettenhoeve (1867–77); Fourrier (1963, 1975); Longnon (1895–9); Scheler (1870–2); (*Chroniques* trans.) Johnes (1803–5), (selections) Brereton (1968); Fyler (1998).

FULGENTIUS, Fabius Planciades (*fl. c.*480–550). His *Mitiologiarum libri III* described the ancient gods and myths, and offered allegorical interpretations and etymologies. Much of his material went into later *mythography.

(ed.) Helm (1970); (trans.) Whitbread (1971).

Furies, Furiis, the Furies or Erinyes (in Chaucer **Herynes** or **Herenus**) the demonic avengers of crime in *classical literature. They were represented as winged women with snaky locks. Their names were Allecto (*Alete), Megaera (*Megera), and Tisiphone (*Thesiphone). Chaucer read about them in Virgil and Ovid (where they are the daughters of Night and denizens of the underworld). He seems also to have been influenced by *Dante's portrayal of them (*Inferno* 9.37–51) as both inflicting torment and suffering torment in hell. There they are the 'handmaidens of the queen of everlasting lamentation' (*Proserpina), rending their breasts with their nails, beating themselves with the palms of their hands, crying so loudly that Dante in terror presses close to Virgil. In *Boece* (III m.12:34) they torment the souls until the music of *Orpheus makes them weep for pity. They are present at the ill-fated marriage feast of *Tereus and Procne (*LGW* 2252). '*Pite' is rather mysteriously called 'thow Herenus quene' (*Pity* 92), where 'Herenus' seems to be a form of Erinyes. Pity is perhaps their 'queen' because she can control vengeance and vindictiveness; or perhaps Chaucer is recalling Dante's 'queen of everlasting lamentation'. The phrase 'this furial pyne of helle' (V.448) seems to mean 'pain such as the Furies suffer'. In *Troilus and Criseyde* Pandarus invokes them in an oath—'O Furies thre of helle, on yow I crye!' (II.436). They seem to preside over the action of that poem. At the beginning Chaucer calls on Tisiphone ('thow goddesse of torment, | Thow cruwel Furie, sorwynge evere in peyne', I.6–9) to help him write his 'woful verses' deliberately summoning up this grim, infernal creature. And at the beginning of the final downturn of the lovers' fortunes, the Furies are again invoked—'O ye Herynes, Nyghtes doughtren thre, | That endeles compleignen evere in pyne'—and solemnly named—Megera, Alete, and ek Thesiphone' (IV.22–4).

FURNIVALL, FREDERICK JAMES (1825–1910), man of letters, an enthusiast who threw himself into many radical causes, and did a great deal to make medieval works available to scholars and readers through his Early English Text Society (founded 1864). His Chaucer Society (1868) published a number of very useful parallel text editions. His own appreciation of Chaucer was enthusiastic and emotional. Without later 20th-c. doubts he endorsed a 'biographical' approach. Chaucer at length became 'the most gracious and tender spirit, the sweetest singer, the best pourtrayer, the most pathetic, and withal the most genial and humourful healthy-souled man that England had ever seen'. Furnivall's great achievement lay in the inspiration and organization of scholarly editorial work by others, which laid the foundations for the later study of Chaucer and of medieval English literature in general.

CH ii. 167–77.

G

Gabriel, the archangel who announced to Mary the coming birth of Christ (Luke 1:25–38), mentioned in *ABC* (115). In the Middle Ages he was regarded as a saint, and churches were sometimes dedicated to him.

GAIUS CESAR, Gaius Caesar Caligula, son of Germanicus, emperor AD 37–4, mentioned in *Boece* (I pr.4:181).

Galathee, Galatea, heroine of the *Pamphilus de amore* (see *Pamphilles), mentioned in *The Frankin's Tale* (V.1110).

Galaxye, the Milky Way (Greek *Galaxias*, L. *Via lactea*), the irregular band of densely distributed stars encircling the sky. The association with milk antedates Homer. (See also *Milky Wey; *Watlynge Strete.)   [JDN]

Galgopheye, probably Gargaphia or Gargaphie, a thickly forested valley in Boeotia, Greece, sacred to the goddess Diana (*Dyane). It was here that the huntsman Actaeon (*Attheon) met his death. Chaucer's allusion to it in *The *Knight's Tale* (I.2626) as a 'vale' and the haunt of tigers suggests that he remembered *Ovid's story (*Met.* 3).

Galice, Galicia, a province in north-western Spain, in which is situated St James, of Compostela, the famous pilgrim centre (Seint *Jame (2); see Map 3).   [PS]

GALYEN (1), Galen of Pergamum (AD 129 or 130–99 or 200). A Greek physician, he studied in various centres, notably Alexandria. Galen wrote copiously, throughout a career that began humbly with him as physician to the gladiators in Pergamum. He was for some years physician at the court of Marcus Aurelius in Rome. Galen surpassed all before him in theory and in practice, in anatomy and physiology, in prognosis and diagnosis, and was an influential teacher. His pathology was heavily enmeshed in a theory of the four *humours, a theory to which Chaucer refers on several occasons. Galen's deeply philosophical style and his monotheistic theology endeared him to the Middle Ages. He was referred to in (*The *General Prologue* as one of those authorities known to the Doctour of Phisik. (See also *medicine.)   [JDN]

GALIEN (2), Gallienus, emperor AD 253–68. 'The Romayn Galien' (perhaps so called to distinguish him from *Galyen (1) = Galen) is mentioned in *The *Monk's Tale* (VII.2336) as one of those who dared not fight with Zenobia (*Cenobia).

Galilee, a northern province of Palestine (III.11; see *Cane).

Gallus, see *Symplicius Gallus.

game (which covers Modern English 'pleasure, happiness, joy'; 'amusement, sport, entertainment' (of various kinds); 'joke, jest'; 'contest, game') is an important word and concept. It overlaps with 'play', an equally important concept, if, as Huizinga says, civilization 'does not come from play like a babe detaching itself from the womb; it arises *in* and *as* play and never leaves it'.

Chaucer refers to a number of the games and pastimes practised in his time. He mentions, for instance, *chess, 'tables' (backgammon), 'raket' (probably 'rackets', a game like squash; *Tr* IV.460), wrestling both ancient (I.2961) and modern (I.548, VII.740), jousting, singing and dancing, and so on. There are references to jugglers (e.g. V.219) and *tregetoures (illusionists). *Absolon (2) in *The *Miller's Tale* acts in dramatic plays. The *portraits of the pilgrims in the *General Prologue* stress their occupations rather than their leisure-time activities, but some interesting pastimes are revealed. Some serious figures seem to devote themselves exclusively to their occupations, whether for good or ill; others have some wider interests, or hobbies. The *Prioress is a pet lover, and the *Monk delights in hunting and coursing. The *Miller wins prizes for wrestling, and is adept in the recondite art of breaking doors with his head. Others have a developed interest in *food, *wine, the pursuit of the opposite sex, or 'wandrynge by the weye'. Chaucer, who likes to present himself as a bookish individual, once says that he thinks a book 'better play | Then playe either at ches or tables' (*BD* 50–1).

His narratives are full of examples of 'game' in the more general sense. Many are connected with *love, or passion, and its curious ways. In The *Miller's Tale Nicholas's scheme for deceiving Alison's husband is called a 'game' (I.3405), and in The *Reeve's Tale *Aleyn calls his exploit in swiving the miller's daughter 'a noble game' (I.4263). 'Game' is associated with *youth (cf. *PF* 226; I.3259). But those of greater age and experience may also find different kinds of 'game' in the observation of love and lovers (I.1806).

Some characters are notable jesters and purveyors of 'game'. *Pandarus is aware of this quality in himself (see *Tr* II.1110). He delights in it. 'A ha!' he exclaims when he is close to discovering Troilus's secret, 'Here bygynneth game' (I.868). Later we are reminded of it: 'When he was com, he gan anon to pleye | As he was wont, and of hymself to jape' (III.554–5). Another is the *Host, introduced as 'right a myrie man', who after the first supper begins to 'pleyen' and speaks 'myrthe amonges othere thynges' (I.757–9). Both like to enjoy jesting relationships with their friends or acquaintances.

When laughter is directed against folly, delight can be mixed with sharpness. When 'the folk' in The Miller's Tale laugh at the 'fantasye' of the carpenter (I.3840), they turn 'al his harm unto a jape'. Fortune's laughter is often bitter: at the death of Nero, she laughed 'and hadde a game' (VII.2550). As the *Parson remarks, people may sometimes speak 'in game and pley, and yet they speke of wikked entente' (X.644). 'Game' is not always present, and does not last forever: even Pandarus can find no more jests at the end of *Troilus*. However, the characteristic liveliness and sprightliness of Chaucerian

narrative is reinforced by a pervasive sense of 'game'. His characters usually do things with zest and delight. Even a merchant's arrival in Bruges is done 'murily' (VII.301; and cf. VII.3267). The voice of the narrator will sometimes betray a sheer delight in a scene. Troilus rides back from battle to great applause, modestly blushing and lowering his eyes, 'that to byholde it was a noble game' (II.647). When Criseyde and her nieces go into the *garden 'to pleyen', 'it joye was to see' (II.817).

Chaucer was particularly interested in the relationship between 'game' and 'ernest'. The two are often opposed (e.g. I.1125). More often, the relationship is complicated or uncertain. 'Game' can turn into 'ernest', as it does when *Dorigen makes a rash promise 'in pley' (V.988). The opposite can happen too. The Manciple's quarrel with the Cook is resolved by a drink: *Bacchus can 'turnen ernest into game' (IX.100).

There is sometimes a certain playfulness about the pairing. The eagle in The *House of Fame remarks 'take it in ernest or in game' in the midst of a long disquisition on the nature of sound (822). We are told that 'bitwixe ernest and game' *January finally chose his bride (IV.1594). The exploitation of ambiguity in the meanings of 'game' is most notable in *Troilus*. Pandarus treats his great task of bringing Troilus and Criseyde together as a serious 'game'. But at one point (*Tr* III.250–5) he expresses a doubt that his 'game' has become 'bitwixen game and ernest' that of a go-between. The word 'game' can refer to the stratagems which Pandarus uses (III.1084) or the noble 'game' of love (as Criseyde uses it in III.1494).

Sometimes 'game' is related to truth-telling (see, for instance, the Host, I.4355; VII.1963–4). A narrator may apologize (with indeterminate seriousness), like the Wife of Bath, 'taketh not agrief [do not be upset] of that I seye, | For myn entente nys but for to pleye' (III.191–2). Chaucer himself quotes the proverbial 'men shal nat maken ernest of game' (I.3186) to excuse the telling of the Miller's fabliau, to alert us to the kind of tale it is to be, and to arouse our expectations. Such remarks often raise questions concerning the nature of literature. One of the defences of 'game' was man's need for recreation and refreshment. The ancient idea that literature should be 'useful' and 'sweet' lived on strongly. Chaucer clearly offers us what his friend *Gower describes as 'somwhat of lust [pleasure], somwhat of lore'. Even his Host, who insists strongly on the entertainment value of stories, is of like mind. The requirement of 'tales of best sentence and moost solaas' (I.798) comes from him. When he reproves the Monk for his soporific performance 'therinne is ther no desport ne game' (VII.2791), he remarks that if a man has lost his audience, 'nought helpeth it to tellen his sentence'.

In all of Chaucer's narrative works 'game' is important, but it is most obviously so in *The Canterbury Tales*. Its centrality is established from the very beginning. The framework has no hint of the darker background which is found at the beginning of some story collections, like the need for Shahrazad to escape death by telling stories for 1001 nights or for the narrators of the *Decameron* to flee from the plague-stricken city. Its opening is strikingly and significantly different from the sombre opening of *Troilus*. There may be dissensions within the company of pilgrim-narrators, and violence and sorrow in the tales, but the surrounding framework is dedicated to 'game'. The 'game' of tale-telling is first referred to by the *Knight: 'syn I shal bigyyne the game'. And when he has ended this is echoed by the Host: 'trewely the game is wel bigonne' (I.3117). And he urges even the austere *Clerk to be an obedient 'player': 'what man that is entred in a pley, | He nedes moot unto the pley assente' (IV.10–11, which he proves to be: 'Hooste ... I am under youre yerde'). As this exchange implies, there appear to be 'rules' in the 'game'. The Host is the arbiter. He is to be 'governor' and 'judge', and the pilgrims are to be 'ruled' by him in 'high and low' (I.813–16). Stories must entertain. The Host goes on to warn the Clerk 'precheth nat, as freres [friars] doon in Lente' (IV.12). Any suggestion of 'preaching' in any form arouses comment. Not surprisingly, perhaps, both *Melibee and The *Parson's Tale are described by their tellers as 'merry tales'. There is an element of contest in the game of storytelling, which sometimes provokes attempts at requital, both good-humoured (as the Miller, I.3318–27) and ill-humoured (as the Reeve, I.3916, 4324).

In his study of play, Huizinga draws attention to the figure of the 'spoilsport'. Where the 'cheat' pretends to be playing the game, the spoilsport deliberately ignores the rules: 'by withdrawing from the game he reveals the relativity and fragility of the play-world', and he must be cast out because he threatens the existence of the play. Perhaps when the Pardoner announces at the end of his Tale that he has forgotten one thing, and proceeds to attempt to sell his relics to the pilgrims, as in real life, he is hovering between these two figures. An angry scene ensues, but he is not 'cast out'. The Knight restores order. Closer to the 'spoilsport' is the *Canon, who joins the company at Boughton. His yeoman says that he is eager to ride with them 'for his desport; he loveth daliaunce' (VIII.590–2). The Host warms to this in a characteristic manner: 'he is ful jocounde also, dar I leye!' Can he tell 'a myrie tale or tweye, | With which he glade may this compaignye?' (VIII.596–8). He certainly can, says the Yeoman, he knows more than enough 'of murthe and eek of jolitee'. What follows is in strong contrast to this build-up. The Canon draws closer to hear the Yeoman's highly critical account of his secret doings, because he always had 'suspecioun | Of mennes speche' (VIII.686–7). He claims slander, tries to silence the yeoman, and when the Host insists that he should 'telle on', the Canon rides away 'for verray sorwe and shame'. At this point, the return of 'game' is announced by the Yeoman with delight: 'heere shal arise game; | Al that I kan anon now wol I telle'. (See also *comedy; *joy.)

Andrew (2000); Huizinga (1949); Strutt (1801).

Gamelyn, a 14th-c. romance in couplets. It is found in a number of MSS of *The Canterbury Tales*, usually assigned to the *Cook. It is not by Chaucer, but it has been suggested that he may have intended to adapt it for the Cook or another pilgrim. However, there is no clear evidence for this. It is a lively story, telling the adventures of Gamelyn, the youngest of three brothers, who has been cheated by his eldest brother of his inheritance. He flees to the forest and lives as an outlaw (see *Robyn (3)) before he finally manages to come into his own. It was used by Thomas Lodge in his prose romance *Rosalynde*, which is the source for Shakespeare's *As You Like It*.

(ed.) Sands (1966); Skeat (1884).

Ganymede, Jove's handsome cupbearer, carried

up to the heavens by an eagle (*Aeneid* 5.252–7, *Met.* 10.155–61), is recalled by Chaucer in a similar situation in *The *House of Fame* (589).

gardens. In the Middle Ages gardens could be found in or close to monasteries, castles, and manor houses, in towns and cities, or in the country. There might be specialized herb gardens, 'physic gardens', orchards or vineyards, but the typical garden often seems to have incorporated these. Although no example of a medieval garden has survived, it is possible to reconstruct its main features from the very frequent descriptions and artistic representations. Characteristically, it was *enclosed*, by walls, hedges, or fences (of wattle or other material). Within it other divisions might be made with low fences, in order to create a shady retreat, for instance. Plants, herbs, and shrubs, chosen for medical as well as aesthetic reasons, would be planted in raised beds. The paths were sometimes covered with sand or gravel, sometimes with low-growing herbs which would give off a fragrance when crushed or brushed against. There were turf seats, benches made of soil or wattle, covered with turf, sometimes mingled with small flowers. Lawns were made from turf beaten and trodden down, mixed with flowers and herbs to give the effect of a 'flowery mead'. The garden might contain turfed mounds, arbours, or mazes. Water was essential. It might be provided by a stream or fishponds. Fountains with the water falling from wellheads into basins were especially prized.

The garden was an inward looking *hortus conclusus* shut off from the rough world outside, representing an ordered compromise between Art and Nature. It had become filled with symbolism and symbolic associations. Gardens were a traditional setting for 'gentil' *love—and for other kinds of erotic encounters presided over by *Priapus 'god of gardyns' (IV.2035). The idyllic garden of love is a mirror of the ideal place of beauty (or *locus amoenus). It is a pleasure garden, devoted to *youth, *beauty, and love. The garden might also recall the paradise garden of Genesis. Its fountain would then symbolize the four rivers of Eden. It might also recall the loss of paradise and the fall of Adam and Eve through the wiles of the serpent. There was also another biblical *hortus conclusus* in the Song of Songs (4:12). This enclosed garden was often taken

to be an allegory of the Virgin Mary (*Marie) or of the Church. Exotic Oriental gardens could be found in romance and in travellers' tales.

The most influential of medieval literary gardens is that in the *Roman de la Rose (see Fig. 10). The dreamer comes upon it as he is walking through a meadow along a river (ll. 136 ff. in the Chaucerian version). It is enclosed 'and walled well | With highe walles enbatailled'—instead of a hedge (481). The walls are decorated with paintings depicting the qualities inimical to love. Common people are kept out too—no shepherd ever got into it. The only entry is through a small wicket gate. When the dreamer is finally allowed in, he thinks that he is in paradise. It is the garden of Mirth, full of *birds and flowers and spices growing on the banks. It is completely shaded by the many trees. When the dreamer goes down a little path 'of mentes [mints] full, and fenell grene' (731), he finds Mirth, beautiful people dancing, and the god of Love himself. There are shady springs (with no frogs!) and at their edges the grass springs up as thick and soft as velvet ('on which men myght his lemman [beloved] leye | As on a fetherbed to pleye'). Under a pine-tree, springing up in a marble stone, is the 'Welle of Love'. This description is frequently echoed in medieval love poetry. And other ideal gardens form the setting for very different literary works—for a *dream vision like *Pearl or for the telling of a series of stories in the *Decameron.

Chaucer certainly knew and used traditional literary descriptions of gardens, but he may well also have drawn on his own experience. While he was Clerk of the Works he paid the king's gardeners, and his assistants paid for seed and turf and rods for tying up the vines. No document records his ownership of a garden, but the tenement he leased at Westminster in the last years of his life is described as 'in the garden of the Lady chapel'. In what *may* be an autobiographical reference in the Prologue to The *Legend of Good Women (200–7) he describes coming home in spring from the fields, and having his resting-place made 'in a litel herber [arbour] that I have, | That benched was on turves fressh ygrave [dug]'.

Such detail is often found even in his frequent brief allusions to gardens. In *Troilus and Criseyde Deiphebus and Helen read a letter in 'an herber grene' which they reach from the house by a 'stair' or steps (II.1705; III.204–5). Pandarus describes walking with Troilus in 'the paleys gardyn, by a welle' (II.508 ff.). In The *Reeve's Tale the clerks' horses are tethered 'bihynde the mille, under a levesel [arbour]' (I.4061). (And there are brief references to gardens with rustics making a fire (VII.2542–4).)

There are also gardens which form significant settings for adventures or meetings, usually erotic ones. In The *Parliament of Fowls within the walled park there is a garden (183) 'ful of blosmy bowes | Upon a ryver, in a grene mede'. It is a *locus amoenus*, with a well beside which Cupid is forging his arrows, and in it the dreamer finds Venus's temple of brass. In The *Shipman's Tale (VII.89 ff.) the amorous monk Daun John is walking in the garden (where he has previously said his devotions) when he meets the merchant's wife. In The *Knight's Tale (I.1051 ff.) the two knights see Emily gathering flowers in the garden whose wall is next to the great tower in which they are imprisoned: here two images associated with love, garden and *prison, are linked in a highly visual way.

A more elaborate garden is found in The *Merchant's Tale (IV.2029 ff.). Old January's garden of erotic delight is described with many ironic literary allusions. It is so beautiful that even 'he that wroot the Romance of the Rose' or the god *Priapus himself could not do justice to it. The ironic echoes of the Song of Songs in January's address to his young wife include the phrase 'the gardyn is enclosed al aboute' (2143). It is 'walled al with stoon', and the only entry is through a small wicket. It has a 'welle' under 'a laurer alwey grene'. It is also inhabited by supernatural creatures, the '*fayerye'. *Pluto, the king, sits 'upon a bench of turves, fressh and grene', and talks to his wife *Proserpina (whom he had 'ravysshed' as she was gathering flowers in the mead, 2230–1). Perhaps when the squire Damyan sits quietly under a bush (2155) or later sits merrily 'among the fresshe leves grene' of the pear-tree (2326–7), we might think of the serpent in Eden—though May has already 'fallen'.

In The *Franklin's Tale, which also has a love-triangle, there is also a garden, in which Dorigen is entertained by her friends (V.902–17). In contrast to the grim rocky cliffs, its beauty is greater than any other 'but if it were the verray paradys'.

But although its sweet-smelling flowers bring delight, it also proves to be the setting for a temptation, and is intended to be the setting for the fulfilment of the rash promise (1504–13).

The scene in Criseyde's garden in the second book of *Troilus* (814 ff.) gives us the clearest and most powerful example of the garden as a setting for 'gentil' love. The details of the brief description are very precise. It is reached by descending a 'steyre': 'this yerd was large, and rayled [bordered, fenced] alle th'aleyes, | And shadewed wel with blosmy bowes grene, | And benched newe, and sonded alle the weyes' (820–2). Here Chaucer sounds rather like a connoisseur, or a Clerk of the Works, commending the newness of the turf benching and the sanding of the paths. This is a peaceful, shady retreat from the life of the city, secluded from war and turmoil. It is the perfect setting for *Antigone's song in praise of ideal love. It is here that on the following morning Pandarus gives Criseyde Troilus's love letter (1114–17). (And, almost as if to complete the pattern, a garden is the setting for Troilus's song of love at the end of the third book (1737–71).)

Finally, the humblest but one of the merriest Chaucerian gardens is that of the widow in The *Nun's Priest's Tale, which is the realm of her cock Chauntecleer, and proves to be the setting for his adventure. She has 'a yard . . . enclosed al aboute | With stikkes, and a drye dych withoute' (VII.2847–8). It does not have fountains of love or turfed benches, but as Pertelote points out at some length (VII.2951–67), the medicinal herbs necessary for her husband's choler and melancholy (including spurge-laurel, hellebore, caper-spurge, or ground ivy) can be found 'growyng in oure yeerd, ther mery is [where it is pleasant]' (VII.2966). But even the most practical garden has its dangers. The fox, having got in, lies low in a bed of cabbages (VII.3221). Perhaps this shows that even the humblest Eden is not safe from intruders.

Crisp (1924); Harvey (1981); McLean (1981); Thacker (1979).

GATESDEN, John of Gaddesden (*c.*1280–1349), physician, author of a widely circulated medical treatise, *Rosa Anglica Medicinæ* (written sometime between 1305 and 1317). A fellow of Merton College, Oxford, Gaddesden was doctor of medicine, and student of theology there. He held several ecclesiastical preferments, and was long in royal service. His book is a medley of sober academic medicine, traditional leechcraft, charms, and religious and astrological invocations. Although it was severely criticized by the surgeon Guy de Chauliac, Chaucer was perhaps playing to the English gallery when he included Gaddesden's name in a list of famous physicians, in describing the Physician in the *General Prologue* to the *Canterbury Tales*. Also on his list were *Bernard Gordon and Gilbertus Anglicus (*Gilbertyn).   [JDN]

GAUFRED, Geoffrey of Vinsauf, a rhetorician who taught in England at 'Hampton' (probably Northampton) at the end of the 12th and the beginning of the 13th c. He wrote a number of poems and treatises, the best known of which is the *Poetria nova* (?*c*.1200–2, with later additions), a guide to the art of poetry written in Latin hexameters. It is indebted to *Horace and to the *Rhetorica ad Herennium* (see *rhetoric). Geoffrey discusses 'invention', the finding or choice of material, and the ordering of it; the techniques of amplification and abbreviation, and the ornaments of style. Chaucer adapts his architectural image for the creation of a poem in *Troilus* I.1065–71, and in *The Nun's Priest's Tale* (VII.3338 ff.) the comically elaborate rhetorical passage on the dreadful fate of Chauntecleer includes a brief parody of Geoffrey's even more elaborate lament for the death of Richard the Lionheart ('kyng *Richard'), a self-conscious display of rhetorical technique. The following lines (3355–73) expatiate on the event according to Geoffrey's instructions about amplification. In *The *Book of the Duchess* too, it is possible that the description of the lady (855–960) is following Geoffrey's model for the description of female *beauty. It has been suggested Chaucer did not know Geoffrey's work in full or directly, but only from passages in compilations. However, the *Poetria nova* exists in numerous MS copies, and, moreover, Chaucer's references seem to point to a close knowledge of his ideas (e.g. on *digression) as well as his text. And an intimate knowledge seems to be implied by the affectionate, teasing tone of his invocation (VII.3347) to 'Gaufred, deere maister soverayn'.

(ed.) Faral (1924), 194–327; (trans.) Nims (1967); Dronke (1974), 169–72.

GAUFRIDE, 'Englyssh Gaufride', who appears in a list of writers who 'bore up' the fame of *Troy in *The *House of Fame* (1470), is usually taken to be Geoffrey of Monmouth (d. 1154). His *Historia regum Britanniae* (History of the Kings of Britain) popularized the legendary history of the British kings (including Arthur). It begins with the founding of *Albion by Brutus (*Brut), the descendent of the Trojan Aeneas (*Eneas). It has been suggested that Chaucer meant himself to be recognized as 'Englyssh Gaufride', but (on the usual dating of *HF*) he had hardly done much at this time to bear up the fame of Troy.

(ed.) Griscom (1929); (trans.) Thorpe (1966).

Gaunt, Ghent in modern Belgium. One of the commercial centres of Flanders (*Flaundres), it was famous for its cloth-making. The *Wife of Bath is said (I.448) to have surpassed in this art those 'of Ypres and of Gaunt'. In *The *Romaunt of the Rose* the robe of Idleness is 'of cloth of Gaunt' (574).

GAUNT, JOHN OF, see *John of Gaunt.

Gawayn, Sir Gawain, the son of King Lot, one of the great heroes of Arthurian romance. He is noted (especially in earlier romances) for his nobility and courtesy (*curteisie). Chaucer alludes to him once in *The *Squire's Tale* (V.95).

Gawain and the Green Knight, see *Sir Gawain and the Green Knight.*

Gawle. The phrase 'folk of Gawle' (in *Dorigen's complaint, V.1411) seems to be translating *Jerome's word *Gallorum*. 'Gawle' could be Gaul, but since the fearful maidens in the allusion are in Miletus (*Milesie) on the coast of Asia Minor, their oppressors are probably from Galatia in central Asia Minor.

Gazan, Gaza, the city in Palestine, whose gates were carried off by Samson (*Sampson, VII.2047). (Possibly the form reflects the L. accusative *Gazam* in the Vulgate (Judges 16:1).)

Geffrey. In *The *House of Fame* (729) the *Eagle familiarly addresses Geoffrey *Chaucer by his first name.

Gemini(s)

Gemini(s), the third sign of the Zodiac, the Twins. (See also *Castor and Pollux; *signe.)

[JDN]

gems, jewels, and jewelry. Gems and precious stones were much prized in the Middle Ages. They were used for ornament and as a sign of status or wealth. In addition, many had symbolic associations, and many were thought to have medicinal or magical virtues (see *Lapidaire). Gems were brought or imported from Byzantium and the East, and, not surprisingly, figure prominently in exotic descriptions in *romance. There is a hint of this when *Alceste's white crown is said to be made of a single exquisite pearl 'oriental' (*LGW* 221). The important place that light held in medieval aesthetics was another reason for the popularity of gems.

Important items of jewelry were the brooch and the finger ring, belt buckles, and pendants. Brooches and rings which were set with precious stones had an added attraction in the magical 'virtue' of the gems, even though they could hardly match the spectacular magic rings of romance, like the rings of *Canacee. Jewels were used in richly embroidered clothes, and were set in women's coronals.

Chaucer mentions a variety of gems, or precious stones (often, but not always, in lists intended to give an impression of splendour or wealth). We find, for example: *adamant*, a very hard, magnetic stone (from which the door of the temple of Mars is made, I.1990 (cf. also I.1305, *PF* 148, *Rom* 1182), and the green *beryl* (from which the House of *Fame is built (see *architecture)), which magnifies everything. There is the *carbuncle*, a red stone which, according to *Bartholomew, 'shineth in dark places, and seemeth as it were flame'. Sir *Thopas has one on his shield (VII.871), appropriately, perhaps, since his name seems to be that of a gem: the *topaz*. *Crystal* is at its most spectacular in the two marvellous crystal stones in the Fountain of Love in the *Romaunt* (1568 ff.): when the sun shines on them then the crystal takes on a hundred hues, and it affords a perfect mirror. The oratory of Diana (I.1910) is made of red *coral* and white alabaster. There are *diamonds*, *emeralds*, and the 'jagounce' or *jacinth* (*Rom* 1117). The green *jasper*, a stone of great 'virtue' (more prized than gold,

according to a proverb, VII.1106), provides the great pillars on which the temple of Venus stands (*PF* 230), and a seat for Criseyde and Pandarus (*Tr* II.1229). *Pearls* are frequently mentioned (see e.g. I.2161), as are *rubies*, which 'shine by night' (*LGW* 1119): the cloak of *Emetreus is full of rubies 'rede as fyr sparklynge' (I.2164). Less common is the highly prized blue *sapphire* (VII.2468, *Rom* 1117), which *Bartholomew says is the best among precious stones.

Much of the lore of gems had become so well known that it could be simply alluded to (e.g. the 'virtue' of precious stones, *Tr* II.344) or used in various metaphorical or symbolic ways. The boy martyr in The *Prioress's Tale* is called 'this gemme of chastite, this emeraude, | And eek of martirdom the ruby bright' (VII.609–10). (The purity of chastity is traditionally likened to a 'gem' (cf. VI.223); emeralds were thought to guard against lechery; the redness of the ruby suggests the blood of martyrdom and the Passion of Christ.)

There are references to ornaments—to rings and brooches (cf. IV.255) or to diadems and crowns (*LGW* 2224). Gems often emphasize magnificence. In Fame's house of beryl the hall (1343 ff.) is plated with gold and set full of the finest stones that are named in the Lapidary. The goddess sits on a seat made of a ruby 'which that a carbuncle ys ycalled' (1361–3). They may also be used in more critical or satirical descriptions of pride or ostentation (cf. *Former Age* 30). *Nero in The *Monk's Tale* wears clothes embroidered with 'rubies, saphires, and of perles white . . . | For he in gemmes greetly gan delite' (VII.2468–70; cf. *Bo* III m.4). A more subtle example is in the description of the *Prioress (I.158–62). She has a very elegant rosary, a set of beads made of 'smal coral' divided by larger beads of green to mark the paternosters. And from it there hangs a golden brooch with a 'crowned A' and the inscription *amor vincit omnia* ('Love conquers all'). Nuns were not supposed to wear brooches.

Sometimes jewels are used for particular emphasis or effect. 'The broche of Thebes . . . so ful of rubies and of stones of Ynde' (see *Mars* 245 ff.) becomes an image of the destructive power of love and beauty. In narratives they may give a special focus. Thus the contrast of poverty and wealth in The *Clerk's Tale* is neatly emphasized by the jewelled ornaments given to Griselda for her wedding (IV.254), by the detail that the new queen was arrayed for marriage 'ful of gemmes cleere' (779), and by Griselda's refusal to take her jewels back home (869–73). In the narrative of *Troilus and Criseyde*, jewel imagery is especially important. Such images seem to be used at high points in the poem. They may be simply allusive or metaphorical (*Tr* II.585; cf. V.549), or references to actual rings (the ruby in his signet that Troilus uses to seal his love letter, II.1086–8, or the 'blue ring' which Criseyde and Pandarus talk about (III.885–93)). Later, the lovers mark a solemn moment when (III.1368–72) they 'pleyinge entrechaungeden hire rynges', and Criseyde gives Troilus 'a broche, gold and asure, | In which a ruby set was like an herte', and fastens it on his shirt. The narrator's remark that he cannot 'tellen no scripture', i.e. give the text of any inscription on the rings, refers to the posies or inscriptions on actual medieval rings (like *bel amie ne me ublie mie*, 'fair beloved, never forget me'). The brooch also sounds like a medieval one (e.g. 'one broche of golde shapyn like an herte writen therinne, *A vous me lie*'). Perhaps to quote such 'scriptures' might have seemed too bitterly ironic in the light of the conclusion. 'The storie telleth us', says the narrator in book V, that Criseyde gave Diomede a brooch which was Troilus's, 'and that was litel nede' (1040). And it is by a brooch that Troilus is at last convinced of his betrayal (V.1660 ff.): in these lines the word 'brooch' is repeated four times. (See also *clothes*.)

Genelloun, Genylon, Ganelon, the French knight in the *Chanson de Roland* who betrayed Roland (*Rowland) and Oliver (*Olyver) to the Saracens. For this he was condemned to be torn apart by four horses. In the Middle Ages he was an archetypal figure of treachery. The vengeance exacted on 'Genylon of France' is mentioned in an oath in *The *Shipman's Tale* (VII.194; cf. 136). In *The *Book of the Duchess* the 'false Genelloun', who 'purchased the tresoun | Of Rowland and of Olyver', appears in a list of great traitors (1121–3); and in a similar list the fox in *The *Nun's Priest's Tale* is addressed as 'newe Genylon' (VII.3227). In *The *Monk's Tale* (VII.2389) Oliver de Mauny, one of those who betrayed King Pedro (*Petro (1)) is

called 'Genylon-Olyver' (as against the faithful 'Charles Olyver').

General Prologue, the 858 lines in couplets which introduce *The *Canterbury Tales* in Fragment I. It is spring: the natural world revives, and 'folk' begin to want to go on pilgrimage, and especially from all parts of England to the shrine of St *Thomas at Canterbury. Chaucer says that he was at the *Tabard Inn in Southwark (*Southwerk) ready to go, and fell in with twenty-nine other 'sondry folk' there. He announces that before continuing his tale he will describe each one of them. There follows a series of *portraits of his fellow pilgrims (see the individual entries): a *Knight, a *Squire, a *Yeoman, a *Prioress (accompanied by a *second nun and 'preestes thre' (probably an unrevised or erroneous phrase disguising the undescribed *Nun's Priest)), a *Monk, a *Friar, a *Merchant, a *Clerk, a Sergeant of Law (*Man of Law), a *Franklin, five *Guildsmen (a haberdasher, a carpenter, a weaver, a dyer, and a tapestry-maker), a *Cook, a *Shipman, a Doctor of Physic (*Physician), a 'good Wif . . . of biside Bathe' (*Wife of Bath), a *Parson, a *Ploughman, a *Miller, a *Manciple, a *Reeve, a *Summoner, and a *Pardoner. After requesting his audience's tolerance for sometimes speaking plainly in reporting his characters' words and behaviour, Chaucer describes how 'oure Hooste' (Harry Bailly) proposes some entertainment for them as they ride along. Each of them must tell two stories going and two on the way back, and whoever 'bereth hym best of alle' will win a supper paid for by all of them. He will accompany them as guide, 'governour', and judge. Anyone who gainsays his judgement must pay for everything spent along the way. They agree, and in the morning the Host gathers them 'in a flok'. When they have ridden as far as the brook called the '*Wateryng of Seint Thomas', he pauses, and makes them draw lots. The lot falls to the *Knight, who proceeds to tell the first tale.

It is usually assumed that Chaucer wrote most of the Prologue early in the period of the composition of *The Canterbury Tales*, perhaps in the late 1380s. It is clear that in one or two cases further revision would have been necessary: there is no description, for instance, of the *Second Nun or of the *Nun's Priest, both of whom tell stories. On the other hand, the deafness of the *Wife of Bath (I.446) is explained in her own later Prologue (III.666 ff.), suggesting that this detail (and probably this portrait) was written at the same time as the Wife's Prologue, or at least with it in mind.

The opening lines of the *General Prologue* are among the most famous in English literature. The *chronographia* or 'statement of time' nicely sets the balance of 'earnest' and '*game' that characterizes the whole collection of stories. The brilliance and originality of the way that the pilgrims are introduced has also long been admired. No exact literary model has been found for this. It is clear that in presenting them as representatives of occupations Chaucer is using a technique of medieval '*estates satire', but they are not simply 'general types'. In different ways each is individualized—and some may well contain echoes of real people (see, for instance, Harry Bailly (*Host), the *Cook, the *Man of Law). Chaucer carefully gives the impression that they are a collection of individuals who have come together by chance. The presentation is full of surprises and odd juxtapositions, both in the details of the individual portraits and in the order in which they presented. In general outline the order is that of a descending social scale, beginning with the Knight and including the highest ecclesiastics soon after, and moving down to the middle classes, and the artisans and the lower ecclesiastics. But the pattern is far from being rigid. It is not clear, for instance, that the Friar deserves his ranking, even though he dresses like 'a maister or a pope'. In those cases where portraits seem to be arranged in pairs there is some contrast or difference. The Knight and the Squire form a nice contrast, both in age and in way of life and the Pardoner and the Summoner are associated in villainy, of different kinds. There are also artistic contrasts: variety in the length of the description, the amount of detail given, the items selected for note, and the narrator's observations on them. The principle of *diversity is firmly established. Furthermore, some techniques serve to unsettle the reader and make him alert. Not only do some portraits give us little vignettes of the character's behaviour in 'real life' (like the Prioress carefully wiping her lip), but some in a proleptic manner seem to imagine the pilgrim already riding on a horse along the way. Most teasing of all are the remarks and the attitudes of the narrator ('myself' (544), not the least important of the pilgrims) notably his enthusiasm, and his apparent approbation of the most surprising things.

(ed.) *Rv* 23–36, 797–826; Bowden (1956); Cooper (1989), 27–60; Mann (1973); Pearsall (1985), 52–71.

Genesis, the biblical Book of Genesis (X.755).

Genylon, Genylon-Olyver, see *Genelloun.

Genoa in Italy (*Ytaille) was in Chaucer's day an independent and prosperous city-state, locked in rivalry with others. The modern word 'jeans' (garments made originally of Genoese fustian material) preserves the memory of its commercial importance. Chaucer uses the word 'jane' (a Genoese coin worth about a halfpenny, IV.999, VII.735). There were close connections between Genoa and England, and a treaty had been made in 1371. A number of Genoese merchants lived in *London. The small Genoese community also included galleymen ('strangers born of Genoa and those parts') who had their own quay near the Tower of London and were parishioners of All Hallows, Barking. Chaucer visited Genoa on his Italian journey of 1372–3 (see Geoffrey *Chaucer: life). He was involved in negotiations concerning the Genoese use of an English port, and, possibly, military matters like the hiring of Genoese mercenaries. In 1376 he had further dealings with Genoese merchants at Dartmouth (*Dertemouthe).

gentilesse is the abstract term for the quality expressed by the various meanings of its etymologically related adj. *gentil*, i.e. (1) 'of noble birth' (2) 'of noble character' (3) 'excellent', 'superior', 'splendid' (as 'a gentil . . . faucon heroner'). Sometimes these senses may overlap (as probably in 'a verray, parfit gentil knyght'). Both words appear very frequently in Chaucer. To a certain extent they overlap with a semantic range of words denoting nobility or goodness of various kinds: *noblesse, nobleye, fredom* (which can also mean 'liberty, generosity'), *franchyse* (which can also mean 'generosity' or 'decency'), *dignitee, goodnesse, bountee* ('goodness, kindness; good qualities; honour'), *worthinesse*, *honestee* ('honour, virtue, decency, dignity'), *honour*, **curteisie* (and its adj. *curteis*), the adj. *hende* ('courteous, polite, gentle'), or *debonairetee* (adj. *debonair(e)*) ('kindness, meekness, graciousness'). With these they share such characteristic qualities as *largesse* ('generosity'), '**pite*', or *trouthe*. Just as *curteisie* often still retains something of its original etymological connection with courts and the world of **chivalry*, so *gentil* and *gentilesse* may sometimes have a class meaning. The Romance descendent of the Latin word *gentilis* 'belonging to the same *gens*' (family or race) had developed the sense of belonging to a noble family. So, when Cecilia in *The *Second Nun's Tale* is asked 'what maner womman artow?', she replies 'I am a gentil womman born'. It seems to be expected that those of noble birth should behave nobly. In *The *Knight's Tale*, which is especially praised by the 'gentils' on the pilgrimage, *gentilesse* is associated with honour and 'good name'; a *gentil* person can be recognized by his words and deeds (Arcite was 'so gentil of condicioun | That thurghout al the court was his renoun | . . . his name is spronge | Bothe of his dedes and his goode tonge'). Duke Theseus, after a struggle, overcomes his anger with the young knights, and decides not to act tyrannically, 'for', as Chaucer is fond of saying, 'pitee renneth sone in gentil herte'. The word *gentil* can be used playfully, as when the **Wife of Bath* describes the biblical text which urges us to 'wax and multiply' as 'that gentil text'; and even the phrase 'pitee renneth sone in gentil herte' is once used sardonically, by the **Merchant* in his account of how the 'gentil' May yielded to the 'gentil' squire, Damyan. But usually these words and the ideas they embody are very serious ones. Indeed, they sometimes have religious overtones: the quality of 'gentilesse' is attributed to the Virgin **Mary* in *The *Man of Law's Tale* and to Christ in *The *Parson's Tale*.

One particular intellectual tradition which went into the making of the complex of ideas Chaucer calls 'gentilesse' seems to have interested him especially. This is the idea of 'nobility of soul', a 'true gentilesse' which is not dependent on noble birth or lineage. The origins of this are to be found partly in Christianity (with its insistence on the equality of human souls before God, or in the paradox that in the Incarnation Christ the most sublime and noble became the most humble and the lowest of men). However, its roots lie also in classical literature. Chaucer seems to have been familiar with statements of the idea in the *Letters* of Seneca (**Senec*) and in the Eighth Satire of **Juvenal*, which is a fierce attack on the decadence of the aristocracy. In Boethius (**Boece*), Lady Philosophy puts the idea of true nobility ('gentilesse' in Chaucer's translation) and of the uselessness of boasting about pedigrees into a Christian-Platonic context: all things have one Father, who brought down souls from heaven to the bodies of mortals on earth; therefore the only man who can be called base or 'ongentil' is he who defaces his origins with vices. Chaucer also knew and used later treatments of the idea in **Jean de Meun* and in **Dante*, who followed **Guinizelli* in associating the 'gentle heart' with love, and in the *Convivio* argues that *gentilezza* has nothing to do with lineage or riches, but is a special grace given by God to a chosen soul which shows itself in nobility throughout its mortal life. Chaucer seems to have been influenced by this mystical and intellectual concept of *gentilesse* as a kind of spiritual perfection.

After Chaucer, the idea is much discussed by the Italian humanists, and affects later ideals of the true 'gentleman'. It has played a role in the development of a non-aristocratic view of society, but although it is potentially egalitarian (as in the verse quoted at the time of the **Peasants' Revolt*, 'When Adam delved and Eve span | Who then was the gentleman?'), in the medieval discussions such implications are not usually developed. Chaucer himself gives a general statement of the idea of 'true nobility' in his poem **Gentilesse*, and in **Troilus and Crilseyde* presents a hero who embodies the noble love, generosity, and open-hearted *pite* that are the essentials of 'gentilesse'. In *The *Canterbury Tales*, where *gentilesse* is an important theme, we find not only discussions of the idea of true nobility but a dramatic portrayal of the varieties of *gentilesse* in the complicated and difficult circumstances of life. Not only do we have the 'chivalric' *gentilesse* of *The Knight's Tale* and the 'Christian' *gentilesse* alluded to in *The Parson's Tale*, but the exemplary and optimistic story of **Melibee*, which celebrates 'ethical' or 'moral' *gentilesse*. In *The *Wife of Bath's Tale*, the ugly old hag lectures her nobly born husband on the nature of true nobility, quoting or referring to Seneca, Juvenal, Boethius, and Dante (a scene which is at once a serious 'persuasion to gentilesse' and in its outcome a demonstration of the rule that women desire '*maistrye*'). In *The* *Clerk's Tale*, the peasant girl Griselda so cruelly treated by the Marquis Walter (who is 'to speke as of lynage, | The gentilleste yborn of Lumbardye) is a saintly exemplum of 'true gentilesse'. In *The* *Franklin's Tale*, it seems to act as a profoundly positive moral quality like grace, encompassing the qualities of 'trouthe' or faithfulness, compassion, generosity, and love: here not only does the 'gentil herte' exhibit 'gentilesse', but a 'gentil' deed will produce a further act of 'gentilesse'. All three show Chaucer exploring a favourite pattern of ideas in stories which blend the realistic and the recognizably human with the extremes of situation or behaviour characteristic of the *exemplum or *folk tale to which they are related. He seems to have combined an admiration of the ideal of true *gentilesse* with an awareness (and sometimes a comic awareness) of the difficulties that many human beings find in achieving it.

Gray (1987).

Gentilesse is a moral *ballade of three stanzas, which survives in ten MSS and the editions of *Caxton and *Thynne. The title is modern; in the MSS it is simply headed 'moral balade' or 'balade' 'of Chaucer'. There is no reason to doubt the attribution. It is attested by *Shirley and *Scogan; and the poem is a statement of the idea of true '*gentilesse' which is discussed elsewhere in Chaucer's works. It echoes the ideas and words of Boethius (*Boece) and *Dante (the phrase 'old richesse' is the exact equivalent of the 'antica richezza' used in Dante's *Convivio*). The poem does not have the intellectual power of the *canzone* on the topic in the *Convivio*, but it is an eloquent philosophical lyric, and the recurring refrain 'Al were he [even though he should wear] mytre, croune, or diademe' reinforces the point that rank or outward show is vain and useless. Gentilesse cannot be inherited, but comes from God: the man who claims to be gentil must follow Christ, practise virtue, and avoid vice.

(ed.) *Rv* 654, 1085; Pace and David (1982), 67–76; Scattergood (1995), 67–76.

GEOFFREY OF MONMOUTH; GEOFFREY OF VINSAUF. See *Gaufride; *Gaufred.

geomancie, geomancy. Divination on the basis of patterns of dots. These are formed according to definite rules on the basis of random figures drawn, for instance, in sand. Geomancy is possibly, but not certainly, of Arab origin. The patterns had names, and there is a reference to two of them—Puella and Rubeus—in *The* *Knight's Tale*. The *Parson (X.603–5) preaches against nigromancy, the conjuring up of spirits, and exorcism, and some versions of the manuscripts have 'geomancie' in place of 'nigromancie'; but the two forms of divination were thought to be accompanied by very different degrees of spiritual danger. Geomancy was a court pastime, and there is still extant a very fine geomantic manuscript prepared for *Richard II in March 1391. There was a relationship established between geomancy and astrology. [JDN]

Gerland, the name of a dog in *The* *Nun's Priest's Tale* (VII.3383).

GERMAYNE, appearing only in the possessive form 'Germaynes sone' in *Boece (I pr.4:181), is the Emperor Germanicus (d. AD 19), the father of *Gaius Caesar Caligula.

Gernade, Granada, formerly the Moorish kingdom (capital city, Granada), comprising the southern half of Andalusia in the south of *Spain (see Map 3), and the last area of the Peninsula to be reconquered by the Christians, under the Catholic kings, in 1492. Algeciras (*Algezir) at whose siege the *Knight was present (I.56–7), then formed part of this kingdom, where the Muslims who had originally occupied nearly the whole of the Peninsula were confined between approximately 1250 and 1492. [PS]

Gerounde, the river Gironde in France, which flows into the Atlantic past Bordeaux (*Burdeux), mentioned with the Seine (*Sayne) in *The* *Franklin's Tale* (V.1222).

Gerveys, the Oxford (*Oxenford) blacksmith in *The* *Miller's Tale* (I.3761ff.). He is busy repairing ploughing equipment at his forge during the night (the first cock has just crowed, but the night is dark as pitch; 3687, 3731), as medieval smiths frequently did. A contemporary *alliterative poem on black-smiths refers satirically to the noise they make. It has been suggested that his smithy was in the old Smithgate near the north end of Catte Street, and close to the city wall—and the fields beyond.

Bennett (1974).

gestures play an important role in Chaucer's nar-rative art, and contribute to its strongly *visual quality. He would have been aware of the way ges-tures were used in painting and sculpture (and especially the dramatic and expressive gestures found in the work of later medieval artists), and on the medieval stage, where the raging tyrant Herod (*Herodes) for example might brandish a sword in a large expressive gesture. The staging of Christ's Passion would involve a visual enactment of the cruel scornful gestures of his tormentors which received much emphasis in devotional literature, like those mentioned by the *Parson: Christ was unmoved by 'the foule spittyng that men spitte in his face . . . the buffettes that men yaven [gave] hym . . . the foule mowes [grimaces]' (X.258). Actors in pageants and mimes would depend even more on gestures. Chaucer also knew the rhetor-ical principle that a speaker's demeanour and gestures should be suited to his matter (V.99–104; Tr I.12–14). And he would have been familiar with some of the literary and visual depictions of alle-gorical figures like virtues, vices, and sins, and their appropriate gestures and attributes.

Discussions of medieval literary 'body language' customarily interpret 'gesture' in a wide sense, and it seems sensible to include physical reactions like weeping, coughing, starting back, etc. The mater-ial can be classified in a variety of ways. Chaucer does not have anything to say about sign language (as used by the deaf and dumb, or in the Middle Ages also by Cistercian monks), but he is aware of this general type of communication. *May makes signs to her lover in the bush ('coughen she bigan, | And with hir fynger signes made she | That Damyan sholde clymbe upon a tree' (IV.2208–10)), and the *Manciple advises that if you hear a chat-terer, you should not speak, 'but with thyn heed thou bekke [nod]. | Dissimule as thou were deef' (IX.346–7). He makes extensive use, however, of

gestures accompanying speech, on the part of speaker and listener, by which meaning is empha-sized and communication established, and even more of gestures which express *emotions and attitudes towards others.

The variety is considerable. A large number involve the face and the *eyes. *Constance cast up her eyes to heaven (II.840); the sleepy god of sleep cast up 'his one eye' (BD 184–5). Eyes are cast down for sorrow (Tr V.1005), or embarrassment (Tr II.648), or humility (Tr III.96). *Fortune makes a 'mow' or grimace (Tr IV.7). But other parts of the body are involved. The head is shaken as a sign of negation (VII.112), and a sign of sorrow (LGW 2344). There is nodding ('becking') with the head. The Pardoner describes his preaching in a grotesque image: he stretches out his neck 'and est and west upon the peple I bekke, | As dooth a dowve sittynge on a berne'. He continues to describe his combination of speech and gesticula-tion with some satisfaction: 'myne handes and my tonge goon so yerne [quickly] | That it is joye to se my bisynesse' (VI.395–9). Lips are wiped, deli-cately by the well-mannered *Prioress (I.133), more urgently by *Absolon (I.3747–8). Heads are wiped for similarly contrasting reasons (III.731; VIII.1186–8). Fists deal out buffets (I.4275; III.792, 795). Hands are wrung (HF 299; Tr IV.1171), clapped (to bring a magical vision to an end, V.1203), lifted or held up (in assent (I.783), in binding agreements (III.1009; III.1404; VI.697–8; V.1328), in prayer (V.1024)).

Characters are taken hold of or seized, with varying degrees of physical and emotional force (cf. I.957; I.3475–6). Close friends, relatives, and lovers are embraced (see Tr I.1045; IV.1100–3; III.1252; III.1803; etc.). Kissing is a sign of love or passion, and also of reverence (HF 1107–8; VI.944) and of the restoring of peace (VI.965). Female bodies are stroked (Tr III.1249; IV.2414) or patted (I.3304). People kneel in prayer (I.2219, etc.), before one of high estate (IV.292), to ask for mercy or to intercede (I.1758), or to express emotion and gratitude (Tr I.1044–5). Characters emit non-verbal noises of various kinds: coughing (to draw attention; like May, Absolon coughs softly with 'a semy soun' (I.3697) under Alison's window, and later 'he cougheth first, and knokketh therwithal | Upon the wyndowe' (I.3788–9))—and farting.

gestures

Sometimes the gestures are involuntary or near-involuntary physical reactions (though they are none the less significant for that, as Absolon's remark 'My mouth hath icched al this longe day; | That is a signe of kissyng atte leeste' (I.3682-3) demonstrates). Fear causes pallor and the hair to stand on end: when Piramus sees the prints of a lion 'pale he wex; therwith his heer aros' (*LGW* 831), and starting back (I.3736, etc.). People 'quake' because of fear (I.3614; IV.358), or anger (I.1762), or amazement (IV.317). Extreme sorrow can cause extreme physical reactions: Troilus 'wel neigh for sorwe adoun ... gan to falle' (*Tr* V.532). A particularly effective example (on the edge between the involuntary and the voluntary) is used to express the despair of Criseyde, 'ful of sorwful piete': 'on hire bed she gan for ded to falle, | In purpos nevere thennes for to rise' (*Tr* IV.733-4).

It is evident that a number of these gestures are traditional and have conventional meanings. Some have a long literary and/or biblical ancestry. Thus, conventional gestures of sorrow include beating the breast (*Tr* I.932-4) and tearing the hair or the face (I.2833-4). Sometimes the significance is so well known that it can become the basis for a metaphorical expression. Characters can speak of committing themselves or something of value to them 'into the hands' of another (*Tr* I.433, 1053), or of 'bowing down the neck' (VI.909; IV.113). At other times the gestures are unusual and vivid, as in the scene at the end of *The House of Fame* in which everyone scrambles to hear news. The rapid enumeration adds to the sense of chaos:

> Tho behynde begunne up lepe,
> And clamben up on other faste,
> And up the nose and yën kaste,
> And troden fast on others heles,
> And stampen, as men doon after eles.
>
> (2150-4)

Thisbe (*Tisbe) finds her dying lover 'betynge with his heles on the grounde' (*LGW* 863).

Sometimes a gesture will be accompanied by an explanatory phrase—'for joye', 'for pitee', etc., making its meaning explicit. Often, however, the gesture is allowed to stand alone, making its point in a dramatic way, or, sometimes, remaining ambiguous and suggestive. In *The *Friar's Tale* when the summoner asks for the name of the mysterious

yeoman he receives an enigmatic smile (III.1446). The fabliaux in particular are full of dramatic gestures. When Nicholas in *The Miller's Tale* makes a 'pass' at Alison, the scene (I.3276-88) consists almost entirely of gestures: 'prively he caughte hire by the queynte ... and heeld hire harde by the haunchebones ... she sprong as a colt ... and with hir heed she wryed faste awey.' To heighten the sense of realism, a further gesture is implied in the ensuing dialogue: 'I wol nat kisse thee'. He manages to kiss her a little later, after he has 'thakked [patted] hire lendes [loins] weel' ('thakked' is an appropriate word for this 'coltish' girl: in III.1559 it is used of patting a horse). A more symbolic gesture is suggested at a turning point in *The *Wife of Bath's Tale* when the old woman says to the knight 'cast up the curtyn, looke how that it is' (III.1249). And at the end of *The *Knight's Tale* a 'ceremonial' gesture is given symbolic significance in the same dramatic way when Theseus says to Emily 'lene [give] me youre hond' (I.3082) and then tells Palamon 'taak youre lady by the hond' (3093). As often, gestures are both realistic and symbolic.

The use of a gesture to point an emotional scene is very common. Towards the end of a 'pitous' scene in *The *Man of Law's Tale* (II.822-75), in which Constance (about to be banished) kneels, covers the eyes of her weeping child with a cloth, soothes it, and raises her eyes to heaven as she prays, comes a telling gesture: 'therwith she looked bakward to the londe, | And seyde, "Farewel, housbonde routhelees!"' (Looking back is a gesture which can be particularly powerful and suggestive: cf. the famous example in the story of *Orpheus (*Bo* III m.12).)

A gesture singled out in a simple narrative can have a curious force. It sometimes seems to crystallize the emotional significance of a scene, as when Pyramus and Thisbe kiss 'the colde wal ... of ston' which separates them (*LGW* 768). At other times it may function as a moment of vision, an 'epiphany', which 'lifts the curtain' to reveal a personality or the significance of a moment in the narrative. Possible examples include the monk who after making suggestive remarks to a wife blushes at 'his own thought' (VII.111), the visiting friar settling himself 'softly' after driving the cat away from the bench (III.1775-7), or the young bride disposing of her lover's letter down the privy (IV.1954).

Troilus and Criseyde demonstrates the range and the skilful use of gestures in an extended dramatic narrative. Long exchanges between the characters are punctuated by them. In one at the beginning of the second book, Criseyde, desperate to know the drift of Pandarus's speech, 'down hire eyghen caste' (II.142), which she does again, perhaps from embarassment, at II.253. Here Pandarus coughs (II.254), and as he speaks, puts pressure on her through his gaze: 'he loked on hire in a bysi wyse' (II.274). Eventually his words cause her to weep (II.408) and to sigh (II.428, 464). When he hears her ask if Troilus can 'wel speke of love', Pandarus 'a litel gan to smyle'. There are many varied examples of the technique of dramatic pointing. Troilus weeps as he seals his love letter and kisses it (II.1086–90). Pandarus thrusts it into Criseyde's bosom (II.1155). Sometimes there is a bold mixture of pathos and comedy. As the lovesick Troilus raises himself up in bed Criseyde lays both her hands on him softly, and he manages for the first time to express his devotion to her, with quaking voice and 'now his hewes rede, | Now pale'. His manly sorrow would have moved a heart of stone, says the narrator, 'and Pandare wep [wept] as he to water wolde, | And poked evere his nece new and newe' (III.71–116). There is a similar scene later, when they have to revive him from a swoon by rubbing his wrists and the palms of his hands, and wetting his temples (III.1114–15). Violent expressive gestures are used in scenes of sorrow and despair. At the beginning of the fourth book, Troilus, alone in his room, rushes about like a wounded bull, 'smytyng his brest ay with his fistes smerte', beating his head against the wall, hurling his body to the ground, and weeping and sobbing so that he can hardly speak (IV.239–59). But when, later, in a 'public' scene he bids farewell to Criseyde, he manages to refrain from weeping, although she is weeping tenderly. He looks at her piteously, and draws near 'to take hire by the honde al sobrely' (V.81). It is a carefully devised moment of dramatic shock to hear this echoed a little later by Diomede (who has noticed Troilus's demeanour) as he promises to be her servant: 'yeve [give] me youre hond' he says (V.152).

R. G. Benson (1980); Gray (1995); Habicht (1959); Schmitt (1984 and 1990); Windeatt (1979).

Gy, hero of the romance *Guy of Warwick*.

GILBERTYN, Gilbert of Aquila, Gilbert del Egle, or Gilbertus Anglicus (*fl.* 1240), physician, author of an extremely popular *Compendium Medicinæ*. There is much biographical confusion, possibly because there were two English physicians of the same name at the time in question. The *Compendium* is the oldest English synthesis of medicine of any importance, however, and was long valued, since it was relatively free from popular remedies and charms, but also because it was presented in a scholastic philosophical style, with definitions, first principles, and syllogistic arguments *pro* and *contra*. It was printed as late as 1608 (Geneva) under the title *Laurea Anglicana*. It was perhaps English pride that caused Chaucer to include Gilbert's name in his list of famous physicians, when describing the pilgrim Physician in the *General Prologue* to the *Canterbury Tales*. Also on Chaucer's list were Bernard Gordon and John of Gaddesden. (See *Bernard* and *Gatesden*.)

GILE, SEINT, St Giles or Aegidius, a 7th-c. hermit, who founded a monastery (later called Saint-Gilles) in Provence. According to legend he protected a hind from hunters. He became a very popular saint in the Middle Ages, being the protector of cripples, lepers, and nursing mothers. He is mentioned twice in Chaucer (VIII.1185; *HF* 1183). Both are asseverations 'by Seint Gile!' and both occur in rhyme. It is not clear that they have any special significance.

Gille, the carpenter's maid in *The *Miller's Tale* (I.3556).

Gysen, the river Gyndes, a tributary of the Tigris. Its destruction by Cyrus (*Cirus*) is mentioned in *The *Summoner's Tale* (III.2080).

gyterne, see *musical instruments*.

GLASCURION. 'The Bret Glascurion' mentioned among harpers in *The *House of Fame* (1208), seems to be the 'Y Bardd Glas Keraint', the Blue Bard (i.e. chief Bard) Keraint (or Geraint) of Wales (*Walys*) who probably lived in the 10th c. Not much is known about him, nor is it known

215

how Chaucer came to hear of him. He is probably the same as Glasgerion, a harper who appears in a ballad (which might possibly go back to the Middle Ages). In a later 18th c. version he is said to be able to harp a fish out of salt water, water out of a stone, or milk out of a maiden's breast.

Glose, glosynge (n.), glose(n) (v.) (from L., ultimately Greek *glossa*, a 'gloss' or explanatory note written in the margin of a text) meant 'interpretation', 'interpret', but had also developed pejorative senses, 'specious interpretation', 'mislead', 'deceive', etc. In the Prologue to The *Legend of Good Women* 'in pleyn text, withouten nede of glose' (328) the word is used in its neutral sense, but in a passage in The *Summoner's Tale* (III.1788–96) both the word and the practice of expounding the true spirit of a text rather than its literal meaning are treated with irony. The friar says that his sermon was 'nat al after the text of hooly writ', because that is hard. He will rather teach 'al the glose', because the letter kills: 'glosynge is a glorious thyng'. He alludes to the technique of 'glosynge' later when he claims that when Christ said 'blessed are the poor in spirit' he particularly meant friars ('I ne have no text of it . . . | But I shal fynde it in a maner glose', III.1920). *Friars were famed (and notorious) for their ingenious feats of interpretation. In Chaucer 'glose' usually has a bad sense, 'mislead' or 'deceive' (e.g. IX.34; VII.2141; X.45), or 'flatter' (Jankin—a 'clerk'—knew how to 'glose' the *Wife of Bath, III.509). The phrase 'withouten glose' in V.166 means 'truthfully'.

GLOUCESTER; Golden Legend. See *Thomas of Gloucester; *Jacobus da Voragine.

GODWIN, WILLIAM (1756–1836), political philosopher and novelist, was educated at Hoxton Academy, and began life as a Dissenting minister. Later he became an atheist, anarchist, and vegetarian. He taught benevolence; man was perfectible, and rational creatures could live harmoniously together without laws. As well as pamphlets and novels, his works include *An Enquiry concerning Political Justice* (1793) and the life of his first wife, Mary Wollstonecraft, the mother of Mary Shelley

(1798). His *Life of Chaucer* appeared in 1803. He describes himself as a 'novice', and while he was able to make use of Dryden, Urry, and Tyrwhitt, he did not make significant contributions to Chaucerian scholarship. As a critic, however, he was one of the most interesting commentators of the period. He recognized the achievements of medieval culture, and insisted on seeing the writer in his own age. He thought, like some of his predecessors, that Chaucer was 'the father of our language', who 'fixed and naturalised the genuine art of poetry in our island'. He had strong views about narrative: he thought The *Knight's Tale* 'full of novelty and surprise' and the 'most powerful portrait of chivalry that was perhaps ever delineated' more to the taste of the age than the 'naked and desolate simplicity of the Troilus', which was 'considerably barren of incident'. The 'falsing' of Criseyde offended him: he thought that if a love story had a tragical conclusion, 'it should not be one which arises out of the total unworthiness of either'. But he praised it for its passages 'of exquisite tenderness' and for its characterization. Chaucer's poem presents real life and human sentiments: 'the love he describes is neither frantic, nor brutal, nor artificial, nor absurd. His hero conducts himself in all respects with the most perfect loyalty and honour; and his heroine, however she deserts her character in the sequel, is in the commencement modest, decorous, affectionate, and prepossessing.' And he gives an excellent summary of the variety found in The *Canterbury Tales*: 'splendour of narrative, richness of fancy, pathetic simplicity of incident and feeling, a powerful style in delineating character and manners, and an animated vein of comic humour'.

CH i. 237–47 (extract).

Golias, the giant Goliath 'unmesurable of lengthe', who was slain by the young David armed only with a sling (I. Sam. 17). This event is mentioned in The *Man of Law's Tale* (II.934–8) as an example of God's providential grace.

Goodelief, the wife of Harry Bailly, the *Host, receives a brief but memorable mention when her husband comments on the tale of *Melibee and its message of *patience (VII.1891–1923). According to him, she is extremely impatient and quick to urge him to take violent revenge. It may well be that the choice of a name signifying 'good dear one' is ironic (the real Harry Bailly's wife seems to have been called Christian).

Gootland, probably Gotland, an island in the Baltic off the coast of Sweden (I.408). Jutland, off Denmark, is possible, but the phrase in which the name occurs suggests the great geographical spread of the harbours which the *Shipman knew, and Gotland is further from 'the cape of *Fynystere'.

Gothes, the Ostrogoths, the eastern group of the Goths, a Germanic people. In the 3rd c. AD they settled in the lands between the rivers Don and Dneister, but the incursions of the Huns drove them westwards. They eventually settled in northern Italy. Chaucer mentions them in a gloss in his *Boece (I pr.4:73). (See **Boethius** (*Boece); *Theodoric.)

GOWER, JOHN (*c.*1330–1408), Chaucer's friend and fellow poet. He is the 'moral Gower' to whom (along with *Strode) *Troilus and Criseyde* is 'directed' for correction (V.1586). Little is known about his life. He seems to have been a man of some means, and connected with the law. In 1398 he married Agnes Groundolf. He was a benefactor of the priory of St Mary Overie in Southwark, and lived in Southwark in the latter part of his life. His tomb is in Southwark Cathedral. He is the author of three long poems. The *Mirour de l'omme* (Mirror of Man; in French, ?1376–9) is a learned, moral work which discusses vices and virtues, contains a vivid description of the *seven deadly sins, and some good examples of *estates satire. The Latin *Vox clamantis* (The Voice of one Crying (in the Wilderness)), in seven books, is also a work of satire which stresses the importance of order in society. A *dream vision in book 1 describes the events of the *Peasants' Revolt of 1381. The best known is his long English poem, the *Confessio Amantis. Here he shows himself to be a writer of elegant English verse and a master of the short narrative. His moral concerns appear here too, in his notion of 'honest' or noble *love, the link between concord in man and in the state, his remarks on the corruption of the world, and the advice he gives to rulers. He also wrote shorter poems in all three languages, and the *Cronica tripertita* (1399–1400), a verse chronicle which justifies the overthrow of *Richard II by *Henry IV.

In the 15th c. Gower was regularly linked with Chaucer (and *Lydgate) as a major English poet, and his popularity continued until the time of *Shakespeare, who takes the plot of *Pericles* from his narrative of *Apollonius of Tyre, and brings him on to the stage as a presenter. After a long period of neglect, there has been some serious reappraisal of Gower, but he remains an unjustly neglected poet.

The nature of his friendship with Chaucer has given rise to some discussion. There is no doubt that they were friends. When Chaucer went abroad in 1378 he gave Gower power of attorney. In addition to Chaucer's reference to Gower in *Troilus, Gower in the first version of the *Confessio Amantis* (1390) makes Venus say 'gret wel Chaucer whan ye mete, | As mi disciple and mi Poete', and says that he has filled the land with 'ditees' and 'songes glade'. It has sometimes been suggested that the friendship cooled in the 1390s, because of the *Man of Law's disparaging remarks about the stories of Canace and Apollonius (both told by Gower) in II.77–89—'of swiche cursed stories I sey fy!' and the fact that in most, though not all, of the MSS of the later version of the *Confessio Amantis* do not have the reference to Chaucer. But this is unproven. It is by no means clear that the Man of Law's remarks are straightforwardly disparaging remarks by Chaucer about Gower, and Gower's revision of the ending of his poem seems likely to have been for structural rather than personal reasons.

(ed.) Macaulay (1899–1902); (selections) Bennett (1968*b*); (trans. of Latin works) Stockton (1962); Fisher (1964); Minnis (1983); Wickert (1981).

GRATIAN (12th c.), collector of the material from the fathers, early conciliar and papal decrees that, together with Gratian's own comments, came to form the first part of canon law, the *Decretum* or *Book of *Decrees. This was put together some time after the 1139 Lateran Council, and quickly gained circulation.   [AH]

(ed.) Friedberg (1879–81).

GRAUNSON, OTON DE

GRAUNSON, OTON DE (*c*.1340–1397), a French poet, 'flour of hem that make [compose] in Fraunce', as Chaucer says in **Venus* (82), which is adapted from three of his **ballades. He was also a famous figure of *chivalry, and was in the service successively of *John of Gaunt, *Richard II, and *Henry of Derby (the future Henry IV). Chaucer certainly knew him. Like Chaucer, he wrote verse '*complaints'. Chaucer may have read his two 'St *Valentine' poems. His *Songe Sainct Valentin* has some similarities with *The *Parliament of Fowls*, though it is not a 'model' for Chaucer's poem.

(ed.) Piaget (1941); Braddy (1947).

GRAY, THOMAS (1716–71). The poet and scholar was an enthusiast for earlier English and European literature. His commonplace books contain some notes intended for a history of English poetry. He admired *Lydgate, in some of whose writing he found 'a stiller kind of majesty'; but, he says, 'in images of horrour and a certain terrible greatness' Lydgate comes 'far behind Chaucer'. He does not elaborate on this, but it is interesting that he should find the 'sublime' (a contemporary and personal literary ideal) in Chaucer. He also has some clear and sensible remarks on Chaucer's metre, in which he notes that there have been changes in accent and the pronunciation of the unstressed *e*.

CH i. 215–20.

Grec, Gre(e)k, Grekyssh, Grekissh, Grykkysche, Greek. The adj. is used to describe the nationality of some famous figures (*Synon, Pythagoras (*Pictagoras)); and also the language. References to the language appear in **Boece* (e.g. I pr.1:30; II pr.2:73)—unlike Chaucer, Boethius was familiar with Greek—and in the **Astrolabe* since 'these noble clerkes Grekes' had been important in the history of *astronomy. Greeks appear in some numbers in *The *Knight's Tale* and **Troilus and Criseyde*.

Grece, Grees. Greece in Chaucer's day was part of the Byzantine empire, with its capital at Constantinople. It was already suffering from the attacks of the Ottoman Turks. An army of European Crusaders attempting to relieve Constantinople was disastrously defeated by the Sultan Bajazet at Nicopolis on the banks of the Danube in 1396. There was a Latin duchy of Athens (*Athenes), and Venetian forts at points on the coast. His references, however, are to ancient Greece. It is the setting for some of his stories, notably *The *Knight's Tale*, and a number of the tales in *The *Legend of Good Women*. (See *classical antiquity.)

Grece, See of, the (eastern) Mediterranean (II.464).

Greek Literature, see *classical literature.

GREGORIE, SEINT, Gregory the Great (*c*.540–604), an important figure in the religious culture of the Middle Ages. The son of a Roman senator, he became a monk, and was later elected Pope. His rule was wise and efficient. He was responsible for sending Augustine to convert the Anglo-Saxons. His voluminous writings were very influential. He is several times quoted by the *Parson, and another (unidentified) saying is attributed to him in **Melibee* (VII.1497).

Grekissh, Grekyssh, see *Grec.

Grenewych, Greenwich, now part of *London, about a half-mile past Deptford (*Depeford). The pilgrims pass it on their way out of London. The *Host's remark, 'Lo Grenewych, ther many a shrewe [rascal] is inne!' (I.3907) is usually taken to be a private joke on the part of Chaucer, who may well have been living there at the time of writing the line. He lived in Kent (see Geoffrey *Chaucer: life), and the fact that in 1390 he was made a commissioner of walls and ditches along the Thames between Greenwich and Woolwich may suggest that he had a particular link with the area. The 'Fowle Ok' in Kent where he was robbed in 1390 was in the parish of Deptford (*Depeford).

Grete Se(e), the, the Mediterranean. Chaucer uses the phrase twice (I.59, *BD* 140; see also **See of** *Grece). As in antiquity, it was the best-known sea, and (as its Latin name implies) close to the centre of the world. (See Maps 1, 3.) *Bartholomew says that 'the Great Sea of middle-earth cometh out of the west and out of Ocean and passeth toward the south and then winds toward the north . . . it is called the Great Sea for other seas are little in comparison thereof, and is called the sea of the middle-earth for he passeth by the middle of the earth anon to the east, and departeth three parts of the earth that are called Asia, Africa, and Europa.' The Hereford Mappa Mundi (see *Mappemounde) shows a number of the ancient wonders associated with it: the pillars of Hercules, Mt. Etna in eruption, Scylla and Charybdis (*Caribdis), the Labyrinth (*Laboryntus) in *Crete, and the Colossus of Rhodes.

Grykkysche, see *Grec.

Grisel in *Lenvoy de Chaucer a *Scogan* (35) is apparently a nickname for a grey-haired old man, or (possibly) a grey horse.

Grisild(e), Grisildis, Griselda, the heroine of Chaucer's *Clerk's Tale*, and of the earlier versions of *Boccaccio and Petrarch (*Petrak). She quickly became the proverbial type of the patient wife. Her story was retold and adapted (from one or more of the early versions) in a variety of forms. She appears in English broadside ballads and in plays (e.g. *Patient Grissil* by Dekker, Chettle and Haughton, 1599–1600). There was a 14th-c. French play, *L'estoire de Griseldis* (based on a French translation of Petrarch). The MS contains a series of interesting drawings. The story produced some fine illustrations—a series from *c.*1500 adorns a *cassone* or dower chest (now in the National Gallery). In the 19th c. it could be seen in the form of puppet plays. Other versions of the story include an opera by Vivaldi, set in the ancient world. In this, Ottone loves Griselda, but the people complain of her low birth: this is the reason for the test. In another, by Massenet, *Grisélidis* (1901), she has an admirer Alain, but refuses the Devil's suggestion that her husband is unfaithful, and rejects Alain. He takes her child, and it is eventually retrieved by the Marquis.

Cooper (1989), 423–4; R. S. Loomis (1965), 151–60.

GROSSETESTE, ROBERT (*c.*1169–1253). Grosseteste was the leading figure in English scholastic life in the first half of the 13th c., and had a considerable influence on European thought—especially in the natural sciences—throughout the later Middle Ages. He was born of humble stock in the county of Suffolk, and was perhaps educated in the schools of Lincoln and Oxford. He was in the household of the bishop of Hereford by 1198, and might later have taught at Oxford until the dispersion of students and masters of 1209–14, but we can say with certainty only that the first fifty years of his life were spent in relative obscurity. From this Grosseteste had emerged by 1225, by which time he was lecturing on theology in Oxford. He left there in 1235 when he was appointed bishop of Lincoln—then England's largest diocese—and he died in that office in 1253.

Although not a Franciscan, already by 1232 Grosseteste had given up all secular positions to live something approximating to the Franciscan life. From about 1229 to 1235 he was lecturer in theology to the Oxford Franciscans, and was largely responsible for turning their interests to the study not only of the Bible but of the natural sciences and *Aristotle. By the early 1220s he had written two or three works on the computus (calendar calculation), and commentaries on Aristotle's *Prior Analytics* and parts of the *Physics*. Before leaving Oxford he had extended the latter, and might also have composed his great *Hexaëmeron*, chief of several commentaries on scripture (in this case, on the six days of the Creation). He had then begun to study Greek, and at Lincoln, with the help of assistants, he secured translations of Aristotle's *Nicomachean Ethics* and *De cœlo* (*On the Heavens*), together with various Neoplatonic works. He knew some Hebrew, and had the Psalms translated directly from that language. He had the skills of medical practitioner and lawyer, but above all was a Christian philosopher, who had been much influenced in early life by a new translation of Avicenna's *On the Soul* and Augustine's *City of God* (see *Avycen; *Austyn). Grosseteste was aptly described by Beryl Smalley as the 'Erasmus of the Middle Ages'.

Grosseteste inherited a *cosmology that was in outline more or less Aristotelian. By the 13th c., however, one of the standard ways of 'reading' the universe was the way of astrology. He used astrological methods in medicine and meteorology, and one of the earliest items of his own handwriting is on a diagram showing an astrologically significant conjunction. Such concerns, and his Neoplatonism, help to explain his recurrent use of the concept of light in philosophical explanation. He decided that light (*lux*) was the fundamental corporeal substance, the first form to be created by God in prime matter, and that optics must therefore be at the foundation of all physics. He introduced these ideas even into his theology; and the hierarchies that he saw in the cosmos he wished to be mirrored in a centralized and hierarchical Church.

Grosseteste wanted the reform not only of the Church but of its calendar, and his writings on this theme were well planned and highly influential (through *Bacon, especially), although the Julian calendar was not to be replaced until 1582—and not in his own country for much longer. His greatest influence on fundamental Western science, however, was achieved through his writings on geometrical optics (refraction, mirrors, the rainbow, vision, and so on) and his vigorous preaching of a scientific method that was primarily Aristotle's. His astronomical and optical knowledge led him to insist on the scientific importance of mathematics—a principle proclaimed repeatedly by his leading advocate, the Franciscan Roger Bacon. (See also *astrology and astronomy; *conjunccio(u)n; *Kalendere; *medicine; Plato; Somer; *weather.) [JDN]
Crombie (1953); McEvoy (1982); Smalley (1955), 96; Southern (1986).

GUYDO (DE COLUMPNIS), Guido delle Colonne, a Sicilian judge who in 1287 completed the *Historia destructionis Troiae*, a Latin prose redaction of the *Roman de Troie* of *Benoît de Sainte-Maure. It was widely regarded as authoritative, and was translated into several languages. Guido reduced the element of the marvellous in Benoît's story, and also his stress on the power of passionate love. He presented the story as a chronicle. In *The House of Fame* (1469) Guido is one of those who 'bear up' the fame of Troy. He is also mentioned in *The Legend of Good Women* (1396, 1464), where Chaucer is using his account of *Jason for the tale of *Hypsipyle and *Medea. He also used him for the Trojan material in *Troilus and Criseyde*. And when he was writing the opening to the *General Prologue* he may have recalled a *chronographia* (or 'setting of time') in the *Historia* in which the sun has just entered Aries, the weather begins to entice

mortals into the air, springs bubble up, seeds sprout, and crops and leaves are renewed.
(ed.) Griffin (1936); (trans.) Meek (1974); C. D. Benson (1980).

Guildsmen and Guilds. In the *General Prologue* (361–78) there is a brief description of a group of five Guildsmen. It consists of a carpenter and four clothworkers—a haberdasher (a dealer in caps and small wares), a 'webbe' (weaver), a dyer, a 'tapycer' (weaver of tapestry). They all belong to the same guild, 'a solempne and a greet fraternitee', and wear its distinctive ceremonial livery. It is not possible to identify any particular historical guild with certainty. The fact that they are not all of the same trade suggests that we are not dealing with a 'craft guild' but rather with a 'parish guild', an association for religious and charitable purposes. The guildsmen have brought their wives along, and have their own *Cook. They cut a grand figure, and their evident desire to impress is shared by their wives ('it is ful fair to been ycleped [called] "madame"'; cf. I.3956).

Guilds played an important role in medieval commercial and economic life. Two important types were the merchant guilds, associations of traders involved in a variety of forms of commerce, and the craft guilds, associations of particular trades (goldsmiths, fishmongers, mercers, butchers, smiths, etc). These were concerned with the commercial interest of the members, but also had social, educational, and religious functions. Craft guilds, which were very prominent in England, were associations of 'masters', established craftsmen who owned shops. They fixed the basic rules of the trade, and operated an apprenticeship system. Young boys were taken on for fixed terms of service during which they worked without wages and were taught the 'mysteries' of the craft. The masters provided food, lodging, and education, and stood *in loco parentis*. Chaucer's *Perkyn is an example of a lively but unsuccessful apprentice in 'a craft of vitailliers [victuallers]'. The successful apprentice would then become a journeyman free to work for wages, and eventually, perhaps, a master.

Guilds appeared in a great variety of forms, ranging from the large and powerful craft guilds of *London (which took a prominent part in civic pageantry) to essentially devotional confraternities. Their social and charitable functions included the distribution of alms to the widows and orphans of their members, and to the deserving poor in general. They could also make a contribution to cultural life: in Venice, the *scuole* (lay charitable fraternities) commissioned important works of art, while in England the craft guilds were closely involved with the staging of the mystery plays (see *drama). There was sometimes considerable rivalry between powerful guilds, but there were also cases of successful cooperation, the most celebrated being the German Hansa or Hanseatic League, a league of urban merchant guilds which fostered trade in the Baltic and the North Sea.

(ed.) *Rv* 29, 813–14; Cooper (1989), 47; Mann (1973), 103–5; S. Reynolds (1984); Unwin (1908).

GUILLAUME DE DEGUILLEVILLE, a French Cistercian monk, the author of three allegorical poems: the *Pélerinage de la vie humaine* (the Pilgrimage of Human Life, 1331 (revised 1355)), followed by the *Pélerinage de l'âme* (the Pilgrimage of the Soul), and the *Pélerinage de Jésus Christ*. The first two were translated into English in the 15th c. The *Pélerinage de la vie humaine* was extremely popular. It survives in many MSS, often illustrated. Its allegorical narrative tells of the journey through life of the Pilgrim, in which he meets both spiritual helpers like Grace Dieu (the Grace of God) or Reason, and enemies, like the *Seven Deadly Sins. Chaucer's *ABC* is an adaptation of a prayer to the Virgin Mary (*Marie) found in it.

GUILLAUME DE LORRIS, the author of the first part of the *Roman de la Rose*, written 1225–40. Almost nothing is known of his life. He was presumably born in Lorris (east of Orléans), and was probably of noble birth. He refers to or uses a number of ancient authors (e.g. Macrobius, Ovid), but does not flourish his learning in the manner of *Jean de Meun, who continued the poem.

GUILLAUME DE MACHAUT (*c*.1300–1377), a French composer and poet. He is known to have been in the service of John of Luxemburg, the king of Bohemia, for a number of years, gaining various ecclesiastical benefices. Other patrons or dedicatees include John's daughter, Bonne of Luxemburg, the wife of King John II of France,

King Charles II of Navarre, and Jean, duke of Berry. In 1337 he became a canon of Rheims, where he was buried after his death in 1377. He was the most important and innovative French composer of the 14th c. His work includes motets, lais, virelais, rondeaux, and ballades, as well as the earliest-known complete setting of the Mass by a single composer. He was a pioneer of the polyphonic style. Most of his music was not written for the Church, but for his secular songs and lyrics, monophonic lais, and polyphonic *ballades and *rondeaux. It shows considerable skill in uniting words and music, and in creating intricate formal structures. His poetry, while less remarkable, was very influential. *Deschamps, *Froissart, and Chaucer all learnt much from him.

In addition to his lyrics he wrote a number of *dits* or narrative poems concerning love. These are influenced by the *Roman de la Rose* but are much shorter and less strictly allegorical. The *Jugement dou Roy de Behaigne* (Judgement of the King of Bohemia), a debate between a knight whose lady has been unfaithful and a lady whose lover has died, poses the question which one of them is the more unhappy. The king declares the knight to be the greater sufferer. That this judgement caused discussion is suggested by the complementary poem the *Jugement dou Roy de Navarre*. This has an autumn setting and begins with some gloomy reflections on the calamities which are afflicting the world, especially the plague. When the poet rides out hunting he meets a lady Bonneurté. She says that the king of Bohemia's judgement was an insult to womankind. Machaut defends himself. In the argument held before the king of Navarre, Bonneurté's ladies give examples of women who have suffered for love. The king finds against Machaut, and he (identified as 'Guillaume') has to do penance by composing three poems. The *Livre dou voir dit* (true story) describes the love affair between the ageing poet and a young lady. A number are *consolations. In the *Remède de Fortune*, which contains lyrics set to music, the lover becomes a victim of Fortune, but is consoled by Hope. The *Confort d'ami* is offered as a consolation for Charles of Navarre in his imprisonment, and the *Fonteinne amoureuse* for the enforced separation of the duke of Berry from his young wife. Machaut also wrote some shorter *dits*, like the *Dit de la marguerite* (Daisy) and the *Dit de la fleur de lis et de la marguerite* (Lily and Daisy).

The reader of Chaucer will already have recognized some suggestive parallels. Chaucer seems to have had an extensive knowledge of Machaut's narrative poetry. Its influence is most obvious in The *Book of the Duchess*, where he used the *Jugement dou Roy de Behaigne* and other *dits* (e.g. the *Fonteinne amoureuse*, which has a passage on *Morpheus and the story of Ceyx (*Seys) and Alcyone (*Alcione). There are echoes of Machaut in other works, e.g. in the Prologue to The *Legend of Good Women* (where *Alceste appears in the likeness of a daisy). For his account in The *Monk's Tale* of Pierre de Lusignan (*Petro (2) kyng of Cipre) Chaucer may have used Machaut's last poem, the *Prise d'Alexandrie* (The Capture of Alexandria (*Alisaundre)), a chronicle of his life and death. It is possible that the lost *Book of the Lion* was an adaptation of Machaut' s *Dit dou Lyon* (which, with its magic boat, enchanted island, and faithful lion, is close to *romance). More generally, Chaucer found a model for his distinctive development of the comic narrator in Machaut, who sometimes presents himself as fearful and uncomprehending.

(ed.) Hoepffner (1908–21); Poirion (1965); Reaney (1971).

GUINIZELLI, GUIDO (*c*.1230–1275) of Bologna, Italian poet. His canzone 'Al cor gentil rempaira sempre Amore' (Love always seeks his dwelling in the gentle heart) insists on the unity of noble love and true '*gentilesse' ('Within the gentle heart love shelters him, | As birds within the green shade of the grove. | Before the gentle heart, in Nature's scheme, | Love was not, nor the gentle heart ere love' (D. G. Rossetti)). This, and the way in which Guido combined passion and intellect to create a philosophical poetry of love, profoundly impressed *Dante, who quotes and echoes the canzone several times. Chaucer's lines in *Troilus and Criseyde* 'Plesance of love, O goodly debonaire, | In gentil hertes ay redy to repaire' (III.4–5) seem to be a clear echo of the poem's opening. It is not certain that Chaucer knew the whole poem at first hand: he could well have picked up this passage from Dante. However, the sentiments of *Antigone's song in *Troilus* are similar to

Guinizelli's. Whether at first hand, or via Dante, Guinizelli's ideas influenced Chaucer.

(ed.) Marti (1969).

Guy of Warwick, a popular English romance (?*c*.1300) deriving ultimately (like *Bevis of Hampton* (*Beves), which it resembles in other ways) from an earlier Anglo-Norman romance. The Middle English poem exists in different versions. In that of the *Auchinleck MS, Guy, the son of Syward of Wallingford, falls in love with Felice, the daughter of the earl of Warwick. When he is rejected, he goes overseas to prove himself in tournaments. Sent away yet again by his beloved, he wins glory in battle, and the emperor of Constantinople offers him his daughter in marriage. He refuses (as he had previously done with a French princess), and after seven years returns to England, where he kills a dragon and marries Felice. After only a short time he leaves his bride, who is now pregnant, and sets out on a pilgrimage to Jerusalem. He has suddenly been struck by the thought that he has never served God in the way he has suffered hardship for the sake of his lady. Felice laments, and gives him a gold ring. After further adventures, disguised as a palmer he returns to England, and saves King Athelstan from Anlaf and the Danes by overcoming the giant Colbrond in an epic battle. He retires to Warwick, and lives as a hermit. On the point of death he reveals his identity to Felice by means of the ring. In grief she follows him to the grave. The romance ends with the adventures of Reinbrun, son of Guy and Felice.

The story is an *exemplum of loyalty and of military lay *piety. It 'had everything' (love, battles, adventures, renunciation, and religion) and not surprisingly became one of the favourite stories of the Middle Ages. It travelled all over Europe, and lived on in popular literature until the 19th c. Supposed relics of Guy are still to be found in Warwick castle; Guy's Cliffe, near Warwick, is the legendary site of his hermitage.

Chaucer seems to have known it well. In *Sir Thopas* he mentions the hero by name (VII.899, linking him with the equally popular hero *Beves), and he made use of it for his parody of popular romance: there are a couple of particularly close verbal similarities (VII.772–4 and 804–6).

(ed.) Zupitza (1883–91).

H

Habradate(s), Abradates, king of the Susi. In her lament, *Dorigen says that when he was killed, his wife killed herself, and let her own blood flow into his wounds (V.1414–18). Chaucer found the story in St *Jerome.

Hayles, Hailes Abbey (Gloucestershire), a Cistercian monastery founded in 1246. It was famous for a *relic, a vial of the Precious Blood of Christ. Hence the oath 'by the blood of Crist that is in Hayles', mentioned by the *Pardoner (VI.652).

HALY, one of the authorities known to the Doctour of Physik (*Physician), according to the *General Prologue. He might have been meant as any one of the following: (1) Abû'l-Hasan 'Alî ibn 'Abbâs al-Majûsi (d. 994). Persian physician, pharmacologist and writer on natural philosophy. Al-Majûsi was employed in the royal household at Shariz, where he wrote a medical compendium that became popular in the West in Latin translation under the title *Liber Regius*. He was known in the West as Haly Abbas. Constantine the African made his work on phlebotomy a standard European source (see *Constantyn). (2) Abû'l-Hasan 'Alî ibn Ridwân (998–c.1069). An Egyptian royal physician, his commentaries on Hippocrates and Galen circulated in the West in Latin translation. His commentaries on Ptolemy's astrological writings and on much of Aristotle were also known there. (3) Abû'l-Hasan 'Alî ibn Abi al-Rijâl (*fl.* 988–1040). Active in Córdoba or Tunis. Little is known of his life. Under such names as Haly Abenragel, Haly, and Albohazen, the Latin translation of a work of his on astrology became one of the most popular of Western texts. It contains an interesting passage of relevance to the thorny problem of the word 'atazir' in The *Man of Law's Tale* (l. 305). It also contains some medical astrology, which was occasionally abstracted and copied in a separate recension.

(See also *astrology and astronomy; *Galyen; medicine; *Ptholomee; *Ypocras.)   [JDN]

HANYBAL, Hannibal (247–183 or 182 BC), the famous Carthaginian general who invaded Italy during the Second Punic War. In The *Man of Law's Tale* (II.290) there is an allusion to the 'harm' caused by his attack on Rome. The remark that he vanquished the Romans 'tymes thre' probably refers to his crushing victories at Trebia (218), Lake Trasimene (217), and Cannae (216).

harp; Harpies; Harry Bailly. See *musical instruments; *Arpies; *Host.

HARVEY, GABRIEL (d. 1631), born at Saffron Walden, the son of a rope-maker, was educated at Cambridge, and became a Fellow of Pembroke Hall. He was a humanist scholar of very wide interests (including rhetoric, mathematics, medicine, and navigation) and a friend of the poet *Spenser. His books and MSS are filled with marginalia. Those concerning Chaucer (one set of which are in his copy of *Speght's edition) show a great admiration for the poet and an awareness of the range of his learning. Others, he says, commend Chaucer and Lydgate 'for their wit, pleasant vein, variety of poetical discourse, and all humanity', but 'I specially note their astronomy, philosophy, and other parts of profound or cunning art'. In these 'few of their time were more exactly learned': 'It is not sufficient for poets to be superficial humanists: but they must be exquisite artists, and curious universal scholars.' As a rhetorician, he clearly relished Chaucer's 'notable descriptions, and not any so artificial in Latin or Greek'. Chaucer is 'excellent in every vein and humour'. Some notes offer brief descriptions of the tales: The *Summoner's Tale* is 'an odd jest in scorn of friars', The *Clerk's Tale* is 'moral and pathetical'; *Troilus and Criseyde* is praised as 'a piece of brave, fine, and sweet poetry'.

CH i. 120–4; (ed.) Moore-Smith (1913).

Hasdrubales wyf, wife of Hasdrubal, the ruler of Carthage when the Romans finally destroyed it in 146 BC. *Dorigen in The *Franklin's Tale* recalls how she took her own life when the Romans took Carthage, throwing herself and her children into the fire to avoid dishonour (V.1399–404). The same episode is mentioned (in mock-heroic vein) in The *Nun's Priest's Tale* (VII.3362–8). Chaucer probably read the story in St *Jerome.

hats, see *clothes.

HAWES, STEPHEN, poet and groom of the chamber to Henry VII. His long allegorical poem *The Passetyme of Pleasure* (printed in 1509) describes the quest of Graunde Amoure for his beloved, La Bell Pucell, and the accomplishments that are necessary for an ideal knight. The *Example of Vertu* (printed 1512) is also a moral didactic work. Hawes was deeply influenced by Chaucer's style, which he attempts to decorate and elaborate. The *Passetyme* contains a praise of the earlier poet for 'kyndlynge our hertes with the fyry leames | Of morall vertue', and singles out some individual works for mention: 'the Boke of Fame which is sentencyous'; 'the tragydyes so pyteous | Of the nyntene ladyes' (The *Legend of Good Women); The *Canterbury Tales* ('some vertuous, and some glade and mery'); and the 'pytous dolour' of Troilus 'for his lady Cresyde full of doublenesse'.

CH i. 81–2; (ed.) Mead (1928).

HAWKWOOD, SIR JOHN (d. 1394), a famous *condottiere* or military captain, 'a fine English knight', according to *Froissart. He fought in Gascony as the leader of a troop of English mercenaries known as the White Company. They moved to Italy, and fought for various cities and princes. The force was a formidable and disciplined one, consisting of a thousand lances and two thousand infantry, and specializing in ruthless night raids. In 1368 he entered the service of the Visconti at Milan, and married a daughter of Bernabò Visconti (*Barnabo Viscounte). He ended his career as commander of the Florentine forces. Hawkwood (or

'Acuto' as he was called in Italy) died in *Florence, received a state funeral, and was buried in the *duomo*, where he can still be seen in a mural painting, riding proudly. The purpose of Chaucer's mission to Italy in 1376 (see Geoffrey *Chaucer: life) was to negotiate with Bernabò and Hawkwood.

HAZLITT, WILLIAM (1778–1830), critic and essayist. His relatively brief remarks about Chaucer are lucid and intelligent. He shared his period's interest in *characterization, arguing (in 'Characters of Shakespeare's Plays', 1817) that compared with Shakespeare's, Chaucer's have little relief or light and shade, and lack the blend of ludicrous and ironical and the stately and impassioned found in Shakespeare. Chaucer is 'the most literal of poets': 'every thing in Chaucer has a downright reality'. He has perceptive remarks on individual characters (Criseyde is 'a grave, sober, considerate personage . . . who has an alternate eye to her character, her interest, and her pleasure') and passages (like Criseyde's first avowal of her love). In *Lectures on the English Poets* (1818) he says that (compared with *Spenser) Chaucer 'was the most practical of all the great poets, the most like a man of business and the world'. He praises the way he 'dwells only on the essential', his precision, and the minuteness of circumstances. Chaucer 'does not affect to shew his power over the reader's mind, but the power which his subject has over his own'. His readers 'feel more nearly what the persons he describes must have felt, than perhaps those of any other poet'. He notes that 'the picturesque and the dramatic are in him closely blended together, and hardly distinguishable; for he principally describes external appearances as indicating character, as symbols of internal sentiment. There is a meaning in what he sees'. Hazlitt responds not only to the comic tales, but, very warmly and sympathetically, to the 'pitous' stories told by the *Clerk, the *Man of Law, and the *Prioress. Chaucer has an imagination 'that reposes entirely on nature' and therefore has strength as well as simplicity: 'in depth of simple pathos, and intensity of conception, never swerving from his subject, I think no other writer comes near him, not even the Greek tragedians'. Hazlitt's *Select Poets of Great Britain*, which appeared in 1825, contains a number of Canterbury tales.

CH i. 272–84.

Heaven and Hell. Chaucer does not, as *Dante does, use heaven and hell, and purgatory, as the imaginative setting for a spiritual journey. Nor do we find in him the extended vivid descriptions of the pains of hell and the joys of heaven frequently found in medieval devotional works. However, incidental references show that he was aware of the common traditional features. Thus, he assumes that heaven is the dwelling-place of God and the angels, and of the saints, and ultimately of all the redeemed who receive the reward of eternal life and bliss. In The *Second Nun's Tale* Maximus sees the souls glide to heaven 'with aungels ful of cleernesse and of light' (VIII.402–3), and earlier, heaven is described as 'swift and round and eek brennynge' (VIII.114). But most references (even in The *Parson's Tale*) are very general: Christ is 'the Kyng of Hevene with his woundes newe' (II.458); the Virgin Mary is the 'blisful hevene quene' (*ABC* 24); heaven is the home of angels (VII.3292), and is a place of 'bliss' (VI.912). *Hevene* is the usual word in ME for 'sky' (a word which Chaucer uses only twice, V.503, and *HF* 1600, there in its older sense of 'cloud'), and the 'heavens' are full of significance (see *astronomy and astrology); cf. II.190–2. It is not therefore surprising that he uses *heven(e)* for the abode of the pagan gods (*Tr* III.590, etc.), and more generally in ancient contexts (*Tr* III.8). Heaven is frequently used figuratively for bliss (IV.1647, *Tr* II.826, etc.) or associated with the exquisite *joy of *love (*Tr* III.1322).

Hell was traditionally the place of punishment for the wicked after death, and in the Middle Ages was thought to be down beneath the earth. It was a place of spiritual and physical torment. Satan was bound there. After his death on the cross Christ descended there to 'harrow' or despoil it, releasing the souls of the Old Testament patriarchs who had died before the Redemption (hence the formulaic phrase 'hym that harwed helle' I.3512, III.2107).

The *Parson talks of the penitential value of remembering the pains of hell, and in the manner of penitential treatises gives a quite detailed account (X.158 ff.), mostly composed of scriptural quotations. It is a place of darkness, but of 'darkness visible'. Job calls it the 'land of darkness': it is 'dark' because of the absence of light, but 'the derke light that shal come out of the fyr that evere shal brenne [burn]' brings pain to the sinner by showing him the devils tormenting him. There, sinners do not have the sight of God, and suffer 'misease' of various kinds. There are no joys or delights for the senses. Hell is the shadow of death because it is like the pain of death, but its inhabitants will never die. Unlike the rest of God's creation, hell has no order. It is a place of eternal horror and 'grisly dread', and a place without hope. Apart from a remark that adulterers suffer in a pool burning with fire and brimstone (X.840), there is (in contrast with Dante) little about the torments reserved for particular groups of sinners.

Chaucer's other works contain allusions to these traditional features. 'The serpent' is 'depe in helle ybounde' (II.361). There fiends lie 'ful lowe adoun' (VII.2464), etc. Such allusions: to the darkness of 'helle-pit' (*BD* 171), to its smell (*HF* 1654), or to its noise (*HF* 1803), are often in the form of similes, and suggest that the lore is familiar and proverbial, and can be treated in a not totally serious way (cf. *NPT* VII.3389, and see The *Friar's Tale* and The *Summoner's Tale*).

The word *helle* is frequently used for the classical underworld. It too is a place of torment: Sisyphus (*Cesiphus) lies there (*BD* 589). When *Orpheus 'wente hym to the houses of helle' he assuaged the torments and made the Furies weep, only to look back when he reached 'the laste boundes of helle' (*Bo* III m.12), etc. Again, it is familiar enough to appear in similes: Troilus suffers woe 'as sharp as he *Ticius in helle' (I.786).

Purgatory, the place where souls were purged through pain before they were admitted to Heaven, is twice mentioned by the Parson (X.715, 808). Elsewhere it is only found in figurative senses, applied to the torments of love (I.1225–6), or wedlock: 'in erthe | was his purgatorie' says the Wife of Bath (III.489), and old January who desires a young wife is warned, 'paraunter she may be youre purgatorie' (IV.1670).

Hector, see *Ector.

hed(e), heed, heved, head. In *A Treatise on the *Astrolabe* and *Equatorie of the Planetis*, the word denotes the first degree or beginning of the sign (L. *caput Arietis*, etc.). It is used in practice of only four signs, but that is because they are of special importance. The four are Aries, Cancer, Libra, and Capricorn. The Sun's entering those signs marks the commencement of the four seasons, spring, summer, autumn, and winter. The head of Aries is the reference point from which *longitudes are measured along the *ecliptic. (See also *months and seasons; *signe.) [JDN]

heyte, height, elevation, altitude, especially of a star or planet above the horizon, measured in degrees, minutes, etc. in *A Treatise on the *Astrolabe*. Chaucer announces his intention of using the word 'altitude' in preference to it, however. (See *astrology and astronomy.) [JDN]

Helie, Eli, the Old Testament priest, whose sons were 'sons of Belial; they knew not the Lord' (I Sam. 2:12). The *Parson says that sinful priests are the sons of Eli (X.897).

Hell, see *Heaven and Hell.

Helowys, Héloïse (d. 1163 or 1164), the lover and later the wife of Abelard, the 12th-c. philosopher, theologian, and poet. After their secret marriage, Abelard was attacked and castrated by followers of her uncle. He tells his story in the *Historia Calamitatum* (History of my Calamities). Héloïse entered a nunnery at Argenteuil near Paris, later becoming its prioress, and ended her life as abbess of the oratory of the Paraclete near Troyes. A series of letters between them survives. Hers show a remarkable passion, sensitivity, and learning. In them she talks about their relationship as well as spiritual matters. She recalls that she argued against 'an ill-starred marriage', saying that she preferred 'love to wedlock and freedom to chains'. When she laments that she was the cause of the disaster, she mentions other (traditional) examples of women who brought great men down. When *Jean de Meun (who translated the *Letters* into French) tells her story in the *Roman de la Rose* he puts it into the mouth of a jealous husband to illustrate the argument that marriage is best avoided (8759–832), and gives a summary of the arguments she had used to Abelard. It is presumably because of these arguments (whether or not Chaucer knew the *Letters* directly) that 'Helowys,

| That was abbesse nat fer fro Parys' is mentioned in *The *Wife of Bath's Prologue* as one of the authors in *Jankyn's (4) anti-feminist book (III.676–7).

(ed.) Muckle (1950–55); (trans.) Radice (1974); Dronke (1976); Mann (1991), 51–4.

Hemonides, Maeon, the son of Haemon, mentioned in *Troilus and Criseyde* (V.1492). He was sent by Eteocles (*Ethiocles), ruler of *Thebes (1), to attack *Tydeus. Tydeus slew all his companions, and he alone escaped.

Hengwrt Manuscript, MS Peniarth 392D in the National Library of Wales, is the earliest extant MS of *The *Canterbury Tales*. It was written apparently by the same scribe who wrote the *Ellesmere MS, but a few years earlier (? *c.*1402–4). Hengwrt and Ellesmere are the most important MSS of the work. In many ways Hengwrt is the better witness to what Chaucer wrote. It is less of an 'edited' production than Ellesmere, and seems to preserve a great many superior readings: it is 'an early and uneditorialized MS of incomparably high quality, with excellent spelling, paragraphing and punctuation' (Pearsall). However, it seems to have been hastily put together, perhaps from a number of separate exemplars. Sections of the text are wanting—e.g. The *Canon Yeoman's *Prologue* and *Tale*, the Merchant's Prologue, and some of the *links—and the order in which the scribe has attempted to arrange the Tales sometimes seems disjointed. Because of the high quality of its individual readings, some editors have argued that it should be the base text. Others, however (including the Riverside editors), have preferred to use Ellesmere, but with substantial emendations from Hengwrt.

(facsimile) Ruggiers (1979); Pearsall (1985), 11–13; Samuels (1983); Blake (1985).

HENRY IV, HENRY OF DERBY (1366–1413), king of England from 1399 following the deposition of *Richard II. Henry was the son of *John of Gaunt and grandson of *Edward III; he became earl of Derby in 1377 and later, following the death of his father early in 1399, duke of Lancaster; his invasion of England later in 1399 to retrieve the estates of his father was followed by the defeat and imprisonment of Richard. In 1395 Chaucer received a scarlet gown and payment of £10 for livery from Henry. On Henry's accession in 1399 he confirmed the grant on a tun of wine yearly made by Richard II, and confirmed and enlarged the monetary grant of his predecessor; it seems possible that Chaucer's *Complaint to his *Purse*, or at least its envoy, was written before this confirmation.   [AH]

LR 118–19, 525–33; Cavanaugh (1985), 408–11.

HENRY OF GROSMONT, first duke of Lancaster (1310–61), the father of *John of Gaunt's wife *Blanche (to whom *The Book of the Duchess* is a memorial). He was a great soldier and a 'flower of *chivalry' who fought against the heathen (like the *Knight, at '*Algezir' and in '*Pruce') and was renowned for his generosity. In 1352 he wrote *Le Livre de seyntz medicines*, a devotional and confessional prose work. It deals (rather like *The *Parson's Tale*) with remedies for the disease of sin and the wounds caused by the *Seven Deadly Sins. The book is attractively personal, and is an interesting example of 14th-c. lay *piety.

(ed.) Arnould (1940); (trans.) Tavormina (1999).

HENRYSON, ROBERT (d. *c.*1500–5), one of the best, if not the best of the Scottish poets of the late Middle Ages. Almost nothing is known of his life, except that he was a university graduate, and probably a schoolmaster at Dunfermline, and a notary public. His works consist of a collection of thirteen *fables, *The *Testament of Cresseid*, *Orpheus and Eurydice*, and a number of shorter poems. He is a highly individual poet, but the influence of Chaucer is evident in his writing. One of his fables is based on the story of *The *Nun's Priest's Tale*, and the whole collection shows a Chaucerian irony and humanity. The prominence of the figure of the narrator also owes much to Chaucer's example. The *Testament of Cresseid* tells the story of the end of Criseyde, which 'worthie Chaucer glorious' had not given in his *Troilus and Criseyde*. The *Testament* was printed in William *Thynne's edition of Chaucer (1532) after *Troilus and Criseyde*, and continued to appear in later editions until the late 18th c. (although Francis Thynne, the editor's son, had pointed out that it was not by Chaucer). The result was that this

poem of Henryson was much more widely known than his other works, and that it had some influence on readers' attitudes to Chaucer's Criseyde.

(ed.) Fox (1981); Gray (1979).

herberwe, herbergage, words for 'lodging'. One of the obvious necessities of life: man, says the *Parson, has need 'of foode . . . of clothyng and herberwe' (X.1030). The need is felt most sharply by those who are away from their own house and have to seek for lodging in a *hostelrye* or an *in(n)* or find hospitality elsewhere: travellers, merchants (see II.146–7), and pilgrims (the itinerary of Chaucer and his companions after they leave the shelter of the *Tabard Inn is not fully worked out, but there is a reference (VIII.589) to another *hostelrie* along the way). There would be considerable variety both in the finding of lodgings and in the quality of the hospitality. The king and his household could instal themselves in a castle or in some of the best houses in a town. Others (usually neither the most powerful nor the poorest) had to pay. Others might find hospitality in a monastery, which had a religious duty to provide it (probably only the most important guests stayed in the monastery itself; the majority would be lodged in the guest-house). There were hostels belonging to the 'Knights Hospitallers' (the Knights of the Order of the Hospital of St John of Jerusalem, or the 'Knights of Rhodes') a knightly order whose members were bound by religious vows, which had been instituted to provide hospitality and protection for Crusaders and pilgrims (these are the 'hospitaliers' mentioned by the Parson, X.891). Hospitality could also be sought in castles, manors, and houses.

In the Middle Ages hospitality was a duty for Christians: 'harbouring the stranger' was the fourth of the bodily works of mercy. It also accorded with ideals of courtesy (*curteisie). But this probably simply reinforced the powerful social obligation of hospitality in a 'traditional' society. In modern secular urbanized societies it is no longer usual to give food and lodging to strangers who knock at your door. The ideals of hospitality are reflected in a number of medieval literary works. In *Sir Gawain and the Green Knight*, for instance, Gawain is welcomed with great ceremonial when he arrives by chance after a long journey at the castle of Sir Bertilak, though here, as in some other romances and folk tales, the narrative pattern arouses some uncertainty about the motives of the (possibly magical) host. In Chaucer, The *Reeve's Tale gives a more homely version of the rituals of hospitality. Here the miller's visitors, the two clerks, are not strangers, and propose to pay: 'for the love of God they hym bisoght | Of herberwe and of ese, as for hir peny' (I.4118–19). Their host provides them with food, drink, and beds: What follows does not accord with the ideal ritual of hospitality, or with the romance pattern of the potentially magical host: here the guests have already been cheated, and it is the host and his family who need to be vigilant.

'Seynt *Julyan, loo, bon hostel!' exclaims the *Eagle, about to deposit Chaucer at the House of Fame after a long aerial journey, appealing to the patron saint of hospitality, travellers, and innkeepers. Travellers and lodgers in the Middle Ages often needed protection, spiritual or physical, against the very real danger of robbers or even murderers. There is a reflection of this in the story told by *Chauntecleer in The *Nun's Priest's Tale about the two pilgrims who found lodgings (with some difficulty) in a town (VII.2984–3062), only for one of them to be murdered by his innkeeper. Other stories highlight dangers of a different kind. Lodgings, or lodgers within one's house often encourage erotic adventures. 'Draweth no monkes moore unto youre in' is Harry Bailly's conclusion after The *Shipman's Tale (VII.442). This notion is especially prominent in the *fabliaux of Fragment I. The *Cook underlines it when he remarks that the miller in The Reeve's Tale 'hadde a sharp conclusion | Upon his argument of herbergage' (I.4328–9). It is evident enough in the plot of that tale (and emphasized by repetition of the word herberwe 4119, 4145). Nicholas in The *Miller's Tale, who has 'a chambre . . . in that hostelrye' (I.3203), causes similar difficulties. It appears also to be developing in The Cook's Tale, where the conclusion as it stands has been called 'the recipe for carefree herbergage'. The proverb of 'Solomon' quoted by the Cook, ' "Ne bryng nat every man into thyn hous," | For herberwynge by nyghte is perilous' (I.4331–2), aptly sums up what has been demonstrated by the preceding tale. It

also suggests the existence of a less altruistic view concerning strangers who knock at your door.

Heal (1990); Stanley (1976).

Hereos, loveris maladye of, love-sickness. In The *Knight's Tale the 'woful lovere, daun *Arcite' is unable to sleep or eat, and weeps constantly; his sprits are low, and his voice can no longer be recognized (I.1361–79). His behaviour suggests 'the loveris maladye of Hereos', and also mania 'engendred of humour malencolik'. Love-sickness (aegritudo amoris) as a disease of the mind was recognized and discussed by medieval authorities on *medicine (e.g. *Bernard Gordon). It still forms a prominent part of Burton's discussion of melancholy in the 17th c. 'Hereos' represents the Greek eros, influenced by L. heros ('hero') and herus ('master'). (See also **love**; **melancholy**.)

Rv 831; Wack (1990).

heresy, the formal denial of a defined orthodox doctrine (the term comes from a Greek word meaning 'choice' or 'thing chosen'), theological error. Throughout the Middle Ages a series of movements questioning points of doctrine or critical of ecclesiastical practice (often by contrast with an ideal of Apostolic poverty) were condemned as heresies. In Chaucer's England the most significant of these movements was that of *Wyclif and his followers (see *Loller; Lollards). Chaucer uses the word only once, as part of the ecclesiastical vocabulary of the religion of *love. The god of love accuses Chaucer of having 'translated the Romaunce of the Rose, | That is an heresye ayeins my lawe' (LGW 329–30).

Hermanno, Heremianus, a son of Zenobia (*Cenobia), in The *Monk's Tale (VII.2345).

Hermengyld, the wife of the constable in The *Man of Law's Tale (II.533 ff.).

Hermyon, Hermione, daughter of Menelaus and Helen. She married Neoptolemus, but he was murdered by Orestes who carried her off. She is mentioned in the list of Cupid's saints in the Introduction to The *Man of Law's Tale (II.66) as one who appears in Chaucer's 'large volume', but her story is not in The *Legend of Good Women as we have it. Chaucer would have read it in Ovid's *Heroides* (***Episteles of Ovyde**).

Hermus, a river (modern Gediz) in western Turkey (ancient Lydia) mentioned in **Boece* (III m.10:4). It has a 'rede brinke' (L. *rutilante ripa*) because of the gold deposited on it.

Herodes, Herod. Medieval legend sometimes conflated Herod the Great (d. 4 BC), the king of the Jews, who, according to Matthew 2:16, ordered the Massacre of the Innocents, and Herod Antipas, the tetrarch (4 BC–AD 34), who beheaded **John the Baptist. In the medieval *drama, Herod was often a melodramatic tyrant who ranted and blustered (cf. Shakespeare's phrase 'out-herods Herod', applied to actors who tear a passion to tatters). This is the part which *Absolon in The **Miller's Tale* plays 'to shewe his lightnesse and maistrye' (I.3383–4). The *Pardoner cites Herod (Antipas) as an example of drunkenness, who, filled with wine at his own table (a later addition to the biblical account), ordered the beheading of the Baptist (VI.488–91). The *Prioress calls the *Jews 'cursed folk of Herodes al newe' (VII.574).

Heroides; **Herry Bailly.** See ***Episteles of Ovyde; *Host**.

Herro, Erro, Hero, a priestess of Venus loved by Leander (*Leandre) of Abydos. He would swim across the Hellespont to meet her, guided by her lighted torch. One stormy night he was drowned, and Hero threw herself into the sea. She is mentioned in the Introduction to The *Man of Law's Tale* among the saints of Cupid (II.69), but her story is not in The **Legend of Good Women* as it stands. She is, however, mentioned in the *ballade 'Hyd, Absolon', in the Prologue to *LGW* (F 263, G 217). Chaucer probably knew the story from Ovid's *Heroides* (18).

Hesperus, the Evening Star (Greek *Esperos*, L. *Vesper*), from Ancient times onwards commonly depicted as a boy carrying a torch. He was sometimes associated with Atlas, as a son or a brother, and legend has it that he was swept off Mount Atlas in a whirlwind, having climbed the mountain to observe the stars. In **Boece* I m.5 and

IV m.6 the identity of Hesperus with the Morning Star *Lucifer is asserted.   [JDN]

Hester, see ***Ester**.

Hierse, Herse, the sister of Aglauros, loved by Mercury. The story is alluded to in Troilus's prayer to the gods for help (*Tr* III.729–30). (See ***Aglawros**.)

HILTON, WALTER (d. 1396) a Cambridge graduate, eventually prior of the house of Augustinian canons at Thurgarton (Notts.), and perhaps the most original of the English spiritual writers of his period. His best-known work is the *Scale of Perfection*, in two books, surviving in numerous manuscripts and printed first in 1494 (*STC* 14042). His acquaintance included Adam de Horsley, baron of the exchequer, to whom he addressed a letter *c*.1384 concerning Horsley's desire to enter the Carthusian order; it is thus possible that Chaucer may have known of him.   [AH]
Dictionnaire de Spiritualité VII.525–30.

HIPPOCRATES; Hippolyta; Hypermnestra. See ***Ypocras; *Ypolita; *Ypermystra**.

HOCCLEVE, THOMAS (*c*.1367–1426), one of the most interesting poets of the earlier 15th c., worked for much of his life as a clerk in the office of the Privy Seal. His works include The *Letter of Cupid* (*c*.1402), a version of a poem by **Christine de Pisan; La Male Regle* (1405–6), which gives an account, of his misspent youth in London; The *Regiment of Princes* (1411–12), an ambitious 'mirror for princes' written for Henry Prince of Wales, and other 'public' poems; petitions and religious poems; and in his later years, the *Series*, a collection of short works, with a long introduction, the *Complaint* and the *Dialogue with a Friend*. A very remarkable feature of Hoccleve's poetry is its strongly personal and autobiographical element: his account of his youthful wildness and adventures in London is highly entertaining (as well as morally instructive), the *Regiment* is preceded by a very long introduction in which he meets an old beadsman in a London field to whom he reveals his anxieties about the impending onset of age and poverty, and in the *Complaint* he gives a vivid and moving account of a mental illness he suffered (probably in 1414). Even more than his master Chaucer he is a poet of London, and memorably evokes its taverns and temptations. His admiration for Chaucer is equally personal and powerful: it is very likely that he was acquainted with the older poet (as the beadsman in the *Regiment* seems to imply clearly), and received advice from him. In that poem he says that he remembers his appearance so vividly that he has caused his likeness to be painted in the book (see Fig. 1). His eulogies and laments ('O maister, maister, god thy soule reste!') sound more than conventional.

(ed.) Furnivall (1897 and 1892, 1970); Gollancz (1925, 1970); Burrow (1994).

Hogge, Hodge, a familiar form of *Roger, the name of the *Cook (I.4336). It was later used as a typical name for rustics and 'country clowns'.

HOLCOT, ROBERT (d. 1349), a learned English Dominican friar, who taught at Oxford for a number of years. He wrote numerous influential works. His *Moralitates historiarum* consists of a series of vividly told metaphorical stories. He was interested in 'pictures', metaphorical representations of abstract ideas and especially in ancient *mythography. Chaucer seems to have derived much of the information on *dreams which he uses in The *Nun's Tale from Holcot's commentary on the Book of Wisdom.

Pratt (1977); Smalley (1960), ch. 7.

Holdernesse, 'a mersshy contree' in Yorkshire in which the friar of The *Summoner's Tale preaches and operates (III.1710). It is a flat area east of Hull (*Hulle), which contains some notable churches. It was the home of Sir Peter Bukton, the possible recipient of Chaucer's *Envoy a Bukton*.

holyday, a religious festival, on which work was forbidden (Chaucer's word is *haliday* or *holyday* (pl. *halydayes*), sometimes spelt as two words). These were Sundays, the great church festivals like Easter or Christmas, the major saints' days, and the feast day of the saint to whom the local parish church was dedicated. They could also be

occasions of 'holiday' merriment: parishes celebrated the festival of their saint by 'wakes' accompanied by feasting and entertainment. In Chaucer they are simply part of the texture of ordinary life, and the setting for some not very holy vignettes: it is on Sunday that the *Wife of Bath puts on her voluminous headgear. The carpenter's wife goes to the parish church 'on an haliday' (I.3309) (possibly a feast to be kept by women) where Absolon censes the 'wyves of the parisshe' (3340–1). *Symkyn and his wife parade with much show 'on halydayes' (I.3951–62). The *Parson, however, rebukes those who make their servants work 'out of tyme, as on haly dayes'. *Cupid also has his 'halydayes' (*LGW* 422; cf. 35). (See also *fairs.)

HOMER, see *Omer.

HORACE, Quintus Horatius Flaccus (65–8 BC), the Roman poet. How much, if any, of his work was known to Chaucer is uncertain. In *Troilus and Criseyde* (II.1037–43) Pandarus warns Troilus to avoid jumbling discordant things together in writing a love letter, illustrating it with an image: if a painter were to paint a pike with asses' feet and a head like an ape, it would be discordant and a jest. This is a clear echo and adaptation of the beginning of Horace's *Art of Poetry*: 'if a painter chose to join a human head to the neck of a horse, and to spread feathers of many a hue over limbs picked up now here now there, so that what at the top is a lovely woman ends below in a black and ugly fish, could you my friends . . . refrain from laughing' (trans. Fairclough). Horace's image sounds like the hybrid monsters of classical art; Pandarus's like a medieval grotesque. It has been claimed that it could be found in *florilegia. However, Horace was a 'curriculum author' (*auctor), known as a satirist (in *Dante, when he appears with the other ancient poets he is called 'Horace the satirist'), and as the author of the *Ars poetica*. It is certainly possible that Chaucer knew the work directly. It has also been strongly argued (Norton-Smith) that Horace provided a model for Chaucer's familiar verse epistles (see *Bukton, *Scogan) and for their personal, calmly jesting style.

(ed.) Klinger (1939); (ed. and trans.) Fairclough (1929); Norton-Smith (1966b).

Horaste, according to *Pandarus, a suitor of *Criseyde (*Tr* III.797). The name seems to have been formed on that of Orestes, which was sometimes spelt Horeste or Horrestes.

Horn child, a hero of English *romance mentioned in a list in *Sir Thopas* (VII.898). 'Child' is commonly used in romances to mean 'a young noble man'. Horn appears in early romance in Anglo-Norman and in ME (*King Horn*), but Chaucer probably read of him in a later version like *Horn Childe and Maiden Rimnild* in the *Auchinleck MS. Horn Child, the son of the king of northern England, and Rimnild, the daughter of the king of the south of England fall in love. Because of a false accusation, Horn is forced into exile, but takes with him Rimnild's magic ring. After various adventures, the ring brings him back to England just in time to rescue Rimnild from being married to a man she does not love, to overthrow the traitors in a tournament, and to marry her. This version does scant justice to a touching story of young love, retelling it in the popular tail-rhyme stanza without much subtlety or skill. This may be why 'Horn child' appears in *Sir Thopas.
   (ed.) M. Mills (1988).

horoscope (Greek *horoskopos*, L. *horoscopus*). The disposition of the heavens as charted for a particular place at a particular time, for example in connection with a birth (when the horoscope is called a *nativity*) or a moment of undertaking an enterprise (when it is called an *election*). Horoscopes were also often computed for anniversaries. As usually performed, this requires the division of the *ecliptic into twelve parts according to one of several mathematical systems. The most common system in use in the Middle Ages is explained in Chaucer's *A Treatise on the *Astrolabe*. The division depends on the geographical latitude of interest. John Walter drew up tables of houses for Oxford, and Chaucer planned to include them in the fifth section of his *Treatise*.
   The houses in a horoscope are numbered from the ascendent in the order of the signs (i.e. of increasing ecliptic *longitude). Roughly speaking they signify, in order: life, money, brothers, parents, children, health, marriage, death, religion, honours, benefits, afflictions. The positions of the planets, in relation to the houses and to each other, were of prime importance. There are several horoscopes implicit in Chaucer's poetry. Explicit examples are to be found in the legend of Hypermnestra and The *Wife of Bath's Prologue*.
   In *A Treatise on the *Astrolabe* Chaucer follows Latin usage in taking *horoscopum* or the phrase *in horoscopo* to refer to the ascendent. (See also ***astrology and astronomy; *face; *hous; *nativitee.)   [JDN]
   North (1986; 1990).

hospitality, see *herberwe.

Host, The, of the *Tabard, introduced at the end of the *General Prologue* later named by the *Cook as 'Herry Bailly'. This is almost certainly the name of a real person. A 'Henri Bayliff, ostyler' in *Southwark is recorded in the early 1380s. Chaucer describes the Host briefly as 'a large man . . . with eyen stepe [? 'prominent' ? 'bright']'. He is said to be 'boold of his speche' as well as 'wys, and wel ytaught', and his manliness is singled out for comment. He is a jovial host, and sets the dominant tone of mirth. This *homme moyen sensuel*, as he reveals himself to be, is one of Chaucer's most interesting characters, and has a vital structural role in *The Canterbury Tales*. It is he who organizes the storytelling, and appoints himself as the presiding figure. 'Oure Hoost', as he is regularly called, keeps the entertainment going with much enthusiasm ('the game is wel bigonne', I.3117), and in some sort of order. In general the pilgrims treat him with deference (e.g. IV.21–5; V.703–8), though there is some rebellion: the drunken *Miller refuses to give way and insists on telling the second tale, and the *Pardoner irritates him mightily. He is brisk and sometimes impatient: at the *Reeve's 'sermonyng' ('what shul we speke alday of hooly writ?') and the *Franklin's musings on nobility ('straw for yore gentillesse', V.695). He likes to keep things moving. In an unusually philosophical passage in the Introduction to The *Man of Law's Tale* he laments the passing of time (II.16–32). He also likes to make suggestions or issue instructions about the tale that is to be told, usually that it should be 'merry', but sometimes in more detail: not only must the *Clerk not put his hearers to sleep but he must avoid rhetorical figures and speak 'pleyn'.

His various reactions to the pilgrims is one of the constant delights of the Tales. As befits an innkeeper, he speaks with bonhomie, and a certain decorum. The 'churls' are addressed familiarly ('abyd, Robyn, my leeve brother', 'telle on, Roger') but to the *Prioress he speaks 'as curteisly as it had been a mayde': 'My lady Prioresse, by youre leve, | So that I wiste I sholde yow nat greve'. In tone he can be severe (he speaks 'as lordly as a kyng' to the Reeve) or contemptuous ('thou beel amy, thou Pardoner'). He is fond of assuming a familiar and joking relationship with some of his fellow pilgrims. This involves much teasing and 'joshing' and an implied licence to be outspoken (as with the Cook I.4345–55). The Monk has to take it, 'in patience' when teased about his unmonastic physical qualities, again with the excuse, 'be nat wrooth . . . though that I playe' (VII.1924–64). He is more gentle with the Clerk ('it is no tyme for to studien heere'), and the *Physician (VI.304–13), and Chaucer (VII.693–706).

These exchanges are always lively, and almost always good-natured. Harry Bailly has a certain amount of calming down to do among his fellow travellers. He silences a squabble between the *Friar and the *Summoner (III.850–3), and again when it erupts later (III.1298), and yet again, this time with a touch of irritation: 'Pees . . . for Cristes mooder deere!' (III.1762–3). (He sounds rather like Dame *Nature and her unruly birds in The *Parliament of Fowls.) He persuades the *Manciple not to reprove the drunken *Cook (IX.56–104). His one failure is with the angry *Pardoner (VI.941–68), where the *Knight has to intervene to restore peace.

His speech is full of oaths, exclamations and colloquialisms, and he delivers opinions on a variety of subjects. His reaction to a story is forthright and immediate, if not subtle: he wishes that his wife could have heard the story of *Griselda's patience (IV.1212a–g; see *epilogues); The *Merchant's Tale causes him to remark on women's 'sleightes and subtiltees' and again on the shrewishness of his wife (IV.2419–40; He expands on his own marital sufferings yet again after the tale of *Melibee. He can respond vehemently to a tale: ' "Harrow!" . . . this was a fals cherl and a fals

justise" (VI.289). He wishes that God would give the monk in The *Shipman's Tale 'a thousand cartloads of bad years'. His mood changes quickly. After the 'pitous tale' of the Physician he needs a drink or a merry tale to restore him, and after the sober mood produced by The *Prioress's Tale, he begins to 'jape' by turning to Chaucer. His literary criticism is militant: he stops the tale of *Sir Thopas because of Chaucer's 'drasty rymyng', and joins in when the Knight stops the Monk (VII.2780–805): 'ye seye right sooth; this Monk he clappeth lowde'. Here yet again he voices his insistence on the need for 'desport' and '*game' in literature: if the audience is put to sleep, the 'sentence' is lost.

Rv 825.

hour, one twenty-fourth part of the natural *day or of the artificial day. For the doctrine of planetary hours, see ***planete**. For the system of canonical hours, which are of longer duration, see ***Pryme**. [JDN]

hous, hows, house (astr.). The word is ambiguous in all languages as between (1) one of the twelve signs of the Zodiac, regarded as the *domicile of a planet, and (2) one of the twelve subdivisions of the Zodiac appropriate to a particular moment for which a *horoscope is cast. The context usually makes the difference clear. The twenty references to houses in A Treatise on the *Astrolabe are all meant in the second sense. (The astrolabe was one of the chief means to calculating the houses in this sense.) In the second book of *Troilus and Criseyde, when Venus is said to be in 'hire seventhe hous of hevene', and when in The *Man of Law's Tale the lord of the *ascendent falls from his angle 'into the derkeste hous', the meaning is the same. In the interrupted lines that end The *Squire's Tale, 'the god Mercurius hous' has the first meaning, for which elsewhere the word '*mansioun' is also used. In *Boece, 'the houses that beren the sterres' might have been understood either as the signs of the Zodiac or as the planetary spheres. The mundane houses were traditionally considered to have their own characters. (See also ***astrology and astronomy**; *signe; *spere; *Zodiak.) [JDN]

House of Fame, The, an unfinished *dream vision of 2,158 lines in couplets. Chaucer calls it 'the book that hight the Hous of Fame' in the Prologue to *The *Legend of Good Women* (417), and 'the book . . . of Fame' in the **Retracciouns* (X.1086). It was probably composed while he was controller of the wool custom (1374–85; see Geoffrey **Chaucer: life*). It cannot be dated more exactly, but most scholars think it likely to have been written *c.*1379–80. A date after Chaucer's journeys to Italy in 1372–3 and 1378 might well account for the extensive use of Dante. Attempts have been made to find an occasion for it, e.g. the 'tidings' of the marriage of **Richard II* and **Anne* of Bohemia, or the expected betrothal of Philippa, the daughter of **John of Gaunt*, but there is no clear evidence. It survives in three MSS and the early printed editions of **Caxton* and **Thynne*.

The work reveals a very wide range of reading: the French love visions (as in *The *Book of the Duchess*), accounts of other celestial journeys, **Virgil* (whose influence is especially pervasive), **Ovid* and other Latin authors, and **Dante*. *The House of Fame* may well be the 'Dante in Inglissh' which appears in a list of Chaucer's works given by **Lydgate*. Chaucer's poem certainly has a number of points in common with Dante's: the division into three books, the precise dating, the **Eagle*, and some features of the landscape. There are shared interests, and Chaucer clearly echoes Dante on occasion. However, *The House of Fame* is neither a straightforward 'imitation' of the *Commedia*, nor a 'parody' of it, although it sometimes seems to present an ironic counterpoint to it.

Book I opens with a proem (1–65) in which Chaucer discusses the nature of **dreams*, and announces that he intends to relate a wonderful dream which came to him on 10 December (the exact significance of this date is not certain; it seems appropriate because it is close to the longest night). There follows an Invocation to the god of sleep (see **Morpheus*), asking for his aid (66–110).

(111–508) The poet dreams that he is in a temple of glass, filled with splendid images and tabernacles. It is the temple of **Venus*. As he walks around he finds a table of brass with the story of the *Aeneid* on it. We are given a brief epitome of the earlier books, with an especial emphasis on the story of **Dido* and her abandonment by Aeneas (**Eneas*). Before her death she laments that her deeds will be spread over the whole land by

Rumour ('wikke Fame'). After some other examples of men's 'untrouthe', we are taken quickly to the end of Virgil's story. When the dreamer goes out from the temple he finds a great sandy desert, with no living creature. Praying to be saved from 'fantome [phantasm, hallucination] and illusion', he raises his eyes to heaven, and sees a great golden **eagle*.

In the proem to book II (509–28) he prays to Venus and the **Muses* for help in writing his wonderful dream. (529–1090) The Eagle swiftly descends, picks up the dreamer in his talons, and carries him up ('as lyghtly as I were a larke'). The dreamer is beside himself with trepidation, but is recalled to his senses when the eagle begins to speak to him ('Awak . . . Seynte Marye, | Thou art noyous [troublesome] for to carye!') and tries to reassure him. Jupiter does not intend to turn him into a star as he fears, but has had pity on him because he has served Venus and Cupid so diligently, yet has no tidings of 'Loves folk'. He has sent the Eagle to bring him to the House of Fame, where he will find a multitude of tidings. Her palace is placed between heaven and earth and sea, and every sound makes its way thither. The Eagle launches into a learned disquisition on the nature of sound, and how it is transmitted. When Chaucer is persuaded to look down he sees the earth beneath receding until it seems no more than a dot. When he looks up he can see the Milky Way and the 'eyryssh bestes' (demons of the air?). Declining further instruction in the stars, because he is 'too old', the dreamer is brought to the House of Fame. As they approach, he hears a great rumbling sound coming from it: it is full of 'tidings'. Whenever any speech comes to the palace it instantly takes the shape of the person who uttered it.

Book III opens with an invocation (1091–109) to **Apollo*. (1110–418) The House of Fame is placed high on a rock of ice with the names of famous people engraved on it. On one side these have almost melted. On the other side, protected from the heat, the names are still fresh. The dreamer climbs the hill, and finds a dwelling made of beryl, curiously and richly ornamented, and full of windows. In the niches of its pinnacles are musicians (harpers, pipers, trumpeters), magicians, and sorcerers. When he enters, he meets crowds of people crying out for gifts. The hall is plated with gold and in the midst is placed an imperial throne. On this sits the strange figure of the goddess of *Fame, changing shape (sometimes less than cubit in length, but then touching heaven with her head) and having many eyes, ears, and tongues. Around her the *Muses sing beautifully (1419–1519). On the sides of the hall stand pillars of metal. First, upon a pillar of lead and iron (the metals of *Saturn and *Mars) stands *Josephus, who told of the great deeds of the Jews. Then the dreamer sees a pillar of iron painted with tigers' blood: on it stand the writers who bear up the fame of *Thebes (1) and *Troy. On a pillar of 'tinned iron' stands *Virgil: next to him on a pillar of copper *Ovid. On other pillars stand *Lucan and *Claudian.

(1520–915) A noise like the murmuring of bees now approaches, and a great company of people enter the hall to kneel before the goddess for a boon, 'good fame'. Although they are deserving, they are rejected. The goddess commands Aeolus (*Eolus), the god of winds to bring his trumpets ('Clere Laude' and 'Sklaundre'). When another company comes in, their good works are of no avail: they will have 'shrewed fame'. The sound of the black trumpet Sklaundre spreads their shame over the whole world. A third group enters. They have deserved fame, and the goddess grants it. The gold trumpet laude rings out. Other companies follow: those that wish their deeds and name to be hidden, idlers who have done nothing but still wish for fame, traitors, and shrews. Each group receives a similarly arbitrary treatment. A man standing just behind the dreamer asks him if he has come to seek fame. No, says the dreamer, but to learn some new tidings, 'of love or suche thynges glade'. The man tells him to come with him to another place where he will hear many.

(1916–2158) Outside, down in a valley, the dreamer sees a strange house made of twigs, perpetually whirling about. A great noise comes from it: there are holes and doors everywhere, and it is full of 'tidings', whispers and gossip about every topic. The eagle, who is perched on a rock nearby, carries him in through a window. Inside it is packed with a crowd of people all passing on 'new tidings' ('"Thus hath he sayd" and "Thus he doth"', etc.). Each tiding increases as it is passed

on from mouth to mouth, until eventually it flies out of the house and comes to Fame, who according to her disposition gives it a name and allots its duration. The house is full of those who are especially known for spreading tidings: shipmen and pilgrims (with bags full of lies mingled with tidings), pardoners, couriers, and messengers. The dreamer hears a commotion in one corner where people are telling love-tidings. Everyone is rushing and clambering up to see. At last he sees a man whom he cannot name, 'but he semed for to be | A man of gret auctorite'. Here the poem breaks off.

This tantalizing ending has occasioned a great deal of speculation. Candidates proposed for the man of great authority (most of them extremely unlikely in the context of the House of Rumour) include Boethius, Christ, Love itself, Richard II, and John of Gaunt. However the text suggests that Chaucer could not identify the person (and the word 'semed' may suggest irony). It may be that the poem has been deliberately left unfinished, for some unknown reason. Perhaps Chaucer had said all that he wanted to say, or a wedding or betrothal had been cancelled. All remains uncertain. The poem has presented larger difficulties as well. The question of its unity (especially the relationship of the first two books to the third) has been constantly discussed. It is a poem (perhaps a loosely meditative one) about ideas. That of Fame is clearly central. The linking of fame with rumour and fortune is found well before Chaucer. Love and fame are found together in the story of Dido, and seem to be linked in Chaucer's mind because he sees himself as a poet of love. The poem poses questions about the nature of love (which Chaucer continues to explore in his later works) and the nature of the *poet's calling, his motivation and his material. There has been general agreement about the poem's incidental felicities, notably the comic exchanges with the Eagle. However, there is more to praise in it than that. It presents a remarkable blend of comedy, fantasy, and a profound interest in *science and natural philosophy. Dante seems to have given a new dimension to Chaucer's imagination, suggesting the scenes of the swirling crowds of suppliants, and the visionary scope of the poem: 'ther myghte y seen | Wynged wondres faste fleen [fly], | Twenty thousand in a route, | As Eolus hem blew aboute.'

(ed.) *Rv* 347–73, 977–90; Havely (1994); Minnis (1995), 161–251; Bennett (1968*a*); Boitani (1984); Clemen (1963), 67–121; Delany (1972); Fyler (1979); North (1990); Norton-Smith (1974), ch. 3.

Huberd, the name of the *Friar in the *General Prologue* (I.269). Various suggestions about Chaucer's choice of this name (some personal allusion, Hubert the kite in the *Roman de *Renart*, etc.) have been put forward, but nothing has been proved.

HUGELYN OF PYZE, Ugolino of Pisa, whose tale is told by the *Monk (VII.2407–62). He plotted with his grandson Nino Visconti for the control of Pisa. He was blamed for a number of Pisan defeats. After quarrelling with Nino, he conspired with his rival, Archbishop Ruggieri. Nino was banished, but Ruggieri stirred up the people against Ugolino. He was committed to prison with his two sons and two grandsons, and died of starvation there in 1289. *Dante tells the story of the gruesome death of Ugolino and his children (now four young sons) in the *Inferno* (33.1–90). It is one of the most terrible and impressive sections in the poem. This is Chaucer's acknowledged source (2459–62), although he may have also had access to other information. Chaucer makes a number of changes. Whereas in Dante Ugolino is placed among the traitors (and finds himself next to Ruggieri), there is no mention of any guilt. He is fitted into the pattern of The *Monk's Tale* as a victim of *Fortune. Other changes are designed to increase the pathos of the episode (the '*pite' is stressed at the outset, 2408). There are exclamations against Fortune from the narrator and from Ugolino. In Dante Ugolino hears his children crying in their sleep for bread. Chaucer makes this into a brief 'pitous' speech from a 3-year-old child. The children place themselves in their father's bosom (2440) or lap (2454) to die. It is a powerful story, which stands out in its context. (See also *children.)

Boitani (1976); Mann (1983).

HUGH OF LYNCOLN (d. 1255), a child saint invoked at the end of The *Prioress's Tale* (VII.684–90). He is sometimes called 'little St Hugh' to distinguish him from the earlier St Hugh of Lincoln (d. 1200), a Carthusian monk who became bishop of that diocese. At the age of 9, he was murdered by unknown persons, and his body was thrown into a well or a stream. It was widely believed (without any evidence) that he had been the victim of a ritual murder by the *Jews, a number of whom were executed. He was buried in the cathedral, where the remains of his shrine can still be seen. The story was, as the Prioress says, 'notable'. It lived on in popular legend: versions of the ballad 'Sir Hugh or the Jew's Daughter' were recorded in the 18th c.

Hulle, Hull, a port on the Yorkshire coast. In the *General Prologue* it appears in the description of the *Shipman in the phrase 'from Hulle to *Cartage' (2) (I.404), i.e. 'anywhere'.

humanism, a word which is sometimes found in discussions of Chaucer, needs careful definition. General senses of the word now current, like 'a non-religious view of the world' or indeed an anti-religious outlook, are of dubious relevance to the late 14th c. In its earlier, stricter sense, which originated in 15th-c. universities, it meant the *studia humanitatis*, the study of 'humanity', i.e. of classical literature. Based on Cicero's remarks on a liberal education, this involved grammar, rhetoric, poetry, history, and moral philosophy, studied through classical texts in Latin and Greek. This 'humanism', which flourished in 15th-c. Italy and spread northwards, owed much to the 14th-c. writer Petrarch (*Petrak) and his enthusiasm for the classical past *as* past. Although Chaucer knew and used some of Petrarch's work, there is no evidence which allows us to call him a 'humanist' in this sense. He does not show the antiquarian urge, the interest in classical philology, or attempt to write 'pure' Latin. However, the memory of the ancient past had never died in the Middle Ages, and it seems as if this highly influential revival of a very specialized scholarly interest is the last of a series of 'renewals' or *renovationes*. It is possible to discern an older, broader tradition of 'medieval' humanism, which may take differing forms: in 14th-c. England, for instance, there is a group of

humour

'classicizing friars' with an interest in ancient stories and *mythography, scholarly figures like the bibliophile *Richard of Bury, as well as writers like *Gower and *Chaucer, who like *Jean de Meun before them, have an enthusiasm for the 'old books' of antiquity and their literary possibilities. Chaucer's writing shows a *humanitas* which owes something to his reading of classical authors. (See also *classical antiquity.)

Gray (1989); Rundle (1996); Smalley (1960); Southern (1970); Wetherbee (1972).

humour, one of the four fluids of the body by the relative proportions of which a person's mental and physical character was supposedly determined. The theory of humours was a part of the 'fourfold scheme' of Galen (see *Galyen (1)). By this, the humours (blood, phlegm, choler, and black bile or melancholy), the elementary qualities (hot, cold, moist, dry), the elements (earth, air, fire, and water), the seasons, human ages, and various other quadruples with a relevance to human life, were interrelated. Galen claimed to have the theory from *Aristotle and Hippocrates in this matter, but this over-generous acknowledgement was evidently to provide it with a respectable pedigree. (Aristotle's *cosmology has the four elements and four qualities.) According to the *General Prologue, Chaucer's *Physician knew the causes of maladies (hot, cold, moist and dry) and the humours they engendered. *Arcite's melancholy humour is used to explain his character in The *Knight's Tale. The most extensive use Chaucer makes of the doctrine is in The *Nun's Priest's Tale, where Chauntecleer's choleric complexion is related to various other medical factors. (See also *medicine.)   [JDN]

Hundred Years War. A series of wars between *France and *England in the period 1337–1453 rather than the continuous conflict the (modern) name implies. The main issues were the sovereignty of Gascony, of which the English king was duke, and under feudal obligation to pay hommage for it to the kings of France, and *Edward III's claim to the French throne through his mother. It is often thought that the conflicts were part of a wider process of development which was ending the Anglo-French past of the area by the growth of separate centralized states. France was the setting for the fighting, and suffered greatly from the devastation of the campaigns. The first campaign by Edward III and the *Black Prince produced spectacular English victories at Crécy (1346) and Poitiers (1356), and ended with the French king in captivity, and the English in control of considerable territories. After some years of peace Edward resumed his claim to the French throne, and his French lands were declared confiscate by Charles V. Under his direction the area held by the English was greatly reduced. They were forced into a largely ineffective defensive war, and the deaths of the Black Prince (1376) and King Edward (1377) further lowered morale. This period of French recovery came to an end with the death of Charles V in 1380. There followed a long period of uneasy truce, in which both countries were preoccupied with internal problems: the intermittent madness of Charles VI, the growth of Burgundian power, the removal of *Richard II from the throne. Hostilities were actively resumed by Henry V in a campaign which culminated with victory at Agincourt (1415). By 1420 most of France north of the Loire was controlled by the English. After Henry's death (1422), the French again began to win back territory, helped (in the area of the Loire) by Joan of Arc. The English decline continued. By 1450 Normandy and much of Gascony were in French hands. Bordeaux (*Burdeux) fell in 1453. The English retained Calais, and mounted some later expeditions, but effectively the war was over.

HUNT, JAMES HENRY LEIGH (1784–1859), poet and essayist, the friend and supporter of *Keats and other Romantic writers. He has been described as perhaps 'the most constant and enthusiastic lover of Chaucer in the early nineteenth century' (Spurgeon). He is unusual in his time in giving extensive technical analyses of Chaucer's *irony, humour, *narrative technique, and the musical quality of his verse. He praises the 'unrivalled perfection' of Chaucer's descriptive portraits, and descriptions like that of the cave of Morpheus, than which nothing has 'a more deep and sullen effect'. In his 'Characteristic Specimens of the English Poets' in the *London Journal* (1835) he remarks that Chaucer combines 'an epic power of grand, comprehensive, and primitive *imagery, with that of being contented with the smallest matter of fact near him'. The greatest poets, like Chaucer, have both fancy and imagination, which is (*Imagination and Fancy*, 1844) 'the feeling of the subtlest and most affecting analogies; the Perception of sympathies in the natures of things, or in their popular attributes': Chaucer was 'one of the profoundest masters of pathos that ever lived'. *Wit and Humour Selected from the Old English Poets* (1846) contains characters from the *General Prologue* and selections from some of the Tales, with a modern English prose version. In the prefatory remarks Hunt discusses the characteristics of Chaucer's humour, which is 'entertaining, profound and good-natured'. In the preface to *Stories in Verse* (1855) he speaks of the musical qualities of Chaucer, and the way in which sound and sense are united. He also produced a number of adaptations and *imitations of Chaucer.

CH ii. 70–88; Clogan (1979); Spurgeon (1925).

hunting. While Chaucer does not have anything as elaborate as the descriptions of the hunts in *Sir Gawain and the Green Knight*, he often refers to hunting. This is not surprising, since it was a very prominent feature of medieval life. It took a variety of forms: hunting or trapping animals, hunting birds with falcons, or catching them by snares. It was an occupation of all social classes (one of the humbler forms is alluded to in *The *House of Fame* (2154) where men stamp as they do to drive eels into the nets). In courtly circles the hunting of animals in *forests or parks was often an occasion of great pageantry and ceremony. It was largely a male activity, but not exclusively so. Women regularly rode out hawking, but this was shared pastime: Troilus is described riding 'with hauk on honde' (*Tr* V.65) (see Fig. 6). A knowledge of the rituals and ceremonies of the hunt was part of a nobleman's training. Hunting manuals provided information on the nature of the quarry, on the method of hunting each kind, and on dogs, weapons, and equipment. These books are often beautifully illustrated. One splendid example is a MS of the late 14th-c. *Livre de chasse* of Gaston 'Phoebus', count of Foix (a work which was translated into English in the early 15th c. by Edward, duke of York, as *The*

Master of Game). Depictions of hunts are frequently found in MSS, murals, and tapestries.

For a medieval writer, hunting was surrounded by literary and symbolic associations. Ancient stories provided the figure of Diana (*Dyane), the huntress (depicted in *The *Knight's Tale* with bow, arrows, and hounds, famous hunts, like those involving *Dido, Actaeon (*Attheon), Adonis (*Adoon), Atalanta and Meleager (*Atthalante, *Meleagre), or episodes (as when *Venus appears as a huntress, like Diana; see *LGW* 971–5, *HF* 225–30). The Middle Ages added the symbolic hunt of the unicorn (which could only be overcome by a virgin) and allegorical narratives in which hunts were images of the pursuit of *love. In some saints' lives supernatural events occurred in the course of a hunt: seeing a crucifix in the horns of a stag (St Eustace, St Hubert), or receiving a prophetic warning from a stag (St Julian). Hunts are sometimes the setting for *dream visions or strange events in *romance.

Two of Chaucer's pilgrims are singled out for their interest in hunting. The *Yeoman as a professional gamekeeper, knew 'al the usage' of 'wodecraft' (which probably includes the ceremonials and practices of the hunt). His equipment is also professional: arrows in good condition, horn, sword, and dagger. The *Monk who is not supposed to be a hunter, did not bother about the dictum that 'hunters ben nat hooly men' (I.178). With his horses, and greyhounds, and his love of hare-hunting, he is an enthusiast.

Chaucer's familiarity with hunting and its terminology is evident. Examples of people who dream about their daytime occupations include the 'weary hunter' ('to wode ayeyn his mynde goth anon', *PF* 99). He frequently uses the cynegetical imagery that is widespread in medieval literature. A bold and recondite example is when Pandarus, referring to the lessening of Troilus's sorrow, says 'algate [at any rate] a foot is hameled of thi sorwe' (II.964): 'hambling' is the maiming of a dog by cutting off the balls of its feet so that it is unfit for hunting. Presumably Troilus's sorrow is imagined as a pursuing hound (see also I.463). More usual are the falconry references: to the 'luring' of hawks (i.e. reclaiming them after flight, III.1340), which a proverb says cannot be done with empty hands (I.4134; III.415), to the *sours*, 'source' or upward flight of the hawk rising on the wing (III.1938; a hawk soars when it 'listeth for to pleye', *Tr* I.671), which is applied to the prayers of friars, to the *mewe* or *muwe* 'pen for a hawk' in both its literal sense (V.643, 646) and in a simile (Criseyde looks out of her window 'as fressh as faukoun comen out of muwe', *Tr* III.1784). In *The *Legend of Good Women* 'the smale foules ... | That from the panter [bird snare] and the net ben scaped' sing in despite of the fowler (130–1). These devices, like the common 'snare', may be applied metaphorically to love.

There are a number of references to hunting and hawking as noble pastimes. It is while Walter is out hunting that he first notices Griselda (IV.232–4); the Clerk's association of his delight in hawking and hunting (IV.80–2) with his lack of thought for the future suggests that it was excessive. Sir Thopas (VII.736–8) 'koude hunte at wilde deer, | And ride an haukyng for river [to hunt for waterfowl] | With grey goshauk on honde'. Theseus enjoys hunting for 'the grete hert in May', 'with hunte and horn and houndes hym bisyde' (I.1673–87), with him are his Amazonian womenfolk, who also serve Diana (1682; cf. 2308).

Sometimes these references become little vignettes. In *The *Franklin's Tale* (V.1189–97) the first of the courtly scenes which the magician produces is the vision of a great hunt, in which a hundred deer are slain by the hounds, and some bleed with bitter wounds from the arrows, followed by falconers hunting the heron along the river bank. In *The *Knight's Tale* an elaborate hunting simile (I.1638–48) conveys the excitement and danger of the moment when the prey (the 'leon or the bere') comes 'russhyng in the greves, | And breketh bothe bowes and the leves'. The hunt of Dido and Aeneas (*LGW* 1188–217), which is interrupted by the storm, is described with considerable verve and in some detail. Chaucer warms to the excitement of Virgil's account, adding some medieval detail to the ancient nets and spears: Dido rides on a sturdy palfrey, Aeneas on a restive 'courser'. When the herd of harts is found, Ascanius's wish for a boar or a lion is replaced by cries of excitement from the 'young folk': '"Hay! Go bet! Pryke thow! Lat gon, lat gon! | Why nyl the leoun comen, or the bere ... ?"'

Longer and more detailed than this is the hunt in *The *Book of the Duchess* (344–86) in which the dreamer becomes involved. His curiosity is aroused by the sound of excited preparations: the huntsman testing his horn, the noise of the men going up and down with their horses and hounds, and talking about the forthcoming hunt. When he decides to go out, he overtakes a great company on its way to the forest. The description here bristles with technical terms: there are *foresteres* 'trackers'; *relayes* 'packs of fresh hounds'; *lymeres* 'leash-hounds'. Chaucer seems fully in control of the procedure: the *mayster-hunte* (chief huntsman) blows three *mot* ('notes') on a great horn at the *uncouplynge* (unleashing) of his hounds. But this dream hunt comes to nothing. The hart *rused* (made a detour to escape the hounds) so that the dogs overshot it. The huntsman blows a *forloyn* (a call which indicates that the hounds are far from the prey), and the hunt fades away until the end of the poem (1311–20), when it (or rather its ending) returns briefly and abruptly, in a dreamlike way, as the huntsmen 'strake forth' (go off, perhaps blowing their horns). Chaucer has written a vivid description of a hunt, and at the same time fitted it into the pattern of his dream narrative, with its strange, frustrated quest. He seems to be drawing on the traditional associations of the hunt in its symbolic association with love (suggested by the apparently punning 'hert-huntyng', 1313) and its use as a setting for mysterious events. (See also *animals; *birds.)

Baillie-Grohman (1904); Rooney (1993); Thiébaux (1974).

Huwe, Sir, Hugh, a nickname for a priest (III.1356).

HUXLEY, ALDOUS (1894–1963), novelist and man of letters, wrote an interesting essay on Chaucer originally published in the *London Mercury* (1920). It is a lively and sympathetic attempt to rescue him from 'literary fossilization'. The Chaucer that emerges is a very secular and sceptical poet (strikingly unlike G. K. *Chesterton's), who 'has no patience with superstitions' like astrology. Where the evidence of experience is lacking, 'he is content to profess a quiet agnosticism', sometimes even questioning the fundamental beliefs of the Church. Huxley's stress on Chaucer's tolerance makes him sound rather bland ('to read Chaucer one would imagine there was nothing in fourteenth-century England to be indignant about'). He praises his naturalism and his 'power of getting into someone else's character': 'when one sees with what certainty and precision Chaucer describes every movement of Cressida's spirit from the first movement she hears of Troilus's love for her to the moment when she is unfaithful to him, one can only wonder why the novel of character should have been so slow to make its appearance'.

CH ii. 354–66.

HYGINUS, Caius Julius (2nd c. AD), Roman author, compiler of *Genealogiæ*, a collection of Greek myths. A shortened version of this was sometimes included in reading for the *Trivium. There is also a manual of astronomy presumed to be by the same writer, and a poem on the images of the constellations.   [JDN]

Hypsipyle, see *Isiphile(e).

I

Note: in Middle English words the letter 'y' when it represents a vowel is treated as 'i'.

Yarbas, King Iarbas, a suitor of *Dido (*LGW* 1245).

IBN AL ZARQUALI, IBN AZ-ZARQELLU; IBN RUSHD; IBN SINA; Iconography. See *Arsechieles; *Averrois; *Avycen; *visual arts.

Idre, Idra, the Lernaean Hydra, a monstrous serpent which lived in the marshes of Lerna, near Argos. It had many heads, and when one was cut off, others grew in its place. It was killed by Hercules (*Ercules). This is 'the firy serpent venymous' of The *Monk's Tale (VII.2105): the 'firy' apparently comes from another monster mentioned by Virgil (*Aen.* 6.288), the Chimaera. It is twice mentioned in *Boece* (IV pr.6:19, m.7:42).

Ykarus, Icarus, the son of Daedalus (*Dedalus). As he was escaping from Crete by flying with the wings his father had made, he flew too near the sun. The wax melted, and he was drowned in the sea. The *Eagle in The *House of Fame refers to the story of 'nyce [foolish] Ykarus' to impress upon Chaucer the height to which he has been taken (920–4). Chaucer would have read the story in Ovid (*Met.* 8. 183–226).

Ilion, Ilyoun, Ilium, the name of the city of *Troy (from Ilus, its founder). Medieval writers regularly used it to refer rather to *Priam's citadel within Troy (often imagined as a medieval castle). Chaucer uses the name a number of times, and sometimes clearly distinguishes the two: 'the noble tour of Ylioun, | that of the cite was the chef dongeoun' (*LGW*), 'the destruccioun | Of Troye and of Ilyoun' (*BD* 1247–8).

illustrations. There is a long tradition of illustrating the works of Chaucer. From the late Middle Ages on there have been illustrations accompanying the texts in MSS and printed books. In more modern times these have been joined by separate works of art inspired by scenes in the tales.

The early 15th-c. *Ellesmere MS of The *Canterbury Tales has a handsome set of miniatures representing the mounted pilgrims, which are placed at the beginning of their respective tales. These are the work of at least two artists. In general, they seem to have been attentive to the poet's descriptions in the *General Prologue, selecting significant details. The *Squire has his short gown embroidered with red and white flowers. The illustrator has attempted to show his curly locks, and has given him a lively horse. The Wife of Bath (Fig. 2) has her broad hat, her large hips, and her spurs (unlike the nuns she is shown riding astride her *amblere*). The excellent miniature of the *Pardoner (Fig. 3) shows his long yellow hair falling over his shoulders, his smooth chin, and the *vernycle sown on his cap. He carries his cross of brass full of stones, and his wallet of pardons is slung around his horse's neck rather than being 'biforn hym in his lappe'. The illustrator has attempted to show the *Prioress's small mouth and broad forehead; she carries her beads on her left wrist.

There is, understandably, no attempt at reproducing all of the details supplied by Chaucer. Thus, the *Monk's horse has gold bells on its bridle, but we miss the fur trimmings on his sleeves, yet the illustrator has allowed two of his greyhounds to accompany him. The *Merchant seems to be wearing his 'Flaundrissh bever hat', but has lost his forked beard. The *Clerk's horse is properly thin (so that its bones stand out), but the Clerk himself is not. He has brought some of his books with him. Other pilgrims carry symbolic signs of their occupation: the Doctor of Physic has a glass urinal, the *Summoner is holding a summons. The illustrators had to represent a number of pilgrims whose appearance is not described in detail, like the *Second Nun (who is made to look like the Prioress), the *Manciple, or the *Parson (who rides with arms crossed, apparently as a sign of piety or humility). The series also contains a picture of Chaucer himself on horseback (see frontispiece). He carries a stylus for writing on wax tablets, and the illustrator makes his figure slightly rotund. As in the other early portraits in three MSS of *Hoccleve (Fig. 1), he has a small forked beard.

No other surviving Chaucer MS has anything comparable. However, some later 15th-c. MSS once had illustrations of the pilgrim narrators. They have survived in fragmentary form. One at present in the Rylands Library has the Miller; another in the Rosenbach Foundation has the Cook and the Manciple. MS Gg. 4. 27, in the Cambridge University Library, is of particular interest in that it is an early attempt to collect Chaucer's major poems together and to accompany them with a programme of illustrations. Among those which survive are depictions of some of the vices and virtues touched on in The *Parson's Tale. These are based on traditional iconography. The sins ride on appropriate animals, Lechery on a goat, Envy on a wolf. The virtues are female figures with symbolic attributes (Charity, for instance, holds a flaming heart). The surviving pilgrim portraits (the Wife of Bath, the Pardoner, the Manciple, the Monk, the Reeve, and the Cook) are energetic and imaginative (see Figs. 5, 7). Other illustrations survive here and there. MS Rawlinson poet. 223 in the Bodleian Library has figures of the Friar and (possibly) Melibeus. A MS containing The Complaint of *Mars and The Complaint of *Venus has pictures of Mars, Venus, and Jupiter (Fig. 9). More famous is the 'Troilus frontispiece' in MS Corpus Christi College, Cambridge 61 (of the first quarter of the 15th c.), which shows a courtly outdoor scene, with a figure (probably Chaucer) in the centre (Fig. 8). There are empty spaces in the MS for other illustrations. An illustration of the group of Canterbury pilgrims all together (a subject which was very popular in later centuries) is found in MS

Royal 18 D ii in the British Library, a copy of *Lydgate's Siege of Thebes, where they are depicted leaving Canterbury on their way home.

Early printed editions often contain illustrations in the form of woodcuts. *Caxton's second edition of The Canterbury Tales has illustrations (including one of the pilgrims at table), and these are used in the editions of Pynson (1492) and Wynkyn de Worde (1498). The tradition continues in later editions: e.g. *Thynne (1542), *Urry (1721), and others in the 18th and 19th c. Later modernizations and children's versions of Chaucer were often illustrated. Cowden Clarke's Riches of Chaucer (1835), for instance, has a series of attractive small illustrations. The frontispiece shows the abbot and the dead child singing, from The *Prioress's Tale; the title page opposite is a small Tabard Inn. A picture is placed at the beginning of each tale or extract. After the procession of pilgrims, we have, for instance, Theseus and the ladies, Constance with her baby about to board the ship, the knight and the ugly old woman from The *Wife of Bath's Tale, Walter, Janicula, and Griselda (looking very demure and well turned out: see Fig. 11), Dorigen and Aurelius in the garden, a sorrowing Troilus and Criseyde, and a grieving Ariadne on the shore. The Routledge Chaucer from the middle of the 19th c. (several times reprinted) is illustrated by Corbould. Leigh *Hunt thought the 'delicate illustrations' were the best 'that ever came from his pencil'. The illustrations in popular editions such as these undoubtedly influenced the way readers responded to the text, and form an important element in the history of the 'reception' of Chaucer.

Not in any way typical, but undoubtedly the most magnificent of the 19th-c. illustrated Chaucers is William *Morris's Kelmscott Chaucer of 1896 (see Figs. 12, 13). For this, as for earlier productions of the press, most of the blocks were engraved on wood by William Harcourt Hooper. There are eighty-seven woodcuts after designs by Burne-Jones, an elaborate title page drawn by Morris, decorated borders, and ornamented initial letters. The effect of one of the elaborate decorated pages is a little overwhelming for the modern reader unused to Morris's medievalism, but many of the pictures are impressive, with a typically Pre-Raphaelite emphasis on idealized beauty and love of drapery. Scenes of pathos are excellently done: Constance in her boat driven by the waves, Griselda standing with humble downcast eyes before Walter, the 'new queen' (her daughter), and her son, Dorigen kneeling before Arveragus. In a striking night scene in the Greek camp (against an austere background of tents under a starlit sky), Diomede is shown (in full armour) entreating Criseyde and leaning towards her: her emotions are registered in the way her left hand clutches the fingertips of the right.

The illustrations catch some dramatic moments in the text: the cruel sergeant carries off Griselda's child while she kneels and prays for mercy; the old woman in *The Wife of Bath's Tale* stands in front of a forest and stops the knight with upraised hand; Cleopatra plunges into the snake-pit. There is much variety in the subjects chosen: the Eagle picks up the poet in his claws, the dreamer sees the names melting on the rock of Fame's house, Dorigen looks out over an almost surreal scene of 'black rocks' and threatening waves, Canacee stands beside the falcon in a strange, desolate landscape. We are shown the suppliants in *The *Knight's Tale* approaching their gods, and the scenes of magic in *The *Franklin's Tale*. Chaucer himself appears (looking rather like a pre-Raphaelite Dante) kneeling before the Virgin and Child at the head of the *ABC, at the beginning of *The Canterbury Tales* in a garden with a book, and above the *Retracciouns, holding a book and taking leave of Poesis in a garden. We miss the Wife of Bath, the portraits of the pilgrims (especially the disreputable ones) and scenes from *fabliaux. While Venus and the old lady in *The Wife of Bath's Tale* after her transformation are shown as shapely nude figures, there is little of the eroticism that Beardsley had developed. The lovers in *Troilus* stand and kiss in an elegant and chaste embrace. The Kelmscott presents a Chaucer who is courtly and idealized, but it also suggests the impressive range of his imagination.

Still in the mainstream of the 19th-c. tradition are the illustrations (photogravures by Gilbert James) for Skeat's modernized *The Story of Patient Griselda* (1906). Characteristically, illustrated Chaucers have since been for the 'art presses'.

Notable here are the illustrations done by Eric Gill for the Golden Cockerell Press editions, of *The Canterbury Tales* and *Troilus and Criseyde* (see Fig. 14).

Paintings and other works of art inspired by Chaucer's poems are not as numerous. A very early (and isolated) example is the carving of three scenes from *The *Pardoner's Tale* on a wooden chest (now in the Museum of London) made about 1400 (see Fig. 4). It shows the buying of the poison from the apothecary and the two consequent death scenes. The *Chaucer Drawings* (1787) of J. H. Mortimer, a set of engravings from his own drawings, may have been intended for an edition. They include 'January and May', 'The Sompnour, the Devil, and Old Woman', 'The Three Gamblers and Time', 'The Departure of the Canterbury Pilgrims', etc. The Pilgrims became the favourites of later painters. In the early years of the 19th c. both Stothard (1786–1821) and *Blake produced versions. An engraver who had seen Blake at work encouraged him, but went to Stothard to propose the same subject as if it were his own idea, and without telling him of Blake's project. In 1807 Stothard's *Canterbury Pilgrims* was exhibited with great success, and was later published as an engraving. Not surprisingly, this aroused Blake's anger. In 1808 Blake finished his fresco of *The Canterbury Pilgrims* (which was also later made into an engraving) and decided to 'appeal to the public' with an exhibition of this and other 'Poetical and Historical Inventions'. This took place in 1809, and for it Blake produced his *Descriptive Catalogue*, with interesting notes on the Pilgrims and some hostile remarks about Stothard. Corbould, the illustrator of the Routledge Chaucer, painted 'The Pilgrims leaving the Tabard Inn', and there have been other examples since. The pilgrims appear in modern stained glass windows in Westminster Abbey and in St Saviour's, Southwark (1900).

R. S. Loomis (1965), 1–2, 68, 80–101, 177–9; Bindman (1978) nos. 477–8; Johnson (1973).

imagery (see also *imagination; *visual arts). Imagery, while it is not as dense or as complex as in Shakespeare, has an important part in Chaucer's poetry. In earlier usage, the word 'image' (L. *imago*) has a wide range of senses. It may be applied to the pictures or figures created by painters, sculptors, etc., like those which were everywhere to be found in the medieval world. Chaucer uses 'ymageries' for the carvings on the House of Fame (*HF* 1304). Images such as these had power. Religious images in particular were often invested with considerable power; people would touch them or kiss them. The word can also mean a 'mental image'. In Chaucer, for instance, *Tarquinius recalls the 'image' of *Lucrece: 'th'ymage of hire recordynge alwey newe: | "Thus lay hire her . . . | Thus sat, thus spak, thus span; this was hire chere"', etc. (*LGW* 1760–3). This image which he recreates by memory also has an affective power. He is deeply moved: just as the water of the sea which has been shaken by a tempest will still toss about for a day or two even after the tempest has passed, 'the plesaunce of hire forme was present' even though her physical form was absent (1765–9). The effects of 'ymaginacioun' on the Carpenter in The *Miller's Tale (I.3611–19) are described in similar terms: he quakes as he seems to see the waves of Noah's flood. The connection of the image with *memory, and its affective power are important.

The discussions in the *rhetorical handbooks are brief, and at first sight disappointing. Geoffrey of Vinsauf (*Gaufred), who considers *imago* separately from metaphor (a distinction not found in many modern studies), calls it 'a comparison of one thing with a similar thing by means of an appropriate image' and relates it to *effictio* (portrayal) 'wherby I depict or represent corporeal appearance in so far as is requisite'. But there is a continual insistence on imaginative vividness (*enargeia*); writers are urged to place things before the very eyes of their readers (*ante oculos ponere*).

The visual and the mental image overlap. Cicero remarks that we not only 'see' but also 'think' *imagines*. Images have symbolic and intellectual overtones of meaning. They are a means of knowing. The created world was thought to be filled with meaningful signs: 'every creature in the world is as a book and picture to us', says Alan of Lille. At the same time, alongside this characteristic emphasis on the significance of images, there is a stress on their visual quality. The sense of sight is regarded as the most powerful of the senses. In affective devotional writing especially, writers try to make their readers *see* the sacred and terrible scenes of Christ's suffering. But most medieval poets try to *portray* (a word used both of writing and painting) their scenes vividly. This quality of vividness in Chaucer's writing was recognized early: later he was praised for his 'images of horror' by *Gray, and as a 'picturesque poet'. Imagery is a central element in this.

Chaucer draws his images from a wide range of experience, and puts them to a variety of uses. His fondness for images from the natural world (see also *animals; *birds) is seen in the *portrait of *Alison (1) in The Miller's Tale (I.3233–70). Here a series of similes and comparisons (weasel, sloe, pear-tree, wool of a wether, swallow's song, kid, calf, apples, etc.) culminating in the description of her as 'a prymerole, a piggesnye' strongly suggest the naturalism and sensuousness of the girl. This is carefully 'counterpointed' with a few images from 'art' (the description of her elegant purse, her face shining like a newly forged coin) and other visual details (her broad brooch, her shoes laced high on her legs, etc.). In the complementary portrait of *Absolon (2) (I.3312–38), where images of 'art' predominate, there are one or two (rather conventional) natural images (eyes as grey as a goose, a surplice as white as a flower on the twig) and the vigour of his dancing hints at a certain physicality which is comically confirmed by the image of the cat and the mouse (I.3346–7).

We may find a religious image full of traditional symbolism, like that put into the *Prioress's mouth, 'O bussh unbrent, brennynge in Moyses sighte' (VII.468; the bush which the shepherd boy Moses saw burning but not consumed had become a common 'type' or foreshadowing of the perpetual virginity of the mother of Christ), or a more straightforwardly expressive one, as when the lively and gaily coloured *Perkin is compared to a goldfinch (I.4367). Vivid, memorable images are used for grotesque or satirical effects: the *Miller's mouth 'as greet . . . as a greet forneys' (I.559), perhaps with suggestions of the gaping mouth of hell (and in *physiognomy thought to be sign of a gluttonous and bold personality); or the *Pardoner's glaring eyes like a hare (I.684), with their eerie suggestion of madness (and also a physiognomical sign of a man given to folly, a glutton, a libertine, and a drunkard). Yet sometimes in the course of one of these portraits, we find an image that is unexpectedly lyrical, like the *Friar's eyes twinkling 'as doon the sterres in the frosty nyght' (I.268).

Images are used in portraits and in descriptions of *landscape and of actions of every kind. Occasionally they come in 'serial' or extended forms: as in the *Reeve's meditation on his passing years (I.3867–98), where a remarkable series of images that concern ageing and decay culminate in an elaborately worked out image of a wine cask and the 'tap of life'. Sometimes they appear with dramatic suddenness in the midst of a narrative, but are always carefully set in their narrative context. The excitement of the arrival of the *Canon's Yeoman is caught in the vivid natural image of the sweating horse and its sweating rider ('it was joye for to seen hym swete!', VIII.579). But this exclamation is followed immediately by an unusual simile which looks forward to the alchemical matter of the tale: 'His forheed dropped as a stillatorie [vessel for distillation] | Were ful of plantayne [the herb plantain] and of paritorie [the herb pellitory].'

Chaucer's images may also have a larger structural function. While they do not produce iterative imagery of the kind which has been discerned in Shakespeare, they sometimes form clear patterns running through a work. In *Troilus and Criseyde, for instance, images (explicit or implicit) of 'binding' recur (see e.g. I.237, 235, 439, 507–9; III.1746–50) expressing both the torments and the concord of the 'chain of love'. In the fourth book especially, imagery concerning the underworld and its torments are prominent. Throughout there are images of the blindness of lovers and of mortals in general. It has also been argued (notably by Kolve) that in The Canterbury Tales each narrative has certain 'dominant' or 'controlling' images—e.g. the prison, the garden, and the amphitheatre in The *Knight's Tale or the rudderless boat and the sea in The *Man of Law's Tale.

Kolve (1984).

ymaginacioun. Imagination in medieval terminology is not the Romantic concept of the 'creative imagination' ('the creative faculty of the mind in its highest aspect . . . poetic genius' (OED)), although the semantic links which led to

that idea are fairly clear. But even when *Hawes uses the word of Chaucer's poetic creation ('upon hys ymaginacyon | He made also the tales of Caunterbury') or Shakespeare's Theseus speaks of imagination 'bodying forth' the 'forms of things unknown' and the poet's pen turning them to 'shapes' (A Midsummer Night's Dream 5.1.12 ff.), we are still close to the traditional medieval psychology of perception and knowledge. In his translation of a passage in Boethius (*Boece), where imagination is discussed (Bo V pr.4), Chaucer says that man is 'sensible', 'ymaginable', and 'resonable'. Man perceives by his 'wits', the five outer senses, and he is also endowed with 'imagination', and also (unlike other animals) with the power of reason. By imagination he can recall the image of something seen in the past or invent an image by combining memories. Chaucer once speaks of the 'eyes of the mind' with which even the blind see (II.551–3). Because the imagination preserves the figure of a thing by separating it from its matter (cf. Bo V pr.4:158–9) it was regarded as a higher faculty than the 'wits'.

There was general agreement as to where the faculty was located. *Bartholomew says that the brain has three 'cells or dens', three 'hollow places that physicians call ventriculos, "small wombs"'. That at the front of the brain is called 'imaginativa, wherein things that the outer wit apprehends are ordained and put together within'. The other two contain *reason and *memory. Imagination is always associated with the creation of images. This may have great affective force, because 'impressions' in the mind are deeply engraved. A comic passage in The Miller's Tale (I.3611–19) illustrates its power: 'men may dyen of ymaginacioun, | So depe may impressioun be take.' In the higher faculty of reason the image can be related to all other associated images, and, ultimately, reason is freed from both matter and images. Higher still, and encompassing all the previous faculties, is the unique faculty of 'intelligence' possessed only by divine Providence (cf. Bo V pr.4:162–6).

Besides the noun ymaginacioun, Chaucer uses a number of other etymologically related words: ymaginatyf (adj. 'using mental images'), in the phrase been ~ (V.1094) = 'speculate', 'be suspicious': ymagynyng (n. 'imagination, fancy', in LGW G 331, where the equivalent passage in F 355 has *ymagynacioun*: but *derke ymaginyng* in I.1995 suggests 'wicked plotting'); and the v. *imagine(n)*.

The word *ymagynacioun* itself is frequently used in the technical sense of 'the faculty of imagination' (or its working), especially in *Boece*, where it regularly translates L. *imaginatio*. On three occasions there Chaucer uses it to translate L. *imago* (e.g. V m.4, where *sensus et imagines* becomes 'sensible ymaginaciouns or ellis ymaginaciouns of sensible thingis'), perhaps in order to emphasize the notion of a mental process. It can also mean 'idea, fancy'. On the one hand this sense covers ideas or notions that are erroneous or uncertain, like the 'veyn ymaginacioun' of I.1094, or the 'sorwful ymagynacioun' which haunts the dreamer's mind (*BD* 14) and suggests the *visum* or meaningless phantasm distinguished by *Macrobius in his discussion of *dreams. On the other hand, it comes close to 'ingenuity', as in *The *Summoner's Tale*: 'How hadde this cherle ymaginacioun | To shewe swich a probleme to the frere?' (III.2218–19). And when it is used of a slanderer (*LGW* 355), 'fancy' has the added implication of a wicked purpose (cf. 'evyl ymagynacioun' *LGW* 1523). The sense of 'scheming' or 'plotting' has been suggested for a problematical case in *The *Nun's Priest's Tale* (VII.3217) where the phrase 'by heigh ymaginacioun forncast' is applied to the fox 'ful of sly iniquitee', which had lived three years in the grove, breaking into the yard 'the same nyght'. The sense would fit with the semantic range of the word (cf. also *imagining*) as well as with the iniquity of the fox. However, the adjective 'high' rather strongly suggests a mock-heroic association with the question of God's foreknowledge and of the truth of dreams which is even more prominent in the tale. It may very well be that we have here a deliberate piece of ambiguity.

Certainly, in Boethius's Neoplatonic vision the divine 'intelligence' which contains 'the symple forme of man' also encompasses images and figures. God, is addressed by Philosophy (III m.9), 'Thow . . . berynge the faire world in thy thought, formedest this world to the lyknesse semblable of that faire world in thy thought' (cf. IV pr.6:82–99). That God made man 'after his image' is recalled at the end of *Troilus* (V.1839). Earlier in the poem in a more secular, and a sadder context, the idea that ideal beauty is a 'memory' of this image

is perhaps the remark that Criseyde's 'face, lik of Paradys the ymage, | Was al ychaunged in another kynde' (IV.864–5; cf. V.817).

Bundy (1927); Burnley (1983), 102–115; Carruthers (1990); Kolve (1984).

Ymeneus, Hymenaeus or Hymen, the god of marriage. He is invoked by Troilus (III.1258), and alluded to in *The *Merchant's Tale* (IV.1730) and *The *Legend of Good Women* (2250). In both these last references he is explicitly identified as the 'god of wedding'.

imitations of Chaucer may be distinguished from *modernizations and translations, although the line is a fine one in the case of some early examples of the latter which paraphrase or add passages or speeches. Imitation in the strict neo-classical sense is (Dr Johnson) 'a method of translating looser than paraphrase, in which modern examples and illustrations are used for ancient, or domestick for foreign'. But, as *Dryden had already remarked, sometimes the 'translator' takes 'only some general hints from the original' and 'runs division on the groundwork'. This can take 'imitation' a long way from 'translation'.

Chaucer, like Shakespeare, was not easily imitated. The best examples come from the period closest to him. The earliest of all are problematic cases of works on the edge of the *canon, such as lyrics of uncertain attribution. A very Chaucerian passage on *'gentilesse' in Fragment B of the *Romaunt of the Rose*, which has no equivalent in the French original, may perhaps have been inspired by Chaucer's lines in *The *Wife of Bath's Tale*. The 15th c. is the great age of Chaucerian 'imitation' in the wide sense. It produces a series of poems which show the influence of his style and his ideas (see *Chauceriana, *Chaucerians), a varied group ranging from *The *Kingis Quair* or *Henryson's 'The Cock and the Fox' to attempts at 'continuations' of *The *Canterbury Tales* (as in *The Tale of *Beryn* or *Lydgate's *Siege of Thebes*).

The urge to finish *The *Squire's Tale* inspired two writers at the end of the 16th and the beginning of the 17th c. In Book IV of *The Faerie Queene* *Spenser picks up the remark in the final lines about *Cambalo fighting in the lists 'with the bretheren two' for *Canacee, and ends it with

'Cambello' and 'Triamond', the only survivor of the brethren (three in number in Spenser), being magically reconciled, and marrying respectively 'Cambina', Triamond's sister, and Canacee. A much less talented writer, John *Lane, wrote a continuation in 1615 (revised and enlarged in 1630). The early 16th-c. The*Pilgrim's Tale is more clearly an 'imitation' of a Canterbury Tale, and the excellent The *Cobler of Canterburie imitates the whole work by setting (prose) tales within a framework. In Greene's Vision (probably but not certainly the work of Robert Greene) Gower and Chaucer appear and argue on gravity and levity in poetry. Greene gives Chaucer a fabliau, but decides in favour of Gower and moral seriousness. And throughout the period there are retellings and reworkings of the popular *Griselda story.

From the 16th c. on there were attempts to write in Chaucer's manner in what was supposed to be early English. These are usually wanting in any sound linguistic knowledge or literary talent. Most are simply of antiquarian interest. Probably the most entertaining is the 'imitation' of Chaucer done by the young *Pope (who also produced some modernizations). That 'women ben full of ragerie' is illustrated by the merry tale (more broad than anything written by Chaucer) of a lad who stuffs a filched duck into his trousers so as not be 'spied of ladies gent'. It thrusts its neck out at the front and utters a quack: 'Te-he cry'd ladies; clerke nought spake: | Miss star'd; and gray Ducke crieth Quaake'. Other 18th-c. imitations include those of Prior ('An Imitation of Chaucer' and 'Erle Robert's Mice, In Chaucer's Stile', 1712) and Fenton, whose 'A Tale devised in the plesaunt manere of gentil maister Jeoffrey Chaucer' (1717), later called 'The Curious Wife', is similar to Pope's in its bawdiness. It concerns a priest, Isaac Wever, and his young bride in the country, where she learns the habits of cocks and chickens and the facts of life. In William Mason's Musaeus, A Monody to the Memory of Mr Pope (1747), Chaucer appears as Tityrus (as in Spenser), and speaks some lines in which he praises Pope for having restored and smoothed his lines that were 'cancred by Time': 'Whanne shallow brooke yrenneth hobling on, | Ovir rough stones it makith full rough song; | But, them stones removen, this lite rivere | Stealith forth by, making plesaunt murmere.'

Rather surprisingly, Chatterton does not produce a Chaucerian imitation. A small part of the archaic vocabulary in his 'Rowley' poems is derived from the glossary of *Speght's edition, and clearly the reading of Chaucer had a formative influence on him (he made extracts from Speght's Chaucer, and has his Rowley say that he was never proud of his verse since he read Master Chaucer). 'An Excelente Balade of Charitie' has been said to show the earlier poet's influence, but this short Rowleyan tale of a poor pilgrim, an uncharitable abbot, and a charitable friar, though it is a much better poem than other 18th-c. 'imitations', is not really very close to Chaucer. Harriet *Lee chose to imitate the framed narrative of The Canterbury Tales (in prose). An interestingly different 19th-c. imitation is 'The Tapiser's Tale' of Leigh *Hunt. This is the brief 'pitous' story based on a legend of a miracle which gave the 'Field Floridus' near Bethlehem its name. A 'poore orphan mayd' is falsely accused of unchastity, and condemned to be burnt at the stake. The narrator exclaims in horror: 'Oh pure blood, swiche feendlich thirst to slake! | Alas for the soft flesche and gentil herte! | Alas, why colde she not fro life asterte | Softlie and sodenlie, with no moe care!' But just as the fire is lit, there is a heavenly smell of flowers, all the faggots are turned into roses, all 'her foes are gone, feeble with dredfull feare', and the crowd kneels before her: 'and there she standeth, shining all abrede, | Like to an angell, paradysed in dede'.

B. Bowden (1991); Hammond (1908), 220–33.

Inde. India in Chaucer's day consisted of a number of kingdoms and states. Prominent among them were the Hindu kingdom of Vijayanagar in the south and the Muslim Sultanate of Delhi which controlled most of the Ganges basin, although it suffered from incursions of Mongols and others from the north, culminating in the invasion of Timur (Tamburlane) in 1398. However, for most people in Europe India was a mysterious area. (See Map 1.) *Bartholomew gives an awesome list of its marvels drawn from Isidore (*Ysidre) and Pliny. There are great elephants and unicorns and parrots, spices, ivory, many precious stones, hills of gold (though it is impossible to come to them because of dragons and griffons and men of wonderful shape). There are men with the feet turned backward, with eight toes on one foot, and others with dogs' heads, clothed in the skins of wild beasts, who bark like dogs and 'speaketh none other wise', etc. Marco *Polo has a fuller and more factual account (embroidered with some travellers' tales). His descriptions of regions from Kashmir to the hot lands of the south and Ceylon note such things as diving for pearls, searching for diamonds, the cultivation of ginger and other spices, the exquisite leather mats and cushions made in Gujerat, etc. He shows a good deal of interest in the practices of exotic societies—the burning of a dead king on a pyre, the use of the right hand only in eating, maidens bringing offerings of food to the temples. The people worship idols, and venerate the ox. There are ascetic naked yogis, who only drink water and will not kill any living creature. He is also interested in the Indian Christians who guard the burial place of St Thomas the apostle (Chaucer's 'Seynt *Thomas of Ynde'). Probably, however, most readers preferred the more heightened account in '*Mandeville'. Here diamonds grow on the rocks: they grow together male and female, nourished by the dew of heaven. He is fascinated by the idols, which he sees as unnatural grotesques, 'as an image that hath four heads', etc. It is a land with serpents, monsters, and other marvels.

In Chaucer, India is a very remote place. It appears in phrases like 'from *Denmark unto Ynde' (III.824) or 'bitwixen *Orkades and Inde' (*Tr* V.971), which signify the furthest extent of the whole world. Similarly, the old man in The *Pardoner's Tale says 'I ne kan nat fynde | A man, though that I walked into Ynde' (VI.721–2; see also *BD* 889, *Bo* III m.5:5, *Rom* 624). It is also exotic. The *Clerk urges wives to be as fierce 'as is a tygre yond in Ynde' (IV.1199). A man transformed by *Circe 'goth debonayrely in the hows as a tigre of Inde' (*Bo* IV m.3:16). Its celebrated *gems appear on 'the broche of Thebes', 'ful of rubies and of stones of Ynde' (*Mars* 246). The blue dye obtained from India, now called 'indigo', had given rise to the adj. *inde* ('(indigo' blue', *Rom* 67). Its rulers are figures of romance. In The *Squire's Tale the strange knight is a messenger from 'the kyng of *Arabe and of Inde' (V.110)— though this is probably 'India Minor' or 'Middle India' i.e. southern Arabia. In The Knight's Tale

'the grete Emetrius, the kynge of Inde' makes a spectacular appearance (I.2155–89), dressed in cote armure of cloth 'of *Tars' with rich gems, bearing a white eagle on his hand, while tame lions and leopards run beside him.

Indulgences, see *Pardoner.

Indus. The great river of the Indian subcontinent flowing from Kashmir through Pakistan is mentioned in *Boece (III m.10). It is 'next the hote partie of the world', and mingles 'the grene stones with the white' (emeralds with pearls).

Inferno, see *Divina Commedia.

INNOCENT III (1160–1216), Pope from 1198; he greatly extended the power and authority of the papacy throughout Western Europe. His insistence on the appointment of Stephen Langton as archbishop of Canterbury in 1206 led King John, after a period of excommunication, to submission and the recognition of Innocent as feudal overlord. Amongst his writings was the *De miseria humanae conditionis* (written in 1195), a widely disseminated and quoted work in the medieval period. In the G version of the Prologue to The Legend of Good Women it is stated that the work was translated by Chaucer as *Of the *Wreched Engendrynge of Mankynde* (G414); the translation does not survive, but Chaucer's familiarity with the work is evident from allusions elsewhere in his writing. Chaucer's translation seems to have been made between the date of the F Prologue to The Legend of Good Women, in which it does not appear, and the writing of the G Prologue, in which it does, that is between 1384–6 and 1394–5. [AH]

(ed. and trans.) R. E. Lewis (1978).

Yole, Iole, the daughter of King Eurytus (*HF* 403). Hercules (*Ercules) fell in love with her and left Deianira (*Dianira).

Ypermystra, Hypermnestra, in classical legend one of the daughters of Danaus (*Danao) who were ordered, under threat of death, to kill their husbands on their wedding night. She spared her husband Lynceus (*Lyno), and became an exemplary figure of the faithful wife (II.75; *LGW* F 268). Her story is the last in *The *Legend of Good Women* (2562–723). Chaucer seems to have based it on Ovid's *Heroides* (14), but rather oddly makes her the daughter of Aegyptus (*Egiste) not Danaus.

YPOCRAS, Hippocrates of Cos (469–399 BC), the most famous of all Greek physicians. Although most of his works are lost, he was so widely and favourably reported (for instance by Plato) that he became the ideal of later physicians, and was still so long after Chaucer's time. He is referred to in the *General Prologue as one of those authorities known to the *Physician. (See also ***medicine**.)   [JDN]

Ypolita, Hippolyta, the queen of the Amazons (*Amazones), 'the faire, hardy queene of *Scithia' in *The *Knight's Tale*, who was overcome by *Theseus and became his wife. Her great beauty is alluded to in **Anelida and Arcite* (36–42).

Ypomedoun, Ipomedon, Hippomedon, one of the seven champions who fought against *Thebes (1). He is listed among the heroes in **Anelida and Arcite* (58), and his death by drowning is mentioned in **Troilus and Criseyde* (V.1502–3). (The ME romance *Ipomadon* is not connected with this story.)

Ypotys, the child hero of a pious legend mentioned in *Sir Thopas (VII.898) among other young heroes of romance. The story was very popular, appearing in Latin and in a number of vernaculars. In it a wise child (whose name is that of Epictetus the stoic philosopher) instructs the Emperor Hadrian through a series of questions and answers. Chaucer is thinking of the ME verse legend, which appears in MSS together with romances.

Sutton (1916).

Ypres, a city in Flanders (*Flaundres) (now Belgium) famous for its cloth-making (I.448).

irony, originally a technical *rhetorical term: 'a figure of speech in which the intended meaning is the opposite of that expressed by the words used' (*OED*). The word is not found in Chaucer's English, but the L. *ironia* is used in early rhetorical treatises. In modern criticism 'irony' may be used in wider senses—'dramatic irony', the 'ironic pattern' of a story, or a writer's 'ironic vision', etc. Types of irony carefully controlled by the writer are sometimes distinguished from 'unstable' irony, which sets up disturbing resonances and ambiguities that go beyond the text or raises questions beyond those posed by the narrative voice.

In the criticism of Chaucer there has been a discernable shift in the importance attributed to irony (see ***criticism of Chaucer II**). Early critics hardly mention it. It begins to attract attention in the 19th c. Leigh *Hunt, for instance, noting that it is 'a mode of speech generally adopted for purposes of satire, but may be made the vehicle of the most exquisite compliment', gives an example of how Chaucer 'with a delightful impudence, has drawn a pretended compliment out of a satire the most outrageous' in Chauntecleer's '*Mulier est hominis confusio*', which insult 'he proceeds to translate into an eulogy' (VII.3163–6). J. W. Hales in 1873 praises Chaucer's blend of pity and irony ('that dissembling, so to speak, that self-retention and reticence, or at least, indirect presentment, that is a frequent characteristic of the consummate dramatist, or the consummate writer of any kind who aims at portraying life in all its breadth'). But it is the criticism of the second half of the 20th c. with its love of ambiguity which has really emphasized his irony.

It has sometimes overemphasized it. A determination to find a pervasive irony has produced some extreme and unconvincing readings (as of *The *Knight's Tale* as a totally ironic and antichivalric work). The idea of the naive and gullible persona of 'Chaucer the Pilgrim' or the use of the 'frame-narrative' of *The Canterbury Tales* as 'an ironically informative clue to the "real" meaning of a tale' have sometimes been taken to dubious extremes. As Pearsall says, the employment of the 'dramatic principle' as a means of ironization allows the appropriation of tales not to modern taste to 'some fashionable modern ideology': 'by this means Chaucer can be recruited to worthy causes, and all need of effort at true understanding is removed.'

There are certainly cases where it is genuinely

difficult to decide if irony is present, or if it is, how sharp it is. Chaucer is fond of combining different tones within the same line, so that it is misleading to suppose that every instance of irony is totally 'reductive'. It is by no means always true that 'the intended meaning is the *opposite* of that expressed by the words used'. Not only are there delicate gradations, but the irony is often intermittent and flickering rather than a consistent presence. It is subtle and shifting, for 'if everything is ironical, nothing is interesting, since the reader has been deprived of those conspiratorial pleasures, those satisfactions of knowing that he has joined an elite fraternity of knowingness' (Pearsall).

Variety is to be found as well as subtlety. Among some fine examples of dramatic irony may be mentioned the moment in The *Pardoner's Tale* when the three rioters, having just been told of the whereabouts of death, *run* to the pile of gold under the tree, or the extended scene between the summoner and the 'yeoman' in The *Friar's Tale*. In *Troilus and Criseyde*, where dramatic irony is frequent, it is very often used not to reveal folly but to enhance the pathos and tragedy of the lovers' situation. In The *Merchant's Tale* we find a powerful undercurrent of irony pointed by sardonic asides. The many ironic or semi-ironic remarks made by Chaucer or his narrators help to produce a shifting perspective or a delightful uncertainty: 'This storie is also trewe . . . | As is the book of *Launcelot de Lake, | That wommen holde in ful greet reverence' (VII.3211–13), 'Thise been the cokkes wordes, and nat myne' (VII.3265), etc. A poetic irony which holds discordant elements together produces a characteristic balance of detachment and sympathy.

Booth (1974); Pearsall (1985), 63; Muecke (1982).

Ysaye. Isaiah, the Old Testament prophet, is several times quoted by the *Parson (X.198, 208, 209, 280). He is mentioned in The *House of Fame* (514) as a famous dreamer (see Isaiah 1 and 6).

Ysaak, Ysaac, Isaac, the Old Testament patriarch (Gen. 21–8), the son of *Abraham and Sarah (*Sarra) after many years of a childless marriage. Abraham demonstrated his total obedience to God's command by being willing to offer his son

in sacrifice (Gen. 22). Isaac was regularly taken as a 'figure' of Christ: 'Ysaac was figure of his deth, certeyn' (*ABC* 169). In *Melibee* (VII.1098) there is an allusion to his blessing of his son *Jacob.

Isaude, Isawde, Ysoude, Iseult, the beloved of Tristan (see *Tristram). Her story appears among those of other lovers in the temple of Venus in The *Parliament of Fowls* (290), and as a paragon of beauty ('bele Isawde') she is mentioned in the Prologue to The *Legend of Good Women* (F 254) and in The *House of Fame* (1796).

Ysidis, Isis, the Egyptian goddess. The reference in The *House of Fame* (1842 ff.) to her temple in Athens being burnt seems to be a version of the story of Herostratus burning the temple of Diana at Ephesus in order to win fame. 'Herostratus lives that burnt the temple of Diana, he is almost lost that built it', says Sir Thomas Browne in *Hydrotaphia*. Herostratus here appears in person, but as an anonymous 'shrewe', and reveals his motive.

YSIDRE, SEYNT, Isidore of Seville (*c.*570–636), bishop of Seville for thirty-six years, and an energetic ecclesiastic and educator. Of his various works, the most famous and influential was the *Etymologiarum Libri XX* or *Etymologies*, an encyclopaedic work in twenty books, a compendium of information relating to the liberal arts, theology, history, and science. It presents also a system of knowledge, based, as its name implies, on etymologies (often incorrect). This view, that the essential meaning of a phenomenon or a thing is revealed by the etymology of its name proved very influential (there is a reflection of it in the *Second Nun's exposition of the meaning of the name *Cecilie). The *Etymologies* passed on much ancient learning to the later Middle Ages. It was a popular storehouse of information. In it readers could find definitions of literary types and terms (like *'tragedy' or 'the theatre'; 'heroes', who are those who 'by their wisdom and courage are worthy of heaven', etc.), a view of universal history, and notes on planets, animals, birds, plants, and much else. Chaucer almost certainly knew the *Etymologies*. He mentions Isidore by name twice in The *Parson's Tale* (X.89, 551), a quotation of a proverbial saying from his *Sententiae*, and a remark about the property of the juniper tree taken from the *Etymologies*.

(ed.) Lindsay (1911); (trans.) Brehaut (1912, selections).

Isiphile(e), Hypsipyle, the daughter of *Thoas, the legendary king of Lemnos (*Lemnon). She rescued her father when the women of the island decided to kill all the men. When the Argonauts came to Lemnos they remained for a year, and Hypsipyle married *Jason, and bore him two sons. She was abandoned, but was always true to him, and 'deyede for his love, of sorwes smerte'. She is an exemplary figure of the faithful woman, betrayed by a man (see *HF* 400; *LGW* F 266, G 220). In *The Legend of Good Women* (1306–1579) Chaucer tells that part of her story which concerns Jason. He found it in *Guido delle Colonne and *Ovid (*Met. 7, Her.* 6).

Isle of Ladies, The, a 15th-c. poem of over 2,000 lines in couplets, surviving in two MSS (in one of which it is ascribed to Chaucer). It appears in *Speght (1598) under the title of 'Chaucers Dreame'. The modern title was given to it by Henry *Bradshaw. As 'Chaucer's Dream' it remained among Chaucer's works until the 19th c. When it was banished from the canon it fell into undeserved obscurity. It is an attractive love vision simply told 'in playne Englishe'.

In May the poet, thinking of the beauty of his lady while he rests after *hunting in a lodge beside a well in a forest, falls into a kind of half-waking vision. He seems to be in an island surrounded with walls and gates made of glass and elaborately decorated. The only creatures he can see are beautiful ladies. They tell him that he cannot dwell among them because of 'the old custome of this lande'. Their queen arrives. Standing beside her is a knight, and the dreamer's own lady.

The fleet of the god of love appears, and the ladies are unable to defend themselves. The god tells the queen to show mercy to the knight, and pierces her heart with an arrow. He also urges the dreamer's lady to show pity. The queen and the ladies present a petition to him asking for forgiveness and promising steadfast service. The god of love says he will be lord of the isle, 'his new conquest'. He summons them all to come the follow-ing day to hear his answer. When they assemble before him, he promises the knight and the dreamer that they will be restored to joy and commends them to their ladies. He leaves, followed next morning by the poet's lady in her ship. The distraught lover rushes into the water and is almost drowned. He is pulled on board and promises to be faithful forever. They arrive in her country, but as they land the dreamer wakes. His room is full of smoke, and his cheeks wet with tears. He goes to another room, where he hopes to sleep more easily, falls on the bed and dreams again.

He is back on the island, where the queen has agreed to marry the knight. It is agreed that he will return home and bring a company of knights who will marry the ladies. This is all to be done within a fixed term. The knight and the dreamer set off in a magic barge, but they are unable to return with their company until after the term has expired. They are met on the shore by a lady in black who says that their 'untrothe' has brought ruin. The queen and many of the ladies have chosen to die rather than live with the shame of betrayal. The knight is overwhelmed with grief and stabs himself. The bodies of the dead prince, the queen and the ladies are placed in an abbey of black nuns. On the following day a brightly coloured bird comes to the queen's bier and sings three songs, but startled by a movement, it crashes against a window and dies. Other birds come to the broken window and one flies in with a herb which he places beside the dead creature. A seed placed in its beak restores it to life. The abbess puts the remaining seeds by the queen's body and the miracle is repeated, and again for the prince and the ladies. After much rejoicing they decide to go back to the island for a great wedding feast. But the noise of the music and rejoicing wakes the dreamer. He is all alone, and in despair. He can only hope for his lady's grace, or else return to his dream and live on the island forever in her service.

(ed.) Jenkins (1980).

ISOPE, Aesop the legendary father of the Western *fable. He is said by Herodotus to have been a slave on the island of Samos in the 6th c. BC. Greek 'Aesopic' fables were collected in the late 4th c. BC, but the medieval Western 'Aesopic' tradition was derived from Latin writers like Phaedrus and

Avianus. Two very important sources were the collection attributed to 'Romulus' (? *c.*350–500) and, especially, a verse redaction of it in the 12th c., perhaps by 'Walter the Englishman'. There were many others in Latin and the vernaculars. The Latin 'Aesop' was a school text, and well known, so that allusions to Aesopic fables came very easily. In *The *Knight's Tale* Chaucer alludes to a fable of two dogs fighting over a bone, only to see a kite carry it away (I.1177–80), and in *The Reeve's Tale* to the fable of the Wolf and the Mare (I.4054–6). There are a number of similar Aesopic stories. In *Melibee* a proverbial remark (VII.1184) is attributed to 'Aesop'.

Ysoude, see *Isaude.

Israel, the land of Israel (VII.2060, 2152, *LGW* 1880).

Ytaille, Itayle. In the 14th c. Italy was both an abstract notion and a reality. On the one hand, the country had long been divided, politically into many regional and city-states (such as, for instance, the Angevin kingdom in the south, the papacy's dominions throughout central Italy, and towns like Lucca and Siena), linguistically into many dialects that appeared as true independent languages. Thus, 'Italy' and 'Italian' had a fairly vague meaning. On the other hand, the geographical notion of Italy carried well-established historical and cultural associations, particularly in connection with the country's classical past and with contemporary claims for a truly 'Italian' language in literature (the eventual success of which after many a struggle against Latin was substantially due to the immense popularity and prestige of *Dante's *Divine Comedy* and, later, of *Boccaccio's *Decameron* and Petrarch's (*Petrak) vernacular poems). As Chaucer knew from Virgil, Aeneas had, 'thurgh his destinee', landed in 'Itayle' (*HF* 145–7); and, although the English poet was aware of Dante's Florentine origins (the Wife of Bath calls him 'the wise poete of *Florence', III.1125), he also realized that Dante could be—and was by most 'Italians'—considered as 'the grete poete of *Ytaille* (VII.2460).

Chaucer's knowledge of Italy seems to mirror this double aspect. As a wine merchant's son, a

courtier, a clerk in charge of customs, and a diplomat. Chaucer was certainly acquainted with the fact that 'Italy' meant *Genoa, Venice (*Venyse), Lombardy (*Lumbardye), Florence, and many other different entities rather than one country as such. He would thus imagine the walls, floor, and roof of Fame's hall as 'plated half a foote thicke— Of gold' 'as fyn as ducat in Venyse' (*HF* 1343–8). Economic and political differences were reflected by linguistic ones, which Chaucer could not have failed to notice. We do not know if, how, and when Chaucer learnt to speak Italian (and which Italian he learnt). The many merchants, bankers, friars, clerics, and university men who went to England from Italy would all have been able to use either French or Latin in their dealings with the English. Amongst themselves, only Tuscans would speak a language coming close to the 'Italian' employed and ennobled by Dante, Boccaccio, and Petrarch. It is, however, clear that at one point in his life Chaucer became capable of reading this kind of literary Italian competently, to the point of playing skilfully with his own 'translations' from it, as in *Troilus* and the *Monk's Tale*.

The moment for getting deeper into the language, becoming more than superficially acquainted with the literary scene, and even acquiring actual manuscripts of Italian works may have come during the first of the two journeys which we know for sure he made to the peninsula and which were directed to specific places rather than to 'Italy'. This, in 1372–3 (Chaucer was away for six months and back by 23 May 1373), brought him to accompany Giovanni di Mari and Jacopo di Provano to Genoa in order to negotiate with the Genoese, who were seeking to obtain the use of a port in England. In the course of this journey, and presumably still in an official diplomatic capacity, Chaucer also visited Florence. The second trip (between 28 May and 19 September, 1378) was a mission to Lombardy, where he and Sir Edward Berkeley were to discuss 'business concerning the king's war' with Bernabò Visconti (*Barnabo Viscounte), then ruler of Milan, and Sir John *Hawkwood, the English commander of Visconti's mercenary army. Thus neither of Chaucer's visits had the quality later to be associated with the 'Italian journey' by northern European men of letters.

Ytakus

We shall never know what impression the reality of Genoa, Florence, and Lombardy made on Chaucer, if and how he reacted to landscape, architecture, sculpture, painting, and even local colour. His writings contain no original description of Italian places. The Clerk's account of 'Pemond', 'Saluces', and the Po valley down 'to Emele-ward, to Ferrare and Venyse' (IV.43–52) explicitly refers the audience back to Petrarch's 'prohemye' to his version of the Griselda story. In *The *Merchant's Tale* we hear no more of Lombardy and Pavia after the first two lines, which mention the former as the tale's setting and the latter as January's birthplace. Only one detail of Italian topography in the whole canon of Chaucer's works seems realistic—the location 'litel out of Pize' of the tower where Hugelyn and his children starved to death (a detail which is not present in Chaucer's source, Dante's *Inferno* 33, nor in Villani's *Chronicle*). But this location is actually mistaken.

In Chaucer's writings Italy, as distinct from her individual regions and cities, seems to be surrounded by a literary aura. Both in book I of *The *House of Fame* and in the Dido episode of *The *Legend of Good Women* the country's name is repeatedly used in connection with Aeneas, often in passages inspired by Virgil (or Ovid) or which constitute summaries of Virgil's narrative. At this stage, then, in Chaucer's mind Italy seems to be tied to the story of the *Aeneid*, to classical poetry, and particularly to Virgil. When, later, Italy enters the *Canterbury Tales* (namely, the Man of Law's, the Merchant's, the Monk's, and above all the Clerk's), the association with literature and learning becomes explicit. This time, contemporary authors such as Dante, the 'grete poete of Ytaille', and Petrarch, the 'maister' 'whos rethorike sweete | Enlumyned al Ytaille of poetrie', dominate the scene (with Giovanni da Legnano, the Clerk's 'Lynyan', whose provinces are philosophy or law 'or oother art particuler'). Padua and Bologna, seats of famous universities, take their place by Rome, Lombardy, Venice, Pisa, Florence, and Piedmont (Campania and Sicily had appeared in *Boece*, southern Italy being otherwise absent in Chaucer's writings).

It is not by chance that literature acquires such prominence in Chaucer's idea of Italy. Of all the exciting experiences he could have had in the field of Italian culture and art (one thinks, for instance, of Giotto's 'narrative' frescoes, of the different sense of space, civic consciousness, and individual pride that secular buildings and statues may have communicated to him), the literary one would be both natural to a poet and most rewarding at the time he came upon it. Trecento literature presented Chaucer with a fascinating mixture of traditional and innovative features in the genres to which he was already attracted (such as dream vision, romance, and story collection), with a powerful sense of the continuity between classical antiquity and the present, with three great and selfconscious personalities—those of Dante, Petrarch, and Boccaccio—who had experimented in all kinds of vernacular poetry and narrative as well as in scholarly writings in Latin. Although Chaucer's works show that he did not ignore contemporary Italian reality (the allusion to 'tirauntz of Lumbardye' in the *Legend of Good Women*, F 374, and the Monk's short 'tragedy' on Bernabò Visconti are witnesses to the contrary), it was literary Italy that he appreciated and worked on. In different ways and to varying degrees the *Parliament of Fowls*, the *Knight's Tale*, the *Clerk's Tale*, the *Monk's Tale*, and above all *Troilus and Criseyde*, indebted as they are to the works of Dante, Petrarch, and Boccaccio, represent the greatest 14th-c. European monuments to this Italy, which thereby began to become a *locus* of the imagination to be transformed into English poetry. [PB]

Boitani (1983); Wallace (2000).

Ytakus, the Ithacan i.e. Ulysses (*Ulixes), who came from Ithaca, an island in the Ionian Sea (*Bo* IV m.7:18).

Iulo, Iulus (or Ascanius (see *Askanius)), the son of Aeneas (*Eneas). He is mentioned only in *The *House of Fame* (177), where it seems that Chaucer thought of him as a different son.

YVE, SEINT, St Ive(s)—though which one is not clear. He appears twice, in a formulaic oath (and in rhyme): 'that lord that clepid is Seint Yve' (III.1943; VII.227). It seems likely (though not absolutely certain) that they both refer to the same saint. On geographical grounds, St Yves or Yve, the patron saint of Brittany, who was canonized in 1347, might be thought to fit the second reference (in *The *Shipman's Tale*, set in France), while St Ives (allegedly a Persian bishop who came to England and died there as a hermit), the patron of St Ives near Huntingdon, and who worked miracles at Ramsey Abbey, might be a little closer to the *Holderness of *The *Summoner's Tale* (and perhaps, more likely to be known to Chaucer). A third possibility (favoured by some) is St Yvo of Chartres (*c.*1140–1216). He was a great canon lawyer, but it is not clear that he was such a familiar saint that the English would swear by him.

Ixion, king of the Lapithae. Although he had obtained purification from Jupiter for the killing of his father-in-law, he ungratefully attempted to win the love of Juno. Jupiter sent a cloud in the shape of Juno, and by her Ixion begot the Centaurs (see *Centauris). As punishment in Hades he was bound to a wheel which turned forever. His torment is stilled by *Orpheus (*Bo* III m.12:37). The grieving Troilus (*Tr* V.212) turns and tosses 'in furie, as doth he Ixion in helle'.

J

Jack Upland, a satirical text based on a series of hostile questions to a friar; the questions circulated in various forms, English and Latin, in the time of Chaucer and shortly afterwards. If not Wycliffite in origin, the questions were taken over by the Lollards. They were answered in Latin by the Franciscan William Woodford; *Jack Upland* itself was answered in English by a Dominican writing under the name of Friar Daw; this latter was in turn rebuffed in rough alliterative lines added to its margins, and known as *Jack Upland's Rejoinder*.   [AH]

(ed.) Heyworth (1968); E. Doyle (1983).

Jacob, the Old Testament patriarch, the son of Isaac (*Ysaak) (see Gen. 25–34). The Merchant (IV.1362) recalls how he tied the kid's skin around his neck to win the blessing of his father (who mistook him for his elder son, the hairy Esau). This was because of the 'good *conseil' of a woman, his mother Rebecca (*Rebekke), a point also made in *Melibee* (VII.1098). In The *Parson's Tale* (X.443) there is a reference to God's blessing of *Laban 'by the service of Jacob' (Gen. 31). The *Wife of Bath notes (III.56) that he had more than two wives (Leah, *Rachel, and their respective handmaids).

JACOBUS DA VORAGINE, a 13th-c. Italian Dominican friar, later archbishop of Genoa, the author of the *Legenda aurea* or *Golden Legend* (1255–66). It is a collection of *saints' lives and treatises on religious festivals arranged according to the liturgical year. The legends are simply and vividly told, and the book's mixture of folklore, romance, and devotion made it very popular. It was translated into a number of vernaculars (including two 15th-c. English versions, one of them by *Caxton). Chaucer used the *Golden Legend* for the story of St Cecilia in The *Second Nun's Tale*.

(ed.) Graesse (1850); Maggioni (1998); (Caxton modernized edn.) F. S. Ellis (1900); (trans.) Ryan and Ripperger (1941); Stace (selections, 1998).

Jaconitos, Jaconites, a city in Colchis (*Colcos, *LGW* 1590). Chaucer, following *Guido, calls it the 'mayster-toun' of the region; historically, apparently, this was Dioscuras.

Jakke of Dovere (I.4347), a familiar name for one of the *Cook's 'delicacies' ('that hath been twies hoot and twies coold'). It may be a twice-cooked pie ('Jack of Paris' is a later term for this) or a fish (cf. 'John Dory'). (In Chaucer's day 'Jack' was already a nickname for 'John'; see III.1357.)

JAKKE STRAW, a leader of the *Peasants' Revolt of 1381. According to *Froissart he was involved in the destruction of the Palace of Westminster and the palace of the Hospitallers and the killing of 'all the Flemings they found in churches, chapels and houses'. This seems to be alluded to in The *Nun's Priest's Tale* (VII.3394). He was later executed.

jalousie, jelousie, jelosye (adj. *jalous(e), jelo(u)s*), jealousy, 'suspicion in love' (Dr Johnson). The words are occasionally used in wider senses (the *Parson speaks of 'jalousie of goodnesse' ('zeal for goodness', X.539); and the 'jealous' swan drives away intruders, *PF* 342), but usually relate to *love. In '*courtly love' in particular, jealousy is inimical to lovers and to love. In the *Roman de la Rose* Jealousy imprisons Belacoil (Fair Welcome) in a castle; in his company are Evil Tongue, *Daunger, Shame, and Fear. Only at the end of the poem is the castle stormed.

Jealousy is regularly opposed to love (cf. *PF* 457–8, *Mars* 36–7). '*Maistrye' and jealousy have no part in the marriage of Arveragus and Dorigen (*FranT*, V.748). The sun is once called 'the candel of jelosye' (*Mars* 7), because lovers have to flee for fear of wicked tongues. Lovers must resort to secret signs: 'swich subtil lookyng and dissymulynges | For drede of jalouse mennes aperceyvynges' (V.285–6). The ways in which 'subtil Jelosie, the deceyvable, | Ful often tyme causeth desturbyng' (*Venus* 43–4) are demonstrated in a number of stories, ranging from the tragic results of confinement (as in the story of Pyramus and Thisbe and their 'wrechede jelos fadres' (*LGW* 900) in '*Babiloyne', where 'maydenes been ykept, for jelosye, | Ful streyte, lest they diden som folye', 722–3) to the comic results of attempted confinement in *fabliaux.

'Suspicion in love' is interestingly treated in a scene in the third book of *Troilus and Criseyde*. Previously in the poem the traditional views of jealousy have been alluded to. Criseyde, musing on husbands, says that they are either 'ful of jalousie, | Or maisterfull, or loven novelrie' (II.755–6). *Antigone's song, as if in answer, celebrates her ideal love 'withouten jalousie or strif' (II.837). But the destructive power of jealousy suddenly becomes evident when Criseyde (falsely rumoured to love Horaste) in a lament bursts out with an exclamation: 'O thow wikked serpent, jalousie, | Thow mysbyleved [faithless] envious folie' (III.837–8). The powerful images are traditional: like envy, jealousy is associated with serpents and venom (cf. *Tr* III.1010); it is also *folie* ('folly', 'madness', 'insanity'), and the enemy of *trouthe* (III.839–40).

This scene (which is Chaucer's invention) is placed in bold contrast with the earlier episode of Antigone's song and with the immediately following scene of the union of the lovers which is a celebration of 'benigne Love, thow holy bond of thynges' (III.1261). After Troilus has come in, Criseyde defends herself in a fervent and 'pitous' speech (981–1057). She recognizes that it is love which is the cause of such 'folie', and gently sets out to cure it. Beginning with the proverb 'Ye, jalousie is love' (III.1024) she goes on to discuss jealousy. Only God knows whether it is more like love, or hate, or anger; what is certain is that some kinds are more excusable than others (e.g. if there is reason, and if the 'fantasie' is repressed so that it

scarcely reveals itself in word or action). But sometimes it is so 'ful of furie and despit' that it cannot be repressed. Troilus, she says, is not in that plight: 'I wol nought calle it but illusioun | Of habundaunce of love and besy cure [anxious care], | That doth youre herte this disese endure.' The scene ends in reconciliation and mutual forgiveness (1177–83). In the last book of the poem jealousy creeps in with the despair Troilus feels when Criseyde has not returned: 'therwith the wikked spirit . . . | Which that men clepeth woode [mad] jalousie, | Gan in hym crepe in al this hevynesse' (V.1212–14). Finally his suspicion is confirmed (1644–66): 'now ful wel he wiste, | His lady nas no lenger on to triste.'

The discord caused by 'subtil Jelosie, the deceyvable' is dramatically shown in *The *Knight's Tale*. When Arcite is to be released from prison, its effects on his rival in love Palamon are intense: 'the fyr of jalousie up sterte | Withinne his brest, and hente him by the herte | So woodly [madly, passionately] that he lyk was to biholde | The boxtree or the asshen dede and colde' (I.1299–302). He suffers because of the jealousy of two goddesses: *Juno 'jalous and eek wood' in her anger against *Thebes (1) and *Venus, who slays him 'for jalousie and fere of hym Arcite' (1332–3). The perception that jealousy is not always simply an enemy of love but is in some ways connected with it (or at least with the kind of passionate love associated with Venus) is very marked in this tale. In the temple of Venus, Jealousy is depicted: she wears a garland of yellow marigolds (her 'jaundiced' colour), and has a cuckoo (the emblem of cuckoldry) sitting on her hand (I.1928–30). (Similarly, in the temple of Venus in *The *Parliament of Fowls* the cause of the sorrows of the unfortunate lovers is said to have come from 'the bittere goddesse Jelosye' (251–2).) In the battle between the two knights, the 'jelous herte' of Arcite incites his cruel onslaught, while Palamon responds so that 'the jelous strokes on hir helmes bete' (2626–35). In the reconciliation at the deathbed of Arcite, jealousy (linked with 'strif and rancour') is specifically mentioned. He confesses to Emily: 'I have heer with my cosyn Palamon | Had strif and rancour . . . For love of yow, and for my jalousye' (2783–5).

The destructiveness and danger of jealousy is

shown in *The *Manciple's Tale*, where the 'jalous' Phoebus, who wished to keep his wife caged, finally kills her. In fabliaux, even though 'jalous folk ben perilous everemo' (I.3961), the potential danger adds zest to attempts to outwit a jealous husband, like the carpenter in *The *Miller's Tale*, who was 'jalous' and tried to keep his Alison 'narwe in cage' (I.3224; see 3294–7, 3404, 3851). The *Wife of Bath is aware of the problem (see III.303–7), but she knows how to use jealousy as a weapon, or rather as a purgatorial pain (III.487–9, and she is echoed by the *Clerk in his advice to wives, IV.1205–6). The Pardoner is selling a potion for 'jalous rage' which is so effective that the husband will never mistrust his wife, even though he knows of her misdeed (even if she has taken 'prestes two or thre', VI.366–71). However, in *The *Merchant's Tale*, where the blind January suffers from the 'fyr of jalousie' in a very intense form (IV.2073–91), the quick-wittedness of his spouse is sufficient to allay the pangs.

Jame (1), Seint, St James the Apostle ('the Great'), who was martyred in AD 44. His shrine at Compostela (see Seint *Jame (2)) was an important pilgrimage site. Images of the saint often have the pilgrim's hat and scallop-shell (supposed to be used as a scoop for water and a plate for food) associated with Compostela. He was a popular saint in England, where over 400 churches are dedicated to him. Reading Abbey claimed to possess his hand. In Chaucer his name is commonly found in oaths (I.4264; III.312; 1443, etc.). It is not clear that he distinguished the Apostle from St James 'the Lord's brother' who was often thought to be the author of the 'Epistle of James'. This book of *consolation is mentioned at the end of *The *Clerk's Tale* (IV.1154). Chaucer here (as often) simply calls the author 'Seint Jame'; both Petrarch (*Petrak) and the French translation attribute it specifically to the Apostle. The *Parson's Tale* (X.348) quotes it as by 'Seint Jame the Apostel'. The book is also quoted in *Melibee* (VII.1119, 1517, 1675, 1869).

Jame (2), Seint, St James of Compostela (Santiago de Compostela), the shrine of what were believed by divine revelation to be the relics of the apostle James, martyred in Jerusalem, and miracu-

lously transported to Spain, which, it was thought, he had formerly evangelized. Transformed by popular belief into a warrior saint, willing to appear in battle on his white charger in order to defeat the Moors, he was to become the patron saint of Spain and his feast day (25 July) a public holiday in that country. Situated as it was in the northern fringe of the Peninsula, the shrine became the rallying point for Christian Spain, and from the 10th c. onwards a place of pilgrimage second only in popularity to Jerusalem and Rome. The *Wife of Bath had visited all three (I.463–6).

[PS]

JAMES I, see *Kingis Quair*.

Janicula, Janicle, the father of *Griselda (IV.208).

Jankin (1), Jenkin (diminutive of John), Johnny; (II.1172) a derisive name for a priest (cf. Sir John, VII.2810).

Jankyn (2), the squire of the lord in *The *Summoner's Tale* (III.2288, 2293).

Jankin (3), Janekyn, 'oure apprentice' in *The *Wife of Bath's Prologue* (III.303, 383).

Jankin (4), 'Jankyn clerk', the *Wife of Bath's fifth husband (III.548, etc.). He is often assumed to be the same as Jankin (3), but the fact that he is constantly called a 'clerk' suggests that he is a different person. His career (a clerk at Oxford, then boarding with the Wife's gossip, Alison) does not seem to be that of an apprentice. The problem is that 'Jankin' is a conventional name for amorous young men, including amorous young clerks. Jankin 'oure clerk', the fifth husband, has a splendid collection of anti-feminist writings. The difficulties which this causes are vividly described in *The *Wife of Bath's Prologue*.

Januarie, the aged knight in *The *Merchant's Tale* (IV.1393, etc.), the husband of the young May. The name is obviously (and in Chaucer, unusually) symbolic. Possibly Chaucer found the suggestion in a *ballade of *Deschamps 'contre les mariages disproportionnés' in which January and April are wed.

Janus, the Roman god of goings out and comings in, gates and doors (L. *janua*), of entry and beginnings (who therefore gave his name to the first month of the year). He was called *bifrons* the two-faced god, looking both before and behind. According to *Macrobius this signifies wisdom: he knew the past and foresaw the future. There is a nice reference to him in *Troilus and Criseyde* (II.77): as Pandarus sets off on his mission to the house of Criseyde, the narrator exclaims 'Now Janus, god of entree, thow hym gyde!' In *The *Franklin's Tale* he appears at the turning point of the year in a little vignette reminiscent of the depictions of the Labours of the *Months: 'Janus sit by the fyr, with double berd, | And drynketh of his bugle [buffalo] horn the wyn; | Biforn hym stant brawen [meat] of the tusked swyn' (V.1252–4).

Jason, Jasoun, Jason the Argonaut, most notable in Chaucer as the unfaithful lover of *Medea and Hypsipyle (*Isiphile(e)). There is a brief and partial account of his doings in their 'Legend' (*LGW* 1368–1679). Jason, the son of Aeson (*Eson), after the death of his father excites the envy of Pelias (*Pelleus), who thinks to destroy him by sending him into a distant country. When the news spreads that in the 'isle' of Colchis (*Colcos) there is a ram with a fleece of gold, guarded by a dragon, Pelias suggests that Jason should win the treasure and the honour. He undertakes the adventure. *Argus (1) builds the ship (the *Argo*), and Jason sets out, accompanied by Hercules (*Ercules) and other knights. At Lemnos (*Lemnon) he meets Hypsipyle, whom he marries but then abandons. At Colchis Medea is enamoured of him, and tells him how to win the fleece. He returns home, and later abandons Medea also. The story of Jason and Medea appears in the windows of the room in which the dreamer finds himself in *The *Book of the Duchess* (330; cf. also 727). Chaucer's other references to Jason are consistently hostile. He was 'of love so fals' (II.74), an exemplary figure of male 'doubleness' in love (V.548 ff.; see also *HF* 400–1; *LGW* 266). The Legend of Hypsipyle and Medea begins with a fierce invocation: 'thow rote of false lovers, Duc Jasoun, | Thow sly devourere and confusioun | Of gentil wemen' and continues in this vein for about thirty lines ('there othere falsen oon,

thow falsest two!', 'Have at thee, Jason! Now thyn horn is blowe!'). The vehemence of the language has suggested to more than one reader that Chaucer may not have been entirely serious. Elsewhere in medieval literature Jason receives more sympathetic treatment. He is regarded as a 'flower of chivalry', and in 1429 Duke Philip the Good of Burgundy founded the Order of the Golden Fleece.

jealousy, see *jalousie.

JEAN D'ANGOULÊME, the brother of Charles d'Orléans the poet, who like him spent years in captivity in England (1412–45). The keepers of both brothers included men who owned Chaucer MSS or were in the circle of Thomas *Chaucer. There survives an incomplete MS of *The *Canterbury Tales* which belonged to Jean d'Angoulême (now MS fonds anglais 39 in the Bibliothèque nationale, Paris). It was written in the first half of 15th c. by a professional scribe under direct supervision, with corrections and comments, some of them in Jean's own hand. The treatment and arrangement of the text also seems to reflect his own taste. Most of *The *Squire's Tale* (described as *valde absurda* (very absurd)) is omitted, as is much of *The Monk's Tale* (*valde dolorosa* (very sorrowful)). He seems to have liked *The *Knight's Tale* (*valde bona* (very good)).

Strohm (1971).

JEAN DE MEUN (Meung), called Clopinel or Chopinel, a French poet of the second half of the 13th c. who completed the *Roman de la Rose* (?c.1275). Very little is known of his life. He seems to have come from Meung-sur-Loire, and was a university graduate, a 'master'. Jean was a scholar and an intellectual, who translated various works from Latin into French. These include a prose translation of the *Consolation of Philosophy* which Chaucer used for his *Boece. Jean's continuation of the *Roman* is both didactic and highly entertaining. It has an encyclopaedic scope, and is full of digressions and expansive disquisitions. Reason has a prominent place in his view of the world; he is interested in science and in many of the intellectual questions of his day. He is an excellent satirist, who attacks the *friars with particular ferocity. He does not see women as the idealized creatures of courtly poetry, and sometimes treats them with marked irreverence. This caused some literary controversy, and he is accused by some taking part (e.g. *Christine de Pisan) of anti-feminism. Whether all his remarks should be taken at face value, or whether he reveals a sardonic and ironic view rather than a strictly anti-feminist one are matters for debate. This, however, is the background to the episode in the Prologue to The *Legend of Good Women in which the god of love condemns Chaucer for having translated the work. What Chaucer thought about this question is not clear, but it is evident that he had read Jean de Meun with great attention and profit. He shared his fascination with ideas, and echoes his remarks on a number of topics (e.g. *Nature and '*gentillesse'). He probably responded also to the strong sense of personality which emerges and to Jean's use of loquacious speakers, his love of digressions, dramatic oppositions, and variety of tone. Fragment C of The *Romaunt of the Rose is a translation of a section of Jean's continuation, but it is not usually thought to be Chaucer's.

jelousie, jelosye. See *jalousie.

Jepte, Jephtha (Judges 11). After a victory, Jephtha vowed to sacrifice whatever or whoever came out of his house on his return. It was his own daughter, who came out to welcome him. She asked for two months' respite from death so that she might lament her virginity. This is alluded to in The *Physician's Tale where Virginia, requesting a little time in order to lament, mentions Jephtha, who gave his daughter 'grace | For to compleyne, er he hir slow' (VI.240–1). The point of this allusion has been debated, some critics finding it 'comically maladroit.' Jephtha's rash vow was often condemned in the Middle Ages, but some writers responded to the '*pite' of the tragic story—notably Abelard, who wrote an eloquent and passionate *complaint of Jephtha's daughter. It seems likely that Chaucer is also invoking the story to increase the pathos of the scene.

Jeremye, Jeremiah, the Old Testament prophet (7th c. BC). His attack on idle swearing (Jeremiah 4:2) is quoted by the *Pardoner (VI.634–7) and by the *Parson (X.592): 'thou shalt swere in trouthe,

in doom [case at law], and in rightwisnesse'. He is quoted on two other occasions in The *Parson's Tale (X.76 (Jeremiah 6:16), 189 (apparently echoing 18:8–10 or I Sam. 2:30)).

JEROME, SEINT (c.342–420). After Augustine (*Austyn), the most influential patristic writer in the medieval period and also the translator of the Hebrew and Greek testaments that became known as the Vulgate, or standard, version of the Latin *Bible. Chaucer's biblical quotations, like those of all his contemporaries, derived from this version. Jerome was also a noted commentator on the Bible, and the writer of numerous letters and polemical tracts. Perhaps the most important text for Chaucer is Jerome agayns Jovynyan (LGW Prol. G 281, PL 23.211–338), one of the main sources of medieval anti-feminist satire and a major contributor to Jankyn's book (WBProl. III.674).

[AH]

Jerusalem, the ancient holy city (of Judaism, Christianity, and Islam) in Palestine, marked in medieval maps as the centre of the world. (See Maps 1, 3.) In the Middle Ages its holy places made it the greatest of the *pilgrimage centres—the *Wife of Bath had visited it three times (I.463; see also III.495). Chaucer also refers to the Old Testament Jerusalem, the site of the temple, conquered by Nebuchadnezzar (*Nabugonosor) and threatened by Holofernes (*Oloferne) (VII.2147, 2196, 2596), and to the allegorical 'Jerusalem celestial' in The *Parson's Tale (X.51, 80), the heavenly 'New Jerusalem' (of Revelation 21:2), the goal of the Christian's spiritual pilgrimage.

Jesus; Jewels; Jewerye, Juerie. See *Jhesus; *Gems; *Jews.

Jews. The destruction of the Temple at *Jerusalem by the Romans in AD 70 led to widespread Jewish emigration. By the Middle Ages, groups were to be found throughout most of Western Europe, especially in Spain, France, and Germany, preserving their religion, culture, and learning. They suffered frequent waves of persecution, but they were also tolerated, notably in Muslim Spain for extended periods. These communities contained merchants and writers and intellectuals, like the

12th-c. philosopher and physician Moses Mai-monides (Mosheh ben Maymun) who was born in Córdoba, but later had to flee to Egypt. For medieval Christianity the Jews were problematic. One view, deriving from the Epistle to the Romans, and endorsed by Augustine and others, thought of a continuing spiritual Israel, which did not include the Jews. Yet, although they had rejected Christianity, they were not rejected by God, and would be converted at the end of time. There was a more negative view, deriving from the Epistles to the Galatians and the Corinthians, which saw them as Ishmael, the son of a slave woman, who must be driven out. They were iden-tified with the Old Testament, which was part of sacred scripture, but also with the Old Law (repre-sented in medieval iconography by the figure of the Synagogue) standing blindfolded on one side of the crucified Christ, while on the other the fig-ure of the Church stood with eyes uplifted and her chalice ready to receive the Redeemer's blood. Above all, they were held to be responsible for Christ's death, and the gospel phrase 'his blood be upon us' was often quoted. On the other hand the Old Testament afforded some heroic figures, e.g. *Judith, *Judas Machabeus, etc.

The Jews were an obvious target for persecu-tion, since they were so clearly different from their Christian neighbours. They carefully preserved their own traditions, and tended to live in tightly knit communities. The difference was empha-sized by the Christians. In the later Middle Ages Jews were required to wear some identification, a yellow cloth or a badge or a hat (in medieval art they are normally represented wearing pointed hats). Their involvement in money-lending and finance (partly because of the Christian Church's hostility to usury) made them both useful and unpopular. Although both secular and ecclesias-tical authorities made attempts to prevent the worst excesses, persecution was often cruel and violent. Popular hatred seems to have been at its worst in periods of religious enthusiasm and nat-ural disaster. Popular suspicion was fuelled by leg-ends of the ritual murder of children (like that *Hugh of Lincoln), of defilement of the conse-crated Host, of involvement in magic, etc. In more intellectual circles the Jewish presence and its challenge to Christianity had the positive effect of provoking the development of sophisticated theological arguments in defence of the Christian faith, and attempts to convert the Jews sometimes led to some knowledge of Hebrew and rabbinic writings.

The Jews had been driven out of England by Edward I in 1290, leaving such memorials as the names of Jewry Street, old Jewry, or the church of St Lawrence in the Jewry, so called, says *Stow, 'because of old time many Jews inhabited there-about'.

In Chaucer, Jews are most prominent in *The *Prioress's Tale*, a story much discussed for its real or supposed anti-Semitism. Its setting, the 'Jew-erye' (apparently around a street which is 'open' at each end) in a 'great city' in Asia, sounds very like what was later called a 'ghetto' (from the example in Venice). The remark that it was maintained by a lord 'for foule usure and lucre of vileynye' perhaps suggests a European Christian rather than an oriental viewpoint. Chaucer himself would not have seen such a community in England, though he might have in France, Italy, or Spain. However, he may well have drawn his information from a lit-erary source. Other references are usually to events or figures in Jewish history, mostly from the Old Testament: Solomon (*Salomon, IV.2277), *Judith and Holofernes (*Oloferne, VII.2551 ff.), the crossing of the Red Sea (II.489–90), etc. 'Ebrayk *Josephus' has a place in the House of Fame (*HF* 1429–36) for bearing up the fame of 'the Jewerye.' But *The *Parson's Tale* refers to 'the cursede Jewes' who dismembered the precious person of Christ (X.590); they hate his name (599), and reproved and despised him (663). The law of the Jews which required death for adultery is opposed to that of Christ 'that is lawe of *pitee' (X.889). The *Pardoner's relic, a bone of 'an hooly Jewes sheep', which will increase the number of a person's animals and goods (VI.351–65), seems to imply the popular connection of Jews with both magic and money. The hauberk of Sir *Thopas (VII.864) is 'ywrought of Jewes werk' (perhaps in Spain?). The old man in *The *Pardoner's Tale* has often been associated with the legendary figure of the wandering Jew, who because he taunted Christ on his way to the crucifixion was doomed to wander over the earth until the Day of Judgment.

Roth (1949, 1964); Rubin (1999).

Jhesus, Jesu(s) (Crist). Jesus Christ is very frequently mentioned, in references to his sayings or to events of the New Testament (e.g. I.698). His name is often found in invocations and oaths (e.g. I.3483, 3711). There are also traditional formulaic titles and descriptions: 'oure soules leche' (VI.916), 'kyng of kynges' (III.1590), 'hevene kyng' (III.1181), etc. Examples of the intense, personal, 'affective' devotion to 'Oure sweete Lord Jhesu Crist' (X.315) characteristic of medieval Christianity can be found: for instance, in Constance's prayer to Mary who saw her son suffer (II.845–8), or the lines at the end of *Troilus and Criseyde* urging 'young folk' to love 'hym the which right for love' died on the cross (V.1841–6). The **Parson's Tale*, which has a passage on the love of Christ (X.944 ff.), is typically Christocentric. His example is often cited as a pattern for human behaviour, e.g. in **Melibee*: he wept for his friend Lazarus (VII.987); he would not give a sudden answer (1033); he suffered patiently (1502–3), etc. (See **piety; *religion*.)

Jhesus Syrak, Jhesus filius Syrak, Jesus, son of Sirach (Joshua the son of Sira of Jerusalem), the author of the book of Ecclesiasticus, one of the 'Wisdom' books of the Old Testament. This is now regarded as apocryphal, but was widely known in the Middle Ages. He is several times quoted, e.g. on women (IV.2250–1), on putting away sorrow from one's heart (VII.995), that 'musik in wepynge is a noyous thyng' (VII.1045), etc. (not all the quotations in fact come from Ecclesiasticus).

Joab, a general of King David, noted for sounding his trumpet (2 Sam. [2 Kings in the Vulgate] 2:28; 18:16, 20:22). Hence at the wedding feast of January and May there is loud minstrelsy 'that nevere tromped Joab for to heere' (IV.1719). He also appears among the minstrels in *The *House of Fame* (1245). In both cases he is associated with the classical **Theodamas*.

Job. The Old Testament book of Job describes the patient sufferings of Job, a man in the land of Uz who was upright and feared God. It raises the problem of the suffering of the innocent, and celebrates Job's total piety. He was already a trad-itional figure of **patience* in the New Testament (James 5:11). In Chaucer he is several times referred to, usually for his proverbial patience, for example, by the **Wife of Bath* (III.436), by the **Clerk* (who says that **Griselda*, a woman, showed greater 'humblesse' than Job, a man, IV.932–8), and by **Prudence* (VII.999–1000), who says to her husband, 'remembre yow upon the pacient Job': when he lost his children and his goods and suffered bodily sickness he said 'the Lord gave, and the Lord hath taken away; blessed be the name of the Lord' (Job 1:21). In *The *Friar's Tale* the fiend mentions his sufferings to demonstrate how devils may torment the body and not the soul (III.1491). He is several times mentioned in *The *Parson's Tale*, where there is a lengthy exposition (X.176 ff.) of the **prayer* Job makes (Job 10:20–2) for a respite to bewail his trespass—verses which are given a poetic translation: 'Suffre, Lord, that I may a while biwaille and wepe, er I go withoute returnyng to the derke lond, covered with the derknesse of deeth, to the lond of mysese and of derknesse, whereas is the shadwe of deeth, whereas ther is noon ordre or ordinaunce but grisly drede that evere shal laste.' He is once called 'Seint Job' (X.223), perhaps meaning simply 'holy', or perhaps giving him sanctity because the image of him sitting covered with sores on a dunghill was taken to be a 'figure' of Christ the Man of Sorrows, sitting covered with wounds.

JOCE, SEINT. St Judoc (Fr. Josse). The **Wife of Bath* swears that she has quit her fourth husband 'by God and by Seint Joce!' (III.483). Judoc (7th c.) was a son of the king of Brittany, who gave up his position and riches to become a priest. He went on pilgrimage to Rome, and returned to live as a hermit near Étaples at a place now called Saint-Josse. There was an early connection with England: in Carolingian times his hermitage was used as a guest-house for English travellers, and his relics were brought to Hyde Abbey, Winchester, c.902. In art he is represented with a pilgrim's staff. This connection with pilgrimage makes him an appropriate saint for the Wife of Bath to swear by. Her words, 'I made hym of the same wode a croce [cross]' seems to imply his emblem. Her fourth husband had a paramour, and she 'quit' him 'nat of my body, in no foul manere', but by arousing his

1. In this early 15th-c. copy of Hoccleve's *Regiment of Princes* (perhaps intended for Henry, Prince of Wales), Chaucer is shown in the margin opposite his disciple's warm praise of his dear master. Although Chaucer is dead, his appearance remains vivid in Hoccleve's mind, and he has instructed this portrait to be made (BL MS Harley 4866, fo. 88).

2. The Wife of Bath as a pilgrim, with her whip and spurs and extremely large hat, is shown riding astride her horse (unlike the Prioress and the Second Nun, who ride side saddle) (Ellesmere MS EL 26 c 9, fo. 72, Huntington Library, San Marino, California).

3. The Pardoner as a pilgrim. The illustration has vividly reproduced some of the details of Chaucer's description. His cap has its badge, his chin is smooth, but his bag of pardons is hanging around his horse's neck (Ellesmere MS EL 26 c 9, fo. 138, Huntington Library, San Marino California).

4. Scenes from *The Pardoner's Tale*, the buying of the poison and the death of the rioters, from a carved wood panel, ?1400–1401. On the left the youngest 'rioter' is buying the pardon from an apothecary; in the centre we see his murder; and on the right the death of his companions (Museum of London).

5. The Pardoner, holding a relic (Cambridge University Library MS Gg. 4.27, fo. 306).

Here begynnyth the Pardoner his tale

6. Criseyde (wearing her black widow's 'habit') rides away from Troy (a medieval walled town with moat and drawbridge) and the sorrowing figure of Troilus. (From a manuscript of the French translation of Boccaccio's *Filostrato*; Bodleian Library, MS Douce 331, fo. 52.)

7. The Wife of Bath, here riding side saddle, with her whip and large hat (Cambridge University Library MS Gg. 4.27, fo. 222).

8. A bearded figure resembling the portraits of Chaucer is at a lectern reading to a company of noble men and ladies (see p. 38). Frontispiece to a manuscript of *Troilus and Criseyde* (Parker Library, Corpus Christi College, Cambridge, MS 61, fr.)

9. Jupiter, Mars, and Venus
(*The Complaint of Mars*;
Bodleian Library,
MS Fairfax 16, fo. 14v).

10. The Garden of the
Rose: the dreamer is
admitted by Idleness;
on the walls can be seen
Covetousness, Avarice,
Envy, Sorrow; inside,
Narcissus; and on the
left Daunger with his
club. (From a manuscript
of the French *Roman de
la Rose*, British Library,
MS Egerton 1069, fo. 1.)

11. Griselda, her father, and Walter, in *The Clerk's Tale* (Charles Cowden Clarke, *The Riches of Chaucer*, 1835). There is some attempt at a kind of 'ancient' garb, though the demure Griselda looks like a 19th-c. heroine (Bodleian Library, 35.216, vol. I, facing p. 203).

12. Criseyde sees Troilus ride past returning from the battle (from the Kelmscott Chaucer (1896), Bodleian Library, Kelmscott Press b.1, p. 482).

Of which the sone of Tydeus took hede,
As he that coude more than the crede
In swich a craft, and by the reyne hir hente;
And Troilus to Troye homward he wente.

This Diomede, that ladde hir by the brydel,
Whan that he saw the folk of Troye aweye,
Thoughte: Al my labour shal not been on ydel,
If that I may, for somwhat shal I seye.
For at the worste it may yet shorte our weye.
I have herd seyd, eek tymes twyès twelve:
He is a fool that wol foryete himselve.

But natheles this thoughte he wel ynough:
That certaynly I am aboute nought
If that I speke of love, or make it tough;
For douteles, if she have in hir thought
Him that I gesse, he may not been ybrought
So sone awey; but I shal finde a mene,
That she not wite as yet shal what I mene.

This Diomede, as he that coude his good,
Whan this was doon, gan fallen forth in speche
Of this and that, and asked why she stood
In swich disese, and gan hir eek biseche,
That if that he encrese mighte or eche
With any thing hir ese, that she sholde

Comaunde it him, and seyde he doon it wolde.

For trewely he swoor hir, as a knight,
That ther nas thing with whiche he mighte hir plese,
That he nolde doon his peyne & al his might
To doon it, for to doon hir herte an ese.
And preyede hir, she wolde hir sorwe apese,
And seyde: Ywis, we Grekes con have joye
To honouren yow, as wel as folk of Troye.

He seyde eek thus: I woot, yow thinketh straunge,
No wonder is, for it is to yow newe,
Thaqueintaunce of these Troianes to chaunge,
For folk of Grece, that ye never knewe.
But wolde never God but if as trewe
A Greek ye shulde among us alle finde
As any Troian is, and eek as kinde.

And by the cause I swoor yow right, lo, now,
To been your freend, and helply, to my might,
And for that more acqueintaunce eek of yow
Have ich had than another straunger wight,
So fro this forth I pray yow, day and night,
Comaundeth me, how sore that me smerte,
To doon al that may lyke unto your herte:

13. A night scene shows Criseyde and Diomede in the Greek camp (from the Kelmscott Chaucer (1896), Bodleian Library, Kelmscott Press b.1, p. 536).

14. *The Reeve's Tale*. A capital shows the nightly manoeuvrings of the clerks, the miller, and the miller's wife (*The Canterbury Tales*, with wood engravings by Eric Gill, Golden Cockerell Press, Waltham St Lawrence, 1929–31; British Library, c.98.99.26, vol. I, p. 132).

For every clerk anon right heeld with other.
They seyde, 'the man is wood, my leve brother';
And every wight gan laughen of this stryf.
Thus swyved was the carpenteres wyf,
For al his keping and his Ialousye;
And Absolon hath kist hir nether ye;
And Nicholas is scalded in the toute.
This tale is doon, and God save al the route!

WHAN folk had laughen at this nyce cas
Of Absolon and hende Nicholas,
Diverse folk diversely they seyde;
But, for the more part, they loughe and pleyde,
Ne at this tale I saugh no man him greve,
But it were only Osewold the Reve,

132

15. Scene from *The Merchant's Tale* (May (Josephine Chaplin) and her husband January (Hugh Griffith)), from Pasolini's *I Racconti di Canterbury* (1972).

jealousy and anger. Possibly she is alluding to the 'staff' in a more indecorous way (cf. I.673).

Haskell (1968).

Joh(a)n (1), Seint, St John the Evangelist. His authorship of the fourth gospel was assumed from an early date. The Apocalypse or Book of Revelation was also traditionally ascribed to him, but this is now thought unlikely. He is several times referred to in Chaucer, as one of the four gospel writers (VII.951), and is quoted in *The *Parson's Tale* (X.216, 349 ('if that we seyn that we be withoute synne, we deceyve us selve, and trouthe is nat in us'), etc.). He is also mentioned as a visionary, 'the grete evaungelist, Seint John' who wrote of the 'white Lamb celestial' (VII.582–3), of the four beasts 'full of eyes before and behind' (*HF* 1385; Rev. 4:6), and of the pains of hell (III.1647; cf. Rev. 19 and 20). His name is frequent in oaths (often in rhyme): e.g. II.18, 1019, III.164, etc., though it is not always clear that it is John the Evangelist rather than John the Baptist.

John (2) 'the Baptist John', St John the Baptist, the forerunner of Christ who baptized him in the river Jordan. There is one certain reference to him, to Herod ordering his execution (VI.491). It is possible that the phrase 'Seint John to borwe [as my guarantor]' (V.596, *Mars* 9) refers to him, and in the context, may have some reference to lovers' rites associated with his day (24 June), a festival connected with the summer solstice which attracted many folk customs.

JOHN (3) CRISOSTOM, SEINT (*c.*347–407), bishop of Constantinople, a learned doctor and an austere moralist. His name ('golden mouth') alludes to the eloquence of his preaching. He is once quoted (on penitence) in *The Parson's Tale* (X.109); the remark comes from a sermon formerly attributed to him.

John (4), the old carpenter in *The *Miller's Tale*. His background is filled in with some detail (he is well off, having a house big enough for two servants and a lodger), and he is a more complex character than the usual old husband of the *fabliaux*.

John (5), one of the high-spirited clerks in *The *Reeve's Tale*.

John (6), the *friar in *The *Summoner's Tale*. He is regularly referred to as 'the/this friar', and is only once named (by the lord) as 'frere John' (III.2171).

John (7), the monk in *The *Shipman's Tale*. 'This noble monk' is identified as 'daun John' early in the tale (VII.43). While this is almost a 'generic name' for a cleric (see *John (8)), it is regularly used throughout, with a certain savour ('my lord daun John', 68, etc.).

John (8), a name (sometimes contemptuous) for a priest (see Jankin (1)). The *Host, who does not know the *Monk's name, asks if he should call him 'daun John' (or 'daun Thomas', etc.; VII.1929). He similarly summons the *Nun's Priest: 'com neer, thou preest, com hyder, thou sir John' (VII.2810). That Chaucer echoes it ('this sweete preest, this goodly man sir John', 2820) is sometimes taken as evidence that it really was his name.

JOHN, see *Gatesden; *Somer.

JOHN OF GAUNT (1340–99), son of *Edward III and father of *Henry IV; earl of Richmond 1342, married *Blanche, daughter of Henry duke of Lancaster 1359 and succeeded to the duchy in 1362. Blanche died in 1368 or 1369, and he married again in September 1371 Constance, daughter of Pedro, king of Leon; following Pedro's death, he attempted to assert his claim to the kingdom. His third wife was Katherine Swynford, his mistress for twenty years. Chaucer's wife Philippa has been claimed as the sister of Katherine Swynford; certainly Philippa was for some time in the service of Constance, and received in 1372 an annuity from John of Gaunt; Chaucer himself received an annuity from 1374. It is generally accepted that the *Book of the Duchess* commemorates the death of Gaunt's first wife Blanche (see the references in *BD* 948, 1318–19 and the naming of the poem as 'the Deeth of Blaunche the Duchesse' in *LGW* Prologue F 418, G 406), though whether as consolation or as memorial poem (a question that affects the *terminus ante quem* of the poem's writing) is less certain.   [AH]

LR; Cavanaugh (1985), 474–6; Goodman (1992).

JOHN OF SALISBURY (*c*.1115–1180), educator, scholar, and humanist, studied in Paris and Chartres. He was in the service of two archbishops of Canterbury, Theobald and Thomas Becket (*Thomas of Kent) (he was in the cathedral at the time of the assassination). In 1176 he was made bishop of Chartres. He wrote works on logic and metaphysics (the *Metalogicon*) and on the theory of the state (the *Policraticus*). Two possible examples of Chaucer's use of the *Policraticus* have been suggested. It seems likely that in *The *Pardoner's Tale* the stories of *Stilboun and *Demetrius (VI.603–20) come from it. It has also been suggested that he might have found there the lines of *Horace which may have been the source of the mysterious '*Lollius'.

(ed.) Webb (1909 and 1929); (trans.) McGarry (1955); Pike (1938); Dickinson (1927).

JOHNSON, SAMUEL (1709–84), writer and literary critic, makes only a few references to Chaucer. In his 'History of the English Language' prefixed to his *Dictionary* (1755). Chaucer is described as 'the first of our versifiers who wrote poetically'. He does not, however, 'appear to have deserved all the praise which he has received, or all the censure that he has suffered'. Remarks on Dryden's modernizations in the *Lives of the Poets* (1779–81) suggest that he had a low opinion of *The Nun's Priest's Tale* ('The tale of the Cock seems hardly worth revival') and of *The Knight's Tale* ('containing an action unsuitable to the times in which it is placed'). However, one of his unaccomplished projects was 'Chaucer, a new edition of him, from manuscripts and old editions, with various readings, conjectures, remarks on his language, and the changes it had undergone from the earliest times to his age, and from his to the present. With notes explanatory of customs, etc., and references to Boccace and other authors from whom he has borrowed; with an account of the liberties he has taken in telling the stories; his life; and an exact etymological glossary.'

Jonas, Jonah the Old Testament prophet. His book tells the story of how he was told to go to Nineveh, how he attempted to evade the command by a sea journey and was punished by being thrown overboard. He was swallowed by a great fish, but delivered after three days and three nights. He is mentioned as an example of God's providential care in *The Man of Law's Tale* (II.486–7).

Jonathas, Jonathan, the friend of David (I Sam. 13 ff.). His 'friendly manere' is mentioned in the *ballade in *The Legend of Good Women* (251).

Joseph (1), the son of Israel in the Old Testament (Gen. 37–50). Because of the enmity of his brothers he fled to Egypt. He was a prophet, and earned the favour of Pharoah by interpreting his dreams. There are a few references to him in Chaucer. God gave his blessing to Pharaoh by the service of Joseph (X.443). He is also quoted in *The *Parson's Tale* as an example of the kind of 'trouthe' or fidelity rarely found nowadays (X.880): the story of Joseph and Potiphar's wife (Gen. 39:8–9) is used to illustrate a passage on the breaking of faith. Joseph is also cited as an authority on *dreams and as proof of their truth (VII.3130–5; *BD* 280).

Joseph (2), the husband of Mary (*Marie) and the foster father of Christ. Although there is some early evidence of a liturgical cult, the full-scale devotion to St Joseph developed after Chaucer's time. He is once mentioned in *The *Parson's Tale* (X.286), simply as 'Joseph'.

JOSEPH OF EXETER, the author of a Latin verse epic on the Trojan War, based on the work of *Dares the Phrygian. Very little is known about his life. He studied at Rheims, and worked, perhaps as a secretary, for his uncle, Baldwin of Exeter, archbishop of Canterbury (1185–90), to whom the poem is dedicated. His epic is variously called *Bellum Trojanum*, *De Bello Trojano*, or the *Frigii Daretis Ylias*. Chaucer's references to 'Dares' may well be to Joseph's poem. There are a couple of instances of direct borrowing. It is likely that some of the epithets applied to the trees in *The *Parliament of Fowls* (176–82) are taken from or suggested by those used by Joseph in his description of the trees at Troy (e.g. 'the olyve of pes' (*oliva concilians*), 'the dronke vyne' (*ebria vitis*)). He is also the main source for the formal *portraits of *Diomede, *Criseyde, and *Troilus which Chaucer places in the last book of *Troilus and Criseyde* (V.799–840).

(ed.) Gompf (1970); (trans.) Roberts (1970); Dronke (1974); Rigg (1992), 99–102.

JOSEPHUS, EBRAYK, Flavius Josephus Ebreacus (AD 37–c.98), the author of the *History of the Jewish Wars* and of the *Jewish Antiquities*, which linked the history of the Jews with that of Rome. A Jewish military commander, he won the esteem of the Roman Vespasian and Titus. He was present at the capture of Jerusalem by Titus in AD 70, and returning to Rome with him was granted Roman citizenship. He appears in The **House of Fame* (1429–36) standing on a pillar of lead and iron, because he is of the 'secte saturnyn' (lead is the metal of Saturn, and as the oldest of the gods, he is associated with 'olde merveiles' and the ancient Jewish religion). Josephus, who told the 'gestes' or great deeds of the **Jews, 'bears up' their fame.

Jove(s), see **Jup(p)iter.*

JOVINYAN, Jovinianus, a 4th-c. monk who denied that virginity was a higher state than marriage, that abstinence was better than grateful eating, and doubted the perpetual virginity of Mary. He was attacked by St Augustine (**Austyn), and (very vehemently) by St **Jerome in his *Epistola adversus Jovinianum*. Jerome's description of him as 'this handsome monk, fat, shining, whitewashed, stepping along like a bridegroom' is the source of the friar's attack in The **Summoner's Tale* on those other clerics 'that swymmen in possessioun', and are, like Jovinian, 'fat as a whale, and walkynge as a swan, | Al vinolent as botel in the spence' (III.1929–31). Jerome, writing from a strictly ascetic viewpoint, incorporates much antifeminist material in his praise of chastity, which is extensively used in The **Wife of Bath's Prologue*. Jerome's 'book agayn Jovinian' forms part of the collection prized by her husband Jankin (III.674–5). It is referred to in the Prologue to The **Legend of Good Women* (G 281ff.) because of its praise of good chaste women, and it provides some of the exemplary figures of virgins and widows who preferred death to dishonour cited by **Dorigen in her speech in The **Franklin's Tale* (V.1367–456).

joy, 'a vivid **emotion of pleasure arising from a sense of well-being or satisfaction; the feeling or state of being highly pleased or delighted; exultation of spirit; gladness, delight' (*OED*). Chaucer's word *joye* exists beside a range of synonyms or near-synonyms, including, e.g. *blis(se)* (with which it is often linked), *delit* ('pleasure, delight'), *felicite(e)* ('happiness'), *gladnesse, wele* ('happiness, prosperity', often opposed to 'woe').

In medieval literature joy is a particularly vivid and intense emotion. This is especially so in contexts of **love, where it still had a suggestion of the *joie d'amour* of the French and Provençal poets, an exhilarating and overwhelming passion. There are many echoes of this in Chaucer, especially in **Troilus and Criseyde*. In The **Knight's Tale* the excitement of the moment when Palamon and Arcite know that there is the possibility of winning Emily's hand: 'who spryngeth up for joye but Arcite? | Who kouthe telle, or who kouthe it endite, | The joye that is maked in the place' (I.1871–3). Chaucer sometimes likes to emphasize the intensity of the joy of love by a metaphorical verb. When the knight in The **Wife of Bath's Tale* sees the new beauty of his lady, 'for joye he hente hire in his armes two. | His herte bathed in a bath of blisse' (III.1252–3). The same idea is alluded to in *Troilus*: 'ye loveres, that bathen in gladnesse' (I.22), 'of al this blisse, in which to bathe I gynne' (II.849), 'he felte his herte in joie flete [float]' (III.1671). The suggestion is perhaps of a sea of happiness. Possibly behind it lie visual images, like those of the Fountains of Love or of Youth, or the depictions of the planetary **Venus and her 'children', the lovers who are shown bathing together. In *Troilus* the joy of love is even called 'this hevene blisse' (III.1322). But the joy of love is not always uncomplicated ecstasy. At the beginning of the *Parliament* it is called 'the dredful joye ... that slit so yerne [slides away so quickly]' (3), a phrase that is used by Criseyde as she broods on the uncertainties of love (*Tr* II.776).

The joy of the soul's union with God celebrated in mystical writing is not found in Chaucer, although he frequently refers to 'hevene blisse', and contrasts it with 'worldly blisse'. However, the end of The **Parson's Tale* speaks eloquently of the eternal joy which is the 'fruit' of penance: 'the endelees blisse of hevene, ther joye hath no contrarioustee of wo ne grevaunce . . . ther as is the blissful compaignye that rejoysen hem everemo, everich of otheres joye' (X.1075–6).

Chaucer regularly associates joy with *nature. In The *Parliament of Fowls it is a 'joy' to see the green trees (175), in the beautiful garden there was 'joye more a thousandfold | Than man can telle' (208–9), and at the end the birds fly off making 'blisse and joye' (669). Even the more domestic birds of The *Nun's Priests's Tale provoke the comment: 'swich a joye was it to here hem synge, | Whan that the brighte sonne gan to sprynge' (VII.2877–8). But 'joy' is occasioned by a variety of experiences: the dreamer has 'gret joye' when he looks at the stained glass windows (BD 325). When Arcite wins the tournament the excited noise of the crowd 'for joye of this' is so loud that it seemed the lists would fall down (I.2661–3): the *Pardoner admires the movement of his hands and tongue: 'it is joye to se my bisynesse' (VI.399), and so on.

Differing views are expressed about the nature of mankind's true happiness. Among the pilgrims in the *General Prologue, we have for instance, the *Franklin who agrees with the view attributed to *Epicurus 'that pleyn delit [pure pleasure] | Was verray felicitee parfit [true perfect happiness]' (I.337–8), a view shared by *January (IV.2021–5). Others take a quite different view. Criseyde exclaims that 'worldly selynesse [happiness], | Which clerkes callen fals felicitee, | Imedled [mixed together] is with many a bitternesse' (Tr III.813–15). After his death, Troilus despises 'this wrecched world' in comparison with 'the pleyn felicite | That is in hevene above' (V.1818–19). It is acknowledged that there are wicked 'joys', like those of the 'shrewes' in The *House of Fame who proudly proclaim that they have 'delyt in wikkednesse, | As goode folk han in godnesse; | And joye to be knowen shrewes' (1830–3), and false joys, like January's living 'deliciously'. 'Mannes foul delit', to which *Dorigen refers (V.1396), is a favourite topic of moralists like the *Parson (e.g. X.298, 330).

We are often reminded that in a world ruled by *Fortune 'to [too] lytel while oure blysse lasteth' (BD 211). Proverbial matter emphasizes that after joy comes woe ('the ende of blisse ay sorwe it occupieth', Tr IV.836), that there may be joy after woe and woe after gladness (I.2841), or that every joy is mixed with its pain. This idea is treated in a variety of contexts and in a variety of tones, ranging from the less than serious in The *Nun's Priest's Tale (see VII.3204 ff.) or The *Merchant's Tale (see IV.2055 ff.) to the tragic and piteous. In Troilus, for instance, the theme of how 'his aventures fellen | Fro wo to wele, and after out of joie' is announced at the beginning (I.3–4), and remains central throughout. The scene of the union of the lovers in book III is Chaucer's most powerful celebration of the joy of love. The word joie and its synonyms are repeated again and again (e.g. 1253, 1310–14, 1317–23, 1376–9, 1398–1407, 1413, 1442). The effect is heightened by a series of remarks on the impossibility of describing the sublimity of the joy, concluding (1688–94): 'Felicite, which that thise clerkes wise | Commenden so, ne may nought here suffise; | This joie may nought writen be with inke . . .'. But only a few lines later a hint of forboding may perhaps be heard ('thus Fortune a tyme ledde in joie', (1714), and the next book opens sombrely: 'But al to litel, weylaway the whyle, | Lasteth swich joie, ythonked be Fortune'.

An alternating pattern of joy and woe is characteristic of The *Man of Law's Tale: a joyous welcome ('with alle joye and blisse . . . in murthe and joye', II.409–10) is quickly followed by a massacre, the 'sodeyn wo' (always 'successour | To worldly blisse . . . | The ende of the joye of oure worldly labour', 421–3), joy at the birth of a child (726–35) by treachery and suffering. The joyous reunions at the end of father and son ('swich a blisse is ther bitwix hem two' that it surpasses anything 'save the joye that lasteth everemo', 1075–6) and between husband and wife and father and daughter restore concord and happiness, but it is mingled with tears. It is a 'pitous joye' (1114; cf. ClT, IV.1080). The Man of Law's Tale, true to its pattern, does not quite leave its personages 'in joye and blisse' (1118), but reminds us of the instability of the 'joye of this world' (1131–41), by recording the death of Alla. The final prayer is to Christ, who can 'sende | Joye after wo' (1160–1). Elsewhere, the 'high bliss' of heaven forms part of the final prayer (see VII.1886, 3444–6). The *Wife of Bath has an individual variation on this, leaving her characters living 'unto hir lyves ende | In parfit joye', and praying to Christ to send us 'housbondes meeke, yonge, and fressh abedde'. (See also *emotions; *game; *love.)

Jubaltare, Gibraltar, forming part of the 'narwe mouth' of the Mediterranean through which *Custance passes in her voyage (II.947).

Judas, Judas Iscariot who betrayed Christ for 30 pieces of silver, and subsequently hanged himself in despair. There were many legends about him, and some of the literary treatments (notably in the plays, or in the ballad 'Judas') are of considerable interest. Chaucer refers to him a few times simply as an exemplary figure. He was the greatest example of treachery: in The *Nun's Priest's Tale (VII.3227) the fox is called 'newe Scariot', and is linked with the other traitors Ganelon (*Genylon) and *Synon. Flatterers are like Judas, says the *Parson: they betray a man to sell him to his enemy (X.616). He is a proverbial figure ('any Judas') of the single wicked 'shrewe' in a company (VIII.1001–9). Other references are to the events of the gospel story: how he 'grucched' because Mary Magdalene (*Maudelayne) used the expensive ointment to anoint Christ's head (X.502; see John 12:4–6), how he despaired of God's mercy (X.695, 1015), or how he was thief (John 12:6). The summoner in The *Friar's Tale 'right as Judas hadde purses smale, | And was a theef' (III.1350–1).

Axton (1990).

Judas Machabeus, Machabee, Judas Maccabeus (d. 161 BC), the leader of the Jewish revolt against the Syrians described in the Books of Maccabees (*Machabee (2)). In *Melibee Prudence quotes him (as 'Goddes knyght') encouraging his little company with the remark that God almighty can as easily give victory to a few folk as to many folk (VII.1658–72). The episode is in I Maccabees 3:18–19.

Judicum, the L. title (*Liber Judicum*) of the Book of Judges, referred to (VII.2046) as the source of the story of Samson.

Judith, the Jewish heroine who saved her people from Holofernes (*Oloferne), who was besieging the city of Bethulia. Inspired by God, she devised a daring strategy: going to his camp, she aroused the tyrant's lust, waited till he was in a drunken sleep, and beheaded him. The story (from the apocryphal OT Book of Judith) was very popular in both literature and art in the Middle Ages. It is briefly told in The *Monk's Tale (VII.2551–74). Judith is cited elsewhere as an example of a weak person given courage by God (II.939), and as an example of women's *counsel (IV.1366 (possibly an ambiguous one in its context), and VII.1099).

Juerie; *Jugement du Roy de Behaigne, Jugement dou Roy de Navarre.* See *Jews; *Guillaume de Machaut.

Julian, Seint, St Julian 'the Hospitaller'. In remorse for having killed his father and mother by mistake (as had been prophesied by a hart that he was hunting), he and his wife built a hostel for the poor at a river crossing. He seems to have been a popular saint, associated especially with travellers, innkeepers, and hospitality. Appropriately, the *Eagle says 'Seynt Julyan, loo, bon hostel [good lodging]' as he brings Chaucer to the House of Fame (1022). And that generous householder, the *Franklin, is described as 'Seint Julian . . . in his contree' (I.340).

JULIAN OF NORWICH (1343–?1415). Her visions on 13 May 1373, when she was sick and apparently near to death, inspired her to compose the shorter text of her *Revelations* and, twenty years later, to enlarge and revise these. She was still alive in 1415, as a recluse at the church of St Julian, Norwich; sometime between 1402 and 1415 Margery Kempe visited her there. She described herself as 'a symple creature unlettyrde', but recent scholars have emphasized her acquaintance with Latin writings and even rhetoric; she may, despite the use of the first-person pronoun throughout, have dictated her *Revelations*. To judge by the paucity of manuscripts of the *Revelations* (only one of the shorter versions, three of the longer but all of the 16th c. or later), circulation was limited; there is no evidence that Chaucer knew her writings. [AH]

(ed.) Colledge and Walsh (1978).

JULIUS, Gaius Julius Caesar (100–44 BC) the great Roman general and statesman. He is the subject of one of the *Monk's tragedies (VII.2671–726). His story (linked with that of

Juno

Pompey (*Pompe)) is couched in rather general terms, and although Chaucer mentions *Lucan, Suetonius (*Swetoun) and *Valerius (Maximus), it is not easy to discover which particular sources he was using. He shares the general medieval admiration for 'Julius, the conquerour', who was one of the *Nine Worthies. A number of details come from medieval tradition rather than history: Caesar is said to have come from 'humble bed', to have been 'emperour', to have been Pompey's son-in-law (rather than father-in-law). The tragedy tells of his conquest of the West and his defeat of Pompey. But Fortune became his adversary, and he fell victim to the conspiracy of 'false' *Brutus (2) (see also *Brutus Cassius). The account of the murder is done with some detail: he was stabbed many times, but only groaned at one stroke, or at most two, as he died he pulled his mantle over his hips 'for no man sholde seen his privetee'. Elsewhere he mentions 'the slaughtre of Julius' depicted in the temple of Mars (I.2031), and that his death was 'written' in the stars (II.199). There is a reference (II.400) to his triumph as described by Lucan, who in The *House of Fame (1502) is said to have borne up his fame. It is also recorded in the *Astrolabe (i.10.9 ff.) that Julius Caesar took two days out of February and put them in his month of July.

Juno, the Roman goddess of women, daughter of Saturn and wife of Jupiter. Her anger against *Thebes (1) (because of Jupiter's adultery with the Thebans Semele and Alcmena) is referred to several times. In *Anelida and Arcite it is called 'the olde wrathe of Juno' (51; see also Tr V.601). *Arcite in The *Knight's Tale laments the destruction she has caused to the city and to his lineage (I.1329–31, 1543–61). She was also hostile to the Trojans. The dreamer in The *House of Fame sees a depiction of the scene from the Aeneid of 'cruel Juno' stirring up a storm against Aeneas and his men (198–211), and refers to her 'sleight and . . . compas' against the hero (461). Her power is alluded to by *Pandarus, who hopes that 'blissful Juno' will send her grace through her great might (Tr IV.1116), and Criseyde alludes to 'Saturnes doughter, Juno' and her power (IV.1538), and prays 'as helpe me Juno, hevenes quene' (IV.1594). In The *Book of the Duchess another woman, *Alcyone, prays to her

goddess Juno to bring her news of her husband, and Juno sends a messenger to *Morpheus, the god of sleep, to ask him to bring the drowned body to her (109 ff.). Juno gives her blessing to brides: it is therefore sinister that at the wedding of Procne (*Progne) she 'lyst nat at the feste to be' (LGW 2249).

Jupiter, (1) Ancient Italian god of the sky, connected with the Greek Zeus. The Jupiter cult assumed great importance in the late Etruscan period, and among the Romans Jupiter assumed the role of principal deity. The god was always to some extent concerned with oath-taking and sanctions against oath-breaking and treachery. He is a hurler of thunderbolts, often in judgement. (*Pandarus speaks of 'Jupiter, that maketh the thondre ring', Tr II.233.) His literary reputation as a magnanimous judge was mirrored in medieval art. Very different is the Greek myth of Europa's abduction by Zeus, who adopted the form of a bull. (In some accounts the bull became the constellation Taurus.) Transferred to Jupiter, as it had been for example in *Ovid's Metamorphoses, the story is referred to by *Troilus. (See also *Bole; *Pheton.)

(2) The planet. Jupiter occupies the sixth sphere of simple Aristotelian *cosmology. In astrology Jupiter was usually deemed temperate, wise, and concerned with law and judgement. There is an example of allegory in the fourth book of *Troilus and Criseyde where Jupiter sits in judgement on Venus. This benevolent planet Jupiter also had strong, albeit often only tacit, affiliations with God and Christ in judgement in Christian art. *Arcite's invocation to Jupiter ('Juppiter so wys . . . have of my soule part') would not be difficult to transform into a Christian prayer. The planet's *domiciles were *Sagittarius and *Pisces, his exaltation was in *Cancer and his dejection in *Capricorn. Jupiter as judge and arbitrator appears in an astrological allegory in the third part of The *Knight's Tale, where he is settling the strife of Mars and Venus. The planet comes into the Legend of Hypermnestra (LGW 2585–8), giving the subject 'conscience, trouthe, and drede of shame'. (3) the metal tin, in alchemical symbolism (as noted by the *Canon's Yeoman). (See also *alchemy.) [JDN]

Justin(us), in *The *Merchant's Tale*, one of *January's 'brethren' of whom he asks advice; as his name implies, he is the 'just' or upright one.

JUVENAL, Decimus Junius Juvenalis (*c.* AD 60–136), the Roman satirist. He is twice mentioned by Chaucer. It is not certain that he had read all of Juvenal's satires. He might have known only one or two, or even simply extracts in *florilegia (see *classical literature), though the latter seems unlikely. Juvenal was a 'curriculum author', and often mentioned in commentaries. Both of Chaucer's references are to the tenth Satire. Juvenal is quoted by the old woman in The *Wife of Bath's Tale in her disquisition on '*gentillesse', speaking of 'glad poverty': 'the povre man, whan he goth by the weye, | Bifore the theves he may synge and pleye' (III.1192–4). In **Troilus and Criseyde* the narrator exclaims, 'O Juvenal, lord, trewe is thy sentence', and quotes a sententious remark from the beginning of the poem, that people are unable in their desires to distinguish what will be harmful because the 'cloude of errour' (L. *erroris nebula*) does not allow them to discern what is best (IV.197–201). Chaucer is clearly translating Juvenal here. Juvenal's advice against marriage in his sixth Satire was summarized by *Jean de Meun in the **Roman de la Rose*, and Chaucer certainly knew this, if not necessarily the original. His *Envoi a *Bukton* treats a similar topic, though in a quite different tone.

(ed. and trans.) G. G. Ramsay (1940).

K

〜〜〜

Kakus, see *Cacus.

Kayrudd, the home of Arveragus in *The *Franklin's Tale* (V.808), near Penmarc'h (*Pedmark) is unidentified. The name seems to represent the Breton Kerru (Welsh Caer-rhudd, 'red house', 'red town', probably referring to the colour of old Roman brickwork). The modern villages called Kerru do not fit Chaucer's description.

Kalendarium; **Karibdous; Kaukasous.** See *Nicholas of Lynn; *Caribdis; *Caucasus.

Kalendere, calendar. The L. *Kalendæ*, the Kalends, was the first day of the Roman month. (Thus a letter from Criseyde was judged by Troilus in book V to be a 'kalendes of chaunge', the mark of a new situation. In book II there was talk of a kalends of hope.) On this first day interest was due, hence a *Kalendarium* was an account book. Its general form was adopted for the ecclesiastical calendar, which listed days of the year, and saints' days. (In the *ABC*, the lines 'Kalenderes enlumyned ben thei | That in this world ben lighted with thi name', addressed to the Virgin, refer to the custom of illuminating or rubricating the names of the chief saints.) Calendars also included information (Golden Numbers, etc.) connected with the lunar and solar cycles that allowed the computation of Easter and of other movable feasts of the Church. The art of such computation was an important part of the *Quadrivium.

Astronomical tables of a more advanced sort were often incorporated in ecclesiastical calendars in the Middle Ages, and this was often true of astrological material, such as the Zodiac Man. (For examples by Nicholas of Lynn and John Somer known to Chaucer, and for the question of calendar reform, see *Lenne; *Somer. See also *Zodiak.) The basic solar calendar used throughout the Middle Ages in the West was the Julian calendar, but Christian scholars were familiar with the lunæ-solar calendar of Islam, and variants of the same, and of the method of converting from one to another.

The back of a normal astrolabe carries a *calendar scale* that allows the user to find the Sun's approximate *ecliptic position on each day of the year. In elaborate examples, this might also be marked with saints' days. (See also *astrology and astronomy; *astrolabe.) [JDN]

Coyne (1983); Eisner and MacEoin (1980); North (1990).

karole, see *Carole.

KEATS, JOHN (1795–1821), the Romantic poet read Chaucer in *Speght's edition, with enjoyment. He also enjoyed the pseudo-Chaucerian poems printed there: he used the title of La *Belle Dame sans Merci*, and wrote a sonnet at the end of 'Chaucer's Tale of "The *Flowre and the Lefe"' praising this 'pleasant tale . . . like a little copse': 'Oh! what a power hath white Simplicity! | What mighty power has this gentle story!' He alludes to Chaucer but does not discuss him. In *Endymion* (I.128–34) he prays his muse to inspire him 'that I may dare, in wayfaring, | To stammer where old Chaucer us'd to sing'. Most of his own archaic forms are derived from *Spenser and Chatterton.

Kelmscott Chaucer, see *illustrations; *Morris.

KENELM, SEINT, St Kenelm (d. 812 or 821), Cynhelm, a Mercian prince of whom almost nothing is known. By the second half of the 10th c. he was regarded as a martyr. The 11th c. saw the development of an imaginative legend. According to this, at the age of 7 he succeeded his father

Coenwulf (*Kenulphus) and reigned for a few months, but was murdered at the instigation of his jealous sister, Quendreda. Before his death he had a prophetic dream in which he climbed a tree which was cut down beneath him, and his soul flew out like a bird. In *The *Nun's Priest's Tale* (VII.3110–21) *Chauntecleer recounts it with some feeling as a warning to *Pertelote to take *dreams seriously.

Kent. In the latter part of his life Chaucer was closely associated with Kent (see Geoffrey *Chaucer: life). In 1388 he is described as 'of Kent', and he was probably living there before that, perhaps at Greenwich (see *Grenewych). He was Justice of the Peace for Kent 1385–9, and a Knight of the Shire for Kent in 1386. In his poetry the name only occurs in conjunction with St *Thomas (I.3291; *HF* 1131).

KENT, SEINT THOMAS OF, see *Thomas of Kent, Seint.

Kenulphus, possessive form of Coenwulf, king of Mercia (796–821), the father of *Kenelm (VII.3111).

KER, WILLIAM PATON (1855–1923), born in Glasgow and educated at Glasgow University and Balliol College, Oxford, from 1889 Quain Professor of English at University College, London. His extraordinary range of reading in the medieval literature of the whole of Western Europe is reflected in his books *Epic and Romance* (1897) and *The Dark Ages* (1904), both of them humane and enthusiastic studies. He wrote a short but important book on medieval English literature, *English Literature: Medieval* (1912). His most extensive discussion of Chaucer is to be found in a long review of *Skeat's edition in the *Quarterly Review* (1895). Among many perceptive remarks, he points out (characteristically) that 'in the case of Chaucer it is peculiarly difficult to draw any line between criticism which is historical and positive, and criticism which is purely aesthetic', and that he poses difficulties 'for a critic who has his own private devices for the solution of all problems': 'the problems in Chaucer are continually altering, and the ground is one that calls for all varieties of

skill if it is to be tracked out and surveyed in all its changes of level.'
CH ii. 233–59.

Kin; Kynde. See *family; *Nature.

Kynges, the Book of, quoted in *The *Parson's Tale* (X.897) is the Vulgate's I Kings, the equivalent of I Samuel in the Authorized Version; 'the secounde Book of Kynges' (VII.1668) is 2 Samuel.

Kingis Quair, The. One of the best of all 15th-c. '*Chaucerian' poems, *The Kingis Quair* (the king's little book) is almost certainly the work of King James I of Scotland (d. 1437). He spent most of his youth in English captivity. In 1424, the year of his release, he married Joan Beaufort, the sister of the earl of Somerset. It is usually thought that the poem represents (no doubt in a heightened and fictionalized form) the experience of his love. But it is more than romantic autobiography: in true Chaucerian style, it is a poem which raises and discusses general ideas concerning *love and *fortune and their place in the universe. Echoes of Chaucer (often recalling situations as well as local contexts) are skilfully woven together to create something new. The poem is very carefully constructed. After a prologue describing how the perplexed and sleepless poet takes up a book to read (the *Consolation of Philosophy* of Boethius (*Boece)) the ringing of a matins bell summons him to tell his 'aventure'. He recalls how Fortune caused his shipwreck and imprisonment, and how, like Palamon and Arcite, he first saw from his prison his beloved as she walked in the garden. He experiences the sudden shock of love and the beginning of a new and different kind of 'thraldom'. The sorrowful prisoner falls asleep and dreams. His dream brings him illumination: he is taken up on a heavenly journey to the abodes of the goddesses *Venus and *Minerva. In Venus's court he sees her (varied) servants, and is sent by her to Minerva, 'the pacient goddess', who tells him that his love must be well grounded and virtuous. Then he is taken down to earth again to seek help from Fortune, who holds court in a beautiful landscape filled with all the sublunary creatures of Nature. She looks favourably upon him and his case. After she has woken him up by mischievously tweaking his ear, a white dove brings him a message of comfort as a sign of the happy conclusion of his 'aventure'. He looks back upon the experience with gratitude, prays for all lovers, and blesses the gods, the nightingale which sang in the garden, and even his prison walls. The golden chain of love is an easy thraldom, and binds all creatures together in concord. The emotional and intellectual movement of the poem, from complaint to illumination and to grace, is complete.

(ed.) Norton-Smith (1971).

KITTREDGE, GEORGE LYMAN (1860–1941), a graduate of Harvard University, and Professor of English there from 1894 to 1936, was one of the most influential Chaucerians of the early 20th c. Kittredge was a learned medievalist, who wrote on a variety of subjects from a historical and comparative point of view. His book on Chaucer, *Chaucer and His Poetry* (1915) has been frequently reprinted. For him The *Canterbury Tales* was 'a human comedy' with the pilgrims as dramatis personae: 'the Pilgrims do not exist for the sake of the stories, but *vice versa* ... the stories are merely long speeches expressing, directly or indirectly, the characters of the several persons.' However, they are not simply monologues, but part of an elaborate dramatic structure. This 'dramatic principle', which Kittredge applied in a thoroughgoing manner, is still influential, although it has been increasingly questioned (see *Criticism of Chaucer II). His earlier studies also left their mark on the criticism of Chaucer: a psychological study of the *Pardoner (1893), and, especially, 'Chaucer's Discussion of Marriage' (1912), which argues that there is a '*Marriage Group' of tales, a debate culminating in The *Franklin's Tale, which offers a 'solution'.

CH ii. 305–29.

Knight, The. The 'verray, parfit gentil knyght' of the *General Prologue (I.43–78) is one of Chaucer's most famous *portraits. He is described as a 'worthy man', who has always loved '*chivalrie' and its virtues, and has seen extensive military service (recorded in a list of resounding names of battles and sieges), especially in *crusades. His simple attire and the fact that his tunic is stained by his coat of mail may suggest that he has come straight on pilgrimage, and that he eschews finery and display. That he is placed first in the list of pilgrims and tells the first tale seems to reflect his high social status, and Chaucer's admiration for him. Most critics have assumed that he is an admirable figure, even an ideal one, but in the 20th c. there have been dissenting voices, suggesting that he is not completely idealized, or that he represents a somewhat outmoded ideal, or even, more severely, that he is simply a mercenary, and that Chaucer meant the whole description to be ironic. The historical evidence for this last view is not convincing: several of the knights with whom Chaucer was associated had campaigned in the same areas, and were proud of it. It has not been possible to find a real-life prototype for the knight, but he seems to be presented as a 'flower of chivalry', like, for instance, *Henry of Grosmont. War and chivalry figure prominently in his own tale, but later we see him in a knightly peacekeeping role, when he quietens the angry quarrel between the *Host and the *Pardoner (VI.960–8). Later, he intervenes to stop, firmly but politely, the apparently interminable flow of the *Monk's *tragedies.

Rv 800; Cooper (1989), 34–6; Pearsall (1985), 64–5; T. Jones (1980); Keen (1983); G. A. Lester (1982).

Knight's Tale, The. The first of the Canterbury Tales, this long poem of over 2,000 lines in couplets begins with *Theseus, duke of *Athens, riding back from conquering the land of the *Amazons with his bride the Queen Hippolita (*Ypolita) and her young sister Emily (*Emelye). Outside the town, he is met by a company of mourning ladies, lamenting that *Creon, the new lord of *Thebes (1), will not allow the bodies of their husbands who died in battle there to be buried or burnt. Theseus has pity on them, and leads his host to Thebes to wreak vengeance. Thebes is taken, and Creon killed. In a heap of dead men are found alive two young knights, *Arcite and *Palamon, of royal blood, and sisters' sons. They are taken to Athens to perpetual imprisonment (I.859–1032).

One May morning the beautiful Emily walks in the *garden next to the great tower in which they are kept. Palamon sees her, and cries out as though pierced to the heart. Arcite too is smitten by love.

Their *friendship is instantly assailed by rivalry. At the instigation of his friend *Perotheus, Theseus allows Arcite to leave, provided that he never enters his lands again, on pain of death. Both the young knights are now plunged into melancholy, for different reasons, and they both make formal *complaints against the workings of *Fortune. This section (formally distinguished in the *Ellesmere MS as the 'first part') ends with a *demande d'amour: which of them, the narrator asks 'lovers', is in the worse plight? (1033–354).

Back in Thebes, Arcite suffers grievously from love-melancholy. Ordered by the god *Mercury to return to Athens, he finds service there under the name of 'Philostrate.' Meanwhile Palamon manages to escape and hides himself in a grove nearby. The next morning Arcite rides past, and Palamon, overhearing his love-lament, bursts out and confronts him angrily as his mortal foe. They agree to settle the matter by battle the following day. They are fighting ferociously when they are interrupted by Theseus, who has ridden out hunting. When they have confessed who they are, and that they are fighting for Emily, he condemns them both to death, but when the ladies plead for them, decides to show mercy, commenting wryly on the mighty power of *love, and remarking that Emily knew nothing at all about their hot passion. The knights swear that they will never war against him, and Theseus decrees that a tournament will be held to decide which of the two will win Emily (1355–880).

The third part (as Ellesmere distinguishes it) begins with a description of the amphitheatre that contains the lists. At the east gate is an oratory of *Venus, at the west one of *Mars, and at the north one of Diana (*Dyane). Portrayed on the walls of these temples are the figures of the gods, their aspects and qualities, and their 'children' (see *mythography). As the day approaches knights desirous of honour assemble, and preparations begin. Palamon is accompanied by Lycurgus (*Lygurge) the king of Thrace, Arcite by *Emetreus, king of India (*Inde), and their companies (1881–2208).

Before daybreak, at the planetary hour of Venus, Palamon arises and goes to her temple to pray, not for victory in battle, but to win his love Emily. If she will not grant this, he would wish to be slain. The statue makes a sign, which he takes to mean that his prayer is accepted. Emily comes at the appropriate hour to the temple of Diana. She prays to be allowed to serve her as a maid. However, there is an eerie reaction: one of the altar fires dies down and then springs up, the other is extinguished, making a whistling sound, with bloody drops coming from the ends of the brands. Emily is terrified. Diana appears as a huntress and tells her that it has been established by the gods that she must be married to one of the knights, and vanishes. Finally, at the hour of Mars, Arcite goes to that temple, to pray for victory. The statue rings its coat of mail, and a low murmuring says 'Victorie!'. Up in the heavens, strife breaks out between Venus and Mars. Jupiter tries to quell it, but it is the cold and sinister god Saturn (*Saturne) with his ancient experience who promises to bring it about that Venus's knight will have his lady, and that Mars will help his knight (2209–482).

'Part Four' opens with a lively scene of busy preparation of armour, shields, weapons, and horses. Theseus announces that the battle is not to be pursued to the death: those who are overcome will be taken as prisoner, and the tournament will end when one of the leaders is taken or killed. Battle is fiercely joined. Palamon is wounded, and dragged off as a prisoner, and Theseus declares Arcite to be the victor. Up in the heavens, this causes great distress to Venus, but Saturn silences her, saying that though Mars's knight has had his reward, she will soon be satisfied. Arcite rides in triumph, looking up to Emily, when suddenly 'a *furie infernal' sent up from *Pluto at Saturn's request bursts out of the ground in front of his horse, which in terror throws his rider. Grievously injured, Arcite is cut out of his armour, and carried to a bed.

His condition rapidly worsens, until it is clear that he will die. He sends for Emily and Palamon, and bids them farewell. He sorrowfully bequeathes the service of his spirit to Emily, and asking her to take him in her arms, tells her that his cousin and rival is more worthy to be loved than anyone he knows and will serve her faithfully for the rest of his life. With the words 'Mercy, Emelye!' he dies. There is great lamentation. Theseus decides to build a great funeral pyre on the spot in the grove where the two knights fought for love. The solemn funeral rites are performed.

After several years have passed, and a parliament is discussing an alliance with Thebes, Palamon (still clad in black) is brought by Theseus to Athens. The duke speaks solemnly to him and Emily, pointing out that mutability has been established in the world by 'the Firste Moevere of the cause above', who is himself stable and eternal. Like the great oak and the hard stone, each man and woman must come to an end. It is therefore wise, he says, 'to maken vertu of necessitee', and accept what we cannot escape. And since it is better for a man to die with *honour, his friends should be happier at such a death. Arcite, the flower of chivalry, has left 'this foule prisoun of this lyf'. Rather than longer mourning, Theseus suggests that out of two sorrows there should be made one perfect joy. He joins Emily and Palamon in wedlock, and they live in happiness and concord (2700–3108).

The story is an adaptation of the *Teseida* of *Boccaccio. The mention of 'al the love of Palamon and Arcite | Of Thebes' in the list of Chaucer's works in the Prologue to The *Legend of Good Women* (420–1) indicates that The Knight's Tale existed in some form before the writing of The Canterbury Tales. The remark in the Prologue that the story is little known has been taken to suggest that it was then a recent composition, done perhaps at about the time Chaucer was adapting another poem of Boccaccio in *Troilus and Criseyde*. It might be simply an allusion to the novelty of his Italian source, but a number of scholars accept a dating in this period (the tale contains a number of astrological references which, according to North, point to 1387/8). Whenever it was written, the Tale is fitted to its teller and to its place in the collection.

Chaucer condensed the *Teseida*, abbreviating (and often remarking on it), or omitting whole sections—e.g. the ascent of Arcite's soul to the spheres (an episode which he preferred to use in *Troilus*). He makes the structure more patterned and symmetrical, with closely parallel episodes and characters (a feature further emphasized by the Ellesmere MS's division into four parts). He deliberately eschews psychological *characterization. Emily has virtually no personality, and although Palamon is consistently a servant of Venus, as Arcite is of Mars, it is often hard to differentiate the two young men. The interests of the tale are in patterns of action and patterns of thought. The Italian romantic epic has been transformed into a kind of philosophical romance.

As the first of the Tales, The Knight's Tale has an important role as an elaborate 'introduction' to the collection. The reader finds here a brilliant demonstration of the variety and subtlety of Chaucer's narrative voice and tone and a number of plot motifs and patterns which recur later—like the pattern of the girl with two lovers, merrily treated in the following tale of the Miller. And as a complex poem concerned with ideas, it also introduces many of the major themes which are prominent in The Canterbury Tales—*death, *fortune, *friendship, *love, *'gentilesse', *'pite'.

The action of the poem raises some large questions concerning the human condition, and the characters involved comment on them. Arcite, Palamon, and Theseus are each given formal speeches which touch on the questions of why the innocent are forced to suffer, whether there is order in the universe, and so on. These speeches are dramatic, rather than strictly philosophical, statements, and arise directly from narrative situations. The influence of Boethius (*Boece) is evident, but since the characters are pagans, Chaucer avoids giving a specifically Christian cast to their reflections, whereas the Christian narrator is allowed to point out in an aside echoing *Dante that 'destiny' is 'ministre general', putting a divine providential scheme into execution (I.1663–72). The laments of the two knights in prison are powerful and moving, particularly Palamon's questioning outcry against the 'crueel goddes' that govern the world. Their actions do indeed seem arbitrary and merciless. Chaucer shares Boccaccio's interest in mythography, but is also interested in the way the planets influence men's lives, and emphasizes the *astrological aspects of the gods. Saturn's role is his own invention. Theseus's final speech has been variously interpreted: as a convincing Boethian answer to the questions raised in the tale, or as an unconvincing and irrelevant attempt at philosophizing. Much depends on the view taken of Theseus, who for some is a wise ruler and an almost divine embodiment of order, but for others a harsh and politically motivated tyrant. However, it is possible to argue that he should be taken (with less strain on the text) as an essentially human figure, prone to anger but capable of mercy, older and more worldly wise than the young lovers, and a ruler who attempts to govern with justice and order. His speech then might be seen less as a grand philosophical 'answer' than as a human attempt to urge a rather stoic acceptance of the mutability and uncertainty of man's life.

The tale is well received by the pilgrims ('a noble storie | And worthy for to drawen to memorie'), and especially praised by the 'gentils'. In the centuries after Chaucer's death its popularity continued, as is shown by the works based on it or which echo it in one way or another by writers such as *Lydgate, *Shakespeare, and *Dryden. Early readers seem to have shared the poem's evident delight in the glittering surfaces of courtly life and *chivalry. In reaction to the very idealized expressions of praise commonly found in the 19th and the early 20th centuries, some modern critics have expressed dissatisfaction with the tale and its teller, even going to the extreme of claiming that it is the tale of a cynical mercenary, and a glorification of violence. However, there seems to be no compelling reason to embrace either extreme. Irony and nobility, tragedy and comedy coexist in the tale. Its splendid tapestry contains many dark threads, and it cannot be said to ignore the destructive forces in the world (of love as well as of war). Opinions will differ as to the final balance it achieves between disorder and order. One view might be that in shifting the story away from what was essentially the tragedy of Arcite, and in emphasizing the attempt to find 'o parfit joye' in the union of Palamon and Emily, Chaucer has achieved something like the tragicomic effect of Shakespeare's last plays, where the survivors find a new harmony after the experience of sorrow and death, an experience which is not obliterated or forgotten but comprehended and understood.

Rv 37–66, 826–41; *S&A* 82–105; Cooper (1989), 61–91; Pearsall (1985), 114–38; Boitani (1977 and 1983), 194–9; Havely (1980); T. Jones (1980); Muscatine (1950); North (1990), 402–21; Norton-Smith (1974), 123–36; Salter (1962).

KYNASTON, SIR FRANCIS (1587–1642), educated at Oriel College, Oxford, and Trinity College, Cambridge, became the centre of a literary coterie at court, and founded an academy, the 'Musaeum Minervae' in London. His Latin translation of the first two books of *Troilus and Criseyde* was published in 1635. He also translated *Henryson's *Testament of Cresseid* into Latin.

L

Laban, son of Nabor and the father of Leah and *Rachel, with whom *Jacob took service (Gen. 29–31), mentioned in *The *Parson's Tale* (X.443).

Label, a rule pivoted about the centre of an astrolabe or equatorium, and providing a diametral reference-line (e.g. for reading a scale at the periphery). (See *Astrolabe.) [JDN]

La belle dame sans merci, see *Belle dame sans merci.*

Laboryntus, the Labyrinth in Crete. The monstrous Minotaur (*Mynotaur) was enclosed in a house designed by the architect Daedalus (*Dedalus). Ovid says that he 'constructed the maze, confusing the usual marks of direction, and leading the eye of the beholder astray by devious paths winding in different directions' (*Met.* 8. 156–8; see also *Aeneid* 5.588–91, 6.27). The labyrinth was well known in the Middle Ages, and is sometimes shown on medieval maps (e.g. on the Hereford Mappa Mundi (*Mapamounde), where it appears in the form of a series of concentric circles). It is often called the 'house of Daedalus': in *Boece* (III pr.12:155–7) Chaucer translates *me inextricabilem labyrinthum rationibus texens* as 'hast so woven me with thi resouns the hous of Didalus, so entrelaced that it is unable to ben unlaced'. In *The *Legend of Good Women* (2014) he says it 'is shapen as the mase is wrought'. Mazes (which do not have the darker suggestions of the Cretan labyrinth) were found in antiquity (the different kinds are discussed by Pliny) and remained popular in the Middle Ages and the Renaissance. The Labyrinth is mentioned by name in a comparison in *The *House of Fame*: 'Domus Dedaly, | That Laboryntus cleped ys' is not so wonderfully or elaborately made as is the House of Rumour (1920–3). It has been claimed that the labyrinth is a dominant image in *The House of Fame,* and that it may be related more generally to Chaucer's liking for 'labyrithine' and deceptive narrative patterns and for *diversity.

Boitani (1982); Doob (1990).

Lacedomye, Lacidomye, Lacedaemon or Sparta in ancient Greece. The Spartan maidens who chose death rather than dishonour are mentioned by *Dorigen in *The *Franklin's Tale* (V.1380), and the Spartan ambassador '*Stilboun' by the *Pardoner (VI.605).

Lachesis, the second of the three Fates (see *Parcas), mentioned at the beginning of the final book of *Troilus and Criseyde* (V.7): 'Troilus shal dwellen forth in pyne | Til Lachesis his thred no lenger twyne.'

Lack of Steadfastness; **Ladies, The book of the xxv.** See *Lak of Stedfastnesse; *Legend of Good Women.*

Lady, A Complaint to His (sometimes called *A Balade of Pity*), a short poem, which survives in two MSS and in *Stowe's edition of 1561. It is attributed to Chaucer by *Shirley, who calls it 'The Balade of Pytee'. This attribution is accepted by most, but not all scholars. The poem begins with two stanzas in rhyme royal (see *versification) expressing the lover's despair. This is continued in the following stanza of eight lines in terza rima—apparently the first time this rhyme scheme appears in English. In the next section of seventeen lines, also in terza rima, the poet 'names' the lady: her surname is 'Faire Rewthelees | The Wyse, yknit unto Good Aventure'. The final part, of nine stanzas, all but one of which are of ten decasyllabic lines, reiterates the poet's sorrow, and humbly pleads for mercy. The poem has an odd, fragmentary feel, and it is hard to know if it is an unfinished, experimental work, or a series of separate lyrical pieces. There is no clear indication of the time of its composition, except that the sections in terza rima cannot presumably antedate Chaucer's reading of *Dante.

(ed.) *Rv* 642–3, 1078; Scattergood (1995), 476–7.

Ladomya, see *Laodomya.

Layus, Laius, a legendary king of *Thebes (1), the husband of Jocasta and father of Oedipus (*Edippe), who killed him without recognizing who he was (*Tr* II.101).

Lak of Stedfastnesse, the modern title of a *ballade of four stanzas in rhyme royal, which survives in fifteen MSS and Thynne's edition of 1532. A striking textual difference in the final line and other variations have suggested the possibility of two 'authentic' texts. The poem laments that the world which 'somtyme . . . was so stedfast and stable | That mannes word was obligacioun' is now 'turned up-so-doun' because of 'mede [bribery] and wilfulnesse'. Nowadays, a man is only esteemed if he can 'by som collusioun | Don his neighbour wrong or oppressioun'. *Trouthe, reason, virtue, and *pite are in low repute; discretion is blinded by covetousness. The refrain emphasizes the gloomy message that 'al is lost for lak of stedfastnesse'. The final stanza is the *envoy, addressed (as is the convention) to a 'prince', urging him to cherish his people and hate extortion, maintain order: 'dred God, do law, love trouthe and worthinesse, | And wed thy folk agein to stedfastnesse.' It is an eloquent and polished example of a 'complaint upon the times', a type of lament on the 'world upside down' very popular in the Middle Ages. It is quite possible that for all its generality it was provoked by a particular situation. The 15th-c. scribe *Shirley says that Chaucer wrote it in his 'laste yeeres' (and heads the envoy 'Lenvoye to kyng Richard'), but the political references are not specific enough to date it certainly.

(ed.) *Rv* 634, 1085–6; Pace and David (1982), 77–89; Scattergood (1995), 489–92; Norton-Smith (1982).

Lamedon, Lameadoun, Laomedon, the father of *Priam, the ruler of Troy, who built its great walls.

He was helped in this by Apollo and Neptune, and incurred their wrath by not paying them. In *Troilus and Criseyde *Calkas alludes to this episode (IV.120–6). Laomedon is also mentioned, as part of the story of Troy, in The *Book of the Duchess (329).

Lamek, Lameth, Lamech, in the Old Testament the descendant of Cain (*Caym) who took two wives (Gen. 4:19). This gave him a certain notoriety as the first bigamist. The falcon in The *Squire's Tale bitterly refers to him ('that alderfirst bigan | To loven two') as an example (*exemplum) of the deceitful lover (V.550–1). However, the *Wife of Bath, who is not averse to numerous spouses, remarks: 'what rekketh me [do I care], thogh folk seye vileynye | Of shrewed [wicked] Lameth and his bigamye?' (III.53–4). His falseness is also referred to in *Anelida and Arcite (150–4)—though it was his son Jabal, not Lamech himself, who 'found tentes first' (Gen. 4:20). He is mentioned as the father of another son, *Tubal (*BD* 1162).

Lament, see *Complaint.

Lamentation of Mary Magdalene, a late 15th-c. religious poem of 714 lines which was included in *Pynson's 1526 Chaucer and some later editions, perhaps because it was thought to be '*Origenes upon the Maudelayne' (*LGW* 428). It was rejected from the canon by *Tyrwhitt. The *Lamentation* is a passionate and rhetorical work in which Mary Magdalene recalls the scenes of the Passion and expresses her love for Christ. It is quite unlike Chaucer in style.

Lameth, see *Lamek.

Lamuel, King Lamuel (AV Lemuel) in the Old Testament, whose wise sayings include (Prov. 31:4) 'Do not give wine to kings, O Lamuel, do not give wine to kings, for there is no secret where drunkenness reigns'. The *Pardoner refers to this advice in his disquisition on drunkenness (VI.584–5), taking extreme care to distinguish Lamuel from Samuel.

landscape (see also *forest, *garden, *nature). The word is not found in Chaucer (it appears in English in the early 17th c. as a technical term from painting). His own descriptions of 'landscapes' draw both on 'experience' of actual scenery and on the 'authority' of his books. His *England was not heavily populated, and its villages and towns were often set in fields and woodlands. There were marshlands and fens, moors and desolate areas. Chaucer sometimes alludes to features of the English landscape: to the brook at *Trumpington (I.3921–2), the (undrained) Cambridgeshire fens where the wild horses run (I.4065), to the 'mersshy contree alled *Holdernesse' (III.1710). His European travels had brought greater variety. He had crossed the Alps to the fertile north Italian plain 'where many a tour and toun thou mayst biholde' (IV.60). But when he refers (IV.45–51, 58) to Monte Viso ('Vesulus the colde') from which the river Po (*Poo) begins its course, or the Apennines (*Apennyn), he is following his 'author', Petrarch (*Petrak). His descriptions of landscapes do not show the intense observation of scenery characteristic of some Romantic writers.

In his books he found a series of literary landscapes, traditional in nature and used primarily for rhetorical purposes (the details or 'circumstances' of a scene often include its topography). These landscapes are usually idealized (see *locus amoenus), fertile (filled with trees, springs, and flowers), and inhabited (by gods or men). He could also find a variety of symbolic or allegorical landscapes. Moralists pictured the dangerous landscape of the world through which the Christian soul journeyed as a desert or the sea. The *Roman de la Rose showed the landscape of the mind in love in a way which in later centuries became formalized in the 'carte du tendre'.

Chaucer will sometimes refer quite generally to 'hills', 'fields,' etc., especially in *Sir Thopas, where he is imitating the formulaic style of popular romance: the hero rides 'by dale and eek by downe', 'prikyng over hill and dale' (VII.796, 837). But he often notes the *diversity, the orderly variety of Nature: the world as seen from the air in The *House of Fame (896–903) has

> feldes and playnes,
> And now hilles, and now mountaynes,
> Now valeyes, now forestes,
> .   .   .   .
> Now tounes, and now grete trees,
> Now shippes seyllynge in the see.

*Pandarus uses a similar proverbial idea, 'next the valley is the hill olofte' (Tr I.950), to illustrate the way men's fortunes change. And, although Chaucer's descriptions are brief, they themselves exhibit a good deal of variety. The high rock of ice on which the house of Fame is built (HF 1116–35) is perhaps his most obviously symbolic landscape feature, but he will often fit a landscape to the mood and meaning of the narrative.

The commonest landscape is the beautiful meadow associated with flowers, spring (e.g. Tr I.155–8), and 'disport' of various kinds—*dancing (III.861) and gathering flowers (IV.2231), and the equally beautiful garden or park (which, in The *Parliament of Fowls includes both the temple of Venus and the 'hill of flowers' where Nature sits). Even in the exotic East, in '*Sarray', Canacee can walk out in a park with trees (with the distinctive detail that the rising vapour makes the sun look 'rody and brood', V.384–98). Chaucer is not drawn to rugged northern scenes in the way that the poet of *Sir Gawain and the Green Knight was, but rougher landscapes, and wildernesses, can be found. Especially striking is the forest in the cold, frosty region of Thrace which is depicted in the temple of *Mars in The *Knight's Tale (I.1975–80), where the roughness is emphasized by alliteration: 'knotty, knarry, bareyne trees olde, | Of stubbes sharpe and hidouse to biholde'. In this forest, significancly, 'ther dwelleth neither man ne best'.

There are a number of references to a 'wilderness'. Aeneas meets Venus in one (LGW 970). The satyrs and fauns are 'halve goddes . . . of wildernesse' (Tr IV.1545). In *Scogan Chaucer imagines himself 'forgete in solytarie wildernesse' (46), and in *Truth he uses it as the traditional symbolic image of the world: 'her is non hoom, her nis but wildernesse' (17). The desert is associated with ascetics like 'the Egipcien *Marie' (II.501) or St *Jerome (X.344). *Solomon is quoted as saying that it is better to dwell in a desert than with a woman who is 'riotous' (VII.1087; Prov. 21:19). More spectacular is the 'large feld . . . Withouten toun or hous, or tree, | or bush, or gras, or eryd [ploughed] lond' in The House of Fame (482–91). It is of sand 'as small as man may se yet lye | In the desert of *Lybye,' and the dreamer can see 'ne no maner creature | That ys yformed be *Nature' (486–91). This desert is both literary and symbolic. It echoes the 'gran diserto' in which *Dante finds himself at the beginning of the *Inferno* (1.64; see also 14.8–13), and possibly *Lucan. Similar deserts in French love visions are places of despair for lovers, the opposite of the gardens of delight. It may suggest the sterility of inordinate erotic love (as in the story of *Dido), and possibly the fear of imaginative sterility. The dreamer prays to be saved from 'fantome and illusion'. The desert was the sort of place where this could happen, as in the legend of the Temptation of St *Antony, or in the stories told by Marco Polo and other travellers of the great Gobi desert in which spirits appear to men or speak to them in order to lure them away from the path.

In Chaucer topographical details are usually primarily significant for the narrative: thus, Hypsipyle sees the ship of Jason while 'romynge on the clyves by the se' (*LGW* 1470; cf. 1497). We sometimes find more elaborate landscape settings. In the story of Ariadne (*Adryane) there is an isle in 'the wilde se, | Ther as there dwelled creature non | Save wilde bestes, and that ful many oon' (*LGW* 2163–5). Her abandonment there by *Theseus is an eerie scene. Her cry is echoed by the hollow rocks (2193); 'no man she saw, and yit shyned the mone', but when she climbs high on a rock she sees his ship sailing away. In *The *Book of the Duchess*, following Ovid, he places the cave of the god of sleep in a dark valley 'wonder depe' (155 ff.), with a few springs running down its cliffs. This makes a nice contrast with the forest and its green glades in which the dreamer later finds himself. An excellent example of how landscape may be invested with emotional as well as suggestive or symbolic qualities can be seen in *The *Franklin's Tale* in the striking contrast between the black rocks on the sea coast (V.857 ff.) which bring despair to *Dorigen (their hostility emphasized by the repetition of phrases like 'the grisly rokkes blake', 'thise grisly feendly rokkes blake') and the garden 'ful of leves and of floures' (908–17) in which she meets the squire *Aurelius. Both scenes have an essential role in the story.

Curtius (1953), ch. 10; Hoskins (1955); Pearsall and Salter (1973).

LANE, JOHN, a minor poet, wrote a continuation of *The *Squire's Tale* (1615, rev. 1630). He added ten cantos, which include the story of Algarsif and Theodora mentioned by the Squire. Algarsif is led astray by a witch Videria, but eventually marries Theodora. Much else happens. Cambuscan dies and is revived by an elixir. There is a singing match, won by Canacee and Theodora, Akafir, Cambuscan's High Admiral, triumphs in a tournament, and marries Canacee. Canacee restores the falcon to the tercelet, and they fly off as lovers. 'This, or like this,' says Lane, 'th' ingenious Chaucer wrought, | but lost or supprest. (See *imitations.)

LANGLAND, WILLIAM, generally accepted to have been the author of the long alliterative poem *Piers Plowman*, probably in all its three or four versions (A, B, C, and arguably Z). Langland was at work during the 1360s–1380s or, according to some datings of the C version, even the 1390s; accepting the account of the dreamer in the C version as in outline autobiographical, it would seem that Langland had spent some time in London. Earlier modern critics emphasized the differences between the interests and satirical techniques of Chaucer and Langland, and, citing the Parson's apparent dislike of alliterative verse (*ParsT*, Prol. 43), dismissed the possibility of contact between them. More recent critics have suggested that this view may need revision, and that Chaucer in *The Canterbury Tales* may at times echo *Piers Plowman*. [AH]

(eds.) Skeat (1886) (all three texts); Kane (1960) (A); Kane and Donaldson (1975); Schmidt (1978) (B); Pearsall (1978); Kane and Russell (1997) (C); C. Brewer and Rigg (1983) (Z); Alford (1988); Bennett (1969); Cooper (1987); Mann (1973).

language. With one arguable exception, none of the manuscripts of Chaucer's writing was written by the poet himself (the possible exception is the Peterhouse manuscript of the doubtfully authentic *Equatorie of the Planets*, and on the implications of this see below). Consequently, most of the details of Chaucer's language are beyond scrutiny. In a period when there was no fixed standard orthography each scribe introduced spellings of his own, along with varying degrees of fidelity to the orthography of his exemplar; in general this means that, for a writer such as Chaucer whose works were steadily copied in his lifetime and in the years after his death, traces of the poet's own language are the more difficult to establish the more distant, whether in time or place, the writing of the manuscript. Least vulnerable to alteration are features of the poet's vocabulary, though scribes modified unfamiliar words; most liable to change are aspects of orthography and morphology. The poet's anxiety about scribal alteration is evident from *Chaucers Wordes unto Adam, his owne Scriveyn* and, with more direct reference to linguistic matters, in *Troilus and Criseyde* V.1793–6:

> And for there is so gret diversite
> In Englisshe and in writyng of oure tonge,
> So prey I God that non myswrite the
>   [i.e. the poem],
> Ne the mysmetre for defaute of tonge.

Modern discernment of the details of Chaucer's language is not aided by the almost universal habit amongst modern editors of producing a text that is to some extent normalized; the continuance of this in editions of Chaucer sets the poet apart from almost every other medieval English writer.

Traditionally the evidence used to establish features of the language of Chaucer has been rhyme and metre: the assumption that the poet aimed at perfect rhyme seems a reasonable one, though the arguments concerning the finer details of Chaucer's metrical practice (in particular in regard to questions concerning unstressed syllables) make the second a less safe guide. This evidence leaves uncertain a very great deal. It seems clear, however, that Chaucer for the most part used the expected language of London of his time, though that language tolerated more variation than is acceptable now; Chaucer took advantage of this variation both for stylistic and for metrical purposes. Chaucer's ear for linguistic variation is shown by the speech of the clerks in *The Reeve's Tale*, where many features of northern English are captured. A fuller account of Chaucer's language may be found in the preface to the Riverside edition; the following only aims to deal with major features.

A number of the major features of Chaucer's morphology can be established from rhyme or unchallenged aspects of the metre. In the present tense of the verbs, Chaucer normally used in the indicative the characteristic Midland and southern *-eth* or *-th* in third-person singular (though using northern *-es* for the clerks in *RvT* and very rarely for rhyme elsewhere), and the normal Midland *-en/-n/-e* for the plural (with *-es* from the clerks in *RvT*); in the imperative the singular was normally endingless, the plural *-eth*, though the spread of the former to the plural is evidenced. Chaucer uses exclusively the form *-ing(e)* in the present participle (unlike his contemporary Gower, who in addition used *-end(e)*. In the past tense the plural may end in *-en/-n/-e*, and the same variation is found in strong past participles; in both the variation is used to avoid or allow elision; an extra syllable was also available in the possibility of initial *y-* before the past participle. In the pronominal system the most noteworthy features are in the third person: here the chief differences from modern English are the use of *his* for the possessive of *it* (modern *its* had not yet emerged), and the use of *hire* and *hem* respectively for the possessive and oblique plural (*their* and *them* were at this date still restricted to dialects more northerly than Chaucer's, though his knowledge of them is shown by the clerks in *The Reeve's Tale*). There is no provable differentiation between the forms of the feminine singular possessive and oblique and the plural possessive: both are normally spelt *hire* in early manuscripts, and both are metrically within the line regularly monosyllabic (but in rhyme a disyllabic form *here* is also found, e.g. *CT* II.460). The possessives *min/my* and *thin/thy* coexist in adjectival use, the first in each pair being used before words beginning with a vowel or *h*; in pronominal use the forms are always *min* and *thin*. Usually simple oblique pronouns function as reflexives. The definite article is invariably *the*; the demonstratives are *that* or *this* singular, *tho* or *thise* plural (the last monosyllabic). The normal relative is *that*, though *which* (sometimes reinforced by *that*), *whom* and *whos* (but not *who*) are used when the antecedent is a person. In nouns plurality is usually shown by *-es* or *-s*, though more survivals of OE *-en* and endingless plurals are found than in modern English (e.g. *foon, shoon, toon; hors, thyng*). In the singular possession is usually shown by *-(e)s*, though *brother, fader, suster* regularly, *herte* and *lady* occasionally are unchanged. In certain frequently occurring prepositional phrases a survival of the OE dative is seen: *to bedde, on fire, with childe*. Adjectives are normally invariable in form; but monosyllabic adjectives may take final *-e* when attached either to plural nouns or in positions where a weak adjective would have been used in OE.

The precise pronunciation of Chaucer's time is unascertainable, though the phonemes are discernable. The vocalic system consisted of the short phonemes /a e i o u/, the long phonemes /a: E: e: i: O: o: u: y:/ and the diphthongs /ai au iu eu ou oi/. This system emerges from rhyme evidence, but is concealed to varying extents by the orthography: the same graph may be used not only for long and short vowels but also for open and closed varieties of the long vowel as in the case of <e> and <o>; the same graph may be used for two different vowels of the same quantity, as with the habit (derived from French and convenient in script as a way of distinguishing minims) of using <o> for /u/ in the neighbourhood of letters such as <n> or <m>; two different graphs may be used for the same sound, as in the case of <i> and <y>, the latter often being used in the neighbourhood of <n> or <m>. In the consonantal system it should be noted that many letters that are now silent were still pronounced (e.g. initial <g>, <k> and <m> in groups, <l> before consonants and <r> in all positions). Most modern editions use the spelling <gh> in words such as *knight* and *doughter* (though manuscripts may use <ʒ> and <h> respectively); these probably reflect a voiceless palatal and velar fricative dependent upon the quality of the preceding vowel. To judge by rhyme evidence, Chaucer's usage reflects pronunciation that was distinctively non-northern (e.g. OE long *a* rhymes on OE short *o*, not on OE short *a*, lengthened in an open syllable), and distinctively non-western (e.g. the reflex of OE *eo* rhymes on the reflex of OE *e*); there is variation in the realization of OE *y* between rhymes with OE *i* and OE *e*, the first of which is characteristically east Midland, whilst the second may reflect south-eastern unrounding or may indicate the further lowering of an earlier east Midland /i(:)/.

Generalizations in regard to syntax are hard to make. Chaucer followed the contemporary habit, derived from French, of using in the second person the plural pronouns, and consequently verbs, to express respect to a single person; the use of the old singular forms (*thou/thee/thin/thi*) was limited to speech between close friends or to subordinates. Thus Troilus and Criseyde, with only rare exceptions (III.1512, IV.1641), always address each other with the plural form; the Black Knight addresses the dreamer with the old singular pronoun, but the dreamer replies with the respectful plural (*BD* 519–24). Use of the old subjunctive forms persists more frequently than in modern English, and the absence of normal indicative verbal endings should be observed since this may indicate difference of meaning (e.g. from expression of fact to one of doubt). Appearance of expanded or progressive tenses is less frequent than in modern English, though the verb *ginne* (especially in its past tense singular *gan*) may be used to form periphrastic tenses. As often in ME, the present tense is often used in reference to past time even in close conjunction with others verbs in the past tense (e.g. *CT* I.975–82). The most frequent negative adverb is *ne*; repeated negatives act for emphasis and do not cancel each other out.

Chaucer's vocabulary was large. Characteristically for its period and for the subject matter with which it often deals, there was a very considerable French element in it; as a Londoner, it is not surprising that the number of Norse-derived words in it is quite small. How far Chaucer was himself responsible for introducing French words into English has been a matter of considerable dispute: it seems likely that early critics overestimated the number of his innovations because of their reliance upon *OED*, whose ME sources of evidence were unduly restricted.

Recently claims have been made that further details about Chaucer's language can be elicited from the usage of a scribe who wrote parts of several manuscripts of the poems, and also copied other works: since the scribe uses regularly certain spellings in Chaucer's works but contrasted spellings of the same words in the other texts, it has been argued that the first must be traced back to Chaucer himself. A comparison was then made with the orthography of the single surviving manuscript of the *Equatorie of the Planets*, MS. Peterhouse 75.1, which was claimed by its first editor as a holograph; it was found that many of these spellings are also to be found there. Distinctive forms of only a very limited number of words can be found in this way. But if the presence of these few in the *Equatorie* is indeed significant, it has been argued that the logical extension is that the entire orthography of the *Equatorie* manuscript can be regarded as Chaucer's. To date no attempt has been made to produce an edition of any of Chaucer's undisputed writings in this orthography. (See also *versification.) [AH]

    Rv pp. xxv–xxxviii; Burnley (1983); Elliott (1974); Samuels (1988); Wild (1915).

Laodomya, Laudomia, Ladomya, Laodamia the wife of Protesilaus (*Prothesalaus), a Thessalian prince who was the first to leap ashore in the attack on Troy, but was instantly killed. Laodamia's grief was so great that the gods allowed him to return to her for three hours; when he left her, she killed herself. Chaucer would have known the version of the story in the *Heroides* (13). Laodamia is one of the heroic *examples mentioned by *Dorigen in *The *Franklin's Tale* (V.1445–7). In the Introduction to *The *Man of Law's Tale* her story is said to be available in Chaucer's '*Seintes Legende of Cupide' (II.71). But although she is mentioned in the *ballade 'Hyd Absolon' in the Prologue to *The *Legend of Good Women* (F 263, G 217), her story does not appear in the collection in the form in which we have it. Perhaps Chaucer recognized it as an appropriate one and thought of including it.

Lapidaire, lapidary, treatise on stones (medieval Latin *lapidarium*, Fr. *lapidaire*). There are numerous medieval treatises on widely differing aspects of the subject of stones—their physical properties, decorative functions, magical properties, economic values, medical potencies, astrological relationships, biblical symbolism and religious significance.

    As judged by surviving artefacts, Greek chemical technology was well developed, but ancient writings on the subject are few. Theophrastus, *Aristotle's successor at the Lyceum, wrote a short book on geology, dealing with a relatively small number of minerals. A text with more useful sections on mineralogy, but containing much misinformation, was Pliny's *Natural History*. The first truly systematic and scientific medieval writer on mineralogy was Albertus Magnus (*c.*1200–1280),

who provided a considerable body of information from his own observations, and also a theoretical structure for the organization of his empirical material. This is not without mystical and magical elements. There were stones that could ensure success in robbery, others that would keep one safe from thieves, stones to test for virginity, and so forth. Albert here had many texts from which to select his material (including one by Bede), but one he certainly used was the *Liber lapidum* of Marbode of Rennes (1035–1123). It is usually assumed that when Chaucer spoke in *The *House of Fame* of 'the fynest stones faire | That men rede in the Lapidaire (1352)' he was referring to Marbode's work, which was certainly much copied and on which many commentaries were written. (See also *alchemy; *gems; *ston.) [JDN]

    Evans (1933); Thorndike (1923–41); Wyckoff (1967).

Latin. The Latin language spread with the growing political importance of Rome, until, by the time of the empire, it was spoken widely throughout Western Europe. Its popular or 'vulgar' forms were the ancestors of the Romance languages. The 'maner Latyn corrupt' of *Constance, the emperor's daughter is probably a 'mixed Latin' or, possibly, Italian. The Latin of the ancient authors (see *classical antiquity; *classical literature) lived on, beyond the end of antiquity, as a spoken and written language, often influenced by local vernacular vocabulary and usage.

    Medieval Latin was a central part of the European literary tradition, used for the description and analysis of every area of human experience. It was, pre-eminently, the language of the Western Church—of its Bible and liturgy and its theology. But it was not only the vehicle of a splendid tradition of religious writing (hymns, dramas, meditations, etc.), but also of a lively secular tradition of satire, story, and song. Latin was the language of the '*clerks', the intellectuals: by learning it one became fully 'literate' (able to read, write, and speak Latin) and could become part of the clerical elite. Chaucer assumes this as the background to his narratives. In *The *Franklin's Tale*, when *Aurelius and his brother, the 'clerk', meet another 'clerk', he greets them in Latin (V.1174). The little boy in *The *Prioress's Tale* is just at the beginning of the learning of this skill: he has to have the meaning of the *Alma Redemptoris explained, since he does not yet know 'what this Latyn was to seye' (VII.523). (Similarly, Chaucer writes the *Astrolabe in English for little Lewis at the 'tendir age of ten yeer', 'for Latyn canst thou yit but small', 27.) The *Parson, who is familiar with it, takes care not to flaunt his learning: he speaks of 'the synne of worldly sorwe, swich as it cleped *tristicia*' and so on. Rather different is the *Summoner, who when he had drunk some wine 'thanne wolde he speke no word but Latyn' (I.638). And since Latin is popularly associated with authority (*auctoritee), philosophy, 'quaint terms', etc., it can be used to impress the non-learned. The *Pardoner does this flagrantly ('in Latyn | speke a wordes fewe')—and Chauntecleer uses a Latin phrase to score off his wife (VII.3163–6).

Latyne, Latinus, the king of Latium, the father of Lavinia (*Lavyne (1)), and the ally of Aeneas (*Eneas), is mentioned in *The House of Fame* (453).

latitude, geographic or celestial latitude. Both coordinates are analogous, but the planes of reference should not be confused. The *ecliptic is the celestial reference plane, and not (in the case of what is usually called latitude) the celestial equator (equinoctial). The equator is midway between the poles and in the same plane as the terrestrial equator. Like its counterpart '*longitude', the word 'latitude' is directly from medieval Latin; but unlike it, 'latitude' was much used by Chaucer as a technical term. (See also **astrology and astronomy**.)   [JDN]

Latona, the Moon. Latona was a Titaness. (Latona is the L. equivalent of the Greek Leto.) The Greek myth made her daughter of Coeus and Phoebe; also mother of Apollo and Artemis. Chaucer's reference to 'Lat(h)ona the clere' in *Troilus and Criseyde* (V.655) is plainly to the Moon, but copyists, glossators, and modern commentators have been perplexed by this, and *Caxton emended the text to 'Lucyna'. Leto gave birth to Apollo leaning against Mount Cynthus; and *Cynthea is an alternative name for Diana. But as Dante knew, Latona was traditionally Diana's mother. Virgil and *Ovid have 'Latonia' as a name

for the Moon, which might explain Chaucer's confusion, if 'Latona' is not a miscopied word. (See also *Apollo; *Dyane; *Lucina.)   [JDN]

Latoun, see *metals.

Latumyus, Latumeus. The *Wife of Bath's *Jankin (4) told her (III.757–64) how 'oon Latumyus' had a tree in his garden on which his three wives had hanged themselves, thus exciting the envy of his friend *Arrius. The story is found in several places, but not the name Latumyus.

Laude, Clere Laude (Praise, Pure Praise) a trumpet used by Aeolus (*Eolus) in *The *House of Fame* (1575, 1673).

Laudomia, see *Laodomya.

Launcelot, Sir Lancelot, the great hero of Arthurian romance, the son of King Ban of Benwick (Brittany), usually called Launcelot 'of the Lake' because of the story that he had been abducted at birth and raised by the Lady of the Lake. He is renowned for his knightliness and courtesy, and for his consuming love for Arthur's queen, Guenevere. Both of Chaucer's references to him are light-hearted. In *The *Squire's Tale* at the dances there is such 'subtil lookyng and dissymulynges | For drede of jalouse mennes aperceyvynges' that no one could relate it, save Lancelot, 'and he is deed' (V.283–7). And the *Nun's Priest remarks slyly that his story is as true as 'the book of Launcelot de Lake, | That wommen holde in ful greet reverence' (VII.3211–13).

Lavyne (1), Lavinia, the daughter of King Latinus (*Latyne), given in marriage to Aeneas (*Eneas), mentioned a number of times (*BD* 331; *HF* 458; *LGW* 257, 1331).

Lavyne (2), a city of Latium, south of Rome (*HF* 148).

law in Chaucer's *England differed in many respects from the institution with which we are familiar today. Most obviously, it was not a unified hierarchical structure with the most powerful courts at the top dealing with only the most serious cases and delegating others to lower courts with more limited powers. It was, rather, a congeries of competing and imperfectly distinguished systems which might at times offer the potential litigant a bewildering range of choices. The most important division was between customary and written law: on one side stood the common law courts (particularly King's Bench and Common Pleas) and on the other the courts of the canon lawyers and civilians. Though it is possible to map out the general jurisdictional territories claimed by each, in practice the boundaries between them were far from stable.

Thus, the king's duty to maintain peace and order in the kingdom required that cases of felony and trespass (what we would call tort) should come before his common law courts (generally King's Bench), and his position as feudal overlord meant that the obvious forum for settling private disputes over land or property was again the common law (generally the court of Common Pleas). The simple and familiar division into public and private spheres of law that this implies is, however, illusory. In theory, for instance, rape was a felony and a suspected rapist might expect to be indicted by a presenting jury, arrested by the sheriff of his county, and prosecuted by the crown; in practice, however, a quasi-private action (an appeal) might also be brought against him by his victim or her family, or his crime might even be treated as a private wrong and prosecuted as a trespass (with the advantage that his victim might then expect damages). On the other hand, if they had been committed within the jurisdiction of a franchisal court, some of the most serious felonies might never come before King's Bench at all; thus, many borough courts were under no obligation to refer a murderer to a higher court, but might try and even execute him themselves.

Between the customary law courts and those following the tradition of written law there were similarly vague lines of demarcation. The right of clerics (*clerks) to an ecclesiastical trial even where they had committed a secular offence was always a potential source of dissension, but there were plenty of others: church jurisdiction over marriages and wills led to clashes with the common lawyers when the passing of property depended on the legitimacy of an heir or when the payment of a

dowry depended upon the authentification of a marriage. Though contractual disputes were generally heard in secular courts as matters of private obligation, canon lawyers, pointing out that contracts were made with God as witness, sometimes claimed jurisdiction over them as matters of broken faith. Generally speaking, church courts had less power in England than on the continent, but they might still rival the king's law in some areas. Civil law, the medieval incarnation of the academic Roman law of Justinian, was taught at the universities, but its practical application in Chaucer's England was comparatively limited. The king's council followed rules of civil procedure and some people suspected Richard II of favouring civilians, at the expense of common lawyers. The major civil law court of the 15th c., the Court of Chancery, was still in its infancy in the late 14th, however, and the only other civilian courts at this period were the Courts of Admiralty and Chivalry.

The difference between medieval customary law and written law is most marked in the kinds of legal records that each has bequeathed us. The common lawyers had few theoretical tracts (and the best, Bracton, has been heavily influenced by the civilians), while the records of their actual proceedings are terse, uninformative, and often inconclusive, consisting mostly of writs and enrolments reduced to the lowest level of bureaucratic formalism. Many an apparent eyewitness account (such as that, given in the *Chaucer Life Records* (*LR* 357–8), concerning Alexander Broadbred found guilty of manslaughter in 1389) turns out to be largely a legalistic fiction (in this case intended to guarantee the accused a pardon for murder). The only common law records to give any sense of forensic life are the Year Books and even they are poor things compared, for instance, to the letters of remission from France with their vivid circumstantial accounts of violent crime. The authors of the Year Books (the 'termes' of Chaucer's *Man of Law) were interested only in the highly technical business of pleading, recording the success or failure of novel lines of argument with almost no concern for the larger human drama of the cases themselves. By contrast, civilians and canon lawyers accepted written depositions and kept careful records of testimony, and a number of recent studies (Le Roy Ladurie's *Montaillou*, for example, or Natalie Zemon Davis's *The Return of Martin Guerre*) have successfully exploited the rich detail of such archives on the continent.

The difference between the two kinds of law is well illustrated by cases in which Chaucer was himself involved. Chaucer's notorious legal entanglement with Cecily Champain in a case of rape illustrates the opacity of the records of customary law perfectly. The case is preserved in five documents whose significance and relationship one to another is far from clear. Two are variant copies in the royal archives of a quitclaim issued by Champain to Chaucer on 1 May, 1380, only one of which specifically releases him from any action 'de raptu meo'. The remaining three are copies in the London Municipal archives of documents drawn up at the end of June, apparently concerning debts settled between Chaucer and two London citizens, Richard Goodchild and John Grove, and, further, between these two citizens and Champain. From this evidence, there seems to be no way of knowing whether or not the charge of rape could have been substantiated, on what terms the action was settled, nor what role Goodchild and Grove may have played in events. Even had the case come to trial, the records would have given us little circumstantial detail and the possibility of legal fiction might have thrown even this into question.

By contrast the one civil case in which Chaucer was involved, the famous dispute between Sir Richard Scrope and Sir Robert Grosvenor over the right to a certain coat of arms, heard by the Court of Chivalry from 1385 to 1390, tells us more about him than any other document in the *Life Records*, yet he was merely a comparatively unimportant witness (*LR* 300–1). The deposition of each witness is meticulously recorded, so that we hear Chaucer tell the court how he was walking along Friday Street in London one day when he was surprised to see Scrope's coat of arms hanging outside an inn and even more surprised to be told that the arms belonged not to Scrope but to a Cheshire knight called Grosvenor, a man he had never heard of before. From the Scrope–Grosvenor records we also discover that Chaucer had been present at the siege of Réthel (December 1359 to January 1360), and, most important, we

learn all we know of his age (that he was *40 years and more* in October 1386 and that he had first been *armed* twenty-seven years earlier). Clearly had Cecily Champain been able to bring her charge against Chaucer in a civilian court we should now know, not only rather more about what had actually gone on between the two in the spring and summer of 1380, but a great deal more about the poet himself and any of his friends summoned as witnesses.

Chaucer's own work reveals considerable familiarity with the law (though no more so than his contemporary William Langland), and it has been suggested that he may himself have been educated at one of the Inns of Court. There are two difficulties with this hypothesis. First, the tradition which links Chaucer with the Inner Temple is very late (first mentioned by Thomas* Speght in 1598), and second, the educational role of the Inns of Court when Chaucer was a young man remains unclear. Like Oxford and Cambridge colleges, the Inns of Court seem to have begun life as simple halls of residence, and though they certainly had an important pedagogic function by the time Fortescue wrote about them *c.*1470, evidence that they were offering regular instruction more than a century earlier is inconclusive. Unfortunately records which might now illuminate the early history of the Inns seem to have been systematically destroyed in the Peasants' Revolt. There is, however, no real need to postulate a formal legal education to explain Chaucer's knowledge of the law. The *Chaucer Life Records* reveal that like most other members of the gentry he was frequently involved in legal disputes, both as principal and as surety, and that he even served on the bench himself alongside such prominent Ricardian lawyers as Robert Belknap, William Rickhill, and Robert Tresilian.

The fundamental division between customary and written law is nicely exemplified by the two legal officers portrayed in the *General Prologue* to the *Canterbury Tales*. The Man of Law represents one of the most important common lawyers in the land, a member of an exclusive order (normally a dozen or so in the late 14th c.) with sole rights to plead in the Court of Common Pleas (the court in which all the interminable, and doubtless lucrative, medieval disputes over land tenure were heard). The *Summoner, on the other hand, was a minor official in the ecclesiastical court system, responsible for dragging before the archdeacon members of the laity who had offended against the moral standards of the Church. The *General Prologue* accurately portrays the enormous social gulf between these two officials, but the implied moral gulf between them offers a telling instance of Chaucer's solidarity with the administrative elite of medieval Westminster. Whilst we are ready to accept that summoners were widely hated for their venality and officiousness, we are less likely to recognize that common lawyers were equally loathed by the people at large. Judges and men of law bore the brunt of the peasants' anger in 1381 when the mob stuck the head of the Chief Justice of King's Bench on a pole and paraded it around Bury St Edmunds. Jostled on the streets and shouted down in their own courtrooms, the royal officials we meet in the 14th-c. *coram rege* rolls bear little resemblance to the aloof professional of Chaucer's *General Prologue*.

In the late 14th c. the common law was distinguished for neither its impartiality nor its equity. More than two centuries of inflexible formalism had produced an institution riddled with recondite procedures that served only the interests of professional lawyers and those who could pay for their services. Langland's fierce denunciation of legal corruption and *Gamelyn's* glorification of the outlaw represent two possible literary responses to this sorry state of affairs, but it might be argued that a saturnian nostalgia for the good old law of an earlier age is a third. Such nostalgia can be sensed in a number of fictional accounts of trials in this period (in *Ywain and Gawain*, for example, or *Athelston*), but that Chaucer's own *Man of Law's Tale* should present the trial of Constance for the murder of Hermengild as a conspicuously archaic process, reminiscent of the proof by ordeal not seen in English law for almost two hundred years, is particularly interesting. (See also **Geoffrey**, *Chaucer: life**)   [RFG]

LR; Pollock and Maitland (1968); Harding (1966); Milsom (1981).

Lazar, Lazarus, in the New Testament parable (Luke 16:19 ff.), the poor beggar full of sores who sat at the gate, desiring to be fed with the crumbs which fell from the rich man's table. When he died, angels carried him into Abraham's bosom, whereas the rich man (*Dives) went to hell. The friar in *The *Summoner's Tale* likens the poverty of *friars to the life of Lazarus (III.1877–8).

Lazarus, Lazarus of Bethany, the brother of Mary and Martha, fell sick and died, but was raised from the grave by Christ (John 11). He is mentioned once by Chaucer, in *Melibee* (VII.987): 'Jhesu Crist . . . himself wepte for the deeth of Lazarus hys freend' (alluding to John 11:35: 'Jesus wept').

Leandre, Leander, a youth of Abydos who loved Hero (*Herro) of Sestos and drowned while swimming across the Hellespont to meet her (II.69).

LEE, HARRIET (1757–1851), novelist and dramatist. With her sister Sophia, also a writer, she ran a private school in Bath. Her most successful work was *The Canterbury Tales* (1797–1805), in which a group of seven travellers in a stagecoach are snowed in at Canterbury, and tell stories (in prose) to pass the time. It was subsequently extended to five volumes, her sister contributing some of the tales. Harriet Lee was admired by *Godwin; Byron based his 'Werner' on one of the stories. (See *imitations.)

Legend of Good Women, The, a poem of about 2,700 lines in couplets consisting of a Prologue (which exists in two versions) and a series of nine tales. The Prologue (579 lines in the F version, 545 in G) has an arresting opening: 'A thousand tymes have I herd men telle | That ther ys joy in hevene and peyne in helle'—but, Chaucer continues, no one living in this country has been to either. The only way he can know about it is by hearsay or writing. We should give credence to the 'olde appreved stories' found in *books: 'yf that olde bokes were aweye, | Yloren were of remembraunce the keye'. He delights in reading so much that hardly anything can tear him from his books, except the coming of May, when he loves to go out to see the daisy, his favourite flower. At the end of one such day, when the sun is setting and the flower is closing, he returns home to his little arbour, where he falls asleep and dreams. He is back in the meadow, and he sees the god of *love approaching with a beautiful queen clad in green, gold, and white. The god has two fiery darts, and his 'gaze' is fearsome. A *ballade, 'Hyd, Absolon, thy gilte tresses clere', is sung in honour of the queen. The god of love catches sight of the poet kneeling by his flower. His reaction is hostile: Chaucer is his enemy, who makes war on him, speaking ill of his old servants. He has translated 'the Romauns of the Rose' (see *Romaunt of the Rose*) and has told the story of *Criseyde. The queen intervenes and tells the god that he must listen to any defence the poet can make. Even though he cannot compose very well, he has made ignorant folk delight in serving love. She lists his other works. He must swear never again to offend, and must make amends. The god agrees. Chaucer must do penance by making 'a glorious legende | Of goode wymmen'. The god of love tells him of the great goodness of the queen, Alcestis (*Alceste) who chose to die for her husband, and was transformed into a daisy. He is set to work, and must begin with Cleopatra (*Cleopatre).

(I) *Cleopatra* (580–705). After the death of King Ptolemy (*Tholome (2)) of Egypt, his Queen Cleopatra reigned. Antony (*Antonius), a senator, comes to conquer 'regnes and honour' for Rome. He proves false to Rome and abandons his wife, the sister of Octavius (*Octovyan). His passion for Cleopatra is so great that he sets no store by 'al the world'. They are married, and Octavius leads a great fleet to destroy Antony. After a sea battle, Antony is worsted and put to flight, and Cleopatra 'with al hire purpre sayl' also flees. Seeing this, Antony in despair kills himself. But the 'faithfulness' of women is shown through Cleopatra, who has a splendid shrine built for Antony's body, and next to it a pit filled with serpents. In a speech she recalls her covenant to share the same fate as Antony, and is determined to fulfil it—it will be seen that there never was 'unto hire love a trewer quene'. She plunges to her death among the snakes.

(II) *Thisbe* (*Tisbe; 706–922). Two lords lived in Babylon (*Babiloigne) with only a stone wall separating their dwellings. One has a daughter, Thisbe, the other a son, Pyramus (*Piramus). The children fall in love, but their fathers are not willing to allow their marriage. There is a tiny hole in the wall through which they can speak without their parents knowing. One day they agree to trick their guardians and steal out of the city in the darkness to meet at the place where king Ninus (*Nynus) was buried beneath a tree. Thisbe makes her way to the place, but is frightened by the appearance of a wild lioness 'with blody mouth'. As she hurries to take shelter in a cave she drops her wimple without realizing it. While she is hiding, Piramus arrives, sees 'the steppes brode of a lyoun', and finds the wimple, now torn by the lion's bloody mouth. Assuming that she is dead, he blames himself for having put her in this mortal danger, and kills himself. Now Thisbe, fearing that Piramus may have come and, not finding her, might think her 'fals and ek unkynde', emerges from the cave, and finds her lover in his death throes. Taking his sword she determines to accompany him ('God forbede but a woman can | Be as trewe in lovynge as a man!'), and stabs herself.

(III) *Dido* (924–1367). After the fall of *Troy, Aeneas (*Eneas) and his company arrive on the shore of Libya (*Lybye). His mother, *Venus, appears to him and tells him to go to Carthage (*Cartage). It is ruled by Dido, a noble queen. She has pity on the unfortunate man, and entertains him and his followers. The queen is seized by a passionate desire for him. That night she tosses and sighs in torment ('as don these lovers, as I have herd seyd'). Finally, she makes her lament to her sister Anna (*Anne (2)) and confesses her desire to be wedded to 'this newe Troyan'. There is no withstanding her: 'love wol love, for nothing wol it wonde [cease]'. The next morning preparations are made for a great *hunt, and the amorous queen and the Trojan prince ride out together. A sudden storm forces them to take shelter in a cave. There Dido 'tok hym for husbonde and becom his wyf | For everemo'. Wicked *fame (rumour) spreads the news, bringing distress to Dido's suitor Iarbas (*Yarbas). What is it, asks the narrator, that makes women 'ful of innocence, | Ful of pite, of trouthe and conscience' trust men so? Although Dido has given Aeneas her body and her kingdom, he secretly prepares to leave. Suspecting something is amiss, she asks what displeases him. Mercury has appeared to him, he says, and has told him that it is his destiny to sail away to conquer Italy, though this breaks his heart. Dido laments bitterly, but to no avail. She orders fire to be brought for a sacrifice but plunges onto the fire herself, piercing her heart with the sword that Aeneas has left behind. It is said that before her death she wrote a letter of lament to him, beginning 'Ryght so . . . as that the white swan | Ayens his deth begynnyth for to synge'.

(IV) *Hypsipyle* (*Isiphile(e)) and *Medea* (1368–679). These two stories begin with a vigorous attack on *Jason. On his quest for the Golden Fleece, he goes to Lemnos (*Lemnon). Hypsipyle, the daughter of the king, sends a messenger to discover if the voyagers need help. Jason and Hercules (*Ercules) deliberately deceive her. Jason marries Hypsipyle, but then abandons her. She remained true to him all her life, and died for his love. He goes on to Colchis (*Colcos), where Medea, the daughter of king Aeëtes (*Oetes) falls in love with him, and enables him to achieve the fleece. He marries her and takes her back to Thessaly (*Tessalie), but then abandons her: this was her reward for 'trouthe' and love, *Ovid records her letter to him.

(V) *Lucretia* (*Lucrece; 1680–885). The last king of Rome, *Tarquinius, becomes bored during the long Roman siege of *Ardea, and jestingly suggests that they should speak about wives. Collatinus (*Colatyn), a knight, says that if they go to Rome they will see the goodness of his wife, Lucrece. They enter the house secretly, and indeed find her a model of devotion. Tarquinius lusts after her, and returns at night with a drawn sword. Threatening her with it, and with the loss of honour she will suffer if he arranges an accusation of adultery, he rapes her. When he has gone she sits weeping in despair. Eventually she is constrained to tell her friends what has happened. She is determined that her husband should not be dishonoured, and rejecting her friends' insistence there is no guilt, seizes a knife and kills herself. Tarquinius and all his kin are banished, and she is honoured as a saint.

(VI) *Ariadne* (*Adriane; 1886–2227). *Theseus, son of the king of Athens, is to be sacrificed to the *Minotaur in Crete. Ariadne and Phaedra (*Phedra), the daughters of king *Minos, hear his lament and take pity on him. They decide to help

him kill the monster, and find his way back through the labyrinth (*Laboryntus). Theseus promises Ariadne to serve her faithfully. He is successful, and takes the woman away to the land of Oenopia, where they hold a great feast. There he has Ariadne who saved him 'in his armes'. But on his way home he puts in to a deserted island in the wild sea, and there he abandons his wife Ariadne 'for that hire syster fayrer was than she'. She laments piteously.

(VII) *Philomela* (*Philomene; 2228–393). The story of the 'grisly deed' of *Tereus, king of Thrace (*Trace), who wedded Procne (*Progne), the beautiful daughter of king *Pandion. After five years she wishes to see her sister, Philomela. Tereus goes to Athens to bring her, but is so taken by her beauty that he determines to have her at any cost. When he arrives in Thrace he leads her into a cave in a forest, rapes her, cuts off her tongue so that she cannot speak, and keeps her imprisoned in a castle. He tells Procne that her sister is dead. Philomela, however, manages to weave her story into a piece of cloth which she secretly sends to her sister. In sorrow and rage Procne goes to Philomela. (With the remark, 'thus I late hem in here sorwe dwelle | The remenaunt is no charge for to telle', Chaucer omits the ending of Ovid's story, in which the sisters serve Tereus with the flesh of his son, and all three are transformed into birds.)

(VIII) *Phyllis* (2394–561). *Demophon, the son of *Theseus, and another false lover, on his way back to Athens after the fall of Troy, is wrecked on the shore of a land ruled by the beautiful queen Phyllis. He goes to her for help and succour. Demophon is famous, and like his father in appearance, but also in his falseness. He promises to wed Phyllis, but says he has to return briefly to his country to make preparations for the wedding. He never returns, and Phyllis kills herself, after writing him a letter of complaint.

(IX) *Hypermnestra* (*Ypermystra; 2562–723). There were once two brothers in Greece, Danaus (*Danao) and Aegyptus (*Egiste). Aegyptus has many daughters, including Hypermnestra, the youngest. The influence of the planets *Venus and *Jupiter has lessened that of *Mars, so that she dares not handle a knife in malice. Unfortunately, the evil influence of *Saturn means that she is to die in prison. The brothers decide that she should be married to Lynceus (*Lyno), the son of Danaus (as was permitted in those days). This is done with great ceremony, but at night before the bride retires, Aegyptus summons her secretly, gives her a knife 'as rasour kene', and tells her that under pain of death she must cut her husband's thoat while he sleeps, because he has been warned in dreams that his nephew will slay him. In great distress Hypermnestra agrees. When her husband is asleep, she rises weeping, and cannot bring herself to do the deed ('Allas! And shal myne hondes blody be? . . . Myne handes ben nat shapen for a knyf'). She awakens him, and helps him to escape. He leaps from a window and runs away quickly. She follows, but cannot keep up with her 'unkind' husband. She is captured by her father and 'fetered in prysoun'. With the line 'this tale is seyd for this conclusioun' it breaks off. Perhaps Chaucer meant to complete it but never did; perhaps a brief ending was written but has been lost.

The Legend of Good Women is both interesting and problematical. It survives in twelve (incomplete) MSS and in the edition of *Thynne. The exact relationship of the MSS is not clear, but MS Gg 4.27 in Cambridge University Library, the only MS to contain the G version of the Prologue, is frequently adopted as a base text, though extensively emended. The title is derived from Alceste's command, but elsewhere Chaucer refers to it as 'the Seintes Legende of Cupide' (II.61) and 'the book of the xxv [or in some MSS xv or xix] Ladies' (X.1086–7).

The date and the manner of its composition are uncertain. A reference to Queen *Anne (of Bohemia) (F 496–7) places that version of the Prologue between 1382 and 7 June 1394). She has been associated with the figure of Alceste and taken to be the patron of the poem. It is possible that it is the result of a royal request, but there is no certain evidence about her role or about a particular occasion. That *Troilus and Criseyde* is prominently mentioned suggests a date after 1385. There is no mention of The *Canterbury Tales*; it has been suggested that since the *Legend* is Chaucer's first work in iambic pentameter couplets, and is a collection of short narratives within a framework, that a date near the inception of the Tales (e.g. 1386–) may be likely. However it is possible that some of the legends were composed

earlier, and some may have circulated separately. The list given in the Introduction to The *Man of Law's Tale* (II.61ff.) differs both from Chaucer's number of 'xxv ladies' (if that is the correct reading), and from what we have, in omitting Cleopatra and Philomela, but includes others (Deianira (*Dianire), Hermione (*Hermyon), Hero (*Erro), Helen (*Eleyne), Laodamia (*Ladomya), Penelope (*Penelopee), and Briseis (*Breseyda), whose stories may have been written but have not survived, or may have been intended or thought possible. Similarly, those good women mentioned in the *ballade in the Prologue (249–69) might have afforded further stories. It seems likely (but not certain) that Chaucer had in mind a larger collection of legends, but if he did it is not clear which stories he would have included, nor why he left the work unfinished. The question of the priority of the two versions of the Prologue cannot be finally settled, but most scholars now are of the opinion that G is the later, revised version (and, since it lacks the references to Queen Anne, coming from or after 1394, the year of her death).

The Prologue, in both versions, draws extensively on Chaucer's reading in French love vision and lyric, especially the poems of *Deschamps. For the individual legends he used material from a variety of literary sources, notably *Ovid, but also *Virgil, *Guido delle Colonne, and other (sometimes unidentified) authors. The general literary model is the *saint's life. The good women are presented as 'martyrs'. In the background there is perhaps the pattern of *Boccaccio's *De claris mulieribus*, a collection of stories of virtuous women which includes most of Chaucer's martyrs. Closer in spirit is Ovid's *Heroides*, which Chaucer probably read in glossed and annotated copies and possibly with the Italian translation by 'Filippo'.

The Legend of Good Women seems to have been popular and influential in the 15th c., but many modern critics have found it unsatisfactory. While the Prologue has been generally admired, the narratives have been criticized as perfunctory. It has often been claimed that Chaucer found his task wearisome, and finally gave it up. The evidence for this, however, is far from clear. A series of statements that the author does not have time or does not wish to relate part of a story (e.g. 994–7,

1002–3, 1564–5, 1678–9, 1692–3, 2454–8, 2470–1, 2490–1) can be taken as examples of the rhetorical technique of 'abbreviation', which is used in other poems where a narrative is being compressed (e. g. The *Knight's Tale). That there is in one or two an undoubted element of joking or irony ('for I am agroted [fed up] . . . | To wryte of hem that ben in love forsworn, | And ek to haste me in my legende', 2454–6) does not necessarily indicate boredom with a task.

The interpretation of the tone and significance of the Legend has provoked a wide variety of opinion, ranging from the commonly expressed view that it is deeply ironic (even to the extent of being a satire against women) to that which would read it straightforwardly, and as a riposte to anti-feminism. A sophisticated example of this view (Mann, 1991) argues that Chaucer's slanting of the stories in order to favour women (e.g. in suppressing the ending of the tale of Medea) need not be interpreted ironically, but is intended to correct the anti-feminist bias of *exempla against women, and that he makes them into 'expressions of a peculiarly female ethos' associated with '*pite' and compassion. There is no doubt of the seriousness of his treatment of the rape of Philomela and Lucretia. And as elsewhere in his work he is very eloquent in scenes of *pathos and in the expression of *emotion. Also characteristic is the mixture of earnest and *game, an Ovidian 'interplay between wit and pathos' (Norton-Smith, 1974). The ironies and jesting asides of the Legend need not be taken as totally reductive. This combination distinguishes it from the consistently serious defence of women in *Christine de Pisan's later Book of the City of Ladies.

The work is the product of Chaucer's maturity, the last of his *dream visions and his first experiment with framed narratives. Neither the framework nor the stories themselves have the range and dramatic variety of The *Canterbury Tales, but some of them (e.g. those of Hypsipyle or Lucretia) are impressive examples of the short tale in verse. As in his longer narratives the voice and attitude of the narrator is prominent. The vividness of some scenes (e.g. the sea battle in Cleopatra, the hunt in Dido, or that of Ariadne waking on her rocky island) is especially memorable. Sometimes a tale seems to be constructed around a carefully placed significant speech or scene. It may well be argued that the early popularity of the Legend was not misplaced.

(ed.) Rv 587–630, 1059–75; Cowan and Kane (1995); Minnis (1995), 322–454; Delany (1994); Frank (1972); Fyler (1979); Mann (1991), 31–47; Norton-Smith (1974), 62–78.

Legenda Aurea; LEIGH HUNT. See *Jacobus da Voragine; *Hunt, James Henry Leigh.

LELAND, JOHN (1506?–1552). In 1533 Leland was given to a commission by Henry VIII to investigate the antiquities of Britain, and between 1534 and 1543 made a number of journeys to seek out manuscripts and documents, especially in the libraries of religious houses. In 1536 he sought to obtain permission to collect such materials for preservation, but gained little support or finance for such an enterprise. He published little in his own lifetime, but the information that he gathered was drawn on by a succession of later antiquaries, notable amongst them John *Bale. In his Commentarii de Scriptoribus Britannicis, written c.1545, Leland provided the first coherent biography of Chaucer (printed Spurgeon) but one that was full of inaccuracies. Though the Commentarii was not printed until 1709, Bale's use of Leland's notes ensured that much of the false detail is found in accounts up to that of Thomas *Tyrwhitt (1775) who grasped the unreliability of Leland's details. Leland drew upon *Thynne's 1532 edition for his list of Chaucer's writings, and it is from that source that he took over most of the apocryphal material. [AH]

Spurgeon (1925), iii. 13–19.

Lemnon, Lemnos, an island in the Aegean, appears in the story of Hypsipyle (*Isiphile(e)) in The *Legend of Good Women (1463).

LENNE, FRER N., Nicholas of Lynn (fl. late 14th c.). A Carmelite friar from the convent of Lynn (now King's Lynn) in Norfolk, he moved to the Oxford convent and became lector in theology. It is possible that he was the Oxford scholar of whom Jacob Cnoyen spoke long afterwards as having travelled in arctic latitudes in 1360, and who was said to have surveyed with an astrolabe. John

Dee and Richard Hakluyt name Nicolas of Lynn explicitly, but in the original story the friar was said to be a Franciscan, and John *Somer's name has been proposed.

In his introduction to *A Treatise on the *Astrolabe*, Chaucer referred to his intention of drawing upon the *calendar of Nicholas of Lynn, as well as from that of John Somer, for Part III of his own treatise; but the promise remained unfulfilled. Nicholas's calendar had been written at the request of John of Gaunt; it was said to be a continuation of that by Walter of Elveden. Like John Somer's, the new calendar commenced at the new lunæ-solar (nineteen-year) cycle that began in 1387. Both contained extensive *tables for the Sun and the Moon, eclipses, *ascensions, and other severely astronomical material, although each had at its core the ecclesiastical calendar. Nicholas's version contained a relatively unusual table correlating day and hour with the altitude of the Sun, as measured by the length of the human shadow. It may be proved that Chaucer made use of this in his *Nun's Priest's Tale*, in the *Host's Introduction to The *Man of Law's Prologue*, and in the Prologue to The *Parson's Tale*. (See also *Kalendere.) [JDN]

Lente, lent, the season of spring, and (ecclesiastical, by extension) the period from Ash Wednesday to the eve of Easter. This time of fasting and penitence includes forty weekdays, and commemorates Christ's fasting in the wilderness. The *Host (in The *Clerk's Prologue*) uses the word in the ecclesiastical sense, and the Wife of Bath in her Prologue seems to use it in the traditional sense, equivalent to our imprecise 'spring'. (See also *months and seasons.) [JDN]

Leo, Leo(u), the fifth sign of the Zodiac, the Lion; also the constellation of the same name. The sign is the *domicile of the Sun. (See also *Aldiran, *Zodiak.) [JDN]

LEONARD, St Leonard, a hermit (of the 6th c.?), one of the most popular saints in the Middle Ages. According to legend he was a Frankish nobleman who was converted to Christianity. His cult spread from his monastery and shrine at Saint-Léonard-de-Noblat near Limoges. Over a hundred English churches were dedicated to him, as was the nunnery at *Stratford atte Bowe. In *The *House of Fame* (115–18) there is an obscure (and apparently joking) reference to the exhausted traveller who had gone two miles on pilgrimage to the shrine of St Leonard 'to make lythe [easy, soft] of that was hard'. Leonard was the patron saint of captives and prisoners, and in the *Roman de la Rose* (8833–8) he is invoked as a help against the chain of marriage.

Leoun, The Book of the, see *Book of the Lion.

Lepe (VI.563, 570), either ancient Illipula, modern Niebla, in south-western Spain between Seville and Huelva, or the modern township of Lepe between Huelva and Ayamonte. A 12th-c. Arabic writer refers to Niebla as an important trading-centre, so Chaucer's *Pardoner may have been thinking of the shipping rather than the actual provenance of the 'white wyn' he refers to in the preamble to his tale. There has been a certain amount of scholarly speculation as to why Chaucer should have used the name Lepe in the general context of Spanish wine, but it is to be supposed that, vintner's son that he was, he would have been familiar with the provenance of imported wines, and, of course, he may have been in need of a suitable rhyme (twice) for *Chepe*. It is worth noting too that, in his *Handbook to Spain* (1845), Richard Ford observes that 'the bad wine' of Lepe 'is sent to San Lucar, and converted for the English market into fine sherry', and, in modern times, white wines from the Lepe area were often imported into Jérez for blending with sherry. The 'fumositee' referred to by the Pardoner would be, as he suggests, the result of mixing this white wine with other, superior French wines; however, it has been likewise suggested, tentatively, that this intoxicating quality of the wine might have been due to fortification, for the Moors certainly distilled alcohol for medicinal purposes, and *if* this is so, the Pardoner's remarks would constitute the first recorded instance of a fortified wine. (See also *wine.) [PS]

Lete, Lethe ('oblivion'), a river in the underworld. According to *Ovid, it flows from the cave of Sleep in the dark land of the Cimmerians

Letter of Dydo to Aeneas, The

(*Cymerie). Chaucer, in his invocation to the god of sleep (*HF* 66–80) describes it as 'a flood of helle unswete'.

Letter of Cupid, The, see *Hoccleve.

Letter of Dydo to Aeneas, The. This poem follows 'The *Lamentation of Mary Magdalen' in the 1526 edition of Chaucer by *Pynson. It is an eloquent rhetorical poem based on the late 15th-c. French translation of Ovid's *Heroides* 7 by Octovien de Saint-Gelais.

letters served a variety of purposes in Chaucer's England. (He uses the words *lettre* or *letter* and for more formal documents *pistel* or *epistel*.) As in the rest of medieval Europe, the letter was an important form of composition. There was much official correspondence (usually in Latin or in French) as well as in literary and didactic epistles and private business or personal letters. In the Middle Ages the art of formal letter-writing in Latin was taught through the *ars dictaminis* or *ars dictandi*, a recognized part of *rhetoric. There were treatises and manuals, and collections of model letters, testifying to a concern for an elegant style, suited to its recipient (including, if necessary, the 'heigh style, as whan men to kynges write', IV.18).

In the later Middle Ages the structural pattern was adapted for letters in the vernacular. MSS written in England in the 14th and 15th c. contain guides to the writing of letters in French. Letters in English survive in considerable numbers from the 15th c., and contain recognizable formulaic patterns very similar to those in French. Respectful letters open with a salutation, commonly beginning 'Right worshipful' (or 'worthy' or 'well-beloved') sir (or 'husband', 'father', etc.), followed by a formula commending the writer to the recipient (sometimes with an expression of humility, an expression of a desire to hear of the recipient's welfare, a prayer asking that his or her well-being may continue, news of the writer's welfare (introduced by a deferential formula—'if it liked you to hear of me', or 'may it please you to have knowledge of my welfare ...', etc.), and an expression of gratitude to God for it. The modern 'hoping this finds you as it leaves me' is a simplification of these formulae. Similarly, there are equivalent closing

formulae: 'written in haste by candle-light', etc. (i.e. 'I must rush now'). Less formal letters occasionally begin with 'dear', although this remains rare until the 17th c. Sir John *Hawkwood writes to a friend, 'Dere, trusty, and welbeloved frend, hertliche I grete you wel ...'. His two letters (from the early 1390s) show that the epistolary conventions were established in English letters by Chaucer's time.

The medieval art of letter-writing owed a considerable debt to antiquity. The structure of the more literary examples is based on that of the ancient oration, often with allusions to classical works and authors (as in the letters of Eloisa (*Heloise) and Abelard). The literary epistles of Cicero and Seneca were widely read. Even more widely known were the Christian adaptations of the epistle as a form of moral instruction. Chaucer, for instance, mentions those of St *Peter (VII.1500) and of St *James (1) (IV.1154), and makes use of St *Paul and of St *Jerome's *Epistula adversus Jovinianum*. Chaucer had a particular interest in the ancient verse epistle. He knew Ovid's *Heroides* (which he calls Ovid's '*Epistel(e)s') very well, and used it frequently. In *Troilus and Criseyde* he refers to the letter of *Oenone (I.656 ff.). In The *Legend of Good Women* he mentions those of *Dido (1354 ff.), Hypsipyle (*Isiphele(e); 1564 ff.), *Medea (1670–9), and *Phyllis (2494 ff.). He will sometimes quote a passage in translation. However, he fits Ovid's heroic epistles into his own narrative pattern, removing their (rather easily separable) letter-writing formulae, and turning them into speeches of lament. Whether or not he knew Horace has been much discussed: it is at least possible that Horace has influenced his own 'envoys' or verse epistles to *Scogan and *Bukton. These do not seem to follow a French tradition. Chaucer's two short verse epistles (that to Bukton is called a 'lytel writ') are familiar in tone and show an urbane blend of playfulness and seriousness.

Letters have a varied and significant role in Chaucer's other works. They are part of the circumstances of everyday life to which he can allude. Thus, *Arveragus writes home to his wife, assuring her of his welfare and promising that he will quickly return (V.837–40), *Walter sends a secret letter of instructions (IV.760–3), and Hector asks for advice (*Tr* II.1697 ff.). In *The* *Summoner's Tale* (III.2128), when the Friar speaks of 'oure letter with oure seel' the reference is to a letter of admission to a confraternity (and, in the eyes of satirists, yet another way of extracting money). Pandarus carries letters to Criseyde when Troilus is absent (III.488); when Criseyde is absent Troilus reads a hundred times the letters 'that she of olde tyme | Hadde hym ysent' (V.470–2). And there are allusions to the appearance of letters. It was customary to sew together the leaves of parchment on which the letter was written: it was folded into the shape of a packet and either stitched through or secured by narrow paper tape, and sealed. Troilus folds and seals his letter (*Tr* II.1085–8), Pandarus offers to sew and fold Criseyde's letter (II.1201). Hector's letter is 'unfolded' (II.1702). The Paston ladies of the 15th c. used amanuenses to write their letters. Criseyde, however, writes hers with her own hand (II.1218, though it is, she says, the first letter that she has written), as does *Anelida (Anel 209).

In some narratives letters play a more prominent part. In *The* *Man of Law's Tale* the wicked *Donegild's substitution of false letters leads to the expulsion of Constance and her young child (II.724 ff.). In *The* *Merchant's Tale* it is clandestine letters rather than 'countrefeted lettres' which are to the fore. There the lovesick squire Damyan 'in a lettre wroot he al his sorwe, | In manere of a compleynt or a lay' to his May. She hides it in her bosom, and then disposes of it. She grants 'verray grace' to her admirer in a letter 'right of hire hand' (IV.1996) which she pushes under his pillow. Her instructions to him about what to do in the garden are conveyed by letter (2215).

Most interesting of all, perhaps, are the letters in books II and V of *Troilus*. Chaucer took the idea of these from his Italian source, but handles them very differently. In book II (1002 ff.) Pandarus, as in Boccaccio, suggests to Troilus the writing of a letter. Chaucer gives him some typically expansive comments on the style required by the occasion, Pandarus forbids Troilus to write in the formal style of a scribe ('scryvenyssh') or with too much art ('craftyly'): 'biblotte it with thi teris ek a lite [little].' (This too is good classical doctrine; cf. Briseis, *Heroides* 3.). He must not harp on one string, nor jumble discordant images together (this literary advice comes ultimately from *Horace). In

the *Filostrato* Troiolo's letter is an intense poetic epistle which in its opening proclaims its difference from traditional love letters. He says that he cannot give his lady 'good health', because he does not have it to give, unless she give it to him. Chaucer presents it in indirect speech, making it sound more formal (with a hint of the conventional formulae: 'first he gan hire his righte lady calle . . . | He gan hym recommaunde unto hire grace'), and allowing the amused detachment of the narrator to come through strongly (1068, 1071, 1077, 1083). But although he cannot resist pointing out that the expression of Troilus's passion is like that of other lovers, he presents it as real and deserving of compassion. And it pleases Criseyde when she reads it: she 'fond no lak, she thoughte he koude good'. Her letter in reply, which is given at length in Boccaccio, is again given in a short (and serious) summary (1218–25).

The letters in book V are given in full (and marked in a number of MSS as *Litera Troili* (1317–421) and *Litera Criseydis* (1590–631)). The second is Chaucer's invention (using some phrases from Boccaccio's earlier letters). It is deliberately careful and stiff (it seems to Troilus 'al straunge'), and full of unconscious ironies and pathos. After it we hear no more from Criseyde. The earlier letter of Troilus corresponds in general to that in Boccaccio, where it is a long, passionate lyric of yearning, but Chaucer uses the formulae of contemporary English and French letters, the 'familiar patterns of the kind of letter that his readers might have planned, or received, themselves' (Davis). He begins with the formulaic *Right* + an adjective of respect—'Right fresshe flour . . .', and continues with formulae commending himself to the recipient with an expression of humility ('I, woful wyght, in everich humble wise . . . | Me recommaunde unto youre noble grace'), the deferential offer of news ('Liketh yow to witen, swete herte', 'And if yow liketh knowen of the fare | Of me'), the desire to hear of the recipient's welfare ('desiryng evere moore | to knowen fully, if youre wille it weere, | How ye han ferd and don whil ye be theere'). When Troilus says that in spite of his sorrow he is 'on-lyve, | Al redy out my woful gost to dryve' (1369 ff.) Chaucer is adapting the well-known formula reporting that the writer is in good health at the time of the making of the letter. As well as being close to the experience of the English audience, Troilus's letter is in its own right a polished courtly lyric (cf. the traditional images of song turned into lament, 'good' into 'harm', joy into woe, 1373–9), which seems to have been a model for later, 15th-c. English verse epistles of sorrowing lovers. The 'signature' *Le vostre T.* seems both to recognize the French courtly tradition to which the lyric owes much and the association of the art of polite letter-writing with French. The letter is less passionate and immediate, and less rambling, than Troiolo's, but its more stately eloquence expresses an intense emotion, heightened by the realism which comes (Davis) from Chaucer's 'individual perception of matters of common experience'. (See also *documents.)

Davis (1965); Norton-Smith (1966*b*).

Lettow, Lithuania, one of the places in which the *Knight had campaigned (I.54) with the Teutonic Knights (see *chivalry). The name refers not only to the land along the Baltic inhabited by ethnic Lithuanians speaking an Indo-European language, but to a much larger political entity extending around the Dneiper and including part of the Ukraine (see Map 3). The Lithuanians were pagan, and from the 13th c. were involved in almost constant warfare with the Teutonic Order. In 1386 its ruler, Prince Jagailo (or Jagiello), was converted to Latin Christianity, but hostilities with the Knights continued.

Liber Aureolus; **Liberal Arts.** See *Theofraste; **Seven Liberal Arts**.

Lybeux, Sir, Lybeaus Desconus, a hero of medieval romance, mentioned in a list of those who cannot match the glory of Sir *Thopas (VII.900). The story of the 'Fair Unknown' was a popular one. Guinglain, the natural son of *Gawain, is brought up in seclusion, but makes his name as an unknown knight.

Lybye, Libya (see Map 3), which is, according to *Bartholomew, a 'full hot land and burning, and breedeth in diverse places many venemous beasts and beasts wonderly shaped'. In *The *House of Fame* there is a reference to its desert of fine sand

(486–8; see also *Bo* IV m.7:52). Libya also contains the 'noble toun' of Carthage (*Cartage), the setting for the story of *Dido (see *LGW* 958 ff.).

Libra, the seventh sign of the Zodiac, the Scales. At the autumnal equinox the Sun is at the head of Libra. In the Prologue to *The *Parson's Tale*, with the pilgrims nearing their destination, Libra is said to have been ascending, and it is likely that this is part of an astrological allusion to Christ's Passion. (See also *hed; *signe; *Zodiak.)   [JDN]

Libraries; *Libro de buen amor.* See *book; *Ruiz, **Juan**.

Lyde, Lydia, an ancient kingdom in the centre of the western part of Asia Minor (present-day Turkey). Its capital was Sardis. A powerful Lydian empire developed in the 7th and 6th c. BC under the dynasty of the Mermnadae. The last of these rulers was the legendary King Croesus (*Cresus), whose tragedy is told in *The Monk's Tale* (VII.2727–66), and is alluded to elsewhere (see VII.3138; *HF* 105; *Bo* II pr.2:58).

Lyeys, Ayas or Ayash, a port mear Antioch, in Cilicia or Lesser Armenia (now in Turkey; see Map 3), a busy trading centre. It was captured by Peter, King of Cyprus (*Petro (1)), in 1367. His force included English knights. Chaucer's *Knight was at Lyeys when it was won (I.58).

Lyf of Seynt Cecile, see *Cecile, *Second Nun's Tale.*

Lygurge. Lycurgus, 'the grete kyng of Trace [Thrace]', who rides with his company to support *Palamon in *The *Knight's Tale* (I.2129 ff.), seems to be a combination of Lycurgus of Nemea, whose child Opheltes was killed by a serpent, when the army of Adrastus (*Adraste) was on its way to Thebes, and Lycurgus, the legendary king of Thrace, who is mentioned in the *Thebaid*. Lygurge is an exotic figure, with black beard and hair, and a fierce look: 'the cercles of his eyen in his heed | . . . gloweden bitwixen yelow and reed.' He wears a black bearskin, and his chariot is drawn by four white bulls, and is accompanied by white wolfhounds. Some of the physiognomical details may suggest *Saturn, who is supporting Palamon, while the white bulls suggest an affiliation with *Venus.

limbe, lymbe, limb (edge of an instrument, graduated or not). In the *Equatorie of the Planetis* the word (also modern English; from L. *limbus*) is used of the rim of both the face and the *epicycle.
[JDN]

Limote (*HF* 1274), probably Elymas the sorcerer in the New Testament (Acts 13:8).

Lyncoln, modern Lincoln, a city in the north-east Midlands dominated by its cathedral which stands on a hill. The Prioress mentions the legend of (Little) St *Hugh of Lincoln (VII.684), said to have been murdered by the Jews of the city in 1255, following her similar story of the *litel child* in *Asye*.
[AH]

LYNYAN, Giovanni da Lignano or Legnano (*c.*1310–1383), a professor of canon law at Bologna, is said by the *Clerk to have 'enlumyned' Italy with philosophy and law, as Petrarch (*Petrak) did with poetry (IV.34). He is said to have preferred simple dress (like the Clerk), and to have been a friend of young poor scholars. He was known in England for his defence of Urban VI at the time of the Great Schism.

links, the general name given to the linking passages in The *Canterbury Tales* which bind individual tales together (see also *epilogues, *prologues). Within the fragments this is sometimes carefully done, and it seems clear that Chaucer envisaged an elaborate frame-narrative, which he was not able to bring to completion. What survives is often remarkably dramatic in nature: in Fragment I after The *Knight's Tale* the exchange between the *Host (who has a very prominent role in the framework), the *Miller, and the *Reeve vividly exhibits the potential disorder in the pilgrim company and signals a change in tone from the courtly idealism of the Knight's narrative to the bawdy world of the *fabliaux, as well as a clash of personalities which is to find expression in the Reeve's 'quitting' of the Miller. Similarly, in Fragment VII, after *Melibee* is

concluded, there is a very neat transition in which the Host's comments on patience and his own wife lead on to a proposal for a different kind of 'mateere' and his bantering 'murye wordes' to the *Monk. The Monk takes 'al in pacience' and gives a careful, and daunting, account of the tragedies he intends to recount. Sometimes the links contain some quite unexpected action: the *Cook falls off his horse, the *Pardoner tries to sell relics to the pilgrims, and the *Canon and his Yeoman join the company.

Lyno, Lynceus, the husband of Hypermnestra (*Ypermystra). (See The *Legend of Good Women.)

LIONEL, earl of Ulster and duke of Clarence (1338–68), the third son of *Edward III, said to be tall and handsome. He married Elizabeth de Burgh, in whose household the young Chaucer was a retainer. Chaucer's military service in France (1359–60) was probably with the prince's company. The last record of Chaucer in Lionel's service was in late 1360 when he was paid for carrying letters from Calais to England. After the death of Elizabeth, Lionel married Violante, the daughter of Bernabò Visconti (*Barnabo Viscounte), in Milan in 1368. A few months later he died of a violent sickness at Alba.

LYVIA, Livia (or Livilla), the sister of Germanicus, caused her husband Drusus to be poisoned (AD 23) at the instigation of Sejanus. She is one of the 'wicked wives' of the anti-feminist tradition (III.747–51).

LIVY, see *Titus Livius.

locus amoenus ('lovely place'), the name applied to the idealized idyllic 'pleasance' of ancient and medieval poetry. It is a beautiful shady place, with trees, a meadow, a spring or brook, flowers and birds. Sometimes it is related to the earthly Paradise. It is a traditional, rhetorical motif, rather than a case of the direct observation of *nature, but it is often vivid and picturesque. A good example (among several) in Chaucer is the setting for the parliament of the goddess Nature in The *Parliament of Fowls* (see also *gardens; *landscape).
Curtius (1953), 192–200.

lodging, see *herberwe.

LOY, SEINTE, by whom the *Prioress swore (I.120; possibly, according to some, because Chaucer needed a rhyme for 'coy'), is almost certainly St Eligius or Éloi (c.588–660), a goldsmith who later became bishop of Noyon (and still later, the patron of goldsmiths, blacksmiths, farriers, and carters). He was especially associated with horses, and his emblem is a horseshoe: he calmed a rearing horse with the sign of the cross, cut off its leg, fastened a horseshoe to it, and then replaced the leg. His cult and legends were widespread, and the scene of the miraculous shoeing is often depicted. It is not clear whether there is any particular point (satirical or otherwise) in associating him with the Prioress: he may have been the object of a fashionable cult. But it is obviously appropriate for a carter to swear by him (III.1564) when his horses get the cart out of the mud.

Loller, Lollard. Apparently in origin based on the Dutch verb lollen 'to mumble', the word was used in late 14th-c. England to mean 'religious eccentric', but was particularly associated after 1382 with the followers of John *Wyclif. It seems to be in this last sense that Loller is used of the Parson in the doubtful *epilogue to The Man of Law's Tale (1173, 1177), where two characteristics of Lollards are mentioned: their dislike of oaths and their emphasis on preaching (though the Parson's participation in the Canterbury pilgrimage and the orthodox emphasis on oral confession within the Parson's own tale make it unlikely that the Host's accusation is accurate). Chaucer's awareness of contemporary Lollard techniques and vocabulary, for instance in The Wife of Bath's Prologue and in the description of the Parson in the General Prologue, has recently been emphasized.   [AH]

Lollius, one of the great Chaucer mysteries. He is named three times as an authority on the Trojan War. In The *House of Fame (1468) he appears among other writers on the subject. In *Troilus and Criseyde (which is derived from *Boccaccio's Italian poem the Filostrato) Chaucer once calls him 'myn auctour' (I.394). Here the immediate reference is to Troilus's song (which is in fact based on Petrarch (*Petrak)). However, a later remark, as telleth Lollius' (V.1653), makes it clear that 'Lollius' is the source of the main narrative. To complicate matters, Chaucer elsewhere (II.13–14) says that his source is Latin. There has been much discussion about why he does not mention Boccaccio, and about who 'Lollius' is. It is possible that there may have been some genuine muddle over the authorship of the Filostrato (at least one MS of the French translation attributes it to Petrarch), but since Chaucer chose to say that his source was in Latin when he knew it was Italian makes this less likely. Of the various candidates suggested, the Lollius mentioned by Horace (Epistles 1.2.1–2) is the most promising. Horace remarks 'while you, Maximus Lollius, are declaiming at Rome, I have been reading again at Praeneste the writer of the Trojan War [i.e. Homer]' ('Troiani belli scriptorem, Maxime Lolli, | dum tu declamas Romae, Praeneste relegi'). If, as actually happens in one MS of John of Salisbury's Policraticus where these lines are quoted, 'scriptorem' were read as 'scriptorum', and the name 'Maxime' taken as an adjective, Lollius would be 'the greatest of the writers of the Trojan war' (an error perpetuated in Jean Foullechat's 14th-c. French translation of the Policraticus). Even if Chaucer thought that Lollius was an ancient 'author' (and shared the view of many medieval writers that his antiquity and Latinity gave him more authority than a modern author), it may well be that attributing the Filostrato to him was a deliberate piece of mystification—and perhaps a private joke.

   Rv 1022; Windeatt (1992), 37–41; Kittredge (1917).

Lombardy, see *Lumbardye.

London, Londoun, Chaucer's birthplace, was the most important town of medieval *England. A later Londoner, *Stow, who edited Chaucer, began his antiquarian Survey of London with Geoffrey of Monmouth's story that it was founded by Brutus as Troynovant or New Troy and was later improved by King Lud (from whom Ludgate takes its name). It was an important mercantile centre from Roman times, enjoying an advantageous position at the first point at which the river Thames, a major highway for trade, could be bridged. Medieval London was a small city, which could be traversed easily on foot. It corresponded roughly to the present 'City of London' around the Norman Tower and London Bridge. See Map 2. Westminster, a newer royal and ecclesiastical centre, was to its west, Southwark (*South-werk) across the river to the south. Besides the Tower and many churches, the city's skyline was dominated by the great Gothic cathedral of Old St Paul's (which was destroyed in the Great Fire of 1666). Because of its commercial and political importance it not only attracted people from other parts of England but also foreign merchants and workers, Italians, Flemings, and others. It was the home of rich and powerful *guilds. A number of medieval writers (notably *Langland, and, after Chaucer, *Hoccleve and the anonymous 15th-c. poet who wrote 'London Lickpenny') give vivid glimpses of its street life. According to Langland, cooks and their servants cried 'hote pies, hote!' and taverners similarly advertised their wines. The narrator of 'London Lickpenny' says that his hood was stolen in Westminster and that he found it later in the day on sale in Cornhill. London in the 14th c. was probably not exactly as *Morris imagined it, 'small and white and clean', since in spite of attempts at sanitary organization, the gutters carrying the refuse must have produced a notable stench in hot weather. However, its smallness (and its closeness to the country) no doubt did much to balance its lack of cleanness. We read of various kinds of entertainment enjoyed by the inhabitants: wrestling and archery and other sports at Moorfields, with Londoners sometimes competing (once or twice violently) against the youths of Westminster, pageants and processions, and jousts like those at Smithfield in 1390 which Chaucer helped to organize. It was also the scene of disorderly violence and riots (see *Jakke Straw; *Peasants' Revolt).

Chaucer's travels, varied experience, and wide reading made him an international poet, but he was also a London poet. He spent his formative years there, worked there (e.g. as controller in the port of London), lived for twelve years over *Aldgate and leased a house in Westminster at the end of his life, and probably wrote much of his poetry in or near London (see Geoffrey *Chaucer: life). London and London life are not as obviously central to his imaginative work as Paris was to

be for Villon, but his allusions show how it forms a significant part of his and his readers' experience. (See also *Chepe, *Fysshstrete, *Newegate). He refers, for instance, to London ale (I.382), which was strong and expensive. His *Parson was not one of those who abandoned their flocks in order to run 'to Londoun unto Seinte *Poules' to find employment as chantry priests singing offices and masses for the dead (I.509–10). (Later we hear in The *Canon's Yeoman's Tale of the cheating of one such chantry priest in London.) One of the Wife of Bath's husbands was in London (presumably on business) during Lent (III.550). A number of the Canterbury Pilgrims have connections with the London area: Harry Bailly is from Southwark; the *Prioress is associated with *Stratford atte Bowe, the *Man of Law with the '*Parvys' (portico) of St Paul's, the *Manciple with a 'temple' or 'Inn of Court'; and the *Pardoner works from the Hospital of St Mary of Rouncesval (*Rouncivale) at *Charing Cross.

It is the *Cook 'of London' (I.4325), whose pies leave much to be desired, who sets his tale in the city, and takes us briefly into the merry life of apprentices 'in oure citee'. His Perkyn sounds like one of the 'common dicers and night walkers' often prosecuted by the authorities, and hurries to see the 'ridings' (perhaps sometimes of Lords of Misrule?) in Cheapside.

Baker (1970); Hanrahan (2000); Myers (1972); Riley (1868); R. H. Robbins (1959), 130–4; Robertson (1968).

longitude, celestial longitude, analogous to geographical longitude. The origin of the celestial coordinate is the head of Aries (see *hed). Although the concept is used frequently by Chaucer in his astronomical writings, the word is not, since he can talk instead of the 'degree' of a star or planet, the 'degree of a sign' at which something is found, the 'degree of the Zodiac with which a planet rises', or the 'true place (etc.) of a planet' (*verrey aux, verrey mote, verrey place*, and so forth). (See also *astrology and astronomy*; *eclyptik*; *latitude*.) [JDN]

Longius, Longinus, the centurion who, according to legend, pierced the side of Christ with his spear (*ABC* 163–4).

Looth, Lot in the Old Testament, who after drinking wine lay with his own two daughters (Gen. 19:30–8). He is cited as an *exemplum by the *Pardoner (VI.485–7).

LORRIS, GUILLAUME DE; lost works. See *Guillaume de Lorris; *Canon of Chaucer's Works, *Book of the Lion, *Lyrics, Origenes upon the Maudeleyne, *Wrecched Engendrynge of Mankynde.

love. Chaucer repeatedly professes to know little or nothing of the ways of love, or to be unable to write about it 'feelingly', but this most complicated of human *emotions is one of his most central topics. It is human love which engages him (although a tale like that of the *Second Nun shows him to have been sensitive to the intense love of God characteristic of much medieval *piety). This is a constant theme from his earliest works onwards, and it is one which is treated with subtlety and great insight, in a variety of contexts and situations and from a variety of viewpoints. In a number of places Chaucer expresses amazement at the diversity of love's ways (e.g. Tr II.27–8; III.33–5). Love seems to cover a variety of emotional experience. However, some ideas recur. It is associated not only with the goddess *Venus, but also with God's vicegerent *Nature, whose task it is to reproduce and maintain his diverse created species. Her basic principles are harmony and moderation ('*mesure'), and these are ideally reflected in noble love and in good marriage. Falling in love is necessary and 'natural', since love is part of the 'lawe of kynde', as Troilus discovers when he tries to scorn it (I.233–8).

Love is part of the divine creation ('God loveth, and to love wol nought werne [deny], | And in this world no lyves creature | Withouten love is worth, or may endure', Tr III.12–14). Boethius (*Boece) sees it as part of the fabric of the universe, binding disparate elements together. This is the theme of Troilus's hymn to 'Love, that of erthe and se hath governaunce' at the end of the third book of *Troilus and Criseyde. The noblest love may reflect that divine love which as *Dante says, 'moves the sun and the other stars'.

But in the sublunary world human love is often imperfect and mutable, and unpredictable in its working. Chaucer takes particular delight in presenting and exploring its contradictions and paradoxes. As the inscription over the gate in The *Parliament of Fowls warns, the lover may experience the greatest joy or the greatest sorrow. Love unites opposites: 'Allas, what is this wondre maladie? | For hote of cold, for cold of hote, I dye' (Tr I.419–20). Love unsatisfied may beget sorrow, anguish, and physical distress: symptoms of 'the loveris maladye of *Hereos'. Chaucer uses some of the proverbial lore concerning the instability and insecurity of human love ('hot love soon cold', 'in great love is great mourning', 'love changes oft', etc.): Criseyde asks 'endeth than love in wo? Ye, or men lieth' (IV.834), and later remarks that 'men rede | That love is a thyng ay ful of bisy drede' (IV.1644–5).

The great power of love is constantly stressed ('in hevene and helle, in erthe and salte see | Is felt thi myght, if that I wel descerne, | As man, brid, best, fissh, herbe, and grene tree | Thee fele in tymes with vapour [influence] eterne', Tr III.8–11). In imperfect human situations this power may sometimes seem dangerous and destructive, and potentially anarchic ('who shall give a lover any law?', I.1164; cf. Bo III m.12). This is especially so when there is a lack of 'mesure', or when the love seems to turn in on itself and exist only in a private and vulnerable world. And yet there is a tragic grandeur in the stories of some of the victims.

At its finest, love (as celebrated in the song of *Antigone, Tr II.827–75) ennobles its subjects, demonstrates generous and open-hearted qualities, '*gentilesse', '*pite', 'trouthe' or faithfulness, and is implacably opposed to such vices as covetousness (coveitise), falseness, jealousy (*jalousie), malice, or pride. 'Love is a thyng as any spirit free', as the *Franklin says (V.767); it will not be constrained by 'mastery'. This reflects Nature's ideal of free choice, as exercised by the courtly lady (so in The Parliament of Fowls the female eagle insists on having her 'choys al fre', 649), but is also associated with an ideal of mutual 'suffraunce' which Chaucer seems to see as the basis of a good *marriage like that of Arveragus and Dorigen in The *Franklin's Tale. The ecstatic *joy of love is balanced by responsibility and the need to live virtuously. Criseyde tells Troilus (IV.1667–82) that she came to love him for such qualities: 'moral vertu, grounded upon trouthe . . . gentil herte and manhood . . . and that youre resoun bridlede youre delit': 'this may lengthe of yeres naught fordo, | Ne remuable Fortune deface'. At the end of the poem the unchanging stability of the love of Christ (often imagined in medieval literature as a lover-knight) is contrasted with the mutability of this world. Elsewhere, noble love is shown to be threatened by wickedness and deception, and although the union of Dorigen and Arveragus seems to reflect Nature's *mesure* and harmony, other marriages (like that of *January and *May) do not.

In his treatment of love, Chaucer will use and adapt proverbial lore about the 'old dance' (as it is called in the *General Prologue* (I.476) and elsewhere) (that 'love can espy all' is demonstrated in the story of Pyramus and Thisbe (*LGW* 742; cf. IV.2167–27), or the terminology of *courtly love, or the language of the religion of love ('Blissed be Love, that kan thus folk converte!', *Tr* I.308, etc.). He constantly finds variations on traditional images and patterns of ideas. Thus, the fire of love, given visual form in the firebrand with which, Venus dances at the marriage of January and May (IV.1727), burns in the hearts of Troilus ('the hote fir of love hym brende', *Tr* I.490) or Arcite (who laments 'Love hath his firy dart so brennyngly | Ystiked thurgh my trewe, careful herte', I.1564–5). This image is so pervasive that it becomes part of the texture of language: the *Squire loves so 'hotly' that he cannot sleep (I.97) and, in a more comic context, Chaucer says of himself 'I brenne ay in an amorous plesaunce' (*Rosemounde* 22). He makes use of it in the most profane context, as when *Absolon's 'hoote love was coold and al yqueynt' (I.3754), as well as in divine, when a man 'brenneth in the love of God and for the love of God' (X.382): St *Cecilia was 'brennynge evere in charite ful brighte' (VIII.118). Similarly, the image of love as a bond or a chain (*vinculum amoris*) ranges from the 'faire cheyne of love' created by the First Mover which binds the elements together (I.2987–93) or 'benigne Love', the 'holy bond of thynges' invoked by Troilus (III.1261) to the anguish of the lover suffering in passion's bonds: 'now artow hent, now gnaw thin owen cheyne!' (*Tr* I.509). He also has variations on the ideas of blindness (see *MchT*) or the madness or folly of

lovers (I.1799). The mythological deities (Venus, and her son *Cupid) are used to objectify the workings of love. And sometimes personified figures from psychological allegory (*Dauger, *Pite, etc.) appear. But Chaucer prefers to treat love in a more realistic narrative mode, recording the flow of thought and emotion through dramatic speeches and scenes.

He seems fascinated with the variety of human love and passion, and by its comic or absurd aspects as well as by its ennobling or tragic ones. Even though it may bring the lover into some spiritual experience of divine harmony, love is a physical experience. Nature's sexual drive is strongly felt by old men like January and by young men like Nicholas and Absolon in *The Miller's Tale* and quickly leads to what the Parson would call lust or lechery. He enumerates the five fingers of the devil's hand (X.851 ff.): foolish looking, wicked touching, foul words, kissing, and the 'stinking deed of lechery'. In sharp contrast to the Parson, the Wife of Bath celebrates physicality and the sexual purpose of 'membres . . . of generacioun'. The distinctly predatory instincts of an Absolon (see I.3342–7) are frustrated, and his 'love-longing' comes to nought in a raucous, comic manner. However, the more sinister passion of *Apius is the cause of *Virginia's death.

The process of wooing or 'making advances' is charted with some detail and subtlety. The process may be hesitant and full of feeling, as in the case of Troilus, or rather more 'sudden', as in the case of *Diomede, or much more sudden, as in the case of Nicholas (I.3271–81). It involves the art or craft of love, which is (*PF* 1) 'so long to lerne'. This may be very noble and refined: Alceste says the god of Love 'taught al the craft of fyn lovynge' as well as 'of wyfhod the lyvynge' (*LGW* 544–5). Sometimes it is Ovidian advice on the techniques of wooing or seduction, or the 'daliaunce and fair langage' that the *Friar was skilled in (I.211). In *The *Parliament of Fowls* Chaucer delights in the comic contrast of styles of wooing: the highly verbal and intricate courting rhythms of the noble birds prove far too leisurely for many of the lower (491–5).

Certainly, as far as the expression of affection is concerned, 'fair langage' is important at all levels. Troilus demonstrates convincingly that he 'can . . . wel speke of love' (Criseyde's first question about him, II.503). The consummation of their love is described in beautiful and touching terms. But 'in sondry londes, sondry ben usages': elsewhere Chaucer shows us the far from lyrical union of January and May, the grotesque coupling of May and Damian in the pear-tree, the hasty 'merry fits' by night in *The *Reeve's Tale*, and other assorted acts of 'swiving'. Relationships may be brief or stable; harmony and disharmony may be found both inside and outside 'the bond | That highte [is called] matrimoigne or mariage' (I.3094–5). (See also ***courtly love; *emotions; *gestures; *jalousie; *joy; *marriage**.

Bayley (1960), ch. 2; Bennett (1957), 181–93; C. S. Lewis (1936); Mann (1991); Phillips (2000).

Lovers' Mass, an anonymous 15th-c. 'Chaucerian' poem found in MS Fairfax 16, a collection of poems including Chaucer's dream visions and some of his lyrics. It is an elegantly written parody of the liturgy, beginning with the 'Introibo' (here signifying 'I will go unto the altar of the god of Love') and proceeding through the stages of the Mass.

LOWYS, see **Lewis *Chaucer**.

Luc. St Luke the Evangelist (VII.951) is twice quoted by the Parson (X.700, 702).

LUCAN, Marcus Annaeus Lucanus, the Roman poet (AD 39–65). The nephew of Seneca (*Senec), he was born in Córdoba in Spain, and was educated in Rome. For a time he enjoyed the patronage of *Nero, but when he was discovered to have been involved in a conspiracy he was forced to commit suicide. His only surviving work is the *Pharsalia*, an epic devoted to the civil war between Caesar and Pompey, which culminates in the death of the latter at the battle of Pharsalia. The poem is eloquent, rhetorical, and vigorous, rich in scenes of pathos. It was greatly admired in the Middle Ages, and was studied as a school text. Chaucer refers to Lucan four times in his poetry, but whether he knew his work directly has been doubted. (A fifth reference, in the translation of Boethius, where Lucan is called by Philosophy *familiaris noster*, which becomes Chaucer's 'Lucan, my famylier' (*Bo* IV pr.6:231), does not help with the problem.)

In *The *House of Fame* (1497–502) Lucan is called 'the grete poete' who 'bears up' the fame of Caesar and Pompey, and at the end of **Troilus and Criseyde* (V.1792) he is listed among the other ancient authors (*auctour). The other two references are in passages concerning Julius Caesar (II.401; VII.2719). The first says that he made a great parade of 'the triumphe of Julius', whereas Lucan says explicitly that Caesar did not hold one. However, it has been noted that other passages in the *Pharsalia* imply that he intended to hold one, and that it may be that medieval readers assumed that he did: in a MS of a commentary by *Trevet it is said that he did; a French version, *Ly histoire de Julius Cesar* by Jehan de Tuim, describes triumphs at the beginning and the end. Similarly, the account of Caesar given by the *Monk may be based on Lucan or on some intermediate version like that of Jehan de Tuim. A couple of further possible echoes have been claimed in *The House of Fame*: in the description of the desert at the end of the first book (possibly from Jehan de Tuim), and in the elaborateness of Fame's house, which may have some affinity with the way Cleopatra's palace is described in the *Pharsalia*. Behind the apotheosis of Troilus's soul, which Chaucer takes from Boccaccio's *Teseide*, there lies the account of Pompey's ascent after his death and his laughter at the preparations for his funeral.

(ed. and trans.) Duff (1928).

Lucye, Lucia or Lucilia, wife of the poet Lucretius, appears in the book of 'wicked wives' which *Jankin (4) reads to the *Wife of Bath (III.747–57). She is said to have given her husband such a powerful love potion that he died from it. Chaucer found this in St *Jerome.

Lucyfer, literally 'light-bringing' (L.), and used with this simple meaning by Lucretius, *Ovid, and other ancient writers. (1) The Morning Star, Venus. Cicero and Ovid used it with this meaning, which occurs also on three occasions in **Boece*. There Lucifer as a star is linked with *Hesperus, that is, with Venus as the Evening Star. Ovid also uses 'Lucifer' as a name for the son of *Aurora and Cephalus (cf. an early Greek tradition that made Hesperus out to be the son of Astræus, or Cephalus, and Eos); Ovid and Propertius even

used it to mean the day itself. In *Troilus and Criseyde* III.1417, Chaucer refers to Lucifer as 'the dayes messager', by which he is generally assumed to have meant the Morning Star: Lucifer there 'Gan for to rise and out hire bemes throwe'. (2) *Satan. The first 'tragedy' in The *Monk's Tale is that of Lucifer, the rebellious archangel whose sin led to his fall to hell. The *Parson's Tale cites Lucifer's (with that of the Antichrist) as the greatest sin. Satan had been given the name of the Morning Star as the result of a peculiar Patristic interpretation of Isaiah 14:12, 'How art thou fallen from heaven, O Lucifer, son of the morning!'
[JDN]

Lucina, an ancient Italian deity who gave the new-born child the light of day. In The *Knight's Tale a woman in labour calls on her help. Lucina was absorbed in the Juno cult. There was anciently a connection of some sort with the Moon, for the calends of every month were sacred to Juno. In The *Franklin's Tale, and in *Troilus and Criseyde, Chaucer gave the name correctly to the Moon, as sister of Phoebus, the Sun. (See also *Apollo; *Cynthea; *Dyane; *Latona.)   [JDN]

Lucrece, Lucresse, Lucretia, the wife of Lucius Tarquinus Collatinus. After her brutal rape by *Tarquin she chose to commit suicide rather than to live in dishonour. It was a popular story in the Middle Ages, appearing, for instance, in the *Roman de la Rose and *Gower. Chaucer tells it in The *Legend of Good Women, apparently following *Ovid, and, possibly, a translation of *Valerius Maximus. Lucretia was a an exemplary figure of wifely virtue and chastity, and as such is several times referred to (V.1405–8; *BD* 1082–7; *Anel* 82; *LGW* 257).

I. Donaldson (1982).

Lumbardes. Bankers from Lombardy were an important part of the medieval European economy. The *Shipman's Tale alludes to them and their work (VII.367). The merchant borrows a large sum of money from them in Bruges, and redeems his 'bond' from their 'branch' in Paris. (See *money.)

Lumbardye, Lombardy, an area in northern Italy (*Ytaille), named after the Lombards or

Langobardi, a Germanic tribe. For Chaucer it is a larger area than the present Italian province, bounded on the east by the Apennines (*Apennyn, IV.46), and including Saluzzo (*Saluces) in present-day Piedmont (its lord, *Walter, was 'the gentilleste yborn of Lumbardye', IV.72). See Map 3. The *Merchant's Tale is also set in Lombardy. It may not be accidental that both Walter and *January are men who insist on having their own way. Lombardy was famous, or notorious, for its tyrants. *Alceste, urging mercy in a lord, says that he should 'nat be lyk tirauntz of Lumbardye, | That han no reward [regard] but at tyrannye' (*LGW* 374–5). Bernabò Visconti (*Barnabo Viscounte) of Milan, 'scourge of Lumbardye', appears in The *Monk's Tale. The region was also noted as a mercantile and financial centre (see *Lumbardes) and for its horses (V.193). Chaucer had first-hand knowledge of it from his visits to Italy: his journey in 1378 was specifically to Lombardy (see **Geoffrey *Chaucer: life**).

Luna, the Moon (L.). Used as an alchemical name for silver in *The Canon's Yeoman's Tale. (See also *alchemy.)   [JDN]

Lute, see *musical instruments.

LYDGATE, JOHN (*c.*1370–1449/50), a Benedictine monk of Bury St Edmunds, and the most voluminous of the 15th-c. English 'Chaucerian' poets. He was held in high esteem in his time and later, and his name was regularly linked with those of Chaucer and Gower. His modern reputation of being prosaic and dull is not entirely justified. His works include *A Complaint of the *Black Knight* (which echoes The *Book of the Duchess), *The Temple of Glass* (indebted to The *House of Fame), *The Flower of Courtesy* (a Valentine's Day poem, like The *Parliament of Fowls), *The Troy Book, The *Siege of Thebes* (in the prologue of which he imagines that he joins the pilgrims at Canterbury and is invited to tell a tale), and *The Fall of Princes* (a series of 'tragedies' of the kind told by Chaucer's *Monk, but much longer). He also wrote an elegant poem to Thomas *Chaucer, the poet's son. Lydgate had steeped himself in Chaucer, and shows an excellent and extensive knowledge of the works (of which he gives a list in *The Fall of

Princes). The dream visions, *Troilus* and *The Knight's Tale* are obvious favourites, but he also refers to the *Wife of Bath. In a number of places he praises Chaucer, 'poete of Brytayne', singling out for special mention his eloquence and rhetorical skills and the way he has 'illumined' 'oure rude langage'. He admires him as a great poet, 'fayrest in our tonge, and as the laurer grene', distinguished by his wisdom and learning.

(ed.) Norton-Smith (1966a, Selections).

lyrics. The medieval lyric tradition was a rich and diverse one, in Latin and in the vernaculars. That songs and lyrics were a feature of everyday life in 14th-c. England is suggested by a number of Chaucerian allusions. 'Com hider, love, to me!', which the *Pardoner sings 'ful loude' (I.672) sounds like a popular song. Another is 'My lief is faren in londe [my love has gone to the country]' which *Chantecleer and *Pertelote sing 'in sweete accord' (VII.2879). In The *Miller's Tale* Nicholas the clerk sings in his room at night the *Angelus ad virginem*, a religious song, and an unidentified song 'the Kynges Noote' (I.3214–17), while Absolon sings a song of love-pleading outside Alison's window. The *Squire, a more courtly lover, 'koude songes make and wel endite': songs were a part of court entertainment, and 'making' them a courtly accomplishment (and one which Chaucer would have learnt). He refers to the fashionable forms of French lyric, the *ballade, the *roundel, the *virelay, the *complaint, and the lay. The squire Damian composes for May a *letter 'in manere of a compleynt or a lay', which he slips into her hand (IV.1880–1, 1936 ff.). The Man in Black in The *Book of the Duchess* expresses his sorrow in a lay: 'he sayd a lay, a maner song, | Withoute noote, withoute song' (471–2), a remark which perhaps suggests that it would normally have been sung. It seems likely also that Chaucer was aware of the *aubade, the lovers' farewell song at dawn.

Chaucer is now best known as a narrative poet, but he is also a distinguished lyric poet. There survives a group of independent lyrics and lyrical pieces which are usually grouped together in modern editions under the title 'Short Poems'. These are the *ABC, The Complaint unto *Pity, A Complaint to his *Lady, The Complaint of *Mars, The Complaint of *Venus, To *Rosemounde, *Womanly

Noblesse, *Chaucer's Wordes unto Adam, his owne Scriveyn* (*Adam (2)), The *Former Age*, *Fortune*, *Truth*, *Gentilesse*, *Lak of Stedfastnesse*, *Lenvoy de Chaucer a *Scogan*, *Lenvoy de Chaucer a *Bukton*, The Complaint of Chaucer to his *Purse*, and the *Proverbs*. To these are sometimes added poems which though not ascribed to Chaucer in MSS may possibly be by him: *Against *Women Unconstant*, *Complaynt d'Amours*, *Merciles Beautee*, and A *Balade of Complaynt* (see individual entries).

These so-called 'Short Poems' (the 'shortness' varies somewhat) probably do not represent the total of Chaucer's lyric output. It seems likely that a number of the songs in praise of love mentioned in the Prologue to The *Legend of Good Women* (422–3, no doubt including some of the 'songs and lecherous lays' he refers to in the *Retractions) and the 'ditees and songes glade' that *Gower says he composed in his youth have been lost. Possibly a number of them were written in French (see '*Ch') as well as in English. Those we have are mostly in the tradition of French courtly lyric as it had been developed by *Guillaume de Machaut, *Deschamps, *Graunson, and others. They show a willingness to experiment with form and technique (e.g. in the use of terza rima in *A Complaint to his Lady*), and some variety in topic and in tone (e.g. the satirical *Adam* or the lighthearted *Purse*). They also include philosophical or 'Boethian' lyrics (such as The Former Age, Gentilesse, Lak of Stedfastnesse, Truth), and familiar verse epistles.

He also makes interesting use of lyrics set within a narrative. In The Book of the Duchess the lay comes at a turning point in the 'plot' and changes the emotional direction of the poem; in the Prologue of The Legend of Good Women the ballade 'Hyd, Absolon, thy gilte tresses clere' (249–69) heralds the arrival of the beautiful *Alceste and her maidens; the roundel 'Now welcome, somer, with thy sonne softe' sung by the birds in The *Parliament of Fowls* 'to don Nature honour and plesaunce' at their departing is a magnificent celebration of spring and brings the poem to a joyous conclusion. Rather different is the *envoy at the end of The *Clerk's Tale*. Although they are not marked formally as lyrics, the Prologue of The *Prioress's Tale* and the 'invocation to Mary' in the Prologue of The *Second Nun's Tale* are ecstatic lyrical prayers of the kind found in the medieval religious lyric (of which the *ABC* is a more elaborate example).

The technique of placing lyrics within the course of a narrative in prose is not uncommon in late antiquity and the Middle Ages: a well-known example is the *Consolation of Philosophy* of Boethius (*Boece). Chaucer's most systematic use is in *Troilus and Criseyde*, where formal lyrics are put into the mouths of characters at crucial points in the story. The first (*Canticus Troili*) comes in Book I after Troilus is wounded by love (I.400–20): 'If no love is, O God, what fele I so?' It is a fairly close translation of a sonnet by Petrarch (*Petrak), expanded into three stanzas of rhyme royal. The song is appropriate to Troilus's emotional state, full of a questioning anguish. It is also neatly fitted into the larger structure, not only expressing the contradictory emotions of an individual, but also suggesting the mysterious and contradictory nature of *Love in general. In the second book, *Antigone sings a 'Trojan song' in Criseyde's garden (II.826–75): 'O Love, to whom I have and shal | Ben humble subgit'. It is a song of ideal love, which provides an answer to Criseyde's worry that love may prove 'the moste stormy lyf', moves her deeply (884 ff.), and leads on to the song of the nightingale and the dream of the eagle (918 ff.). Towards the end of the third book, another *Canticus Troili* celebrates the cosmic power of love ('Love, that of erthe and se hath governaunce', 1744–71). This is a Boethian philosophical lyric appropriate to the markedly intellectual nature of the hero; it also ends with a characteristically 'gentil' prayer that even those with 'hertes colde' should be encircled in the bond of Love. Book IV, which announces the end of this idyllic love, does not have a formal song, but perhaps an equivalent is found in the passage (958–1082), a kind of philosophical 'complaint' in which Troilus bitterly disputes with himself the nature of free will and necessity ('For al that comth, comth by necessitee'). (The densely philosophical style, which though the product of a deep emotion, eschews the direct expression of emotion until the final prayer, is not unlike that of *Dante's ode on '*gentilesse' in the *Convivio*.) Finally, in the fifth book yet another *Canticus Troili* 'of his lady deere, | That absent was' ('O sterre, of which I lost have al the light', 638–44) is sung 'with soft voice'. A much longer lament in Boccaccio has been replaced by a single stanza which is a powerful expression of despair. (See also **carole**; **envoy**).

M

Mabely (a form of Mabel), the name of the old woman in The *Friar's Tale (III.1626).

Macchabee (1), see *Judas Machabeus.

Machabee (2), the four books of the Maccabees (included in the Vulgate but part of the Apocrypha in AV). The first two tell the story of the resistance led by the famous Jewish family (see *Judas Machabeus). The source of the story of *Antiochus in The *Monk's Tale (VII.2579) is 2 Maccabees 9. The Monk also refers to 1 Maccabees 1 in his story of Alexander (*Alisaundre) (VII.2655).

MACEDO the Macedonian (HF 915), Alexander the Great (see *Alisaundre).

Macedoyne, Macidoyne, Macidonye, Macedonia. Chaucer's references are to the ancient kingdom, to the north of Greece (V.1435, VII.2656; BD 1062).

MACHAUT see *Guillaume de Machaut.

MACROBES, MACROBEUS, MACROBYE Macrobius Theodosius (fl. c.400). Almost nothing is known of the life of this Latin author. He was apparently not of Roman birth: he says he was 'born under another sky' (perhaps in Africa). His commentary on the Somnium Scipionis (*Drem of Scipioun) sets out Cicero's narrative (thus preserving it for us), and discusses the questions it raises about the nature and destiny of the soul and the structure of the universe. It is a strongly Neoplatonic work, which owes much to Plato's Timaeus. In the Middle Ages it was taken as a source-book for information about *cosmology and *dreams. To justify Cicero's choice of the 'fabulous' device of the dream Macrobius discusses dreams in some detail, offering an elaborate classification of the kinds, and arguing that the fiction of the dream is a 'fabulous narrative' in which philosophical truths are concealed (see *dream vision, dreams). Chaucer refers to Macrobius a number of times. In The *Parliament of Fowls (110–11) he makes the author of the Somnium appear and praise him for 'lokynge of myn olde bok totorn, | Of which Macrobye roughte [cared] nat a lyte [little]', probably alluding to Macrobius's concluding remark that 'there is nothing more complete than this work, which embraces the entire body of philosophy'. When he says in The *Book of the Duchess that Macrobius 'wrot al th'avysioun' of 'kyng Scipioun' (284–6), he presumably means 'wrote down' or perhaps 'wrote a commentary on'. Chauntecleer also refers to it in The Nun's Priest's Tale (VII.3123–6), a tale which makes use of Macrobius's discussion of dreams.

(trans.) Stahl (1952).

Madrian. At the end of *Melibee Harry Bailly, the *Host, swears 'by that precious corpus Madrian' (VII.1892), apparently a reference to the body of a saint. He or she remains unidentified. St Madron (or Madern), or St Madrun (or Materiana), both Cornish saints, may be (remote) possibilities. It may be one of the Host's malapropisms (cf. 'by corpus bones', VII.1906). Possibly it is a mistake for St Hadrian (or Adrian), an early Roman martyr who was supported by a constant and patient wife.

Magdale(y)ne, Maudelayne (always called by Chaucer 'the Magadalene'), St Mary Magdalene. Mary of Magdala, a woman from whom Christ cast out seven devils (Luke 8:2) was identified in the Middle Ages with Mary the sister of Martha and with the unnamed female sinner who anointed Christ's feet (Luke 7:37). In art a pot of ointment was her emblem. Other legendary details were added, e.g. that she brought the gospel to

Provence and died there. Many churches were dedicated to her. The *Shipman's barge, 'the Maudelayne' (I.410), is named after her. One of Chaucer's lost works is '*Origenes upon the Maudeleyne'. His other references are all found in The *Parson's Tale: X.502 (anointing); 504 (weeping at Christ's feet); 947 (chaste widows are the vessel of the blessed Magdalene); 995 (her confession to Christ).

magic ('the art of putting in action the power of spirits' and 'the secret operations of natural powers' (Dr Johnson)), also included in the Middle Ages various kinds of illusionistic techniques. It overlapped both with *science (notably in *astrology and *alchemy) and with *religion (where some popular practices and beliefs were difficult to distinguish from magic). The medieval Church shared a belief in the supernatural power of spirits, but condemned practices which involved demons, the use of spells for harmful effects, fortune-telling, etc. 'Superstitious' practices were essentially those of which the Church disapproved. Alongside an intellectual bookish tradition of ancient and Arabic magic and the ʻnatural magic' (magic as applied knowledge of the secret operations of natural powers) propounded by Roger *Bacon and Albert the Great, there was a vast area of popular magic, involving the use of charms or prayer charms and ritual practices for healing, defending one's property or livestock, protection from thieves or evil spirits, producing love, etc.

In Chaucer's work we find a familiarity with the world of popular magic. 'Charms' are part of common parlance (Tr II.1314, 1580; I.2712). His characters use the term 'enchant' metaphorically (III.575, Tr IV.1395)—though it seems to be more pointedly 'magical' in suggestion than its modern English equivalent is. Magic seems to have an ambiguous status. It is sometimes linked with 'sorcery' (II.755) or deception (II.214), and 'sorceress' is used as a term of abuse to the seer Cassandra by Troilus (Tr V.1520). When the 'subtil clerk' in The *Franklin's Tale begins his magical work the narrator refers to 'swich a supersticious [Chaucer's only use of this word] cursednesse' (V.1272), but describes the process in informed detail. The most hostile attitude is in The *Parson's Tale, which refers to the 'malefice of sorcerie' (X.340), and makes a fierce attack (X.603ff.) on false enchanters or necro-

mancers who practise exorcism and the conjuring of spirits 'in bacyns ful of water, or in a bright swerd, in a cercle, or in a fir, or in a shulder-boon of a sheep'. The Parson also lists various methods of divination: 'as by flight or by noyse of briddes or of beestes . . . by dremes, by chirkynge of dores . . . by gnawynge of rattes', etc. (Our knowledge of medieval magical beliefs often depends on such detailed attacks.) He takes a sceptical view of 'the art of putting in action the power of spirits': 'charmes for woundes or maladie of men or of beestes, if they taken any effect, it may be peraventure that God suffreth it, for folk sholden yeve [give] the moore feith and reverence to his name' (X.606). Other characters are less detached. The *Pardoner assumes that he has a market for his magical relics (VI.347–76). The carpenter in The *Miller's Tale pronounces a charm, a 'white paternoster'; to cure his clerkly lodger of despair (I.3472–86). His 'night-spell' is in the form of a prayer (hence it is 'white' rather than 'black' magic, directed against evil spirits: it invokes Christ, 'Seinte *Benedight' and 'St *Peter's sister'.

Elsewhere we find references to ancient magicians, to 'Circes the enchaunteresse' (Bo IV m.3:32) and 'th'enchauntementz of Medea and Circes' (I.1944), though not much is made in Chaucer's story of Medea of 'the sleyghte of hire enchauntement' which helped Jason (LGW 1650). These two appear along with other practitioners, ancient and modern, of the magic arts in The *House of Fame (1259–81). The list includes jugglers and '*tregetours' (illusionists) as well as 'charmeresses, | Olde wiches, sorceresses', and 'clerkes . . . which konne [know] wel | Al this magik naturel'. The names of seven (perhaps a significant number) are given: the other five are Calypso (*Calipsa), Hermes, *Simon Magus, and '*Colle [I] tregetour'. 'Magik naturel' ('the secret operations of natural powers') is practised by the *Physician (I.416), but most spectacularly by the clerk of Orléans in The Franklin's Tale (V.1123–296), who after demonstrating his magical skills in producing illusions or 'apparences' (V.1140; see also V.218), turns to serious and precise astrological observation and brings it about 'thurgh his magik, for a wyke [week] or tweye [two], | It semed that alle the rokkes were aweye'.

Thorndike (1923–41).

MAHOUN, MAKOMETE, Muhammad (c.570–632), the prophet who founded Islam. The legends of medieval Christian propagandists, fearful of the challenge presented by the spread of this rival religion, caricatured its founder: he is sometimes portrayed as a magician, a schismatic, or a renegade cardinal. Rare cases of a more tolerant understanding of Islam among Christian intellectuals are outweighed by a widespread popular ignorance, symbolized by the odd way in which the name of the founder of a religion fiercely opposed to idolatry is enshrined in the common French and English words *mawmet* and *mawmettrie* ('idol' and 'idolatry'; both used by Chaucer, X.749, 860; II.236; X.750). Rather more accurately, in *The *Man of Law's Tale* the Syrians are made to call Muhammad 'our prophet' and 'God's messenger' (II.224, 333).

maistrye is the same word as the modern 'mastery', but it has wider connotations. Besides 'mastery' it can mean 'skill' (I.3383) or 'master-stroke, achievement' (VIII.1060). Chaucer uses it frequently in the senses of 'mastery, upper hand', 'control', and 'dominion' (where it overlaps with *soveraynete* 'sovereignty'), and seems particularly interested in it as a concept when he treats the relationship between men and women. In *The *Wife of Bath's Prologue* she describes how she won from *Jankin (4) the 'bridle' and 'the governaunce of hous and land' and 'by maistrie, al the soveraynete' (III.813–18). The answer to the question put in her *Tale* is that 'wommen desiren to have sovereynetee | As wel over hir housbond as hir love, | And for to been in maistrie hym above' (III.1038–40), but the tale began with a crude example of male *maistrye*, a rape. There are joking references to the 'heigh maistrie' advocated and achieved by the Wife of Bath (IV.1172), but Chaucer often seems to be suggesting the need for some voluntary and mutual surrender of *maistrye*. This is especially so in the marriage of Dorigen and Arveragus in *The *Franklin's Tale* (see IV.738–86). (See also ***marriage.**)

MAKOMETE, see ***Mahoun.**

Malencolie, see ***Melancholy.**

Malyne, Malkyn, Malle, three names which are diminutives of 'Matilda' (L. = English Maud). Malyne (a form of Malkyn) is the name of the miller's daughter in *The *Reeve's Tale.* Malkyn is the name of a serving girl in *The *Nun's Priest's Tale* (VII.3384). The name is used proverbially to indicate a lower-class girl of low morals: 'Malkynnes maydenhede' (II.30) will never come again. Another variant, Malle, is the name of a sheep in *The Nun's Priest's Tale* (VII.2831).

Manciple, Maunciple. A manciple was an officer or servant who purchased provisions for a college or a legal inn of court (or 'temple', I.567). It is for such a legal establishment that the 'gentil' Manciple of the *General Prologue (I.567–86) works. We are not told much else about him. The tone of the portrait (if it can be called a portrait, since it contains no visual detail and concentrates exclusively on his business activities) is ironic. He is an expert buyer, and though he is unlearned he can deceive his learned masters. It may be significant that he rides next to the *Reeve, another very shrewd businessman. The only other manciple mentioned in Chaucer occurs in *The *Reeve's Tale.* He is the manciple of a Cambridge college, and suffers grievously from toothache.

Rv 821; Cooper (1989), 55; Mann (1973), 174.

Manciple's Tale, The. The Manciple's Prologue and Tale (362 lines in couplets) form Fragment IX of *The *Canterbury Tales.* The Prologue describes how the Host calls for a tale from the *Cook who looks sleepy and ready to fall from his horse. The Manciple intervenes ('I wol as now excuse thee of thy tale') and speaks sharply about the Cook's drunkenness. The latter becomes angry, is thrown by his horse, and has to be restored to his seat with difficulty. The Host reproves the Manciple and warns him that the Cook may make trouble for him: 'as for to pynchen at [find fault with] thy rekenynges, | That were nat honest, if it cam to preef.' The Manciple gives the Cook a drink and harmony is restored, by Bacchus (*Bacus), as the Host remarks. The Manciple begins his story.

When Phoebus lived on earth he was a fine young man, who excelled in chivalry and in every kind of minstrelsy. In his house he kept a crow in a cage, which he had taught to speak. It was white as snow, and besides being able to counterfeit the speech of every man, it could sing merrily. Phoebus also had a wife to whom he was very attentive. But he was also very jealous. However, it is impossible to restrain natural desire: a well-fed caged bird will prefer to eat worms in a forest, and when a cat sees a mouse it forgets milk and 'every deyntee'. Appetite puts discretion to flight. Phoebus was deceived: his wife took a lover, a man of little reputation. So when he was away she sent for her 'lemman'. I am a plain man, says the Manciple, and I see no difference between a wife of high estate who takes a lover, who is called 'his lady, as in love', and a poor woman, who is called 'his wenche or his lemman'. The same is true of the tyrant with a large retinue, who is called 'a capitayn', and the robber with only a small company, who is called 'an outlawe or a theef'. The white crow observes the doings of Phoebus's wife, but says never a word. When Phoebus returns, the crow sings 'cuckoo! cuckoo!' The crow tells him what has happened, and Phoebus in his wrath kills his wife with an arrow. In great sorrow he breaks his musical instruments and his arrows and his bow. In anger he turns on the crow, curses him for his scorpion tongue, and decrees that from henceforth he will be black and lose his sweet song and his power of speech.

This 'ensample' warns men to be careful what they say. The Manciple elaborates this with proverbial lore from his mother: 'my sone, keep wel thy tonge, and keep thy freend. | A wikked tonge is worse than a feend', etc. He concludes with her advice to be 'noon auctour newe | Of tidynges, wheither they been false or trewe': wherever you are, 'kepe wel thy tonge and thenk upon the crowe'.

The Prologue presents an obvious problem with the Host's request to the Cook, who has already told a tale in Fragment I (see *Cook's Tale*), but its liveliness makes a fitting introduction to the sophisticated and worldly story which follows. The date of the Tale is not known, but modern opinion tends to place it in the Canterbury period. The sardonic tone of the story and its stress on caution and expediency seems appropriate to the Manciple of the *General Prologue*. The *fable of the tell-tale bird is widespread. Chaucer found it in *Ovid (*Met.* 2.531–632). He may also have known other related versions (in the *Ovide moralisé*,

*Guillaume de Machaut, and *Gower). He makes a number of changes: e.g. a warning against gossip is extended by the discussion of words and their meanings which shows how dangerous and untruthful language can be, and the practical and non-altruistic advice (that talking too much and too truthfully can get you into trouble), which is common in fables, is made more consistently cynical in tone: one should be economical with the truth. In the surviving pattern of the Tales, this tale is the last piece of fiction (and as an animal fable an extreme form of fiction). Perhaps the stern advice with which it ends, to be 'noon auctour' of tidings, looks forward to the austere dismissal of 'fables' by the *Parson in the Prologue which follows.

(ed.) *Rv* 282–8, 952–5; *S&A* 699–722; Cooper (1989), 383–94; Pearsall (1985), 238–43; Scattergood (1974); Severs (1952).

Manes, in Roman religion the spirits of the dead, the gods of the lower world (mentioned in *Troilus and Criseyde*, V.892).

Man of Law, the name usually given to the narrator of The *Man of Law's Tale*, who is addressed by the Host as 'sire Man of Lawe' (II.33), and whose tale is described by the rubric in the *Ellesmere MS as 'the Man of Lawe his tale'. However, a more precise title is given in the formal *portrait devoted to him in the *General Prologue (I.309–30): 'a Sergeant of the Lawe'. This indicates that he was a lawyer of very high rank. The Sergeants formed a small and prestigious group ('the Order of the Coif') of experienced lawyers. His attire is, however, 'hoomly'—a parti-coloured robe with a silken belt. We are given no details of his physical appearance, nor a name, though the remark 'ther koude no wight pynche at his writyng' has suggested a pun on the name of Thomas Pynchbek, a Sergeant in Chaucer's time who was noted for his acquisition of land (and who had signed a writ for the poet's arrest in a case of debt in 1388). But it is not clear that he was in any exact sense a model for the character. The portrait concentrates on the Sergeant's professional skills ('he knows every statute by heart, etc.), and bristles with legal terms (*assise, patente* [royal letter of appointment], *pleyn commissioun* [full jurisdiction]', etc.). It is apparently complimentary about

his personal qualities ('discreet,' 'of greet reverence', etc.), but there is a certain ambiguity: the
phrase 'of greet reverence' is followed by 'he semed
swich [such]'; the remark that he was a very busy
man is followed by 'and yet he semed bisier than
he was'; there seems to be a hint that he has done
well out of his skill in 'purchasyng' (buying land).
Some read the satire as sharp and damning, but it
is notable that he is not charged with the greed,
bribery, and corruption that are commonplace in
medieval satires against lawyers. Chaucer seems
rather to be gently but pointedly drawing attention to a concern with appearances. (See also
*law.)

   Rv 811–12; Cooper (1989), 44; Mann (1973),
86–91.

Man of Law's Tale, The, preceded by an Introduction and a Prologue and followed by an *Epilogue, forms an independent unit in the sequence
of the surviving *Canterbury Tales. Its exact place
has been a matter of dispute, but its usual modern
position as Fragment II (which it has in the
*Ellesmere MS) seems quite reasonable.

   In the Introduction the Man of Law agrees to
tell a tale, but says that it is hard to find a 'thrifty
tale' which Chaucer has not told ('thogh he kan
but lewedly | On metres and on rymyng craftily'),
especially about lovers, whereupon he lists 'thise
noble wyves and thise loveris' which appear in 'the
*Seyntes Legende of Cupide' (see *Legend of Good
Women). But he begins 'with a sobre cheere' with a
Prologue, five stanzas (99–133) in rhyme royal,
which is to be the metrical form for the remainder
of the Tale. It starts as a vehement invective
against poverty, and ends with an address to merchants, who seek land and sea for their winnings
and are 'fathers of tidings and tales'. He would not
have a tale to tell if it were not for a merchant who
taught him one many years ago.

   The Tale (over 1,000 lines long) is divided in
the Ellesmere MS into three parts.

   (134–385) A company of rich merchants in Syria
(*Surrye) come to Rome and hear reports of the
goodness and beauty of the emperor's daughter,
Custance. When they return they tell the Sultan
about her, and he falls in love. He summons his
council and declares his intention of marrying her,
and of converting to Christianity. This is agreed,

and Custance departs sorrowfully from Rome,
committing herself to Christ. Meanwhile, the
Sultan's mother urges her councillors not to give
up their holy laws for a new law which will mean
thraldom and penance. She suggests that they
should pretend to become Christians ('coold
water shal nat greve us but a lite!'), and announces
to her son that she will accept Christianity.

   (386–875) The Christians arrive and are greeted
with great magnificence. The Sultaness invites
them with the Sultan and his men to a splendid
feast. There they are all murdered, with the exception of Custance, who is set adrift in a rudderless
boat. She prays to the holy cross and her boat carries her 'yeres and dayes' from the Mediterranean
into 'oure wilde see' until she is cast ashore in
Northumberland, where 'the wyl of Crist was that
she sholde abyde'. She is found by the constable of
King Alla, and he and his wife Hermengild take
pity on her. They are converted from paganism.
But Satan tries to destroy Custance, inspiring a
knight to lust for her. When he is rejected, he cuts
the throat of Hermengild and falsely places the
bloody knife near Custance. She is accused before
King Alla, but the false knight is miraculously
smitten down, and Alla is converted. He marries
Custance, but his wicked mother, Donegild is dis-
pleased by this. When Alla goes off to make war in
Scotland, Custance is left in the care of the constable. She bears a son, who is baptized Mauricius
(or *Maurice). A messenger is dispatched to Alla
with the news, but Donegild makes him drunk,
steals his letters, and substitutes one which says
that the queen has given birth to a horrible 'fiend-
ly creature'. Alla, though sorrowful, writes back in
his own hand that they should both be kept safely.
But again Donegild makes the messenger drunk
and gives him a counterfeited letter instructing
the constable to banish Custance from the land in
the ship in which she arrived. Sorrowfully the
constable does this, and Custance with her little
child weeping on her arm prays to the Virgin
Mary, goes into the ship, and 'in the see she
dryveth forth hir weye'.

   (876–1162) Alla returns, discovers Donegild's
treachery, and kills her. Custance meanwhile sails
on for five years and more. When she comes to
land, she has to fight off the lord's steward: the
Virgin Mary helps her and he falls overboard. Her

ship takes her back into the Mediterranean. The Roman emperor has sent a senator to take vengeance on the Syrians for the massacre of the Christians. He is returning in triumph to Rome and chances to meet Custance's ship. He entrusts her and her young son to his wife, and she remains there for a long time. King Alla comes to Rome on pilgrimage. Custance's son accompanies the senator to a feast with King Alla, and stands 'lookynge in the kynges face'. The senator tells Alla how the child and his mother were found. The boy's face reminds the king of Custance, and he goes home with the senator to find her. In a tearful scene of reunion all the misunderstandings are resolved. Then the emperor is invited by Alla to dinner, and the sight of the child makes him think of his lost daughter. She reveals herself to him in a scene of 'pitous joye'. Maurice is later made emperor. Alla and Custance return to England, and when Alla dies Custance comes back to Rome to live with her father 'in vertu and in hooly almus-dede' until death separates them.

As a whole Fragment II presents some problems. The status of the epilogue is questionable. Both Introduction and Prologue also contain puzzling features. The Man of Law's statement 'I speke in prose, and lat him [Chaucer] rymes make' seems to imply that a tale in prose is to follow. It has been suggested that this was Chaucer's original intention, and that possibly either *Melibee* or the lost *Wreched Engendrynge of Mankynde* (the L. original of which is the source for much of the Prologue) was destined for the Man of Law. There have been various attempts to find another meaning for the statement: e.g. 'I usually speak in prose', or that 'prose' may be used for some other kind of verse, or for a specific kind of verse narrative, a Christian legend, or in some more general sense. But since Chaucer elsewhere uses 'prose' to describe the prose tales of *Melibee* and the Parson, most scholars are inclined to accept the difficulty. There has also been argument about the purpose of the comments on Chaucer and on the 'Seintes Legende of Cupide' (though Custance is like a saint, and is a Christian example of a suffering heroine), and about the relevance of the remarks on poverty and on merchants.

The Tale itself has also proved problematic, although it may be that some difficulties are of critics' making. It is not now thought to be an early work, and is often dated *c.*1390 (the calculation of time in the Introduction is based on the *Kalendarium* of Nicholas of Lynn (*Lenne)). Its main source is a story in an early 14th-c. Anglo-Norman chronicle by Nicholas *Trevet. It seems likely that Chaucer also knew *Gower's version of this story. Behind this lie folk tales, especially that of the 'calumniated wife', accused of giving birth to a monster, etc. Such stories were widespread and popular.

The Man of Law's Tale does not fit neatly into any genre. It has similarities to a *saint's life, and to a *romance (especially those like *Apollonius of Tyre* which are related to the Greek romances with separated families, extensive wanderings and supposed deaths). But it is notable that although everything ends happily, the reader is reminded of the inevitability of death. This is consistent with the moral and didactic tone of the story. It is an 'exemplary' story, and one of those in which (like *The Clerk's Tale*) Chaucer takes every opportunity to emphasize scenes of '*pite' and pathos. But unlike *The Clerk's Tale* it is self-consciously rhetorical. The heroine is given a number of eloquent formal laments and prayers. The narrator's voice is constantly heard, commenting on sudden turns in the plot, exclaiming against villainy or misery, praying for his heroine.

Not all modern critics are happy with its sentiment or its rhetoric. Some claim that the deficiencies of the tale expose the deficiencies of the narrator. He is over-emotional and sentimental, his heroine is a flawed ideal of womanliness, and so on. It can be objected that Chaucer is more sensitive to the power of pathos than many modern readers are, that he responds to the heroic and spiritual qualities of *patience and suffering. And while nothing in the portrait of the Man of Law in the *General Prologue* would lead us to expect him to tell this kind of story, there is nothing inconsistent about it. As in other serious and moral stories (e.g. *The *Franklin's Tale*) Chaucer sometimes likes to experiment with a deliberate inconsistency of tone: after the piteous scene of Custance's departure from Rome, the narrator remarks ironically, 'housbondes been alle goode, and han ben yoore; | That knowen wyves; I dar sey yow na moore. 'And on Custance's wedding night with Alla he says that married folk must 'leye a lite [little] hir hoolynesse aside, | As for the tyme'.

We can recognize in this tale the interest in patience and power, in *marriage and family relationships which will figure prominently in Fragments III, IV, and V. There is also a good deal to connect it thematically with what (probably) precedes it in Fragment I, notably in the question of fate and providence and of why the innocent suffer (see I.1313–14, II.814–16). The world of *The Man of Law's Tale* at first seems to be ruled by the stars, then by an explicitly Christian pattern of providence. No neat philosophical resolution is offered: the central human figure is patient, but not weakly passive, she demonstrates a fortitude equal to that of Griselda. Unlike Griselda, Custance is a 'far traveller', and her wanderings in the rudderless boat offer an image of man's pilgrimage in the 'thurghfare ful of wo' (I.2846–7).

(ed.) *Rv* 87–104, 854–63; *S&A* 155–206; Cooper (1989), 123–37; Mann (1991), 128–43; Pearsall (1985), 256–65.

'MANDEVILLE, SIR JOHN'. The book now known as *Mandeville's Travels* was apparently written first in French in the mid-14th c. It was translated into English and into other European vernaculars, and remained a popular work for centuries. The author presents himself as a widely travelled English knight from St Albans. He seems, however, to have been more of an 'armchair traveller', since much of the book is compiled from earlier sources. The first part, based on pilgrim guides, describes the way to the Holy Land, and the holy places there. The second part continues beyond Jerusalem to the more exotic regions of India (*Inde) and Asia (*Asye (1)). (See Map 1.) This uses the accounts of earlier travellers, the friars sent on embassies to the Great Khan, John of Plano Carpini, William of Rubruck, and Odoric of Pordenone, for the road to Cathay and realms of the great Khan. Of these realms 'Mandeville' gives an entrancing account, combining an enthusiastic wonder with a detached scepticism. He shows a surprising tolerance ('we know not whom God loveth ne whom God hateth') and a genuine curiosity about 'strange things and other diversities'. He even expresses his wish to be able to 'go more beyond', for 'new things and new tidings be pleasant to hear'. His book continued to be read by later generations of explorers, including Columbus. Chaucer drew on this kind of writing in his description of the wonders of the court of *Cambyuskan (Genghis Khan) in The *Squire's Tale*, and it may be that when he mentions (V.67–71) the strange foods of the Mongols 'as tellen knyghtes olde' that he is referring to 'John Mandeville, knight'.

(ed.) Seymour (1968, modernized); (trans.) Moseley (1983).

manners (see also **curteisie**). Contemporary manners, especially but not exclusively, in the sense defined by Dr Johnson as 'ceremonious behaviour, studied civility', are often alluded to in Chaucer, and sometimes form part of the texture of a scene. He uses the singular form *manere* to mean 'manners, behaviour'; sometimes it has the sense of 'demeanour' or 'deportment' (e.g. I.140; V.546): Hypsipyle recognizes Jason and Hercules as 'gentil men of gret degre' by 'hyre manere, | By hire aray, by wordes, and by chere' (*LGW* 1504–5). He also uses a number of other terms, such as *fare* ('behaviour, conduct'; *strange fare*, VII.263, seems to mean 'elaborate courtesies'), *port* ('bearing, manner'), *thewes* ('good qualities'). People may be *gracious* or *hautein* ('haughty') in speech or 'port', or *hende* ('courteous, polite'). The courtly Squire is 'of his port as meeke as is a mayde' (I.69). Manners are inculcated by 'nurture'. It is remarkable and worthy of note that the humbly born *Griselda did not appear to have been 'born and fed in rudenesse, | As in a cote [cottage] or in an oxe-stalle, | But norissed in an emperoures halle' (IV.396–9). The halls of rulers and of other rich and powerful persons were of course the settings for the public display of the ceremonious behaviour and studied civility taught by the books of 'nurture'. More frequently we find characters addressing one another (with varying degrees of politeness) by the common terms ('dame', 'madame', 'sir(e)', 'sires'), greeting (with 'hayl' or 'al hayl' or 'hayl, and wel atake [well met]', III.1384), sending greeting and bidding farewell ('Grete wel oure dame . . . | And fare wel, deere cosyn, til we meete!', VII.363–4). One may greet another 'fairly' (II.1051), 'reverently and wisely' (and kneeling, IV.952), 'meekly' (VI.714), 'in his best wise' (*Tr* III.955), 'soberly'

(*Tr* III.1588). Ceremonious partings similarly range from the loving ('Farwel, dere herte swete; | Ther God us graunte sownde and soone to mete!', *Tr* III.1525–6) to the sorrowful ('Farewel, housbonde routhelees!', II.863).

In a few cases manners are singled out for special emphasis. The description of the virtuous and well-brought-up girl *Virginia (VI.30–82), for instance, illustrates that outward *beauty reflects an inner beauty which also reveals itself in gracious manners. Virginia shows moderation ('*mesure') in bearing and dress, is 'discreet' in answering, avoids 'countrefeted termes', and has the 'shamefastnesse' (modesty) proper to maidens. Among the Canterbury pilgrims, the *Prioress is singled out for her exquisite (and perhaps overexquisite) table manners (I.127–36). And she is not only 'at mete wel ytaught', her whole demeanour suggests good breeding: 'she was of greet desport [dignified in manner], | And ful plesaunt, and amyable of port, | And peyned hire to countrefete cheere | Of court, and to been estatlich of manere [dignified in behaviour]' (I.137–41). The contrast with the description of Virginia is striking. Sharper satire is found in the description of the social pretensions of the miller's wife and her husband in *The Reeve's Tale* ('ther dorste no wight clepen hire but "dame"', I.3956). At the climax of the tale the miller expresses his mortification in a self-revelatory exclamation: 'Who dorste be so boold to disparage [degrade, dishonour] | My doghter, that is come of swich lynage?'

mansio(u)n (astrology) (1) planetary *domicile; as when in *The *Squire's Tale* the *Sun is said to be in the mansion of *Mars. (2) lunar mansion; as in the '*Moones mansiouns' of *The *Franklin's Tale*. *Aurelius' brother hoped that some scholar of Orleans might be familiar with the art of using them for the purposes of natural *magic. (See also *astrology and astronomy; *hows; *planete.)

[JDN]

Mantoan 'of Mantua', the town in northern Italy. *Virgil, born there, is formally invoked at the beginning of the story of *Dido as 'Virgil Mantoan' (*LGW* 924).

MANUEL, DON JUAN (1282–1349), Spanish nobleman, nephew of Alfonso X the Learned, generally considered the foremost Spanish prose writer of the Middle Ages, author of some twelve books, of which five have been lost, an irony of fate considering the great and, for the period, unusual pains he took to preserve his manuscripts for fear of careless copyists (cf. Chaucer's *Adam (2)). These include historical works, treatises on falconry, on chivalry (based on Llull's *Order of Chivalry*), on education, and his most famous work, *Count Lucanor* (El conde Lucanor), written between 1328 and 1335. Clearly influenced by Petrus Alphonsus's (*Pier Alfonce) *Disciplina Clericalis*, this work consists of an attractive collection of tales, shot through with irony and humour, and imbued with the spirit of Jewish and Muslim wisdom, which are presented in the form of a series of exempla, which Count Lucanor's counsellor, Patronio, narrates in answer to the former's requests for advice. Unlike his most distinguished Spanish contemporary, Juan *Ruiz, and *Boccaccio, to whose *Decameron Count Lucanor* has often been compared, love plays no significant role in these stories, although *Example XXXV* provided the germ, via Italy, of the plot of *Shakespeare's *Taming of the Shrew*. Richard Lionheart, on the Third Crusade, 1190, is the hero of *Example III*, in which a bigoted hermit is put in his place. [PS]
England (1987).

manuscripts, see *book.

Mapamounde, Mappemounde, the Mappa Mundi or map of the world, alluded to in *Rosemounde: 'as fer as cercled is the mapamounde'. The word *cercled* refers to the circular shape of medieval world maps rather than to the roundness of the earth's globe (though the idea that everyone in the Middle Ages thought that the world was flat is erroneous). Many medieval examples of the Mappa Mundi survive. The common pattern is sometimes called the 'T/O' map (see Map 1). As in ancient geography, the world is surrounded by the Ocean. On this 'O' shape can be seen a 'T', dividing it into three continents. North is not placed at the top as in the modern convention, but at the left-hand side: at the top is East, often with the Earthly Paradise depicted there. Above the top of the 'T' is the large continent of Asia (*Asye (1));

the downward stroke of the 'T' represents the Mediterranean ('See of *Grece') dividing *Europe (2) to the left from Africa (*Affrike) to the right. *Jerusalem is usually placed at or near the centre of the world. The scheme explains why navigators like Columbus expected to reach Asia by sailing across the Ocean. This schematic world map was increasingly refined by the use of 'portolans' or 'portulanos', navigational guides prepared and used by navigators. These were much more accurate in detail.

The Mappa Mundi often included illustrations of real and fabulous animals and sundry 'wonders'. A famous map now in Hereford Cathedral (late 13th c.), for instance, contains pictures of Adam and Eve and their expulsion from the Garden of Eden, dragons and giants, the elephant, the unicorn, the lynx, Noah's Ark, the Golden Fleece, pygmies and monsters, and much else.

Chaucer seems to have shared this general picture of the world, though he would have had a more detailed geographical knowledge of those parts of England and of Europe in which he had worked or travelled (see Geoffrey *Chaucer: life). In his narratives he makes use of a wide variety of geopraphical settings, ranging from Trumpington to the more exotic regions of the East. His Canterbury pilgrims include a number who have travelled extensively, notably the *Knight, the *Shipman, and the *Wife of Bath.

Crone (1978); P. D. A. Harvey (1991, 1996); Magoun (1961).

Marcia, Marsyas, a satyr who became an accomplished flute player and challenged the god Apollo to a contest. When the Muses gave the victory to Apollo, the god flayed Marsyas alive. Marsyas is mentioned among the minstrels and musicians in The *House of Fame (1229–32), though Chaucer, perhaps misled by the Italian form Marsia in *Dante (or possibly the Fr. Marsie), here makes him female.

MARCIA CATOUN, a faithful Roman wife mentioned in the Prologue to The *Legend of Good Women (252). She may be the wife of Cato of Utica, who returned to him after having been divorced, or possibly his daughter, who was also true to her love. Chaucer could have found the first in *Lucan and *Dante, the second in St *Jerome.

MARCIAN, Martianus Capella (early 5th c.), the author of the De nuptiis Mercurii et Philologiae (the Marriage of Mercury and Philology), a Latin cosmological epic in a mixture of prose and verse. It describes how the Philology, the learned bride of Mercury, ascends to heaven accompanied by the nine *Muses and the *Seven Liberal Arts. It is an encyclopaedic work which transmits much ancient learning to the medieval West. Chaucer refers to Martianus twice. In The *House of Fame (985) he is cited as an authority on the celestial regions. In The *Merchant's Tale (IV.1732–7) he appears in a more ironic context. Although he describes 'that ilke weddyng murie | Of hire Philologie and hym Mercurie, | And of the songes that the Muses songe' he must hold his peace, because he is not able to describe the splendid wedding of January and May.

(ed.) Dick (1978); (trans.) Stahl (1977).

MARCO POLO; MARCUS TULYUS, MARCUS TULLIUS SCITHERO. See *Polo; *Tul(l)ius.

Mardochee, Mordecai, the uncle and guardian of Esther (*Ester) in the Old Testament. Because of her 'good conseil' he was given advancement (IV.1373).

MARIE DE FRANCE, a 12th-c. author, wrote in French a number of verse tales and a set of *fables. She seems to have done most of her literary work in England. The tales or Lais (see *Breton lays) are elegant narratives, usually about love, often set in Brittany and claiming to be come from stories told by the Bretons. Middle English versions of two of them survive (see *Sir Launfal). It is not certain that Chaucer knew her work at first hand: he could have derived his knowledge of Breton lays from elsewhere.

(ed.) Ewert (1947); (ed. and trans.) Spiegel (1987); (trans.) Burgess and Busby (1986).

Marie, Egipcien, St Mary the Egyptian (5th c.?). According to legend an Alexandrian prostitute who was converted on pilgrimage. She lived for many years as a solitary in a cave in the desert, eating dates and berries; when her clothes wore out her long hair covered her. She is cited as an example of God's providential care in The *Man of Law's Tale (II.500–1).

Marie, Seinte, the Blessed Virgin Mary, daughter of Anna (*Anne (1)), and the mother of Jesus Christ, was by Chaucer's time the most powerful and the most popular of all the *saints. Her cult began in the early Church, and reached a point of great intensity in the high and late Middle Ages. Not only are a large number of churches dedicated to her, but her cult sometimes affected the very architecture of a church by the building of a 'Lady Chapel'. There was a series of Marian feast days, the most important being those of the Annunciation (Lady Day, 25 March) and the Assumption (15 August). Veneration of the Virgin Mary is found across the whole social and intellectual scale, expressed ecstatically by theologians and mystics like St *Bernard or with simple devotion by those who could only repeat the Ave Maria or 'Hail Mary', the prayer based on the Angelic Salutation. Her life and legends are celebrated in art and literature. She is presented as the tender loving mother of the Christ child, the sorrowing mother (Mater dolorosa) at the scene of her son's death, as the powerful and magnificent queen of heaven (her part in the scheme of Redemption made her the 'second Eve' who reversed the damage caused by mankind's first mother). She is most frequently invoked as an intercessor and as a kindly protector: a popular series of legends, the '*Miracles of the Virgin', demonstrates how she will intervene to rescue her devotees from every kind of danger. A number of traditional paradoxes seem to intensify her appeal. She is both maiden and mother, and represents the perfection of both states. She is a humble creature who bore the creator of all things. In her blessed state too 'Our Lady', as she is so often called, is a great and powerful lady, but ready to hear the prayers of the most humble because she herself is humble ('humble, and heigh over every creature').

Chaucer's most obviously 'Marian' work is the *ABC, translated from *Deguilleville. This prayer to the Virgin ('lady bright', 'blisful hevene queene', Crystes blisful mooder deere', 'glorious mayde and mooder') makes lyrical use of her various traditional attributes and images: she is the queen of mercy who shows '*pite' to man and acts as an intercessor against God's just wrath; she is the temple in which God dwelt; the fountain which washes the sinful soul; the burning bush which Moses (*Moyses) saw was not consumed; she is the sorrowing mother at the foot of the cross, etc. In two of the Canterbury Tales (both from female religious) we find intensely lyrical Marian invocations. That of the *Second Nun, which is largely based on *Dante, boldly puts the traditional paradox: 'thow mayde and mooder, doghter of thy sone'. Similarly the *Prioress addresses her as 'O mooder Mayde, O mayde Mooder free!' The tale which the Prioress tells is a 'miracle of the Virgin'.

Outside these explicitly 'Marian' works, there is one striking case where an innocent woman and mother, *Custance in The *Man of Law's Tale, shows a deep devotion to the Virgin. When she is banished from Northumberland with her small child in a ship she makes an eloquent prayer to Mary (II.841–54), alluding to her as the 'second Eve', and to her as the mother who suffered more than anyone by seeing her son slain before her eyes. Addressing Mary, very appropriately, as 'thow glorie of wommanhede', and using two traditional images which also have a particular point in this context ('Thow haven of refut, brighte sterre of day') she appeals to her qualities of 'pite' and '*gentilesse': 'Rewe on my child, that of thy gentilesse | Rewest on every reweful in distresse.' Her prayer is answered. She sails on 'til Cristes mooder—blessed be she ay!— | Hath shapen, thurgh hir endelees goodnesse, | To make an ende of al hir hevynesse' (II.950–2).

The way in which Mary and Marian devotion were accepted as part of ordinary life is shown in a number of allusions. The 'litel clergeon' had already learnt to say his 'Ave Marie', and hears the Marian antiphon O *alma redemptoris at school (VII.508, 518). In a less innocent context, Nicholas in The *Miller's Tale likes singing the Marian *Angelus ad virginem. And the *Pardoner claims to have among his *relics 'Oure Lady veyl' (I.695). Other characters swear by Mary: 'Seynte Marie!', 'By Seinte Marie!', 'Marie' (IV.1899; VI.685; VII.402), etc. One example (in a notably ironic context, seems to have some appropriateness: 'A wyf! a, Seinte Marie, benedicite!' (IV.1337).

Mark. St Mark the evangelist is quoted by the *Wife of Bath (III.145–6) and mentioned with the other gospel writers (VII.951) by Chaucer.

Marmoryke, Marmarica in northern Africa (eastern Libya), mentioned in *Boece (IV m.3:12).

marriage (see also *love, *women). Chaucer's interest in marriage is evident, and some scholars have held that in The *Canterbury Tales, a number of stories form a distinct unit, the 'Marriage Group', in which the topic is raised by the *Wife of Bath, and continued (with a couple of interludes) in the tales of the *Clerk and the *Merchant, and concluded by the *Franklin. Any rigid idea of a formal 'Marriage Group' or 'Marriage Debate' is open to serious objections: these tales are not the only ones concerned with marriage, for instance, nor is marriage their only unifying theme. However, they are concerned (in common with some other tales) with varying examples of what the Wife of Bath describes as the 'wo that is in mariage', and throw up a number of ideas about sovereignty or '*maistrye'. But Chaucer's interest is seen throughout his works. The treatment of *Nature and 'common profit' in The *Parliament of Fowls, for instance, has an obvious bearing on his ideas about marriage. He seems fascinated by the variety of human emotions and problems which are highlighted in this relationship.

Marriages in the Middle Ages were normally arranged marriages, but consent was necessary. Marriage was not at all incompatible with love, but probably many people thought of marriage less as the culmination of a romantic relationship than as a kind of job (one of the rewards of which might be love and mutual affection). Parents played a major role in the arrangement of marriages (and there could be considerable family pressure brought to bear upon a daughter) and in settling the financial details, but the Church insisted on the consent of the partners. Marriages were sometimes arranged between small children, and it was possible to be married by proxy, but such arrangements had to be confirmed when the partners reached the age of consent (12 for girls, 14 for boys).

The ceremonials of marriage also differed from modern Western practice. Of great importance was the ceremony of betrothal, in which the man and the woman took each other's hand, and declared before witnesses their intention of marrying, usually exchanging gifts. This was a very solemn agreement: if a betrothed woman married another man the betrothed man could legally claim her back. The marriage ceremony took place before a priest at the church porch, when the ring was placed on the bride's finger. The party might then enter the church for Mass and prayers, though marriage in church was not a legal necessity. The ceremony was followed by feasting and singing and dancing.

There was not a simple or totally consistent medieval theory of marriage. Some elements came from Roman law, some from social practice, but increasingly the most important were those deriving from Christianity. Even here different views and emphases were possible. The text 'what God hath joined together let no man put asunder' apparently ruled out divorce. But some held that it could be justified by adultery, though others took a more rigorous view. Annulment could be permitted on various grounds, notably of consanguinity, or of failure to consummate the union. Emphasis might be placed on the importance of mutual consent in marriage (as in Roman law) or on consummation and the procreation of children. There was a Christian model of marriage as chaste companionship based on consent in the marriage of the Virgin Mary and Joseph, but increasingly the stress came to be placed on the end of marriage being to beget children. The emphasis on celibacy and the ascetic tradition was another complicating factor, leading to the widespread view that marriage was second best to virginity. In the eyes of many clerics sexual union almost always involved sin, and this could be reduced by marriage: 'better to marry than burn' (a text gleefully used by the Wife of Bath). Another strand was the idea that husband and wife owed each other a debt (which included sexual union) and that they each had rights to this. The text, 'the husband is the head of the wife, as Christ is the head of the Church', is frequently quoted, and it seems to have been generally agreed that the duty of a wife was to be meek and obedient.

In Chaucer an ecclesiastical model of marriage is clearly put by the *Parson. It is a sacrament made in Paradise which 'bitokneth the knyttynge togidre of Crist and of hooly chirche' (X.842), and a lifelong bond. The 'trewe effect of mariage clenseth fornicacioun and replenyssheth hooly chirche of good lynage, for that is the ende of mariage; and it chaungeth deedly synne into venial synne bitwixe hem that been ywedded, and maketh the hertes al oon of hem that been ywedded, as wel as the bodies'. The husband has lordship, but he 'sholde bere hym to his wyf in feith, in trouthe, and in love'. They should each love each other with heart and body. But there are different kinds of sexual intercourse: (1) for the engendering of children (meritorious); (2) 'to yelden everich of hem to oother the dette of hire bodies' (meritorious); (3) to avoid lechery and sin (turning it into venial sin); but (4) 'oonly for amorous love' and 'to accomplice thilke brennynge delit, they rekke nevere how ofte' is deadly sin. This ideal of chaste marriage differs from the practice of *January ('a man may do no synne with his wyf', IV.1839; cf. ParsT X.859) and of *Chauntecleer, who served Venus 'moore for delit than world to multiplye' (VII.3345).

Chaucer alludes to a number of contemporary marriage practices: to having husbands 'at chirche dore' (III.4–6), to the 'bridale' or wedding party with its dancing and singing (I.4375). The festivities in The *Merchant's Tale (IV.1709 ff.) are especially elaborate, and are graced by the mythological figures of Bacchus (*Bacus), *Venus and '*Ymeneus [Hymen], that god of weddyng is'. They follow the church ceremony (1700–9—described with some irony), which itself follows the necessary legal formalities by which May was 'feffed' (endowed) with January's land (1696–8). The marriage of Palamon and Emily at the end of The *Knight's Tale involves a political agreement, but also the consent (and the love) of the partners; it is celebrated 'with alle blisse and melodye'. Elsewhere the role of parents is assumed (I.3980–2, Tr V.863). At the end of The *Clerk's Tale the marquis Walter marries his daughter 'richely' to a worthy lord (IV.1130–1). For his own marriage, however, he had insisted on his absolute freedom of choice, but when he chooses Griselda he at least observes the formalities, approaching her father,

his liege man, for his agreement (IV.302–15), and insists on asking Griselda for her consent after the negotiations. His words ('it liketh to youre fader and to me', etc.) leave no doubt about his determination and his position of power, but she has a formal choice (though the demands he makes are closer to *folk tale than to canon law). She is 'spoused with a ryng' (IV.386; cf. 868 and II.712; Anel 131), and the wedding is followed by 'revel'. When he pretends to put her away for a new wife (799 ff.; with the alleged agreement of the Pope, 'rancour for to slake') in a particularly monstrous way, he says he is willing to allow her to take back the dowry that she brought; as she points out, it consists only of her wretched clothes.

Chaucer makes extensive use of what seems to be common lore. The proverbs concerning marriage (and especially wives) which are quoted in a variety of contexts are usually distinctly unidealistic: a good wife should not be watched, and it is useless to watch a shrew (IX.148 ff.); 'suffer thy wife's tongue' (IV.1377; cf. X.630 ff.); 'who has no wife is no cuckold' (I.3152); wives hide their vices till they are married (III.282); 'a man should wed his similitude' (I.3228). And there is an ironic reference to the legendary monster *Chichevache, which fed on patient wives. Exemplary wives, both good and bad, are cited. The good qualities associated with the adjective 'wifely' include homeliness (IV.429), patience (IV.919), steadfastness (IV.1050), and chastity (V.1453, LGW 1737); of *Lucrece it is said 'hir herte was so wyfly and so trewe' (LGW 1843). Emily's desire 'noght to ben a wyf and be with childe' (I.2310) echoes the normal assumption. The Wife of Bath puts special emphasis on the duty of a husband to pay his 'debt' to his wife (e.g. III.129–32, 152–5); husbands, moreover, should be 'fressh abedde' (1259). The wife in The *Shipman's Tale echoes these sentiments (VII.174–7). The Wife of Bath does not exactly conform to the Parson's ideal of widowly chastity: to be 'a clene wydewe, and eschue the embracynges of man, and desiren the embracynge of Jhesu Crist' (X.944). Dismissing the clerical lauding of virginity, she is enthusiastic about sex: 'I nyl envye no virginitee . . . In wyfhod I wol use myn instrument | As frely as my Makere hath it sent' (III.142 ff.).

The idea that marriage is a 'bond' or a 'yoke' ('the bond | That highte matrimoigne or mariage',

I.3094–5; 'that blisful yok | Of soveraynetee, noght of servyse, | Which that men clepe spousaille or wedlok', IV.113–15, etc.) is treated in a variety of ways (see The *Merchant's Tale, *Bukton, etc.). The Wife of Bath gives a vivid account of her own marital experience. In the *fabliau world the marriage of those that are 'dissimilar' (especially in age) is likely to end in comic disaster, and the treatment there of love triangles and the subterfuges of lovers is in a kind of carnival spirit (and far removed from the Parson's severe condemnation of 'avowtrie' or adultery (X.840 ff.). But alongside all his comedy and irony, Chaucer seems to have a serious view of marriage, which is consistent with his view of *love. Like the relationship of the Man in Black and the Lady White in The *Book of the Duchess (which seems to be a kind of mirror image of marriage) and perhaps of Troilus and Criseyde (which has been seen, though not to everyone's satisfaction, as a kind of pagan 'marriage' or state of betrothal, though remaining clandestine) the good marriage involves love, '*gentilesse', friendship and companionship. He is especially interested in the relationship of 'soveraynetee' and 'servyse'. The common assumption that the husband is the 'lord' (e.g. I.3081; X.930) is adapted (notably in The *Franklin's Tale) to include his submission and patience, and the 'yoke' of marriage is seen as a loving mutuality.

Brooke (1989); Brundage (1993); Cartlidge (1997); Kelly (1975); ('marriage group') Kittredge (1912); Rv 863–4.

Marrok, Strayte of, The strait of Gibraltar or Morocco, through which *Constance sails (II.464–5).

Mars, Marte, (1) ancient Italian god, second only to Jupiter, and always connected with rites of war. The month of March was named after him. The mythology of Mars is largely borrowed from that of the Greek war god Ares, who for the Greeks, however, was never accorded the same importance. As a violent lover and a ferocious fighter, often on the side of an enemy, he has a questionable, if not always fearsome character. In keeping with their martial themes he is a central figure in The *Knight's Tale ('with spere and targe', 'the god

of armes') and in *Troilus and Criseyde ('the god that helmed is of steel', 'that god is of bataille'). With the progression of time, the ancient image of the bearded warrior was exchanged for that of a younger man, often Venus's lover. He has this role in Chaucer's Complaint of *Mars. He remained, however, in the words of The *Man of Law's Tale, 'crueel Mars'. (2) the planet. Mars occupies the sixth sphere of simple Aristotelian *cosmology, and is the first superior planet (that is, above the Sun). In keeping with Greek and Roman mythology, the planet's astrological character is generally maleficent, and always warlike. As the *Wife of Bath affirms in her Prologue, 'Mars gaf me my sturdy hardynesse'. Even with Venus, Mars may modify love, turning it into violent love and lechery. At the Wife's nativity, Venus provided her 'lust' and 'likerousnesse'; as she points out, although Taurus, *domicile of Venus, was then *ascendent, Mars was in that sign. The domiciles of Mars are Aries and Scorpio. The planet's exaltation is in Capricorn, and his dejection in Cancer. (See also *astrology and astronomy; *exaltacio(u)n; *planete; *signe; *sper(e).) (3) the metal iron, in alchemical symbolism, as noted by the *Canon's Yeoman. (See also *alchemy.)

[JDN]

Mars, Complaint of, a poem of 298 lines, which falls into three parts (the first two in rhyme royal): (1) a Proem beginning 'Gladeth, ye foules, of the morowe gray' sung by a bird on St Valentine's day, overheard by a narrator, who announces that he will sing 'in . . . briddes wise' the 'sentence' of the complaint which 'woful Mars' made at departing from Venus in the morning when Phoebus 'with his firy torches rede' searched out the lovers. (2) The Narrative: Mars wins the love of Venus and becomes her servant. She restrains his propensity to cruelty and tyranny. The two mythological lovers are also the two planets that move into conjunction: the warlike planet is governed by the planet of love. While they are together they are in the greatest joy: 'this worthi Mars, that is of knyghthod welle, | The flour of feyrnesse lappeth in his armes, | And Venus kysseth Mars, the god of armes.' But they are threatened in their chamber by the approaching Sun. Mars prepares for battle, and tells Venus to flee 'lest

Phebus her espye'. Venus flees to the tower of Mercury and hides in a dark cave. Mars is enfeebled, and follows Venus. But *Cilenius (Mercury) riding in his course, sees Venus, greets her warmly, 'and her receyveth as his frend ful dere'. Mars is left in his adversity, and makes a *complaint. (3) The long and eloquent Complaint, in nine-line stanzas, follows. Mars will never cease to be the truest servant of his lady of great excellence, and will die in her service. Alas, that lovers must endure for love 'so many a perilous aventure'. To what end does God constrain people to love, when their joy is so quickly followed by sorrow? What is the meaning of 'this mystihed'? It seems that he bears enmity to lovers, like the fisherman who baits his hook 'with som plesaunce' so that the maddened fish seizes it and then has all his desire and 'therwith al myschaunce'. The brooch of Thebes was like this: the beauty of its gems drove everyone who looked on it out of his mind, but when he had it he had to suffer fear, and when he lost it his sorrow was doubled. 'So fareth hyt by lovers and by me'—yet his lady was not the cause of his adversity, but he who created her and put such beauty in her face. Let all knights, ladies, and lovers join him in lamenting.

The poem survives in eight MSS and the early printed editions of Julian Notary (1499–1501) and Thynne (1532). (For the illustration in MS Fairfax 16, see Fig. 9.) It is attributed to Chaucer by *Shirley and *Lydgate (see also *Brooch of Thebes). The astrological details (see below) point clearly to the date of 1385. According to Shirley's rubric it was made at the commandment of *John of Gaunt; in his colophon he records what seems to be a 15th-c. rumour concerning an actual affair at court, and this has led to attempts to find a particular allusion in the poem, but nothing has been proven. The story comes from Ovid's *Metamorphoses* (4.171–89), and had also been told by *Jean de Meun in the *Roman de la Rose. The *Complaint of Mars* is one of Chaucer's most interesting works, which puts together in a very original way a variety of literary material, highly complex in its structure, finely combining the mythographical and the astrological, raising questions concerning the perplexities of human *love and its role in God's creation. The pattern of tragic love which it establishes is very reminiscent of the longer

narrative poem Chaucer wrote about this time: the *Complaint* has indeed been called 'a miniature *Troilus'*.

Note on the astrology

The astrological meaning is very thinly veiled, and conforms to the movements of the planets Mars and Venus, and the Sun, between 14 February and 12 April 1385. At the outset, Venus is at her exaltation. Mars enters Taurus, her *domicile, on 12 March, and by 17 March the two are abed. Phebus, the Sun, knocks on the palace gates on 27 March— an event that would have been perfectly intelligible to those aware of the astrological doctrine of rays and combustion. The rays of the Sun and Mars touched on 3 April; Venus left for Gemini five days later. A second stage in the combustive process began on 12 April, a date actually named in the poem.

There is much use of technical vocabulary, with such ideas as that of 'valance' (a well-dignified place), reception, anger, and burning of the planets. Chaucer has no difficulty in combining such abstractions with the conventional and more readily understood imagery of the signs of the Zodiac, and with the traditions of the classical pantheon.   [JDN]

Rv 643–7, 1078–81; Scattergood (1995), 473–6; Eade (1984); North (1990), 304–25; Clemen (1963), 188–97; Norton-Smith (1974), 23–34.

MARTIANUS CAPELLA; MARY THE VIRGIN. See *Marcian; *Marie, Seinte.

MARTYN, SEINT, St Martin of Tours (*c.*316–397). Serving as a Roman soldier in Gaul he is said to have given half his cloak to a poor beggar in Amiens. That night Christ appeared to him in a dream wearing the part of the cloak he had given away. He founded the first monastery in Gaul, and became a widely venerated saint. The Monk in The *Shipman's Tale* (which is set in northern France) swears by him (VII.148).

MÂSHÂ'ALLÂH (*fl. c.*762–815), prolific Jewish writer on astrology, from Basra. He is usually known in the West as **Massahalla**. There were at least a score of Latin astrological works ascribed to him and based on writings in Arabic, but not all

were by him. The Latin treatise on the astrolabe that went under his name was perhaps the most widely diffused of all that dealt with that instrument in the Middle Ages, and Chaucer made extensive use of it for *A Treatise on the *Astrolabe*. It was not written by Mâshâ'allâh, however, but was apparently a composite work. The first part (on making the instrument) is a Western Latin compilation from the mid- or late-13th c., from as many as four or five sources. The second part (on the use of the instrument) is a Western compilation based on John of Spain's Latin translation of an Arabic original by a Spanish-Muslim, Ibn al-Saffâr (a pupil of Maslama al-Majrîtî, to whom some manuscripts ascribe it). The Latin material uses an Arabic vocabulary, but one that had long been in use in Europe by the time the compilations were made.   [JDN]
    Kunitzsch (1981).

MASSYNISSE, Masinissa (*c.*238–149 BC), a king of Numidia (in north Africa) who first fought with the Carthaginians against the Romans, but became the friend and ally of Scipio Africanus (*Affrycan (1)) (*PF* 37–40).

MATHEOLUS, a cleric from Boulogne wrote in Latin his *Lamentationes* towards the end of the 13th c. A fiercely anti-feminist work, it was later translated into French (and answered) by Jean le Fèvre. Chaucer may well have known it in this form. It is the reading of Matheolus which provokes the writing of *Christine de Pisan's *Livre de la cité des dames*. It belongs to the category of works which also provoked the *Wife of Bath, and is echoed in her Prologue.
    (ed.) Van Hamel (1892–1905); (trans.) Blamires (1992).

Mathew, Seint. St Matthew the evangelist is quoted by the *Pardoner on swearing (VI.633–4), several times by the *Parson (X.588, 842, 845, 1036–7), and is mentioned with the other gospel writers (VII.951) by Chaucer.

MATTHEW OF VENDOME, see *rhetoric.

Maudelayne, the name of the *Shipman's barge (I.410) (see *Magdele(y)ne).

Maunciple, see *Manciple.

MAURE, St Maurus (6th c.), a disciple of St Benedict (*Beneit), with whom he is associated in a satirical remark about the *Monk (I.173).

Maurice, Mauricius, the son of Custance and Alla in The *Man of Law's Tale.

Maxime, Maximus the Roman prefect converted by St Cecilia in the *Second Nun's Tale.

MAXIMIAN, MAXIMIANUS, a 6th-c. Roman poet, and a friend of Boethius (*Boece), wrote a series of elegies on old age. These were well known in the Middle Ages (he was regarded as an authority on old age), and one was adapted in a 13th-c. Middle English version. The lines in The *Pardoner's Tale (VI.727–36) in which the old man says that he knocks on the ground with his staff and calls 'leeve [dear] mooder, leet me in!' are based on a passage in his first elegy.

May (1), Maius the young wife of January in The *Merchant's Tale.

May (2), see *months and seasons.

Mecene, Messenia, in Greece, in the south-west Peloponnese (V.1379).

Medea, daughter of Aeëtes, king of Colchis (*Colcos), loved by *Jason, and betrayed by him. Her story is told in The *Legend of Good Women (1580–670). This version concentrates on her as a betrayed heroine and omits the revenge she took by killing the new bride and her own children (as does Christine de Pisan in the *Cité des Dames*), although Chaucer mentions it when he refers to the *Legend* in the Introduction to The *Man of Law's Tale (II.72–3: see also *BD* 725–7). The story of Jason and Medea is mentioned elsewhere (*BD* 330; *HF* 401), and there are references to Medea's magic power, which helped Jason gain the Golden Fleece (I.1944, *HF* 1271).

Medes, the people of the ancient realm of Media (in north-western Iran), associated with the Persians (*Perses) in the story of Belshazzar (*Balthasar) (VII.2235).

medicine. Unlike most of the sciences, medieval medicine cannot be studied entirely from its books: Galen (see *Galyen) himself emphasized that it was a conjectural art in which practice was of equal importance to reason. Although there were a few great centres of academic medicine, it was mostly learned through apprenticeship, and favourite texts were always diagnostic and therapeutic, that is, were concerned with practice—with heart, pulse, blood-letting, urine, the cure of fevers, surgery, and so on, rather than with theories about the cause of disease. When long classical medical texts were abbreviated, the theoretical and the practical tended to be separated into different treatises, often into several. This happened with the translation by Cælius Aurelianus in the 5th c. of the work of Soranus of Ephesus, a vital link between ancient and medieval medicine. Some of this found its way into encyclopaedias, such as those by Isidore of Seville (*Ysidre) and Rhabanus Maurus, and most after them. These were valued in the European monastic world for their practical value, for use inside and outside the monastery. Since herbal information often becomes redundant (where the climate is unfavourable to a plant), the monasteries became centres of experiment on substitute remedies. New texts included not only these, but an admixture of folklore and magic.

A distinctly new phase began with the translation by Constantine the African (d. 1085) of many classical and Arabic treatises into Latin (*Constantyn). In the course of the next century this put new life into the most important European school of medicine, that at Salerno, where an interest in theoretical matters then developed, especially in anatomy. Salernitan medicine had always been predominantly pragmatic: its most influential product was its versified *Regimen Salernitanum*, which was to become the practical dietary handbook of all Europe, available in many vernaculars. In the mid-12th c. its curriculum now expanded to include much more use of theories of the *humours and complexions, and the first European universities—Bologna, Paris, Oxford—soon followed suit. A new demand for this kind of knowledge was created, and new schools of translators supplied books in which it was to be found, one group in Spain, working from Arabic and

Hebrew, and another in Italy working with newly found Greek manuscripts. This is the period when '*Serapion, *Razis and *Avycen' were translated, and '*Haly' too, all among the *Doctour of Phisik's authorities (I.429–34). Others were 'Deyscorides, and eek Rufus': Dioscorides had been available in Latin from the 7th c., and this is true of Rufus of Ephesus, but there is a distinct possibility that Chaucer had in mind not Rufus but a medical herbal by Rufinus (*fl.* 1290), in which Dioscorides is repeatedly quoted at length. The authorities Hippocrates (or pseudo-Hippocrates) and Galen were translated in some measure at every historical phase.

In the universities, the emphasis changed yet again in the direction of speculative science. This trend was aided by a reading of Avicenna's *Canon of Medicine*, which in turn directed attention to *Aristotle's work. Aristotle's *De anima* (*On the Soul*), a work of psychology, was made part of the curriculum, and although the entry of Aristotle, Avicenna, and Averroes to the universities of Paris and Oxford received a number of setbacks, those writers were fairly securely entrenched by the 1230s, and made their presence visible through the style of medical writing in the centuries that followed—witness the scholastic style of '*Gilbertyn'. (This style was less typical of Bologna, but by Chaucer's time it had spread eventually to all of Italy too.)

The more familiar the translated texts became, the more scholars recognized how many remained to be translated. Texts were obtained from Constantinople, and between 1308 and 1348 Niccoló da Reggio, physician to the king of Naples, produced translations of around fifty of them. One of the consequences of this flood of texts—added to the old—was that there were now many inconsistencies in medical literature that could not be easily resolved. University disputation was one way of finding a solution. Mystery was added to mystery, however, when astrological medicine took root in the universities. It had been there as long as astrological texts had been there, which is to say since their foundation; but it assumed an important role in the more 'theoretical' phase of medical study, especially in the 14th and 15th c.

It would be easy, however, to exaggerate the numbers educated in the Faculty of Medicine in the universities. In Oxford and Cambridge numbers were certainly small, and in terms of healing the sick far more good (and perhaps harm) was done by barber-surgeons, physicians attached to hospitals, and village leeches. Surgeons were often highly expert, and operated successfully on hernia and cut for stone. In some parts of Europe women found employment as surgeons. They had always, of course, held a near-monopoly in gynaecology. Dissections were rare, and generally frowned upon. The surgeons had the best knowledge of anatomy, but were not thereby the most esteemed authorities. Guy de Chauliac (1298–1368), whose work was popular enough to be translated into English, probably had little practical experience by comparison with the many army surgeons of the time.

Against the great catastrophe of the 14th c., the *Black Death, medical science was helpless. Even the interest in public health stirred by Avicenna's *Canon* was to no avail. Under the circumstances it is not surprising that astrological medicine grew in importance. The Doctour of Phisik carried his astrolabe; he knew how to cast an *ascendent. The notion that heavenly influence could be astrologically directed, while never forgotten, was rejuvenated, and thereafter magic stones and talismans are much discussed in medical texts without any sense of impropriety. The health of the medical sciences generally was not as poor as this fact might suggest, however. It was sustained by the practical experience of the bulk of its practitioners, most of whom were not overly educated.   [JDN]

Grant (1974); P. M. Jones (1984); O'Malley (1970); Talbot and Hammond (1965).

Megera, Megaera, one of the *Furies (*Tr* IV.24).

Melan, Milan in northern Italy is mentioned (VII.2399) in the *Monk's account of its ruler Bernabò Visconti (*Barnabo Viscounte), whom Chaucer had visited in 1378. It was an important political, commercial, and cultural centre.

Melancholy (malencolie). Melancholy (Greek: 'black bile') was the condition, arising from an imbalance in the body's '*humours', of having too much black bile. *Bartholomew (4.11) lists some of its symptoms: the sufferer is faint and fearful

without cause (some fear enmity; some think that they will soon die; some desire death); he will dream fearful dreams. The condition may lead to *passio melancolia*, a kind of madness, in which a person laughs at sorrowful things and sorrows because of joyful things, is silent when he should speak, and speaks too much when he should be silent. Some think they are earthenware vessels and are afraid of being touched in case they break (rather like the later story that Tchaikovsky felt he had to hold his head up while conducting in case it fell off); some think they have the world contained in their fist and are afraid to put out their hand to take food; some hearing cocks crow raise up their arms and crow; others become violent towards their friends. It produces many wonderful passions: Nebuchadnezzar thought he was an animal and ate grass; a nobleman fell into such a madness from melancholy that he believed he was a cat, and would rest nowhere except under beds where cats watched for mice. Despair is the most malignant and destructive form of melancholy. More generally, melancholy is associated with tears and sighs, with blackness and darkness, with sullenness and anger as well as sloth and dejection or 'litargie', but also (like *Saturn, the father of melancholy) with a subtle imagination.

Chaucer's melancholics do not show the more extravagant symptoms, but the nature of the condition is often alluded to. Melancholy is a cause of *dreams (see *HF* 30, *Tr* V.360). *Pertelote, analysing the dream of *Chantecleer as the result of a combination of red choler and melancholy, is very specific: 'the humour of malencolie | Causeth ful many a man in sleep to crie | For feere of blake beres, or boles blake, | Or elles blake develes wole hem take' (VII.2933–6). The humour also engenders 'the loveris maladye | Of *Hereos' which afflicts *Arcite (he is solitary, sorrowful, and tearful). Lovers are particularly prone to melancholy, and to despair. In this context both terms may sometimes be used in an attenuated sense (overlapping with *tho(u)ght* 'anxiety; sorrow, grief'), but the sufferings of melancholy lovers like Troilus are extreme and desperate. The more strictly medical sense is found in The *Miller's Tale* when the carpenter thinks that Nicholas is 'in despeir' (I.3474): he has found him sitting 'stille as stoon', gaping up into the air. His treatment is both physical and spiritual: he shakes him and urges him to think on Christ's passion (a traditional remedy for despair). Despair can lead to suicide (as in the cases of *Antony and *Dido (*LGW* 660–1, 2557). The *Parson puts the theological view (X.692) of 'wanhope, that is despeir of the mercy of God, that comth somtyme of to muche outrageous sorwe, and somtyme of to muche drede', which can become a sin against the Holy Ghost. It is a 'horrible sin', associated with 'sompnolence, that is sloggy slombrynge' which comes from sloth. No one should despair, because no sin is so horrible that it may not be destroyed through penitence.

Especially interesting portrayals of melancholy are found in The *Book of the Duchess and in *Troilus and Criseyde. In the former, the narrator before he dreams says (in a not completely serious vein) that he is suffering from melancholy: he does not care about anything, joy and sorrow is the same to him, his spirit has lost its liveliness, and he has 'fantasies'. This is echoed in the sorrow of the Queen Alcione in the book he reads. And in his dream he comes upon what seems to be the very image of melancholy, 'a man in blak' with his head bowed, making a complaint 'with a dedly sorwful soun'. It was a wonder that *Nature might suffer any creature to have such sorrow and remain alive. As he sets about discovering the cause of the sorrow, the dreamer is fearful that the man may destroy himself (724). And perhaps, as he attempts to bring some consolation through the recollection of the story of his love and loss, he is exploiting for this purpose one of the characteristics of melancholy—a particularly sharp and heightened *memory (the melancholic received the impressions of images more clearly and retained them longer). Troilus suffers the anguish of love as a suppliant, but these pains are as nothing compared to the sorrow that comes when Criseyde must leave Troy. In book V especially, Chaucer gives a poignant depiction of his melancholy. He returns from bidding her farewell 'in sorwe aboven alle sorwes smerte, | With feloun look and face dispitous'. He is afflicted with terrible dreams (246–59) and thoughts of death (295 ff.). He too recalls in obsessive detail the places associated with his love (561–81, 603–16). He imagines himself to be 'defet [disfigured] and pale, and waxen

lesse', and that people are talking about him— 'and al this nas but his malencolie, | That he hadde of hymself swich fantasie' (622–3). The sequence is brought to a close with his lyric of despair, 'O sterre, of which I lost have al the light'.

Kilbansky et al. (1964).

Meleagre, Meleager, the son of Oeneus, king of Calydon (*Calydoigne). At his birth he was destined to live as long as a brand on the fire remained unconsumed. His mother Althaea snatched it out and kept it in safety. Later, when a great boar was sent to ravage Calydon by Diana (*Dyane) who had been affronted by Oeneus. Meleager gathered a band of heroes to hunt it and destroy it. They succeeded, and Meleager gave its hide and head to the virgin huntress Atalanta (*Athalante), whom he loved and who had been the first to wound it. His brothers were angry at this, and he killed them. Hearing of their death Althaea threw the brand into the fire, and brought about Meleager's death. The story would have been known to Chaucer from the eighth book of *Ovid's *Metamorphoses* (260–546). In The *Knight's Tale the hunting of the boar by Atalanta and Meleager is painted on the wall of the temple of Diana (who 'wroghte hym care and wo') (I.2069–72). *Diomede in *Troilus and Criseyde is descended from Meleager; hence the story of the hunting of the Calydonian boar is told by *Cassandra in *Troilus* (V.1464–84) to interpret Troilus's dream of the boar and *Criseyde.

Melibee, Melibeus, the hero of Chaucer's Tale of *Melibee. His name is explained as meaning 'a man that drynketh hony' (VII.1410).

Melibee (in Fragment VII of The *Canterbury Tales) a prose tale told by Chaucer himself after the Host has interrupted his tale of *Sir Thopas. Melibee, a young man, 'mighty and riche', begat on his wife Prudence a daughter, who was called Sophie. While he was out, three of his enemies managed to enter his house, beat his wife, wounded his daughter with five mortal wounds, and left her for dead. When Melibee returns he weeps and laments 'lyk a mad man rentynge his clothes'. Prudence counsels him to cease from his excessive weeping. He does not know what to do, and she advises him to call his friends together, listen to what they say, and follow their advice. He sets out his problem, his words revealing 'a crueel ire, redy to doon vengeaunce upon his foes'. Some of his friends and neighbours counsel vengeance, others oppose it. An advocate urges caution and further deliberation: he should ensure that his house is defended, but should not take vengeance rashly ('for the commune proverbe seith thus: "He that soone deemeth [judges], soone shal repente"'). At this the young people rise up, together with the greater part of the company, and say that just as men should strike while the iron is hot so they should avenge wrongs while they are fresh and new—'and with loude voys they criden "Werre! Werre!"' A wise man warns that many who cry for war do not know what it involves. Seeing her husband intent on revenge Prudence humbly advises him to wait. He is not inclined to accept her advice (1) because it would involve changing something established and (2) because it would involve yielding '*maistrye' to a woman, and Solomon says that they are all wicked. Prudence 'ful debonairly and with greet pacience', and quoting many authorities, succeeds in persuading him to accept her counsel. She discourses on the nature of 'counsel' and of friends who offer it. He has made errors: in gathering too many together, of revealing to them his wish to take revenge, in listening to the majority rather than to his 'trewe frendes olde and wise', etc. She continues at some length to urge him against taking vengeance, and to show patience, reproving him for his trust in worldly power and riches. He should make peace with his enemies. Melibee objects that he would lose his honour, but finally succumbs to the arguments of Prudence, and agrees to follow her counsel. She calls the enemies to her, tells them of the benefits of peace and urges them to repent. They do this and commit themselves to her disposition. They submit themselves to Melibee, who, at Prudence's instigation, forgives them for the wrongs that they have done.

Melibee is a close translation of the French version (by Renaud de Louens) of *Albertanus of Brescia's *Liber consolationis et consilii*. The date of the Tale is unknown. There have been attempts to find in it a contemporary political allegory or an anti-war tract of the late 1380s. This also remains uncertain. That its advice is of very general appli-

cation and that it is taken from earlier works has been adduced as an argument against such interpretations, but general advice may be given particular application. The suggestion that it may have been written with Richard II in mind is not impossible. Chaucer describes it as 'a litel thyng in prose' and as 'a moral tale vertuous'. It is certainly the second, belonging to the category of moral treatises more popular with medieval readers than with modern, who find the ceaseless citing of authorities especially unfamiliar and irritating. However, the extreme reactions of either dismissing it completely or rewriting as an ironical parody of the moral treatise both seem untenable. The allegorical framework suggested at the beginning of the tale is lost sight of, the prose is not exhilarating, and there are very few dramatic moments. It seems likely that Chaucer's choice of such a work for himself at this point is a humorous one, but he does not produce a burlesque as he did with *Sir Thopas*, and the 'sentence' of *Melibee* is certainly consistent with the patterns of ideas that run through the Tales. In particular we can recognize the emphasis on prudence and wisdom in secular life, the interest in *consolation, in *patience, and in '*gentilesse' (which here as in *The Franklin's Tale* brings about a happy conclusion). It presents, moreover, earnest and serious treatments of 'counsel' (*conseil), the role of wives in *marriage, and the question of *maistrye* which are elsewhere more lightheartedly or ironically portrayed.

(ed.) *Rv* 217–39, 923–8; *S&A* 560–614 [321–408]; Cooper (1989), 310–22; Pearsall (1985), 285–8.

memory, 'the power of retaining or recollecting things past' (Johnson), has such an obvious importance in the life of individuals and of societies and cultures that it is not surprising to find that in the Middle Ages it has many significant and interesting ramifications. It finds a place in theological, scientific, and rhetorical discussions. It was, according to St Augustine, one of the three great powers of the soul. In scientific works (like that of *Bartholomew) it is placed in one of the three cells of the brain—*imaginativa, logica, memorativa*. He calls it 'the virtue of mind' (in ME 'mind' can mean 'memory' as well as 'mind'). This stores images, forms, and intentions apprehended by the imaginative and rational powers. According to Boncampagno da Signa (13th c.) memory is 'a glorious and admirable gift of nature by which we recall past things, we embrace present things, and we contemplate future things through their likeness to past things' (Yates, 70). This is close to the idea of Cicero (*Tullius) that 'the treasure-house of all things' is one of the three parts of *Prudence, an idea which is endorsed by later medieval philosophers. It is usual to distinguish 'natural' memory, given to everyone, and 'artificial' memory, which aids it, and can be learnt and trained. Memory is one of the five divisions of the art of *rhetoric, and rhetorical works sometimes contain 'arts of memory' which demonstrate how the memory may be consciously exercised. These seem to have been influential. In devotional and didactic literature, for instance, we find mnemonic schemes (e.g. virtues or vices displayed or enumerated as branches of a tree), numerical patterns (seven deadly sins, four cardinal virtues, etc.). Meditative poems and treatises recall the memory of Christ's passion. More generally the art of memory may have influenced *imagery by its preference for odd, grotesque (and thus memorable) images. The literary importance of memory went well beyond the arts of memory and the rhetorical books. In Greek myth Mnemosyne was the mother of the Muses. Memory underpins the whole idea of literary tradition, of literary *fame, of stories preserving the famous deeds of the past, of achieving what Johnson calls 'exemption from oblivion'.

In Chaucer there are many references to the general lore concerning memory (*memorie, remembraunce, mynde*). Memory is one of the three parts of the soul: 'memorie, engyn, and intellect also' (VIII.339). The Parson includes 'good memorie' among the 'goodes of nature of the soule' (X.452). Chaucer is also aware of the Platonic idea of memory which is found in Boethius (*Boece). Lady Philosophy tells Boethius that he has forgotten his true nature, and that he is confused by lack of memory (I pr.6). Man has a 'dyrkyd memorie' (III pr.2:85). His mind always seeks the sovereign good, but he does not know by which path he may return home 'ryght as a dronke man not nat [does not know] by whiche path he may retourne hom to his hous' (echoed in *The *Knight's*

Tale, I.1260–7). The memory of his original felicity is lost by 'the contagious conjunccioun of the body with the soule' (III pr.12:5). Learning is really 'anamnesis' or the reawakening of memory (cf. III m.11:43–7).

Memory is often associated with literature, with books and the making of books: the opinion is expressed that *The *Knight's Tale* is a 'noble storie | And worthy for to drawen to memorie' (I.3111–12): see also *LGW* 1685–6, 1888–9). Troilus, recalling the course of his love ('whan I the proces have in my memorie'), remarks that 'men myght a book make of it, lik a storie' (V.583–5). That books preserve the memory of the past is implied in phrases such as 'as olde bookes maken us memorie' (VII.1974) and 'bokes . . . Thurgh whiche that olde thinges ben in mynde' (*LGW* 18; see also *BD* 52–5). The idea is made powerfully explicit at the beginning of *The *Legend of Good Women*: 'yf that olde bokes were aweye, | Yloren were of remembraunce the keye' (25–6). One of the daughters of Memory, the muse Polyhymnia (*Polymya) sings on Parnassus 'with vois memorial (i.e. inspired by memory) in the shade' (*Anel* 18). In *The *House of Fame* Chaucer considers the various and sometimes curious ways in which men are remembered for their writings and their deeds (see Fame).

Memory's essential role in human consciousness and social life is indicated in a phrase used of the mortally wounded Arcite: he was brought to his bed 'for he was yet in memorie and alyve' (I.2698). In Chaucer's narratives it is put to a variety of uses. Those who speak in didactic tones often like to make their hearers 'call things to mind' (usually traditional *exempla or sayings preserved from the past) by using the instructional formula 'remember you': 'remembre yow that Jhesus Syrak seith', 'remembre yow upon the pacient Job', 'remembre yow of Socrates', etc. In a religious context, the Parson will urge man to 'remembre hym of his synnes', and the Man of Law will beseech God to have 'som mynde' on his heroine and her child (II.908). There are also variations on the ancient connection of memory with rhetoric. In the midst of the Wife of Bath's superb 'autobiographical' display of memory there is a fine example of comic forgetfulness (for rhetorical effect) when she is made to lose the thread of her discourse (III.585–6). Similarly, the *Pardoner affects to have forgotten 'one word' in his tale, that he has relics and pardons all ready in his bag (VI.919). 'Forgetting' is used cynically by Pandarus when he tries to persuade Troilus to find a new love to drive out the old (*Tr* IV.414–20): since love is but 'casuel plesaunce', 'som cas shal putte it out of remembraunce'. But we might set against this a serious, lyrical metaphorical use in The *Book of the Duchess* (appropriate to its treatment of sorrow and consolation), where the meadow filled with flowers had forgotten (the word is twice repeated) the poverty and sorrows of winter (410–15).

Sometimes there is an interest in the complexities of human memory. It can bring pain: as Criseyde says, if a person knows that joy is transitory, then every time 'he that hath in memorie', the fear of losing it means that he cannot be in perfect felicity (*Tr* III.827–31). But the Wife of Bath's delicious memory of the days when she had youth and jollity 'tickles' her 'heart-root' even though age has now come upon her (III.469–79). The mysterious mingling of joy and pain which memory can produce is well illustrated in the case of lovers. *Melancholy was a condition which was thought to be characterized by an acute memory. When the sorrowful Troilus rides around the city which Criseyde has left, 'every thyng com hym to remembraunce' at the places 'in which he whilom [formerly] hadde al his plesaunce', and he recalls his joys in detail (V.561–81). Similarly, in The Book of the Duchess the Man in Black is encouraged to recall the places and the moments of his past sorrows and joys, which he does vividly. The purpose here is to bring him some *consolation. Yet another narrative situation in which memory figures prominently is the *recognition scene. In one case, in The *Man of Law's Tale Alla, long separated from his wife Custance, looks at the face of the 'fair child' who serves him (his son in fact), and 'hath the face in remembrance | Of dame Custance'. Here a conclusion of 'pitous joye' is triggered by the recollection of things past.

Carruthers (1990); Yates (1966).

men, like *women, are central to Chaucer's work. They appear in considerable numbers, and show considerable variety. The group of male pilgrims described in the *General Prologue is an obvious example, but we should not forget the many male figures, ranging from heroes to villains, who populate Chaucer's narratives. They appear in a variety of roles, as lovers, husbands, fathers, warriors, cheats, rogues, and much else. While it may be thought that none of Chaucer's male characters have quite the psychological subtlety of *Criseyde or the *Wife of Bath, a number are of considerable interest—like the strongly contrasting characters of Troilus, Pandarus, and Diomede in *Troilus and Criseyde. It is noticeable that while Chaucer's wicked women like *Donegild remain simple figures in a narrative, wicked men like the *Pardoner can develop a strange complexity.

As in the case of women there are traditional medieval attitudes and stereotypes which affect Chaucer's treatment, but which he will sometimes transform, invert, or make fun of. It was usually assumed that men had been given authority and sovereignty over women, and especially over their wives. Chaucer considers this critically and in some depth in his treatment of '*maistrye' and *marriage. *Bartholomew associates man (L. *vir*) with might and strength, and says that he has been given the virtues of shaping and working (whereas the woman is 'material, suffering and passive'). The status of man is apparently secure. But while there is nothing in the traditional accounts of the nature of man exactly equivalent to the debate over the nature of woman, it might be argued that Chaucer, like *Boccaccio before him in another *comédie humaine*, raises just this question in the implications of his stories, and treats it with his usual subtlety, irony, and wit.

Just as the difference between men and women was emphasized by distinctive dress, so Chaucer will sometimes give a clear (and obviously traditional) demarcation of their roles and characteristics, contrasting 'womanly' qualities with 'manly' ones. Thus when Criseyde is first introduced, it is remarked that her limbs 'so wel answerynge | Weren to wommanhod, that creature | Was nevere lesse mannysh in semynge' (*Tr* I.282–4), where the contrastive word 'mannysh' is used to emphasize (approvingly) her essential femininity. When 'mannish' is applied to the cruel and tyrannical Donegild ('Fy, mannysh, fy!', II.782) it has the condemnatory sense of 'unwomanly'. Less extreme examples of the contrasting of men with women are found frequently, sometimes in asides (as when

Pandarus, addressing Troilus, speaks of 'us men' (*Tr* III.322)), sometimes more formally (as when at the end of that poem the narrator warns women to beware of men). Sometimes the rivalry between the sexes is presented in a spirit of *game, sometimes it is rather more confrontational: the Wife of Bath has a merry time not only with husbands, but with male writers and with the male sex in general ('the mark of Adam', III.696) and its status.

No one is formally asked the question 'what is it that men most desire?', but some answers are suggested to the question 'what do men desire?' The Wife of Bath attributes to an old husband a number of the reasons for which men desire women (III.257–61). Men's desires often lack foresight: as Arcite, musing on *Fortune, says, 'Som man desireth for to han richesse, | That cause is of his mordre or greet siknesse' (I.1255 ff.). Other narratives illustrate and enact a wide variety of masculine desires: to possess a young wife, to test a wife, to have treasure or power or vengeance.

In general, the men come off poorly in comparison with the women, and not only in the legends of those 'good women', the telling of which Chaucer says was imposed on him. He says much worse things about men than about women, and shows men doing much worse things. Men reveal characteristic (though not exclusively male) vices as violence, anger, treason, deceit, cruelty, 'newfangleness' (especially in love). At the same time, the curious urges and obsessions of men furnish Chaucer with a splendid range of comic and satirical figures, which go well beyond the traditional stereotypes of, for example, the jealous husband (cf. John the carpenter in *MilT*), or the *senex amans* (old man in love: cf. January in *MchT*).

There are some good men (the *Parson is 'a good man . . . of religioun', I.477), but Chaucer is not much interested in ideal heroes, and certainly not in 'macho' heroes. It would be hard to produce a list of masculine virtues to match the vices, but some traditional qualities can excite admiration: the courage and the martial skill of men like the *Knight, or *Theseus, or *Troilus, for instance, who show themselves to be 'manly as a knyght' (I.987). But since 'manliness' is a physical as well as an 'ethical' idea (cf. the 'manly voice' (III.1036; V.99) or the 'manly face' (I.2130), as well as the manly heart' (VII.2711)), it too may be comically inappro-

priate: the monk is 'a manly man, to been an abbot able' (I.167). 'Manly' is used as a term of approbation by *January of his squire (IV.1911); similarly in *Troilus* Pandarus says of Troilus 'God woot where he was lik a manly knyght!' (II.1263; see also IV.622). Later, when Criseyde has to leave Troy, Troilus 'gan his wo ful manly for to hide' (V.30), at least in public (an interestingly different emphasis from the way the narrator describes his earlier dissimulation when smitten by love in the temple, I.318–22). In these sort of contexts, 'manly' behaviour or demeanour is associated with ideas of honour, courage, and fortitude. In others we may find a contrast between true and supposed 'manly' behaviour (like the boisterous rowdiness and aggressiveness exemplified by the *Miller, among others): thus, the Parson is critical of those who delight in swearing 'and holden it a gentrie or a manly dede to swere grete othes' (X.601); possibly there is a hint of this when Philosophy sharply reminds Boethius how, when Fortune was flattering him, he used to attack and scorn her 'with manly woordes' (*Bo* II pr.1:28–9). What is very remarkable is the way in which 'manly' and knightly characters are either made to learn the need for gentler qualities, which are found in abundance in Chaucer's women—the wrathful Theseus is persuaded to allow '*pite' to 'run' in his 'gentil herte' (and comes to despise the 'lord that wol have no mercy' and stubbornly remains 'a proud despitous man', I.1742 ff.)—or are endowed with them. Troilus, 'gentil and . . . tendre of herte' (III.904), has been described by Jill Mann as a 'feminised hero'. It seems that Chaucer is shifting traditional demarcation lines, changing traditional stereotypes, and suggesting that the qualities he admires so much ('*pite', '*gentilesse', '*trouthe') transcend gender boundaries.

Beidler (1998); Mann (1991), ch. 5.

Menelaus, the brother of Agamemnon (*Agamenoun) and the husband of Helen (*Eleyne) of Troy, is mentioned in one of Chaucer's glosses in *Boece* (IV m.7:7).

Mercenrike, the Anglo-Saxon kingdom of Mercia, home of St *Kenelm (VII.3112).

Merchant, The, and merchants. The *portrait in the *General Prologue* (I.270–84) is a brief one, singling out a few salient features: e.g. he has a (fashionable) forked beard and Flemish beaver hat; he speaks 'ful solempnely', and constantly, about his profits (a common failing of merchants according to *estates satire). He is clever in his financial dealings, no one knows that he is in debt (a carefully ambiguous statement). There is a cluster of financial and mercantile terms—*eschaunge, sheeldes* (monetary units of exchange: see *money), *bargaynes* (buying and selling), *chevyssaunce* (dealing, lending)—which perhaps hint at a certain 'shadiness' (fraud and dishonesty are common charges in estates satire). The narrator says that he does not know his name—and there may be other things, perhaps, that are hidden from us. The reference to the ports of *Middelburgh and Orwell (*Orewelle) not only reinforces his connection with Flanders (*Flaundres), but indicates that he was engaged in the export and import trade, possibly a Merchant of the Staple or one of the Merchant Adventurers (whose headquarters were at Middleburgh from 1384 to 1444). Gilbert Maghfield (Mawfield), a wealthy London merchant who engaged in a great variety of 'bargaynes', advanced money to a number of prominent men (and to Chaucer himself in 1392), and was briefly a 'keeper of the sea', has been suggested as a model for the Merchant. Whether he is or not, there is no doubt about Chaucer's close connections with the world of merchants (see Geoffrey *Chaucer: life). Not only did he have a mercantile family background, but his work brought him into contact with some of the most powerful English 'merchant-princes'—Brenbre, Philipot, Walworth. His familiarity with this world is evident in his writings.

The terms and the phraseology come easily: 'this bargain is ful dryve [firmly concluded], for we been knyt' (V.1230). The *Wife of Bath discusses the caution with which women must market their 'wares' (III.521–3). There is a great deal of buying and selling, and a great deal of interest in various forms of income, both among the Canterbury pilgrims (e.g. the Sergeant of Law (*Man of Law; I.318–20), the *Guildsmen (I.373) or the *Friar, whose 'purchas' (takings or ill-gotten gains) was better than his 'rente' (proper income)), and characters in their tales (cf. such small businessmen as the carpenter in The *Miller's Tale or the miller in

The *Reeve's Tale). The world of the great merchants is evoked in The *Shipman's Tale, where 'chevisaunce' and mercantilism have a central role.

Besides being rich and interested in profit, merchants are great travellers, who 'seken lond and see' for their 'wynnynges' (II.127). They 'knowen al th'astaat | Of regnes', and carry not only 'chaffare', but stories: they are 'fadres of tidynges | And tales' (II.128 ff.). Though their vices and pretensions may be sharply satirized, the trade of merchants ('money is their plough', VII.288) is accepted as part of life. The *Parson gives an interesting defence of it (X.775 ff.): he distinguishes 'bodily' and 'goostly' (spiritual) 'marchandise'. If a land is self-sufficient then it is 'honest and leveful (permissible)' to help another land that is needy, 'and therfore ther moote been marchantz to bryngen fro that o contree to that oother marchandises', whereas spiritual trade involves fraud and deceit, and is nothing but *simony. However, his comparison of a merchant and the devil ('right as a marchant deliteth hym moost in chaffare that he hath moost avantage of, right so deliteth the fend in this ordure') (i.e. lechery, X.850) is perhaps a less than complimentary one. And Chaucer records the ancient tradition that there were no merchants in the Golden Age: in those times people had not yet begun to search for 'newe stroondes to leden marchandise into diverse contrees' (*Bo* II m.5:20–2), and 'no marchaunt yit ne fette outlandish ware' (*Former Age* 22).

Rv 809–10; Cooper (1989), 42; Mann (1973), 99–103; Thrupp (1948).

Merchant's Tale, The (of just over 1200 lines, in couplets) follows The *Clerk's Tale in Fragment IV. It begins with a short Prologue (1213–44), in which the *Merchant complains bitterly about his wife of two months, contrasting her sharply with *Griselda, and concluding that 'we wedded men lyven in sorwe and care'.

(1245–688) January, a knight of Lombardy (*Lumbardye) who has indulged his lusts but remained unmarried, decides when he has passed the age of 60 to find himself a wife ('were it for hoolynesse or for dotage | I kan nat seye'). A long and ironic disquisition on the theme 'to take a wyf it is a glorious thyng', extols the excellence of *marriage and of wives, and in particular of their faithfulness, wisdom, and good counsel (*coun-seil). January announces his intention to marry, stressing that he must have a young wife ('she shal nat passe twenty yeer'). Two of his friends fall into debate. Placebo [L. 'I shall please'] praises January's wisdom. Though Solomon said 'wirk alle thyng by conseil', he holds January's counsel to be the best. He has been a 'court-man' all his life, and has learnt not to contradict a lord. It is an excellent idea for an older man to take a young wife. Just-inus (cf. L. *justus* 'just') argues that a man should carefully consider to whom he gives his property or his land. One should make enquiries about a prospective wife's character. Married life may be praised, but it can bring 'cost and care'. January will not be able to please a young and beautiful wife for long. January dismisses this advice, sup-ported again by Placebo. In his mind he considers the appearance and qualities of the maidens living near, and finally he settles on one, 'and chees [chose] hire of his owene auctoritee; | For love is blynd alday, and may nat see'. In bed at night he imagines her beauty and excellence, and convinces himself that his choice cannot be 'amended' nor opposed. He tells his friends that he has deter-mined on a maiden of great beauty (although of 'smal degree'). His only worry is that since no man can have 'blisses two' (both in earth and in heaven) and since heaven is bought with tribula-tion and penance, how can it be that he will come through the perfect happiness of his marriage to the bliss of heaven? Justinus mockingly answers that his wife may turn out to be his purgatory, so that his soul will 'skip' quickly to heaven; he should consider the teaching of the *Wife of Bath.

(1689–2020) Arrangements are quickly made, and the chosen maiden, May, is married to Janu-ary with great magnificence. Her old husband ('ravysshed in a traunce' whenever he looks upon her) is eager to bring her to bed. A young squire, Damyan, is also 'ravysshed' by May's beauty, but he has to suffer the pain of love in silence. The aged husband is 'al coltissh, ful of ragerye'; his young bride 'preyseth nat his pleyyng worth a bene'. Meanwhile, the lovesick Damyan writes a *letter to May 'in manere of a compleynt or a lay' and keeps it in a silken purse next to his heart. January, hearing that his squire is sick, sends May and her ladies to visit him. He passes the purse to

her secretly; later, she finds an opportunity to read it and to destroy it—in the privy. May suffers Janu-ary's amorous demands, but begins to take *pite* on Damyan. 'Fulfilled of pitee', she writes a letter granting him 'hire verray grace', and slips it under his pillow: 'al passed was his siknesse and his sorwe'.

(2021–418) The voluptuous January has a walled pleasure garden made, fairer than any other. It is said that around its spring *Pluto and *Proserpina 'and al hire fayerye' often disport themselves and dance. January brings May there in the summer—but in the midst of all his joy, suddenly he becomes blind. In time he comes to bear his affliction with patience, but he is consumed with intense jealousy (*jalousie). He insists on keeping his hand on May at all times—to her and to Damyan's great distress. However, love will always find a way. They contrive to make a copy of January's key to the gate of the garden, and May urges him to take her to the garden 'for to pleye', making a sign to Damyan to go in first. January takes her in and closes the gate, thinking that they are alone. May assures him that she will never be false—and signals to Damyan to climb up into a fruit-tree. Meanwhile, Pluto and Proserpina are in the garden, and the king holds forth to his wife on the innumerable treasons which women do to men, quoting Solomon, who says that he found one good man among a thousand 'but of wommen alle foond I noon'; since there is an example before them, he will give January his sight back when his wife deceives him. 'Wol ye so?' says Proserpina. She will give May 'suffisant answere, | And alle wommen after, for hir sake'—and Solomon was nothing but a lecher and an idolater. In the garden January is singing merrily. When he and May are under the tree, she says that she is longing to have one of the pears that she can see, and if she can climb up on his back she will get some. Up she goes, to the waiting Damyan, who 'gan pullen up the smok, and in he throng [thrust].' At this very moment January can see again, and gives 'a roryng and a cry'—but May maintains that she is simply helping to cure him by causing him to see her struggle with a man up in a tree. When he queries the term 'struggle', she replies that her medicine must not have worked since if he could see he would not say such words: 'ye han som glymsyng, and no parfit sighte.' Many a man, she says, thinks that he has seen something, but it is quite different from what it seems—and she jumps down. January is 'glad', and kisses her and takes her home, stroking her 'wombe' (stomach, or, possibly, pudendum). 'Now, goode men,' says the narrator to the audience, 'I pray yow to be glad.'

The Merchant's Tale is so clearly linked with its predecessor (by its northern Italian setting, its differing treatment of the trials of marriage, and its allusions to the earlier discussions of the Wife of Bath) that it seems almost certainly to have been composed at the time of *The Canterbury Tales.* However, remarks such as 'thise fooles that been seculeer', 'I speke of folk in seculer estaat' (IV.1251, 1322) suggest that it was originally intended for a clerical narrator, perhaps the *Monk (in answer to *The *Shipman's Tale?*) or the *Friar. While it is not the kind of story that the description of the Merchant in the *General Prologue* might lead us to expect, and not especially 'mercantile', it fits the embittered narrator briefly sketched in its prologue (which may possibly have been written when the placing of the story was changed).

No exact literary source has been discovered, but the pear-tree story is widespread. Chaucer could have read it; he might also have heard it. But in his hands it becomes a highly literary piece of work. The opening section uses some of the same material as *The Wife of Bath's Prologue* and the whole tale has a characteristically dense texture of literary and scriptural allusion (ranging from the *Roman de la Rose* to the Song of Songs).

It is a *fabliau, with the common love-triangle situation and involving an old husband (*senex amans*) and a young wife. But it has been transformed and elaborated, both by the long 'preamble' on marriage involving a mock-encomium and a kind of *debate, and by the continual rhetorical flourishes in the story itself. It mixes different styles and genres, suggesting now an *exemplum, now a courtly *romance. The narrative rhythm is unlike that of Chaucer's other fabliaux, with a slow, elaborate opening, and the pace of the 'comic' plot being artfully delayed by expansions, asides, and *digressions.

The irony is omnipresent and usually mordant. Sometimes it is startling in its depth. Before he leads May into his pleasure garden, January addresses her in the very words of the Song of Songs: 'Rys up, my wyf, my love, my lady free! | The turtles voys is herd . . . | Com forth now, with thyne eyen columbyn [dove-like]!' (2138–41). The narrator remarks: 'swich olde lewed [?foolish ?lascivious] wordes used he,' There are ironic variations on the proverbial dictum that 'love is blind'. Self-delusion is ruthlessly presented and exposed. The tone of the narrator's voice is characteristically sardonic and cynical: when January and May are married, 'forth comth the preest, with stole aboute his nekke, | And bad hire be lyk *Sarra and *Rebekke . . . | And seyde his orisons, as is usage . . . | And made al siker ynogh with hoolynesse' (1703–8). There has been much argument about how far this is a 'reflection' of the Merchant-narrator, whether it should be seen as an elaborate piece of psychological self-revelation or as a more rhetorical device of a misanthropic narrative voice (like that of the misogynistic works which are echoed at the beginning) in sharp contrast to that of *The Clerk's Tale.* Readers have also disagreed vehemently over the question of whether the Tale is entirely dark, sardonic, and cynical. It has been pointed out, with some justification, that there is a curious alternation between grimly realistic details like the 'thikke brustles' of January's beard on his wedding night ('lyk to the skyn of houndfyssh') and the more generalizing effect of the symbolic names and the involvement of the gods Pluto and Proserpina. And though the folly of January is mercilessly demonstrated, it has a 'perverse romantic idealism'. Our sympathy for May is not allowed to survive for long. The ending is curiously ambiguous, even by Chaucerian standards. This tale may arouse disgust and contempt, and yet wit and comedy are by no means totally absent. If it is not every reader's favourite among the tales, it is certainly one of the most original and the most powerful.

(ed.) *Rv* 154–68, 884–90; *S&A* 333–56; Cooper (1989), 202–16; Burrow (1957); David (1976), 179–81; Pearsall (1985), 193–209.

Merciles Beaute, a lyric (beginning 'Your yen [eyes] two wol slee me sodenly') usually thought to be by Chaucer, although it is not attributed to him by the scribe of the single MS (Pepys 2006) in which it occurs (and which contains a number of works by him). It is an accomplished triple *roundel, possibly meant to be sung. It uses the topics of French love poetry (the lady's eyes, '*pite' and '*daunger') deftly, and the third section, in which the lover celebrates his escape from love, has some Chaucerian-sounding images and phraseology: love has stricken my name from his slate, and the refrain 'Sin I fro Love escaped am so fat, | I never thenk to ben in his prison lene; | Sin I am free, I counte him not a bene'.

(ed.) *Rv* 659, 1090–1; Pace and David (1982), 171–8; Scattergood (1995), 480–1.

Mercurye, Mercurius, (1) Mercury, the Roman god of merchants, the equivalent of the Greek Hermes. In Greek mythology he was the son of Zeus and Maia, and was born on Mt. Cyllene. Mercury was renowned for his cunning. He carries a herald's staff (L. *caduceus*) which explains the planet's symbol, and connects with his reputation for oratory and fluency of speech. This is evident even from the title of Martianus Capella's *Marriage of Philology and Mercury*. (See *Marcian.) In ancient and medieval art he usually carries the caduceus and wears a wynged cap and boots or sandals. (He is 'the winged god Mercurye' in *The *Knight's Tale.) He escorts heroes, and this is his persona when he assigns the soul of *Troilus its final resting place in the closing stanzas of *Troilus and Criseyde. (The stanzas are essentially taken from *Boccaccio's *Teseida*, where the soul is Arcite's.) (2) Mercury, the planet. This occupies the sphere beyond the Moon, the second in all, counting outwards from the Earth. In Ptolemaic astronomy, Mercury has the most complex model: the centre of its deferent circle is not fixed, but is carried round a small auxiliary circle. Mercury never wanders far from the Sun, and is consequently lost in the Sun's rays for much of the time. (See also *Cylenios.)

The conventional astrological properties of the planet are more or less those of the god. The (domiciles of Mercury are the signs Gemini and Virgo; its exaltation is in Virgo and its dejection in Pisces. The Wife of Bath makes a point of the fact that the case of Venus is exactly the reverse. A reference to 'the children of Mercurie and Venus', also in *The *Wife of Bath's Prologue*, is to people who fall under those planets' influence at birth,

scholars and lovers respectively. In *The *Squire's Tale*, Chaucer makes much play with the astrological and astronomical properties of the planet. (See also *astrology and astronomy; *exaltacio(u)n; *planete; *signe; *sper(e).) (3) mercury, the metal, quicksilver, in alchemical symbolism, as noted by the *Canon's Yeoman. (See also *alchemy; *dragon.)   [JDN]

Meridian, meridian (n.). The great circle through the zenith and southern point of the horizon, crossed by the Sun at local noon; or the corresponding line on an astrolabe. Chaucer also uses the word (as is still done) as an adj. (from L. *meridianus, -a, -um*), as in the phrase 'altitude meridian', the altitude of the Sun at noon. (See also *astrology and astronomy, *Cenyth, *heyte, *midnyght, *oriso(u)nte.)   [JDN]

mermaids, commonly identified with Sirens, are, according to *Bartholomew, sea-beasts wonderfully shaped, which draw shipmen to peril by the sweetness of their song. He records various views concerning their shape, including (from *Physiologus) the familiar woman-fish form. Mermaids are said to be merry in a tempest and sorrowful in fair weather. The song lulls the sailors asleep, and the mermaid comes aboard and takes whichever one she pleases to a dry place where she makes him 'do the deed of lechery': if he will not or cannot, she slays him and eats his flesh. In Chaucer they appear briefly in *Boece (I pr.1:69), rendering L. *Sirenes*, and in the *Romaunt of the Rose (679–84), where the singing of the birds is compared to their clear song. In *The *Nun's Priest's Tale* (VII.3270–3) Chauntecleer is said to sing more merrily than 'the mermayde in the see | (For Phisiologus seith sikerly | How that they syngen wel and myrily)'. This is just before he himself falls victim to the flattering words of the fox.

Merton College, see *Oxenford.

Messenus, Misenus, the son of Aeolus (*Eolus), trumpeter to Hector (*Ector) and Aeneas (*Eneas; see *Aeneid* 6.162–76), appears among those 'that maken blody soun | In trumpe, beme, and clarioun' in *The House of Fame* (1243–4).

'mesure' (modern English *measure*) is used by Chaucer to mean 'measurement' (e.g. IV.256–7), but regularly has the sense of 'moderation'. Thus *Prudence speaks of 'mesure of wepyng' (VII.990); *Virginia has 'mesure . . . of beryng and array' (VI.47). Moderation in behaviour is praised (with a lover's hyperbole by the Man in Black: his lady was not 'to sobre ne to glad; | In alle thynges more mesure | Had never, I trowe, creature' (*BD* 880–2). *Criseyde quotes the proverbial 'in every thyng . . . ther lith mesure' (*Tr* II.715). The opposite of 'mesure' (in Fr., *démesure*) is *excesse* or *outrage* ('excess, extravagance', 'disorder, violence'). 'Mesure' is contrasted with what is *disordinat* or *inordinat* 'out of mesure' or 'over mesure'.

In addition to *mesure*, Chaucer uses a number of other words (*mene, attempraunce, suffisaunce*) to cover the ancient notions of 'moderation' (Greek *sophrosyne*, L. *moderatio, mediocritas, temperantia,* etc.). These range from 'self-restraint' to the philosophical notion of 'moderation' as a 'mean' between the extremes ('vertu is the mene' as '*Etik' says (*LGW* 165)). They were transmitted to the Middle Ages in a number of forms: the ancient pagan Four Virtues were Christianized (producing an emphasis on temperance, the self-restraining aspect of moderation); there was a Neoplatonic tradition of moderation, both cosmological and ethical (which again stressed self-control); and an Aristotelian pattern of 'mediocritas' and the idea of the 'mean' in a proportional ethical system. The different systems were often blended. Chaucer seems to have derived his ideas from Boethius (*Boece), *Macrobius, Alan of Lille (*Aleyn (1)) and *Jean de Meun. Cosmologically, moderation is associated with *Nature, who joins the elements 'by evene noumbres of acord' (*PF* 381). It is found in the detail of her creation—as in the eyes of the lady in *The *Book of the Duchess*: 'the goddesse, Dame Nature, | Had mad hem opene by mesure | And close (871'–3). 'Mesure' is an ethical ideal also, but one of some complexity, and one which is usually implied rather than stated explicitly. Some of his characters (like Prudence) seem to embody it, many have to learn it from experience, and many ignore it in various 'disordinat' ways.

Norton-Smith (1974), 226–60.

metals are frequently alluded to. The Middle Ages prized the art of metal-working, especially 'goldsmythrye' (I.2498). The working of humbler metals (as in the blacksmith's shop briefly pictured in *The *Miller's Tale*) was an even more necessary part of life. Metals may have symbolic or medicinal value, and may be used metaphorically or proverbially. The *Canon's Yeoman gives a vivid account of the chemistry used in the 'slidynge science' of *alchemy (VIII.898 ff.), and gives the planetary equivalents of the metals—gold/Sun; silver/Moon; iron/Mars; quicksilver/Mercury; lead/Saturn; tin/Jupiter; copper/Venus (VIII.825 ff.). The symbolic association of metals and planetary gods is also used in *The *House of Fame* (1419 ff.). There *Josephus stands on a pillar of lead and iron ('for yren Martes metal ys, | Which that god is of bataylle; | And the led . . . | . . . the metal of Saturne', who, as the oldest of the gods and the 'father of the planets' is associated with the Jewish religion), and the writers of the ancient wars stand upon iron pillars. *Virgil is on a pillar of 'tynned yren cler', perhaps suggesting Jupiter, the patron of Aeneas; *Ovid, 'Venus clerk', stands on a pillar of copper; and *Claudian, who wrote of the underworld, on a pillar of sulphur.

Even when their symbolic associations are less obvious, metals often carry some kind of 'charge'. In the case of the 'precious' metals it may be ambiguous, since medieval moralists liked to expand on the vice of covetousness, which, as *The *Former Age* tells us, began when men 'first dide hir swety bysinesse | To grobbe up metal, lurkinge in derknesse'. Thus *gold*, traditionally of highest value (see *The *Wife of Bath*, III.100–1; and cf. 'if gold ruste, what shal iren do?', I.500) is used for splendid decoration (like the golden chariot of King *Lygurge, I.2138, etc.). Beautiful hair shines like gold (I.3314, etc.). Gold is used for rich ornaments (sometimes owned by those dedicated to religious poverty like the *Prioress (I.160) or the *Monk (I.196). Gold is sometimes synonymous with 'money': the disastrous passion for treasure finds a memorable image in the effect of the heap of gold coins in *The *Pardoner's Tale*. Gold has a medicinal 'virtue': it could cleanse superfluities and was good for leprosy, and for the heart. Ironically, it is remarked of the *Physician that since 'gold in phisik is a cordial [medicine for the heart], | Therefore he lovede gold in special' (I.443–4). And as the proverb, aptly quoted in *HF* (272), says, 'hyt is not al gold that glareth'. Similarly *silver* is used for images and ornaments (I.115), and the word can mean money in general (I.713). The proverbial 'bright as silver', is adapted in 'out goon the swerdes as the silver brighte' (I.2608), and imaginatively used of small fish, 'with fynnes rede and skales sylver bryghte' (*PF* 189). In 'the silver dropes hangynge on the leves' (I.1496) the adjective perhaps gives a hint that Nature has her own art.

Of the non-precious metals, *iron* and its working gives a common proverb: 'whil that iren is hoot men sholden smyte' (VII.1035; cf. *Tr* II.1276). *Steel*, which is frequently associated with arms and armour, also generates a common proverb 'true as steel' (IV.2426, *PF* 395, etc.) which underlies the phrase 'love of stiel' (*Tr* IV.325, *HF* 683). There is a nice allusion to this in the remark that Criseyde felt that Troilus was 'to hire a wal | Of stiel' (*Tr* III.479–80), *Brass* is the material of pans (I.3944) and trumpets (*HF* 1637). More spectacular creations are the horse of brass in The *Squire's Tale* (V.81 ff.) and the temple of brass in The *Parliament of Fowls* (231). This is the temple of Venus: brass and copper, her metal, were closely linked in the Middle Ages, (*Boccaccio, who here has a temple of copper, explains in a note that he means copper and brass, which are in general the same metal 'born of the planet Venus'.) The *Clerk, lamenting the decline of patient wives, alludes to the practice of alloying gold with brass in coins (IV.1167–9): it looks good, but it will break rather than bend. Another similar alloy *latoun* (latten), which had the appearance of gold, was widely used for decorative purposes (I.699, 3251) and for armour (Sir Thopas's helm is of 'latoun bright', VII.877). The ageing sun has the colour of 'latoun' (V.1245).

Metellius, a 'foule cherl', according to the *Wife of Bath, who killed his wife for drinking wine (III.460–2). This is a version of a story told by Valerius Maximus (*Valerie) and others.

Methamorphosios, the *Metamorphoses* of *Ovid II.93.

metre, metrical forms; Meun, Jean de. See *versification; *Jean de Meun.

Michelmesse, Michaelmas, the feast of St Michael and All Angels (29 September), one of the quarter-days of the administrative year, when *Scogan gave up his lady (*Scogan* 19).

Michias, the Old Testament prophet Micah, quoted by the *Parson (X.201).

Myda, Midas, the legendary king of Phrygia, who was granted his wish that all he touched would turn to gold (see, for example, *Ovid's *Metamorphoses* 11.100 ff.). In the Middle Ages he was often associated with avarice (e.g. by *Gower, *Confessio Amantis* 5.153 ff.) and covetousness (by both *Dante, *Purgatorio* 20, and Chaucer, *Tr* III.1387–93, where Midas 'ful of coveytise' is linked with *Crassus, as an example of those opposed to the 'gentil' servants of love). The wish (1387–9) that wretches who despise the service of love should have ears as long as Midas did alludes to a further episode in his legend, that Apollo changed his ears into those of an ass. He attempted to conceal this, but his barber, who knew his secret and was afraid to reveal it could not resist the urge to whisper it into a hole in the ground. But whenever the wind blew, the reeds which later sprang up there murmured the words that had been 'buried'. The *Wife of Bath tells a version of this story (III.951–82) in which Midas's wife replaces his barber.

Middleburgh, Middelburg, a port in Holland, on the island of Walcheren. The *Merchant in the *General Prologue* (I.276–7) is said to desire that the passage from Orwell (*Orewelle) to Middelburg should be protected at all costs. It was an important centre for English trade: it was the headquarters of the Merchant Adventurers, and from 1384 to 1388 was a 'staple port', through which wool was licensed to be exported.

midnyght, line of, the lower half of the vertical diameter on the plate of an astrolabe (also called 'the north lyne') representing the continuation of the meridian line (the upper half of the diameter). (See also *A Treatise on the *Astrolabe.*) [JDN]

Midsummer Night's Dream, A. Shakespeare's play (1593–94?) is indebted to Chaucer in its relation to The *Knight's Tale* and, to a lesser extent, to three other Chaucerian works: *The *Merchant's Tale*, *The Tale of *Sir Thopas*, and the story of *Pyramus and Thisbe as told in *The *Legend of Good Women*. The influence of *The Knight's Tale* and *The Merchant's Tale* in *A Midsummer Night's Dream* lies not so much in specific instances of resemblance but in the principal theme which they all share of the irresponsibility and randomness of romantic love, how quickly lovers surrender themselves to it, and how in these works the lovers are assisted or hindered in their affairs by supernatural powers (Venus and Saturn, Pluto and Proserpina, Oberon and Titania) who are as irresponsible as the mortals.

The play's action is presided over by Theseus, duke of Athens, and Hippolyta his Amazon queen, whom Shakespeare could have read about both in North's *Plutarch* (1597) and in *The Knight's Tale*. Shakespeare's Theseus inherits from Chaucer the strife of irrational lovers, not this time a triangle of Palamon, Arcite, and Emily but two pairs of lovers. (Cf. a similar situation, again with *The Knight's Tale* as influence, in *Two Gentlemen of Verona*.) Out hunting, in both, Theseus discovers the rival lovers: the prison-breaker Palamon and the eloping Lysander. The climax of jealous discord in *A Midsummer Night's Dream*, as in *The Knight's Tale*, is reached in a wood, Lysander and Demetrius seeking 'a place to fight' and the women Hermia and Helena quarrelling in parallel. Puck's famous exclamation at the behaviour of the lovers, 'Lord, what fools these mortals be!' (3.2.115) has its antecedent in the response of Chaucer's Theseus to the knights fighting over Emily: 'Who may be a foole, but if he love?' (I.1799).

The literary parody and romance clichés of *The Tale of Sir Thopas* are reflected, both stylistically and thematically, in Peter Quince's play of Pyramus and Thisbe, though it also derives from Golding's translation of Ovid's *Metamorphoses* (1567). There are relationships too with Chaucer's telling of the story in *The Legend of Good Women*. The Chaucerian connection is reinforced by the fact that the lovers are also alluded to in *The Merchant's Tale* and, in a serious context, in *Troilus and Criseyde* (IV).   [RB]

Bethurum (1945); Brooks (1979); Bullough (1957); E.T Donaldson (1985); Muir (1957); A. Thompson (1978).

Milesie, Miletus, a city in western Asia Minor, the home of the seven maidens who slew themselves rather than be raped (V.1409).

Myle-wey, twenty minutes, the time to walk a mile. In *A Treatise of the *Astrolabe* Chaucer uses the expression to indicate the equivalence of the Sun's daily movement in twenty minutes and the angle of 5 degrees that separates the long strokes on the astrolabe's outer scale.   [JDN]

Milky Wey, the Milky Way, or Galaxy. The irregular band of densely distributed stars encircling the sky. It has been described in many different cultures as a path, and the association with milk is pre-Homeric. (See also *Galaxye; *Watlynge strete.)   [JDN]

Miller, The. The portrait of the Miller (I.545–66) is one of the most vivid in the *General Prologue. He is 'ful byg of brawn and eek of bones', of great strength, an expert wrestler, and able to break a door with his head. Like the traditional stereotype of millers in *estates satire, he is a swaggerer (armed with a sword and buckler) and a thief. His strength is matched by his grossness—of appearance (his beard red like a sow or a fox and broad as a spade; his wide black nostrils, the wart on his nose with a tuft of red hairs, his mouth large as a great cauldron) and of behaviour (a buffoon and a teller of obscene stories). He plays the bagpipe (see *music), and we learn later that he is called Robyn (I.3129). He is not the only miller in Chaucer. The *Reeve, who is annoyed by his tale, describes a proud and swaggering miller in *Trumpington, and deliberately endows him with some of the characteristics of the Miller in the *Prologue*. Not only is he violent and a wrestler, but he is even more obviously dishonest.

The Reeve's Tale gives a momentary glimpse of the working of a medieval mill (where 'the hopur wagges til and fra'). Mills were operated by water power as there, or by animals or the wind. (Windmills, which were relatively late in developing, were common enough in Chaucer's day for him to allude to a magician doing a trick with one; *HF* 1280–1.) The mill was important in medieval life; it was a place for collecting news and gossip as well as corn, and its owner, the miller, was an important tenant of the manor. Its ubiquity is shown by the frequency with which it was depicted in MS illustrations, and by the number of common proverbial sayings relating to milling. Besides those which touch on the dishonesty of millers (I.562–3), the *Wife of Bath quotes 'whoso comes to the mill first grinds first' (III.389), and the phrase 'to clap [chatter noisily] like a mill' is twice used (IV.1200; X.406).

Rv 820–1; Cooper (1989), 53–5; Mann (1973), 160–2; Bennett (1974), 120–3.

Miller's Prologue and Tale, The (746 lines in couplets) follow *The *Knight's Tale* in Fragment I. The drunken *Miller interrupts the *Host's request to the *Monk to produce 'somwhat to quite the Knyghtes tale', and insists on telling a story about a carpenter and his wife and a clerk— to the irritation of the *Reeve, who is a carpenter.

*John (4), a rich carpenter, lives in Oxford (*Oxenford), and has a lodger, a student called *Nicholas, who is fascinated by astrology. He also has a young and extremely attractive wife, *Alison (1). Nicholas makes known his passion for her, and she promises to do what he wishes whenever she can find an opportunity: her husband is jealous, and dangerous, and it must be secret. Nicholas, confident that a clerk should be able to beguile a carpenter, bides his time. Alison has another young admirer, *Absolon a parish clerk, with beautiful golden hair and dandyish tastes. The sight of Alison 'propre [handsome] and sweete and likerous [sexy]' in a church service fills him with 'lovelonging'. He sets about wooing her, coming to sing under the window, sending her presents, and ('for she was of town') offering her money—but all to no avail. Nicholas now begins his 'wile'. He stays in his room until the carpenter becomes worried and sends his servant up to call him or knock. When there is no response, the servant peers in through a hole and sees Nicholas sitting and gaping up, as if he were gazing on the new moon. John, who prides himself on being a practical man who does not meddle with understanding 'Goddes pryvetee [secrets, private affairs]', thinks that the clerk has fallen into some madness through his astronomy. Breaking down the door, he shakes him and says a protective charm over him. Eventually, Nicholas 'comes to', and announces that it has been revealed

to him through his astrology that another Flood is imminent which will destroy the world. They can be saved, however, as Noah was. John, Alison, and Nicholas must provide themselves with three tubs, furnished with food and hung up in the roof, in which they can float until the water subsides. In the evening there must be complete silence, and the carpenter must hang well away from his wife to avoid sin.

The carpenter believes all this, and makes the necessary preparations. He is soon deeply asleep in his tub, and Alison and Nicholas climb down and disport themselves all night in the carpenter's bed. Absolon, who has not seen the carpenter about, has decided that the moment has come to tell Alison of his love-longing, and at the first cockcrow he comes and stands beneath the window, and calls Alison. His avowals of love are not well received, but when Alison discovers that a kiss will send him on his way she promises him one and devises a jape. Absolon kneels down and makes ready; Alison opens the window and sticks out her bottom. Absolon kisses her naked arse and starts back in considerable discomfiture. Alison and Nicholas are in high delight, while Absolon is consumed with mortification and the desire for revenge: his hot love is now cold and quenched. He goes across the street to where the blacksmith, Gerveys, is already at work in his forge. He borrows a red-hot coulter, and, returning to the window, calls Alison again. Nicholas now decides to follow Alison's behaviour, except that instead of a kiss he gives a colossal fart. But Absolon strikes with his hot coulter, and Nicholas's agonized cry. 'Help! Water! Water! Help . . . !'—arouses the carpenter, who thinks that the flood has arrived. With his axe he cuts his cord and plunges to the ground, breaking his arm. The ensuing hubbub brings in the neighbours. Alison and Nicholas tell them that he is mad, and they laugh at his 'fantasye' and turn his 'harm' into a 'jape'.

There is no way of establishing the date of composition of *The Miller's Tale*, but it is likely that it was written in the 'Canterbury period' with its place after *The Knight's Tale* in mind. Nor is any direct source known, though there are analogues, and the individual motifs (a man who is made to fear a second flood, a 'misdirected kiss', branding with a hot iron) are widespread, and could have been found in written or oral form. The Tale belongs to the genre of the *fabliau, but it transforms the fabliau pattern and raises it to the level of high art. The expansive treatment of the story allows passages of brilliant dialogue, formal *portraits, and clever characterization. The main figures are neatly differentiated, and intriguing in the facets (suspected or unsuspected) that are dramatically revealed. The carpenter's combination of stupidity, anti-intellectualism, credulity, and a touching affection for his 'hony deere' ('and shal she drenche [drown]? Allas, myn Alisoun!') makes him an easy victim for Nicholas's scheming. Nicholas, who rarely acts without forethought, has a rash moment of hubris when he suddenly tries to 'amenden al the jape'. Absolon's sudden and intense mortification and passionate urge to vengeance is related to his vanity. Most remarkable is the thoroughness with which Chaucer gives the tale a local setting. The Oxford references are numerous and detailed, ranging from references to local saints like St *Frideswide and parishes (St *Thomas's), monasteries (at *Oseney) and friaries to the evocation of a student's room and belongings (I.3203–18). The fantastic plot is set in the midst of images of real life: Alison goes off to church with the other wives of the parish; Gerveys works at night, as smiths did, probably repairing farm implements for the morning.

After the leisurely presentation of the characters the complicated plot moves rapidly in a series of scenes, with its ingenious denouement triggered by the cry for water. The tale is full of irreverent *ironies and *parodies, with references to or echoes of biblical material and the religious *drama (Noah, Herod): the aptly named *Absolon is made to echo the Song of Songs in his wooing, and Nicholas sings *Angelus ad Virginem with a delight which seems to be erotic. In particular there are a number of comic echoes of *The Knight's Tale* verbal, structural (e.g. the girl with two lovers), and thematic. The courtly world of the Knight is in effect turned upside down. What emerges is a kind of festive comedy, celebrating the energy of sex and life.

(ed.) *Rv* 66–77, 841–9; *S&A* 106–23; Cooper (1989), 92–107; Bennett (1974), 26–57; David (1976), ch. 6; Muscatine (1957); Norton-Smith (1974), 136–45; Pearsall (1985), 171–85.

Mylner of Abington. *A Mery Jest of the Mylner of Abington* (printed *c.*1533) is a version of *The *Reeve's Tale* in tail-rhyme stanzas. The setting is moved a little further from Cambridge, and most of Chaucer's ironic detachment and satire is lost. Some differences in the plot (e.g. a framework telling how the penniless mother of the students came to Cambridge to ask her sons to beg some food for her) suggest that the author knew other forms of the story.

MILTON, JOHN (1608–74) seems not to have been as excited by Chaucer as he was by Chaucer's follower *Spenser, but he mentions him several times in his Commonplace Book (referring, for instance, to *MchT* and *WBProl* on 'the discommodities of marriage', and to *PhysT* on the bad effect feasts, revels, and dances have on children). There is an allusion to Chaucer in *Il Penseroso*: 'call up him that left half-told | The story of Cambuscan bold' (109 ff.). This is the unfinished *Squire's Tale* (Milton may have known John *Lane's continuation). (It has been claimed that 'thick . . . | As the gay motes that people the sunbeams' in the same poem (7–8) may be an echo of a similar phrase in *The *Wife of Bath's Tale* (III.868), but the underlying phrase is proverbial.) In the Latin poem *Mansus* Chaucer (called Tityrus—as he had been by Spenser in *The Shepheardes Calendar*) is said (rightly) to have visited the shores of Italy. The tower of *Fame in another Latin poem *In Quintum Novembris* may possibly owe something to *The *House of Fame*. In his prose works Milton also refers to him as 'wise', 'renowned', 'learned'. He had read Chaucer in the edition of *Speght, which also includes *The *Plowman's Tale*, which Milton quotes as Chaucer's, evidently relishing its anti-clerical and reforming spirit. Some lines from the description of 'The Merry Friar' in the *General Prologue* are also used in a passage of anti-episcopal satire. Speght's edition also contains *The *Cuckoo and the Nightingale*, in which Milton probably read that hearing the nightingale before the cuckoo is a good omen for a lover, and the opposite a bad one: see *Sonnet*, 1.9–10.

Mynerva, Mynerve, Minerva, the Roman goddess of wisdom, identified with the Greek Pallas Athene, the daughter of Zeus (the meaning of her title Pallas is not known). Chaucer uses the names Minerva and Pallas interchangeably. The goddess is the protector of Troy (the wooden horse is 'offered unto Mynerve', *LGW* 932; see also *Palladion*). She is several times mentioned in *Troilus and Criseyde*. Pandarus swears by 'the goddesse Mynerve' (*Tr* II.232); Pallas is invoked by Criseyde (II.425; V.977, 999). Elsewhere we find the proverbial phrases 'as wis as Mynerva' (*BD* 1072), 'wis as Pallas' (VI.49). In the invocation at the beginning *Anelida and Arcite* Pallas is mentioned along with *Mars and *Bellona (1–5). It is sometimes claimed that here Chaucer has confused her with Bellona, but it seems more likely that he is deliberately equating the two, and is thinking of Pallas as the armed goddess. Athene was associated with war as well as with wisdom, and was generally represented with armour and a shield. In *Troilus* (V.308) Troilus wishes to bequeath to her his shield.

Mynos (1), the legendary king of ancient *Crete, the husband of Pasiphaë and the father of Ariadne and Phaedra, who demanded a tribute of Athenians for the monstrous Minotaur (*Mynotaur) (see The *Legend of Good Women*). Chaucer calls him both 'the myghty kyng of Crete' (1894) and 'juge infernal . . . of Crete kyng' (1886), i.e. Mynos (2). This identification had been made by *Boccaccio and others.

Mynos (2), a judge of the dead in classical literature. He is mentioned in *Troilus and Criseyde* (IV.1188). The context of an intended suicide suggests that Chaucer may have been recalling *Dante, who in the *Inferno* not only has Minos as a terrible judge (5.4–6), but also (13.94–6) associates him with suicides.

Mynotaur, the Minotaur, a monstrous hybrid. When Minos (1) offended Poseidon, the god caused the king's wife, Pasiphaë, to mate with a bull. Her offspring, known as the Minotaur, was kept in a labyrinth (*Laboryntus) in Crete. It was destroyed by *Theseus. Chaucer refers to the monster in The *Knight's Tale* (I.980) and in The *Legend of Good Women* (1928 ff.).

Miracles of the Virgin Mary are devotional tales of

miracles wrought by the Virgin Mary or through her intercession, which demonstrate her power and her benevolence to her devotees (even though they may have sinned very grievously). Although individual stories are found earlier, the compilation of collections of them begin to appear in the 12th c. Such stories seem to have been very popular, and are often very attractive (like the well-known 'Tumbler of Our Lady'). The story of the monk Theophilus, who made a pact with the devil, is one of the forerunners of the Faust legend. There are ME examples from the 13th c. to the eve of the Reformation. They then came under attack: one Reformer mentions 'a book of Our Ladys miracles well able to match the Canterbury tales. Such a book of dreams as ye never saw'. Yet one, the story of the child slain by the Jews, appears as a popular ballad ('Sir Hugh, or the Jew's Daughter') in versions recorded from the 18th c. Chaucer's *Prioress's Tale*, which tells a variant of this story, is by far the most sophisticated example of the genre in English.

Boyd (1964); Whiteford (1990).

Miroir de Mariage, see *Deschamps.

Mirra, Myrrha, the daughter of Cinyras king of Cyprus fell in love with her father. When he attempted to kill her, she fled, and after nine months' wandering her desperate prayer to be changed into another form was heard. She was transformed into a myrrh tree and wept tears through the bark. From the tree her child Adonis (*Adoun) was born. Chaucer knew the story from *Ovid (*Met.* 10.311 ff.) and alludes to Myrrha's 'bitter tears' in *Troilus and Criseyde* (IV.1135–9).

mirror. Mirrors (which were made of 'polished glass' or polished metal) appear frequently. Thus, *Arcite sees from one that his appearance is altered (I.1399; cf. *Tr* II.404–5). The mirror may be used figuratively: *Troilus 'gan . . . make a mirour of his mynde', in which he sees the figure of Criseyde (*Tr* I.365). It may be used as an image: Chaucer in his gloss to *Boece V m.4 says that the Stoics thought that the soul was 'naked of itself' like a mirror or a clean parchment, on which were impressed images from without; and in *Against *Women Unconstant* (if it is his) the mirror is something on which no permanent impression can be made (8–9). The mirror had significant and symbolic potential. Mirrors like eyes (the mirrors of the soul) may do more than simply reflect, they may have magic or prophetic power: Chaucer gives an excellent example in the magic 'brood mirour of glas' which appears in The *Squire's Tale (V.82; see 132–6, 225–35). (Possibly the idea of the face as the 'mirror' of the soul underlies Pandarus's remark as he looks intently at Criseyde's face: 'on swich a mirour goode grace!', Tr II.266.) But the symbolism of the mirror is not simple. It is associated with beauty (especially female beauty) and is a regular attribute of *Venus and Luxuria (Lechery). Perhaps therefore it is appropriate that the image of the 'mirror of the mind' is used of the lecherous old knight *January who imagines in his mind the figures of the desirable maidens of his neighbourhood 'as whoso tooke a mirour, polisshed bryght' (IV.1582 ff.). In the *Romaunt of the Rose the beautiful Idleness carries a mirror in her hand (567); more unusually, the unstable *Fortune has one (Fort 10). A mirror can encourage self-regard, as in the notorious case of *Narcissus in the Romaunt, for whom the two crystal stones in the spring (*eyes) form 'the mirroure perilous' in which he saw his face and fell in love, with fatal consequences. But, on the other hand, the mirror is a source of knowledge (e.g. Fort 10), and especially self-knowledge. In this positive sense it is commonly used in the titles of medieval works: The Mirror of Man's Salvation, the Speculum Stultorum (Mirror of Fools), the Speculum Historiale (*Vincent of Beauvais's '*Estoryal Myrour', LGW G 307), etc. 'Mirror' in ME may mean 'example', 'exemplar', or 'paragon'. Thus the virtuous *Custance is described as 'mirrour of alle curteisye' (II.166; see also V.1454; BD 973–4).

Moder, mother (of an astrolabe; L. mater). The 'thikkest plate', as Chaucer describes it in A Treatise of the *Astrolabe, that has a concavity ('hir wombe') that holds the plates of horizons and the rete. The back of the mother carries a calendar scale, a shadow square, and often other ancillary scales. (See also *clymat, *Kalendere, *riet.)

[JDN]

moderation, see 'mesure'.

modernizations and translations of Chaucer (as against *imitations) have been common since the time of *Dryden. They begin in the period when the difficulties of Chaucer's language (often commented on) had for ordinary readers become acute. About 1630 one 'J.S.', apparently Jonathan Sidnam, produced a verse paraphrase of the first three books of *Troilus and Criseyde for those 'who either cannot, or will not, take the pains to understand the excellent author's far more exquisite and significant expressions though now grown obsolete and out of use'.

Dryden's versions of The *Knight's Tale, The *Nun's Priest's Tale and The *Wife of Bath's Tale remain the most ambitious and, in purely literary terms, the most successful. Dryden caught well the verve and the zest of Chaucer's narrative, and produced a translation that is never slavish but confident and eloquent. Thus, he opens his 'Palamon and Arcite':

> In days of old, there liv'd, of mighty fame,
> A valiant prince, and Theseus was his name:
> A chief, who more in feats of arms excell'd,
> The rising nor the setting sun beheld.
> Of Athens he was lord; much land he won,
> And added foreign countries to his crown

He will expand, or paraphrase freely, and will bring allusions up to date. Sometimes his 'polishing' of the 'rough diamond' (as he calls Chaucer) means the loss of the very characteristic sudden changes of register. The description of the temple of Mars (which he turns into resonant verse) contains, for instance, among the scenes of violence and mischance, 'the sowe freten [devour] the child right in the cradel; | The cook yscalded, for al his longe ladel'. The horror of the first line is rather softened, and the humble cook is given a more epic end: 'the newborn babe by nurses overlaid; | And the cook caught within the raging fire he made'. As the epic quality of this tale is impressively realized, so Dryden shows himself to be at ease with the mock-heroic qualities of The Nun's Priest's Tale.

A few years after Dryden, the young *Pope wrote (c.1704) two modernizations: 'January and May; or, the Merchant's Tale' and 'The Wife of Bath her Prologue' (which begins 'Behold the woes of matrimonial life, | And hear with rev'rence an experienc'd wife!'). The weaknesses of these are evident: Chaucer's sharp realism is lost (when May and January are in bed together 'the lumpish husband snor'd away the night, | Till coughs awak'd him near the morning light'), as is his directness in describing sexual experience. But at their best they show wit and liveliness.

A more distinguished translator is *Wordsworth, whose interest in and knowledge of Chaucer is often underestimated. His versions, notably that of The *Prioress's Tale remain close to Chaucer's text, and show a remarkable sensitivity to his language and his lyrical qualities. He is in many ways at the opposite pole of 'translation' from Dryden: he says that in his rendering of the Prioress 'no further deviation from the original has been made than was necessary for the fluent reading and instant understanding of the author'. The result is a very close rendering which catches the essential simplicity of the language of the tale:

> Among these children was a widow's son,
> A little scholar, scarcely seven years old,
> Who day by day unto this school hath gone,
> And eke, when he the image did behold
> Of Jesu's Mother, as he had been told,
> This child was wont to kneel adown and say
> Ave Marie, as he goeth by the way.

He also modernized a passage from Troilus and Criseyde, including Troilus's despairing lyric: 'O star, of which I lost have all the light'.

Between Dryden and Wordsworth, and into the later 19th c. many minor poets attempted modernizations of Chaucer. Of these Leigh *Hunt (who did part of The Squire's Tale and The *Pardoner's Tale) is the best known to literary historians, but some of the more obscure figures are not without some interest. These include such figures as the Revd Henry Travers (d. 1754, who did versions of the Shipman and the Reeve), Mrs Elizabeth Cooper, George Ogle, Samuel Cobb (a teacher at Christ's Hospital who modernized The Miller's Tale for Ogle's collection), Charles Cowden Clarke, and others. Chaucer's 'indelicacy' sometimes produces arch or evasive translations, but by no means always. An anonymous translation of The Miller's Tale in 1791 which is exceptional in offering a forthright defence against the charge of indelicacy ('it may shock, at

first sight; but on consideration, will be found not a whit more injurious to morality, than the customary vein of luscious phraseology and description, which abounds among our modern poets') shows an evident enjoyment of some of its scenes: Nicholas

> with this gay wife in wanton dalliance toy'd:
> They kiss'd, caress'd—the mounting blood
>   grew warm —
> Beneath her stays he thrust his letcherous arm —
> Fast round her supple loins one hand he prest,
> And with the other grasp'd her heaving breast . . .

and later '. . . Absolom, before he smoak'd the jest, | Ev'n on her bum a luscious kiss imprest'. But The Canterbury Tales of the Reverend William Lipscomb (1795), which contains most of the tales (except the Parson's which is too 'dry and unentertaining'), omits the tales of the Miller and the Reeve. Careful 'editing' is also a characteristic of 19th-c. children's versions.

A very interesting 19th-c. collection is The Poems of Chaucer Modernized of 1841 (see *Wordsworth), with an introduction by R. H. Horne, who provided three of the pieces. Richard Henry Horne or Richard Hengist Horne as he was later known (he had apparently taken the name from a Mr Hengist whom he met in the Australian bush) was a colourful character as well as a voluminous writer. Among other youthful adventures he had apparently served in the Mexican navy and had a narrow escape from a shark in the bay of Vera Cruz. He gives a critical account of earlier modernizations: 'Dryden's version of the "Knight's Tale" would be most appropriately read by the towering shade of one of Virgil's heroes, walking up and down a battlement and waving a long gleaming spear to the roll and sweep of his sonorous numbers'; Pope by divesting the licentious humour of its quaintness and obscurity makes it 'yet more licentious in proportion to the fine touches of skill with which it is brought into the light'. He complains (rightly) of the way Samuel Cobb turned Absolon playing Herod upon a scaffold high into 'Sometimes he scaramouch'd it all on hie, | And harlequin'd it with activity'. But Wordsworth's Prioress's Tale is praised for 'the severe poetical fidelity of its execution'. Horne says that there are two extremes in

335

the practice of modernizing Chaucer. On the one hand the view that the spirit rather than the letter should be preserved may lead to rewriting everything thought to be obsolete. On the other, a more reverent attitude to the letter will insist that 'all the substantial material and various rhythm of Chaucer should be adopted as far as possible; his obsolete phrases, words, terminations, and grammatical construction, translated, modernized, and humoured, to the best of the writer's ability'. He thinks that the best course lies between the extremes, but leaning to the latter.

Subsequent modernizations have usually been practical and often literal, producing a 'severe fidelity' less poetical than Wordsworth's. Of the long list of 20th-c. attempts, from those of Skeat (1904–6) onwards, the version of the Canterbury Tales by Nevill Coghill (1951) is still the best known in Britain. This is a close and flowing translation (significantly, like his translation of *Troilus* (1961), having its origin in radio readings), which imitates the liveliness of Chaucer's narratives. Comic and slapstick scenes are treated with particular verve ('. . . Absalon, so fortune framed the farce, | Put up his mouth and kissed her naked arse | Most savorously . . .'), though solemn or lyrical passages do not match Dryden or Wordsworth:

> Among these children was a widow's son,
> A little chorister of seven years old,
> And day by day to school he used to run
> And had the custom (for he had been told
> To do so) should he happen to behold
> An image of Christ's mother, to kneel and say
> *Hail Mary* as he went upon his way.

The introduction sets out clearly the many problems confronting a translator of Chaucer, and his own aims: to lose as little of Chaucer's meaning as possible, to follow his 'tone of voice' as far as possible.

Another smaller category of translations deserves a mention. The first three books of *Troilus* were translated into Latin in the 17th c. by Sir Francis *Kynaston, and from the 19th c. various Chaucerian works have been translated into other languages, including German, French, Italian, and Polish. But Chaucer has never been 'exported' through translations as thoroughly as Shakespeare.

Hammond (1908), 220–33; B. Bowden (1991).

Moyses, Moses, the Old Testament leader of the children of Israel, is twice mentioned by the *Parson (X.195, 355). Events from his well-known story are also alluded to: he fasted forty days and forty nights before God spoke with him on Mt. Sinai (III.1885–7; Exod. 34:28); he saw a burning bush which remained miraculously unconsumed (Exod. 3:2), commonly taken as a figure of the Virgin Mary (*Marie; VII.468, *ABC 89–94). Because he was a figure of spiritual power, surrounded by supernatural events and 'learned in the wisdom of the Egyptians' (Exod. 7:10–11, Acts 7:22), he became in medieval legend a notable magician who made a ring of memory and a ring of oblivion: this is alluded to in The *Squire's Tale (V.250).

Mone, Moone, Moon. The Moon occupies the nearest sphere to the Earth, in simple Aristotleian *cosmology. Astrologically the Moon is feminine, cold and moist, signifies childhood, and has much to do with matters relating to water. There exist, however, long catalogues of the Moon's influence in different places in the Zodiac, and in different aspects with other planets. The Moon's *domicile is Cancer; her exaltation is in Taurus and her dejection in Scorpio.

The word 'Moone' is used in The *Knight's Tale of a painted Moon under Dyane's feet, one that was said to be waxing, but that would soon wane. It is used in the phrase 'Moone's mansions', the lunar *mansions. Except in his scientific writings, and his reference (in the *General Prologue to The *Canterbury Tales) to the Shipman's lunar (tidal) calculation, Chaucer seldom used the word of the Moon itself. There are examples in The *Miller's Tale and The *Legend of Good Women, but he preferred to raid the language of mythology for alternatives: *Cynthea, *Dyane, *Latona, *Lucina. He used the Latin *Luna for silver.

In Chaucer's A Treatise of the *Astrolabe, stellar, solar lunar, and planetary positions are either accepted as given or are all derived from observation in more or less the same way, regardless of any theory of their movement. The Moon thus requires little by way of special treatment. Chaucer makes it clear that he was anxious to have accurate values for its position—which changes rapidly, of course. He shows an awareness of the need to take the Moon's *latitude into account, and criticizes common treatises on the astrolabe for failing to do so. In the *Equatorie, which is concerned with the calculation of longitudes and (lunar) latitudes from a prior theory, the Moon occupies a more important place. It differs from the planets in that (in the Ptolemaic theory) it moves around its *epicycle in the opposite sense to that of the epicycle on the *deferent; and the treatment of the *equant centre is also different, for that of the Moon rotates, whereas those of the planets (other than Mercury) are fixed. Chaucer incorporates in his equatorium a subsidiary instrument for determining the Moon's ecliptic latitude. (See also *astrology and astronomy; *exaltacio(u)n; *scorpio; *taur.)   [JDN]

Monesteo, Mnestheus, son of Priam and Hecuba (*Tr* IV.51).

money is of great importance in Chaucer's narratives. There are many allusions to coins and currency. By modern standards medieval coins were light and rather insubstantial, but they were made of gold or silver or 'billon' (silver mixed with a baser metal). The merchant Marco *Polo, who takes a great interest in currency, describes the paper money used in the realms of the great Khan, but for Western Europe that was still an exotic wonder. There were two types of money: the notional 'money of account' used for exchange (like the English or French pound, consisting of 20 shillings made up of 12 pennies), and the actual local coinage. The relationship between them fluctuated. Because of the fluctuation in exchange rates merchants had to compile elaborate and detailed lists. Coins made of good metals were often accepted internationally.

It is impossible to translate medieval currency accurately into modern equivalents. As a rough guide it has been estimated that in 14th-c. England a few of the highest nobility had annual incomes from land of about £3,000, whereas the majority of knights made only about £60. A knight in the king's army was paid 2 shillings a day, which was quite high, but out of it he had to support a page and/or a valet and maintain two or three horses. In 1351 the Statute of Labourers tried to fix the maximum yearly wage of 10 shillings for a skilled labourer (e.g. a ploughman), but this was more often than not exceeded.

Chaucer mentions the coins most frequently found in his day. His *peny* (pl. *pens*) is the English silver penny, which was a 'money of account', always worth 1/240th of a pound, although its silver content varied, and a basic coin. Silver pennies were called *sterlynges* (VI.907; *HF* 1315); they circulated widely in France and northern Europe. In Chaucer the penny is extremely common, sometimes in formulaic expressions ('for peny ne for pound', VIII.707), sometimes synonymous with 'money'. He also refers (III.1749) to 'a Goddes halfpeny, or a masse peny', i.e. a halfpenny given as alms, or a penny offered at mass. Besides the *halfpeny* there is the *ferthyng* (I.255), a small coin worth 1/4 of a penny. The *grote* or groat ('pens or elles grotes', VI.376, etc.) is worth 4 pennies. The *pound* (orig. a unit of weight) corresponded to 240 pennies (20 shillings of 12 pennies each) of the local coin. The *mark* (an old Germanic unit of weight) is also a money of account, worth in England 13s. 4d. or two-thirds of a pound. The Pardoner prides himself on having made 'an hundred mark' in his career (VI.390; cf. also *CYT*, VIII.1026–30). The *noble* (VI.907, etc.) was an English gold coin introduced by Edward III in 1344; it was worth 6s. 8d. (half a mark).

The *floryn* (I.2088) or florin was a gold coin first minted in *Florence in 1252, and continuously produced in the same weight and design until 1533. Initially it was worth £1 in local money of account, but the inflation of silver and billon coinage increased its value considerably. It was in widespread use because of the dealings of the Florentine merchants and bankers, and in Chaucer's time it had become the most generally accepted international means of exchange. It was imitated in other countries so that there were German or Flemish 'florins'. It is not clear whether the *floryns* which appear so spectacularly in the heap of 'floryns fyne of gold ycoyned rounde' in The *Pardoner's Tale* (VI.770 ff.) are of Florentine or Flemish origin.

Among other coins mentioned are the *frankes* which appear prominently in The Shipman's Tale (VII.181, etc.), but only there. The franc was a French gold coin, and therefore appropriate to the setting of the tale. It was worth approximately half an English noble (3s. 4d.). The she(e)ld is another French gold coin, the escu or écu, or its Flemish equivalent (24 silver Flemish groats; 25d. sterling). It was a 'money of account' used in currency exchange (e.g. by the *Merchant, I.278). The merchant in The Shipman's Tale spends 20,000 'shields' on credit in Bruges (VII.329–31). The ducat is associated with Venice (*Venyse), HF 1348. The jane (yet another coin taking its name from its place of origin) is a Genoese coin worth a halfpenny. Hence the expression 'deere ynough a jane!' (expensive enough at a halfpenny, IV.999) means 'without value'. Sir Thopas's robe 'coste many a jane' (VII.735). Even humbler is the myte, originally a Flemish coin of very small value, frequently and proverbially used to mean a thing of little or no value, the equivalent of 'not worth a bean'. The lussheburghes referred to slightingly by the *Host (VII.1962) are imported coins of inferior metal from Luxemburg.

Even this list does not fully suggest the importance of the role of money in Chaucer. In The *Canterbury Tales the realism of his writing ensures that it is seen to be part of the texture of life. People are continually buying and selling, borrowing, getting into debt (I.280; VIII.734, etc.). Proverbs and colloquial phrases reinforce this impression: (of merchants) 'money is their plough' (VII.288); the image of the coin which looks beautiful but the gold is so mixed with brass that it will break (IV.1167–9); or more cynically, the saying of Solomon (Eccles. 10:19), 'alle thynges obeyen to moneye' (VII.1550). Even the financial arrangements for the game of storytelling have their place (I.803–6, 815, 834). Of all the Tales, The *Shipman's Tale stands out for the role it assigns to money and financial dealings (the loan which is central to the plot, for instance) and for the close association it makes between sex and money.

The dangers of money and its misuse and the wickedness of covetousness and avarice are rehearsed by a chorus of moralists using material both classical and Christian. The old woman in The *Wife of Bath's Tale quotes Seneca (*Senec) and *Juvenal: 'glad poverte is an honest thyng'; the poor man as he goes by the way can sing 'bifore the theves' (III.1183, 1192–4). The covetous, like Midas (*Myda) and *Crassus, are hostile to love and its generous instincts (Tr III.1373 ff.). The

avaricious man, says the *Parson, 'dooth moore observance in kepynge of his tresor than he dooth to the service of Jhesu Crist': he is simply an idolater, 'for certes, every floryn in his cofre is his mawmet [idol]' (X.747–9). The *Prioress remarks sharply that a ghetto is maintained by a lord 'for foule usure and lucre of vileynye' (i.e. excessive profits, VII.490–1).

In spite of this a good number of the pilgrims and the characters in the stories they tell are keenly, and sometimes excessively interested in money. Often the satire is that traditionally levelled at their '*estates': the *Physician who 'loved gold in special', the Merchant or *Man of Law with their exaggerated professional interest in making money. Lesser businessmen feather their nests with varying degrees of dishonesty, being sometimes sharp, like the *Manciple, sometimes clever, like the *Reeve, or straightforwardly dishonest like the *Miller, another traditional trait found in a much more flagrant form in the Cambridge miller described by the Reeve, who 'therbiforn . . . stal but curteisly, | But now he was a theef outrageously' (I.3996–7).

The clerical figures are as bad, if not worse. In sharp contrast to the poor Parson, who 'koude in lytel thyng have suffisaunce', and the otherworldly *Clerk, who 'had but litel gold in cofre', stand those who are a little more than comfortably off, like the *Monk, who would spare no cost for greyhounds, those that have a nose for money (the *Friar, that distinguished beggar, whose manner became courteous and humble 'ther as profit sholde arise'), and those who are simply corrupt (the *Pardoner and the *Summoner). The Pardoner makes money by selling indulgences and fake relics, and preaches 'to wynne silver'. Later, in his Prologue, he analyses his techniques of salesmanship, how his relics are efficacious (if one offers 'pens or elles grotes', VI.376) and how he preaches to encourage his congregation 'to yeven hir pens, and namely [especially] unto me', then tells a tale which offers the most vivid moral emblem of the destructive power of gold, and then tries to make money from his fellow pilgrims by encouraging them to buy his relics and pardons—'so that ye offren, alwey newe and newe, | Nobles or pens, whiche that be goode and trewe' (929–30). The Summoner, it is clear, takes bribes, and has a cynical view of his ecclesiastical functions ('Purs is the ercedekenes helle'). This traditional satire is later given dramatic form by the Friar, an expert money-raiser, in his account of the extortion practised by a summoner who 'knew of briberyes mo | Than possible is to telle in yeres two' (III.1367–8). One of the many comic moments turns on the repetition of the exact sum he is determined to extract from the old woman (III.1598–607); '"pay anon—lat se—| twelf pens to me, and I wol thee acquite" . . . "yif me twelf pens, I may no lenger tarye" . . . "Twelf pens!" . . . "Now, lady Seinte Marie . . . Ne have I nat twelf pens withinne myn hoold."' (See also *Lumbardes*.)

Monk, The. The description of the Monk (I.165–207, placed between those of the *Prioress and the *Friar) is one of the most memorable satiric portraits in the *General Prologue*. It uses in a masterly way the traditional topics of anti-monastic *estates satire: e.g. that monks, who are supposed to be leading an ascetic life of prayer and labour, are lazy, worldly, fond of good food and rich clothing, of hunting, and of travelling about outside their monasteries. The technique is one of suggestion rather than denunciation. The details of his supple boots, his well-fed look and his delight in a roasted swan suggest his un-ascetic style of life. And by apparently uniting his point of view with that of the monk ('and I seyde his opinion was good') Chaucer makes the monk reveal himself unconsciously as he self-approvingly demonstrates the traditional vices, and ignores the old strict rule. The way that the 'description' slides into the Monk's own speech ('How shal the world be served? | Lat *Austyn have his swynk [work] to hym reserved!') gives a dramatic sense of an individual. Much later (VII.2792) he is given a name: 'Daun Piers'. In The *Shipman's Tale there is another monk, Daun John, who is introduced with considerable irony, a 'gentil monk', who proves to be splendidly lustful.

Even if they did not all ride around the countryside in the manner of Daun Piers, monks would have still been prominent in Chaucer's England. Their great abbeys were impressive monuments (as can still be seen from the ruined remains at Bury St Edmunds) with rich and extensive estates and fine libraries. The long tradition of monasticism, developing from the ascetic hermits of the desert like St *Antony into the organized communal life associated with the names of St Basil (*Basilie) and St Benedict (*Beneit) had made a remarkable contribution to learning and piety. At various times (especially in the 10th and 12th c.) dissatisfaction with the wealth and worldliness led to movements of reform, and the establishment of new stricter orders such as the Cistercians (founded in 1098 by St Robert of Molesme, and famous for its son St *Bernard) or the Carthusians (founded in 1084 by St Bruno). In the high Middle Ages the monks and their privileges were challenged by the new mendicant orders of *friars. Chaucer seems to be critical of the failings of monks rather than of the institution itself (as followers of *Wyclif were)—and he spent his last days close to the monks of Westminster. It is difficult to assess how accurate an historical picture the extensive anti-monastic satire of the later Middle Ages presents. There certainly was corruption, and some cause for the criticism and discontent.

Rv 806–7; Cooper (1989), 39–40; Mann (1973), 17–37.

Monk's Tale, The (1776 lines in the eight-line stanza (*ababbcbc*) used in the *ABC*) follows *Melibee* in Fragment VII. It begins with a Prologue in couplets in which the *Host first gives an entertaining disquisition on the difference between his wife and *Prudence, and then turns to the Monk for a story. He expresses his admiration for him in terms which recall the more un-monkly characteristics singled out in the *General Prologue*, lamenting that he has entered a religious order rather than using his fine physique in engendering ('religioun hath take up al the corn | Of tredyng, and we borel [lay] men been shrympes'—probably a satirical reference to the supposed sexual prowess of clerics). The Monk says that he will tell 'a tale, or two, or three', the life of St *Edward, or else some tragedies, of which, he says meaningfully, 'I have an hundred in my celle'. After giving a definition of *tragedy, and announcing that he will not tell the stories in order, but 'tellen hem som bifore and som bihynde', he launches in.

He will 'biwaille in manere of tragedie | The harm of hem that stoode in heigh degree, | And fillen so that ther nas no remedie | To brynge hem out of hir adversitee'. No one can withstand *Fortune: let no man trust in 'blynd prosperitee'. Seventeen 'tragedies', varying in length from one stanza to sixteen, follow (for the stories see entries under individual names): *Lucifer; *Adam; Samson (*Sampsoun); Hercules (*Ercules); Nebuchadnezzar (*Nabugodonosor); *Balthasar; Zenobia (*Cenobia); Pedro of Castile (*Petro (1)); Pierre de Lusignan (*Petro (2)); Bernabò Visconti (*Barnabo Viscounte); Ugolino of Pisa (*Hugelyn); *Nero; Holofernes (*Oloferne); *Antiochus; Alexander (*Alisaundre); *Julius Caesar; and Croesus (*Cresus). (The order here is that of most modern editions, following that of the majority of the MSS: some very good MSS, like *Ellesmere and *Hengwrt place the so-called 'modern instances'—Pedro of Castile d. 1369, Pierre de Lusignan d. 1369, Bernabò Visconti d. 1385, Ugolino d. 1289—at the end rather than between Zenobia and Nero.) The tale of Croesus comes to a fine climax with his death because of Fortune, who will always 'assaille | With unwar strook the regnes that been proude; For whan men trusteth hire, thanne wol she faille, | And covere hire brighte face with a clowde'. At this point the *Knight intervenes, saying that 'litel hevynesse | Is right ynough to muche folk', and that it is much more pleasing to hear stories which portray the rise of those that have been in 'poor estate'. This is the opening of the Prologue to The *Nun's Priest's Tale.

It is often assumed that The Monk's Tale is an early work which was in existence before The Canterbury Tales, except for the four 'modern instances' which were added later. It would then be an early experiment with a collection of short tales (like The *Legend of Good Women, which also has 'pitous' stories). However, there is no clear evidence for this, and, whenever it was written, it seems to have been fitted to its teller and fitted neatly in its place before The Nun's Priest's Tale.

The general plan seems to come from *Boccaccio's De casibus virorum illustrium (On the Falls of Famous Men), and it establishes a pattern which appears in the 15th c. in *Lydgate's Fall of Princes and in the 16th-c. Mirror for Magistrates. The sources are very varied, including *Dante (Ugolino), Boccaccio—both the De casibus and the De claris mulieribus (On Famous Women—for Zenobia), Boethius (*Boece), *Ovid, *Vincent of Beauvais, the Roman de la Rose, and the Bible. It seems likely that for the stories ot the two Peters and Bernabò Visconti Chaucer drew on his own knowledge.

We are clearly meant to be relieved by the interruption of this succession of tragedies, and to smile when the Host joins in ('he spak how Fortune covered with a clowde | I noot nevere what'), but the comic detachment is quite subtle. It is not the case that Chaucer wrote a series of bad and dull stories to demonstrate the Monk's inadequacies. It is too easy to underestimate The Monk's Tale. In fact, the story of Ugolino is excellently told, and a number of the others are good brief examples of 'pitous tales', and many have moments of lyrical eloquence. Even those very short items which seem almost bare chronicle entries or the simplest kind of *exempla may well be deliberately designed to achieve a kind of detachment and to contribute to an underlying comic feeling of boredom by highlighting the cryptic style imposed by the limitations of an apparently endless catalogue. It is largely the relentless march of 'tragedies', the repeated rhetorical laments, and the unremitting gloom of the view of the world they suggest which becomes overwhelming and eventually demands some kind of comic release. It is intensified by the simplicity of the Monk's intellectual framework: the repeated demonstration of the arbitrariness of the goddess Fortune suggests a world subject to a grim determinism. This, and other aspects of the Tale, are picked up and treated with hilarious and generous comedy in the following tale, that of the Nun's Priest.

(ed.) Rv 240–53; S&A 615–44 [409–47]; Cooper (1989), 323–37; Pearsall (1985), 279–85.

months and seasons. Chaucer's divisions of the year were in part informal, and in part those of the astronomer. Important to him as a poet of the formal scheme were the moments of the Sun's entry into the signs of the Zodiac, four of which are cardinal points in the Sun's annual motion: our spring and autumn begin at the equinoxes, and our summer and winter at the solstices. He used the names for the four seasons loosely: *lente was ambiguous as between the Church's Lent and (the common usage) spring; somer and winter are in A Treatise on the *Astrolabe attached by name to the solstices, but not in definitions of the kind now adopted. In fact Chaucer's *somer* and *somer-sesoun* in **Boece* are used loosely to cover times that, on our definition, are within spring and even early autumn; but *autumpne* is used there too for the harvest period.

His scheme of months was of course a precise one, even though it had slipped out of key with its creators' intentions. Chaucer was a poet of the calendar. His affections were drawn towards the spring and summer seasons in general, but to the months of March, April, and May more particularly, and May above all. A favourite description, offered especially of the young, was 'fressh as is the month of May' (the *Squire); thus '*May' was a name chosen for the young wife of *Januarie in **The Merchant's Tale*. Indeed, Chaucer's description of their behaviour, and of *Damian's, probably owed something to a type of illustration used to ornament ecclesiastical calendars of the day.

It is clear that many dates within the months had a special attraction for him: the most notorious is 3 May, a day of near-disaster in *The *Nun's Priest's Tale* but also used elsewhere. The poet's fascination with the calendar did not stop at the months and days: he took precise astronomical information from the calendars of John *Somer and Nicholas of Lynn (see *Lenne), and made serious structural use of it.

Like virtually all contemporary astronomers, Chaucer accepted the year beginning at 1 January (rather than 25 March, or any other civil convention). Typical manuscript spellings for the months were, in addition to the Latin forms: *Januarie, Februarie, March, Aprill, May, Juyn, Juyll, August, Septembre, Octobre, Novembre, Decembre*. His calendar was of course Julian, and in his lifetime the vernal equinox occurred in the neighbourhood of 12 March, nine days removed from ours. This presented a problem for those such as *Grosseteste, *Bacon, and Somer, who wished to reform the calendar. Their main concern was a different one: it was that Easter was being calculated wrongly. (See also *Equinoxiall; *hed(e); *Kalendere; *signe; *solsticioun; *weather; *yer(e); *Zodiak.)

[JDN]

MORE, SIR THOMAS (1478–1535). Educated as a lawyer, More entered the service of Henry VIII in 1517 and became Speaker of the House of Commons in 1523 and Chancellor of England in 1529, a post he resigned in May 1532. He remained loyal to Katherine of Aragon throughout Henry's attempts to divorce her, and on his persistent refusal to take an oath that involved denial of papal supremacy and approval of that divorce he was imprisoned, accused of high treason, and executed. Friend of numerous humanists, including Erasmus, he was the author of extensive writings on religious and social questions (notably *Utopia*) and polemical tracts against the religious reformers and their ideas. More refers to Chaucer in his discussion of images in *A Dialogue concerning Heresies*, particularly alluding to the Pardoner's prologue (VI.351). [AH]

(ed.) Lawler, Marchadour and Marius (1981), i. 98, 217.

MORELL, THOMAS (1703–84) of Turnham Green, one of Chaucer's earlier 18th-c. editors, was a cleric, a classical scholar, and an antiquarian. He was also a musician and a friend of Handel, for whom he wrote the libretti of a number of oratorios (it is to Morell that we owe 'See the conquering hero comes'). He seems to have been a merry soul, 'who loved a jest, told a good story, and sang a good song', was 'careless of his own interests', 'dressed ill', and 'always poor and in debt' (*DNB*). His edition of *The Canterbury Tales* (1737) contains only the **General Prologue* and *The *Knight's Tale* (in ME, with modernized versions by Dryden and others), but it is the first attempt at a critical text of Chaucer. Morell (who believed, like *Tyrwhitt, that Chaucer's metre was not 'lame') says that he proposes to restore 'him to his own true shape, and not by servilely following any one particular MS, but by collating several of the best authority'.

CH i. 187–97.

Morpheus, the god of sleep, who figures prominently in the earlier part of *The *Book of the Duchess* (136 ff.) was in antiquity the god of *dreams (dreams were the daughters of Night). Ovid (whom Chaucer is following) says that he was particularly skilled in imitating the human shape of men (*Met.* 11). In Chaucer he 'takes up' the drowned body of Ceyx (*Seys) and bears it to his wife.

MORRIS, WILLIAM (1834–96), artist, poet, storyteller, and Socialist activist, was one of the leading, and most attractive figures of Victorian medievalism. Educated at Marlborough School and Exeter College, Oxford, he was seized with a passion for the Middle Ages, and his intense delight in the art, craft, and literature of the period is evident throughout his career. Malory and the Arthurian legends and Froissart are the inspiration for much of his early verse; later, he found a spiritual affinity with the heroic qualities of the Icelandic sagas. Although he admired and liked Chaucer, there is little sign of any significant direct influence. The plan of his poem *The Earthly Paradise* (1868–70), with a prologue and twenty-four tales, in Chaucerian metres, is clearly modelled on *The Canterbury Tales*, but the tales do not use Chaucerian material, the narrators are not differentiated, and the framework remains very static. A very brief critical mention of Chaucer in 'Signs of Change' (1888) notes that his muse is 'kindly and human', and that he created a 'sunny world'. Morris's admiration for 14th-c. England, in particular its craftsmanship and its radical ideas, infuses his Utopian visions *A Dream of John Ball* (1888) and *News from Nowhere* (1890). His greatest contribution to the appreciation of Chaucer was the conception and the making of the famous 'Kelmscott Chaucer' which was completed just before his death, in 1896, and remains one of the most beautiful books of the period (see ***illustrations**, Figs. 12, 13).

CH ii.226–7.

Mot(e), motus, motus (L. *motus*), motion; in the sense of an angular distance moved (rather than the act of moving) with respect to a reference point, usually the head of Aries. In **Equatorie of the Planetis*, when the motus is based on an average angular velocity (it may, for example, be a mean motus per day multiplied by an appropriate number of days) it is a 'mean mot'; and when this is corrected by the incorporation of equations it is called a true motus, a 'verrey mot'. (See also ***astrology and astronomy**; ***equacio(u)n**; ***first moeving**; ***hed(e)**.)   [JDN]

Mum and the Sothsegger, an editorial title given to two fragments of satirical alliterative poetry influenced by Langland's *Piers Plowman*, each of which is found in a single manuscript. The first, known to early critics as *Richard the Redeless*, deals with contemporary abuses at the court of *Richard II in the late 1380s and 1390s, though parts of it, at least, may originate after Richard's deposition; the second, to which the title *Mum and the Sothsegger* should probably be limited, was written in the reign of *Henry IV, almost certainly after 1406; both share the view that an important cause of corruption is the reluctance of subjects to tell the ruler the unvarnished truth. The two fragments are linked by John *Bale, who in his *Index Britanniae Scriptorum* gives the title of the second with the incipit of the first; doubt remains concerning the precise relation, if any, of the two fragments.   [AH]

(ed.) Day and Steele (1936); Barr (1993).

Muses, in ancient mythology the nine daughters of Mnemosyne or *Memory, who were associated with the different arts, usually as follows: Calliope (epic poetry), Clio (history), Euterpe (flute-playing), Melpomene (tragedy), Terpsichore (dancing), Erato (playing the lyre), Polyhymnia (sacred song), Urania (astronomy), Thalia (comedy). (Chaucer refers to three by name; see *Caliope, *Cleo, *Polymya.) They were venerated especially at Pieria near Mt. Olympus in Thessaly, their supposed dwelling-place (hence the name Pierian)—Chaucer refers (II.92) to the 'Muses that men clepe *Pierides—and at Mt. Helicon (*Elicon) in Boeotia, and Mt. Parnassus (*Pernaso).

The early Christian poets sometimes rejected the Muses in favour of strictly biblical poetics, but they return in the more humanistic poetry of the Carolingian period and remain prominent in learned poetry for centuries as a powerful metaphor for poetic inspiration. *Boccaccio associates their singing with the eloquence that brings memory and fame. For *Dante they are 'our nurses', 'most holy virgins', who nourish poets with their sweet milk (*Paradiso* 23.55–8).

They appear in Chaucer's translation of Boethius (*Boece) (where the 'poetical Muses' are firmly driven away by Lady Philosophy) and in a number of references, e.g. to their singing ('the songes that the Muses songe', IV.1735). He will sometimes call upon them for help in composition. Thus at the beginning of the second book of *The *House of Fame* invokes them: 'ye, me to endite and ryme | Helpeth, that on Parnaso duelle . . . O Thought, that wrot al that I mette [dreamed]' (520–3), echoing both Boccaccio and Dante (*Inf.* 2.7–9—'O Muses, O lofty genius, aid me . . . O memory [*mente*]' that noted what I saw). Similarly in **Troilus and Criseyde* Clio is called upon to be 'my Muse' (II.9). And at the end of the third book he uses the traditional rhetorical technique of a special invocation of the muses at a climactic moment (cf. e.g. *Inferno* 32.10–12): 'yee sustren nyne ek, that by Elicone | In hil Pernaso listen for t'abide' (III.1809–10). The sorrowful fourth book begins with an invocation to the *Furies, rather than to the Muses, perhaps an echo of another traditional device, the 'rejection' of the Muses in favour of some other source of inspiration (at the beginning of the *Filostrato*, for example, Boccaccio gives his lady this role: 'thou art my Jove, thou art my Apollo, thou art my muse'). In the invocations in the religious tales of the *Prioress and the *Second Nun the Virgin Mary takes the place of the Muse.

Curtius (1953), 228–46.

music and musical instruments. The Middle Ages enjoyed a rich and varied musical tradition. Theoretical writing on music went back to the treatise *De musica* of Boethius and earlier. In quite non-technical contexts we may find echoes of the three types of music distinguished by him: *musica mundana* (the music of the universe; the perfect mathematical harmonies of the music of the spheres); *musica humana* (the harmony within the microcosm of man, of body and soul, of the equilibrium of the 'temperament', of sense and reason); and *musica instrumentalis* (the music made by men, which should imitate the harmony and proportion of the music of the universe). By Chaucer's time the music made by men, for both sacred and secular use, was developed and complex. There was the music of the Church—chanted plainsong, polyphonic music for several voices, traditional sung forms like the hymn or the sequence, etc.; the music of courtly entertainment—for dancing or for various sung forms like the lay, the complaint, or the virelay (see *lyrics). There was also a vast body of popular music and

song, often known only from passing allusions (by preaching friars and moralists as well as more literary men or from the illustrations in manuscript margins (where we see humble folk dancing ringdances or *caroles, shepherds with their bagpipes and flutes, etc.). Music was played by ensembles and by individuals, by professionals and by amateurs. In the 14th c. it was France rather than England (which enjoyed a renaissance in the following century) that was the centre of the most impressive developments in sophisticated music. It was the period of *Guillaume de Machaut and the 'Ars Nova' (or 'new art' of notation and its developments by 14th-c. composers).

Chaucer makes numerous references to music, which while they suggest the variety and the richness of contemporary musical life, do not reveal the extent of his technical knowledge or skill. He alludes to the well-known music of the spheres: Scipio heard the melody that comes from the nine spheres, 'that welle is of musik and melodye | In this world here, and cause of armonye' (*PF* 60–3); and similarly the spirit of Troilus going up through the spheres hears 'armonye | With sownes ful of hevenyssh melodie' (*Tr* V.1812–13). There is not much evident interest in musical theory. There is one reference to Boethius in *The Nun's Priest's Tale*, when the fox flattering Chauntecleer praises his heavenly voice, saying 'ye han in musyk moore feelynge | Than hadde Boece, or any that kan synge' (VII.3293–5)—since Boethius's interest seems to have been exclusively theoretical this is probably ironic. There are reflections of the celestial harmony in the way the birds 'maken melodye' (I.9) or sing 'with voys of aungel in here armonye' (*PF* 190–1). That the melancholy Troilus cannot bear to hear music (V.459–62) and that the sound of 'song or instrument' makes the sorrowful Arcite weep (I.1367–8) testify both to the disharmony of 'temperament' that *melancholy produces and to the long-acknowledged emotive power of music.

Some of Chaucer's figurative expressions connected with music and singing, often apparently proverbial or colloquial, show how familiar music must have been to his contemporaries. These include the formulaic 'forth she moot [must], wher-so she wepe or singe' (II.294) or the proverbial association of trumpets with loudness: 'his

voys was as a trompe thonderynge' (I.2174), or colloquial expressions: 'blow the buck's horn' (I.3386),
or 'pipe in an ivy leaf' (*Tr* V.1432), both meaning
'go whistle', 'go off and do what you like'. We
already find 'harping on one string' (*Tr* II.1030).
Pandarus alludes to the proverbial ass who is deaf
to the harp (*Tr* I.729). *Burdoun*, the bass part or
ground melody, must have been familiar enough
for it to be used comically of snoring (I.4165); the
*Summoner's loud 'stif burdoun' which accompan-
ies the *Pardoner's song (I.672–3) may possibly
contain a sexual pun (on *burdoun* = staff).

Behind some expressions perhaps lie allusions
to contemporary uses of music not only to celebrate and to express joy, but to condemn and
mock. *Perkyn, like other disorderly characters,
was sometimes 'lad with revel to Newegate',
accompanied on his way to the prison by minstrels
proclaiming his disgrace, rather like the satirical
procession of the 'charivari' or 'skimmity ride' with
its 'rough music' of pots, pans, horns, pipes, etc.,
well documented in England later. Are these
uses of music implied in 'he rong hem out a
proces [argument] like a belle | Upon hire foo'
(*Tr* II.1615–16; cf. II.804–5), or Criseyde's exclam-
ation, 'O, rolled shal I ben on many a tonge! |
Thoroughout the world my belle shal be ronge!'
(*Tr* V.1061–2), or the taunt launched at *Jason:
'Have at thee, Jason! Now thyn horn is blowe!'
(*LGW* 1383)?

Chaucer makes few allusions to sacred music,
and most of them appear in slightly comic or ironic contexts. However, the '*Alma redemptoris
mater' which the little boy learns at his elementary
school has a serious role in the devotional story
told by the *Prioress, and 'organs' play at St *Cecilia's wedding (VIII.134). Less straightforward, is
*Nicholas's singing of *Angelus ad Virginem, or
the comparison of *Chauntecleer's voice to 'the
murie orgon | On messe-dayes that in the chirche
gon' (VII.2851–2). The detail that the Prioress 'ful
weel . . . soong the service dyvyne, | Entuned in hir
nose ful semely' (I.122–3) may well refer to an
approved method of voice production, yet there
seems a hint of comic incongruity in its selection.

There are many more references to the role of
music in secular society: the friends of *Dorigen
dance and sing in the garden (V.918–19); lyrics and
songs are sung (both in public and in private) by

*Antigone and Troilus and others. In the Pro-
logue to The *Legend of Good Women (G version)
the ladies sing a balade in 'carole-wise' (G 200 ff.).
It seems to be assumed that ladies are skilled in
singing and dancing (see *BD* 848–9; I.2197–202,
etc.). Emily sings as she walks in the garden
(I.1051–5), and the *Wife of Bath recalls that when
she had had some wine she could 'daunce to an
harpe smal, | And synge, ywis, as any nyghtyngale'
(III.457–8). But men sing as fervently, especially if
they are lovers—like the *Squire of the *General
Prologue (I.91, 95), or *Arcite (I.1509–12), or *Aurelius who 'syngeth, daunceth, passynge any man'
(V.929) and composes a variety of lyrics (947–9).

Music regularly accompanies great feasts and
festivals: the king *Cambyuskan (V.266 ff.) is preceded by 'loude mynstralcye' in his procession to
his 'presence chamber', 'ther as they sownen
diverse instrumentz'; at the house of *Sarpedoun
(*Tr* V.442–8) 'delicious' instruments are played
'thorugh wynd or touche of corde' (see also *LGW*
2157, I.2197, etc.). There is music at weddings and
wedding feasts (e.g. II.703–8 or IV.1709 ff., where
there is elaborate 'minstrelsy' with every course),
and on other ceremonial occasions: the Marquis
Walter goes in procession with his retinue and his
minstrels 'with many a soun of sondry melodye'
(IV.267–73); Sir *Thopas summons his minstrels
and tale-tellers to be present at his arming
(VII.845–7).

Music is also found in less formal circumstances. The revellers who haunt stews and taverns in The *Pardoner's Tale 'with harpes, lutes and
gyternes [citterns]' are entertained by dancing
girls, and 'syngeres with harpes' (VI.463 ff.). The
apprentice Perkyn in The *Cook's Tale is fond of
dancing, singing, and 'minstrelsy' (I.4375, 4395).
The *Friar sings 'yeddynges' (songs or ballads) and
plays the harp and the 'rote' (I.236–7, 266). There
are one or two references to what seem to be
well-known popular songs: 'com hider, love, to
me' (I.672) sung by the Pardoner and the Summoner; the unidentified 'Kynges Noote' sung by
Nicholas (I.3217); 'My lief is faren in londe', which
Chauntecleer and Pertelote sing 'in sweete accord'
(VII.2879); and what the *Parson calls this 'newe
Frenshe song', 'Jay tout perdu mon temps et mon
labour' (X.247; see also *Fortune 6–7). (The Parson
takes an austere view of music, remarking that

too great 'curiositee [elaborate performance] of mynstralcie' stirs a man to lechery, X.445.)

Musical references in stories with ancient settings (like Troilus or *The Knight's Tale*, etc.) are normally given a contemporary medieval colour. Aeneas makes songs for Dido (*LGW* 1269 ff.; cf.1100–1); Phoebus is skilled in every 'mynstralcie' (IX.113–18; his instruments are thoroughly medieval, 268). *Proserpina's retinue 'makes melody' in the manner of the medieval *"fayerye' into which they have been transformed (IV.2039–40). Chaucer also alludes to a number of classical and biblical figures associated with music: *Apollo, *Amphion, *Orpheus, Marsyas (*Marcia), *Tubal, and others (a number of them among the group of minstrels, harpers, and musicians who appear in *HF* 1195–259).

A wide variety of musical instruments are mentioned: (string) the *rubible* (I.3331, 4396) a rebeck, an early fiddle with three strings played with a bow; (stringed instruments which were plucked): the *citole* 'cithara' (held by Venus in *KnT* I.1959); the *giterne* 'cithern', an instrument of the guitar kind strung with wire and resembling the *citole* (I.3333, 4396; VI.466; IX.268); the *sautrie* or 'psaltery', resembling the dulcimer, but played by plucking the strings with the fingers or a plectrum (I.296, 3213, 3305; IX.268); the *harpe* (VII.815, etc.); the *rote* perhaps a 'harp-psaltery' of triangular shape (I.236); the *lute* (VI.466, IX.268).

The *simphonye* which accompanies the queen of Faery in *Sir Thopas* (along with 'harpe and pipe' VII.815) is usually thought to be a 'hurdy-gurdy', a kind of mechanical fiddle with the strings sounded by a wheel turned by a handle, not a bow. However, the early use of the word is often vague, and the 'symphony' may be a kind of tabor or drum (*Bartholomew says it is made of hollow tree enclosed in leather and minstrels beat it with sticks: this would certainly fit the context in *Sir Thopas*).

Among the wind instruments are the *baggepipe* played by the *Miller in the *General Prologue* (I.565; cf. I.3927). This was a widespread folk-instrument, and seems sometimes to have retained the ancient associations of wind instruments with passion—though sometimes angels are depicted playing it. The French form *cornemuse* is found in *HF* 1218. Other unspecified

pipes are quite often mentioned (I.2511; VII.815; *HF* 773–5, 1219, etc.). The 'pipes made of grene corn' (*HF* 1224) are simple home-made pipes used by shepherds ('as han thise lytel herde-gromes'). *Shalemyes* (*HF* 1218) are 'shawms', loud reed instruments which were the predecessors of the modern oboe. Smaller shawms would make a piercing sound like the bagpipe (Chaucer links them with *cornemuse*). The *flowte* 'flute' and the *doucet*, a similar wind instrument, are mentioned in the same passage.

The varieties of trumpet (*trompe, beme, clarioun*) are found in martial and ceremonial contexts. In *HF* the players of the three instruments are said to make 'blody soun' (1239–42; cf. I.2511–12); the clarioun is used there also as if by a herald (cf. I.2600) to praise and to dispraise (1573–82). In more humble surroundings, in pursuit of the fox in *The Nun's Priest's Tale* the villagers shout and yell, and 'of bras they broghten bemes, and of box [boxwood], | Of horn, of boon, in whiche they blewe and powped' (VII.3398–9). Elsewhere the *horn* is linked with the trumpet in a description of a marriage feast (II.705). The horn is also associated with hunting (e.g. I.116, 1678). The *liltyng horn* mentioned (in conjunction with flutes) in *HF* (1223) seems to be some kind of trumpet: elsewhere it glosses L. *lituus* 'clarion, trumpet'.

Percussion instruments include the *belle*, the *tabour* (tabor, small drum; III.2268), and the *naker* (kettle-drum; mentioned with other instruments in a martial context, I.2511). Chaucer also refers the *organ*, the oldest of keyboard instruments, which was known both in large versions (the 'great organ' played in church: this kind is probably implied in the comparison with the mighty crowing of Chauntecleer and in small (the 'portative organ' which could be played in processions and courtly entertainments, and the slightly larger 'positive organ').

Carter (1961); Stevens (1986); Wilkins (1995); Winternitz (1967).

Mutability; Mystery Plays. See *Fortune; *drama.

mythography, the representation of ancient myths, and the study of this representation. There was considerable interest in the Middle Ages in the attributes and characteristics of the ancient gods, and in the myths told about them. Early examples are to be found in the works of *Fulgentius, Isidore of Seville (*Ysidre), and 'Albericus of London' (also called 'Mythographus Vaticanus Tertius'), who wrote *c.*1200. Closer to Chaucer's time stand *Boccaccio (*De genealogiis deorum gentilium*, the 'genealogies of the pagan gods') and *Bersuire. The gods had gradually been 'astrologized', and the planets which bore their names had developed 'personalities' from the characteristics of the planets and from the myths about the gods (so that the red and fiery *Mars was thought to be warlike, and the distant, slow-moving *Saturn was perceived as a slow old man). Pictures showed the planetary gods surrounded by their 'children': thus, *Venus's children may be shown as lovers, in a bathhouse, or making music or dancing; Mars, who often rides in a chariot, accompanied by a wolf (see I.2041–8), presides over soldiers, killers and murderers. Chaucer (who seems to have known Bersuire's work) clearly shared the late medieval interest in mythography. It is most evident in his descriptions of Venus in the *Parliament of Fowls* and of Venus, Mars, Diana (*Dyane) and Saturn in The *Knight's Tale*.

Kolve (1984); Panofsky (1939); Seznec (1953); Tuycross (1972).

N

Nabal, the husband of *Abigail (1 Sam. 25) (IV.1370, VII.1100).

NABUGODONOSOR, Nebuchadnezzar, king of Babylon (c.605–652 BC). His story (based on Dan. 1–5) is told in The *Monk's Tale (VII.2143–82). Twice conqueror of Jerusalem, he carried off the vessels of the temple, and oppressed the children of Israel. His prophetic *dreams were interpreted by *Daniel. He set up a great statue of gold to be worshipped, and cast Daniel and his companions into 'a fourneys, ful of flambes rede' when they refused. God punished his pride by driving him mad. He lived outdoors like an animal, eating grass and letting his hair and nails grow, until God finally released him from his sickness. For this he thanked God and did no further wrong. The episode of his humbling was influential in some medieval accounts of madness and *melancholy. He is elsewhere cited as a famous dreamer (X.125, HF 515).

Nadir, nader, nadyr, nadir (Arabic nadír). A diametrically opposed point, whether on a sphere or a circle. The word is used in A Treatise on the *Astrolabe and *Equatorie of the Planetis of points on scales; in the first text the word is used often in the phrase 'nadir of the Sonne', that is, on the other side of the *ecliptic. Note that this is not the modern sense of a lowest point, a nadir of the zenith. (See also *astrology and astronomy; *Cenyth.)

[JDN]

Narcisus, Narcissus, son of the river-god Cephisus, a beautiful youth, loved by the nymph *Echo. When he repulsed her he was punished by being made to fall in love with his reflection in a clear pool. He wasted away for unrequited love. The story was a popular one in the Middle Ages; Chaucer read it in *Ovid (Met. 3.339–510) and in the *Roman de la Rose (see Rom 1439–638) (see Fig. 10). Narcissus appears in the temple of *Venus in The Knight's Tale (I.1941), and is mentioned twice elsewhere (V.952 and BD 735).

Narice. Ulysses (*Ulixes) is called 'duc of the cuntre of Narice' (Bo IV m.3:2; L. Neritii (or Nericii) ducis). The 'cuntre' is Ithaca; the name is derived from Mt. Neriton, on the island.

narratives and narrators. In a period which prized, and excelled in the art of narrative Chaucer stands out as a master. He conducts his narratives (which come in a variety of shapes and forms) vividly and dramatically, with much use of direct speech, *dialogue, significant *visual details and *gestures. He will often use dramatic scenes to suggest character and personality. In more complex narratives (like Troilus and Criseyde) larger patterns of *irony and *imagery are established. He shows considerable technical skill in the handling of beginnings, endings ('th'ende is every tales strengthe'), and climaxes. The tempo, pace, and mood of the narrative is carefully controlled. Chaucer likes to experiment with *digressions and pauses, which by holding up the narrative 'flow' increase its dramatic effect and emphasize the presence and the personality of the narrator. There is considerable variation. Some passages of narrative are conducted in a leisurely and expansive fashion ('I wol no lenger tarien in this cas, | But to kyng Alla . . . | I wol retourne, and lete [leave] I wol Custaunce', II.983–6), others move quickly and remorselessly to a conclusion. A 'turn' in the narrative may be gentle and explanatory ('Now lat hem rede, and torne we anon | To Pandarus', Tr II.1709) or it may be abrupt and emotional, as at the end of the fourth book of Troilus: 'whan he saugh that she ne myghte dwelle, | Which that his soule out of his herte rente, | Withouten more out of the chaumbre he wente'.

Nativitee

His narrative art is highly self-conscious. From time to time he will give us comments (not always equally serious) on the nature of his storytelling: we must forgive him for speaking broadly, for a reporter must record speech as closely as he can (I.725–42); if women rather than clerks had told stories (he makes the Wife of Bath say) the wickedness of men would be made very evident; one should not delay the 'knotte' [main point] of a story too long in case the 'savour' is lost 'for fulsomnesse of his prolixitee' (as he makes the prolix Squire say at some length (V.401–8)), and so on. Like his Monk's tale, one of his own is judged to be inadequate, and is interrupted. He seems very interested in the relationship between fiction and truth (seen in extreme form in the Pardoner's insistence that an immoral man may tell a moral tale and in the Parson's refusal to tell any fictitious tale at all).

Very characteristic is the self-conscious development of what seems to be a close and intimate relationship with his *audience. As early as *The *Book of the Duchess* we find him experimenting with a talkative and sometimes apparently uncomprehending narrator, and he goes on to develop a whole range of narrative voices. Thus in *Troilus* he will sometimes simply 'present' the narrative action in a series of dramatic scenes in direct speech, while at other times he will adopt a 'choric' role, making direct interventions, commenting on the narrative and on the characters' reactions. In *The *Canterbury Tales* we have a more complicated arrangement with a variety of very different narrators and, both 'behind' them and 'among' them a Chaucer who imagines himself to be in the company of the pilgrims. Modern critics, responding to these experiments with voices and personae, have sometimes oversimplified them, suggesting that 'Chaucer the Pilgrim' or 'the narrator of *Troilus*' are somehow distinct characters quite separate from their creator. The technique, however, is more subtle and complex: the creative mind of the poet will sometimes project an attitude or a voice or assume different 'parts' in the course of narrative. Rather than a fixed and separate ingenuous narrator-character, Chaucer prefers to use a variety of voices, constantly shifting and changing the tone of the narrative and the audience's reactions to it, and creating a *mélange* of 'ernest' and '*game'.

Naso, see *Ovide.

Nativitee, nativity, birth *horoscope. This might denote either the stellar and planetary situation at birth, in regard to the houses, or the diagram summarizing that situation. As an example: Venus was not altogether hostile to *Troilus 'in his nativitee' (*Tr* II.684–5). (See also *astrology and astronomy.)   [JDN]

nature, kynde. Scholastic writers frequently personified nature even when writing scientific texts: they regularly distinguished, for example, between what is known to us and what is known to nature. What they said about nature, however, was generally compounded from a variety of different sources, of which they were often scarcely aware. The God of the Old Testament was not in any pronounced sense a God of nature; as a consequence, in both Jewish and Christian thought, there arose the theological notion of a world as an independent reality separate from God. The world remained subject to God's will: miracles were witness to the fact, and presented intellectual difficulties only for the most philosophical of theologians. Angels were deemed to be able to manipulate the world on God's behalf. Christ's attitude to nature was in keeping with this view: nature was something admirable, something in which to glory because it was of God's making.

Early medieval Western writers on nature enlarged on this nucleus of Christian doctrine. They dwelt on God's involvement in the creative act: the classical but always controversial source was John Scotus Erigena's chief work (*On the Division of Nature*), which advocated a form of pantheism, all reality being identified with God. Much subsequent debate centred on the implications of the presence of evil in the world. Scientific discussion in the early Middle Ages generally suffered to some extent from a fear of the implications of spiritual involvement in the world. It was often thought that all natural science was an extension of magic and sorcery, witchcraft and *alchemy, all of which were the province of evil spirits on the Earth. This fear was not helped by the Platonic conception of nature as a living organism (see *Plato), and yet that particular notion more than any other was responsible for the idea that nature-as-a-whole could be personified.

Another fundamental source of a very different kind, and one on which many scholastic commentaries were written, was *Aristotle's discussion of nature in his *Physics* II.i. He asks there whether only the *matter* of a natural object should be called its nature, or whether we may include its *form* under this heading; and he decides that both are admissible. First, however, he needs a definition of nature. He decides that natural objects are distinguished from others by the fact that they have within them whatever it is that is responsible for their changing, and for their remaining changed. (He did not think that this could be said of artefacts.) In short, his starting point is the nature of separate things, rather than a universal natural force. (Of course many things may share the same internal natures.) The Aristotelian view is not conducive to the idea of a personified Nature, although Aristotelians could personify the Primum Mobile without difficulty (see *First Moeving*).

Even in late antiquity, and certainly by the Middle Ages, several of these traditions were inextricably interwoven. The sublunary world, the world below the sphere of the Moon (see *cosmology*), is in a state of flux, and the agent of its change, its nature, was spoken of as Natura, sometimes a goddess, queen of the entire mundane region. On many occasions Chaucer introduces scientific theories into his descriptive poetry, and this art he learned from various sources in which just such a character played a central role.

In Jean de *Meun's *Roman de la Rose*, it is given to Nature (in her confession to Genius) to describe the universe, its creation, the elements, humours, planetary influence, the theory of dreams, and in fact everything that might be considered her own workings. The metaphysics owes much to Plato, but the cosmology is largely that of Aristotle and such followers as Galen (*Galyen (1)*). In the encyclopedic commentary by Macrobius on Cicero's *Somnium Scipionis*, it is explained how the divine Creator uses Pythagorean numerical ratios in weaving the fabric of the World-Soul, and the idea is also conveyed that the harmony present in the human soul derives from that of the World-Soul. Human and natural actions alike are thus explained in one of Chaucer's main scientific sources on the basis of Platonic principles. Macrobius also uses borrowed Neoplatonic arguments to refute Aristotle on the self-movement of things. He does not know Aristotle at first hand, but is indebted to him in ways he does not appreciate.

That personification is not incompatible with an Aristotelian cosmology is evident from Boethius. There, half-concealed under an overlay of poetry, is Aristotle's idea that things have within themselves a power that causes them to seek out their natural places; and one relevant passage is quoted in *The *Squire's Tale* from *Boece*: 'alle thyng, repeirynge to his kynde, | Gladeth hymself'. The section in question in *Boece* (III m.2:39–42) opens with a statement of intent: to show what great control Nature in all her power exerts over things, and by what laws she, in her foresight, keeps the great world. As against this perspective on Nature, Chaucer very often speaks of the intrinsic natures ('kyndes') of objects and human individuals as determining their characters and patterns of behaviour. The Eagle, in his lesson in physics in *The *House of Fame*, explains how speech or sound 'of pure kynde' is inclined to move naturally upwards, and how everything, indeed, has an inclination to return to its natural place, its 'kyndelyche stede'. The pedantic bird actually uses this Aristotelian notion of individual natures no fewer than eight times in thirty lines. While lending itself less to poetry than the personification of Nature as a whole, it is to the Eagle's perspective that we must look for the marked rise of natural science in Chaucer's century. (See also *science*; *technology*.) [JDN]

Nature, the Goddess (see also *Nature, kynde*), appears in *The *Parliament of Fowls*, where she is found sitting in a glade 'upon an hil of floures', her 'hall' and 'bower' made of branches, and surrounded by a vast concourse of birds of every species. Like her antecedents in the philosophical and cosmological poetry of the 12th c., in Alan of Lille's *De planctu Naturae* or the 'Pleynt of Kynd' (*PF* 316) and in Jean de Meun's part of the *Roman de la Rose*, she is a natural force ordained by God to carry out his purpose of continuing creation ('the vicaire of the almyghty Lord, *PF* 379). She is associated with plenitude and with life, but also with law ('the law of kind'), order and reason. Nature and her domain reflect God's ordering power. She observes the principles of moderation and harmony, holding together 'hot, cold, hevy, lyght, moyst, and dreye | . . . by evene noumbres of acord' (380–1), and speaks with an 'esy voys', as she presides over her assembly. There is a striking contrast between her 'halls' and 'bowers' made of branches, and the magnificently 'artful' temple of *Venus, with its depictions of the disastrous tales of passion.

Navarre, a Spanish kingdom in the north of the Iberian Peninsula, under French rule from 1234 until 1512, when it was reincorporated into Spain by the Catholic monarchs, Ferdinand and Isabella. In the spring of 1366, Chaucer was granted a safe conduct by Charles II of Navarre, permitting him to travel through the latter's kingdom, with three companions and their equipment, a document which suggests that Chaucer may have visited Spain that year (see *Spaigne). [PS]

Nazarenus, the Nazarene (i.e. '(Jesus) of Nazareth'). The *Parson explains the meaning of the word as 'florisshynge' (X.288–9).

NECKHAM, NEQUAM, ALEXANDER (1157–1215). Born at St Albans on the same night as Richard I, Alexander's mother suckled both children. A precocious scholar, he had charge of schools in Dunstable and St Albans, before and after studying in Paris, where he acquired the name Nequam ('bad' or 'worthless') from fellow students. He wrote two popular works on natural science, both showing a close acquaintance with classical authors. The second (*De laudibus divinæ sapientiæ*, in elegiacs) is a restrained version of the first (*De naturis rerum*, in prose), an anecdotal work showing no real feeling for scientific method. *Bacon was justifiably critical of him. He also turned Aesop's Fables into elegiac verse, wrote commentaries on parts of the Bible, *Ovid, *Aristotle, and Martianus Capella (*Marcian). In his own day he was an influential grammarian. He was much at court, and eventually became abbot of Cirencester, a house of Augustinian canons. [JDN]

Nembrot, Nimrod, the 'mighty hunter' of Genesis (10:8–12). In medieval tradition he was thought to be a tyrant and the builder of the tower of Babel. The *Former Age* describes him as 'desirous to regne' and a builder of 'toures hye' (58–9).

Neptune, Neptunus, the Roman god of the sea (V.1047, *LGW* 2421, *Tr* II.443). His resentment at the Trojans because of Laomedon's refusal to pay him and Apollo for building the walls of the city is alluded to in *Troilus* IV.120.

NEQUAM, ALEXANDER, see **Alexander** *Neckam.

NERO, NEROUN, Roman emperor (reigned 54–68). His story is told by the *Monk (VII.2463–50). He is presented there as the exemplar of a vicious tyrant, 'pompous of array', and devoted to pleasure, who burnt Rome, and slew the senators 'to heere how that men wolde wepe and crie'. He killed his brother, lay with his sister, and mutilated his mother. His tutor Seneca (*Senec) who reproved his vices was forced to commit suicide. *Fortune turns against his pride: there is rebellion, and Nero kills himself. Chaucer refers to the account of Suetonius (*Swetonius), but it is not certain that he really knew it directly: he could have found the material in the *Roman de la Rose* and elsewhere. In the following *Nun's Priest's Tale* the burning of Rome and the cries of the senators' wives appear in a more comic context (see VII.3369–73). Nero's cruelty and tyranny are emphasized a number of times by Boethius (*Boece) (see *Bo* II m.6:3; III m.4 and pr.5). His death is depicted on the walls of the temple of *Mars in *The Knight's Tale* (I.2032).

Nessus, a centaur who was killed by Hercules (*Ercules) for attempting to rape Deianira (*Dianira). The *Monk refers to the story that he advised her to use his blood to regain Hercules's love (VII.2127–8).

Newegate, Newgate prison in London (I.4402), the city's principal gaol from the 13th c. See Map 2. Rebuilt in the 18th c., it was pulled down in 1902. Part of its wall was incorporated into the Old Bailey.

Nicerates wyf, wife of the Athenian Niceratus (*fl.* 5th c. BC) who was put to death in the time of the Thirty Tyrants. According to *Jerome she killed herself rather than submit to their lust. *Dorigen refers to her (V.1437).

Nichanore (1), Nicanor, defeated by Judas Maccabeus (2 Macc. 8), mentioned by the *Monk (VII.2591).

Nichanore (2), one of the generals of Alexander (*Alisaundre), for love of whom a Theban maiden slew herself (V.1432).

NICHOLAS OF LYNN, see **Frer N. *Lenne**.

Nicholas, Nicholay, the Oxford student in *The *Miller's Tale*, who becomes the lover of Alison. He is repeatedly described as 'hende' (gracious, charming); he is a musician, and is fascinated by astrology.

Nicholas, Seint, said to have been bishop of Myra in the 4th c., although there are no historical records. His cult was ancient and widespread. His piety in youth made him the patron of children and clerks. Hence he is mentioned by the *Prioress in her tale of the 'clergeoun', 'for he so yong to Crist dide reverence' (VII.514).

NICOLE DE MARGIVAL (13th c.), the author of *La panthère d'Amours* which contains a description of the house of Fortune. It is placed on a mountain of ice, a detail which Chaucer adapts for his house of Fame.

NIGEL WIREKER, see *Speculum Stultorum*.

Nine Worthies, the legendary Nine Heroes (Fr. *les Neuf Preux*) made famous by Jacques de Longuyon's early 14th-c. poem, *Les voeux du paon* (the Vows of the Peacock). There are three sets of three: three pagans, Hector (*Ector), Alexander (*Alisaundre), *Julius Caesar; three Jews, *David, Joshua, *Judas Maccabeus; and three Christians, Arthur (*Arthour), Charlemagne (*Charles), and Godfrey of Bouillon, the crusader. The Nine Worthies became a popular subject in the visual arts, especially in tapestries.

Nynyve(e), Nineveh, capital of Assyria, is several times mentioned (II.487, in connection with Jonah (*Jonas); VIII.974; *BD* 1063, as a great city).

NYNUS, king of Assyria in the 9th c. BC and husband of Semiramis (*Semyrame). His tomb appears in the story of Thisbe (*Tisbe; *LGW* 785).

Nyobe, Niobe, daughter of Tantalus (*Tantale) and queen of Thebes. When her seven sons and seven daughters were killed by Apollo and Diana, she wept until she turned into a column of stone from which her tears continued to flow. She is mentioned by *Pandarus (*Tr* I.699; see 759).

Nysus, Nisus, king of Megara, near Athens (*LGW* 1904). Described by *Ovid as a venerable white-haired man who had one tress of bright purple hair in the middle of his head. He was the father of Scylla (*Silla). For his story, see *Silla**.

Nysus doughter, see *Silla**.

Noe, Noah (Gen. 5–9). He is once mentioned by the *Parson (X.766), but appears most frequently in *The *Miller's Tale*, where a repetition of 'Noah's flood' is threatened. Here at one point (I.3534–43) Chaucer seems clearly to be thinking of the way he was presented in the mystery plays, as one who had 'sorwe' 'er that he myghte gete his wyf to shipe'. In the plays she is sometimes an obstreperous and shrewish woman. (The Miller's 'Nowelis flood' (I.3818, 3834) instead of the usual 'Noe(e)s flood' (3518, 3616) may be a malapropism.)

Nonyus, Nonius, a (wicked) Roman politician mentioned in *Boece (III pr.4:12, 15).

Noote, the Kynges an unidentified song sung by *Nicholas in *The *Miller's Tale* (I.3217).

Northfolk, Norfolk, where the *Reeve comes from (I.619). (There seems to have been a tradition that people from Norfolk were crafty and treacherous.)

Northhumberlond, Northhumbrelond, Northumberland, scene of part of *The *Man of Law's Tale* (II.508 ff.).

NOTE, SEINTE, St Neot (d. *c.*877) a monk and hermit, after whom the towns of St Neot (Cornwall) and St Neots (Cambridgeshire) are named, because of their proximity to his hermitage and to a shrine with relics respectively. *Gerveys in *The *Miller's Tale,* the Oxford smith who works by night, swears by him (I.3771). It is not clear that there is any special significance in the oath, although it has been suggested that Chaucer may have known of the saint's connection with King Alfred's legendary foundation of Oxford or his practice of rising in the dead of night in order to say his prayers.

Nothus, the south wind (*Bo* II m.6:25; III m.1:8); see *Auster.

Nun's Priest's Tale, The, preceded by a Prologue and followed by an *Epilogue (found only in nine MSS), forming in all nearly 700 lines in couplets, is the final tale of Fragment VII. The Prologue (VII.2767–820) begins with the interruption of *The *Monk's Tale* by the *Knight. He would prefer something 'gladsom', 'as whan a man hath been in povre estaat, | And clymbeth up and wexeth fortunat, | And there abideth in prosperitee'. The Host joins in, and when the Monk refuses to tell another story, he accosts the Nun's Priest, who agrees.

(2821–3186) A poor widow lived humbly and temperately in a small cottage, providing for herself and her two daughters. She owned three sows, three cows, and a sheep. In her yard she had a splendid cock called *Chauntecleer, peerless in crowing and magnificent in appearance. 'This gentil cok' had seven hens, of whom his favourite was 'faire damoysele Pertelote'. One dawn Pertelote is alarmed to hear him 'gronen in his throte': he has had a frightening dream in which he met in the yard a hostile beast like a hound, with glowing eyes. Pertelote is scornful of his fear: *dreams simply come from a disordered 'temperament' and digestion. The wise Cato (*Catoun) said 'do no fors of dremes'. A purging laxative is all that is needed, and the herbs for it are growing in the yard. Chauntecleer does not agree. Wiser men than Cato give an opposite opinion, that 'dremes been significaciouns'. He tells Pertelote stories involving dreams which accurately prophesy death and he quotes a string of authorities in support of the view that one should take heed of dreams. He concludes that some adversity will come to him—as for laxatives, 'I love hem never a deel!' But his mood changes: the beauty of Pertelote's face drives his fear away. Flying down to the yard, he feathers her twenty times, and 'on his toos he rometh up and doun'.

(3187–3446) On 3 May, while he is walking in the yard with his seven hens, a fox 'ful of sly iniquitee' has crept into the yard and is hiding among the cabbages. When Chauntecleer sees the fox he is about to flee, but the fox reassures him—he has only come to hear his beautiful singing. His father ('God his soule blesse!'), also a peerless singer, when he sang used to close his eyes and stretch out his neck. Can Chauntecleer imitate his father? Deceived by treacherous flattery, Chauntecleer does just this, whereupon the fox seizes him by the throat and makes off with him towards the wood. The clamour of the hens rouses the widow and her daughters, who set off in noisy pursuit accompanied by dogs, cow and calf, hogs, ducks, geese, and a swarm of bees. Fortune suddenly changes. Chauntecleer says to the fox, 'if I were you, I would say "Turn back, all you proud cherls—the cock will stay here."' He does so, and Chauntecleer, flies up to a tree. Now wise through experience he refuses a request to come down: may the man 'that wynketh whan he sholde see' never prosper. And the fox curses the person 'that is so undiscreet of governaunce | That jangleth whan he sholde holde his pees'. The narrator points a moral ('Lo, swich it is for to be recchelees | And necligent, and truste on flaterye'), and urges us not to despise this tale 'as of a fox, or of a cok and hen', for St Paul says that everything that is written is written 'to oure doctrine'.

It is generally agreed that the tale was composed in the period of the *Canterbury Tales* with its narrator in mind. The astronomical references in ll. 3187–97 seem to indicate (Friday) 3 May 1392. The narrator who gives such a brilliant performance is scarcely mentioned in the *General Prologue (as one of the 'preestes thre' accompanying the Prioress?). Possibly a fuller portrait might have been provided later, possibly Chaucer deliberately left the figure vague in order to allow the satire full scope. The remarks there and in the Prologue to the Tale itself perhaps give two hints: the connection with the Prioress (which may have some bearing on the narrator's treatment of women) and the contrast with the rich and worldly monk (the Nun's Priest's horse is only a 'jade' and 'foul and lene'), but it is not clear how far these may be taken.

A brief synopsis of the tale gives no indication of the rich elaboration of its telling. It is a version of a popular *fable which Chaucer could have found in *Marie de France and in 'Branche' II of the *Roman de Renart*, but the simple structure is elaborated with *digressions, exclamations, asides, and a display of rhetorical techniques. The 'hovering' relationship of animal to human which is characteristic of the beast fable is exploited to the full and used to give a serio-comic treatment of a number of favourite Chaucerian themes: *women and *marriage, the significance of *dreams, *fortune and predestination. The principle of incongruity is however taken much further than is usual in the beast fable and the tale becomes an extended exercise in the mock-heroic. The beauty of the birds is described in terms reminiscent of those used of courtly heroes and heroines, the learned cock discourses on a variety of high matters, the narrator deploys immense rhetorical hyperbole in his laments over the 'pitous cas' of the unfortunate Chauntecleer. There is a strong suggestion as he stands earlier 'roial, as a prince is in his halle', that he is a likely victim for the sudden turns of Fortune which produce the tragedies of *The *Monk's Tale* (and other parallels, notably prophetic dreams and the counsels of women, are wickedly brought to mind). But to treat it simply as a '*parody' would be too reductive. Similarly, it resists ingenious attempts to read it as a solemn allegory (of the Fall of Man, of slothful secular priests and guileful friars, etc.). The suggestion of a clever underlying astronomical 'allegory' with Chauntecleer as the sun and his seven hens as the Pleiades is much more attractive. Like other beast fables it has a morality—or perhaps too many moralities. It seems to remain preeminently and triumphantly a story which demonstrates all of Chaucer's *narrative techniques. And it certainly fulfils the requirements of the Knight and the Host: in the end it is a story of one who 'hath been in povre estaat, | And clymbeth up and wexeth fortunat, | And there abideth in prosperitee' and it does 'sey somwhat of huntyng'.

(ed.) *Rv* 252–61, 935–41; Pearsall (1984); *S&A* 645–63 [449–89]; Petersen (1898); Cooper (1989), 338–56; North (1990), ch. 15; David (1976), ch. 15; Mann (1974–5); Pearsall (1985), 228–38.

nuns, see *Prioress.

O

oaths, swearing. For legal purposes it was customary throughout the medieval period (as it still is in Britain) at the beginning of testimony to administer an oath, usually by God, Christ or the Trinity with the speaker's hand on the Bible, to confirm the veracity of his statements. Biblical precept would seem to discourage, if not actually prohibit, swearing: the Pardoner mentions the standard proof texts of Exodus 20:7, Jeremiah 4:2, and Matthew 5:34 (VI.629–47). The standard orthodox view accepted oaths for legal purposes or in great necessity, as does the Parson (X.592): 'And if so be that the lawe compelle yow to swere, thanne rule yow after the lawe of God in youre sweryng, as seith Jeremye, *quarto capitulo*: Thou shalt kepe three condicions: thou shalt swere "in trouthe, in doom and in rightwisnesse".'

From the legal context, where oaths were held to guarantee a statement's veracity, the habit grew of adding an abbreviated oath to any statement, and the use of an oath as exclamation. In these extra-legal contexts the names of various saints and their attributes, or of parts of Christ's body or sufferings, might be substituted for the name of God. Promiscuous swearing is regularly condemned by confessional manuals (e.g. by that underlying the Parson's tale, X.587 ff. where it is treated as a subdivision of anger) and by preachers (e.g. by the Pardoner VI.629–59). The frequency with which preachers condemned swearing reflects the strength of the habit in ordinary speech. Chaucer mirrors this habit in the persistent oaths of characters such as the Host (e.g. I.854; IV.7; 1213a); the Host also demonstrates the linguistic perversions that frequent oaths produced (e.g. X.29 'for cockes bones'). Such oaths, to judge by Chaucer's usage, were particularly characteristic of men and women of low rank (see, for instance, figures in the Miller's and Reeve's tales, I.3291, 3425, 3449, 3461, 4127, etc.). The comment on the Prioress (*GP* I.120 'Hire gretteste ooth was but by Seinte Loy') shows that even one who had social pretensions to gentility might use them; Chaucer portrays himself, at least in the anxiety of his aerial journey in the eagle's claws, resorting to them (*HF* 1131, 1183). As Cleopatra in *The Legend of Good Women* 666 indicates ('Ye men that falsly sweren many an oath | That ye wol deye if that youre love be wroth'), lovers were also especially prone to using oaths to affirm their claims (as, for instance, the tercel eagle does at *PF* 451). The Pardoner in his tale expostulates against swearing, and gives some characteristic examples (VI.651–5): 'By Goddes precious herte', and 'By his nayles', and 'By the blood of Crist that is in Hayles', 'By Goddes armes'. Chaucer, like most medieval writers, describes pagans as using similar oaths, though he largely avoids the anachronism of specifying in them Christian saints (e.g. *Tr* III.705, *LGW* F 338 *seynt Venus*, with which compare *The Romaunt of the Rose* 5953).

In the Epilogue to *The Man of Law's Tale*, a passage which, to judge by its absence from both Hengwrt and Ellesmere manuscripts, Chaucer may have cancelled or intended to transfer, the Host's oaths 'for Goddes bones . . . by Goddes dignitee' draw objection from the Parson '"Benedicite! | What eyleth the man, so synfully to swere?" ' (II.1166–71). This in turn leads the Host to his observation '"O Jankin, be ye there? | I smelle a Lollere in the wynd"' (II.1172). In fact, as is obvious from the views of the Pardoner already quoted, objection to casual swearing was entirely traditional and orthodox. Characteristic of the *Lollards and in medieval England virtually peculiar to them, however, was an extensive refusal of oaths in the original legal context; this refusal became more widely known in the early 15th c., but Henry Knighton, writing about the same time as Chaucer, records Lollard preference for formulae such as 'I am sykyr, It is soth, Withoute doute it is so' (*Chronicon* ii. 262). (See also *ejaculations*.)

[AH]

OCKHAM, WILLIAM OF (*c*.1300–49), an influential Franciscan philosopher noted for his strict and precise logical method. His radical (and anti-papal) views on the question of poverty brought excommunication, and he had to find refuge with Louis of Bavaria. His philosophical writings, with a nominalist distrust of universals and a markedly Augustinian stress on the divine will and on the pre-eminence of faith, are often thought to have played an important role in the breakdown of the Thomist synthesis between Christian theology and Aristotelian *philosophy.

OCTOVYAN, OCTOVYEN, Gaius Octavius (63 BC–AD 14), the nephew of *Julius Caesar, adopted by him and hence called Caesar, later the Emperor Augustus (see *Augustus Cesar). His defeat of *Antony at Actium is described in the legend of Cleopatra (*Cleopataras) in *The *Legend of Good Women*. He is probably 'th' emperour Octovyen' mentioned in *The *Book of the Duchess*, 368). It has been suggested that (if he is 'this kyng' of l. 1314) this may be a delicate compliment to Edward III. It is not clear how he is related, except by name, to the legendary 'emperor Octavian', the hero of a very popular romance.

Odenake, Odenathus, the ruler of Palmyra and husband of Zenobia (*Cenobia) in *The *Monk's Tale*.

Oenone, a nymph of Mt. Ida who was deserted by her lover *Paris (1) (*HF* 399). Her *letter of 'complaint' (*Heroides* 5) is alluded to in *Troilus and Criseyde* (I.654 ff.).

Oetes, Aeëtes, king of Colchis (*Colcos), the father of *Medea (*LGW* 1438, 1593).

Oyse, the river Oise, in northern France (*HF* 1928).

old age, elde (see *Ages of Man). Medieval literature often seems to take a gloomy view of old age, stressing its decrepitude and proximity to death,

but this is not always the case. *Bartholomew cites the view of Isidore (*Ysidre) that 'the end of age and of life' has both good and bad qualities. Old age frees one from the power of tyrants, puts an end to lust, has wit and wisdom, and has the ability to give good counsel ('as many old men do'). It is the end of life's wretchedness and woe. (This positive view of age is eloquently presented in Cicero's *De senectute* (Of Old Age) and lies behind the wise old figures such as 'Cato' (*Catoun) to whom collections of saws are attributed.) But old age, says Isidore, has its drawbacks: it brings sickness; strength fails, the sinews shrink, the body bends and grows crooked, and all its fairness is brought to nought; 'all men despise the old man'.

These varying views are found in Chaucer. In *The *Clerk's Tale* Walter is presented with the commonplace that old age will come inevitably and that death follows: 'thogh youre grene youthe floure as yit, | In crepeth age alwey, as stille as stoon, | And deeth manaceth every age' (IV.120–2). (This proverbial-sounding disquisition on the theme 'ay fleeth the tyme; it nyl no man abyde' is sharpened by the appropriate word 'crepeth'.) *Pandarus warns *Criseyde that 'elde wasteth every houre | . . . a partie of beautee' (*Tr* II.393 ff.), mentioning, *inter alia*, crows' feet growing under the eyes. Less precise is the traditional 'crookedness' used in an almost formulaic way to characterize a blind beggar: 'croked and oold, with eyen faste yshette' (II.560). On the other hand, the connection of old age with long experience and wisdom can be equally formulaic. There are many approving references to old books or stories or clerks, to 'thise olde wyse' (e.g. VIII.1067; *LGW* 19). In *Melibee* wise old men play their traditional role as counsellors. In *The *Knight's Tale* the idea that 'elde hath grete avantage' is expanded with a proverb—'in elde is bothe wysdom and usage; | Men may the olde atrenne [outrun] and nought atrede [outwit]' (I.2447–9)— though it is apropos of the 'olde experience' of the sinister *Saturn.

In *Melibee* the hot-headed young folk scorn the counsel of the old. The opposition of *youth and age is proverbial: 'youthe and age is often at debaat' (I.3230). This is especially so where love is concerned. In *The *Romaunt of the Rose* where the walled garden of love is for the beautiful young folk alone, a portrait of 'Elde' is found outside the wall, next to those of Envy and Sorrow (349–412). The description of this foul and wrinkled female figure is a rhetorical tour de force, in which the characteristics of female *beauty are transformed: she is wizened, feeble, sallow, white-haired, can only walk with a staff, is doting and helpless, perpetually cold, etc. In *fabliaux there is little sympathy for the old husband or old lover (*senex amans*) with a young wife, figures like Chaucer's *January in The *Merchant's Tale (in which 'tendre youthe hath wedded stoupyng age', IV.1738), or the carpenter in The *Miller's Tale who was not aware of the wise advice of 'Catoun' that 'man sholde wedde his simylitude' (I.3228). Moralists join in the mockery of aged lechers. The *Parson vehemently attacks 'thise olde dotardes holours [lechers]', who 'kisse, though they may nat do', comparing them to dogs that make a pretence of pissing by a rosebush even when they are not able to (X.857ff.).

Chaucer's elderly or ageing characters are in fact a varied and interesting group. They include the old widow in The Friar's Tale (slangily referred to as a *ribibe* or *rebekke* 'fiddle'), the widow 'somdeel stape [advanced] in age' of the Nun's Priest's Tale, the 'olde Sowdanesse' and 'olde Donegild' in The Man of Law's Tale, *Egeus in The Knight's Tale, Griselda's father *Janicula, 'good *Urban the olde' in the Second Nun's Tale, *Priam and Calchas (*Calkas, of whom his daughter quotes the proverb 'elde is ful of coveytise', Tr IV.1369). More prominent roles are played by the old woman in The Wife of Bath's Tale (who besides giving the knight instruction in a number of vital matters, reproves him for his lack of deference to the aged: 'men sholde an oold wight doon favour', III.1210), by January in The Merchant's Tale, whose vigour contrasts with his appearance, and by the strange old man in The Pardoner's Tale, who has the traditional attributes (a staff, a pale and withered face) and who wanders the world yearning for death and unable to find a man who will change youth for his age. He too provokes a hostile and arrogant reaction from the young, and he reproves them: 'Ne dooth unto an oold man noon harm now, | Namoore than that ye wolde men did to yow | In age, if that ye so longe abyde' (VI.745–7). The last phrase has a sinister ring: he is both a *memento mori* and a messenger of death. Finally,

two of Chaucer's pilgrims touch on the problems of ageing. The *Reeve eloquently laments his age and 'white top' (I.3867–88) and the curse of the old, to have lost the 'myght' but not the 'wyl': 'yet ik have alwey a coltes tooth'. And the *Wife of Bath, after describing her treatment of her old husbands (which involves reminding them of their age; see III.235, 242, 281, 291, 302, 331, 357) herself laments that age has bereft her of her beauty and her 'pith'. But her reflections on her lost youth are less of a 'sermoning' than the Reeve's speech: 'Lat go. Farewell! The devel go therwith! | The flour is goon; ther is namoore to telle; | The bren, as I best kan, now moste I selle; | But yet to be right myrie wol I fonde [try]' (III.476–9).

Burrow (1986); Shahar (1997); Steadman (1964).

Oliphaunt, sire, a giant in *Sir Thopas (VII.808) with a suitably comic name ('Sir Elephant') modelled on similar giant names in romances (Amoraunt, Guymerraunt).

Olyver, the friend and comrade of Roland (*Rowland) in the Charlemagne legends, famous for his loyalty and wisdom. The two are linked in BD 1123. Oliver is an example of true *friendship as against the false traitor Ganelon (see Charles, *Genelloun, *Genylon-Olyver).

Oloferne, Olofernus, Holofernes, the general of Nebuchadnezzar (*Nabugonosor) who laid siege to *Bethulia but was killed as he lay in a drunken stupour by *Judith a Jewish woman whom he hoped to seduce. The story (from the apocryphal book of Judith) is briefly told in The *Monk's Tale (VII.2551–74), and is alluded to elsewhere (II.939–40; IV.1368; VII.1099).

OMER, Homer the Greek poet to whom the Iliad and the Odyssey are attributed, and who is usually placed in the 9th c. BC, is several times mentioned by Chaucer. But the story of *Troy was known from Latin sources, from *Virgil, from the Ilias Latina, or the books of *Dares and Dictys (*Dite). Chaucer, however, thinks of 'Homer' as a great author: in *Troilus and Criseyde he is listed at the beginning as one of the authorities on Troy (I.146), and at the end among the great poets

(V.1792). 'The gret Omer' appears in *HF* (1466) with other historians of Troy, although there is a reference there (deriving from Dares and others) to the charge of partiality to the Greeks and of 'feigning', 1477–9). His celebration of chaste *Penelope is alluded to in *The Franklin's Tale* (V.1443). This reference comes from St *Jerome, a man who still had a knowledge of Greek. Similarly, Boethius (*Boece) quotes Homer and refers to his poetic skill: 'Homer with the hony mouth (that is to seyn, Homer with the swete ditees)', as Chaucer turns *melliflui canit oris Homerus* (*Bo* V m.2:1–2). (See *classical literature.)

Opilion, Opilio, an informer and enemy of Boethius (*Boece) (*Bo* I pr.4:114).

Oreb, the Old Testament Mt. Horeb or Mt. Sinai (*Synay), where Moses (*Moyses) fasted (III.1891).

Orewelle, Orwell, in Suffolk, the seaport for Ipswich (I.277).

organ, see *musical instruments.

'Origenes upon the Maudeleyne', which appears in a list of Chaucer's works given in the Prologue to *The *Legend of Good Women* (F 428, G 418), seems to refer to a lost translation of a 13th-c. Latin homily *De Maria Magdalena* which was wrongly attributed to the Greek Father Origen (*c.*186–255).

ORION, Arion (*fl.* 625 BC), Greek poet and harpist, mentioned in *The *House of Fame* (1205), as is the constellation named after his harp (*Arionis harpe). [JDN]

oriso(u)nte, horizon (from Greek). Unqualified, this is the common modern concept, but was known more precisely to the medieval astronomer as the *oblique* horizon, for which Chaucer uses the phrase 'embelif orisonte'. This distinguishes it from his 'orison rectum' or 'right orisonte', namely the great circle passing through the poles and the eastern and western points of the other (oblique) horizon. These lines are drawn on all ordinary astrolabe plates, the 'embelif orisonte' as

an arc of a certain circle, varying according to the geographical latitude for which the plate is drawn, the 'right orisonte' as a straight line through the astrolabe's centre. See *clymat. [JDN]

Orkades, Orkney, to the north of Scotland, used in a phrase 'bitwixen Orkades and *Inde' to suggest the extreme limits of the known world (*Tr* V.971). In Chaucer's time Orkney was still part of the realm of the kings of Norway, though by that time the jarls or earls of Orkney were Scots.

Orliens, Orléans, in France, where the university was not only famous for its school of law, but was in Chaucer's time renowned for the study of 'magyk natureel'. It is from here that the clerk in *The *Franklin's Tale* comes (V.1118 ff.).

Orpheus. The story of the legendary poet and musician, the son of *Caliope the *Muse, who went down to the underworld in search of his wife Eurydice (*Erudice), but lost her because he could not refrain from looking back as he led her upwards, was extremely popular in the Middle Ages. It was known from the versions of the ancient 'authors', *Virgil, *Ovid, and Boethius (*Boece), but around these there grew up a mass of commentary, and many retellings, often (like the ME *Sir Orfeo*) of a less learned kind. Orpheus is not only the discoverer of *music and the first player of the lyre (which was transformed into the medieval harp), but also a famous lover. When Boethius tells the story (III m.12) there is a Neoplatonic opposition between the ability to see 'the clere welle of good' and the downward pull of the 'the boondes of the hevy erthe'. The lyric is an exemplum, but it also expresses powerfully the intensity of earthly *love. It is love which both inspires Orpheus to his heroic quest, and causes his failure. Chaucer's sensitivity to this is reflected in the eloquence of his translation:

but what is he that may yeven [give] a lawe to loverys? Love is a gretter lawe and a strengere [stronger] to hymself thanne any lawe that men may yyven. Allas! Whanne Orpheus and his wif weren almest at the termes of the nyght (that is to seyn, at the laste boundes of helle), Orpheus lokede abakward on Erudyce his wif, and lost hire, and was deed.

Elsewhere he alludes to Orpheus as 'god of

melodye' (*BD* 569) and as a famous musician (IV.1716; *HF* 1201–3). A more pathetic allusion to the love story is placed in the mouth of Criseyde (*Tr* IV.788–91) about to be parted from Troilus: 'for though in erthe ytwynned [separated] be we tweyne, | Yet in the feld of pite, out of peyne. | That highte *Elisos, shal we ben yfeere [together], | As Orpheus and Erudice, his feere [companion].' The phrase 'ytwynned be we tweyne', which echoes an earlier lament by Troilus (IV.476) is later the sorrowful message brought to him by the wind 'that sowneth so lik peyne' (V.673–9).

Oseneye, Osenay, Osney, now part of Oxford (*Oxenford), but then outside the town, was the site of an abbey of Augustinian canons. Its magnificent buildings have now vanished. It afforded work for the carpenter in The *Miller's Tale* (I.3274, 3400, 3659).

Osewolde, the name of the *Reeve.

OTON DE GRAUNSON, see *Graunson.

OVIDE, Ovid, Publius Ovidius Naso (43 BC–AD 18), Roman poet. He was born at Sulmo, and studied rhetoric and law before devoting himself to poetry. He died in exile at Tomi, by the Black Sea. His earliest works seem to have been the *Amores*, a collection of love elegies. The *Heroides* or *Heroidum Epistulae* ('Letters of Heroines') casts the stories of legendary lovers in the form of verse letters (see *Episteles (of Ovyde)*). The *Ars amatoria* ('Art of Love') is a mock didactic verse handbook on love, with the *Remedia amoris* ('Remedies of Love') purporting to offer antidotes. His narrative skills are seen at their best in the *Metamorphoses*, a work of epic scope in fifteen books, in which many mythological tales involving love and various transformations are cleverly linked together. The *Fasti* (uncompleted, in six books) uses legends to explain the origins of various rites in the Roman calendar, and narrates legends connected with particular dates. From the end of his life come elegies of complaint, the *Tristia* and *Epistulae ex Ponto*.

Ovid's influence on medieval literature was immense. His 'immorality' troubled some, especially in the earlier periods, but his works were copied, his popularity was soon established, and he became a 'curriculum author'. Various *sententiae* or wise sayings are collected in *florilegia* and are often quoted. A desire to find allegorical meanings in his stories is seen as early as *Fulgentius (5th c.) and culminates in the *Ovide moralisé* and *Bersuire's *Ovidius Moralizatus*. Writers were fascinated by Ovid's blend of wit and sensuousness, his rhetorical skills, his treatment of myths and mythography, or by his narrative art. Among many poets, *Chrétien de Troyes, *Dante, *Gower, and Chaucer responded to him with enthusiasm.

It is evident that Chaucer read widely in Ovid and was deeply influenced by him. He seems to have used 'glossed' copies, and besides the Latin texts to have read an Italian translation of the *Heroides* by Filippo, and, probably, the *Ovide moralisé* (though he does not use its allegorizations). He makes many references to Ovid (or 'Naso') by name. Ovid is listed among the great poets in *Troilus and Criseyde* (V.1792), and in The *House of Fame* (1486–92) he stands on a pillar of copper. Chaucer also mentions some individual works: the 'Episteles of Ovyde' (i.e. the *Heroides*; *HF* 379; *LGW* G 305, 1465; II.55); 'Methamorphosios' (II.93 (a variant of the possessive sing. form)); 'Ovides Art' (the *Ars amatoria*: III.680, as part of *Jankin's (4) 'book of wicked wives' (it was in fact sometimes included in anti-feminist collections)); and the 'book that cleped [called] is the Remedie of Love', from which *Prudence quotes a 'sentence' (VII.976). Chaucer is also fond of sending his readers off to consult Ovid for further details: 'rede Ovyde' (for Dido's letter, *LGW* 1367; see also *HF* 379), and the *Wife of Bath says (III.981–2) 'redeth Ovyde' for the rest of the tale of Midas (*Myda). And there are quotations and allusions: 'noble Ovid', says the *Merchant, was right to say, of Pyramus (*Piramus) and Thisbe (*Tisbe), that love will always find a way (IV.2125); Troilus alludes to the story of Adonis (*Adoun; III.720 ff.), and so on.

In spite of the evidence of his familiarity with Ovid, it would be rash to suppose that Chaucer had read all of the poet's works, even if he sometimes mentions them (see *classical literature). His direct knowledge of the *Ars amatoria*, the *Remedia amoris*, and the *Amores*, for instance, has been doubted. Of the first, however, it may be said that it was both extremely popular and easily accessible, and that there are lines which could well be echoes of it (e.g. IX.97–9, 105–8). The 'sentences' from the *Remedia* quoted by Prudence (VII.976, 1325) are both in the French original of *Melibee*. But the remark in The *Book of the Duchess* that 'nought al the remedyes of Ovyde' can remove the Man in Black's sorrows suggests that it was familiar. And confidants (like the dreamer in *BD* or *Pandarus in *Troilus*) seem sometimes to be using Ovidian 'remedies' (e.g. that one strong emotion drives out another). Possible echoes include *Tr* I.760, 857–8, 946–9; IV.414–15. The quotation from the *Amores* in *Melibee* (VII.1414–15) is in the French text, but there seem to be clear echoes in *Troilus and Criseyde*, in the passage in which Troilus laments the coming of the day (III.1422–35; cf. *Amores* 1.13; see *Aubade) and that in which Pandarus alludes to the variety of ladies (IV.407–12; cf. *Amores* 2.4.9–48). The evidence for his knowledge of Ovid's last poems is less secure, but there are possible echoes. Troilus's sorrowful address to 'lovers' (IV.323–9) sounds like Ovid's epitaph for himself as a lover (*Tristia* 3.3.73–6) but Chaucer may have picked it up from *Boccaccio's *Teseida* (11.91). Another from the *Tristia* (V.220–4) may have become proverbial. But it is possible that the germ of Chaucer's favourite line '*pitee renneth soone in gentil herte' (e.g. I.1761) may have been Ovid's 'the greater a man, the more his wrath can be appeased; a noble mind is easily capable of kindly impulses' (*Tristia* 3.5.31–2). A glossator noted in one MS of *Troilus* a reference to Ovid at I.712–14, probably to *Ex Ponto* 2.7.41–2 ('I am so wounded by the continual blows of Fortune that there is scarcely room on me for a new wound').

In the case of three major poems we are on more certain ground. The story of *Lucrece in The Legend of Good Women* follows the narrative in Ovid's *Fasti* (2.685–852), and the allusion to the story of *Priapus in *PF* 253–9 seems to show a knowledge of the same work (1.415–40) as well as of Boccaccio's version in the *Teseida*. The *Metamorphoses* provide Chaucer with a number of tales—Ceyx (*Seys) in *BD* (*Met.* 11); Pyramus and Thisbe (*Met.* 4) and Philomela (*Met.* 6) in The *Legend of Good Women*; and that of the crow in The *Manciple's Tale* (*Met.* 2). The story of Ariadne (*Adriane) in *House of Fame*

405–26 and *Legend of Good Women* 1886–2227 is based on the versions in *Metamorphoses* 8 and *Heroides* 10. Ovid's vivid descriptions of the dwelling of the god of sleep (*Met.* 11) and of the house of Rumour (*Met.* 12) inspire similar passages in The *Book of the Duchess* and *House of Fame*. The *Legend of Good Women* is especially indebted to the *Heroides*, for Dido's letter (*Heroides* 7), for the stories of *Phyllis (*Her.* 2), Hypermnestra (*Ypermystra; *Her.* 14), and to some extent in the stories of Ariadne and Hypsipyle (*Isiphele(e)) and *Medea (*Her.* 6, 12).

Chaucer's treatment of Ovid is never slavish. His retellings of the stories are lively, embellished with new and vivid details (e.g. in Pyramus and Thisbe: 'the *colde* wal they wolden kysse *of ston'*, *LGW* 768). He adds comedy to the scenes of the houses of Sleep and Rumour. He sees Ovid as a poet of *love (in *HF* he is called 'Venus clerk'), and is himself compared to him in the Introduction to The *Man of Law's Tale*: 'he hath toold of loveris up and doun | Mo than Ovide made of mencioun | In his Episteles, that been ful olde' (II.53–5). He learnt much from Ovid in the portrayal of women in love, in the conduct of dramatic narrative, in the clever and graceful use of *allusion and *digression, in the easy treatment of social life, and in the art of achieving a 'continuous interplay between wit and pathos'.

In an interesting passage *Dryden drew attention to a number of resemblances between Chaucer and Ovid, some of which would still be endorsed: 'both of them were well-bred, well-natured, amorous, and libertine, at least in their writings; it may be, also, in their lives. Their studies were the same, philosophy and philology. Both of them were knowing in astronomy . . . Both writ with wonderful facility and clearness . . . Both of them built on the inventions of other men . . . Both of them understood the manners; under which name I comprehend the passions, and, in a larger sense, the descriptions of persons and their habits', and portrayed them vividly, though 'Chaucer's figures are more lively'. Dryden also says approvingly that Chaucer 'writ with more simplicity and followed nature more closely' and avoided using Ovid's conceits: Ovid, he says, would 'certainly have made Arcite witty on his deathbed'.

(eds.) Miller (1916); Mozley (1979); Showerman and Goold (1977); Martindale (1988); Fyler (1979).

Oxenford

Oxenford, Oxford, in Chaucer's day a walled town (with its Norman castle), but already spreading out beyond the walls. It was a city of churches and monasteries, and a busy market centre with its own annual *fair. It had also become a 'university town' (from about the end of the 12th c. masters with their students are recorded). The characteristic colleges of Oxford were still, however, the exception rather than the rule. (Of the present institutions, Balliol, Merton, and University Colleges date from the 13th c., Exeter, New, Oriel, and Queen's from the 14th.) Most students lived in 'halls' or private houses or in hostels (like Tackley's Inn). Halls were very numerous, and although only one (St Edmund's Hall) has survived, a number of others later became colleges. Halls usually provided some lectures. In them students would share a room or have separate studies which led off from a communal bedroom. Chaucer's *Nicholas, who has a bedroom to himself in his 'digs' was probably relatively well-off: the formulaic phrase 'a poure scoler' applied to him may be ironic. Because of the behaviour of *clerks' like Nicholas the University eventually decreed that all scholars should reside in hall or in college. Life in medieval Oxford could be turbulent. Not only was there rivalry between the 'town' and the 'gown' (often more violent than that between Chaucer's Nicholas and *Absolon), but also between the different 'nations' (northerners, southerners, Welsh, etc.). There were some spectacular riots in the 13th c. Students, who by modern standards were very young, followed a traditional course of studies (see **Seven Liberal Arts**; **university**). Oxford was a lively intellectual centre, noted for science and for theology and philosophy (such diverse figures as Duns Scotus, *Bradwardine, *Ockham, and *Wyclif lectured there).

In Chaucer the most learned representative of the university is the *Clerk: he is addressed by the Host with a certain deference as 'Sire Clerk of Oxenford' (IV.1). Another Oxford clerk becomes the *Wife of Bath's fifth husband, *Jankin (4) (III.527). Especially notable however is the Oxford setting devised for The *Miller's Tale. Here we have a number of local references (to the abbey of Osney (*Oseneye)), St *Frideswide the town's patron saint, possibly to the parish church of St *Thomas) and detailed descriptions of the room of the 'poor scholar' and of the skills of the parish clerk. The night work of *Gerveys may, it has been suggested, have taken place at a smithy in Smithgate just inside the town wall at the north end of Catte Street. It is significant that at the end of the tale it is remarked that 'every clerk . . . heeld with oother' against the townsman. Chaucer seems to be well acquainted with Oxford. It is quite likely that he had a connection with Merton College, which was a major centre of scientific study (see *science) and had a fine library, rich in astronomical books. He mentions two Fellows of Merton College by name: Bradwardine was a prominent and well-known figure, but the other, Radulphus (Ralph) Strode, a logician who is almost certainly the 'philosophical *Strode' referred to at the end of *Troilus and Criseyde, sounds like a personal friend.

Bennett (1974).

P

Padowe, Padua (Padova), in northern Italy (IV.27), where the Clerk says he learned the story of Griselda from Petrarch (*Petrak). Petrarch was archdeacon of Padua, and lived there or at Arquà nearby from 1368 to 1374. His association with the town was well known and the remark need not imply that he met Chaucer there. Oxford clerks studied at Padua and Bologna.

Palamon, Palamoun, one of the heroes of *The *Knight's Tale*.

Palamon and Arcite, Love of, apparently an early version of The *Knight's Tale* mentioned in the Prologue of *The Legend of Good Women* (420).

Palatye, Balat, on the south western coast of Turkey. In the 14th c. it was an independent emirate. The *Knight is said to have fought with its 'lord' against another heathen in Turkey (I.65–6).

Palymerie, Palmyra, a city in Syria ruled by Zenobia (VII.2247).

Palinode, a song in which a writer recants something he has previously written, a recantation in general (see *Andreas Capellanus). Possible examples in Chaucer are the ending of *Troilus and Criseyde* and the '*Retracciouns'.

Palinurus, the pilot of Aeneas's ship. Aeneas meets his spirit in the underworld (*HF* 443).

Palladion, Palladium, the ancient image of Pallas Athene (*Mynerva) which ensured the safety of *Troy. Chaucer calls it a 'relic' (*Tr* I.153): he perhaps imagined it as a splendid reliquary—in one 15th-c. depiction of it in a tapestry Pallas looks remarkably like a crowned Virgin Mary in a tabernacle.
Scherer (1963), pl. 87.

Pallas, see *Mynerva.

Pamphilles, Pamphilus, the hero of the medieval Latin comedy *Pamphilus de amore* who loves Galatea (*Galathee). *Aurelius's love for *Dorigen is said to be more secret than Pamphilus's (V.1110). *Prudence quotes 'Pamphilus' three times (VII.1556, 1558, 1561), but only the first is genuine.

Pan was originally an Arcadian god of shepherds, but because his name was (wrongly) associated with Greek *pan* 'all', he became a universal god of *nature ('that men clepeth god of kynde', *BD* 512).

Pandarus, Pandare in *Troilus and Criseyde*, the uncle of Criseyde and the friend of Troilus. He is based on Boccaccio's Pandaro, 'a Trojan youth of high lineage and very bold spirit'. (His name goes back to classical sources, but the conception is Boccaccio's.) Because of his role as a go-between his name later became the word 'pander' (see *Tr* III.252–5). His character in Chaucer's poem has been much discussed. His liveliness and his love of manipulation and of the art of persuasion is often highly entertaining and comic, but some have seen in him a more sinister figure of treachery and deceit. He is first introduced as a 'friend', and such he remains throughout Troilus's adversities (he probably owes something to the character of Amis or 'Frend' in the *Roman de la Rose* and to the ancient idea of *friendship). Chaucer, unlike Boccaccio, does not give any indication of his age.

Pandyon, king of Athens and father of Philomela (*Philomene) and Procne (*Progne).

Panik, Panico, near Bologna in Italy (IV.939).

PAPYNION

Panthère d'Amours; Paradiso. See **Nicole de Margival*; **Divina Commedia*.

PAPYNION, Aemilianus Papinianus, a famous Roman jurist executed in 212 on the orders of the Emperor Caracalla for objecting to his intention to murder his brother Geta (*Bo* III pr.5:50).

Parables of Salomon, The, anti-feminist proverbs attributed to Solomon, an item in Jankyn's book of wicked wives (III.679).

Parcas. The 'angry Parcas, sustren thre' (invoked at the beginning of book V of *Troilus and Criseyde*) are the three Fates, elsewhere called the 'fatal sustren' (*Tr* III.733; *LGW* 2630) or the 'Wirdes' (*LGW* 2580; from OE *wyrd* 'fate'). Chaucer's 'Parcas' represents the accusative form or an anglicization of L. Parcae. The Parcae were represented as three old women spinning: Clotho ('spinner') who held the distaff with the thread of life, **Lachesis* ('apportioner') who drew off the thread and allotted life's span, and Atropos (**Attropos*) who cut it.

Pardoner, Pardoners. In Latin *questor*, a pardoner, usually ordained at least in the lower orders, was employed by the Church to take round indulgences to the faithful within a certain area. As the Parson (X.108 ff.) makes clear, the medieval Church taught that each Christian, to obtain forgiveness of sin, required contrition of heart, oral confession to a priest, and the performance of satisfaction. This satisfaction should be regarded as restitution—directly and practically in the case of material damage done to a neighbour, but indirectly in the case of sin against God or where no reparation was possible to a fellow human being. In the second case, satisfaction might be made either by compensatory extra good deeds on earth or in purgatory. The theory developed by theologians and canonists, chiefly in the period around the Fourth Lateran Council of 1215, taught that the Pope and his subordinates could grant to a sinner an indulgence that remitted part of the penalty for sin (*pena*) in purgatory in exchange for the donation of money to the Church for good purposes. This theory presupposed the sinner's contrition and confession of his sin to a priest, which expunged the *culpa* for sin, and was invalid without these. Gradually, however, indulgences came to be seen as a substitute for the whole penitential process, and the purchase of a pardon was often understood as absolving the purchaser from all guilt and punishment (*a pena et a culpa*). This misunderstanding was fostered by the prolific issue of indulgences by the Pope and religious institutions largely to raise money for their own support. The abuses are accurately described in the *General Prologue* account of the Pardoner (I.669–714) and in his own description in his prologue (VI.329–422) and the conclusion to his tale (VI.904–68); in all of these the association between indulgences and **relics* is emphasized, though the association was originally only that acquisition of either required payment. The Pardoner's association with **Rouncivale* (I.670) places him as employed by one of the English houses that most notoriously at this date exploited the fund-raising possibilities of indulgences, the Hospital of St Mary Rouncesval at Charing Cross in London. The fact that he 'streight was comen fro the court of Rome' (I.671) would validate the indulgences he offered, since all such documents theoretically had to be authorized by the Pope ('His walet . . . | Bretful of pardoun comen from Rome al hoot', I.686). Whether the association between the Pardoner and the Summoner involves more than their sexuality is not altogether clear: there is no necessary link between the professional activities of the two men, though the frequent corruption of the ecclesiastical courts by bribery might reasonably be considered parallel to the disruption of correct penitential processes fostered by indulgences. The mention of pardoners in the house of rumour at *The House of Fame* 2127 emphasizes their role as purveyors of stories as they travelled.   [AH]

Rv 823–5; Cooper (1989), 57–9; Mann (1973).

Pardoner's Prologue and Tale, The (640 lines in couplets) follows *The *Physician's Tale* in Fragment VI of *The *Canterbury Tales*. It is preceded by a forty-two-line Introduction in which the Host laments the fate of **Virginia* in *The Physician's Tale* ('Allas, so pitously as she was slayn!'), and asks the Pardoner for a tale—a merry one, he insists, for his heart 'is lost for pitee of this mayde'. The Pardoner agrees, but the 'gentils' become alarmed when he announces that first he will drink and eat some bread 'heere at this alestake' (the sign of a tavern): they demand 'som moral thyng', not 'ribaudye'. And this is what (eventually) they get. First, however, he gives a long monologue (329–462) in which he explains the techniques and the motivation of his preaching. The constant theme of his preaching is '*radix malorum est cupiditas*' ('greed is the root of all evils'), a text from I Timothy 6:10. He begins by showing his official indulgences (see *Pardoner), then shows his false *relics, expounding their remarkable virtues. Those who 'offer to' his relics are absolved, and by his trickery he makes a steady income. He preaches with enthusiasm on the wickedness of avarice in order to stir his audience not to abandon sin but to give him money. He does not care what happens to their souls. Thus, he says proudly, 'kan I preche agayn that same vice | Which that I use'. He does not see why he should imitate the poverty or the virtue of the apostles. He is in the habit of telling 'ensamples . . . of olde stories', since 'lewed [unlearned] peple loven tales olde'. One of these he will tell to the pilgrims—'for though myself be a ful vicious man, | A moral tale yet I yow telle kan'.

The Tale is set in Flanders (*Flaundres), where a company of young 'rioters' or rakes spend their time drinking, wenching, gambling, and swearing. The Pardoner pauses, and attacks the vices of drunkenness and gluttony, gambling and swearing in turn in an expansive and homiletic style (483–660). Returning to his narrative, he tells how the three 'rioters' are drinking at a tavern in the early morning when they see a corpse being carried to burial. It turns out to be a former companion of theirs who has been taken by *Death, who is slaying all the people in the region ('he hath a thousand slayn this pestilence'). When the taverner mentions that in a neighbouring village he has killed 'bothe man and womman, child, and hyne [servant], and page'—'I trowe [believe] his habitacioun be there'—the three swear brotherhood in order to slay 'this false traytour Deeth', and drunkenly set out towards the village. On the way they meet an old man, who tells them that he wanders the world restlessly, longing for death. Rudely, they accuse him of being in league with death 'to slay us yonge folk'. The old man tells them that if they want to find Death they should

turn up 'this crooked way' to a grove where he is under a tree. They run to the tree and find there a heap of gold coins. It is decided to carry the gold away at night, and the youngest of the three is chosen by lot to go to the town to bring food and wine while the others guard the treasure. The other two begin to discuss how they may keep the gold for themselves, and decide that when their companion returns he should be killed. Meanwhile, the youngest on his way to the town, thinking of the 'beautee of thise floryns newe and brighte', yearns to have them for himself, and quickly yields to the temptation to kill his companions. He buys poison from an apothecary and puts it into two of the three bottles he has borrowed. When he returns he is murdered, and the two survivors settle down: 'now lat us sitte and drynke, and make us merie, | And afterward we wol his body berie'. They drink the poison and both die (see Fig. 4). The Pardoner concludes with a warning against avarice and with an invitation to come up and buy his pardons. The Tale and the demonstration of his preaching technique apparently end—'And lo, sires, thus I preche'. But there is a further twist ('But, sires, o [one] word forgat I in my tale . . . '): he now offers his pardons to the Pilgrims themselves, beginning with the *Host 'for he is moost envoluped [enwrapped] in synne'. This provokes a violent and crude reaction, and the *Knight has to intervene to bring peace.

Because of the unity of Prologue and Tale and because of the high literary quality, the work is thought to come from 'the Canterbury period'. Both are remarkable rhetorical tours de force. The Prologue, a long monologue which resembles the *Wife of Bath's in being apparently confessional, owes much to the self-exposure of Faux Semblant ('False Seeming') in the *Roman de la Rose, though it is more realistic and more cynical in the flaunting of the vice of cupidity. The Tale is an *exemplum of the kind the Pardoner uses in his sermons on this very theme. It is also a remarkable piece of narrative art ('a matchless short story' says *Kittredge) which combines homiletic digression with rapid dramatic action in a series of vivid scenes. The story of the three companions and death is a widespread *folk tale, possibly ultimately of Eastern origin. The powerful moral idea of

Paris (1)

treasure-hunters or criminals destroying each other because of cupidity has remained popular.

While the tale has been constantly praised (and sometimes suggested as a likely contender for the prize), a number of passages and aspects of it have occasioned considerable discussion. The mysterious old man, for instance, has been identified or associated with a variety of figures ranging from Death to the Wandering Jew and has been variously (but not very convincingly) allegorized. Even more ink has been spilt over the question of what it reveals of the Pardoner's personality and motives. It was formerly often suggested that the tale was told in a tavern and that the Pardoner was drunk, but the text can hardly bear this interpretation. Very many explanations have been offered of his revelation of his techniques of persuasion, of his final attempt to sell his pardons, and of the Host's reaction. Because of the clearly dramatic quality of the whole performance and the links it has, or may have, with the *portrait of the Pardoner in the *General Prologue (taken by some to suggest that he was a born eunuch or homosexual) it has been seen as an extended psychological self-revelation, a demonstration of character in action. Kittredge, for instance saw him as the 'one lost soul' on the pilgrimage who showed for a moment at the end a 'paroxysm of agonised sincerity'. Others have seen it as an expression of a need for approval, or for compassion. In reaction to the extremes of psychological interpretation, it has been argued that the Pardoner simply sets out to entertain his hearers, either jokingly or cynically. More convincing is the suggestion that we should treat him as a more conventionally constructed dramatic figure like Faux Semblant or the 'Vice' of the late morality plays, though, as with the Wife of Bath, Chaucer has transformed a conventional type into a figure of great vitality and individuality. What is clear is that the tale firmly draws attention to the question of the morality of art by making a 'ful vicious man' tell a powerful moral tale.

(ed.) *Rv* 193–202, 904–10; *S&A* 409–38 [265–319]; Cooper (1989), 260–75; Faulkner (1973); Kittredge (1893); Minnis (1986).

Paris (1), the son of Priam and Hecuba. He was left outside to die when he was born because of a dream prophesying that he would cause the destruction of *Troy, but was rescued and brought up by shepherds. He married the nymph *Oenone, whom he later abandoned. When asked by the goddesses Juno, Minerva, and Venus to choose which was most beautiful he gave the golden apple to Venus, who had promised him the most beautiful woman in the world. Juno was henceforth implacably hostile to Troy (see *HF* 200–1). Eventually recognized by *Cassandra, he was sent by his father on a mission to Menelaus, king of Sparta, fell in love with Helen (*Eleyne) Menelaus' wife and carried her off to Troy, causing the great war. He appears a number of times in Chaucer, notably in *Troilus and Criseyde* (I.57–63, 652ff.; II.1449; IV.608–9). Elsewhere he is mentioned as a false lover, the betrayer of Oenone (*HF* 399; see also V.548), and as prominent in the Trojan story (*BD* 331). As a pair of famous lovers, Paris and Helen appear in the temple of Venus (*PF* 290–1). January's ardour for May in The *Merchant's Tale* is incongruously compared to that of Paris for Helen (IV.1753–4).

Paris (2), the city in *France, visited by Chaucer in 1377. Medieval Paris was an important mercantile, political, and intellectual centre. Its *university was especially famous and influential. It was a large and attractive city, with gardens and open spaces within the walls. In Chaucer it is most prominent in The *Shipman's Tale*, which is set at Saint-Denis (Seynt *Denys), then a separate town just to the north: the merchant goes to Paris on business (VII.332, 366). The *Wife of Bath notes that the abbey of Héloise (*Helowys) was not far from Paris (III.678). The *Prioress's French was not the French of Paris (I.126).

parish clergy; Parlement. See *Parson; *politics.

Parliament of Fowls or *Parlement of Foules* (called by Chaucer 'the Parlement of Foules' (*LGW* 419) and 'the book of Seint Valentynes day of the Parlement of Briddes' (X.1086)), a *dream vision in 699 lines of rhyme royal. It was written before The *Legend of Good Women* but its precise date is uncertain. Attempts have been made to link it with a particular royal betrothal or marriage, notably the negotiations in 1380 for the betrothal of Richard II to Anne of Bohemia (whom he married in 1382), but these are not proven. The poem would fit such an occasion, but it is entirely autonomous. It is usually thought to come between The *House of Fame* and *Troilus and Criseyde* in the late 1370s or early 1380s (though J. D. North argues that the astronomical references suggest that the time of the editing was 1 May, or possibly 3 May 1385). It survives in fourteen MSS and in Caxton (1477) and other early printed editions. It draws on a variety of sources, including besides the named *"Drem of Scipioun"* and the comments of 'Macrobye' and Alan of Lille (*Aleyn (1), in the 'Pleynt of Kynde'), *Claudian, *Dante, and *Boccaccio. It is one of the earliest known Valentine poems (others are written by *Gower and *Graunson).

The poem opens with musings on the mystery and the 'wonderful werkynge' of love. The poet does not know Love 'in dede' but has read about his 'myrakles and his crewel yre'. He describes how he avidly read a book, *"Tullyus of the *Drem of Scipioun', which tells how Scipio was visited by his ancestor *"Affrican' (Scipio Africanus Major) who took him up to the heavens and told him of the heavenly reward of the virtuous souls 'that lovede commune profyt', and warned him against delighting in the deceitful things of earth. The way to the bliss of heaven is 'Know thyself first immortal, | And loke ay besyly thow werche and wysse | To commune profit'. Night falls, and the poet's weary spirit finds rest in sleep. He dreams that Affrican stands at his bed-side, and praises him for reading his 'olde bok totorn'.

(113–234) With an invocation to *Venus to help him in his work, the poet tells of his dream. Affrican takes him to the gate of a park. Over the gate is a double inscription. One side says that it is the entrance to the 'blysful place' where 'grene and lusty May shal evere endure' and urges the reader to enter into its joy. The other announces that it is the entrance to a place of sorrow where Disdain and *Daunger inflict 'mortal strokes', and that the only remedy is to avoid it. These inscriptions written in gold and black throw the dreamer into confusion and uncertainty. His guide pushes him in, telling him not to be afraid since the inscriptions are not meant for him but only for the servants of Love. He can be an observer and, he will see 'mater

of to wryte'. They come into a beautiful landscape, with a river, trees, and many flowers, where rabbits, deer, and squirrels disport themselves and *birds sing with angelic voice. The air is temperate, without extremes of hot or cold. Under a tree, beside a spring, *Cupid is making his arrows, which are tempered in the water by his daughter, Wille. With them are the allegorical personages of love allegory, including *Curteysie, Craft, Delyt, *Beauty, and *Youth. There is a temple of brass set on pillars of jasper: women dance around it and on it sit many white doves. Inside the temple the dreamer hears the sound of sighs, and sees the god *Priapus and 'in a prive corner in disport' *Venus and her porter Richesse. Beside Venus are Bacchus and Ceres. The walls of the temple are painted with stories of famous lovers—'al here love, and in what plyt they dyde'.

(295–699) Returning to the park, the dreamer sees the goddess *Nature sitting on a hill of flowers. Before her sits a multitude of birds of all kinds: it is St Valentine's day and they have come to hear Nature's judgements and to choose their mates. She has them sit in order, the birds of prey highest, then those that eat worms and the water fowl, and on the ground the seed-eaters. On Nature's hand sits a beautiful female eagle. Nature announces that the birds shall choose their mates, beginning with the tercel eagle, and on condition that the female birds agree with the choice: 'this is oure usage alwey, fro yer to yeere'. The royal tercel announces that his choice is for the female eagle and pleads his case. But a second and then a third tercel urge their claims. This 'gentil ple [noble suit] in love' lasts most of the day, and the rest of the birds become impatient, crying 'have don, and lat us wende!' Nature quietens them, and decides that a spokesman should give the verdict for each group of birds. On behalf of the birds of prey a young falcon says that since it cannot be proved by reason which of the suitors loves the female eagle best, and a trial by battle (which they would welcome) is ruled out, the noblest of the three ('the worthieste | Of knyghthod . . . of blod the gentilleste') would be most fitting for her, and she herself must know which this is. The remarks of the goose on behalf of the waterfowl ('but she wol love hym, lat hym love another!') excite the scorn of the noble birds; the turtle dove's belief in long and true service is scoffed at by the duck, who is in turn rebuked by the falcon. Finally the cuckoo's 'if they can't make up their mind let them stay single all their lives' provokes an angry reply from the merlin. Nature intervenes again, and announces her judgement, that the female eagle herself shall choose between the three. If she were *Reason, Nature says, she would advise her to take the royal tercel 'as for the gentilleste and most worthi'. The female eagle humbly asks for a boon: that she should be allowed respite for a year before she makes her choice. Nature agrees, and gives all the other birds their mates. They rejoice and are eager to go, but first, in accordance with their custom, a number are chosen to sing a *roundel in Nature's honour. When this is over, the noise they make as they leave awakes the dreamer, who turns back to other books.

The liveliness of the *Parliament* makes it a favourite with readers. Critics in the earlier part of the 20th c. sometimes rather undervalued it, seeing it primarily as one step in an upward progress towards The *Canterbury Tales* and stressing the comedy of the parliament scene at the expense of other aspects. More recently it has been taken seriously as a poem in its own right with its own structure and coherence, which through a series of scenes and images explores the nature of *love and its relation with nature and society. The contrasting images and ideas (the austere devotion to '*commune profyt', the verdant park with its contradictory inscriptions which contains both the sensuous temple of Venus and the figure of God's vicar Nature presiding over the continuation of her species with the birds choosing their mates, whether in an elegant courtly style or more hastily and directly) seem to work together in a dialectic manner. Comedy and social satire coexist with seriousness and learning in a work of great variety and sophistication.

(ed.) *Rv* 383–94, 994–1002; Brewer (1960); Minnis (1995), 252–321; North (1990), 326–66; Aers (1981); Bennett (1957 and 1979); Clemen (1963), ch. 3.

PARMANYDES, Parmenides of Elea (*c.*515–after 450 BC), the founder of the *Eleatic school of philosophy, mentioned in *Boece* (III pr.12:193). Boethius quotes Parmenides as saying

that the divine substance turns the world and the moving sphere.

Parnaso, Pernaso, Mt. Parnassus, north of Delphi, sacred to the *Muses. Chaucer's references allude to it as the dwelling of the Muses (*HF* 521; *Anel* 16; *Tr* III.1810), or associate it with the skills of *rhetoric: 'I sleep nevere on the Mount of Pernaso,' says the *Franklin (V.721).

parody and burlesque. Parody and burlesque are both forms of mocking imitation. The two are not clearly distinguishable; but burlesque is commonly held to lean more towards sheer fun, whereas 'parody' implies a rather more serious attempt to ridicule its object. The *OED* describes parody as 'a composition in prose or verse in which the characteristic turns of thought and phrase in an author or class of authors are imitated in such a way as to make them appear ridiculous, especially by applying them to ludicrously inappropriate subjects'. Chaucer is an author much given to imitating the 'turns of thought and phrase' characteristic of voices other than his own, and he also has a keen sense of the ridiculous. So, in his work, the possibility of a parodic or burlesque intention is commonly to be reckoned with.

It is, however, not always easy to determine, in a particular poem or passage, whether an imitation is indeed intended to make its object 'appear ridiculous'. What appears ridiculous to a modern reader may not have seemed so to Chaucer or his original audience. So the identification of parody or burlesque in his work requires a certain exercise of the historical imagination. Thus, to many modern readers it may appear that the high-flown love speeches of the three eagles in The *Parliament of Fowls* must be read as parodic of the artificial language of courtly love; but it is hard to find anything in either the content or the context of these speeches to support such a reading. The eagles represent just that class of human society, the aristocracy, to which such sentiments were considered appropriate—Criseyde dreams of Troilus in the form of an eagle (*Tr* II.926)—and the goddess Nature herself, so far from regarding their behaviour as unnatural, treats them with special favour. By contrast, a burlesque intention is clearly signalled in the love speech which the parish clerk

Absolon addresses to the carpenter's wife Alison in The *Miller's Tale* (I.3698–707). *Absolon's (2) language is itself suspect, as the eagles' is not. He blends rich biblical imagery (honeycomb, cinnamon, turtle dove) with bathetic references to sweat and sheep's udders; and when he addresses his beloved as 'lemman' (I.3700, 3705) he employs a term which in Chaucer's English was evidently marked as vulgar: the Manciple calls it 'a knavyssh speche' (IX.205). In any case, the whole social context of Absolon's utterance, as well as its ridiculous outcome, serve to establish its burlesque character. He and Alison are 'ludicrously inappropriate subjects' for the expression of such sentiments.

It was in *The Canterbury Tales* that Chaucer's talent for burlesque or parodic imitation found most scope. Because the pilgrims tell so many differing types of tale, the collection fostered an awareness of genre which could, on occasion, turn to mockery. The joke may arise from the juxtaposition of sharply contrasting genres, as in the case of The *Monk's Tale* and The *Nun's Priest's Tale*. The story of Chantecleer unfolds in a farmyard world utterly remote from the world of the Monk's lofty 'tragedies'; yet when Chantecleer is threatened by the fox, the Nun's Priest treats the case with full tragic gravity. The sudden fall of the proud fox prompts reflections on the transience of worldly joy—'For evere the latter ende of joye is wo'—and on the mysteries of predestination; and a series of piteous exclamations links the affair with the great tragedies of Greece and Rome and with the death of King Richard I of England. This last was the subject of a grand lamentation by the rhetorician Geoffrey of Vinsauf (*Gaufred), which the Priest invokes as a model of what he himself would have wished to produce in the present case. All this, like much more in the Tale, is burlesque writing: the application of lofty ideas and sentiments to a ludicrously inappropriate subject. The presence of the Monk's immediately preceding tale points up the joke, so far as 'tragedy' is concerned. It may even be thought that the Nun's Priest's 'mock-heroic tragedy', as the poem has been called, was designed to make The *Monk's Tale* itself look ridiculous. But this would be to mistake the nature of burlesque—or at least burlesque such as this, where the joke seems to lie simply in the free-

wheeling absurdity of responding 'tragically' to the adventure of a cock (who does, after all, survive the experience).

The case is somewhat different with the prime example of mocking imitation in Chaucer's work, his Tale of *Sir Thopas*; for here there is a definite intention to hit and damage a target, albeit in a light and humorous fashion. The target is romance—not the kind of romance represented by the tales of the Knight or the Squire, but the more popular or minstrelesque romances of the day. In much detail and with considerable relish, Chaucer imitates the metre, rhymes, and diction of these rather inartistic productions. Their characteristic tail-rhyme stanza (which he himself employs only here) becomes ridiculous in his hands, with its curt three-stress tail-lines and the even curter one-stress bobs ('In towne', 'With mace'); and this would have alerted readers to look for other non-Chaucerian things in the Tale. They would not have had far to look. The opening lines—'Listeth, lordes, in good entent, | And I wol telle verayment | Of myrthe and of solas'— make their minstrelesque appeal to the 'lords' in the audience with a word, 'listeth', that Chaucer never uses outside *Sir Thopas* ('herkneth' would be his usual word), and with a rhyme which suppresses the final -e which 'entente' always has elsewhere in Chaucer. Nor is the telling of the story better handled. There are several extensive passages of description—of Sir Thopas himself, of the forest through which he rides, and of his arming for battle—but the main events of the action are treated either cursorily ('Sire Thopas fil in love-longynge') or not at all. When Thopas does finally come upon the three-headed giant, he has to turn back home to fetch his armour, and the promised encounter in fact never takes place. The Host can stand no more of such time-wasting: 'Namoore of this, for Goddes dignitee'.

However, the authors of *Guy of Warwick*, *Bevis of Hampton*, *Lybeaus Desconus*, and the other target romances might well have objected that, considered as a parodic imitation of their work, *Sir Thopas* was grossly unfair. Chaucer does imitate, with deadly precision, many of what he regarded as the infelicities in their manner; but there is also in the poem a vein of pure burlesque comedy—a comedy which leaves the popular romances quite unscathed. It is a case, again, of the 'ludicrously inappropriate subject'. For Sir Thopas, unlike Sir Guy, Sir Bevis, and the rest, is no proper hero of romance, however popular—no more than Absolon is a proper courtly lover or Chantecleer a proper tragic hero. His unheroic birthplace, Poperyng in Flanders, arouses suspicions which are to be borne out by such things as his effeminate appearance (white face and 'lippes rede as rose'), his ride through a forest peopled by 'many a wilde best | Ye, bothe bukke and hare', and his prudent withdrawal in the face of the giant. Jokes like these quite fail to hit the target, and indeed can never have been meant to do so: Guy of Warwick is no pale-faced bourgeois knight. Rather, they add to the parodic imitation an element of sheer, self-delighting absurdity. And it is this latter characteristic—so prominent in The Nun's Priest's Tale—which is most distinctively Chaucerian in those places where the poet turns to what we call parody or—in his case, better—burlesque. [JAB]

parson, parish clergy. The word *parson* in Middle English usually denotes a cleric who held the right to the tithes of a parish as rector rather than as vicar (see *MED persoun(e)* n. (2)), though this distinction is not always clear. The parson held the primary responsibility for the pastoral care of the parishioners, though might delegate this with permission to a curate. The geographical extent of a parish varied considerably, from a very small area in a city such as London where numerous parishes are to be found, to a very large area in sparsely populated rural districts; normally each parish had at least one church but it might also contain subordinate chapels separate from this church. The parson was instituted by the diocesan bishop, though was usually nominated by the patron of the living (a religious house or a member of the gentry who had endowed the church). Parsons might be licensed by the bishop to hold more than one living, or to take leave of absence for a specified time for legitimate purposes such as study, but were expected to provide and pay for a substitute. The Parson of *The Canterbury Tales*, perhaps the only figure in the *General Prologue* in whose description no trace of irony is perceptible, portrays the ideal of the parish priest at the end of the 14th c.; but the description

in largely negative terms gives a good picture of the normal abuses of the office. [AH]

Heath (1969); A. H. Thompson (1947); *Rv* 819.

Parson's Tale, The, forms Fragment X of *The *Canterbury Tales* and brings that work, at least in the form in which it has survived, to its conclusion. A verse Prologue of seventy-four lines introduces a long prose work. In the Prologue, which is linked to the preceding Fragment by the opening line 'By that the Maunciple hadde his tale al ended', The *Host, remarking 'now lakketh us no tales mo than oon', asks the Parson for his story. The instant reply is 'Thou getest fable noon ytoold for me'. Quoting Paul's letter to Timothy, he asks why he should sow chaff rather than wheat. If they would like to hear 'moralitee and vertuous mateere' he will provide it. Since he cannot 'geeste "rum, ram, ruf," by lettre' and holds 'rym' to be 'but litel bettre', he will tell 'a myrie tale in prose | To knytte up al this feeste and make an ende'. His tale will be a 'meditacioun'. The pilgrims agree, for it seemed appropriate 'to enden in som vertuous sentence', and the Host requests that he tell his 'meditacioun'—'but hasteth yow; the sonne wole adoun; | Beth fructuous, and that in litel space'.

He begins with a verse from Jeremiah: 'Stondeth upon the weyes, and seeth and axeth [ask] of olde pathes (that is to seyn, of olde sentences) which is the goode wey, and walketh in that wey, and ye shal fynde refresshynge for youre soules.' There are many spiritual ways which lead folk to Jesus Christ and to the reign of glory: the way of Penitence (see *penance, penitence) is a noble one 'which may nat fayle to man ne to womman that thurgh synne hath mysgoon fro the righte wey of Jerusalem celestiall'. He proceeds to expound the nature of penitence, and especially the things which are necessary to perfect penitence: contrition, confession, and satisfaction. Each of these is treated in detail, and the section on confession involves a long exposition of the sources of sin, and of the *Seven Deadly Sins with their appropriate remedies. Finally after a brief account of the things which 'disturb' penitence, the treatise ends with the 'fruit' of penitence: 'the endelees blisse of hevene', which 'blisful regne may men purchace by poverte espirituel, and the glorie by lowenesse, the plentee of joye by hunger and thurst, and the reste by travaille, and the lyf by deeth and mortificacion of synne'.

It is impossible to determine the date of the tale. Some think that it may have been an independent work from an earlier period which was worked into *The Canterbury Tales*, others that it was written at a late stage with the Tales in mind (a view supported by a number of links with the preceding tales), others that it comes from a very late stage and is intimately connected with the *Retractions, yet others that it is not by Chaucer at all but was added by an editor (a view for which there is no textual evidence). It is not, as is sometimes said, a sermon, but an example of another common medieval type, a treatise on penance. It is based on two well-known 13th-c. handbooks, Raymond de Pennaforte's *Summa de poenitentia* and a treatise on the Seven Deadly Sins, the *Summa vitiorum* of William *Peraldus, and draws on similar didactic works.

As benefits a didactic work (and the character of the Parson as described in the *General Prologue*) the style is simple and direct. But although only the single voice of an expositor is heard, there are some vivid similitudes and brief descriptions in colloquial style, and some passages which achieve a grave eloquence. The question of its significance in the overall structure of the *Tales* has been much debated. It is clearly in some sense a conclusion, and is indicated as such by various closural remarks in the Prologue, but it is far from clear that it represents 'the Conclusion' claimed by some critics, a kind of religious 'key' to the whole meaning of Chaucer's work. But, on the other hand, even though it moves us out of the world of fiction and indeed questions the validity of fiction, it should not be ignored (as it often is) as a dull and unfortunate coda. The Parson gives orthodox clerical views on a wide range of topics and themes (such as *marriage for *gentilesse') which are given dramatic treatment in the preceding narratives, and these not only illuminate their background, but add yet another viewpoint in an encyclopaedic work. The Parson is one voice among others. 'Ne breke thou nat oure pley' the Host says to him, and although he seems in one way to break the play of competing narratives, in another his 'myrie tale in prose' adds a new dimension by its earnest direction of the listeners to the

way 'of thilke parfit glorious pilgrimage | That hight Jerusalem celestial'.

(ed.) *Rv* 287–327, 956–65; *S&A* 723–60 [529–611]; Petersen (1910); Cooper (1989), 395–409; Bestul (1989); Howard (1976), 376–87; Patterson (1976).

Parthes, Parthians, a warlike people who established an empire in Northern Persia and fought a series of wars against the Romans. They are mentioned in *The *Pardoner's Tale* (VI.622) and *Boece* (II pr.7:65).

Parthonope, Parthenopaeus, one of the Seven against *Thebes (1) (*Anel* 58, *Tr* V.1503), who died of his wounds.

Parvys, the Sergeant of the Law 'often hadde been at the Parvys' (I.310). A *parvis* was the porch or forecourt of a church. The reference here is almost certainly to the porch of St Paul's Cathedral in London, which was a meeting-place for lawyers and for their clients.

Passetyme of Pleasure, see *Hawes.

Pathmos, the Greek island of Patmos off the coast of Turkey, where St *John (1) saw his vision (VII.583).

pathos, see *pite(e).

patience, defined in a modern dictionary as 'tolerant and even-tempered perseverence' and 'the capacity for calmly enduring pain, trying situations, etc.', has in Chaucer both wider and stronger connotations. Sometimes it is a spiritual quality: 'pacience' is, says *Prudence, quoting Solomon and St James, 'a gret vertu of perfeccioun' (VII.1516), 'this vertu', says the Parson, 'maketh a man lyk to God, and maketh hym Goddes owene deere child'. Sometimes its close association with suffering (with which it is etymologically connected (L. *patior*: suffer) is unusual or disturbing to a modern reader, as when Virginia's father, about, to kill her says, 'O gemme of chastitee, in pacience | Take thou thy deeth' (VI.223–4). The proverbial *vincit qui patitur* (he who suffers conquers) underlines what is perhaps the greatest difference in the medieval idea of patience, that it is often regarded as a very positive virtue, and not simply as totally passive suffering. In Prudentius's allegorical *Psychomachia* Patience or Longanimity 'fights' against Wrath by receiving imperturbedly all the blows on her impenetrable armour, so that Wrath is driven to kill herself in frenzy. In the 15th-c. play *The Castle of Perseverance* she fights with roses. A 16th-c. emblem of Jean Cousin shows her with armour and shield but without weapons trampling on the wheel of *Fortune, whose slings and arrows she has survived. Patience is sometimes close to Fortitude: 'patience as the truest fortitude' in Milton's phrase. Medieval ideas about patience derive from both classical and Christian roots. They owe a good deal to stoicism with its stress on the virtuous indifference to the storm or *perturbatio* of passions or external tribulations. A strictly Christian view of it would not be a simple celebration of human endurance but would involve the imitation of Christ (who, according to St Bernard, 'had in life a passive action and underwent in death an active passion, doing the work of salvation on earth'). In practice, however, and especially if the idea of imitation is not made explicit, the two merge easily. Biblical and Senecan texts are found side by side in *Melibee*. And Chaucer's reading of Boethius probably influenced his ideal of 'patient suffraunce'.

The most extensive descriptions of the virtue are to be found in *Melibee* and *The Parson's Tale*, and have a distinctly religious cast. From the Old Testament came not only proverbial matter from 'Solomon', but the exemplary figure of the patient *Job, who became a 'figure' of Christ the suffering Man of Sorrows. Prudence urges her husband to imitate Christ (VII.1500 ff.). Another argument in her persuasion of her husband is the Christian hope of a later reward. You should strive, she says, to have patience, for the tribulations of this world soon pass, and the joy that a man seeks to have through patience is eternal. The Parson speaks of it as a remedy against the Sin of Wrath. He comes to it after discussing 'mansuetude [meekness], that is debonairetee [meekness, kindness]' (X.659 ff.). Patience is a virtue 'that suffreth swetely every mannes goodnesse, and is not wrooth for noon harm that is doon to hym'. He adds other

definitions from various authorities: it is the virtue 'that suffreth debonairely alle the outrages of adversitee and every wikked word', and it is powerful, for it defeats an enemy (as 'the wise man' says 'If thow wolt venquysse thyn enemy, lerne to suffre').

It is with 'the outrages of adversitee' that Patience is associated: it is a remedy against the vicissitudes of *Fortune. In *The *Parliament of Fowls* the dreamer finds outside the temple of Venus Peace, and beside her 'Dame Pacience syttynge . . . | With face pale, upon an hil of sond'. The hill of sand appears to be Chaucer's iconographical addition. It seems to suggest the instability of the world (and there does not seem to be much room for patience inside Venus's temple). The image of the heroic suffering of those who are 'constant in heart' (cf. VI.56; IV.668, 1047) sometimes excite the wicked to new excesses of cruelty (IV.622–3), but the sight of patient suffering should excite '*pite' and wonder. Patience (the enemy of Wrath) is regularly linked in Chaucer with the gentler human emotions—'*gentillesse', 'pite', and kindness. It is closely associated with goodness ('pacient benyngnytee', IV.929; *Griselda is 'pacient *and kynde', IV.1187). Perhaps this connection has something to do with the sense of 'suffer' as 'allow' (as in 'suffer little children').

'Suffer' is of course one of the words which often appear in contexts to do with patience. Even more interesting perhaps is 'endure', which illustrates some of the nuances of the concept in different contexts. Its meanings range from 'continue, last, remain, stay' to (the transitive) 'suffer, put up with' a variety of 'tribulaciouns'. Often it is 'sorwe' (*Anel* 327) or 'wo' (V.1484) or, especially, the adversity of Fortune (as in *The *Clerk's Tale*, IV.756, 811, 1042). In stories set in the ancient world, like *The *Knight's Tale*, 'enduring' often seems a kind of stoic acceptance which is sometimes close to fatalism. Arcite says that he and Palamon must endure the adversity of prison, caused by Fortune and some wicked disposition of Saturn (I.1091), a thought that is echoed later (1185–6), with the addition 'and everich of us take his aventure'. Elsewhere it can refer to the pains of love ('swich peyne and wo as Loves folk endure', *Tr* I.34).

As always in Chaucer, a general concept is used

dramatically. Alongside exemplary figures like Griselda or *Custance, or the *Parson of the *General Prologue* who was 'in adversitee ful pacient' (I.484) there are some less willing sufferers, like the old husband with a young wife, who 'moste endure, as other folk, his care' (I.3232). Prudence's husband is at first very resistant to her doctrines, and other characters are decidedly *im*patient, as the *Wife of Bath, who unlike Griselda, 'this flour of wyfly pacience' (IV.919), chides her third husband (who has had the temerity to 'preche of Jobes pacience') and tells him that *he* must do the suffering: 'suffreth alwey, syn ye so wel kan preche', and, since a man is 'moore resonable' than a woman, 'ye moste been suffrable' (III.436–42).

Of the Tales in which Patience has a particularly significant role, it is perhaps *The Franklin's Tale* which presents the ideal of 'pacient suffraunce' in its most original form. Here patience, strongly opposed to 'rigour', is praised in the most positive terms by the narrator: 'pacience is an heigh vertu, certeyn, | For it vanquysseth, as thise clerkes seyn, | Thynges that rigour sholde nevere atteyne.' 'Lerneth to suffre,' he continues—because in life you will have to, whether you want to or not (V.773 ff.). In the tale, in a secular context of love, patience emerges as a state of the soul which prizes a mutual and submissive tolerance—'a willing forbearance, a voluntary embrace of some constraint upon or diminution of the self' (Pearsall). And, of course, it illustrates the old maxim that those who suffer conquer.

Crampton (1974); Schiffhorst (1978); Pearsall (1985), 160.

patrons and patronage. A patron of art or letters is (Johnson) 'one who countenances, supports, or protects', a meaning derived from L. *patronus* 'protector, defender, patron'. Chaucer uses the word *patroun* only twice (*Mars* 275, *Anel* 4), of the god Mars, in the sense of tutelary deity or protector. In the Middle Ages, writers could benefit from patronage from a variety of sources: from the Church, guilds, confraternities, civic bodies, or private individuals. Royal patronage of the arts seems to have been more extensive and official in *France than in England (where there were no great royal libraries that could match those of the French kings). In general, painters or sculptors could receive financial support in a direct way from commissions (especially at the hands of great patrons like Jean, duke of Berry), whereas writers and scholars, unless they owed their living to the Church, usually could expect to benefit from support or protection in more indirect ways, through influence which might lead to various kinds of preferment. There is no evidence that Chaucer received financial reward for his poetry. The payments recorded (see Geoffrey *Chaucer: life) are for public service and duties. It is, no doubt, very possible that he received indirect help or preferment through influence, but there is no evidence that this was due to his distinction as a poet rather than as a civil servant. What is more remarkable is the absence of reference to patrons or patronage in his works, compared with *Gower, *Hoccleve, or *Lydgate—though they do not seem to have been financially dependent on patronage. Nor is there much external evidence. Allusions suggest that *The *Book of the Duchess* is connected with the bereavement of John of Gaunt, but the poem contains no reference to its having been received or having been approved by him. The 16th-c. note that it was 'made by Geffrey Chawcyer at ye request of ye duke of Lancastar' has no real authority. Similarly attempts to find occasions, much less patrons, for the other dream visions have not won acceptance. The allusion in the Prologue of the *Legend of Good Women* (496–7) where Alceste says that when the book is finished he should 'give it to the queen' (there is no evidence that this was ever done) may well be a quite general allusion to a common practice in the world of court poetry. The famous Troilus frontispiece (see *audience and Fig. 8) seems rather to suggest a listening group of the elegant and mighty rather than to identify 'Chaucer reading to the Court of Richard II'. It is possible that he read his poems to the court or to individual members of it (just as Froissart read to Gaston Count of Foix), but there is no hard evidence for it. Many of his poems seem rather to be addressed to his friends. There is a notable absence of effusive dedications to great patrons, such as are commonly found, and nothing to suggest that as a poet he sees himself as a 'client': his 'habitual manner (as author or poet figure) maintains a bland indifference to, and independence from, the usage of clientship'

Paul, Poul, Paulus (Seint)

(Norton-Smith). Perhaps he might have been sympathetic to the later remark of Francis Bacon, that 'books (such as are worthy of the name of books) ought to have no patrons but truth or reason'.

Green (1980); Holzknecht (1923); Norton-Smith (1974), 3; Pearsall (1977).

Paul, Poul, Paulus (Seint), St Paul the Apostle (sometimes simply called 'the Apostle', e.g. by the Wife of Bath, III.49, 64, etc.). He is quoted frequently (especially, though not exclusively, by the *Parson), and on a variety of topics: the *Wife of Bath discusses his remarks on virginity (III.73ff.), the Nun's Priest quotes his statement that everything that is written is written for our doctrine (VII.3441–2), the Parson quotes his warning against 'fables and swich wrecchednesse' (X.31–4). *Prudence quotes him on rejoicing with the joyful and weeping with the sorrowful (VII.939), on not returning evil for evil (VII.1292), and on the duty of judges to punish misdoers (VII.1440). The *Pardoner is enthusiastic about his treatment of gluttony: 'of this matiere, O Paul, wel kanstow trete' (VI.517–23). The Parson finds matter in him for this and for other sins (covetousness, avarice, lechery, adultery, etc.), and cites him on the need for wives to be subject to their husbands (X.634) and for a man to love his wife as Christ loved the Church (X.929). Warning against the misuse of penitential garments (see *clothes), he quotes Paul to prove that Christ is more pleased by the spiritual clothing of 'misericorde, debonairetee, suffraunce, and swich manere of clothynge' than by hair shirts and the like (X.1054). (For the cathedral in London dedicated to him, see *Poules, Seinte.)

PAULYN, Decius Paulinus, consul in 498, defended by Boethius (*Boece) from the rapacity of the imperial courtiers ('the howndes of the paleys', *Bo* I pr.4, 92–3).

Paulus, see *Paul.

PAULUS, Lucius Aemilius Paulus 'Macedonicus', so called because of his defeat of Perseus the last king of Macedonia in 168 BC, a Roman general and consul. He is mentioned in a passage on Fortune's mutability because he wept piteously for the captivity of the king (*Bo* II pr.2:64).

Pavye, Pavia, in northern Italy, the birthplace of *January in *The Merchant's Tale* (IV.1246); also mentioned in *Rom* A (1654).

Pearl, poem found in BL Cotton Hero A.1, in eleven-line stanzas with heavy but not structural alliteration, the stanzas being linked by concatenation and grouped by means of the recurrence of this into groups of five (or in one case six). This, and the other poems in the manuscript (*Patience, Purity* or *Cleanness,* *Sir Gawain and the Green Knight*) are usually regarded as deriving from a single author from the borders of Staffordshire / Cheshire / Derbyshire in the period *c*.1360–90. *Pearl* provides an instructive comparison with Chaucer's *Book of the Duchess,* even though no influence can be proved in either direction, since both are dream poems dealing with the loss of a beloved relation through death and the possible sources of consolation for this bereavement.

[AH]

(ed.) E.V. Gordon (1953).

Peasants' Revolt, the name given by modern historians to a series of attempts in 1381, some of them certainly coordinated but some probably independent, by those below the rank of the gentry to redress social grievances. The immediate focus of discontent was the proclamation of a poll tax in 1380, but other factors of rural life since the *Black Death added to the strength of the revolt. The main participants in the movements, contrary to the revolt's popular name, seem to have come not from the lowest ranks of society but from those, such as minor landholders, free tenants, and artisans, with some education and standing. Two of the main areas of revolt were Essex and Kent; forces from these counties with their leader *Wat Tyler converged on London in June 1381 and broke open and burned documents from the New Temple and other lodgings of lawyers and clerics; the Londoners meanwhile destroyed Gaunt's palace of the Savoy in the Strand, and a band of rebels led by Jack Straw (*Jakke Straw) raided in the western suburbs of London. The young Richard II met some of the rebels at Mile End, and succeeded in gaining their agreement to disperse with a promise of redress for some of their grievances. During the meeting or shortly after, another group of rebels succeeded in breaking into the Tower of London where they dragged out and killed Simon Sudbury, archbishop of Canterbury and three others. The following day when Richard again confronted the rebels, their leader Wat Tyler was killed. Other disturbances occurred outside London in a number of places, and the property of religious houses such as St Albans and Bury St Edmunds was often the target of the rioters. Chaucer refers to Jack Straw, and to the mob's dislike of the *Flemings, in *The Nun's Priest's Tale* VII.3394–7.   [AH]

Dobson (1983); Hilton and Aston (1984).

Pedmark, Penmarch, on the rugged coast of Brittany, not far from Quimper (V.801). The 'contré' of Arveragus in *The Franklin's Tale* is nearby. It has been suggested that this area may have been 'in the news' because in 1386 John Hawley, a famous buccaneer, seized three ships there.

Pegasee, the, the Pegasean horse, i.e. Pegasus, the legendary winged horse (V.207).

Pelleus, Pelias, the uncle of *Jason, who usurped the throne of Iolchos from his half-brother Aeson (*Eson) (*LGW* 1397ff.).

Pemond, Piedmont, the province in northern Italy (IV.44).

penance, penitence, penitential literature. Following on from early medieval ideas concerning the process by which a man might secure release from the consequences of his sin and obtain God's mercy, the Lateran Council of 1215 distinguished between three stages: first contrition, ME *penitence*, the repentance or revulsion within a man's own soul from the sin committed; second, confession or acknowledgment of that sin, usually to a priest and normally to a man's parish priest; third, atonement for the sin done, *penance*, by restitution if this were possible (e.g. of property stolen) or, if restitution were impracticable (e.g. in the case of rape, or if the offence were against God rather than against a neighbour), by the performance of

some virtuous action that would not normally be undertaken. Because these three stages were so closely connected in medieval thought and practice, the terms penitence and especially *penance* often cover all three. The Lateran Council laid the requirement for annual confession to the parish priest on each Christian; this was reinforced by local legislation. Consequently a whole genre of penitential literature grew up to counsel the clergy on the details of their obligations regarding confession, with particular emphasis on the analysis of sin; in some cases these texts were used by, and adapted for, the literate laity. Chaucer's *Parson's Tale* gives a good example of such a text. Inevitably in such works the first stage of the process described above receives the least attention, since it was hard for even the most expert confessor to discover the inward state of a man's soul; this neglect of the need for a revulsion from sin (satirized by *Langland, for instance, in *Piers Plowman* B 20, 305–80) was encouraged by the Church's fostering of the purchase of indulgences as a form of penance (see *pardoners).   [AH]

Pene, the contre of, Carthage (L. adj. *Poeni* (*leones*) 'Phoenician' or 'Carthaginian' (lions)). (*Bo* III m.2:8).

Penelope(e), Penalopee, Penelope, the wife of Ulysses, who faithfully waited for him during his twenty years' absence. She became an exemplary figure of wifely steadfastness. Chaucer several times cites 'good Penelope' as an example of female *trouthe* (II.75; V.1443; *BD* 1081; *Anel* 82; *Tr* V.1778; *LGW* 252).

Penneus, Peneus, a river god (the river Pinios in Thessaly) who was father of Daphne (*Dane; I.2064).

PEPYS, SAMUEL (1633–1703), the diarist, was an admirer of Chaucer ('a very fine poet'). He suggested to *Dryden 'the character of the good Parson' which appeared in the *Fables*. Pepys owned a copy of *Speght's edition and some MSS of Chaucer (his Speght and MS Pepys 2006 are still in the Pepysian Library, Magdalene College Cambridge).

CH i. 153–5.

PERALDUS, WILLIAM (*c.*1200–*c.*1271), sometimes known in the medieval period as *Parisiensis* (though he is not the only recipient of that surname). Dominican friar of Paris, best known as the author of the *penitential handbook, *Summa virtutum ac viciorum*; there are numerous derivatives from this, such as the French *Miroir du monde / Somme le roi* and its English versions (e.g. the *Ayenbite of Inwit*). Chaucer's *Parson's Tale* draws ultimately much of its material from Peraldus. [AH]

Perce. Persia in Chaucer's day consisted of a number of realms under Mongol lordship, part of what he called *Tartarye. His references are all to ancient Persia and its inhabitants (Percyens, Perses, Persien). They occur mostly in the story of Zenobia (*Cenobia) in The *Monk's Tale* (VII.2247–374). (See also III.2079; VII.2235; the reference in *Boece* (II pr.2:65) to 'the kyng of the Percyens' is a mistake (from the French translation) for 'King Perseus' who was defeated by *Paulus.)

Percyvell, see *Sir Perceval of Galles*.

Perkyn Revelour, the apprentice in The *Cook's Tale*.

Pernaso, see *Parnaso.

Perotheus, Pirithous, the childhood friend, and 'felawe' or sworn brother, of *Theseus in The *Knight's Tale* who visits him and intercedes for *Arcite (I.1191 ff.). The *friendship was legendary: their attempt to abduct Proserpina from the underworld to be Pirithous's bride is mentioned in classical sources; Chaucer refers to a non-classical story (found in the *Roman de la Rose*) that when Pirithous died Theseus sought him 'doun in helle'.

PERRERS, ALICE, notorious as the mistress of the ageing *Edward III, at whose court she exerted great influence and patronage; she fled abroad following Edward's death, and her property was confiscated. It is usually thought that *Langland based his portrayal of Lady Meed (B passus 2–4) on Alice Perrers. Chaucer's name appears along with hers in a document of 1379. [AH]

LR 115–16.

Perses, Persien, see *Perce.

PERSIUS, Aulus Persius Flaccus (34–62), Roman satirical poet. The *Franklin's remark (V.721) that he never slept on Mount Parnassus (*Parnaso) is a quotation from the Prologue to Persius's Satires. That it is not an exact quotation ('nor dreamed that I slept on twin-peaked Parnassus') and that it is the only one from Persius in Chaucer is usually taken to indicate that he did not know the Latin poet at first hand but picked the phrase up from a *florilegium or some other source.

Pertelote, Chauntecleer's favourite hen in *The *Nun's Priest's Tale*. The name is not found before Chaucer. It lives on after him in the form 'Partlet' as a name for any hen.

Peter, Petre, St Peter the Apostle, the leader of the disciples, traditionally the first bishop of *Rome, and the author of two New Testament Epistles. These are sometimes quoted or referred to (III.1819; VII.1501–3 (on Christ's *patience); X.141; X.930 (on the obedience of wives); X.988 (on humility in confession)). Similarly there are references to his sayings (on the name of Jesus, X.287, 597) or to the events of life in the gospels or the Acts of the Apostles (his dealings with *Simon Magus, X.781–3; his weeping after his denial of Christ, X.994). He was a very popular saint in the Middle Ages. A testimony to this is the number of times his name is used as an *oath ('Peter!') by a variety of Chaucerian characters (III.446, 1332; VII.214; VIII.665; *HF* 1034, 2000). We also find him appearing twice in contexts where popular religion slides into magic. The Pardoner's relics include a piece of St Peter's sail (I.696–7; see Matt. 14:29), and 'St Peter's sister' figures in the charm spoken by the carpenter (in other charms not only his sister, but his brother and his daughter share his spiritual power).

PETER ALFONCE, see *Piers Alfonce*.

PETER OF RIGA (*c.*1140–1209), a native of Reims, was the author of *Aurora*, a popular and influential versification of parts of the Bible. Chaucer mentions it in *The Book of the Duchess* as the source for the statement that the Greeks say that Pythagoras invented the art of song (1167–70). Possibly the detail of *Absolon's golden hair (I.3314) comes from Peter's description of the beauty of the Old Testament character.

(ed.) Beichner (1965).

PETRAK, FRAUNCEYS. Francesco Petrarca or Petrarch (1304–74), the Italian poet and humanist, was born in Arezzo and spent his youth in Avignon. He devoted himself to literary pursuits, indulging his passion for books and for classical antiquity, and writing with elegance and passion in both Latin and Italian, and playing a central role in the development of Italian *humanism. In 1341 he was crowned poet laureate in Rome. From 1353 he lived mostly in Italy, and died at Arquà near Padua (*Padowe) in the Euganean Hills. His works in Latin include the *Africa*, a Latin epic, the *De remediis utriusque fortunae* (Remedies of Fortune), the *Secretum*, a dialogue with St Augustine, and a much revised collection of letters owing much to his favourite author Cicero; in Italian, the *Rime* or *Canzoniere*, a sequence of love poems addressed to Laura, and the *Trionfi* (Triumphs). He was an immensely influential figure in the literary culture of the Renaissance.

Chaucer's debt to Petrarch is not as extensive or as profound as that to *Dante and *Boccaccio, but it is none the less a significant one. The connection is superficially surprising, since Petrarch was less a dramatic artist than an introspective one, much given to careful self-presentation and self-fashioning. And although Chaucer loved 'olde bokes', he did not devote himself to an intensely scholarly life, and although he celebrated the Golden Age in The *Former Age, he did not constantly express a deep dislike of the present age in the way Petrarch did ('I am alive now yet I would rather have been born at some other time'). But he clearly found some of his work challenging and inspiring. He mentions Petrarch twice. In The *Monk's Tale (VII.2325–6) he appears to credit the story of Zenobia (*Cenobia) to his 'master' Petrarch, whereas it comes in fact from Boccaccio (though Petrarch did mention her in the 'Triumph of Fame'). This remains mysterious; possibly he confused Petrarch and Boccaccio (see

*Lollius); possibly he recalled the passage in the *Trionfi* and conflated it with his knowledge of the skill with which Petrarch had written of the 'meschief and . . . wo' of another woman, Griselda. The references earlier in The *Canterbury Tales (IV.31, 1147) are more accurate and revealing. The *Clerk says rightly that his story of Griselda comes from Petrarch. Although his words do not necessarily imply an actual meeting between the two poets in Padua or Arquà, they show that Chaucer knew a good deal about the Italian writer (who, he says, is now dead, IV.29). He refers to him as 'the lauriat poete' and to the 'prohemium' of his tale. Petrarch wrote his Latin prose *De obedientia ac fide uxoria mythologia* in 1373 and placed it at the end of his *Epistolae seniles*; a year later he revised it and added another letter. Chaucer seems to have had the final version.

This 'clerkly' work represents the aspect of Petrarch which was most influential in northern Europe in the late Middle Ages. Rather than his more deliberately humanistic writings, it seems to have been his moral and generally philosophical writings like this story and the *De remediis* which had the greatest appeal, the work of Petrarch the 'worthy clerk' rather than Petrarch the humanist or Petrarch the love poet. Indeed, his vernacular Italian love poetry, although it is reasonable to see it as the culmination of medieval love lyric, seems to have been ignored in France and England before the early 16th c. when it became a dominant fashion. This makes Chaucer's earlier borrowing from Petrarch, in *Troilus and Criseyde, all the more exciting. In the 'Canticus Troili', the song which Troilus 'seyde in his song' after his return from the temple where he has seen and fallen in love with Criseyde, Chaucer gives him (I.400–20) what is a translation of one of Petrarch's sonnets, 'S'amor non è' ('if this be not love'). Chaucer expands the sonnet into three stanzas of rhyme royal, but although he does not attempt to reproduce the form, he seems to have understood its structure: two stanzas are devoted to the first two quatrains, and the third to the sestet. Some divergences from the Italian may be mistranslations, or due to textual variants, but in some cases (e.g. in the opening phrase 'if no love is . . .') they could well be deliberate alterations: Chaucer is concerned to fit the song into his larger structure, and to emphasize not only the contradictory emotions of love felt by one individual, but also to suggest something of the mysterious and contradictory nature of *love in general. The song with its oxymorons is remarkably appropriate to Troilus's emotional state, helpless in the turmoil of love, full of a searching and questioning anguish. The characteristically Petrarchan combination of intense private emotion, intelligent introspection, and precise scholastic logic, with the arguing of propositions and the balancing of opposed points of view, is typical of Troilus's mode of thought. Troilus is a more introspective and 'Petrarchan' character than Boccaccio's Troiolo. This is, as far as is known, the first adaptation of a Petrarch sonnet in English, and although Chaucer's lyric is sometimes copied separately, English Petrarchanism does not flourish until much later. We cannot be sure that Chaucer knew the rest of the *Canzoniere* in whole or in part. It is possible, but not certain, that Troilus's later song (V.638–44) may echo the beginning of Petrarch's sonnet 189 ('Passa la nave mia colma d'oblio', later translated by Wyat as 'My galey charged with forgetfulness'. (See also *Ytaille.)

(ed.) Buffano (1975); Durling (1976); Neri (1951); S&A 288–331 [104–5]; N. Mann (1984).

PETRO (1). Pedro, king of Castile (1350–69), known to Spanish historians as Peter the Cruel, was the legal successor to Alfonso XI. The latter, however, had had twins by his mistress, Leonora Guzmán, whose murder in 1351 Peter is thought to have connived at. His entire reign was taken up with the civil war between himself and his half-brothers, one of whom, Henry (Enrique), count of Trastamara, killed Peter 'with his owene hand'. The episode constitutes the eighth 'ensample' of the tragic shifts of Fortune illustrated by The *Monk's Tale (VIII.2375–90). This Castilian king is, presumably, viewed favourably by Chaucer, because of his alliance with the Black Prince, who fought on Peter's side at the battle of Nájera in 1367, receiving on that account the great ruby which was to become the chief jewel in the English crown (see also *Spayne).   [PS]
Galvan (1989).

PETRO (2) KYNG OF CIPRE, Pierre de Lusignan, king of Cyprus (*Cipre), crusader and the conqueror of Alexandria (*Alisaundre). Famed for his chivalry, he was well known in England (which he visited in 1363) and counted Englishmen among his followers. He was assassinated by three of his knights in 1369. His 'tragedy' is briefly recounted by the *Monk (VII.2391–8). However, the reason for his murder seems to have been his cruel behaviour rather than any envy of his fame. It has been suggested that Chaucer knew *Guillaume de Machaut's poem La prise d'Alexandrie (1369) which presents him in a very favourable light.

Phanye, Phanie the daughter of Croesus (*Cresus), who expounded his dream (VII.2758).

Pharao, Pharoo 'of Egypte the kyng', the Pharoah of the Old Testament, whose dreams (and those of his baker and his butler) were interpreted by *Joseph (1) (see Gen. 40–1). He is mentioned several times (VII.3133; X.443; BD 282; HF 516) always in connection with *dreams.

PHARSALIA, see *Lucan.

Phasipha, Pasiphaë, the daughter of the Sun and the wife of Minos. When he refused to sacrifice a fine bull to the god Poseidon as he had promised, the god caused Pasiphaë to fall in love with the bull. The result was the monstrous Minotaur (*Mynotaur). The story of 'hire horrible lust' is one of those which Jankin reads to the Wife of Bath (III.733–6)—he finds the tale sweet.

Phebus, Phoebus, an alternative name for *Apollo, often called Phoebus Apollo by the Greeks. (1) Chaucer uses both names for the god. For example, as explained near the beginning of *Troilus and Criseyde, *Calkas knew that Troy should be destroyed 'by answer' of the god named 'Daun Phebus or Apollo Delphicus'. (2) Chaucer tends to prefer the name 'Phebus' when speaking of the Sun. (As it happens, this is in keeping with its original meaning, 'the shining one'.) (3) The god Phebus is the principal character in The *Manciple's Tale. The tale concerns the period when Phebus lived on earth, when he was a remarkable archer, musician, and singer—all in keeping with one branch of the Apollo tradition.   [JDN]

Phebuseo, a Trojan hero, apparently invented by Chaucer (*Tr* IV.54).

Phedra, Phaedra, the daughter of Minos and Pasiphaë and the sister of Ariadne (*Adriane). Theseus abandoned Ariadne for her and made her his wife. (See the Legend of Ariadne in *LGW* and *HF* 405–20.)

Pheton, Phæthon, in Greek mythology the son of Helios and Clymene. Discovering the identity of his father, he searched him out and, when granted a favour, asked to drive the Sun's chariot for a day. Losing control of the horses, he would have set the Earth on fire had Zeus not killed him with a thunderbolt. In *Troilus and Criseyde*, as the days lengthen and the absent Criseyde does not return, Troilus fears that Pheton is again in charge of the chariot. Chaucer retells the story in *The *House of Fame*, and there blames the bolting of the horses on the sight of the sign *Scorpio. Pheton is now thrown from the chariot, by *Jupiter. (See also *signe; *Sonne.) [JDN]

Phidon, an Athenian slain at a feast by the Thirty Tyrants of Athens (*c.*404–403 BC). *Dorigen records that his daughters were forced to dance naked over his blood, but that they drowned themselves rather than lose their virginity (V.1369 ff.).

Philipenses, (ad) (X.598) L. = (Paul's Epistle to the) Philippians.

PHILIPOT, JOHN (d. 1384) a rich London merchant, a member of the Grocers' Company, one of the powerful victuallers' *guilds, member of parliament and Lord Mayor of London in 1378–9. With *Brenbre and Walworth he was one of the collectors at the Customhouse in the period when Chaucer was working there as controller. He seems to have been a powerful friend. His name appears as a witness to Cecily Champain's release to Chaucer in 1380 (see Geoffrey *Chaucer: life). He was an important figure in London—at the death of Edward III he acted as spokesman for the city and assured the young Prince Richard of its loyalty. With Walworth he was appointed a treasurer of war. Along with other merchants he made a large loan to the king. His effective action in the aftermath of a French raid on the Isle of Wight and the seizure of a number of English merchant vessels in equipping a large force which pursued and recovered them was much praised, though not by all the nobles: he is said to have defended himself to the earl of Stafford by saying that if the nobles had not left the country open to invasion he would not have interfered. As Lord Mayor he seems to have been generous and effective. In 1381 with Brenbre and Walworth he took a prominent part in restoring order in the city, for which all three were knighted. He was praised for his 'zeal for the king and the realm'.

Philippes (VII.2656), possessive form of Philip, the name of Alexander's father.

Philistiens, Philistines, in the Old Testament a non-Semitic people inhabiting Philistia, the enemies of Samson (VII.2048).

Phillis, Phyllis, who loved *Demophon. Her story is told in *The *Legend of Good Women*. She is also mentioned elsewhere as a martyr of love (*BD* 728; *HF* 390; *LGW* 264).

Philologie, see *Marcian.

Philomene, Philomela, the sister of Procne. Her story is told in *The *Legend of Good Women*. In Ovid's *Metamorphoses* she was transformed into a nightingale.

philosophy, the pursuit of speculative truth, was an important element in the intellectual life of the Middle Ages. The term was used more widely than in the modern period, to cover, for instance, as 'natural philosophy', the sciences (see *science). Thus in the discussion of *alchemy in *The *Canon's Yeoman's Tale*, 'philosophers' are extensively quoted. Its methods were also applied to law and politics. The reconciliation of reason (in a philosophical system of knowledge) and faith (a body of revealed truth held on faith, analysed by theology) formed a distinctively Christian philosophy, but this was never a completely monolithic set of doctrines. Its sources were varied: the Bible, patristic writings, some of the philosophical traditions of antiquity, such as Neoplatonism or Stoicism, mediated through writers like St Augustine (*Austyn) or Boethius (*Boece), and from the 12th c. onwards many of the works of *Aristotle—as were the schools and systems which it developed. Philosophy became the object of formal study, first in the cathedral schools and then in the *universities of the 13th c. Systematic metaphysical systems were developed: problematic questions like that of 'universals' (the relation of genera and species to individuals) were fiercely debated. Dialectic was developed into a characteristic system of argument using syllogisms and distinctions. Philosophy was now pre-eminently the domain of the academic clerisy, of the 'schools' and 'scholasticism'. In the Aristotelian philosophy of the 13th c., St Thomas Aquinas is a figure of central importance, but other schools of thought developed: Scotism (based on the work of Duns Scotus) or Nominalism (in the 14th c. associated with William of *Ockham and his attempt to separate faith and reason). Nominalism held, in opposition to 'realism' that universals or abstract conceptions were simply names, rather than having any objective or absolute existence. In Chaucer's own time *Wyclif, a radical theologian, is also one of the last masters of medieval philosophy.

Just how much of this long and complex tradition was known to Chaucer is not an easy question to answer. He did not have a university training, but could, of course, have picked up a good deal of knowledge from academic friends (like 'philosophical *Strode', perhaps), or from what had become generally known, or from his own reading (of Boethius, for example). The indirectness and detachment of his own writing makes it impossible to label him with any certainty as an adherent of any single philosophical 'school'. He makes no reference to Aquinas, Scotus, or Ockham (though he does to *Bradwardine), but many to the older moral philosophers, Boethius and Seneca (*Senek). Other references seem to come either from 'general knowledge' (Aristotle or Plato) or from the pages of Boethius, rather than from first-hand acquaintance with philosophical texts. He uses some technical, or more or less technical, terms, but these too tend to be picked up from his originals (like *ambages* ('ambiguities') in *Tr* V.897, from Boccaccio), or are sometimes ancient rather than scholastic terms (like *amphibologies* ('ambigu-

ities') *Tr* IV.1406), or seem likely to have passed into common usage. *Sophyme*—sophism or trick of logic, a plausible but fallacious argument (as it means in V.554) had come to mean a question disputed in logic. In IV.5 it is associated, significantly, with the *Clerk (*sophistrye* had already acquired the more general meaning of 'cunning' or 'trickery' (*LGW* 137)). The scholastic distinction between '*accident' (attribute or surface quality) and 'substance' had become familiar enough for it to be made into a joke (VI.539). Similarly, Chaucer sometimes makes his characters refer to the various types of 'cause' distinguished in philosophical discourse. Pandarus speaks of the 'final cause' of Troilus's sorrow (*Tr* I.682); the philosophical Prudence applies Cicero on 'causes' to her husband: there are causes for his wrong, that 'clerks' call '*Causa longinqua* and *Causa propinqua*; this is to seyn, the fer cause and the ny cause'. The 'far' cause was almighty God, the cause of all things; the 'near cause' was his three enemies, the 'cause accidental' was hate; the 'cause material' was the five wounds inflicted, the 'cause formal' the way they proceeded, by climbing through the windows, the 'cause final' was to kill his daughter (VII.1395–401). We also find 'propositions' and 'disputation'—which is what 'clerks' do in 'school' (V.890; VII.3235–9).

The few 'philosophers' who appear as characters in Chaucer include Lady Philosophy in *Boece*, but also the 'philosophre' in *The *Franklin's Tale*, the wonder-working clerk or 'magician'. Even his Oxford Clerk who had studied logic and possessed copies of Aristotle, is the subject of a joke on two senses of 'philosopher': 'al be that he was a philosophre, | Yet hadde he but litel gold in cofre'. Non-intellectuals believe that clerks, following the legendary Friar *Bacon, dabble in 'artes that been curious' (V.1120), hence the carpenter's concern for the psychological health of *Nicholas in *The *Miller's Tale*. Yet there is no doubt that Chaucer was, as *Usk described him, 'the noble philosophical poete in Englissh' in that he was passionately interested in ideas, an interest which appears again and again, in his treatment of *love, of *Nature, of true nobility or *'gentilesse', of *free will and predestination, and of the problem of the suffering of the innocent.

Burnley (1979); Kretzmann et al. (1982); Leff (1958).

Philostrate, the name assumed by Arcite in *The *Knight's Tale* (I.1428 ff.). In the *Teseida* Arcita calls himself Penteo. Chaucer took the name from the title of Boccaccio's *Filostrato* ('[the man] overthrown by love').

Philotetes, Philoctetes, the pilot of the Argonauts (*LGW* 1459).

Phisic, *Aristotle's *Physics*, referred to by Philosophy in *Boece*: 'Myn Aristotle . . . in the book of his Phisic' (V pr.1:63).

Phisik, see *medicine.

Physician, The, or 'Doctour of Phisik' is described in lines 411–44 of the *General Prologue* in an ambiguous combination of apparent praise and irony. Ideas from the medieval tradition of medical satire (that doctors are greedy, ignorant, incompetent, and dangerous) are clearly in the background, but are not made explicit. Indeed, Chaucer transforms 'the features which other writers attack into evidence of professional skill' (Mann). We are first given a list of his technical skills (he is no simple physician but a 'doctour', a man with an advanced degree), 'a verray, parfit praktisour'. His practical skills include a relationship with his apothecary who supplied him with drugs and medicines in an arrangement which was of financial benefit to them both. The ambiguity is so consistent that for most of the time 'we cannot be absolutely sure about anything in the Doctor's character' (Curry). How much knowledge of the imposing medical authorities which are listed did he actually have? And there are a number of asides containing apparently matter-of-fact statements, about his careful and moderate diet, for instance, which may be interpreted in different ways. The remark that 'his studie was but litel on the Bible' may be a proverbial criticism of physicians, but it is just possible to take it in a literal and neutral sense. Satirical undertones become more pointed towards the end of the portrait; he wears rich and sumptuous dress, but is careful with his money ('he kepte that he wan in pestilence'), and for him gold does not have a simply medical power ('For gold in phisik is a cordial [medicine], | Therefore he lovede gold in special'). (See also *medicine.)

Rv 815–17; Cooper (1989), 49–50; Curry (1960), 3–36; Mann (1973), 91–9; Ussery (1971).

Physician's Tale, The (of 286 lines in decasyllabic couplets) is the first tale of Fragment VI, and is followed by *The *Pardoner's Tale*. Its date of composition is uncertain. It is often thought to have been written before or just at the beginning of the period in which Chaucer began *The Canterbury Tales*. Perhaps it was written when he was working on *The *Legend of Good Women*, with its short tales of suffering women, like that of *Lucrece. It has been suggested that the digression on the guardians of lords' daughters may refer to a contemporary scandal, the elopement of John of Gaunt's daughter Elizabeth in 1386, but there is no supporting evidence for this. The story of Virginia was a popular one in the Middle Ages, told by *Jean de Meun, *Gower, and others. Chaucer begins the tale, 'Ther was, as telleth *Titus Livius . . .' The story derives ultimately from Livy's Roman history, although it is unlikely that he knew that work at first hand. Chaucer's basic source was Jean de Meun's version in the *Roman de la Rose*.

Virginius, an honourable knight, has an only daughter, aged 14, called Virginia (though we are not told her name until line 213). She is of great beauty and virtue. The teller's elaborate description (7–71) leads into a disquisition on governesses and the duty of parents to bring up children well (72–103). One day when she goes to the temple with her mother, Apius, a judge and governor of the region, sees her, and struck by her beauty, says to himself 'This mayde shal be myn'. Realizing that he will not be able to satisfy his lust easily, he secretly arranges that an accomplice, Claudius, should summon Virginius on a false charge before him. Claudius claims that Virginia is a servant of his who has been stolen from him while she was very young. Before Virginius can deny it, the judge rules that Virginia must be surrendered to him. Returning home, Virginius 'with a face deed as asshen colde' calls his daughter to him and tells her that the judge has determined to live in lechery with her, and that the choice is between death or shame. The latter is out of the question, and he must strike off her head. After a brief intense scene Virginia prepares for death (or martyrdom).

'Blissed be God that I shal dye a mayde!' she exclaims, asks her father to kill her before she is shamed, and prays him to smite softly. Her father cuts off her head and sends it to Apius. The judge orders him to be taken and hanged. But the people rush in to save the knight. Apius, his iniquity now revealed, is thrown into prison, where he takes his own life. Claudius is condemned to be hanged but Virginius intercedes and he is exiled. The others involved are hanged. The tale ends with a brief moral. Sin has its reward, and no one knows whom God will strike nor how: 'Forsaketh synne, er synne yow forsake.'

This violent and disturbing tale has never been a favourite with readers, and critics have often condemned it as confused and unsuccessful. It has been criticized for the long *digression at the beginning, where, it has been argued, the advice to parents and guardians is irrelevant to the case of Virginia, since the narrator says she needed no mistress but was an example to others. It is apparently an exemplary tale, but (Cooper) 'if the tale as a whole is an exemplum, it is very hard to see what it exemplifies'. Some have found the final moral inappropriate to the story.

These points may be answered, in part at least. Thus, it may be that the tale is not meant to be totally or consistently 'exemplary', but contains examples of those Ovidian changes of tone which Chaucer uses in *The Legend of Good Women*, and elsewhere. The worldly-wise remark (70–1), 'al to soone may she lerne loore | Of booldnesse, whan she woxen is a wyf', may be an example of this, as may the sudden dismissal of the hyperbolic and exemplary advice: 'hir neded no maistresse'. Chaucer took trouble to change some emphases of the story in order to increase its pathos and horror. The wickedness of the judge is found in all versions, but Chaucer makes the victim the central character. The long description of Virginia highlights the grim fact that in this cruel world her virtue is of no avail, and increases the horror. He makes the scene between Virginia and her father a very domestic one: it takes place not in the courtrooom but at home. (A contrast between public and private scenes is characteristic of this tale.) He adds the scene in which in tears she begs her father to kill her. That the decapitation takes place in private, and after reflection, and not in the public courtroom (which might allow us to think of a moment of passion) not only increases its horror, but confronts us directly with the full rigour and absolute demands of honour. (It is also one of several repeated patterns: like Apius, Virginius sentences her, but from love, not for lechery.)

There is no doubt that the scene is an extremely disturbing one. Modern readers often feel that it is unfair that only Virginia should die, and that Virginius might also have taken his own life for honour's sake. But that is not what the inherited story allows. It is similar to other tales involving the sacrifice of a child by a parent, like that of Iphigenia by Agamemnon, or that of Isaac which Abraham is commanded to carry out. In these an explicit divine command is present. Virginius acts from honour, but not from a narrow code of honour, rather from a moral revulsion, in which Chaucer has blended ancient Roman honour and sense of justice with a hatred of lechery and an admiration for chastity which would have been familiar to the audience used to medieval Christian religious writing. At one point the story seems to be almost beginning to modulate into a narrative of martyrdom. The father's agonized feelings (eloquently expressed in the first direct speech in the Tale) lead into an intense private scene between father and daughter in which 'the tragic conflict between action and feeling is stressed by the insistent repetition of "father" and "doghter"' (Mann), and the pathos increased by the action of Virginia throwing her arms around her father's neck 'as she was wont to do'. As in the medieval proverb, love is as strong as death. The uncompromising emphasis on the father's *pite' and love ('with fadres pitee stikynge thurgh his herte' 'my pitous hand moot smyten of thyn heed') makes it into a terrible scene of pathos. It is, as the *Host says at the end, 'a pitous tale', and has similarities with another of Chaucer's experiments in that kind, The *Prioress's Tale, an equally disturbing story, in which the central figure is also a child (and which in its allusion to another child martyr, Hugh of Lincoln, may remind us of Virginia's reference to the daughter of Jephtha (*Jepte)).

Jean de Meun quotes an ancient dictum that virtue and great power are never seen together. In Chaucer's tale the power of Apius seems absolute and arbitrary, and he is entirely vicious. The popular revolt 'for routhe and for pitee' which comes too late to save Virginia, avenges the wickedness but does not obliterate its memory. It is very hard to explain or contain the horror we feel at the unjust fate of an innocent victim. Perhaps the Host's emotional exclamation is the proper human response: 'Allas, so pitously as she was slayn!' (VI.298).

(ed.) *Rv* (190–4, 901–4); Corsa (1987); *S&A* 398–408; Cooper (1989), 248–59; E. Brown (1981); Ellis (1986), ch. 8; Hirsh (1993); Mann (1991), 143–6; Middleton (1973–4); Pearsall (1985), 277–9; Ramsay (1972).

physiognomy, 'the art of judging character and disposition from the features of the face or lineaments of the body generally' (*OED*), and also of foretelling a person's destiny, was much discussed from *Aristotle on. Western medieval scientists, like Albert the Great or Michael Scot, continued the work of the Greeks and Arabs. It was part of the system in which the fundamental 'complexion' or physical constitution of the human body was determined by celestial influences at conception and at birth. The physical appearance of the 'sanguine' *Franklin and the 'choleric' *Reeve reflect their dominant *'humour'. The *Wife of Bath says that she has the mark of Mars on her face ('and also in another privee place' III.619–20). In later centuries scientific interest waned, but popular interest did not. The extensively illustrated essays of Lavater in the 18th c. were widely read, and in the 19th there was considerable interest in the physical characteristics of criminals. We still hear echoes of it in popular talk, 'I don't like the cut of his jib' or 'his eyes are too close together,' both, in traditional manner, being attempts to interpret appearance as a guide to character and to possible future behaviour. Perhaps, as one 19th-c. practitioner (Woolnoth, 1865) said 'we are all physiognomists by nature': it is a natural tendency 'to be ever speculating upon character'. (He remarked that children were especially so—just as Chaucer recorded that the children were afraid of the *Summoner's red and ugly face, I.628.) It might seem easier to interpret facial appearance as an expression of emotion rather than as an expression of character or 'disposition' (according to Woolnoth 'indelibly fixed at the earliest stage of the susceptibilities'),

but attempts are still made. One problem which was evident even in early proverbial lore is that interpretations may differ. This problem confronts readers of Chaucer who wish to find some further significance in the fact that Criseyde's brows were joined together (*Tr* V.813). Physiognomic treatises offer so many possible significances for this that it seems safest to accept Chaucer's literal remark that it was the only 'lak' or blemish in her beauty.

Chaucer was certainly aware of physiognomic lore, and uses it extensively, especially in the *General Prologue*. A study by W. C. Curry extensively documents this. The Pardoner's glaring eyes indicate a man given to folly and a glutton, a shameless libertine and a drunkard. The Miller's physical characteristics would variously suggest a gluttonous, talkative, lecherous, and quarrelsome disposition. That the Wife of Bath is 'gat-tothed' ('with teeth set wide apart') could indicate a nature that was envious, irreverent, luxurious, bold, faithless, and suspicious, and her red face immodesty, loquaciousness, and drunkenness. Sometimes the material probably comes from popular physiognomical lore as much as from the learned treatises quoted by Curry—the red beard of the Miller suggesting treachery or deceit, for instance. Such popular lore sometimes lives on, and can be instantly recognized: that ears 'glow' when the owner is being talked about (*Tr* II.1022), or that blushing is a sign of embarrassment or shame (*Tr* II.1198; VIII.1095). Physiognomic details are often accompanied by other satiric pointers (*animal images, for instance: the Miller's beard is red like a fox, the Pardoner's eyes like those of the hare, believed to sleep with eyes open and to be hermaphroditic), or other salient details of appearance and *clothing. Such details impressed Leigh *Hunt, who praised Chaucer's fondness for seeing the spiritual in the material, the mind in the man's aspect, and remarked that 'he is as studious of physiognomy as Lavater, and far truer'. (See also **beauty; *emotions; *eyes; *science.)

Curry (1960); Woolnoth (1865).

Phisiologus, *Physiologus* ('the Naturalist') a popular compilation from late antiquity. A curious blend of Christian allegory and ancient mystical science, it contains descriptions of *animals real and legendary and also presents them as divine emblems which illustrate the mysteries of the faith and give instruction to Christian souls on their journey through life. The sections are often introduced by the phrase `Physiologus says'. In the course of the Middle Ages a large body of such works developed, usually called '*bestiaries*', in both verse and prose, in Latin and in various vernaculars. The *Nun's Priest quotes Physiologus ('Phisiologus seith sikerly') to the effect that *mermaids sing (VII.3271–2).

Phitonissa (III.1510), the biblical Witch of Endor (Vulgate: 1 Chr. 10:13; 1 Sam. 28:7).

Phitoun, the Python, the great serpent slain by Apollo (IX.109, 128). *Ovid describes the episode (*Met.* 1.438–51).

Pycardie, Picardy, a province in northern France in which the *Squire had fought (I.86; see *Artoys).

PICTAGORAS, PICTAGORES, PICTIGORAS, Pythagoras of Samos (*c.*560–*c.*480 BC) a renowned mathematician, astronomer, mystic, and investigator of the mathematics of musical harmony.

Outside *Boece*, Chaucer names Pythagoras twice in *The *Book of the Duchess*, once virtually in the middle, and again 500 lines later. These facts may be part of a deliberate numerological scheme.

Pythagoras travelled in Egypt and Babylonia, and eventually left Samos for southern Italy, where he had a large following. Thirty years or so after his death his followers were dispersed by a democratic uprising there, and various sects were set up, some content to retail the (largely secret) teachings of the master, others insisting on developing them. As a result, much doubt attaches to the extent of Pythagoras' own contribution to the body of doctrine known under his name. The Pythagorean theorem (see *Dulcarnoun*), was known in Babylonia long before him, but perhaps he was the first to provide a proof. He seems to have discovered geometrical incommensurability and some properties of the regular solids. In Pythagorean arithmetic, figurate numbers and the theory of means were important.   [JDN]

Pierce the Plowmans Crede, poem in alliterative long lines, strongly influenced by *Langland's *Piers Plowman*, but with a much narrower scope. The primary target of the satire is the fraternal orders, and the author is sympathetic to many of the ideas of the *Lollards. The author of *The *Plowmans Tale* (1065–6) claims that he also wrote the *Crede*.   [AH]

(ed.) Skeat (1867); Barr (1993).

Pierides, the *Muses, so called from Pieria on the slopes of Mt. Olympus. The remark in the *The *Man of Law's Prologue* that the teller (who has just been praising Chaucer) would hate to be likened 'to Muses that men clepe Pierides' is also an allusion (indicated by the reference to *Methamorphosios) to the story told by Ovid (*Met.* 5) of the other Pierides, the nine daughters of King Pierus who challenged the Muses to a song contest, and were changed into magpies.

Piers, Daun the *Monk (VII.2792).

PIERS ALFONCE, PETER ALFONCE, Petrus Alphonsus, a Spanish Jew and Islamic scholar who was converted to the Catholic faith in 1106, on the feast of SS Peter and Paul, under the influence of King Alfonso I of *Aragon who acted as his godfather—hence the name. He is the author, amongst other works, of a theological treatise, the *Conversations of Petrus Alphonsus*, in which he refutes the false views of the Jews, which may have motivated his leaving Spain for England where, in about 1111, he became physician to Henry I, and an active influence on the scientific life of the time. He is likewise the author of the extremely popular *Disciplina clericalis*, a work, he says in his Prologue, made up 'partly from the sayings of wise men and their advice, partly from Arab proverbs, counsels, fables and poems, and partly from bird and animal similes', offering thus a fund of stories, forms, attitudes, and images that in the Middle Ages were common to both East and West. The *Disciplina clericalis* was copied all over Europe, and French translations, both in verse and prose, were made in the 12th c. Chaucer includes several quotations from this work in his *Tale of *Melibee*, and the story told in *Exemplum XIII* forms the basis of the 13th-c. English fabliau, *Dame Sirith*.   [PS]

(trans.) Quarrie (1977).

Piers Plowman, see *Langland.

piety, which means faithfulness to religious duties, describes a range of observances, often private, but also those manifested in public. It carries with it the connotation of duties which are beyond but usually not opposed to conventional religious behaviour or to reason, and which the subject undertakes unreservedly, conscious of a felt dedication to a supernatural authority. Public expressions of piety—at masses, observances associated with *saints and saints' days, gifts to ecclesiastical foundations of money and land, and events like *pilgrimages and processions—were much in use in the late 14th c. and continued to be so, though not without expressions of distrust among those who considered such things. But increasingly the word *piety* came to mean private devotion, a wide range of activities, practices, and observances encouraged by an extraordinary range of devotional texts, many not yet edited, through which the Christian deepened his or (more often) her spiritual life, sometimes attesting to the faith in the process.

The 'ful devout corage' with which the narrator of The *Canterbury Tales* begins his pilgrimage shows an attitude of mind to which many aspired, even those who did not cultivate a 'spiced conscience', a problematic phrase in the *General Prologue* which probably implies a degree of fashionable effort but not of hypocrisy. Meditation on religious topics (the best known ones in English were ascribed to Richard *Rolle; many concerned Christ's Passion) was both encouraged and cultivated, and in some cases became associated with a sense of divine presence which seemed to some a kind of paramystical awareness.

There are several kinds of piety in Chaucer, ranging from the 'heigh devocioun' Arcite brings to Mars in The *Knight's Tale*, through the 'greet devocioun' the public is called upon to observe in The *Man of Law's Tale*, to the evidently private 'devocioun' John recites in The *Miller's Tale*. All bespeak in inner attitude, most often one that issues in action.

Four of Chaucer's tales engage piety directly, though it figures in others, sometimes prominently. The protagonists in The Man of Law's Tale and The *Second Nun's Tales* show a depth of religious devotion which manifests itself in their lives, and which gives them strength in adversity. In The Man of Law's Tale Constance's piety sustains her as she is driven from one vicissitude to another; in The Second Nun's Tale Cecilia's piety supports the motivating energy by which she remakes the world around her. In each case the protagonist is a noble woman, though Griselda in The *Clerk's Tale* shares, if allegorically, Constance's piety and fortunes, and comes from the working class. In each case the piety which Chaucer praises emerges as a personal religious quality which issues in action, whether by obedience or initiative. There seems too to be the assumption that piety will manifest itself in an attitude towards others, for example, by a mother's continuing care for her child, or by a saint's concern for the spiritual welfare of all, though such expressions are not themselves piety.

Two other tales, The *Prioress's Tale* and The *Pardoner's Tale*, also treat piety, though with considerable irony. The Prioress's piety, like the *Monk's, is selective and self-serving, designed to accommodate a self-image of use in public, but finally indifferent to the condition of others. Her approval in the tale of 'the white lamb celestial' is one of the few allusions in Chaucer to the general topic of mysticism, though there is considerable ambiguity in its implications. It is not simply that the child's death is taken as a justification for killing others, or that his mother's search for her son 'half out of hir mynde' contrasts with Constance's fortitude, as that the terms in which this religiousness is cast seem plainly mistaken, a creation of sentiment and self, engaging in secular, but hardly in sacred, terms.

This same astringent attitude is apparent in The Pardoner's Tale, both in the cynical and grasping behaviour of the Pardoner himself, and in the naïve and self-centred attitudes apparent in his prologue and tale. Like the Prioress, the Pardoner makes an easy link between innocence and piety, and like her invests a high degree of interest in the delineation and preservation of appearances. The *oaths '"By Goddes precious herte," and "By his nayles," | And "By the blood of Grist that is in *Hayles"' register authorial irony towards certain popular devotions (the *Arma Christi*, the nails by which Christ was fastened to the cross, the Holy

Pigmalion

Blood preserved at Hayles Abbey in Gloucestershire, a popular place of pilgrimage until the Reformation), though Chaucer avoids the wholesale condemnations which were becoming current as he wrote.

In some ways the most problematic reference to piety is the tale and the person of the admirable *Parson. The man himself is as energetic as Cecilia, but with Constance's regard for duty and reverence, and his public life seems based upon a felt religious conviction which manifests itself in his concern for the spiritual welfare of his flock. His tale, offered as a 'meditacioun', is an English translation of parts of the Summa de poenitentia of St Raymund of Pennaforte and the Summa vitiorum of the Dominican William *Peraldus, from which certain important, and possibly authorial, deviations have been made. The tale embraces such traditional devotional topics as, in the third part, the seven deadly sins, and also the newer affective devotions, many added to the source, though by whose hand is uncertain. Though the placing of the text seems somewhat problematic, it has had cogent defences made for it, and may well represent an important authorial attitude.

It is difficult to be certain that any particular pious practice may have been one that Chaucer himself observed (references to saints seem largely conventional, and recorded for artistic purposes, frequently with irony), but the invocation to the Virgin in the Prioress's and the Second Nun's prologues, the prayer to Mary Chaucer added to The Man of Law's Tale and the 'ABC', may indicate a more than conventional attitude; devotion to Mary (see *Marie) was widespread, but perhaps more among men than women. If the alterations to The Parson's Tale are indeed authorial, that tale may also offer important insight into Chaucer's own piety showing a certain sympathy for popular affective devotions not otherwise commended in his work. But it is evident too that, in devotion as in other things, Chaucer was inclined to test the current formulations, and was attracted towards a piety which moved outward as well as in. (See also *religion; *prayer.) [JCH]

Bestul (1989); Cuming and Baker (1972); Duffy (1992); Hirsh (1989 and 1996); L. Patterson (1978); Powicke (1935); Sargent (1989); R. Whiting (1989).

Pigmalion, Pygmalion, the famous Greek sculptor, a legendary king of Cyprus who fell in love with the statue of a woman he had made, more beautiful than any real woman. In answer to his prayer for a wife like the statue Venus gave the statue life, and Pygmalion married her. The story is told by Ovid (Met. 10). In the Middle Ages Pygmalion is cited as one of the examples of the supreme artist. Chaucer's only reference imagines *Nature saying that his work cannot match hers in the creation of the beautiful *Virginia (VI.14).

Pilates, possessive form of 'Pilate' i.e. Pontius Pilate, the governor of Judaea who according to the New Testament condemned Christ to death. The drunken *Miller, interrupting the Host, 'in Pilates voys he gan to crie' (I.3124). This probably means in a loud ranting voice like that of Pilate in some mystery plays.

pilgrimage. The habit of visiting places with religious associations, found in many religions, was from an early period common in Christianity; it was fostered by the conversion of Constantine, and by the finding of the true cross by his mother Helena in 326. The practice was often declaredly undertaken as an act of either *piety or *penance. The establishment of shrines with images at those places to which pilgrimage was taken further encouraged the habit; indulgences were often available to those who completed such pilgrimage. The favourite destinations for pilgrimage throughout Christendom were Jerusalem, with its many places associated with the life of Christ, and Rome with its shrines to the memory of the early martyrs and of those associated with the establishment of the Church; the Wife of Bath had visited both and had also undertaken another common pilgrimage, that to the shrine of St James at Compostella (I.462ff.). There were numerous shrines in England to which pilgrimages were made, the most renowned certainly being that of Thomas à Becket at Canterbury. Though the purpose of pilgrimage was supposedly entirely religious, the journeys were often undertaken for various other reasons: desire for travel, for companionship, and simply for change. Since travel was slow, arduous, and often dangerous, groups of pilgrims often journeyed together; it was common for individuals, if not the whole group, to stop for various lengths of time on the way to earn further money for the next stage. The varied aims and attitudes of pilgrims are well represented by Chaucer in the *General Prologue*, and in the pilgrims' own comments later; many of them are frivolous, worldly, or unthinking, and only the Parson (X.50) reminds the group of 'thilke parfit glorious pilgrymage | That highte Jerusalem celestial' on which they should be engaged. Awareness of the contemporary abuses of worldly pilgrimage, along with an insistence that spiritual goals could not be achieved by devotion to physical means, led the *Lollards to complete condemnation of the habit, and of the related devotion to images; the Parson's participation in the Canterbury pilgrimage is evidence enough that Chaucer did not intend to portray him as a wholehearted follower of *Wyclif.   [AH]

Pilgrims Tale, The, written probably between 1536 and 1538 (it refers to the Lincolnshire rising of 1536 but also to the shrine at Walsingham, destroyed in 1538), and surviving only in the single incomplete copy of the *Courte of Venus* ([1538?], *STC* 24650). The tale is written in imitation rather than completion of *The Canterbury Tales*, since its narrator is on a pilgrimage to Sempringham not Canterbury; its outlook is anti-fraternal in a more specifically radical way than Chaucer's.   [AH]
  (ed.) Kingsley (1865), 77–98; R. A. Fraser (1955).

PYNSON RICHARD (d. 1530) a London printer of Norman extraction. He produced editions of *The *Canterbury Tales* (c.1492) and of Chaucer's Works (1526), both apparently from Caxton's second edition. The Works contain a number of non-Chaucerian pieces (see *Chauceriana) and is arranged in three parts.

Piramus, Pyramus the lover of Thisbe (*Tisbe). Their story is told in *The *Legend of Good Women*. It is alluded to as proof that love will find a way (IV.2128) and the two lovers appear in the temple of *Venus (*PF* 289).

Piros, Pyrois, one of the four horses that draw the chariot of the sun (*Tr* III.1703).

Pirrus, Pyrrhus (or Neoptolemus), the son of *Achilles and the slayer of *Priam in a scene vividly described in the second book of *Virgil's *Aeneid* (533 ff.). This scene of '*pite' was evidently a memorable one. Chaucer alludes to it several times: in *HF* (159–61) noting that the old king was slain 'despitously', and as the cause of lamentation (the 'tendre wepyng' when Pyrrhus 'brak the wall', II.288). In a less serious context in *The Nun's Priest's Tale* the 'cry and lamentacioun' exceeded any Trojan weeping when the city fell and 'Pirrus with his streite swerd, | . . . hadde hent kyng Priam by the berd, | And slayn hym' (VII.3357–9). (Chaucer's 'beard' rather than Virgil's 'hair' may well echo Pertelote's earlier remark to her husband 'Have ye no mannes herte, and han a berd?')

Pisces, the twelfth and last sign of the Zodiac, the Fishes. The sign is the *domicile of Jupiter. In *The *Wife of Bath's Prologue* it is explained that Venus has her exaltation in this sign, whereas Mercury has there his dejection ('is desolat'); and that their roles are reversed in (by implication) *Virgo. (See also *exaltacioun; *Fyssh; *signe.)   [JDN]

pite(e) (routhe). The frequency of these words is evidence of Chaucer's consistent interest in the nature and the portrayal of pity and compassion. Middle English *pite* is ultimately derived (as is modern 'piety') from L. *pietas*, which in later L. was extended from its meanings of 'duty' and 'natural affection' to include those of 'gentleness, tenderness, pity, compassion'. The less common word *routhe* ('pity, compassion, mercy') is almost synonymous with it, and the senses of both words often overlap with those of *mercy* (or *misericorde*) and *compassioun*, words with which they are often found in association. Both *pite* and *routhe* can mean both the emotion of pity and the object or cause of the emotion (and similarly, the adj. *pitous*).
  In Chaucer *pite* is characteristically a generous and outgoing emotion and sometimes a very intense one: Canacee in *The Squire's Tale* after hearing the pitiful lament of the falcon 'wel neigh for the routhe almoost . . . deyde' (V.438), just as *Dante after hearing the story of Paolo and Francesca fell like a dead man because of his pity (*pietade*). It is associated with tears and weeping

'pitously': Canacee wept 'as she to water wolde'. In
*Melibee (VII.985 ff.) moderation in weeping is
urged, supported by texts from Seneca (*Senek):
'whan that thy frend is deed . . . lat nat thyne eyen
to moyste been of teeris, ne to muche drye;
although the teeris come to thyne eyen, lat hem
nat falle' (VII.991). However most of Chaucer's
characters ignore this stoic advice and weep copiously, as it seems (to judge from scenes in chronicles) many people in the Middle Ages did.
Opposed to the generously *pitous* person is the
hard-hearted man with the proverbial heart of
stone or the 'proud despitous man' (I.1779) 'that
wol mayntene that [what] he first bigan', who is
linked in this speech by Theseus with 'a lord that
wol have no mercy'. The need for a prince to show
mercy and *pite* is often emphasized. The *Parson
quotes Seneca: 'ther is no thing moore covenable
to a man of heigh estaat than debonairetee and
pitee' (X.465). A *pitous* heart is a sign of the truly
noble man (cf. I.953).

Pite is regularly linked with noble generous
*love and with '*gentilesse'. Chaucer is fond of the
dictum that 'pitee renneth soone in gentil herte'
(I.1761; V.479; *LGW* 503). In *The* **Man of Law's
Tale* the good King Alla feels pity for the falsely
accused Custance: he 'hath swich compassioun, |
As gentil herte is fulfild of pitee, | That from his
eyen ran the water doun' (II.659–61). As often in
Chaucer, noble qualities such as *pite* and *gentilesse*
are especially associated with women. In medieval
love poetry the idea that the lady should show pity
for the suffering lover and grant him grace was a
traditional one. This is found, for example, in *The
Complaint unto* *Pity. In an allegorical work like
the *Roman de la Rose the personified Pitié is
opposed to such enemies of love as Cruelty or
*Daunger (and overwhelms Daunger in battle by
floods of tears). But this traditional pattern is not
always simply conventional. If *daunger* suggests a
holding back, a defensive refusal of love, *pite* may
imply a giving of one's self, or a generous self-
sacrifice. The struggle between the two emotions
is treated non-allegorically in the case of *Criseyde
until the moment when she 'opened her heart'. On
behalf of Palamon Theseus appeals to Emily's
'womanly pitee' (I.3083). 'Womanly pitee' can be a
source of weakness as well as a sign of moral
strength. It leads such figures as Ariadne or Dido

into an over-generous trust in deceitful men. A
mother's pity is an especially intense emotion: the
mother of the child in *The* **Prioress's Tale* searches
for him 'with moodres pitee in hir brest enclosed |
. . . as she were half out of hir mynde' (VII.593–4).

This noble human quality is a reflection of the
divine. *Pite* is sometimes close to Caritas. The
word appears frequently in specifically religious
contexts. The Parson (X.805) says that *pite* is followed by *misericorde*, which performs charitable
deeds of mercy. It mirrors the *pite* shown to man
by Christ and the Virgin Mary. The Parson refers
to Christ's 'teeres whan that he weep for pitee of
good peple' (X.255). In *The Man of Law's Tale*
Custance prays to the cross, 'reed of the Lambes
blood ful of pitee' (II.453). Mary, traditionally the
'mother of mercy', *mater misericordiae*, is called in
the *ABC the 'well' of *pite* (cf. also VIII.50–6).

Pite and compassion are evident in much
Chaucerian narrative, not only in comments given
to his narrators but in his attitude to characters
and their situations. He will usually elaborate or
emphasize a 'pitous cas', a moment of great pathos
or high emotion. Examples of his fondness for
scenes of pathos or extreme sorrow can be found
throughout his work (notably in *KnT, SqT, LGW*,
or books IV and V of *Tr*), and he devotes much art
to the 'pitous tale' (which is how the Host
describes the story of *Virginia), tales of extreme
suffering and emotion, often involving separated
families, cruelly imposed suffering, false accusations, and deeds of horror. Some end cruelly and
disastrously; others, like *The* **Clerk's Tale* or *The
Man of Law's Tale* end in reconciliation, with
*recognition scenes which are both tearful and
joyful, marked by what Chaucer describes as
'pitous joye'. He is one of the medieval masters of
this kind of writing.

Irony, however, is by no means always absent.
The word *pite* may refer to an emotion which is
less than noble. In *The* **Merchant's Tale*
(IV.1977–97) old January's young wife feels *pite* for
her lovesick admirer Damian, and the narrator
exclaims, 'Lo, pitee renneth soone in gentil herte'.
Then 'this gentil May, fulfilled of pitee' writes a
letter to Damian setting the day and place for a
meeting. More characteristically, Chaucer weaves
ironies delicately into moments of pathos and *pite*,
without destroying them, as when in *The* **Knight's*

Tale Emily's sorrow at the death of Arcite occasions the narrator to reflect on the way in which women sorrow at the parting from their husbands, 'that for the moore part they sorwen so, | Or ellis fallen in swich maladye, | That at the laste certeinly they dye' (I.2824–6). But we instantly return to a grand choric scene of lamentation for the fallen hero: 'Allas, the pitee that was ther'.

Gray (1979).

PITS, JOHN (1550–1616). Pits was born and educated in England until in 1580 he went into voluntary exile as a Catholic; after study in Rome, he was ordained, and worked mainly in France but also in a number of other continental countries. In the third part of his *Relationes historicae de rebus Anglicis* (Paris, 1619), pp. 572–5, Pits, despite his abhorrence for its compiler, took over the biography of Chaucer and the list of his works printed by *Bale, themselves derived largely from *Leland. [AH]

Spurgeon (1925), iii. 63–5.

Pity, Complaint unto, or, as it is called in two MSS, 'A Complaint of *Pitee', is one of Chaucer's short poems (ascribed to him by *Shirley). It survives in nine MSS and in *Thynne's edition. It consists of 119 lines in rhyme royal (see *versification). The date is uncertain, though it has often been regarded as an early poem. Possibly it shows Chaucer's first use of the rhyme royal stanza. Like other *complaints it is introduced by a narrative section. The poet, who has long sought Pity 'with herte soore and ful of besy peyne', wishes to complain to her 'upon the crueltee and tirannye | Of love', but finds her dead 'and buried in an herte'. Her hearse (the frame which supported the candles) is surrounded by Bounte 'and fresshe Beaute, Lust, and Jolyte' and other figures 'confedered alle by bond of Cruelte', the contrary and foe of Pity. He would have presented to her 'compleynt', but seeing this company ranged against him, he decides to keep it in his hand 'for to that folk . . . | Withoute Pitee ther may no bille availe'. However, he gives us the 'effect' of his complaint. It warns her of Crueltee's alliance against her authority: she will be deprived of her heritage by Crueltee, 'and we despeyred that seken to your grace'. He is in despair, but will maintain his *trouthe until his

death: 'thus for your deth I may wel wepe and playne | With herte sore and ful of besy peyne'. The poem is from the world of the courtly French love allegory; it is polished and graceful (notably in its structure and echoic technique), and yet passionate and intense.

(ed.) *Rv* 640–1, 1077–8; Scattergood (1995), 468–9, 478.

Pize, Pisa, in Italy, is mentioned in the Monk's tragedy of Ugolino (*Hugelyn) the 'myghty Erl of Pize' (VII.2407, 2416, 2456).

Placebo (L. 'I will please'), the name of the flattering adviser of January in *The Merchant's Tale*.

Plague, see *Black Death.**

Planete, planet (Late L. *planeta*, from Greek *planetes*, wanderer; (Old Fr. *planete*). The wandering character of the planets underlies the name 'erratik sterres' in *Troilus and Criseyde*. (See also *retrograde.) By the nature of the work, the word 'planete' occurs often in the *Equatorie of the Planetis*. It occurs even more often in *A Treatise on the *Astrolabe*. There also the ancient astrological doctrine of planetary hours, 'houres of planetes', is fully explained. According to this, each hour of the day, beginning on Saturday, is governed by one of the planets, taken in the traditional order *Saturne, *Jupiter, *Mars, *Sonne, *Venus, *Mercurius, *Mone. The eighth hour belongs again to Saturn, and so on through the 168 hours of the week. The names of the *days of the week then correspond to the planets governing their first *hour: Saturn, Sun, Moon, Mars, Mercury, Jupiter, and finally Venus for Friday—something of which Chaucer makes use in *The *Nun's Priest's Tale*. (See also *sterre.) [JDN]

PLATO(N), Plato, the Greek philosopher (427–347 BC), author of twenty-five dialogues, of which the *Timaeus* was the only one well known in the Middle Ages, in the 4th-c. Latin translation and commentary by Chalcidius. Nevertheless there was a strong Platonic element in medieval thought, in religious writing mediated by St Augustine (*Austyn) and other Fathers, and in philosophical writing via Cicero (*Tullius) and

Boethius (*Boece). Platonic ideas come to Chaucer from Boethius, *Macrobius, and the 12th-c. cosmological poets Bernard Silvestris and Alan of Lille. Chaucer's references to Plato are mostly in his translation of Boethius (e.g. I pr.3:23, pr.4:26; IV pr.2:260 ff.; V pr.6:52 ff., etc.). The *Consolation* is a deeply Platonic work, in form (a dialogue) and in its ideas: see especially book III, metrum 9 (based on the *Timaeus*) and metrum 11 (the idea of the soul's 'recollection' of what it once knew). Philosophy describes him as 'my Plato' (I pr.3:23) 'my disciple' (III pr.9:190–1, referring to his *Timaeus* (in *Thymeo*). Elsewhere he quotes the dictum 'the wordes moote be cosyn to the dede' (I.741–2; IX.207–10) from the *Timaeus* (298). He may have derived this from Boethius (III, end of prose 12). It later became proverbial. Chaucer's ascription of it in *The Manciple's Tale* to 'the wise Plato' perhaps suggests that it may already have been a maxim. The philosopher appears in an alchemical context in *The Canon's Yeoman's Tale* (VIII.1448–71), where the dialogue between Plato and a disciple seems to have been expanded by Chaucer from a passage in a Latin version of a commentary by *'Senior'. Here Chaucer makes Plato refer to Christ. In *The House of Fame* there are two cosmological references. 'Daun Platon' is linked with Aristotle and other philosophers as an authority for the idea that everything 'hath his propre mansyon' (753 ff.), an idea which Chaucer could have found in Boethius (III pr.11) and Dante (*Paradiso* 1) and on 'the eyryssh bestes' (929–32) which had bean discussed by Alan (*Aleyn (1)) (and on which St Augustine had cited Plato in *The City of God*). For a possible reference to the *Symposium* (*LGW* 521–6) see *Agaton.

Pleyndamour is mentioned in *Sir Thopas* (VII.900) as an (apparently) well-known romance hero. He has not been identified. In Malory a 'Sir Playne de Amoris' is mentioned, but he seems very obscure compared with the other famous names in the Chaucerian passage (*Horn child, *Beves, etc.). Perhaps Chaucer invented the name on the model of Sir Eglamour. It is probably the origin of *Spenser's Sir Blandamour, a 'jollie youthfull knight' in book IV of *The Faerie Queene*.

Pleynt; Pleynt of Kynd. See *Complaint; *Aleyn (1).

ploughman. Any general agricultural labourer could be described by this term, but his wealth and status might vary from complete penury and virtual enslavement to the possession of some land and hence of some independence. Chaucer's Plowman of the *General Prologue*, judging by I.539–41, was of the latter type as were an increasing number following the *Black Death. Because of the use of ploughing and associated activities in parables in the New Testament, the figure of the ploughman was often used as a type of labourer crucial to the survival of civil society, and his activity well performed as the quintessence of secular Christian behaviour. Such an attitude is implicit in Chaucer's praise of the Plowman, brother it should be noted to the Parson, and is much more explicit in *Langland's *Piers Plowman*. [AH]
Rv 820.

Plowmans Tale, The. As Chaucer left *The Canterbury Tales*, no tale is provided for the Ploughman; at later dates two tales, neither written by Chaucer, were assigned to him. One is Hoccleve's *Miracle of the Virgin* (ed. I. Gollancz EETS ES 73 no. 7) found in one manuscript of *The Canterbury Tales*, Christ Church Oxford 152. The other is a work no longer extant in manuscript, that was first printed by Thomas Godfrey in [1536?], *STC* 5099.5; this was incorporated by William *Thynne into his 1542 reprint of Chaucer's works and subsequently appeared in all 16th-c. editions. The tale as it stands consists of 700 lines in eight-line stanzas; it may be a composite of a core of early 15th-c. Lollard material, with later amplification and the provision of an early 16th-c. prologue. The explicit link with the Ploughman is only made in this prologue. The author's affiliations are clearly Wycliffite, and he refers sympathetically to Sir John Oldcastle (whose execution in 1417 provides a *terminus post quem* for the composition of the core); he also claims (1965–6) to have written *Pierce the Plowmans Crede*. [AH]
(ed.) Skeat (1897).

Pluto, god of the underworld (Greek Hades), who abducted *Proserpina to be his queen. Like other medieval writers Chaucer associates the underworld with hell. The poet *Claudian, who told the story of the rape of Proserpina, is said to have 'borne up' 'al the fame of helle, | Of Pluto, and of Proserpyne, | That quene ys of the derke pyne' (*HF* 1507–12). There are a number of references to him and to the 'dirke regioun | Under the ground, ther Pluto dwelleth inne' (V.1074–5). Pandarus swears vehemently to Criseyde that he will see that all is well, or else he would rather be 'with Pluto kyng as depe ben in helle | As Tantalus' (*Tr* III.592–3). In two of the *Canterbury Tales* he plays an active role. In The *Knight's Tale* he sends from his 'derke regioun' (I.2082; see also I.2299) a fury which terrifies Arcite's horse (I.2685). In The *Merchant's Tale* he appears in a very entertaining episode (IV.2225 ff.). Here he is 'kyng of *fayerye', like the fairy king of the Otherworld in *Sir Orfeo, and with his wife and her retinue disports himself in *January's garden. They observe the situation of the mortals there, discuss it, and intervene. Chaucer generates much comedy from the domestic squabble of the divine husband and wife, and the apparent contrast between the sinister memory of the lord of the 'dark region' who 'ravysshed' Proserpina and carried her off his 'grisely carte' and the bright morning scene of the 'kyng of fayerye' seating himself on a 'bench of turves, fressh and grene.' (But fairies too were renowned for their abduction or dishonouring of mortal ladies; see the beginning of The *Wife of Bath's Tale.) It is smug, to say the least, for Pluto, seated on his bench of turves, to lecture his wife on wickedness of women. He gets a sharp response.

poets and poetry (see also *auctour and auctoritee; *fame; *rhetoric). Chaucer rarely accords the title of 'poet'. He so names *Virgil and *Lucan, (and in the list of those he implies are great poets in *Tr* V.1790–2, also includes *Ovid, Homer (*Omer) and Statius (*Stace)). Apart from the ancients, only *Dante and Petrarch (*Petrak) are so honoured. However, he does use the word in a general sense; an unidentified 'poet' is once cited in *Melibee (VII.1495), and the book in which Chaucer reads an Ovidian story (*BD* 52–6) contains fables put in rhyme by 'clerks' and 'other poetes'. It may be significant that he does not call

himself a poet, but the word 'maker' which he applies to himself (*Tr* V.1787) seems close to a medieval definition of 'poet' ('a poet is called a maker, or one who gives shape to things', Conrad of Hirsau). He tells his book of *Troilus* to be 'subgit . . . to alle poesye', but beneath the humility we may sense a certain pride: the book is at least to kiss the steps where the poets walk. He certainly seems to show a self-conscious interest in the poet's calling, and in his 'art poetical'. We should not take too seriously the comically self-deprecating portrait he has the Eagle give of the poet at work in his 'study' (*HF* 613–40), devoting his small wit to the making of numerous works in praise of Love, making his head ache, and reading until he is dazed, or the strange figure he presents in The *Canterbury Tales* (VII.613–704), abstracted and remote, constantly looking at the ground and 'elvish' in his appearance. These seem like typically Chaucerian variations on the topic of 'poetic madness' or the divine frenzy, *furor divinus sive poeticus*.

Burrow (1995); Ebin (1988); Minnis and Scott (1988).

Poilleys (adj.), Apulian (from Apulia in southern Italy), V.195.

Polydamas, a Trojan the son of *Antenor (*Tr* IV.51).

Polymya, Polyhymnia, the *Muse of sacred song, who is invoked at the beginning of *Anelida and Arcite* (15). She sings 'with vois memorial.' The adjective comes from her association with *memory. Her name (the Muse of many songs) was sometimes etymologized as 'the Muse of many memories'; possibly Chaucer found this in Boccaccio's commentary on Dante. But Chaucer's 'memorial' is rich in its suggestiveness: 'partaking of the quality of remembrance'; 'conferring memorableness'; 'memorable in its quality of expression'.

Norton-Smith (1981), 92–3.

Polymyte(s), Polynices the son of Oedipus (*Edippe) and Jocasta, who besieged *Thebes (1). He is mentioned in *Troilus and Criseyde* (V.938, 1488, 1507).

Polynestore

Polynestore, Polymnestor, a Trojan warrior, the king of Thracian Chersonese (the peninsula on the western side of the Hellespont on which Gallipoli stands) (*Tr* IV.52).

Poliphemus, Polyphemus, a Cyclops, one of the one-eyed giants who captured Ulysses (*Ulixes) and was blinded by him. The story is alluded to in *Boece* (IV m.7:20–8).

Poliphete, a Trojan who, according to Pandarus, intends to bring a legal action against Criseyde (*Tr* II.1467ff.). The episode and the character are Chaucer's invention. He perhaps took the name from Polyphoetes (or Polyboetes), a Trojan priest in the *Aeneid* (6.484).

Polite(s), a son of *Priam, killed by Pyrrhus (*Pirrus) (*HF* 160; *Tr* IV.53).

politics and political themes do not, at first sight, occupy a prominent place in Chaucer's writing. He produced no theoretical treatise like *Dante's book on monarchy, and although the Canterbury Pilgrims represent many of the occupations and 'estates' of medieval England, the purpose of the *General Prologue* is not primarily to provide sociological or political analysis. The great crises through which he lived in England (and about which, given his administrative posts, he must have been reasonably well informed) must certainly have affected his life, but he does not write about them in any direct or 'topical' way. (It is certainly possible, indeed likely, that his works may contain topical allusions or echoes, but attempts to identify them (even very sophisticated ones— e.g. in *Melibee* (see *Rv* 923–4)) have not always convinced sceptical readers.) The *Peasants' Revolt, for instance, occasions only an apparently joking reference to *Jakke Straw (and, perhaps, two very uncertain ones in *KnT* I.2459, *Tr* IV.183). However, in the light of the uncertainty and anxiety of the life of a late medieval official, largely dependent on *patronage and favour, this is hardly surprising. Critics have often speculated that his experience in the Parliament of 1386 (see Geoffrey *Chaucer: life) may have coloured his accounts of the parliaments in *The Parliament of Fowls* and in book IV of *Troilus* but this has to remain specula-

tion. Knowledge and connections resulting from his experience on embassies abroad may lie behind his references to Bernabò Visconti and Pedro of Castile in *The *Monk's Tale*, and may have sharpened Alceste's advice in the Prologue to *The *Legend of Good Women* to the God of Love not to be like 'tirauntz of Lumbardye | That kan no reward but at tyrannye' (*LGW* 374–5), although in general her insistence that a king or lord ought not to be 'tiraunt ne crewel' sounds rather like the traditional advice to princes material found in works like the *Secreta Secretorum* attributed to *Aristotle ('the Philosophre', 381) and other 'mirrors for princes', which emphasized the need for virtue and wisdom in the ruler. This material was widespread and influential, and we find echoes of it in Chaucer, sometimes in different contexts, as love and marriage in *The *Franklin's Tale*: 'after the tyme moste be temperaunce | To every wight [person] that kan on [knows about] governaunce' (V.785–6). A wicked tyrant like *Nero in *The *Monk's Tale*, in spite of the instruction of the wise Seneca (*Senek) that an emperor should 'be vertuous and hate tirannye' (VII.2508), yielded to the vice of tyranny. The Middle Ages had both a political definition of a tyrant (as a wicked ruler who cruelly oppresses the people, Isidore of Seville (*Ysidre)), and a more general religious one (as any man who exercises dominion without humility, whether in the state, the province, the congregation, his own house, or himself, Pope Gregory the Great). 'Political' tyrants appear in *The Monk's Tale*, and in *The Knight's Tale* where *Creon, 'fulfild of ire and of iniquitee', refuses 'for despit and for his tirannye' to allow the dead to be buried or burnt (I.940–7), and 'the tiraunt, with the pray by force yraft' (I.2015) is listed as one of children of Mars. One of the marks of a good ruler is that he should be 'benigne to his goode subgetis' (*Parson's Tale*, X.466, where Seneca is quoted on the need for clemency or, in Chaucer, '*pite').

Chaucer's narratives take place against a background of society, and its political structures are often alluded to. There are many kings and rulers, with their symbols of power (crowns, sceptres, thrones): they consult with counsellors or hold parliaments (e.g. in *KnT* I.2970, 3076), they receive pleas for help (e.g. *KnT* I.893–951), hold court, feasts and tournaments. Ambassadors and messengers come and go, and in *The *House of Fame* there is an apparently light-hearted allusion to spies; 'though that Fame had alle the pies [magpies]| In a realme, and alle the spies' (703–4). This poem gives a heightened and satirical description of a court, with all its suppliants and all its gossip. Although theoretical political statements are absent, Chaucer clearly shows a thoughtful interest in questions about the good life in society. In Boethius (*Boece) he had read some powerful laments on the instability and injustice of the sublunary world, where instead of Plato's wise men, tyrants and corrupt men rule and oppress the innocent in bitter contrast to the order and harmony ordained by God in the cosmos. When he is adapting Cicero's *Somnium Scipionis* for *The Parliament of Fowls*, he turns *patria* and *res publica* as '*commune profyt' (47; cf. 75, 507), a phrase which he uses several times elsewhere, sometimes contrasting it with 'singuler profite' (for an individual, and sometimes self-seeking), to suggest a state of general peace and harmony, a reflection of divine charity. The idea that *love holds 'regne and hous in unitee' (*Tr* III.29; cf. III.1746–7) is similar to that expressed by his friend *Gower. The humbly born but virtuous *Griselda puts this into practice as a good ruler:

> whan that the cas required it,
> The commune profit koude she redresse.
> Ther nas discord, rancour, ne hevynesse
> In al that land that she ne koude apese,
> And wisely brynge hem alle in reste and ese.

(IV.430–4)

There is a constant interest in 'governaunce' of all kinds, ranging from that of God over his creatures, to that of realms, households, *families, and the individual. Here Prudence's wise words to Melibee on how to govern himself may be set against an example of bitter self-knowledge: 'God yeve him meschaunce,' says the tricked fox in *The Nun's Priest's Tale*, 'That is so undiscreet of governaunce | That jangleth whan he sholde holde his pees' (VII.3433–5). Statements of the ideal order of things are made, or urged (fathers and mothers must give a good example to the children under their 'governaunce', VI.93–102), and quite often questioned or disputed (e.g. Dorigen on the 'governaunce' of God (V.865ff.)). The dictum of *Custance that women are born to be 'under mannes governance' (II.287) is contradicted by the triumphant words of the *Wife of Bath: 'He yaf me al the bridel in myn hond, | To han the governance of hous and lond, | And of his tonge, and of his hond also' (III.813–15; cf. III.1231, 1262; IV.1192–4), and leads to a serious discussion of '*maistrie' (and patience and 'rigour' in a relationship, V.773–86). The world of the Canterbury tale-tellers is presided over by a superb example of a 'play' ruler, the *Host, 'oure governour' who is generally obeyed by his 'subjects' ('I am under youre yerde', says the Clerk, 'Ye han of us as now the governance', IV.22–3), but has to threaten those who may be 'rebel' to his judgement (I.833), or to reprove those who indulge in 'sermonyng', like the Reeve, to whom (I.3900) 'he gan to speke as lordly as a kyng'.

Aers (1986); Benson (1990); Knight (1986); P. A. Olson (1986); Patterson (1990); Strohm (1989); Swanson (2000); Wallace (1997).

Polixena, Polixene, Polyxena, a beautiful daughter of *Priam, the sister of Troilus (*Tr* I.455; III.409). According to the medieval *Troy books *Achilles fell in love with her and was ambushed and killed in the temple of Apollo to which he had gone to arrange a marriage: he died 'for love of Polixena' (*BD* 1071). The ghost of Achilles claimed her and she was sacrificed at his tomb; hence she is one of those heroines 'that boghten love so dere' (*LGW* 258).

Pollux, see *Castor.

POLO, MARCO (1254–?1323), a Venetian who in 1271 accompanied his father and uncle on an embassy from the Pope to the Great Khan, Kubilai, in China. He apparently became a trusted servant of the Khan, and it was twenty-four years before he returned to Venice. His vivid and detailed account of the great journey and of the realms of *Tartary was written in French while he was in a Genoese prison. He was probably helped by Rustichello of Pisa, a writer of romances. The book contains some 'travellers' tales' (and was called the 'book of marvels') but many fewer than the more popular *Mandeville. It is a remarkable description of a very different civilization.

Whether Chaucer knew it is not certain: it does not seem to have been a common book in 14th-c. England.

(trans.) Latham (1958).

POMPE, POMPEI, POMPEYE, POMPEUS, Pompey 'the Great', Gnaius Pompeius Magnus (106–48 BC) a Roman general who became a member, with Caesar (*Cesar) and Crassus, of the 'first triumvirate'. He won great victories in the east. In 49 BC civil war broke out between him and Caesar, and in the following year he was defeated and killed at the battle of Pharsalus. The *Pharsalia* of *Lucan celebrates Pompey as a hero. In Chaucer Pompey appears in the *Monk's tragedy of Caesar (VII.2679–94), as Caesar's father-in-law (he was actually his son-in-law; the mistake is found in other medieval writers). He is a 'noble governour' of Rome, whose 'knyghthod' was once favoured by Fortune who made him 'of th'orient conquerour' before turning against him. One of his own men killed him and took his head to Caesar. His death, it is said in *The *Man of Law's Tale* (II.199) is one of those which were written in the stars.

Poo, the river Po in northern Italy (IV.48).

Pool, pole (*astron.*). In *Boece, the north pole is 'the sovereyne centre or poynt', 'the sovereyne pool of the firmament', near which the stars of *Arctour turn. Both 'poles of this world' are recognized in *The Treatise on the *Astrolabe. (See also *astrology and astronomy.)   [JDN]

POPE, ALEXANDER (1688–1744), poet and man of letters, was an admirer of Chaucer. In his youth he wrote *modernizations of *The *Merchant's Tale* (c.1704, published 1709) and *The *Wife of Bath's Prologue* (c.1704, pub. 1713), and a bawdy *imitation of Chaucer (before 1709, pub. 1727). It has also been claimed that the version of the *General Prologue* ('Chaucer's Characters') which appeared under the name of the actor and dramatist Thomas Betterton in Lintot's *Miscellaneous Poems and Translations* (1712) was written by Pope. Of his *The Temple of Fame* (written 1711, pub. 1715) he remarks that 'the hint . . . was taken from Chaucer's *House of Fame* (the third book),

but that 'the design is in a manner entirely alter'd, the descriptions and most of the particular thoughts my own'. In his note he defends allegorical poetry, and says that Chaucer produced some 'masterpieces of this sort'. A passage in *An Essay on Criticism* (written 1709, pub. 1711) on the impermanence of the English language has the famous couplet: 'Our sons their fathers' failing language see, | And such as Chaucer is, shall Dryden be.' Later (1728–30), in conversation Pope is recorded as saying, 'I read Chaucer still with as much pleasure as any of our poets. He is a master of manners, of description, and the first tale-teller in the true enlivened natural way.'

Poperyng, Poperinghe, a town in Flanders, the birthplace of *Sir Thopas (VII.720). It was noted for its cloth and its pears. Perhaps Chaucer chose on it because it sounded distinctly and comically unromantic.

PORCIA, Portia, wife of Marcus *Brutus (d. 42 BC). Chaucer knew a tradition, probably from St *Jerome, that she died when she heard of Brutus's death. She therefore appears in *Dorigen's catalogue of noble wives (V.1448): 'withoute Brutus koude she nat lyve'.

Portyngale, Portugal, a kingdom on the western seaboard of the Iberian Peninsula, which was recognized as sovereign by Castile and León in 1143, and which reaffirmed its independence at the decisive battle of Aljubarrota in 1385, where English archers likewise made their contribution to the victory. Chaucer once mentions a 'greyn [crimson dye] of Portyngale' (VII.3459).   [PS]

'portraits' is a word frequently used in a figurative sense to describe Chaucer's verbal 'pictures' or descriptions of characters, especially in the *General Prologue. It is not used by Chaucer himself (it is attested later, in the 16th c.), but he uses *portreye* ('draw' I.96; *BD* 783; 'depict', 'picture' *ABC* 81; *Tr* V.716) and *portreiture* ('painting'; I.1968, 2036; *HF* 131. See *visual arts). The formal description of persons (*effictio, notatio*) has an extensive background in ancient and medieval *rhetoric, where it is one of the techniques of amplification used either for praise or blame. In *De inventione* Cicero suggests a number of topics for the orator to discuss, including a person's name, gender, his native land, the excellences or faults of his appearance, his type of life (education, occupation, friends), his affections and emotions, his tastes, plans, deeds, and words. In the Middle Ages Matthew of Vendôme in his *Ars versificatoria* gives quite elaborate illustrative examples of the description of a person's nature (both physical and moral). A servile following of the rhetoricians' 'rules' could result in a rather rigid catalogue of features listed from the head down to the feet, which became a common pattern in medieval poetry for the description of feminine *beauty. Chaucer's treatment is typically imaginative and original—and not always clearly related to either praise or blame. The portraits of the *General Prologue* are visual, and have inspired painters and illustrators, and also vivid, and have been much praised for their 'realism' (although there has been controversy over whether they are 'individuals' or 'types' or 'rhetorical constructs': see *characterization, *estates satire, *physiognomy). One of their most striking characteristics is a quality of unexpectedness. We meet the pilgrims in the hostelry, but are made sometimes to imagine them already riding along the road. There is no cataloguing of features, and indeed no single set pattern of description: the 'ordering of detail is quite unsystematic, and comment on different aspects of physical appearance, behaviour, array, opinion, attitude, inward moral life and professional occupation is presented in the order in which it seems to have occurred to the memory of the observer' (Pearsall, 58). Throughout the amazing flow of detail (the Cook's 'mormal', the Wife of Bath's large hat, the Pardoner's yellow hair, etc.) runs the voice of the narrator, with its comments, suppositions, or studied refusals to comment. The same variety is found throughout the rest of Chaucer's work, ranging from the grotesque figure of *Fame in *The *House of Fame* to the Saturnian portrait of *Lygurge in The *Knight's Tale*, and to the parodic description of the noble knight *Sir Thopas. In *Troilus and Criseyde* (V.799–840) just before the final action he inserts formal portraits of Troilus, Criseyde, and Diomede. These, taken from *Joseph of Exeter, sound a little old-fashioned in a poem which has concerned itself so markedly with

psychology and the workings of the inner mind, and perhaps signal a shift to a more detached, more chronicle-like mode of narration. Some narratives will have no formal portraits (in *The Franklin's Tale* the heroine Dorigen is simply the most beautiful lady on earth: 'oon the faireste [= the fairest] under sonne'), others quite elaborate ones (like the description in *The Physician's Tale* of Virginia, whose beauty is the cause of her death). Some of the most impressive examples are to be found in the *fabliaux, a form in which traditionally the storyline is of the highest importance and descriptions of persons are usually non-existent or highly stereotyped. Chaucer's *The *Shipman's Tale* with its trio of a merchant, a wife, and a monk follows this pattern, but in the fabliaux of Fragment I he produces a dazzling array—of *Alisoun (1), *Nicholas, and *Absolon (2) in *The *Miller's Tale*, Symkyn and his wife and daughter in *The *Reeve's Tale*, and Perkyn Revelour in *The *Cook's Tale*.

S&A 3–5; Faral (1924), 75–82; Haselmayer (1938); Mann (1973); Pearsall (1985), ch. 3.

Poul, *see* *Paul.

Poules, Seinte (or simply Poules) St *Paul's Cathedral in *London (see Map 2). This is 'Old St Paul's', the great Gothic church, one of the largest in Europe, which in Chaucer's day had a tall spire of at least 480 ft (160 m) and must have dominated the landscape of the city. It was damaged beyond repair in the Great Fire of 1666. Chaucer's references show how familiar it must have been: the *Parson did not run 'unto Seinte Poules' to find a position as a chantry priest (I.509), the elegant *Absolon (2) had 'Poules wyndow' carved on his shoes (I.3318, i.e. they were cut and latticed so that they looked like the cathedral's windows), the *Host swears by 'Seint Poules belle' (VII.2780).

poverty and its effects are not a central theme in Chaucer, but are the subject of some powerful passages concerned with two traditional (almost proverbial) topics. The *Man of Law launches into a bitter diatribe 'O hateful harm, condicioun of poverte!' (II.99–121), based on *Innocent III's *De miseria condicionis humane*. If you are poor you must steal, beg, or borrow; you blame Christ and your neighbour; you are despised and hated: the wise say that it is better to die than to live in poverty. Similar sentiments are expressed in one of *Prudence's speeches in *Melibee* (VII.1560–75), in which she argues that riches properly gained bring great benefits whereas poverty is the cause of much distress and evil. She quotes Innocent, who says that the lot of a poor beggar is especially miserable, since if he does not ask for food he dies of hunger, and if he does he dies of shame, as well as other authorities. But we also find the opposed idea that poverty may be the cause of happiness: 'glad poverte is an honest thyng, certeyn' exclaims the old woman in The *Wife of Bath's Tale* (III.1183). This is part of her argument that true nobility or '*gentilesse' does not depend on riches. The stoic dictum derives from Seneca (*Senec) and had become proverbial. He who does not have possessions does not covet them. She quotes a remark of *Juvenal, which had also become proverbial: 'the povre man, whan he goth by the wey, | Bifore the theves he may synge and pleye.' The extreme poverty of the virtuous *Griselda and her family and village, which is heavily stressed (NB the repetition of 'povre' IV.200, 204, 205, 213, 222, 232), while perhaps infused by the Christian ideals of apostolic poverty, again forms the background to an examplum of 'gentilesse'. The 'narwe cotage' of the poor and very temperate widow at the beginning of The *Nun's Priest's Tale* might suggest the setting for a similar exemplum, but the tale takes off in a rather different direction. Many other allusions to or mentions of poverty suggest that it is part of life (with accompanying obligations to give alms to the poor—'he has treasure who gives to the poor' says a medieval proverb. The Pardoner, however, exploits the poor, I.702ff.). Some social groups are described as 'poor' in an almost formulaic way: poor scholars or poor clerks, for instance (I.3190, 4002). While Nicholas in The *Miller's Tale* with his scientific equipment and a room of his own clearly falls short of the stereotype, the Clerk of the *General Prologue*, with his threadbare coat is just as clearly the real thing, as is the poor parson serving his poor parishioners. The friars ('povre freres', I.232), committed to an ideal of apostolic poverty, were often the target of satirists for their hypocrisy: the *Friar, 'the beste beggere in his hous' (I.252), spurned poor lepers in favour of profit and splendid clothing—not for

him the threadbare cloak of a poor scholar. Finally, there is Chaucer's own witty poem on the lack of money, the *Complaint to his *Purse*.

prayer (in the religious sense of an address, petition or expression of adoration directed to God or a saint) is found in some interesting contexts. The words *preye* and *preyere* are also frequently used in their more general secular senses. Chaucer also uses a number of other terms: *orisoun* 'prayer', and the older words *bidde* 'beg, pray' (as well as 'command') and *blesse* 'bless, cross oneself'. The Old Testament *Job prays, Chaucer's pagans pray to their gods, and prayer forms part of the 'religion of *Love' (e.g. *Tr* I.15–49), but in general, prayer takes place within a Christian context. It is very frequent, and very varied in its nature and intensity. 'Prayers' are often very brief, and sometimes formulaic; it may be significant that a number of characters are not represented as praying at all. But we are made to feel that whether heartfelt, conventional, or ironic, prayer is part of contemporary life. The *Clerk dutifully prays for the souls of his benefactors (I.301). In a more comic context in The *Reeve's Tale* (I.4286–7) the startled wife of the miller cries out for aid to a famous relic, 'Help hooly croys of Bromeholm', adding '*In manus tuas!* Lord, to thee I calle', a verse from Luke (23:46) that was used as a prayer before sleep or at the hour of death. Very brief prayers like these are sometimes used as *ejaculations, *oaths, curses, expressions of goodwill or devices of emphasis. They are commonly used by narrators to mark the closure of a tale: 'Thus endeth Palamon and Emelye; | And God save al this faire campaigne!' (I.3107–8; cf. 'This tale is doon, and God save at the rowte!' I.3854); 'God blesse us, and his mooder Seinte Marie!' (IV.2418), etc. They are usually formulaic, but are sometimes given a particular twist by the narrator, most obviously and elaborately by the *Wife of Bath:

> and Jhesu Crist us sende
> Housbondes meeke, yonge, and fressh abedde,
> And grace t'overbyde hem that we wedde,
> And eek I praye Jhesu shorte hir [their] lyves
> That noght wol be governed by hir wyves;
>
> (III.1258–62)

see also I.4322–4 and VII.433–4. More earnest and devout examples are also found (II.1160–2;

VII.684–90). The finest is Chaucer's prayer to the Trinity at the end of *Troilus* (V.1863–9), a solemn and eloquent stanza based on *Dante. Within narratives formal prayers may be used both as devout petitions and as moments of emotional outpouring which heighten scenes of '*pite' or pathos. The *Man of Law's Tale* contains a number of good examples: Custance's eloquent prayers to the cross (II.451–62), to God and the Virgin Mary (639–44), and to Mary (841–54). At the end of the second part the narrator prays for his heroine. The prologues of two tales have prayers which are almost self-contained religious *lyrics. The *Prioress's Prologue* is an ecstatic prayer in five stanzas addressed to God and the Virgin Mary, with echoes of traditional Marian imagery, the psalms, Dante, and the Mass of the Holy Innocents. After her song of adoration, the Prioress associates herself with innocent children (one of whom is to be the subject of her tale) and beseeches the Virgin for help, 'Gydeth my song that I shal of yow seye'. The *Second Nun's Prologue* contains a prayer of seven stanzas, an invocation to Mary. Some of it is based on St Bernard's prayer to the Virgin in Dante's *Paradiso*. An even more elaborate Marian prayer is Chaucer's devotional alphabetical poem, the *ABC*, in which an ecstatic list of the qualities, attributes, and symbols of the Virgin is combined with a series of emotional petitions. (See *piety*.)

preaching/preachers. The duty of preaching had been encouraged and to some extent codified by the provisions of the 1215 Lateran Council and ensuing local legislation. To persuade the congregation to the fulfilment of the obligation of at least annual confession and reception of the Eucharist, the parish priest was urged to preach weekly to his flock expounding the gospel lection and especially the elements of *religion: the commandments, the sins and virtues, the sacraments, creed, *Pater noster* and *Ave*, etc. The difficulties found by the parish clergy in fulfilling this duty were in various ways alleviated: by provision of written material in the form of *penitential handbooks, of model sermons, handbooks of sermon construction, and (though this came to be regarded as a potential infringement upon the rights of the *parish clergy) by the assistance of peripatetic friars. Because of

the popularity of the more radical preachers, and because of fear of heresy, regulation of preaching (who could preach? when and where? under whose licence?) became increasingly strict at the end of the 14th and the beginning of the 15th c. It has been customary to distinguish two types of sermon at the end of the medieval period: 'ancient', which discussed the lection in the fashion of an exposition, following narrative order, and 'modern' which proceeded by an elaborate series of subdivisions and usually was based on only a single biblical verse; 'modern' is generally characteristic of academic sermons, 'ancient' of more popular productions. But it has been realized that this distinction, made in many late medieval handbooks, whilst it may characterize the subdivided sermons well, leaves as 'ancient' a wide variety of sermons.

In Chaucer's *Canterbury Tales* the Parson would be obliged to preach and evidently did so (I.481 'Cristes gospel trewely wolde preche'); the Friar apparently preferred the confessional to preaching as a way of pursuing his dubious ends. A number of the tales have been loosely described as 'sermons': apart from the Parson's tale, those also of the Prioress, the Second Nun, the Monk, and the Pardoner. This description seems inaccurate and unhelpful: the Parson's is a penitential handbook, the next two saints' lives, the third a series of tragedies. Only the Pardoner's has a text (*Radix malorum est cupiditas* VI.heading, 334, 426), which the tale demonstrates; but the digressions and the lack of biblical exegesis, let alone the flamboyantly self-congratulatory style, would make it a poor introduction to other medieval sermons; Chaucer has adopted some of the characteristic features of medieval preaching without composing a sermon. Similar adoption of these features are found in little elsewhere, for instance, as the Friar twits her, in the discourse of the Wife of Bath (III.165). [AH]

Priam(us), Priam, the son of Laomedon and king of Troy. He is mentioned a number of times, especially in *Troilus and Criseyde* (I.2; IV.139 ff., 194–5, 921, 1206; V.284, 1226; see also *BD* 328). His death at the hands of Pyrrhus (*Pirrus) at the fall of Troy (*LGW* 935–9) is vividly recalled (*HF* 159; VII.3358).

Priapus

Priapus, an ancient god of *gardens and fertility (images of him as a small misshapen man with an enormous phallus were often placed in gardens). Chaucer probably knew of him from *Ovid's *Fasti*. He is, appropriately, mentioned in connection with *January's pleasure garden (IV.2034), and is the subject of one of Chaucer's more recondite *allusions in *The* *Parliament of Fowls* (253–9), to the story of how, rejected by the nymph Lotis, he came by night to take her, but was betrayed by the braying of Silenus's ass, and exposed (with 'his member well prepared') to the scorn of the nymphs and gods (*Fasti* I).

Pryme, Prime, one of the canonical hours used to regulate worship during the Church's day. The names of the so-called canonical hours (with the commencement of each) were traditionally Matins (midnight or later), Prime (6 a.m.), Terce (9 a.m.), Sext (noon), None (3 p.m., often said with Sext), Vespers (6 p.m.), and Compline (9 p.m.). They were originally kept using the system of seasonal (unequal) *hours, but with the introduction of the mechanical clock the situation changed. From internal astronomical evidence it seems that in The *Nun's Priest's Tale and The *Merchant's Tale Chaucer took prime (when its completion is understood) to be 9 a.m. in hours of the clock; in The *Knight's Tale 'not fully pryme' meant not yet 9 a.m., and The* Squire's Tale 'pryme large' meant the same. That he meant a stretch of time and not a point of time is clear from the usage 'half-wey pryme' in The *Reeve's Prologue. (See also **clokke**; *day.) [JDN]

primer meant in Chaucer's time a devotional book of prayers used by the laity, and also a small prayer book from which children were taught to read. It is one of these that the little school boy in The *Prioress's Tale studies from (VII.517, 541).

Prioress, The, described in the *General Prologue to The *Canterbury Tales (118–62) in a way that is both vivid and delicately ambiguous. She is a nun, who sang her service 'entuned in hir nose ful semely', but has the appearance and the manners of a beautiful courtly lady, or of one who would be courtly (she 'peyned hire to countrefete cheere | Of court'). She has the grey eyes of the traditional heroine of romance, and her table manners are exquisite, or a shade over-exquisite (hyperbole often trembles on the edge of bathos). She is a lady of feeling, whose sensibility is so refined and directed to such specialized objects of pity as a mouse caught in a trap or the suffering of one of her pet hounds that it is on the edge of sentimentality: 'al was conscience [here 'sensiblity', but perhaps with a lingering echo of another meaning, 'moral sense'?] and tendre herte'. She is given a name ('madame *Eglentyne') and a local setting in the nunnery of St Leonard's at 'Stratford-atte-Bowe' (which contained some well-connected ladies, like the sister of Elisabeth de Burgh, the countess of Ulster, in whose household Chaucer served). There are comic or semi-comic provisos (concerning her French, which is not that of Paris) and ambiguities (like the inscription on her brooch, *amor vincit omnia*—'love conquers all'). Nuns were not supposed to wear brooches; nor were they supposed to go on pilgrimages, although this, like other rules, could be waived or ignored. There is no doubt that Chaucer is playing with the discrepancies between her religious profession and her more secular inclinations, like her taste for fine clothes, but there has been much argument about the severity of his satire here, ranging from the view that it is so gentle as to be virtually non-existent to the view that it is a sharp exposé of ecclesiastical inadequacy and of her moral shortcomings (this is generally based on the anti-Semitism of The *Prioress's Tale). She does not have many of the more spectacular failings that nuns are accused of in traditional *estates satire, and Chaucer seems to insist on her pleasantness, and refrains from any expression of judgement—though this might seem simply to add to the ambiguity of the portrait.

Rv 803–6; Cooper (1989), 37–9; Mann (1973), 128–37; Ridley (1965).

Prioress's Prologue and Tale, The (238 lines in rhyme royal) is the second story in Fragment VII, and follows The* Shipman's Tale (to which it probably alludes in lines 642–3). Its date is not certain, but it is usually thought to have been written for *The Canterbury Tales*. It has been suggested that it was read on the occasion of a visit made on 26 March 1387 by Richard II and Queen Anne to

Lincoln Cathedral, which had the shrine of St *Hugh. But if it were composed for this occasion it is strange that St Hugh does not figure more prominently in it. That the tale ends with a prayer to this child saint may reflect a particular devotion on the part of Chaucer (whose wife Philippa had been admitted to the fraternity of the cathedral in 1386), but it seems quite appropriate for the Prioress to end with an invocation to another child martyr. The tale as we have it is clearly intended for a female speaker ('quod she', 454, 581). The Prologue makes use of scripture and the liturgy, with echoes of the Little Office of the Virgin Mary and the Mass of the Holy Innocents (an emphasis on childlike innocence continues through the Tale). Lines 474–80 are based on the prayer in *Dante, *Paradiso* 33.1–21, which Chaucer had earlier used in *The *Second Nun's Prologue*. The tale itself is called a 'miracle' (691): it belongs to the popular genre of *miracles of the Virgin, stories of the way in which Mary (*Marie) rescued or rewarded her faithful devotees. This particular story is widespread.

The Prologue is a fervent prayer to the Virgin in five stanzas (five, perhaps, because of the traditional Five Joys or Five Sorrows of Mary), praising her power and goodness, and asking for her aid. The Tale is set in a city in Asia (*Asye). There, in the midst of a Jewish quarter, is a little Christian school. One of the children, a 7-year-old widow's son, is especially devoted to the Virgin Mary, and learns by heart the antiphon *Alma redemptoris mater*, which he would sing as he passed through the 'Jewerye' on his way to and from school. Satan stirs up the hatred of the Jews, and they hire a murderer to kill him. His throat is cut, and his body thrown into a privy. His mother searches for him everywhere without success, until, inspired by Christ, she comes to the place where his body lies, and the child begins to sing *Alma redemptoris* loudly. The Christians wonder at the miracle, and the boy is taken, still singing, to the nearest abbey. The guilty Jews are put to a cruel death. In response to the abbot's entreaty the child explains that at what would have been the moment of his death the Virgin Mary came and told him to sing the antiphon. She placed a seed on his tongue, and promised to come and take him when it was removed. The abbot removes it, the child

dies gently, and his body is placed in a marble tomb.

Its effect on its fictional listeners is powerful: Chaucer says that at the end of the tale 'every man | As sobre was that wonder was to se'. It seems to have been popular with early readers, but has had a mixed reception in modern times. It is an extreme example of Chaucer's 'pitous' writing (see '*pite'), and has sometimes been criticized as sentimental. It certainly makes a direct assault on the emotions, emphasizing the pathos and horror of the events. But tenderness (as seen in the evocation of the innocence of the 'litel clergeon') is not necessarily sentimentality, and the scene in which the despairing mother searches for her child is genuinely moving. The tale owes much to the tradition of medieval 'affective' religious devotion, which is deeply emotional, and concentrates on the human qualities of Christ and the Virgin. It is also very consistent with the passionate Marian devotion of the Prioress shown in the Prologue: indeed, the narrator's presence is strongly felt. It also contains writing of a powerful, limpid eloquence. It is carefully constructed: the emotional exclamations (579–85, 607–13) and the final prayer mark the culmination of distinct stages in the narrative. Modern readers are disturbed not only by the violence (which is also often found in saints' lives), but by the anti-Semitism of the story evident from the beginning (see *Jews). Attempts to shift the blame for this from Chaucer to the Prioress and to present the tale as a demonstration of her moral limitations are not really convincing: that the Tale appears in independent MS copies without any connection with the *General Prologue* suggests that it was not read then in this modern 'ironic' way. We should certainly now expect a story turning on racial or religious hatred to treat this in a more even-handed way, but it would be difficult to find many examples of this from Chaucer's time, and especially in this kind of genre, which is not primarily 'realistic' and wishes to present a sharp opposition between the innocent victim and the wicked, demonized persecutors. It is a disturbing but strangely beautiful tale of pathos. (See also *piety.)

(ed.) *Rv* 209–12, 913–16; Boyd (1987); *S&A* 447–85; Cooper (1989), 287–98; Collette (1980–1); Hirsh (1975–6); Mann (1983); Pearsall (1985), 246–53.

prisons and prisoners. As far as we know, Chaucer's only first-hand experience of imprisonment was his brief spell as a prisoner of war in 1359–60 (see Geoffrey *Chaucer: life). He presumably had, like others, a general knowledge of prisons and prison conditions. The confinement of prisoners (for custodial, coercive, or penal reasons) varied considerably. At best a prisoner (especially a well-connected one) might enjoy a private 'chamber'; at worst, he might be committed to the depths of the prison, shackled, and subject to other forms of duress. There was an elaborate system of fees and payments: gaolers, who had no stable income, could sell food and other goods to prisoners or even quittance from 'irons'. Escapes were frequent, and were often severely punished. Probably most prisoners had to endure discomfort, cold, smells, and boredom (alleviated for some by the carving of graffiti on the walls, as at Carlisle Castle).

Chaucer's most horrific prison scene is the brief account of Ugolino (*Hugelyn) being starved to death in a tower (*MkT* VII.2407–62). There are a number of references to modes of imprisonment. In the legend of Ariadne (*Adriane) Theseus is thrown by Minos 'into a prysoun, fetered' (*LGW* 1950) before he is to be devoured by the Minotaur, in a tower 'doun in the botom derk and wonder lowe' but he is helped to escape. Other victims include Hypermnestra (*Ypermystra) (*LGW* 2722). Samson (*Sampson) (VII.2073). The Parson alludes to the duty of helping the needy, including 'visitynge in prisone' (X.1030–1).

The most extended account is the imprisonment of Palamon and Arcite in *The Knight's Tale*, who are condemned to remain in prison perpetually, since Theseus 'nolde no raunsoun'. They are kept in a tower, but Palamon by leave of his gaoler is allowed to go up to a higher chamber from which he can see the city and garden (in which Emily is walking). Other remarks ('in cheynes and in fettres' (I.1343) or 'in derknesse and horrible and strong prisoun', 1451) suggest the severer forms of imprisonment. Thanks to the intervention of *Perotheus, Arcite is allowed to leave prison, but never to return to Theseus's lands (1204–15). After seven more years Palamon, helped by a friend, gives a narcotic to his gaoler, and manages to break out ('brak his prisoun': the term 'break' is

found in medieval documents). Confinement in prison is a dominant image in the first half of the tale. It is also used to further Chaucer's larger literary and philosophical purposes. The two young knights fall to musing on their lot and on questions of providence and justice. Imprisonment may encourage philosophical reflection and/or literary composition. Two later examples are the author of the *Kingis Quair* and the 'knight prisoner', Sir Thomas Malory. Boethius (*Boece), writing his *Consolation of Philosophy* in prison was an especially powerful model. He is not mentioned by name in *The Knight's Tale* but provides much of the material for the knights' speeches. In this tale there is also a hint of a grim cosmic dimension, in that the planet-god *Saturn in his malign aspect is especially associated with imprisonment (elsewhere, Chaucer says that his 'badde aspectes' caused Hypermnestra to die in prison, *LGW* 2597–8). Arcite alludes to his 'wikke aspect or disposicioun' as responsible for their fate (1087–9), as does Palamon (1328). Later, Saturn himself announces 'myn is the prison in the derke cote [cell]' (2457). In the earlier part of the story the theme of imprisonment is intricately connected with that of *love. The opening contrasts the beautiful garden in which Emily walks and the tower which confines the two prisoners. Arcite is released from prison but condemned to exile away from Emily ('now is my prisoun worse than biforn', 1224). The question is posed as to which of the two had the worse in suffering 'the peynes stronge | Both of the lovere and the prisoner' (1338–9).

The metaphorical and symbolic association of imprisonment and love is implied in the common phrases 'bound by love' ('Love is he that alle thing may bynde' *Tr* I.237; cf. 255) and 'the chain of love', which may be sweet or painful, as Troilus finds: 'he seyde, "O fool, now artow in the snare, | That whilom japedest at loves peyne, | Now artow hent, now gnaw thin owen cheyne!"', *Tr* I.507–9. Chaucer alludes to the 'chain' of marriage in *Lenvoy de Chaucer a *Bukton*; and to the 'prison' of Disdain (Criseyde 'gan hire herte unfettre | Out of desdeynes prisoun but a lite', *Tr* II.1216–17). Other metaphorical uses include the Parson's 'prisoun of helle' (X.310), and (from St Paul) 'the prisoun of my caytyf body' (X.343; cf. VIII.71–4). From ancient and sometimes Platonic sources come Theseus's 'this foul prisoun of this lyf' (I.3061) and Boethius's 'the prysone of the erthe' (*Bo* II pr.7:154).

Hanawalt (1979); C. Harding (1985); Pugh (1968).

Progne, Proigne, Procne, the wife of *Tereus and the sister of Philomela (*Philomene), whose story is told in The *Legend of Good Women*. In *Troilus and Criseyde* the swallow Procne 'with a sorowful lay' laments her transformation (II.64–6).

Prologues. 'Let the poem's beginning, like a courteous attendant, introduce the subject with grace [*honeste*]' says Geoffrey of Vinsauf (*Gaufred). Other writers on ancient and medieval *rhetoric offer more detailed advice to orators and poets on the introductory discourse, often more formally called a prologue or a proem or prohemium. A variety of topics may be used: devices to win the goodwill and attentiveness of the audience (by the writer modestly excusing himself or commending himself, by announcing the bringing of things never said before, or by using invocations or prayers (to the Muses, God, a saint). A work may be dedicated to an earthly or a heavenly patron. We find many examples of these techniques in the prologues in Chaucer's work.

The more academic prologues of medieval commentators on biblical or ancient texts may be an 'extrinsic' prologue, which discusses the nature of the art or science in question or an 'intrinsic' prologue, on the rules or precepts which have to be known in order to practise the art, the intention of the author, his manner of writing, his reason for writing, etc. Introductions (or *accessus*) to such commentaries may analyse the title of the book, its subject matter, its stylistic treatment, or give some information on the life of the author. The closest to an 'academic prologue' in Chaucer is found (appropriately) in the words of the *Clerk when he announces (IV.26–56) that he will tell a tale which he learned from Petrarch: he briefly remarks on his life and achievement, comments on the 'prohemye', written in 'heigh stile', which describes the geographical setting, gently suggesting that this may be a *digression.

Chaucer prefers the literary prologue, which he uses (and transforms) in a variety of ways. It is not at all surprising that a writer who is so interested in the creation of strong, insistent narrative voices should have shown such a marked interest in the ways that beginnings may introduce the subject. The *Book of the Duchess* already has an introductory section, not formally marked as a 'prologue', which describes the circumstances of the dream which is the poem's subject matter, and introduces the reader to the highly distinctive voice of the poet/narrator. A similar pattern is found in other *dream visions, from the *Parliament of Fowls* to the elaborate example in The *Legend of Good Women*. This latter is now always entitled the 'Prologue', which is justified by its structure and by early scribal rubrics ('the Prologue of ix goode wymmen', 'explicit prohemium'), but the fact that the proems and invocations of The *House of Fame* are marked as such only by modern editors might suggest that for early readers such clear demarcations were not necessary or always usual. Each of the first four books of *Troilus and Criseyde* is preceded by an introductory proem, the first shading into narrative (signalled by the remark 'now wil I gon streght to my matere'), the others more formally self-contained. All are elegant and informative.

After the elaborate introduction given in the *General Prologue* to The *Canterbury Tales*, individual tellers are often introduced by the Host, and a number of them use introductions or introductory material. There is a good deal of variety in what may be called 'prologues', and in the nature of the prologues. As Helen Cooper says, 'most manuscripts designate the *links between the tales as 'prologues' to the following tales, and it seems likely that the terminology is in most instances Chaucer's own, but it can on occasion be misleading. Many of the links function as epilogues as much as prologues: they both sign off the preceding tale and introduce the next, and in the process they often serve to indicate a relationship between the two' (Cooper, 92). Early examples in the collection are the prologue to the Miller's tale—really the 'words between' the Host and the Miller, with a literary comment from the poet, and the Reeve's more elaborate melancholy confessional introduction. Some, like the Miller's, consist of an exchange of words. But these often alert us to clashes of personality or the nature of the tale which is to follow): see, for instance, the prologue of the Friar or the Monk (who like the Reeve announces his intention) or the Nun's Priest. The Summoner's prologue (he uses the word itself) is fiercely personal and combative like the Reeve's. The Merchant's prologue again is a short personal lament which the Host uses to invite him to tell on, a neat example of the way in which Chaucer can fuse prologue with dramatic situation and conversation. The Prioress's prologue is, appropriately, an eloquent prayer. After his words with the Host, the Franklin gives a brief formal 'literary' prologue which indicates the genre to which his story belongs. A more elaborate example is found in the Introduction and Prologue of The *Man of Law's Tale*. That Chaucer was deliberately experimenting with prologues, introductions, and the beginnings of *narratives seems confirmed by the Canon Yeoman's Prologue with its dramatic action, and by the ambitious monologues given to the Pardoner and the Wife of Bath. As our text stands, the wife simply begins talking in her distinctive voice and continues until she announces that she will tell her tale, at which point the Friar interrupts with a joke—'Now dame . . . | This is a long preamble of a tale' (III. 831). It illustrates both Chaucer's self-consciousness (he knows the terminology ('preamble' and 'preambulacioun', 'prohemye', 'prologe', 'preface' (VIII.271), 'introduccion' (VIII. 1386)), and his originality. He had learnt how to introduce a subject not only with grace but with wit and verve.

Cooper (1989); Hunt (1948); Minnis and Scott (1988), ch. 1.

pronunciation, see *language.

prophecy. Although in the medieval period the identification in the Old Testament of prophecy concerning the events following the incarnation was the commonest form (and is found in Chaucer's *Parson's Tale*, X.75 ff. etc.), similar predictions about the future in pagan stories were described by the same name (e.g. in *Tr* V.1494, 1521 Cassandra's prediction from Troilus's dream of the boar are described by her and by Troilus as *prophecie*). Similarly, *prophete* might be used both of an Old Testament figure such as Jeremiah, of

Mahomet (*MLT* II.224) or of a bird such as the owl (*LGW* 2254). [AH]

Proserpina, Proserpyne Proserpina (Greek Persephone), the wife of *Pluto and the queen of the underworld. She appears with him in *The Merchant's Tale* (IV.2038 ff.), and in her own right as 'quene of the dark peyne' (*HF* 1511–12) a phrase which seems to be a variant of *Dante's 'regina dell'eterno pianto' (queen of everlasting lamentation); see also *Troilus* IV.473–6.

Protheslaus, Protesilaus, killed at Troy (V.1446), the husband of Laodamia (see *Laodamya).

proverbs. The proverb, 'a short pithy saying in common and recognized use . . . which is held to express some truth ascertained by experience or observation and familiar to all' (*OED*), is an ancient and widespread form, still common in 'traditional' societies throughout the world. Proverbs are rarely used by modern Western writers, but their predecessors in the Middle Ages and the Renaissance make extensive use of them. They appear in various forms—popular adages, *sententiae* or 'sentences' usually originating from a more learned tradition, 'sayings' or proverbial expressions, proverbial phrases and similes (like 'make a virtue of necessity' or 'swim like a fish'). In the Middle Ages they are both 'popular' and 'learned' (moving in and out of various social, cultural, and literary levels), often associated with 'old wives' and 'rustics' but also with figures of wisdom like Solomon, Cato, and others. Their use (as persuasive literary 'arguments' and ornaments) is encouraged by rhetoricians such as *Geoffrey of Vinsauf (*Gaufred). Proverbs recommend norms of behaviour and offer a guide to wisdom and practical living. However, any corpus of proverbial lore is not always as fixed and universally truthful as some of its users imagine. There will often be pairs of opposed proverbs (in medieval English we find 'children are unlike their elders' but also 'such father, such son'; 'dreams are true' but also 'dreams are false'). That they easily take their colour from the circumstances of their use suggests that their wisdom may sometimes be relative, and clearly offers considerable possibilities for a writer such as Chaucer. His works contain a great number and show a great range: they often pass unnoticed by modern readers, but were noted and prized by earlier ones. To describe their various forms he uses the word 'proverb', 'sentence' (often attributed to ancient authors or 'the wise'), 'ensaumple' (see *exemplum), 'saw' ('saying'): in 'the old clerkes sawe, | That "who shal yeve [give] a lovere any lawe?"' (I.1163–4) the old clerks include Boethius, but the sentiment was proverbial. And there are many proverbial similes; 'brown as a berry', 'black as a crow', 'like a busy bee', etc.

Proverbs are used for various kinds of rhetorical emphasis. At the end of his tale the Reeve triumphantly quotes one to prove his moral: 'a gylour shal hymself bigyled be.' Lamenting her desertion by the lover who has stolen her heart, the falcon in *The Squire's Tale* makes a point with 'Sooth is seyd, goon sithen many a day | "A trewe wight and a theef thenken nat oon"' (V.536–7). At a tense emotional moment in *The Franklin's Tale* Arveragus consoles Dorigen; '"Ye, wyf," quod he, "lat slepen that is stille"' (V.1472). Boldly, Chaucer puts one in Criseyde's mouth in a despairing speech: 'To what fyn [end] sholde I lyve and sorwen thus? | How sholde a fissh withouten water dure? | What is Criseyde worth, from Troilus?' (*Tr* IV.764–6). This common proverb is used in quite a different context, satirically, of the Monk, who had no time for such old ideas as 'that a monk, whan he is recchelees [careless of rules], | Is likned til a fissh that is waterlees' (I.179–80). Chaucer is aware that proverbial truths may be limited and relative. He shows this in dramatic form in exchanges between characters. When they use a proverb they will often insist on its truth, by saying 'it is very true that' or by investing it with authority by describing it as 'common' or 'old'. Not everyone is convinced, however. 'Wel may that be a proverbe of a shrewe!' exclaims the Wife of Bath (III.284), and remarks of a later husband, 'I sette noght an hawe [hawthorn berry, i.e. nothing] | Of his proverbes n'of his olde sawe' (III.659–60). Pertelote, using a proverb of 'Cato' in support of her view of the untrustworthiness of dreams, provokes a riposte from Chauntecleer that there are many men of greater authority than 'daun Catoun'. In *The Merchant's Tale* the proverbial advice of Justinus does not suit old January, who exclaims 'Straw for thy Senec, and for thy

proverbes!' (IV.1567); and the young lover Troilus rebels against the flow of sententious advice from Pandarus: 'thi proverbes may me naught availle . . . Lat be thyne olde ensaumples. I the preye' (*Tr* I.756, 760).

*The *Wife of Bath's Prologue* is almost a 'proverb war'. It reaches a crisis with Jankin's great collection of examples of wicked wives, which contains 'sentences' to be quoted. He would seek out, for instance, 'that ilke proverbe of Ecclesiaste | Where he comandeth and forbedeth faste | Man shal nat suffre his wyf go roule [wander] aboute', to which he adds a humbler proverbial 'commination' of such folly: 'Whoso that buyldeth his hous al of salwes [willow branches], | And priketh his blynde hors over the falwes [unused arable land], | And suffreth his wyf to go seken halwes, | Is worthy to be hanged on the galwes!' (III.650–8). The Wife says that 'he knew of mo proverbes | Than in this world ther growen gras or herbes' (illustrated by four anti-feminist examples; III.773–85). She cites others used by her earlier husbands (III.278–84, 348–56). However she seems to know at least as many proverbs herself, which she uses throughout her discourse; 'I shal telle ensamples mo than ten'. They range from texts and sentences from biblical and anti-feminist writers (better to be wedded than burn, for instance), to Ptolemy, 'the wise astrologien', from an allusion to the classical Argus with his proverbial hundred eyes, to more homely examples ('ne noon so grey goose gooth ther in the lake | As seistow, wol been withoute make [mate]' III.269–70), often with sexual undertones: 'Whoso that first to mille comth, first grynt [grinds]' (389), 'Wynne whoso may, for al is for to selle; | With empty hand men may none haukes lure' (414–15). Her remarks often have a distinctly proverbial cast: of her fourth husband she says, 'in his owene grece I made hym frye | For angre, and for verray jalousye'.

Even a courtly work like *Troilus and Criseyde* contains great numbers of proverbs. Pandarus, of course, who is especially skilled in persuasive techniques, uses them continually. His persuasion of Criseyde becomes pressure: 'Lat this proverbe a loore [doctrine] unto yow be; | To late ywar [aware], quod Beaute, whan it passe' (II.397–8). In consoling Troilus in book IV he quotes a series of proverbs to convince him that he should find a new lady to replace Criseyde (e.g. 'the newe love out chaceth ofte the olde', IV.415). But Criseyde uses them too: for instance in a passage of self-persuasion (II.703 ff.) in which she argues with herself about love (in favour, cautiously, 'in every thing . . . ther lith mesure'; and against, 'harm ydoon is doon', 'ful sharp beginning breketh ofte at ende'; to a final resolve, 'he which that nothing undertaketh | Nothyng n'acheveth'). And the narrator also uses many, sometimes to reassure, approve, encourage, or build a relationship with his audience. In book I, as Troilus approaches Criseyde 'ay the ner [nearer] he was the more he brende [burnt]', and the narrator continues with a proverb and an appeal to a shared common experience; 'For ay the ner the fir, the hotter is—| This, trowe I, knoweth al this compaignye' (I.449–50). Allusions to proverbs often have the effect of bringing them 'back to life':—Pandarus 'felte iron hoot and he bygan to smyte' (II.1276).

Chaucer's style is often strongly proverbial. He often gives common proverbial phrases a curious unexpectedness, clarity, and vigour: the Franklin's beard white as a daisy; the dying Arcite 'as blak he lay as any cole or crowe, | So was the blood yronnen [run] in his face' (I.2692–3). He seems to relish the vividness that some proverbs have: 'Therfore bihoveth hire a ful long spoon | That shal ete with a feend' (V.602–3). He has favourite proverbs and maxims: 'pite renneth sone in gentil herte', 'vincit qui patitur' or 'pacience is a heigh vertu, certain, | For it venquysseth, as thise clerkes seyn, | Thynges that rigour sholde nevere atteyne' (V.773–5). Proverbs cluster around favourite topics like *love or *Fortune. They can be expanded, adapted, used for various dramatic, satiric, or ironic purposes, 'werk al by *conseil, and thou shalt nat rewe' says Nicholas in The *Miller's Tale to the carpenter he is about to deceive. This proverb, attributed to 'Solomon', is also used by Placebo the flattering counsellor in The *Merchant's Tale (IV.1478–90), and, more straightforwardly, by Prudence to Melibee (VII.1003). Proverbs like 'diverse men diversely they said' and 'men shal nat maken ernest of game', and the ironies that can be woven around them, seem to embody major controlling ideas in The Canterbury Tales.

Lumiansky (1950); B. J. Whiting (1968).

Proverbs (of Chaucer) eight lines of verse, usually divided by editors into two quatrains, containing proverbial matter. They appear in four MSS and the *Stowe edition. In two MSS (but not that of *Shirley) they are attributed to Chaucer. Modern editors are divided over accepting them as Chaucer's or making them 'doubtful'.

(ed.) Rv 657, 1089, Pace and David (1982), 195–200; Scattergood (1995), 496–7, 503.

Pruce, Pruyse, Prussia, a land along the Baltic coast between the rivers Vistula and Niemen. The name was originally applied to the home of a pagan people around the mouth of the Vistula; by the 14th c. it referred to a larger area, a monastic republic administered by the Knights of the Teutonic Order. Chaucer's *Knight fought there with the Teutonic Knights (I.53; see *crusades). Some of Palamon's knights have 'a Pruce sheeld' (a Prussian shield; I.2122). The land is also mentioned in The *Book of the Duchess (1025) as a remote region.

Prudence, the wife of Melibee in *Melibee.

Prudence, the quality embodied in Melibee's wife, was in medieval moral philosophy one of the four cardinal virtues (the others being Justice, Fortitude, and Temperance). The tradition that Prudence considers past, present, and future led to her depiction as a (female) figure with three eyes. Criseyde alludes to this: 'Prudence, allas, oon of thyne eyen thre | Me lakked alwey' (Tr V.744–5). Chaucer probably picked this up from an even more allusive reference in *Dante's Purgatorio (29.130–2), perhaps aided by a commentary and an illustration. In Chaucer prudence is much admired. It is urged throughout Melibee; the Parson quotes a remark on its use from Seneca (X.759). It is a quality of such virtuous figures as *Griselda (IV.1022) and *Virginia (VI.110). In The *Man of Law's Tale Christ's 'purveiance' [providence] is described as 'prudent' (II.483)—although we ignorant mortals cannot always recognize it. The potential for human error or uncertainty in the attribution of prudence to other humans also sometimes lurks (with attendant ironies) in the background: at the beginning of The Clerk's Tale Griselda's husband Walter was regarded by his subjects as a 'prudent man' because he saw that virtue was often hidden under low degree (IV.427). A more worldly judgement describes merchants as 'prudent folk' (II.123). The monk in The *Shipman's Tale is called a man 'of heigh prudence' (VII.64), and the same phrase is used of the *Canon (VIII.630) and of *January (by the flatterer Placebo, IV.1482). Related to 'prudence' is 'discrecioun', a quality of a good prince (I.1779, 2537) as well as of a prudent lover ('I ne loved nevere by no discrecioun' confesses the *Wife of Bath, III.622). The adjective 'discreet' may sometimes also have a gentle ambiguity: it is used of the Sergeant of Law, who was 'war [wary, prudent] and wys' (I.309). There is much advice, often of a homely and proverbial kind, to be 'ware'.

Matthews (1976).

Pseustis (Falsehood), a shepherd who contends unsuccessfully with Alithia (Truth) in the 10th-c. *Ecloga Theoduli*, a common school text in the Middle Ages. He is an Athenian, who plays on the pipes of Rumour, and there represents the pagan poet, who is artful but false. 'Of Athenes daun Pseustis' appears as one of the pipers in The *House of Fame* (1228).

PTHOLOMEE, Claudius Ptolemæus (c.100–c.170), Ptolemy. Ptolemy, a Roman citizen of Greek-Egyptian extraction, was the greatest mathematical astronomer of antiquity. The only place mentioned in connection with his observations is Alexandria. His most important and influential astronomical work was originally entitled 'Mathematical Synthesis', which in turn became 'The Great (megiste) Synthesis', and eventually, through Arabic al-majisti, our Almagest (L. Almagestum). This work provided the structure and much of the detail for all mathematical astronomy, including even that of Copernicus (1473–1543). There can be little doubt that Chaucer knew the general character and much of the content of Almagest, although he might have had no copy. (If so, the clerk *Nicholas in The *Miller's Tale was more fortunate.) There were many digests of it to be had, and the *canons to astronomical *tables were also capable of providing an alternative introduction to its contents. The one quotation Chaucer claims to draw from it is in fact

an apothegm from an Arabic collection that had found its way into a preface to the Latin translation of Almagest by Gerard of Cremona (1114–87). The planetary theory in *Equatorie of the Planetis is thoroughly Ptolemaic, but with a set of newer planetary parameters assembled for the Alfonsine tables in 13th-c. Spain.

There is in Almagest a catalogue of over a thousand stars, and there is reason to think that Chaucer made use of an appropriately modified version of it for allegories in The *Legend of Good Women, The *Nun's Priest's Tale, The *Squire's Tale, and The *Parliament of Fowls.

Ptolemy wrote other important works, including an Optics (see *Alocen), a Geography, and other astronomical studies, some of them related to the theory of astrolabe projection. He greatly influenced medieval astrology with his four-part Tetrabiblos, and many of the astrological doctrines to be found in Chaucer's writings may be traced to that work, although not necessarily directly. (See also *astrology and astronomy.)   [JDN]
(ed.) Heiberg (1898–1919); (ed. and trans.) Toomer (1984); (ed. and trans.) F. E. Robbins (1940); Pedersen (1974).

PUBLIUS SYRUS, 1st-c. mime and collector of moral maxims. A number of those attributed by Chaucer to Seneca (*Senec) are from him.

puns and word-play (ancient techniques, common in many linguistic communities) are found in Chaucer, as in other medieval writers. Rhetoricians noted adnominatio or paronomasia as an ornament of style. The term 'word-play', it should be stressed, does not imply that the use of puns was always simply for comic effect. It could involve similar or identical sound effects and/or the meaning of words, especially those which contain a potential ambiguity. The study of Chaucer's puns raises some problems, and needs to be approached with some caution. Modern readers in hot pursuit of them may overestimate the number (they are not as frequent as they are in Shakespeare) and need to be careful not to make them depend on post-Chaucerian sounds or senses. Others that were possible in Chaucer's day raise questions about intention or appropriateness. When the forlorn Troilus in a fine lyric speech addresses Criseyde's empty palace as 'thow lanterne of which queynt [extinguished] is the light' (*Tr* V.543) it seems most unlikely that in this context we should hear (as has been suggested) a pun on the noun 'queynte' (pudendum or cunt). It is totally out of keeping with the register of Troilus's speech here or elsewhere, and a crude ironic intrusion by the poet here seems equally unlikely. A number of other supposed cases are disputable. The suggestion that when in the *General Prologue* (I.673) the Pardoner is singing and 'this Summonour bar to hym a stif burdoun' we have besides the literal musical sense of 'burdoun' as 'ground-bass' an obscene play on the homonym 'burdoun' = 'pilgrim's staff', with the implication of a homosexual relationship has been very widely—but not universally—accepted. Among other possible bawdy puns the Summoner's 'arsmetrike' (III.2222) (arithmetic, but with a pun 'ers' (arse)) seems appropriate in its context, as does the Miller's 'An housbonde shal nat been inquisityf | Of Goddes pryvetee, nor of his wyf' (I.3163–4) (secrets/private parts). Sometimes it is hard to see a clear purpose behind a pun, as in 'fro Paradys first . . . | Was man out chaced for his glotonye; | And chaast was man in Paradys, certeyn' (III.1915–17). Chaucer's 'chacèd'/'chaast' are not identical in sound, but certainly close enough. Tatlock's comment 'Chased out, and chaste in, what a beautiful thought! Of course the friar does not know he is punning, it is merely the way his mind works' is nice, but perhaps somewhat fanciful. Perhaps Chaucer was just enjoying the acoustic fun—as he seems to be with 'whan this Calkas with his calkulynge' (*Tr* I.71). The friar's lines in *The Summoner's Tale* do, however, have an earlier parallel in *The Friar's Tale* when the teller remarks 'for though this Somonour wood were as an hare, | To telle his harlotrye I wol nat spare' (III.1327–8), where sense as well as sound is involved (the appearance and the behaviour of the hare being perhaps appropriate to the Summoner's harlotry). Both Friar and Summoner are involved in a little verbal play at the end of the Wife of Bath's Prologue. When the Friar jokingly calls it 'a long preamble of a tale' (III.831), the angry Summoner produces a kind of malapropism: 'What spekestow of preambulacioun?' No doubt we are meant to recall that the Wife was

riding an 'amblere' (or ambling horse, I.469). Serious and significant puns probably include that on 'hart/heart' in 'the hert-huntyng' (*BD* 1312); and in the word 'makeles' ('peerless', and also 'without a mate') applied to the beautiful Criseyde as she stands in the temple (*Tr* I.172). An undisputable pun is the joke about the messenger's elevated address in the **Squire's Tale*: 'Al be that I kan nat sowne his stile, | Ne kan nat clymben over so heigh a style' (V.105–6). Others are in the thinly disguised names of Richmond and Lancaster in *BD* 1318–19, or the more recondite 'wikked nest' (*mau ni* [modern Fr. *nid*] Oliver Mauny), VII.2386 (see **Petro* (1)). When Chaucer says of the Clerk that although he was a 'philosophre' he had but little gold (I.297) he is playing with that word's other sense of 'alchemist'. An excellent example is in his own complaint to his **Purse*, 'his lady dere': 'I am so sory, now that ye been light, | For certes but yf ye make me hevy chere', where he suggestively plays with some of the various sense of 'lyght' (light in weight, cheerful, fickle, wanton, graceful) and 'hevy' (heavy in weight, sad, serious, clumsy, pregnant).

Baum (1956, 1958); Kökeritz (1954).

Purgatorio; purgatory. See **Divina Commedia*; **heaven and hell*.

Purse, Complaint of Chaucer to his, a short poem of three rhyme royal stanzas and an envoy of five lines addressed to Henry IV, surviving in a number of manuscripts, and first finding its way into print in **Caxton's Anelida and Arcite* (1477–8). The envoy can be dated towards the end of Chaucer's life, after the acceptance of Henry as king on 30 September 1399. He reconfirmed Richard II's annuity in a document which was issued in mid-February 1400, and partial payments were made. It may be that Chaucer was short of money in this period, and that, as is often assumed, the poem with its envoy was directed to the king, although there is no independent evidence that it was presented to him. Since the envoy is not found in all of the manuscripts, it has sometimes been thought that it may have been a later addition to an already existing poem. With the envoy the *Complaint* is a clear example of a 'begging poem', of which there are earlier French examples; without it it would be a more general lament about the lack of money, of which there are examples in both French and English. Chaucer's poem stands out for its wit and originality. The purse is addressed as 'my lady dere' and the poem is a mock love complaint. He beseeches her (with clever playing on the words 'light' and 'hevy') for mercy—'beth hevy ageyn, or elles mot I dye', repeated as a refrain. Let me hear your 'blissful soun', and see 'your colour lyk the sonne bright | That of yellownesse hadde never pere', he prays. As his emotion rises she becomes (like the Virgin Mary) his heart's guide and 'quene of comfort and of good companye', the light of his life and his saviour 'doun in this world' where he is 'shave as nye as any frere'—shaven (of money) as closely as a friar's tonsure.

(ed.) *Rv* 656, 1088–9; Pace and David (1982), 121–32; Scattergood (1995), 510–12; Ferris (1967–8); Strohm (1992).

Purveiaunce ('providence, foresight') see *free will and predestination.

Q

Quadrivium, Arithmetic, Geometry, Astronomy and Music, namely the four more advanced of the *Seven Liberal Arts. (See also ***Trivium**.)

Quyryne, Quirinus, a name of *Romulus in *Troilus* (IV.25). Quirinus was originally the local deity of the Sabines who lived on the Quirinal hill. He was later identified with the deified Romulus.

quotation. 'Quotation', says the compiler of a modern 'Dictionary of Quotations', 'brings to many people one of the intensest joys of living.' It would be rash to claim that this was true of Chaucer, who himself provided the English language with a number: 'gladly wol he lerne and gladly teche,' 'and yet he semed bisier than he was', etc., but he certainly indulged in the practice. The practice, of citing a memorable phrase of passage from a book or an author, 'especially to illustrate succinctly or support a point or an argument' (a quotation from another dictionary) was in the Middle Ages in essence very similar to today's, but there were some differences. We should not assume that because a medieval writer quotes another writer he has actually read that writer's work (he might have got the phrase of passage from a *florilegium, his equivalent of a 'dictionary of quotations'). Because medieval 'quotations' may be paraphrases, it is sometimes difficult to distinguish them from *allusions, and it is more difficult to speak of deliberate 'misquotation'. In Chaucer, quotations are regularly used to further a rhetorical argument and to claim authority (*auctoritee) for what is being said. As with allusions, his range of reference is very wide. Biblical quotations, *proverbs, maxims ('sentences' or *sententiae*), and 'ensaumples' (*exempla) are all common. There are some from *classical literature ('O *Juvenal, lord, trewe is thy sentence', *Tr* IV.197–201). An example of an extended quotation is the paraphrase of a section of Boethius put into the mouth of Troilus (*Tr* IV.958–1078). Many of Chaucer's characters or narrators use quotations. In the case of some it is made into a characteristic pattern of speech. *Prudence in *Melibee* supports her discourse with ample quotation: she begins by recalling a 'sentence' of *Ovid, and progresses through Seneca (*Senec), Paul, '*Jhesus Syrak', Solomon (*Salomon), Cicero (*Tullius), and others. *Pandarus uses a great store of proverbs and 'olde ensaumples'. Sometimes very familiar quotations become 'tags' and only a word or two is needed ('"Now, *Pater noster,* clom!" seyde Nicholay,' I.3638). The Latin formula used at the end of prayers to Christ ('who with the Father and the Holy Spirit lives and reigns for ever and ever') is used in full at the end of the '*Retractions' (X.1091), but in a more offhand way by the friar in The *Summoner's Tale*—'with *qui cum patre* forth his wey he wente' (III.1734). The practice of *friars in quoting the beginning of the Gospel of John ('in the beginning was the Word') when they entered houses lies behind the satirical remark about the *Friar in the *General Prologue*: 'for thogh a wydwe hadde noght a sho [shoe], | So plesaunt was his "*In principio,*" | Yet wolde he have a ferthyng, er he wente' (I.253–5). The *Pardoner likes to use a few words of Latin, and the *Summoner in his cups repeats the few Latin tags 'that he had lerned out of som decree': '"*Questio quid iuris* [the question is what point of the law]" wolde he crie' (I.646).

R

Rachel, the daughter of Laban won by *Jacob as his wife (Gen. 29–35). Rachel weeping for her children (Jer. 31:15) is interpreted by Matthew (2:18) as a prophecy of the lamentation of the mothers of the children murdered by Herod. It was part of the gospel for the Mass of the Holy Innocents. Chaucer alludes to this by calling the grieving mother of the murdered child in The *Prioress's Tale 'this newe Rachel' (VII.627).

Radix, root, radix (L.); pl. radices. In medieval astronomy, the initial value of a quantity that changes with time, such as mean *longitude ('mean *mote'). This is quoted at the 'radix date', the fundamental epoch of any *table used to evaluate the quantity at later times (for example, by adding appropriate multiples of the mean motion to the radix of mean motion). In the tables bound with the text of *Equatorie of the Planetis there are several radices quoted, and a statement is made giving the number of days between the beginning of the Christian era and what is called 'Radix Chaucer' (1392). This is at the heart of the claim that Chaucer wrote the Equatorie. (See also *astrology and astronomy; *tables.)
[JDN]

Ram, see *Aries.

Raphael, the archangel (Tobit 6:16) (X.906).

Rauf (a popular form of Ralph), the name of a fornicator (III.1357).

Raven, the constellation Corvus (HF 1004).

Ravenne, Ravenna in northern Italy, close to the Adriatic. From the beginning of the 5th c. it was the capital of the Western Empire. Chaucer's only reference is in *Boece (I pr.4:123).

RAZIS, Rhazes, Abû Bakr Muhammad ibn Zakariyyâ al-Râzî (c.854–c.935). This famous medical writer, who also wrote on natural philosophy, ethics, religion, and alchemy, directed a hospital in Baghdad. Although much influenced by Galen, he took issue with him in an intelligent way on many points. Latin translations of his works were much valued in the West, and he is listed in the *General Prologue as one whose works were known to the *Physician (I.432). [JDN]

reason. The rational faculty ('man is a resonable two-foted beest' Boece V pr.4:196–7) holds a high place in medieval thought and literature. Aquinas says that 'the root of all human goodness lies in the reason'. A personified Reason is a prominent character in *Jean de Meun's part of the *Roman de la Rose. It is always associated with moderation ('*mesure'): a tyrant (like *Nero) or one who yields to an excess of rage is 'unreasonable'. It is also associated with *Nature in her work of creation, as the vicegerent of God ('that is so just and resonable', VII.3054). It is therefore a sign of *Dorigen's extreme despair when she questions why 'a parfit wys God' could make 'this werk unresonable' in the dangerous black rocks (V.868–72). It is also associated with love, but this association is a more uneasy one. Even in the matter of advice about the choice of lovers, where Nature can say 'if I were Resoun, thanne wolde I | Conseyle yow the royal tercel take' (PF 632–3), one of the suppliants has already announced 'ful hard were it to preve by resoun | Who loveth best this gentil formel . . . | I can not se that argumentes avayle' (PF 534 ff.). And blind desire, as in The *Merchant's Tale, is even less amenable to reason. Lovers may be torn between love and reason, as in the dilemma of Troilus when it has been decided that Criseyde must leave Troy: 'Love hym made al prest [prompt] to don hire byde [to cause her to stay] . . . But

Resoun seyde hym, on that other syde, | "Withouten assent of hire ne do nat do so"' (*Tr*IV.162–8). Later in that book he says 'thus am I with desir and reson twight [pulled]' (IV.572); when he suggests that they escape together, she argues against that course and concludes 'forthi [therefore] sle wil resoun al this hete!' (IV.1583). Reason has a part in noble 'gentil' love: one of the reasons Criseyde gives when she tells Troilus why she loved him is 'that youre resoun bridled youre delit' (IV.1678). Similarly, the speech of the lady in The *Book of the Duchess* was gentle and friendly and 'well founded on reason' (922). Reason and arguments are prominent in the philosophical tale of *Melibee*, and in works like The *Parson's Tale* and *Boece*. Not surprisingly, however, many characters in the narratives are shown to act without much regard for reason, and the anti-intellectuals among them distrust the 'art' of logic as practised by professionals. The miller in The *Reeve's Tale*, 'apologizing' for the smallness of his house, says to the *clerks: 'ye konne by argumentes make a place | A myle brood of twenty foot of space' (I.4123–4). The notion that men are particularly associated with reason is bitterly alluded to by *Anelida appealing to the 'manly resoun' of her false lover (*Anel* 259), and ironically by the *Wife of Bath: 'sith a man is moore reasonable | Than womman is, ye moste been suffrable [able to bear suffering]' (III.441–2).

A. Murray (1978).

Rebekka, Rebekke, Rebecca, the wife of Isaac (Gen. 27), and the mother of Esau and *Jacob. She disguised Jacob as Esau so that the blind old Isaac gave him the firstborn's blessing. In the Middle Ages she was often taken as a model of wifely 'good *counsel'. Chaucer refers to her twice—in *Melibee* (VII.1098), and possibly in a more ironic way in The *Merchant's Tale* (IV.1363–5; and 1704, where she is cited in the marriage service).

recognition scenes, which have produced some of the most memorable moments in European literature (e.g. the recognition of Odysseus by his nurse Eurycleia), are frequent in medieval literature—a famous example occurs in *Henryson's *Testament of Cresseid*. Chaucer's are not so well known, but are both subtle and powerful. He did not know Aristotle's extended discussion of

anagnorisis [recognition], but he clearly was aware of some of the qualities and effects which Aristotle noted such scenes produce—(the shock of surprise and *emotion and wonder, the profound and overwhelming change from ignorance to knowledge) and the ways in which recognition is brought about (through 'signs', through *memory or the use of *reason, through the combination of events, etc.).

His most elaborate scenes are found in his 'pitous' tales of the *Man of Law and the *Clerk. Both involve the reunion of separated families and the rediscovery of persons who are thought to be dead, and both produce an intense mixture of '*pite' and *joy. In The *Man of Law's Tale* there is a double recognition, brought about, it is suggested, both by the workings of Providence and the apparently chance 'aventure' of romance. King Alla first sees the fair child whom we know to be his son, and 'hath of this child greet wonder'. His resemblance to his lost wife Custaunce reminds Alla of her face, and he sorrowfully muses 'if that the childes mooder were aught she | That is his wyf'. Disbelief ('fantome is in myn heed!'), since she must have been drowned in the sea, gives way to the thought that possibly Christ may have brought her here as he had brought her to Northumberland. When later he sees his wife, 'at the firste look he on hire sette | He knew wel verraily that it was she', and the emotions are released. In the tearful but joyful scene Custance too comes to a new knowledge, that Alla was not guilty of 'unkindness'. The scene in The *Clerk's Tale* differs in that it is a 'gradual' recognition scene, since the long-suffering Griselda does not at first recognize the new young wife to be her own daughter. Here the denouement is brought about by a human agency, the marquis Walter, who acts like a presiding figure in a folk tale or a magician: 'this is thy doghter, which thou hast supposed | To be my wyf.' But the element of wonder, which here refers to Griselda's realization that she has not in fact been dismissed ('and she for wonder took of it no keep; | She herde nat what thyng he to hire seyde; | She ferde as she had stert out of a sleep'), and of 'pitous joye' is powerfully felt, and her physical reunion with her children is, after the cruel test, much more intense. The last book of *Troilus and Criseyde* offers a tragic moment of recognition. It is carefully prepared. Troilus has had a dream which shows him Criseyde's betrayal, but although his perception is confirmed by Cassandra, part of his mind refuses to accept it. Criseyde's letter seems 'al straunge' to him but he cannot accept that she will not keep her promise. The awful moment of recognition comes (V.1653 ff.) when he examines the tunic taken from Diomede and finds on the collar a brooch that he has given her: 'as he gan byholde, | Ful sodeynly his herte gan to colde.'

We also find some comic variations upon the recognition scene. In the *fabliaux, for instance, there is the moment when *Symkyn the miller finds the lusty clerk has climbed into his bed by mistake and is telling him what has been done to his daughter, or that when the blind *January is suddenly given back his sight (recognition scenes usually depend upon the *eyes) and sees his young wife up in the tree with her lover. The traditional pattern underlies the denouement of the *Wife of Bath's Prologue, when finally she recovers from her swoon and speaks to Jankin, 'O! hastow slayn me', and he responds 'Deere suster Alisoun, | . . . I shal thee nevere smyte!', a scene which is a 'figure' of the later scene in the Tale, when the knight sees his bride transformed: '"Cast up the curtyn, looke how that it is"! And whan the knyght saugh . . . | That she so fair was . . . | For joye he hente hire in his armes two.' There is a hilarious 'lack of recognition scene' in The *Friar's Tale when the stranger announces 'I am a feend', and the summoner solemnly responds 'I wende ye were a yeman [yeoman] trewely' and questions him about the shape of spirits in hell. Perhaps, if Chaucer deliberately left The *House of Fame unfinished, he was giving us an example of a 'thwarted recognition scene': we would all want to know who the 'man of gret auctorite' was.

Rede See, the Red Sea, famous for precious stones (*Bo* III m.3:5).

Reeve. A Reeve was a general foreman on a manor, who looked after the upkeep of the estate, oversaw the work, collected the dues, and presented the accounts. The portrait of the Reeve in the *General Prologue concentrates on his appearance and on his behaviour in business. He is 'a sclendre

coleric man' [i.e. dominated by the *humour called choler]. He is remarkably thin, closely shaven, with closely cropped hair 'like a priest'. His efficiency is equally remarkable. He knows everything about the estate he manages. The auditors cannot catch him out, and he terrifies the stewards, shepherds, and servants whom he supervises. Perhaps the pressures on a reeve from both above and below may account for some of his tetchiness. Some guarded and ambiguous remarks strongly suggest that he 'makes a bit on the side' for himself, and cheats his lord. Reeves had a reputation for dishonesty and thieving—as did, it seems, people from Norfolk, where he lives in a handsomely sited house. Oswald (as we later learn his name to be) is further individualized: we are told the name of his town, Bawdeswell (*Baldeswelle), and the situation of his house. It has been suggested that Chaucer may have been drawing on some personal knowledge. Bawdeswell lay partly in the manor of Foxley, which belonged to the earls of Pembroke, and Chaucer had some connection with Sir William de Beauchamp, the cousin of the second earl, but there is no certain evidence. The final detail, that he always rode at the end of the group of pilgrims, seems significant. It may suggest an instinctive craftiness and watchfulness, and perhaps has the advantage for him of keeping as far away as possible from the *Miller. Millers and reeves are likely to be opponents, and a quarrel soon erupts between this pair. Another aspect of the Reeve is revealed by the powerful monologue he delivers in his own Prologue, in which he grumblingly complains of the onset of *old age in a way which suggests that he may be both a lecher and a moralist, an intriguing introduction to the story he tells.

Rv 821–2; Cooper (1989), 55–6; Mann (1973), 163–7.

Reeve's Prologue and Tale, The (470 lines in couplets) follow The *Miller's Tale* in Fragment I. The Reeve does not share in the merriment it causes in 'the moore part' of the pilgrims, 'by cause he was of carpenteris craft'. He says that he could answer him with the tricking of a proud miller if he wished to speak of 'ribaudye', but he is old. Thereupon he launches into a remarkable 'grucchyng' lament on the way *old age has left him with 'an hoor heed and a grene tayl' like a leek. Though he still has 'a coltes tooth', the barrel of life is almost spent. After a while the *Host interrupts his 'sermonyng' and urges him on to the tale. He leaves no doubt about his intentions. The drunken Miller has told a story about the beguiling of a carpenter, 'peraventure in scorn, for I am oon'. He will be 'quited' in his own 'cherles termes'.

At *Trumpington near Cambridge (*Cantebrigge) there lived a proud and swaggering miller called 'deynous [haughty] Symkyn', thievish and sly. He has a round face, a snub nose, and his skull is hairless like an ape's. He has a wife 'of noble kin' (the parson of the town was her father, and she was brought up in a nunnery). She is just as proud. When she walks behind her husband on holydays 'ther dorste no wight clepen hire but "dame"' and no one dares to make advances to her; 'she was as digne [honourable] as water in a dich.' They have two children, a daughter (Malyne) of 20, who is 'thikke and wel ygrowen' and has her father's snub nose ('but right fair was hire heer [hair]'), and a child who is only six months. The parson is minded to make the girl his heir, and will not have her married to anyone: 'his purpos was for to bistowe hire hye [nobly] | Into som worthy blood of auncetrye.' One of the miller's customers is a Cambridge college, '*Soler Halle'. When its manciple is ill, the miller steals even more meal and corn than usual. Two poor northern scholars (John and Aleyn) ask the warden's permission to go and keep a watch on the milling. The miller receives them with some amusement, and while they are watching the corn being ground, slips out and lets their horse run loose to the wild mares in the fens. When they discover this and rush after it, the miller removes half a bushel of their corn and has his wife knead it into a loaf. At last 'weary and wet' the clerks return with the horse, now realizing that their corn will have been stolen, and that everyone will call them fools. It is now night, and they have to ask the miller for food and lodging. The daughter is sent into town for provisions, and a bed is prepared for them in the bedroom which they must share with the family: the room also contains a bed for the miller and his wife with the child's cradle at its foot, and another for the daughter. After much drinking they retire. The clerks suffer more irritation from the snoring of

the miller and the wife and the daughter. Aleyn decides that even though, as John warns him, the miller 'is a perilous man', he must have some 'amendement' for their loss, and so he creeps into the girl's bed, giving her no time to cry out—'and shortly for to seyn, they were aton [at one]'. John now begins to feel even more of a fool, and deciding to take the risk, gets up and moves the cradle from the bottom of the wife's bed to his. Soon after, the wife 'gan awake, and wente hire out to pisse'. Coming back, she misses the cradle, and groping around in the dark (and telling herself that she had almost got into the clerks' bed) eventually finds it and climbs into the bed occupied by John. He leaps upon her, and she enjoys a 'myrie . . . fit' such as she has not had for a long time. As dawn comes Aleyn bids farewell to Malyne (who tells him about the loaf) and tries to return to his bed. But finding the cradle there, he hastily gets into the other, clasps the miller, and addressing him as John ('thou swynes-heed') tells him of his exploit with the daughter. This provokes a predictably violent reaction, and blood starts to pour from Aleyn's nose. As they struggle, the miller falls backward upon his wife who has dropped off to sleep with John. She cries out for help ('ther lyth oon upon my wombe and on myn heed . . . the false clerkes fighte!'), and finds a staff. By a 'litel shymeryng of a light' she can see something white, which she takes to be Aleyn's nightcap, and delivers a blow, which falls squarely on the miller's bald skull. He falls crying 'Harrow! I dye!', and the clerks beat him, take their horse and their corn, and depart, stopping at the mill to pick up their loaf. The Reeve ends triumphantly: 'thus is the proude millere wel ybete . . . His wyf is swyved, and his doghter als | Lo, swich it is a millere to be fals!'

We have no indication of the date of composition of the Tale, but it was clearly written with *The Miller's Tale* in mind. It may well be based on a French *fabliau: the closest of several analogues is one known as *Le meunier et les ii clers* (the Miller and the Two Clerks). Whatever the source, the story has been carefully adapted to the teller and to its context in Fragment I. The 'quiting' of the Miller is thoroughly carried through: Symkyn's wickedness and folly and his undoing are described with gleeful vehemence. Like *The*

Miller's Tale it has an unusually precise local setting (there was a bridge and a brook and a mill and a parson at Trumpington), but it lacks its more relaxed characterization and general expansiveness. It is a fine piece of satirical writing, vitriolic but controlled, which concentrates its attack on 'deynous Symkyn', who in so many obvious aspects of appearance and personality bears an unmistakable close resemblance to the Miller. Even an apparently offhand remark about class and status made by the Miller, that Alison was a poppet 'for any lord to leggen in his bedde, | Or yet for any good yeman to wedde' (I.3269–70), seems to be taken up and heightened into Symkyn's immense sense of social importance in respect of himself and his family: he 'wolde no wyf . . . | But she were wel ynorissed [brought up] and a mayde, | To saven his estaat of yomanrye'. When he learns of the dishonouring of his daughter it seems to be the low birth of the seducer which affects him most, 'who dorste be so boold to disparage [dishonor] | My doghter, that is come of swich lynage?' Yet this strongly developed social satire is wider in its implications, taking in the pretensions of Symkyn's wife and of her father the parson (here with more than a hint of anti-clericalism: 'for hooly chirches good moot been despended | On hooly chirches blood, that is descended'). It would be too limiting to see the tale simply as an attack on the Miller or a revelation of the Reeve's own personality, however. It is a brilliant comic performance, with the skilful plotting that is needed in farce (e.g. the placing of the cradle) and a finely controlled narrative rhythm. The introduction of Symkyn and his family is superbly done. The (probably) comic use of northern dialect in the speech of the clerks seems to be the earliest extended example in English literature. The Tale offers a tough and sharp view of life, in which sexual necessity, animal instinct, and violent passion seem dominant (and are underlined by a consistent use of *animal imagery: the miller's ape-like skull, the 'wehee' of the horse as it gallops towards the mares, the snoring of the miller 'as an hors', etc.). The one moment when a gentler human feeling seems to emerge is also mingled with sardonic irony: when Malyne says goodbye to her 'deere lemman'; '"And, goode lemman, God thee save and kepe!" | And with that word

almoost she gan to wepe.' It would be hard to find a 'moral' in the Miller's tale, but the Reeve provides one, a kind of fabliau moral that is consistent with his mixture of 'ribaudye' and 'sermonyng' and presents a kind of poetic justice: 'a gylour [trickster] shal hymself bigyled be.'

(ed.) *Rv* 77–84, 848–53; *S&A* 124–47 [23–73]; Cooper (1989), 108–17; Bennett (1974), ch. 4; Copland (1962); G. Olson (1974); Pearsall (1985), 183–93; Tolkien (1934).

REGULUS, Marcus Atilius Regulus a Roman general of the 3rd c. BC. During his second consulship in 256 he defeated the Carthaginians, but in the following year was himself defeated and captured. (A later famous, and perhaps apocryphal, story says that he was sent on by them to Rome to negotiate a successful peace, and was made to swear that he would return if the negotiations were unsuccessful, but he urged the Romans to continue the war and returned to face death in captivity.) Lady Philosophy cites him as an example of the instability of *Fortune: he cast many Carthaginians into fetters but soon after he had to hold out his own hands to receive the chains (*Bo* II pr.6:70).

Reynes, Rennes in Brittany, France. It was famous for its fine linen: hence the reference in *The *Book of the Duchess* (255) to a pillowcase 'of cloth of Reynes'. The expressions 'cloth of Raines' or simply 'Raines' remained in use to the 16th c. and beyond.

relics. The veneration of the earthly remains of a holy person is traceable to Old Testament times (e.g. 2 Kings 2:14, 13:21), but was greatly extended throughout the medieval period, despite occasional expressions of unease at this attachment to the physical rather than the spiritual aspect, and at the dangers of idolatry. Relics of Christ, the Virgin and saints were eagerly sought by kings, popes, and religious houses, were preserved in elaborate shrines and formed the objective for most pilgrimages. This stress on physical remains is evident at the start of *The Canterbury Tales* 'The hooly blisful martir for to seke' (I.17). In addition, however, to the institutionalization of relics, and because of this attachment to physical signs, small fragments of such relics might be sold to the faithful, or carried around and shown in exchange for money: the *Pardoner describes this process (VI.341 ff.) and attempts unsuccessfully to practise it (VI.919 ff.).   [AH]

religion means a form of life bound by rules which are maintained with a view to an ultimate reality, but often it has been by the rules rather than the reality that it has become known. In Chaucer's period, those rules took many forms.

The only public religion widely practised in England throughout the 14th c. was Christianity, Jews having been expelled from the kingdom by King Edward I in July 1290, and Christianity meant an ecclesiastical hierarchy at whose head stood the Pope. Early in the century the relative weakness of the Crown helped to keep relations between England and the papacy correct, even though in 1309 the papacy had moved from Rome to Avignon, thus placing it in an enemy nation at the beginning of what was to become known as the Hundred Years War. With the coming of 'Great Schism' in 1378, during the election, in Rome, of Pope Urban VI, national attitudes changed, and the English took Urban's side; Chaucer may allude to this support in the *Second Nun's Tale, which was probably associated with the English Cardinal Adam Easton, a sometime adviser of Pope Urban.

In England, the Ecclesia Anglicana was governed by the archbishops of Canterbury and York. Canterbury contained eighteen dioceses (including four in Wales), York only three, and during Chaucer's lifetime the primacy of Canterbury became increasingly apparent. Below these came the bishops, who like the archbishops, Chaucer passes over in silence, though there is a perceptive if passing allusion in the *Nun's Priest's Tale to the greatest scholar among them, Thomas *Bradwardine, archbishop of Canterbury, who died of the plague in 1349 soon after his consecration in Avignon. Below the bishop (and his vicar) stood the sometimes unpopular archdeacon, intimately connected (in England) with the cathedral church, whose administrative duties included holding annual visitations at the archdeaconries and convening the archdeacon's court, but by the late 14th c. practices associated with the courts had become notorious, as Chaucer's scathing description of the *Summoner in the *General Prologue makes clear.

But if the hierarchy did not engage Chaucer's affection the lowest rung of the ecclesiastical ladder did. Rectors of churches could be powerful (and taxable) individuals who handed their church over to a vicar in favour of a comfortable chantry in London, where they derived income by saying masses for the wealthy deceased, but Chaucer represents instead as one of his most attractive pilgrims a country *Parson, who would have been approved by orthodox and *Lollard alike, a man whose sole concern is for the souls of his parish, and for whom no effort is too great to win them. The secular clergy apart, there was too the regular clergy, men (like the *Friar and the *Monk) and women (like the *Prioress and the Second Nun) bound by the rules of their order. As with the Parson, Chaucer's treatment is general rather than specific. His Monk may be a Benedictine, his Friar a Franciscan, but these distinctions are not insisted upon, and their representations depend both upon literary models and upon empirical observation.

Thus although the extent to which each pilgrim actually represents his estate varies, Chaucer's pilgrims do represent some of the realities and the ecclesiastical corruptions apparent to a perceptive observer. By the 14th c. the economic power and sometimes the ostentation of the monastic orders was apparent, though their political influence, as evidenced by appointment to high ecclesiastical office, was declining, and the important abbots tended to be those who could maintain physical holdings and fulfil the rule, not broaden spiritual horizons. The fraternal orders were no longer growing in numbers or in influence (their assumption of high church office was also declining, in part because royal influence over such appointments, which was increasing, favoured the secular clergy), but their associations with universities ran deep, and their contribution to the spiritual life of the period was evident and lasting. In a large city like London the influences of the regular orders mixed with others and was less readily apparent, but in a city like Norwich, almost a test-tube example of late medieval spirituality, it emerged in the many foundations, the churches and chantries, the guilds and the confraternities, and in such unusual features as houses of religion dedicated to devout women unattached to a regular order, as near to Béguine foundations as the English experience allowed. The presence in the city of the anchoress and mystic *Julian of Norwich suggests too something of the powerful spirituality which flourished in late medieval England, but which finds only an occasional echo in Chaucer's poetry.

Among lay persons religious practices took many forms, but the extent of their devotions have yet to be thoroughly measured. Most knew the Creed, the Paternoster, the Ave Maria, the three theological and four cardinal virtues and the *seven deadly sins, and many went to confession and took the Eucharist at least once a year, as the Fourth Lateran Council had directed in 1215. In 1281 the Franciscan Archbishop John Pecham convened the Lambeth Council which enjoined the clergy to improve knowledge of faith, and which produced the *De informatione* (sometimes miscalled the *Ignorantia sacerdotum*), a work which commended to the laity a range of *prayers and uncomplicated theological ideas. Among affluent lay persons who undertook significant gift-giving to religious houses, usually with a view to chantries or masses after death, family feeling tended to be vertical, with prayers stipulated for parents and spouses, as well as for the donor; it was not customary for such feeling to reach out to other relatives in the same generation. The public attestation of a procession or *pilgrimage involved a much broader range of society, though here too a series of rules and conventions structured the experience and suggested the circumstances which would contribute to a successful completion. Even more complicated arrangements were proposed in increasingly detailed spiritual guidebooks, many in the vernacular, intended primarily for women (but also for some men) of the upper and noble classes, which delineated a demanding but apparently satisfying way of life.

The question as to what Chaucer himself intended by the representations he introduced into such works as the *Canterbury Tales* does not admit of a simple answer. In general, it is deviation from the rule which he reprehends, but it would be a mistake simply to describe him as a religious conservative, for whom all is corruption. His contemporary *Wyclif would make ecclesiastical corruption a key point in his teaching, and although Chaucer does not share the radical point of view already sounded by contemporary *Lollards, there is a sceptical turn to his mind which resists final definition, but which seems to imply that the failures he chronicles lie as much in some of the institutions he describes as in human nature, or the conditions of the hour. It is significant that he does not much concern himself with those religious attitudes which found expression outside communal interchange. Hermits do not appear in his work, nor anchorites, nor mystics, nor (for the most part) the more extreme forms of *piety. Among his Canterbury pilgrims those whose religious attitudes he most endorses seem to be the Parson and perhaps the Second Nun, both religious, both faithful to their vows. As a man and a courtier he would not have been inclined to regard the Church as a protection against a secular power it was sometimes his office to represent, and his sympathy for women usually did not extend to regarding religion, as some did, as an ally against the encroachments of secular authority. And while the distinction between the holy and the ecclesiastical was, in the 14th c., apparent to many observers, it is clear that Chaucer conceived of religion as distinguishable from any human agency, and as representing a different, and probably a more lasting order than any he had written about, experienced, or observed. (See also *piety.)
[JCH]

C. D. Benson and E. Robertson (1990); Bynum (1982); Finucane (1977); Giffin (1956); Haines (1989); Hirsh (1989); Hudson (1988); Knowles (1940, 1955); Pantin (1955); Swanson (1989); Szittya (1986); Tanner (1984); A. H. Thompson (1947); J. A. F. Thomson (1983); Warren (1985).

Remedie of Love, see *Ovid.

Renard, Reynard, by Chaucer's time a common name for a fox. The French *Roman de Renart*, a composite work from the latter part of the 12th c., which was very popular and influential, had established him as a superbly cunning and deceitful 'anti-hero'. Versions of this work and stories from it (like that of the fox Daun *Russell in *The *Nun's Priest's Tale*) are common throughout the Middle Ages. Chaucer uses the name only once, when remarking that *Demophon was false like his father: 'it com hym of nature | As doth the fox Renard, the foxes sone' (*LGW* 2448).

Réthel, a town near Reims, famous for its cattle market and its medieval church, deserves also to be remembered as the place near which Chaucer was captured on active service in 1359–60.

Retracciouns, often called 'Chaucer's Retraction (or Retractation)', a passage which appears in the MSS at the end of *The *Parson's Tale*. Chaucer himself uses the phrase 'my retracciouns' (X.1085) so that the plural form, which strongly suggests the title of St Augustine's (*Austyn) *Retractationes*, seems preferable. It presents a number of problems, and has been much discussed. In modern editions it is usually separated from *The Parson's Tale* by a rubric from the *Ellesmere MS: 'Heere taketh the makere of this book his leve'. If this is authentic, it identifies the speaker of the first sentence ('now preye I to hem alle that herkne this litel tretys or rede') as Chaucer. If it is not, then this opening part (which asks readers to thank Christ for anything that has pleased them in it and to ascribe anything displeasing to his ignorance, and quotes the verse 'al that is writen is writen for oure doctrine') could be read as being spoken by the Parson, whose tale would otherwise seem to lack a formal conclusion, in which case the next part would be an insertion into the ending by Chaucer or somebody else. In this the 'I' speaker asks for prayers for the forgiveness of his sins, 'and namely [especially] of my translacions and enditynges of worldly vanitees, the whiche I revoke in my retracciouns; as is . . .' There follows a list of Chaucer's works in which we can identify *Troilus, The *House of Fame, The *Legend of Good Women, The *Book of the Duchess, The *Parliament of Fowls, The *Canterbury Tales* 'thilke that sownen [those that tend] unto synne', the (lost) 'book of the *Leoun', 'and many another book, if they were in my remembrance, and many a song and many a leccherous lay'. But, it continues, 'of the translacion of Boece . . . and othere bookes of legendes of seintes, and omelies, and moralitee, and

devocioun, that thanke I oure Lord Jhesu Crist and his blisful Mooder, and alle the seintes of hevene', and prays that they may send the grace of true repentance so that 'I may been oon of hem at the day of doom that shulle be saved'. *If* the list of works is an insertion, most or all of the final prayer would be quite suitable as the end of the Parson's conclusion.

It is not easy to reach a decision about the status of the central section. Some have felt that it might well be something which has strayed in by accident, since it seems to be a farewell to the writing of literature rather than to the writing of *The Canterbury Tales*. Its authenticity has also been questioned, but the MS evidence seems overwhelming. One view is that while it is the work of Chaucer, it is less an expression of personal remorse than the dramatically necessary response of the poet-narrator to the Parson's stirring words on repentance. Others have thought that it does represent a late conversion or sense of remorse, citing Thomas Gascoigne's 15th-c. story of Chaucer's deathbed repentance (though this account could well come from the passage in question). It would not be at all unusual for a medieval (or Renaissance) writer to express some regret for the writing of worldly books. In fact there seem to be enough examples to speak of a tradition of such statements, serious or less serious, which are sometimes similar to the *palinode. It has been suggested that Chaucer's remarks are an ironic reflection on this convention, less a serious statement of repentance than a statement of the canon of his works. It must be said that the phrase 'and many another book, if they were in my remembrance' does not sound deeply penitential, though some of the surrounding language does (though the tone is hard to establish). The word 'revoke' does not necessarily mean 'retract'. It seems clear that Chaucer is thinking of St Augustine's work, which is not a formal 'retractation', but rather a 'revision'. It may be that he is inventing a work of his own 'my *Retracciouns*' and giving a list of his works (see also *LGW* and Introduction to *MLT*) putting them not in chronological order but in a deliberately random order, to give them impression of a spontaneous recollection. But it is impossible to be certain.

(ed.) *Rv* 328, 965; *LR* 547; Cooper (1989),

410–12; Norton-Smith (1974), 80; Sayce (1971); Wurtele (1980).

retrograd, retrograde (L. *retrogradus*). The general direction of the planetary motion, as seen against the background of the stars, follows that of the Sun (in its annual motion). This is the direction in which the signs of the *Zodiac are usually taken. Any motion in the opposite sense is described as retrograde. From time to time, the planets are seen to move with retrograde motions. In Ptolemaic astronomy, the Moon's motion on its *epicycle is retrograde, but the apparent motion of the Moon is of course always direct. (See also *astrology and astronomy.) [JDN]

rhetoric, the art of persuasion, originally in the legal advocacy of the ancient world, but later more generally the art of speaking and writing well, was highly prized in the Middle Ages. Its devices and techniques were not simply ornamental; they were intended to give elegance to the discourse and bring pleasure to the hearers, but were above all means to affect and persuade the audience. Argument rather than ornament for its own sake is central. Over the centuries rhetoric has been very closely associated with dialectic. Its relationship with morality and moralists has not always been straightforward, since it may be used in the service of evil and falsehood as well as in that of goodness and truth. There has been, therefore, a traditional insistence that rhetoric must be linked with wisdom, from the ancient world (where this was originally a defence against Platonic attacks) to the Middle Ages and the Renaissance. Rhetoric is the whole art of speaking and writing well, and not just a list of rules and figures, but it is an art, which may be taught, practised, and perfected.

A number of treatises offered instruction and advice (sometimes citing literary as well as oratorical examples), for example, the *De oratore* and the *De inventione rhetorica* of Cicero (*Tullius), the *Ad Herennium* (*Ad Caium Herennium libri iv de arte dicendi*) which during the Middle Ages was thought to be by Cicero, and the *Institutio oratoria* of Quintilian (*c.*35–*c.*95). Some of this Roman tradition survived the fall of the empire and provided an important basis for medieval rhetoric. Not every work was available everywhere—Quintilian,

for instance, seems to have been known in part or in extracts to some, but his complete text was not discovered until the end of the Middle Ages. Two texts were especially influential—Cicero's *De inventione* and the *Ad Herennium*. From them came a traditional structure and a number of ideas and patterns: the five parts of rhetoric, namely (1) invention (the finding of arguments or matter), (2) arrangement or disposition (their ordering, division, and distribution), (3) style (the choice of words, appropriateness and decorum, levels of style—high or grand, middle, or simple), (4) *memory (by which subject, words and arrangement could be held in the mind, and (5) delivery (the skilful use of voice, expression, and gesture). The structure of the discourse was analysed, from its exordium or introduction (where the orator might attempt to win the audience's goodwill (*captatio benevolentiae*) by a modest apology or statement of his inadequacy) through to the conclusion or peroration which will sum up the argument, and bring it to a persuasive conclusion. Ornaments and techniques of style are discussed, sometimes (as in the *Ad Herennium*) divided into figures of diction (e.g. *epanaphora* (or *anaphora*) the repetition of the first word in successive phrases) or tropes or figurative uses of language (like metaphor or metonymy), and figures of thought (such as simile, personification, etc.).

From ancient rhetoric also came an interest in the topics and general ideas which might be used to persuade and prove. These 'topics' or *topoi* are 'places', *loci communes* or 'common places' (i.e. recognized and responded to by many, not 'commonplace' or ordinary). They cover a wide range—there are topics of the opening, of the conclusion, of consolatory discourse, and so on. Christian authors develop inherited topics ('all must die', the 'world upside down', 'life as a pilgrimage', 'fortitude and wisdom', etc.) in their own distinctive ways. For many Christians fine words and the potentially amoral nature of rhetoric were highly suspect, but St Augustine (*Austyn) (himself a former teacher of rhetoric) in his *De doctrina christiana* established a genuinely Christian rhetoric. He pointed to the combination of wisdom and eloquence in the Bible, and emphasized imagination rather than the learning of rules; for him true grandeur lay in the power of the matter, the *vis rerum*. The Christian sermon may be seen as a modified form of the ancient oration, and medieval preachers were instructed in the techniques of eloquence by 'arts of preaching' (*artes predicandi*) and were provided with collections of *exempla, instructive stories and figures from history and legend. Another specialized development was the *ars dictaminis* which gave instruction in the composition of *letters.

The medieval books of rhetoric, which flourish especially in the 12th and 13th centuries, are directly in the tradition of the earlier manuals, but increasingly concern themselves with poetry. Well-known examples include the *Ars versificatoria* of Matthew of Vendôme and the *Poetria nova* of Geoffrey of Vinsauf (see *Gaufred). Geoffrey insists that the poet needs to conceive the whole work in his mind before commencing. He discusses *digression, and the order of narrative as well as amplification and abbreviation, and the traditional figures and ornaments of style.

Skill in rhetoric could be acquired by precept, drawn from the manuals studied in school or later, by the imitation of literary models and by practice. It is not easy to isolate the sources of Chaucer's undoubted skill. It is very likely that much of it comes from imitation of authors whom he had read (and perhaps from observing the persuasive techniques of other speakers), and was developed by practice in writing. We can be fairly sure that he did not compose at his desk surrounded by rhetorical handbooks, but he certainly shows a knowledge of that tradition. Some of it probably goes back to schooldays when he would have learnt (Latin) grammar, from elementary textbooks like the *Graecismus* of Eberhard of Béthune or the primers of Donatus (whose name, as 'Donet', became a common term for '*primer'). Both authors include some examples of tropes and figures, and elementary grammar was not unliterary: the boundary between rhetoric and grammar was a fluid one. He quotes, and parodies Geoffrey of Vinsauf, and may well have read other rhetorical works or anthologies.

It is easy to identify figures which Chaucer uses, but sometimes less easy, in the case of common figures like *exclamatio* ('Allas, allas! That evere love was synne!') to say whether he is using them self-consciously as figures which he recognized. With others it is difficult to tell if they have been picked up from rhetorical manuals or from his reading of poets. The listing of impossibilities (*impossibilia* or *adynata*), for instance, is a figure used for emphasis in both ancient and medieval literature. It may be used in comic or satiric contexts (as in Donne's 'Goe and catche a falling starre') or in serious ones. It is used at two solemn moments in *Troilus and Criseyde*: when the lovers part in book III (1495–8), Criseyde says that sooner shall the sun fall from its sphere, the eagle be the mate of the dove, and every rock start from its place before Troilus shall leave her heart, and in a more desperate farewell later she swears that she will return to him, adjuring the river Simois to run backwards to its source if she is false (IV.1551–4). The latter example is probably echoing *Ovid; the earlier is probably indebted to the general literary tradition. What is most important is the effect Chaucer achieves with the figure, as a persuasive device within her speech, in heightening the emotion (and in building up a potential pattern of dramatic irony).

Chaucer certainly reveals a knowledge of the terminology of rhetoric and of the questions raised by the art. A number of the terms he uses had probably become part of the common literary language ('invocacion' or '*prologe') or were used not simply as technical words but in wider senses (as 'descripsioun'). But a number of words and a number of contexts clearly suggest a special and a self-conscious interest in rhetoric. The Clerk says that the poet Petrarch's 'rethorike sweete | Enlumined al Ytaille of poetrie' (IV.32–3). Technical terms, like 'colours' (figures or ornaments) are common. The narrator of The *Squire's Tale (V.38) protests his inability (the traditional 'modesty-topos', an especial favourite with Chaucer) to describe every part of the beauty of the lady (another topic): 'It moste been a rethor excellent | That koude his colours longynge for that art, | If he sholde hire discryven every part. | I am noon swich, I moot speke as I kan'. The *Franklin also modestly disclaims any learning in rhetoric (but refers to Parnassus and Cicero), and jokes that the only colours he knows are those which grow in the meadow or those that men dye or paint (V.719–26). In The *Clerk's Prologue (IV.16) 'colours' are linked with 'figures' and 'termes' (i. e.

technical terms: here of rhetoric, elsewhere of law, astrology, alchemy, philosophy, and love (*Tr* II.1038–9)). Perhaps there is a more recondite allusion to the 'colours' of rhetoric when the Pardoner remarks that he uses a few Latin words 'to saffron with [flavour with saffron] my predicacioun' (VI.345)—suggesting that he imagines his sermon as a well-spiced and colourful dish. In *The *Squire's Tale*, when the strange knight arrives and begins to speak, his delivery (the fifth part of rhetoric) is praised:

> He with a manly voys seide his message,
>
> .   .   .   .   .   .
>
> Withouten vice of silable or of lettre;
> And for his tale sholde seme the bettre,
> Accordant to his wordes was his cheere
>   [behaviour, demeanour],
> As techeth art of speche . . .
>
> V.99–104)

It is already evident that passages concerning rhetoric often contain irony, humour, and jokes. More extreme examples, like the clever parody in *The *Nun's Priest's Tale* of Geoffrey of Vinsauf's virtuoso lament on the death of Richard the Lionheart (Kyng *Richard), or what may seem to be comic deflations ('til that the brighte sonne loste loste his hewe; | For th'orisonte hath reft the sonne his lyght—| This is as muche to seye as it was nyght' (V.1016–18) or 'the dayes honour, and the hevenes ye [eye], | The nyghtes foo—al this clepe I the sonne' (*Tr* II.904–5)) have sometimes been taken as proof that Chaucer was making fun of rhetoric, or that having begun as a youthful disciple of rhetoric he later became more independent and critical. This is almost certainly too simple. In fact the examples remain firmly within the rhetorical tradition. A more likely explanation is that Chaucer was so skilled in the art that he could practise it with a self-conscious playfulness. When the Host asks the Clerk to tell a tale he forbids preaching or dullness, and insists on a plain style:

> Telle us som murie thyng of aventures.
> Youre termes, youre colours, and youre figures,
> Keepe hem in stoor til so be ye endite
> Heigh style, as whan that men to kynges write.
> Speketh so pleyn at this tyme, we yow preye,
> That we may understonde what ye seye
>
> (IV.15–20)

The joking aside to the *ars dictaminis* and the high style thought (according to the Host) to be necessary in addressing kings is only one element in a half-comic scene in which the Host is teasing the Clerk as a 'typical intellectual'. Harry Bailly is a lover of plain (and sometimes blunt) speech. It is characteristic that soon after he is introduced in the *General Prologue* he uses the formulaic phrase 'to speken short and pleyn' (I.790). The Clerk, of course, has been described in the *General Prologue* (I.304–7) as one whose speech was 'short and quyk and ful of hy sentence'. Not surprisingly, his tale is markedly plain and simple (and, perhaps by way of a gentle rejoinder, he includes a couple of references to his author Petrarch's 'high style'. Underlying it all is a good rhetorical point concerning appropriateness and levels of style, but it is lightly done—just as when the Eagle in *The House of Fame* 854–62 delightedly claims credit for speaking simply, without subtlety of speech, prolixity or 'termes', 'figures' and 'colours').

Chaucer's own practice is skilful and flexible. His awareness of stylistic decorum (also found in the passage in which Pandarus advises Troilus on the appropriate style for a love letter (*Tr* II.1023–43), alluding to the opening of Horace's *Ars poetica*, and in his fondness for quoting the dictum going back ultimately to Plato's *Timaeus*, 'the wordes moote be cosyn to the dede' (I.741–2; IX.207–10, *Bo* III pr.12:206)), is reflected everywhere. In *Troilus* for example, characters sometimes (especially in scenes of high emotion) give speeches that are verbally elaborate, almost like arias in opera; at other moments familiar dialogue will give a sense of spontaneity. In *The Parliament of Fowls* Nature speaks with 'esy voys' (382). This accords with her character but is also a persuasive technique. Chaucer's contemporary *Usk in his *Testament of Love* (I, ch. 4) praises the 'esy manner'. The wise commonly speak 'esily and softe', for various reasons: their words are the better believed, and men may take heed 'what to putte forth and what to holden in'.

Chaucer often draws attention to the way his characters talk, as in the significant idiosyncrasies of the Prioress, the Friar, or the Pardoner (who makes a living through his 'sales talk'). He is obviously very interested in the rhetorical structure of narratives, in amplification and abbreviation, *digression, and in the techniques of opening and closing. It is possible that a knowledge of the theory and practice of rhetoric may have encouraged other interests and tendencies in his work. If he knew of the rhetorical training in arguing both sides of a case, for instance, it might well have encouraged his marked tendency to present or entertain more than one aspect or level of a scene or a speech, and a liking for using the art of persuasion playfully as well as in earnest. There is no doubt that he enjoyed presenting arguments, disputes, and other attempts at persuasion. Powerful persuaders appear again and again. Pandarus, the Pardoner, and the Wife of Bath are very obvious examples. Along with this goes an interest in the variety of ways that rhetoric may persuade to less than altruistic or noble ends, an interest in feigning and deceit. We are presented with many cases where the ideal union of eloquence with wisdom is imperfectly realized, from the 'wordes white' (the misleading or specious words) of Pandarus (*Tr* III.901, 1567), that arch-persuader, who will use such oblique methods of persuasion as well as more traditionally direct ones, to the outright 'feigning' of the false Arcite in *Anel* (e.g. lines 155 ff.) or the systematic flaunting of the ideal by the 'ful vicious' Pardoner, who, for all his 'feyned flaterye and japes' still maintains that he can tell a moral tale. Chaucer's early readers were quick to recognize his skill in the art of rhetoric and to praise it: *Deschamps describes him as 'saiges [wise, skilled] en rethorique', *Dunbar as 'rose of rethoris all'. (See also *debate; *digression; *exemplum; *portraits; *Ubi Sunt.)

(eds.) Butler (1963); Caplan (1954); Faral (1924); Murphy (1971); Sutton and Rackham (1942); Wrobel (1887); (studies) Caplan (1970); Curtius (1953), 95–8; Dronke (1973); Manly (1926); Murphy (1974); Payne (1963).

RICHARD, KYNG (I) (1157–99). King of England 1189–99, son of Henry II and Eleanor of Acquitaine. Richard spent much of his life, and most of his reign abroad especially in France, where he was a friend and patron of a number of troubadours and, according to apparently reliable testimony, a poet himself. His death is mentioned in *The Nun's Priest's Tale* (VII.3348).

[AH]

RICHARD II (1367–1400). King of England 1377–99, son of the Black Prince and grandson of *Edward III; he came to the throne as a minor, was deposed following the invasion in 1399 by Henry Bolingbroke (*Henry of Derby), son of *John of Gaunt, and murdered a few months later. Much discussion of Richard's actions, character, and the circumstances that led to his deposition has not produced an entirely convincing or coherent account; neither is it clear whether the flowering of the arts during his reign owed anything directly to his patronage or instigation. *Gower dedicated the first version of his *Confessio Amantis* to Richard, and seems to suggest that it was written at the king's prompting; it is less clear that any work of Chaucer's should be connected with the king, though a colophon in one manuscript of *Lack of Steadfastness* (Harley 7333) states that it was sent to Richard II, and the envoy to the poem in Trinity College Cambridge R.3.20 is headed 'Lenvoye to Kyng Richard'. For Richard's confirmation of his grandfather's grants to Chaucer, and his various appointments of, grants to and dealings with Chaucer see *Life Records passim*. [AH]

Cavanaugh (1985), 724–33.

RICHARD OF BURY (1287–1345). He held numerous benefices, and posts associated with the court of Edward III; he was a scholar and book-collector, leaving a large library at his death some of which is detailed in his *Philobiblon*. As bishop of Durham 1333–45 he collected around him a notable group of scholars. [AH]

N. Denholm-Young (1973).

riet, (1) *rete*, net (L. *rete*). The pierced metal disc on an astrolabe. Its most important attributes are the pointers, the tips of which represent the stars, and the eccentric graduated circle that represents the *ecliptic, the Sun's annual path. The decorative style of the rete changes steadily with period, and those illustrated in *A Treatise on the *Astrolabe*, with a pronounced Y-shape across the middle, are quite typical of Chaucer's time, and not of his source. (See also *astrelabie; *clymat; *Mâshâ'allâh.) (2) At one place in *Equatorie of the Planetis* the pierced disc known as the *epicycle (in reality it serves as a multiple epicycle) is referred to as *riet*. [JDN]

RIGA, PETER OF, see *Peter of Riga.

Robert, Sir, a name for a fornicator, probably a priest, possibly a knight (III.1356).

Robyn (1), the *Miller (I.3129).

Robyn (2), John's servant in *The Miller's Tale* (I.3466, 3555).

Robyn (3) appears in a phrase spoken by Pandarus to himself when Troilus is convinced that he can see Criseyde coming back (*Tr* V.1174): 'From haselwode, there joly Robyn pleyde, | Shal come al that that thow abidest heere'. It seems to be an English expression of incredulity that Chaucer has substituted for an Italian one ('this poor wretch expects a wind from Mongibello'). The exact reference is uncertain. Robin is the traditional name of a shepherd or rustic in the French *pastourelles*, lyrical poems which describe how the shepherdess, Marion, (usually) repulses the advances of an amorous knight in favour of the charms of her rustic lover. Possibly the phrase means therefore 'from the unreal world of Arcadia', 'from the land of fancy'. Perhaps Pandarus is thinking of some jovially erotic pastourelles where the new knight overcomes the maiden's resistance (cf. Feste's 'Hey, Robin, jolly Robin, | Tell me how thy lady does' (*Twelfth Night* 4.2)). Possibly the reference is to Robin Hood, whose legends were current in some form in Chaucer's time. Chaucer does not refer to him directly, as does Langland, but the proverb he uses in *Troilus* II.861 'thei speken, but thei benten nevere his bowe' is frequently used of the outlaw (which the note in two MSS, 'of robyn hod', recognizes), and in the meeting in *The Friar's Tale* with the yeoman in green 'under this grene-wode shawe' (III.1386) the phrase is similar to a formula of the outlaw ballads.

Rochele, the, La Rochelle, a port on the Atlantic coast of France from which *wine was exported to England (VI.571).

Rodogone, Rhodogune, a daughter of Darius mentioned by *Dorigen (V.1456). St *Jerome says that she killed her nurse for suggesting that after her husband's death she should marry again.

Rodopeya, Rodopeye, the country near Rhodope (Rodopi), a mountain range in Thrace (*LGW* 2438, 2498).

ROET, PHILLIPA, see **Philippa *Chaucer**.

Roger (1) (or Hogge) the *Cook.

ROGER (2), Ruggieri degli Ubaldini, bishop of Pisa (1278–1335), who conspired with Ugolino (*Hugelyn) and betrayed him (VII.2416).

ROLLE, RICHARD (d. 1349), educated briefly at Oxford, but spent most of his life in Yorkshire as a hermit and spiritual director. The first of the major English mystical writers, using both English and Latin, verse and prose, often with heavy alliteration. His writings were widely disseminated, and his influence on spirituality in England in the late medieval period was enormous.   [AH]
  H. E. Allen (1927); *Dictionnarie de Spiritualité* XIII.572–90.

Romayn(s), see *Rome.

Roman de la Rose (called by Chaucer 'the Roma(u)nce (or Romauns) of the Rose' (IV.2032; *BD* 334; *LGW* 329) or simply 'the Rose' (*LGW* 441, 470)), a long French poem of which the first part (*c.*4,000 lines) was written *c.*1230 by *Guillaume de Lorris. It begins as an allegorical narrative. The poet dreams that in May he finds a *garden surrounded by a wall painted with images (Avarice, Envy, Sorrow, *Old Age, etc.) (see Fig. 10). He is allowed in by a maiden, Idleness. It is the Garden of Mirth (Deduit), of extraordinary beauty. There he meets Mirth and his companions, Courtesy, Gladness, Beauty, and others, all beautiful young people dancing and singing. The God of *Love himself is there, and he follows the dreamer like a skilful hunter. Coming to the the well of Narcissus (*Narcisus), the dreamer sees a beautiful rosebud. The God of Love sends an arrow which enters his eye and pierces his heart. He becomes the liegeman of the God of Love and is instructed in Love's commandments. He also learns the pains of love. He is encouraged by Fair Welcome (Bialacoil), but Fair Welcome is driven away by a churlish gardener, *Daunger. *Reason tries to persuade the lover to give up his service to Love, but without success. The lover is helped by Friend, and Franchise and Pity ('*Pite') intercede for him. He manages to kiss the Rose, but Shame and Wicked Tongue arouse Jealousy, who imprisons Fair Welcome and the Rose in a castle. The lover laments. At this point Guillaume's poem ends. About forty years later it was taken up by *Jean de Meun, a scholarly intellectual known as a translator and commentator. In his continuation, the allegorical framework remains, but it is pushed into the background, and the idea of love is given a much wider encyclopaedic and philosophical discussion, with many *digressions and ramifications. Reason discourses on *old age, *fortune, true happiness, justice and injustice (illustrating this with the story of *Virginia). The lover claims that what she calls plain speaking about evil is bawdy and lewd, but Reason defends her use of words. The lover's Friend gives him some worldly advice on the art of winning love. Eventually the God of Love promises to try to rescue Fair Welcome, and with the aid of False Seeming and an Old Woman who acts as go-between for the lover and Fair Welcome, the lover gets into the castle of Jealousy. (These sections contain much satirical material—against friars, a cynical account of how women gain men's love, etc.—of a kind which is not found in Guillaume's part.) Once again Daunger opposes the lover, and a battle ensues. We are told how *Nature wars against death. Nature herself discourses on free will and destiny, the influence of the stars, dreams, true nobility, etc., and finally sends her priest Genius to urge on the God of Love. He and his barons storm the castle, the lover enters and at last (after nearly 22,000 lines), in a thinly veiled and detailed sexual allegory, wins his rose.

Both parts of the *Roman de la Rose* were immensely influential. Guillaume's elegant and graceful psychological allegory made the love vision one of the most fashionable forms in later medieval literature, and Jean de Meun's encyclopaedic learning and much less courtly view of love and ladies delighted many. Not everyone, however, was an admirer of the *Roman*. It provoked intense discussion and debate in French literary circles in Chaucer's time. *Christine de Pisan thought it was a handbook for lechers, and the

querelle de la Rose continued in the 15th c. There is a clear hint of this argument in the hostile comments which the God of Love in the Prologue of *The *Legend of Good Women* makes about the poem ('that is an heresye ayeins my lawe'). Whether or not any part of the surviving Middle English *Romaunt of the Rose* is by Chaucer, there is no doubt that the *Roman* was a major influence on his work. Echoes and allusions can be found everywhere. Guillaume's work pervades the landscapes of the dream visions, and the descriptions of the experiences and the sufferings of courtly lovers. Chaucer also evidently appreciated Jean de Meun's variety of tone and detachment and his obsession with the poetic expression of ideas: Chaucer's own ideas about Nature and love owe much to this part of the *Roman*.

(ed.) Langlois (1914–24); Lecoy (1966–70); Poirion (1974); (trans.) Dahlberg (1971); Horgan (1994); H. W. Robbins (1962); Fansler (1914); Fleming (1969); Gunn (1952); Kay (1995); C. S. Lewis (1936); Tuve (1966); Wimsatt (1970).

Roman de Thèbes, a 12th-c. French verse romance which tells the story of *Thebes (1). Chaucer knew the French romance (which was commonly associated with *Benoît's *Roman de Troie* and sometimes bound together with it). It is probably the 'the geste | Of the siege of Thebes' which the maiden reads to the ladies in *Troilus and Criseyde* (II.80–111); Criseyde calls it the 'romaunce . . . of Thebes'. Pandarus's reference to the 'bookes twelve' (108) shows that he is thinking of the *Thebaid* of Statius (*Stace).

(ed.) Raynaud de Lage (1966–7).

Roman de Troie, see *Benoît.

romance (see also *Breton lay). The word 'romance' originally simply meant a poem written in French, a 'Romance' language deriving from the popular Latin spoken by the inhabitants of that part of the Roman empire. In the 12th c. romances were written for French-speaking courtly audiences in France and in England. These included stories of the ancient world (like the *Roman de Troie*) and stories from Celtic tradition, especially those concerning Arthur

(*Arthour), the legendary ruler of the Britons. Later, romances were written in English for those not able to understand French. Most of these seem intended for less courtly audiences: they were probably read by 'clerks', merchants, and other literate laymen, and would also be recited or read aloud. As the prestige of the English language increased, writers of considerable literary talents (like the author of *Sir Gawain and the Green Knight*) began using the genre. English romances appear in a number of metrical forms: in couplets (like their French ancestors) and also in stanzaic (like *tail-rhyme) or *alliterative verse. It is difficult to define 'romance'. Medieval terminology was not exact: what modern scholars class as romances are sometimes called that, sometimes 'tales' or 'gests' (literally 'deeds'). Indeed, the romance sometimes overlaps with a variety of other literary forms (chronicles, epics, moral tales, *saints' lives, *folk tales, ballads). However, many attempts at a definition would include the words 'story', 'adventures', and 'chivalry.' The romance is pre-eminently a narrative kind. It characteristically consists of a series of 'adventures' which befall its hero, and it is usually (even in its more 'popular' forms) infused by and concerned with the ideals of knightly behaviour or *chivalry. It has often been described as 'remote', and it is normally set in the remote past (which it sometimes contrasts with the present). It is also sometimes set in a remote and mysterious land, and often contains magic or supernatural incidents and elements. Much in it is heightened and idealized. At the same time it is in other ways close to the medieval world and to medieval experience. Characters and settings are 'medievalized', and sometimes it will concern itself with patterns and problems of contemporary ideology and behaviour. While it sets out to entertain with its adventures, and often with the strange and the fantastic, it also often claims, and often has, a moral purpose. Some romances are clearly 'didactic', others are 'moral' in a more general sense. The more sophisticated examples often explore the problems of noble behaviour or of noble love. *Love indeed is very often the central theme. Noble knights are usually noble lovers as well as great warriors. Women, often left on the margin in earlier epics, take on in the romance a central role, as inspirers or as testers. Knights have

to prove themselves through the many adventures they meet on their quests. Generally the heroes are successful, and their story has a happy end, but there are a number of tragic romances, notably those which deal with the death of Arthur, or Alexander, or the story of *Tristram. The literary quality ranges from the highly sophisticated to the flat and banal. Some of the English popular romances seem only interested in a flow of adventures, conventional and sometimes absurd. This kind of work is superbly parodied and burlesqued by Chaucer in his own *Sir Thopas. It is clear that he had a wide knowledge of such romances. Some have argued that they may have had a formative influence on his narratorial style. He had certainly read other kinds of romances. He would have come across examples of 'hagiographic romances', stories on the border between the genre of romance and that of the saint's life, a pattern which seems to underlie his own *Man of Law's Tale. He also knew French romances, such as the *Roman de Thèbes. Much more unusual was his acquaintance with the newer Italian romances (or narrative poems on the edge of that genre). Boccaccio's *Teseida* and *Il Filostrato*.

Chaucer's attitude to romances and chivalry has been much debated. Modern critics impatient with this favourite medieval genre sometime claim that it is a dismissive one, but this is oversimple. There are clear hints of a certain detachment about some aspects of the genre. That Chaucer uses the title 'Sir' of his hero Thopas, a traditional feature of Middle English popular romance not found elsewhere in his romances, may not only suggest its 'Englishness' but also perhaps a slightly old-fashioned quality (though the main drive of the attack seems to be on its style and its vacuity). Two remarks about heightened and exotic behaviour in The *Squire's Tale* may suggest a similar sense of the 'passé' (though they are not necessarily dismissive): the strange knight's courtly behaviour was such that 'Gawayn, with his olde curteisye, | Though he were comen ayeyn out of Fairye [Fairyland], | Ne koude hym nat amende with a worde'; and the dances at court were so strange that no man could tell their 'form' except Launcelot—'and he is dead' (V.95, 287). When Pandarus in *Troilus and Criseyde* (III.980) brings the lovers together, and draws away to the fire, takes a light, and assumes the attitude or pretence 'as for to looke upon an old romaunce', the tone is more ambiguous. The Wife of Bath thinks that fairies existed only long ago in King Arthur's time (III.857–72), but perhaps Chaucer, for all his concern with 'real life', was not entirely out of sympathy with Fairyland (*fayerye). A clearer (but still playful) doubt concerning the 'truth' of romances is found in the Nun's Priest's claim that his story is as true 'as is the book of Launcelot de Lake, | That wommen holde in ful greet reverence' (VII.3212–3). And in *Rosemounde Chaucer makes an offhand comparison of himself to *Tristram.

Chaucer's own romances differ markedly from the mainstream Middle English popular romances he made fun of in *Thopas*, and they are a very varied group. The *Squire's Tale* is called by some 'pure romance', by others a parody of romance. If it is deliberately left unfinished this may possibly suggest a feeling on Chaucer's part that this kind of romance with its exotic Oriental setting and marvels was just too extravagant, or perhaps that the Squire is lost in a labyrinth of his own making (the tale has the interlaced plots fashionable in contemporary French romances, and promises more of the same). On the other hand, Chaucer seems to enjoy the marvels and the pathos offered by the story as far as it goes. In The *Wife of Bath's Tale*, which is on the border between romance and folk tale, like a number of English popular romances and *Breton lays. Chaucer again seems quite at ease with the supernatural element, which he uses as a part of a pattern of moral ideas. Similarly in The *Franklin's Tale*, which announces itself as a Breton lay (and like other examples of the kind has a basis in folktale, a central theme of love, and a strong element of wonder), he is concerned to emphasize the ideas of 'gentilesse' and patience, and to show noble ideals under strain. The *Knight's Tale* is totally unlike any previous English romance. Like the *Teseida* on which it is based it is a kind of romantic epic, showing a new interest in mythographical and astrological matter. Chaucer uses the story to explore the uneasy relationship between love and friendship, and to raise serious philosophical questions about the human condition. His greatest achievement is in *Troilus and Criseyde*, a work which has clear affinities with romance, but transcends it to become, as W. P. Ker said 'that form of story which is not restricted in its matter in any way, but is capable of taking in comprehensively all or any part of the aspects and humours of life' (1905, 83). Chaucer was more interested in romance and the challenges it offered to his creative imagination than many of his critics allow. As with other literary genres, his method is one of bold exploration and transformation.

Everett (1929); Ker (1897, 1905); Stevens (1973); Vinaver (1971).

Romance of the Rose, see *Roman de la Rose*.

Romaunt of the Rose. A Middle English translation (7,692 lines in four-stress couplets) of about one third of the *Roman de la Rose* exists in one MS, which was printed and attributed to Chaucer in Thynne's 1532 edition. His attribution was based on the statement of the God of Love to Chaucer in the Prologue to The *Legend of Good Women*: 'Thou hast translated the Romaunce of the Rose, | That is an heresye ayeins my lawe' (329–30). *Lydgate also says (perhaps echoing *LGW*) that Chaucer translated the work. However, it is by no means certain that the extant text is the Chaucer translation (if indeed he ever made one). Even after a long controversy about language, style, and rhyme the question has not been finally decided. The Middle English translation may be the work of two, or possibly three different authors. The general consensus is that it is extremely unlikely that the whole work is by Chaucer. Concerning the three 'fragments' which have been distinguished within the work opinions differ. Fragment A (1–1705), a literal translation, is generally 'Chaucerian' in language and style and is accepted as an early work by some editors though not by all. Fragment B (1706–5810), a freer translation, has northern forms and un-Chaucerian rhymes, and is not thought to be Chaucer's, or the work of the authors of either A or C. However, the poet was a 'Chaucerian' who knew the master's work (he adds a passage on '*gentilesse' (2185–202) which sounds very like the section in The *Wife of Bath's Tale*). While these first fragments cover the work of *Guillaume de Lorris and the first part of *Jean de Meun's continuation, Fragment C (5811–7696), a fairly literal translation, picks up Jean de Meun's continuation after a gap of some 5,000 lines. It is more 'Chaucerian' than B, but has more uncharacteristic rhymes than A, and has generally not been accepted as Chaucer's. One attractive hypothesis (David, *Rv*) is that A, either by Chaucer or thought to be by him, was continued, perhaps for commercial reasons, with two translators, both 'Chaucerians', working simultaneously (if B had continued to the point where C begins, and C had continued to the end, both would have had a stint of *c*.10,000–11,000 lines). The enterprise was abandoned, but someone combined the three sections. The text is of considerable interest in providing a contemporary version, even if not all by Chaucer, of the influential French poem.

(ed.) *Rv* 685–767, 1103–16.

Rome (Chaucer's adj. is Romayn; he calls the inhabitants Romayns) had been for most of the Middle Ages the principal city of Italy (*Ytaille) and of medieval Europe, and, although in the 14th c. it suffered from internal dissensions, the exile of the papacy to Avignon (whence the Pope returned in 1378), and the mercantile competition of other Italian cities, it still remained important. It was famed for its classical past, the ruins of which were still evident and which were noted in the *Mirabilia Romae Urbis* (Wonders of the City of Rome), a 12th-c. guide, a mixture of information and legend. Because of the memory of the heroic days of early Christianity preserved in churches, shrines, and relics, Rome was visited by many pilgrims, and it had become the administrative and spiritual centre of Western Christianity.

Chaucer's many references reflect various aspects of the city's history and significance. There is no evidence that he visited it, but it clearly has an important part in his literary and symbolic landscape. He lists it as an example of a great and rich town, along with Nineveh (*Nynyvee), Alexandria (*Alisaundre), *Troy and others (VIII.975; *BD* 1063). He refers to figures and episodes from its ancient history and legends (*Hannibal, *Claudius, *Nero, etc., the magic mirror of Virgil, V.231), to institutions and places (senators, and senators' wives, VII.3371), the Capitol (*Capitolie)). And from ancient or later sources (including what he rather vaguely calls once 'the olde Romayn

geestes', II.1126) he draws a number of stories: Lucretia (*Lucrece), *Virginia, Julius Caesar (*Cesar), *Nero. Early Christian Rome of the persecutions and the catacombs is the setting for the story of St Cecilia (*SNT*). Then comes the time of St *Jerome, 'a clerk at Rome' (III.673), and Boethius (*Boece). From the 6th c. (apparently) come the legendary figures of *Custance and her father the emperor (*MLT*). Contemporary Rome is represented too. The *Wife of Bath had been there on pilgrimage (I.465), and the *Pardoner has just come 'fro the court of Rome' with his indulgences (I.671, 687). In the eyes of satirists Rome was a hotbed of corruption: 'at the court of Rome all things are bought and sold' says a contemporary proverb. It would probably not have surprised readers of the *Griselda story (in Boccaccio, Petrarch, and Chaucer) to find Walter sending to Rome for counterfeit bulls to enable him to marry a new wife (IV.736–49). A final example of the city's centrality is seen in the way in which the proverbial diversity of the paths which lead to Rome is adapted to the ways of lovers: 'for every wight which that to Rome went | Halt nat o path' (*Tr* II.36–7).

***Romeo and Juliet*.** The melodramatic love stories of *Troilus and Criseyde* and *Romeo and Juliet* have often been thought of together, but the relationship is perhaps one of analogy or similarity rather than of influence. It has been said that *Shakespeare's play succeeded Chaucer's poem as 'the single most important and influential lovetragedy in English poetry, the archetype to which situations in both life and literature [are] referred' (Thompson). The chief immediate source of Shakespeare's play was Arthur Brooke's poem *The Tragical History of Romeus and Juliet* (1562), itself a free rehandling of a French version of a novel by Bandello, and any relation between Shakespeare and Chaucer here must be in the ways in which the tragic love stories are narrated and dramatized, and in their shared vision that human love at its most passionate and most fulfilling cannot last in the real world. In neither story is the tragedy the result of moral principles ranging themselves against the lovers: mischance and the world destroy Romeo and Juliet; in Chaucer's poem the love is flawed and Criseyde, victim to mischance and the world, drifts into other arms. Both works

carry too a heavy freight of determinism: the role of destiny and fickle Fortune in *Troilus and Criseyde*, and Shakespeare's 'pair of star-cross'd lovers'. Pandarus and Friar Lawrence may be seen as spokesmen for conventional morality, but they are rapidly overwhelmed by the march of events beyond any apparent control. Some scholars believe Shakespeare borrowed Friar Lawrence's image in 'These violent delights have violent ends, | And in their triumph die like fire and powder, | Which as they kiss consume' (2.6.9–11) from Chaucer's Criseyde's meditation. 'Ful sharp beginning breaketh oft at ende' (II.791).   [RB]
     Bullough (1957); E. T. Donaldson (1985); A. Thompson (1978).

Romulus (also known as Quirinus; see *Quyryne), the legendary founder of *Rome, said to be the son of Mars. He disappeared from the earth in a cloud during a storm (hence the reference in *HF* 589). The 'moder of Romulus' (*PF* 292) mentioned among the unfortunate lovers in the temple of Venus was Rhea Silvia, a Vestal virgin. After the birth of the twins Romulus and Remus she was put in chains, and died.

Rondeau, see *Roundel.

Ronyan, Ronyon, Seint. The *Host swears by this saint when he addresses the *Pardoner (VI.310) and the Pardoner repeats the oath (apparently with a slight change of pronunciation as 'Ronyon') when he replies (320). The identification is not certain. The most likely explanation is that it is a form of St Ronan, a 7th-c. Scottish hermit. It has been suggested that it represents a popular variant form of St Ninian, a widely known Scottish saint. Or possibly it is an invention of the Host, perhaps a nonsense word, perhaps based on some obscene term. ('Runnion' (an abusive term for a woman; also meaning 'male member') has been suggested: this word of obscure origin is recorded only at the end of the 16th and in the 17th c., but words of this kind are often only intermittently recorded in literary texts.)

Rosarie, see *Arnold of the Newe Toun.

Rosemounde, To, a *ballade of three stanzas, ascribed to Chaucer in the sole MS copy that survives. There is no indication of date, and the identity of Rosemounde (if she existed) is unknown. Lady Alice de Bryenne, betrothed as a child to Richard II, and the Princess Isabelle of Valois. Richard II's child bride, who made an entry into London in 1396, have been suggested, but there is no convincing evidence. It is one of the most attractive and graceful of Chaucer's short poems, blending the conventional praise of a lady ('Madame, ye ben of al beaute shryne', etc.) with self-deprecating humour. The poet twisting in the throes of love compares himself to a pike steeped in sauce; because of the constancy of his love he is 'trewe *Tristam the secounde'.
     (ed.) *Rv* 649, 1082; Pace and David (1982), 161–71; Scattergood (1995), 479–80.

rote, see *musical instruments.

Rouchestre, Rochester in Kent, about 30 miles (48 km) from London on the way to Canterbury. Its fine medieval cathedral has a wall-painting of *Fortune's wheel. The *Host's remark (VII.1926), 'Loo Rouchestre stant [stands] heer faste by!', has occasioned some argument in the question of the order of the fragments of The *Canterbury Tales, but it may simply be there because Chaucer knew the town and wanted to give a general air of verisimilitude.

Rouncivale, the Hospital of St Mary Rouncesval at Charing Cross in *London, where the *Pardoner was employed (I.670). It was a dependency or cell of the Augustinian Hospital of Our Lady of Roncesvalles in the Pyrenees on the pilgrim route to Compostela. It was notorious for the zeal with which it sold indulgences.

Roundel, a rondeau, a French verse-form, a short *lyric in which the opening line or lines recur as a refrain in the middle and at the end. In Chaucer's time the number of lines varied from eight to fourteen or more. Like the *carole it was originally a dance song (with a clerical equivalent in the *rondellus*). It was much elaborated, but retained its connection with music. Chaucer refers to the singing of roundels (I.1529; *PF* 673–93), and to their 'making' (V.948). He also says that he wrote them himself (*LGW* 423); the two surviving examples are the roundel sung by the birds at the end of The *Parliament of Fowls* ('Now welcome, somer, with thy sonne softe') and *Merciles Beaute.*

Stevens (1986), 159–98.

routhe, see *pite(e).

Rowland, Roland, the nephew of Charlemagne (*Charles), who, according to legend died fighting heroically against the Saracens at Roncesvalles, the hero of the *Chanson de Roland* (*BD* 1123).

rubible, see *musical instruments.

Ruce, Russye, Russia. The *Knight campaigned in 'Russia' (I.54), presumably in a part adjacent to medieval Lithuania (*Lettow), perhaps the principalities of Pskov and Novgorod, on the borders of Livonia (the area north of Lithuania on the Baltic), or Rossenia, between Livonia and Prussia (*Pruce). The Mongol raids into Russia are referred to in The *Squire's Tale* (V.10).

RUFUS, Rufus of Ephesus (1st c. AD), a famous Greek physician and anatomist, cited as a medical authority (I.430).

RUIZ, JUAN, archpriest of Hita (*c.*1280–*c.*1350), Spanish ecclesiastic, undoubtedly the most outstanding and most original poet of the Spanish Middle Ages, author of one work, *The Book of Good Love,* a collection of narrative and lyrical poems, composed in a variety of styles and metres, united by a common autobiographical thread. Showing more Arabic than Latin influence, the book, (possibly composed in prison), according to its prose preface, has a didactic aim, that of distinguishing 'good love'—the love of God—from 'foolish love', i.e. 'that of worldly sin', but then proceeds to exemplify the ways of this 'foolish love' for those 'all too human' readers unable to resist it! The poet then presents himself as the ironical, humorous, and tolerant protagonist of a series of what might be considered (priest as he was) scandalous love affairs, in which he plays the varying roles of rejected lover, seducer, and victim of the amorous attentions of lascivious cow-girls. A fair amount of speculation exists as to the possibility of Chaucer's being familiar with this Spanish book, since a number of resemblances may be perceived between the work of both authors (see *Spaigne). [PS]

(trans.) E. K. Kane (1968); Mignani (1970).

Rumour, see *fame.

Rupheo, Ripheus (or Rhipeus) a Trojan hero (*Tr* IV.53). Chaucer took the name from *Boccaccio, who probably took it from *Virgil.

Russell, daun, the name (Fr. red-haired) of the fox in *The Nun's Priest's Tale* (VII.3334).

Russye, see *Ruce.

S

⚭

Sagittarius, Sagittarie, the ninth sign of the Zodiac, the Archer. The sign (following representations of the corresponding constellation) is commonly depicted as a Centaur with bow and arrow. (See also *Centauris; *signe; Zodiak.)

[JDN]

Sayne, Seyne, the river Seine in France (V.1222, *Rom* 118).

saints and saints' lives. Saints (Chaucer also uses the older English word 'halwes', which survives in 'Allhallows') were persons whose extraordinary holiness of life had ensured them, according to the Church's teaching, an exalted place in heaven. Devotion to the saints was especially intense in the Middle Ages. Saints were powerful: they were able to intercede for the living, to help them in all kinds of ways, to protect them from danger and disease, and heal their sicknesses. St Thomas of Canterbury, the first of many saints mentioned in *The *Canterbury Tales* helped folk 'whan that they were seeke': 'optimus egrorum medicus fit Thoma bonorum' [Thomas is the best healer of the virtuous sick'] says an inscription on an ampulla now in the Museum of London. Some specialized in particular ailments or occupations. They could work miracles: their shrines were places of *pilgrimage. The saints which surrounded God in heaven included martyrs (like 'the hooly blisful martir' Thomas) rewarded like victors with the 'palm of martirdom' (VIII.240) and 'confessors', women as well as men. The Virgin Mary (*Marie) had a preeminent place. Saints were not only close to God, they were close to their earthly devotees. Theologians distinguished between a proper veneration of saints and the worship due to God, but in popular devotion this distinction was sometimes unclear. In some cases veneration of the images of saints or of their *relics or of the healing wells at some of their shrines could be almost indistinguishable from magic. Saints were such a prominent feature of the medieval spiritual landscape that they could be adapted to less orthodox purposes. The religion of *Love could have its saints and martyrs (the suffering of the imprisoned lover Palamon is called a martyrdom (I.1460)). Saints could be treated with a rather secular familiarity: 'men moste axe at seyntes if it is | Aught fair in hevene' says Antigone to Criseyde (*Tr* II.894), and Pandarus produces a less proverbial-sounding offhand remark, 'and if thow deye a martyr, go to hevene' (*Tr* IV.623).

The saints had their own literature. Chaucer uses two kinds—the *Miracles of the Virgin Mary, in *The *Prioress's Tale*, and Saints' Lives or Legends, in *The *Second Nun's Tale* ('the lyf of Seint *Cecile'). The writing of saints' lives (or hagiography) flourished throughout the Middle Ages. These developed their own conventions, originally based on the rules of ancient rhetorical biography or eulogy. The hero or heroine usually followed a set pattern, sometimes saintly from infancy, sometimes a sinner who was converted. Miracles were common; devils tempted and attacked the faithful soul, wicked persecutors tormented the body. There was not usually much attempt to set the story in any historical context. It was largely 'dateless', and its veracity was taken for granted. There was a strongly providential pattern in the story, with the hero, a pilgrim in a hostile world, moving towards a spiritual apotheosis, often aided along the way by Christ and the saints. Increasingly the genre used material from folk tale and folklore, as is evident in many examples in the influential *Golden Legend* of *Jacobus da Voragine. The saint's life was often close to the *romance, and it also sometimes provided a pattern for history and biography. Its patterns have been detected in Chaucer's tales of 'secular saints', the providential background of The *Man of Law's Tale or the 'passion' of Griselda in The *Clerk's Tale (called 'legend' in a following *link in some MSS). As with the saints themselves, their legends were familiar (cf. III.690, Tr II.118) and adaptable, as in The *Legend of Good Women (the 'Seintes Legende of Cupide). 'Legend' is sometimes used more generally (III.742), or more pointedly of a secular wife's suffering (VII.145). The religious sense (cf. VII.3121) gives a piquancy to the announcement of the Miller (who has supplanted the Monk in the order of storytelling) that he will 'telle a legend and a lyf | Bothe of a carpenter and of his wyf'. See individual saints: *Anne (1); *Anselm; *Antony; *Basilie; *Beneit; *Bernard; *Cecilie; *Cutberd; *Damasie; *Denys; *Dunstan; *Edward; *Eleyne; *Frydeswyde; *Gile; *Gregorie; *Hugh; *Ysidre; *Yve; *Jame; *Jerome; *Joce; *John (1); *Julian; *Kenelm; *Leonard; *Loy; *Luc; *Madrian; *Magdaleyne; *Marie; *Marie (Egipcien); *Mark; *Martyn; *Mathew; *Maure; *Nicholas; *Note; *Paul; *Peter; *Ronyan; *Symoun; *Thomas. See also *pilgrimage; *relics; *religion.

Delehaye (1998).

Salomon, Salamon, Solomon, the Old Testament king of Israel, renowned for his wisdom and for his many wives. He is frequently quoted as a sage (especially in *Melibee and The *Parson's Tale). The *proverbial sayings come from the Wisdom books of the Old Testament (Proverbs, Ecclesiastes, or Ecclesiasticus (see *Jhesu Syrak)). Among those attributed to him are 'werk al by conseil, and thou shalt nat rewe' (I.3530) and 'every thing hath tyme' (Tr II.989, etc.). Solomon had already become the proverbial figure of the wise man: 'and whan we been togidres everichoon, | Every man semeth a Salomon' (VIII.961). He was also celebrated as a magician: in The *Squire's Tale it is remarked apropos of making magic rings that he 'hadde a name of konnyng in swich art' (V.251). The wisdom and the wives are sometimes linked together for comic purposes. The *Wife of Bath calls Solomon 'the wise kyng' and, remarking 'I trowe he hadde wyves mo than oon', wonders at the many joys he must have had and wishes that she were allowed 'to be refresshed half so ofte as he' (III.36–43). But the '*Parables of Salomon' are

in her *Jankyn's (4) misogynistic book (III.679). When Pluto, in The *Merchant's Tale quotes a saying about the wickedness of women; that he found one good man among a thousand men, but out of all women not a single one (Eccles. 7:28/9; cf. VII.1057), his wife is briskly dismissive: 'he was a lecchour and an ydolastre' (IV.2242–8, 2276–302).

Saluce(s), Saluzzo in Piedmont, northern Italy, the setting of The *Clerk's Tale.

Samaritan, the woman of Samaria (John 4:7–18), to whom Christ said 'thou hast had five husbands; and he whom thou now hast is not thy husband'. This is mentioned by the *Wife of Bath (III.16 ff.)—'what that he mente therby, I kan nat seyn'.

Sampson, Sampsoun, Samson in the Old Testament (Judg. 14–16), famous for his strength, which lay in his hair, a secret that was betrayed to the Philistines by his lover Delilah (*Dalida). This led to his imprisonment and eventually to his death when he pulled down the temple on himself and his captors. The *Monk tells his story (which Chaucer could have found in the Bible and in *Boccaccio's De casibus virorum illustrium) rather well, drawing the moral from it that men should be wary of telling their '*conseil' to their wives. Delilah's role in the story accounts for its appearance in Jankyn's book of wicked wives (III.721–3). His strength was proverbial: no man should trust in his own perfection, says the *Parson, unless he is 'stronger than Sampson' (X.955). The *Pardoner describes the drunk man making a noise through his nose as if he were saying 'Sampsoun, Sampsoun!'—and yet Samson never drank wine (VI.554–5). He is used by the dreamer in The *Book of Duchess as an example of the folly of killing oneself for love (738–41). *Saturn says that he slew him 'shakynge the piler' (I.2466). His death is one of those written in the stars (II.201).

Samuel, the Old Testament judge and adviser of King Saul. After his death Saul visited the witch of Endor (*Phitonissa), who raised the spirit of Samuel for him (1 Sam. 28:3–20). This is alluded to by the fiend in The Friar's Tale (III.1510). The *Pardoner very carefully distinguishes Samuel from *Lamuel (VI.585).

Santippe

Santippe (from Boccaccio's Santippo), Xantippus, an ally of the Trojans (*Tr* IV.52).

SAPOR, Shapur I, king of Persia (3rd c. AD), appears in the story of Zenobia (*Cenobia; VII.2320).

Sarpedo(u)n, Sarpedon, the leader of the Lycians, an ally of the Trojans (*Tr* IV.52; V.402–501).

Sarra, Sarah, wife of *Abraham (Gen. 12–23). Her wifely obedience (1 Pet. 3:6) made her an exemplary figure, who was used with Rebecca (Rebekke) in a prayer in the marriage service. Hence she is cited as a model for *May (IV.1704).

Sarray, in *The *Squire's Tale (V.9, 46), the capital of *Tartary. Marco *Polo visited Sarai (on the Volga), which was a centre for the court of Barka Khan. Sarray has been identified with the modern Tsarev.

Satalye, Antalya (in modern southern Turkey), a Turcoman principality where the *Knight saw service (I.58). It was attacked by Peter of Cyprus (*Petro (2)) in 1361.

Sathan, Sathanas, Satan, the name of the *devil.

Satiry, satyrs, mythological creatures of the woods and hills, attendants of Dionysus, partly of human form, but partly animal, e.g. with the legs of a goat (*Tr* IV.1544).

Saturne, Saturnus, (1) Saturn (L. *Saturnus*), the Roman deity, anciently identified with the Greek Kronos. In the historical period, his festival in Rome in December (Saturnalia) was the most exuberant of the year. By the 4th c. this was transferred to a feast of the New Year, and later, under Christian influence, to the feast of Christmas. (2) the planet Saturn. The outermost planet known to the Middle Ages (Uranus, the next higher planet, was not to be discovered until 1781). Saturn moved on the seventh sphere in the simple version of Aristotelian *cosmology. In *alchemy, Saturn denotes the metal lead: a complete planetary catalogue is given in *The *Canon's Yeoman's Tale*. The Saturn-lead case is implicit in a passage in *The *House of Fame* (1429–50), and at the same point a standard astrological association of the planet with the Jews is made.

One of Saturn's most notorious powers was that of causing *melancholy. Like *Mars, he has a generally maleficent influence, but it is that of the embittered old man rather than the man of war. The two planets are named together in *Troilus and Criseyde* as producing 'aspectes badde' (III.716). In the same poem, the occurrence of Saturn with *Jupiter in *Cancer is given responsibility for heavy rain (III.625–8), following standard doctrine. The dismal events of *The *Knight's Tale* hinge on the tradition of the planet Saturn's general malevolence: the god's statement of his powers is fully in accordance with astrological principles, although not described as such. His association with *prison, as there stated, plays a central part in *The Legend of Hypermnestra*. (See also *astrology and astronomy*; *exaltacio(u)n*; *planete*; *signe*; *sper(e)*.) (3) the metal lead, in alchemical symbolism (as noted by the *Canon's Yeoman). (See also *alchemy*.)   [JDN]

sautrye; Scariot. See *musical instruments*; *Judas.

science. Chaucer's use of the word is fully in keeping with Latin *scientia* and Old French *science*, denoting knowledge, learning, or skill, usually over a wide range, implying preparation or training. *Mercury is the deity (or planetary deity) governing wisdom and science. The word might be used of knowledge in general (in *The *House of Fame* *Apollo is 'God of science and of lyght'), or of knowledge of a wide-ranging subject (such as that practised by the *Sergeant of the Lawe, or the *Canon's Yeoman's *alchemy, or the 'particuler sciences' studied in Orleans). Use of the word was not confined to the natural sciences, but in what follows we restrict our attention to them, and to what are in continental usage called the 'exact' sciences (roughly mathematics and those sciences such as *astronomy and astrology with a large mathematical component). (See *arsmetrik*; *augrym*.)

A substantial part of medieval Western scientific knowledge was derived from Greek sources, obtained in Latin translation, often through Arabic and other intermediaries, especially from the 12th c. onwards. The main routes of transmission were through Italy and Spain. The translated material entered into a Christian theological milieu that had more tenuous but essentially continuous links with sections of Greek and Latin learning, and much of Chaucer's knowledge reached him through this older and scientifically less well-informed tradition. (It knew translations of only limited parts of *Plato and *Aristotle, for example; and see *Boece; *Macrobes; *Marcian.) Boethius had translated parts of Euclid's *Elements*, an important text for the lessons it tacitly gave in the axiomatic method (see *Euclide). Perhaps more typical of attitudes in late antiquity and the early Middle Ages were those of Cassiodorus (*Cassidore), friend of Boethius, who valued ancient learning chiefly for its application in biblical commentary.

Other kinds of scientific knowledge were transmitted for reasons of practical utility, but utility of a different sort: in medicine, alchemy, and *technology, there was a strong pragmatic component. On the theoretical side, all of these subjects had an involvement with astrology.

*Astronomy and astrology were by far the most highly developed of the exact sciences from ancient times until the 19th c. Astronomy gave its mathematical style to other scientific subjects, whether at the simple geometrical level of *cosmology (see *sper(e)), or through its use of *tables to embody mathematical functions (see *cano(u)n), or through its having provided techniques of instrumentation. All three types of influence are visible in the optical work of Ptolemy (*Ptholomee).

Optics assumed an important position in the hierarchy of the natural sciences after the change of mood brought about by the translations of the 12th c., largely because *Grosseteste and *Bacon valued it so highly. Chaucer's awareness of this scientific fashion is clear from his references in The *Squire's Tale (see also *Alocen and *Vitulon). Optics had an affinity with experimental sciences described as 'natural magic', which must be sharply distinguished from the doctrinally dangerous spiritual magic that invoked demonic assistance. Most of medieval ray-optics, even

physiological optics, would be readily recognizable as 'science' by a modern observer.

The correctness of the description is less obvious in regard to natural philosophy, often judged to have been the most important ingredient in medieval progress towards the scientific revolution of the 17th c. Following the recovery of the text of most of Aristotle by the early 13th c., and for about a century and a half thereafter, there was a period of Aristotelian 'scholasticism': the sciences were studied in the context of the philosophical writings not only of Aristotle but of his commentators, Islamic, Jewish, and Christian. This period of intellectual history is marked by a great breadth of vision: there was an ambition to reach truth in every branch of knowledge by the procedures laid down in Aristotle's *Prior Analytics* and *Posterior Analytics*. At first (for instance in Grosseteste) Aristotelianism was allied with Augustinian philosophy, but this element faded away as time progressed.

Grosseteste was influential among the Franciscans in England, especially Roger Bacon and John Pecham, and they in turn influenced the important group of scholars at Merton College, Oxford, in the 14th c. What distinguishes the Oxford tendency from the Aristotelianism of such great Dominicans as Albertus Magnus and Thomas Aquinas was its great attention to the mathematical structure that nature was assumed to have. Albertus Magnus was a man with much sound empirical knowledge (see *Lapidaire) but he, and many lesser writers who resembled him in this respect, added little of theoretical importance to the scientific structures they inherited. The Merton philosophers, on the other hand, managed to add materially to them, in ways that had repercussions on the science of motion for almost three centuries.

The basis for their work was Aristotle's *Physics*, his assertion that motion (change) is involved in the very definition of nature, his analysis of motions in terms of four types of cause (material, efficient, material, and final), and his analysis of the continuum. Scholastic writers generally accepted his account of natural and forced motion (see *cosmology), but they introduced many new arguments into their accounts of how projectile motion takes place, new ideas of spatial and temporal continuity, and new forms of mathematical proportionality that are needed for the analysis of constant and accelerated motions. (The astronomers dealt with similar problems, but for the most part very differently.) Great conceptual advances were made by Thomas *Bradwardine, and his work was later much advanced by such men as Richard Swynshed and Nicole Oresme. Where the Mertonians were generally restricted to a difficult verbal calculus—one much used, for instance, in university debate—Oresme, in Paris, introduced graphical methods into the study of motion. These theories, which were designed to handle what were known as 'latitudes of forms' (as it were numerical strengths of qualities), had antecedents in medicine and pharmacology, in combination with the doctrine of the four *humours; but now they were found a rich variety of application to new problems. Most of these new problems were admittedly without any useful scientific application, but those dealing with uniformly accelerated motion were known to Galileo, and of great potential value to him.

At the other extreme of theoretical sophistication in science came biology, better described as natural history; but its greater accessibility and hence its greater popularity is not in doubt, and is part of the reason for the popularity of encyclopaedias, in which it had always been accorded a conspicuous place. Medieval accounts of flora and fauna have their main sources in ancient texts, such as the anonymous bestiary *Physiologus, and works by Aristotle, Pliny, and Dioscorides (*Deyscorides), in which fact and fantasy were mixed to various degrees. (We recall that biology was Aristotle's forte, however.) Exotic *animals were difficult to transport, and animals generally were studied less critically than plants, with their potential pharmacological value. Herbals were enlarged substantially in northern lands, to include plants unavailable in Mediterranean countries.

The usual divisions within bestiaries are into mammals, birds, fish, reptiles, and *vermes* (worms, insects, spiders, and more or less anything that will not fit elsewhere). Fabulous creatures were included in all classes. One particular type of bestiary includes a short etymology on the name of each animal, and ultimately derives from Isidore of Seville (*Ysidre). Bestiaries were often used in moral teaching, in the manner of Aesop, and to this tradition Chaucer was no stranger (see *Isope). They, like herbals, often listed the 'virtues' or properties of what they described, and occasionally incorporated information from astrological and mineralogical sources, especially when used for talismanic or magical purposes. Herbals were if anything less well classified than bestiaries. Unfortunately the alphabetical format most useful to the physician was of no taxonomic value, and impeded the development of both pharmacological and botanical theories.

It would be mistaken to characterize the medieval sciences as entirely bookish, although even those who proclaimed most often the importance of experience performed relatively few systematic experiments. Broadly speaking, they were likely to perform more, the further they were from a university environment (such as those concerned with alchemy and pharmacology). Within the universities, the greatest scientific contributions were made in regard to the exploration of alternative conceptual schemes: in astronomy, much new mathematics was developed, and instrumentation was improved; in natural philosophy new conceptual networks were often investigated with great rigour as exercises in logic, but it must be admitted that they were often entirely barren. If the greatest theoretical advances were made in astronomy, this is not unconnected with the fact that there the standard of inherited theoretical knowledge was highest. (See also *Astrolabe; *Avycen; *Bartholomew the Englishman; *clokke; *cosmology; *Equatorie of the planetis*; *Galyen (1); *geomancie; *Nature; *Neckham; *Razis; *Secreta secretorum; *Senior, *seven liberal arts; *sound.) [JDN]

Clagett (1959); Crombie (1969); E. Grant (1974); Klingender (1971); McCulloch (1962); Manzaloui (1974); Murdoch (1987); North (1990); Stannard (1974); Thorndike (1923–41).

SCIPIO(N), SCIPIOUN, CIPIOUN, Scipio Africanus Minor (*c.*185–129 BC), the grandson by adoption of Scipio Africanus Major (see *Affrican). Scipio Africanus Minor was a distinguished general in the Third Punic War, and destroyed

Carthage. He was famous as an orator and a patron of learning. Cicero (*Tullius) regarded him as the ideal statesman, and made him a central figure in his works on *friendship and *old age, and in the *De re publica*, in the last book of which is told the story of Scipio' s dream (see *Drem of Scipioun). Chaucer refers to him several times as a famous dreamer (VII.3124; *BD* 286; *PF* 31 ff.; *HF* 514–17, 914–18).

Scithero, see *Tul(l)ius.

Scithia, Cithe, Cithia, Scythia, the land of the Scythians, a nomadic Indo-European people famed for archery and horsemanship. After being driven out of Asia Minor by the Medes they established kingdoms in southern Russia which traded with Greek cities on the Black Sea. About the 2nd c. BC they were forced to move into the Crimea. They fought with success against the Persians and against the Macedonian troops of Alexander the Great (*Alisaundre). In Chaucer 'the aspre [harsh] folk of Cithe' are overcome by *Theseus, a campaign referred to both in *The *Knight's Tale* (I.865–82) and *Anelida and Arcite* (23, 37). He takes to wife Hippolyta (*Ypolita), 'queene of Scithia' (I.882). It is explained that the land of the Amazons (*Femenye) was formerly called Scythia (I.867), perhaps thought of as being in the region of the river Don in southern Russia.

Scogan, Lenvoy de Chaucer a Scogan, a short poem of seven stanzas in rhyme royal, survives in three manuscripts (one written by *Shirley) and the editions of Caxton (1477–8) and Thynne (1532). It is a witty sophisticated verse epistle, somewhat Horatian in tone, perhaps written in the later 1390s. Because Scogan has not been faithful in love, Venus is weeping so copiously that we shall all be drowned by her tears. Chaucer fears that Cupid will take revenge on all those 'that ben hoor and rounde of shap'. Scogan, he imagines, will say 'Lo, olde Grisel [?old grey horse?] lyst to ryme and playe.' But no, to this Chaucer replies that he is not able or willing to write verse: 'ne thinke I never of slep to wake my muse, | That rusteth in my shethe stille in pees.' The envoy asks Scogan, who kneels 'at the stremes hed | Of grace' (at the end of which stream Chaucer is 'dul as ded, | Forgete in

solytarie wildernesse') to remember his friend, and never defy love again. There has been much speculation about what if any ulterior purpose the poem may have: perhaps the best suggestion is that Scogan is being reminded of 'Tullius Kyndenesse', Cicero's advice that a true friend should help another in adversity (like living in obscurity without reward?). The recipient is almost certainly Henry Scogan (*c.*1361–1407), a Norfolk gentleman who succeeded his brother John as lord of the manor of Haviles, near Great Rainham in 1391. He was in the service of Richard II and lived at some time in London. He is probably the Henri Scoggan who in 1390 had a loan from the merchant Gilbert Mawfield (Maghfield), like Chaucer and others associated with Chaucer. He became tutor to the four sons of Henry IV, to whom he addressed, according to Shirley, A Moral Balade, written after Chaucer's death, in which he cites the poet's views on virtue and nobility and quotes his balade of '*Gentilesse'.

(ed.) *Rv* 655, 1086–7; Pace and David (1982), 149–60; Scattergood (1995), 506–11; Lenaghan (1975); Norton-Smith (1974), 213–35; Scattergood (1991).

Scorpio, Scorpio(u)n, the eighth sign of the Zodiac, the Scorpion. Also the constellation of the Scorpion. In *The *House of Fame* the Eagle draws attention to the Scorpion as something to be seen, calling it also a sign. (See also *signe.)

[JDN]

Scot, the name of the *Reeve's horse (I.616). It was apparently a common name then and later in East Anglia. Another horse in the unlocalized *Friar's Tale* is also called Scot (III.1543).

Scotland was in Chaucer's day an independent kingdom with uneasy political relations with England, which had its own cultural and literary traditions. Chaucer mentions Scotland and the Scots only in *The *Man of Law's Tale* (II.580, 718), as the enemies of King *Alla.

Scottish Chaucerians; Scrope-Grosvenor Trial; sculpture; seasons. See *Chaucerians, Scottish; Geoffrey *Chaucer: life; *visual arts; *months and seasons.

Second Nun's Tale, The, with the *Canon Yeoman's Tale*, to which it is explicitly linked, makes up Fragment VIII of The *Canterbury Tales*. Its Prologue (written, like the tale itself, in rhyme royal) contains an invocation to the Virgin *Mary (based on *Dante's *Paradiso* 33.1–51) and some pious etymologies of the name of the heroine, *Cecilie (Cecilia). The brief Tale (of just over 400 lines) relates how this 'mayden bright', a nobly born Roman Christian devoted to virginity, is married to Valerian, and tells him that her angel will not suffer him to touch her. Valerian says that he will believe her if he can see the angel. He is sent out to the Via Appia to the aged *Urban, and is converted. When he returns, he finds Cecilia with an angel, who gives them garlands of roses and lilies brought from Paradise, and promises that they will die martyrs. Valerian's brother Tiburce is also converted. But this is the period of the persecutions: Urban has often been condemned to death, and has to live in hiding in the catacombs. At last Valerian and Tiburce are brought before the prefect, Almache (Almachius), who sends them to do sacrifice before the statue of Jupiter. Supported by Cecilia, they steadfastly refuse and are both beheaded. Maximus, one of the prefect's officers, is moved by '*pite', and converts others by his account of how he saw their souls glide to heaven 'with aungels ful of cleernesse and of light'. He too is killed, and is buried beside them by Cecilia. She is now summoned by Almachius and (having converted some of his ministers on the way) questioned. She answers bravely and firmly, and is cruelly put to death. Urban and his deacons bury her in what is now called the church of St Cecilia (in Trastevere) in Rome, where she is still venerated.

The tale, based on the *Golden Legend*, is a fine example of the *saint's life, and is obviously appropriate to a nun. A reference to the 'lyf of Seynt Cecile' in the list of Chaucer's works in the Prologue to The *Legend of Good Women* indicates that it existed in some form before 1386–7; it was presumably adapted for The *Canterbury Tales* (although there is no portrait of its teller in the *General Prologue*). It has rarely been a favourite with modern readers (although there have recently been some sympathetic studies). It deserves attention for the powerful lyrical writing in the Invocation (one of Chaucer's best versions of

*Dante), and for the simple strong lines of Cecilia (who, like other saintly women in Chaucer, is a figure of considerable strength of spirit) when she refutes Almachius, or when she heartens the martyrs to be 'Cristes owene knyghtes leeve and deere', to cast away 'the werkes of derknesse', and to arm themselves in 'armure of brightnesse'. (See *religion; *saints.)

(ed.) *Rv* 262–9, 942–6; *S&A* 664–84 [491–527]; Cooper (1989), 358–67; Clogan (1972); Collette (1975–6; 2001); Hirsh (1977–8); Kolve (1981).

Secreta Secretorum, *The Secret of Secrets* (*Sirr al-asrâr*), an Arabic pseudo-Aristotelian treatise with considerable influence in Europe. The medical parts were translated into Latin in the 12th c., and all was translated in the first half of the 13th. Roger *Bacon, Thomas *Bradwardine, and John *Wyclif all made use of it. The Latin was widely circulated, and was turned into many vernaculars in the Middle Ages. The many references to physiognomy in The *Canterbury Tales* have sometimes been held to imply an acquaintance with the *Secret of Secrets*. The *Canon's Yeoman seems to refer to it when he speaks of the 'secree of the secretes', but this is uncertain, since the phrase is a common figure of speech in alchemical literature. (See also *alchemy; *Senior.) [JDN]

Seyne, see *Sayne.

Seint-Denys, Saint-Denis, a town north of *Paris (of which it is now a suburb). Its basilica, then an abbey church, is one of the earliest examples of Gothic art. The town is the setting for The *Shipman's Tale* (VII.1).

Seintes Legende of Cupide; Seint-Jame; Seint Thomas, Wateryng of. See *Legend of Good Women; Seint *Jame (2); *Wateryng of Seint Thomas.

Seys, Ceys, Ceyx, king of Trachis and husband of *Alcyone. His story is briefly told in The *Book of the Duchess*.

Semyrame, Semyramis, Semyramus, Semiramis, queen of Assyria (*c*.800 BC), famed as a warrior of great strength (who wore men's clothes), the fortifier of Babylon, and as a legendary lover. For the moralists of the Middle Ages she became an example of licentiousness. *Christine de Pisan, however, praises her courage and forcefulness as a general and ruler, and excuses her marriage with her son on the grounds that it was before 'our law' and under the law of Nature. Chaucer alludes to her building of the walls of Babylon (*LGW* 706–9), and she appears among the lovers in the temple of *Venus (*PF* 288). The Sultan's mother in The *Man of Law's Tale* who murders her son is addressed as 'Virago [probably a woman who does the office of a man], thou Semyrame the secounde!'.

SENEC, SENEK, SENECA, SENEKKE, Lucius Annaeus Seneca (4 BC–AD 65) born at Córdoba in Spain. He was brought up in Rome, and became a well-known orator and philosopher. His uneasy relationship with the Emperors Caligula and Claudius culminated in his exile by the latter. He was recalled by Agrippina in AD 49 to be the tutor of her son *Nero. When his influence over the emperor waned, and Nero's conduct deteriorated, Seneca asked permission to retire from the court. However, a few years later he was charged with complicity in a conspiracy and ordered to kill himself—which he did by opening his veins in a hot bath. Chaucer records his death in the *Monk's tragedy of Nero (VII.2496–518; cf. *Bo* III pr.5). Seneca's dialogues, treatises, and letters were very popular in the Middle Ages, partly because of a tradition that he was a Christian who had corresponded with St Paul, but also because his Stoicism was attractive, and his humane reflections on life's problems, and on consolation, peace of mind, and virtue were found useful. Chaucer is very fond of quoting Seneca, but it is often difficult to know whether he is quoting from complete works or from *florilegia*. Furthermore, some aphorisms attributed to Seneca are not actually from him but from intermediate sources such as *Albertanus, *Publius Syrus, or pseudo-Senecan texts. However there is a strong Senecan presence in Chaucer. General proverbial aphorisms attributed to him, e.g. on loss of time ('Los of catel [goods] may recovered be, | But los of tyme shendeth [ruins] us' (II.27; cf. *Tr* IV.1283)) often have similarities with a Senecan text (here *Epistulae morales* 1.3). The story

of the wrathful potentates, Cambises and Cyrus (III.2017–88) are from Seneca's *De Ira*, although Chaucer may have found them in the *Communiloquium* of John of Wales. The Pardoner quotes a 'good word' on drunkenness (VI.492). In *Melibee* and The *Parson's Tale* we also find Senecan ideas, coming through from translated texts. At the beginning of the first, for instance, we have a distinctly Stoic doctrine: 'the wise man shal nat take to greet disconfort for the deeth of his children, but, certes, he sholde suffren it in pacience as wel as abideth the deeth of his owene propre persone' (VII.984) ultimately from the *Ad Lucilium*, and another on moderation in grieving (991). Others follow (1328, 1481–3, 1857), from the epistles and the treatises on wrath and clemency. The Parson, noting that one of the signs of '*gentilesse' is for a man to be gentle to his good subjects (X.466–8), quotes Seneca (via *Peraldus), 'ther is no thing moore covenable [fitting] to a man of heigh estate than debonairetee and pitee' (Chaucer uses his favourite word 'pite' for clemency). The advice to lords to be gentle with their thralls (who are God's people and Christ's friends, X.759–63) echoes Seneca (*Epist.* 47) on the treatment of slaves. Chaucer's ideas on 'gentilesse' owe something to Seneca. His Epistle 44 is one of the texts that lie behind the old wife's remarks on true nobility ('Reedeth Senek' she tells the knight, III.1168), and her praise of 'glad poverte' (1183 ff.) is also Senecan in tone. Whether Chaucer knew Seneca's tragedies is not absolutely certain. Texts, and the commentary of *Trivet were available, and John Norton-Smith has argued that they profoundly influenced the scenic structure of *Troilus and Criseyde* and medieval ideas of *tragedy in general.

(ed. and trans.) Basore (1951); Gummere (1917); Miller (1917); (ed.) L. D. Reynolds (1965); L. D. Reynolds (1955); L. D. Reynolds, Marshal, and Mynors (1983, 1986); Norton-Smith (1974), ch. 6; Pratt (1966).

Seneciens (*Bo* I pr.3:57), apparently 'the followers of Seneca' (L. 'men like Seneca').

Senex Amans, see *old age.

SENIOR, Abû 'Abdallâh Muhammad ibn Umail al-Tamîmî (*c.*900–*c.*960), called al-Sadiq.

This influential alchemist was known in the Latin West as Senior Zadith, to which could be added 'filius Hamuelis', from 'ibn Umail'). He is referred to at the end of The *Canon's Yeoman's Tale in a discussion of the Philosopher's Stone. The Latin treatise by him known as the Tabula Chemica is a 'letter from the Sun to the waxing Moon'. ('Sol' and 'Luna', referring to gold and silver, occur in Chaucer ten lines earlier.) Senior was a follower of Plato, and some Western manuscripts of the 'letter' actually identify him with the Greek philosopher.

Other treatises circulating in Europe under Senior's name include the popular Secret of Secrets, a pseudo-Aristotelian work to which the Canon's Yeoman also seems to refer three lines earlier— although it has been argued that 'the secree of the secretes' means only 'the best of secrets', and is a name for alchemy. (See also *alchemy; *Secreta Secretorum.) [JDN]

Septe, Ceuta, the seaport in Morocco opposite Gibraltar (*Jubaltare) (situated below seven peaks called the 'seven brothers' (L. Septem Fratres), II.947).

Septemtryones, the stars of the constellation Ursa Minor, the Lesser Bear. (See *Bere.) The septem referred to the seven ploughing oxen (L. triones), the seven stars near the North Pole, hence the adj. septentrionalis, ME septemtryoun, northern. [JDN]

SERAPION, Sarâbiyûn, Arabic physician of the late 8th or early 9th c., author of a work translated into Latin as Liber de medicamentis simplicibus, presumably what Chaucer had in mind as one of the Doctour of Phisik's authorities (GP I.432). There might be a confusion of the man with Yûhannâ ibn Sarâbiyûn, his son, however. [JDN]

Sergeant of the Lawe; sermons. See *Man of Law; *preaching.

Seryens, the Chinese (Bo II m.5:11; adj. Syrien Bo II m.5:13).

Seven Deadly Sins. Sin 'the purposeful disobedience of a creature to the known will of God' (Oxford Dictionary of the Christian Church) can obviously take a variety of forms, and theologians and confessors were at pains to analyse and classify them. The worst type was the mortal or deadly sin, or cardinal sin, a deliberate act of turning away from God and seeking satisfaction in a creature, committed with a clear knowledge of guilt and full consent of the will: it could lead to the loss of grace and eternal damnation. Each deadly sin could be used a heading for the classification of related and lesser varieties of sin. By Chaucer's time Seven had become the fixed traditional number of the Deadly Sins. The seven were: Pride (L. Superbia); Envy (Invidia); Anger (Ira); Sloth (Acedia); Avarice (Avaritia) or Covetousness; Gluttony (Gula); Lust (Luxuria). The order sometimes varied, but generally fell into three main groups. That quoted is the very popular Gregorian order, which is used in Chaucer's *Parson's Tale. There was also much diversity in the classification of the 'branches' or subdivisions. By the early 13th c. and the growth of penitential practice and literature the Deadly Sins had become part of daily life, 'as real as the parish church itself' (Bloomfield). The arrangement of the Sins in both literature and the visual arts tended to follow standard systems: a ladder, a wheel, a tree, a procession of animals. A complex iconography sometimes overlaps with that of the Vices (in the Virtues and Vices series). The famous depiction of Envy by Giotto in the Arena chapel in Padua as a woman with horns coming out of her head, and a snake issuing from her mouth and turning back to sting her is actually part of a Virtues and Vices pattern, but one which includes Envy and Wrath. The association of sin with venom, sickness and disease and animals encouraged grotesque images and scenes. The tradition had much to offer the satirist, in details, and in the association of certain sins with certain estates (sloth with monks, for instance). The terms, sometimes reverting to their non-theological senses (as psychological states rather than as sins) are found everywhere, as in proverbs: 'pride will have a fall', 'envy is the lavender [laundress] of the court', 'wrath said never well', 'sloth is the mother of vice', 'covetise [avarice] is the root of all evils', 'gluttony wakens lechery', 'lechery is no sin'. Penitential literature and sermons make extensive use of the Seven Deadly Sins, sometimes as a structural principle. In *The *Parson's Tale* each sin and its branches are given detailed treatment, with appropriate spiritual 'remedies'. Elsewhere in *The Canterbury Tales* there are references and outbursts (against wrath in *The *Summoner's Tale*, against avarice in *The *Pardoner's Tale*), but there is no evidence that the Seven Deadly Sins are used as an organizing principle for the *Tales* as a whole. They are, however, in Gower's *Confessio Amantis*, where the pattern is adapted to the 'religion of Love', with exemplary stories and penitential advice. In Gower's *Mirour de l'homme*, a lament on the wretched state of the world, the Sins are the daughters of Death and Sin and are vividly pictured riding on animals (Pride on a lion, Wrath on a boar, lechery on a goat, etc.) in a grotesque procession (as they are later in Spenser's *Faerie Queene*). Surviving *illustrations in a Cambridge manuscript of *The Canterbury Tales* show sins mounted on animals. The most imaginative treatment in medieval English literature, however, is found in Langland's *Piers Plowman*, in a 'confession' scene, in which, stirred by Reason and Repentance, the Sins themselves (vividly described) attempt to repent, but without a great deal of success: Gluttony, for instance is lured into a tavern and becomes drunk.

Bloomfield (1952); Wenzel (1967); Katzenellenbogen (1939); R. S. Loomis (1965), 177–9; Tuve (1966), 57–143.

Seven Liberal Arts, seven subjects of central importance to the medieval university curriculum, comprising the three introductory subjects of the Trivium (originally Grammar, Rhetoric, and Logic), and the four mathematically founded subjects of the Quadrivium (Arithmetic, Geometry, Astronomy, and Music).

The Trivium had been taught in more or less the same form from the time of *Aristotle, and later in the Roman world, but it reached its summit in the cathedral schools of the 11th and 12th c., notably at Chartres. In these, its earliest phases, the Trivium was primarily a grouping of literary subjects—at times little more than reading, writing, and speaking—but this changed with the rise of the *universities. University students were older and generally more literate than those of the cathedral schools, so that the teaching of grammar

and rhetoric was restricted to short introductory courses. Added to this, great advances were made in logic itself in the schools of northern Europe in the 13th and 14th c., especially at the universities of Paris and Oxford, with the result that the Logic component replaced parts of the teaching in Grammar and Rhetoric. At this stage, the Trivium was commonly described as Grammar, Rhetoric, and Dialectic—a branch of Logic. Logic became more abstruse, and was directed towards higher studies, for example in natural philosophy and theology.

The subjects of the Quadrivium were individually taught from before the time of Aristotle, but their medieval grouping originates primarily with Martianus Capella's *De Nuptiis Philologiæ et Mercurii* (see ***Marcian**). In this he was echoed by Boethius (*Boece) and Cassiodorus, and the cathedral schools of Europe followed their plan. In the absence of strong mathematical and scientific traditions, and dominated by Platonic and Augustinian influences, the universities taught the Quadrivium in a somewhat literary way—well illustrated by the highly influential astronomical textbook of John of Sacrobosco. Several factors contrived to change this situation, especially from the mid-13th c. onwards. Most of the work of Aristotle became available, and that of his commentator Averroes. Many hitherto unknown Greek texts became available, largely through Arabic intermediaries. Many original Muslim contributions to the sciences became known in the West, largely through Spain. Astronomical writings and *tables were particularly important for raising the European scientific consciousness, even in other subjects—such as arithmetic and natural philosophy, through the introduction of similar formal techniques.

The universities of Paris and Oxford had long been the principal centres of activity in the subjects of the Quadrivium in Chaucer's day. Merton College in Oxford was the most important English centre of such activities in the 14th c., and it is likely that he was familiar with, and influenced by, several scholars other than Ralph *Strode from that college. (See also ***astrology and astronomy**.)

[JDN]

Catto (1984 and 1992); H. de Ridder-Symoens (1996); Bishop (1979).

Seven Sages of Rome, collection of tales within a frame: each of the 'seven sages' tells a tale to the Emperor Diocletian to save the life of the emperor's son, falsely accused of treachery by his stepmother, who herself narrates further tales between those of the sages. The English version in short rhyming couplets survives in nine manuscripts, five of them closely related, whose origins on linguistic grounds seem to be in or near London; one of these manuscripts is the *Auchinleck MS which may have been known to Chaucer. The English text derives from a French prose version.

[AH]

ed. Brunner (1933).

SHAKESPEARE, WILLIAM (1564–1616), dramatist and poet, left no extended formal criticism of Chaucer (although the Prologue of *Two Noble Kinsmen* remarks that he is 'of all admired') but evidently read his poetry with care and understanding. It is easier to indicate general parallels than to identify precise echoes or allusions, but of a number of Chaucer's poems that he made use of, two in particular stand out. *Troilus and Criseyde* with its dramatic telling of a story of doomed love invited transformation into a play, and the story had become a widely known and popular one. Already at the beginning of the 16th c. the Children of the Chapel Royal presented the 'Story of Troylous and Pandor' and there are references to a number of later plays now lost, as well as allusions in extant plays to the story. Shakespeare's *Troilus and Cressida* differs in many ways from Chaucer's poem, but an earlier critical scepticism about his knowledge and understanding of it has given way to a more informed and sympathetic approach. Shakespeare made use of other 'Trojan' material in his story of war and love, but it is deeply indebted to Chaucer. He responded to the ambiguity and the vulnerability of Chaucer's heroine, and recent criticism has argued that he went some way toward rescuing her from the bad reputation she had acquired by the end of the 16th c. Chaucer's *Troilus* also seems to have played an important imaginative role in the making of *Romeo and Juliet,* although it is not the main 'source' of the story. The *Knight's Tale,* which was very popular in the 16th and 17th c. is the direct source of Shakespeare and Fletcher's *Two Noble Kinsmen.* The story of Palamon and Arcite had previously been given dramatic form by Richard Edwardes (1566) and in a play recorded as having been presented by the Admiral's Men in 1594. Shakespeare brings out the darker and pessimistic qualities in this tale of the uneasy relationship of love and friendship. *The Knight's Tale* probably also influenced *The Two Gentlemen of Verona,* another story of love and friendship, and certainly *A *Midsummer Night's Dream,* to which it gives the figures of Theseus and Hippolyta and their relationship to young lovers. The story of *Pyramus and Thisbe, told by *Ovid and by Chaucer, is the subject of the mechanicals' play, and it has been argued (by Donaldson) that this is an 'inspired re-creation' of Chaucer's *Sir Thopas,* a burlesque of old-fashioned style and literary form. Unlike Thopas, Bottom wins the 'elf-queen'. It may well be that the less than romantic presentation of Pluto, the king of 'Fayerye', and his wife Proserpina in *The *Merchant's Tale* provided Shakespeare with models for his Oberon and Titania. Interestingly, just before they are introduced in that tale, there is a reference to Pyramus and Thisbe as an example of how love will always contrive to find a way (IV.2125–31). There is a touch of cynicism in the play's treatment of love, but as in Chaucer disparate tones are held together. Both writers show an awareness of the irresponsibilities, absurdities, and extremes of romantic *love ('Who may been a fool but if he love?'; 'Lord, what fools these mortal be!'), but with it a tolerance and sympathy for young love.

Shakespeare in his last plays also shares Chaucer's interest in fortitude and *patience in the face of great and undeserved suffering. It is possible that *The *Clerk's Tale* and *The *Man of Law's Tale* may have influenced *The Winter's Tale* and *Pericles* (which is based on a story in *Gower, but recalls the sufferings of Custance in *MLT*). Other echoes may be more elusive or fleeting—'mine host of the garter' in *The Merry Wives of Windsor* may recall Chaucer's Host of Southwark, and some intriguing similarities between Falstaff and the *Wife of Bath have been noted—but we should not underestimate the effects of Shakespeare's reading of Chaucer or his knowledge of his general medieval inheritance. He may not have known that the story of *As You Like It* which he

found in Lodge's romance *Rosalynde* derived ultimately from the medieval romance of *Gamelyn*,
but he was aware of earlier literary forms (like the
*romance) or images (like those of *death). Simi-
larities with Chaucer in his treatment of topics
such as love, or *nature, or *fortune suggest a
world-view still not radically different (and, if
recent suggestions of an early involvement with
Catholicism are correct, one which was very close
indeed). In later criticism he was linked with
Chaucer as part of a great tradition of poetry, and
similarities as well as differences were constantly
noted: in *characterization, in the use of both
*irony and pathos, in a delight in human variety, in
the mingling of 'earnest' and '*game'.

    E. T. Donaldson (1985); A. Thompson (1978);
Cooper (1989), 420–4; Windeatt (1992), 360–82.

Sheene (*LGW* 497), the royal residence at Sheen
(now part of Richmond, Surrey). After the death
of Queen *Anne (of Bohemia), *Richard II
ordered it to be demolished.

Sheffeld, Sheffield, already famous for its steel, of
which the knife of the miller in *The Reeve's Tale*
was made (I.3933).

Shipman, The, described in lines 388–410 of the
General Prologue. Only a few details of his
appearance are given (e.g. that he has a dagger
around his neck and under his arm, and that the
hot summer had made his complexion brown),
but a vivid personality emerges. As sailors were
sometimes reputed to be, he is skilled in thieving
(of wine, while the merchant slept)—'of nyce
[scrupulous] conscience took he no kepe'. He has
an abrupt and ruthless way of dealing with his
defeated enemies: 'by water he sente hem hoom to
every lond.' He is a very experienced and skilled
mariner, who knew all the techniques of navigation. The remarks that he lived 'fer by weste' and
was 'of Dartmouth' (*Dertemouthe) (perhaps
because it was a haunt of pirates) and that his ship
was called 'the Maudelayne' (a ship of that name is
recorded as sailing out of Dartmouth) have
encouraged commentators to look for possible
connections with real-life 14th-c. mariners with
piratical records or tendencies, such as Piers Risshenden or Risselden, associated with a notorious

buccaneer John Hawley, or John Piers of Teign-
mouth, who in 1383 captured a ship called the
Magdeleyn. It may well be that men such as these
gave Chaucer some hints for the portrait.

    Rv 815; Cooper (1989), 48–9; Mann (1973),
170–2.

Shipman's Tale, The (434 lines in couplets), the
opening tale of Fragment VII. A rich *merchant
lives at Saint-Denis (*Seint-Denys) with his
beautiful wife. He is a hospitable man, and among
his frequent guests is a *monk, Daun John, a close
friend who claims kinship since he was born in the
same village. The merchant has to go to Bruges
(*Brugges) on business, and invites the monk to
visit him and his wife before he leaves. On the
third day while the merchant is in his counting-
house doing his accounts, Daun John walks in the
garden and meets the wife. She complains of
the miserable life she has with her husband, and
the monk confesses that he had only claimed to
be the merchant's cousin in order to be close to
her. She has a debt, she says, which must be paid
by the following Sunday, and pleads with the
monk to lend her the 100 franks needed to save her
from dishonour. The monk promises to produce
the money while her husband is away, and kisses
the wife passionately. Before the husband leaves,
Daun John takes him aside and asks him for a loan
of 100 marks for a week or two for the purchase
of some animals. The merchant generously
agrees. The monk returns to his abbey and the
merchant goes off to Bruges. On Sunday Daun
John comes back to Saint-Denis, and in exchange
for the 100 francs spends the night with the wife,
and returns to the abbey. The husband comes
home, and tells his wife that he has had to make
a pledge for 20,000 'shields' (*écus*) and to raise
the money he will need to go to friends in Paris.
His first call is on Daun John, who receives him
warmly, and tells him that he is not rich but
that he has returned the merchant's 100 francs
to the wife. The merchant manages to raise his
loan, and returns home in high spirits. In bed with
his wife he confesses to being a little annoyed that
she did not tell him about Daun John's repayment.
She brazenly curses the wicked monk—she had
thought that it was a gift intended for her and she
has spent it all. Do not be angry, she says,

'ye shal my joly body have to wedde [pledge]'. She will only pay him in bed. The merchant sees that there is no remedy, and tells her not to be so generous in future.

The tale is not obviously appropriate (or inappropriate) to the *Shipman, and it is often thought to have been originally intended for a female narrator, probably the Wife of Bath. The feminine pronouns in the passage about 'the sely housbonde' near the beginning (10–19) ('he moot *us* clothe, he moot *us* arraye', etc.) have been taken as evidence of a not completely revised text, although it is just possible that they may be part of a male narrator's impersonation or imitation of a woman's voice. The tale is a *fabliau, and one closer to the usual model than the other examples in *The Canterbury Tales* with their various elaborations and transformations. In particular, the plot is of prime importance. The story is an example of the narrative motif of 'the lover's gift returned', with a clever addition in the conclusion, when the wife proves herself as tricky as her lover, and gives an original twist to the notion of the 'marriage debt'. It is an excellent example of Chaucer's narrative art. The plain unfussy style allows the neatness of the plot, and its various ironies, to emerge clearly. Everything is carefully controlled. The emotions of the characters are normally hidden beneath a proper and undramatic exterior, but occasionally break out in moments of great excitement. When the wife has received the monk's promise of money, and his embrace, she goes off 'as jolif as a pye [magpie]' to hurry the cooks up and to knock on her husband's office door 'boldly' to get him down to dine (208–23). When he has been successful in raising money, her husband's sexual excitement is aroused (373 ff.). It is never cruel or violent: for all their trickiness the figures remain surprisingly human. There are no bravura passages, but the brief dramatic scenes are highly sophisticated. In the exchange between the monk and the wife in the garden, the emotions beneath the surface are delicately suggested: the monk blushes at his own slightly risqué remarks on old husbands (111), and stares at the wife when she then speaks vehemently (124). The satirical stereotype of the avaricious merchant is transformed in the evocation of the counting-house into which he retreats, shutting the door and shutting out the world, to place his books and bags before him, like a small-town Volpone (75–88) or in his slightly aggrieved and patient exposition to his wife of the 'curious bisynesse' of merchants and how they stand in fear of 'hap and fortune' in their 'chapmanhede' (224–38). Money and sex together dominate the tale. It is perhaps over-crude to say that they are identified: rather, they lovingly (or lustfully) embrace. Sexual puns and inuendoes flow as easily as the favours and friendships oiled by generosity and well-timed gifts. It is an amoral world in which cleverness seems to be the one essential virtue, but the tale is outrageously funny—not least (Copland) in the exhilarating 'impudence of the wife's totally materialistic challenge to familiar pieties and decencies'.

(ed.) *Rv* 203–8, 910–13; *S&A* 439–46; Cooper (1989), 278–86; Copland (1966); Hahn (1986); Pearsall (1985), 209–17; Scattergood (1976–7).

SHIRLEY, JOHN (?c.1366–1456), a scribe whose copies of the poems of Chaucer and Lydgate were important for the dissemination of these texts in the later 15th and the 16th c. He was an esquire in the service of Richard Beauchamp, earl of Warwick, and maintained his connection with the household after he settled in London in the 1430s. He was familiar with courtly life and literature, and in his rubrics and annotations gives information on attributions and contexts of poems, sometimes probably gossip, and sometimes of variable reliability. Probably his copying was a personal rather than a commercial activity: there seems to be no certain evidence to support the theory that he was a kind of stationer or publisher.

Connolly (1998); A. I. Doyle (1961).

Sibyle, the Sibyl at Cumae, a prophetess who accompanied Aeneas to the underworld (*HF* 439).

Sibille, apparently used as another name for Cassandra (*Cassandre) rather than as a generic description ('prophetess') (*Tr* V.1450).

Sidyngbourne, Sittingbourne, a town in Kent between Rochester and Canterbury (III.847).

SIDNEY, SIR PHILIP (1554–86) in his *An Apology for Poetry* (?1581–3) makes a number of references to Chaucer, whom he sees as a 'fore-goer', with Gower, of the poets who have beauti-fied 'our mother tongue', notably his (somewhat qualified) praise of *Troilus and Criseyde*, a poem especially popular in the 16th c.: 'Chaucer, undoubtedly, did excellently in his *Troilus and Criseyde*: of whom, truly, I know not whether to marvel more, either that he in that misty time could see so clearly, or that we in this clear age walk so stumblingly after him. Yet had he great wants, fit to be forgiven in so reverent antiquity'.

    (ed.) Shepherd (1965).

Siege of Thebes, The, a poem by John *Lydgate (perhaps more appropriately entitled, as it is in a number of MSS, 'The Destruction of Thebes'), usually dated 1420–2, is a dark retelling of the tragic story, with many scenes of pathos, and passages which show an anxious awareness of the horrors of war and disruption. It is introduced by a prologue, lighter in tone, in which Lydgate imagines himself at Canterbury with the pilgrims, and being asked by the Host to tell the first tale on the return journey— 'some tale of myrth or of gladnesse'. Lydgate offers instead a rather pessimistic parallel to and excursus on the Theban history behind *The *Knight's Tale*, the first of the original set of stories.

    (ed.) Erdmann and Ekwall (1911, 1930); Pearsall (1970); Simpson (1997).

signe, sign (of the Zodiac). The Zodiac (see **Zodiak**) or *ecliptic had from ancient times been divided into twelve equal parts, or signs, each of 30 degrees extent, commencing from the head of Aries and continuing in the direction of the Sun's annual motion. (The Sun is at head of Aries at the spring equinox. The ecliptic crosses the celestial equator there.) The names of the divisions were taken from the constellations that were situated in them at the time. With the precession of the equinoxes (known in the Middle Ages as the 'movement of the eighth sphere') the constella-tions drifted away from the twelve signs to which they had given their names, although the original names were always retained—thus giving rise to ambiguity (see *Scorpio). Chaucer refers in due course to each of the twelve signs, typically using the following names (the order here is that of the signs themselves): *Aries (also *Ram); *Taur (see

also *Bole); *Gemini; *Cancre; *Leo; *Virgo; *Libra; *Scorpio; Sagittarius; *Capricorne; *Aquarie; *Pisces (see also *Fyssh). (See also **astrology and astronomy;** *constellacio(u)n.)   [JDN]

Signifer, the *Zodiac (L. 'a bearer of signs'), *Troilus* V.1020.

Silla, Scylla, who became infatuated with Minos of Crete who was besieging *Alcathoe, the city of her father *Nisus. She cut off a purple lock of her father's hair on which the safety of his realm depended, and offered it to Minos. He refused it in horror and forbade her to come to Crete. She leapt into the water to swim after his ship, and was attacked by her father, transformed into an osprey. She too was changed into a bird called *ciris* (or shearer). The story is told by Ovid in *Metamor-phoses* 8. Chaucer tells it briefly in *The Legend of Good Women* 1908–20, emphasizing Minos's cruelty, and omitting the transformation. That however is alluded to in *Tr* V.1110, where 'Nysus doughter song with fressh entente' at dawn. Here she seems to be a lark (a detail which Chaucer may have found in a gloss or in the *Ovide moralisé*). Scylla also appears among the lovers in the temple of *Venus (*PF* 292).

SYMACHUS, Quintus Aurelius Memmius Symmachus, consul in 485, the father-in-law of Boethius (*Boece), who puts a warm praise of his virtue and wisdom into the mouth of Lady Philosophy (*Bo* II pr.4:26).

Symkyn (diminutive form of) Symond. Simon, the miller in *The *Reeve's Tale*.

Symois, Simoïs, a river near *Troy (*Tr* IV.1548).

Simon Magus, a sorcerer (Acts 8) who was con-verted to Christianity, but later offered the apos-tles money for the power of the Spirit (8: 18–24). In *The *House of Fame* (1274) he is among the sorcer-ers. It is possible that he is, or is lurking beneath, the 'Seint *Symoun' of the exasperated sick man confronted by the grasping friar in *The *Summoner's Tale* (III.2094).

Simon the Pharisee (Luke 7:37–50), who invited Jesus to his house but complained about the sinful

Simony

woman who washed and anointed his feet. She was later identified with Mary *Magdalene. The *Parson refers to this episode in his discussion of 'grucchyng' or murmuring (X.504).

Symond, see *Symkyn.

Simony, named from *Simon Magus, Acts 8:9–24, who attempted to obtain spiritual power from Peter and the apostles for money; hence *simony* describes any action of obtaining advancement in the Church or any spiritual advantage (e.g. absolution) by means of payment or bribery of any sort; both the payer and the recipient in such a transaction were regarded as guilty of the crime. The Parson (X.780–90) gives an account similar to the above, and adds the opinion of Pope Damasus that, after the sin of Lucifer and Antichrist, simony is the worst. Almost every writer in the medieval period condemns the sin, which, they all agree, was rife in almost every transaction involving the Church or its members. [AH]

Symoun, Seint, by whom Thomas in The *Summoner's Tale* swears (III.2094), may be St Simon the apostle, but may well be, or contain an ironic punning reference to, *Simon Magus.

simphonye, see *musical instruments.

Symplicius Gallus, Sulpicius Gallus, a Roman who, according to the story in *Valerius Maximus, left his wife because he found her looking out of the door with her head uncovered. *Jankyn (4) tells it to the *Wife of Bath (III.643–6).

Synay, the Old Testament Mt. Sinai, where Moses (*Moyses) fasted (III.1887).

Syno(u)n, Sinon, the Greek who persuaded the Trojans to take the great horse inside the walls of Troy. Like *Judas and Ganelon (*Genelloun), he became a standard exemplary figure of treachery. Chaucer refers to him a number of times (V.209; *HF* 152; *LGW* 931); the fox in The Nun's Priest's Tale is called 'false dissymulour . . . Greke Synon' (VII.3228).

Sir Eglamour, a 14th-c. romance in tail-rhyme stanzas which seems to have been extremely popular. It concerns the love of Eglamour for Christabelle, the daughter of the earl of Artois, and the three quests he must perform before he can win her father's consent. It is full of wonderful (and traditional) motifs—magic swords and rings, the falsely accused princess, etc. It is related to the type of story found in The *Man of Law's Tale* and may well have been one of the romances which Chaucer echoes in *Sir Thopas.
  (ed.) F. Richardson (1965).

Sir Gawain and the Green Knight, found, together with *Pearl, Patience* and *Purity* (or *Cleanness*) in British Library Cotton Nero A.x; a *romance in alliterative long lines, divided into stanzas by use of a concluding 'bob and wheel' (a short line with single stress, followed by three rhyming lines with two stresses). It has been suggested that in Chaucer's *Squire's Tale* the description of the arrival of 'a knyght upon a steede of bras' (V.76–109), especially because of its comparison of the knight's behaviour with that of Gawain, may have been influenced by the description of the arrival of the Green Knight at the beginning of this poem. [AH]
  (ed.) Tolkien and Gordon, rev. Davis (1968).

Sir Launfal, one of the subgroup of Middle English romances described as a Breton lay; this is one of only two for which the French source (though not the Breton original, if such ever existed) survives. Parallels have been noted with Chaucer's tale of *Sir Thopas, and the poem may have provided the model for Chaucer's form of the tail-rhyme stanza in this poem. [AH]
  (ed.) Bliss (1960); R. S. Loomis in *S&A* 486 ff.

Sir Orfeo, like *Sir Launfal, one of the subgroup of Middle English romances described as a *Breton lay, in this case telling a version of the classical Orpheus legend crossed with a Celtic story of similar type; it survives in three manuscripts, the earliest being the *Auchinleck MS, which, it has been suggested, Chaucer may have seen. The beginning of the text is now missing from Auchinleck, because of the excision of columns containing illuminated initials, but it may have included a description of the nature of Breton lays similar to that attached to *Sir Orfeo* in the other two copies; this could have given Chaucer some of the information found in the *Franklin's Prologue* (V.709–15).   [AH]

(ed.) Bliss (1966); R. S. Loomis in *S&A* 486 ff.

Sir Perceval of Galles, a 14th-c. Middle English *romance in *tail-rhyme stanzas, tells the story of the youthful hero, who is not here connected with the Holy Grail as he usually is. When his father is killed by the Red Knight, his mother brings up her infant son in the woods in an attempt to prevent him from ever learning about the knightly life. This is, predictably, not successful. Perceval goes to Arthur's court, kills the Red Knight, becomes a knight himself, and rescues and marries Lufamour of Maydenlande. Other exploits include the killing of the Black Knight, and a giant, and the rescue of his mother, who, thinking her son dead, has gone mad with grief in the woods. Chaucer's reference to 'the knight sire Percyvell' in *Sir Thopas* is probably an allusion to this romance.

(ed.) French and Hale (1930).

Sir Thopas (206 lines in *tail-rhyme stanza) follows *The *Prioress's Tale* in Fragment VII, and is told by Chaucer himself—until he is interrupted by the Host. In the manner of popular minstrel romances, of which it is a burlesque imitation, it is divided into 'fits' or sections, each beginning with a call to attention. The first ('Listeth, lordes, in good entent') introduces the hero, Sir Thopas, and gives a gently comic description of his appearance. Many maidens yearn for him 'paramour', but he is chaste 'and no lechour'. One day he rides out through a fair forest and is suddenly smitten with love-longing (apparently brought on by the singing of the thrush). He decides that he will love an 'elf-queene', for no woman in this world is worthy to be his mate, and goes off in search of one. He is challenged by a great giant, Sir Olifaunt. The Second Fit sees Thopas preparing for battle. Minstrels and tale-tellers are summoned, wine and sweetmeats brought, and the knight is armed. The third Fit begins with a promise of battle, chivalry and 'love-drury' [courtship], and a list of famous heroes of romance, who are all eclipsed by Thopas who bears the flower of royal chivalry. As

'a knyght auntrous' he preferred to sleep out of doors with his bright helm as pillow: like Sir Perceval he drank water from the spring, until one day . . . But here the Host has had enough and abruptly stops Chaucer, complaining of his 'rym dogerel'. The Host is literally right, but (as we the readers are allowed to see) has missed the main point: the tale is deliberately and exquisitely awful. No plot summary can give a real sense of the delicate and clever comedy. It is never too obvious: indeed it is possible to argue about the exact point of some apparent jokes. It seems likely, for instance, that Chaucer thought '"Poperyng', the name of Thopas's birthplace, comic sounding: it may be that he thought Flanders (*Flaundres) a mundane and mercantile place for the setting of a romance (the phrase 'in fer contree' would arouse expectations of a more exotic land). There seems to be a mixture of plausible and absurd detail, so that in context everything (or almost everything) comes to sound slightly off-key and comic. Sometimes it is the ponderous listing of detail after detail (as in the ceremonial arming of the hero), sometimes it is the use of a final (and banal) short line to underline a detail not usually noticed in romance ('he hadde a semely nose') to achieve the 'art of sinking' in poetry. It is a burlesque, but a loving burlesque. Chaucer carefully imitates the metre, the diction, and style (using set formulae 'bright in bour') and the story motifs (lover knight, giant, the arming of the hero, the mysterious elf-queen) of popular romances. It seems to be full of echoes of such romances as *Guy of Warwick, Bevis of Hamton, *Sir Launfal, *Sir Perceval of Galles, *Sir Eglamour, and others. In the 18th c. Bishop Hurd (*Letters on Chivalry and Romance*, 1762) recognized the tale as 'a sort of prelude to the adventures of Don Quixot': Chaucer 'not only discerned the absurdity of the old romances, but has even ridiculed them with incomparable spirit'. (See also *parody and burlesque.)

(ed.) *Rv* 212–17, 917–22; *S&A* 486–560; Cooper (1989), 299–309; Burrow (1971); Pearsall (1985), 160–5.

Syrien, see *Seryens.

Syrius, Sirius, the Dog Star (*Bo* I m.5:28) (see *Alhabor).

Sysile, Sicily, mentioned only in the translation of Boethius (*Boece), as the realm of the tyrant Dionysius of Syracuse (*Bo* III pr.5:24).

Sytheo, Sychaeus, the deceased husband of *Dido (*LGW* 1005).

Sytho, strem of (*LGW* 2508), the Thracian current (Ovid's 'Sythonis unda', after Sithon, King of Thrace, who was in fact the father of Phyllis). The name caused the scribes great trouble: the form 'sytho' is an emendation, not found in any MS. Cowan and Kane (1995) read 'Sito[nie]'.

SKEAT, W. W. (1835–1912), from 1878 Professor of Anglo-Saxon at Cambridge, was encouraged by *Furnivall to work for the Early English Text Society. He went on to produce monumental editions of Langland and Chaucer. Six volumes of *The Complete Works of Geoffrey Chaucer* appeared in 1894. Volume vii (1897) containing 'Chaucerian and Other pieces' printed texts of Thomas *Usk and of 15th-c. 'Chaucerian poems' which were not easily available (his *The Chaucer Canon* (1900) was a major contribution to the task of establishing the authentic works). Skeat's was undoubtedly the best edition of Chaucer hitherto produced, and became the basis for all subsequent work. The Notes are especially learned and still very useful. His somewhat eclectic treatment of the text is open to criticism. Though he consulted many (but not all) manuscripts, the reasons for some (usually intuitive) editorial decisions were not always made clear. Nevertheless it 'marks the beginning of a new epoch in Chaucer scholarship, signalling the beginning of its modern age'.

A. S. G. Edwards (1984).

SKELTON, JOHN, the Tudor poet and satirist (?1460–1529), places an elaborate praise of Chaucer 'that famus clerke' in the mouth of Jane Scrope in *Philip Sparowe*, one of his earlier poems: 'His mater is delectable, | Solacyous and commendable ... | His termes were not darke, | But plesaunt, easy and playne; | Ne worde he wrote in vayne.' She is made to show a good knowledge of Chaucer's poetry and of its diversity—'the Tales of Caunterbury | Some sad [serious] storyes, some mery'. She comments on the Wife of Bath,

Troilus and Criseyde, and Pandarus, and refers to other Chaucerian figures. Skelton had obviously read Chaucer *in extenso*. The *House of Fame* is part of the literary background of *The Garlande of Laurell*. In that poem, among the poets that appear are three English ones, Gower, Chaucer, and Lydgate, who promise to bring Skelton before the Queen of Fame (386–448). Skelton praises Chaucer for his polished eloquence that 'oure Englysshe rude so fresschely hath set out'.

(ed.) Scattergood (1983).

SOCRATES, the Greek philosopher (*c*.469–399 BC) who was charged with introducing new deities and corrupting the youth of Athens, and condemned to death by drinking poison. From Plato, medieval writers knew in general of him as a great philosopher, and as an example of *patience in adversity. In Chaucer, he appears in *Boece: in I pr.3 Lady Philosophy says he won victory in his 'unryghtful deth' with her at his side, and that he suffered for despising vain pursuits according to her teaching; and in the following prose she records approvingly his ruling that it is wrong to assent to falsehood and conceal truth. Elsewhere, his death is written in the stars (II.194–203). He appears as an example of steadfastness and of indifference to Fortune. The dreamer in The *Book of the Duchess* urges the man in black to remember Socrates 'for he counted nat thre strees [straws] | Of noght that Fortune koude doo' (717–19). In *Fortune* (17–24) there is an invocation to him as a steadfast champion who never feared the oppression and torments of Fortune. A less solemn example occurs in The *Wife of Bath's Prologue* (III.727–32) when Jankin recalls the care and the woe that Socrates had with his wives, and how when *Xantippa 'caste pisse upon his heed', he 'sat stille as he were deed', wiped his head, and only dared say 'Er the thonder stynte [stops], comth a reyn'.

Sol, the Sun (L.), the metal gold, in alchemical symbolism (as noted by the *Canon's Yeoman). (See also *alchemy.) [JDN]

Soler Halle, the Cambridge college in The *Reeve's Tale* is probably King's Hall, later merged in Trinity College. The name refers to the number of solars (rooms admitting sunlight) which it contained. The introductory phrase 'men clepen' ('which people call', I.3990) may suggest that Chaucer is deliberately giving it a name which is not the official one.

Bennett (1974); Cobban (1988).

Solomon, see *Salomon.

solsticioun, solsticium, the solstice (L. *solstitium*). Either of the two points in the year at which the sun reaches its greatest distance from the celestial equator: it is furthest north at the summer solstice (marking the beginning of summer) and furthest south at the winter solstice (the beginning of winter). (See also *equinoxiall; *months and seasons; *yere.)   [JDN]

SOMER, J., John Somer (*fl.* 1380–1403), a Franciscan friar who had entered the order at the Bridgwater convent (Somerset), but who was at the Oxford convent by 1380 and was still there in 1395. A star *table of his is extant, dated 1403. (It is of a Ptolemaic type that Chaucer may be shown to have used in another recension.) There is an outside chance that John Somer was the Franciscan of whom Jacob Cnoyen spoke long afterwards as having travelled in arctic latitudes in 1360; he is purported to have surveyed with an astrolabe.

In a treatise standing in a long tradition of calendar reform, John Somer criticized the state of the ecclesiastical calendar, but he also composed his own calendar for Joan, princess of Wales, mother of Richard II. In his introduction to *A Treatise on the *Astrolabe*, Chaucer referred to his intention of drawing from this, and from the calendar of Nicholas of Lynn (see *Lenne), for the third part of his own treatise; but the promise seems to have remained unfulfilled.

Like Nicholas of Lynn's, the new calendar was occasioned by the fact that a new lunæ-solar (nineteen-year) cycle began in 1387. Both calendars contained extensive tables for the Sun and Moon, eclipses, *ascensions, and other astronomical material, in addition to the conventional ecclesiastical calendar. (See also *Kalendere.)   [JDN]

Somnium Scipionis; songs. See *Drem of Scipioun*; *lyrics.

Sonne, Sunne, Sun (possessive Sonnes). In the Aristotelian and Ptolemaic cosmological systems, working outwards from the Earth, the Sun came next after Venus. In Ptolemaic astronomy its annual motion is well described by a single eccentric, that is, without an *epicycle. It is not surprising that of the three hundred or so references to the Sun in Chaucer's writings, nearly half of them are in *A Treatise on the *Astrolabe*. There are also many in *Boece and *Equatorie of the Planetis*. An equatorium provides the solar positions during the year; the astrolabe can do almost as well (with the calendar scale on the back). It is also capable of providing the Sun's *longitude from observation, but is primarily used for determining the hour and minute of the day, the solar longitude having been found from the calendar scale or from tables.

There are in Chaucer's poetry many simple comparisons drawn with the Sun—the shining of a golden bridle, of coin, and so forth—and with everyday situations involving the Sun; but quite apart from them, there are numerous occasions when the Sun is used, either straightforwardly or with periphrasis, to provide a season, a date, or a time. (The best-known example comes near the beginning of the *General Prologue*, where the Sun's position in Aries is stated obliquely.) On occasion this is done with considerable astronomical precision, as when Chaucer tacitly makes use of *Kalendarium* of Nicholas of Lynn (see *Lenne) in quoting a solar altitude, in *The *Nun's Priest's Tale*.

Astrologically, the Sun is hot and dry. It has its *domicile in *Cancer and its exaltation in *Aries. Astrologically speaking, the Sun is a neutral object under the sway of other planets, and generally Chaucer relies on its innate brilliance, rather than any familiar astrological doctrine, to give colour in solar personification. A good example of this is in the Proem to the *The Complaint of *Mars*, where the Sun is described merely as a '*candel* of jelosye'. In the *Complaint* itself, however, the Sun—as Phebus—plays a very precise astrological role, and there is a similarly hidden solar allegory in *The *Nun's Priest's Tale*, involving the Sun's position in the Zodiac, adjacent to the Pleiades, and representing his wives. (See also *day; *exaltacioun; *hed; *months and seasons; *Phebus; *yere.)   [JDN]

sons, see ***families**; ***children**.

Sophie ('Wisdom') the daughter of *Melibeus and *Prudence.

Soranas (*Bo* I pr.3:57). The reference alludes to men like Marcus Barea Soranus, a just and virtuous governor of Asia who was forced to commit suicide by *Nero.

sound. Chaucer makes much play with sound, whether it be the 'soun of minstralsye' and 'songes amorous of maryage' at one extreme of politeness or, at the other, the Summoner's recurrent reference to sounds produced at the other end of the body. In his *Complaint to his *Purse*, Chaucer looks forward to the sound it may make; in The Legend of Cleopatra the canon goes off with 'grysely soun'; and the pleasures of harmonious sound are occasionally emphasized by the introduction of *Venus, since she is traditionally responsible for all melody. It is in *The *House of Fame*, however, that Chaucer treats sound almost as a subject in its own right—using the word more than a score of times. The Eagle treats of sounds in his lecture: sounds, on his account, being of the nature of air, travel naturally upwards (in an Aristotelian *cosmology) to the House of Fame. This is not entirely conventional, but the Middle Ages did not have much to say of the theory of sound. In practical respects, it did much: witness the bells and organs, and the resonance chambers of large churches. The *Pardoner, however, did not need such an aid to make his 'hauteyn speche . . . rynge out as round as gooth a belle'. (See also *clokke; *science.) [JDN]

Southwerk, Southwark, across London Bridge on the south side of the Thames, where the *Tabard was situated (I.20), and where the road to Canterbury began.

Spaigne, Spayne. Spain occupies the second largest peninsula in Europe, named by the Greeks Iberia, and by the Romans Hispania, a legendary land with its gold-bearing River Tagus (*Bo* III m.10:12–13), its siren-infested Pillars of Hercules, and its giants, a particularly ferocious specimen of which, we are informed by Geoffrey of Monmouth (*Gaufride) in 1155, was vanquished by King

*Arthur on the Mont-Saint-Michel. The high percentage of mountainous areas in the Iberian Peninsula explains perhaps why Chaucer should have remembered this aspect of Spanish physical geography when situating his *House of Fame upon '"so hygh a roche | Hier stant ther none in Spayne"' (1116–17), nor is it surprising, considering that seven-eighths of the Peninsula's boundaries are washed by the seas, that his *Shipman should be well acquainted with 'every cryke . . . in Spayne' (I.409), such creeks (Spanish *rías*) being particularly characteristic of Galicia (*Galice, I.466), where one of the westernmost promontories of Europe, Cape Finisterre is situated, a locality likewise familiar to the Shipman (*Fynystere, I.408). Chaucer was probably aware too that Spain's finest natural harbour is that of Cartagena (*Cartage, I.404) in the Spanish Levant, *Cartago Nova* being established by one of the many peoples who have in turn, and sometimes simultaneously, partially occupied the Iberian Peninsula: Phoenicians, Celts, Greeks, Carthaginians, Romans, Visigoths, and Moors, these latter occupying and ruling over some parts of Spain for almost 800 years, 711–1492. For the final 250 years, however, the Muslims were confined to the kingdom of Granada (*Gernade, I.56), certain areas of which were gradually being reconquered: Chaucer's *Knight, for example, was present in 1344, when Alfonso XI of Castile, after a prolonged siege, finally recaptured the town of Algeciras (*Algezir, I.57). The last enclave of Iberian Islam, the city of Granada itself, however, fell to the Christians under the Catholic monarchs Ferdinand and Isabella of Aragon and Castile, as late as 1492.

The Moors, however, left behind then a cultural heritage many aspects of which are still patent in modern Iberian tastes and customs, not the least important being the large number of Arabic loanwords incorporated into the Peninsular languages, some of which, generally through French, in some instances perhaps directly from Spanish, found their way into Middle English. Thus, Chaucer's *Summoner's pimples are proof against *boras* and *tartre*, lexical items which likewise appear, together with *alkali* and *elixir in the *Canon's Yeoman's alchemical discourse. *Azimutz* (I.19.6), *cenyth* (I.18.6), *nadir* (II.6.1), and *almenak (Intro., 93) appear in the *Treatise on the *Astrolabe*, and Nicholas in *The *Miller's Tale* has his *Almageste* (I.3208) at his 'beddes heed'.

By the 14th c., Spanish *Navarre having been under French rule since 1234, the various kingdoms of the Iberian Peninsula had been reduced to the Moorish kingdom of Granada, and the Christian kingdoms of Portugal (independent of Castile since 1143), Aragon and Castile, this last thus named for the large number of castles (late L. *castella*) built on its borders against possible encroachments by the Moors, a characteristic feature subsequently associated with Spain in general, and reflected in the metaphorical expression already incorporated into the *Roman de la Rose*, c.1290, (2430), and translated by Chaucer (?) as 'Thou shalt make castels thanne in Spayne' (*Rom*. B. 2573). Only in 1479 was the union between Aragon and Castile finally achieved under the joint reign of Ferdinand and Isabella.

Politically speaking, a certain parallelism may be observed between the constitutional development of *England and that of Spain, where, as early as the 12th c., the kings of the different kingdoms would occasionally call to their *Cortes*, or parliaments, representatives of the towns, who thus constituted a third estate to be added to the nobles and the churchmen. From 1295, these representatives of the moneyed middle classes were invariably included in the Castilian *Cortes*, often meeting annually, the situation being similar in Aragon, where, however, a subdivision was established between the higher and the lesser nobility. As in England too, the vernacular tongue replaced Latin as the vehicle of records and literature in the 13th c., due, above all, to the influence of the celebrated and scholarly king of Castile, Alfonso X 'the Learned' (1221–84), who actively contributed to the achievements of the famous school of translators at Toledo, and was largely responsible for the composition of the *General Chronicle* of the Spanish people, of the '*tables tolletanes*' consulted by the magician in *The *Franklin's Tale* (V.1273) and personal author of 417 lyrical *Songs of the Virgin Mary* (see *Miracles of the Virgin Mary*), one of which (*Cantiga* 6) offers a number of striking similarities to *The *Prioress's Tale*.

Throughout the century, the two Spanish kingdoms produced, and traded with, their most characteristic commodities: commercially enterprising Aragon selling Catalan coral, wheat, textiles, leather, spices, and Valencian fruit and nuts, Castile, poorer and less commercially adventurous, dedicated to subsistence-level agriculture, but, particularly in the 14th c., exporting raw wool to England and Flanders (*Flaundres) (which Chaucer as customs Controller in the port of London would be familiar with), and developing a number of artisan industries such as ship-building, mercury-mining, the manufacture of arms and ceramics in Toledo, of soap and leather in Andalusia—no lesser a personage than Sir *Thopas wore 'shoon of cordowane' (VII.732), i.e. made of Cordovan leather—and, we have Chaucer's word for it, vintner's son as he was, likewise exporting Andalusian wines, such as the 'white wyn' of *Lepe, used to adulterate the choicer and more expensive French wines of Gascony and Guienne.

Castilian literature, like English literature, comes fully of age in the 14th c., in which a number of outstanding works are produced. As early as the 12th c., however, lyrical poetry of great refinement was being composed in Andalusia, whilst the first major work in Castilian, the epic *Poem of the Cid*, narrating the adventures of a real-life hero, a simple but enterprising Castilian knight, Don Rodrigo Díaz de Vivar (the 'Cid'), was composed in about 1140. (See also *Piers Alfonce*.) The 13th c. witnessed the rise of lyrical poetry in Castile in the verse translations of the monk, Gonzalo de Berceo (*c*.1200–1265), and in his charming *Miracles of Our Lady*, similar to the *Songs of the Virgin Mary* by Alfonso X mentioned above. These latter, however, were composed in the gentle Galician dialect, as were a large number of anonymous love poems, showing Provençal influence, dedicated to peasant girls, or to their laments for their absent lovers. In the mid-13th c., two anonymous Spanish verse translations were made of classical 'novels', *The Book of Apollonius* (*Appollonius) and that of *Alexander* (*Alysaundre), whilst towards the end, a characteristic Spanish prose style was being forged in Toledo for the translation of scholarly works from the Hebrew, Arabic, and Latin. In this period the major literary achievements in Catalan are the works of the polymath, Ramón Llull.

The lyrical tradition was carried on into the 14th c. by the Jewish poet, Don Semtob de Carrión (*fl.* 1340) whose delicate and sensuous verses were dedicated to the future Peter the Cruel of Castile (*Petro (1)), whose troubled reign likewise witnessed the rise of the *romance*, or ballad. The literary giants of the period, in all styles and metres, are, however, Juan *Ruiz, Don Juan *Manuel and Pero López de *Ayala, certain resemblances to all three of whom may be perceived in the life and works of Chaucer. Thus, both Chaucer's narrative poems, and Juan Ruiz's *Book of Good Love*, are characterized by the presence of the author as a participant in the action, and, therefore, by a conversational approach to the reader; similar too are their realistic, humorous, and often ironical attitudes to life, and, above all, to love, which figures prominently in the work of both writers, as is their deep-seated respect, in spite of this, for love and for its power to improve and refine the lover (cf. *Troilus) even where such love is unrequited (the Archpriest is rarely successful, the narrator of *Troilus and Criseyde* 'ne dar to Love . . . preyen'); both incorporate into their narratives characters from all walks of life, including a go-between in a major role (Trota-conventos and *Pandarus), as well as allegorical figures such as Don Amor and Doña Venus or Daun Cupido and Seynt Venus.

With Don Juan Manuel, Chaucer shares a familiarity with court life, possibly a preoccupation concerning careless copyists (cf. *Adam Scriveyn*—(*Adam (2)), and his choice, for his greatest work, of a specific narrative framework into which to insert a series of tales of varied provenance. Chaucer and Chancellor Ayala have in common their active professional life as courtiers and diplomats, in the service of a series of monarchs, their satire of ecclesiastical corruption, combined with a deep respect for authentic religious values (Ayala's Job, Chaucer's *Parson), their satire, indeed, of corruption at all social levels: if Chaucer's innkeepers adulterate their wine and his cooks reheat their pies, Ayala's merchants, in deliberately darkened shops, sell Rouen lace for Mechlin! Doctors and lawyers, according to both authors, try to show off their book-learning, but their 'finos amores', says the Spaniard, are really directed exclusively to money. The two writers obviously have similar literary interests, both translating Boethius's (*Boece) *De consolatione* into the vernacular, both attracted to *Boccaccio, whose *De casibus virorum illustrium* the Chancellor translated into Spanish, and whose *Filostrato* Chaucer adapted for his Trojan love story, this latter providing another bond, since, in fact, López de Ayala translated *Guido delle Colonne's *Historia Trojana* into Spanish. Finally, Ayala's most celebrated *Chronicle* is that of King Peter the Cruel, a character in whose fate Chaucer was obviously profoundly interested (cf. *Petro (1)).

Indeed, it has been suggested that Chaucer and López de Ayala might actually have met, when the latter was captured by the English at the battle of Nájera, for the discovery of Chaucer's safe-conduct, dated 1366, to travel through *Navarre, has naturally led to speculation as to what he might have been doing in Spain. Going on a pilgrimage to Seint-Jame (2) is one possibility, but, his interest, precisely, in the affairs of Peter the Cruel would seem to suggest a diplomatic motive: recalling English mercenaries from the service of Peter's half-brother and enemy, the count of Trastámara perhaps, or preparing the way for the passage through Navarre of the Black Prince's troops who, in 1367, were to support King Peter's cause and be victorious at Nájera. Indeed, since John of Gaunt likewise formed part of this Spanish expedition, and Chaucer was in his service, it is not entirely impossible that he may himself have been present at the battle. His interest in Petro may have been due to this circumstance therefore, (although this is mere speculation!), or to the fact that, John of Gaunt having married King Peter's daughter, Costanza, she may well have talked to her lady-in-waiting, Philippa Chaucer, of her father, whose 'pitous deeth' thus became immortalized not only in López de Ayala's magnificent *Chronicle*, but also in The *Canterbury Tales*.   [PS]

Shaw (1992).

Speculum Stultorum ('The Mirror of Fools'), a Latin verse satire by Nigel Whiteacre (later corrupted to Wireker), a Benedictine monk of Canterbury (b. *c.*1140), against other religious orders. It tells of the adventures of an ass, Burnellus, who wants a longer tail. At one point he is told the story of a cock who takes revenge on Gundulfus a priest's son who has damaged its leg. Chaucer alludes to this in the lines on 'Daun Burnel the Asse' in The *Nun's Priest's Tale (VII.3312–19), placed in the mouth of the fox. Later Burnellus decides to become a monk, but after reviewing the orders on offer, decides to found his own. It is very likely that this lively and irreverent satire was an important inspiration for Chaucer's imagination and technique.

(ed.) Mozley and Raymo (1960); (trans.) Mozley (1961); Regenos (1959); Rigg (1992), 102–5; Mann (1974–5).

SPEGHT, THOMAS (*fl.* 1600), read Chaucer when a student at Peterhouse, Cambridge. He later became a schoolmaster and a canon of Ely Cathedral. In 1598 he produced an edition of Chaucer, *The Workes of our Antient and Learned English Poet, Geffrey Chaucer*, with a life of the poet, and a list of 'old and obscure words explained'. It contained, as previous editions had done, some non-Chaucerian works, including The *Flour and the Leafe* and The *Isle of Ladies*. A further edition in 1602 incorporated some corrections from a letter of Francis Thynne, son of William Thynne, editor of the 1532 edition, and also Chaucer's *ABC* and the non-Chaucerian *Jack Upland*. Another edition followed in 1687.

E. P. Hammond (1908), 122; Pearsall (1984).

SPENSER, EDMUND (*c.*1552–99), Renaissance poet, the author of *The Faerie Queene*, was educated at Pembroke College, Cambridge, where he met Gabriel *Harvey. He served in the household of the earl of Leicester, and later as secretary to Lord Grey of Wilton and an administrator in Ireland. He was buried in Westminster near his admired Chaucer, 'that old Dan Geffrey (in whose gentle spright | The pure well head of Poesie did dwell)' (*Faerie Queene* 7, canto 7, stanza 9). Chaucer appears in his *The Shepheardes Calendar* (1579) as Tityrus who 'many meete tales of youth did . . . make, | And some of love, and some of chevalrie' (February eclogue). In the June eclogue (81–96) there is an eloquent lament for his death, in which Spenser in the person of Collin says that he 'taught me homely, as I can, to make [compose]'. He refers to or alludes to a number of Chaucer's poems, and in *Faerie Queene* book 4.2

continues the narrative hint at the end of the unfinished *Squire's Tale* of the rivalry between Cambalo and the 'brethren' for Canacee. Like other 16th-c. readers, he warmed to *romance and to Chaucer's 'warlike numbers and heroicke sound'. His opening 'whylome as antique stories tellen us' suggests that he also had The *Knight's Tale* in mind here (in canto 1 the house of Ate or Discord seems to echo the description of the temple of Mars in that poem). It is here that he describes Chaucer as 'well of English undefyled', an idea which is not very accurate linguistically, but indicates the nature of Spenser's indebtedness. He seems to have wished to draw on the resources of the 'pure' and 'old' language to enhance the contemporary vernacular. To this end he uses echoes of Chaucer's diction and style and experiments with dialect terms (in *The Shepheardes Calender*) and with archaisms. However, he seems to have been equally influenced by a number of Chaucer's dominant ideas and themes, notably *Nature and '*gentilesse'. Thus he opens *The Faerie Queene* 6.3 with a Chaucerian 'sentence' (from the old woman's speech in *The Wife of Bath's Tale* III.1170—and cf. 1113–16): 'True is, that whilome that good poet sayd, | The gentle minde by gentle deeds is knowne.'

CH i. 114–16; Cooper (1989), 414, 424–5.

sper(e), speer(e), *pl.* **speres, speeris,** (1) sphere, celestial sphere. The planets were usually supposed to be carried round the sky on spheres. Some spoke as though they were of a crystalline substance, the fifth essence; astronomers might explicitly disavow the idea, and insist that the circles and spheres of astronomy had a purely hypothetical function. The former view was clearly of more value to the poet: *Phebus may fall from his sphere; *Latona should run fast round hers; and the ancient tradition that a harmonious melody was created by their rotation was used by Chaucer twice (at the end of *Troilus and Criseyde* and at the beginning of The *Parliament of Fowls*, reporting the dream of *Scipio).

(2) the eighth sphere ('the 8 speer' of *A Treatise on the *Astrolabe* 1.17.39). On the simplest medieval astronomical theory, this is the sphere next beyond that of Saturn, and holding the fixed stars. *Troilus, on his death, ascended to the 'houghnesse' of the eighth sphere and looked down on

the planets. It had been discovered by Hipparchus, as explained in Ptolemy's *Almagest*, that the *longitudes of the stars actually increase very slowly with time. It was as though the stars were drifting slowly round the *ecliptic: in the terminology of the Middle Ages, there was a 'movement of the eighth sphere'. (Since we now know that this is due to a slow precessional (conical) motion of the Earth's axis, which changes the reference frame with respect to which longitudes are measured, we now speak rather of the 'precession of the equinoxes'.) The *Franklin refers to one of the several theories by which the shift in longitudes was calculated when he relates how the clerk of Orleans knew how far 'Alnath was shove | Fro the heed of thilke fixe Aries above' (V.1281–2). (See *Alnath; *Aries; *hed.)

(3) as in 'speer solide', an astronomical instrument for demonstration and rough calculation. (L. *sphœra solida*, medieval L. *spera solida*.) When Chaucer uses the phrase in *Astr* 1.17.19–20, and 2.26.1 he is clearly referring to one of the many books describing it, rather than to the instrument itself. It was 'solid' in the sense of being three-dimensional, and was usually only a framework of metal rings, each representing one of the principal circles of the celestial sphere. Although large examples (then usually called 'armillary spheres') incorporated a stand, it is frequently depicted as small, say 10 or 20 cm across, and held in the hand by the university lecturer in front of his class. (See also *astrology and astronomy.) [JDN]

Squire, The, described in lines 79–100 of the *General Prologue*, after the portrait of his father the *Knight. He embodies however the romantic rather than the religious patterns of *chivalry. He is a young and handsome lover, who has already seen military action, in which he acquitted himself well ('in hope to stonden in his lady grace'). His care for his clothing and appearance is perhaps made to sound just a little excessive, but he is an attractive figure, 'as fressh as is the month of May', with an impressive list of courtly accomplishments. He is musical, and a poet, and able to joust and dance. He could also 'weel purtreye and write'. 'Purtreye' literally means 'draw' or 'represent', but many scholars think that since art was not a formal part of noble education, we should here gloss it

figuratively as 'mentally conceive and put down on paper'. However, it seems churlish to deprive him of a possible, if unusual skill. Like other literary squires he is hotly amorous (as are *Damyan and *Aurelius). (Some of these 'squirely' characteristics are found in ardent young men from different social classes: *Absolon (2) in *The Miller's Tale* for example. The Wife of Bath says that suspicion is aroused when *Jankin (3) the apprentice 'with his crispe heer, shynynge as gold so fyn | ... squiereth me bothe up and doun', (III.305).) The Squire certainly belongs to a familiar literary type, which owes much to the descriptions of the lover and of Mirth in the *Roman de La Rose*. Yet he is also properly mindful of his responsibilities and duties: 'Curteis he was, lowely, and servysable, | And carf biforn his fader at the table'. Chaucer himself had been a squire, and had made war as well as love poetry, and though there seems no reason to find an autobiographical sketch in the portrait, perhaps his earlier experience helped to give it an affectionate blend of detachment and sympathy.

Rv 802; Cooper (1989), 36–7; Mann (1973).

Squire's Tale, The (664 lines in couplets) is the first tale in Fragment V, with a brief introduction that seems to follow closely on the Epilogue to *The *Merchant's Tale*. It is unfinished. (Part 1) In the land of the Mongols (*Tartarye) there is a great king called *Cambyuskan. He was two sons, *Algarsyf and *Cambalo, and a daughter of great beauty, *Canacee. To celebrate twenty years of his reign Cambyuskan holds a great birthday feast. It is interrupted by entry of a knight riding on a steed of brass, with a *mirror in his hand, a gold ring on his thumb and a sword by his side. He delivers his message: the king of Arabia and India sends you this steed in honour of the feast. It can carry you anywhere you wish in the space of one natural day. The *mirror and the ring are for Canacee: the mirror can see any adversity about to occur, and in it a lady can see treachery of a lover; the ring gives knowledge of the language of *birds. The sword will cut through armour, and anyone wounded by it will never be healed until the wound is stroked with the flat of the sword. The strange knight is led to his chamber and disarmed. People wonder at the steed and the other magic gifts, and the festivity continues almost to dawn. (Part 2) Everyone sleeps heavily except Canacee, who goes to the park in the early morning. She hears the birds and, thanks to the ring, can understand what they are saying. She overhears the sorrowful and eloquent lament of a female falcon, who has been betrayed by her false lover. The bird swoons in Canacee's lap. Moved by pity she treats it with herbs and salves and places it in a pen beside her bed. The narrator promises to return to this story and tell how the falcon regained her love, but ends the section by giving an ambitious account of what he proposes to tell first. (Part 3) After only two lines the tale breaks off. In the MSS it is followed immediately by the words of the Franklin, 'In feith, Squier, thow hast thee wel yquit | And gentilly . . .', which is sometimes read as a gentle 'interruption'. It is not clear whether Chaucer really did intend to complete the tale (which could have been very long indeed).

The Tale seems very appropriate to its teller: 'as *gentil*, as promising, and as unfinished as the Squire himself is' (Phillips). It is an oriental *romance, with magic and wonders. In spite of 'as the storie telleth us' (655) there does not seem to be any single 'source'. Chaucer seems to have assembled a miscellany of motifs and story patterns, some perhaps ultimately of Eastern origin (there is, for instance, an analogue to the story of the magic gifts in the *Thousand and One Nights*) and of hints and reminiscences from travel books like *Mandeville or the letter of 'Prester John'. Chaucer goes to some trouble to make the setting sound oriental. Cambyuskan's name is a version of Genghis Khan, and the other names sound suitably exotic, whatever their exact origin (one suggestion (among others) for Cambalo is that it may be from Cambaluc, a form of a Mongol name for Beijing). There is no clear evidence for the date of composition. Modern critics have often dismissed the Tale, or, sometimes, tried to excuse it by claiming that it is determinedly parodic or ironic or that its absurdities show up the inadequacies of the teller. These arguments are both dubious and dangerous (in rewriting Chaucer to make him conform to modern taste or fashion). Two distinguished early readers, Spenser and Milton, were enthusiastic about it, probably because they found its air of 'wonder' encouraged a freedom of imagination. We should perhaps be more seriously attentive to this. The tale contains some fine scenes (like that in which the crowd gathers round and marvels at the magic gifts), and in the episode of Canacee and the falcon an excellent example of Chaucer's pathetic writing (see '**pite**'). At the same time there is sometimes a gentle flickering irony and some discreet hints of mockery (a premonition of Ariosto's treatment of romance, perhaps). Perhaps the Squire is gradually becoming lost in the labyrinth of his extremely leisurely and digressive romance, but any irony is probably detached and controlled, and certainly not destructive.

(ed.) *Rv* 169–77, 890–5; Baker (1990); *S&A* 357–76 [169–209]; Cooper (1989), 217–29; Pearsall (1985), 138–44; Phillips (2000), 135.

STACE, Publius Papinius Statius (d. AD 40–96), a Roman poet, born in Naples, who lived for a period in Rome in the time of the Emperor Domitian. Chaucer's description of him as 'the Tholosan' (a native of Toulouse, *HF* 1460) comes from Dante who seems to have confused him with a rhetorician of the same name who did live in that city. Statius won a number of prizes for poetry, and retired to Naples, where he died. His surviving works are the *Silvae*, and two epics—the *Thebaid*, and the *Achilleid*, which he left uncompleted. Statius was a popular writer during the Middle Ages, and one of the 'curriculum authors'. A bizarre legend had it that he was a Christian. In Dante's *Purgatorio* 22 his shade explains that he was led to Christianity by reading a prophetic passage in the fourth *Eclogue* of *Virgil, his poetic master: 'per te poeta fui, per te cristiano' ('through thee I was a poet, through thee Christian') he says to him. The *Thebaid* in particular was influential. It offered a vivid narrative of the tragic story of *Thebes (1), a sententious pictorial style, and a series of fine scenes of pathos: the blind Oedipus, the doomed priest Amphiaraus, and others. Chaucer mentions Statius by name several times: he is one of the five ancient poets listed at the end of *Troilus* (V.1792). He is closely associated with Thebes (*Anel* 21; I.2294): in The *House of Fame* (1460–3) he 'bar up' the fame of Thebes upon his shoulders, 'and the name | also of cruel Achilles' (an indication that Chaucer knew of the *Achilleid* though not necessarily that he had read it). It does seem, however, that he knew the *Thebaid* well. There are some close parallels: for instance, in the passage in *The Complaint of *Mars* (245–62) on the 'broche of Thebes' and its discordant power, based on *Theb.* 2.265 ff., or the opening of the 'story' in *Anel* (22–42) with the return of Theseus, based on *Theb.* 12.519–35. The *Knight's Tale* is based on Boccaccio's *Teseida*, but Chaucer seems sometimes to recall the *Thebaid* which lies behind it. In the description of the temple of Mars, for instance, where the idea of Discord is prominent, he has 'Conquest' sitting in honour, with a sword hanging over his head (perhaps echoing Discordia's two-edged blade in Statius). Perhaps too Statius's bleak view of human life has left its mark on the tale. In *Troilus and Criseyde*, where the parallel story of Thebes is often alluded to, *Cassandra gives (V.1485–1510) a summary of the action of the epic. Before this, in book II (80 ff.), Criseyde and her ladies are listening to the reading of a 'romaunce' of Thebes. The word 'romance' might suggest rather a French version, but Pandarus's (perhaps rather superior?) comment that he knows the story and that 'herof ben ther maked bookes twelve' refers to the epic. It has been pointed out that Pandarus's interruption is exactly at the mid-point of the Theban story, at the end of book VI where a rubric would announce the impending death of Amphiaraus, and that it is left almost to the end of Chaucer's tale for Cassandra to announce the end of the epic. Possibly there is even an allusion to Statius at the beginning of the poem in the phrase the 'double sorwe' of Troilus. This is likely to be an echo of Dante's 'doppia tristizia' (of Jocasta), a phrase used by Virgil to Statius in Canto 22 of *Purgatorio*.

(ed. and tr.) Mozley (1928); Harbert (1974); Norton-Smith (1974), 32–4, 131–2; Vessey (1973); Wise (1911).

Stedfastnesse, Lak of, see *Lak of Stedfastnesse.*

sterre (pl. sterres, gen. pl. sterres), star, planet. The word occurs most frequently in *Boece* and *A Treatise on the *Astrolabe*. In The *Man of Law's Tale* there is an astrological statement concerning the way the book of heaven was written with stars (that is, to their configuration) at birth. The death of every man is written in them 'clerer than is glass'. Chaucer frequently alludes to the transference of persons into stars—the subject on which the Eagle wishes to discourse in The *House of Fame*. The 'loode-sterre' in The *Knight's Tale* is the pole star. (See *septemtryones.) Troilus three times alludes to Criseyde as his star: she is his lodestar. By 'sterres seven' in The *Book of the Duchess* Chaucer might have referred to either the Greater or Lesser Bear, or to the Pleiades. He always draws a conventional distinction between 'sterre fixe', fixed star, and star in general, which includes *planete. (See also *astrology and astronomy; Athalantes doughtres; *Bere.)   [JDN]

Stilboun, in The *Pardoner's Tale* (VI.603–20), a Spartan ambassador to Corinth, who when he found all the leaders there gambling returned to advise against an alliance with them. In *John of Salisbury's *Policraticus* the name of the ambassador is Chilon; possibly Chaucer had in mind the philosopher Stilbo, mentioned in Seneca.

Stymphalides, Stymphalis, a virgin murdered by the tyrant *Aristoclides as she clung to the altar in the temple of *Diana. The story (from *Jerome) is told by *Dorigen (V.1387–94).

Stix, Styx the principal river of the underworld. Chaucer, like other medieval writers, calls it the pit of hell (*Tr* IV.1540); in *Dante it is a marsh.

Stoyciens, Stoics (*Bo* I pr.3:33 etc.).

ston, stoon, pl. **stones,** (1) stone, piece of stone, (fig.) rock giving security; frequently in comparisons, as something blind, cold, dead, dumb, hard, silent. (2) testicle; the Host chaffed the Nun's Priest: 'I-blessed be thy breche, and every stoon'. (3) *gem; 'cristal stones' in The *Pardoner's Prologue* were cases of glass or rock crystal for holding religious relics. (See also *Lapidaire.) (4) the 'privee stoon' (secret stone) in The *Canon's Yeoman's Tale* is the Philosopher's Stone of *alchemy.   [JDN]

STOW, JOHN (1525?–1605), known during his lifetime chiefly as a chronicler, and in modern times for his *Survey of London* (1598). Stow produced in 1561 an edition of Chaucer's works,

STC 5076. Based largely upon the 1532 edition of *Thynne or a reprint of this, but adding a further twenty-three short poems and, after the colophon 'Thus endeth the workes of Geffray Chaucer' Lydgate's *Siege of Thebes*. Of the twenty-three poems three are now generally accepted to be by Chaucer: *Gentilesse, A *Complaint to his Lady* and the address to *Adam (2) scriveyn; two others, *Proverbs* and *Against *Women Unconstant* have been variously regarded. Stow saw a number of surviving Chaucer manuscripts, as is evident from his distinctive hand in annotations; but it seems likely that a fair number of these notes derive from a time later than his edition.   [AH]

Hudson (1984); Kingsford (1971).

Stratford atte Bowe (I.125) was in Chaucer's day a town a few miles from London. It was the site of the Benedectine nunnery of St Leonard's (see *Prioress).

Straw, see *Jakke Straw.

STRODE, Ralph Strode (d. 1387?). Oxford philosopher and logician. A fellow of Merton College (1359–60), very probably identical with a London lawyer of the name who died in 1387, survived by a wife Emma and a son who also bore the name Ralph. Among Strode's extensive logical writings are *Consequentiæ* and *Obligationes* that were required texts at several universities in the late Middle Ages, and that were later printed in many editions. He was the friend, the 'philosophical Strode', to whom (with John Gower) Chaucer dedicated *Troilus and Criseyde*. On the authority of a note written a century later on a Merton document, Strode was a 'noble poet' who had written a work in elegiac metre called *Phantasma Radulphi* ('Ralph's Vision'), but this is lost. An end-note added at a later date to the copy of *A Treatise on the *Astrolabe* in Cambridge University MS Dd.3.53 suggests that N. Strode (the initial is already a plain mistake) was Lewis Chaucer's tutor at Oxford. The dating of the work makes this impossible. The note, however, could be read as indicating that Chaucer's own work was done under the care (*sub tutela*) of Strode, and this may be its meaning. The two men were neighbours in London.   [JDN]

Strother, an unidentified town in the north of England (I.4014).

Summoner, The, described in lines 623–68 of the *General Prologue*. He rides beside the 'gentil' *Pardoner, and they make a fine pair of ecclesiastical villains. In one of his most vivid portraits Chaucer details his revolting and fearsome appearance (fiery face, narrow eyes, black brows, scraggy beard, white pustules) which makes children afraid of him. It seems that he has the symptoms of alopicia, a form of leprosy, but the symptoms arouse no sympathy. When he is in his cups, he speaks Latin—but he can only parrot the legal tags of his trade. A summoner was a minor official who delivered citations to appear before an ecclesiastical court. This Summoner is himself guilty of the sins he is supposed to be bringing to correction, notably lechery and venality. He is deceitful and cynical. His moral *ugliness matches his appearance. At the end the portrait is not exactly lightened, but is enlivened by a wildly grotesque visual detail: on his head the Summoner wears a huge garland, and he carries a little shield made of bread.

Rv 822–3; Cooper (1989), 56; Curry (1960), 37–53; Bowden (1956), 269–72; Mann (1973), 139–40.

Summoner's Tale, The (just under 600 lines in couplets) in Fragment III follows *The *Friar's Tale*, to which it is a riposte. A brief Prologue describes how the Summoner is so infuriated by what he has just heard that he stood high in his stirrups and 'lyk an aspen leef he quook [shook] for ire'. The friar was right, he says, to boast of his knowledge of hell, because that is where friars are: there is a nest of them under Satan's tail. 'God save you alle' he says to his hearers in conclusion, 'save [except] this cursed Frere'. His passion is felt in his Tale. In Holderness, in Yorkshire, there is a begging friar (later called John) who in his preaching encourages people to pay the friars for 'trentals' (sets of thirty masses for the dead) and for the building of their holy houses. As he goes about, followed by a servant with a sack to collect whatever has been given, he keeps a list of the names of those who have given something, as if he would pray for them, but as soon as he has left he wipes them out. At this point the Friar bursts out angrily 'thou liest!', but is calmed by the Host, and the Summoner continues. The friar comes to a house where he has dined well in the past. Thomas, the owner, is bedridden. The friar drives away the cat from the bench, and 'sette hym softe adoun'. When the wife enters, he greets her courteously, embracing her closely and kissing her. He says he could like a few words with Thomas, and she advises him to chide him well because he is angry, even though he has everything. The friar begins to reprove him, pausing only to order a rich and elaborate dinner, even though he is, he says, a man who is weakened by prayer and fasting. The wife tells him that her child has just died, and he says that he saw his death by revelation, and his soul carried into bliss. He praises at some length the poverty and abstinence of friars and the efficacy of their prayers. Thomas remarks testily that though he has given a great deal to different kinds of friars he is none the better for it. He is told not to be inconstant and to be faithful (and generous) to one convent. The friar goes on to warn of the dangers of anger, with examples. He asks Thomas to make his confession. Thomas says he has already done so, to his curate. Give us gold then, says the friar, or else we will have to sell our books. As he pleads, he kneels. Thomas is now almost mad with rage ('he wolde that the frere had been on-fire | With his false dissymulacioun'), and says that he will give him what is in his possession. It is in his bed under his buttocks. The friar, as instructed, puts his hand there in the hope of finding a gift, but receives instead a great fart: 'ther nys no capul [horse], drawynge in a cart, | That myghte have lete [released] a fart of swich a soun.' The friar flies into a furious rage, which increases when he is chased out: 'he looked as it were a wild boor, | He grynte with [ground] his teeth, so was he wrooth'. He hurries to the house of a lord to whom he was confessor, who placates him and discovers the story of the 'odious meschief', and that Thomas has told the friar to share it equally with his fellows. The lord broods on the mathematical problem that has been set ('in *arsmetryke shal ther no man fynde, | Biforn this day, of swich a questioun'). It is solved by his squire, who suggests that a cartwheel be brought in with twelve spokes. Twelve friars shall put their noses

to them, and the friar confessor's nose under the hub. Thus both sound and stink may be shared out equally. The squire is held to have spoken as well as Euclid or Ptolemy.

The *fabliau has no known source (although there are stories involving humiliating gifts). It is possibly based on some current joke, or Chaucer may very well have invented some or all of it. The image of the cartwheel may be a *parodic allusion to representations of the descent of the Holy Spirit to the twelve apostles at Pentecost. The tale obviously owes much to the tradition of anti-fraternal satire, but in the figure of the monstrously unctuous and hypocritical friar transforms and transcends its topics. It is often neglected by modern readers, perhaps because of the earthiness of its finale. It should be noted, however, that early satire often prefers a direct and heavy blow below the belt to indirect glancing darts, so that the nemesis of the fart is an appropriately humiliating one for this self-satisfied figure—and its crude combination of wind and sound is appropriate to a preacher who makes a living by his words. Beside the earthiness there are some delicate ironies of language and *narrative. It contains some of Chaucer's best writing, especially in his imitations of speech and casual conversations (e.g. in 1797 ff.). The rhetorical variation is exciting: at the beginning (1746–53) we are suddenly, without syntactic warning, given an example of the hurried, colloquial speech of the friar to a popular audience; later, of his rotund expository style, urgent persuasive *rhetoric (1954 ff.) and his violent outburst of anger. The speech of the other characters is nicely distinguished—that of the irritable Thomas and his wife, and of the apparently straight-faced lord and lady. Throughout the tale Chaucer plays variations on the language of rage: that of the narrator is succeeded by that of Thomas and the friar. The tale is a kind of 'flyting' answering The *Friar's Tale, and it is hard to say which climax—the summoner taken to hell or the friar's humiliating 'gift'—is the more crushing. The two tales make a brilliant pair and were almost certainly written together to complement each other.

(ed.) *Rv* 128–36, 876–79; *S&A* 275–87; Cooper (1989), 176–83; Pearsall (1985), 222–8.

Sunne, see *sonne.

Surrye, Syria (adj. Surrien 'Syrian'). According to *Bartholomew Syria stretches from the Euphrates to Egypt and from Armenia down to the Arabian sea. It is a rich land with noble harbours; its inhabitants are warriors and merchants. Chaucer (who gives no geographical detail) makes it the setting of the first part of The *Man of Law's Tale*: it is a company of rich Syrian merchants which sets the plot in motion.

Susanne, Susanna, the heroine of the (apocryphal) biblical Book of Susannah. She was falsely accused of adultery by two lustful elders whose advances she had rejected, but was saved by God. *Custance mentions this providential intervention in her prayer in *The Man of Law's Tale* (II.639–40); the *Parson mentions the story to illustrate false witness (X.797).

SWETONIUS, SWETOUN, Gaius Suetonius Tranquillus (b. *c.*70). Roman biographer. His surviving works are *De vita Caesarum* (Lives of the Caesars) and part of *De viris illustribus* (Of Illustrious Men—including lives of the poets). The *De vita Caesarum* in particular was admired and imitated in the Middle Ages. Suetonius is referred to twice as an authority by the *Monk: for the tragedy of *Nero (VII.2465) and for that of Julius Caesar (*Cesar), but it seems unlikely that he was the direct source for either.

swearing, see *oaths.**

T

Tabard, an inn in Southwark, so called from its sign, a jacket embroidered with a coat of arms, or perhaps, a tank (of ale). The name was common, but there was an inn (apparently a large one) called The Tabard in Southwark.

Wright (1992).

table, table (L. *tabula*, Fr. *table*). (1) tablet (e.g. of stone or brass), to receive writing or an inscription; (2) table (an item of furniture); (3) (pl.) the game of backgammon; (4) tablet or plate of an astrolabe, as in 'tables of the *clymates' of *A Treatise on the *Astrolabe*; (5) a tabulated list of astronomical, mathematical or other data. The 'table of centris' in *Equatorie of the Planetis*, for example, listed the distances of the *equant and *deferent centres from *Aryn for each planet separately, and was specific to that work. The many astronomical tables with which that text is bound are more typical of advanced astronomical manuscripts of the period: for the most part they are drawn from, or based on, recensions of the Alfonsine tables. Among them are tables of the general character of those mentioned in *A Treatise on the *Astrolabe* and *The *Franklin's Tale*, although the latter were perhaps meant to be the more antiquated Toledan tables. (See also *almenak; *astrology and astronomy; *Tolletanes.) [JDN]

tabour, see *musical instruments.

Tagus, the river Tajo in Spain, famous in antiquity for its gold (*Bo* III m.10:12).

tail-rhyme, a stanza form consisting of pattern made up from the repetition of a pair of rhyming lines (often four-stress) followed by a single line of different length (often three-stress). It is found in a number of Middle English romances, in a variety of patterns of which aabccbddbeeb is

common. Chaucer uses it only in *Sir Thopas*, in a shorter stanza (aabaab or aabccb). He seems to relish the comic banality which can be emphasized by the final short line.

Talbot, the name of a dog, used in *The Nun's Priest's Tale* (VII.3383).

Tantale, Tantalus, Tantalus, son of Jupiter and father of Niobe (*Nyobe) and Pelops, offended the gods (according to one account by dismembering his son and serving his flesh to them), and was punished in Hades by being placed in a pool of water which always receded when he tried to drink (*Bo* III m.12:38). Chaucer alludes to his torment in Hades (*BD* 709; *Tr* III.593).

Tarbe, see Tharbe.

TARQUINIUS, Tarquinius Superbus, the last of the (semi-legendary) kings of Rome (reigned 534–510 BC), father of *Tarquinius the yonge (*LGW* 1682).

TARQUINIUS THE YONGE, TARQUYN, TARQUINY, Tarquinius Sextus, son of Tarquinius Superbus, who brutally raped *Lucrece. He was banished with all his family. The story is told in *The *Legend of Good Women*, and alluded to by *Dorigen in *The *Franklin's Tale* (V.1407).

Tars, Tarsia, in Chinese Turkestan. The name occurs in the common phrase 'clooth of Tars' (i.e. silk from Turkestan; I.2160).

Tartarye, the land of the Tartars or Mongols. In *The *Squire's Tale* (V.9) the word seems to refer specifically to the Mongol empire in southern Russia; in *The *Book of the Duchess* (1025) it is used more generally for outer Mongolia. See Map 3.

Taur, Taurus, Tawr, Taurus, the Bull, the second sign of the Zodiac—a *domicile of Venus. The Wife of Bath's *ascendent was in this sign. The Moon's exaltation is there, a fact that is implicit in The *Parson's Prologue. (See also *Aldeberan; *Bole; *signe.)   [JDN]

technology. Some of the greatest of all human achievements in the Middle Ages were of a technological sort, but all too often documentary evidence for them is wanting. New techniques and inventions were often jealously safeguarded by guild or individual for economic reasons, but they were presumably often produced without documentary support, even highly complex machines being often built from designs passed on from one generation to the next with only an earlier exemplar as guide. Any practical text or drawing tends to disappear quickly from view. One of the most obvious examples is in ecclesiastical building (see *architecture), where plans that undoubtedly existed for some of the most ambitious architectural achievements of all time have very rarely survived. This does not imply the absence of an underlying rationale. The Roman architect Vitruvius asserted the importance of both *fabrica and ratiocinatio*, of making and of theorizing, but this would not have astonished the average medieval architect, ignorant though he probably was of Vitruvius.

Following classical precedents, medieval writers attached much importance to the division between art and *nature. *Aristotle in his *Meteorology* and *Physics*, Plato in the *Timaeus*, and Chalcidius in his commentary on the latter, touched on the relations between art and nature, and there was a general belief that the mechanical arts were originally learned by man copying natural processes. In a classification by Hugh of St Victor, the arts of cloth-making, armament, commerce, agriculture, hunting, navigation, medicine, and theatre—all of which he thought began with the copying of nature—were placed below the *Seven Liberal Arts, but at least they were in the same hierarchy.

The intellectual element in the practical arts was recognized, as it had been in the ancient world, and yet modern writers often criticize both for failing to make use of their intellectual inventions. There are famous technical treatises

from antiquity, such as the pseudo-Aristotelian *Mechanical Problems*, and the works of Ctesibios, Archimedes, and Hero, that describe hydraulic devices, machines for opening temple doors automatically, water organs, fire pumps, and so forth; but there is rarely any suggestion in them of serious economic application. The modern criticism appears just, but only because we are now steeped in a materialistic view of technology, and believe that human labour is something to be spared. Ancient and medieval inventions were frequently meant to amuse, mystify, or astonish, rather than to offer material help. Some practical inventions were clearly meant to offer material help, and then it comes as a surprise to find how restricted in distribution these often were, except where labour was scarce: the wheeled plough and the water mill are notorious examples from late antiquity.

The Arabs strengthened the Greek link between technology and science. They excelled in the decorative arts, and in metal- and glass-working, for example, and *alchemy is the scientific correlate of many of these activities. Particularly important economically was something quite different, namely the agricultural revolution that followed the rise of Islam. The key to this was the introduction of many new crops—rice, hard wheat, citrus fruit, and many vegetables—from India and Persia. These were disseminated to places as far away as North Africa and the Iberian peninsula. With this revolution came much attention to techniques of cookery, and to irrigation, although there the ancient devices were still usually employed—the Archimedean screw and the water wheel.

The Arabs took over the Greek technology of devices for show. Water clocks fall more or less under this heading, but there the Arabs transformed their inheritance out of all recognition. As the Greeks had done, they coupled their clocks not only to the ringing of bells on the hour but to sophisticated displays of the moving heavens, in the form of an *astrolabe dial. Such clocks might also incorporate a geared and automated planetarium, so as to show the planetary movements (see *Equatorie of the Planetis for a comparable computing device, that was not driven by wheel work). A planetary clock of this kind was the great gift of al-Ashrâf, Sultan of Damascus, to the Emperor Frederick II in 1232, the heaven on this device being of gold stellated with gems. From such astronomical machinery the mechanical clock was derived in Europe, probably in England, about half a century later (see *clokke). It has to be emphasized here, however, that there was a long-standing European tradition, perhaps continuous from late Roman times, of driving an astronomical dial by a water clock (the 'anaphoric clock'). The other principal element in the ancestry of the mechanical clock was the simple monastic alarm, again water-driven (see *day).

Such precision machinery did not assume real economic importance until long after Chaucer's time. Commercial advantage lay, as ever, with goods of everyday importance. After the collapse of the Roman empire there had been a gradual northward drift away from Italy of the main centres of production of metals, pottery, and glassware. Such places as Lyons and Cologne grew steadily in importance, and commerce often went hand-in-glove with the arts of war: the pattern-welded steel of the Merovingian long-sword had made those warriors who possessed it much more efficient, and the medieval literary attention given to the sword should come as no surprise. Sword and spear became still more formidable weapons when wielded by cavalrymen made more secure in the saddle by the use of the stirrup, a small but influential invention gradually brought into use in war between say 800 and 1100, with great effect.

The plough was much improved from about the 6th c. onwards: from prehistoric times until then, ploughs had cut into the soil without turning it. The new *carruca* type of plough could include such components as a coulter and ploughshare (blades for cutting the soil), a mouldboard (for turning the furrow), and wheels (for adjusting the depth of cut). (We recall that the smith Gerveys in The *Miller's Tale smithed 'plough harneys' in his forge and sharpened 'shaar and kultour bisily'.) There was a shift to more efficient draught animals—to the horse rather than the ox—for ploughing. New crops such as barley and rye were introduced as a consequence, and medieval experiments in improving agricultural productivity are not unknown.

The spread of such improvements in agricultural techniques owed much to the Cistercians, from the 12th c. onwards, with their commitment to the practical life. A Cistercian monastery was a veritable technological microcosm, with corn mill, brewery, a wine-press perhaps, a weaving shed, fulling mill, tannery, and smithy. The famous architect-engineer of the 13th c., Villard d'Honnecourt, was a Cistercian. One should not undervalue the role of the other religious orders in technological matters, however: Richard of Wallingford (c.1292–1336) was abbot of England's premier abbey, the Benedictine foundation at St Albans, where he built the most ambitious item of precision technology of the Middle Ages up to that time, an immense astronomical clock embodying subtle theoretical principles that scarcely half a dozen people in Europe would have properly understood, had they been privy to them. His practical credentials were enhanced in two different ways: his father had been a blacksmith; and at Oxford he had learned to make his own astronomical instruments (rule, quadrant, astrolabe, sphere, and so forth), as did almost all the most serious astronomers, and he had written treatises on new types (albion and rectangulus).

The economic importance of the techniques of the millwright were of a different order. Watermills rapidly multiplied after the 10th c. The windmill reached Europe by various routes, for instance from China through Persia and Arab lands, and thence through Italy; and also through North Africa and Spain. Various different types were developed, but all shared the advantage that they were not restricted to places adjacent to running water. Mills of all kinds saved labour and improved productivity. They were costly enterprises but they yielded great profits, and both of these facts help to explain the large numbers of lawsuits involving them. From an early stage there were attempts by feudal lords to control their use, and take a tithe from those they controlled. That millers nevertheless had much scope for profiteering is clear from Chaucer's account of the Miller *Robin of The *Canterbury Tales, who well knew how to steal corn and take his toll three times, so illustrating the proverb that 'an honest miller has a golden thumb' (meaning that there were no honest millers).

The Miller, however, was the mere operator of a machine that was built by others. At first these skilled millwrights, like those who built large clocks and jacquemarts, who cast bells and cannon, built organs, and undertook many similar large-scale activities for which high expertise was necessary, were tied into the feudal system; but their skills were called upon from far and wide, so that they often became itinerant. This fact, like the *guild systems they developed, helped to give them a large measure of independence, and especially in the towns they became a counterpoise to the feudal powers. By Chaucer's time the guilds had become powerful enough for Parliament to take measures to check their advancement. Chaucer's five *guildsmen were a haberdasher, a carpenter, a weaver, a dyer, and a tapestry weaver. Neither they nor their cook were given a central part in The Canterbury Tales, but it is amusing to note that Chaucer made them out to be dressed in expensive livery, for in 1389 Parliament had petitioned the king to restrict this show of their strength. Equally noteworthy is the fact that none of the pilgrims aspired to any of the higher reaches of technology, except Chaucer himself, in the sense that he was sometime Master of the King's Works. (See also *alchemy; *Bacon; *Secreta Secretorum.) [JDN]

Drachmann (1963); North (1989), chs. 11, 12; Singer et al. (1954–74); Lynn White (1962).

Tereus, king of Thrace (*Trace), the husband of Procne (*Progne), who raped her sister Philomela (*Philomene). The story is told in The *Legend of Good Women and is alluded to in *Troilus and Criseyde (II.69).

Termagaunt, a supposed Saracen god (VII.810).

TERTULAN, Tertullian (c.160–c.220), a native of Carthage, became the foremost Christian theologian before St Augustine. *Jankyn's (4) 'book of wicked wives' contains an unidentified work by him (III.676).

Tesbee, see *Tisbe.

Teseida, a romantic epic of almost 10,000 lines telling of the love of Palemone and Arcita for Emilia, written (c.1340–1) by *Boccaccio, which is the main source of The *Knight's Tale. It is divided into twelve books and uses pagan gods and classical epic machinery. The Thebaid of Statius (*Stace) lies behind much of it. Boccaccio also wrote glosses for it, and these were possibly known to Chaucer. Chaucer shortened it and made significant changes, removing, for instance, the apotheosis of Arcita's soul (which he used in *Troilus and Criseyde), and making the two heroes more equal.

(ed.) Limentani (1964); Boitani (1977); Havely (1980).

Tessalie, Tessaly, Thessalie, Thessaly, in northeastern Greece, mentioned as the land of *Jason (LGW 1396ff.); here also, at Pharsalus, Pompey was defeated by Caesar (VII.2679).

Testament of Cresseid, The, a poem by Robert *Henryson (d. by 1505–6) tells the story of the end of Chaucer's *Criseyde. Its date is not certain, nor is it clear whether it was invented or was based on the (unknown) 'other book' that he says he found it in. It appeared in *Thynne's 1532 Chaucer and in subsequent editions. The action begins with the rejection of Cresseid by *Diomede, and her isolation and despair, which culminates in a bitter outcry against Venus and Cupid, and an eerie dream in which the planetary gods assemble and lay a judgement on her for her blasphemy: she becomes a leper, and must live in the leper-house. The horror of her fate is eloquently expressed through description and through her own formal laments. One day a company of Trojans led by *Troilus is returning from battle, and the lepers beg for alms. Troilus has pity, and looking at Cresseid, does not recognize her in her present condition, but something suggests to him that he has seen her face before. A spark of love moves his heart and 'for knichtlie pietie and memoriall | Of fair Cresseid' he gives her a rich gift—but neither recognizes the other. When she is told who he was, she swoons, and, overwhelmed by sorrow, gives a final lament, writes her testament, and dies. It is a powerful and disturbing poem.

(ed.) Fox (1981).

Testament of Love, see *Usk.

Teuta, a warrior queen of Illyria (3rd c. BC) who defied the Romans. *Dorigen says that her 'wyfly chastitee' (mentioned by St *Jerome) is a mirror to all wives (V.1453–4).

Tewnes, Tunis (*BD* 310).

Tharbe, Tarbe, sister of *Antigone the niece of Criseyde (*Tr* II.816, 1563).

Thebes (1), Thebes, the chief city of ancient Boeotia in Greece, renowned in ancient myth and legend. Chaucer refers to a number of famous events and figures: its founding by Cadmus (*Cadme; I.1546–7), the building of its walls by Amphion (*Amphioun) the king and a famous harper (IV.1716–21; IX.116), or the madness of King Athamas (*Athamante; *Tr* IV.1539–40), but above all to the story of the expedition of the Seven against Thebes in support of Polynices (*Polymyte(s)) against his brother Eteocles (*Ethiocles) who had seized the throne. This was known in the Middle Ages from the *Thebaid* of Statius (*Stace) and the *Roman de Thèbes*. Chaucer seems to have been familiar with both works, and was clearly very interested in the story. He refers to the individual heroes (*Adrastus, the leader, *Tydeus the father of *Diomede, Parthenopaeus (*Parthonope), *Capaneus, Hippomedon (*Ypomedoun), Amphiarus (*Amphiorax) and Polynices (*Polymyte(s)), and to a number of the more spectacular events of the expedition: the death of Amphiarus, the '*broche of Thebes', etc. The story was so well known that it could provide exemplary material. 'The strif of Thebes' was one of those 'written in the stars' (II.200); the fall of the city (like that of *Troy) caused great lamentation (II.289). In a quite different context, the treachery of Eriphyle (*Eriphilem), the wife of Amphiarus, could be recounted to the *Wife of Bath (III.742–6). The expedition is briefly touched on at the beginning of *Anelida and Arcite (50 ff.). Thebes plays a much more important role in The *Knight's Tale and in *Troilus and Criseyde. In the first we are told of the intervention of *Theseus, the ruler of Athens, when *Creon refused to allow the burial of the bodies of the seven heroes (I.893 ff.), and the heroes of the tale, Palamon and Arcite, are of the royal blood of Thebes. In *Troilus and Criseyde we have a series of allusions to the Theban war,

with two obvious high points—the reading of 'the geste | Of the siege of Thebes' to Criseyde and her maidens at the beginning of the second book, and the genealogy of Diomede (V.1485 ff.), which indicates that the fathers and grandfathers of those engaged in the siege of Troy had fought in the war of the Seven against Thebes. Chaucer strongly suggests a parallel between the doomed city of Troy and Thebes.

Thebes (2), the city in ancient Egypt (on the site of which Luxor now stands) (I.1472), the origin of a narcotic drug.

Thelophus, Telephus, son of Hercules, who became king of Mysia. Wounded by *Achilles then on his way to *Troy, he was sent by the oracle to seek a cure from 'the wounder'. This turned out to be the spear of Achilles. It is alluded to in The *Squire's Tale (V.238–40).

Theodamas, Thiodamas, the augur of the army at *Thebes (1). His first prayer was followed by the trumpet blasts of the attacking army (*Thebaid* 8.276–347), and he is later (10.160–553) associated with the trumpets of battle. Chaucer makes him into a trumpeter (IV.1720–1; *HF* 1246).

Theodora, the wife of *Algarsif in The *Squire's Tale (V.664).

THEODORIC, THEODORIK, Theodoric the Great, king of the Ostrogoths from 490 to 526. In the name of the Emperor Zeno at Constantinople he invaded Italy and defeated Odoacer. He ruled as a king, without making imperial claims. He was an admirer of Roman civilization, and at his court in Ravenna (*Ravenne) employed Romans as his officials (with his Goths in the military posts). Among others, Boethius (*Boece) found favour with him for many years. Theodoric was an Arian (i.e. a Christian who believed that the Father and the Son were not 'one substance'), but in general he maintained good relations with the Catholics, although towards the end of his reign anti-Arian feeling and persecution made him suspicious of conspiracies; and led to the condemnation and death of Boethius. The king is not mentioned by name in the *Consolation of*

Philosophy, but Chaucer names him twice in the explanatory glosses (*Bo* I pr.4:73; III pr.4:25).

'Theodulus' (possibly Gottschalk of Orbais), the author of a 9th-c. Eclogue which became a popular and widespread school text. In it a shepherd *Pseustis sings of pagan myths and is answered by the shepherdess Alithia. Not only does the shepherd's name appear in *The *House of Fame* (1228), but other possible echoes of the *Ecloga Theoduli* have been detected in that work (e.g. 588–92).

Theofraste, Theophrastus, said to be the author of the *Liber aureolus de nuptiis*, an anti-feminist tract preserved in St *Jerome's *Adversus Jovinianum*. It finds a place in *Jankyn's (4) book (III.671), and is referred to in *The *Merchant's Tale* (IV.1294–310).

Theorik(e), theory (L. *theorica*). In *Equatorie of the Planetis* the word is applied to a particular theory from a type of treatise with the generic name *Theorica planetarum*. The promised fourth part of *A Treatise on the *Astrolabe* was to have been just such a work, 'a theorike to declare the moevyng of the celestiall bodies with the causes'. The fifth part was to have abstracted from among the 'general rules of theorik in astrologie'. (See also *astrology and astronomy.) [JDN]

Thesbee, see *Tisbe.

Theseus, the legendary hero, son of Aegeus, king of Athens. A friend of Hercules, he performed a number of great deeds in his youth. By the help of Ariadne (*Adriane) he killed the *Minotaur in Crete, and on his return became king (in Chaucer duke) of Athens (*Athenes). With his friend Pirithous (*Perotheus) he attempted to carry off *Proserpina. He overcame and married Hippolyta (*Ypolita) the queen of the Amazons, and defeated and destroyed *Creon the tyrant of *Thebes (1). In The *Knight's Tale, where he is based on *Boccaccio's Teseo in the *Teseida*, he is presented as a wise ruler and a good man who, though prone to irascibility can take a relaxed and worldly view of the excesses of young love and can console the survivors at the end of the tale with grave stoic advice. (This is the generally held view—some

critics are much more severe in their judgement of him as ruler and as philosopher.) *Anelida and Arcite* opens with the triumphant return of 'this noble prince Theseus' to Athens. However, in the story of Ariadne in The *Legend of Good Women* the younger Theseus (aged 23 and 'semely . . . to se') is shown to be a false lover, who abandons the faithful Ariadne for her sister Phaedra (*Phedra; see also *HF* 405–26).

Thesiphone, Tisiphone, one of the *Furies (*Tr* I.6; IV.24).

Thessalie, see *Tessalie.

Thetis, the mother of Achilles, a Nereid (the daughter of Nereus a sea-god). She helps to rescue *Demophon from the waves (*LGW* 2421–3).

Thymalao, Timolaus, one of the sons of Zenobia (*Cenobia; VII.2345).

In Thymeo (L. in the *Timaeus* (of *Plato)) *Bo* III pr.9:191.

Thymothee (1), one of the generals defeated by *Judas Maccabeus (VII.2591).

Thymothee (2), Timothy, the recipient of Paul's Epistles. St Paul's caution against fables (1 Tim. 1:4; cf. 4:4) is quoted by the *Parson (X.32). Later in the Tale (X.739) the verse 'the roote of alle harmes is coveitise' (see also VI.334; VII.1130, 1840) is correctly designated '*Ad Thimotheum sexto*' (I Tim. 6:10).

Thisbe, see *Tisbe.

Thoas, king of Lemnos and father of Hypsipyle (*Isiphile) (*LGW* 1468).

Thobie (1), Tobit or Tobias, the pious old exile in the apocryphal Book of Tobit) (VII.1117).

Thobie (2), Tobias the son of Tobit (Thobie (1)); instructed by the angel Raphael (X.906; Tobit 6:17).

THOLOME (1), see *Ptholome(e).

THOLOME (2), 'the kyng' (*LGW* 580) Ptolemy of Egypt, either Ptolemy XII, the father of Cleopatra (d. 51 BC), or one of her two brothers of that name: Ptolemy XIII (d. 47 BC), whom she married, and who was defeated by Caesar, or Ptolemy XIV (d. 44 BC), also her consort and co-ruler, whom she ordered to be murdered.

Tholosan, a native of Toulouse (see *Stace).

Thomas (1), the householder in *The *Summoner's Tale.*

Thomas (2), a name the *Host uses for the *Monk (VII.1930).

THOMAS OF GLOUCESTER (1355–97), often known as Thomas of Woodstock; the youngest son of Edward III, created duke of Gloucester 1385. His growing hostility to Richard II, his nephew, culminated in his participation in the group of 'Appellants' (see *Brenbre); he returned, however, to loyalty, was in Ireland with Richard in 1394, but was in 1397 arrested on Richard's command and taken to Calais where he died, probably murdered at Richard's behest. His library was extensive.   [AH]
    Cavanaugh (1985), 844–51.

Thomas of Ynde, Seint, St Thomas, the doubting apostle who insisted on touching the wounds of the risen Christ (John 20:25–8). The legend that he spread the word of God in India was widely accepted from the early Middle Ages. Travellers found Nestorian Christians in India, and (at various places) the apostle's tomb. Marco Polo recounts some vivid legends connected with it; Mandeville says that the relic of his arm and hand decides between true and false causes. Chaucer's most pointed allusion is in *The *Summoner's Tale* (III.1978–80), where the friar refers the doubtful householder (called Thomas) to the life of the saint for evidence of the benefits of 'buyldynge up of chirches'. The saint's name is also found in *oaths (IV.1230 and (probably) III.666).

THOMAS OF KENT, SEINT, Thomas Becket, St Thomas of Canterbury (*Caunterbury) (1117–70). After studying at Paris, and working as a merchant's clerk, Becket entered the service of Archbishop Theobald, and quickly rose to become Henry II's royal chancellor (1154) and archbishop of Canterbury (1162). His vigorous opposition to royal encroachments on ecclesiastical liberties led to a rift with the king, exile, and a reconciliation which proved temporary. After another dispute, Becket was murdered in the cathedral at Canterbury by four knights who thought that they had been encouraged by the king's angry words. The shock which the murder produced was quickly exploited by the Church. The king was forced to do public penance, and Becket was canonized in 1173. His cult spread quickly, and Canterbury became an important pilgrimage centre. His shrine there was destroyed by Henry VIII. He is the 'hooly blisful martir . . . | That hem hath holpen whan that they were seke' referred to at the beginning of the *General Prologue. He was a healer, and a holy well near his shrine was especially famed for its powers. The other references in Chaucer to his name are in *oaths (*HF* 1131; I.3291, 3425, 3461—the last three in *The *Miller's Tale,* possibly as deliberate local colour, since there was a church and parish of St Thomas in Oxford (*Oxenford)).

Thopas, sire, the hero of *Sir Thopas.*

Thorus (MSS) or Chorus (*Thynne's reading, accepted by some editors) unidentified, but presumably a sea god (*LGW* 2422). If *Chorus* is correct it may come from a misunderstanding of Virgil's *chorus* ('band, troop') in a passage listing sea-creatures (*Aeneid* 5.823) as a proper name.

THYNNE, WILLIAM (d. 1546). An official in the household of Henry VIII, Thynne produced in 1532 the first single volume collection of Chaucer's works (*STC* 5068); it was reprinted in two slightly differing forms in 1542 (5069–70) and in four more in [1550?] (*STC* 5071–4). Thynne's text was largely derived from the earlier editions of *Caxton, *Pynson, and *Wynkyn de Worde, but with limited use for some poems of manuscripts (including Glasgow University Hunterian V.3.7 and Longleat House 258); the 1532 edition added several works to the Chaucer canon (*Henryson's *Testament of Cresseid, The Flower of Courtesy, The*

Assembly of Ladies), whilst those of 1542 added *The *Plowman's Tale*. Thynne's edition was the basis for that issued by *Stowe in 1561, and Stow's in turn was the model for *Speght's of 1598 and 1602; the last was the basis for the 1687 edition.   [AH]
    Blodgett (1984).

Tybre, the river Tiber in Rome (VII.2476).

Tiburce, Tiburtius, in *The *Second Nun's Tale* the brother of Valerian, the husband of St Cecilia, who converts him. He is martyred with his brother.

Ticius, Tityus, a giant punished in Hades by the gods for assaulting the goddess Leto by being bound on his back while a vulture tore at his liver (*Bo* III m.12:42; *Tr* I.786).

Tydeus, king of Calydon, the father of *Diomede (*Anel* 57; *Tr* V.88, etc.).

Tigrys, the river Tigris in Mesopotamia (*Bo* V m.1:1, 6).

Tyle, Ultima Thule ('the laste ile in the see') (*Bo* III m.5:7).

time, see *clokke; *day; *hour; *Kalendere; *myle-wey; *months and seasons; *mot(e); *Pryme; *radix; *yer(e).

Tyrene, Tyrrhenian (sea), to the west of Italy (*Bo* III m.8:9).

Tyresie, Tiresias, the blind Theban seer (*Bo* V pr.3: 134).

Tyrie, the ancient Tyre, in Phoenicia (along the coast of Syria and Lebanon) (*Bo* II m.5:11, 14; III m.4:3).

Tyro, see *Appollonius.

Tisbe, Thisbe(e), Tesbe(e), Thesbe(e), Thisbe, the story of whose ill-fated love for Pyramus is told in *The *Legend of Good Women*, and is alluded to elsewhere (II.63; IV.2128; *PF* 289; *LGW* 261).

Titan, the sun (*Tr* III.1464).

TYTUS, see *Dite.

TITUS LIVIUS, TYTUS, the Roman historian Livy (59 BC–AD 17). He is cited as the source of *The *Physician's Tale* (VI.1), but although the story is told by Livy, it seems likely that Chaucer found it in an intermediate source, probably the *Roman de la Rose* (where it is also attributed to Livy). Livy is also claimed as a source for the story of *Lucrece (*LGW* 1683, 1873; cf. *BD* 1084), where again Chaucer does not seem to be following him directly.

Toas, Thoas, king of Aetolia, an ally of the Greeks (*Tr* IV.138).

Tolletanes, Toledan. An adjective applied to certain astronomical *tables assembled at Toledo. Such tables were used by the Clerk of Orléans in *The *Franklin's Tale*, and Chaucer's brief listing of the sort of technical terms to be found in them is faultless. Azarchel wrote *canons to the set of tables usually known by this description. (See *Arsechieles; *astrology and astronomy.)
                                            [JDN]

Trace, Thrace, a region in northern Greece, is several times mentioned in Chaucer's 'classical' tales. The ancient idea of it as a primitive area is reflected in the way Chaucer seems to think of it as a cold and rugged place. It is in the 'frosty contree called Trace' that *Mars has his 'grisly temple' (*Anel* 1–4): the description of this in *The *Knight's Tale* (I.1970 ff.) stresses the roughness of 'thilke colde, frosty regioun' (see *landscape) and the eeriness of the temple and its setting. It is the home of winds (*Bo* I m.3:11–13); Aeolus (*Eolus) the god of wind is to be found in a cave there (*HF* 1571–85). Its king Lycurgus (*Lygurge) who appears in *The Knight's Tale* (I.2128–54) is a strong, fearsome, exotic figure wearing a bear's skin. The violent rapist *Tereus was 'lord of Thrace and kin to Mars' (*LGW* 2244); his crime is performed in a dark cave in a Thracian forest (2309 ff.). Less alarming inhabitants are *Phyllis, the daughter of the king of Thrace, and *Orpheus 'the poete of Trace' (*Bo* III m.12:4).

tragedy. In medieval literature the word normally means a narrative poem (rather than a play) with a disastrous end. Chaucer applies it both to the short verse examples in *The *Monk's Tale* and to the long and much more impressive poem **Troilus and Criseyde*, which he humbly describes as 'lytel myn tragedye' (V.1786). The Monk's somewhat pedestrian definition is often quoted: 'tragedie is to seyn a certeyn storie . . . | Of hym that stood in greet prosperitee, | And is yfallen out of heigh decree | Into myserie, and endeth wrecchedly' (VII.1973–7). A similar gloss in *Boece* (II pr.2:70–2) ('tragedie is to seyn a dite [composition in verse] of a prosperitee for a tyme, that endeth in wrecchidnesse') is equally well known. But these isolated quotations do not give much sense of the emotional power and the horror which medieval tragedy could have. The Monk begins his Tale 'I wol bewaille in manere of tragedie' and repeats 'crie' and 'bewaille' at the end, only to be scoffed at by the Host, who does not see any use in bewailing what has already happened. And the definition in *Boece* quoted above is preceded by a reference to the 'cryings' of tragedies—'what other thynge bywaylen the cryinges of tragedyes but oonly the dedes of Fortune, that with an unwar strook overturneth the realmes of greet nobleye?' But Philosophy's purpose is to offer a firm consolation (it is not clear that there is room for 'tragedy' of any kind in her scheme). However the two opening stanzas of the *Troilus* have a quite different emotional power, with words like 'the double sorwe of Troilus', the repetition of 'sorwynge', 'sorwful', and with an invocation to a Fury ('goddesse of torment', 'sorwynge evere in peyne' as muse, to help the poet compose 'thise woful vers, that wepen as I write'. After the joy of book III, the descent is grim and terrible: tragedy 'is in its beginning admirable and tranquil but in its end fetid and horrible' says the Epistle to Can Grande, often attributed to *Dante. The concept (and perhaps the techniques) of medieval tragedy are likely to have been influenced by the tragedies of Seneca (*Senec). There seems to have been an expectation of scenes of pathos and horror, violently strained emotions, eloquent rhetorical speeches and laments, and urgent moral 'sentence'. The workings of Fortune are important, but individual character and personal choice are by no means excluded (even in the brief and gloomy tragedies of the Monk). The narrator may act as a dramaturge or presenter of the action (which is how *Lydgate seems to have imagined the ancient tragic poet) or in a choric role, offering philosophical reflections or consolations, or expressing anxiety. Chaucer's *Troilus* and Henryson's *The *Testament of Cresseid* are impressive examples. (See also '***pite**'.)

Boitani (1989); Dante in Moore and Toynbee (1924), 416; Kelly (1997); Minnis and Scott (1988).

Tramyssene, Tlemcen in north-west Algeria. Here the *Knight fought for 'oure feith' (I.62).

tregetoures, magicians or illusionists, some of whose feats are described in *The Franklin's Tale* (V.1141–51). Artificers produced similar wonders for medieval monarchs in their great halls. In *HF* (1260) they are coupled with magicians in a list of various kinds of enchanters, and one of them, *Colle tregetour, is mentioned by name (1277).

L. Loomis (1958); R. S. Loomis (1965), 165; Wickham (1991).

TREVET, TRIVET, Nicholas, a Dominican friar (?d. *c.*1334), who studied and taught at Oxford, Paris and London, was a man of considerable learning ('a true polymath' (Smalley)), with a notable interest in classical texts. His numerous works include commentaries on the Psalter, on Augustine's *City of God*, Boethius, Livy, Ovid's *Metamorphoses*, the elder Seneca's *Declamations*, and the plays of the younger Seneca (written *c.*1315, for his friend Cardinal Nicolas of Prato), and possibly commentaries (now lost) on other classical works. A section of his Anglo-Norman chronicle (written in the early 14th c. for Marie the daughter of Edward I who had become a nun) provided Chaucer with an account of the life of Constance on which he based *The *Man of Law's Tale*. He also used Trevet's commentary on Boethius for his *Boece*, and may have used the commentary on Seneca's plays.

Emden (1957–9); Minnis and Scott (1988), 316 ff.; Smalley (1960), 58.

TREVISA, JOHN (d. *c.*1401). Spent many years in Oxford, mostly at Queen's College where he may have known *John Wyclif. By 1387 he was vicar of Berkeley (Glos.), where he was chaplain to Thomas, 9th Lord Berkeley. He translated into English, in some cases at the instigation of Thomas, a number of works including Higden's *Polychronicon*, Bartholomeus Anglicus (*Bartholomew) *De proprietatibus rerum*, *FitzRalph's *Defensio curatorum*; Caxton credited him with a translation of the Bible, but, unless Trevisa was involved in the processes that led to the versions of the Wycliffite Bible, this has not survived.   [AH]

A. S. G. Edwards (1984).

Trygwille, Triguilla, a Goth hostile to Boethius (*Bo* I pr.4:58).

Tristram, Tristam, Tristan, the lover of Iseult or Isolde (*Isaude) in a series of romances which were immensely popular in the Middle Ages. He is depicted among the lovers in the temple of *Venus (*PF* 290). Chaucer (gallantly? jocularly?) calls himself 'trewe Tristam the secounde' in *To *Rosemounde* (20).

Triton, a merman, the son of Neptune (*LGW* 2422), portrayed blowing a conch shell and hence associated with trumpets (*HF* 1595–604).

TRIVET, see *Trevet.

Trivium, Grammar, Rhetoric, and Logic (later called Dialectic), namely the three introductory of the *Seven Liberal Arts. The adjective *trivialis* of university Latin was at first more or less descriptive, but gradually took on the meaning of our 'trivial', which seems not to have been used before the late 16th century, however.   [JDN]

Troilus, the hero of *Troilus and Criseyde* is a Trojan prince, the youngest son of Priam and Hecuba. He does not have a prominent role in ancient literature, although Virgil mentions him and records his death at the hands of Achilles (*Aeneid* I.474–8). It is *Benoît de Sainte-Maure who tells the story of his love for *Briseida, who later becomes Criseida or Criseyde in the elaborated stories of *Boccaccio and Chaucer. Late in his poem (V.827–40) Chaucer gives a brief

description of him; tall, well formed, 'yong, fresh, strong, and hardy as lyoun'. He does not specify an exact age, though most readers would endorse the adjective 'young', which comes from earlier tradition (in Virgil he is an 'unfortunate boy' ['infelix puer']). The importance of Troilus the warrior, pre-eminent in 'durryng don that longeth to a knyght [daring to perform knightly deeds] (V.837) is emphasized throughout (cf. for instance the 'knightly sight' of Troilus riding back from battle in II.624–48)—the adjective 'manly' is several times applied to him (II.1263; III.113; V.30). It is easy to forget this because of the great fame of Troilus the lover. And Troilus seen exclusively as lover has also suffered from unsympathetic and careless readings. Modern students are particularly impatient with his tears, swoons, and uncertainties. Chaucer, however, like Shakespeare, was more sympathetic to young love, even though he too could see its occasional absurdities as well as its sometimes tragic excess. Troilus has something in common with the lover in the *Roman de la Rose*, but he is far from being just a conventional courtly lover. Chaucer presents dramatically the agonies and despair as well as the ecstasy of his experience in love. Love comes to him as an overwhelming force, which brings a genuine 'conversion', and his words at the end of the third book, 'now I feele a newe qualitee— | Yee, al another than I dide er this' (III.1654–5), suggest that the union has been a profound experience, and signal a new maturity and assurance (soon to be cruelly tested). Love for him is a serious and noble thing, and not selfish desire. Chaucer also takes pains to set the love in a social situation with its own *mores* and demands. One of the main reasons Troilus in the fourth book does not act as some of his critics would wish him to and make his love public or run away with Criseyde is his regard for her honour (the value which she not only places upon herself but which she feels is placed on her by society— see, for instance, III.162–8; IV.554–74). Troilus has an essential nobility of spirit, marked by those qualities that Chaucer admired, '*gentillesse' and '*pite'. The expression of these qualities can certainly be highly emotional, but Chaucer seems to find this a sign of generosity of spirit and an admirable quality in a man rather than a fault. It has indeed been convincingly argued that Troilus is an example of an ideal 'feminised hero' (Mann). Chaucer added yet another element to this far from simple figure. Troilus is also an intellectual, more concerned than the other characters to analyse and understand the philosophical implications of their situation. It is most appropriate that the philosophical love sonnet of Petrarch (I.400–20) is put in his mouth, and this urgent questioning is found throughout, in his reflections on free will and determinism, and elsewhere. In IV.1667–80 Criseyde describes the qualities which led her to love him: they include 'moral vertu, grounded upon trouthe' and 'gentil herte and manhod'. Troilus is in every sense the hero of the poem.

David (1962); Mann (1991).

Troilus and Criseyde (also called by Chaucer 'The Book of Troilus' in his *Retractions* and simply 'Troylus' in *Adam*, see *Adam (2)), a poem in rhyme royal, in five books, the first four of which are introduced by a formal proem or *prologue. (These are of considerable interest, suggesting a number of dominant ideas and images and establishing the voice of the narrator. In the briefest outline: (1) states the subject and asks the Fury Tisiphone (*Thesiphone) for aid in his sorrowful task. He is simply the servant of the servants of love, and asks them to pray for him and for other lovers; (2) signals the beginnings of hope for Troilus, asks the *muse Clio (*Cleo) for aid, and touches on mutability and diversity in language and in love; (3) is a prayer to and praise of *Venus, the 'blisful' planet and the goddess of love; (4) reflects that joy lasts all too shortly, thanks to *Fortune, and asks the Furies and Mars to help him bring the story he must tell to its unhappy end.)

Book I (1092 lines). (57–154) The scene is set in the Trojan War, with the defection of Calchas (*Calkas) and the plight of his daughter Criseyde. (155–322) In April the Trojans celebrate the feast of *Palladion. In the temple Troilus sees Criseyde, and falls in love with her. (323–546) Troilus returns to his palace. Alone in his chamber he sings a song of love. He suffers the throes of love-melancholy, and makes an anguished '*complaint'. (547–1092) His friend Pandarus enters, and in a long scene Troilus confesses his love and finally admits the name of his lady. Pandarus promises to help him.

Book II (1757 lines) (50–595) Pandarus goes to Criseyde and begins his campaign of persuasion. The episode begins after a May introduction, with Pandarus discovering Criseyde and her ladies listening to the story of *Thebes (1). In a long scene Pandarus teases and mystifies Criseyde with his promise of news, and his hints. A new stage is prefaced by his self-conscious musings on persuasive tactics. He looks at Criseyde 'in a bysi wyse' and finally satisfies her curiosity: Troilus the king's son loves her. He urges her to show pity or else he will die, 'love of friendship' will not incur any scandal. She must love, before her beauty is wasted by age. She agrees to try to please Troilus ('myn honour sauf') but nothing more. He leaves Criseyde fearful, worried, curious, and prepared to entertain the thought of love. (596–931) Criseyde alone in her room recalls everything that has been said and done. She is interrupted by the sight of Troilus riding back from battle, which sets off a long argument within her mind as to what she feels and what she should do. She goes into her garden and hears *Antigone's song of ideal love. Night falls, the nightingale sings under her chamber, and she dreams how a white eagle tore out her heart and replaced it with his own. (932–1302) On the same night Troilus is visited by Pandarus, who suggests writing a letter to Criseyde, and on the next day riding past her palace. He takes the letter to her, and persuades her to reply to it. She again sees Troilus as he comes riding past. (1303–757) Pandarus brings her letter back to Troilus, and encourages him. Pandarus is now ready to begin his 'grete empryse [undertaking]'. He tells Deiphebus, Troilus's brother, that Criseyde is being persecuted, and arranges a dinner (a midday meal) for her friends at Deiphebus's house. Criseyde is invited, but not told that Troilus will be there. Returning to Troilus, Pandarus urges him to 'bear him well' on the following day, and, to cover his fear and nervousness, devises a further sleight: Troilus is to feign illness, and stay over night in Deiphebus's house. Everything goes according to Pandarus's plan, and finally, after dinner, Pandarus contrives to bring Criseyde alone into the room where the 'sick' Troilus lies.

Book III (1820 lines). (50–231) The scene between Troilus and Criseyde at Deiphebus's house is resumed. Troilus manages to say 'Mercy,

mercy, swete herte', and then an eloquent plea. Criseyde looks on him 'ful esily and ful debonairly [graciously]' and says that, 'myn honour sauf', she will receive him to her service, and kisses him. (232–504) Pandarus speaks earnestly to Troilus about the 'game' he has begun and his part in it as a go-between, and urges him to be discreet. Troilus, filled with joy, reassures him (he has done it all for friendship), and says that he would willingly do the same for him. Time passes and Troilus shows himself to be discreet and faithful. (505–693) Pandarus invites Criseyde to have supper at his house, and arranges for Troilus to be there, hidden. A terrible 'smoky' rain falls, and she is prevailed upon to stay the night. (694–1190) After much emotion and yet another stratagem, Pandarus brings the lovers together. (1191–414) In a fine lyrical scene their union is celebrated: Criseyde's fearfulness is overcome and she 'opens her heart'. Both, for a time at least, find assurance and 'sikernes' in a love that is noble, spiritual, and physical. (1415–554) Dawn comes and the lovers must part, and return to the ordinary world. (1555–820) Pandarus comes to Criseyde, and teases her. Troilus sends for him and expresses his gratitude and joy. The lovers meet again, and are again separated by the coming of day, and 'thus Fortune a tyme ledde in joie | Criseyde and ek the kynges sone of Troie'. Troilus sings a song of praise to Love, and the book ends with him 'in lust [delight] and in quiete | . . . with Criseyde, his owen herte swete.'

Book IV (1701 lines). (29–217) There is a battle, and *Antenor is captured. There is discussion of an exchange of prisoners, and Calchas pleads with the Greeks to propose the exchange of Antenor for his daughter. This is done, and there is a tense scene at the Trojan parliament, at which Troilus is present. At the news he almost dies, but does not show his emotion. In spite of Hector's objection that Criseyde is not a prisoner, 'the noyse of peple' clamouring for the warrior Antenor seals her fate. (218–658) Troilus returns alone to his palace, and vents his feelings in a passionate lament. Pandarus hurries to him and attempts to console him, but his suggestions are firmly refused. (659–945) News of the exchange reaches Criseyde. When her women friends leave, she goes into her chamber and bitterly laments.

Pandarus arrives, and tries to calm her. (946–1127) Pandarus finds Troilus in a temple, despairing, praying to the gods, and disputing with himself the philosophical idea that 'al that comth, comth by necessitee'. Pandarus points out that Criseyde has not yet had to leave, and urges him to visit her. (1128–701) In a long, intense scene the lovers meet privately for what is to be the last time. Criseyde faints, and Troilus, thinking her dead, laments and prepares to kill himself. She revives before he is able to, and as they lie together she attempts to console him by finding a remedy for their plight. She will attempt to return quickly and they can be reunited. Her father is avaricious and she can trick him. Troilus is not convinced. Her father is too cunning to be deceived. He will marry her off to some Greek: indeed, among the Greeks she will come to despise the Trojans. She swears that she will return on the tenth day. They lament and kiss and embrace. When dawn comes Troilus leaves.

Book V (1869 lines) (1–196) Diomede comes to lead Criseyde to the Greek camp. Troilus and a large group of knights are in attendance, and he bids her farewell. She is reunited with her father. (197–686) Troilus waits for her to return. He is assailed by terrible dreams. Pandarus takes him to visit *Sarpedon, where they are splendidly entertained, but nothing can relieve Troilus's melancholy. He visits the empty palace of Criseyde and the gates from which she rode out. He sings a sorrowful song, and looks out from the walls to the Greek camp. He desperately endures 'til fully passed was the nynthe nyght'. (687–1099) Criseyde stands sorrowfully among the Greeks looking back at the walls of Troy, still determined to find some way to go back. Diomede determines to win her. At this turning point we are given brief portraits of the main characters, Diomede, Criseyde, and Troilus. (799–840) On the tenth day Diomede makes an opportunity to speak to Criseyde. He talks of the war but moves on to more personal matters and questions. Troy is doomed, he insists. She should forget the Trojans, recover her beauty, and find a more perfect love among the Greeks. Criseyde responds to this politely, but agrees to speak with him further. However, thinking over his words, a change begins in her. Diomede returns, she gives him gifts, and, says the poet, 'men seyn—I not—that she yaf[gave] hym hire herte'. She reproaches herself in a final farewell speech. (1100–869) Troilus waits with Pandarus through the tenth day, and as the days pass he is plunged into profound melancholy. He dreams of a boar lying with Criseyde, which he interprets as a sign that she has betrayed him. Pandarus tries to dismiss the dream, and persuades him to write a letter to her. His sister *Cassandra confirms his interpretation of the dream. He receives a letter from Criseyde which seems to him 'al straunge', and finally he discovers his brooch on a tunic taken from Diomede. He makes a bitter lament but cannot find it in his heart to 'unloven' Criseyde. He tries to seek out Diomede in battle and kill him, but without success, and at the end he is himself killed by *Achilles. His spirit goes up to the eighth sphere. The poet gives a final address to his readers and to 'yonge, fresshe folkes' and ends with a prayer to God in Trinity.

The poem survives in sixteen manuscripts, and a number of fragments, and in the prints of *Caxton (*c.*1483), Wynkyn de Worde (1517) and Thynne (1532). There is some evidence of revision (thus, the Proem to book IV seems to suggest that the story will end in that book, and is presumably an unrevised relic from an earlier plan), but the nature and extent of revision remains uncertain. Nor is the date of the poem certain. It was written before The *Legend of Good Women. It must have been completed before the death of Thomas *Usk (4 March 1388), who refers to it in his *Testament of Love* written in prison (either his final imprisonment or, possibly, an earlier one from December 1384 to June 1385). If 'philosophical *Strode' is Ralph Strode, it would have been written before his death in 1387. If the remark 'right as oure firste lettre is now an A' (I.171) alludes to Anne of Bohemia, who married Richard II on 14 January 1382, it would have been written after that date. Other possible guides are suggestive, if their significance is not always certain. There is a clear astronomical reference (III.624–5) to an event which took place on 9 June 1385, when the new moon was almost invisible and near Jupiter, and Jupiter and Saturn were in the sign of Cancer (see North for this and for a possible astrological 'timetable'). Less clear is the question of whether the Trojan parliament at the beginning of book IV has any topical relevance: it has been suggested that it reflects the English parliament which Chaucer attended in October and November of 1386. A tentative period of composition from ?1382 to 1385, 1386, or 1387 is suggested. The latter part of the period corresponds to what seems to have been a difficult time in Chaucer's life, in which he lost both of his controllerships, and in which his wife died (see Geoffrey *Chaucer: life).

Chaucer's main source is *Boccaccio's poem *Il *Filostrato*, written in the late 1330s. He may also have used a French prose translation of it, the *Roman de Troyle* by a 'Beauvau', seneschal of Anjou. The *Filostrato* is a very good poem (offering a model of dramatic narrative with vivid scenes and dialogue and songs, and of a thoughtful treatment of love in an eloquent vernacular style), and clearly sparked Chaucer's imagination. He follows the main lines of its plot, but treats it freely and boldly, transforming a good poem into a masterpiece. He invents whole scenes (like the dinner party at the house of Deiphebus), characters are deepened, philosophical implications and questions widened and pursued. He presents Criseyde, and her progress towards love, as more uncertain and less straightforward than in Boccaccio, and he shows much greater *pite* for her at the end. *Troilus* is a very literary poem, full of *allusions to Chaucer's remarkably wide reading. He makes use (sometimes extensive use) of Boethius (*Boece) and *Dante, *Ovid and Statius (*Stace), the *Roman de la Rose* and *Guillaume de Machaut, stories of Troy by *Benoît de Sainte-Maure, *Guido, and *Joseph of Exeter, Petrarch (*Petrak), and other works of Boccaccio, the *Teseida* (from which he took the apotheosis) and perhaps the *Filocolo*.

The poem has sometimes been compared to the later novel, because of its psychological realism, the interaction of character and situation, and the way in which a reader comes to 'inhabit' the little world of the lovers and Pandarus. Perhaps a comparison with the *drama would be more cogent. It is a markedly dramatic narrative. It has been calculated that about seven out of every eight lines in the poem are in direct speech. Whole scenes are conducted in dialogue, many of the scenes are conceived visually, and there is a dramatic imagination behind the structural contrasting of scene with scene. Yet it remains a narrative poem, with its own proper techniques. It does not seem to fit easily into any single one of the genres with which it has affinities—epic, *romance, or 'history'. Chaucer calls it a 'tale' and a 'story', but also significantly a '*tragedy'. At the beginning the sorrow of the story is emphasized, and the sudden destruction of the lovers' joy has the intense pathos and horror expected in medieval tragedy (probably reflecting the patterns of Senecan drama). Emotions are stretched and torn; speeches and laments are rhetorical and sometimes operatic. The poet-narrator sometimes speaks as a kind of dramaturge, simply presenting the scene, sometimes as a kind of chorus, commenting, expressing hope, anxiety, or sympathy. It may even be that the poem's five-book structure (which allows Chaucer to use a deliberate symmetry of organization, using contrasting parallels in situation, imagery, etc., to achieve pathos and irony) was suggested to him by the five-act structure of Roman drama.

Troilus and Criseyde has occasioned much discussion, and has sometimes been the victim of limited and limiting critical approaches which exaggerate one aspect or idea (the 'narrator' as against Chaucer, 'irony', 'courtly love', etc.) at the expense of everything else, and at the expense of the poem's genuine complexity. It is a complex and sometimes a difficult poem, and it is possible to hold different and conflicting views about a range of issues which it raises—the interpretation of the 'Christian' ending and its relationship with what has gone before, for instance. What readers unite in admiring is the sheer power of the writing, the narrative skill, the weaving of patterns of imagery, the blending of the serious with the comic, of high tragedy with the humble 'common rhythm of life' (the arrangement of the rooms in Pandarus's house for instance, or the medieval night-light by which Criseyde tells the time, IV.1245–6). It has long been admired—praised by *Sidney, imitated in various ways by *Henryson, *Shakespeare and *Dryden. In the Middle Ages it was a valued (and probably a valuable) book. Under the words of the inventory of the 15th-c. gentleman, John Paston II, lurks an intriguing story. He possessed 'a Boke of Troylus', which a

certain William 'has had nearly ten years', and not only that, but had lent it to 'Dame Wyngfelde'—'and I saw it there!' (*CH* i. 71).

(ed.) *Rv* 471–585, 1020–58; Root (1926); Windeatt (1984*b*); Windeatt (1992); North (1990), ch. 11; R. K. Gordon (1934); Bayley (1960); Boitani (1989); Donaldson (1963); Dronke (1964); Dunning (1962); C. S. Lewis (1932); Meech (1959); Norton-Smith (1974), ch. 6; Payne (1963), ch. 6; Wetherbee (1984).

Troilus and Cressida, Shakespeare's main source for the material of *Troilus and Cressida* was *The Recuyell of the Historyes of Troy* in Caxton's translation (*c*.1475) rather than either Homer or Chaucer, and Shakespeare's focus in the play is not solely on the love story of Troilus and Cressida. The play is a hard-edged anti-heroic treatment of the harebrained Trojans and beef-witted Greeks, ranging the characters of the *Iliad* against each other, and effectively concludes with the brutal slaughter of the unarmed Hector by Achilles and his Myrmidons rather than Troilus's disillusion.

Some have disputed whether Shakespeare had read Chaucer's poem at all. Others have claimed that if he had he could not have understood it very well, and in any case would have read it together with *The Testament of Cresseid* printed in Tudor and Elizabethan editions after the last book of *Troilus and Criseyde*, with no indication of change of authorship. It has also been pointed out that any exploration of Shakespeare's relationship with Chaucer's version would be hampered by the fact that before the end of the 16th c. Cressida was proverbial for her faithlessness, and Pandar had become a common noun, a bawd or pimp. The Chaucer story and its sequel had been balladed in the 1560s and several plays on the story staged before Shakespeare's, thus making any immediate debt to Chaucer difficult to judge.

Others have objected to this kind of literary determinism and resisted the suggestion that the deterioration of the Cressida figure (and with it that of Troilus) forced Shakespeare into depicting her as a whore, if a witty one. In Chaucer's poem Criseyde, after she has decided to accept Diomede as her lover in place of Troilus, acknowledges the role she will play in literary history, and Cressida in the play is aware of her function as the unforgivable heroine of a sour love story: 'As false as Cressid'. Donaldson (1985) in particular asserts the attractiveness and vitality of Shakespeare's Cressida, and carefully assesses the similarities and differences between Chaucer's and Shakespeare's characterizations of them, pursuing the transformation of Criseyde into Cressida on the assumption that Shakespeare did indeed form his Cressida from Chaucer.

Several scenes and incidents in the play parallel those in the poem and invite comparison and contrast: for example, the lovers kiss to Pandarus's verbal accompaniment; both Pandaruses visit Criseyde/Cressida after the night of love-making; both women lament at the prospect of leaving Troy; both Troiluses make their farewells. In rehabilitating Cressida as a more attractively ambiguous character than merely one of the 'daughters of the game' the possibilities for comparison and contrast with Chaucer's heroine increase. [RB]

Burns (1980); E. T. Donaldson (1982; 1985); Hillerbrand (1953); Kimbrough (1964); A. Thompson (1978).

Trophee in *The Monk's Tale* (VII.2117) is said to have written that Hercules set pillars at both ends of the world. He remains unidentified. Glosses in the Ellesmere and Hengwrt MSS identifying 'Tropheus' as 'a prophet of the Chaldees' seem to be puzzled guesses.

Tropic, the 'turning point' of the Sun (Greek *tropikos*) at either of the solstices; or a circle on an astrolabe centred on the north pole (at the pin) and drawn through one of the solsticial points, the head of Cancer or the head of Capricorn; or the corresponding circle on the Earth's surface, along which the Sun may be in the zenith at the time of the solstice. (See also *astrology and astronomy; *Cenyth; *hed; *solsticioun.) [JDN]

TROTULA appears among the anti-feminist writings in *Jankin's (4) 'book of wicked wives' (III.677). She is probably Trotula or Trota, a woman physician at Salerno in the late 11th or 12th c. The only work that can be safely attributed to her is the *Practica secundum Trotam* ('the Practice according to Trotula'), but later a number of other treatises on obstetrics and gynaecology were associated with her name. She probably appears in the list of Jankin's texts because she was thought to endorse the idea of women's physical inferiority to men. (See also *medicine.)

Barratt (1992), 27–39 and references.

Troy(e) (see also **Ilio(u)n**) Troy, the ancient city on the eastern shore of the Hellespont, in modern Turkey, said in legend to have been founded by Dardanus the son of Zeus, and celebrated in literature because of the Trojan War. The story of how it was besieged by the Greeks under Agamemnon (*Agemeno(u)n) in order to recapture Helen (*Eleyne) who had been abducted by *Paris the son of King *Priam, of the series of great battles involving especially the champions, the Trojan Hector (*Ector) and the Greek *Achilles, the stratagem of the 'Trojan Horse' and the deceit of Sinon (*Syno(u)n) and the consequent fall and destruction of the city was immensely popular. Chaucer had not read Homer (*Omer), but he knew that he was one of those who 'bore up' the fame of Troy (*HF* 1477): the others included the authors of what he calls the 'Troian gestes [tales of exploits]'. *Dares (see also *Joseph of Exeter), Dictys (*Dite), *Guido, Chaucer's own mysterious '*Lollius', and of course *Virgil. Most of this literature had a markedly Trojan bias: England, like other nations, claimed descent from Brutus, the great grandson of Aeneas, who founded 'New Troy' there (in Chaucer's lifetime there was talk of renaming London 'Troynovaunt'). The stories were told in French (see *Benoît de Sainte-Maure), in English, and in many other vernaculars. Chaucer knew them well, making passing allusions to the city, the war, and its heroes, and evidently expected his audience to be familiar with them: 'yt is wel wist [known] how that the Grekes stronge | In armes with a thousand shippes wente | To Troiewardes' (*Tr* I.57–9). He refers several times to the 'grete sege' and to the 'destruccion' of the city (clearly a deeply emotional event) and to the scenes of pathos associated with it: the weeping when the dead body of Hector is brought back to Troy (I.2833) or the death of Priam (*HF* 158–61, and, in a mock-heroic context, VII.3355–61). In *Troilus and Criseyde* he made his own distinguished contribution to the literature of Troy.

The city and the siege are the sharply realized background for his love story. Although it has a temple, the city has become a medieval walled town (as it is depicted in contemporary illustrations) (see Fig. 6): at night the 'warden of the gates' calls on people outside to drive in their beasts. Its great figures (like Hector) and its physical features are referred to easily and familiarly: Criseyde calls on the river Simois to bear witness to what she says (IV.1548–50). The characters allude to its history as something commonly known: replying to Pandarus's taunt (an attempt at consolation), 'Artow in Troie, and hast non hardyment | to take a woman which that loveth the' (IV.533–4), Troilus says soberly, 'thow woost [know] this town hath al this werre | For ravysshyng of wommen so by myght' (547–8), the plural 'wommen' neatly alluding to two fatal abductions (Telamon's abduction of Hesione of Troy and Paris's retaliation). The war is always there, and the prophetic reminders of the fate of the city ('the tyme is faste by | That fire and flaumbe on al the town shal sprede, | And thus shal Troie torne to asshen dede', IV.117–19, etc.) build up a powerful sense of doom. The 'peril of the town' (V.1025) is one factor in Criseyde's change of heart.

C. D. Benson (1980); Scherer (1963).

Trumpyngton, Trumpington, near Cambridge (I.3921).

Truth, one of Chaucer's philosophical short poems, Boethian in tone (in some MSS headed 'Balade de Bon Conseyl'). It consists of three stanzas in rhyme royal (see *versification), followed (in one MS only) by an *Envoy, also in rhyme royal. It is an eloquent address to an individual (called 'thou' throughout) and apparently a friend. From the beginning ('Flee fro the prees [crowd] and dwelle with sothfastnesse' [truth]) it is a stirring series of imperatives, urging contentment with few possessions, the obedient acceptance of what is sent, and a withdrawal from the turmoil of the 'prees' ('gret reste stant in litel besinesse'). The emphasis on fruitless struggle ('the wrastling for this world axeth a fal') shifts to one on the idea of a pilgrim in this world, which is not a 'home' but a wilderness ('Forth, pilgrim, forth! | . . . know thy contree, look up, thank God of al'), and this is continued in the Envoy. Each stanza ends on a note of consolation and hope with the refrain, 'and trouthe thee shal delivere, it is no drede [fear]'. ('Trouthe' here signifies both 'truth' ('sothfastnesse') and faithfulness or fidelity, a highly prized virtue in the Middle Ages.) The poem was apparently popular, surviving in over twenty MS copies and two early prints. The only possible hint as to its date may come from the Envoy, which is almost certainly Chaucer's (though he could well have added it to an earlier version). Its opening, 'therfore, thou Vache, leve thyn old wrecchednesse', seems certainly an address to Sir Philip de la Vache (1346–1408), a courtier and son-in-law of Sir Lewis *Clifford, a friend of Chaucer. In 1386–9, because of the Lords Appellant, he was out of favour (as Chaucer was). The poem (or the unique version with the Envoy) may come from this period, although absolute certainty is impossible. Matters improved for Vache when Richard resumed power, and he was eventually made a Knight of the Garter. The poem can be read on various levels, and the 'prees' and the 'world' almost certainly refer to the court as well as having a more general sense. It is a good example of Chaucer's epistolary style, witty and sympathetic, and sometimes very familiar— as when Vache is not only identified with a 'pilgrim' but with a 'beast' in a stall (18), and has an outrageous pun made on his name ('vache' Fr. 'cow').

(ed.) *Rv* 653, 1084–5; Pace and David (1982), 49–65; Scattergood (1995), 492–6, 502–3.

Tubal, The Man in Black (*BD* 1162 ff.) refers to

> Lamekes sone Tubal,
> That found out first the art of songe;
> For as hys brothres hamers ronge
> Upon hys anvelt [anvil] . . .
> Therof he took the firste soun

although the Greeks say that the inventor was Pythagoras (*Pictagoras). In Genesis (4:22) Lamech's son Tubal-Cain is said to be 'an instructor, of every artificer in brass and iron'; another son (by another wife), Jubal is described in the preceding verse as 'the father of all such as sing to the harp and the organ'. The two were often confused.

TUL(L)IUS (also called **Marcus Tulyus** or **Marcus Tullius Scithero** (V.722, apparently from a spelling Cithero)), Marcus Tullius Cicero (106–43 BC) Roman orator, writer, and statesman. Among his many works the best known were *De oratore*, *De re publica* (book 6 of which was the *Somnium Scipionis*, Chaucer's *Drem of Scipioun*), *De officiis*, *De senectute*, *De amicitia*, and his letters to his friends. He was celebrated for his rhetorical skill. As well as his genuine treatise *De oratore*, the popular *Rhetorica ad Herennium* was attributed to him in the Middle Ages (see *rhetoric). The Franklin refers to him as a rhetorical authority (V.722). General philosophical 'sentences' were also often quoted: these often come through intermediaries, and (as with Seneca (*Senec)) not all the sayings attributed to Cicero are actually from his works. There are a large number in *Melibee (via the *Livre de Melibee*), mostly from *De officiis* (VII.1180, 1192, etc.), but also from *De senectute* (1165), the Tusculan Disputations (1174), and the *De amicitia* (1176)—on the danger of flattery to friendship. *Boece (V. pr.4:3–5) refers to *De divinatione*. Chaucer reads that very influential book, the 'Drem of Scipioun', at the beginning of *The *Parliament of Fowls*, and it lies in the background of the ascents to the heavens of himself in *HF* and of the spirit of Troilus.

(ed. and trans.) Falconer (1923); Keyes (1928); King (1927); W. Miller (1913); W. G. Williams (1927).

TULLIUS HOSTILLIUS, Tullus Hostilius, the legendary third king of Rome (673–642 BC). He is cited by the old woman in *The *Wife of Bath's Tale* (III.1165–7) as an example of one who rose to 'heigh noblesse' from poverty, according to *Valerius Maximus. The 'Tullius' whose 'kyndenesse' is mentioned in *Scogan (47) may be the king, but more probably is Cicero.

Turk(e)ye, Turkey, which in Chaucer's time (see Map 3) was firmly under the control of the Ottomans, who were steadily advancing into south-eastern Europe and gradually isolating Constantinople. Under Murad I (1362–89) the south Serbian states were conquered, and at Kosovo (1386) the north Serbian states were defeated. Bajazet I (1389–1403) effectively blockaded Constantinople and at Nicopolis (1396) destroyed the Christian army that was attempting to relieve it. The *Knight had fought in Turkey (I.66; see *Palatye); in *The *Book of the Duchess* (1026) it is mentioned as a distant realm. The 'bowe turkeys' (I.2895) and 'Turke bowes' (*Rom* 923) refer to the short powerful Turkish bow (the first may have been suggested by a gloss 'turcassi' ('quivers') in Boccaccio).

Turnus in the *Aeneid* (books 7–12) the king of the Rutuli and the suitor of Lavinia, the daughter of *King Latinus. He was eventually defeated and killed by Aeneas. Chaucer refers to him several times. He appears in the temple of *Venus in *The *Knight's Tale* (I.1945) 'with hardy fiers corage'; and his fate was one of those written in the stars (II.201). On the walls of the temple in *The *House of Fame* there is a depiction of how Aeneas slew him and won Lavinia (457–8). And at the beginning of the second book there is an allusion (516) to one of his prophetic dreams (*Aen* 7.413–59 or 9.1–13).

Two Noble Kinsmen, The. Shakespeare's and John Fletcher's collaborative play signals its Chaucerian source with unusual frankness in its Prologue: 'Chaucer, of all admired, the story gives', and *The *Knight's Tale* forms the basis of the story. The play follows the main action of the poem fairly closely, with the addition of a sub-plot, mostly contributed by Fletcher. The question of the attribution of the various parts of the play to either Shakespeare or Fletcher can be pursued in, for example, Waith's edition of the play in The Oxford Shakespeare series (1989), and the relationship between the play and its source has been treated in depth by Thompson (1978) and Donaldson (1985). Fletcher presumably read Chaucer in Thomas Speght's edition, first published in 1598; Shakespeare, as when he drew on *The Knight's Tale* in *A Midsummer Night's Dream*, probably used Stow's 1561 printing of Thynne's edition (1532), but there is no clear indication of which edition he was following for *The Two Noble Kinsmen*.

The similarities and differences in treatment between Chaucer's telling of the story and that of the later play—granting the generic differences between a medieval philosophical romance and a

Jacobean play staged at Blackfriars—have naturally occupied commentators. It has been suggested that the issue that interests Chaucer is the dominant role of chance in determining the course of human life, and there is a weighty pessimism underlying the tale, despite Theseus's fine speech arguing for a divine plan behind the randomness of events and despite the description of Palamon and Emily as living happily ever after. Whereas the misfortunes in Chaucer's tale seem to be mostly charged to the gods above, Shakespeare's and Fletcher's recreation, in which the gods (with the exception of Hymen) do not appear on stage, seems to show characters manipulated not from above but from within. The play's Palamon and Arcite may be more or less indistinguishable in their characters and desires, and less interesting than they are in the tale, but Emily is fleshed out in the play in a way which makes her more than a poetic image and whose dilemma of choice between the suitors generates much of the dramatic interest of the final part of the play.

In *The Knight's Tale* no one asks Emily what she wants. In the play Emilia is consulted but is offered only a cruelly conditional choice between the knights. When Theseus finds the lovers fighting in the woods and sentences them to immediate death Emilia, like Emily in the tale, is one of the women who pray to Theseus to spare them and, in the play, it is her prayer that finally moves him, though only perhaps because he is reminded that he had promised her a favour. He rejects, though, her suggestion that the knights be banished to separate countries—a plan which they reject too. Emilia is then asked to choose between them, the loser to be put to death. She refuses, but the knights agree enthusiastically. Theseus then proposes a tournament between them, each supported by three knights (instead of Chaucer's one hundred). The tournament is supposed to be non-lethal but the losers, all four of them, will be judicially executed and the winner will get Emilia. If She were to refuse to serve as a prize, Theseus would carry out his original sentence of death on them both.

In depicting Theseus's merciless all-or-nothing kind of 'justice' in the play it seems clear that Shakespeare and Fletcher are especially interested in the classical idea of *friendship and loyalty

between kinsmen (perhaps reflecting the revival in Prince Henry's court of the Elizabethan enthusiasm for *chivalry) and its conflict with law and, especially, the power of love. One of the larger designs of the play may be seen as the passage from the innocence of friendship between members of the same sex—not only that between the two captive knights but also between Emilia and her childhood friend Flavina—to the experience of love between the sexes, leading to marriage where it can and often to death or madness where it cannot. (In stage performances of the play it is evident that the non-Chaucerian material of the sub-plot concerning the jailer's daughter who is passionately but hopelessly drawn to Palamon and Ophelia-like, goes mad, has been the most popular part of the play.)

As in *The Knight's Tale*, Palamon prays to Venus, Arcite to Mars, and Emilia to Diana before the tournament. Emilia initially prays to remain unwed, but adds that if she must marry one may it be the one who loves her best. Throughout the final scenes she is not provoked into a preference, but her mind constantly dwells on the fact that one of the young men must die. She refuses to watch the tournament. It is clear that her cruel position, which the drama emphasizes, is not one devised by the gods but by Theseus's edict. The Theseus of the play is very different from Chaucer's: he appears to have neither tolerance nor humour, is a harsher, more remote figure than the earlier Theseus, and is less evidently a duke of chivalric 'gentilesse' and 'pitee'. Palamon wins Emilia, but only after a last-minute reprieve from execution following the news that Arcite, having won the tournament and been awarded the prize, rode round the city on the horse Emilia had given him (an irony the play adds to the tale): frightened not by a fury sent by Pluto at Saturn's request, as in *The Knight's Tale*, but by sparks caused by its own hooves, the horse had reared up and fallen backwards upon its rider.

Chaucer's tale concludes with Arcite's long death scene, his long and splendid funeral, the passing of years, the summoning of Palamon back from Thebes, and his final marriage to Emily. The play disposes of the finale in fifty lines, most of them assigned to Theseus. Some readers of the play see a congruence between the play's ending and Chaucer's tale, finding in the same irony of chance and coincidence pointing to Theseus's 'O you heavenly charmers, | What things you make of us!' Others find a different kind of irony, deriving from Shakespeare's imputed awareness that his and Fletcher's play is *not* about the chance-laden interaction of gods and mortals but is about the hearts and wills of the contestants, so that actually only Emilia is helpless before chance in the same sense that the heroes of *The Knight's Tale* are.   [RB]

(ed.) Waith 1989; Bertram (1965); E. T. Donaldson (1985); P. Edwards (1964); Ferguson (1986), 66–82, 140–2; A. Thompson (1978); Wickham (1980).

Tyrants, see *politics.

TYRWHITT, THOMAS (1730–86), educated at Eton and Queen's, Oxford, had a brief political career as clerk of the House of Commons (1762–8). He became a learned and distinguished classical scholar and commentator, and then used his skills on English texts. He edited Chatteron's 'Rowley' poems and pronounced them modern not ancient (1777–8). His critical notes on Shakespeare insisted on the careful collation of early texts. The edition of *The *Canterbury Tales* (4 vols. (1775), vol. v with Glossary 1778) explained Chaucer's *versification (his recognition of the pronunciation of unstressed -*e* rescued Chaucer from the charges of 'roughness') and began the task of establishing the canon. Tyrwhitt observed that several of the poems printed in previous editions of Chaucer were ascribed in MSS or prints to other writers: he therefore eliminated *La *Belle Dame Sans Merci, The *Letter of Cupid, The *Testament of Cresseid* and others. He also removed *The *Assembly of Ladies, *Beryn, *Gamelyn, *Jack Upland, The *Plowman's Tale,* etc. (including most of the 'heap of rubbish' added by *Stow), apparently on literary and stylistic grounds. He still accepted *The *Court of Love, The Complaint of the *Black Knight, The *Cuckoo and the Nightingale, The *Flower and the Leaf* (hesitantly), *The *Isle of Ladies,* and *The *Romaunt of the Rose.* His text formed the basis for most of the editions for the next seventy years. It was a genuine attempt to restore the text of *The Canterbury Tales.* Tyrwhitt collated or consulted over twenty MSS (although he used them in an unsystematic way), and added useful notes and glosses. His knowledge of early English was exceptional for his time.

CH i. 230–3; Windeatt (1984*a*).

U

ubi sunt [L. 'where are they'] a *rhetorical device consisting of a series of questions concerning the vanished riches or the vanished great men or women of the world, used characteristically in a poem on death or a lament. The most famous example is Villon's 'mais où sont les neiges d'antan?' ('but where are the snows of yesteryear?'), but the 'ubi sunt' is widely found in Latin and in both Old and Middle English. Chaucer translates a brief example in Boethius (*Boece): 'Where wonen [dwell] now the bones of trewe Fabricius? What is now Brutus or stierne Catoun? The thynne fame yit lastynge of here idel names is marked with a fewe lettres' (Bo II m.7:17–21). The *Parson meditating on the fate of the rich uses it (as was often done) in a more homiletic way: 'where been thanne the gaye robes, and the softe shetes, and the smale [thin, delicate] shertes?' (X.197). Chaucer has two excellent examples in the last book of *Troilus and Criseyde: at the opening of Troilus's lament (V.218–21) 'Wher is myn owene lady, lief and deere? | Wher is hire white brest? Wher is it, where? | Wher ben hire armes and hire eyen cleere | That yesternyght this tyme with me were?'; and later, more bitterly, when Troilus finds that Criseyde has abandoned him: 'O lady myn, Criseyde, | Where is youre feith, and where is youre biheste [promise]? | Where is youre love? Where is youre trouthe?' (V.1674–6).

ugliness. Just as there was a standard *rhetorical description of human *beauty, so there were formulae for the description of ugliness—often involving the reversal of the details of the former. This is found especially in satirical writing (vituperatio), where the ugliness of the person expresses the ugliness of the soul within. Some medieval writers are fond of the long set formal description of ugliness (a famous example is the gigantic herdsman in the Yvain of *Chrétien de Troyes). Gower rises to the description of an old hag in his story of Florent, but it is interesting that in Chaucer's version of this story in The Wife of Bath's Tale the narrator simply remarks that 'a fouler wight ther may no man devyse' (III.999): the reader is left to imagine the extent of her ugliness from the reactions of the knight. It seems that Chaucer was not interested in a display of rhetorical bravura. He notes rather examples of physical flaws or deviations from the ideal of beauty (the widely spaced teeth of the Wife of Bath or the joined eyebrows of Criseyde), details which give a sense of the 'thisness' of persons and of a pervasive realism (like the 'crows' feet' which Pandarus says age will bring (Tr II.403), the disfiguration caused by drunkenness (VI.551–4), or the purple ring with which sorrow encircles Criseyde's beautiful eyes (Tr IV.869) (see *eyes). Characteristically such details are used to emphasize a narrative and/or a moral point in a scene, like the gruesome moment in The *Merchant's Tale when old January's 'slakke skyn aboute his nekke shaketh' (IV.1849). They are used tellingly in some of the *portraits in the *General Prologue (like the 'mormal' on the *Cooks's shin). Here ugliness is usually obliquely or allusively suggested. The *Monk, for instance, is not exactly ugly but the cumulative effect of the details of the appearance of this 'fair prelaat' (the shining bald head, the shining face, the fatness, gleaming prominent eyes) is a highly unpleasant one. Even the descriptions of the *Pardoner with his glaring eyes or the even more repulsive *Summoner with fiery face, 'scalled browes', etc., who makes the children afraid, depend more on the careful selection of details of ugliness rather than on the overwhelmingly direct method of the vituperatio. The most extended examples are to be found in the descriptions of the images on the wall in the translated Romaunt of the Rose—Hate with 'frounced' face, grinning for rage, her nose 'snorted up [turned up] for tene [vexation]', Coveitise with crooked hands, Avarice green as a leek, 'yvel hewed' and in ragged clothing, Envy looking awry, Sorrow as if jaundiced, 'ful fade, pale, and megre [thin]', and Elde (Age), dried up to 'a foul forwelked [wrinkled] thyng', with her ears hanging from her head. But the most interesting is Chaucer's own 'grotesque' which he puts in the mouth of Pandarus (*Tr* II.1037–43), where *Horace's classical hybrid monster ('if a painter chose to join a human head to the neck of a horse, and to spread feathers of many a hue over limbs picked up now here now there, so that what at the top is a lovely woman ends below in a black and ugly fish') is transformed into what might have appeared in the margins of a medieval MS: 'if a peyntour wolde peynte a pyk | With asses feet, and hedde it [give it the head] as an ape'. Yet again it is fitted to the narrative and rhetorical context: this is advice on not jumbling together 'discordant thyng' in the writing of a love letter.

Ziolkowski (1984).

UGOLINO, see *Hugelyn.

Ulixes, Ulysses, the wandering Greek hero, who finally returned to his faithful wife *Penelope. In the Middle Ages his adventures were known from Latin sources. In Chaucer he appears only in the translation of Boethius (*Boece), who alludes to his adventures with Circe (*Cerces; *Bo* IV m.3) and Polyphemus (*Poliphemus; IV m.7).

university. In the medieval period an institution for advanced education, to which boys went after school at approximately 14; exercises were prescribed for the various degrees, and in England study for the degree of Master of Arts was required of all students first (apart from members of the fraternal orders who claimed exemption on the ground that they had covered the subjects in their own schools) before advancement to the study of theology, law, or medicine; study for the various degrees might take a variable, but often extensive, number of years. At Chaucer's time the only English universities were those of Oxford (with which Nicholas of *The Miller's Tale* was connected) and Cambridge (of which Alan and

John of *The Reeve's Tale* were members); on the continent Paris was still pre-eminent, but because of the wars between England and France was not so popular as in previous times. *Leland, followed by *Bale, stated that Chaucer had studied at Oxford, but for this no documentary confirmation has been found; Chaucer certainly knew Ralph *Strode who was at Merton College 1359–60 and maintained connections much later.   [AH]

A. B. Cobban (1988).

URBAN, Pope Urban I, of whom very little is known, except that he was elected Pope in 222, and was martyred in Rome in 230. In *The *Second Nun's Tale* Chaucer presents him as the leader of the persecuted early Christians, hiding 'among the seintes buryeles', the catacombs. At the time of the Tale's probable composition the Pope in Rome was Urban VI (1378–87), and it has been suggested (but not universally accepted) that Chaucer was alluding to this, and expressing a hope for the ending of the Schism.

URRY, JOHN (1666–1715), a friend of the antiquary Hearne, worked for some years on an edition of Chaucer's works, but died before it was completed. It was published in 1721 with a life of Chaucer by John Dart revised by William Thomas. It also contains the non-Chaucerian works found in earlier editions. Urry attempted to 'restore Chaucer to his feet again', i.e. to straighten out the metre by 'the discreet addition or omission of several initial or final syllables'.

Alderson (1984).

Ursa, one of the constellations, the Greater or Lesser Bear (note that *ursa* is strictly a she-bear), or a star. When Chaucer translated *Boece he was probably thinking of the star with Arabic name al-Dubb, alpha Ursae Majoris, which in some star-lists is glossed 'id est ursa'. (See also *Bere.)   [JDN]

USK, THOMAS, clerk to John of Northampton, mayor of London 1381–3; in 1384 Usk was arrested, but was released when he produced incriminating statements concerning Northampton; Usk joined himself then to Sir Nicholas *Brenbre, but together with Brenbre was in 1387 accused of treason by the duke of Gloucester and his associates (the 'appellants'), was condemned and executed on 4 March 1388. Usk acted as collector of customs in 1381–3, whilst Chaucer was Controller of Customs. Two of his writings survive: his Appeal in 1384, and the *Testament of Love*. The latter is a long and rambling prose work, dwelling at length upon his own misfortunes and the possible consolations that might be found for these: as the final chapter rightly says 'In this boke be many privy thinges wimpled and folde; unneth shul leude men the plites unwinde'

(3.9.76). The *Testament* only survives in the edition of Chaucer's works by William *Thynne, from which all later copies derive; the text in that edition seems to be corrupted in numerous ways. Usk in the *Testament* praises Chaucer, though without naming him, as 'the noble philosophical poete in Englissh' and the author of 'the boke of Troilus' (3.4.249 ff.); echoes of *Troilus* and of *The House of Fame* and *The Book of the Duchess* are found in the work, together with extensive use of Chaucer's translation of Boethius.   [AH]

(ed.) Skeat (1897).

V

VACHE, Sir Philip de la Vache (1346–1408), a member of the king's household, who married the daughter of Sir Lewis *Clifford, a friend of Chaucer. His reputation for hospitality has led to the suggestion that he may have provided a model for the *Franklin. He is addressed in the envoy to *Truth (22).

Valence, in France, famous for its textiles (*PF* 272).

VALENTYN(E), SEINT, one of the several Christian saints of this name, most probably the first of the following, the three strongest candidates: (1) Roman priest martyred on the Flaminian Way, supposedly under Claudius (his Feast is on 14 February); (2) Bishop of Terni, martyred at Rome (his Feast is also on 14 February); (3) first bishop of Genoa (Feast: 2 May, or possibly 3 May). The tradition of St Valentine as a patron of mating birds (as introduced into The *Parliament of Fowls) may be no older than Chaucer, although his contemporaries *Gower, *Clanvowe, and Oton de *Graunson also wrote Valentine poems.   [JDN]
   North (1990); Kelly (1986).

Valeria, cited by *Dorigen as an example of wifely faithfulness (V.1456), refused to remarry after the death of her husband Servius (she is mentioned by St *Jerome).

Valerian, the husband of St Cecilia in The *Second Nun's Tale; converted by her, he died a martyr.

VALERIE, Valerius, supposed author of the Dissuasio Valerii ad Rufinum philosophum ne uxorem ducat or Epistola Valerii ad Rufinum, an anti-feminist tract which was included in the De nugis curialium ('Courtiers trifles', 1180–93), a collection of entertaining tales by Walter Map, archdeacon of Oxford, but circulated separately earlier. In it 'Valerius', a fictional character, argues against his friend Rufinus's plan to marry. The work is included in *Jankyn's (4) book of 'wicked wives' (III.671), and the 'Valerie' mentioned in The *Legend of Good Women (G 280) is probably its 'author'.

VALERIUS FLACCUS, see *Argonautycon.

VALERIUS, Valerius Maximus (early 1st c. AD), compiler of the Facta et dicta memorabilia, a collection of anecdotes and *exempla for the use of orators. The book was popular in the Middle Ages; epitomes were made, and excerpts from it appear in other works. It has been suggested that Chaucer read the story of *Lucrece (see *Legend of Good Women) in Simon of Hesdin's expanded translation of it. The stories of *Metellius and *Simplicius Gallus which the *Wife of Bath mentions (III.460–4, 643–6) are found in Valerius. That of *Tullius Hostillius which is attributed to Valerius by the old woman in the Tale (III.1165–7) is also in the Facta, but Chaucer may have found all three stories in the 13th-c. Communiloquium of John of Wales. The *Monk (VII.2720) cites Valerius as an authority for his tale of Caesar (*Cesar). The story which *Chauntecleer attributes to 'oon of the grettest auctour that men rede' (VII.2984–3049) may also come from Valerius (with a possible punning reference to his name), but it is also told by Cicero (*Tullius).
   (ed.) C. Kempf (1888); Pratt (1966).

Venyse, Venice, the powerful maritime and commercial centre in Italy (*Ytaille), is mentioned in the geographical introduction to The *Clerk's Tale (IV.51) and in connection with the ducat, a Venetian coin (*HF* 1348).

Venus (1) goddess of love. Venus was an ancient Italian goddess who at an unknown but early date became identified with the Greek Aphrodite, goddess of love, beauty, and fertility and generation. By Chaucer's time much astrological imagery had been mingled with mythology as reported by Greek and Roman poets, but when in The *House of Fame Chaucer refers to *Ovid as Venus's clerk, he is naming his most important single source, and a title he would not have declined himself.

(2) the planet. In traditional order, Venus occupies the third sphere, counting outwards from the Earth (after the spheres of the *Moon and *Mercury). Venus, 'the brighte Venus', is by far the brightest planet; in astrology she is generally benevolent (the 'wel-willy planete' of *Troilus and Criseyde, book III), and has control over love, and indeed all that was traditionally in the province of the goddess. She is exalted in *Pisces. In *alchemy she is associated with the metal copper, as we are told in The *Canon's Yeoman's Tale. By her 'valaunse' (The Complaint of *Mars) we must understand a particularly well-dignified place in a term in *Taurus. (See *dignite(e).)

The majority of references to Venus as goddess raise the question of an allegorical reference to the planet. Chaucer could be said to have followed either astrology or mythology when he made Venus out to be responsible for love and beauty, music and dance. In The Complaint of *Mars she is 'The faire Venus, causer of plesaunce', and the most transparent case of allegory is in that poem, where the terms describing the movements of the goddess Venus are precisely those astrology used to describe the movements of the planet. In fact the correspondence with those movements in 1385 is precise. There are many comparable allegories elsewhere in Chaucer's writings, however, notably those in which they might have been suspected from the sheer frequency of reference to Venus: The *Knight's Tale (20 references); The *Wife of Bath's Prologue (9); *Troilus and Criseyde (14, of which 7 are in book III, in a very marked sense Venus' book); The House of Fame (8); and The *Legend of Good Women (9). Chaucer's allegiance to the planet is even evident from A Treatise on the *Astrolabe, where he gives examples of the determination of the planet's *latitude and longi-

tude. The determination of Venus's position was naturally an aim of *Equatorie of the Planetis, and is of no special significance. (See also *astrology and astronomy; *exaltacio(u)n; *planete; *signe; *sper(e).)

(3) the metal copper, in alchemical symbolism (as noted by the *Canon's Yeoman). (See also *alchemy.)   [JDN]
  Twycross (1972).

Venus, Complaint of, a poem consisting of three *ballades and an *envoy which survives in eight MSS and the prints of Julian Notary (1499–1501) and Thynne (1532). It is a free reworking of a series of ballades by Oton de *Graunson. The date is uncertain: if Chaucer's remarks about the effects of old age (76–8) are taken literally, they would suggest a date towards the end of his life. The title may well be editorial (the Fairfax MS has 'here endith the Compleynt of Venus and Mars'). The scribe John *Shirley also links it with The Complaint of *Mars—though there does not appear to be any internal evidence to support this—and furthermore records a tradition associating it with a court scandal (with Mars being John Holland and Venus Isabel of York (d. 1392)). That Chaucer changed Graunson's speaker to a woman could well suggest that he had a particular lady in mind. Graunson's 'lady' was an 'Isabel': it has also been suggested that Chaucer made the poem for Isabella of France after her enforced separation from Richard in 1399. Chaucer says that he is following 'word by word'—which he is not. Of the five ballades in the French sequence, he omits the second and the third. Besides changing the male speaker to a woman, he simplifies the allegorical personifications into the single hostile figure of Jealousy (*Jalousie). The poem is a polished and eloquent work, interesting as an example of Chaucer's experiments with the *complaint and of his treatment of *love: here the lovers are presented as enjoying a complete mutual happiness threatened only by the external figure of 'subtil Jelosie, the deceyvable'.

  (ed.) Rv 648–9, 1081–2; Scattergood (1995), 465–8; Braddy (1947), 77–83; Norton-Smith (1974), 17–21.

vernycle, which the *Pardoner wears on his cap (I.685), a pilgrim badge with a representation of

Verone

St Veronica's veil on which an image of the face of Christ was believed to have been imprinted.

Verone, Verona, in northern Italy (*Bo* I pr.4:213).

versification. Flexibility characterizes Chaucer's handling of prosody. Prosodic flexibility gives expression to the sense of syntactical units exceeding the line. That flexibility is to be heard against a system of metrical lines, unusually regular for Middle English, in the alternation of unstress (given the notation ×) and stress (given the notation /) and in the count of syllables.

No manuscript survives with Chaucer's verse written in Chaucer's own hand, so that Chaucer's versification has always to be seen through scribal practice, at a time when many words had more than one form, often affecting the number of syllables. At the time of Chaucer's scribes final unstressed -*e* was ceasing to be sounded in speech, whereas in his poetry it was in use and provided an unstress to alternate with a stress. Many Middle English scribes had no great respect for the integrity of the text they were copying; but the best scribes who copied Chaucer's verse seem to have had some regard for his authorial will. He himself reminded them that they had a duty towards his text: 'And for ther is so gret diversite | In Englissh and in writyng of oure tonge | So prey I God that non myswrite the, | Ne the mysmetre for defaute of tonge' (*Tr* V.1793–6).

Chaucer's lines in some poems have regularly four stresses: × / × / × / × / (×), in other poems, regularly five stresses: × / × / × / × / × / (×).

Not every line has a final unstressed syllable.

He combined his lines of both measures into rhyming couplets:

>   ×   / ×   /   ×   / × /
>   She gan to wringe hir hondes two.
>   × /   ×   /   ×   /   ×   /
>   "Allas," quod she, "what me ys woo!"
>   (*HF* 299–300)

>   × /   ×   / × / × /   ×   /×
>   In Flaundres whilom was a compaignye
>   × /   ×   /   ×   /   × / ×/×
>   Of yonge folk that haunteden folye.
>   (VI.463–4)

In some poems Chaucer combined five-stress lines into stanzaic forms, most often consisting of stanzas seven lines long, usually rhyming ababbcc, a form which is sometimes given the name 'rhyme royal', earlier 'rhythm royal', perhaps from its post-Chaucerian employment in *The* **Kingis Quair*. Chaucer uses rhyme royal in some of *The Canterbury Tales* and in *Troilus and Criseyde*. Other stanzaic forms are rarely used. *ABC* and *The Monk's Tale* are written in stanzas of eight lines, rhyming ababbcbc.

Sir Thopas combines four-and three-stress lines (with, in a small number of stanzas, an additional one-stress line, known as a 'bob') mainly in a six-line stanzaic form parodying its use in the versified popular romances '*tail-rhyme' (or *rime couée*), rhyming aabaab or aabccb, where the *b* lines have three stresses, the *a* and *c* lines have four stresses. The literary parody of *Sir Thopas* may provide an insight into Chaucer's preference for the five-stress line, and his abandoning the use of shorter lines. The additional foot, usually an iamb consisting of unstress followed by stress, delays the incidence of rhyme, and rhyming in *Sir Thopas* is made to sound obtrusive, especially in the scheme aabaab, as it is not elsewhere in Chaucer's handling, not even in poems written in four-stress lines. In Chaucer's lines the last stress is strong, that preceding it often weak, leaving in four-stress lines only two stresses outside the predictable pattern of the second half. The feel of the longer line is therefore of greater fluency and ease, partly because its stress patterns are less predictable.

The count of syllables is complicated by two very different features, elision and spelling. Both features can be demonstrated even in the very small number of lines quoted so far. In the following lines final -*e* of *defaute* is not sounded before the vowel of *of* and final -*e* of *wringe* is not sounded before the *h*- of unstressed *hir*: 'Ne the mysmetre for defaute of tonge' (*Tr* V.1796), 'She gan to wringe hir hondes two' (*HF* 299). Elision is not invariable before *h*- of an unstressed word; for example *hadde he*, but with elision of final -*e* of *shyne*: 'That on his shyne a mormal hadde he' (I.386). A different form of losing an unstressed syllable occurs in the common phrase *many a*, in which by converting the final vocalic -*y* into the semi-vowel pronounced like the *y* in modern English *young*, the pronunciation is not of three syllables, namely /mani a/, but of two, namely

/man ya/; for example, twice in *GP* 350 (with elision also of final -*e* of *luce*):

× / × / × / × / × / ×
And many a breem and many a luce in stuwe.

Even in these few examples the complexity of Middle English spelling and accentuation requires a more complicated explanation of the rhythm of the lines. The French loan-word *defaute* is occasionally spelt without final -*e* in Middle English, though after the preposition *for* final -*e* is probably better than omitting it. The matter is far from clear, and it is possible that the word existed in two forms trisyllabic (× / ×) and dissyllabic (× /). Chaucer's verse has many examples with elision, but otherwise provides evidence only for the trisyllabic form (both lines quoted from *Hengwrt with its virgules to mark a syntactic pause, often called 'caesura'):

× / × / × / × / × / ×
Thogh he the soothe / of hir defaute wiste
(VI.370)

× / × / × / × / × / ×
That no defaute / no man aperceyueth
(IV.1018)

In VI.370 there is elision at the syntactic pause as is usual in Chaucer, though not invariable. Hiatus (the opposite of elision) may occur where the pause coincides with a major break for a new sentence; for example:

× / × / × / × / ×
Com forth my white spouse / out of doute
Thow hast me wounded . . .
(IV.2144–5)

Chaucer has no fixed place in the line at which he introduces the syntactic pause: no regular caesura. The virgule of the manuscripts does not always coincide with the position where most metrists would place the pause, and in some lines the manuscripts have more than one virgule.

Spelling may introduce what looks like a syllabic -*e*- but only serves to indicate that the *u* preceding it is the consonant now represented by letter *v*, and that it is not the vowel now represented by letter *u*. In modern editions manuscript letters *u* and *v* are often brought into conformity with Modern English orthographic practice. As a result of that modernization the Middle English use of -*e*- as a

consonant marker is turned into an apparent syllable; for example, *heuene(s)* and *heuenissch*, *louede*:

× / × / × / × / × /×
That myghty God is in hise heuenes hye
(VIII.508)

The line, both in *Hengwyrt and *Ellesmere, has the spelling *hise* (not uncommon for the plural), but the word is never dissyllabic in Chaucer, and many editors print *his*. Editors also print *hevenes* and *hevenissch* though that confusingly invites the unlikely trisyllabic pronunciation, for example, in:

× / × / × / × / ×
With sownes ful of heuenyssch melodie
(*Tr* V.1813)

A good example of the confusion created by spelling in the various manuscripts is provided by *louede*. Ellesmere at *The General Prologue*, line 444 has *louede* (against Hengwrt *loued*):

× / × / × / × / × /
Therfore he louede gold in special

Most editors turn *louede* into *lovede*, again inviting a trisyllabic pronunciation; editorial modernization should lead to the form *lovde* which does not look like Middle English, but would lead to the correct scansion. When *louede* has elision of final -*e* the word is monosyllabic, as in

× /× / × / × / × /
For paramour I loued hire first er thow
(I.1155)

where both Hengwyrt and Ellesmere have *loued hire* often followed by the editors with modernization to *loved hire* though the scansion is *lovd hir* (the form for the pronoun being invariably monosyllabic in Chaucer). Words of French, ultimately Latin, origin, for example *reuerence*, behave differently in syllabicity:

× / × / × / × / × / ×
That child may doon to fadres reuerence
(IV.231)

There is argument about the syllabicity and accentuation of some longer words; for example, *housbondes*. In Middle English verse, the most heavily stressed syllable is not necessarily the first; thus

× / × / × / × / × / ×
Housbondes meke / yonge / and fressh abedde
(III.1259)

but the main stress of *housbondes* can be on the first syllable, and final *-es* non-syllabic (exceptionally so in Chaucer):

/ ×　　×　/　×　/ ×　/ ×　　/ ×
Housbondes at chirche dore / she hadde fyue

(I.460)

Preterite *hadde* may be scanned either dissyllabically or, as here, monosyllabically.

Chaucer's metre is usually iambic, unstress followed by stress; but he often begins a line with inversion of that order, trochaic, with stress followed by unstress, as at the head of *The General Prologue*, line 460. That is done for striking effects, and it is best to see Chaucer's metre not line by line, but as part of a larger sense unit (as punctuated in Ellesmere):

/ ×　　×　×　/ ×　/ ×　/ ×　/ ×
Boold was hir face / and fair and reed of hewe
× / ×　/ ×　/ ×　/ ×　/ ×
She was a worthy woman al hir lyue
/ ×　　×　/　×　/ ×　　/ ×　　/ ×
Housbondes at chirche dore / she hadde fyue

(I.458–60)

Flexibility is achieved by Chaucer also in four-stress verse, as at the climax of *The Book of the Duchess* (MS F, with MS virgules and paragraphs, but otherwise modern punctuation):

× / ×/　×/ ×　/ × / ×
'And thus we lyued / ful many a yere
/ × × /　×　/ × /
So wel I kan / nat telle how.'
/ × × /　×　/ ×　/
¶ 'Sir' quod I / 'where is she now?'
/ ×　/ ×　/ ×　× /
'Now?' quod he / and stynte anoon,
× / ×　/ ×　/ ×　/
Therwith he waxe / as dede as stoon
× / ×　/ × / ×　/
And seyde 'Allas / that I was bore,
/ × × /　× / × /×
That was the losse / that herebefore
×/ ×　/ ×　/ ×
I tolde the that / I hadde lorne.
× / ×　/ ×　/ × /
Bethenke how / I seyde herebeforne,
× /　×　/× 　/ ×　/ ×
"Thow wost / ful lytel / what thow menyst:
/ ×　/ ×　/ ×　/ ×
I haue lost more / than thow wenyst."
× / × /　×　/ ×　/
¶ God wote allas! / Ryght that was she.'
× / ×　/ ×　/ × /
'Allas sir how? / What may that be?'
× ×　/　/ × × / ×
'She ys ded.' / 'Nay.' / 'Yis be my trouthe.'

× / ×　/　×　/ × × / ×
'Is that youre losse? / Be God hyt ys routhe.'

(*BD* 1296–310)

Rightly or wrongly (how can we tell?), I have given exceptional stress to *So* in line 1297, to *That* in line 1302, to *more* line 1306. Lines 1298 and 1299 are 'headless', that is, they lack the initial unstress. Line 1309 twice switches speaker, and twice has two unstressed syllables where one would be more normal; yet that irregularity gives point and poignancy to the piece. Line 1310 has two unstresses together after the exclamatory *Be God!*, and that too is satisfactory because it throws into prominence *routhe*—the pity of it.

Line 1304 is irregular, and none of the variant readings gives an ideal line metrically, but perhaps the scansion attempted above is not impossible. A better reading, by emendation *metri causa*, would be:

× / ×/ × / × /
Bethenk the: I seyde herbeforn

But emendation *metri causa* is out of fashion among editors, precisely because the skill of Chaucer's art of flexible metrics makes the modern reader hesitate before he tries to improve.

Headless lines are not very rare in Chaucer, especially in four-stress metre; yet at one time their very existence in his five-stress metre (or heroic metre) was disputed. A distinguished metrist puts his denial of their existence in terms that make overt the subjectiveness of that denial: 'For my own part, as I read a poem by Chaucer in heroic metre I have the feeling every time I come upon a line without its initial unstressed syllable as if I had been forcibly derailed, and I am careful not to make Chaucer responsible for that feeling, all the more so since in most cases an easy emendation will remove it.' An example is: 'Twenty bookes clad in blak or reed' (I.294).

Chaucer's art is shown in his mastery of rhyme royal, and that may be exemplifed by two stanzas, very different in tone and scansion, the first very regular except for line 840 (unless *durre don* is dissyllabic with *don* unstressed and stress on *that*), the second showing many metrical varieties skilfully used to give the rhythms of direct speech. They come close together near the end of *Troilus and Criseyde* (quoted with modern punctuation and with | to mark where a pause might fall, and with | for a further possible pause or break); line 834 perhaps with elision of *storye it is* (as if *story 'tis*):

```
 ×   / ×  /|×  /  ×  / × / ×
```
And certeynly in storye it is yfounde
```
 ×   /×/ | ×    /    ×  / ×
```
That Troilus was neuere vnto no wight
```
× / ×   / |×   /  × / × /
```
As in his tyme in no degree secounde
```
×  / ×   /  | × /  ×   /× /
```
In duryng don that longeth to a knyght.
```
 ×  /   × /×  | / ×   /   × /
```
Al myghte a geant passen hym of myght,
```
 ×   / × | / ×   /   ×    / × /
```
His herte ay with the first and with the beste
```
 ×   / ×  / × / (×)  | | ×   ×   / ×
```
Stood paregal to durre don that hym leste

(*Tr* V.834–40)

```
  × /   ×    / × |/ × / × /
```
'We han naught elles for to don ywis,
```
 ×    / × / | ×   /  ×  / ×  /
```
And, Pandarus, now woltow trowen me?
```
 ×  / ×    /×|× / × / ×  /
```
Haue here my trouthe: I se hire! ȝond she is!
```
 ×  /  ×  /×   / | ×  / × ×
```
Heue vp thyn eyen, man! maistow nat se?
```
/  ×  / ×    × | /  |× /   × /
```
Pandare answerede, 'Nay, so mote I the!
```
 ×   / × /   ×  /  ×   /  |   ×   / × ×
```
Al wronge, by God! What saistow, man? Where arte?
```
 ×  /×   /   |× /  × /×  / ,
```
That I se ȝond nys but a fare-carte.'

(*Tr* V.1156–62)

Enjambment is common in Chaucer's verse; the end of the line is not the variable end of a clause, and the pause in mid-line assumes an important role in the sentence structure; for example, in *The Knight's Tale* lines 1767–78 (with modern punctuation, but the virgules of Hg):

```
  ×   /   ×  /  ×  /  × / × /
```
¶ As thus / he thoghte wel that euery man
```
  ×  /    ×  / × /   ×  / × /
```
Wol helpe hymself in loue / if that he kan,
```
  ×  /  ×  /  × /   × /  ×/
```
And eek / deliuere hymself / out of prisoun.
```
 ×  /    ×  / × / ×   /  ×/
```
And eek / his herte had compassioun
```
 ×  / ×     / ×   /  × /   × /
```
Of wommen / for they wepen euere in oon,
```
×   /   × /×  / ×   /    × /
```
And in his gentil herte / he thoghte anoon,
```
× / ×   ×/× /  ×  /  × /
```
And softe vnto hymself / he seyde, 'Fy
```
×/  × /  × / ×  /   × /
```
Vpon a lord / that wol haue no mercy,
```
×  /   ×/×  /  × /  ×   / × /
```
But be a leoun / bothe in word / and dede

```
 ×  /   ×  / × / ×   /  ×    / ×
```
To hem / that been in repentaunce and drede
```
 ×  /  ×  /×  /  ×/×  /
```
As wel / as to a proud despitous man
```
 ×   / ×   /×    /  × /   × /
```
That wol mayntene / that he first began.

Chaucer's rhymes are very exact by the variable standards of Middle English rhyming. Rhymes may be on the last stressed syllable of the line: *fy/mercy*; or on the last stress followed by an unstressed syllable: *dede/drede*. The former are called masculine rhymes, the latter feminine. It is thought that he sometimes availed himself of dialect forms that provide an exact rhyme where most other dialects would not; for example *kiste/liste* (general in Middle English), as well as *kestel/reste* (south-east England only). Occasionally he plays with rhymes on homophones. These identical rhymes are sometimes called *rimes riches*: they are more common in French than in English verse. The following is a Chaucerian example, elegantly bridging within the couplet the transition to what in Hengwrt and Ellesmere is marked ¶: 'Therfore I passe as lightly as I may. | ¶ It fil that in that seuenthe yeer, of May' (I.1461–2). *Rimes riches* often involve words with identical stems, but one of the pair having a prefix; for example, *forbede/bede*, *biholde/holde*. Very rarely *rime riche* involves a form of rhyme in which one rhyme position is occupied by two words; for example: 'Hym wolde he snybben sharply for the nonys. | A bettre preest I trowe nowher noon ys' (I.523–4). One word rhyming with two is not uncommon, especially when the second of the two words is *is* (or *ys*): 'Of katapuce or of gaitrys berys, | Of herbe yue, growyng in oure yeerd ther mery is' (VII.2965–6). In Alisoun's preliminary refusal of Absolon's advances, made lively by Chaucer's metrical flexibility (including two unstressed syllables at the mid-line pause of lines 3707 and 3710, and twice in line 3708) he, within this kind of rhyme, uses of slang *pa* (or *ba* 'to kiss') to introduce us strikingly to the notion of kissing:

```
 ×  / ×  /  × / ×    / ×    /  ×
```
'I may nat ete, namoore than a mayde.'
```
/    × × × /  × /  ×   × / ×
```
'Go fro the wyndow, Jack fool!' she sayde,
```
 ×   /  ×   / ×  /  × / × / ×
```
'As help me God, it wol nat be "com-pa-me!"
```
×  / ×/ × ×   /   ×   /  × / ×
```
I loue another, and ellis I were to blame,

```
        ×  /   ×    /   × / × /   × /
Wel bet than thee, by Iesu, Absolon.
        ×  /   ×  / × / ×  /   /   /
Go forth thy wey, or I wol caste a stoon.'
```

(I.3707–12)

Rarely Chaucer uses a run of lines on the same rhyme for special effect. He does so at the beginning of the envoy of *Troilus and Criseyde*:

Go, litel bok! go, litel myn tragedie,
Ther God thi makere yet, er that he dye,
So sende myght to make in som comedye!
But, litel book, no makyng thow nenuie,
But subgit be to alle poesye!

(*Tr* V.1786–90)

Alliteration was used by Chaucer as an occasional ornament, but not in a manner reminiscent of alliterative verse, for example: 'Oure firste foo, the serpent Sathanas' (VII.558); 'Of bras they broghten bemys, and of box' (VII.3398). In the describing the battle of Actium, however, Chaucer seems quite deliberately to recall Middle English *alliterative verse, both in some of the words introduced and in the use of alliteration:

With grysely soun out goth the grete gonne,
And heterly they hurtelyn al atones:
From the top doun comyth the grete stonys.
In goth the grapenel so ful of crokis.
Among the ropis rennyth the scherynge hokys.
In with the polax presith he & sche.

(*LGW* 637–42, MS Gg)

Throughout most modern discussions of Chaucer's metre the assumption is made that Chaucer aimed at and achieved a high degree of regularity, and the witness of the best manuscripts supports that view. The less good manuscripts (and the definition of 'best' and 'less good' is heavily influenced by how well their lines scan), have often metrically irregular variants, and are rightly disregarded by the editors. Some of the very best manuscripts, Ellesmere pre-eminently, give variant readings metrically smoother than Chaucer may have written. The editorial choice is not easy.

It is certain, however, that the regularity usually assumed by modern prosodists of Middle English verse cannot have been felt by readers of the 15th c. Even if they had Ellesmere in their hands, they would have read it without understanding that final -*e* was syllabic. Caxton's print of 1483, in fact his second edition, is conveniently available in facsimile, and it is worth quoting from it *The Miller's Tale* lines 3707–12:

```
×  /    ×   /   × /    ×  ×  /
'I may not ete, nomore than a mayde.'
 /  ×   ×  /   ×   /   ×    × /
'Go fro the wyndow, Jacke fool!' she sayde,
×   /    ×  /  ×  / × /  ×   / ×
'As helpe me God, it wol nat be "com-ba-me!"
× / × /  ×  / ×  /  ×   /
I loue another, and ellis I were to blame,
   ×  /    ×   /   × / × /   × /
Wel bet than the, by Ihesu, Absolon.
   × /    ×  / × / ×  /   /   /
Go forth thy wey, or I wyl throwe a stoon.'
```

(I.3707–12)

Caxton's print is not careless, but the scansion I have attempted shows far more irregularities than do the best manuscripts. If a more regular piece of verse is taken, for example *The Knight's Tale*, lines 1767–78, the difference is even more noticeable, with only lines 1772 and 1775 remaining regular:

```
×    /  ×   /       /   × / × /
As thus he thoughte wel that euery man
× /   ×   / ×  /  ×  /   /  ×
Wyl helpe hymself in loue as he can,
×   × / ×   /   ×  / ×  / ×
And delyuer hymself out of pryson.
×   /  ×   ×  /   ×  / × × /
And eke in hys herte he hadde compassion
×   /   ×  ×  / ×  / × × /
Of wommen for they were euer in one,
×   /  ×  / ×  /  ×  / ×   /
And in his gentil herte he thoughte anon,
×   /  × /  ×  / ×  /   /
And softe vnto hymself he sayde, 'Fy
× / × /   ×   × /   × / ×
Vpon a lord that wyl haue no mercy,
\× / × /×   /   ×  / ×    /
But be a lyoun bothe in word and dede
× /  ×  /   × × / ×   /
To hem that ben in repentaunce and drede
×   / × × /   ×  / ×    /
As wel as a proud dyspytous man
×  / × /   × /  × /   /
That wyl mayntene that he first began.
```

The scansion attempted here is doubtful in many ways. It does, however, clearly demonstrate that the smooth regularity of Chaucer's verse has been replaced by a roughness, quite un-Chaucerian, yet shaping the perception of his poetry not only in the 15th c., but for long thereafter. Dryden, commenting on the last printing of an unscholarly edition of Chaucer—editorial scholarship of Chaucer beginning with *Tyrwhitt—summarizes the perception of Chaucer's verse throughout the period from the 15th c. to the 19th, and still not quite dead:

The Verse of *Chaucer*, I confess, is not Harmonious to us; but 'tis like the Eloquence of one whome Tacitus commends, it was *auribus istius temporis accommodata*: They who liv'd with him, and some time after him, thought it Musical; and it continues so even in our Judgment . . . There is the rude Sweetness of a *Scotch* Tune in it, which is natural and pleasing, though not perfect. 'Tis true, I cannot go so far as he who published the last Edition of him; for he would make us believe the Fault is on our Ears, and that there were really Ten Syllables where we find but Nine: But this Opinion is not worth confuting; 'tis so gross and obvious an Errour, that common Sense (which is a Rule in every thing but Matters of Faith and Revelation) must convince the Reader, that Equality of Numbers in every Verse which we call *Heroick*, was either not known, or not always practis'd in *Chaucer*'s Age. It were an easie Matter to produce some thousands of his Verses, which are lame for want of half a Foot, and sometimes a whole one, and which no Pronunciation can make otherwise.

Common sense is not a good guide in scanning Chaucer's verse as it would have been scanned by his earliest readers: flexibly to some extent, but basically with each line consisting of ten (or, in four-stress lines, of eight) syllables, five (or four) of them stressed; that is not how Dryden would have scanned Chaucer's verse, lame for want of half a foot or a foot in thousands of lines. Dryden's condescension in recognizing merits as one might in a Scotch Tune is insufficiently informed: but that must have been the perception of Chaucerian prosody from the 15th c. onwards. There is no justification for it.   [EGS]

Vesulus, Mount, Monte Viso, in northern Italy 'at the west syde' where the river Po (*Poo) begins (IV.47, 58).

Via Apia, the Appian Way, the road from south Italy to Rome (VIII.172).

VINCENT, Vincent of Beauvais (*c*.1190–*c*.1264), French Dominican encyclopaedic writer and philosopher. His *Speculum maius* was in three parts: a 'mirror of nature', a 'mirror of history', and 'a mirror of teaching'. (A spurious fourth part was added between 1310 and 1325.) Chaucer refers to the second, which covers the history of mankind from Creation to 1254, in *The *Legend of Good Women*. (See ***Estoryal Myrour**.)   [JDN]

VINSAUF, see ***Gaufred**.

Virelay, a French *lyric form usually consisting of short lines arranged in stanzas with only two rhymes, the end-rhyme of one stanza providing the main rhyme of the next. Chaucer is said (*LGW* 422–3) to have written but no example has survived.

VIRGIL(E), VIRGILIUS, Publius Vergilius Maro or Virgil, the Roman poet (70–19 BC). He was born at Andes near Mantua (Mantova), and studied at Cremona, Milan, and Rome. He enjoyed the patronage of Maecenas, and became a friend of Horace. After his *Eclogues* and *Georgics* he devoted the last years of his life to the *Aeneid* (***Eneyde**). After some initial Christian distrust because of his paganism (though he was often thought to have prophesied the coming of Christ in the *Eclogues*: see *Stace) he found a secure place as a 'curriculum author'. His works were frequently copied, accompanied by various commentaries. For *Dante he was 'our greatest poet' and his guide during the first two parts of the *Commedia*. In many ways he came to represent the *poet for the Middle Ages. Although his influence on Chaucer is not as profound or as obvious as that of *Ovid, it is nevertheless important. He is mentioned (along with Dante, III.1519) as one who described the underworld, as one of the writers who 'bore up' the fame of Troy (*HF* 1482–5), as one of the great ancient poets (*Tr* V.1792). In the first book of *The *House of Fame* (143–465) Chaucer summarizes the whole action of the *Aeneid*, mostly condensing it, but expanding the story of *Dido, which is of particular interest to his themes: the role of *love in an epic poem, and that of *Fame itself. Not only does he emphasize her lament on 'wicked fame', but Virgil's description of Fama underlies his own allegorical figure of the goddess Fame in the third book. Virgil as the great poet links books I and III as part of the idea or the writing of lasting and philosophical poetry. When he tells the story of Dido again in

The *Legend of Good Women* he opens with a solemn apostrophe to Virgil (924–7) in an appropriately sonorous style: 'Glorye and honour, Virgil Mantoan, | Be to thy name! and I shal, as I can, | Folwe thy lanterns, as thow gost byforn.' Elsewhere there are allusions and echoes, sometimes close, sometimes distant. In *Troilus and Criseyde*, book IV, for instance, when the despairing Troilus throws himself on his bed Chaucer adds (and adapts) a famous simile from Dante ('and as in wynter leves ben biraft, | Ech after other, til the tre be bare', 225–6) and it seems very likely that he was also thinking of its Virgilian antecedent used of the souls of the dead (*Aen.* 6.309–12). There are other instances in this book. Other possible influences—on Chaucer's use of simile, or on the strongly visual element in his poetry—are possible, but difficult to prove. However, it has been suggested (Norton-Smith) that one aspect of his style may owe much to Virgil's 'subjective style' in which the author passes imperceptibly in and out of a character's speech or mind using the character's 'thought' or 'words', but qualifying them. This would suggest that Chaucer had read Virgil with close attention.

(ed.) Mynors (1969); (ed. and trans.) Fairclough (1930–2); (trans.) Day Lewis (1952); Baswell (1995); Norton-Smith (1974), 104.

Virgin Mary, see **Seint *Marie**.

Virginia, the heroine of *The *Physician's Tale*.

Virginius, the father of *Virginia in *The *Physician's Tale*.

Virgo, the sixth sign of the Zodiac, a *domicile and exaltation of Mercury, and dejection of Venus. (See also *exaltacioun; *pisces; *signe.)
[JDN]

VISCOUNTE, see *Barnabo.

Visevus, Mt. Vesuvius, the volcano (*Bo* I m.4:8).

visual qualities and visual arts. Readers are instantly struck by the vividness and the often sharply visual quality of Chaucer's writing, which evokes the surface appearance as well as the spirit

of medieval life. We need to become familiar with the common images which he took for granted, and also with the symbolic language they often embody. His age was one in which the visual image was omnipresent and of great importance. He frequently uses words like 'depeynted' or 'image', and makes allusions to the art and artefacts of the time, to *architecture, to sculpture, and to painting. There were statues above the porches and doors of medieval churches, and images of saints and crucifixes inside. There was stone carving in the capitals of columns, and wood carving in the rood screens. Under the seats of the choir stalls were often 'misericords', corbels projecting from the hinged seats to afford some unseen comfort for clerics obliged to stand for long periods. These were often decorated with carvings depicting less solemn and edifying scenes and figures than those more publicly displayed in the church: monsters, grotesques, scenes of domestic life and strife which suggest the world of the *fabliaux. Stained-glass windows and wall-paintings portrayed biblical scenes and saints, and served as 'books' for the illiterate laity. Illuminated manuscripts, sometimes splendidly illustrated, were available for the rich. The funeral effigy of the Black Prince is a fine example of late medieval tomb sculpture. Chaucer seems to imagine the House of Fame, adorned with 'babewynnes' [grotesques], carvings, and 'tabernacles' and 'habitacles' [niches for statues], with supports for arches and cornices 'ful of ymageries', as an elaborate hall. Visual images played a part in different kinds of public ceremonial, religious and secular (royal entries, coronations, executions, processions) as well as in the *drama. Pagan images or idols are scorned by St *Cecilia: (they are clearly not as spiritually efficacious as the image of the Virgin Mary venerated by the pious child in *The *Prioress's Tale*). Chaucer himself takes a less austere view when he is imagining a pagan world in *Troilus or *The *Knight's Tale*. He describes the image of Pallas (*Palladion), in Troy as a 'relik', thinking of it as a splendidly medieval shrined relic on an altar, and warms to the descriptions of the temples in Athens and their 'oratories' with 'noble kervyng' and 'portreitures' and statues of the gods.

Images referred to a world of things, but they also referred to a world of ideas. The created universe was a book written by God, and in it *animals, plants, and jewels had significances which could be discovered and learnt from. Scenes and images from the Old Testament had more than a literal or historical significance: they were also foreshadowings of events in the New, so that the *Prioress can address the Virgin Mary (*Marie) as the 'bussh unbrent' seen by Moses. There was what has been called 'a language of sign' (the analysis of which is now called iconography). It included the attributes of saints (St Catherine with a wheel, etc.) and of legendary and historical figures (cf. *Samson slaying himself with a pillar; I.2466; *BD* 738–9). These are often used in an 'emblematic' or mnemonic way, but it is important to remember that such images do not have one fixed significance in all contexts—a dove may stand for the Holy Spirit, but in a different context it may be associated with *Venus. There are allegorical figures—like *Fortune as a female figure (often blindfolded) with a wheel. These are sometimes so well known that Chaucer simply alludes to them: he seems to expect us to know that *Prudence was sometimes depicted with three eyes (*Tr* V.744). In the depiction of scenes, especially religious ones such as the Nativity or the Crucifixion, artists very often followed or adapted formulaic patterns. There developed a number of popular traditional topics or subjects. When Chaucer describes the winter scene in *The Franklin's Tale* (V.1250–5) with Janus sitting by the fire, drinking wine and with the meat of a boar in front of him, he is probably thinking of a scene from the 'Labours of the Months', a series of scenes appropriate to each of the calendar months (see *months and seasons).

Medieval theory held that the *memory received and stored both visual and mental images, and that they could be recalled, transformed, and used by the faculty of *imagination. The sense of sight was held in especially high esteem by both philosophers and rhetoricians (see *rhetoric). The latter constantly urged vividness of representation. Quintilian praised that *enargia* 'which makes us seem not so much to narrate as to show'. The idea that the rhetorical figure of *demonstratio* 'sets forth the whole incident and virtually brings it before our eyes' became almost proverbial, and was adapted to become a standard

topic in early art criticism (with such laudatory remarks as 'faces that live' or 'statues that want only a voice'). An early example is *Dante's praise of the sculptured scenes on the wall of the first terrace in Purgatory: in the first, the Annunciation (*Purgatorio* 10.31–45), the angel appeared 'so truly graven there in a gracious attitude that it did not seem a silent image. One would have sworn he said: "*Ave*", for she was imaged there who turned the key to open the supreme love, and in her bearing she had this word imprinted: "*Ecce ancilla Dei*" as clearly as a figure is stamped in wax' (trans. Sinclair). Chaucer not only read this passage, but probably saw some of the works of the Pisan and Florentine sculptors that were in Dante's mind when he wrote it.

Chaucer's own poetry does not seem to have attracted the attention of numerous talented illustrators in its own time in the way that Dante's Commedia did, although much may have been lost (see *illustrations). However, it does often recall the vividness and the pictorial qualities of Dante's style. He uses a range of 'topics' and techniques—formal descriptions of persons and places (see *portraits, *landscapes), *imagery *gestures. Images vary from the gentle and lyrical to the violent and bloody (like those on the temple of Mars in *The Knight's Tale*). Often it is a reference to very familiar things which achieves visual and emotional vividness: the glorious golden hair of *Absolon (2) 'strouted [stretched out] as a fanne large and brode' (I.3315); the despairing Troilus sitting 'ful lik a ded ymage, pale and wan' (*Tr* IV.235). The ancient rhetorical ideal of the orator bringing about 'seeing through hearing' moved easily into medieval poetry, which was normally spoken or read aloud and 'performed'. The visual and the dramatic are often united in Chaucer's poetry. Probably then 'seeing' and 'hearing' were not so radically opposed as they are now. It has been argued (Kolve 1974) that 'the verbal, the visual, and the memorial were linked in Chaucer's mind' and that the description of the scenes for the *Aeneid* in book I of *The House of Fame*, where the verb 'graven' moves between 'engraved with letters' and 'engraved in pictures', 'offers a medieval paradigm of how narrative poems are made, responded to, and remembered'.

Chaucer's skill in bringing his matter 'before our eyes' was recognized by some early readers. Francis *Beaumont in an often-quoted passage praised him for this gift: much earlier a 15th-c. courtesy book had also detected it—'his langage was so fayr and pertynente | It semeth unto mannys heerynge | Not only the worde | but verily the thynge'. (See also *allegory; *beauty; *dreams; *mythography; *physiognomy; *ugliness.)

Kolve (1974, 1984); Camille (1992); J. Evans (1949); Loomis (1965); Randall (1966); Stanbury (2000).

VITULON (*c.*1230–*c.*1275), Witelo (*c.*1230–*post* 1275). (Manuscripts and early printings use such spellings as 'Vitellio' and 'Vitello'.) Polish writer on natural philosophy, famous for a highly influential treatise on optics (*Perspectiva*) written not long after 1270. He probably came from the Wrocław district. Witelo studied in Paris and Padua. Parts of his *Perspectiva* were adopted for university teaching in many European universities. The whole is extremely long: books VI to IX deal with the formation of images in mirrors, to which subject there is an allusion in *The *Squire's Tale* (V.228–35). Witelo's work shows the influence of Ibn al-Haytham (see *Alocen); *Grosseteste; and *Bacon. (See also *science.)

[JDN]

VORAGINE, JACOBUS DA, see *Jacobus da Voragine.

Vulcano, Vulcanus, Vulcan, the Roman god of fire and smiths, and the husband of *Venus. Chaucer calls her 'spouse of Vulcanus' in *The *Knight's Tale* (I.2222); he knew *Ovid's story (*Met.* 4) of how Vulcan trapped Venus and her lover *Mars in a net he had forged, and alludes to it later in the Tale (I.2389–92). An image of Vulcan stands in the temple of Venus in *The *House of Fame* (138–9); his face is 'ful broun', blackened from his work at the forge ('charbonez de sa forge' in the *Roman de la Rose*).

W

(decorative flourish)

Wade, an obscure legendary hero, to whom Chaucer refers twice: *Pandarus entertains Criseyde by telling his story (*Tr* III.614), and the *Merchant, insisting that he will only marry a young woman, says of 'thise olde wydwes' that 'they konne so muchel craft on Wades boot [boat]' (IV.1423–4). *Speght, in a famously exasperating note, says of the latter, 'concerning Wade and his bote called Guingelot, as also his strange exploits in the same, because the matter is long and fabulous, I passe it over'. At least it probably indicates that the fabulous story of his exploits was known in the 16th c. In early Germanic legend Wade was the father of Wayland the smith; he appears as a giant, or as a famous warrior. There are cryptic references to him in Old English and Middle English (e.g. in the phrase 'wight [strong, valiant] as Wade', a phrase which Caxton apparently added to his text of Malory). In the Middle High German *Kudrun* the warrior 'old Wate' leads an expedition to Ireland to win the princess Hild for his king, Hetel: she is abducted by boat. This has led to the suggestions that Wate as a go-between might be an appropriate parallel to Pandarus, or that 'old widows' know all the tricks of wedlock. It is possible that some fantastic story may be in question. It all remains mysterious.

Rv 886.

Walakye, Wallachia, then an independent principality, in what is now southern Romania, mentioned (*BD* 1024) in a list of distant and war-torn countries. See Map 3.

Walys, Wales, which Chaucer mentions only once (*MLT* II.544), remarking that the Christian Britons fled there from the pagans. Although under English rule from the time of Edward I, it retained its cultural independence, its language, and its rich and varied literary tradition—though

Chaucer probably did not know this at first hand. (See also *Dafydd ap Gwilym; *Glascurion.)

WALSINGHAM, THOMAS, Benedictine monk of St Alban's Abbey from 1364 almost without interruption until at least 1422. Chiefly known as a chronicler both of his house and of the kingdom, he constantly revised and extended his chronicles. He also wrote a commentary on *Ovid's *Metamorphoses* called the *Archana Deorum*, a version of *Dictys's history of the Trojan War (*Ditis Ditatus*) and a *Historia Magni Principis Alexandri*, but there is no evidence that Chaucer knew any of these. [AH]

Walter, the husband of Griselda in The *Clerk's Tale.

Ware, a town in Hertfordshire about 30 miles (48 km) north of London (I.692, 4336).

WARTON, THOMAS (1728–90), poet and scholar, educated at Trinity College, Oxford, of which he became a Fellow. He was professor of poetry at Oxford (1757–67), and was made poet laureate in 1785. His *The History of English Poetry* (3 vols., 1774–81) is justly famed for its learned and sympathetic account of earlier English Literature. Remarkably for his age, he prefers Chaucer's *House of Fame* to *Pope's *imitation of it. A long section on Chaucer notes the importance of his literary contact with Italy and the advantages which came from his being a man of the world, not a reclusive scholar, and praises his talent for satire. Like others of his time Warton admires the way in which Chaucer's humour is displayed in the characters of The *Canterbury Tales*, with their manners 'copied from the life'. More unusually, he also remarks, apropos of *Sir Thopas* that 'genuine humour, the concomitant of true taste, consists in discerning improprieties in books as well as characters', and sensibly maintains that the design is to

ridicule the frivolous descriptions and other tedious impertinencies, so common in the volumes of chivalry . . . not to degrade in general or expose a mode of fabling, whose sublime extravagancies constitute the marvellous graces of his own Cambuscan; a composition which at the same time abundantly demonstrates that the manners of romance are better calculated to answer the purposes of pure poetry, to captivate the imagination, and to produce surprise, than the fictions of classical antiquity.

CH i. 226–30 (extracts).

WAT TYLER, leader of the Kentish rebels in the 1381 *Peasants' Revolt; he was killed by a follower of the king during the meeting between *Richard II and the rebels at Smithfield on 15 June 1381.   [AH]

Wateryng of Seint Thomas, a spring or brook about two miles from London on the road to Canterbury (I.826).

Watlynge Strete, Watling Street (Wætlinga Stræt is the Anglo-Saxon name for a Roman road across southern Britain), in The *House of Fame used to refer to the Milky Way. (See *Galaxye; *Milky Wey.)   [JDN]

Watte, diminutive form of the name Walter (I.643).

weather. Chaucer's references to the weather are of two sorts: when he uses the word 'weder', as in The *Franklin's Tale, The *Summoner's Tale, and *Troilus and Criseyde, the word 'wind' is not far to seek, and he is referring to the state of the local atmosphere in familiar terms. Elsewhere he elevates the question to a higher level, to what we might call 'the state of the times' (cf. Fr. *temps* and L. *tempus*); and this was something astrology was believed capable of predicting. A typical work on the subject written in 14th-c. England was Richard of Wallingford's *De prognosticatione temporum*. In book III of *Troilus and Criseyde*, the rain that fell so heavily is said to have been a direct consequence of a *conjunction of the *Moon, *Saturn, and *Jupiter in the sign of *Cancer. There

were close parallels between this kind of scientific prediction or explanation of the weather and that of history on a large scale—in this case the fall of Troy is at issue. (See also *astrology and astronomy; *months and seasons.)   [JDN]

Wife of Bath, The. (See Figs. 2, 7.) The portrait of the Wife of Bath (whose name, we later learn, was Alison) in the *General Prologue (445–76) is supplemented by her own confessional *Prologue*, to which it is a careful introduction. It begins with a somewhat unsettling and suggestive detail 'but she was somdel deef, and that was scathe [pity]'. The reason for her deafness is given later in her *Prologue*; no explicit hint is given here as to any further significance. It goes on to remark on her skill in her occupation—weaving—and on her well-developed sense of her own status (whether this was entirely justified or not is left unsaid). Details of her dress, like her headdress of extravagant size and her red stockings, might lead us to expect a conventional satire on the vanity of women, but again nothing reproachful is said, and we are given rather a hint of a flamboyant personality, larger than life, and perhaps something of a comic caricature. This is supported by the details of physical appearance that are singled out, her widely spaced teeth and her broad hips. Her many pilgrimages (another topic of anti-feminist satirists) are simply recorded, with the apparently bland remark: 'she koude muchel [knew much] of wandrynge by the weye.' Similarly the fact that she had had five husbands is accompanied by the sly remark 'withouten [not counting] oother compaignye in youthe'. This is returned to at the end, when after a reference to her joviality and conviviality ('in felaweshipe wel koude she laughe and carpe [talk]'), we are told that she was skilled in love's old dance. It seems that we are encouraged to be intrigued rather than to judge. The portrait is individual and original, and at the same time plays with and transforms traditional topics. Whether an actual woman lies behind it, perhaps one of a number of Alisons recorded in the parish of St Michael, where cloth-weaving was an important occupation, is debatable—and unprovable. But it also owes something to the literary figure of the old woman ('la Vieille') in the *Roman de la Rose. The old woman acts as a go-between for the lover and Fair Welcome. She tells the story of her life (eloquently expressing the topic of 'je ne regrette rien', and nostalgically recalling the past good times when she had her fun, memories which reinvigorate her). She teaches Fair Welcome the craft of love (with exemplary tales and reminiscences of how she treated her lovers). There is much here that is also found in the wife of Bath's *Prologue*, but there are considerable differences. The Wife is not a 'false and servile crone' nor a bawd nor a temptress. Chaucer has taken some hints and gone his own way. The character of his Wife of Bath, especially as revealed in the *Prologue*, has been endlessly discussed (sometimes with highly bizarre interpretations; ranging from a martyr to patriarchy to a frigid nymphomaniac or 'sociopath' or the Samaritan woman whom Christ met beside a well). Her own suggestion is that she was born under the influence of Venus and Mars, and (by implication) encouraged by experience. To say, in a severe reaction against the search for a psychological 'key' to her character, that she has no real personality at all, but is simply a bundle of traditional attributes and attitudes, is probably to go too far. It hardly does justice to her vitality and individuality, which have made her one of the most famous figures in English literature. Her larger than life presence is there from the beginning. Within *The Canterbury Tales* she is referred to or quoted as an authority (in tones ranging from awe to irony) by the Friar who follows her in the tale-telling, by the Clerk (IV.1170–2), and even by a character in *The *Merchant's Tale* (IV.1685–7). Chaucer himself in *Lenvoy de Chaucer a *Bukton* advises his friend to read her.

Rv 817–19; Cooper (1989), 50–2; Mann (1973), 121–7.

Wife of Bath's Prologue and Tale, The (1264 lines in couplets) is the first contribution in Fragment III.

The *Prologue* (1–856) is a confessional monologue. It opens directly: 'Experience, though noon auctoritee | Were in this world, is right ynough for me | To speke of wo that is in mariage'. The Wife of Bath justifies herself for having five successive husbands: 'God bad us for to wexe [increase] and multiplye'. The sixth will be welcome. Virginity may be 'great perfection' but it is not obligatory for

everyone. What were our genital organs created for? Brushing off an interruption by the *Pardoner, she continues with an account of her five husbands ('thre of hem were goode, and two were badde'). The three good ones were rich and old (and had given her their gold and land), but could scarcely pay their sexual 'debt' to her—and she made them suffer for it. They were glad when she spoke graciously to them because they were usually cruelly scolded. For the instruction of 'wise wives' she gives an entertaining demonstration of how she would speak to them, reproving them variously for desiring a neighbour's wife, for complaining about her friends (here she begins a tirade with the repeated phrase 'thou sayest'), for maligning women, and urging them not to be niggardly, or complain about women's love of fine clothes, or the force of women's love. 'O Lord! the peyne I dide hem and the wo!' she exclaims in delight, glorying in her '*maistrye'. Her fourth husband was a reveller and had a paramour, but she got her own back on him. She looks back to her earlier days ('I have had my world as in my tyme' she says), but now devouring age has taken her beauty and vigour. The final section is a short narrative which looks forward to her Tale. Her fifth husband is remembered with some affection though he behaved badly to her (and was the cause of her deafness). She loved him because he was hard to get. He was Jankin, an Oxford '*clerk', young and lively, but, being a clerk, he did not speak well of women. He kept up a flow of anti-feminist proverbs and stories, and had a large book 'of wicked wives' from which he used to read as he sat by the fire at night. Once, thinking that he would never stop, she pulled a leaf out of the book and punched him so that he fell backwards into the fire. In fury he hit her on the head, and she lay in a swoon. The quarrel, which the Wife won not by aggression but by pathos ('now wol I dye, I may no lenger speke') eventually ended in harmony, with Jankin forgiven, but having to surrender sovereignty and burn his book. She lived faithfully and happily with him for the rest of his life.

From its confident opening to its unexpected conclusion the *Prologue* is a genuine tour de force, at once amusing and outrageous, a persuasive flow of speech with *digressions, asides, and interjections. Its date is not known, but the general assumption that it is a late work seems very likely. It uses an extraordinary range of sources. Apart from the Bible and the *Roman de la Rose*, it is mainly derived from the extensive array of anti-feminist treatises that Jankin loved to read: *Jerome, Theophrastus (*Theophraste), Map's *Dissuasio Valerii de uxore non ducenda* (*Valerie), the *Lamentations* of *Matheolus, and perhaps the *Miroir de Mariage* of *Deschamps. All are in the Wife of Bath's voice ('authority is reprocessed as experience' (Cooper)), and all are carefully misused. In her tirade the commonplaces of the anti-feminist tradition are placed in her husbands' mouths in what is a vigorous interaction with the stereotypes. Later, with Jankin's book, where she is not in control, she has to suffer and confront them. Anti-feminist satire is not endorsed by her (although she sometimes seems to embody some of its charges) or by Chaucer. Not surprisingly the *Prologue* has sometimes provoked extreme reactions in critics. Some have been mesmerized by the wife's eloquent self-justification and praised her for her life-affirming endorsement of sexuality; others, more resistant, point out contradictions and faults, and see the *Prologue* as an indictment of her from her own mouth. It seems too clever, too elusive, and too subtle to be so neatly pinned down. She presents herself as a larger than life figure: ironies, mockery, and parody weave themselves round her 'counter-official' views on virginity, marriage, and its woes (unlike La Vieille she is all for marriage, provided she rules). There is a certain ambiguity left around her shrewdness or cynicism and the ways in which she exploits her would-be exploiters. In short, Chaucer makes her emerge as such a fascinating figure that it is perilously easy for a critic to forget that she is after all a fictional character.

Her *Tale* (857–1264) follows a brief exchange between the *Friar and the *Summoner. In the days of King Arthur, when this land was filled with fairies (nowadays there are only friars lurking everywhere), a young knight from his household rides out. He sees a maiden and rapes her. For this he is condemned to death, but the queen and other ladies intercede and the king leaves it to her to decide his fate. She tells the knight that he can have his life if after a twelvemonth and a day he can answer the question 'what thing is it that

wommen most desire'. He goes off asking everywhere, receiving a variety of answers. (To illustrate, or rather refute, one of these, that women like to be thought 'stable, and eek secree [also secret]' we are told Ovid's story of Midas (*Myda), who had asses' ears. Only his wife knew, and had promised never to reveal it, but the strain proved too much, and she went down to a marsh and told it to the water.) The knight happens to ride by the side of a forest, where he sees twenty-four ladies dancing, when he approaches they vanish, and only an ugly old woman is left. He asks her the question. She will tell him the answer, but on condition that he promises to do the next thing she requires. They go to court, and with manly voice he gives the answer: 'Wommen desiren to have sovereyntee | As wel over hir housbond as hir love, | And for to been in maistrie hym above.' No one in the court can contradict this. The old woman now speaks up and announces the request which he must accept: he must take her as his wife. Sorrowfully and reluctantly he agrees. As he lies in bed with her in the evening she asks why he is grieving. He answers that it is because she is ugly, and old, and sprung from a low stock. Calmly but firmly she gives him a lesson on the nature of true '*gentilesse', answering his three objections to her in turn. Finally she offers him a choice between having her as she is and being a true, humble wife, or young and fair, with unpredictable consequences. He sighs, and places himself in her 'wise governance': he will accept whichever she chooses, and confirms that she now has 'maistrie'. She promises that she will be both fair and good, and is transformed into a beautiful young woman. And so they live happily till their lives' end. The tale closes with a prayer to Christ to send us 'housbondes meeke, yonge, and fressh abedde' and grace to outlive them: cursed be those who refuse to be governed by their wives, and may God send a plague on old and angry misers.

The *Tale* is a kind of folk-tale romance, and was probably written for, or adapted to the Wife of Bath, perhaps as a substitute for The *Shipman's Tale*, which is often thought to have been originally intended for her. The story of the 'Loathly Lady' who promises to tell what women most desire in return for marriage seems to have been a popular one in England: versions of it are found in the romance *The Weddynge of Sir Gawen and Dame Ragnell*, a ballad, and *Gower's tale of Florent. None of the analogues contain anything corresponding to the rape, the story of Midas or the passage on 'gentilesse'. At first sight it seems surprising that the Wife of Bath should tell a fairy tale, and should 'digress' on the nature of true nobility. On the other hand, even if it was not Chaucer's original choice for her, it has been carefully adapted, not only at the beginning and at the end, where her distinctive voice is clearly heard, but in the central role given to 'maistrie', and even in the way, when the question of what women really want is being variously answered, the narrator shifts to personal pronouns: 'somme seyde wommen loven best richesse | . . . Somme seyde that oure hertes been moost esed | What that we been yflatered'. It is now often said that the Tale adds another aspect to what has already been revealed of the Wife's personality in the Prologue, a softer, more 'romantic' one perhaps, with a yearning for fulfilment. It may also be argued that it continues and expands the theme of sovereignty. Here the surrender of 'maistrye' by the knight brings about a reconciliation and a transformation more startling than that of the Wife's own Jankin. The knight has been changed from a casual rapist and a nobleman with a very fixed and limited view of nobility and beauty into a submissive husband and a truly 'gentle' man. This fairy-tale transformation is, as Mann points out, initiated by the queen's clever punishment for him. It is the undergoing of an educative process completed by his wife's words on 'gentilesse' that brings about a change in him which is as miraculous as her physical transformation. We are given a glimpse of the mutuality that is so prominent in The *Franklin's Tale*. It is one of the most charming and moving of the *Canterbury Tales*.

(ed.) *Rv* 105–22, 864–74; *S&A* 207–68; Cooper (1989), 139–66; Beidler (1996); David (1976), ch. 9; Donaldson (1977); Mann (1991), 87–93; Muscatine (1957), 204–13; Pearsall (1985), 71–91.

Wilkyn, a diminutive form of the name William (III.432).

WILLIAM, KYNG, William the Conqueror (reigned 1066–87) (I.324). The Sergeant of the Law knew all the cases and judgements recorded in the Year Books since his time.

WILLIAM OF WYKEHAM, bishop of Winchester 1366–1404, founder of Winchester College and of New College Oxford. He served as clerk of the King's works from 1356 to 1361, a post held by Chaucer from 1389 to 1391; later he was chancellor from 1367–71 and 1389–91.   [AH]

(for his books) Cavanaugh (1985), 931–3.

Wyndesore, Windsor, about 20 miles (32 km) west of London. It is mentioned only in the *Romaunt of the Rose* (1250), but Chaucer knew it well from his time as Clerk of the Works (see Geoffrey *Chaucer: life). The great stone castle, originally begun by William I as a wooden structure, was a favourite residence of Edward III, who liked to celebrate the feast of St George there. It is likely that Chaucer had visited it earlier in his life as part of the entourage of the countess of Ulster, and perhaps on St George's day in 1374, when the king granted him a daily gallon pitcher of wine.

wine. Chaucer must have acquired his intimate knowledge of wine and the wine trade in his youth: his father and his grandfather were among the most important vintners in London. Both held the office of deputy to the king's butler. (The king's butler was responsible for the collection of taxes on imported wines.)

Wine is a perishable commodity: exposure to air or dirt turns it into vinegar. In the Middle Ages there were no glass bottles and corks, and wine was kept in large wooden casks. Wood is permeable and difficult to clean; once broached, the cask had to be finished as quickly as possible, or the wine would go off. As a result, most wines did not last from one year to the next. Sweet wines and wines that were high in alcohol lasted longer, because sugar and alcohol are natural preservatives, and these were the wines that medieval writers praise most highly. Good wine in Chaucer is always called strong or sweet. 'He served us with vitaille at the beste; | Strong was the wyn, and wel to drynke us leste' (I.750), he says of the Host. In her younger days the Wife of Bath would dance and sing when she had 'dronke a draughte of sweete wyn' (III.459).

Although the great majority of the wines imported into England in Chaucer's day were dry wines from France (mainly from Bordeaux but also from La Rochelle), sweet wines had been imported from Italy and Greece since the beginning of the 14th c. They were carried by Venetian and Genoese galleys. The most highly prized of these sweet wines was *vernage*, Italian *vernaccia*, from Vernaccia (near Florence). To *Dante, a Florentine, vernaccia signified excess. He places Pope Martin IV in purgatory, where he has to do penance for his prodigality. Martin IV died of a surfeit of eels which, it was said, he used to cook in vernaccia; Dante remarks snidely that by fasting Martin is purging the eels of Lake Bolsena and the vernaccia (*Purgatorio* 24.23–24). Chaucer mentions vernaccia in *The Shipman's Tale*: With hym broghte he a jubbe of malvesye, | And eek another ful of fyn vernage, | And volatyl, as ay was his usage (VII.70–72). *Malvesye*, from French *malvoisie*, is malmsey, another strong sweet wine. Its name is a corruption of Monemvasia (in the south-western corner of the Peloponnese), the port from which this wine was shipped; it was produced all over the eastern Mediterranean, but the chief suppliers were Cyprus and Crete. The wine is made from a single grape variety, which is still known as malmsey. These two wines, but vernaccia in particular, were considered luxuries, and fetched much higher prices than the short-lived wines of Bordeaux and La Rochelle. Hence a jug (*jubbe*) of malmsey and a jug of vernaccia are appropriate wines for the wordly and ostentatiously open-handed monk to bring when visiting his generous friend the merchant.

Dry wines did not last: they had to be drunk young of necessity. The red wines must have been 'hard', i.e. full of tannin, when in good condition, and off if kept too long. In order to disguise either of these defects, wines were sometimes served flavoured with spices and sweetened. These spiced wines were known variously as 'hippocras', 'clary', and 'piment'. Once the spices had been added, the wine needed to be strained; this was done through a linen bag known as 'Hippocrates' sleeve', hence *hippocras*. *Clary* is from the French; *piment* is French, ultimately from Latin *pigmentum*, 'an ingredient (in an ointment, lotion etc.); a drug' (*Oxford Latin Dictionary* s.v.). Honey and spices were expensive, however: hippocras, clary,

and piment were luxuries, and wine was normally drunk neat. On his wedding night, only the best will do for January so he drinks 'ypocras, clarree, and vernage | Of spices hoote t'encressen his corage' (*CT* IV.1807–8), and spiced wine plays a part in another dubious liaison, when Nicholas woos Alison with 'pyment, meeth [mead], and spiced ale' (I.3378). In the lyric *The *Former Age*, the spices needed for 'clary' and 'sause of galantyne' are among the luxuries that had no place in the Golden Age (line 16). The source, Boethius's *Consolation of Philosophy*, book II metre 5, has 'Non Bacchica munera norant | Liquido confundere melle', 'they did not know how to mix Bacchus' gifts with clear honey': Boethius is referring to *mulsum*. In his own translation of these lines, Chaucer adds an explanatory note, 'that is to seyn, they coude make no pyment or clarree'. Strictly speaking, this is wrong, because *mulsum* does not contain spices. Chaucer's gloss is not his own but derives from the commentary of Nicholas Trevet, who adds 'ad faciendum pigmentum et claretum', 'in order to make piment and clary'. Unfamiliar with classical *mulsum*, Chaucer adopts Trevet's medievalization of Boethius.

Innkeepers often adulterated their good wines with cheaper ones. Numerous royal writs and proclamations survive forbidding this practice, insisting that customers should be allowed to see their wine drawn and, less practicably, that different kinds of wine should be kept in different cellars. The frequency with which these writs and proclamations were issued shows that they continued to be disregarded. In his rant against the evils of drink the Pardoner warns:

> Now kepe yow fro the white and fro the rede,
> And namely fro the white wyn of Lepe
> That is to selle in Fyshstrete or in Chepe.
> This wyn of Spaigne crepeth subtilly
> In othere wynes, growynge faste by,
> Of which ther ryseth swich fumositee
> That whan a man hath dronken draughtes thre,
> And weneth that he be at hoom in Chepe,
> He is in Spaigne, right at the toun of Lepe,
> Nat at the Rochele, ne at Burdeux toun.
>
> (VI.562–71)

The wines of La Rochelle and Bordeaux are adulterated with the more alcoholic wine of *Lepe because strength was a virtue and perhaps also to make the wines keep better. Lepe is in the south of Spain, on the coast between Jerez and the Algarve. This had been Moorish territory, and it has been claimed that the white wines of Lepe were fortified, since the Moors knew the art of distillation. Unfortunately there is no evidence that the wine of Lepe was indeed an ancestor of sherry; in any case, the hot climate would have produced wines that were stronger than those of Bordeaux and La Rochelle. But the offending inn keepers' motive was of course the vice that the Pardoner castigates, for the white wine of Lepe was cheaper than good-quality French wines such as Bordeaux and La Rochelle—never mind the headaches that this vile mixture would have given their undiscerning customers. [HW]

Wireker; Witelo. See *Speculum Stultorum*; *Vitulon.

Womanly Noblesse, a short poem ('so hath myn herte caught in remembraunce | Your beaute hoole and stidefast governaunce') of three stanzas and an *envoy, surviving in only one MS, where it is entitled 'Balade that Chaucier made'. It is accepted as Chaucer's by Skeat, Robinson, and Benson, but not by all modern editors. A polished *ballade, but conventional in its sentiments, it offers no conclusive internal evidence. In form, however, it is unusual in having nine-line stanzas and no refrain, and in using only two rhymes throughout the stanzas and continuing one of them into the envoy.

(ed.) *Rv* 649–50, 1082–3; Pace and David (1982), 179–86; Scattergood (1995), 479, 482.

women are central to much of Chaucer's poetry, and his treatment is remarkable both for the unparalleled psychological subtlety of many of his portrayals and for the inventiveness of his contribution to the debate on their status. He was thoroughly conversant with the literature of medieval anti-feminism and cannibalized it voraciously; but a century after his death Gavin Douglas could chide him for bias in being 'ever womenis frend'. Almost all his works, from the *ABC forwards, contain major women characters, but their further function in a larger debate on women develops only gradually.

Chaucer works within deep cultural assumptions that define women by relation to men, but he does so with unusual awareness. The imaginative centre of The *Book of the Duchess*, the Lady White, is presented entirely through her lover's idealizing perceptions of her, as the perfect courtly lady. The poem is at once an elegy for and a celebration of Blanche, duchess of Lancaster, and, through the generalization of dream, a study of love and bereavement; White is therefore not confined to her historical prototype but is made a model of all that is lovely in mortal femininity. There is more polemic in the treatment of *Dido, in the first part of The *House of Fame*: Chaucer presents her as a true lover abandoned by a faithless seducer, so that she becomes the stable centre of the narrative in contrast to the fickle and wandering Aeneas and the rival and unverifiable versions of her story told by Virgil and Ovid. The *Parliament of Fowls* is a study of the various mating habits of both birds and humans; the males do the wooing, but it is stressed that the formel eagle courted by three rival birds of prey has the right to choose her own mate. Two female figures are especially significant, both personifications rather than women: *Venus, who is lying half-naked in the temple of Priapus, and *Nature, God's vicegerent on earth. With their allegorical charges of lust versus divinely sanctioned plenitude, they embody two aspects of the debate over women and sexuality that becomes explicit in The *Canterbury Tales*.

Chaucer's first great psychological portrait of a woman, *Criseyde, represents a revolutionary departure from tradition. His main source, Boccaccio's *Filostrato*, treats her as charming but shallow, and well capable of running her own sexual affairs; like the earlier treatments of the story by * Benoît de Saint-Maure and *Guido delle Colonne, it draws a moral about the inconstancy and untrustworthiness of women. Chaucer chooses to emphasize rather Criseyde's attractiveness (she is repeatedly described in terms of the strongly favourable impression she makes on other people); her vulnerability, as shown in her desire for protection (her first appearance in the poem is as a suppliant for Hector's goodwill, she takes both Troilus and Diomede as lovers on the grounds that they will shield her); and her sensitivity to the society and circumstances in which she finds herself (she is playful with Pandarus, is the ideal courtly lady to Troilus, is devastated by grief at the thought of leaving him, and falls an easy prey to Diomede's techniques of sexual conquest). Her traditional fickleness is thus grounded for much of the poem in qualities resembling virtues, and only her implied association with *Fortune suggests a more dangerous mutability. Chaucer offers various concluding morals, but none condemns her, or women with her; rather, women are warned to 'beth war of men' (*Troilus* V.1785). The wider, gender-inclusive, conclusion of the poem is that 'yonge fresshe folkes, he or she' should alike turn to the unfailing love of God.

Despite this sympathetic treatment of his heroine, Chaucer was blamed for presenting the 'wikednesse' of women in Criseyde, or so he describes the God of Love as saying in the Prologue to The*Legend of Good Women*. Whether the lines constitute a fictional justification for the *Legend* or represent actual audience reaction is impossible to say, but the poem itself, which grants even its potentially powerful heroines such as Cleopatra and Medea extraordinarily little autonomy, makes odd reparation. Female goodness and wickedness are defined as truth or unfaithfulness to men who are mostly cast as villains. The women are almost all abused and abandoned by lovers or rapists; many kill themselves. Anything near perfect love is presented only in the Prologue, by Alcestis, who was willing to die for her husband. He, interestingly, is not present, his place as her partner being taken by the God of Love.

Despite their potential ethical range, from exemplars of chastity to sorceresses, the women of the *Legend* are presented in a monotone of both style and moral treatment. *The Canterbury Tales*, by contrast, makes the most of its multiplicity of genres, styles, speakers, and points of view to turn the whole question of the status of women into a lively and wide-ranging debate. This is carried on at several levels: through dramatic interplay between the pilgrims; through the rival portrayals of women in the stories; through opposing generalizations; and in terms of active engagement with anti-feminist texts from the Bible forwards. The debate focuses on two main issues: whether women are good; and the related question of the

rights and wrongs of sexual activity. Chaucer treats both questions part seriously, part with a good deal of mischief—with both wisdom and wit.

The wit is to the fore over the question of good and bad in womankind, a question generally posed in the Middle Ages not in terms of most women's being a mixture of the two, but rather of there being some of each sort; the issue therefore focuses on the proportion of good to bad. A favourite authority on the subject was Solomon (*Salomon), who found one good man in a thousand but no woman at all (Eccles. 7:29; cited by Pluto, IV.2242–8, and Melibee, VII.1057; refuted by Proserpina, IV.2276–90, and Prudence, VII.1057, 1076–80). The God of Love in the *Legend*, by contrast, had stated that women—or at least, stories about women—run at 'evere an hundred goode ageyn oon badde' (G 277); the Miller, still more optimistically, insists that there are a thousand good wives for every bad one, but also that it helps to keep the statistics favourable if husbands do not look into the matter too closely (I.3154–66)—a principle endorsed by his own story of a cuckolded carpenter.

The *Bible itself contains the material for both negative and positive readings of women, and a standard selection of examples and texts was used by proponents of each attitude. Eve was commonly regarded as responsible for the Fall; the Virgin had been instrumental in the Redemption. Against Solomon's denial of the existence of good women is his portrayal of the ideal wife (Prov. 31:10–31). Several texts are more equivocal: Rebecca (*Rebekka) deceived her aged husband, but is cited in the marriage service as a model wife; St *Paul insisted that husbands should love their wives and wives their husbands, but also that wives owed their husbands obedience. Sexuality itself could likewise be given contradictory valuations. The principle of plenitude and regeneration is inherent in the Creation, the patriarchs were frequently polygamists and Solomon rather more than that; but the Fall was often associated in exegesis with sexual activity, both Mary and Christ were virgin, and St Paul advocated continence over marriage. The Song of Songs, read allegorically, is a love song of the marriage of Christ and His Church, or a hymn in honour of the Virgin, but read literally was the most erotic text available to Western Christendom.

Chaucer uses all these examples, and uses them with a sharp awareness of their contradictions. In particular, he shows how the Bible's neutral or favourable statements on women and sex had often been given deeply anti-feminist interpretations by celibate male authorities. St Jerome, who set himself against all sexual activity in his treatise *Adversus Jovinianum*, was a notorious offender. His bias appears at its most undisguised when he abandons the Bible altogether to quote with evident glee the whole of a lengthy diatribe against women by the pagan author Theophrastus. In *The *Wife of Bath's Prologue*, Chaucer turns the ground for debate upside down by presenting the same material from the woman's point of view. He sets her to offer a rival, female reading of women and sexuality based on the biblical text, not the gloss, and he gives her a diatribe of her own that amounts to an *Adversus Hieronymum*. Her appropriation of misogynist arguments for herself threatens to leave her opponents weaponless. Such material determines both what she says and what she is. Two passages in Jean de Meun's section of the *Roman de la Rose* are crucial for her portrayal: the jealous husband's account of wives, derived from Jerome-Theophrastus; and the autobiography of the elderly bawd, La Vieille. Chaucer's extraordinary achievement is to turn an embodiment of the worst dreams of every henpecked husband or celibate cleric into such a vibrant personality. With her outsize hat, her spurs and red stockings, her garrulity, her will to dominate her five husbands and her eagerness for a sixth (she is as much a wife by profession and calling as the Parson is a priest), she has consistently captivated her fellow pilgrims, Chaucer's associates, scribes, and later readers.

Within the *Tales*, the *Clerk is given the most direct response to her challenge that no clerk can speak good of wives. His tale of Griselda's patient endurance of the mental torture inflicted on her by her husband at once praises good women and insults the Wife. Chaucer radically changes the moral balance of his Petrarchan original, intensifying its comments on the husband's behaviour into outrage, and removing the parallels between him and God to stress the parallels between Griselda and Christ or the Virgin. The Tale's overt message of wifely submissiveness is sabotaged by its potential for calling patriarchal ideology into question through its demonstration of the abuse of male power, and by Grisilde's moral and spiritual superiority.

Like Grisilde, Custance (*Man of Law's Tale*) and Cecilia (*Second Nun's Tale*) are associated by language and imagery with the Virgin; Virginia (*Physician's Tale*) and Prudence (*Melibee*) are also striking as images of virtuous women—almost, indeed, of specific virtues: Prudence is on the borderlines of personification, and the names of Custance/Constance and Virginia (in fact derived from their fathers) imply their distinctive qualities of constancy and temperance or chastity. Cecilia's name is given an elaborate series of moralizing etymologies. Like Prudence and the Wife, but in contrast to the model of female submissiveness, she exercises dominance over the men of her Tale, though she does so in the name of God. Although she is martyred, she is in no sense a victim—in strong contrast to Virginia, killed by her father to protect her from rape by an unjust Judge.

Cecilia and Virginia are defined in part by their avoidance of sexual activity; Cecilia's virginity is protected by an angel. Such heroines are counterbalanced by women whose main plot function is sexual, notably adulterous wives—the *Miller's Alison, the *Cook's whore, the Merchant's May, the *Shipman's unnamed protagonist, Phoebus's wife of The *Manciple's Tale. The heroines of the secular romances, the *Knight's Emily, the *Squire's Canacee, and the *Franklin's Dorigen, offer more positive images of courtship and marriage. Chaucer's presentation of all these women goes beyond stereotyping. Emily comes closest, as the courtly lady *par excellence*, but she can also therefore work as a foil for Alison's animal energies. Cecilia's spiritual transcendence of the temporal world, or May's corruption of romance ideals.

Other women in the *Tales* relate in various ways to these images of courtly lady, pious virgin, and shrewish wife. Offstage characters include the Merchant's wife, whom he regards as a living warning against marriage, and the Host's, a virago regarded with both pride and awe by her husband. Among the pilgrims, the *Prioress is famous for the degree to which the woman in her compromises her religious calling. In The *Nun's Priest's

Tale there is Pertelote, in whom the woman—courtly heroine, fussy wife, distant cousin of Eve—is seriously compromised by the hen. And *The*Wife of Bath's Tale* predicts Freud's question, 'What do women want?', and provides the answer he failed to find. [HC]

Dinshaw 1989 (see also *criticism of Chaucer II).

Women Unconstant, Against, a *ballade ('Madame, for your newefangelnesse | Many a servaunt have ye put out of grace') of three rhyme royal stanzas (see *versification) which survives in three MSS but is not by them ascribed to Chaucer (in one it is headed 'The Newfangilnes of a Lady', in another simply 'Balade'). *Stowe included it in his edition of 1561, with the rubric 'A balade whiche Chaucer made ageynst women inconstaunt'. Skeat was certain that it was Chaucer's, Robinson, though almost certain, cautiously placed it among the poems of dubious authorship, where it usually remains. It is a lively 'farewell' to the inconstant lady, who turns like a weathercock, and might better be enshrined for her 'brotelnesse' than 'Dalyda, Creseyde or Candace', with an accusatory refrain using colour symbolism: 'in stede or blew [blue, the colour of constancy], thus may ye were al grene.'

(ed.) *Rv* 657, 1089–90; Pace and David (1982), 187–93; Scattergood (1995), 481–3.

WOOLF, VIRGINIA (1882–1941), novelist and critic, in her essay on 'The Pastons and Chaucer' (*The Common Reader*, 1925), makes a number of perceptive points about Chaucer's narrative technique. Like a true storyteller he has the gift of 'making us wish to learn the end of the story', and he knows how to 'tell his story craftily'. She admires 'the solidity which plumps it out, the conviction which animates the characters'. The 'simple faithfulness to his own conceptions' which allows him to write frankly gives a special stability to his characters: 'it does not occur to him that his Griselda might be improved or altered. There is no blur about her, no hesitation; she proves nothing; she is content to be herself.' He is a profoundly moral poet: 'questions press upon him; he asks questions, but he is too true a poet to answer them'—'his morality lies in the way men and women behave to each other.' Chaucer 'has some

art by which the most ordinary words and the simplest feelings when laid side by side make each other shine; when separated, lose their lustre'.

CH ii. 377–84.

WORDSWORTH, WILLIAM (1770–1850), the poet, had known Chaucer in imitation and translation since youth, when he committed large parts of *Dryden and *Pope to memory, and it is probable that he had dipped into the 1561 edition of Chaucer in the library of his grammar school at Hawkshead. But until the Grasmere household acquired a set of Robert Anderson's *The Works of the British Poets* (13 vols., Edinburgh and London, 1792–95), sometime in 1800, Wordsworth had had no occasion for close study. Late in 1801, just when the winter evenings were longest, Wordsworth was reading in a generous selection from *The Canterbury Tales* and other poems, in a text drawn from Thomas *Tyrwhitt's 1775–8 edition. Wordsworth immersed himself in them, not just as a pastime, but as a poetic opportunity, even as a challenge; he was soon at work translating *The Manciple's Tale*.

Commentators rarely linger over Wordsworth's work on Chaucer, since it is generally assumed that he was marking time, either because he was in holiday mood, or in the doldrums. This notion is mistaken. Wordsworth declared that when he first gave himself up 'to the profession of poet for life', he was 'impressed with a conviction, that there were four English poets whom I must have continually before me as examples—Chaucer, Shakespeare, Spenser, and Milton. These I must study, and equal *if I could*.' By 1801 Wordsworth had written (but not published) a long narrative in Spenserian stanzas, a Shakespearian tragedy, and many philosophical passages in a blank verse which evokes, but is not overwhelmed by, Milton. Now at last he could encounter the poet he later hymned as 'great Precursor, genuine Morning Star'.

What did Chaucer mean to Wordsworth at this early stage in his career? That he was 'the morning star of [England's] literature' and therefore to be reverenced, went without saying. He excited emulation, too, as a consummate artist, skilled in the technicalities of narrative, dialogue, and description, a poet capable of a range of emotional effects equalled only by Shakespeare. But, more specifically, he appealed to Wordsworth as a poetic example because he seemed in two ways to prefigure his own current concerns. First, he offered proof, in Wordsworth's judgement, that poetic language could attain permanence, if the poet honoured the 'repeated experience and regular feelings' of common humanity rather than the 'arbitrary and capricious habits of expression' to which they too often resort. As a buttress to this cornerstone of his own poetic intention, Wordsworth added a footnote to the Preface to *Lyrical Ballads* (1800), which contended that 'the affecting parts of Chaucer are almost always expressed in language pure and universally intelligible even to this day'. Second, Chaucer evidently shared Wordsworth's conviction, voiced in the 1802 additions to the Preface, that the 'objects of the Poet's thoughts are every where', that is, that a coarse miller or a Cumbrian shepherd is a fit subject for poetry. With his breadth of human sympathy, Chaucer would have endorsed, so Wordsworth believed, his simple, universalizing defence of *Michael* and *The Brothers*: 'men who do not wear fine cloaths can feel deeply.'

Wordsworth rapidly composed versions of *The *Manciple's Tale, The *Prioress's Tale, *Troilus and Criseyde*, V.519–686, and *The *Cuckoo and the Nightingale*, which was attributed to Chaucer in Anderson. He retained the verse form of the originals and translated what he took to be the meaning as faithfully as possible, consciously deviating only when 'necessary for the fluent reading and instant understanding of the Author' (Wordsworth's note, 1820). There is some evidence to suggest that he thought of publishing them, but once he became absorbed in lyric composition in 1802 Wordsworth put Chaucer aside. *The Prioress's Tale* helped plump out *The River Duddon* volume of 1820, but the rest lay unpublished for nearly forty years.

In 1840 Thomas Powell solicited contributions for a volume to be called *The Poems of Geoffrey Chaucer, Modernized*. The following year Wordsworth's *Troilus and Cressida* and *The Cuckoo and the Nightingale* appeared alongside translations by Leigh *Hunt, Elizabeth Barrett, Richard Hengist Horne, and Powell himself, in an attractive volume, whose new-technology cloth binding was stamped with a 'Gothick' motif, thus neatly suggesting both modernity and the Middle Ages. Powell was a literary adventurer and tuft-hunter, whose first letter to Wordsworth in 1836 was so oleaginous that Uriah Heep might have blushed to write it. He was also devious, and when Wordsworth began to suspect that Powell hoped to float the book on his famous name, relations between them became very strained. But *Chaucer, Modernized* was, nonetheless, a good project. In a long introduction Horne declares it scandalous that while Greek and Latin poets are read, Chaucer is not. It is not true that his language is unintelligible, or that he is coarse. Chaucer's metrical accomplishment is of the highest order, an achievement which would have been recognized had not the meretricious productions of Dryden and Pope blotted it out. Powell's collection, Wordsworth thought, had its defects, but these notwithstanding, he was glad of it, 'so great is my admiration of Chaucer's genius, & so profound my reverence for him', because it was 'a means for making many acquainted with the original, who would otherwise be ignorant of everything about him, but his name'.

Much could be said about *Chaucer, Modernized*, but what is relevant here is that it elicited from Wordsworth a number of impromptu remarks which add up to an apologia for Chaucer, addressed to readers exhibiting early Victorian sensitivities. Three points of especial interest must be summarized.

The first is that Wordsworth approaches problems in Chaucer historically. Claims for his greatness are, of course, universalist: his broad human sympathy speaks to readers independent of time, geography, and so on. Whenever the poetry presents difficulties, however, historical factors are invoked. Chaucer's attitudes to women, Wordsworth assured Isabella Fenwick, were 'as exquisite and pure' as any man's, and his expression of them is beautiful, though 'in the language of his age'. *The Reeve's Tale* Wordsworth declares 'intolerable', but what he reveals is that he means it is intolerable to the present age. Wordsworth makes no objection to the 'spirit of that humour, gross & farcical, that pervades the original'.

The second concerns Chaucer's coarseness, a topic which also moved Powell to an eloquent defence of Chaucerian manly directness against *Pope's sly lubricity. Some of Wordsworth's friends were so exercised by the possibility of indelicacy that he conceded his own judgement and withdrew *The Manciple's Tale* from Powell's collection. But he continued to insist that though 'in his comic tales indecent', Chaucer is never 'insidiously or openly voluptuous', which is more than can be said, Wordsworth adds, for some popular writers nowadays.

When a tale does present problems, moreover, one must look, he insists, to the dramatic context before rushing to judgement. This is the third and perhaps most interesting point. In a note to the 1827 printing of *The Prioress's Tale* he had pointed out that the poem must be understood as an expression of 'the fierce bigotry of the Prioress', and in 1840 he chided his son-in-law, Edward Quillinan, for failing to respond to *The Manciple's Tale* as dramatic utterance. Quillinan, himself a poet, ought to have recognized that the 'formal prosing at the end and the selfishness that pervades it flows from the genius of Chaucer, mainly as characteristic of the Narrator whom he describes in the Prologue as eminent for shrewdness and clever worldly Prudence. The main lesson, and the most important one, is inculcated as a Poet ought chiefly to inculcate his lessons, not formally, but by implication.'

This is off-the-cuff, but so perceptive that one cannot but regret that Thomas Powell did not persuade Wordsworth rather than Horne to write the introduction to *Poems of Geoffrey Chaucer, Modernised*. A formal piece by him might have been one of the better 19th-c. assessments of the poet he regarded as 'one of the greatest poets the world has ever seen'. [SG]

(For full texts and a scrupulous discussion of the circumstances of their composition and publication see Graver (1998). (See also *modernizations and translations.)

Worthies, Nine, see *Nine Worthies.

Wrecched Engendrynge of Mankynde, Of the, mentioned in the Prologue (G version only) of *The *Legend of Good Women* (G 414) as one of Chaucer's works is apparently a lost translation of the whole or a part of the *De miseria condicionis

humanae of Pope *Innocent III ('as man may in Pope Innocent yfynde'). The syntax, apparently linking it with 'he hath in prose translated Boece, | And Of the Wreched', could (but need not) imply that it too was a prose work (possibly, it has been suggested, once intended for the *Man of Law). No attempt to identify it with any surviving prose or verse work has been successful.

WYCLIF, JOHN (*c.*1330–84), spent much of his life until 1381 as teacher in Oxford, but preached in London frequently in the late 1370s; was employed by the Crown in 1374 on an embassy to Bruges, and less officially provided materials in 1378 in defence of royal infringement of the sanctuary rights of Westminster Abbey; seems to have been protected to some extent until 1381 by *John of Gaunt. He first fell into disfavour with the ecclesiastical authorities for his teaching on dominion and for his castigation of the worldliness of all aspects of the Church; in 1381 he was finally condemned for his views on the Eucharist (in which he denied the accepted view that only the accidents of bread and wine remained after the consecration whilst the substance was changed or replaced by the body of Christ). He was forced to leave Oxford, and spent the remaining years of his life in Lutterworth (Leics.), where he continued writing. Though he certainly encouraged the production of a vernacular translation of the Bible, it is less certain that he took any part in the complicated activities that led to the two versions of the Wycliffite Bible; it is also not clear that any surviving English work is directly from his pen. His followers, known as *Lollards, spread his teaching and extended his ideas far beyond the academic circles in which they originated. It is not clear that Chaucer knew Wyclif, though they shared a patron in Gaunt, a friend in Ralph *Strode, and many interests such as *free will and predestination. [AH]

Emden (1957–9), iii. 2103–6.

WYNKYN DE WORDE (d. 1535), from Wörth in Alsace, was brought by *Caxton to London and worked with him as his principal assistant. On Caxton's death he succeeded to the printing business. In 1498 he published an edition of *The *Canterbury Tales.

X

Xantippa, Xantippe, the second wife of Socrates, widely thought in the Middle Ages to have been shrewish. One of the stories *Jankyn (4) reads to the *Wife of Bath describes how she 'caste pisse' on the philosopher's head (III.729–32): in *Jerome, its source, it was simply 'dirty water',

*Christine de Pisan in the *City of Ladies* (2.21.1) gives a much more favourable account of her.

Xristus, spelling of Christus found in the alphabetical *ABC*.

Y

Middle English names beginning with *Y* or *y* as a vowel are listed under the letter *I*.

Yeoman, The. A yeoman was a servant ranking in a feudal household below a squire. The Yeoman (unnamed) of the *General Prologue* (101–17) accompanies the *Knight and the *Squire. He is a forester and a gamekeeper, skilled in 'wodecraft', dressed in green and equipped with a mighty bow.

yer(e), yeer(e), year. Chaucer uses the word in most of the ways customary in common speech, but also (especially *A Treatise on the *Astrolabe* and *Equatorie of the Planetis*) in the more precise ways of the astronomer. In the former case there is often an implication of at least rough measure, as in such phrases as 'this yeer' (during the current year), 'A doghter . . . Of twenty yeer', and 'a child that was of half yeer age'. Often there is a wish to do no more than convey the idea of a long period of time: 'gone sithen many yeres', 'so many a yere', 'yeer by yere' (for many years). Occasionally he specifies a number of years in terms of winters past, without using the word at all, as in *The *Parliament of Fowls*, 'This twenty wynter' (for the last twenty years); elsewhere he uses the word to refer to the year's *harvest*, where the harvest is now implicit.

The reference in *Equatorie of the Planetis* to 'the yer of Crist 1392 complet, the last meridie of Decembre' illustrates the astronomer's way of specifying a standard epoch with the notion of the completed year, *annus completus*. (Here the epoch is noon of 31 December 1392.) This, the astronomer's way of specifying a time, is used by Chaucer to introduce the 'aventure' of Chauntecleer *The *Nun's Priest's Tale* (VII.3187–90). In *A Treatise on the Astrolabe* he refers to the year 1391 of his example in the familiar way of civil reckoning, since there was no computational reason for doing otherwise. Such reasons have to do with the addition of the component parts of mean motions (etc.), and are explained in one of the Supplementary

Propositions (II.45). (See also *astrology and astronomy; *months and seasons; *radix.) [JDN]

Yorkshire, the county in northern England (III.1709).

youth (see *ages of man; *children; *old age). Chaucer often does not give a specific age for those characters he calls 'young': the cases where he does range from 14 (*Virginia) to 30 (the monk in The *Shipman's Tale). Medieval proverbs say that youth is frail, reckless, seldom takes heed of perils. Others sound different kinds of warning notes: 'he that in youth no virtue uses, in age all honour him refuses', 'youth will to youth' and 'youth and age are often at debate', or 'after warm youth cometh cold age'. Literary texts make use of these and other stereotypes, but 'warm youth' is often given more sympathetic treatment. It is regularly associated with *love and springtime. In Chaucer a personified Youth 'ful of *game and jolyte' appears as a companion of Cupid love outside the temple of Venus (*PF* 226), and inside her temple in The Knight's Tale (1926), and as one of the attendants of the dead *Pite (*Pity* 40). Behind these lies the *Roman de la Rose (*Romaunt of the Rose* 1281–302), where Youth is female (and as not yet 12 years old even younger than Virginia). In the Middle English version she is of 'herte wylde and thought volage [flighty, foolish]' but she means no harm ('for yonge folk, wel witen [know] ye, | Have lytel thought but on her play'). Her attentive lover kisses her frequently and openly. They kiss without shame, like two young doves. This is inside the Garden of Mirth, which is no country for old men—or old women (cf. the painting of Elde or *Old Age on the wall outside, 349–412). Chaucer's portrait of the *Squire is a detached but affectionate view of a courtly young romantic. He is sympathetic to the passions and sorrows of young lovers: Palamon, Arcite, and Emily; Piramus and Thisbe; and especially Troilus and Criseyde. In The *Book of the Duchess the Man in Black looking back confesses that in his 'first youth' (when his thoughts and deeds were variable and 'flitting') and Youth his mistress governed him in idleness, he chose love as his first craft (789–802). The beauty and the virtue of the lady he saw in the dance took his heart, and love began its work: he needed to learn ('I was ryght

yong') and tried, to love her as best he could ('after my yonge childly wyt', 1095). Not all young male lovers are so serious and devoted: in The *Legend of Good Women *Jason 'yong and lusty of corage' abandons Hypsipyle and Medea; *Theseus, aged 23 and 'seemly', betrays Ariadne; *Tarquinius, young and 'light of tongue' rapes *Lucrece. In the world of the *fabliaux lechery flourishes among the young of both sexes, although in Chaucer's tales this does not cause lasting damage. It is sometimes intensified by the presence of an elderly husband like the carpenter in The Miller's Tale. The dangers and faults of youth are occasionally mentioned in passing in descriptions of the virtuous young. The traditional (and not wholly inaccurate) thought, 'wyn and youthe dooth Venus encresse' (VI.59), occurs in the description of Virginia, who dutifully avoids revelries and dances where there is likely to be 'folly'. Among the attractive virtues of *Custance (who unlike Virginia is allowed to grow up to become a wife and mother) is 'Yowthe, withoute grenehede [immaturity] or folye' (II.163). The virtues of the young *Griselda are recognized by the young lord *Walter (IV.240–1). As she grows up, he changes, and she suffers. When she is driven away one element in the pathos of the scene is the contrast between earlier happiness and present sorrow: she remembers how 'gentil and kind' he seemed when he married her, and takes with her her old smock, a reminder of the days when she was young and poor. The proverbial 'grenehede or folye' of youth is illustrated in *Melibee (VII.1035–6), where the young folk want instant vengeance and call out for 'war' (the *counsel of young folk is not 'ripe', 1199). Sharper conflicts of youth and age are found in the rudeness of the young knight to the old woman in The Wife of Bath's Tale (III.1098–103, 1207–12) and, more violently, of the young revellers to the old man in The Pardoner's Tale (VI.718–39). Youth is always threatened by age ('in crepeth age alwey', IV.121), and Chaucer's imagination is stirred by those older folk who look back on their former youth—bitterly, like the *Reeve (I.3867–98), or rather more nostalgically, as when Alison the *Wife of Bath recalls her earlier days when she was 'yong and ful of ragerie' (III.455–79). But it is also stirred by the vision of another Alison, the young wife of The Miller's Tale, full of sensuousness and 'ragerie'.

Z

Zakarie, Zacharie, Zechariah, the Old Testament prophet. He is once quoted by the *Parson (X.434), and his prophecy of 'a well opened to the house of David' (13:1) is the source of the image of the Virgin Mary as 'the open welle | To wasshe sinful soule out of his gilt' (*ABC* 177).

ZANZIS (1), Zeuxis of Heraclea, a famous painter of the late 5th c. BC. He is cited by *Nature in *The *Physician's Tale* (VI.15–18) to show that even the greatest artist is unable to match her in the forming and 'painting' of creatures (in this case *Virginia). Behind this contrast of Art and Nature lies the story in the *Roman de la Rose* (going back to Cicero) that when Zeuxis had examined five beautiful girls and found no defect in them even he, skilled as he was in painting, was unable by combining their features to imitate the perfection of Nature's *beauty.

Zanzis (2), 'that was ful wys', to whom is attributed the proverbial remark (deriving ultimately from *Ovid) that 'the new love often chases out the old' (*Tr* IV.414), has been identified with Zanzis (1). They share the unusual name, but the painter's interest in individual characteristics does not seem to provide convincing enough evidence for the connection. Zanzis (2) probably has to remain unidentified: possibly Chaucer invented him.

ZENO, Zeno of Elea (*Eleaticis), the 5th-c. philosopher and disciple of Parmenides (*Parmanydes), said to be the inventor of dialectic. He is named only in the translation of Boethius (*Boece) (*Bo* I pr.3:55) by Lady Philosophy who

refers to the tortures he suffered (at the hands of a tyrant).

Zenith, see *Cenyth.

Zepherus, Zephirus the west wind (I.5; *BD* 402; *Bo* I m.5:22; II m.3:10; *Tr* V.10; *LGW* 171, 2681).

Zodiak, Zodiac, Zodiaacus, Zodiac (Greek *Zodiakos kuklos*, 'circle of animals'; L. *Zodiacus*). The band of sky (through the middle of which runs the *ecliptic) to which the Sun, Moon, and planets are restricted. The Moon's passage through the stars is easily seen and recorded, but the Sun's is less obvious. No matter which came first in (pre-)history, it was natural that the stars and constellations along the way should assume a special importance. The establishment of the Zodiac in its final form (with twelve constellations) took many centuries. With the mathematization of astronomy in Mesopotamia the constellation names were transferred to the signs, twelve uniform divisions each of 30° extent. (See *signe.) In Cicero and many other Latin writers the Zodiac is *Orbis signiferus* or *Circulus signifer* ('Sign-bearing circle'), which explains Chaucer's 'Signifer' in *Troilus and Criseyde*.

The Zodiac Man is an illustration commonly found in medical and astrological texts and calendars (*Kalendere). It shows the parts of the body that are related to the various zodiacal signs— Aries with the head, Taurus with the neck, and so forth. Chaucer makes play with the Taurus/neck relation in *The *Nun's Priest's Tale* and in *The *Wife of Bath's Prologue*. (See also *astrology and astronomy; *Mansio(u)n.) [JDN]

References

The following list of references cited is not intended to be a complete Chaucer bibliography. Fuller information is to be found in *The Riverside Chaucer*, ed. Larry D. Benson (Cambridge, Mass. 1987; Oxford 1988) and in J. Leyerle and A. Quick, *Chaucer, A Bibliographical Introduction* (Toronto, 1986); D. D. Griffith, *Bibliography of Chaucer 1908–53* (Washington, 1955); W. R. Crawford, *Bibliography of Chaucer 1954–63* (Washington, 1967); L. Y. Baird, *Bibliography of Chaucer 1964–73* (Boston, 1977); L.Y. Baird and H. Schnuttgen, *Bibliography of Chaucer 1974–85* (Hamden, Conn., 1988); The periodical *Studies in the Age of Chaucer* has an annual list.

AARNE, ANTTI, and THOMPSON, STITH (1961), *The Types of the Folktale* (rev. edn. Helsinki, 1964).

AERS, DAVID (1980), *Chaucer, Langland and the Creative Imagination* (London).

—— (1981), 'The *Parliament of Fowls*: Authority, the Knower and Known', *ChR* 16:1–17.

—— (1986), *Chaucer* (Brighton).

—— (1988), *Community, Gender and Individual Identity: English Writing 1360–1430* (London).

ALDERSON, WILLIAM L. (1984), 'John Urry', in Ruggiers (1984), 93–115.

ALFORD, J. A. (1988) (ed.), *A Companion to Piers Plowman* (Berkeley).

ALLEN, HOPE EMILY (1927), *Writings ascribed to Richard Rolle . . . and Material for his Biography* (New York, London).

ALLEN, JUDSON BOYCE (1982), *The Ethical Poetic of the Later Middle Ages* (Toronto).

ANDREW, M., et al. (1993) (eds.), *The General Prologue*, 2 vols. (Variorum edn., Norman, Okla.).

—— (2000), 'Games', in P. Brown (2000).

ARIÈS, PHILIPPE (1962), *Centuries of Childhood* (trans. Robert Baldick, London).

Aristoteles Latinus (1952–) (Corpus philosophorum medii aevi, Bruges, Paris).

ARMSTRONG, EDWARD A. (1956), *The Folklore of Birds* (London; rev. edn. New York, 1970).

ARNOULD, E. J. (1940) (ed.), *Le livre de seyntz medicines* (Oxford).

ASTELL, ANN W. (2000), 'The Monk's Tragical "Seint Edward"', *SAC* 22:399–405.

AXTON, RICHARD (1990), 'Interpretations of Judas in Middle English Literature', in Boitani and Torti (1990), 179–97.

BAILLIE-GROHMAN, W. A. and F. (1904) (eds.), Edward Duke of York, *The Master of Game* (London).

BAKER, DONALD C. (1984) (ed.), *The Manciple's Tale* (Variorum edn., Norman, Okla.).

—— (1990) (ed.), *The Squire's Tale* (Variorum edn., Norman, Okla.).

BAKER, TIMOTHY (1970), *Medieval London* (London).

BARBI, M. (1975) (ed.), Dante *Vita Nuova* (Florence).

BARR, HELEN (1993) (ed.), *The Piers Plowman Tradition* (London).

BARRATT, ALEXANDRA (1983) (ed.), *The Book of Tribulation* (Heidelberg).

—— (1992) (ed.), *Women's Writing in Middle English* (London).

BARTHOLOMEW, *see* SEYMOUR.

BASORE, JOHN W. (1951) (ed. and trans.), Seneca, *Moral Essays*, 3 vols. (rev. edn., London, Cambridge, Mass.).

BASWELL, CHRISTOPHER (1995), *Virgil in Medieval England* (Cambridge).

BAUM, PAULL F. (1956), 'Chaucer's Puns', *PMLA* 71:225–46.

—— (1958), 'Chaucer's Puns: A Supplemental List', *PMLA* 73:167–70.

BAWCUTT, PRISCILLA (1967) (ed.), *The Shorter Poems of Gavin Douglas* (STS 4th ser. 3, Edinburgh and London).

—— (1976), *Gavin Douglas: A Critical Study* (Edinburgh).

—— (1992), *Dunbar the Makar* (Oxford).

—— (1998) (ed.), *The Poems of William Dunbar*, 2 vols. (Glasgow).

BAYLEY, J. O. (1960), *The Characters of Love* (London).

BEADLE, RICHARD (1994) (ed.), *The Cambridge Companion to Medieval English Theatre* (Cambridge).

BEICHNER, PAUL E. (1965) (ed.), Peter of Riga, *Aurora*, 2 vols. (Notre Dame, Ill.).

BEIDLER, PETER G. (1996) (ed.), *The Wife of Bath* (Boston, Mass.).

—— (1998) (ed.), *Masculinities in Chaucer. Approaches to Maleness in The Canterbury Tales and Troilus and Criseyde* (Cambridge).

BENNETT, J. A. W. (1957), *The Parlement of Foules: An Interpretation* (Oxford).

—— (1968*a*) *Chaucer's Book of Fame* (Oxford).

—— (1968*b*) (ed.), *Selections from John Gower* (Oxford).

—— (1969), 'Chaucer's Contemporary', in S. S. Hussey (ed.), *Piers Plowman: Critical Approaches* (London).

—— (1974), *Chaucer at Oxford and at Cambridge* (Oxford).

—— (1977), 'Chaucer, Dante, and Boccaccio', *Accademia Nazionale dei Lincei. Quaderno N. 234* (Rome) (repr. in Boitani 1983*a*).

—— (1979), 'Some Second Thoughts on *The Parlement of Foules*', in E. Vasta and A. P. Thundy (eds.), *Chaucerian Problems and Perspectives. Essays Presented to Paul E. Beichner* (Notre Dame, Ind., and London), 132–46.

BENSON, C. DAVID (1980), *The History of Troy in Middle English Literature* (Woodbridge).

—— (1986), *Chaucer's Drama of Style* (Durham, NC).

—— and ELIZABETH ROBERTSON (1990) (eds.), *Chaucer's Religious Tales* (Cambridge).

—— (1990), 'The Aesthetic of Chaucer's Religious Tales in Rhyme Royal', in Boitani and Torti (1990), 101–17.

BENSON, LARRY D. (1987–8) (ed.), *The Riverside Chaucer* (Cambridge, Mass. 1987, Oxford 1988).

BENSON, ROBERT G. (1980) (ed.), *Medieval Body Language. A Study of the Use of Gesture in Chaucer's Poetry* (Copenhagen).

BERTRAM, PAUL (1965), *Shakespeare and the Two Noble Kinsmen* (New Brunswick, NJ).

BESTUL, THOMAS H. (1989), 'Chaucer's *Parson's Tale* and the Late Medieval Tradition of Religious Meditation', *Speculum* 64:600–14.

BETHURUM, DOROTHY (1945), 'Shakespeare's Comment on Medieval Romance in *Midsummer Night's Dream*', *MLN* 60:85–94.

BIELER, LUDWIG (1957) (ed.), Boethius, *De consolatione Philosophiae* (Turnhout).

BINDMAN, DAVID (1978), *The Complete Graphic Works of William Blake* (London).

BISHOP, IAN (1979), 'The Nun's Priest's Tale and the Liberal Arts', *RES* NS 30:257–67.

References

BLAKE, N. F. (1980) (ed.), *The Canterbury Tales by Geoffrey Chaucer edited form the Hengwrt Manuscript* (London).

—— (1985), *The Textual Tradition of The Canterbury Tales* (London).

BLAMIRES, ALCUIN (1992) (ed.), *Woman Defamed and Woman Defended: An Anthology of Medieval Texts* (Oxford).

BLISS, A. J. (1960) (ed.), *Sir Launfal* (London).

—— (1966) (ed.), *Sir Orfeo* (2nd edn., Oxford).

BLODGETT, J. (1984), 'William Thynne', in Ruggiers (1984), 35–52.

BLOOMFIELD, MORTON W. (1952), *The Seven Deadly Sins* (East Lansing, Mich.).

BOAS, M., and BOTSCHUYVER, H. J. (1952) (eds.), *Disticha Catonis* (Amsterdam).

BOITANI, P. (1976), 'The *Monk's Tale*: Dante and Boccaccio', *Medium Evum* 45:50–69.

—— (1977), *Chaucer and Boccaccio* (Oxford).

—— (1982), 'Chaucer's Labyrinth: Fourteenth-Century Literature and Language', *ChR* 17:197–220.

—— (1983*a*) (ed.), *Chaucer and the Italian Trecento* (Cambridge) (contains 'What Dante Meant to Chaucer' by PB).

—— and TORTI, ANNA (1983*b*) (eds.), *Literature in Fourteenth-Century England* (Tübingen and Cambridge).

—— (1984), *Chaucer and the Imaginary World of Fame* (Cambridge).

—— and MANN, JILL (1986) (eds.), *The Cambridge Chaucer Companion* (Cambridge).

—— (1989), *The Tragic and the Sublime in Medieval Literature* (Cambridge).

—— (1989) (ed.), *The European Tragedy of Troilus* (Oxford).

—— and TORTI, ANNA (1990) (eds.), *Religion in the Poetry and Drama of the Late Middle Ages in England* (Cambridge).

BOOTH, WAYNE C. (1974), *A Rhetoric of Irony* (Chicago).

BOSSUAT, R. (1955) (ed.), Alan of Lille, *Anticlaudianus* (Paris).

BOWDEN, BETSY (1991) (ed.), *Eighteenth-century Modernizations from The Canterbury Tales* (Woodbridge).

BOWDEN, MURIEL A. (1956), *A Commentary on the General Prologue to the Canterbury Tales* (New York).

BOYD, BEVERLY M. (1964) (ed.), *The Middle English Miracles of the Virgin* (San Marino, Calif.).

—— (1973), *Chaucer and the Medieval Book* (San Marino, Calif.).

—— (1984), 'William Caxton', in Ruggiers (1984), 13–34.

—— (1987) (ed.), *The Prioress's Tale* (Variorum edn., Norman, Okla.).

BRADDY, HALDEEN (1947), *Chaucer and the French Poet Graunson* (Baton Rouge, La.).

BRANCA, V. (1951–2) (ed.), *Decameron* (Florence).

—— (1964–98) (ed.), *Tutte le opere di Giovanni Boccaccio* (Milan).

—— (1964) (ed.), *Il Filostrato* (Milan).

BREHAUT, ERNEST (1912), *An Encyclopedia of the Dark Ages* (New York).

BRERETON, GEOFFREY (1968) (trans.), Froissart, *Chronicles* (Harmondsworth).

BREWER, CHARLOTTE, and RIGG, A. G. (1983) (eds.), *The Z Text of Piers Plowman* (Toronto).

BREWER, DEREK S. (1955), 'The Ideal of Feminine Beauty in Medieval Literature', *MLR* 50:257–69.

—— (1960) (ed.), Chaucer, *The Parlement of Foulys* (Manchester; repr. 1972).

—— (1964), 'Children in Chaucer', *Review of English Literature* 5 (July), 52–60.

—— (1972), 'Notes towards a Theory of Medieval Comedy', Afterword to Brewer (ed.), *Medieval Comic Tales* (Cambridge; rev. edn., 1996).

—— (1974) (ed.), *Geoffrey Chaucer* (London).

—— (1978*a*) (ed.), *Chaucer: The Critical Heritage*, 2 vols. (London).

—— (1978*b*), *Chaucer and his World* (London).

—— (1984), *An Introduction to Chaucer* (London).

—— (2000), 'Chivalry', in P. Brown (2000).

BROMWICH, RACHEL (1985) (ed. and trans.), *Selected Poems of Dafydd Ap Gwilym* (2nd edn., Harmondsworth).

BRONSON, BERTRAND H. (1952), '*The Book of the Duchess* re-opened', *PMLA* 67:863–81; repr. in Wagenknecht (1959).

BROOKE, C. N. L. (1989), *The Medieval Idea of Marriage* (Oxford).

BROOKS, HAROLD (1979) (ed.), *A Midsummer Night's Dream* (London).

BROWN, EMERSON, Jr. (1981), 'What is Chaucer doing with the Physician and his Tale?', *PQ* 60: 129–49.

BROWN, PETER (1999) (ed.), *Reading Dreams* (Oxford).

—— (2000) (ed.), *A Companion to Chaucer* (Oxford).

BRUNDAGE, J. A. (1993), *Sex, Law, and Marriage in the Middle Ages* (Aldershot).

BRUNNER, KARL (1933) (ed.), *The Seven Sages of Rome* (EETS 191).

BRUSENDORFF, AAGE (1925), *The Chaucer Tradition* (London).

BRUYNE, EDGAR DE (1946; 1969), *Etudes d'ésthétique mediévale* (Bruges); English trans. Eileen Hennessy, *The Aesthetics of the Middle Ages*.

BRYAN, W. F., and DEMPSTER, GERMAINE (1958) (eds.), *Sources and Analogues of Chaucer's Canterbury Tales* (London; first pub. 1941).

BUFFANO, A. (1975) (ed.), *Opere latine di Francesco Petrarca*, 2 vols. (Turin).

BULLOUGH, GEOFFREY (1957), *Narrative and Dramatic Sources of Shakespeare* (London, 1957–75), vol. i.

BUNDY, M. W. (1927), *The Theory of Imagination in Classical and Medieval Thought* (Urbana, Ill.).

BURGESS, GLYN S., and BUSBY, KEITH (1986) (trans.), *The Lais of Marie de France* (Harmondsworth).

BURNLEY, J. D. (1979), *Chaucer's Language and the Philosophers' Tradition* (Cambridge).

—— (1983), *A Guide to Chaucer's Language* (London).

BURNS, M. M. (1980), '*Troilus and Cressida*: the Worst of Both Worlds', *Shakespeare Studies* 13:105–30.

BURROW, J. A. (1957), 'Irony in *The Merchant's Tale*', *Anglia* 75:199–205.

—— (1971), *Ricardian Poetry: Chaucer, Gower, Langland and the Gawain Poet* (London).

—— (1971), '"Sir Thopas": an Agony in Three Fits', *RES* NS 22:54–8.

—— (1986), *The Ages of Man. A Study in Medieval Writing and Thought* (Oxford).

—— (1994), *Thomas Hoccleve* (Aldershot).

—— (1995), 'Elvish Chaucer', in M. T. Tavormina and R. F. Yeager (eds.), *The Endless Knot: Essays on Old and Middle English in Honor of Marie Borroff* (Cambridge).

BUTLER, H. E. (1963) (ed.), Quintilian *Institutio oratoria*, 4 vols. (London).

BYNUM, CAROLINE WALKER (1982), *Jesus as Mother. Studies in the Spirituality of the High Middle Ages* (Berkeley, Los Angeles, and London).

References

CAMILLE, MICHAEL (1992), *Image on the Edge: The Margins of Medieval Art* (Cambridge, Mass.).

CANNON, CHRISTOPHER (1993), '*Raptus* in the Chaumpaigne Release and a Newly Discovered Document concerning the Life of Geoffrey Chaucer', *Speculum* 68:74–94.

—— (2000), 'Chaucer and Rape: Uncertainty's Certainties', *SAC* 22:67–92.

CAPLAN, H. (1954) (ed. and trans.), *Ad Herennium* (London and Cambridge, Mass.).

—— (1970), *Of Eloquence: Studies in Ancient and Medieval Rhetoric* (Ithaca, NY).

CARRUTHERS, MARY (1990), *The Book of Memory. A Study of Memory in Medieval Culture* (Cambridge).

CARTER, H. H. (1961), *A Dictionary of Middle English Musical Terms* (Bloomington, Ind.).

CARTLIDGE, NEIL (1997), *Medieval Marriage: Literary Approaches 1100–1300* (Woodbridge).

CARY, GEORGE (1956), *The Medieval 'Alexander'* (Cambridge).

CATTO, J. I. (1984; 1992) (ed.), *The History of the University of Oxford* vols. i and ii (with R. Evans) (Oxford).

CAVANAUGH, SUSAN (1985), *A Study of Books Privately Owned in England* (Ann Arbor, Mich.).

CH [Critical Heritage] *see* Brewer (1978).

CHADWICK, HENRY (1981), *Boethius* (Oxford).

CHESTERTON, G. K. (1932), *Geoffrey Chaucer* (London).

—— (1933), *All I Survey* (London).

CHRISTIANSEN, ERIC (1980), *The Northern Crusades: The Baltic and the Catholic Frontier 1100–1525* (London).

CLAGETT, M. (1959), *The Science of Mechanics in the Middle Ages* (Madison, Wis.).

CLEMEN, WOLFGANG (1963), *Chaucer's Early Poetry* (trans. C. A. M. Sym, London; *Der junge Chaucer*, Bochum-Langendreer, 1938).

CLOGAN, PAUL M. (1972), 'The Figural Style and Meaning of *The Second Nun's Prologue and Tale*', *Medievalia et Humanistica* NS 3:213–40.

—— (1979), 'Chaucer and Leigh Hunt', *Medievalia et Humanistica* NS 9:163–74.

COBBAN, A. B. (1988), *The Medieval English Universities: Oxford and Cambridge to c.1500* (London).

COLDWELL, DAVID F. C. (1957–64) (ed.), *Virgil's Aeneid Translated into Scottish Verse by Gavin Douglas*, 4 vols. (STS 3rd ser., Edinburgh and London).

COLLEDGE, EDMUND, and WALSH, J. (1978) (eds.), *A Book of Showings to the anchoress Julian of Norwich* (Toronto).

COLLETTE, CAROLYN P. (1975–6), 'A Closer Look at Seinte Cecile's Special Vision', *ChR* 10:337–49.

—— (1980–1), 'Sense and Sensibility in *The Prioress's Tale*', *ChR* 15:138–50.

—— (2001), *Species and Images: Vision and Medieval Psychology in The Canterbury Tales* (Ann Arbor, Mich.).

CONNOLLY, MARGARET (1998), *John Shirley: Book Production and the Noble Household in Fifteenth-Century England* (Aldershot).

CONRAD, PETER (1995), *To Be Continued: Four Stories and their Survival* (Oxford).

CONSTANS, L. (1904–12) (ed.), Benoit de Sainte-Maure *Roman de Troie*, 6 vols. (Paris).

COOKE, THOMAS D. (1978), *The Old French and Chaucerian Fabliaux* (Colombia, Miss.).

COOLEY, F. D. (1948), 'Two Notes on the Chess Terms in the *Book of the Duchess*', *MLN* 63:30–5.

COOPER, HELEN (1983), *The Structure of the Canterbury Tales* (London).

—— (1987), 'Langland's and Chaucer's Prologues', *Yearbook of Langland Studies* 1:71–81.

—— (1989), *The Canterbury Tales* (Oxford Guides to Chaucer, Oxford).

—— and MAPSTONE, SALLY (1997) (eds.), *The Long Fifteenth Century. Essays for Douglas Gray* (Oxford).

COPLAND, MURRAY (1962), '*The Reeve's Tale*: Harlotrie or Sermonyng?', *Medium Evum* 31:14–32.

—— (1966), '*The Shipman's Tale*: Chaucer And Boccaccio', *Medium Evum* 35:11–28.

CORREALE, ROBERT M., and HAMEL, MARY (2002) (eds.), *Sources and Analogues of the Canterbury Tales*, vol. i (Cambridge).

CORSA, HELEN STORM (1987) (ed.), *The Physician's Tale* (Variorum edn., Norman, Okla.)

COYNE, G. V., et al. (1983) (eds.), *Gregorian Reform of the Calendar* (Vatican City).

COWAN, J., and KANE, G. (1995) (eds.), Chaucer *The Legend of Good Women* (East Lansing, Mich.).

CRAMPTON, G. R. (1974), *The Condition of Creatures: Suffering and Acton in Chaucer and Spenser* (New Haven).

CRANE, SUSAN (1994), *Gender and Romance in Chaucer's Canterbury Tales* (Princeton).

CRISP, SIR FRANK (1924), *Medieval Gardens* (London).

CROMBIE, A. C. (1953), *Robert Grosseteste and the Origins of Experimental Science, 1100–1700* (Oxford).

—— (1969), *Augustine to Galileo*, 2 vols. (rev. edn., London).

—— and NORTH, J. D. (1970), 'Bacon, Roger', in C. C. Gillispie (ed.), *Dictionary of Scientific Biography* vol. i (New York), 377–85.

CRONE, GERALD R. (1978), *Maps and their Makers* (Folkestone, Hamden, Conn.).

CROW, MARTIN M., and OLSON, CLAIR C. (1966) (eds.), *Chaucer Life Records* (Oxford).

CROWLEY, T. (1950), *Roger Bacon: The Problem of the Soul in his Philosophical Commentaries* (Louvain and Dublin). (Contains a critical biography.)

CUMING, G. J., and BAKER, DEREK (1972), *Popular Belief and Practice* (Studies in Church History, vol. viii (Cambridge).

CURNOW, Maureen (1975) (ed.), *The Livre de la cité des dames of Christine de Pisan* (Nashville, Tenn.).

CURRY, WALTER CLYDE (1960), *Chaucer and the Medieval Sciences* (rev. edn., New York; 1st edn., Oxford, 1926).

CURTIUS, ERNST ROBERT (1953), *European Literature and the Latin Middle Ages* (trans. Willard R. Trask, London; *Europäische Literatur und lateinische Mittelalter*, Bern, 1948).

DAHLBERG, C. R. (1971) (trans.) *The Romance of the Rose* (Princeton).

—— (1999) (ed.), *The Romaunt of the Rose* (Variorum edn., Norman, Okla.).

DANIELL, CHRISTOPHER (1997), *Death and Burial in Medieval England 1066–1550* (London).

DAVENPORT, W. A. (1988), *Chaucer: Complaint and Narrative* (Cambridge).

DAVID, ALFRED (1962), 'The Hero of the *Troilus*', *Speculum* 37:566–81.

—— (1976), *The Strumpet Muse: Art and Morals in Chaucer's Poetry* (Bloomington, Ind.).

DAVIS, NORMAN (1965), 'The *Litera Troili* and English Letters', *RES* NS 16:233–44.

—— et al. (1979), *A Chaucer Glossary* (Oxford).

DAY, MABEL, and STEELE, R. (1936) (eds.), *Mum and Sothsegger* (EETS 199).

DAY LEWIS, C. (1986) (trans.), Virgil *The Aeneid* (Oxford; 1st pub. 1952).

DE BRUYNE, EDGAR, *see* Bruyne.

DELANY, SHEILA (1972), *Chaucer's 'House of Fame': The Poetics of Skeptical Fideism* (Chicago).

—— (1983), *Writing Woman: Women Writers and Women in Literature. Medieval to Modern* (New York).

References

DELANY, SHEILA (1994), *The Naked Text: Chaucer's 'Legend of Good Women'* (Berkeley and Los Angeles).

DELEHAYE, HIPPOLYTE (1998), *The Legends of the Saints* (trans. D. Attwater, Dublin; 1st Fr. edn., 1905).

DENHOLM-YOUNG, N. (1937), 'Richard de Bury', *Transactions of the Royal Historical Society* 11th ser. 20:135–68.

DICK, A. (1978) (ed.), Martianus Capella (Leipzig, 1925; rev. J. Préaux, Stuttgart).

DICKINSON, JOHN (1927) (trans.), [John of Salisbury] *The Statesman's Book* (New York). (selections)

Dictionnaire de Spiritualité (1937–), ed. M. Viller et al. (Paris).

DINSHAW, CAROLYN (1989), *Chaucer's Sexual Poetics* (Madison, Wis.).

DOBSON, R. B. (1983), *The Peasants' Revolt of 1381* (2nd edn., London; 1st edn. 1970).

DONALDSON, E. Talbot (1954), 'Chaucer the Pilgrim', *PMLA* 69:928–36 (repr. in Donaldson, *Speaking of Chaucer*, New York, London, 1970).

—— (1958) (ed.), *Chaucer's Poetry: An Anthology for the Modern Reader* (New York).

—— (1963), 'The Ending of Chaucer's *Troilus*', in A. Brown and P. Foote (eds.), *Early English and Norse Studies Presented to Hugh Smith* (London; repr. in Donaldson, *Speaking of Chaucer*, London, 1970).

—— (1977), 'Designing a Camel: or Generalizing the Middle Ages', *Tennessee Studies in Literature* 22:1–16.

—— (1982), '*Troilus and Cressida*', in Maynard Mack and George de F. Lord (eds.), *Poetic Traditions of the English Renaissance* (New Haven).

—— (1985), *The Swan at the Well* (New Haven).

DONALDSON, IAN (1982), *The Rapes of Lucretia: A Myth and Its Transformations* (Oxford).

DOOB, PENELOPE (1990), *The Idea of the Labyrinth from Classical Antiquity through the Middle Ages* (Ithaca, NY).

DOYLE, A. I. (1961), 'More Light on John Shirley', *Medium Evum* 30:93–101.

DOYLE, E. (1983) (ed.), 'William Woodford O. F. M.', *Franciscan Studies* 43:76–89.

DRACHMANN, A. G. (1963), *The Mechanical Technology of Greek and Roman Antiquity* (Copenhagen).

DRONKE, PETER (1964), 'The Conclusion of *Troilus and Criseyde*', *Medium Evum* 33:47–55.

—— (1965, 1966), *Medieval Latin and the Rise of European Love Lyric*, 2 vols. (Oxford).

—— (1973), 'The Rise of the Medieval Fabliau', *Romanische Forschungen* 85:275–97 (repr. in Dronke, *The Medieval Poet and his World*, Rome, 1984).

—— (1978), *The Medieval Lyric* (2nd edn., London; 1st edn. 1968).

—— (1973), 'Medieval Rhetoric', in D. Daiches and A. K. Thorlby (eds.), *Literature and Western Civilisation* vol. ii (London; repr. in Dronke, *The Medieval Poet and his World*, Rome, 1984).

—— (1974), 'Chaucer and the Medieval Latin Poets', in Brewer (1974), 154–83.

—— (1976), *Abelard and Heloise in Medieval Testimonies* (Glasgow).

—— (1978) (ed.), Bernardus Silvestris *Cosmographia* (Leiden).

—— (1994), 'Andreas Capellanus', *Journal of Medieval Latin* 4:51–63 (repr. in Dronke, *Sources of Inspiration* (Rome, 1997).

—— (1997), 'Poetic Originality in *The Wars of Alexander*', in Cooper and Mapstone (1997), 123–39.

DU BOULAY, F. R. H. (1970), *An Age of Ambition. English Society in the Late Middle Ages* (London).

—— (1974), 'The Historical Chaucer', in Brewer (1974), 33–57.

DUFF, J. D. (1928) (ed. and trans.), Lucan *The Civil War* (London, Cambridge, Mass.).

DUFFY, EAMON (1992), *The Stripping of the Altars* (New Haven).

DUNNING, T. P. (1962), 'God and Man in *Troilus and Criseyde*', in N. Davis and C. L. Wrenn (eds.), *English and Medieval Studies presented to J. R. R. Tolkien* (London).

DURLING, R. M. (1976) (ed. and trans.), *Petrarch's Lyric Poems* (Cambridge, Mass. and London).

EADE, J. C. (1984), *The Forgotten Sky* (Oxford).

EBIN, LOIS (1988), *Illuminator, Makar, Vates* (Lincoln, Nebr.).

EDWARDS, A. S. G. (1984), 'John Trevisa', in Edwards (ed.), *Middle English Prose* (New Brunswick, NJ), 133–46.

—— (1984), 'Walter Skeat', in Ruggiers (1984), 171–89.

EDWARDS, PHILIP (1964), 'On the Design of *The Two Noble Kinsmen*', *A Review of English Literature* 5 (Oct.): 89–108.

EGERTON, ALIX (intro.) (1911), *The Ellesmere Chaucer: reproduced in facsimile*, 2 vols. (Manchester).

EISENHUT, WERNER (1958) (ed.), *Ephemeridos belli Troiani* (Leipzig).

EISNER, S., and MACEOIN, G. (1980) (eds. and trans.), *The Kalendarium of Nicholas of Lynn* (Athens, Ga.).

ELLIOTT, R. W. V. (1974), *Chaucer's English* (London).

ELLIS, F. S. (1900) (ed.), *The Golden Legend or Lives of the Saints . . . by William Caxton* (London).

ELLIS, R. (1986), *Patterns of Religious Narrative in The Canterbury Tales* (London).

EMDEN, A. B. (1957–9), *A Biographical Register of the University of Oxford to AD 1500* (Oxford).

EMMERSON, R. K. (1984), *Antichrist in the Middle Ages. A Study of Medieval Apocaypticism* (Seattle).

ENGLAND, JOHN (1987) (ed. and trans.), Juan Manuel *El Conde Lucanor* (Warminster).

ERDMANN, AXEL, and EKWALL, EILERT (1911, 1930) (eds.), *Lydgate's 'Siege of Thebes'* 2 vols. (EETS Extra Series 108, 125).

EVANS, JOAN (1933) (ed.), *English Medieval Lapidaries* (EETS 190).

—— (1949), *English Art 1307–1461* (Oxford).

EVERETT, DOROTHY (1929), 'A Characterization of the English Medieval Romances', *Essays and Studies* 15:98–121 (repr. in Everett, *Essays on Middle English Literature*, Oxford, 1955).

EWERT, A. (1947) (ed.), Marie de France *Lais* (Oxford).

FAIRCLOUGH, H. RUSHTON (1929) (ed. and trans.), Horace *Satires, Epistles, Ars Poetica* (rev. edn., London, New York).

—— (1930–2) (ed. and trans.), Virgil, 2 vols. (London, New York).

FAIRHOLT, F. W. (1840), *Satirical Songs and Poems on Costume from the Thirteenth to the Nineteenth Centuries* (Percy Society 27).

FALCONER, WILLIAM A. (1923) (ed. and trans.), Cicero *De senectute, de amicitia, de divinatione* (London, New York).

FANSLER, DEAN S. (1914), *Chaucer and the Roman de la Rose* (New York).

FARAL, EDMOND (1924) (ed.), *Les arts poétiques du xiie et du xiiie siècle* (Paris).

FAULKNER, DEWEY R. (1973) (ed.), *Twentieth Century Interpretations of the Pardoner's Tale* (Englewood Cliffs, NJ).

FERGUSON, ARTHUR B. (1960), *The Indian Summer of English Chivalry* (Durham, NC).

—— (1986), *The Chivalric Tradition in Renaissance England* (Washington, London, Toronto).

FERRIS, SUMNER (1967–8), 'The Date of Chaucer's Final Annuity and of the "Complaint to his Empty Purse"', *MP* 65:45–52.

References

FERSTER, JUDITH (1985), *Chaucer on Interpretation* (Cambridge).

FINUCANE, RONALD C. (1977), *Miracles and Pilgrims. Popular Beliefs in Medieval England* (London).

FISHER, JOHN H. (1964), *John Gower: Moral Philosopher and Friend of Chaucer* (London).

FLEMING, JOHN V. (1969), *The Roman de la Rose: A Study in Allegory and Iconography* (Princeton).

—— (1990), *Classical Imitation and Interpretation in Chaucer's Troilus* (Lincoln, Nebr.).

FOERSTER, WENDELIN (1884–99) (ed.), Christian von Troyes *Sämtliche Werke*, 5 vols. (Halle).

FOSTER, K., and BOYDE, P. (1976) (eds.), *Dante's Lyric Poetry*, 2 vols. (Oxford).

FOURRIER, ANTHIME (1963) (ed.), Froissart *L'Espinette amoureux* (Paris).

—— (1975) (ed.), Froissart *Joli Buisson de Jeunesse* (Geneva).

FOWLER, KENNETH (1967), *The Age of Plantagenet and Valois* (London).

FOX, DENTON (1981) (ed.), *The Poems of Robert Henryson* (Oxford).

FRANK, R. W. (1972), *Chaucer and 'The Legend of Good Women'* (Cambridge, Mass.).

FRAPPIER, JEAN (1976), 'Le thème de la lumière de la "Chanson de Roland" au "Roman de la Rose"', in Frappier, *Histoire, Mythes et Symboles* (Geneva).

FRASER, R. A. (1955) (ed.), *The Court of Venus* (Durham, NC).

FRAZER, RICHARD M. (1966) (trans.), *The Trojan War: The Chronicles of Dictys of Crete and Dares the Phrygian* (Bloomington, Ind.).

FRENCH, W. H., and HALE, C. B. (1930) (eds.), *Middle English Metrical Romances* (New York).

—— (1949), 'Medieval Chess and the *Book of the Duchess*', *MLN* 64:261–4.

FRIEDBERG, E. (1879–81) (ed.), *Corpus Iuris Canonici*, 2 vols. (Leipzig).

FRIEND, A. C. (1953), 'Chaucer's Version of the *Aeneid*', *Speculum* 28:317–23.

FURNIVALL, F. J. (1868) (ed.), *The Babees Book* (EETS 32).

—— (1892) (ed.), Hoccleve, *Minor Poems* (EETS Extra Series 61; rev. edn. J. Mitchell and A. I. Doyle, 1970).

—— (1897) (ed.), Hoccleve, *The Regement of Princes* (EETS Extra Series 72).

—— (1909) (ed.), *The Tale of Beryn* (EETS Extra Series 105).

FYLER, JOHN M. (1979), *Chaucer and Ovid* (New Haven).

—— (1998), 'Froissart and Chaucer', in Donald Maddox and Sara Sturm-Maddox (eds.), *Froissart Across the Genres* (Gainesville, Fla.).

—— (2000), 'Pagan Survivals', in P. Brown (2000).

GALVAN REULA, FERNANDO (1989), 'Medieval English Literature: A Spanish Approach', in Patricia Shaw and others (eds.), *Actas del Primer Congreso Internacional de la Sociedad Española de Lengua y Literatura Ingles Medieval* (Oviedo), 98–111.

GANIM, JOHN M. (1990), *Chaucerian Theatricality* (Princeton).

GIBSON, MARGARET (1981) (ed.), *Boethius: His Life, Thought and Influence* (Oxford).

GIFFIN, MARY (1956), *Studies in Chaucer and his Audience* (Quebec).

GILL, ERIC (1929–31), *The Canterbury Tales with Wood Engravings by Eric Gill* (Waltham St Lawrence).

—— (1927), *Troilus and Criseyde* (Waltham St Lawrence).

GLUNZ, H. H. (1937), *Die Literarästhetik des europäischen Mittelalters: Wolfram, Chaucer, Dante* (Bochum-Langendreer).

GOLLANCZ, SIR ISRAEL (1925) (ed.), Hoccleve, *Minor Poems* (EETS Extra Series 73; rev. edn. J. Mitchell and A. I. Doyle, 1970).

GOLOMBEK, HARRY (1976), *A History of Chess* (London).

GOMPF, LUDWIG (1970) (ed.), Joseph Iscanus *Werke und Briefe* (Leiden).

GOODMAN, ANTHONY (1922), *John of Gaunt. The Exercise of Princely Power in Fourteenth-Century Europe* (London).

GORDON, E. V. (1953) (ed.), *Pearl* (Oxford).

GORDON, R. K. (1934), *The Story of Troilus* (London).

GOTTFRIED, R. S. (1983), *The Black Death: Nature and Disaster in Medieval Europe* (London).

GOUGAUD, L. (1914), 'La Danse dans les églises', *Revue d'histoire ecclésiastique* 15:5–22, 229–45.

GRAESSE, TH. (1850) (ed.), *Legenda aurea* (Leipzig).

GRANT, EDWARD (1974) (ed.), *A Source Book in Medical Science* (Cambridge, Mass.).

GRAVER, BRUCE E. (1998), *Translations of Chaucer and Virgil by William Wordsworth* (Ithaca, NY, and London).

GRAY, DOUGLAS (1979), 'Chaucer and "Pite"', in M. Salu and R. T. Farrell (eds.), *J. R. R. Tolkien, Scholar and Storyteller: Essays in Memoriam* (Ithaca, NY), 173–203.

—— (1979), *Robert Henryson* (Leiden).

—— (1984), 'Chaucer and Allusion', in S. Rossi (ed.), *Saggi sul Rinascimento* (Milan), 7–26.

—— (1986), 'Books of Comfort', in Greg Kratzmann and James Simpson (eds.), *Medieval English Religious and Ethical Literature: Essays in Honour of G. H. Russell* (Cambridge), 209–21.

—— (1987), 'Chaucer and Gentilesse', in G. H. V. Bunt, E. S. Kooper, et al. (eds.), *One Hundred Years of English Studies in Dutch Universities* (Amsterdam), 1–27.

—— (1989), 'Humanism and Humanisms in Late Medieval English Literature', in S. Rossi and D. Savoia (eds.), *Italy and the English Renaissance* (Milan), 25–44.

—— (1995), '"Pite for to here—Pite for to se": Some Scenes of Pathos in Late Medieval English Literature', *Proceedings of the British Academy* 87:67–99.

—— (1996), 'Chaucer and the Art of Digression', *Studies in Medieval Language and Literature* 11:21–47.

GREEN, RICHARD FIRTH (1980), *Poets and Princepleasers: Literature and the English Court in the Late Middle Ages* (Toronto).

—— (1998), *A Crisis of Truth. Literature and Law in Ricardian England* (Philadelphia).

GREENE, R. L. (1977) (ed.), *The Early English Carols* (2nd edn., Oxford).

GRIFFIN, NATHANIEL E. (1907), *Dares and Dictys: An Introduction to the Study of Medieval Versions of the Story of Troy* (Baltimore).

—— (1936) (ed.), Guido delle Colonne, *Historia destructionis Troiae* (Cambridge, Mass.).

—— and MYRICK, A. B. (1929) (ed. and trans.), Boccaccio *Il Filostrato* (Philadelphia).

GRISCOM, ACTON (1929) (ed.), Geoffrey of Monmouth, *Historia regum Britanniae* (London).

GUMMERE, R. M. (1917–25) (ed. and trans.), Seneca *Ad Lucilium epistulae morales*, 3 vols. (London, Cambridge, Mass.).

GUNN, ALAN M. F. (1952), *The Mirror of Love* (Lubbock, Tex.).

HABICHT, W. (1959), *Die Gebärde in englischen Dichtungen des Mitelalters* (Munich).

HAHN, THOMAS (1986), 'Money, Sexuality, Wordplay and Context in the *Shipman's Tale*', in Julian N. Wasserman and Robert J. Blanch (eds.), *Chaucer in the Eighties* (Syracuse, NY), 235–49.

HAINES, ROY MARTIN (1989), *Ecclesia anglicana: Studies in the English Church of the Later Middle Ages* (Toronto, Buffalo, and London).

References

HALLEUX, R. (1979), *Les Textes alchimiques* (Turnhout).

HAMMOND, ELEANOR PRESCOTT (1908), *Chaucer. A Bibliographical Manual* (New York).

HANAWALT, BARBARA (1979), *Crime and Conflict in English Communities 1300–48* (Cambridge, Mass.).

HANNA, R. (1989), (intro.), *The Ellesmere Manuscript of Chaucer's Canterbury Tales. A Working Facsimile* (Cambridge).

HANRAHAN, M. (2000), 'London', in P. Brown (2000).

HARBERT, BRUCE (1974), 'Chaucer and the Latin Classics', in Brewer (1974), 137–53.

HARDING, ALAN (1966), *A Social History of English Law* (Harmondsworth).

HARDING, CHRISTOPHER (1985), et al., *Imprisonment in England and Wales* (London).

HÄRING, NIKOLAUS (1978) (ed.), Alan of Lille *De planctu Naturae*, *Studi Medievali* 3a serie, 19/2.

HARRISON, T. P. (1956), *They Tell of Birds: Chaucer, Spenser, Milton, Drayton* (Austin, Tex).

HARVEY, JOHN H. (1981), *Mediaeval Gardens* (London).

HARVEY, P. D. A. (1991), *Medieval Maps* (London).

—— (1996), *Mappa Mundi: The Hereford World Map* (London).

HASELMAYER, L. A. (1938), 'The Portraits in Chaucer's Fabliaux', *RES* NS 14:310–14.

HASKELL, ANN T. (1968), 'The St Joce Oath in the Wife of Bath's Prologue', *ChR* 1:85–7.

HATTO, A. T. (1965), *Eos. An Enquiry into the Theme of Lovers' Meetings and Partings at Dawn in Poetry* (The Hague).

HAVELY, N. R. (1980), *Chaucer's Boccaccio* (Cambridge).

—— (1994) (ed.), Chaucer *The House of Fame* (Durham).

HAZELTON, R. (1960), 'Chaucer and Cato', *Speculum* 35:357–80.

HEAL, FELICITY (1990), *Hospitality in Early Modern England* (Oxford).

HEATH, P. (1969), *English Parish Clergy on the Eve of the Reformation* (London).

HEIBERG, J. L. (1898–1919) (ed.), *Claudii Ptolemaei opera quae extant omnia*.

HELLINGA, LOTTE (1982), *Caxton in Focus* (London).

HELM, RUDOLF (1898) (ed.), Fulgentius *Opera* (Leipzig; new edn. J. Préaux, Stuttgart, 1970).

HEYWORTH, P. L. (1968) (ed.), *Jack Upland, Friar Daw's Reply, and Upland's Rejoinder* (Oxford).

—— (1981) (ed.), *Medieval Studies for J. A. W. Bennett* (Oxford).

HIEATT, C. B. (1967), *The Realism of Dream Visions* (The Hague, Paris).

—— and BUTLER, S. (1976) (eds.), *Pleyn Delit* (Toronto).

HILLERBRAND, H. N. (1953) (ed.), Shakespeare *Troilus and Cressida* (New Variorum edn., Philadelphia).

HILTON, R. H., and ASTON, T. H. (1984), *The English Rising of 1381* (Cambridge).

HIRSH, JOHN C. (1975–6), 'Reopening the *Prioress's Tale*, *ChR* 10:30–45.

—— (1977–8), 'The Politics of Spirituality: The Second Nun and the Manciple', *ChR* 12:129–46.

—— (1989), *The Revelations of Margery Kempe. Paramystical Practices in Late Medieval England* (Leiden).

—— (1993), 'Modern Times: The Discourse of the *Physician's Tale*', *ChR* 27:387–95.

—— (1996), *The Boundaries of Faith: The Development and Transmission of Medieval Spirituality* (Leiden).

HODGES, LAURA F. (2000), *Chaucer and Costume* (Cambridge).

HODGETT, G. A. J. (1972), *Stere hit well* (London) (with notes on recipes by Delia Smith).

HOEPFFNER, ERNST (ed.), *Oeuvres de Guillaume de Machaut*, 3 vols. (Paris).

HOLLANDER, JOHN (1981), *The Figure of Echo* (Berkeley).

HOLMYARD, E. J. (1957), *Alchemy* (Harmondsworth).

HOLZKNECHT, H. J. (1923), *Literary Patronage in the Middle Ages* (Philadelphia).

HORGAN, FRANCES (1994) (trans.), *The Romance of the Rose* (Oxford).

HOSKINS, W. G. (1955), *The Making of the English Landscape* (London).

HOWARD, DONALD R. (1976), *The Idea of the Canterbury Tales* (Berkeley and Los Angeles).

—— (1987), *Chaucer: His Life, his Works, his World* (New York).

HUBBELL, H. M. (1939) (ed. and trans.), Cicero, *De inventione* (London, Cambridge, Mass.).

HUDSON, ANNE (1984), 'John Stow', in Ruggiers (1984), 52–70.

—— (1988), *The Premature Reformation. Wycliffite Texts and Lollard History* (Oxford).

HUIZINGA, JOHANN (1949), *Homo Ludens. A Study of the Play Element in Culture* (London).

HUNT, R. W. (1948), 'Introductions to the *Artes* in the Twelfth Century', in (ed.) *Studia Medievalia in honorem R. M. Martin, O. P.* (Bruges: repr. in Hunt, *The History of Grammar in the Middle Ages*, Oxford, 1980).

HUTTON, EDWARD (1927) (ed.), *Thirteene most pleasaunt and delectable questions*. Englished by H.G. (1566) (London).

JACKSON, KENNETH HURLSTONE (1961), *The International Popular Tale and Early Welsh Tradition* (Cardiff).

JACKSON, WILLIAM W. (1909) (trans.), *Convivio* (Oxford).

JAEGER, W. (1948), *Aristotle* (2nd English edn., Oxford).

JANSON, H. W. (1952), *Apes and Ape Lore in the Middle Ages and the Renaissance* (London).

JEFFERSON, BERNARD (1917), *Chaucer and the Consolation of Philosophy* (Princeton).

JENKINS, ANTHONY (1980) (ed.), *The Isle of Ladies* (New York, London).

JODOGNE, O. (1975), 'Le Fabliau' in *Typologie des sources du moyen age occidental*, fasc. 13 (Turnhout).

JOHNES, THOMAS (1803–5) (trans.), *Chronicles of Froissart* 4 vols. (rev. edn. 1901).

JOHNSON, FRIDOLF (1973) (ed.), William Morris. *Ornamentation and Illustrations from the Kelmscott Chaucer* (New York).

JONES, L. W. (1949) (trans.), Cassiodorus *An Introduction to Divine and Human Readings* (New York).

JONES, P. M. (1984), *Medieval Medical Miniatures* (London).

JONES, TERRY (1980), *Chaucer's Knight: The Portrait of a Medieval Mercenary* (London).

JORDAN, ROBERT M. (1967), *Chaucer and the Shape of Creation: The Aesthetic Possibilities of Inorganic Structure* (Cambridge, Mass.).

—— (1987), *Chaucer's Poetics and the Modern Reader* (Berkeley and Los Angeles).

KANE, ELISHA K. (1968) (trans.), *The Book of Good Love by Juan Ruiz* (Chapel Hill, NC).

KANE, GEORGE (1960) (ed.), *Piers Plowman: The A Version* (London).

—— and DONALDSON, E. TALBOT (1975) (eds.), *Piers Plowman: The B Version* (London).

—— (1984), *Geoffrey Chaucer* (Oxford).

—— and RUSSELL, G. H. (1997) (eds.), *Piers Plowman: The C Version* (London).

KATZENELLENBOGEN, A. (1939), *Allegories of the Virtues and Vices in Medieval Art* (London).

KAY, SARAH (1995), *The Romance of the Rose* (London).

KEAN, PATRICIA M. (1972), *Chaucer and the Making of English Poetry*, 2 vols. (London).

KEEN, MAURICE (1962), 'Brotherhood in Arms', *History* 47:1–17.

References

KEEN, MAURICE (1983), 'Chaucer's Knight, the English Aristocracy and the Crusade', in V. J. Scattergood and J. W. Sherborne (eds.), *English Court Culture in the Later Middle Ages* (London).

—— (1984), *Chivalry* (New Haven).

KELLY, HENRY ANSGAR (1975), *Love and Marriage in the Age of Chaucer* (Ithaca, NY).

—— (1986), *Chaucer and the Cult of St Valentine* (Leiden).

—— (1987), *Medieval Tragedy* (Woodbridge).

—— (1998), 'Meanings and Uses of *Raptus* in Chaucer's Time', *SAC*: 101–65.

KEMPF, C. (1888) (ed.), Valerius Maximus *Factorum et dictorum memorabilium libri IX* (Leipzig).

KENDRICK, LAURA (1988), *Chaucerian Play: Comedy and Control in the Canterbury Tales* (Berkeley and Los Angeles).

KER, W. P. (1897), *Epic and Romance* (London).

—— (1905), *Essays on Medieval Literature* (London).

—— (1912), *English Literature: Medieval* (London; repr. Oxford, 1969).

KERVYN DE LETTENHOVE (1870–6) (ed.), Froissart *Oeuvres*, 25 vols. (Brussels).

KEYES, CLINTON W. (1928) (ed. and trans.), Cicero *De republica, de legibus* (London, New York).

KIMBROUGH, ROBERT (1964), *Shakespeare's Troilus and Cressida and its Setting* (Cambridge, Mass.).

KING, J. E. (1927) (ed. and trans.), Cicero *The Tusculan Disputations* (London, Cambridge, Mass.).

KINGSFORD, C. L. (1971) (ed.), *Stow's Survey of London* (Oxford).

KINGSLEY, G. H. (1865) (ed.), *The Pilgrim's Tale* (EETS 9), 77–98 (also in Chaucer Soc. 2nd series, 13 (1876)).

KINSLEY, JAMES (1979) (ed.), *The Poems of William Dunbar* (Oxford).

KISER, LISA J. (1983), *Telling Classical Tales: Chaucer and the Legend of Good Women* (Ithaca, NY).

KITTREDGE, GEORGE LYMAN (1893), 'Chaucer's Pardoner', *Atlantic Monthly* 72: repr. in Wagenknecht, 1958.

—— (1983–4), 'Chaucer and Some of his Friends', *MP* 1:1–18.

—— (1912), 'Chaucer's Discussion of Marriage', *MP* 8:435–67.

—— (1915), *Chaucer and his Poetry* (Cambridge, Mass.).

—— (1917), 'Chaucer's Lollius', *Harvard Studies in Classical Philology* 28:47–133.

KLASSEN, NORMAN (1995), *Chaucer on Love, Knowledge and Sight* (Cambridge).

KLIBANSKY, R., PANOFSKY, E., and SAXL, F. (1964), *Saturn and Melancholy* (London).

KLINGENDER, F. (1971), *Animals in Art and Thought to the End of the Middle Ages* (Cambridge, Mass.).

KLINGER, F. (1959) (ed.), Horace *Carmina* (Leipzig).

KNIGHT, STEPHEN (1986), *Geoffrey Chaucer* (Oxford).

—— (1989), 'Chaucer's British Rival', *Leeds Studies in English* NS 20:87–98.

KNOWLES, DAVID (1940), *The Monastic Order in England* (Cambridge).

—— (1955), *The Religious Orders in England*, vol. ii: *The End of the Middle Ages* (Cambridge).

—— (1988), *The Evolution of Medieval Thought* (2nd edn., London).

KÖKERITZ, HELGE (1954), 'Rhetorical Word Play in Chaucer', *PMLA* 69:937–62.

KÖLBING, E. (1885–9) (ed.), *Bevis of Hampton* (EETS Extra Series 46, 48, 65).

KOLVE, V. A. (1974), 'Chaucer and the Visual Arts', in Brewer (1974), 290–320.

—— (1981), 'Chaucer's *Second Nun's Tale* and the Iconography of St Cecilia', in Donald M. Rose (ed.), *New Perspectives in Chaucer Criticism* (Norman, Okla.), 137–58.

—— (1984), *Chaucer and the Imagery of Narrative: The First Five Canterbury Tales* (Stanford, Calif.).

KRAMER, O. (1913) (ed.), C. Valerius Flaccus, *Argonauticon* (Leipzig).

KRETZMANN, NORMAN, KENNY, A. J. P., and PINBORG, JAN (1982), *The Cambridge History of Later Medieval Philosophy 1100–1500* (Cambridge).

KRUGER, STEVEN F. (1992), *Dreaming in the Middle Ages* (Cambridge).

KUNITZSCH, P. (1981), 'On the Authenticity of the Treatise on the Composition and Use of the Astrolabe ascribed to Messahalla', *Archives internationales d'histoire des sciences* 31:42–62.

LANGLOIS, E. (1914–24) (ed.), *Le Roman de la Rose*, 5 vols. (Paris).

LATHAM, ARNOLD (1958) (trans.), *The Travels of Marco Polo* (Harmondsworth).

LAWLER, T. M. C., MARC'HADOUR, G., and MARIUS, R. C. (1981) (eds.), Thomas More, *A Dialogue Concerning Heresies*, 2 vols. (New Haven).

LAWRENCE, W. W. (1950), *Chaucer and the Canterbury Tales* (New York).

LAWTON, DAVID (1986), *Chaucer's Narrators* (Woodbridge).

LECOY, F. (1965–70) (ed.), *Le Roman de la Rose*, 3 vols. (Paris).

LEFF, GORDON (1958), *Augustine to Ockham* (Harmondsworth).

LEICESTER, H. MARSHALL (1990), *The Disenchanted Self: Representing the Subject in the Canterbury Tales* (Berkeley and Los Angeles).

LENAGHAN, R. T. (1975), 'Chaucer's *Envoy to Scogan*: Uses of Literary Convention', *ChR* 10:46–61.

LESTER, G. A. (1982), 'Chaucer's Knight and the Medieval Tournament', *Neophilologus* 66:460–8.

LETTENHOVE, *see* KERVYN DE LETTENHOVE.

LEVY, B. J. (2000), *The Comic Text. Patterns and Images in the Old French Fabliaux* (Amsterdam).

LEWIS, C. DAY, *see* DAY LEWIS.

LEWIS, C. S. (1932), 'What Chaucer really did to *Il Filostrato*', *Essays and Studies* 17:56–72.

—— (1936), *The Allegory of Love* (Oxford).

LEWIS, R. E. (1978) (ed. and trans.), Innocent III *De miseria condicionis humane* (London).

LIMENTANI, U. (1964) (ed.), Boccaccio *Teseida* (Milan).

LINDSAY, WALLACE M. (1911) (ed.), Isidore of Seville *Etymologiae*, 2 vols. (Oxford).

LONGNON, AUGUSTE (1895–7) (ed.), Froissart *Méliador*, 3 vols. (Paris).

LOOMIS, L. H. (1958), 'Secular Dramatics in the Royal Palace, Paris, and Chaucer's Tregetoures', *Speculum* 32:242–55.

LOOMIS, ROGER SHERMAN (1965), *A Mirror of Chaucer's World* (Princeton).

LOWES, JOHN LIVINGSTON (1934), *Geoffrey Chaucer* (Oxford).

LR, see Crow and Olson (1966).

LUKE, DAVID (1982) (trans.), Jacob and Wilhelm Grimm, *Selected Tales* (Harmondsworth).

LUMIANSKY, R. M. (1950), 'The Function of the Proverbial Monitory Elements in Chaucer's *Troilus and Criseyde*', *Tulane Studies in English* 2:5–48.

—— (1955), *Of Sondry Folk: The Dramatic Principle in the Canterbury Tales* (Austin, Tex.).

LÜTHI, MAX (1976), *Once upon a Time: on the Nature of Fairy Tales*, trans. L. Chadeayne and P. Gottwald (Bloomington, Ind.).

LYNCH, KATHRYN L. (1988), *The High Medieval Dream Vision: Philosophy and Literary Form* (Stanford, Calif.).

McCALL, JOHN P. (1979), *Chaucer among the Gods: the Poetics of Classical Myth* (University Park, Pa.).

References

MACAULAY, G. C. (1899–1902) (ed.), *The Complete Works of John Gower*, 4 vols. (Oxford); vols. ii, iii repr. as *The English Works of John Gower*, EETS Extra Series 81–2 (1900–1).

McCULLOCH, F. (1962), *Medieval Latin and French Bestiaries* (Chapel Hill, NC).

McEVOY, J. (1982), *The Philosophy of Robert Grosseteste* (Oxford).

MacFARLANE, K. B. (1972), *Lancastrian Kings and Lollard Knights* (Oxford).

McGARRY, DANIEL C. (1955) (trans.), *The Metalogicon of John of Salisbury* (Berkeley, Los Angeles).

McLEAN, TERESA, *Medieval English Gardens* (London, 1981).

McWILLIAM, G. H. (trans.), Boccaccio *The Decameron* (Harmondsworth, 1972).

MAGGIONI, G. P. (1988) (ed.), *Legenda Aurea* (2nd edn., Florence).

MAGOUN, F. P. (1961), *A Chaucer Gazetteer* (Stockholm).

MANLY, J. M. (1926), *Some New Light on Chaucer* (London).

—— (1926), 'Chaucer and the Rhetoricians', *Proceedings of the British Academy* 12:95–113.

—— and RICKERT, EDITH (1940) (eds.), *The Text of the Canterbury Tales*, 8 vols. (Chicago).

MANN, JILL (1973), *Chaucer and Medieval Estates Satire* (Cambridge).

—— (1974–5), 'The *Speculum Stultorum* and *The Nun's Priest's Tale*', *ChR* 8:262–82.

—— (1983), 'Parents and Children in "The Canterbury Tales"', in Boitani and Torti (1983), 165–83.

—— (1991), *Geoffrey Chaucer* (London).

MANN, NICHOLAS (1984), *Petrarch* (Oxford).

MANZALOUI, M. (1974), 'Chaucer and Science', in Brewer (1974), 224–61.

MAPSTONE, S. (2000), 'The Origins of Criseyde', in J. Wogan Browne et al. (eds.), *Medieval Women: Texts and Contexts in Late Medieval Britain. Essays for Felicity Riddy* (Turnhout), 131–47.

MARTI, MARIO (1969) (ed.), *Poeti del dolce stil nuovo* (Florence).

MARTINDALE, CHARLES (1988) (ed.), *Ovid Renewed* (Cambridge).

MATTHEWS, LLOYD J. (1976), 'Chaucer's Personification of Prudence in Troilus 5.743–9', *English Language Notes* 13:249–55.

MAYER, H. E. (1972), *The Crusades* (Oxford).

MEAD, W. E. (1928) (ed.), Stephen Hawes *The Pastime of Pleasure* (EETS 173).

—— (1931), *The English Medieval Feast* (London).

MEECH, S. B. (1959), *Design in Chaucer's Troilus* (Syracuse, NY).

MEEK, M. E. (1974) (trans.), Guido delle Colonne *Historia destructionis Troiae* (Bloomington, Ind.).

MEHL, DIETER (1974), 'The Audience of Chaucer's *Troilus and Criseyde*', in Beryl Rowland (ed.), *Chaucer and Middle English Studies in honour of Rossell Hope Robbins* (London).

MEISTER, F. (1873) (ed.), *Dares Phrygii de excidio Trojae historia* (Leipzig).

MICHEL, H. (1947), *Traité de l'Astrolabe* (Paris).

MIDDLETON, ANNE (1973–4), 'The *Physician's Tale* and Love's Martyrs: "Ensaumples Mo than Ten" as a method in the Canterbury Tales', *ChR* 8:9–52.

MIGNANI, RIGO, and DI CESARE, MARIO A. (1970) (trans.), Juan Ruiz *The Book of Good Love* (Albany, NY).

MILLER, F. J. (1917) (ed. and trans.), Seneca *Tragedies*, 2 vols. (London, New York).

—— (1916) (ed. and trans.), Ovid *Metamorphoses*, 2 vols. (Cambridge, Mass., and London).

MILLER, W. (1913) (ed. and trans.), Cicero, *De Officiis* (Cambridge, Mass., and London).

MILLS, L. J. (1937), *One Soul in Bodies Twain* (Bloomington, Ind.).

MILLS, MALDWYN (1988) (ed.), *Horn Childe and Maiden Rimnild* (Heidelberg).

MILSOM, S. F. C. (1981), *Historical Foundations of the Common Law* (2nd edn., London).

MINNIS, A. J. (1982), *Chaucer and Pagan Antiquity* (Cambridge).

—— (1983) (ed.), *Gower's 'Confessio Amantis': Responses and Reassessments* (Cambridge).

—— (1984), *Medieval Theory of Authorship: Scholastic Literary Attitudes in the Later Middle Ages* (London).

—— (1986), 'Chaucer's Pardoner and the "Office of Preacher"', in P. Boitani and A. Torti (eds.), *Intellectuals and Writers in Fourteenth-Century Europe* (Tübingen and Cambridge), 88–119.

—— and SCOTT, A. B. (1988) (eds.), *Medieval Literary Theory and Criticism c.1100–c.1375* (Oxford).

—— (1993) (ed.), *Chaucer's 'Boece' and the Medieval Tradition of Boethius* (Cambridge).

—— (with V. J. SCATTERGOOD and J. J. SMITH) (1995), *The Shorter Poems* (Oxford Guides to Chaucer, Oxford).

MOHL, R. (1933), *The Three Estates in Medieval and Renaissance Literature* (New York).

MONFRIN, J., and SAMARAN, C. (1962), 'Pierre Bersuire Prieur de Saint-Eloi de Paris', in *Histoire littéraire de la France* 39.

MOORE, E., and TOYNBEE, PAGET (1924) (eds.), *Le Opere di Dante Alighieri* (4th edn., Oxford).

MOORE-SMITH, G. C. (1913), *Gabriel Harvey's Marginalia* (Stratford-on-Avon).

MOSELEY, C. W. R. D. (1983) (trans.), *The Travels of Sir John Mandeville* (Harmondsworth).

MOSHER, J. A. (1911), *The Exemplum in the Early Religious and Didactic Literature of England* (New York).

MOZLEY, J. H. (1928) (ed. and trans.), Statius *Works* (London, New York).

—— (1934) (ed. and trans.), Valerius Flaccus, *Argonauticon* (London, Cambridge, Mass.).

—— and R. R. RAYMO (1960) (eds.), *Speculum Stultorum* (Berkeley, Los Angeles).

—— (1961) (trans.), *A Mirror for Fools* (Oxford).

—— (1979) (ed. and trans.), Ovid *The Art of Love and Other Poems*, rev. G. P. Goold (Cambridge, Mass., London).

MUCKLE, J. T., and McLAUGHLIN, T. P. (1950, 1953, 1955, 1956) (eds.), '*Historia Calamitatum* and Letters 1–7', *Medieval Studies* 12; 15; 17; 18.

MUCKLE, J. T. (1953) (ed.), 'The Personal Letters between Abelard and Heloise', *Medieval Studies* 15:47–94.

—— (1955) (ed.), 'The Letter of Heloise on Religious Life and Abelard's First Reply', *Medieval Studies* 17:240–81.

MUECKE, D. C. (1982), *Irony and the Ironic* (2nd edn., London).

MUIR, KENNETH (1957) (ed.), *Shakespeare's Sources* (London).

MURDOCH, J. E. (1987), *Album of Science: Antiquity and the Middle Ages* (New York).

MURPHY, J. J. (1971) (ed.), *Three Medieval Rhetorical Arts* (Berkeley, Los Angeles, London).

—— (1974), *Rhetoric in the Middle Ages* (Berkeley).

MURRAY, ALEXANDER (1978), *Reason and Society in the Middle Ages* (Oxford).

—— (1998, 2000), *Suicide in the Middle Ages*, 2 vols. (Oxford).

MURRAY, H. J. R. (1913), *A History of Chess* (Oxford).

MUSCATINE, CHARLES (1950), 'Form, Texture and Meaning in Chaucer's *Knight's Tale*', *PMLA* 65:911–29.

—— (1957), *Chaucer and the French Tradition* (Berkeley and Los Angeles).

References

MYERS, A. R. (1972), *London in the Age of Chaucer* (Norman, Okla.).

MYNORS, R. A. B. (1937) (ed.), Cassiodorus, *Institutiones* (Oxford).

—— (1969) (ed.), Virgil, *Works* (Oxford).

NERI, F., et al. (1951) (eds.), Francesco Petrarcha, *Rime, Trionfi e poesie latine* (Milan, Naples).

NEWMAN, F. X. (1968) (ed.), *The Meaning of Courtly Love* (Albany, NY).

NEWTON, STELLA (1980), *Fashion in the Age of the Black Prince* (Woodbridge).

NICHOLLS, JONATHAN (1983), *The Matter of Courtesy* (Woodbridge).

NIMS, MARGARET F. (1967) (trans.), *Poetria Nova of Geoffrey of Vinsauf* (Toronto).

NORTH, J. D. (1976) (ed.), *Richard of Wallingford*, 3 vols. (Oxford).

—— (1986), *Horoscopes in History* (London).

—— (1989), *Stars, Minds, and Fate* (London and Donceverte).

—— (1990), *Chaucer's Universe* (Oxford; 1st edn., 1988).

NORTON-SMITH, JOHN (1963), 'Chaucer's Etas Prima', *Medium Ævum* 32:117–24.

—— (1966*b*), 'Chaucer's Epistolary Style', in R. Fowler (ed.), *Essays on Style and Language* (London), 157–65.

—— (1971) (ed.), James I of Scotland *The Kingis Quair* (Oxford).

—— (1974), *Geoffrey Chaucer* (London).

—— (1976), 'Chaucer's Boethius and Fortune', *Reading Medieval Studies* 2:63–76.

—— (1981), 'Chaucer's *Anelida and Arcite*', in P. L. Heyworth (ed.), *Medieval Studies for J. A. W. Bennett* (Oxford), 81–99.

—— (1982), 'Textual Tradition, Monarchy and Chaucer's *Lak of Stedfastnes*', *Reading Medieval Studies* 8:3–11.

—— (1996*a*) (ed.), John Lydgate *Poems* (Oxford).

OAKDEN, J. P. (1930, 1935), *Alliterative Poetry in Middle English*, 2 vols. (Manchester).

OBERMAN, H. A. (1957), *Archbishop Thomas Bradwardine: A Fourteenth-Century Augustinian* (Utrecht).

—— (1967), *The Harvest of Medieval Theology* (2nd edn., Grand Rapids, Mich.).

O'DONOGHUE, J. B. (1982), *The Courtly Love Tradition* (Manchester).

OLSON, GLENDING (1974), 'The Medieval Theory of Literature for Refreshment and its Use in the Fabliau Tradition', *Studies in Philology* 71:219–313.

—— (1974), 'The *Reeve's Tale* as a Fabliau', *Modern Language Quarterly* 35:219–30.

OLSON, PAUL A. (1986), *The Canterbury Tales and the Good Society* (Princeton).

O'MALLEY, C. D. (1970), *The History of Medical Education* (Los Angeles).

ORME, NICHOLAS (2001), *Medieval Children* (New Haven).

OWEN, CHARLES A. (1977), *Pilgrimage and Storytelling: the Dialectic of 'Ernest' and 'Game'* (Norman, Okla.).

—— (1990), *The Manuscripts of the Canterbury Tales* (Cambridge).

OWEN, D. D. R. (1987) (trans.), Chrétien de Troyes *Arthurian Romances* (London).

PACE, GEORGE B., and DAVID, ALFRED (1982) (eds.), *The Minor Poems* Part One (Variorum edn., Norman, Okla.).

PAINTER, S. (1940), *French Chivalry* (Baltimore).

PALMER, JOHN N. (1974–5), 'The Historical Context of the *Book of the Duchess*: A Revision', *ChR* 8:253–61.

PANOFSKY, E. (1939), *Studies in Iconology* (Oxford).

PANTIN, W. A. (1955), *The English Church in the Fourteenth Century* (Cambridge).

PARRY, JOHN JAY (1941) (trans.), Andreas Capellanus *The Art of Courtly Love* (New York).

PATCH, H. R. (1927), *The Goddess Fortuna in Medieval Literature* (Cambridge, Mass.).

PATTERSON, LEE W. (1976), ' "The Parson's Tale" and the Quitting of the "Canterbury Tales" ', *Traditio* 34:331–80.

—— (1987), *Negotiating the Past: The Historical Understanding of Medieval Literature* (Madison, Wis.).

—— (1990) (ed.), *Literary Practice and Social Change in Britain 1380–1530* (Berkeley and Los Angeles).

—— (1991), *Chaucer and the Subject of History* (Madison, Wis.).

PAYNE, ROBERT O. (1963), *The Key of Remembrance: A Study of Chaucer's Poetics* (New Haven).

PEARSALL, DEREK (1962) (ed.), *The Floure and the Leafe and The Assembly of Ladies* (London, Edinburgh).

—— (1970), *John Lydgate* (London).

—— and SALTER, ELIZABETH (1973), *Landscapes and Seasons of the Medieval World* (London).

—— (1977), 'The *Troilus* Frontispiece and Chaucer's Audience', *Yearbook of English Studies*, 68–74.

—— and CUNNINGHAM, I. C. (1977) (intro.), *The Auchinleck Manuscript* (London).

—— (1978) (ed.), *Piers Plowman: The C Text* (London).

—— (1984), 'Thomas Speght', in Ruggiers (1984).

—— (1985), *The Canterbury Tales* (London).

—— (1992), *The Life of Geoffrey Chaucer* (Oxford).

PEDERSEN, O. (1974), *A Survey of the Almagest* (Odense).

PETERSEN, KATE O. (1898), *On the Sources of the Nonne Prestes Tale* (Boston).

—— (1910), *The Sources of the Parson's Tale* (Boston).

PETROCCHI, G. (1986–7) (ed.), Dante *La Commedia*, 4 vols. (Milan).

PHILLIPS, HELEN (1984) (ed.), Chaucer *The Book of the Duchess* (rev. edn., Durham and St Andrews).

—— (1993), 'Chaucer's French Translations', *Nottingham Medieval Studies* 37:67–82.

—— (2000), *An Introduction to the Canterbury Tales* (London).

—— (2000), 'Love', in P. Brown (2000).

PIAGET, A. (1941) (ed.), *Oton de Grandson: Sa vie et ses poésies* (Lausanne).

PIEHLER, PAUL (1971), *The Visionary Landscape: A Study in Medieval Allegory* (London).

PIKE, JOSEPH B. (1938) (trans.), *The Frivolities of Courtiers and Footprints of Philosophers* (Minneapolis) (Books 1–3 and selections from Books 7–8 of John of Salisbury's *Policraticus*).

PINTELON, P. (1940), *Chaucer's Treatise on the Astrolabe, MS 4862–4869 of the Royal Library in Brussels* (Antwerp).

PLATNAUER, MAURICE (1922) (ed. and trans.), Claudian *Works*, 2 vols. (London, New York).

PLATT, COLIN (1996), *King Death: the Black Death and its Aftermath in Later Medieval England* (London).

PLUMMER, J. F. (1995) (ed.), *The Summoner's Tale* (Variorum edn., Norman, Okla.).

POIRION, D. (1965), *Le poète et le prince* (Paris).

—— (1974) (ed.), *Le Roman de la Rose* (Paris).

POLLOCK, FREDERICK, and MAITLAND, WILLIAM (1968), *The History of English Law before the Time of Edward I*, 2 vols. (2nd edn. rev. S. F. C. Milsom, Cambridge).

References

POWICKE, SIR MAURICE (1935), *The Christian Life in the Middle Ages* (Oxford).

PRATT, R. A. (1947), 'Chaucer's Claudian', *Speculum* 22:419–29.

—— (1966), 'Chaucer and the Hand that Fed Him', *Speculum* 41:619–42.

—— (1977), 'Some Latin Sources of the Nonne Preest on Dreams', *Speculum* 52:538–70.

PRICE, D. J. (1955) (ed.), *The Equatorie of the Planets, edited from Peterhouse MS 75. I* (with a linguistic analysis by R. M. Wilson; Cambridge).

PUGH, RALPH B. (1968), *Imprisonment in Medieval England* (Cambridge).

QUAGLIO, ANTONIO E. (1964) (ed.), *Il Filocolo* (Milan).

QUARRIE, P. D. (1977) (trans.), *The Disciplina Clericalis of Petrus Alfonsi* (London: trans. from the edn. of Eberhard Hermes, Zürich, 1970).

QUEUX DE SAINT-HILAIRE, AUGUSTE H. E., and RAYNAUD, G. (1878–1903) (eds.), Deschamps *Oeuvres complètes*, 11 vols. (Paris).

RADICE, BETTY (1974) (trans.) *The letters of Abelard and Heloise* (Harmondsworth).

RAMSAY, G. G. (1940) (ed. and trans.), Juvenal and Persius *Satires* (rev. edn., London, Cambridge, Mass.).

RAMSAY, LEE C. (1972), '"The Sentence of it sooth is"; Chaucer's *Physician's Tale*', *ChR* 6:185–98.

RANDALL, LILLIAN C. (1966), *Images in the Margins of Gothic Manuscripts* (Berkeley).

RAYNAUD DE LAGE (1966–7) (ed.), *Le Roman de Thèbes*, 2 vols. (Paris).

REANEY, GILBERT (1971), *Guillaume de Machaut* (Oxford).

REGENOS, GRAYDON W. (1959) (trans.), *The Book of Daun Burnel the Ass* (Austin, Tex.).

REYNOLDS, B. (1969) (trans.), Dante *La Vita Nuova* (Harmondsworth).

REYNOLDS, L. D. (1955), *The Medieval Tradition of Seneca's Letters* (Oxford).

—— (1965) (ed.), Seneca *Ad Lucilium* (Oxford).

—— MARSHAL, P. K., and MYNORS, R. A. B. (1983, 1986) (eds.), *Texts and Transmissions: A Survey of the Latin Classics* (Oxford).

REYNOLDS, SUSAN (1984), *Kingdoms and Communities in Western Europe* (Oxford).

RICHARDS, EARL JEFFREY (1983) (trans.), Christine de Pizan *The Book of the City of Ladies* (London).

RICHARDSON, FRANCES (1965) (ed.), *Sir Eglamour* (EETS 256).

RICHARDSON, JANETTE (1970), *'Blameth Nat Me': A Study of Imagery in Chaucer's Fabliaux* (The Hague).

RIDDER-SYMOENS, H. DE (1996) (ed.), *A History of the European University*, vol. i: *Universities in the Middle Ages* (Cambridge).

RIDLEY, FLORENCE (1965), *The Prioress and the Critics* (Berkeley).

RIGG, A. G. (1992), *A History of Anglo-Latin Literature* (Cambridge).

RILEY, H. T. (1868) (ed.), *Memorials of London and London Life in the 13th, 14th, and 15th Centuries* (London).

RILEY-SMITH, J. (1987), *The Crusades* (London).

ROBBINS, F. E. (1940) (ed. and trans.), Ptolemy *Tetrabiblos* (London, Cambridge, Mass.; repr. 1964).

ROBBINS, H. W. (1962) (trans.), *The Romance of the Rose* (New York).

ROBBINS, ROSSELL HOPE (1959) (ed.), *Historical Poems of the XIVth and XVth Centuries* (New York).

ROBERTS, GILDAS (1970) (trans.), *The Iliad of Dares Phrygius* (Cape Town).

Robertson, D. W. (1962), *A Preface to Chaucer: Studies in Medieval Perspectives* (Princeton).

—— (1968), *Chaucer's London* (New York).

Robinson, Ian (1972), *Chaucer and the English Tradition* (Cambridge).

Rooney, Anne (1993), *Hunting in Middle English Literature* (Woodbridge).

Root, R. K. (1917–18), 'Chaucer's "Dares"', *MP* 15:1–22.

—— (1926) (ed.), *Troilus and Criseyde* (Princeton).

Ross, D. J. A. (1963), *Alexander Historiatus* (London).

Ross, Sir David [W. D.], et al. (1909–52), *The Works of Aristotle Translated into English* (Oxford).

—— (1945), *Aristotle* (4th edn., London).

Ross, T. W. (1983) (ed.), *The Miller's Tale* (Variorum edn., Norman, Okla.).

Roth, Cecil (1964), *A History of the Jews in England* (Oxford).

—— (1949), *The Intellectual Activities of Medieval English Jewry* (British Academy Supplemental Papers No. 8, Oxford).

Rouse, R. H., and M. A. (1979), *Preachers, Florilegia and Sermons* (Toronto).

Rowland, Beryl (1971), *Blind Beasts, Chaucer's Animal World* (Kent, Oh.).

—— (1968) (ed.), *Companion to Chaucer Studies* (Toronto).

Roy, Maurice (1986–96) (ed.), *Oeuvres poétiques de Christine de Pizan*, 3 vols. (Paris).

Rubin, Miri (1999), *Gentile Tales* (New Haven).

Ruggiers, Paul G. (1979) (ed.), Geoffrey Chaucer *The Canterbury Tales. A Facsimile and Transcription of the Hengwrt Manuscript* (with introductions by Donald C. Baker and A. I. Doyle and M. B. Parkes, Norman, Okla.).

—— (1984) (ed.), *Editing Chaucer: The Great Tradition* (Norman, Okla.).

Rundle, David (1996), 'Humanist Texts in England during the Fifteenth Century', in Diane Dunn (ed.), *Courts, Counties and the Capital in the Later Middle Ages* (London), 181–204.

Ruud, Martin (1926), *Thomas Chaucer* (Minneapolis).

Rv, see Benson, Larry D.

Ryan, Granger, and Ripperger, Helmut (1941) (trans.), *The Golden Legend*, 2 vols. (London).

S&A, see Bryan and Dempster (1958), Correale and Hamel (2002).

Sahlin, Margit (1940), *Étude sur la carole médiévale* (Uppsala).

Salter, Elizabeth (1962), Chaucer *The Knight's Tale and The Clerk's Tale* (London).

—— (1983), *Fourteenth-Century English Poetry: Contexts and Readings* (Oxford).

Samuels, M. L. (1988), 'The Scribe of the Hengwrt and Ellesmere Manuscripts of *The Canterbury Tales*', *SAC* 5 (1983) 49–58 (repr. in J. J. Smith (ed.), *The English Of Chaucer and his Contemporaries*, Aberdeen).

Sands, D. B. (1966) (ed.), *Middle English Verse Romances* (New York).

Sargent, Michael G. (1989) (ed.), *De Cella in Seculum. Religious and Secular Life and Devotion in Late Medieval England* (Cambridge).

Saul, Nigel (1983), 'The Social Status of Chaucer's Franklin: A Reconsideration', *Medium Ævum* 52:10–26.

Sayce, Olive (1971), 'Chaucer's Retractions', *Medium Evum* 40:230–48.

Scanlon, Larry (1994), *Narrative, Authority and Power: The Medieval Exemplum and the Chaucerian Tradition* (Cambridge).

Scattergood, V. J. (1974), 'The Manciple's Way of Speaking', *Essays in Criticism* 14:124–46.

—— (1975) (ed.), Sir John Clanvowe, *Works* (2nd edn., Cambridge).

References

SCATTERGOOD, V. J. (1976–7), 'The Originality of the *Shipman's Tale*', *ChR* 11:210–31.

—— (1983) (ed.), John Skelton, *The Complete English Poems* (Harmondsworth).

—— (1991), 'Olde Age, Love and Friendship in Chaucer's *Envoy to Scogan*', *Nottingham Medieval Studies* 35:92–101.

—— (1995), 'The Short Poems', in Minnis (1995).

SCHELER, AUGUSTE (1870–2) (ed.), *Œuvres de Froissart: Poésies*, 3 vols. (Brussels).

SCHERER, MARGARET R. (1963), *The Legends of Troy in Art and Literature* (New York, London).

SCHIFFHORST, GERALD J. (1978) (ed.), *The Triumph of Patience: Medieval and Renaissance Studies* (Orlando, Fla.).

SCHLESS, HOWARD (1974), 'Chaucer's Use of Italian', in Brewer (1974), 184–223.

SCHMIDT, A. V. C. (1976), 'Chaucer and the Golden Age', *Essays in Criticism* 26:99–115.

—— (1978) (ed.), William Langland *Piers Plowman. A Complete Edition of the B-Text* (London).

SCHMITT, J.-C. (1984) (ed.), *Gestures* (*History and Anthropology* I, London).

—— (1990), *La raison des gestes dans l'Occident médiéval* (Paris).

SEVERS, J. BURKE (1952), 'Is the *Manciple's Tale* a Success?', *Journal of English and Germanic Philology* 51:1–16.

SEYMOUR, M. C. (1968) (ed.), *Mandeville's Travels* (Oxford).

—— et al. (1975) (eds.), *On the Properties of Things. John Trevisa's Translation of Bartholomaeus Anglicus. De Proprietatibus Rerum*, 2 vols. (Oxford).

SEZNEC, JEAN (1953), *The Survival of the Ancient Gods* (trans. Barbara F. Sessions, London) (*La Survivance des dieux antiques*, 1940).

SHAHAR, SHULAMITH (1990), *Childhood in the Middle Ages* (London).

—— (1997), *Growing Old in the Middle Ages* (London).

SHANNON, EDGAR FINLEY (1929), *Chaucer and the Roman Poets* (Cambridge, Mass.).

SHAW, PATRICIA (1992), 'The Presence of Spain in Middle English Literature', *Archiv für das Studium der neueren Sprachen und Literaturen* 229:41–54.

SHEPHERD, GEOFFREY (1965) (ed.), Sidney *Apology for Poetry* (London).

SHERIDAN, JAMES J. (1973) (trans.), Alan of Lille *Anticlaudianus, or the Good and Perfect Man* (Toronto).

—— (1980) (trans.), *The Plaint of Nature* (Toronto).

SHOWERMAN, J. GRANT (1977) (ed. and trans.), Ovid, *Heroides and Amores* (rev. G. P. Goold, Cambridge, Mass., London).

SHREWSBURY, J. F. (1970), *The History of the Bubonic Plague in the British Isles* (Cambridge).

SIMONELLI, M. (1966) (ed.), Dante *Convivio* (Bologna).

SIMPSON, James (1997), 'Dysemol daies and fatal houres': Lydgate's *Destruction of Thebes* and Chaucer's *Knight's Tale*', in Cooper and Mapstone (1997), 15–33.

SINCLAIR, J. D. (1939–46) (trans.), *The Divine Comedy of Dante Alighieri*, 3 vols. (London).

SINGER, C. (1954–74), et al. (eds.), *A History of Technology*, 6 vols. (Oxford).

SKEAT, W. W. (1867) (ed.), *Pierce the Plowmans Crede* (EETS 30).

—— (1884) (ed.), *The Tale of Gamelyn* (Oxford).

—— (1886) (ed.), *Piers Plowman* (parallel texts) (Oxford).

—— (1894) (ed.), *The Complete Works of Geoffrey Chaucer*, 6 vols. (Oxford, 1894); vol. vii *Chaucerian and Other Pieces* (Oxford, 1897).

SKLUTE, LARRY (1984), *Virtue of Necessity: Inconclusiveness and Narrative Form in Chaucer's Poetry* (Columbus, Oh.).

SLEDD, JAMES (1951), 'The Clerk's Tale: The Monsters and the Critics', *MP* 51:73–82.

SMALLEY, BERYL (1952), *The Study of the Bible in the Middle Ages* (Oxford).

—— (1955), 'The Bible Scholar', in D. A. Callus (ed.), *Robert Grosseteste: Scholar and Bishop* (Oxford), 70–97.

—— (1960), *English Friars and Antiquity in the Early Fourteenth Century* (Oxford).

SOUTHERN, R. W. (1970), 'Medieval Humanism', in Southern, *Medieval Humanism and Other Studies* (Oxford), 29–60.

—— (1986), *Robert Grosseteste: The Growth of an English Mind in Medieval Europe* (Oxford).

SPEARING, A. C. (1972), *Criticism and Medieval Poetry* (2nd edn., London).

—— (1976), *Medieval Dream Poetry* (Cambridge).

—— (1983), 'Chaucerian Authority and Inheritance', in Boitani and Torti (1983), 185–202.

SPEIRS, JOHN (1951), *Chaucer the Maker* (London).

SPIEGEL, HARRIET (1987) (ed. and trans.), Marie de France *Fables* (Toronto).

SPURGEON, C. F. E. (1901) (ed.), Richard Brathwait, *Comments upon Chaucer's Tales of the Miller and the Wife of Bath* (Chaucer Society, London).

—— (1925) (ed.), *Five Hundred Years of Chaucer Criticism and Allusion 1557–1900*, 3 vols. (Cambridge).

STACE, C. (1998) (trans.), Jacobus de Voragine. *The Golden Legend* (Harmondsworth).

STAHL, W. H. (1952) (trans.), Macrobius *Commentary on the Dream of Scipio* (New York).

—— JOHNSON, R., and BURGE, E. L. (1977) (eds. and trans.), *Martianus Capella and the Seven Liberal Arts* (New York).

STANBURY, SARAH (2000), 'Visualizing', in P. Brown (2000).

STANLEY, E. G. (1976), 'Of This Cokes Tale Maked Chaucer Na Moore', *Poetica* 5:36–59.

STANNARD, J. (1974), 'Medieval Herbals and their Development', *Clio Medica* 9:23–33.

STEADMAN, JOHN M. (1964), 'Old Age and *Contemptus Mundi* in *The Pardoner's Tale,' Medium Ævum* 33:121–30.

STEVENS, JOHN (1973), *Medieval Romance* (London).

—— (1986), *Words and Music in the Middle Ages: Song, Narrative, Dance and Drama 1050–1350* (Cambridge).

STEWART, H. F., and RAND, E. K. (1918) (ed. and trans), Boethius *Tractates and Consolation of Philosophy* (London, New York).

STOCKTON, E. W. (1962) (trans.), *The Major Latin Works of John Gower* (Stockton).

STROHM, PAUL (1971), 'Jean D'Angoulême: A Fifteenth-Centry Reader of Chaucer', *Neuphilologische Mitteilungen* 72:69–76.

—— (1977), 'Chaucer's Audience', *Literature and History* 5:26–41.

—— (1989), *Social Chaucer* (Cambridge, Mass.).

—— (1992), 'Saving the Appearances: Chaucer's *Purse* and the Fabrication of the Lancastrian Claim', in Barbara A. Hanawalt (ed.), *Chaucer's England Literature in Historical Context* (Minneapolis), 21–40 (repr. in Strohm, *Hochon's Arrow: The Social Imagination of Fourteenth-Century Texts*, Princeton, 1992).

STRUTT, JOSEPH (1903), *The Sports and Pastimes of the People of England* (1801; rev. and enlarged edn. by J. Charles Cox, London).

References

SUTTON, E. W., and RACKHAM, H. (1942) (ed. and trans.), Cicero *De Oratore*, 2 vols. (London, Cambridge, Mass.).

SUTTON, J. D. (1916), 'Hitherto Unprinted Manuscripts of the Middle English Ipotis', *PMLA* 31:114–53.

SWANSON, R. N. (1989), *Church and Society in Later Medieval England* (Oxford).

—— (2000), 'Social Structures', in P. Brown (2000).

SZITTYA, PENN (1975), 'The Green Yeoman as Loathly Lady: The Friar's Parody of the Wife of Bath's Tale', *PMLA* 90:386–94.

—— (1986), *The Antifraternal Tradition in Medieval Literature* (Princeton).

TALBOT, C. H., and HAMMOND, E. A. (1965), *The Medical Practitioners in Medieval England* (London).

TANNER, NORMAN P. (1984), *The Church in Late Medieval Norwich 1370–1532* (Toronto).

TAVORMINA, M. TERESA (1999) (trans.), *Le Livre de Seyntz Medicines*, in Anne C. Bartlett and Thomas Bestul (eds.), *Cultures of Piety. Medieval English Devotional Literature in Translation* (Ithaca, NY), 8–40.

THACKER, C. (1979), *The History of Gardens* (London).

THIÉBAUX, MARCELLE (1974), *The Stag of Love: The Chase in Medieval Literature* (Ithaca, NY, and London).

THOMPSON, A. HAMILTON (1947), *The English Clergy and their Organization in the Later Middle Ages* (Oxford).

THOMPSON, ANN (1978), *Shakespeare's Chaucer: A Study in Literary Origins* (Liverpool).

THOMPSON, NIGEL (1996), *Chaucer, Boccaccio, and the Debate of Love. A Comparative Study of the Decameron and the Canterbury Tales* (Oxford).

THOMSON, JOHN A. F. (1983), *The Transformation of Medieval England 1370–1529* (London, New York).

THORNDIKE, LYNN (1923–41), *A History of Magic and Experimental Science*, 5 vols. (New York).

THORPE, LEWIS (1966) (trans.), Geoffrey of Monmouth, *History of the Kings of Britain* (Harmondsworth).

THRUPP, SYLVIA L. (1948), *The Merchant Class of Medieval London* (Chicago).

TOLKIEN, J. R. R. (1934), 'Chaucer as a Philologist', *Transactions of the Philological Society*, 1–70.

—— and GORDON, E. V. (1968) (eds.), *Sir Gawain and the Green Knight* (rev. N. Davis, Oxford).

TOOMER, G. J. (1984) (ed. and trans.), *Ptolemy's Almagest* (New York, Boston).

TRISTRAM, PHILIPPA (1976), *Figures of Life and Death in Medieval English Literature* (London).

TROJEL, E. (1964) (ed.), Andreas Capellanus *De arte honesti amandi* (Copenhagen, 1892; repr. Munich).

TURVILLE-PETRE, THORLAC (1977), *The Alliterative Revival* (Cambridge).

TUVE, ROSEMOND (1966), *Allegorical Imagery: Some Medieval Books and their Posterity* (Princeton).

TWYCROSS, MEG (1972), *The Medieval Anadyomene. A Study in Chaucer's Mythography* (Medium Ævum Monographs NS 1, Oxford).

UNWIN, GEORGE (1908), *The Gilds and Companies of London* (London).

USSERY, HULING (1971), *Chaucer's Physician: medicine and literature in fourteenth-century England* (New Orleans).

VAN HAMEL, A. G. (1892–1905) (ed.), *Les Lamentations de Mathéolus et le livre de Leesce de Jehan le Fèvre, de Resson*, 2 vols. (Paris).

VESSEY, S. (1973), *Statius and the Thebaid* (Cambridge).

VINAVER, E. (1971), *The Rise of Romance* (Oxford).

WACK, MARY F. (1990), *Lovesickness in the Middle Ages. The "Viaticum" and its Commentaries* (Philadelphia).

WAITH, EUGENE M. (1989) (ed.), *Two Noble Kinsmen* (Oxford).

WALLACE, DAVID (1997*a*), *Chaucerian Polity. Absolute Lineages and Associational Forms in England and Italy* (Stanford, Calif.).

—— (1997*b*), 'In Flaundres', *SAC* 19:63–91.

—— (2000), 'Italy', in P. Brown (2000).

WALSH, K. (1981), *A Fourteenth-century Scholar and Primate: Richard Fitzralph in Oxford, Avignon and Armagh* (Oxford).

WALSH, P. G. (1982) (ed. and trans.), *Andreas Capellanus on Love* (London).

WARREN, ANN K. (1985), *Anchorites and their Patrons in Medieval England* (Berkeley, Los Angeles, London).

WATTS, V. E. (1969) (trans.), Boethius *The Consolation of Philosophy* (Harmondsworth).

WEBB, C. C. J. (1909) (ed.), John of Salisbury *Policratici siue De nugis curialium*, 2 vols. (Oxford).

—— (1929) (ed.), John of Salisbury *Metalogicon* (Oxford).

WELTHER, J. TH. (1927), *L'Exemplum dans la littérature religieuse et didactique du moyen âge* (Paris, Toulouse).

WENZEL, SIEGFRIED (1967), *The Sin of Sloth: Acedia in medieval thought and literature* (Chapel Hill, NC).

WETHERBEE, WINTHROP (1972), *Platonism and Poetry in the Twelfth Century* (Princeton).

—— (1973) (trans.), *The Cosmographia of Bernardus Silvestris* (New York).

—— (1984), *Chaucer and the Poets. An Essay on Troilus and Criseyde* (Ithaca, NY).

WHITBREAD, LESLIE G. (1971) (trans.), *Fulgentius the Mythographer* (Columbus, Oh.).

WHITE, LYNN T. (1962), *Medieval Technology and Social Change* (Oxford).

WHITEFORD, PETER (1990) (ed.), *The Myracles of Oure Lady* (Heidelberg).

WHITING, B. J., and WHITING, H. W. (1968), *Proverbs. Sentences and proverbial Phrases from English Writings Mainly before 1500* (Cambridge, Mass.).

WHITING, ROBERT (1989), *The Blind Devotion of the People. Popular Religion and the English Reformation* (Cambridge).

WHITTOCK, TREVOR (1968), *A Reading of the Canterbury Tales* (Cambridge).

WICKERT, MARIA (1981), *Studies in John Gower* (trans. R. J. Meindl, Washington) (*Studien zu John Gower*, Cologne, 1953).

WICKHAM, GLYNNE (1980), 'The Two Noble Kinsmen, or A Midsummer Night's Dream Part III', *Elizabethan Theatre* 7:167–96.

—— (1991), '"Speaking Pictures", "Dumb Poesie" and Chaucer's Tregetours: Court Theatre in Chaucer's England', in Robert G. Benson and Eric W. Naylor (eds.), *Essays in Honor of Edward B. King* (Sewanee, Tenn.).

WICKSTEAD, P. H. (1903) (trans.), Dante *Convivio* (London).

WIGHT, J., and DUFF, ARNOLD M. (1934) (ed. and trans.), *Minor Latin Poets* (London, Cambridge, Mass.).

WILD, F. (1915), *Die sprachlichen Eigentümlichkeiten der wichtigeren Chaucer Handschriften* (Vienna).

References

WILKINS, N. (1995), *Music in the Age of Chaucer* (2nd edn., Cambridge).

WILLARD, CHARITY C. (1984), *Christine de Pizan: Her Life and Works* (New York).

WILLIAMS, ARNOLD (1953), 'Chaucer and the Friars', *Speculum* 28:499–512.

WILLIAMS, GWYN A. (1963), *Medieval London: From Commune to Capital* (London).

WILLIAMS, W. GLYNN (1927) (ed. and trans.), Cicero, *Epistolae ad familiares*, 3 vols. (London, New York).

WIMSATT, JAMES I. (1968), *Chaucer and the French Love Poets* (Chapel Hill, NC).

—— (1970), *Allegory and Mirror* (New York).

—— (1974), 'Chaucer and French Poetry', in Brewer (1974), 109–36.

—— (1982), *Chaucer and the Poems of 'Ch' in University of Pennsylvania MS French 15* (Cambridge).

—— (1991), *Chaucer and his French Contemporaries: Natural Music in the Fourteenth Century* (Toronto).

WINDEATT, BARRY (1979), 'Gesture in Chaucer', *Medievalia et Humanistica* 9:143–61.

—— (1982), *Chaucer's Dream Poetry. Sources and Analogues* (Cambridge).

—— (1984a), 'Thomas Tyrwhitt', in Ruggiers (1984), 117–43.

—— (1984b) (ed.), *Troilus and Criseyde: A New edition of 'The Book of Troilus'* (London; 2nd edn., 1990).

—— (1992), *Troilus and Criseyde* (Oxford Guides to Chaucer, Oxford).

WINTERNITZ, E. (1967, 1979), *Musical Instruments and their Symbolism in Western Art* (London).

WISE, B. A. (1911), *The Influence of Statius upon Chaucer* (Baltimore).

WOOD, CHAUNCY (1970), *Chaucer and the Country of the Stars* (Princeton).

—— (1984), *The Elements of Chaucer's Troilus* (Durham, NC).

WOOLNOTH, THOMAS (1865), *The Study of the Human Face* (London).

WRIGHT, LAURA (1992), *OED*'s Tabard 4.(?); *Notes and Queries* 237:155–7.

WROBEL, J. (1887) (ed.), Eberhard of Béthune *Graecismus* (Bratislava).

WURTELE, DOUGLAS (1980), 'The Penitence of Geoffrey Chaucer', *Viator* 11:335–59.

WYCKOFF, D. (1967) (trans.), Albertus Magnus *Book of Minerals* (Oxford).

YAMAMOTO, DOROTHY (2000), *The Boundaries of the Human in Medieval English Literature* (Oxford).

YATES, FRANCES (1966), *The Art of Memory* (London).

ZIEGLER, PHILIP (1969), *The Black Death* (London).

ZIOLKOWSKI, J. (1984), 'Avatars of Ugliness in Medieval Literature', *MLR* 79:1–20.

ZIPES, JACK (2000) (ed.), *The Oxford Companion to Fairy Tales* (Oxford).

ZUMTHOR, PAUL (1972), *Essai de poétique mediévale* (Paris).

ZUPITZA, J. (1875, 1883, 1887, 1891) (ed.), *Guy of Warwick* (EETS Extra Series 25–6, 42, 49, 59).

FOR REFERENCE
Do Not Take From This Room